GRADUATE STUDY IN CRIMINOLOGY AND CRIMINAL JUSTICE

GRADUATE STUDY IN CRIMINOLOGY AND CRIMINAL JUSTICE

A Program Guide

NICOLE PRIOR

Routledge
Taylor & Francis Group

LONDON AND NEW YORK

First published 2015 by Anderson Publishing

Published 2015 by Routledge
2 Park Square, Milton Park, Abingdon, Oxon OX14 4RN

and by Routledge
711 Third Avenue, New York, NY 10017, USA

Routledge is an imprint of the Taylor & Francis Group, an informa business

Acquiring Editor: Pam Chester
Editorial Project Manager: Ellen S. Boyne
Project Manager: Priya Kumaraguruparan
Designer: Russell Purdy

Library of Congress Cataloging-in-Publication Data
Prior, Nicole M. (Nicole Mary)
    Graduate study in criminology and criminal justice : a program guide / Nicole Prior.
        pages cm
    1.Criminology–Study and teaching (Graduate) 2. Criminal justice, Administration of–Study and teaching
(Graduate) I. Title.

HV6024.P75 2015
364.071'1--dc23

2014017843

British Library Cataloguing in Publication Data
A catalogue record for this book is available from the British Library

ISBN 978-1-4557-7555-2 (pbk)

CONTENTS

Part III List of Graduate Programs in Criminal Justice and Criminology in Canada Alphabetical by School Name 445

Part IV Potential Employment Options with a Master's or Doctoral Degree in Criminology or Criminal Justice........ 459

PART I

INTRODUCTION

Criminology is the scientific study of deviant and/or criminal behavior. The field of criminology views crime as a social phenomenon and seeks to understand the origins, prevention, and treatment of criminal and deviant behavior. The criminal justice system involves law enforcement agencies. the courts, and correctional systems, which all work together to apprehend, prosecute, defend, sentence, incarcerate, supervise, and treat criminal offenders. As an academic field, criminal justice examines topics such as criminal investigation procedures, evidence-gathering procedures, arrest procedures, criminal-charging selection, defense preparation, trial procedures, sentence selection, and offender treatment. While these two disciplines—criminology and criminal justice—are different, they are interdependent. Education in either field prepares students for employment in a multitude of professions and occupations.

Many students who wish to work in the fields of law enforcement, the legal profession, or corrections pursue graduate degrees in either criminology or criminal justice. Numerous individuals who are already employed within these fields find it necessary to obtain a graduate degree in order to continue to move forward in their field. Additionally, many students simply find these disciplines intriguing and wish to understand the above phenomena more fully, while others wish eventually to teach the topic to future criminal justice professionals. Graduate programs will fulfill each of these objectives. With many types of graduate programs within criminology and criminal justice, selecting a graduate program that is best for the prospective student takes persistence, research, and careful deliberation. Some programs focus on preparing students for an academic research and teaching career in either discipline, while others may focus on providing students with the necessary information that is needed to work within a specific component or agency of the criminal justice system. Information about the student's career aspirations and goals, coupled with his or her personal preferences, must be weighed against each program's strengths, weaknesses, and specializations to find the program that is the best fit.

What Exactly is Graduate School? And What Does a Graduate Program Entail?

Graduate school is not simply an extension of undergraduate studies with more challenging assignments. The purpose and goals of a graduate education are distinctly different from those of an undergraduate education. While many undergraduate criminology and criminal justice programs seek simply to expose students to a diverse assortment of information and research within the field, doctorate and—to some degree—master's programs strive to provide their students with a fluency in research techniques and an expertise of information within the discipline of criminology and/or criminal justice. The manner and structure of how each program reaches these objectives will vary.

Each program will be uniquely arranged. The required coursework will typically depend upon the specialization of the program and its faculty. A master's degree may have anywhere from two to four semesters of coursework, whereas a doctoral program will involve additional coursework past the requirements of a master's degree that is more specialized. Many master's degrees will have two options: a thesis and a non-thesis alternative. If a student wishes to pursue a doctorate after completing his or her master's degree, he or she should select the thesis option. Additionally, it would be optimal for the student to choose research for his or her master's thesis that could be carried over to his or her doctoral dissertation, although this might not always be accomplishable. For the non-thesis option, students may be required to complete additional requirements beyond their coursework in lieu of writing a thesis, such as an exam. A majority of doctoral programs will also use examinations to assess the student's completion of coursework. These exams are referred to by many names, including preliminary, comprehensive, qualifying, or candidacy exams. With both the master's and doctoral programs, students have to pass these examinations in order to receive their degree or move on in the program respectively. Often, students are given two attempts to pass the exam; if they fail both, they are not allowed to continue in the program. The student will also be required to defend either his or her master's thesis (if the thesis option is chosen) or the doctoral dissertation. Both defenses are viewed as a type of examination on the subject that was researched. As a rule, a thesis is viewed as a thorough evaluation of a particular area, while a dissertation is an original contribution to the literature of the field.

What Should a Student Consider When Selecting a Graduate School?

Given the current economic conditions, cost should be one of the principal elements considered when selecting a graduate program. Due to the fact that financial aid, whether it be federal aid or a fellowship, scholarship, or assistantship, is not always available or given to every student, the amount of both tuition and living costs must be taken into account. A common solution for many students is to attend school part-time while continuing to work full-time, but some schools may frown upon or outright ban students from working, especially if a student is receiving aid. In regard to tuition and associated fees, public schools typically have lower tuition costs than private schools, but the total will still be more than undergraduate tuition fees. Many public schools will waive out-of-state fees for nonresidents, while private schools rarely make a distinction between resident and nonresident students. Concerning living costs, the largest portion will be the student's housing expenses. The fees associated with housing will vary greatly depending upon the location of the school. Students must factor in whether the program is in an urban or rural setting and the area of the country where it is located. Additionally, the student's accustomed standard of living must also be taken into account when calculating housing costs.

The size and quality of the program must also be considered when making a decision about what program to attend. Although program size is an important factor, it must be interpreted with caution. While the size of the program may help to determine the faculty–student relations and class size, many programs with large enrollments can offer small classes and close student–faculty rapport. Another aspect to bear in mind is that larger institutions generally offer more extensive facilities and research opportunities, while smaller institutions may provide fewer but more focused specializations. In regard to assessing a program's quality, there is no thoroughly reliable measure of quality in education, mostly due to the fact that no two students are uniformly benefitted by the same program. That being said, several criteria factor into a program's caliber and merit that a student can consider: faculty resources, facilities, reputation, and placement success.

Faculty resources include the highest degree held by each faculty member, the institution from which each faculty member received his or her highest degree, and the number of publications and professional honors each faculty member has received. Additionally, students may wish to consider the availability of certain faculty members for mentorship and advising during their course of study, especially if they are interested in studying a specific topic. With respect to a program's facilities, students may wish to inspect the number of courses open to graduate students, the scope of the information covered by the program's required courses, and the level of outside funding that the department has been awarded. Furthermore, students may want to evaluate the size of relevant library holdings and their availability to students. Moreover, looking at how the university prioritizes its funds will provide an indication of the importance of the department to the university at large. A program's perceived quality or prestige is typically reflected in its reputation, although this may not always hold true. Countless students believe that there is a correlation between the competitiveness of a program's admission standards and the quality of the program, but one should be cautioned in interpreting difficulty of admission as indicative of a superior program. Smaller programs may have more permissive admissions policies in order to increase enrollment, while larger departments may curb admissions solely because of limited facilities and faculty. Lastly, the placement success of students and alumni may not directly associate with the program's quality, but students would be wise to factor this element into their decision, especially when the program has had great success with placing previous students and alumni within the specialization or agency in which the student is interested.

One additional element that must be considered when selecting a graduate program is accreditation. Accrediting agencies are nongovernmental agencies that ensure colleges, universities, and individual academic and professional programs meet "acceptable levels of quality" (USDOE). Regional and national agencies grant accreditation to an institution or department based on whether the university or program has set forth and fulfilled an educational purpose and has adequate financial capital and other resources, and based on the quality and level of education offerings and services provided. If a student chooses to attend a graduate school that is not accredited, he or she may not receive federal or state financial aid, may not be able to transfer credits another program/university, and may find it difficult to get a job. Employers are more likely to recognize degrees offered by accredited programs and universities. In general, universities and graduate programs are accredited by one of the following six agencies of accreditation: Middle State Association of Colleges and Schools, New England Association of Schools and Colleges, North Central Association of Colleges and Schools, Northwest Commission on Colleges and Universities, Southern Association of Colleges and Schools, and Western Association of Schools and Colleges. Students should ensure that the program they wish to attend is accredited before enrolling.

Students should always perform their own research to gauge a program's fit. Speaking with some of the program's alumni and inquiring as to how the program prepared them for work in the field and finding out their opinions about the program can prove beneficial. Also, talking with the department's faculty members and graduate advisors can offer the student a chance to get a sense of the program. Additionally, students should familiarize themselves with the most up-to-date information attainable, as programs frequently change. Students should routinely inspect the websites of the graduate schools and departments that are in contention. Lastly, they should visit as many campuses as possible. Students should make an appointment to speak with the graduate advisor, talk to the current students, sit in on a class, check out the facilities, evaluate potential housing situations, and get an overall feel for the program, department, university, and local area. These actions can assist students in making the best decision possible about what program to attend.

How to Apply to Graduate School

In order to qualify for graduate school, a student must possess a bachelor's degree from an accredited institution at the time of entrance into the program. Some programs will require the student's undergraduate degree to be in the fields of either criminology, criminal justice, or a related discipline such as sociology, while others may only require a set number of coursework credit hours from a specified discipline. The student's undergraduate GPA is evaluated by the graduate school and the departmental admissions committee. Many universities and programs will not take a student with an overall GPA below the equivalent of a B. The GPA requirement can be based on a student's cumulative GPA for all undergraduate study or may only apply to a discipline-specific GPA. In addition to the university's application for graduate school, many departments will have a supplemental application that must be submitted. A student will also be asked to furnish an official transcript from each institution that he or she attended while acquiring his or her undergraduate degree. The conferring undergraduate institution will have a procedure and fee in place for sending an official transcript.

Most programs will require between one and three letters of recommendation. Students should carefully choose the individuals whom they request to write their letters of recommendation, as they should not ask someone who they are not confident will give them a positive recommendation. Letters of recommendation ought to be written by a current or former professor who can substantiate the student's intellectual ability and motivation for graduate study. The student should provide a stamped, preaddressed envelope if the program does not utilize an online system for letters of recommendation. Students will sometimes be asked to write a statement of purpose or a personal essay on topics such as the student's projected plans for research or why he or she wishes to study criminology or criminal justice. Be advised that the admissions committee will evaluate not only the content of the essay but also how well the student expresses him or herself. Students should keep their essays brief while also including all of the pertinent information necessary to address the question fully.

Most graduate programs will require an entrance examination, typically the Graduate Record Examination (GRE), sponsored by the GRE Board and administered by Educational Testing Service, Princeton, New Jersey. This examination is offered year-round as a computer-based test. The paper version is administered three times per year and is only offered where computer-based testing is not available. According to the GRE website, a student "can take the GRE revised General Test once every 21 days, and up to five times within any continuous rolling 12-month period ... may take the paper-based GRE Revised General Test as often as it is offered." The General Test, which takes approximately two and one-half hours to take, comprises three sections that are scored separately: verbal reasoning, quantitative reasoning, and analytical writing. Additionally, students will take one unidentified verbal or quantitative section that is being assessed for future testing that does not count toward their score. Despite the fact that computer-based General Test scores are typically reported within 10–15 days, the GRE should be taken well in advance of the application deadline to allow enough time for the delivery of the scores and processing by the institution.

Students must be well informed of each university and program's application deadline. Students should begin their inquiries into the programs in which they are interested a minimum of one year in advance of the desired enrollment. Many programs will have application deadlines in mid-winter, but some will have deadlines as early as late fall. Most admissions committees will not make decisions until all of the information has been obtained; therefore, it is up to the student to ensure that all application materials are received prior to the application deadline. It should be noted that many times the same data are used to award fellowships and assistantships, but the deadlines may differ.

Financial Assistance

There are many types of financial assistance available through federal and state governmental agencies, private foundations, and civic organizations. Each will have its own application policies and procedures. Additionally, many graduate programs offer financial aid via fellowships, scholarships, grants, and assistantships. Some university/departmental aid packages may provide health benefits. These opportunities are commonly awarded on merit and are highly competitive. Their availability is frequently based upon the graduation of the current recipient. Fellowships (traditionally reserved for doctoral students) and scholarships typically include a tuition waiver, a large stipend, and carry no obligation other than academic performance. Grants are usually given based on either financial need or a specialized talent within the field, and can contain a tuition waiver, stipend, or combination of the two. Students should read the terms of the awards carefully, as some will restrict the recipients and not allow them to supplement their income via other methods. Assistantships are awarded based on need, on merit, or on both. Assistantships typically involve either research or teaching duties and are accompanied by a tuition waiver and/ or stipend. Assistantship positions should be recognized as both employment and financial opportunities and as an indispensable part of the student's education. Teaching assistantships require the recipient to assist with the department's undergraduate program by teaching classes, grading papers, or monitoring laboratories. Research assistantships are similar to teaching assistantships but have assignments pertaining to departmental research. Students should consider exploring assistantships and openings for financial help in other departments, residence halls, and administrative offices at the university if not granted departmental aid. Many of these positions will carry the same awards as departmental assistantships.

PART II

LIST OF GRADUATE PROGRAMS IN CRIMINAL JUSTICE AND CRIMINOLOGY IN THE UNITED STATES, ALPHABETICAL BY SCHOOL NAME

(Information taken directly from school/department websites)

Albany State University

Address: 504 College Drive
Albany, GA 31705
Phone Number: (229) 430-4600
Website: https://www.asurams.edu/

Department: Criminal Justice and Forensic Science
Albany State University
117 Harnett Hall
Phone: (229) 430-4864
Website: http://www.asurams.edu/web/academics-college-of-science-and-health-professions/programs#mscj

Type of Program: MS in Criminal Justice

Application Deadline: Fall semester: July 31; Spring semester: December 13

Requirements: All applicants must meet the general requirements for admission to the Graduate School, which include completion of a baccalaureate degree from an accredited college or university and submission of official copies of transcripts forwarded from degree-granting institutions with a cumulative grade point average of 2.5 out of the 4.0 quality points for all courses taken in the last degree program. Applicants whose undergraduate degree was not in criminal justice may be required to complete six semester hours in undergraduate criminal justice courses. Three semester hours must be completed in research or statistics and three hours in criminology or social theory. Students seeking admission to the master of criminal justice program must submit the results of the Miller Analogies Test (MAT) or Graduate Record Exam (GRE) and two letters of recommendation. An MAT score of 27 or GRE score of 700 is required for provisional admission, an MAT score of 44 or GRE score of 800 for regular admission. Applicants who do not fully meet the requirements for regular admission because of grade point average or standardized test score may be considered for provisional admission. Upon completion of the first nine semester hours of study with a grade of B or better, the provisional student is granted full admission to the master of science in criminal justice program. Otherwise, the student's enrollment is terminated. Note: In addition to 18 credit hours of core classes, students must also satisfy the requirements for 9 credit hours in one of the following specialties: corrections, forensic science, law enforcement, and public administration.

Information Required for Application: Application, application fee of $20, transcripts from all institutions attended, GRE or MAT scores, two professional letters of recommendation

Admission Date: Fall, Spring

In-state and Out-of-state Tuition Costs: In-state full time: $2,156; Out-of-state full time: $8,533

Availability of Internships and Scholarships: Not available

Orientation and Emphasis of Department/Program (Program Description): The MS degree program in criminal justice offered by the Albany State University Criminal Justice Institute is designed to prepare students for professional careers within the criminal justice system. Theoretical, methodological, and philosophical understanding of the criminal justice system is stressed during the matriculation process. As a result, students are well prepared for careers in criminal justice. Those seeking advanced graduate education beyond the master's degree level will be able to compete successfully with graduates from other schools and disciplines. The master of science in criminal justice program requires a minimum of 36 hours of classroom study and thesis research. In addition, all students must successfully complete a comprehensive examination on core, statistics/methodology, and a chosen specialty area.

Number of Faculty: 8

Accreditation: Albany State University is accredited by the Commission on Colleges of the Southern Association of Colleges and Schools to award, baccalaureate, master's, and education specialist degrees.

Average Length of Time to Complete the Program: Not available

American University

Address: American University School of Public Affairs
Office of Graduate Admissions
Ward Building, Suite 310
4400 Massachusetts Avenue NW
Washington, DC 20016
Website: http://www.american.edu/
Phone: (202) 885-1000

Department: Justice, Law, and Society
Ward, Room 270
Phone: (202) 885-2948
Fax: (202) 885-2907
E-mail: jls@american.edu
Website: http://www.american.edu/spa/jlc/

Type of Program: MS in Justice, Law, and Society; PhD in Justice, Law, and Society

Application Deadline: January 1: PhD deadline (Fall only)
February 1: Fall merit award consideration deadline (traditional masters programs)
May 1: Fall international admission deadline
June 1: Fall final deadline
November 1: Spring deadline

Requirements: Applicants are evaluated on their undergraduate coursework and grade point average, Graduate Record Examination (GRE) scores, career interests, recommendations, and breadth of background and experience. The admission committee reviews applications on a rolling basis and applicants are notified of the committee's decision as soon as possible thereafter. Before applying, carefully review the admission requirements.

Information Required for Application:
- $55 application fee. The fee is waived for current students, AU alumni, former PPIA/IIPP participants, Teach for American participants, Peace Corps participants, AmeriCorps participants, FAMU Scholars, and McNair scholars. There are no other exceptions. Prospective candidates completing the online application can select "pay by check" as the payment method to complete the application but are not required to provide any payment;
- Academic record or scanned unofficial transcript uploaded prior to submitting the application (Illegible scans will not be accepted. Do not mail in a copy of a transcript or academic

record which you have uploaded to your online application, unless requested by the School of Public Affairs.);

- Personal statement;
- Two letters of recommendation for MS applicants. Three letters of recommendation are required for PhD applicants;
- Résumé;
- GRE scores (Required for all traditional degree programs at the School of Public Affairs. The GRE may be waived for applicants to the MPA and MPP programs who have been out of under-grad for at least eight years and also have eight years or more of related work experience. LSAT scores may be substituted for MSJ, MPA, and MPP. GMAT may be substituted for MPA and MPP. There are no other exceptions. GRE Scores should be sent officially from the Educational Testing Service to American University [Institutional code: 5733]);
- TOEFL, IELTS, or Pearson Test of English test scores for international students (the institutional code for the TOEFL is 5007). The preferred minimum TOEFL score is 250 on the computer test and 100 on the IBT. The preferred minimum IELTS score is 7. The preferred minimum on Pearson Test of English is 68. The University code for PTE is X1Q-K6-10. The Certification of Finances for International Students (CFIS) and a bank statement are also required but may be submitted after admission; and
- Writing sample (required for PhD applicants).

Admission Date: Fall, Spring

In-state and Out-of-state Tuition Costs: $1,440 per credit hour

Availability of Internships and Scholarships:
The university has established the following merit-based awards to assist full-time graduate degree students. Merit-based graduate awards are awarded to students by their respective departments using traditional merit indicators such as GPA, test scores, strength of recommendation letters, and experience. Only full-time students are eligible to receive merit-based assistance, which includes fellowships, assistantships, and study grants. The deadline for merit award consideration is February 1.
Assistantships: Graduate assistantships are merit-based awards that provide the recipient with a monetary stipend and tuition remission for degree-related courses. Students selected for a graduate assistantship are required to work with a faculty member.
Graduate Study Grants: Graduate study grants are merit-based awards that provide the recipient with tuition remission for degree-related courses.

Hall of Nations Scholarships: These awards are available to international students who do not have permanent resident status or U.S. citizenship. The Hall of Nations Scholarships are assistantships and graduate study grants.

Special Opportunity Awards: These assistantships and graduate study grants are for U.S.-born minority students.

Hart A. Massey Fellowship: This fellowship is awarded each academic year to one or more incoming Canadian students pursuing graduate studies full-time at American University. The fellowship is applied to tuition charges.

United Methodist Graduate Scholarship: This scholarship is awarded each academic year to new full-time graduate students who have held membership in the United Methodist Church for at least two years, have strong academic skills, and are either U.S. citizens or permanent residents. The scholarship is applied to tuition charges.

Orientation and Emphasis of Department/Program (Program Description): The MS in justice, law and society is an interdisciplinary program focusing on the foundations and structure of institutions of justice and law. Students receive a thorough grounding in empirical and theoretical approaches to public policy issues. Four concentrations are offered. The concentration in Justice and Public Policy provides theoretical grounding in criminology and coursework in criminal justice, including corrections and policing. This concentration prepares students for a variety of practitioner and research positions in criminal justice or for advanced graduate work in criminology or criminal justice. The concentration in Terrorism and Security Policy focuses on issues of national security from the perspectives of criminology and criminal justice. This concentration prepares students for a variety of practitioner and research positions in the area of the prevention and control of terrorism. The concentration in law and society provides interdisciplinary perspectives on the role of law in society, including the theoretical foundations of law, the relationship between law and the social sciences, and broad issues of social justice. This concentration prepares students for positions in policy research and analysis or for advanced graduate work in law and society. The concentration in jurisprudence and social thought emphasizes philosophical and comparative perspectives on law, providing students with an appreciation of the nature and structural foundations of law and a firm grounding in analytical thought. This concentration serves students who have a background in either the liberal arts or law and are interested in combining the two.

Number of Faculty: 47

Accreditation: American University is accredited by the Middle States Association of Colleges and Secondary Schools and recognized by the University Senate of the United Methodist Church.

Average Length of Time to Complete the Program: Approximately two years

Anna Maria College

Address: 50 Sunset Lane
Paxton, MA 01612
Phone: (508) 849-3330
Website: http://www.annamaria.edu/

Department: Criminal Justice Specialization
Website: http://online.annamaria.edu/mpa/criminal-justice-mpa-specialization/

Type of Program: Master of Public Administration with a Criminal Justice specialization (online)

Application Deadline: Not available

Requirements: Not available (Links will not work to provide more information)

Information Required for Application: Not available

Admission Date: Not available

In-state and Out-of-state Tuition Costs: Not available

Availability of Internships and Scholarships: Not available

Orientation and Emphasis of Department/Program (Program Description): The master of science in criminal justice program is designed to prepare students for professions in criminal justice while enhancing the academic and professional knowledge of those who are already employed in the field. The curriculum engages students in the exploration of the relationship between theory and practice, the issues inherent in focusing on one over the other, and the complexities of searching for answers to crime problems in an area so closely tied to social, political, and economic factors. Students study both ethics and theory throughout the curriculum, integrating the two as they inform policy and decision-making. Anna Maria College recognizes that criminal justice professionals face increasing challenges that demand knowledge and an appreciation of our diverse society. Over the years, Anna Maria College's criminal justice programs have changed with the national scene, contributing to and living within some of the highest academic standards in the field. As the field of criminal justice has gown and evolved, so have our programs, which continue to stand as a model for academic change and excellence. Collaborations and partnerships have allowed the programs to provide education and leadership beyond the traditional classroom walls. Emphasis on intellectual involvement, career preparation, social awareness, and dedication to peace and justice are cornerstones of our programs. The faculty bring a broad spectrum of educational achievements and professional experiences to the classroom. Faculty and students come together as a community of scholars and learners to acquire knowledge in an ever-changing field and to explore the boundaries of that knowledge through research and analytical thought. Anna Maria College-educated criminal justice professionals have a commitment to professionalism and excellence, and are cognizant of their responsibilities to their community. The Criminal Justice Program at AMC is approved by the Massachusetts Department of Higher Education for participation in the Police Career Incentive Pay program established by the Quinn Bill.

Number of Faculty: Not available (not listed, aside from program coordinator)

Accreditation: New England Association of Schools and Colleges

Average Length of Time to Complete the Program: Twelve courses; approximately two years

Arizona State University

Address: 1151 South Forest Avenue
Tempe, AZ 85281
Phone: (480) 965-2100
Website: http://www.asu.edu/

Department: School of Criminology and Criminal Justice
Mail Code 4420
411 North Central Avenue
Phoenix, AZ 85004
Phone: (602) 496-2369
Website: http://ccj.asu.edu/

Type of Program: MA in Criminal Justice (online); MS in Criminology and Criminal Justice; PhD in Criminology and Criminal Justice

Application Deadline: February 1

Requirements:
Master's
- A baccalaureate degree from an institution with regional accreditation;
- A minimum undergraduate GPA of 3.0;
- The applicant's scores on the Graduate Record Examination (GRE);
- Two letters of recommendation from faculty members or others qualified to evaluate the applicant's potential for graduate study;
- A personal statement, not exceeding five pages, that describes the applicant's prior education, relevant professional experience, and career goals; and
- A résumé.

Doctoral
- An earned master's degree or a juris doctor degree from an accredited institution.
    The master's degree may be a degree in criminal justice, criminology, or another field (e.g., sociology, political science, history, social work, public administration, psychology, or philosophy). Outstanding students with a baccalaureate degree may be admitted directly into the PhD program. Admitted students' work will be reviewed after completion of thirty hours of graduate coursework. Students whose work passes the review are awarded the master of arts in passing;
- The applicant's scores on the Graduate Record Examination (GRE);

- Two letters of recommendation from faculty members or others qualified to evaluate the applicant's potential for graduate study;
- A personal statement, not exceeding five pages, that describes the applicant's prior education, relevant professional experience, and career goals;
- A résumé; and
- A writing sample. A sample of the applicant's written work should be submitted electronically. The writing sample may be an article (published or unpublished), a research paper, or any other extended sample of expository skill. The sample must be no longer than thirty-five pages in length. Longer writing samples should not be submitted without first consulting the graduate director. Documents should not be password protected.

International students seeking admission to the program must meet ASU graduate education requirements governing the admission of international students.

Information Required for Application: Stated above

Admission Date: Fall only

In-state and Out-of-state Tuition Costs: In-state: $5,001 per semester; Out-of-state: $11,827 per semester

Availability of Internships and Scholarships: Internships

Orientation and Emphasis of Department/Program (Program Description): The master of arts in criminal justice is a 33-hour professional degree offered completely online. Students gain an advanced training in program planning, management, policy analysis, and program evaluation. The graduate-degree program is tailored to prepare and enhance criminal justice professionals with coursework in criminology and the operation of the criminal justice system. The master of science in criminology and criminal justice (MSCCJ) degree program is designed to provide students with a high level of theoretical and empirical knowledge about crime and criminal justice. Students will gain the advanced research skills needed to prepare them for careers as criminal justice researchers and/or continued study in doctoral programs in criminology and/or criminal justice. Each student will write a thesis that reflects original research and scholarship, that makes a contribution to knowledge in the field, and that demonstrates his or her ability to design and carry out an independent research project. The School of Criminology and Criminal Justice at Arizona State University offers a program of coursework and research leading to the PhD in criminology and criminal justice.

This program emphasizes criminal justice theory, research, and policy. The program is designed to produce highly skilled criminology and criminal justice faculty and agency researchers and administrators.

The PhD program is organized around five components:
1. A core of required courses in theory and research on crime and the criminal justice system;
2. A core of required courses on research methods and analytical techniques;
3. Elective courses in criminology, criminal justice and related fields;
4. A comprehensive examination; and
5. A dissertation.

Number of Faculty: 24 full time, 5 visiting professors, 26 faculty associates, and 5 online faculty members

Accreditation: North Central Association Higher Learning Commission

Average Length of Time to Complete the Program: Online: eighteen months; MSCJC: two years; PhD: not available

Arkansas State University

Address: 2105 Aggie Road
Jonesboro, AR 72401
Phone: (870) 972-2100
Website: http://www.astate.edu/

Department: Department of Criminology, Sociology, and Geography
Room 218
International Student Center
P.O. Box 2410
State University, AR 72467
Phone: (870) 972-3705
Website: http://www.astate.edu/college/humanities-and-social-sciences/departments/criminology-sociology-and-geography/

Type of Program: MA in Criminal Justice

Application Deadline: April 1, November 1

Requirements:
- Submitted a completed online application for admission and the designated nonrefundable application fee to Graduate School Admissions, along with the required program documents, by the deadline on the department website;
- Earned a baccalaureate degree from an accredited institution (or its equivalent as determined by the Graduate School);
- Achieved a minimum cumulative undergraduate grade point average of 2.75 on a 4.00 scale or a 3.00 GPA on the last sixty hours;
- Achieved a minimum 3.00 GPA on any previous graduate courses completed at either Arkansas State University or another accredited university; and
- Submitted official transcripts from each college or university as requested by the Graduate School. Official transcripts must be submitted directly from the registrar of other institutions to the office of the Graduate School at Arkansas State University.

Information Required for Application: Stated above

Admission Date: Fall, Spring

In-state and Out-of-state Tuition Costs: In-state: $238 per credit hour; Out-of-state: $476 per credit hour

Availability of Internships and Scholarships: Not available

Orientation and Emphasis of Department/Program (Program Description): This program is designed to be consistent with the nationally accepted standard in the field set out by the Academy of Criminal Justice Sciences. It is intended to serve two broad constituents. First, the program will assist in developing additional analytical skills for in-service practitioners with BA/BS in the field or in a closely related field. Second, the program will provide a good foundation for students who wish to pursue doctoral studies.

Number of Faculty: 8

Accreditation: The Higher Learning Commission of the North Central Association

Average Length of Time to Complete the Program: Not available

Armstrong Atlantic State University

Address: 11935 Abercorn Street
Savannah, GA 31419
Phone: (912) 344-2576
Website: http://www.armstrong.edu/

Department: Department of Criminal Justice, Social and Political Science
University Hall 226
Phone: (912) 344-2593
Fax: (912) 344-3438
Website:http://www.armstrong.edu/Liberal_Arts/criminal_justice_soc_and_pol_science/cjsocpols_welcome/

Type of Program: MS in Criminal Justice (online)

Application Deadline: Not available

Requirements: All required courses are delivered 100% online
- A 2.5 overall grade point average or higher on completed requirements for a baccalaureate degree from a regionally accredited institution and a 2.75 grade point average over the last two years of undergraduate study (last sixty semester hours);
- A score of no less than 150 on the verbal section and a 141 on the quantitative section or a 3.5-4.0 on the analytical section of the Graduate Record Examination; or, a score of no less than 44 (402-407) on the Miller Analogies Test;
- Letter of Intent, approximately 500 to 1,000 words in length, to the MSCJ coordinator indicating applicant's intent to enroll if selected, a brief paragraph about applicant's academic background and professional credentials, and a statement concerning applicant's reasons for desired enrollment in the program; and
- Two letters of recommendation addressing applicant's (1) academic work; (2) professional experience, if any; (3) ability to handle master's level curriculum; and (4) how the applicant can be expected to contribute to the program.

While an undergraduate degree in criminal justice is not a prerequisite to admission, newly-admitted students must be deemed adequately prepared for graduate study in this essentially multidisciplinary area. Students who lack the necessary background may be required to complete additional undergraduate course work. However, with a major in social science or a minor in criminal justice, and at least a C in a course in statistics, no additional course work will be required.

Information Required for Application:

- A 2.5 overall grade point average or higher on completed requirements for a baccalaureate degree from a regionally accredited institution and a 2.75 grade point average over the last two years of undergraduate study (last sixty semester hours);
- A score of no less than 150 on the verbal section and a 141 on the quantitative section or a 3.5-4.0 on the analytical section of the Graduate Record Examination; or, a score of no less than 44 (402-407) on the Miller Analogies Test;
- Letter of Intent, approximately 500 to 1,000 words in length, to the MSCJ coordinator indicating applicant's intent to enroll if selected, a brief paragraph about applicant's academic background and professional credentials, and a statement concerning applicant's reasons for desired enrollment in the program; and
- Two letters of recommendation addressing applicant's (1) academic work; (2) professional experience, if any; (3) ability to handle master's level curriculum; and (4) how the applicant can be expected to contribute to the program.

Admission Date: Fall, Spring

In-state and Out-of-state Tuition Costs: $400 per credit hour (not including fees)

Availability of Internships and Scholarships: Most scholarships listed are for undergraduates. However, there is a page dedicated to grants.

Orientation and Emphasis of Department/Program (Program Description): Armstrong Atlantic State University's master's degree in criminal justice provides qualified professionals in criminal justice for southeast Georgia and the nation. The program prepares graduates with:

- Sophisticated knowledge of the criminal justice system and understanding of the administration of individual criminal justice agencies;
- Skills to apply advanced research methods to collect, analyze, synthesize, and report information and empirical data; and
- Sensitivity prerequisite to ethical practice and professionalism as a criminal justice practitioner.

The master of science in criminal justice at Armstrong is one of only three such programs in Georgia. Armstrong offers a comfortable, friendly university setting with emphasis on small class sizes and personalized instruction. The criminal justice program is housed in the Department of Criminal Justice, Social and Political

Science within University Hall, in the same building with the Law Enforcement Training Center (Regional Police Academy) and across the street from the regional office of the Georgia Bureau of Investigation and State Crime Lab. A modern library supports the programs of the department.

Number of Faculty: 3

Accreditation: Armstrong Atlantic State University is accredited by the Southern Association of Colleges and Schools Commission on Colleges to award associate's, baccalaureate, master's, and doctoral degrees

Average Length of Time to Complete the Program: Not available (not stated, online courses)

Bellevue University

Address: 1000 Galvin Road South
Bellevue, NE 68005
Phone: (402) 293-2000
Website: http://www.bellevue.edu/

Department: Justice Administration and Crime Management Degree
Website: http://www.bellevue.edu/degrees/graduate/justice-admin-and-crime-mgmt-ms/

Type of Program: MS in Justice Administration and Crime Management; PhD in Justice Administration and Crime Management

Application Deadline: Not available

Requirements:
Master's
- Possess an undergraduate degree from a regionally accredited college or university; or a U.S. equivalent degree from a nationally or internationally accredited college or university.
- Have maintained a GPA of 2.5 or higher from the most recent sixty credits of coursework earned toward the bachelor's degree.
- Have a cumulative GPA of 3.0 or higher for prior graduate work.
- Colleges may require letters of recommendation and essays in certain circumstances.

Doctoral
- Students can take Modules 1 and 2, which will be correlated to Certificates of Completion if the student chooses not to pursue their PhD Modules 1 and 2 prerequisites for admission into Modules 3 and 4 and the full PhD program.
- Possess a graduate degree from a regionally accredited college or university, or a U.S. equivalent degree from a nationally or internationally accredited college or university.
- All applicants for graduate admission to Bellevue University are required to submit an application for admission accompanied by a one-time application fee of $75 for graduate programs (this fee is waived for Bellevue University alumni). International students go to http://www.bellevue.edu/international/future-students/grad-admissions.aspx for Admission information.
- Provide all official transcripts for graduate coursework.

- Have maintained a GPA of 3.0 or higher in previous graduate level coursework earned toward the graduate degree.
- Have five years of professional experience.
- International students who do not possess a degree from a postsecondary institution where English is the principal language of instruction must have a minimum score of 575 on the Test of English as a Foreign Language (TOEFL).
- International credentials must be submitted to World Educational Services (at the applicant's expense) for a formal course by course evaluation at http://www.wes.org/.
- The GMAT and GRE are not required.

Information Required for Application:
Master's
- Possess an undergraduate degree from a regionally accredited college or university; or a U.S. equivalent degree from a nationally or internationally accredited college or university.
- Have maintained a GPA of 2.5 or higher from the most recent sixty credits of coursework earned toward the bachelor's degree.
- Have a cumulative GPA of 3.0 or higher for prior graduate work.
- Colleges may require letters of recommendation and essays in certain circumstances.

Application materials required when applying for the PhD program are outlined below and must be completed prior to admittance into the program:
- Submit a résumé.
- Write a 1,000-word statement of interest describing your interest in the study of human capital.
- Submit one letter of nomination from an employer.
- Submit one letter of recommendation from a peer or personal reference.

Admission Date: Fall, Spring

In-state and Out-of-state Tuition Costs: $495 per credit hour (in class and online)

Availability of Internships and Scholarships: Not available

Orientation and Emphasis of Department/Program (Program Description): The master of science in Justice Administration and Crime Management, offered in class and online, allows you to develop the knowledge and competencies needed to assume leadership roles within the field of criminal justice. The courses in this cohort program are designed to be taken in the order listed.

Number of Faculty: Not available

Accreditation: Higher Learning Commission of the North Central Association of Colleges and Schools.

Average Length of Time to Complete the Program: Not available

Boise State University

Address: Department of Criminal Justice
Boise State University
1910 University Drive, MS1955
Boise, ID 83725-1955
Phone: (208) 426-1000
Website: http://www.boisestate.edu/

Department: Criminal Justice
Albertson's Library Building L166
Phone: (208) 426-4114
Website: http://sspa.boisestate.edu/criminaljustice/

Type of Program: MA in Criminal Justice

Application Deadline: Applicants who wish to enroll in the Summer or Fall semester have the option to send application materials by the priority deadline (February 15) or the final deadline (April 1). The priority deadline is recommended for students seeking financial aid, as most aid decisions are made prior to April 1. The deadline for Spring admission consideration is October 1.

Requirements: An undergraduate degree in criminal justice or related social or behavioral science with at least a 3.0 average is required for admission to graduate study.
- Successful completion of an undergraduate statistics course;
- Successful completion of an undergraduate criminal justice theories course; and
- Introduction to Criminal Justice (CJ101) or its equivalent (required for all entering students)

Applicants with a cumulative GPA lower than 3.0 may still apply to the program with submission of Graduate Record Exam (GRE) scores of 152 or higher on each of the verbal and quantitative reasoning sections and a score of 4 or higher on the analytical writing section.

Information Required for Application:
Concurrent to the application process at the Graduate College, the prospective student should send the following items directly to Department of Criminal Justice:
- A statement of purpose. This statement should explain the student's reasons for seeking admission and what they hope to achieve in the program; and
- Three letters of recommendation from professors/instructors competent to judge the student's likelihood of success in a graduate course of study.

Admission Date: Fall, Spring, Summer

In-state and Out-of-state Tuition Costs:

Per Credit Rate (1-8 credits)	$324
Flat rate (9-17 credits)	$3,716
Non-resident tuition per credit rate (1-8 credits)	$112+Per Credit Rate
Non-resident tuition flat rate (9+ credits)	$6,300+Flat Rate
Overload fee per credit enrolled in 18 or more credits	$166

Availability of Internships and Scholarships: Scholarship applications are now online at http://financialaid.boisestate.edu/scholarships/boise-state-scholarship-application/. Applications for the FBI Scholarship, the Ted Hopfenbeck Scholarship, and the Michael Blankenship Social Justice Scholarship are completed online at the link. Application deadline for scholarships is March 15. There are four opportunities for criminal justice students attending Boise State University to receive scholarships from the Department of Criminal Justice. General departmental scholarships require no application.

General Departmental Scholarships
The names of eligible criminal justice students, GPAs, and class rankings are forwarded to the department for consideration in February. The dollar amount the department has to distribute varies with the current number of criminal justice majors. We typically make several awards ranging from over $1,000 (for the Academic Excellence Award) down to $200 (minimum allowed), and amounts in between, for general scholarships. The department will take the following criteria into consideration when making an award:

- Grade point average: Typically awardees must have a 3.0 plus GPA, but that does not guarantee that a person will receive an award. Award for GPAs above 3.0 in any given year depend on who is eligible that year and on the applicability of the other criteria.
- Either senior standing (at least ninety completed credits) as a criminal justice Major at the time the award will be used, or one or more awards of varying amounts to an outstanding criminal justice graduate student who has completed at least nine hours of graduate credit in the department.
- For undergraduate awards, completion of at least fifteen credit hours at Boise State University.
- Involvement in departmental service, leadership, and research (LAE, APS, volunteer work, research endeavors with faculty, etc.).
- Faculty familiarity with student from in-class involvement.

Orientation and Emphasis of Department/Program (Program Description): The master's in criminal justice is designed to provide a foundation in applied research and theory, seminars in substantive areas of criminal justice activity, and focused scholarship on issues of importance in Idaho. Curricula are organized into three sections. The Foundation Series is a set of core classes that will provide students with the intellectual skills needed for the study of more complex material. The Seminar Series promotes the development of scholarship in particular substantive areas in criminal justice. The Elective Series is intended to provide practical application of skills acquired in the core and seminar series. Students also are required to write either a thesis relevant to issues, policy, or practice in criminal justice, or pass a comprehensive examination.

Number of Faculty: 15

Accreditation: Northwest Commission on Colleges and Universities

Average Length of Time to Complete the Program: Not available

Boston University

Address: 1 Silber Way
Boston, MA 02215
Phone: (617) 353-2000
Website: http://www.bu.edu/

Department: Criminal Justice
Boston University Distance Education
1010 Commonwealth Avenue
Boston, MA 02215
Phone: (888) 883-0218 or (617) 358-1960
Website: http://www.bu.edu/online/programs/graduate-degree/
master-criminal-justice/courses.shtml

Type of Program: Master of Criminal Justice (online)

Application Deadline: Spring deadline is October 1

Requirements: The Boston University Online master of criminal justice consists of ten courses that will provide students with an in-depth examination of crime and justice, to include its theories, trends, and policies in less than two years of study. Students focus on only one course at a time by taking two seven-week courses per semester. This course delivery method is designed for working professionals to make the most efficient use of their time and to maximize the learning experience.

Information Required for Application:
- Application;
- $80 application fee;
- Official transcripts (photocopies and other facsimiles, such as scanned/e-mailed or faxed documents will not be considered official);
- Two official letters of recommendation. Recommendations should be submitted through the online recommendation system or with the paper recommendation form through the mail. Photocopies and other facsimiles, such as scanned/e-mailed or faxed documents will not be considered official. Most departments ask for three letters. Check your department's requirements under Application Requirements and Deadlines;
- Official GRE general scores, sent by ETS to institution code 3087 (some departments may also require the subject test; contact your department for details);
- Personal statement;
- Résumé or CV; and
- A writing sample (required by some but not all departments).

Admission Date: Fall, Spring

In-state and Out-of-state Tuition Costs:

Full-Time Students (12 to 18 Credits Per Semester)

Tuition	$43,970
Student Services Fee	$145 per semester (full-time and certified full-time)
Health and Wellness Fee	$160 per semester (full-time and certified full-time)

Part-Time Students (1/2 to 11 1/2 Credits Per Semester)

Tuition	$1,374 per credit
Student Services Fee	$60 per semester

Availability of Internships and Scholarships: Student employment, loans, and fellowships.

Orientation and Emphasis of Department/Program (Program Description): The master of criminal justice program is designed for those who want to advance in the field of criminal justice, enter it, or simply gain a deeper understanding of this fascinating discipline. An MCJ degree from Boston University's Metropolitan College will give you a competitive edge whether you plan to enhance your career, teach, apply to law school, or pursue a doctorate. Degree candidates will take courses where they will analyze criminal behavior, apply principles of leadership in organizational settings, learn theories of social control, and gain an informed perspective of law enforcement, the judicial system, and corrections. Ever evolving and often misunderstood, crime and justice are central to the moral fabric and social cohesion of society. Taught by leading criminal justice faculty who have extensive experience and scholarship in policing, the judicial system, and corrections, the online master of criminal justice will provide you with the knowledge and preparation to:
- Advance your career;
- Lead the criminal justice community;
- Assess and analyze criminal justice issues using improved critical thinking;
- Expand both your competencies and networking affiliations in criminal justice administration;
- Teach in the field of criminal justice, and/or
- Pursue doctoral studies or law school.

Number of Faculty: 8

Accreditation: New England Association of Schools and Colleges

Average Length of Time to Complete the Program: Less than two years

Bowling Green State University

Address: Bowling Green State University
Bowling Green, OH 43403
Phone: (419) 372-2531
Website: http://www.bgsu.edu/

Department: Department of Human Services
223 Health Center
Bowling Green State University
Bowling Green, OH 43403-0148
Phone: (419) 372-2326
Website: http://www.bgsu.edu/college-of-health-and-human-services/department-of-human-services/criminal-justice.html

Type of Program: MS in Criminal Justice

Application Deadline: Review of applications begins as soon as completed applications are received and continues until all positions are filled. We cannot process a student's application until we receive *all* supporting materials. We urge students to send them promptly. We will begin notifying students of admissions decisions immediately.

Requirements:
Undergraduate study: To gain regular status admission to the MSCJ program, you must have a minimum undergraduate grade point average of 3.00 (on a four-point scale) or 3.00 in at least nine credit hours of graduate-level courses. Students with undergraduate GPA between 2.70 and 2.99 are eligible for regular status admission but not funding through assistantships. Students with an undergraduate cumulative GPA between 2.50 and 2.69 may be considered for conditional admission and no funding through assistantships. Students admitted under conditional status will be required to achieve an overall 3.00 GPA in the first twelve credit hours of graduate study. Failure to meet this requirement will result in dismissal from the program.

Applicants who meet one of the following criteria do not need to take the Graduate Record Exam (GRE):
- GPA of 3.0 in the last sixty semester hours of undergraduate study;
- Overall undergraduate GPA of 2.75;
- 2.5 GPA in the last sixty semester hours of undergraduate study and five or more years of work experience in the criminal justice field; or
- 3.0 GPA in nine credit hours of graduate credit

For applicants who do not meet any of the above criteria, a GRE combined score of 900 on the verbal and quantitative sections will be required.

Information Required for Application:
- Letters of recommendation: Students must submit three letters of recommendation from individuals with knowledge of the applicant's qualifications and ability to complete graduate study. Examples of individuals typically asked to write letters of recommendation are past professors, former supervisors, or colleagues holding a graduate degree.
- Personal letter of application: Applicants must supply a written statement outlining their interests in graduate study and their expectations and future goals. This letter is extremely important since the graduate admissions committee will base many decisions on its content and quality.

Admission Date: Fall, Spring

In-state and Out-of-state Tuition Costs:

	Instructional Fee	Non-Resident
12-18 credit hours	$5,084 per semester	$8,738 per semester
More than 18 credit hours	$200 per credit hour	$200 per credit hour
Fewer than 12 credit hours	$424 per credit hour	$729 per credit hour

Availability of Internships and Scholarships: Graduate assistantships and tuition scholarships

Orientation and Emphasis of Department/Program (Program Description): Prepare to lead.
Take the next step in your criminal justice career with BGSU's master of science in criminal justice. This high-caliber program will equip you for leadership roles in criminal justice agencies, as well as provide a solid base for the pursuit of a doctoral degree. Bowling Green's highly qualified faculty are well respected nationally in their field and bring real-world experience to their teaching. Their areas of specialization include victimology, police organizations, corrections, juvenile justice, criminal law, crime prevention, and more. The program's small class settings foster a dynamic relationship with these professionals.

Number of Faculty: 9

Accreditation: Higher Learning Commission and a member of the North Central Association

Average Length of Time to Complete the Program: Full-time status: one calendar year; part-time: up to two calendar years.

Bridgewater State College

Address: 131 Summer Street
Bridgewater, MA 02324
Phone: (508) 531-1000
Website: http://www.bridgew.edu/

Department: Department of Criminal Justice
Maxwell Library
Room 311
Phone: (508) 531-2107
Website: http://www2.bridgew.edu/content/department-criminal-justice/

Type of Program: MS in Criminal Justice

Application Deadline: April 1, October 1, February 1

Requirements:
- An undergraduate degree with a minimum GPA of 3.0 based upon four years of course work; and
- A composite score of 1,000 on the quantitative and verbal parts of the GRE general test if taken before August 1, 2011, or a comparable composite score on the quantitative and verbal parts of the GRE general test if taken on or after August 1, 2011.

Information Required for Application:
- Completed application and $50 application fee;
- Official transcripts of all undergraduate and graduate course work;
- Official GRE exam scores;
- Three appropriate letters of recommendation;
- Résumé; and
- Personal statement. Prepare a brief but careful statement regarding the reasons you want to pursue graduate work in this field, your specific interest and experiences in this field, and your career goals.

Admission Date: Fall, Spring, Summer

In-state and Out-of-state Tuition Costs: In-state and out-of-state: $362.21 per credit

Availability of Internships and Scholarships: Not available

Orientation and Emphasis of Department/Program (Program Description): Taught by leading criminal justice faculty who have extensive experience as attorneys, law enforcement officers, corrections experts, and investigators, the MS in criminal justice program prepares you for continued study or the pursuit of a variety of careers, including leadership roles within the judicial system, law enforcement agencies, legal firms, correctional facilities and the field of criminal justice education. The MS in criminal justice program offers you:

- Diverse faculty with extensive experience in a variety of criminal justice settings;
- Development of critical thinking skills, as well as oral and written communication capabilities;
- Small classes, facilitating a more personalized learning experience;
- Professional leadership skills and development; and
- Affordable tuition, whether you live in state or out of state

Number of Faculty: 11

Accreditation: New England Association of Schools and Colleges

Average Length of Time to Complete the Program: Not available

Buffalo State College, State University of New York

Address: 1300 Elmwood Avenue
Buffalo, NY 14222
Phone Number: (716) 878-4000
Website: http://www.buffalostate.edu/

Department: Criminal Justice Department
Classroom Building C114
Buffalo State
1300 Elmwood Avenue
Buffalo, NY 14222
Phone: (716) 878-4517
Website: http://www.buffalostate.edu/criminaljustice/

Type of Program: MS in Criminal Justice

Application Deadline: Applications are reviewed on a continual basis for the Fall and Spring semesters.

Requirements:
- Hold an approved baccalaureate degree granted by an institution that is accredited by an approved regional accrediting agency or its equivalent (for international applicants).
- Hold a bachelor's degree from an accredited college or university with a minimum cumulative GPA of 3.0 (4.0 scale) in the last sixty credit hours.

Information Required for Application: A written statement of intent that includes the applicant's preparation for graduate study (guidelines available from the department).
If minimum requirements are not met, the graduate faculty may grant an applicant conditional admission to the program as a premajor if the applicant has a minimum cumulative GPA of 2.75 (4.0 scale) *and* (a.) a minimum of five years of full-time work experience in the criminal justice field *or* (b.) a minimum combined score of 290 on the verbal and quantitative sections of the Graduate Record Examination (GRE).

Admission Date: Not available

In-state and Out-of-state Tuition Costs: $4,935 per semester for New York State residents and $9,175 per semester for out-of-state students

Availability of Internships and Scholarships: Assistantships, scholarships, fellowships

Orientation and Emphasis of Department/Program (Program Description): The department provides a comprehensive education in criminal justice through an academically rigorous, multi-disciplinary program of study. The curriculum, which is grounded in the social sciences, integrates theory, research, and practice with a goal of preparing students for leadership positions in the criminal justice profession and/or for advanced graduate study. The department is committed to fostering an intellectual climate that encourages faculty research, thus enhancing the understanding of criminal justice issues. The department also provides the state and local criminal justice community with expertise across a wide range of specialties represented among the faculty.

Number of Faculty: 12

Accreditation: Commission on Higher Education of the Middle States Association of Colleges and Schools

Average Length of Time to Complete the Program: Not available

California State University, Fresno

Address: 5241 North Maple Avenue
Fresno, CA 93740
Phone: (559) 278-4240
Website: http://www.fresnostate.edu/

Department: Department of Criminology
2576 East San Ramon, MS/ST104
Fresno, CA 93740
Phone: (559) 278-2305
Department Website: http://www.fresnostate.edu/
socialsciences/criminology/

Type of Program: MS in Criminology

Application Deadline: Applications for Fall admission are accepted October 1 through April 1. Admission to graduate standing is prerequisite to admission to the Department of Criminology graduate program. Note: a University graduate admission application must also be completed and submitted. This is in addition to the application that is required for admission into the criminology graduate program. Students interested in applying for Fall admission: applications for graduate work in criminology will be accepted from August through March. Review of application materials will begin in March. All applications received throughout the admittance period will receive full consideration. Please contact Dr. Toni DuPont-Morales at tdupontmorales@csufresno.edu for further information.

Requirements:
- A baccalaureate degree from an accredited institution with a grade point average (GPA) of at least a 3.0 (on a 4.0-point scale); and
- Completion of the general aptitude portion of the Graduate Records Examination (GRE). We require that the general aptitude portion of the GRE be taken prior to a student being admitted into graduate criminology course work or graduate status.

Information Required for Application:
- A completed application for graduate study for the criminology program at California State University, Fresno;
- Three completed recommendation forms for graduate study in criminology;
- A personal essay focusing on a student's "statement of purpose"; and

- An interview may be required by the criminology graduate committee.

Admission Date: Fall

In-state and Out-of-state Tuition Costs: Graduate/post-baccalaureate (for out-of-state residents, add $372 for each unit of credit taken):

0-6 units	7+ units
$2,360.50	$3,776.50

Availability of Internships and Scholarships: The graduate criminology degree offers selective internships.

Orientation and Emphasis of Department/Program (Program Description): The master in criminology is a flexible program that provides a solid core in the field of criminology, while permitting students to pursue specialized areas of interest. The master's program is designed to prepare students for service and responsible administrative and professional positions in agencies within the criminal justice system. The master's program also prepares students for a wide variety of occupations including in-service education, administrative education and management, community college teaching, counseling, doctoral studies, and research. Since offering our first graduate criminology course in 1957, the master's program has become the most comprehensive master's degree program in the discipline between Sacramento and Los Angeles. It is an advanced program that now draws students from all over the United States.

Number of Faculty: 19

Accreditation: The California State Board of Education and the Western Association of Schools and Colleges.

Average Length of Time to Complete the Program: Not specified

California State University, Long Beach

Address: 1250 Bellflower Boulevard
Long Beach, CA 90840
Phone: (562) 985-4111
Website: http://www.csulb.edu/

Department: Department of Criminal Justice
California State University, Long Beach
1250 Bellflower Boulevard, ET-232
Long Beach, CA 90840
Phone: (562) 985-8965
Department Website: http://www.csulb.edu/colleges/chhs/departments/criminal-justice/

Type of Program: MS in Criminal Justice

Application Deadline: The Department of Criminal Justice admits students once per year for Fall start dates. Only those applicants who have earned a bachelor's degree from a regionally-accredited college or university are eligible for admission. The deadlines are as follows:
- CSU Mentor and program application deadline: February 15
- Application fee deadline: February 22
- Transcript and supporting documents deadline: March 8

Requirements:
- A baccalaureate degree from an accredited institution with a grade point average (GPA) of at least a 3.0 (on a 4.0-point scale); and
- Completion of the general aptitude portion of the Graduate Records Examination (GRE). We require that the general aptitude portion of the GRE be taken prior to a student being admitted into graduate criminology course work or graduate status.

Information Required for Application: Students must apply through both the Graduate School and the department.
- Complete a university application via CSU Mentor.
- Send official GRE scores to CSULB directly from Educational Testing Service (ETS).
- Send an official transcript from each college and/or university you attended (including transcripts from community colleges) to CSULB's Enrollment Services.
- Submit three letters of recommendation directly to the Department of Criminal Justice graduate advisor.
- Send a résumé directly to the Department of Criminal Justice graduate advisor.

- Write a typewritten letter of intent (a formal application essay) between three and five double-spaced pages in length (i.e., 750 word minimum; 1,250 word maximum) and send it directly to the Department of Criminal Justice graduate advisor.

Admission Date: Fall

In-state and Out-of-state Tuition Costs: (for out-of-state residents: add $372 for each unit of credit taken)

0-6 units	7+ units
$2,360.50	$3,776.50

Availability of Internships and Scholarships: No assistantships, internships, or scholarships listed for graduate students.

Orientation and Emphasis of Department/Program (Program Description): The master of science in criminal justice will expand and increase individual competency, develop and mature thought processes, aid in gaining insights into professional leadership and knowledge, permit an exchange between students and faculty, and further the spirit of research and scholarship to enhance professional and personal development. The curriculum is designed to offer a balance of theory and practical application that will prove to be challenging to students and useful in the field. The MS provides the requisite knowledge and opportunity for individuals: (1) to be competitive for administrative positions in the courts, corrections, law enforcement, security, probation, and parole; (2) to fill research positions in criminal justice agencies; (3) to pursue advanced degrees (JD or PhD); and (4) to fill community college teaching positions in criminal justice.

Number of Faculty: 44

Accreditation: Western Association of Schools and Colleges

Average Length of Time to Complete the Program: The Department of Criminal Justice offers the MS in two formats:
1. A full-time traditional program on CSULB's campus that is designed to be completed in two academic years (i.e., this program is not designed for students with full-time jobs); and
2. An off-campus accelerated master's program for students will full-time jobs that is designed to be completed in eighteen to nineteen months of classes offered on Saturdays.

California State University, Los Angeles

Address: 5151 State University Drive
Los Angeles, CA 90032
Phone: (323) 343-3000
Website: http://www.calstatela.edu/

Department: School of Criminal Justice and Criminalistics
Hertzberg-Davis Forensic Science Center
Main Office: Room 244
Phone: (323) 343-4610
Fax: (323) 343-4646
Website: http://www.calstatela.edu/academic/hhs/crim_jus/

Type of Program: MS in Criminal Justice; MS in Criminalistics

Application Deadline: Not available

Requirements: To gain maximum benefit from post-baccalaureate or graduate study, students should possess the following:
- Sufficient knowledge and understanding of their chosen field of study to pursue it effectively at an advanced level;
- Basic techniques, skills, and methods necessary for research investigation and other practical applications of knowledge;
- Sufficient maturity and intellectual curiosity to pursue independent study and learning beyond regular assignments; and
- Achievements, aptitudes, and abilities at superior levels to ensure scholarly performance considerably above the average.

Information Required for Application:
- Have completed a four-year college course of study and hold an acceptable baccalaureate degree from an institution accredited by a regional accrediting association, or have completed equivalent academic preparation as determined by appropriate campus authorities;
- Be in good academic standing at the last college or university attended;
- Have earned a grade point average of at least 2.5 on the last degree completed by the candidate or have attained a grade point average of at least 2.5 (A = 4.0) in the last sixty semester (ninety quarter) units attempted; and
- Satisfactorily meet the professional, personal, scholastic, and other standards for graduate study, including qualifying examinations, as appropriate campus authorities may prescribe. In unusual circumstances, a campus may make exceptions to these criteria.

Admission Date: Not available

In-state and Out-of-state Tuition Costs: In-state: graduate/post-baccalaureate tuition and mandatory fees total $7,601; out-of-state: graduate/post-baccalaureate tuition and mandatory fees total $16,529.

Availability of Internships and Scholarships: A link of available scholarships is provided (http://www.calstatela.edu/univ/finaid/scholar.php).

Orientation and Emphasis of Department/Program (Program Description): None provided

Number of Faculty: 19

Accreditation: Accrediting Commission for Senior Colleges and Universities of the Western Association of Schools and Colleges.

Average Length of Time to Complete the Program: Not available

California State University, Sacramento

Address: 6000 J Street
Sacramento, CA 95819
Phone: (916) 278-6011
Website: http://www.csus.edu/

Department: Division of Criminal Justice
Alpine 137
6000 J Street
Sacramento, CA 95819
Phone: (916) 278-6487
Website: http://www.csus.edu/HHS/cj/

Type of Program: MS in Criminal Justice

Application Deadline: The application filing period for the Fall semester begins on October 1.

Requirements:
- A baccalaureate degree in criminal justice. Applicants with degrees in related fields (sociology, psychology, public administration, political science, government, or the like) will be considered on a case-by-case basis, and may be required to complete a course of study or a pro-seminar course in criminal justice as a prerequisite to being admitted to the criminal justice graduate program; and
- A GPA of 3.0 in the major and 3.0 in the last sixty units attempted.

Information Required for Application:
- A letter outlining in some detail the applicant's experience, interests, goals, and expectations in pursuing the MS in criminal justice (this will assist us in assigning an initial advisor);
- Submission of Graduate Record Examination scores including the analytical writing scores of 4.0 or higher; and
- Three letters of recommendation from the student's former faculty who can evaluate the applicant's potential for graduate study. Applicants applying after having been out of college for several years may have recommendations submitted by their employers or other professionals.

Admission Date: Fall

In-state and Out-of-state Tuition Costs: Post-baccalaureate (for out-of-state residents, add $372 for each unit of credit taken)

0-6 units	6+ units
$2,518	$3,934

Availability of Internships and Scholarships: Not listed

Orientation and Emphasis of Department/Program (Program Description): The master of science program in criminal justice offers a generalist degree focused on a variety of areas within the field of criminal justice. It is a mature program that has already made efforts to adapt to anticipated changing demands. The breadth of the curriculum and faculty training is evident in the variety of courses taught by instructors with training in criminal justice, criminology, sociology, psychology, political science, public administration, social work, and law. Faculty members teaching in criminal justice have both academic training as well as practical experience in the criminal justice system. This training enhances the depth of knowledge that is shared with students. In addition, all faculty members that teach in the graduate program have earned doctorates in their respective disciplines. Graduate students in criminal justice progress toward graduation/degree completion as a cohort. They attend weekly evening classes part-time, completing six units each semester. During their first year, students complete twelve units of core classes. In their second year, they complete twelve units of selective/elective courses. In their third year, they complete their culminating experience courses.

Number of Faculty: 23

Accreditation: Western Association of Schools and Colleges

Average Length of Time to Complete the Program: Three years

California State University, San Bernardino

Address: 5500 University Parkway
San Bernardino, CA 92407-2318
Phone: (909) 537-5000
Website: http://www.csusb.edu/

Department: Criminal Justice
5500 University Parkway
San Bernardino, CA 92407
Phone: (909) 537-5506
Fax: (909) 537-7025
Website: http://criminaljustice.csusb.edu/majorsprograms/ma_criminal_justice.htm

Type of Program: MA in Criminal Justice; MA in Criminal Justice (online)

Application Deadline: April 1

Requirements:
- A baccalaureate degree from an accredited college or university;
- Completion of an undergraduate major in criminal justice, criminology, sociology, or an allied field such as psychology, administration, or another social science, or recommendation for admission to the program by the graduate admissions committee;
- Competence in the following prerequisite areas: criminological theory, law enforcement, institutional and community corrections, research methods, and statistics;
- Completion of the graduate entrance writing requirement; and
- A minimum undergraduate grade point average of at least 3.0 overall and 3.0 (B) in the major.

Information Required for Application:
- Completion of the graduate entrance writing requirement;
- Submission of any available GRE or MAT (Miller Analogies Test) scores, in the event the applicant feels that such scores would enhance their chances of admission (submission of such scores is not mandatory); and
- Submission to the Criminal Justice Program of three letters of recommendation from individuals who are familiar with the student's academic work and potential to complete the program successfully. Letters must come directly from the writer or be included in a placement file, and will be evaluated by criminal justice faculty members.

Admission Date: Fall

In-state and Out-of-state Tuition Costs:
Residents

TUITION (All required)	Fall 0-6 Units	Fall 6.010+ Units	Winter 0-6 Units	Winter 6.010+ Units	Spring 0-6 Units	Spring 6.010+ Units
Tuition Fee	$1302	$2246	$1302	$2246	$1302	$2246
Mandatory Campus Charges	$365	$365	$356	$356	$356	$356
TOTAL	$1667	$2611	$1658	$2602	$1658	$2602

All nonresidents are charged an additional $248 per unit.

Availability of Internships and Scholarships: Internship information provided at http://criminaljustice.csusb.edu/majorsprograms/internship.htm.

Orientation and Emphasis of Department/Program (Program Description): The master of arts in criminal justice is designed to serve the growing number of individuals in the criminal justice system who desire post-baccalaureate education, as well as those in more traditional public and private employment who may wish to acquire further education in criminal justice. The degree program offers two options. One is a thesis option designed for students who intend to pursue graduate studies beyond the MA level and those students who have special research interests in the criminal justice system. The examination option is for those with administrative and management goals. The program can serve a variety of student interests. It has been designed with a limited prerequisite requirement to enable students with baccalaureate degrees in related fields such as psychology, administration, anthropology, sociology or social sciences to enroll along with students with undergraduate degrees in criminal justice. The program is intended for evening students primarily and, therefore, classes will be predominately scheduled between 4:00 and 10:00 PM.

Number of Faculty: 12

Accreditation: Western Association of Schools and Colleges

Average Length of Time to Complete the Program: Not available

California State University, Stanislaus

Address: One University Circle
Turlock, CA 95382
Phone: (209) 667-3122
Website: http://www.csustan.edu/

Department: Criminal Justice
Contact: Dr. Peter Nelligan, Program Director
Phone: (209) 667-3030
Website: http://catalog.csustan.edu/preview_program.php?
catoid=9&poid=807

Type of Program: MA in Criminal Justice

Application Deadline: Preference date is April 1

Requirements:
- Completion of a bachelor's degree at an accredited college or university;
- At least fifteen pre-baccalaureate units in criminal justice, criminology, and/or a related discipline as approved by the program director;
- An undergraduate GPA of 3.0;
- A grade of B or better in an upper-division research and methodology course;
- Three letters of reference;
- A one- to two-page letter of intent specifying the applicant's interest in the program, academic and professional background in preparation of graduate study, motivation to advance in the field of criminal justice through study, and intent to study full-time or part-time;
- A sample of the applicant's written work (ideally a library research paper, a theoretical research paper, or an empirical research paper/proposal in the undergraduate major); and
- International students who have not received their undergraduate degrees from institutions in which English is the principal method of instruction must submit minimum scores of 550 total and part scores of 54 on the Test of Written English as a Second Language (TOEFL) or 213 total and part scores of 21 on the computer TOEFL.

Applications for the criminal justice program received by April 1 will receive priority consideration for admission the following Fall semester. Notification of acceptance will be issued by June 1.

Information Required for Application: See above

Admission Date: Fall

In-state and Out-of-state Tuition Costs: On campus: $23,872/academic year; off campus: $23,522/academic year

Availability of Internships and Scholarships: Not available

Orientation and Emphasis of Department/Program (Program Description): The master's in criminal justice builds upon the strong preparatory undergraduate criminal justice program with its blending of liberal arts, sciences, and applied components. Further, the relationship between the criminal justice undergraduate and graduate programs is integral in serving the educational goals of the region and the state of California, and in contributing in complementary ways to building an excellent comprehensive university. Building upon its commitment to excellence of teaching and learning in the undergraduate program, the primary responsibilities of the master's program in criminal justice include, but are not limited to, the advancement of scholarly research and preparation for students to teach in higher education. In accordance with the philosophical underpinning and institutional commitments, the primary goals of the graduate program in criminal justice are to:

- meet the public and private demand for academically-prepared and professionally-competent criminal justice practitioners;
- provide academic emphases in research and data analysis as well as criminology while adding a unique emphasis on teaching criminal justice at the post-secondary level;
- increase cultural, linguistic, and gender diversity among criminal justice practitioners in order to address the needs of a culturally and linguistically diverse community; and
- advance the university's mission by expanding students' intellectual horizons, helping them reach their potentials, and encouraging a passion for lifelong learning.

Number of Faculty: 12

Accreditation: Western Association of Schools and Colleges

Average Length of Time to Complete the Program: Not available

California University of Pennsylvania

Address: 250 University Avenue
California, PA 15419
Phone: (724) 938-4000
Website: http://www.calu.edu/

Department: Department of Justice, Law, and Society
Azorsky Hall, Rooms 117 and 118
Phone Number: (724) 938-4424 and (724) 938-4042
Fax: (724) 938-4265
Website: http://www.calu.edu/academics/colleges/liberal-arts/justice-law-society/

Type of Program: MS in Legal Studies with three concentrations from which to choose: Law and Public Policy, Homeland Security, and Criminal Justice (also available online); MA in Social Science Applied Criminology.

Application Deadline: Not available

Requirements: To be considered for admission into the legal studies program, students must have a baccalaureate degree from an accredited college or university with a minimum quality point average of 3.0 on a 4.0 scale. Those applicants possessing a GPA between 2.5 and 2.99 may be considered for admission if they submit two professional letters of recommendation as well as a current résumé indicating field experience and a listing of three references. All students who do not have a minimum 3.0 undergraduate GPA may be admitted conditionally and will be required to achieve a grade of B (3.0) or higher in each of the first two courses taken during the first semester of study.

Information Required for Application:
- Final official sealed transcripts from all colleges and universities attended;
- Online application;
- Nonrefundable $25 application fee; and
- An official transcript reflecting a baccalaureate degree from an accredited institution. Official transcripts from institutions where a degree was not conferred will only be required in cases where the student wishes to have a transfer of credit evaluation completed.

Admission Date: Not available

In-state and Out-of-state Tuition Costs:

Graduate Student Tuition (per Semester), Pennsylvania Residents	
Type of Student	Cost
Graduate Student	$442 per credit

Graduate Student Tuition (per Semester), Non-Pennsylvania Residents	
Type of Student	Cost
Graduate Student	$663 per credit

Availability of Internships and Scholarships: Graduate as well as undergraduate students may be eligible for a variety of university and endowed scholarships. Each scholarship has special selection and awarding criteria that were agreed upon by the university and the scholarship donor (if applicable). In order to streamline the selection process, California University of Pennsylvania does not use a scholarship application. Rather, all accepted students and currently enrolled students are considered for all possible university scholarships. However, selected applicants for some of the scholarship awards may be required to complete additional information for final determination of the award. If a scholarship application is required for a particular scholarship, it must be submitted to the Financial Aid Office by May 1. The scholarships offered range from $100 to full tuition for an academic year. Many of the scholarships are renewable awards based on the student maintaining minimum academic standards and demonstrating financial need, if applicable. The Financial Aid Office or designated selection committee will select the best applicant(s) from the pool of students who meet the minimum qualifications for the scholarship. Website: http://www.calu.edu/prospective/graduate/tuition-and-financial-aid/types-of-financial-aid/scholarships/index.htm.

Orientation and Emphasis of Department/Program (Program Description): Student in our online legal studies program are part of a community of scholars who yearn for further knowledge about law and public policy in a local, regional, and international sense. In law and legal systems, both individuals and the collectives come to depend on the promise of order and communal stability. In jurisprudence and legal analysis, students will become adept at the real purpose of law in modern life: not only the maintenance of order and the regulation of things but also the assurance that communities and nations can live in harmony and with due respect for the rights of individuals and sovereignties. We offer three concentrations:

- Law and Public Policy: This concentration is directed at those who labor in law beyond the usual targets of judges and lawyers, and delivers a highly sophisticated legal education that leads to greater levels of understanding and responsibility. The program will help you strive for personal, intellectual, occupational, and professional perfection.
- Homeland Security: This concentration prepares students to tackle the many challenges inherent in the protection of a nation. It allows justice professionals, health specialists and legal specialists to concentrate on the methodology of security in this narrow context. Aside from the recurring demands of professional justice duty, homeland security delivers another slant and perspective to harried and often over-tasked public servants.
- Criminal Justice: This concentration prepares learned and erudite justice practitioners who will assume leadership positions in the justice sector and make substantial contributions to the betterment of the legal and justice systems and the community served.

Number of Faculty: 12

Accreditation: The Middle States Association. The program is approved by the Pennsylvania State System of Higher Education Board of Governors.

Average Length of Time to Complete the Program: Not available

Calumet College of Saint Joseph

Address: Calumet College of St. Joseph
Whiting, IN 46394
Phone: (219) 473-4215
Website: http://www.ccsj.edu/

Department: Public Safety Administration
Room 100A
Phone: (219) 473-4274
Fax: (219) 473-4610
Website: http://www.ccsj.edu/academics/graduate/psa/

Type of Program: MS in Public Safety Administration

Application Deadline: Not available

Requirements:
- Have graduated from an accredited post-secondary institution with a baccalaureate degree;
- Present evidence of a 3.0 grade point average on a 4.0 scale for all undergraduate course work;
- Submit a one-page typed statement of purpose indicating interest in the graduate program; and
- Complete the application process.

Information Required for Application:
- Secure an application packet from the coordinator of Graduate Student Services at (219) 473-4295; and
- Complete the application form and submit it with the $25 application fee and appropriate accompanying documents at least two months prior to the cohort start date. Accompanying documents would include a written statement of purpose indicating interest in the program and official transcripts reflecting all undergraduate and/or graduate coursework completed.

Admission Date: Not available

In-state and Out-of-state Tuition Costs: Not listed for graduate programs

Availability of Internships and Scholarships:
To be eligible for an assistantship, the student must first gain admission to graduate study. He or she must register and maintain at least six semester credits of graduate coursework. Full-time assistantships are awarded for each academic year but can be awarded for up to two years. Students must apply each academic year.

- There is a limit of two graduate assistants per a graduate program (certain conditions apply).
- Graduate assistants receive a full tuition waiver for up to twelve credits per semester (fees not included).
- Graduate assistants work approximately fifteen hours a week while school is in session during the academic year.
- Only students in good academic standing with a minimum graduate GPA of 3.0 are eligible for selection as graduate assistants.
- The GPA of 3.0 must be maintained during the assistantship process.

Orientation and Emphasis of Department/Program (Program Description): The master of science in public safety administration is an innovative and practitioner-oriented degree offering. The program complements and expands the institution's historic commitment to addressing the educational need of individuals engaged in law enforcement and related fields. Structured as an accelerated, adult-learning initiative, the degree program removes the time and space barriers that often prevent working professionals from completing graduate level education.

Number of Faculty: 10

Accreditation: Higher Learning Commission, a member of North Central Association

Average Length of Time to Complete the Program: Not available

Capella University

Address: Online
Phone: (866) 679-9682
Website: http://www.capella.edu/

Department: School of Public Service Leadership
Phone: (866) 933-5943
Website: http://www.capella.edu/online-degrees/phd-criminal-justice/

Type of Program: MS in Public Safety; PhD in Public Safety

Application Deadline: Not available

Requirements:
Master's
- Bachelor's degree from an institution accredited by a U.S. Department of Education–recognized accrediting agency or an internationally recognized institution;
- Grade point average of 2.3 or higher on a 4.0 scale; and
- A $50 nonrefundable application fee for initiating an application for admission (may be paid as part of the application process).

Doctoral
- Master's degree from an institution accredited by a U.S. Department of Education–recognized accrediting agency or an internationally recognized institution;
- Grade point average of 3.0 or higher on a 4.0 scale; and
- A $50 nonrefundable application fee for initiating an application for admission (may be paid as part of the application process).

Information Required for Application: See above

Admission Date: Fall: October 7

In-state and Out-of-state Tuition Costs:
Master's: $473 per credit

Doctoral
- Quarterly tuition: $4,665;
- Quarterly tuition for comprehensive examination and dissertation courses: $4,175; and
- Tuition per colloquium: $1,495.

Learners in this program have the option of taking PSL8002, the first required course in the program, at the discounted tuition rate of $3,732 if they take that course alone in the initial quarter of their program.

This tuition estimate is effective July 8, 2013, and is subject to change. Students may take one to three courses per quarter.

Availability of Internships and Scholarships: For the master's program, the MS in Public Safety Grant **pays** $3,000, distributed evenly over seven consecutive quarters. New students seeking the MS in Public Safety with specializations in criminal justice, emergency management, or public safety leadership are eligible. Students must start their program between October 7 and December 2 and pass their first course. The grant is available until December 2. To receive the grant, students must apply before their first course begins and no later than December 2. Late applications will not be accepted.

Orientation and Emphasis of Department/Program (Program Description):

Master's: Advance your career and increase your effectiveness in the fields of corrections, criminal justice, or the judicial system by broadening your skill set and deepening your understanding of the complex issues surrounding criminal behavior. This online master's in criminal justice covers such topics as human behavior, the corrections and judicial systems, social change and public policy, ethnic and cultural awareness, and contributing factors such as addiction.

Doctoral: Make a difference in your career and your community through this criminal justice PhD, designed to prepare you to initiate positive change in the criminal justice system. The intensive program includes online course work, residencies, and research that address the complex issues surrounding criminal behavior, prevention and intervention, the penal system, and the development of public policy strategies at the community, state, and national levels. People who choose this doctoral specialization are often pursuing high-level positions in higher education, a research or consulting agency, a public policy group, or other criminal justice-related organizations.

Number of Faculty: 2

Accreditation: The Higher Learning Commission, a member of the North Central Association of Colleges and Schools

Average Length of Time to Complete the Program: Not available

Carnegie Mellon University

Address: 5000 Forbes Avenue
Pittsburgh, PA 15213
Phone: (412) 268-2000
Website: http://www.cmu.edu/

Department: Philosophy
Baker Hall 135
Carnegie Mellon University
Pittsburgh, PA 15213-3890
Phone: (412) 268-8568
Fax: (412) 268-1440
Website: http://www.hss.cmu.edu/philosophy/

Type of Program: MA in Philosophy (research area of criminal justice)

Application Deadline: Fall: early January

Requirements: No specifics listed

Information Required for Application:
Applications for MA degrees must include:
• Graduate application;
• Sample of original written work;
• Personal research statement;
• Three (or more) letters of recommendation;
• Transcripts from all previously attended colleges or universities;
• GRE scores (institution code: 2074; department code: 2801);
• TOEFL or IELTS scores for non-native English speaking applicants; and $50 application fee.

Scanned versions of official GRE and TOEFL/IELTS scores can be uploaded in place of sending official score reports.

Admission Date: Fall, Spring

In-state and Out-of-state Tuition Costs: Total year: $59,616; Fall semester: $30,353; Spring semester: $29,263

Availability of Internships and Scholarships: Grants and unpaid internships: http://www.cmu.edu/hss/globalstudies/images/Summer-grant-opps-for-unpaid-internships.pdf

Orientation and Emphasis of Department/Program (Program Description): Criminal justice policy is one of the interdisciplinary areas of research and teaching in the department. Criminal justice is concerned with the institutions that administer and enforce the criminal law and the norms that govern—or should govern—those institutions, their policies, and the criminal law itself. Criminal justice is informed by criminology, a multidisciplinary field partaking of the social, cognitive, behavioral, and forensic sciences. Other aspects of criminal justice are concerned with non-criminals as victims and resistors as well as with non-criminal activities (such as legal firearms commerce and ownership). Moral-political philosophy and philosophic jurisprudence are concerned with criminal justice and the criminal law in at least the following respects: (1) What is justice?; 2) What is just (criminal) law?; and (3) What are justifiable policies for enforcing the criminal law and effecting justice in society by means of criminal law? There are several theories of justice (distributive, compensatory, retributive) and several theories of the justifiability of enforcement of—or penalty for—infractions of the criminal law (incapacitation, deterrence, rehabilitation, retribution). And there are a variety of moral philosophic theories one might appeal to in trying to justify specific criminal laws or criminal justice policies (utilitarian, deontological, social contractarian). Research topics in criminal justice or criminal law that Department faculty pursue include the following:

1. Controversy over the putative right to die underlying the issue of medically assisted suicide in the criminal law (Cavalier, Covey);
2. The public policy issue of gun control (Covey);
3. The law and ethics that govern law enforcement officers (Covey, London); and
4. The law and ethics of self-defense, as apply to victims or potential victims of criminal violence (Covey).

Number of Faculty: 28

Accreditation: Middle States Commission on Higher Education

Average Length of Time to Complete the Program: Not available

Central Connecticut State University

Address: 1615 Stanley Street
New Britain, CT 06053
Phone: (860) 832-2278
Website: http://www.ccsu.edu/

Department: Department of Criminology and Criminal Justice
RVAC 208
Phone: (860) 832-3005
Fax: (860) 832-3014
E-mail: oteroca@ccsu.edu
Website: http://www.ccsu.edu/page.cfm?p=4830

Type of Program: MS in Criminal Justice

Application Deadline: June 1, November 1

Requirements:
In addition to standard University graduate admission requirements, the department requires:
- A minimum grade point average (GPA) of 3.00 on a 4.00 scale;
- One undergraduate social science research methods course with a grade of C or better;
- One undergraduate elementary statistics course with a grade of C or better;
- A formal application essay that focuses on (a) academic and work history, (b) reasons for pursuing graduate studies in criminal justice, and (c) future career goals; and
- A résumé.

Information Required for Application:
- Have your previous college(s) and university(ies) send directly to Graduate Recruitment and Admissions Office official transcripts for each course you have taken. We cannot accept hand-delivered transcripts.
- Sign and date the back page of the application.
- Submit the $50 processing fee (this fee is nonrefundable).
- Specify your complete address and telephone number.
- Contact your academic department for information about specific program and admissions requirements.
- Submit required additional materials to the academic department (e.g., departmental packet, essay). See additional materials list at http://finalsite.ccsu.edu/page.cfm?p=1116.

Admission Date: Spring, Fall

In-state and Out-of-state Tuition Costs: Connecticut resident (graduate): $3,919.50; non-resident (graduate) $8,467.50

Availability of Internships and Scholarships: Not listed

Orientation and Emphasis of Department/Program (Program Description): The master of science degree is designed to provide students with the knowledge and skills required for leadership positions in the criminal justice system and continued study at the doctoral level. The criminal justice graduate program strongly emphasizes the application of theory and research in executive decision-making, policy development and analysis, and the treatment of offenders.

Number of Faculty: 9

Accreditation: New England Association of Schools and Colleges

Average Length of Time to Complete the Program: Not available

Chaminade University of Honolulu

Address: 3140 Waialae Avenue
Honolulu, HI 96816
Phone: (808) 735-4711
Website: http://www.chaminade.edu/

Department: Department of Criminal Justice
Behavioral Sciences Division
Behavioral Sciences Building 105A
3140 Waialae Avenue
Honolulu, HI 96816
Phone: (808) 735-4751
Website: http://www.chaminade.edu/criminal-justice/

Type of Program: MS in Criminal Justice Administration (online)

Application Deadline: Not available

Requirements:
- Bachelor's degree earned from an accredited university or college;
- Grade point average of 3.0 or higher (on a 4.0 scale). The applicant must have achieved a cumulative GPA of 3.0 or higher in one of the following ways: (1) a cumulative GPA of 3.0 or higher (on a 4.0 scale) in all coursework; or (2) a cumulative GPA of 3.0 or higher in a minimum of nine graduate hours of coursework from an accredited university or college.
- Completed graduate application; and
- Interview. Upon receipt of the completed graduate application file, all applicants will participate in a formal interview with a member of the MSCJA faculty. If deemed necessary, a second interview with the program director and/or another MSCJA faculty member may be required. If the completed graduate application file is not received in a timely manner, this will delay the interview process, thus delaying the applicant's possible entry into the program.

Information Required for Application:
- Non-refundable application fee of $50 (paper application) or $25 (online application);
- Official transcripts from all previous universities or colleges attended. Sealed official transcripts must be sent directly to the Graduate Services Office at Chaminade University of Honolulu. Official transcripts are defined as being generated by the Registrar's or Records Office, with the signature and/or seal of the Registrar;

- Letters of recommendation. Three letters of recommendation from individuals who are qualified to comment on the student's potential for successful graduate study in criminal justice administration are required. Letters from previous instructors are preferable; however, letters from other qualified individuals (i.e. employers) may be submitted. Letters of Recommendation should be submitted to the Graduate Services Office;
- Test of English as a Foreign Language (TOEFL). An applicant from a foreign country for whom English is a second language must submit a Test of English as a Foreign Language (TOEFL) score of at least 550. The TOEFL is waived for foreign students who have graduated from an accredited American university or college.; and
- Interview. Upon receipt of the completed graduate application file, all applicants will participate in a formal interview with a member of the MSCJA faculty. If deemed necessary, a second interview with the program director and/or another MSCJA faculty member may be required. If the completed graduate application file is not received in a timely manner, this will delay the interview process, thus delaying the applicant's possible entry into the program.

Admission Date: Fall, Winter, Spring, and Summer

In-state and Out-of-state Tuition Costs: Off-campus graduate costs: $35,896 per year. Tuition is $655 per credit hour

Availability of Internships and Scholarships: Not available

Orientation and Emphasis of Department/Program (Program Description): The goals of the master of science in criminal justice administration (MSCJA) program are to enable students to develop critical thinking skills, and the ability to review, analyze, and disseminate applied theoretical knowledge pertaining to criminal justice administration. In addition, the MSCJA program prepares students for instructional positions within the academic community as well as admission to other graduate programs. The MSCJA degree is recommended for those individuals who are pursuing careers or further education in the following:
- Federal, state, county, and municipal law enforcement;
- Homeland security and leadership development;
- Private security and investigation;
- Probation, parole, and community corrections; and
- Law school.

Number of Faculty: 16 in the Behavioral Sciences Department (no specific list for Criminal Justice only)

Accreditation: Accrediting Commission for Senior Colleges and Universities of the Western Association of Schools and Colleges

Average Length of Time to Complete the Program: Not available. Time limit to complete the degree is five years.

Charleston Southern University

Address: 9200 University Boulevard
North Charleston, SC 29406
Phone: (843) 863-7000
Website: http://www.csuniv.edu/

Department: Department of Criminal Justice
Contact: Jordan Katie Stauffer, Graduate Enrollment Counselor
E-mail: jstauffer@csuniv.edu
Phone: (843) 863-5501
Website: http://csuniv.edu/criminaljustice/master/
curriculum.html

Type of Program: MS in Criminal Justice

Application Deadline: Not available

Requirements: Regular admission requires that the student has met all of the following requirements:
- The applicant has submitted a completed application for admission and résumé to the Graduate Center.
- The applicant has taken the Graduate Record Examination (GRE) or Miller Analogies Test (MAT) within the last five years, and the scores have been received by the Graduate Center. An undergraduate GPA of 3.5 may be substituted for the graduate school entry examination.
- The student has earned a baccalaureate degree from a regionally accredited senior institution.

Information Required for Application:
- The student has provided the Graduate Center with official transcripts from all institutions where undergraduate or graduate courses have been taken.
- The student has provided the Graduate Center with two letters of recommendation from individuals familiar with the student's work or academic record. Recommendations from family members are not acceptable.
- The student has provided the Graduate Center with a personal letter of work experience no more than 500 words outlining his or her academic and career goals.

Admission Date: Not available

In-state and Out-of-state Tuition Costs: $470 per credit hour

Availability of Internships and Scholarships: Internships and employment have been offered through the following:
- 15th Solicitor's Office (Horry and Georgetown Counties, SC);
- Charleston, SC, Police;
- Dorchester County, SC, Sheriff's Office;
- Federal Law Enforcement Training Center;
- Georgetown, SC, Sheriff's Office;
- Horry County, SC, Police;
- Myrtle Beach, SC, Police;
- North Charleston, SC, Police;
- North Myrtle Beach, SC, Police;
- Pawleys Island, SC, Police;
- South Carolina Department of Juvenile Justice;
- South Carolina Department of Probation and Parole;
- Summerville, SC, Police;
- United States Bureau of Alcohol, Tobacco, Firearms, and Explosives;
- United States Central Intelligence Agency;
- United States Department of Homeland Security;
- United States Department of Justice;
- United States Department of Labor;
- United States Department of Treasury;
- United States Drug Enforcement Administration;
- United States Federal Bureau of Investigation; and
- United States Secret Service.

Orientation and Emphasis of Department/Program (Program Description): The master of science in criminal justice degree is designed to provide an advanced understanding of the nature of crime, society's reaction to it, and the various components of the criminal justice system. The program of study enhances professional development for those seeking managerial and leadership roles as well as preparing students seeking to enter law school or complete a doctoral degree.

Number of Faculty: 6

Accreditation: Southern Association of Colleges and Schools

Average Length of Time to Complete the Program: Not available

Chicago State University

Address: 9501 South King Drive
Chicago, IL 60628
Phone: (773) 995-2000
Website: http://www.csu.edu/

Department: Department of Criminal Justice
329 Harold Washington Hall
Phone: (773) 995-2108
Fax: (773) 995-3819
Website: http://www.csu.edu/cas/criminalphilosophypolitical/
criminaljustice/

Type of Program: MS in Criminal Justice

Application Deadline: June 21, October 15

Requirements:
- Proof of a bachelor's degree from a regionally accredited college or university is required. Applicants must ensure that each college or university of previous or current attendance (other than Chicago State University) sends the Graduate School an official transcript.
- Certain graduate programs have additional requirements, such as the Graduate Record Examination (GRE), verification of teaching experience, and/or letters of recommendation, among others.

Information Required for Application:
- Nonrefundable application processing fee of $30;
- Completed application for admission, via mail or online;
- Official transcripts;
- Statement of goals and objectives: The applicant must provide a typed, double-spaced career statement indicating the applicant's reason for graduate study in the program selected; and
- Program-specific Requirements. Certain graduate programs have additional requirements, such as the Graduate Record Examination (GRE), verification of teaching experience. and/or letters of recommendation, among others.

Admission Date: Fall, Spring

In-state and Out-of-state Tuition Costs:

Tuition per Credit Hour	Number Credit Hours	Total
$276	1-11	$699 - $3459
$276	12-15+	$4519 - $5347

Availability of Internships and Scholarships: Not available

Orientation and Emphasis of Department/Program (Program Description): The Department of Criminal Justice offers the bachelor of science degree and the master of science degree in criminal justice. The program provides students with a broad foundation in the social sciences while emphasizing restorative justice, social and economic justice, fairness, community involvement, and public safety.

Number of Faculty: 13

Accreditation: Higher Learning Commission

Average Length of Time to Complete the Program: Not available

Clark Atlanta University

Address: 223 James P. Brawley Drive Southwest
Atlanta, GA 30314
Phone: (404) 880-8000
Website: http://www.cau.edu/

Department: Department of Sociology and Criminal Justice
Oglethorpe Hall, Room 219
Phone: (404) 880-6659
Website: http://www.cau.edu/Academics_Sociology_and_J_Welcome.aspx

Type of Program: MA in Criminal Justice

Application Deadline: April 1, October 1

Requirements: Candidates seeking admission to the graduate program of criminal justice must meet the general requirements of the university and of the School of Arts and Sciences. Students must have taken the Graduate Record Examination aptitude test and should have a broadly based background in the social and behavioral sciences. Applicants must have a grade point average of 3.0 in their area of specialization. The undergraduate major should include at least one course in criminal justice theory. At the discretion of the departmental graduate committee, deficiencies in the above areas may be removed by other course work in the graduate program. Persons admitted into the program without an undergraduate degree or experience in criminal justice will be required to take undergraduate prerequisites (six to nine semester hours) as deemed appropriate by the department.

Information Required for Application: Not available

Admission Date: Fall, Spring, Summer

In-state and Out-of-state Tuition Costs: $719 per credit hour

Availability of Internships and Scholarships: Not available

Orientation and Emphasis of Department/Program (Program Description): The Department of Sociology and Criminal Justice houses two programs. Four degrees are offered from these programs: two undergraduate degrees (bachelor of arts in Sociology and bachelor of arts in criminal justice) and two graduate degrees (master of arts in Sociology and master of arts in criminal justice). The department consists of ten full time faculty members with substantive research and teaching backgrounds and training. With an emphasis on teaching, this diversity facilitates comprehensive learning. In addition to core theoretical foundations in sociology, criminology, and criminal justice, departmental strengths include quantitative methodology and analysis. However, environmental justice, medical sociology, law enforcement and corrections are the primary areas of faculty research activity and service. Over the years, the faculty have obtained and administered several grants from federal, state and local governments and private organizations.

Number of Faculty: 10

Accreditation: Southern Association of Colleges and Schools Commission

Average Length of Time to Complete the Program: Two years

Colorado Technical University, Colorado Springs, Denver, Sioux Falls

Address: 4435 North Chestnut Street
Colorado Springs, CO 80907
Phone: (855) 230-0555
Website: http://www.coloradotech.edu/colorado-Springs/

Department: Criminal Justice
Website: http://www.coloradotech.edu/degrees/masters/criminal-justice/

Type of Program: MS in Criminal Justice

Application Deadline: Not available

Requirements: Not available

Information Required for Application: Not available

Admission Date: Not available

In-state and Out-of-state Tuition Costs: $585 per credit; total cost is $30,420 for fifty-two credits

Availability of Internships and Scholarships: Not available

Orientation and Emphasis of Department/Program (Program Description): Develop essential leadership skills relevant to the areas of law enforcement, corrections, the court systems and criminal justice education as you build a strong foundation in public policy, research and legal precedent. Colorado Technical University's master of science in criminal justice degree program is designed for professionals seeking new skills in law enforcement, corrections and the court systems. Coursework for this degree provides a foundation for students interested in pursuing roles throughout the criminal justice industry. This program is structured specifically to develop the knowledge base and skills essential to those who strive to pursue opportunities in policy development, planning, and decision-making in the criminal justice system. The curriculum also serves as preparation for students interested in leadership and teaching roles in criminal justice settings. Concentrations are offered to allow students the opportunity to specialize their master of science in criminal justice degree in order to better prepare for their future. Students can choose from a general concentrations or a concentration in homeland security.

Number of Faculty: 3

Accreditation: Colorado Technical University is accredited by the Higher Learning Commission and a member of the North Central Association of Colleges and Schools

Average Length of Time to Complete the Program: Not available

Columbia College (MO)

Address: 1001 Rogers Street
Columbia, MO 65201
Phone: (573) 875-8700
Website: http://www.ccis.edu/

Department: Not available (under Graduate Studies)
Website: http://www.ccis.edu/graduate/

Type of Program: MS in Criminal Justice Administration

Application Deadline: Not available

Requirements: In general, the admission requirement for full admission to Columbia College graduate programs is a cumulative undergraduate grade point average of 3.0. The MS in criminal justice administration also requires:
- A baccalaureate degree in criminal justice with a minimum cumulative GPA of 3.0 from an accredited college or university; and
- Official transcripts of all college coursework.

Information Required for Application:
- Completed application including narrative component;
- Three completed recommendation forms; and
- Professional goal statement.

Admission Date: Not available

In-state and Out-of-state Tuition Costs: On-campus graduate tuition: $325per credit hour

Availability of Internships and Scholarships: Not available

Orientation and Emphasis of Department/Program (Program Description): You have the option of pursuing the Online MSCJ via the Online Campus or through any one of our thirty-five nationwide campuses. The benefits of being affiliated with a physical campus near you are in-person academic advising, local proctors for online exams, the option to take a mix of online and on-campus courses (where available), and more. The following campuses offer on-campus graduate coursework leading to completion of a master of science in criminal justice administration degree:
- Columbia, MO (main campus)
- Hancock Field, NY
- Orlando, FL

Number of Faculty: Not available

Accreditation: The Higher Learning Commission and a member of the North Central Association

Average Length of Time to Complete the Program: Not available

Concordia University, St. Paul

Address: 1282 Concordia Avenue
St. Paul, MN 55104
Phone: (651) 641-8278
Website: http://www.csp.edu/

Department: Department of Criminal Justice
Contact: Michael Conner
E-mail: conner@csp.edu
Phone: (651) 641-8249
Website: http://www.csp.edu/academics/areas-of-study/
criminal-justice/

Type of Program: MA in Criminal Justice Leadership (online)

Application Deadline: Not available

Requirements:
- Apply online.
- Submit official transcripts from the regionally accredited institution stating the conferral of a bachelor's degree with a minimum cumulative GPA of 3.0 based on a 4.0 system.
- Submit a typed personal statement that answers the questions listed below. Completed statements should be labeled with your name, academic program, and your contact information and submitted via mail, e-mail or fax. Each question should be answered in a minimum of 300 words (one page). Questions: Why are you choosing to pursue a graduate program at this time in your career, and what are you hoping to accomplish by doing so? What strengths do you feel make you a strong candidate for the program? Describe a past or present personal/professional experience that you believe positively influenced your potential to succeed in a graduate program.
- Submit a current, professional résumé.

Information Required for Application: Listed above

Admission Date: Spring, Summer

In-state and Out-of-state Tuition Costs: $475 per credit hour (thirty-six total hours)

Availability of Internships and Scholarships: Not available

Orientation and Emphasis of Department/Program (Program Description): The master of arts in criminal justice leadership program consists of thirty-six credit hours and is offered fully online. The online master's in criminal justice format is designed for busy adult students who are interested in obtaining their degree and require the flexibility of attending class on their schedule. The online masters in criminal justice coursework is more challenging, self-directed, and creative than its undergraduate counterpart. The courses are designed to enhance current professionalism and to position students for leadership opportunities. Current students in the program come from a variety of backgrounds, including law enforcement, military and social service, and corrections.

Number of Faculty: 5

Accreditation: Higher Learning Commission and a member of the North Central Association

Average Length of Time to Complete the Program: Seven weeks

Coppin State University

Address: 2500 West North Avenue
Baltimore, MD 21216
Phone: (410) 951-3000
Website: http://www.coppin.edu/

Department: Department of Criminal Justice and Law
Enforcement
HHSB, Room 518
Phone: (410)951-3044
Website: http://www.coppin.edu/info/200131/academic_
programs/59/all_academic_programs/40/

Type of Program: MS in Criminal Justice

Application Deadline: Not available

Requirements:
- Complete the application for admission and return it with the nonrefundable application fee of $50 to the Office of Admissions, Coppin State University, School of Graduate Studies, 2500 West North Avenue, Baltimore, MD 21216-3698.
- Arrange to have official copies of test scores, if applicable, and official transcripts sent from all college and universities attended, and three letters of recommendation sent to the director of the Office of Admissions at the above address. Transcripts sent by the student are not acceptable.

Information Required for Application:
- Official transcripts from the undergraduate degree granting institution and all other colleges and universities attended; and
- Three current letters of reference from the current employer, instructors, or other persons who can attest to the student's character, integrity, and academic potential.

Admission Date: Not available

In-state and Out-of-state Tuition Costs: In-state residents: $270 per credit hour; out-of state: $490 per credit hour

Availability of Internships and Scholarships: Each student working toward a master's degree in Criminal Justice is encouraged to complete a minimum of three credit hours in either field training or an internship in a criminal justice setting related to the area of specialization. The field training/internship experience consists of a minimum of ninety clock hours of field-related experience for one full semester. The primary objective of the field training/internship is to enable the student to experience criminal justice system practices in action. Field training/internship involves placement in agencies that agree to provide supervised experience at a level corresponding to the student's academic development and career goals. Because field training/internship is viewed as an opportunity to integrate concepts acquired in the classroom with the practical problems of the criminal justice field, students will normally not be approved for enrollment in the field training/internship prior to completion of a minimum of twenty-five hours of graduate credit.

Federal Work-Study: The Federal Work-Study program provides jobs to graduate students who have demonstrated financial need. These jobs are assigned as part of the financial package.

Loans: Loans include the Federal Perkins Loan (formally National Direct Student Loan), which is a long-term low interest loan available in amounts up to $1,500 per year. The Federal Direct Loan program includes both federal subsidized and the federal unsubsidized loans, which can provide up to $20,500 per year for graduate students. Further information about the Federal Direct Loans can be obtained from the Coppin Financial Aid Office.

Student Emergency Loan Fund (SELF): The SELF is intended to assist students attending Coppin with emergency financial assistance in time of need. The loan is specifically earmarked to cover such emergencies as rent evictions, gas and electric turn-off notices, carfare, childcare, and food. The student must be due a financial aid refund.

Bookstore Charge Authorization: The bookstore charge authorization allows financial aid recipients to charge books and supplies at the university bookstore. This service is available only to students due refund monies after their semester charges have been applied. Graduate students are limited to a $500 charge per semester.

Orientation and Emphasis of Department/Program (Program Description): The Department of Criminal Justice offers a program leading to the MS degree. The primary purpose of the program is to provide the criminal justice student with a broad knowledge base and specialized technical training in criminal justice. Course work in the program is designed to increase individual competency, develop analytical thought processes, and facilitate the development of abilities and skills. Course work focuses on examination of contemporary issues in the administration of justice counseling, research, and management problems in the fields of criminal justice and correctional education. Through the advanced study of theoretical and applied issues the master's degree student will be prepared to assume leadership positions in the field of criminal justice.

Number of Faculty: 7

Accreditation: Middle States Association of Colleges and Schools

Average Length of Time to Complete the Program: Not available

Delta State University

Address: 1003 West Sunflower Road
Cleveland, MS 38733
Phone: (662) 846-3000
Website: http://www.deltastate.edu/

Department: Department of Social Justice and Criminology
Contact: Dr. Gavin Lee, Graduate Program Coordinator
210 Kethley Hall
Phone: (662) 846-4093
E-mail: glee@deltastate.edu
Website: http://www.deltastate.edu/college-of-arts-and-sciences/social-sciences-history/undergraduate-programs/social-justice-criminlology/

Type of Program: MS in Social Justice and Criminology

Application Deadline: Not available

Requirements:
- An undergraduate degree in the proposed area of study or a related area;
- A minimum acceptable overall undergraduate grade point average of 3.00 with a 3.00 GPA minimum on all major and other relevant coursework completed during the applicant's last sixty-four undergraduate hours. Applicants may be considered for conditional admission to the program if they have at least three years of successful relevant experience supported by three letters of recommendation from practitioners in the field. In addition, candidates must also be interviewed by the social justice and criminology graduate committee to determine eligibility; and
- A satisfactory score on a nationally recognized, standardized test of verbal skills. (e.g., a minimum score of 3 on the CAAP exam).

Information Required for Application: Not listed

Admission Date: Summer, Fall, Spring

In-state and Out-of-state Tuition Costs: $3,006 (9-13 credits)

Availability of Internships and Scholarships: Not available

Orientation and Emphasis of Department/Program (Program Description): The master of science degree in social justice and criminology is a graduate degree designed for students who wish to pursue academic and/or professional roles in the criminal justice system. Whether you are an experienced professional in the criminal justice field or a recent college graduate considering a career in criminal justice, the social justice and criminology program at Delta State has something to offer you. Delta State is unique in that it provides students with both small class size and matches each student with a faculty advisor to oversee their progress through the program.

Number of Faculty: 3

Accreditation: Southern Association of Colleges and Schools

Average Length of Time to Complete the Program: Not available

DeSales University

Address: 2755 Station Avenue
Center Valley, PA 18034-9568
Phone: (610) 282-1100
Website: http://www.desales.edu/

Department: Department of Criminal Justice
Center Valley Campus
Dooling Hall
2755 Station Avenue
Center Valley, PA 18034
Phone: (610) 282-4361
Website: http://www.desales.edu/home/academics/access/
programs-of-study/in-class-hybrid-degrees/criminal-justice/

Type of Program: MA in Criminal Justice

Application Deadline: Rolling

Requirements:
- A bachelor's degree from a college or university accredited by one of the six regional accrediting bodies (Middle States, New England, North Central, Northwest, Southern, and Western Association of Schools and Colleges) or its equivalent from a foreign institution;
- Background or interest in the field of criminal justice;
- Evidence of potential for graduate work. A personal statement must be submitted that will serve as a demonstration of your ability to write at the graduate level. It should state your personal and professional goals, as well as how an MACJ degree from DeSales University can assist you in achieving them; and
- Three letters of recommendation.

Information Required for Application:
- Recommended way to apply: Online
- Application Fee: $50
- Standardized Exam Required: No
- Official Transcripts Required: Yes
- Personal Statement Required: Yes
- Letters of Recommendation: Three required
- Résumé Required: No

Admission Date: Rolling

In-state and Out-of-state Tuition Costs: $765 per credit hour

Availability of Internships and Scholarships: Not available

Orientation and Emphasis of Department/Program (Program Description): Criminal justice continues to dominate the news and challenge those who study and work in this arena. Science and technology have transformed the criminal justice field. The DeSales University master of arts in criminal justice (MACJ) program addresses these new realities. There are three MACJ program options; all have a strong focus on high ethical standards. A traditional, in-class approach is available if you are interested in a fundamental graduate education in criminal justice. If you have specific interests in investigative forensics or digital forensics, we offer two online MACJ degree programs.

Number of Faculty: 13

Accreditation: Middle States Commission on Higher Education

Average Length of Time to Complete the Program: Not available

Drury University

Address: 900 North Benton Avenue
Springfield, MO 65802
Phone: (417) 873-7879
Website: http://www.drury.edu/

Department: Department of Behavioral Sciences
Contact: Dr. Vickie Luttrell, Chair of Behavioral Sciences and Professor of Psychology
Phone: (417) 873-7254
Website: http://www.drury.edu/section/section.cfm?sid=316

Type of Program: MA in Criminology; MS in Criminal Justice

Application Deadline: Not available

Requirements:
- A completed application form;
- $25 nonrefundable application fee; and
- Official transcripts of all college work (sent to the Graduate Programs Office by the issuing institution).

Information Required for Application:
- Unless previously accepted into a graduate program, each applicant must take the Graduate Record Examination (GRE) or Miller Analogies Test (MAT). The tests are used as a guide for determining full admission to the program and for advisor counseling. The MAT is given at Drury University and the GRE is a computer-based test. Foreign applicants are also required to take the Test of English as a Foreign Language (TOEFL). Information regarding the MAT may be obtained from the testing center, Findlay Student Center, Room 120, (417) 873-7419.
- Two letters of recommendation are required of all applicants and should be sent to the Graduate Programs Office.
- A personal statement indicating the applicant's desire to pursue a graduate degree in education must be submitted to the Graduate Programs Office.

Admission Date: Fall, Spring, Summer

In-state and Out-of-state Tuition Costs: $440 per credit hour

Availability of Internships and Scholarships: The Archie and Marion Russell Scholarship (amounts vary) is available to undergraduate or graduate students who have completed a minimum of thirty college credit hours, have a 3.0 cumulative GPA and are admitted into a degree-seeking program. Scholarships are nonrenewable, but students may re-apply. Apply online for the Archie and Marion Russell Scholarship prior to the semester in which you would like to receive it (deadline is one week prior to the start of classes). Students may also apply for additional outside scholarships or additional loans, if necessary.

Orientation and Emphasis of Department/Program (Program Description): The master of arts in criminology and the master of science in criminal justice programs are carefully integrated with the undergraduate program and grows out of the institutional commitment to the liberal arts. It is intended to provide sound preparation for careers while explaining the breadth of perspective and flexibility that characterize the liberal arts graduate. The master of arts in criminology degree is especially recommended for students who will eventually pursue a PhD

Number of Faculty: 6

Accreditation: Higher Learning Commission and a member of the North Central Association

Average Length of Time to Complete the Program: Not available

East Carolina University

Address: 1001 East 5th Street
Greenville, NC 27858
Phone: (252) 328-6131
Website: http://www.ecu.edu/

Department: Department of Criminal Justice
Contact: William P. Bloss, Chair
247 Rivers Building
Website: http://www.ecu.edu/cs-acad/grcat/programJUST.cfm

Type of Program: MS in Criminal Justice

Application Deadline: April 1, October 1

Requirements: Each applicant is reviewed individually by the admissions committee. No single criterion determines acceptance or rejection. A bachelor's degree from an accredited academic institution with a minimum overall undergraduate grade point average of 2.7 on a 4.0 scale is required. Transfer credit must be established at the time of admittance.

Information Required for Application:
- Three letters of recommendation;
- Purpose statement;
- GRE scores;
- Official transcript(s); and
- A paid and completed application

Admission Date: Fall, Spring

In-state and Out-of-state Tuition Costs: Residents: $4,223 per year; non-residents: $16,540 per year

Availability of Internships and Scholarships: Not available

Orientation and Emphasis of Department/Program (Program Description): The master's program in criminal justice prepares students to become highly skilled and competent professionals who are equipped to seek advancements in the criminal justice profession, teach on the community college level, or pursue a terminal degree in criminal justice or a closely related field. Students must complete twenty-one semester hours of core courses and fifteen semester hours of electives, and can choose to obtain certification in security studies. A comprehensive examination is required for completion of the master's in criminal justice and can be taken after the completion of twenty-seven semester hours and all core courses. Students are allowed a maximum of two attempts to successfully pass the examination.

Number of Faculty: 12

Accreditation: Southern Association of Colleges and Schools Commission on Colleges

Average Length of Time to Complete the Program: Not available

Eastern Kentucky University

Address: 521 Lancaster Avenue
Richmond, KY 40475
Phone: (859) 622-1000
Website: http://www.eku.edu/

Department: College of Justice and Safety
521 Lancaster Avenue
Stratton 354
Richmond, KY 40475
Phone: (859) 622-3565
Website: http://www.justice.eku.edu/

Type of Program: MS in Criminal Justice

Application Deadline: March 15, July 1, November 1

Requirements:
- Hold a baccalaureate degree from an accredited institution of higher learning;
- A 3.0 GPA overall in the last sixty hours of undergraduate course work'
- Have a combined score of at least 286 on the verbal and quantitative portions of the GRE and an analytical writing score of 4.0;
- Apply to and meet the admission requirements of the EKU Graduate School
- Submit a personal statement to the EKU Graduate School (including personal and professional objectives in pursuing a master's degree in criminal justice, primary and secondary motivations for pursuing this degree, your educational interests, potential research interests, and what you hope to accomplish); and
- Submit two letters of recommendation directly to the criminal justice graduate program Coordinator in the College of Justice and Safety.

Information Required for Application: See above

Admission Date: Summer, Fall, Spring

In-state and Out-of-state Tuition Costs: Resident semester: $8,192; non-resident semester: $10,642

Availability of Internships and Scholarships: Due to being designated a Program of Distinction by the state of Kentucky, we are able to award up to twenty research assistant positions—more than any other master's program in the country. These generous awards provide a full two years' worth of funding, tuition waivers, and unparalleled financial support for travel to conferences and conducting research.

Orientation and Emphasis of Department/Program (Program Description): The following specializations are designed to give the student a better idea of the various areas of emphasis in our program, as well as a guide them in creating a coherent curriculum beyond the core courses. (These are not offered as concentrations).

- Leadership and Administration: criminal justice administration and leadership, criminology and public policy, funding/grants in criminal justice, advanced crime and justice theory, globalization and crime justice;
- Social Justice: race, gender and justice, environmental crime and justice, ideology and criminal justice, state crime, human traffic, punishment and society;
- Research Specialist: criminal justice data analysis (statistics), qualitative methods, funding/grants in criminal justice, research internship, thesis option; and
- Security and Surveillance in a Global Environment: policing global insecurity, state crime, globalization and criminal justice, human trafficking, surveillance and advanced technology in criminal justice, comparative criminal justice.

Number of Faculty: 23

Accreditation: Commission on Colleges of the Southern Association of Colleges and Schools

Average Length of Time to Complete the Program: Not available

Eastern Michigan University

Address: 900 Oakwood Street
Ypsilanti, MI 48197
Phone: (734) 487-1849
Website: https://www.emich.edu/

Department: Department of Sociology, Anthropology, and Criminology
Eastern Michigan University
712 Pray Harrold
Ypsilanti, MI 48197
Phone: (734) 487-0012
Website: http://www.emich.edu/sac/

Type of Program: MA in Criminology and Criminal Justice (online)

Application Deadline: May 15, October 15, March 15

Requirements:
- Completed graduate application;
- Application fee ($35);
- A personal statement;
- Official transcripts from all previously attended colleges/universities;
- Additional requirements, such as standardized test scores or teacher certification, determined by each academic department; and
- Have at least a 3.0 undergraduate GPA, and have completed the following courses or equivalent:
  - CRM 300, Criminal Justice
  - CRM 301, Criminology
  - SOCL 250, Quantitative Applications in Sociology
  - SOCL 304, Methods in Sociological Research

Note: If you have a previous degree from EMU and want to apply to another EMU program and you finished your undergraduate or graduate program within the last two years, you do not need to send new transcripts. if you finished your degree more than two years ago, you will need to resubmit transcripts from all universities. The transcripts from other universities are needed to calculate a cumulative undergraduate GPA for graduate admissions and for graduate faculty to check course prerequisites.

Information Required for Application: Listed above

Admission Date: Fall, Winter, Spring

In-state and Out-of-state Tuition Costs:

Course Level	Resident Tuition	Non-Resident Tuition	General Fee	Technology Fee	Student Union Fee
Up to 499	$256.70	$756.10	$25.40	$12.00	$3.55
500 - 699	$449.00	$885.10	$25.40	$12.00	$3.55
700 and Above	$516.65	$997.75	$25.40	$12.00	$3.55

Availability of Internships and Scholarships:

The Barton Scholarship is a one-time competitive award that pays up to $4,000 to new graduate students. To be considered for this award, students must have earned their baccalaureate from EMU with a minimum 3.5 cumulative GPA. The applicant must be admitted to their first graduate program and will need to enroll in and complete four graduate credit hours in both Fall and Winter semesters. Application deadlines are February 15 and October 15.

The Brenner Scholarship is a one-time award of $500 to recognize outstanding academics and personal achievement by graduate students at EMU. Applicants must have completed ten graduate credit hours by the end of the current semester with a 3.5 GPA. They must enroll in and complete a minimum of four credit hours. The deadline to apply is February 15 for Fall awards.

The University Fellowship is a distinction of honor awarded to select graduate students on the basis of academic merit. Fellowship awards may range from $500 to $4,000 per year for full-time (eight credit hours per semester) or part-time enrollment (four credit hours per semester). New graduate students must have a minimum 3.6 cumulative undergraduate GPA for consideration. Current students must have a 3.8 GPA in their program of study. Priority is given to students not receiving other kinds of aid such as a graduate assistantship. Awards are competitive and distributed among all graduate academic programs.

The Martin Luther King, Jr.–César Chavez–Rosa Parks (KCP) Future Faculty Fellowship Program was created to increase the number of under-represented candidates pursuing full-time teaching careers in postsecondary educational institutions within the state. Eligible applicants may receive fellowship awards of up to $20,000 for master's study and $35,000 for doctoral study at Michigan institutions. As a condition of the award, recipients are required to make a commitment to work in higher education institutions for three years. A fellow who defaults on this commitment is required to repay the award sum, which is then treated as a loan. Applications are accepted in the Fall for January awards based on state budget that is finalized in October. Typically, five to seven new awards are offered each year; therefore, the application process is very competitive.

National Scholars Program scholarship is awarded through your admissions application to your first master's degree program, and is only awarded to non-resident students. To be awarded, graduate students must have at least a 3.6 undergraduate GPA and cannot have previously earned master's degree. To receive payment, graduate students must enroll in at least eight credit hours each semester and maintain a 3.2 cumulative EMU GPA. The graduate award is renewable for up to two years or for a maximum of thirty-two credit hours. The NSP is only awarded upon admission to students with non-resident admission status and only applies to courses that are charged non-resident tuition (i.e., not online classes). If students receive another award that pays tuition and fees (such as athletic aid or a graduate assistantship) or their residency status changes, the NSP offer is null and void.

EMU Success Scholarship is a grant awarded through your admissions application to your first master's degree program, and is only awarded upon admission to EMU to non-resident students. To be awarded, graduate students must have at least a 3.2 undergraduate GPA and cannot have a previous earned master's. To receive payment, students must enroll in at least eight credit hours each semester and maintain at least a 3.0 cumulative EMU GPA. The award is renewable for up to two years or for a maximum of thirty-two credit hours. The EMU Success Scholarship is only awarded upon admission to students with non-resident admission status and the award only applies to courses that are charged non-resident tuition (i.e., not online classes). If students receive another award that pays tuition and fees (such as a graduate assistantship) or their residency status changes, the EMU Success offer is null and void.

Orientation and Emphasis of Department/Program (Program Description):
Objectives
1. Attainment of advanced education for persons who wish to enter careers in post-secondary education;
2. Development of skills in research and in program planning and evaluation in criminology and criminal justice;
3. Strengthening of the professional qualifications of persons employed in the fields of criminal justice; and

4. Preparation for doctoral study in a behavioral or social science. The analytical and evaluative skills stressed by this program enable students to identify and assess the often conflicting objectives of criminal justice and to investigate basic issues and practical problems in criminology and the administration of criminal justice. The MA in criminology and criminal justice program requires either a thesis or two essays for the non-thesis option.

- Option I: Thesis students must complete a thesis on a subject determined in consultation with their advisor, in light of their interests. The completed thesis must be approved by the department. Four hours of thesis credit are earned.

- Option II: Non-thesis students must submit two essays dealing with methodological, substantive, or theoretical issues in criminology and criminal justice. These may be based on papers completed in graduate courses, but must be of higher quality than usual term papers, meet departmental requirements through a scheduled meeting with the graduate advisor, and be approved by the department. No credit hours are earned for these essays.

Number of Faculty: 29

Accreditation: Higher Learning Commission, a commission of the North Central Association

Average Length of Time to Complete the Program: Not available

East Tennessee State University

Address: 807 University Parkway
Johnson City, TN 37604
Phone: (423) 439-1000
Website: http://www.etsu.edu/etsuhome/

Department: Department of Criminal Justice and Criminology
201 Rogers-Stout
P.O. Box 70555
Johnson City, TN 37614
Phone: (423) 439-5346
E-mail: ketelaar@etsu.edu
Website: http://www.etsu.edu/cas/cj/

Type of Program: MA in Criminal Justice and Criminology

Application Deadline: June 1, November 1, March 15. In order to be considered for a graduate assistant/tuition scholar position, applications must be completed and received no later than March 1 for Fall consideration.

Requirements: Admission decisions are based on the applicant's combined verbal and quantitative scores on the GRE and the applicant's undergraduate grade point average. The applicant's grade point average during the last two years of undergraduate study will be taken into consideration.
- A bachelor's degree from a regionally accredited institution. Degrees from non-accredited institutions will be evaluated on an individual basis;
- A nonrefundable application fee of $35 ($45 for international students); and
- An undergraduate GPA of 2.5 on a 4.0 scale (some programs require a higher GPA).

Information Required for Application:
- A completed application form;
- One official transcript from every college or university where the applicant has taken courses, except for previous course work at ETSU (applications will not be considered without all transcripts); and
- A personal essay of 150–300 words detailing your interests in a graduate program at ETSU.

Admission Date: Fall, Spring, Summer

In-state and Out-of-state Tuition Costs: In-state: $479 per credit hour; out-of-state: $1,182 per credit hour

Availability of Internships and Scholarships: Graduate assistantships, tuition scholars, and scholarships are available. Scholarships are listed online at http://www.etsu.edu/gradstud/ Scholarships.aspx.

Orientation and Emphasis of Department/Program (Program Description): The Department of Criminal Justice and criminology offers the master of arts degree, which is designed to enhance student understanding of crime, societal reaction to crime, and efforts to control it. It prepares the student for advancement in criminal justice professions, teaching at the community college level, and study at the doctoral level.

Number of Faculty: 18

Accreditation: Commission on Colleges, Southern Association of Colleges and Schools

Average Length of Time to Complete the Program: Two years

Fayetteville State University

Address: 1200 Murchison Road
Fayetteville, NC 28301
Phone: (910) 672-1111
Website: http://www.uncfsu.edu/

Department: Department of Criminal Justice
1200 Murchison Road
Fayetteville, NC 28301
Lauretta J. Taylor Building, 3rd Floor
Phone: (910) 672-1478
Fax: (910) 672-1908
Website: http://www.uncfsu.edu/criminal-justice

Type of Program: MS in Criminal Justice (online)

Application Deadline: April 15, October 15

Requirements: To be considered for admission into the master of science in criminal justice program, applicants must meet the following three criteria:
- Possess a cumulative undergraduate GPA of 2.75 or higher;
- Have a combined score of at least 700 on the verbal and quantitative Graduate Record Examination (GRE) tests; and
- Score at least 3.0 on the GRE analytical writing test.

Information Required for Application:
- Fayetteville State University application for graduate study;
- Official transcripts from all undergraduate and graduate colleges and universities attended, and showing award of the baccalaureate degree (official transcripts should be sent from the university, not from the applicant);
- Official GRE scores sent from Educational Testing Service;
- Two letters of recommendation from people who are qualified to assess the applicant's academic potential. These letters must not be from relatives, nor should they be personal or character references;
- One- to two-page admissions essay detailing the applicant's future goals and explaining how earning a master of science in criminal justice from Fayetteville State University will help achieve those goals; and
- Nonrefundable $35 application fee, in cash, check, or money order.

Admission Date: Fall, Spring

In-state and Out-of-state Tuition Costs: Resident: $2,701 per semester; non-resident: $8,125 per semester

Availability of Internships and Scholarships: Not available

Orientation and Emphasis of Department/Program (Program Description): The Department of Criminal Justice offers a graduate course of study leading to the degree of master of science in criminal justice. The program of study is designed to produce graduates who have the research skills and theoretical knowledge to obtain professional, managerial, and research positions in a variety of justice-related fields and/or pursue doctoral degrees in criminal justice or criminology. The program requires a minimum of thirty-three semester hours of graduate study in criminal justice. The master of science in criminal justice program can be either completely online, completely in-residence, or a combination of both.

Number of Faculty: 17

Accreditation: Southern Association of Colleges and Schools Commission on Colleges

Average Length of Time to Complete the Program: Not available

Ferris State University

Address: 1201 South State Street
Big Rapids, MI 49307
Phone: (231) 591-2000
Website: http://www.ferris.edu/

Department: School of Criminal Justice
Greg Vanderkooi, Graduate Program Coordinator
Phone: (231) 591-3652
Website: http://www.ferris.edu/HTMLS/colleges/educatio/cj/CJAD/

Type of Program: MS in Criminal Justice Administration

Application Deadline: Not available

Requirements:
- A baccalaureate degree—perferably in criminal justice or related field—from an accredited institution with an earned cumulative GPA of 3.0 or higher. Students who do not meet this requirement may be admitted provisionally, but must have a 3.0 GPA at the end of their first twelve semester hours;
- An official transcript (if not a Ferris graduate) from the school granting the baccalaureate;
- Three letters of reference,
- A personal statement indicating why the individual is interested in pursuing a master of science degree; and
- An application fee of $30, which is waived for Ferris graduates and those applying online.

Students are encouraged to apply early in order to facilitate financial aid requests if needed. Applications are available at all sites or by calling (231) 591-3652 or e-mailing the graduate coordinator at vanderkg@ferris.edu.

Information Required for Application: Stated above

Admission Date: Not available

In-state and Out-of-state Tuition Costs: $497 per credit hour (classroom); $507 per credit hour (online)

Availability of Internships and Scholarships: Law enforcement internships and correction, generalist, and statewide agency internships

Orientation and Emphasis of Department/Program (Program Description): As you move through the curriculum, you will gain valuable knowledge through core courses in areas such as legal issues and the nature of crime, enhance your skills through criminal justice research methods and evaluation, and focus on administration through leadership, budgeting and personnel management courses. You will then use what you have learned as you complete either a thesis or graduate topics and comprehensive critique/exam. The master of science in criminal justice administration requires thirty semester hours for graduation. The master's degree emphasizes four core areas:

- Administrative and Leadership Skills
- Personnel and Budgeting Management
- Research and Evaluation
- Crime and Violence

Number of Faculty: 22

Accreditation: Higher Learning Commission

Average Length of Time to Complete the Program: For full-time students, the degree will take one year (Fall, Spring, and Summer semesters). For students taking just two classes per semester, the degree can be completed in two years. Completion will require four years when taking one course per semester.

Florida Agricultural and Mechanical University

Address: School of Graduate Studies and Research
515 Orr Drive
Tucker Hall, Room 469
Tallahassee, FL 32307
Phone: (850) 599-3000
Website: http://www.famu.edu/

Department: Department of History and Political Science
515 Orr Drive
Tucker Hall, Room 462
Tallahassee, FL 32307
Departmental Number: (850) 599-3447
Fax Number: (850) 599-3950
Website: http://www.famu.edu/index.cfm?histpol&MASSGenera
lInformation

Type of Program: Master of Applied Social Sciences

Application Deadline: Not available

Requirements:
- A baccalaureate degree from an accredited institution of higher education;
- Potential for successful graduate study; and
- A combined score of at least 1,000 on the verbal and quantitative sections of the Graduate Record Examination (GRE) and/or earned a GPA of 3.0 or higher in the last sixty hours of undergraduate coursework.

Information Required for Application: The admission application fee is $30 for all applicants.

Admission Date: Not available

In-state and Out-of-state Tuition Costs: Resident: $151.78 per credit hour; non-resident: $549.80 per credit hour

Availability of Internships and Scholarships: All students must complete an approved internship or a thesis to qualify for graduation. Internships will be with a government agency—local, state, or federal—or with a private concern. Internships should be related as nearly as possible to the student's major area and must have the prior approval of the coordinator and the professor supervising the internships. The internship should be a new, professional experience for the student. If a proposed internship does not violate internship criteria, a student may intern in another department of the agency where he or she is employed. The internship must not be simply a continuation of regular duties. The appropriateness of all internships will be determined on an individual basis by the chair of the department of the student's major and the coordinator of the MASS program. A student wishing to write a thesis must select a committee of at least three faculty members. The committee chair must be from the student's major emphasis; the second member must be from the area of the concentration; and the third member may be from the outside the student's area of concentration.

Orientation and Emphasis of Department/Program (Program Description): The following departments in the College of Arts and Sciences participate in the interdisciplinary degree master of applied social science (MASS).
- History
- Political Science
- Public Administration (Summer and Fall acceptance only)
- Criminal Justice

Courses are available in the MASS program from the disciplines of political science, public administration, history and criminal justice. The unique feature of this applied, interdisciplinary program is its flexibility. Building upon a required core of three courses (nine semester hours), the student—in consultation with an advisor—may design the remainder of the program to address his or her own interests. The degree is designed for those who wish to pursue further graduate work in the social sciences and for those who wish to work immediately following completion of the MASS degree.

Number of Faculty: 19

Accreditation: Commission on Colleges of the Southern Association of Colleges and Schools

Average Length of Time to Complete the Program: For the full-time student, the course of study will likely span two semesters plus one Summer, totaling thirty-three hours. Some students may be required to take several prerequisites before commencing their academic program.

Florida Atlantic University

Address: 777 Glades Road
Boca Raton, FL 33431
Phone: (561) 297-3000
Website: http://www.fau.edu/

Department: College for Design and Social Inquiry
777 Glades Road
Boca Raton, FL 33431
Phone: (561) 297-4174
Fax: (561) 297-4172
Website: http://www.fau.edu/cdsi/

Type of Program: MS in Criminology and Criminal Justice

Application Deadline: July 1, November 1, April 1

Requirements:
- Bachelor's degree;
- Undergraduate GPA of 3.0;
- B or better in research methods class; and
- B or better in statistics class.

Information Required for Application:
- Personal letter of intent;
- Résumé; and
- Academic writing sample.

Admission Date: Fall, Summer, Spring

In-state and Out-of-state Tuition Costs: In-state: $369.82 per credit hour; out-of-state: $1024.81 per credit hour

Availability of Internships and Scholarships: The Gubernatorial Fellows Program offers an unparalleled experience in leadership and public service to Florida's best and brightest college and university students. This nonpartisan program provides students interested in public service with the opportunity to gain experience and exposure by working in key areas of government. Fellows travel to Tallahassee for two semesters and are assigned to work in the Executive Office of the Governor or the Governor's agencies, based on their major or area of concentration. Fellows work a minimum of twenty hours per week and are paid for their time on the job, while maintaining full-time status in their academic programs. Fellows participate in a weekly lecture series, where they meet face-to-face with prominent leaders, including the Governor, Lt. Governor, cabinet officers, agency heads, or other top officials. Fellows also travel throughout Florida and to Washington, DC, to meet with local and federal government officials. This is an outstanding opportunity for students interested in public service. In most cases, fellows receive free tuition throughout the academic year.

Orientation and Emphasis of Department/Program (Program Description): Students will acquire a foundation of theoretical knowledge, evidence-based practices, implementation strategies, and professional values necessary to succeed in the criminal justice field, either as practitioners, policy-makers, or researchers. Coursework focuses on understanding theoretical explanations of crime, applying theory to real-life crime problems, as well as evaluating criminal justice policies and practices. In addition to a substantive focus on policing, the correctional system, and juvenile justice, coursework addresses such critical contemporary issues as progressive leadership, organizational culture, examination of ethical considerations, and the role of gender, race/ethnicity, and class in the criminal justice system. The purpose of the program is to prepare well-informed and highly qualified graduates who can effectively:

- Apply their knowledge of theory, evaluation research, evidence-based practices, and implementation strategies to promote both their personal ambitions and the progressive advancement of the criminal justice system;
- Serve as practitioners, future leaders, administrators, managers, policy-makers, evaluators, and research analysts in the criminal justice field;
- Contribute to the development of research, the implementation of policies, and the evaluation of programs designed to advance knowledge and practice in the criminal justice system; and
- Be academically equipped for advanced studies in the field of criminology and criminal justice.

Number of Faculty: 13

Accreditation: Southern Association of Colleges and Schools Commission on Colleges

Average Length of Time to Complete the Program: Not available

Florida Gulf Coast University

Address: 10501 FGCU Boulevard South
Fort Myers, FL 33965
Phone: (239) 590-1000
Website: http://www.fgcu.edu/

Department: Department of Justice Studies
Contact: Jeffrey Kleeger Associate Professor and Chair
Phone: (239) 590-7861
E-mail: jkleeger@fgcu.edu
Website: http://www.fgcu.edu/CAS/Departments/JS/

Type of Program: MS in Criminal Justice

Application Deadline: Not available

Requirements:
- A baccalaureate degree from an accredited institution of higher learning;
- Completion of the Graduate Record Exam (GRE) within the last five years with a combined score of quantitative and verbal sections of 900;
- An undergraduate GPA of 3.0 (scale of 4.0); and
- A score of 550 or higher on the Test of English as a Foreign Language (TOEFL) for international applicants for whom English is a second language.

Information Required for Application:
- A completed FGCU graduate application;
- One official transcript from each baccalaureate and/or graduate institution attended;
- One official copy of test scores on the GRE;
- Three completed reference rating forms/letters of recommendation from persons qualified to judge the applicant's academic and professional potential;
- An immunization history form;
- A Personal Aspiration Statement (300-500 words); and
- An interview.

Admission Date: Not available

In-state and Out-of-state Tuition Costs: Resident: $373.38 per hour; non-resident: $1,300.66 per hour

Availability of Internships and Scholarships: Tuition waiver

Orientation and Emphasis of Department/Program (Program Description): The master of science in criminal justice is designed to prepare graduates for advancement in justice-related professions, particularly as administrative and management level officers in law enforcement, corrections, and juvenile justice. The program will provide graduates with an in-depth understanding of management of criminal justice agencies as it relates to the agency, the law, the courts, and the public. The curriculum consists of thirty-six semester credit hours in foundational criminal justice and administration of justice courses. The MS in criminal justice advances the theoretical perspectives and practical applications of the BS degree in the development of advanced administrative skills that increase the effectiveness and professionalism of criminal justice personnel. As noted by numerous agency heads, a graduate degree is particularly beneficial to those seeking advancement in their current agencies as well as those seeking employment in federal law enforcement agencies and federal courts.

Number of Faculty: 5

Accreditation: Southern Association of Colleges and Schools Commission on Colleges

Average Length of Time to Complete the Program: Not available

Florida International University

Address: 11200 Southwest 8th Street
Miami, FL 33174
Phone: (305) 348-2000
Website: http://www.fiu.edu/

Department: Department of Criminal Justice
Modesto A. Maidique Campus
11200 Southwest 8th Street, PCA-257
Miami, FL 33199
Phone: (305) 348-5890
Fax: (305) 348-5848
Website: http://cj.fiu.edu/?id=1141

Type of Program: MS in Criminal Justice (online)

Application Deadline: June 1, October 1, March 1

Requirements: To be admitted into the master's degree program in criminal justice, a student must have:
• A bachelor's degree from an accredited institution;
• A GPA of 3.0 or higher in the last sixty credits of undergraduate coursework; and
• Graduate Record Exam (GRE) scores taken within the last five years.

Information Required for Application: Above

Admission Date: Fall, Spring, Summer

In-state and Out-of-state Tuition Costs: Contact the college/school for online graduate (5000 level and above) tuition information.

Availability of Internships and Scholarships: Not available

Orientation and Emphasis of Department/Program (Program Description): The master of science in criminal justice requires thirty-six credit hours (twelve courses). All students entering the program are required to complete five courses (fifteen credits) of core requirements, four electives (twelve credits) in criminal justice, and three courses (nine credits) in general electives. The MSCJ program is available at University Park campus and fully online.

Number of Faculty: 19

Accreditation: Southern Association of Colleges and Schools Commission on Colleges

Average Length of Time to Complete the Program: Not available

Florida State University

Address: 600 West College Avenue
Tallahassee, FL 32306
Phone: (850) 644-2525
Website: http://www.fsu.edu/

Department: College of Criminology and Criminal Justice
Eppes Hall
145 Convocation Way
Tallahassee, FL 32306-1273
Phone: (850) 644-4050
Website: http://criminology.fsu.edu/p/academic-grad.php

Type of Program: MS in Criminology and Criminal Justice (also online); MA in Criminology and Criminal Justice; PhD in Criminology

Application Deadline: November 1, March 1, July 1

Requirements:
- A baccalaureate degree from an accredited college or university;
- A 3.25 GPA or higher for the final two years of undergraduate study;
- Most students accepted into our program have GRE scores between 148 and 160 on both the verbal and quantitative tests. Please note that the GRE score is one element of your application and the program considers the entire file in making a determination of admission;
- Three letters of recommendation, preferably from professors familiar with your academic qualifications;
- A 300-500 word statement of interest that describes your interests in pursuing an advanced degree in criminology (including any specific research interests), as well as your ultimate career goals; and
- International students whose native language is not English must take the Test of English as a Foreign Language (TOEFL) and score at least 600 on the paper-based test, or at least 250 on the computer-based test, or at least 100 on the new Internet-based ibTOEFL test. Applicants may be asked to confirm their scores by retaking the exam when they arrive at FSU.

Information Required for Application:
- Official transcripts from all colleges and universities attended;
- Official GRE scores (FSU institution code is 5219);
- Three letters of recommendation (preferably academic references);
- Personal statement;

- Completed graduate application. This can be found on the FSU website at http://admissions.fsu.edu/gradapp/;
- Application fees (can be paid online); and
- Test of English as a Foreign Language (TOEFL) score (for international students).

Admission Date: Fall, Spring, Summer

In-state and Out-of-state Tuition Costs: Graduate resident: $428.44 per credit hour; graduate non-resident: $1059.84 per credit hour; out-of-state online master's student: $513.34 per credit hour

Availability of Internships and Scholarships:
Teaching and Research Assistantships: Teaching and research assistantships are awarded to our most qualified doctoral students each academic year. Students are assigned to assistantships in the College and in the Center for Criminology and Public Policy Research.

Gordon P. Waldo Fellowship: Provides $16,500 a year plus out-of-state tuition waivers. Awarded to highly motivated FSU criminology doctoral students with the intellectual curiosity necessary to challenge popular ideas about the causes, consequences, and control of crime. The Waldo Fellow partners with college faculty who are leading researchers in a field the fellow is interested in pursuing.

Criminology and Public Policy and Social Problems Fellowships: Funded by their related associations, these fellowships provide a Fall, Spring, and Summer stipend of $19,000–$22,000 in addition to tuition waivers. They provide each fellow with valuable editorial experience and exposure to the publication process as the managing editor for each journal.

Richard L. Rachin Fellowship: Established in memory of Richard L. Rachin, founder of the *Journal of Drug Issues*, this fellowship is awarded annually to an academically ambitious and successful student pursuing a PhD in criminology. It presents tuition waivers and a Fall, Spring, and Summer stipend of approximately $16,000 per year. It also provides the fellow with valuable editorial experience and exposure to cutting-edge drug research experience as the assistant editor for the *Journal of Drug Issues.*

University Fellowships (application deadline is January 15 for these fellowships):
- The University Fellowship Program, administered by the Office of Graduate Studies, is a university-wide competition open to new and continuing graduate students. It provides a stipend of $18,000 plus a tuition waiver of up to twelve hours for Fall and Spring.

- Presidential University Fellowships are awarded to newly enrolling PhD students. These awards are multi-year and provide a stipend of $23,000 for the first and fourth years each, plus a tuition waiver of up to twelve hours for each Fall and Spring, funded by the Office of Graduate Studies. The second and third year stipends and tuition waivers are funded by the college.
- The college also awards a one-year, $11,000 university fellowship to an outstanding incoming graduate student. Additionally, the University Fellow receives a tuition waiver of up to twelve hours for Fall and Spring.
- The Delores Auzenne Fellowship for Minorities awards a $5,000 stipend for the academic year, which is distributed in equal increments at the beginning of the Fall and Spring semesters. It is awarded to minority students enrolled as regular full-time graduate students or currently accepted for study in the graduate program.
- The McKnight Doctoral Fellow receives a $12,000 annual stipend plus tuition waivers. The fellowship is awarded to newly enrolling African-American students seeking a doctoral degree. It is renewable up to five years.
- The Leslie N. Wilson Assistantship provides $5,000 per year plus tuition waivers for newly enrolling Black American graduate students. Application forms are available in the office of the dean of graduate studies or from the director of graduate studies of the student's program. The application deadline is February 1.

Find additional fellowship and funding opportunities on the graduate studies website, http://www.gradschool.fsu.edu/Funding-Awards/Graduate-School-Fellowships-and-Grants

National Fellowships
- The American Society of Criminology (http://www.asc41.com/awards.htm) offers several award and fellowship opportunities for graduate students. ASC is an international organization whose members pursue scholarly, scientific, and professional knowledge concerning the measurement, etiology, consequences, prevention, control, and treatment of crime and delinquency.
- The National Institute of Justice Graduate Research Fellowship Program (http://www.nij.gov/funding/fellowships/graduate-research-fellowship/pages/welcome.aspx) is an annual program that provides assistance to universities for dissertation research support to outstanding doctoral students undertaking independent research on issues related to crime and justice.
- Ford Foundation Fellowship Awards are offered at the predoctoral, dissertation, and postdoctoral levels (http://sites.nationalacademies.org/PGA/FordFellowships/). Through its Fellowship programs, the Ford Foundation seeks to increase the diversity of the

nation's college and university faculties by increasing their ethnic and racial diversity, maximizing the educational benefits of diversity, and increasing the number of professors who can and will use diversity as a resource for enriching the education of all students.

- The American Association of University Women (http://www. aauw.org/learn/fellows_directory/) offers fellowship and grant opportunities for graduate students. AAUW has a long and distinguished history of advancing educational and professional opportunities for women in the United States and around the globe.

Orientation and Emphasis of Department/Program (Program Description):

Master of Science: The general requirement for the MS degree includes thirty-three hours of coursework. Of these, at least twenty-four hours must be taken within the College, and twenty-one of the twenty-four hours must be graded (not S/U). Students must earn at least a B (3.0) in each of the five required courses or they will have to be repeated. They also must earn an overall GPA of at least a 3.0 for their master's level work in order to graduate.

Master of Arts: The MA degree includes the same credit and grade point average requirements as the master of science. However, these students must complete six semester hours in humanities courses (non-CCJ elective courses). They must also demonstrate proficiency in a foreign language, which may be accomplished in any of the following ways:

- Four years of a single language in high school;
- Twelve semester hours of a single foreign language in a college or university with an earned average of 3.0 in those courses;
- Satisfactory performance on the Graduate School Foreign Language Test; or
- Certification of proficiency by the appropriate FSU language department core, criminology electives, administration electives, internship, professional paper, and general electives. Those interested in learning more about this option should contact the college's graduate coordinator.

PhD: The doctor of philosophy in criminology and criminal justice is only granted to students who have demonstrated the following:

- Mastery of the body of knowledge in criminology and criminal justice;
- The capacity to do original and independent thinking in the fields of criminology and criminal justice; and
- The ability to do significant independent research in criminology and criminal justice.

Number of Faculty: 20

Accreditation: Southern Association of Colleges and Schools Commission on Colleges

Average Length of Time to Complete the Program: Not available

George Mason University

Address: 4400 University Drive
Fairfax, VA 22030
Phone: (703) 993-1000
Website: http://www.gmu.edu/

Department: Criminology, Law, and Society
George Mason University
4400 University Drive, 4F4
Fairfax, VA 22030
Phone: (703) 993-8315
Fax: (703) 993-8316
Website: http://cls.gmu.edu/

Type of Program: MA in Criminology, Law, and Society; PhD

Application Deadline: MA: February 1; PhD: December 1

Requirements:
- Completed online application for graduate study;
- Nonrefundable application fee;
- Application for Virginia in-state tuition rates, if claiming entitlement to these rates;
- One official transcript from all institutions attended for each program applied to unless the programs are in the same college or school; and
- Other materials specified by the program, which may include departmental forms, writing sample, portfolio, or interview.

Information Required for Application:
- Three letters of recommendation from faculty members or individuals with first-hand knowledge of academic or professional capabilities;
- Goals statement;
- GRE scores on verbal, quantitative, and analytical tests taken within five years prior to application submission;
- Writing sample of a recent sole-authored work of at least 2,500 words;
- Résumé or CV; and
- Interview (may be required for some applicants).

Admission Date: Fall

In-state and Out-of-state Tuition Costs: In-state: $493.25 per credit hour; out-of-state: $1,176.75 per credit hour

Availability of Internships and Scholarships: Not available

Orientation and Emphasis of Department/Program (Program Description):

MA: The MA in criminology, law, and society brings cutting-edge social science methods to the disciplines of criminology and law and society. The program is designed for students who seek to make a difference in the development and evaluation of policy in these fields. The MA program provides students with enhanced skills in analysis and policy evaluation for their further career development and helps them prepare for competitive, sought-after positions. The program draws on a multidisciplinary departmental faculty for required core courses and electives. Students can also take a wide range of other electives from different university programs, including those in computational social science, conflict analysis and resolution, economics, government, law, philosophy, psychology, public administration, sociology, and statistics. The program takes advantage of the university's proximity to many justice organizations at the federal, state, and local levels in the capital region. The curriculum is structured to give students the skills to do policy-relevant research and work with justice and security agencies in the region to exercise those skills and serve the needs of those agencies.

PhD: The PhD program in criminology, law, and society is designed to produce top academic scholars and leaders in policy and applied settings. It brings cutting edge social science methods to the disciplines of criminology and law and society. Students coming to this program seek to make a difference in the development and evaluation of policy in these fields. The goal of this program is to provide a rigorous course of study that will prepare students to do research, teach, develop and test policies, and administer agencies and programs designed to administer law, deliver justice, reduce crime, and enhance domestic security.

Number of Faculty: 14

Accreditation: Commission on Colleges of the Southern Association of Colleges and Schools

Average Length of Time to Complete the Program: Not available

The George Washington University

Address: 2121 I Street Northwest
Washington, DC 20052
Phone: (202) 994-1000
Website: http://www.gwu.edu/

Department: Department of Sociology
801 22nd Street Northwest, Suite 409
Washington, DC 20052
Phone: (202) 994-6345
Fax: (202) 994-3239
E-mail: soc@gwu.edu
Website: http://departments.columbian.gwu.edu/sociology/academics/graduate/macriminology/

Type of Program: MA in Criminology

Application Deadline: April 1 (January 5 for applicants applying for assistantships/fellowships), November 1 (October 1 for international applicants)

Requirements: Stated below

Information Required for Application:
- GRE general test (institutional code 5246; waived for applicants who hold a JD, MD, or PhD);
- Three academic letters of recommendation;
- Transcripts from all colleges and universities attended, whether or not credit was earned, the program was completed, or the credit appears as transfer credit on another transcript. Unofficial transcripts from all colleges and universities attended must be uploaded to your online application. Official transcripts are required only of applicants who are offered admission. If transcripts are in a language other than English, English language translations must be provided. The English translation alone should be uploaded into your application; and
- Statement of Purpose: In an essay of 250–500 words, state your purpose in undertaking graduate study in your chosen field. Include your academic objectives, research interests, and career plans. Also discuss your related qualifications, including collegiate, professional, and community activities, and any other substantial accomplishments not already mentioned on the application. If you are applying for an assistantship or fellowship, you should also describe any teaching or research experience you have had.

Admission Date: Fall, Spring

In-state and Out-of-state Tuition Costs: $1,340 per credit hour

Availability of Internships and Scholarships: Fellowships and assistantships

Orientation and Emphasis of Department/Program (Program Description): An MA degree in criminology is offered in a joint program by the Sociology Department and the Forensic Sciences Department at GWU. The program is unique in combining training in traditional criminology, criminal justice, and forensic sciences. The MA in criminology is an academic program, weighted toward traditional criminology (with some forensic science training as well), and is not intended to train practitioners who wish to work in criminal justice or security agencies. Students interested in pursuing an MA in forensic sciences fields (e.g., traditional forensics, security management, crime in commerce, computer fraud) should consult the Forensic Sciences website. One of the social and behavioral sciences disciplines in the Columbian College of Arts and Sciences, the program looks at the historical development of criminal justice, its evolution into modern legal systems and ongoing problems and reforms in policing, the courts, and corrections. Students develop an understanding of the causes of criminal behavior and the social conditions that contribute to crime, and they analyze how the criminal justice system operates. Students who complete the program and receive an MA degree may continue to pursue training in a PhD program, or they may secure a position in a research organization, government agency, or related job in the criminal justice field. The MA in criminology is a joint program between GW's sociology and forensic sciences departments. Requirements include courses in research methods, statistics, criminology, criminal law, and forensic sciences.

Number of Faculty: 25

Accreditation: Middle States Association of Colleges and Schools

Average Length of Time to Complete the Program: Not available

Georgia College and State University

Address: 231 West Hancock Street
Milledgeville, GA 31061
Phone: (478) 445-5004
Website: http://www.gcsu.edu/

Department: Department of Government and Sociology
Contact: Dr. Sara Doude, MSCJ Program Coordinator
Georgia Campus
College Box 018
Milledgeville, GA 31061
Phone: (478) 445-4527
Website: http://www.gcsu.edu/gov/criminaljustice.htm

Type of Program: MS in Criminal Justice

Application Deadline: July 1, November 15, April 1

Requirements: Stated below

Information Required for Application:
- Application for Admission: Students may apply online or by mail;
- Transcripts: One official copy of all transcripts from undergraduate and graduate institutions should be submitted to the Graduate Admissions Office at the time of application or at least eight weeks prior to the start of classes;
- Standardized Tests: The criminal justice program requires the GRE (general test only) or MAT for admission. To be granted regular admission status, the applicant must score at least 1200 on the admissions formula using the GRE or at least 670 on the formula using the MAT. Applicants who score under 1200 using the GRE admissions formula or 670 using the MAT admissions formula may be granted provisional status. The formulas are:
  - GRE verbal + GRE quantitative + (100 × undergraduate grade point average)
  - MAT scaled score + (GPA × 100)
- Letters of Recommendation: Submit three letters of recommendation to the Graduate Admissions Office (letters may be faxed or mailed); and
- Health Forms: Students are required to submit immunization records. The Certificate of Immunization requires a physician's signature.

Admission Date: Fall, Spring, May semester, Summer

In-state and Out-of-state Tuition Costs: In-state: $283 per credit hour; out-of-state: $1,027 per credit hour

Availability of Internships and Scholarships: Graduate assistant-ships. (This information is for regular graduate assistantships. If you are a prospective MFA student, see MFA requirements.)

A limited number of graduate assistantships are offered to departments with graduate degree programs, as well as to other administrative offices. Graduate assistants provide educationally beneficial assistance to the departments that award the assistant-ships. By policy, graduate assistantship duties should be relevant to students' major field of study and shall be of academic value. Students are only eligible for the financial assistance provided by a graduate assistantship for two years (twenty-four months) appli-cable to the completion of one graduate degree. Once a student has completed a graduate degree, whether that program of study required one year or two, the student is no longer eligible for a graduate assistantship.

Applications for graduate assistantships should be directed to the graduate coordinator of the degree program to which the student has applied. Approval will be granted by the academic school dean, upon the recommendation of the chair or director of the hiring department and the student's graduate coordinator. To obtain a graduate assistantship a student must meet the following requirements:

- Be approved for regular admission to a graduate degree pro-gram; and
- Maintain academic good standing. If a student's grade point average Falls below a 3.00 (academic warning), the student will have next semester or Summer term to improve and return to good standing before termination of the assistantship. Should a student fail to return to good standing after the next semester or Summer term, or should a student receive academic exclu-sion and be dismissed from the degree program, the assistant-ship will be terminated at once.

Graduate assistants are required to work between ten and twenty hours per week (depending on their contracts) for a total of 150-300 hours during the Fall and Spring semesters. Course loads for graduate assistants must be at least six graduate semester hours.

Number of Faculty: 27

Accreditation: Commission on Colleges of the Southern Associa-tion of Colleges and Schools

Average Length of Time to Complete the Program: Not available

Georgia State University

Address: 33 Gilmer Street Southeast
Atlanta, GA 30303
Phone: (404) 413-2000
Website: http://www.gsu.edu/

Department: Department of Criminal Justice and Criminology
140 Decatur Street, Suite 1201
Atlanta, GA 30303
Phone: (404) 413-0021
Website: http://criminaljustice.gsu.edu/

Type of Program: MS in Criminal Justice; PhD in Criminal Justice and Criminology (online)

Application Deadline: October 1, February 15

Requirements: Listed below

Information Required for Application:
- Have a baccalaureate degree from an accredited institution.
- Complete a graduate application and submit the $50 application fee online.
- Supply two copies of official transcripts from all colleges and universities attended.
- Provide official scores from the Graduate Record Examination (GRE). Applicants should take the GRE at least six weeks prior to the admission deadline. Scores must be five years old or less.
- Submit a two- to three-page typed statement of professional and academic goals containing fields of interest and how the degree program will contribute to those goals.
- Provide three letters of recommendation from people who are qualified to assess your academic potential in graduate school.
- International applicants may also be required to submit official scores on the TOEFL and Georgia State University's International Applicant

Admission Date: Spring, Fall

In-state and Out-of-state Tuition Costs: In-state: $6,934; out-of-state: $19,930

Availability of Internships and Scholarships: A limited number of university- and grant-funded graduate research assistantships are available in the department. The department also provides tuition waivers to qualified out-of-state students. The Phil Peters Scholarship is a competitive award aimed at students who have indicated career goals in law enforcement or students who are already in the law enforcement field. The Office of Student Financial Aid provides financial assistance to students who, without such help, would be unable to attend Georgia State University. The assistance available includes scholarships, grants, loans, and employment.

Orientation and Emphasis of Department/Program (Program Description): The master of science (MS) degree represents a broad range of study designed to meet the academic needs of both pre-professional students and those already employed in the wide range of agencies that make up the criminal justice and juvenile justice systems. The master's program focuses on the preparation of criminal justice professionals with advanced competencies in their respective specialties and areas of interest, and emphasizes excellence in practice, problem-solving, critical thinking, inquiry, and leadership. The PhD in criminal justice and criminology is designed to train researchers and teacher-scholars in criminal justice and criminology. The program provides intensive one-on-one mentorship, a flexible curriculum, and core teaching and research skills that enable graduates to excel in university settings and research think tanks. Current and former doctoral students are actively involved in presenting their research at regional and national conferences. Faculty members in the department have actively involved doctoral students in their research projects, resulting in numerous publications with students. In addition, graduate students are actively involved in planning and attending research colloquia and participate in student governance.

Number of Faculty: 17

Accreditation: Southern Association of Colleges and Schools Commission on Colleges

Average Length of Time to Complete the Program: Not available

Graduate School and University Center of the City University of New York

Address: The Graduate Center, CUNY
365 Fifth Avenue
New York, NY 10016
Phone: (877) 428-6942
Website: http://www.gc.cuny.edu/

Department: The Criminal Justice Doctoral Program
524 West 59th Street
Suite 2103 North Hall
New York, NY 10019
Phone: (212) 237-8988
Fax: (212) 237-8940
E-mail: crjphd@jjay.cuny.edu
Website: http://www.gc.cuny.edu/Page-Elements/Academics-Research-Centers-Initiatives/Doctoral-Programs/Criminal-Justice/

Type of Program: PhD in Criminal Justice

Application Deadline: January 1

Requirements: The policy of the doctoral program is to consider students who show considerable promise of succeeding in the program. The admissions committee evaluates each applicant's scholastic record, paying attention to previous academic work, results from the GRE, career goals, professional experience, and evidence of academic potential. Consideration for admission into the PhD program is based on the applicant's completion of a bachelor's degree from an accredited college or university, with a cumulative overall GPA of at least 3.00 (B) on a scale of 4.00. Applicants with a master's degree should have a 3.50 GPA in their graduate work. Some background in criminal justice and in social or behavioral sciences is preferred, but not absolutely required.

Information Required for Application: Not specified

Admission Date: Fall

In-state and Out-of-state Tuition Costs: New York state residents: $4,585 per semester, $385 per credit; out-of-state residents and foreign students on temporary visas: $710 per credit

Availability of Internships and Scholarships: Not available

Orientation and Emphasis of Department/Program (Program Description): The PhD program in criminal justice offers an interdisciplinary education in the field of criminology and criminal

justice. It prepares students for careers of research, scholarship and teaching. In addition, the program offers two unique specializations: forensic science; and policy, oversight, and administration. Our doctoral students work with leading criminal justice researchers on a number of ongoing data collection efforts and research projects. Recently, our faculty has received grants from the:
- National Institute of Health
- Department of Homeland Security
- National Institute of Justice
- National Science Foundation
- Bureau of Justice Assistance
- Guggenheim Foundation
- Robert Wood Johnson Foundation
- Other federal agencies and leading foundations

John Jay College also houses a number of research centers where doctoral students are employed, such as the Center for Crime Prevention and Control, and the Prisoner Reentry Institute.

Number of Faculty: 6 core professors, 18 admissions faculty

Accreditation: New York State Department of Education: Office of Higher Education and Professions

Average Length of Time to Complete the Program: Not available

Grambling State University

Address: 403 Main Street
Grambling, LA 71245
Phone: (318) 247-3811
Website: http://www.gram.edu/

Department: Criminal Justice Department
Contact: Dr. Mahendra Singh, Department Head
Old Alma J. Brown, Room 107
403 Main Street GSU, Box 4226
Grambling, LA 71245
Phone: (318) 274-3310
Fax: (318) 274-3101
Website: http://www.gram.edu/academics/majors/profess-
ional%20studies/departments/criminal%20justice/

Type of Program: MS in Criminal Justice

Application Deadline: Not available

Requirements:
- Evidence of admission to the School of Graduate Studies;
- Evidence of at least a baccalaureate degree from an accred-
  ited institution and a 2.5 (on a 4.0 scale) or better grade point
  average;
- Official transcripts from all colleges and universities in which
  previously enrolled (must be on file in the School of Graduate
  Studies); and
- Scores from the Graduate Record Examination (GRE) taken
  within the last five years.

Information Required for Application:
- Submit a completed application for graduate admission. All
  questions must be answered. Incomplete applications will be
  returned.
- Hold a bachelor's degree from a regionally accredited college
  or university.
- Submit two official transcripts of work completed at each
  accredited college or university attended, including GSU. If
  work is in progress, a supplementary transcript must be sent at
  the end of the term. International applicants must submit official transcripts to World Education Services (WES) for course-
  by-course evaluation.
- Have three completed recommendation forms sent directly
  from the sources, who should be individuals who can attest
  to academic ability, critical thinking skills, communication
  skills, etc.

- Submit official results of the Graduate Record Examination (GRE). All scores must be sent directly from the Educational Testing Service (ETS).
- Foreign students must submit scores on the Test of English as a Foreign Language (TOEFL) and an affidavit of sponsorship in addition to the information requested above.

Admission Date: Not available

In-state and Out-of-state Tuition Costs: $954 per credit hour

Availability of Internships and Scholarships: A limited number of graduate assistantships are available. Graduate assistants must be enrolled full time (a minimum of nine semester hours of graduate credit) during any semester in which they hold an assistantship. To be eligible for an assistantship, a candidate must have a minimum overall undergraduate GPA of 3.0 and regular admission status. The renewal of graduate assistantships is based upon the satisfactory performance of assigned duties and the maintenance of a minimum 3.0 GPA. Graduate students who are interested in assistantships must submit completed graduate assistantship applications to the Graduate School. Applicants must also submit three recommendations from individuals who can attest to their academic abilities, character, and work ethic (e.g., faculty members and former employers). Graduate students should also contact their department and express their interest in working as graduate assistants.

Orientation and Emphasis of Department/Program (Program Description): The interdisciplinary master of science program with a major in criminal justice is designed to provide students with a high quality education through intensive study under the tutelage of a dedicated and professional faculty. The purpose of the program is to provide students with the latest theories and methods that will be of benefit to both practitioners and researchers as they pursue career and educational objectives. A major effort of the program is devoted toward teaching students how to analyze complex problems and research innovative but practical solutions to those problems.

Number of Faculty: 8

Accreditation: Southern Association of Colleges and Schools Commission on Colleges

Average Length of Time to Complete the Program: Not available

Grand Valley State University

Address: 1 North Campus Drive
Allendale, MI 49401
Phone: (616) 331-5000
Website: http://www.gvsu.edu/

Department: School of Criminal Justice
Phone: (616) 331-7130
Website: http://www.gvsu.edu/cj/

Type of Program: MS in Criminal Justice

Application Deadline: May 1, November 1

Requirements:

University Requirements
- A baccalaureate degree from an accredited institution of higher education
- Submission of all required admission materials, including:
  - Completed graduate application for admission;
  - $30 nonrefundable application fee (unless you have previously applied to Grand Valley);
  - Official copies of transcripts from all institutions of higher education previously attended. Transcripts must be sent from those institutions directly to the GVSU Admissions Office. Note: We do not require official transcripts from Grand Valley; and
  - For those whose native language is not English, scores from either the TOEFL (Test of English as a Foreign Language) or CELT (Comprehensive English Language Test).

Program Requirements
In addition to the university requirements of admission, all students seeking a degree for the MS in criminal justice must also meet the following requirements:
- Grade point average of 3.0 (B) from all undergraduate coursework or a 3.0 or higher calculated on the last sixty hours of course work;
- Personal statement detailing academic preparation, background experiences, and professional, educational, and career goals; and
- Three recommendations. Applicants can provide the e-mails of three references at http://www.gvsu.edu/gradapply/, and they will be sent a link to fill out for their online recommendation.

Information Required for Application: Listed above

Admission Date: Fall, Spring

In-state and Out-of-state Tuition Costs: Michigan resident: $541 per credit hour; non-Michigan resident: $731 per credit hour

Availability of Internships and Scholarships: Grants, scholarships, and loans located at http://www.gvsu.edu/financialaid/scholarships-157.htm

Orientation and Emphasis of Department/Program (Program Description): The master of science in criminal justice (MS) degree is designed to prepare students to become highly capable criminal justice leaders, planners, practitioners, and academicians who will continually improve the criminal justice system and profession. The program is also designed to prepare those students who are planning to pursue doctoral degrees. Visit http://www.gvsu.edu/grad/cj/ for admission details. Students study a variety of criminal justice topics, including:
- Advanced criminology
- Criminal justice leadership
- Criminal justice policy
- Data analysis
- Legal and ethical issues
- Research methodology

Number of Faculty: 20

Accreditation: Higher Learning Commission, North Central Association

Average Length of Time to Complete the Program: Not available

Hodges University

Address: 2655 Northbrooke Drive
Naples, FL 34119
Phone: (800) 466-8017
Website: http://www.hodges.edu/

Department: Not specified
Website: http://www.hodges.edu/spDetails.aspx?Channel=
%2FChannels%2FAdmissions+Content&WorkflowItemID=3cc
66700-4351-47a0-bd56-7f449e7c5f16

Type of Program: MS in Criminal Justice

Application Deadline: Not available

Requirements: After the interview process is completed, an application for admission needs to be filed with the university along with a nonrefundable application fee. A bachelor's degree from an accredited college or university is required along with official transcripts from all previous colleges and universities. These transcripts must demonstrate at least a 2.75 GPA in the last sixty credits of college level work. Two letters of recommendation are to be included with the application for admission.

Information Required for Application: The committee reviews applicants on a basis of three components and combines them into a graduate admissions index score. Students are expected to have an index score of 3.0 or above to be admitted into a graduate program at the university.
• Grade point average
• Entrance essay score
• Computer test score

Admission Date: Not available

In-state and Out-of-state Tuition Costs: $660 per credit hour

Availability of Internships and Scholarships: Not available

Orientation and Emphasis of Department/Program (Program Description): The master of science in criminal justice (MCJ) is designed as a comprehensive and contemporary study of the criminal justice system. The program is conceptually based, thereby offering students the opportunity to develop a theoretical understanding of criminal and deviant behavior that is applicable to the practical realities of the criminal justice professional.

Number of Faculty: 13

Accreditation: Southern Association of Colleges and Schools Commission on Colleges

Average Length of Time to Complete the Program: Four terms (two years)

Holy Family University

Address: 9801 Frankford Avenue
Philadelphia, PA 19114
Phone: (215) 637-7700
Website: http://www.holyfamily.edu/

Department: Social and Behavioral Sciences
Website: http://www.holyfamily.edu/choosing-holy-family-u/academics/schools-of-study/school-of-arts-sciences/graduate-programs/162-criminal-justice/

Type of Program: MA in Criminal Justice

Application Deadline: Not available

Requirements: Graduate students seeking full admission to the master of arts program must submit an application to the Office of Graduate Admissions and meet the following requirements:
- Submit application with statement of goals.
- Submit official transcripts from all institutions attended.
- Submit two letters of reference.
- Submit an example of scholarly writing, such as an undergraduate paper or an article authored by the applicant.
- Submit a $25 application fee.

Information Required for Application: Stated above

Admission Date: Not available

In-state and Out-of-state Tuition Costs: $670 per credit hour

Availability of Internships and Scholarships: Not available

Orientation and Emphasis of Department/Program (Program Description): The program's capstone course applies knowledge and practical skills to a specific justice-related issue or problem and sharpens students' writing, research, and communication skills, thereby preparing them either for doctoral-level study or for professional growth and advancement. Students have conducted research on such topics as school shootings, social-structural consequences of incarceration, the relationship between drug use and violent crime, the effectiveness of halfway houses, and the truth behind religious conversion in prisons. Close collaboration and consultation with a faculty mentor allow students to work independently and to tailor the amount of supervision received to their individual needs.

Number of Faculty: 3

Accreditation: Middle States Commission on Higher Education

Average Length of Time to Complete the Program: Not specified
(ten courses)

Husson University

Address: 1 Husson Circle
Bangor, ME 04401
Phone: (207) 941-7000
Website: http://www.husson.edu/

Department: Department of Criminal Justice
Website:http://www.husson.edu/content/6107/criminal-justice/

Type of Program: MS in Criminal Justice Administration

Application Deadline: Rolling admissions

Requirements: To be admitted to the master of science in criminal justice administration program, an applicant must have earned a baccalaureate degree from an accredited institution and must show promise of ability and motivation to pursue graduate-level work. This requirement is determined by the graduate committee based on the following factors:
- A personal interview with the director of the MS in criminal justice administration program;
- Two letters of recommendation;
- Previous college or university transcript;
- Score on the Graduate Records Exam (GRE) or Graduate Management Admission Test (GMAT); and
- Previous work experience.

Information Required for Application:
- Statement of purpose essay;
- Résumé (optional);
- An application with the $40 application fee (nonrefundable);
- Official transcripts of all previous college work;
- Two letters of recommendation;
- Immunization records;
- Graduate Record Examination (GRE). For information concerning this examination, contact the School of Graduate Studies.

Admission Date: Rolling admissions

In-state and Out-of-state Tuition Costs: $410 per credit hour.

Availability of Internships and Scholarships: The Husson University criminal justice program internship involves both didactic and practical work experience that meets the needs of students both academically and professionally as they prepare for graduation and vocational pathways. Interns work closely with practitioners in the criminal justice field, gaining valuable experience while also earning college credit. A minimum of 120 hours must be accrued during a semester for undergraduate students and 150 hours for graduate students to obtain three credits. Further credit hours may be obtained with specific approval. Our goal is to place you in an organization with practitioners in the field who can provide learning experiences and supervision, and where you can contribute. The Criminal Justice Department will assist you in locating quality internships.

Orientation and Emphasis of Department/Program (Program Description): The master of science in criminal justice administration program is a thirty-six credit graduate management curriculum designed to develop and strengthen skills in analysis, decision-making, and implementation. The program balances strengths in the traditional areas of law, budgeting, and policy-making, with careful attention to the development of skills in communication, interpersonal relations, psychology and leadership essential to effective performance in organizations. Students also have the opportunity to participate in experiential internships with organizations related to the criminal justice field that they choose.

Number of Faculty: Not available

Accreditation: New England Association of Schools and Colleges, Inc.

Average Length of Time to Complete the Program: Not available

Illinois State University

Address: 100 North University Street
Normal, IL 61761
Phone: (309) 438-2111
Website: http://illinoisstate.edu/

Department: Department of Criminal Justice Sciences
Normal, IL 61790-5250
Phone: (309) 438-7626
Website: http://criminaljustice.illinoisstate.edu/

Type of Program: MA in Criminal Justice; MS in Criminal Justice

Application Deadline: March 15, October 15

Requirements: The Department of Criminal Justice Sciences offers a program leading to the MA or MS degree. The master of arts degree requirements include:
- A minimum of four semesters (or its equivalent) in one foreign language; and
- A satisfactory score on a university administered language examination approved by the Graduate School.

GPA Admission Criteria (last sixty semester hours of undergraduate work)

3.20 and higher	3.00 to 3.19	2.60 to 2.99	below 2.60
Admitted on a space available basis.	Admitted on a space available basis. Preference given to those with degrees in criminal justice or related disciplines.	Only admitted under special circumstances, such as substantial practical experience in the field and/or exceptional scores on the verbal and quantitative sections of the GRE. Admission contingent upon availability.	Will not be admitted.

Information Required for Application:
- An online graduate application form and submit it to the Office of Graduate Admissions;
- A goals statement to be sent directly to the Criminal Justice Sciences Department;
- Two letters of recommendation are required for any student who is not a graduate of Illinois State University's criminal justice sciences undergraduate program. These letters should be sent directly to the Department of Criminal Justice Sciences.

To assure full consideration, all required documents must be submitted on or before March 15 for Fall semester and October 15 for Spring semester; and

- GRE scores (required only for students who are applying for graduate assistantships).

Admission Date: Fall, Spring

In-state and Out-of-state Tuition Costs: In-state: $345 per credit hour; out-of-state: $716 per credit hour

Availability of Internships and Scholarships: Students interested in applying for a graduate assistantship should use the Graduate Research Assistant and Graduate Practicum. Graduate assistants help with faculty research, support faculty with the administration of undergraduate courses, and help supervise student testing. Typically each assistant is assigned to two faculty members, each for ten hours per week. Some graduate assistants can be placed with criminal justice agencies as part of their assistantship (Practica). Practica students work twenty hours per week, including days while school is not in session. Graduate assistantships cover full-tuition plus a monthly stipend.

Orientation and Emphasis of Department/Program (Program Description): Coursework in the program is designed to increase individual competency, develop analytical thought processes, and promote the development of professional skills. Coursework focuses on examination of contemporary issues in the administration of justice, theories, research, statistical reasoning, and management problems in the field of criminal justice. First year, full-time graduate assistants are required to take a minimum of nine credit hours and not more than twelve credit hours.

Number of Faculty: 18

Accreditation: Higher Learning Commission of the North Central Association of Colleges and Schools

Average Length of Time to Complete the Program: Not available

Indiana State University

Address: 200 North 7th Street
Terre Haute, IN 47809
Phone: (812) 237-6311
Website: http://cms.indstate.edu/

Department: Department of Criminology and Criminal Justice
Holmstedt Hall 210
Terre Haute, IN 47809
Phone: (812) 237-2192
Fax: (812) 237-2407
Website: http://www.indstate.edu/ccj/

Type of Program: MA in Criminology and Criminal Justice; MS in Criminology and Criminal Justice

Application Deadline: Not available

Requirements: The general requirements governing admission, standards of work, and admission to candidacy, which are established by the School of Graduate and Professional Studies, apply to all students working toward the master of arts and master of science degrees in criminology and criminal justice. In addition, applicants for the master of arts in criminology and criminal justice must have an undergraduate cumulative grade point average of 2.75 (based on a 4.00 scale).

Information Required for Application: Applicants must submit a one- to two-page typewritten personal statement that minimally includes the following: career goals, including professional achievement; academic experience to date; and how a master's in criminology from Indiana State University will assist the applicant in achieving personal and professional goals. The applicant must provide three letters of recommendation from academic/ professional resources. Not more than one of the letters can be from the Indiana State University Department of Criminology and Criminal Justice. While the applicant need not have completed an undergraduate major in criminology, he/she should have graduated from an accredited undergraduate institution, and must have completed the following courses or their equivalents: Criminology 200 (three credits) and Juvenile Delinquency 423 (three credits); and twelve credits of courses in sociology, psychology, and political science.

Admission Date: Not available

In-state and Out-of-state Tuition Costs: In-state: $373 per credit hour; out-of-state: $466 per credit hour

Availability of Internships and Scholarships: A student receiving an assistantship in the Department of Criminology and Criminal Justice may be expected to complete any or all of the following tasks: lead small group discussions and presentations in class under the supervision of an instructor, utilize computer resources to present material in class or in leading group discussions, proctor exams, grade exams, record grades in grade book or on spreadsheet, show videos in classes, conduct library and internet research, do data entry, filing, make copies/transparencies, assist other teaching/graduate assistants or professors, assist in the CCJ office, and assist with the CCJ annual career fair. Graduate students may be eligible for federal student loans if they are admitted into graduate degrees (or first-time teacher certification programs) and meet other eligibility requirements. Certificate programs are not eligible for financial aid. Private alternative loans can help students pay college expenses that may not be covered by federal loan programs or other financial aid. For more information, visit financial aid. In addition, students may be eligible for payment plans and veterans benefits. On-campus degree-seeking students may be eligible for special scholarships for residents of Illinois, Kentucky, Ohio, and the Midwest Consortium.

Orientation and Emphasis of Department/Program (Program Description):

Master of Science: The purpose of the MS degree is to provide professional education for those interested in careers in:

- Adult and juvenile probation and parole supervision and administration;
- Adult and juvenile correctional institutional work (classification);
- Adult and juvenile institutional program management;
- Juvenile delinquency prevention and control programs in the community;
- Law enforcement at the federal, state, and local level; and
- Police-community relations, juvenile work, and police personnel and training activities.

Master of Arts: The purpose of the master of arts degree in criminology and criminal justice is to provide education in criminology and criminal justice with a special emphasis on:

- Preparing students for the doctoral degree;
- Teaching at the college or university level; and
- Research, statistics, and planning in the university or any federal, state, or local criminal justice agency dealing with the prevention, control, and/or correctionalization of crime and delinquency

Number of Faculty: 23

Accreditation: Higher Learning Commission of the North Central Association of Colleges and Schools

Average Length of Time to Complete the Program: Not available

Indiana University Bloomington

Address: 107 South Indiana Avenue
Bloomington, IN 47405
Phone: (812) 855-4848
Website: http://www.iub.edu/

Department: Department of Criminal Justice
302 Sycamore Hall
Bloomington, IN 47405
Phone: (812) 855-9325
E-mail: crimjust@indiana.edu
Website: http://www.indiana.edu/~crimjust/about_dept.php

Type of Program: MA in Criminal Justice; PhD in Criminal Justice

Application Deadline: January 15

Requirements:
Doctorate
- Sixty hours course credit;
- Completion of P594 and two graduate-level courses in statistics;
- Reading knowledge of a foreign language or research skills requirement (P599, Research Practicum, or their equivalent); and
- At least one minor area of study from outside the Criminal Justice Department. Requirements for the outside minor will be specified by that unit.

Information Required for Application:
- An official transcript from all previously attended undergraduate, graduate and professional programs;
- A personal statement of approximately 500 words that identifies your academic goals, career objectives, why you are applying to our program, and the qualifications you have that make you a strong candidate;
- GRE scores from the analytical writing, verbal reasoning, and quantitative reasoning sections. Scores from the Personal Potential Index (ETS PPI) on the newly revised GRE are optional. You may submit scores from the previous version of the GRE, if the test was taken within the last two years;
- Three letters of recommendation from faculty members familiar with your prior academic performance and potential for success in graduate work;
- A résumé identifying and describing past academic achievements and activities (e.g., research assistantships, fellowships, internships, awards); and

- Copies of published articles and book chapters, master thesis, and papers presented at conferences. The applicant, at her or his discretion, may also submit course papers.

Admission Date: Fall

In-state and Out-of-state Tuition Costs: In-state: $359.37 per credit hour; out-of-state: $1,087.66 per credit hour

Availability of Internships and Scholarships: Most full time doctoral students and some master's students in the Department of Criminal Justice receive financial support. Associate instructorships, fellowships, and research assistantships are available on a competitive basis. Such positions provide a stipend for living expenses and tuition fee remission; they may also include a Summer tuition fee remission. All full-time graduate students who have either associate instructorships or fellowships are covered by health insurance. This health insurance plan is also available at an additional cost to our students' spouses and their dependent children.

Orientation and Emphasis of Department/Program (Program Description): The Department of Criminal Justice promotes interdisciplinary approaches to studying the nature and causes of crime, the administration of justice (both civil and criminal), and the relationship between law and society. We embrace the importance of cross-cultural inquiry and interdisciplinary by applying insights from other disciplines (anthropology, developmental science, law, political science, psychology, public health, and sociology) to issues in law, crime, and justice. In addition, several of our faculty members do research abroad, including in Central and South America, the Philippines, India, Russia, and Eastern Europe. Given the department's scholarly orientation, we expect students to pursue new and emerging areas of inquiry, and we seek to provide them with the theoretical and methodological skills needed to do so. Moreover, the department provides an excellent environment for graduate study, with our graduates going on to careers in academia, government, and the private sector. Part of our success in graduate training is due to our setting and location, which provide unique resources for graduate study. Indiana University—Bloomington is a Research I University that ranks nationally among top research institutions. IU has outstanding research support and infrastructure. The Herman B. Wells Library is one of the top research libraries in the country, and PC Magazine ranked IU first among public universities in providing students and faculty with an advanced technological environment for learning and research. With over sixty departments and programs in IU's

College of Arts and Sciences, our graduate students are free to explore their interests in other social sciences related to criminology and criminal justice. The college has leading psychology and sociology departments, for example, and anthropology and political science are also very popular. Graduate students interested in carrying out criminological research in other cultures will find amazing resources here, as the college boasts world class language and area studies programs. For those who want to sharpen their quantitative and methodological skills, the college's Department of Statistics, as well as the above mentioned disciplinary departments, provides advanced courses on numerous topics.

Number of Faculty: 13

Accreditation: The Higher Learning Commission, North Central Association

Average Length of Time to Complete the Program: Not available

Indiana University of Pennsylvania

Address: 1011 South Drive
Indiana, PA 15705
Phone: (724) 357-2100
Website: http://www.iup.edu/

Department: Department of Criminology
Wilson Hall, Room 200
411 North Walk
Indiana, PA 15705
Phone: (724) 357-2720
Fax: (724) 357-4018
Website: http://www.iup.edu/criminology/

Type of Program: MA in Criminology (also online); PhD in Criminology

Application Deadline: March 15

Requirements:
Master of Arts: In addition to meeting the requirements for admission to the School of Graduate Studies and Research, a student intending to work toward a master of arts in criminology will be required to have the following prerequisite academic and/or professional preparation:

• Be able to demonstrate a sound understanding of criminological theory and the criminal justice system (generally satisfied by a bachelor's degree in criminology, criminal justice, or related fields); or

• Have knowledge gained through experience within the justice system or by specialized training or completed graduate or undergraduate studies in a related field.

Doctor of Philosophy: It is expected that most students entering the PhD program in criminology will have already completed a master's degree in either criminology or a closely related discipline., In exceptional cases, however a highly qualified applicant may enter the doctoral track with a baccalaureate degree. Such a student would obtain the MA degree en route to the PhD.

Information Required for Application: Applicants must meet all School of Graduate Studies and Research admission requirements. Additionally, the doctoral coordinator, after consulting with the department screening committee, will submit a recommendation regarding applicants to the School of Graduate Studies and Research. The following criteria are reviewed:

- All official college transcripts;
- Three letters of recommendation;
- Statement of goals;
- Example of written work (thesis, articles, reports, etc.);
- GRE scores (A combined score of 900 on the verbal and quantitative sections is expected. Some flexibility may be granted at the discretion of the screening committee.);
- Skill requirement (foreign language, computer or statistical ability, or other skills approved by the screening committee or the department's graduate curriculum committee); and
- Personal interview (may be requested by department screening committee or by applicant.)

Admission Date: Fall

In-state and Out-of-state Tuition Costs: In-state: $442 per credit; out-of-state: $663 per credit

Availability of Internships and Scholarships: Students may apply for student loans, competitive graduate assistantships (awarded in the Fall), scholarships, and university- or grant-funded employment. Assistantship applications must be received by March 15 prior to the year of study.

Orientation and Emphasis of Department/Program (Program Description):

MA: Indiana University of Pennsylvania offers a program of study leading to a master of arts in criminology. For over twenty years, the program has prepared students for administrative and research careers in the criminal justice system and related fields. The criminology MA program also provides a solid foundation for students planning to pursue doctoral studies.

PhD: Informed opinion, including that of the Council of Graduate Schools, the Association of American Colleges and Universities, and the Carnegie Foundation for the Advancement of Teaching, indicates that many PhD programs are imbalanced and do not adequately prepare students for academic life as college and university professors. Many programs narrowly focus on training researchers. More broadly defined aspects of scholarship, especially the link between teaching and research, seldom get the attention they deserve. Our program is designed to educate those who will become what the late Ernest L. Boyer of the Carnegie Foundation called the "new generation of scholars" or "teacher/scholars." Our objective is to provide solid instruction in all aspects of scholarship. We want to produce graduates who are well suited for professional life—men and women who do not juggle research, teaching, and service commitments but rather synthesize them into useful and productive careers. In 1994, our faculty passed a resolution to broaden the emphasis of our PhD program. The purpose of the proposal was to move away for the traditional model of a PhD as exclusively a research degree to a program that incorporates some of the ideas represented in the Preparing Future Faculty program promoted by the American Association of Colleges and Universities and supported by the Pew Foundation.

Number of Faculty: 32

Accreditation: Middle States Commission on Higher Education

Average Length of Time to Complete the Program: Not available

Indiana University—Purdue University Indianapolis

Address: 420 University Boulevard
Indianapolis, IN 46202
Phone: (317) 274-5555
Website: http://www.iupui.edu/

Department: School of Public and Environmental Affairs (SPEA)
Indiana University—Purdue University Indianapolis
801 West Michigan Street, BS 3025
Indianapolis, IN 46202
Phone: (317) 274-4656
Fax: (317) 274-5153
Website: http://www.spea.iupui.edu/contact/

Type of Program: MS in Criminal Justice and Public Safety

Application Deadline: Not available

Requirements: Not available

Information Required for Application:
- Application form;
- Academic record;
- Transcripts of all undergraduate work;
- Admissions test scores (GRE, MCAT, LSAT, DAT, GMAT)
- Letters of recommendation;
- Personal statement; and
- Admissions interview.

Admission Date: Not available

In-state and Out-of-state Tuition Costs: In-state: $379.03 per credit hour; out-of-state: $927.80 per credit hour

Availability of Internships and Scholarships: SPEA offers assistantships, scholarships, and merit-based awards to SPEA graduate students. SPEA IUPUI offers graduate assistantships and university fellowships through a competitive application process. The graduate assistants work twenty hours per week during the academic year. These are research assistantships and not teaching assistantships. In exchange for the twenty hours per week, GAs receive full tuition, most fees, student health insurance, and a stipend of $9,000 that is paid out monthly over the academic year. Graduate assistantships are awarded in March for students who will attend full time. Applications are accepted year-round, but priority deadline is February 1.

Orientation and Emphasis of Department/Program (Program Description): The master of science in criminal justice and public safety (MSCJPS) combines coursework in criminal justice, public safety, and management. Its graduates are increasingly in demand among agencies, organizations, and private companies seeking people with a practical and philosophical understanding of criminal justice and public safety. The program offers experiential learning and internship opportunities for those students seeking additional experience, plus a project-based capstone course in which students demonstrate the kind of knowledge required by state and local agencies.

Number of Faculty: 34

Accreditation: Higher Learning Commission, a commission of the North Central Association

Average Length of Time to Complete the Program: Two years or less for full-time students

Iona College

Address: 715 North Avenue
New Rochelle, NY 10801
Phone: (914) 633-2000
Website: http://www.iona.edu/

Department: Department of Criminal Justice
Contact: Catheryn Lavery, Department Chair
715 North Avenue
New Rochelle, NY 10801-1890
Phone: (914) 633-2597
E-mail: clavery@iona.edu
Website: http://www.iona.edu/Academics/School-of-Arts-Science/Departments/Criminal-Justice.aspx

Type of Program: MS in Criminal Justice

Application Deadline: Not available

Requirements: Not available

Information Required for Application:
- Completed application form;
- Completed undergraduate degree;
- Official transcripts from all colleges attended;
- Current résumé; and
- Two letters of recommendation from a professor and/or supervisor.

Admission Date: Fall, Spring, some Summer classes

In-state and Out-of-state Tuition Costs: $30,670 per year

Availability of Internships and Scholarships: Not available

Orientation and Emphasis of Department/Program (Program Description): Our curriculum covers the full range of the criminal justice system. Students explore the root causes of crime, law enforcement policies, correctional institutions, and the court system, and focus on timely issues like corporate and white-collar crime, profiling violent crime, and victimology. Our new security threat assessment minor builds on the growing interest in the areas of terrorism and intelligence gathering. Students learn firsthand from faculty who are current practitioners and published scholars in the field.

Number of Faculty: 4

Accreditation: Commission on Higher Education of the Middle States Association of Colleges

Average Length of Time to Complete the Program: Not available

Jackson State University

Address: 1400 John R. Lynch Street
Jackson, MS 39217
Phone: (601) 979-2121
Website: http://www.jsums.edu/

Department: Department of Sociology and Criminal Justice
Phone: (601) 979-2591
Website: http://www.jsums.edu/sociology/

Type of Program: MA in Criminal Justice and Sociology

Application Deadline: March 1, March 15, October 15

Requirements:
- An application for admission to the Graduate School;
- Two official copies of transcripts from all regionally accredited colleges and universities attended (one transcript will be retained by the Office of Graduate Admissions and one copy will be forwarded to the academic program);
- Immunization records (send to JSU, Health Services Center, P.O. Box 17097, Jackson, MS 39217); and
- Out-of-state and international applicants must submit a $25 application fee (money orders only).

Information Required for Application: Stated above

Admission Date: Fall, Summer, Spring

In-state and Out-of-state Tuition Costs:
- 1.0-8.0 hours: $353 per credit hour
- 9.0-13.0 hours: $3,174
- Over 13.0 hours: $3,174 + $353 per credit hour
- Out-of-state fees: $4,602

Availability of Internships and Scholarships: Not available

Orientation and Emphasis of Department/Program (Program Description):
Our objectives are:
- To teach students to think critically as they learn about institutions and processes;
- To identify the value choices and ethical considerations involved in decision making in the administration of justice and justice systems; and
- To give students information and skills needed for employment in public and private areas related to the administration of justice and justice systems.

Number of Faculty: Not available

Accreditation: Commission on Colleges of the Southern Association of Colleges and Schools

Average Length of Time to Complete the Program: Not available

Jacksonville State University

Address: 700 Pelham Road North
Jacksonville, AL 36265
Phone: (256) 782-5781
Website: http://www.jsu.edu/

Department: Department of Criminal Justice
126 Brewer Hall
700 Pelham Road North
Jacksonville, AL 36265
Phone: (256) 782-5335
E-mail: cjjsu@jsu.edu
Website: http://www.jsu.edu/criminaljustice/

Type of Program: MS in Criminal Justice

Application Deadline: Not available

Requirements: To be considered for admission to a master's degree program, students need to submit the following:
- Completed application for admission;
- Nonrefundable $35 application processing fee;
- Official transcript(s) from all postsecondary institutions attended;
- Official GMAT, GRE, or MAT test scores;
- Background check; and
- Three completed graduate reference forms (These need to be completed by individuals who can provide qualitative assessment of the potential for success in graduate course work.)

Information Required for Application: Applicants for the MS with a major in criminal justice will be permitted to enroll for one semester of graduate course work while completing all other general application procedure requirements. Applicants for the MS with a major in criminal justice must submit the following documentation to the College of Graduate Studies, Jacksonville State University, 700 Pelham Road North, Jacksonville, AL 36265-1602, to be considered for admission:
1. Completed JSU graduate application for admission;
2. Nonrefundable $35 application processing fee;
3. Official transcripts(s) from all postsecondary institutions attended (students who have previously attended JSU do not need to request a transcript from the university);
4. Official tests scores on the general test of the GRE or the MAT; and

5. Three graduate reference forms completed by individuals who can provide qualitative assessment of the applicant's potential for success in graduate course work.

Admission Date: Not available

In-state and Out-of-state Tuition Costs: In-state: $349 per hour; out-of-state: $698 per hour

Availability of Internships and Scholarships: Criminal Justice Alumni Association Scholarship
Jacksonville State University—in conjunction with the Department of Criminal Justice Alumni Association—is providing scholarship opportunities for students in criminal justice degree programs. Students must meet all of the following criteria:
- Be a United States citizen, national, or alien admitted as a refugee at the time of application;
- Be enrolled full time as a Department of Criminal Justice student either in the undergraduate or graduate program; and
- Possess a cumulative grade point average (GPA) of at least 2.75 based on a 4.0 scale and/or a 3.0 GPA on a 4.0 scale in their major studies.

Orientation and Emphasis of Department/Program (Program Description): The Criminal Justice Department offers courses leading to the master of science with a major in criminal justice. The department also offers an area of concentration in criminal justice within the master of public administration degree program.

Number of Faculty: 23

Accreditation: Southern Association of Colleges and Schools Commission on Colleges

Average Length of Time to Complete the Program: Not available

John Jay College of Criminal Justice of the City University of New York

Address: 899 10th Avenue
New York, NY 10019
Phone: (212) 237-8000
Website: http://www.jjay.cuny.edu/

Department: Criminal Justice
Phone: (212) 237-8988
E-mail: crjphd@jjay.cuny.edu
Website: Master's program: http://www.jjay.cuny.edu/academics/688.php.

Doctoral program: http://www.jjay.cuny.edu/academics/744.php

Type of Program: MA in Criminal Justice

Application Deadline: Not available

Requirements: You should have a minimum cumulative undergraduate grade point average of B (3.0 on 4.0 scale) to apply for graduate programs at John Jay College; however, there are exceptions for certain degree programs. The Graduate Record Examination is required for admission to the forensic science, forensic psychology, forensic mental health counseling and forensic computing programs. The GRE is also required for criminal justice and international crime and justice. The graduate admissions committee will evaluate the GRE scores as one component of the application profile. Applicants to those programs not requiring the GRE general test (public administration and protection management) whose overall undergraduate grade point average Falls below 3.0 are strongly encouraged to submit GRE scores as part of their application. Please consult with a graduate admissions counselor for further information.

Information Required for Application:
- A nonrefundable application fee of $125 in the form of a check or money order made payable to "John Jay College" (do not send cash) must accompany your application for admission. John Jay College alumni who include a copy of their valid alumni card with their application are waived from the application fee. This courtesy is limited to one application fee waiver.
- An undergraduate course in statistics is required for all majors except protection management. Twelve credits of psychology as well as an undergraduate course in experimental psychology is required for forensic psychology and forensic mental health

counseling. However, applicants without these requirements may be accepted on the condition they register and pass the above mentioned courses within the first year of their program. At least eighteen hours of undergraduate work in the social sciences are required for admissions to the MPA program.

- Three academic references or letters of recommendation are required (for students who graduated more than two years ago, professional references are acceptable).
- Applicants should submit a personal statement of approximately 200-350 words indicating the reasons for pursuing graduate study with reference to career objectives.

Admission Date: Not available

In-state and Out-of-state Tuition Costs: In-state: $4,585 per semester (twelve credits): out-of-state: $710 per credit hour

Availability of Internships and Scholarships:
The Scholarship Office
524 West 59th Street
North Hall, Room 1280N
New York, NY 10019
Contact: Michael Scaduto, Scholarship Coordinator
Phone: (212) 237-8872
E-mail: scholarships@jjay.cuny.edu

Orientation and Emphasis of Department/Program (Program Description):
Master's: Criminal justice is a rapidly expanding field of academic study central to the mission of the college. The aim of the master of arts in criminal justice program is to broaden the perspective of those already in the criminal justice profession and prepare students for further graduate work and scholarship. Its courses provide a general survey of the field covering research methods, causes of crime, and analyses of the police, courts and the correctional system. In addition, courses are offered in criminal law, crime mapping, cybercrime, information security and technology, drug abuse, and terrorism.
Doctoral: The doctoral program in criminal justice at the Graduate Center, City University of New York, is housed at John Jay College. The program offers an interdisciplinary education in the field of criminology and criminal justice. It prepares students for careers of research, scholarship and teaching. The program also offers two unique specializations: (1) forensic science, and (2) policy, oversight and administration. The PhD program requires at least sixty credits of coursework, including at least five courses in statistics and research methods. Students are required to pass

three qualifying examinations in criminology, criminal justice, and statistics and research methods. The program culminates in a dissertation in the area of a student's interest.

Number of Faculty: 75+

Accreditation: Middle States Association of Colleges and Secondary Schools

Average Length of Time to Complete the Program: Not available

The Johns Hopkins University

Address: 3400 North Charles Street
Baltimore, MD 21287
Phone: (410) 516-8000
Website: http://www.jhu.edu/

Department: Division of Public Safety Leadership
Website: http://psl.jhu.edu/

Type of Program: MS in Management (also online)

Application Deadline: Not available

Requirements: To be eligible for consideration, applicants must have earned a four-year bachelor's degree (or the equivalent) from a regionally accredited college or university and a minimum 3.0 GPA for the MS programs, and must possess associate in arts degree or sixty transferable credits from a regionally accredited college or university with a minimum cumulative grade point average of a 3.0.

Information Required for Application:
- Official transcripts from all postsecondary schools attended;
- Professional résumé;
- Essay; and
- Two letters of recommendation.

Admission Date: Spring, Summer

In-state and Out-of-state Tuition Costs: $39,000 per year

Availability of Internships and Scholarships: Not available

Orientation and Emphasis of Department/Program (Program Description): The master of science in management program at the Johns Hopkins University prepares today's public safety professionals for their expanding roles. This award-winning program is the first of its kind in the country to bring together current and future public safety leaders from the region and beyond for class sessions that explore the latest, most relevant leadership issues. Students who successfully complete the program are awarded the master of science in management degree. The curriculum covers such diverse topics as leadership, change management, building quality organizations, management decision-making, and ethics and integrity. Both the in-person and online programs can be completed in less than two years.

Number of Faculty: 5 main, 5 adjuncts

Accreditation: Middle States Commission on Higher Education

Average Length of Time to Complete the Program: Less than two years

Kean University

Address: 1000 Morris Avenue
Union, NJ 07083
Phone: (908) 737-5326
Website: http://www.kean.edu/

Department: Department of Criminal Justice
305 Willis Hall
Phone: (908) 737-4230
Fax: (908) 737-4232
Website: http://www.kean.edu/~crimjust/

Type of Program: MA in Criminal Justice

Application Deadline: June 1, December 1

Requirements:
- Baccalaureate degree from an accredited college or university in criminal justice or a related field (including political science, sociology, psychology, and legal studies; students without an undergraduate degree in criminal justice or a related field may be admitted to the program at the discretion of the criminal justice faculty); and
- Cumulative grade point average (GPA) of 3.0 (lower GPAs will be considered based on strength of overall application).

Information Required for Application:
- Official transcripts from all institutions attended;
- Graduate Record Exam (GRE) with a minimum analytical writing score of 3.5 (applicants with a cumulative undergraduate GPA of 3.2 or higher do not need to take the GRE);
- Sample of scholarly work from undergraduate studies. Students who do not have a sample from their undergraduate studies will be assigned a topic by the program coordinator and will need to submit a 1,250-word sample;
- Three letters of recommendation from individuals who can attest to the applicant's professional and/or academic abilities and accomplishments;
- Professional résumé or CV; and
- Personal statement.

Admission Date: Fall, Spring

In-state and Out-of-state Tuition Costs: In-state: $728 per credit; out-of-state: $861 per credit

Availability of Internships and Scholarships: Not available

Orientation and Emphasis of Department/Program (Program Description): The Kean University master's degree program in criminal justice studies the various systems within the criminal justice system, the current theoretical models explaining crime and delinquency, their practical use in addressing crime and enforcement, and the use of scientific inquiry to research and address the theoretical and practical problems facing the criminal justice system currently and in the future. The criminal justice program is designed to ensure that students keep pace with the changing environment and are prepared to be productive, engaged contributors to the debate on policy and practice through instruction in the three major components of the system: police, courts, and corrections.

Number of Faculty: 5

Accreditation: Middle States Commission on Higher Education

Average Length of Time to Complete the Program: Not available

Lewis University

Address: 1 University Parkway
Romeoville, IL 60446
Phone: (815) 838-0500
Website: http://www.lewisu.edu/

Department: Department of Justice, Law, and Public Safety Science
Contact: Michelle Mega, Director of Recruitment and External Relations
Phone: (815) 836-5342
E-mail: megami@lewisu.edu
Website: http://www.lewisu.edu/academics/jlpss/

Type of Program: MS in Criminal/Social Justice (also online)

Application Deadline: Not available

Requirements:
- Possess a bachelor's degree from a regionally accredited institution of higher education with a major in criminal/social justice or with twelve semester hours of credit related to criminal/social justice, or be currently serving as a criminal/social justice practitioner. If the bachelor's degree is not criminal/social justice related and if not currently serving as a criminal justice practitioner, successfully complete two criminal justice courses selected by the program director with a grade of B or better prior to admission as a degree candidate.
- Submit two letters of recommendation.
- Submit a completed application.
- Pay a nonrefundable application fee with the completed application.
- Submit official academic transcripts from each institution attended.
- Have earned an undergraduate GPA of 3.0 or higher on a scale of 4.0, calculated on the most recent sixty semester hours.
- Obtain acceptance by the graduate council.
- Submit a three- to four-page personal statement describing academic/professional background and reason for applying to the program.

Information Required for Application: Stated above

Admission Date: Not available

In-state and Out-of-state Tuition Costs: $740 per credit hour

Availability of Internships and Scholarships: Not available

Orientation and Emphasis of Department/Program (Program Description): Designed specifically for the convenience of working adults, this master's program curriculum combines theoretical understanding with practical application to develop key skills and help accelerate your professional goals within administration, law enforcement, homeland security and more.

Number of Faculty: 9

Accreditation: The Higher Learning Commission and a member of the North Central Association

Average Length of Time to Complete the Program: Two years

Lindenwood University

Address: 209 South Kingshighway
St. Charles, MO 63301
Phone: (636) 949-2000
Website: http://www.lindenwood.edu/

Department: Criminal Justice Program
209 South Kingshighway
St. Charles, MO 63301
Website: http://www.lindenwood.edu/humanServices/cj/

Type of Program: MS in Criminal Justice Administration

Application Deadline: Not available

Requirements: To be considered for admission to the university, an applicant's file must include a completed and signed application form with the $30 application fee (nonrefundable; checks or money orders should be made payable to Lindenwood University) and official transcripts from the school granting the undergraduate degree, as well as official transcript(s) from any graduate school(s) attended. Individual academic schools may have additional documents needed for admission into that school.

Information Required for Application: Not available

Admission Date: Not available

In-state and Out-of-state Tuition Costs: $428 per credit hour

Availability of Internships and Scholarships: Not available

Orientation and Emphasis of Department/Program (Program Description): The master of science in criminal justice administration is designed for practicing professionals in the field of law enforcement and criminal justice administration. The degree is designed for both younger professionals who intend to pursue a career in the field and for seasoned professionals who wish to expand their knowledge and skills in criminal justice administration.

Number of Faculty: 2

Accreditation: Higher Learning Commission of the North Central Association of Colleges and Schools

Average Length of Time to Complete the Program: Not available

Long Island University, Brentwood Campus

Address: 100 Second Avenue
Brentwood, NY 11717
Phone: (631) 287-8500
Website: http://www.liu.edu/brentwood/

Department: Department of Criminal Justice
100 Second Avenue
Brentwood, NY 11717
Phone: (631) 273-5112
Fax: (631) 273-3155
E-mail: brentwood-info@liu.edu
Website: http://www.liu.edu/Brentwood/Academics/Schools/CLAS/CrimJustice/

Type of Program: MS in Criminal Justice

Application Deadline: Not available

Requirements: Stated below

Information Required for Application:
- Application for admission (online or print);
- Official copies of undergraduate and/or graduate transcripts from any colleges or universities attended;
- A bachelor's degree in a related area with a minimum 3.0 undergraduate cumulative average (students whose GPA is 2.5 or better will be considered on an individual basis; students without a background in a related area may petition the department chair for consideration); and
- Two professional and/or academic letters of recommendation that address the applicant's potential in the profession and ability to complete a graduate program.

Admission Date: Not available

In-state and Out-of-state Tuition Costs: $1,068 per semester hour

Availability of Internships and Scholarships: Not available

Orientation and Emphasis of Department/Program (Program Description): The thirty-six-credit master of science in criminal justice is designed to provide the skills and understanding necessary to address the emerging public interest problems of the twenty-first century. The program offers a core curriculum that lays the foundation for the understanding of crime and high technology and the ability to think critically. Graduates of the program are equipped to pursue careers such as working at research institutes, with juveniles, with alternative-to-incarceration programs, with victims' rights groups, for corporate security, with defendants' rights groups, and in treatment and rehabilitation programs, in addition to traditional law enforcement positions at the federal, state, and local levels.

Number of Faculty: 5

Accreditation: Commission on Higher Education of the Middle States Association of Colleges and Schools

Average Length of Time to Complete the Program: Not available

Long Island University, C.W. Post Campus

Address: 720 Northern Boulevard
Brookville, NY 11548
Phone: (516) 299-2900
Website: http://www.liu.edu/cwpost/

Department: Department of Criminal Justice
Contact: Dr. Harvey Kushner, Chair
LIU Post
720 Northern Boulevard
Brookville, NY 11548-1300
Phone: (516) 299-2467
E-mail: harvey.kushner@liu.edu
Website: http://www.liu.edu/CWPost/Academics/Schools/
CLAS/Dept/Criminal-Justice/

Type of Program: MS in Criminal Justice

Application Deadline: Not available

Requirements: See below

Information Required for Application:
- Application for admission;
- Application fee of $40 (nonrefundable);
- Official copies of undergraduate and/or graduate transcripts from any colleges or universities attended;
- A bachelor's degree in a related area with a minimum 3.0 undergraduate cumulative average (a student without a background in a related area may petition the department chair for consideration);
- Two professional and/or academic letters of recommendation that address the applicant's potential in the profession and ability to complete a graduate program; and
- A personal statement that addresses the reason the student is interested in pursuing graduate work in this area of study.

Admission Date: Not available

In-state and Out-of-state Tuition Costs: $1,068 per semester hour

Availability of Internships and Scholarships: Not available

Orientation and Emphasis of Department/Program (Program Description): The thirty-six-credit master of science in criminal justice offers an in-depth, twenty-first century curriculum geared toward forensics, law and society, criminal behavior, cybercrime, terrorism, and criminological theory. In addition to our core curriculum, specializations are available in fraud examination and security administration. The program prepares students for modern-day careers in criminal justice, including cyberspace crime detection, law enforcement management systems, and homeland security. Courses are taught by a distinguished faculty that includes published authors, researchers, and widely-consulted authorities on the American and world criminal justice systems. Adjunct faculty members are working professionals in the field and include attorneys, judges, and law enforcements officials. Our professors will engage and inspire you to exceed your expectations.

Number of Faculty: 3

Accreditation: Commission on Higher Education of the Middle States Association of Colleges and Schools

Average Length of Time to Complete the Program: Not available

Longwood University

Address: 201 High Street
Farmville, VA 23909
Phone: (434) 395-2000
Website: http://www.longwood.edu/

Department: Department of Sociology, Anthropology, and Criminal Justice Studies
Longwood University
West Ruffner 202
201 High Street
Farmville, VA 23909
Phone: (434) 395-2241
Fax: (434) 395-2200
Website: http://www.longwood.edu/sacjs/

Type of Program: MS in Sociology with Criminal Justice Concentration (BS/MS five-year program)

Application Deadline: October 1 (Fall semester of junior year)

Requirements:
- Be in good standing with the university;
- Cumulative grade point average (GPA) of at least 3.00;
- Apply in the Fall semester of junior year;
- Have completed at least sixty undergraduate credit hours (transfer students may apply after the completion of twelve credit hours earned at Longwood);
- Three faculty recommendations; and
- A 1,000-word essay.

Information Required for Application: Stated above

Admission Date: Fall

In-state and Out-of-state Tuition Costs: In-state: $289 per credit hour; out-of-state: $799 per credit hour

Availability of Internships and Scholarships: There is a directory of internships. Faculty or a staff member who wishes to request a graduate assistant position must submit their request for a graduate assistant by March 1 for an assistantship beginning the next Fall term. Students admitted to a degree program may apply for a graduate assistantship by May 1 for an assistantship beginning the next Fall term by submitting the graduate assistantship application. Students are encouraged to browse through the graduate assistantship positions and indicate a preference on their application.

Orientation and Emphasis of Department/Program (Program Description): Criminology/criminal justice and sociology majors can expand their career opportunities by choosing to apply for the combined five-year BS/MS program.

- Earn the BS degree in criminology/criminal justice or sociology in four years.
- Earn the MS degree in sociology with criminal justice concentration in the fifth year.

Number of Faculty: 11

Accreditation: Southern Association of Colleges and Schools Commission on Colleges

Average Length of Time to Complete the Program: Five years (four of undergraduate studies, one of graduate studies)

Loyola University Chicago

Address: 1052 West Loyola Avenue
Chicago, IL 60626
Phone: (773) 274-3000
Website: http://www.luc.edu/

Department: Department of Criminal Justice and Criminology
Loyola University Chicago
820 North Michigan Avenue
Chicago, IL 60611
Phone: (312) 915-7564
Website: http://www.luc.edu/criminaljustice/

Type of Program: MA in Criminal Justice and Criminology

Application Deadline: February 1

Requirements: Applicants for admission to graduate study must hold a bachelor's degree, although not necessarily in criminal justice or criminology. Students with limited or no background in criminal justice or criminology may be required to remediate such deficiencies through additional coursework either prior to or concomitant with enrollment in graduate courses. Acceptance into the master's program is based on a combination of academic and professional factors. Students with a GPA lower than 3.3 must take the GRE test. All students should submit a writing sample and complete the statement of purpose. The statement of purpose should describe the student's career aspirations, educational and practical experience that were critical in their preparation for graduate studies, their research interests, and any additional information that may assess their preparedness for graduate studies.

Information Required for Application: Stated above

Admission Date: Fall

In-state and Out-of-state Tuition Costs: $930 per credit hour

Availability of Internships and Scholarships: Graduate assistantships and merit-based fellowships

Orientation and Emphasis of Department/Program (Program Description): The faculty members invite you to explore our supportive and stimulating educational environment. The department offers a general MA degree that prepares students to excel in today's evidence-based criminal justice system. A supportive environment accommodates the diversity of our students' lives with evening classes, the option of part-time or full-time status, and flexible tailoring of electives. The department is well connected to local and federal agencies. Graduates have been placed in all areas of the criminal justice system including state and county agencies, and federal agencies such as the FBI, Secret Service, Federal Probation, Homeland Security, Federal Pretrial Services, and DEA. Graduates also have been admitted into PhD programs or law schools.

Number of Faculty: 12

Accreditation: Higher Learning Commission of the North Central Association of Colleges and Schools

Average Length of Time to Complete the Program: Not available

Loyola University New Orleans

Address: 1700 Calhoun Street
New Orleans, LA 70118
Phone: (504) 865-3240
Website: http://www.loyno.edu/

Department: Department of Criminal Justice
Stallings Hall, Room 122
6363 St. Charles Avenue, Box 55
New Orleans, LA 70118
Phone: (504) 865-3323
Fax: (504) 865-3612
Website: http://css.loyno.edu/criminaljustice/

Type of Program: Master's in Criminal Justice; MS in Criminal Justice Administration (fully online)

Application Deadline: Not available

Requirements: Stated below

Information Required for Application:
- $20 application fee (check made out to Loyola University New Orleans);
- To apply for Loyola's online degree program in criminal justice administration, please complete the following forms:
- Personal Statements on both of the following: (1) Reflect on your career to date or past educational experience and how that has prepared you to succeed in the MSCJA program at Loyola University New Orleans; and (2) What do you expect to gain from this program? How will you impact those around you based on the knowledge gained in this program?
- Official transcripts from each college/university attended (Loyola University recommends "course-by-course" Educational Credential Evaluators [http://www.ece.org/] for all international transcripts);
- Three letters of recommendation (using the form provided by Loyola) from persons knowledgeable about the applicant's aptitude for master's level study and professional experience relevant to the MSCJA program; and
- A formal interview.

Admission Date: January, April, July, October

In-state and Out-of-state Tuition Costs: $818 per hour

Availability of Internships and Scholarships: Internships are listed, but most are for undergraduate level studies.

Orientation and Emphasis of Department/Program (Program Description):

Master's in Criminal Justice: Criminal justice and private security are two of the fastest growing areas in terms of employment, and an advanced degree is becoming a necessity. The master of criminal justice program responds to the need for professionally-trained criminal justice administrators, planners, and researchers, as well as private security professionals. The master of criminal justice curriculum at Loyola is thirty credit hours. Courses are taught year-round (Spring, Summer, and Fall semesters) with courses available at night in an eight-week format (one night a week per course).

Master of Science in Criminal Justice Administration: The MSCJA degree program consists of a rigorous graduate-level curriculum that integrates the overlapping skills of public- and private-sector law enforcement and corporate risk practitioners into a common framework. This framework makes it possible for those practitioners to obtain the specialized education and skills in their particular sub-area(s) of interest. Moreover, this program consciously and purposefully embeds core Jesuit concepts, spreading social justice into both the traditional venues of criminal justice and private sector risk mitigation, a domain that is not frequently thought to be part of the social justice paradigm.

Number of Faculty: 20

Accreditation: Southern Association of Colleges and Schools Commission on Colleges

Average Length of Time to Complete the Program: Not available

Lynn University

Address: 3601 North Military Trail
Boca Raton, FL 33431
Phone: (561) 237-7000
Website: http://www.lynn.edu/

Department: College of Arts and Sciences
Website: http://www.lynn.edu/academics/colleges/arts-and-sciences/programs/ms-administration-criminal-justice-administration/

Type of Program: MS in Criminal Justice Administration (online)

Application Deadline: Not available

Requirements: Students are urged to apply as early as possible before the start of each term to allow sufficient time for application evaluation and meeting with program coordinator to register for classes.

Information Required for Application:
• Application;
• $45 nonrefundable application fee;
• Essay or statement of professional goals;
• Official transcripts from all previous institutions attended; and
• Letter of recommendation from previous professor or employer.

Admission Date: Fall, Spring, Summer

In-state and Out-of-state Tuition Costs: $660 per credit (criminal justice discount: $125 per credit)

Availability of Internships and Scholarships: Graduate assistant/administrative fellow program.
Students selected for the graduate assistant/administrative fellow program will be required to work eighty hours per eight-week term for each course they take. The typical course load is six credits every term. All graduate assistants/administrative fellows are required to pay all fees every eight weeks and maintain a cumulative GPA of 3.0 in order to participate. Administrative fellows only work their hours and do not receive a stipend. Graduate assistants work required hours per week and receive a $1,000 stipend every eight weeks.

Orientation and Emphasis of Department/Program (Program Description): Our master of science in administration degree program will hone the skills you've already developed as an undergraduate, while at the same time broadening your professional network and opportunities.

By specializing in criminal justice administration, you'll study alongside system experts, working together with your peers and professors to discuss and debate current problems within the field. You'll be given the tools you need to develop solutions to those problems—and you'll be challenged to implement them in the workplace, too. Assignments are field-based, so you can combine theoretical knowledge with practical experience. You'll follow current criminal cases and investigations, and you'll analyze the criminal justice system in order to develop your own perspectives of the field.

Number of Faculty: 3

Accreditation: Southern Association of Colleges and Schools

Average Length of Time to Complete the Program: Not available

Madonna University

Address: 36600 Schoolcraft Road
Livonia, MI 48150
Phone: (800) 852-4951
Website: http://www.madonna.edu/

Department: School of Business
Phone: (734) 432-5354
Website: http://www.madonna.edu/academics/colleges-and-schools/school-of-business/

Type of Program: MSBA Leadership in Criminal Justice; Graduate Certificate in Criminal Justice Leadership

Application Deadline: May 1

Requirements: Not available

Information Required for Application: Not available

Admission Date: Fall

In-state and Out-of-state Tuition Costs: $610 per credit hour

Availability of Internships and Scholarships: Tuition grants are available.

Orientation and Emphasis of Department/Program (Program Description): Not available

Number of Faculty: Not available

Accreditation: Higher Learning Commission of the North Central Association of Colleges and Schools

Average Length of Time to Complete the Program: Not available

Marshall University

Address: 1 John Marshall Drive
Huntington, WV 25755
Phone: (304) 696-3170
Website: http://www.marshall.edu/

Department: Department of Criminal Justice and Criminology
Smith Hall 731
Phone: (304) 696-3196
Website: http://www.marshall.edu/isat/cjc/

Type of Program: MS in Criminal Justice

Application Deadline: July 1, November 1

Requirements:
- A baccalaureate degree from an accredited college or university (preference will be given to applicants with undergraduate majors in criminal justice or closely related social science discipline);
- An undergraduate grade point average (GPA) of 3.0 or higher on a 4.0 scale for all previously completed undergraduate university work;
- GRE scores (will be evaluated in combination with the undergraduate GPA);
- A score of 550 or higher on the TOEFL (for international students only); and
- A C or better in an undergraduate research methods course or equivalent (documentation of course content may be required).

Information Required for Application:
- Two letters of recommendation (college instructors strongly preferred); and
- A personal statement (one- to two-page essay regarding the student's interest in criminal justice and how the MS in criminal justice degree will benefit him or her).

Admission Date: Fall, Spring

In-state and Out-of-state Tuition Costs: In-state: $6,540; out of state: $15,922

Availability of Internships and Scholarships: Graduate internship

Orientation and Emphasis of Department/Program (Program Description): This program will provide students with the conceptual and research skills needed to undertake advanced analyses of the criminal justice system; serve criminal justice professionals and others who are interested in pursuing professional careers in management and administration; furnish law enforcement, corrections, and court practitioners with knowledge of justice administration, theoretical perspectives of human behavior, policy analysis, and criminal justice theory; and prepare social scientists to pursue careers in university and research settings.

Number of Faculty: 10

Accreditation: Higher Learning Commission of the North Central Association of Colleges and Schools

Average Length of Time to Complete the Program: Two years

Marywood University

Address: 2300 Adams Avenue
Scranton, PA 18509
Phone: (570) 348-6211
Website: http://www.marywood.edu/

Department: Department of Criminal Justice
Social Sciences Department
82 Liberal Arts Center
Phone: (570) 348-6211 ext. 2242
Website: http://www.marywood.edu/socsci/criminaljustice/

Type of Program: MS in Criminal Justice

Application Deadline: April 1, November 1

Requirements: Listed below

Information Required for Application:
- Official transcripts from all institutions attended (except Marywood);
- Two letters of recommendation from college/university faculty members (may also include recommendations from supervisors in a criminal justice agency); and
- A two- to four-page expository essay discussing your career objectives and how a master's degree in criminal justice from Marywood will contribute to these objectives.

Admission Date: Fall, Spring

In-state and Out-of-state Tuition Costs: $775 per credit hour

Availability of Internships and Scholarships: Graduate students who are not employed by a criminal justice agency must complete a 240-hour internship.

Orientation and Emphasis of Department/Program (Program Description): This interdisciplinary program combines criminal justice and management course work. Students are encouraged also to select electives from such related fields as psychology and social work. The program has close working relationships with federal Middle District criminal justice agencies located in Scranton. It is the only graduate criminal justice program within a 150-mile radius of Scranton. The program is designed for criminal justice administrators or those who wish to prepare for management positions in this field.

Number of Faculty: 11

Accreditation: Middle States Association of Colleges and Schools

Average Length of Time to Complete the Program: Not available

Mercyhurst College

Address: 501 East 38th Street
Erie, PA 16546
Phone Number: (814) 824-2000
Website: http://www.mercyhurst.edu/

Department: Administration of Justice
Phone: (814) 824-2265
Website: http://www.mercyhurst.edu/academics/graduate/
administration%20of%20justice/

Type of Program: Administration of Justice Graduate Program

Application Deadline: Accepted throughout the year

Requirements: Listed below

Information Required for Application:
- A completed application form (online or hard copy; there is a nominal processing fee to submit hard copy applications);
- Three letters of recommendations;
- Official transcripts from all postsecondary institutions send directly to Mercyhurst University;
- A résumé or curriculum vitae;
- An essay of 300 to 500 words outlining the student's personal, professional and educational goals; and
- Graduate Record Exam (GRE) or Miller Analogies Test (MAT).

Admission Date: Fall, Spring

In-state and Out-of-state Tuition Costs: $1,338 per three-credit course

Availability of Internships and Scholarships: Graduate assistant-ships and fellowships, in addition to internships.

Orientation and Emphasis of Department/Program (Program Description): The oldest Mercyhurst University graduate pro-gram—the administration of justice (AOJ) program—was cre-ated in 1978 under the assumption that criminal justice is a true profession dedicated to serving society and preserving the basic rights and freedoms of all people. The AOJ program is built on a common core of courses involving a broad overview of govern-ment management, organizational and interpersonal dynamics, professional ethics, and research competence.

Number of Faculty: 4

Accreditation: Not available, listed for other individual programs

Average Length of Time to Complete the Program: Two years

Michigan State University

Address: 220 Trowbridge Road
East Lansing, MI 48824
Phone: (517) 355-1855
Website: http://www.msu.edu/

Department: School of Criminal Justice
Baker Hall, Room 560
655 Auditorium Road
East Lansing, MI 48824
Phone: (517) 355-2197
Website: http://criminaljustice.msu.edu/

Type of Program: MS in Criminal Justice; PhD in Criminal Justice; Master's in Criminal Justice (CJ, online); Master's in Law Enforcement Intelligence Analysis (LEIA, online); and Master's in Judicial Administration (JA, online)

Application Deadline: End of December

Requirements: If you are applying to the criminal justice master's program and your overall undergraduate GPA is 3.2 or higher (or you have already completed a graduate degree), you do not need to submit GRE scores. Otherwise, no requirements were specified.

Information Required for Application: See above

Admission Date: Not available

In-state and Out-of-state Tuition Costs: Not available.

Availability of Internships and Scholarships: Fellowships, scholarships, assistantships.
Louis A. Radelet Graduate Diversity Scholarship Fund: Provides assistantship and fellowship funding to minority graduate students in criminal justice.
Michael J. Rutherford Endowed Scholarship: Provides tuition support for juniors, seniors, and graduate students in criminal justice.
Private and Industrial Security Endowed Scholarship: Provides tuition support for upper-level undergraduate and graduate students with career interests in private and corporate security.
Tournament of Friendship Scholarship: Provides support for tuition and textbooks for undergraduate and graduate students in criminal justice. It is designed to promote multicultural diversity, and preference is given to Michigan residents.
Walter E. Bothe Memorial Scholarship: Provides tuition assistance to graduate or undergraduate students pursuing careers in law enforcement.

Zolton Ferency Endowed Scholarship: Awarded to students enrolled in the MSU College of Social Science, School of Criminal Justice.

Orientation and Emphasis of Department/Program (Program Description):
The first residential program is a thirty-credit hour master's degree in criminal justice (CJ) designed to prepare and enhance criminal justice professionals with coursework in the operation and management of different areas of the criminal justice system. The program provides students with analytic skills, an interdisciplinary knowledge base, and practical understanding of the settings where law enforcement, courts, correctional, and corporate security policies are implemented. There is also an option for an international focus that allows students to explore criminal justice systems in other countries.

The doctoral program in criminal justice is designed to support the interdisciplinary study of crime and criminal justice. The program permits students to design an individualized a curriculum that can focus on traditional issues of crime, violence, law and society, and the administration of justice, as well as emerging areas such as conservation criminology, cybercrime, prevention of product counterfeiting, security, and terrorism. Students develop a cognate area of study, building on the strengths of Michigan State University and developing a strong foundation in social science theory and research methods. The doctoral program prepares students for careers in college and university teaching and research, as well as advanced public-policy positions.

Number of Faculty: 32 professors

Accreditation: Higher Learning Commission of the North Central Association of Colleges and Schools

Average Length of Time to Complete the Program: Not available.

Midwestern State University

Address: 3410 Taft Boulevard
Wichita Falls, TX 76308
Phone: (940) 397-4000
Website: http://www.mwsu.edu/

Department: Criminal Justice Department
3410 Taft Boulevard
Wichita Falls, TX 76308
Phone: (940) 397-4752
Website: http://www.mwsu.edu/academics/hs2/criminal justice/

Type of Program: MA in Criminal Justice

Application Deadline: August 7, December 15, May 15, June 15

Requirements: Admission considerations include the following: (1) that the applicant has, or will soon have, an undergraduate degree from an accredited institution in an allied field; (2) official transcripts of all academic work previously undertaken; (3) at least two letters of recommendation from undergraduate professors; (5) a personal essay of the applicant's career goals and aspirations; and (6) international students are required to take the Test of English as a Foreign Language (TOEFL).

Information Required for Application:
- Complete an application online by visiting http://www.apply-texas.org/ before the deadlines. There is an application fee of $35 for domestic students and $50 for international students.
- Take the GRE or GMAT, and request that scores be sent to the MSU Graduate Admissions Office. International students must also take the TOEFL and IELTS, which test proficiency of the English language.
- Request official transcripts from each institution attended other than MSU.

Admission Date: Fall, Spring, Summer sessions

In-state and Out-of-state Tuition Costs: In-state: $115 per credit hour; out-of-state: $404 per credit hour

Availability of Internships and Scholarships: Not available

Orientation and Emphasis of Department/Program (Program Description): The master of arts in criminal justice is designed to prepare graduate students in conducting research and actively participating in the development of knowledge in the areas of criminological theory, crime control, and correctional and police administration. The curriculum has the breadth and depth to fulfill these various interests. Students who are planning careers in law enforcement, corrections, or rehabilitation or who wish to pursue a deeper understanding of crime and the criminal justice system should confer with the graduate program advisor to develop a combination of elective courses that will support their particular career interests.

Number of Faculty: 15

Accreditation: Southern Association of Colleges and Schools Commission on Colleges

Average Length of Time to Complete the Program: Not available

Mississippi College

Address: 200 S. Capitol Street
Clinton, MS 39058
Phone: (601) 925-3000
Website: http://www.mc.edu/

Department: Department of History and Political Science
Jennings Hall 203
Phone: (601) 925-3221
Website: http://www.mc.edu/academics/departments/history/

Type of Program: Master of Social Sciences (MSS) in Criminal Justice

Application Deadline: Not available

Requirements:
- All general requirements for admission to the Graduate School of Mississippi College must be met.
- Must have a baccalaureate degree from an accredited institution.
- Must have a minimum of thirty semester hours of undergraduate work in the social sciences (economics, history, administration of justice, political science, and sociology), fifteen hours of which are in one field.
- Must have undergraduate credit for History 101-102 or 211-212, Economics, and Sociology.
- A verbal score beginning in the range of 146-150 (equivalent to 400-450) and a quantitative score beginning in the range of 140-141 (equivalent to 400-450), or a score within these ranges on either section and a score of 2.5 on the writing assessment of the General Record Examination (GRE) are required. The verbal and quantitative scores will not be combined. Departments may exercise discretion for students who score below this range.

Information Required for Application:
- Application for admission;
- A $35 application fee (nonrefundable; must accompany application);
- One copy of all the official transcript(s) from previous collegiate work (associate's, bachelor's, master's, doctorate), and any transferable graduate credit (official transcripts are those mailed from the college or university directly to the dean of the Graduate School, Box 4029, Clinton, MS 39058; those brought in by applicant, relative, etc. or marked "issued to student" are not considered official);

- For residential students a $100 nonrefundable room reservation fee;
- All applicants seeking the Class AA Standard Educator License must provide a photocopy of their Class A Standard Educator License issued from the State of Mississippi. Applications will not be processed without this documentation.
- A standardized test score should be filed with your application. Lacking this standardized test automatically results in provisional admission. Non-degree-seeking graduate students are exempt from filing standardized test scores unless they are pursuing educator licensure.
- Consult specific degree descriptions for additional admissions

Admission Date: Not available

In-state and Out-of-state Tuition Costs: $504 per credit hour

Availability of Internships and Scholarships: Not available

Orientation and Emphasis of Department/Program (Program Description): Welcome to the Administration of Justice program at Mississippi College. I am Dr. Harry Porter, Director of the Administration of Justice program. Our program is the home of quality, caring professional faculty members who emphasize ethical values in the fields of criminal justice, homeland security/emergency management, and loss prevention. Since its inception in 1984, the Mississippi College administration of justice program has provided its students with exceptional faculty members from diverse backgrounds who help students develop the necessary critical thinking skills to compete in the multifaceted world of criminal justice. Our program graduates outstanding individuals who secure top jobs and become leaders at the local, state, and federal levels of law enforcement and in the private security industry.

Number of Faculty: 14

Accreditation: Commission on Colleges of the Southern Association of Colleges and Schools

Average Length of Time to Complete the Program: Not available

Missouri State University

Address: 901 South National Avenue
Springfield, MO 65897
Phone: (417) 836-5000
Website: http://www.missouristate.edu/

Department: Department of Criminology and Criminal Justice
901 South National Avenue
Springfield, MO 65897
Phone: (417) 836-3799
Fax: (417) 836-3200
E-mail: criminology@missouristate.edu
Website: http://criminology.missouristate.edu/

Type of Program: MSAS in Criminal Justice; Certificate in Homeland Security and Defense

Application Deadline: July 20 for Fall semester, December 20 for Spring semester

Requirements:
- Have earned a bachelor's degree in sociology, criminology, or criminal justice;
- Maintained an overall 3.0 GPA on a 4.0 scale or received a score of 475 or higher on either the verbal or quantitative section of the GRE, and a score no less than 400 on the other section. Please note that, even though admission is based on GRE scores, students must meet the 2.75 GPA minimum required by the Graduate College.

Information Required for Application: Acceptance into a graduate program at Missouri State requires admission into both the Graduate College and the specific master's program. Therefore, acceptance into the Graduate College does not automatically provide acceptance into the specific graduate program.
- Apply to the Graduate College online or by completing a paper copy, which is available in the University's Graduate Catalog.
- Pay the application fee of $35.
- Submit two official copies of your transcript to the Graduate College
- Submit your GRE scores to the university
- Write a statement of intent describing your reasons for applying to the program, what you hope to gain from this educational experience, and your post-graduate plans.
- Provide three letters of reference discussing your academic potential, preferably from academic sources.

Statement of intent and three letters of reference should be sent directly to the Department of Criminology and Criminal Justice at Graduate Admissions, Department of Criminology and Criminal Justice, Missouri State University, 901 South National Avenue, Springfield, MO 65897

Admission Date: Fall and Spring semesters only.

In-state and Out-of-state Tuition Costs: Resident: $5234 (based on eighteen credit hours); nonresident: $9,680 (based on eighteen credit hours); both also include an (estimated) additional $1,000 in supplemental course fees and supplies.

Availability of Internships and Scholarships: Don Ivie Scholarship is awarded annually to graduate students in the department, based on academic merit and student contributions to the department. Scholarship amount varies depending on funding. Graduate assistantships are also available based on academic merit.

Orientation and Emphasis of Department/Program (Program Description): Our goal is to provide students with an education to lead criminal justice agencies through the challenges of the twenty-first century. We offer a curriculum which gives you the tools to sharpen decision making, policy analysis, and managerial skills.

Number of Faculty: 11

Accreditation: Higher Learning Commission of North Central Association of Colleges and Schools

Average Length of Time to Complete the Program: Thesis option: thirty-three semester hours and a written thesis. Non-thesis option: thirty-six semester hours and a 270-hour practicum experience, plus comprehensive exams.

Molloy College

Address: 1000 Hempstead Avenue
Rockville Centre, NY 11570
Phone: (516) 323-3000
Website: http://www.molloy.edu/

Department: Criminal Justice
1000 Hempstead Avenue
Siena Hall, Room 108
Rockville Centre, NY 11571-5002
Phone: (516) 323-3804
E-mail: crj@molloy.edu
Website: http://www.molloy.edu/academics/undergraduate-majors/criminal-justice/

Type of Program: MS in Criminal Justice

Application Deadline: Not available

Requirements: Not available

Information Required for Application: Not available

Admission Date: Not available

In-state and Out-of-state Tuition Costs: $940 per credit

Availability of Internships and Scholarships: Not available

Orientation and Emphasis of Department/Program (Program Description): It's an exciting time to be pursuing a graduate degree in criminal justice and Molloy College is the place for you. Since 9/11, the demand for criminal justice majors—who have an understanding of the criminal system and the minds of criminals—is enormous. Earning your graduate degree will help advance your current career and enable entry into higher level positions, and for many criminal justice agencies an advanced degree is a requirement. As a graduate of the Molloy criminal justice MS program, you will not only qualify for higher-level positions but also stand out as a leader and future expert in your chosen specialty. Your master's in criminal justice from Molloy College will also pave the way for you to pursue your PhD.

Number of Faculty: 28

Accreditation: Middle States Association of Colleges and Schools and Board of Regents of the University of the State of New York

Average Length of Time to Complete the Program: Not available

Monmouth University

Address: 400 Cedar Avenue
West Long Branch, NJ 07764-1898
Phone: (732) 571-3400
Website: http://www.monmouth.edu/

Department: Department of Criminal Justice
Phone: (732) 571-3448
Website: http://www.monmouth.edu/school-of-humanities-social-sciences/criminal-justice.aspx

Type of Program: MA in Criminal Justice; MS in Homeland Security

Application Deadline: July 15, November 15, May 1

Requirements:
Master of Arts
- Possession of a baccalaureate degree with a minimum 2.5 overall GPA and a minimum 3.0 GPA in the undergraduate major;
- Two letters of recommendation for graduate study; and
- Personal essay of 250-300 words that describes your preparation for study in the program and personal objectives for graduate study in criminal justice.

Master of Science
- Possession of a baccalaureate degree with a minimum 2.5 overall GPA;
- Personal essay; and
- Two professional letters of recommendation.

Information Required for Application:
- A nonrefundable $50 application fee must accompany all applications.
- Official transcripts of the undergraduate record, along with transcripts of any graduate work done elsewhere, must be forwarded directly to the Office of Admission Processing.
- Include your Social Security number on all documentation submitted to the Office of Admission Processing.
- Submit your GRE or GMAT scores.

Admission Date: Fall, Spring, Summer

In-state and Out-of-state Tuition Costs: $963 per credit

Availability of Internships and Scholarships: A graduate fellowship award is available to provide scholarship assistance to students who have demonstrated outstanding academic achievement in the completion of the baccalaureate degree. Partial-tuition scholarships are awarded to matriculated students by the Office of Graduate Admission and are made on the basis of the student's cumulative undergraduate grade point average. Graduate scholarships are also awarded to eligible international graduate students. Awards are based on undergraduate grade point average. (International candidates' undergraduate grade point averages are converted to the American grading system.) All applicants for admission are automatically evaluated for scholarship eligibility; the student need not complete a separate scholarship application.

Orientation and Emphasis of Department/Program (Program Description): The thirty-credit master of arts in criminal justice program offers a broad perspective on the justice system and its various institutions and processes. It develops the critical and research skills needed for problem solving and policy making in the profession. Core courses focus on criminal procedure, psychopathology of the offender, research procedures, the use of psychosocial variables, systems thinking, and the development of policy. Students may choose from thesis track or non-thesis track options. The homeland security track will prepare individuals to assist in preventing, anticipating, and preparing for natural and human-made catastrophic events. This concentration will also provide opportunities for criminal justice professionals to work with federal, state, and local governmental agencies. In addition, trained professionals are finding many new opportunities in the private sector, protecting large multinational companies and organizations. Our curriculum provides a solid foundation for a broad liberal arts education and a balanced perspective on the study and practices of the criminal justice system.

Number of Faculty: 8

Accreditation: The Middle States Commission on Higher Education

Average Length of Time to Complete the Program: Thesis option: thirty hours; non-thesis option: thirty hours, plus comprehensive exams

Morehead State University

Address: 150 University Boulevard
Morehead, KY 40351
Phone: (800) 585-6781
Website: http://www.moreheadstate.edu/

Department: Department of Sociology, Social Work, and Criminology
335 Rader Hall
Morehead, KY 40351
Phone: (606) 783-2656
Fax: (606) 783-5070
Website: http://www.moreheadstate.edu/sswc/

Type of Program: MA in Sociology with a focus in Criminology

Application Deadline: Not available

Requirements: Not available

Information Required for Application:
- Create an account through the admissions site and complete the application for admission to Graduate School.
- Pay a $30 nonrefundable application processing fee.
- Submit an official transcript from all institutions attended.
- Submit official general aptitude GRE, MAT, or GMAT scores (if necessary).

Admission Date: Not available

In-state and Out-of-state Tuition Costs: $535 per credit hour (not including fees)

Availability of Internships and Scholarships: Over ninety assistantships are offered each year to graduate students. These assistantships provide a stipend of $10,000 for the academic year (Fall and Spring). If you have any questions regarding the graduate assistantship program at Morehead State University, please contact Ollie Floyd.

Orientation and Emphasis of Department/Program (Program Description): This program focuses on understanding the causes of crime, the structure of the criminal justice system, and how this system operates with regard to both sentencing and innovative treatment in the twenty-first century.

Number of Faculty: 5

Accreditation: Southern Association of Colleges and Schools

Average Length of Time to Complete the Program: Not available

National University

Address: 9388 Lightwave Avenue
San Diego, CA 92123
Phone: (858) 541-7700
Website: http://www.nu.edu/

Department: Department of Professional Studies
Website: http://www.nu.edu/OurPrograms/School-of-Profes-sional-Studies/ProfessionalStudies/Programs/MasterofCriminal-Justice.html

Type of Program: Master of Criminal Justice (MCJ; online)

Application Deadline: Not available

Requirements: Not available

Information Required for Application: Not available

Admission Date: Not available

In-state and Out-of-state Tuition Costs: $384 per quarter unit

Availability of Internships and Scholarships: Not available

Orientation and Emphasis of Department/Program (Program Description): The master of criminal justice (MCJ) is designed to provide students with the required knowledge and competence in administration, management, and problem solving skills for challenging and demanding careers in criminal justice in the fields of criminal justice administration and criminal justice research and development. Students completing the master in criminal justice are exposed to both theoretical and applied models and concepts in criminal justice administration, as well as qualitative and quantitative research methods. The master of criminal justice program integrates theory with practice to provide graduates with the skills and knowledge needed to address the complex issues and challenges of criminal justice in the twenty-first century. Students in this program develop the problem solving and research skills as well as technological expertise necessary to analyze reality-based cases and assignments to develop strategies and solutions that are both practical and effective. Challenging and demanding careers in government at the local, state, and federal level in the administration of justice, law enforcement management, correctional administration, security administration, and criminal justice research, as well as teaching and training assignments await graduates with a master's degree in criminal justice.

Number of Faculty: Not available

Accreditation: Accrediting Commission for Senior Colleges and Universities of the Western Association of Schools and Colleges

Average Length of Time to Complete the Program: Not available

New Jersey City University

Address: 2039 Kennedy Boulevard
Jersey City, NJ 07305-1597
Phone: (201) 200-2000
Website: http://www.njcu.edu/

Department: Department of Criminal Justice
Phone: (201) 200-2419
Fax: (201) 200-3482
Website: http://www.njcu.edu/criminaljustice/gprogram/

Type of Program: MS in Criminal Justice

Application Deadline: Not available

Requirements: Must have a minimum GPA of 2.75; meet all minimum requirements of the Graduate Studies Office, which includes a completed application, transcripts, recommendation letters, essay, résumé, and GMAT results. Supplemental supporting evidence, such as an interview, writing sample, or portfolio, may be required.

Information Required for Application: An application for admission to graduate study and an application for matriculation; a nonrefundable $55 application fee; a 250-500-word essay discussing your goals and objectives for pursuing admission to a degree program; official transcripts from all colleges attended; two letters of recommendation, preferably from previous instructors; and an official copy of the standardized test score report required by the program should all be submitted to the Graduate Admissions Office.

Admission Date: Not available

In-state and Out-of-state Tuition Costs: $628.60 per credit hour

Availability of Internships and Scholarships: A limited number of graduate assistantships are available each year to highly-qualified graduate students. The graduate assistantship covers tuition and fees for full-time study (nine to fifteen credits per semester). Graduate assistants are required to work in a university department or office for eighteen hours each week, for which they receive a stipend of $3,500 over the academic year ($1,750 per semester).

Orientation and Emphasis of Department/Program (Program Description): A master of science in criminal justice—increasingly important for advancement in the field—prepares students in the nature and causes of crime, the management of correctional systems, and the techniques and applications of research. In addition this program provides opportunities for in-depth study in specific areas of interest.

Number of Faculty: 6

Accreditation: Middle States Commission on Higher Education

Average Length of Time to Complete the Program: Thirty credit hours, plus a master's project worth three credit hours

New Mexico State University

Address: P.O. Box 30001, MSC 3-RRGS
Las Cruces, NM 88003-8001
Phone: (575) 646-0111
Website: http://www.nmsu.edu/

Department: Department of Criminal Justice
Phone: (575) 646-3316
E-mail: cjustice@nmsu.edu
Website: http://crimjust.nmsu.edu/

Type of Program: MA in Criminal Justice

Application Deadline: March 1 (for Fall)

Requirements: A minimum overall undergraduate cumulative GPA of 3.0 or minimum 3.5 cumulative GPA for last sixty hours of learned credit; three letters of recommendation from individuals able to comment upon your ability to complete graduate work; and a three- to five-page essay that introduces you and discusses the following topic, "The most important change needed in the criminal justice system is …," to be evaluated by the MCJ admission committee.

Information Required for Application: Apply to the Graduate School at NMSU online; send three letters of recommendation directly to the director of the MCJ program; send the essay described above directly to the director of the MCJ program. The address for letters of recommendation and essay is Dr. Carlos Posadas, Director, Master of Criminal Justice Program, Department of Criminal Justice, MSC 3487, New Mexico State University, P.O. Box 30001, Las Cruces, NM 88003-8001.

Admission Date: Fall only

In-state and Out-of-state Tuition Costs: Residents: one to eighteen credits = $223.25 per credit; nonresidents: one to six credits = $223.25 per credit, seven to eleven credits = $647.25 per credit (not including course fees).

Availability of Internships and Scholarships: NMSU provides the Department of Criminal Justice with a small number of graduate assistantships each year. Each Spring these graduate assistantships are awarded to students for the upcoming academic year on a competitive basis. If you wish to be considered for a graduate assistantship award you must indicate in writing your desire to be considered for a graduate assistantship. For full consideration, the director of the MCJ must be in receipt of all materials for admission, including your written request to be considered for a graduate assistantship, by March 1. The formal allocation of graduate assistantships occurs after the Graduate School informs the Department of Criminal Justice of the number of graduate assistantship allocations. Only campus-based students are eligible for graduate assistantships in the Department of Criminal Justice.

Orientation and Emphasis of Department/Program (Program Description): The mission of the department is based upon our understanding of criminal justice as an interdisciplinary social science field. Our goals are to prepare students for careers at the federal, state, and local levels throughout the criminal justice profession and to deliver the highest quality education to our undergraduate and graduate students, helping them develop critical thinking skills, imparting knowledge of theoretical perspectives and methodological techniques, and providing experiential learning opportunities that give students first-hand exposure to the complexities of the professional environment.

Number of Faculty: 15

Accreditation: The Higher Learning Commission of the North Central Association of Colleges and Schools

Average Length of Time to Complete the Program: Thesis option: thirty-three hours plus a written thesis; non-thesis option: thirty-six hours, plus comprehensive exams.

Niagara University

Address: Niagara University, NY 14109
Phone: (716) 285-1212
Website: http://www.niagara.edu/

Department: Department of Criminology and Criminal Justice
Website: http://www.niagara.edu/crj/

Type of Program: MA in Criminal Justice Administration

Application Deadline: Niagara University has a rolling admissions policy. Applications are considered as they are received and evaluated in a holistic fashion in keeping with the mission of the university. The earlier you apply, the sooner your application will be considered.

Requirements: Not available

Information Required for Application: All application information can be found after creating an account through the graduate admissions portal.

Admission Date: Fall, Spring, and Summer

In-state and Out-of-state Tuition Costs: $655 per credit hour (not including fees)

Availability of Internships and Scholarships: Not available

Orientation and Emphasis of Department/Program (Program Description): This program strives to provide advanced education and professional development in criminal justice administration for those currently working in the criminal justice system, and to provide advanced education for those seeking future leadership positions in the criminal justice field.

Number of Faculty: 11

Accreditation: Middle States Association of Colleges and Schools

Average Length of Time to Complete the Program: The master's degree program consists of eleven three-credit courses. The sequence totals thirty-three semester hours. Full-time students can complete the program in one calendar year (including Summer sessions), while part-time students finish in two.

Norfolk State University

Address: 700 Park Avenue
Norfolk, VA 23504
Phone: (757) 823-8600
Website: http://www.nsu.edu/

Department: Department of Criminal Justice
Phone: (757) 368-6369
Website: http://sola.nsu.edu/macj/

Type of Program: MA in Criminal Justice

Application Deadline: Not available

Requirements: Not available

Information Required for Application: Not available

Admission Date: Fall and Spring

In-state and Out-of-state Tuition Costs: In-state: $459 per credit hour; out-of-state: $1,182 per credit hour

Availability of Internships and Scholarships: Assistantships

Orientation and Emphasis of Department/Program (Program Description): The master of arts in criminal justice (MACJ) program addresses the diverse needs of professionals who provide leadership in the justice system. Two [areas] of concentration permit students to develop specialized skills and expertise. The aim of the MACJ is to provide a coordinated and systematic approach, attracting top quality student into the program. The goal and objectives will focus on skills development and knowledge that reflects the changes in criminal justice education toward professional development.

Number of Faculty: Not available

Accreditation: Commission on Colleges of the Southern Association of Colleges and Schools

Average Length of Time to Complete the Program: Not available

North Carolina Central University

Address: 1801 Fayetteville Street
Durham, NC 27707
Phone: (919) 530-6100
Website: http://www.nccu.edu/

Department: Department of Criminal Justice
301 Whiting Criminal Justice Building
P.O. Box 19772
Durham, NC 27707
Phone: (919) 530-5204
Fax: (919) 530-5195
Website: http://www.nccu.edu/academics/sc/socialsciences/
criminaljustice/

Type of Program: MS in Criminal Justice Law Enforcement

Application Deadline: Not available

Requirements: A minimum overall undergraduate GPA of 2.75, or a 3.0 average for the last four semesters of study from the bachelor's degree; one official transcript from each institution attended; two application evaluation and recommendation forms completed by persons familiar with applicant's academic work; and official GRE scores. Prospective student's application packet and $40 nonrefundable application fee should be mailed to the School of Graduate Studies or the appropriate admitting office.

Admission Date: Not available

In-state and Out-of-state Tuition Costs: resident: $3,852.27 (for twelve credit hours); non-resident: $9,676.77 (for twelve credit hours)

Availability of Internships and Scholarships: Limited funding is available for students. This funding is awarded on a competitive basis. Students are advised to contact the director of graduate programs for the Criminal Justice Department for more information. In addition, students should contact the University Financial Aid Office for information on other funding sources.

Orientation and Emphasis of Department/Program (Program Description): This program prepares students with skills and knowledge, including such aspects of criminal justice as law enforcement, courts, corrections, and crime prevention. The goals of the program are to prepare graduates who are able to: assess and understand criminal justice problems and issues; conduct basic and applied research in criminal justice, particularly evaluation research; use computer technology to locate information and use statistics and software to analyze problems, particularly with respect to criminal justice agencies; understand legal issues that affect criminal justice professionals; and integrate the findings concerning the psychological, sociological, economic, and cultural roots of crime.

Number of Faculty: 11+

Accreditation: Commission on Colleges of the Southern Association of Colleges and Schools

Average Length of Time to Complete the Program: Not available

North Dakota State University

Address: 1340 Administration Avenue
Fargo, ND 58102
Mailing: P.O. Box 6050
Fargo, ND 58108-6050
Phone: (701) 231-8011
Website: http://www.ndsu.edu/

Department: Department of Criminal Justice and Political Science;
North Dakota State University
Department of Criminal Justice and Political Science
NDSU Department 2315
1616 12th Avenue North
P.O. Box 6050
Fargo, ND 58108-6050
Website: http://www.ndsu.edu/cjps/criminal_justice/

Type of Program: MS in Criminal Justice Administration; PhD in Criminal Justice

Application Deadline: Not available

Requirements: Students will need to enter the program with a baccalaureate degree. Students will be required to have had one course in research methods, one course in statistics, and should document adequate background preparation or demonstrated potential in the field of criminology or criminal justice. For admission to full-standing, students are required to achieve a minimum grade point average of 3.0 over their last sixty credit hours. Students not meeting these standards will be evaluated and possibly placed on conditional status.

Information Required for Application: Applicants will be required to submit the following:
- Application for admission;
- Official transcript(s) (grade report);
- A $35 application fee and $10 processing fee (international applicants must pay an additional $15 transcript evaluation fee);
- Statement of purpose outlining your reasons for pursuing graduate study;
- Three letters of recommendation; at least one must be from a person who can evaluate the student's academic work; and
- Official GRE scores and—for international students—official TOEFL or IELTS scores.

Admission Date: Fall, Spring, and Summer

In-state and Out-of-state Tuition Costs: Resident: $3,999.98 (full-time) or $333.34 per credit hour (part-time), plus all applicable fees; nonresident: $9,674.48 (full-time) or $806.21 per credit hour (part-time), plus all applicable fees

Availability of Internships and Scholarships: Not available

Orientation and Emphasis of Department/Program (Program Description): The education and training of master's degree students in this field will (1) furnish practicing professionals with advanced knowledge of justice administration, criminal justice policy, behavioral elements of crime, and research skills; (2) provide students with conceptual and research skills that would facilitate coursework in a subsequent PhD program; and (3) enhance the thinking skills of leaders in the criminal justice system by improving supervisory standards, facilitating critical thinking, and promoting ideas of social change. Doctoral students are prepared to conduct research in the various areas of criminological theory, crime control, and correctional and police administration, and to pursue teaching and/or research positions in academia or research positions within the criminal justice system itself. The curriculum will afford training to students in four areas: (1) criminological theory, (2) advanced research skills, (3) teaching in academia, and (4) specialization in one of three areas: criminology, corrections, and policing.

Number of Faculty: 5

Accreditation: Higher Learning Commission

Average Length of Time to Complete the Program: Thirty credit hours, plus a written thesis or policy-based paper

Northeastern State University

Address: 3100 East New Orleans
Broken Arrow, OK 74014
Phone: (918) 456-5511
Website: http://www.nsuok.edu/

Department: Department of Criminal Justice and Legal Studies
Tahlequah Campus
Seminary Hall 320
Phone: (918) 444-3538
Fax: (918) 458-2348
Website: http://academics.nsuok.edu/criminaljustice/CJLS
Home.aspx

Type of Program: MS in Criminal Justice

Application Deadline: Not available

Requirements: A minimum cumulative GPA of 2.5 based on a 4.0 scale on all undergraduate coursework attempted, or a 2.75 in the last sixty semester hours of undergraduate coursework, or a score in the upper three-fourths of national norms on the GRE. A bachelor's degree in criminal justice or paralegal studies is a prerequisite.

Information Required for Application: A completed application for graduate admission; an official transcript of all previous college coursework; and two references from professional or academic sources.

Admission Date: Fall and Spring

In-state and Out-of-state Tuition Costs: Resident: $204.15 per credit hour; nonresident: $464.15 per credit hour

Availability of Internships and Scholarships: NSU's financial aid program for graduate students is designed to recognize excellence in academics and leadership, and also assists those who otherwise would be unable to attend the university. NSU participates in all traditional types of financial assistance available through the state and the federal government. Graduate students at NSU receive funds from a variety of sources to pay for their education, including scholarships, graduate assistantships, tuition waivers, part-time jobs, and educational loans. This money comes from federal and state agencies, as well as private donors. Assistance from the federal student aid programs is based on the belief that students should make every effort possible to invest in their education. We are committed to working with students to make a graduate degree from NSU affordable. However, please be aware that graduate students are not eligible for subsidized student loans or grant assistance from the Federal Title IV programs.

Orientation and Emphasis of Department/Program (Program Description): The master of science degree in criminal justice is a thirty-six-hour program designed to provide the student with a foundation in five specific areas: criminal justice systems; crime theory; criminal justice administration; legal aspects; and research methods. Additional elective courses offer the student an opportunity to acquire some background in forensics and investigative techniques. The student who successfully completes this program should be adequately prepared to assume administrative, managerial, training, or research responsibilities in the applied criminal justice arena, or to pursue doctoral level education in criminal justice or a related discipline.

Number of Faculty: Not available

Accreditation: Higher Learning Commission of the North Central Association

Average Length of Time to Complete the Program: Two years

Northeastern University

Address: 360 Huntington Avenue
Boston, MA 02115
Phone: (617) 373-2000
Website: http://www.northeastern.edu/

Department: School of Criminology and Criminal Justice
Phone: (617) 373-3327
Website: https://www.northeastern.edu/sccj/

Type of Program: Master's in Criminal Justice (online),

Application Deadline: February 1 (for priority Fall), October 1,
August 1

Requirements: Stated below

Information Required for Application:
- Application form (the entire application form must be completed, and the applicant must submit the $75 application fee online);
- Personal goal statement. The personal statement should briefly describe the student's background, interests, and reasons (expectations, goals, etc.) for wanting to pursue graduate study in the School of Criminology and Criminal Justice. Students may include any other information they feel may be useful in considering their application for admission. We do ask, however, that you limit your personal statement to approximately 500 words;
- Transcripts (unofficial transcripts from all institutions attended should be uploaded);
- Official scores on the Graduate Record Examination (GRE) are required, and must be sent directly to the Graduate School from Educational Testing Services (ETS). Only scores from the past five years will be accepted. No application for admission will be considered prior to receipt of official scores from ETS. Our school code is 3682. For additional information on the GRE please visit their website at http://ets.org/gre/;
- International applicants must also submit evidence of English proficiency: TOEFL, IELTS, or a degree earned at a U.S. institution;
- Three letters of recommendation. Letters should be of an academic and/or professional nature, and not from friends, relatives, or neighbors. Letters of recommendation must also be submitted online as part of your application;
- Résumé; and
- Writing sample.

Admission Date: Fall and Spring

In-state and Out-of-state Tuition Costs: $25,740 per year

Availability of Internships and Scholarships: A variety of opportunities exist for financial assistance through the graduate program in criminal justice. There are teaching and research assistantships that provide a stipend and the remission of tuition, and in turn students work twenty hours per week for the School of Criminology and Criminal Justice. In addition, there is a George Lewis Ruffin Fellowship for minority students that provides tuition remission and a stipend. These awards are made on the basis of scholarly merit and professional experience rather than financial need. The number of these awards is limited and early application is recommended. Decisions regarding assistantship awards are made at the same time as admissions decisions. Graduate student scholarships are available to master's applicants and offer tuition remission with no work requirement. These awards are based on scholarly achievement and are limited to the top applicants. The Dean's Scholarship awards provide a 1/3 tuition discount to full-time students or a 1/4 tuition discount to part-time students. These awards are based on scholarly achievement and are limited to the top applicants.

Orientation and Emphasis of Department/Program (Program Description): The master's program in criminal justice concentrates on both the problem of crime as a form of deviant behavior and the criminal justice and private security systems that deal with it. The program emphasizes a systems approach to criminal justice, stressing policy development and analysis, as well as the impact these policies have on the individuals and organizations charged with delivering justice in a fair and equitable manner. Broad in concept and scope, it encompasses such related disciplines as law, sociology, political science, psychology, criminology, and public administration. The professional master of science in criminal justice is distinguished by its balanced emphasis on leadership and best policies and practices in criminal justice, while providing its students with a rigorous intellectual and philosophical foundation in an adult learning format. In conjunction with the College of Professional Studies, the program combines experiential, urban, and global career-oriented learning through a combination of online courses and a weeklong on-campus Summer workshop. The program emphasizes themes of leadership, communication, integrity, and ethics, as well as best practices in the disciplines of policing/law enforcement, private security, corrections, and community corrections. The School of Criminology and Criminal Justice at Northeastern University offers a PhD in criminology and justice policy. This program prepares students for academic careers as well as careers in research and policy development. The program is small and student-centered with the goal of preparing students for academic and policy placements.

Number of Faculty: 23

Accreditation: New England Association of Schools and Colleges

Average Length of Time to Complete the Program: With a full-time course load, students generally complete the master's program in eighteen months. Part-time students complete their degree in three to four years depending on their pace and course selection. For full-time doctoral students, it is expected that students entering the program with a bachelor's degree will be able to complete the program in five to six years, while students entering with a master's degree will be able to complete the program in four years.

Northern Arizona University

Address: South San Francisco Street
Flagstaff, AZ 86011
Phone: (928) 523-9011
Website: http://www.nau.edu/

Department: Department of Criminology and Criminal Justice
Phone: (928) 523-9519
E-mail: criminal.justice@nau.edu
Website: http://www.nau.edu/sbs/ccj/

Type of Program: MS in Applied Criminology

Application Deadline: Fall: February 15; Spring: October 15

Requirements: Acceptance by the Graduate College and the Department of Criminology and Criminal Justice; a minimum undergraduate GPA of 3.0 on 4.0 scale.

Information Required for Application: In addition to the online completion of admissions forms, the following materials must be submitted to the department through the online application:
* Official transcripts;
* Three letters of recommendation, preferably from academic references;
* A personal statement that describes your interest in the program, your educational and career goals, information regarding your academic and professional preparation for entry into the program, and any special topic areas you would like to pursue at the master's level; and
* A professional writing sample in the English language, such as a professional paper, research paper, or class paper (preferably with instructor's comments included).

Admission Date: Not listed

In-state and Out-of-state Tuition Costs: Tuition at NAU is dependent upon what campus you attend, and what semester you matriculate. A breakdown of tuition and fees can be found at http://www.nau.edu/SDAS/Tuition-Fees/.

Availability of Internships and Scholarships: Departmental graduate assistantships are awarded based on academic merit and student ability to support faculty teaching and research efforts. State-supported graduate assistantships are awarded annually to students by the graduate program committee. Students who receive these awards are assigned to individual faculty members based on the recommendation of the graduate program director. These assistantships include funds for a stipend and a tuition waiver. The nature of the service requirement for the assistantship will be determined by the graduate program director and by the individual faculty member to whom the student is assigned.

Number of Faculty: 20

Accreditation: Higher Learning Commission of the North Central Association

Average Length of Time to Complete the Program: Not available

Northern Michigan University

Address: 1401 Presque Avenue
Marquette, MI 49855-5301
Phone: (906) 227-1000
Website: http://www.nmu.edu/

Department: Department of Criminal Justice
Northern Michigan University
1401 Presque Isle Avenue
Marquette, MI 49855
Phone: (906) 227-2660
Fax: (906) 227-1754
E-mail: cj@nmu.edu
Website: http://www.nmu.edu/criminaljustice/

Type of Program: MA in Criminal Justice (online)

Application Deadline: Not available

Requirements: Not available

Information Required for Application: An application and official transcripts must be submitted to the College of Graduate Education. The following must be submitted to the criminal justice master's program: application to the program; an essay that explains your interest in pursuing a graduate degree in criminal justice; an essay that explains your views on a specific topic; and two recommendations, preferably from academic sources who can comment on your academic ability.

Admission Date: Not available

Tuition costs: $427 per credit hour

Availability of Internships and Scholarships: Graduate assistantships are available based on academic merit.

Number of Faculty: 6

Accreditation: Higher Learning Commission

Average Length of Time to Complete the Program: Not available

Nova Southeastern University

Address: 3301 College Avenue
Fort Lauderdale-Davie, FL 33314-7796
Phone: (800) 541-6682
Website: http://www.nova.edu/

Department: Institute for the Study of Human Service, Health, and Justice
Website: http://www.nova.edu/humanservices/criminaljusticems/

Type of Program: MS in Criminal Justice

Application Deadline: Winter: December 15; Summer: April 21

Requirements: A minimum GPA of 2.5 or higher in the last sixty semester hours of undergraduate coursework, or a master's degree with an overall GPA of 3.0 or better.

Information Required for Application: An online application form must be completed; a $50 application fee with be charged for each application submitted. Official transcripts, two letters of recommendation, and a personal statement indicating your goals in pursuing a degree should all be submitted to: Nova Southeastern University, Enrollment Processing Services, ATTN: Criminal Justice, 3301 College Avenue, P.O. Box 2299000, Fort Lauderdale-Davie, FL 33314-7796.

Admission Date: Summer and Winter

Tuition costs: $628 per credit hour, not including applicable fees

Availability of Internships and Scholarships: Not available

Orientation and Emphasis of Department/Program (Program Description): The MS in criminal justice trains individuals through an interdisciplinary focus in an online environment. The program prepares students through the core curriculum and allows for specialty training through various tracks.

Number of Faculty: 20+

Accreditation: Commission on Colleges of the Southern Association of Colleges and Schools

Average Length of Time to Complete the Program: Not available

Oklahoma City University

Address: 2501 North Blackwelder
Oklahoma, OK 73106-1493
Phone Number: (405) 208-5000
Website: http://www.okcu.edu/

Department: Department of Sociology and Justice Studies
Website: http://www2.okcu.edu/petree/soc/

Type of Program: Masters of Science in Criminology

Application Deadline: Not listed

Requirements: Admission to Oklahoma City University's master's degree programs is open to all students holding bachelor's degrees from regionally accredited colleges or universities and meeting the criteria indicating high potential to succeed in graduate-level work.

- Apply online at www.okcu.edu/admissions/graduate/apply/ Include a statement of purpose of 150 to 200 words describing your reasons for pursuing graduate study and your academic and professional interests and goals.
- All graduate programs require a minimum cumulative 3.0 GPA for admission, based on the undergraduate or most recent degree.
- Submit a typed, doubled-spaced response to the following question, with a minimum of one page typed per social issue: What are the three most significant social issues currently facing us today, and what are the solutions you would suggest?
- Attach a nonrefundable fee of $50.
- Unofficial or photocopies of transcripts from all colleges or universities attended may be included with the application; however, official transcripts must be mailed directly to the Office of Admissions from all colleges and universities attended.
- Two letters of recommendation are required for admission from persons able to comment on professional and academic ability. They may submit the letters electronically at www.okcu.edu/graduate/recommendation/ or by mail to the Office of Admissions.

Admission Date: Not listed

In-state and out-of-state tuition costs: resident: $936 per credit hour not including applicable fees (http://www.okcu.edu/financialaid/tuition/graduate/criminology/)

Availability of internships and scholarships: Information available at http://www.okcu.edu/financialaid/assistance/ and http://www.okcu.edu/financialaid/scholarships/graduate/.

Orientation and emphasis of department/program (Program Description): The Master of Science in Criminology program at OCU offers a curriculum that promotes the development of skills required in the workforce. Students study with faculty working on contemporary issues facing Oklahoma, the United States and the world. We can accomplish this with the assistance of our connections to various local, state, and federal agencies like Oklahoma City Police Department, Oklahoma State Bureau of Investigation, and the U.S. Marshals Service. This advisory board provides direct connections for our students with potential employers as well as developing critical analysis skills for contemporary social issues. Graduates of our program can be found working across the country in these and other agencies: CARE Child Abuse and Response Evaluation Center, Federal Bureau of Investigation, Oklahoma Department of Corrections and U.S. Marshals Service to name a few. The majority of our classes are on an eight-week rotating basis, which means that you take two classes at a time and four classes a semester. We are offering Advanced Research Methods, Serial Homicide Investigation, Law and Social Sciences, and Critical Issues in Justice. With a degree from OCU, you will learn the science, theory, and research of the entire criminal justice process.

Number of faculty: Not available

Accreditation: The Higher Learning Commission of the North Central Association of Schools and Colleges.

Average length of time to complete the program: They are currently developing a fast-track option where you can complete your Master's degree in one year, attending two nights a week.

Old Dominion University

Address: 1 Old Dominion University
Norfolk, VA 23529
Physical address: 5115 Hampton Blvd., Norfolk, VA 23529
Phone Number: (405) 208-5000
Website: www.odu.edu

Department: Department of Sociology and Criminal Justice
Phone: (757) 683-3791
Website: http://al.odu.edu/sociology/

Type of Program: PhD Criminology and Criminal Justice

Application Deadline: January 15

Requirements: A completed master's degree (or equivalent) in criminology, criminal justice, or in an appropriate filed (e.g., administration of justice, sociology, or political science) from a regionally accredited institution of higher education — a thesis is generally expected; a minimum grade point average (GPA) of 3.25 (on a 4.0 scale) overall for the master's degree; a combined minimum score of 1,000 on the GRE general knowledge tests (verbal and quantitative) and 4.5 on the writing test; successful completion of prior coursework in research methodology and statistics at least equivalent to that required by the ODU B.A. in sociology/criminal justice (statistics, research methods, capstone group research project) and M.A. degree in applied sociology (research methods, statistics, computer and data analysis); three letters of reference from sources capable of commenting on the applicant's readiness for advanced graduate study in criminology & criminal justice; a writing sample of at least 20 double-spaced pages on a topic related to the applicant's expertise or area of interest; and a typed statement of approximately 1,000 words summarizing the individual's motivation for applying to the program as well as the professional contributions the student intends to make assuming successful completion of the degree.

Admission Date: Fall

In-state and out-of-state tuition costs: resident: $412/credit hour, not including applicable fees; non-resident: $1,048/credit hour, not including applicable fees.

Availability of internships and scholarships: Not Available

Orientation and emphasis of department/program (Program Description): The PhD in Criminology and Criminal Justice is a sociological criminology program that highlights social inequality and public policy in the study of crime and justice issues. The program produces scholars with strong backgrounds in the substantive areas of criminology, criminal justice, theory, inequality and policy as well as in research methods and statistics. Designed primarily for students who are interested in pursuing careers in higher education, the course offerings also provide students the education and skills needed to be employed as researchers in public and private agencies. Graduates are prepared as scholars able to conduct research, teach college and university courses in their areas of specialization, and to provide service to the discipline and community.

Number of faculty: 19

Accreditation: Southern Association of Colleges and Schools Commission on Colleges

Average length of time to complete the program: Not listed; 48-hour program

Penn State Harrisburg

Address: 777 West Harrisburg Pike
Middletown, PA 17057
Phone: (717) 948-6250
Website: http://harrisburg.psu.edu/

Department: Department of Criminal Justice
School of Public Affairs
Phone: (717) 948-6050
E-mail: L-SPA-STAFF@lists.psu.edu
Website: http://harrisburg.psu.edu/public-affairs/

Type of Program: MA in Criminal Justice

Application Deadline: Fall: May 31; Spring: November 1

Requirements: A minimum undergraduate degree of 3.0, a satisfactory score on the GRE, three letters of recommendation, and a brief statement of purpose.

Admission Date: Fall and Spring

Tuition costs: $9,135 per semester (if enrolled full time)

Availability of Internships and Scholarships: Graduate assistantships are available based on academic merit.

Orientation and Emphasis of Department/Program (Program Description): The program reflects the numerous complexities of the discipline. It provides academic leadership for students to work within corrections, institutionalized and non-institutionalized settings, victim services, adult and juvenile services, policing and law enforcement, private security, courts, and other human service organizations serving the clients of these institutions. It also helps develop research abilities for those students who may wish to consider doctoral studies.

Number of Faculty: 9

Average Length of Time to Complete the Program: Not available

Penn State University Park

Address: University Park
State College, PA 16801
Phone: (814) 865-4700
Website: http://www.psu.edu/

Department: Department of Sociology and Criminology
211 Oswald Tower
The Pennsylvania State University
University Park, PA 16802
Phone: (814) 865-2527
Website: http://sociology.la.psu.edu/

Type of Program: MA in Criminology; PhD in Criminology. The program does not offer a terminal master's degree. All of their students earn a master's degree as they fulfill the requirements for the PhD.

Application Deadline: January 10

Requirements:
- U.S. applicants must have a baccalaureate degree from an accredited institution to apply for admission.
- International applicants must have a tertiary (postsecondary) degree that is deemed comparable to a four-year U.S. bachelor's degree to apply for admission. This degree must be from an officially recognized degree-granting institution in the country in which it operates.
- You may only apply to one graduate program and campus at a time.
- If you currently hold a doctorate, you are not encouraged to apply for a second doctorate.

Information Required for Application: Selection is based on transcripts, three letters of recommendation from persons familiar with the applicant's academic performance, a statement of goals, a sample of written work such as a term paper or thesis, and Graduate Record Examination (GRE) scores. International applicants must also submit TOEFL scores.

Admission Date: Fall only

In-state and Out-of-state Tuition Costs: In-state: $761 per credit hour; out-of-state: $1,302 per credit hour

Availability of Internships and Scholarships: All students admitted to the program receive research assistantships or teaching assistantships. This funding package includes a stipend and a tuition waiver. We also have a strong record of providing Summer support.

Orientation and Emphasis of Department/Program (Program Description): The MA program is intended for students who plan to go on to pursue a PhD. Over thirty credits of course work and a master's thesis are required for the master's degree. This course work includes four 500-level methods courses (two in statistical methods, one in general research methods, and one in research methods for crime, law, and justice); a crime theory course; a course on the criminal justice system; a seminar covering a range of sociological topics; and at least two 500-level substantive crime, law, and justice courses. Finally, the Graduate School requires that MA candidates complete six thesis credits. These are earned while the student writes his or her MA thesis. Doctoral students must complete all courses required for the MA degree or their equivalents. In addition, they must take at least four 500-level courses in crime, law, and justice and a one-credit lab in teaching. Doctoral students must also select—in consultation with their advisory committees—twelve credits of course work outside the criminology program. This concentration must consist of 500-level courses that provide a solid grounding in a social science discipline that can be applied to the study of crime, law, or justice. Examples would include urban sociology, social psychology, human development, and American government institutions, among many other possibilities. All PhD candidates must pass a comprehensive exam and complete a high-quality scholarly dissertation.

Number of Faculty: 88

Accreditation: Middle States Commission on Higher Education

Average Length of Time to Complete the Program: Five years for those entering with a bachelor's degree; four years for those entering with a master's degree.

Point Park University

Address: 201 Wood Street
Pittsburgh, PA 15222
Phone: (412) 391-4100
Website: http://www.pointpark.edu/

Department: Department of Criminal Justice and Intelligence Studies
Phone: (412) 392-8136
Website: http://www.pointpark.edu/Academics/Schools/
SchoolofArtsandSciences/Departments/Criminal
JusticeandIntelligenceStudies/

Type of Program: MS in Criminal Justice Administration

Application Deadline: No application deadline; rolling admissions

Information Required for Application: Transcripts from all previous schools attended, with a minimum undergraduate GPA of 2.75; a 500-word essay explaining the applicant's motivation for seeking graduate education, professional experience, and career goals; a current résumé; and two letters of recommendation, one from an academic source and one from an employer.

Tuition costs: $791 per credit hour (plus all applicable fees)

Availability of Internships and Scholarships: The School of Arts and Sciences offers a graduate assistantship during the academic year (September through April) with all tuition and fees paid along with an annual stipend of $6,400. The graduate assistant must be a full-time incoming or current Point Park University master's degree student and must work in the School of Arts and Sciences for a minimum of twenty hours per week.

Orientation and Emphasis of Department/Program (Program Description): Point Park University's master of science in criminal justice administration provides a strong foundation in business, administration, law, policy, economics, and criminological theory. Our criminal justice master's program is designed for the well-educated criminal justice professional that must be armed with diverse skills.

Number of Faculty: 6

Accreditation: Middle States Commission on Higher Education

Average Length of Time to Complete the Program: Not available

Portland State University

Address: P.O. Box 751
Portland, OR 97207-0751
Phone: (503) 725-3000
Website: http://www.pdx.edu/

Department: Department of Criminology and Criminal Justice
Phone: (503) 725-4014
Website: http://www.pdx.edu/hatfieldschool/criminology-criminal-justice/

Type of Program: MS in Criminal Justice

Application Deadline: February 1 (priority deadline), April 1 (final deadline)

Requirements: A bachelor's degree from an accredited college or university; a total undergraduate GPA of 3.20 or higher, or a graduate GPA of 3.20 or higher for a minimum of 9 credit hours.

Information Required for Application: Portland State University requires that an applicant submit two different application packets: one to the PSU Office of Admissions and the other directly to the Division of Criminology and Criminal Justice. Application instructions, including the required forms, can be obtained from the Office of Graduate Studies. The application forms provide detailed information about what is required by the university to apply. The CCJ Division requires that applicants provide some additional documents: a departmental application form; transcripts from each post-secondary institution attended; two or more letters of recommendation; GRE scores; a 500-word statement of purpose describing academic and professional career goals; and a résumé or curriculum vita (optional).

Admission Date: Fall

In-state and Out-of-state Tuition Costs: Resident: $341 per credit hour (not including applicable fees); nonresident: $533 per credit hour (not including applicable fees)

Availability of Internships and Scholarships: Prospective and returning students are encouraged to complete the application for the graduate assistantship. Graduate assistants (GAs) work with faculty members and receive other benefits—in particular, a tuition remission and modest stipend. GAs must be registered for, and compete, at least nine credits of coursework during each term of their appointment.

Orientation and Emphasis of Department/Program (Program Description): The Division of Criminology and Criminal Justice offers a program of study designed to provide students a broad-based understanding of the criminal justice system and society's response to crime. A major goal of the program is to develop understanding of the applied and theoretical aspects of crime and criminal justice. The program provides a high degree of flexibility and allows students to tailor the program to match their own career interests. Core coursework consists of classes in the theoretical foundations of criminology and criminal justice, methodology, and criminal justice policy analysis.

Number of Faculty: 10+

Accreditation: Northwest Commission on Colleges and Universities

Average Length of Time to Complete the Program: Two years

Radford University

Address: 801 East Main Street
Radford, VA 24142
Phone: (540) 831-5000
Website: http://www.radford.edu/

Department: Department of Criminal Justice
307 Adams Street
P.O. Box 6934
Radford, VA 24142
Phone: (540) 831-6148
Fax: (540) 831-6075
Website: http://www.radford.edu/content/chbs/home/criminal-justice.html

Type of Program: MA in Criminal Justice

Application Deadline: March 1

Requirements: A minimum overall GPA of 2.9; two letters of recommendation; and an original writing sample consisting of five typed pages with peer-reviewed references on the most important current problem in criminal justice.

Admission Date: Not available

In-state and Out-of-state Tuition Costs: Resident: $4,872 per semester; nonresident: $9,500 per semester

Availability of Internships and Scholarships: Not available

Orientation and Emphasis of Department/Program (Program Description): The graduate program in criminal justice allows students to prepare for management and other careers in criminal justice and related fields. The program is designed both to enhance students' existing capabilities and to develop unique competencies and skills for future academic and career goals.

Number of Faculty: 10+

Accreditation: Not available

Average Length of Time to Complete the Program: Not available

Regis University

Address: 3333 Regis Boulevard
Denver, CO 80221-1099
Phone: (800) 388-2366
Website: http://www.regis.edu/

Department: Department of Criminology
Website: http://criminology.regis.edu/criminology-degree/masters-criminology/

Type of Program: MS in Criminology

Application Deadline: Not available

Information Required for Application: Two professional recommendations; two admissions essays; a current résumé; official transcripts from all previous colleges; completed graduate application form; and a $75 nonrefundable application fee are all required during the application process.

Admission Date: Not available

Tuition costs: $535 per credit hour

Availability of Internships and Scholarships: Not listed

Orientation and Emphasis of Department/Program (Program Description): Understanding, predicting, and preventing crime is the goal of master's-level study in criminology. The curriculum of the master's program explores the societal, political, and cultural factors that can cause or contribute to crime, as well as topics related to leadership and ethics, crime policy and prevention, and decision-making. Students are encouraged to personalize the course by using a subject of special interest as an area of research and study. In both the online and on-campus programs, students take the same classes taught by the same distinguished staff of Regis professors.

Number of Faculty: 3

Accreditation: Higher Learning Commission

Average Length of Time to Complete the Program: Not available

The Richard Stockton College of New Jersey

Address: 101 Vera King Farris Drive
Galloway, NJ 08205-9441
Phone: (609) 652-1776
Website: http://www.stockton.edu/

Department: The School of Social and Behavioral Sciences,
Department of Criminal Justice
Phone: (609) 652-4512
Fax: (609) 626-5559
E-mail: SOBL@stockton.edu
Website: http://intraweb.stockton.edu/eyos/page.cfm?siteID=
163&pageID=8

Type of Program: MA in Criminal Justice

Application Deadline: Fall: July 1; Spring: December 1

Requirements: Minimum 3.0 GPA

Information Required for Application: Stockton's online graduate application, three letters of recommendation, an essay, a
résumé, official GRE test scores, and official transcriptions from
all universities or colleges attended must be submitted during the
application process.

Admission Date: Fall and Spring

In-state and Out-of-state Tuition Costs: Resident: $727.63 per
credit hour (including fees); nonresident: $1,029.35 per credit
hour (including fees)

Availability of Internships and Scholarships: Assistantships are
granted in the form of tuition waiver and can vary from a one-
credit waiver to nine credits or the maximum tuition charge per
semester, whichever is applicable. Awards are made on a semester
basis during the academic year (August–May). Nominations are
made by the faculty and program director of each graduate program and are then forwarded to the dean of the School of Graduate and Continuing Studies for final approval. Students who are
approved for an assistantship will receive an offer-of-appointment
letter from the dean.

**Orientation and Emphasis of Department/Program (Program
Description):** The master of arts in criminal justice program
(MACJ) is designed to offer students a broad and multidisciplinary
perspective on the criminal justice system. The work of criminal
justice practitioners is complex, and it requires knowledge of how

and why people engage in crime, as well as an understanding of the issues faced by practitioners in the criminal justice system.

Number of Faculty: 8

Accreditation: Middle States Association of Colleges and Schools

Average Length of Time to Complete the Program: Not available

Rochester Institute of Technology

Address: One Lomb Memorial Drive
Rochester, NY 14623-5603
Phone: (585) 475-2411
Website: http://www.rit.edu/

Department: Department of Criminal Justice
Website: http://www.rit.edu/cla/criminaljustice/

Type of Program: MS in Criminal Justice

Application Deadline: Spring (date not specified)

Requirements: A cumulative GPA of 3.0 or better; completion of a bachelor's degree from an accredited university; two writing samples, one of which is a personal statement; two letters of recommendation; and official GRE scores are all required to be considered for admission into the program.

Admission Date: All academic semesters

Tuition costs: Full-time: $18,618 per semester; part-time: $1,552 per credit hour

Availability of Internships and Scholarships: An internship program is available that is designed to give students the opportunity to interact with criminal justice professionals in a work environment. Students will be closely supervised at the selected agency, developing their professional skills while learning the agency's organization, programs, and methods.

Orientation and Emphasis of Department/Program (Program Description): The objective of the program is to provide students with a strong foundation in criminological and criminal justice theory and social scientific research skills, thus enabling graduates to have successful careers in the policy analysis arena or to be able to easily transfer into a criminal justice doctoral program.

Number of Faculty: 14

Accreditation: Middle States Commission on Higher Education

Average Length of Time to Complete the Program: Not available

Roger Williams University

Address: One Old Ferry Road
Bristol, RI 02809
Phone: (401) 253-1040
Website: http://www.rwu.edu/

Department: School of Justice Studies
Website: http://rwu.edu/academics/schools-colleges/sjs/
degree-offerings/criminal-justice/

Type of Program: MS in Criminal Justice

Application Deadline: Fall: August 1; Spring: January 1;
Summer: May 1

Information Required for Application: Completed online application, a $50 application fee, official transcripts of all undergraduate and graduate coursework, a personal statement, and two letters of recommendation are all required during the application process.

Admission Date: Fall, Spring, and Summer

Tuition costs: $749 per credit hour

Availability of Internships and Scholarships: Not available

Orientation and Emphasis of Department/Program (Program Description): The master of science degree in criminal justice program prepares graduates to formulate justice system policy and serve effectively as administrators to United States justice system agencies. The master's program permits students to explore the fields of criminology, examining the nature and causes of crime, and learn justice system management, which focuses on modern administrative theory, legal issues in personnel administration, and the management of criminal justice agencies.

Number of Faculty: Not available

Accreditation: New England Association of Schools and Colleges, Commission on Institutions of Higher Education

Average Length of Time to Complete the Program: Not available

Rowan University

Address: 201 Mullica Hill Road
Glassboro, NJ 08028
Phone: (856) 256-4000
Website: http://www.rowan.edu/

Department: Department of Law and Justice
Website: http://www.rowan.edu/colleges/chss/departments/
lawjustice/

Type of Program: MA in Criminal Justice

Application Deadline: Fall: August 1; Spring: December 1

Requirements: Not available

Admission Date: Fall and Spring

Tuition costs: $779.90 per credit hour

Availability of Internships and Scholarships: Graduate assistantships are available on a competitive basis.

**Orientation and Emphasis of Department/Program (Program
Description):** This degree prepares students for professional
careers by providing an understanding of the causes of crime, the
impact of law on society, and contemporary issues in policing,
courts, and corrections.

Number of Faculty: Not available

Accreditation: Middle States Commission on Higher Education

Average Length of Time to Complete the Program: Not available

Rutgers, The State University of New Jersey, Camden

Address: 303 Cooper Street
Camden, NJ 08102-1519
Phone: (856) 225-1766
Website: http://www.camden.rutgers.edu/

Department: Department of Sociology, Anthropology, and Criminal Justice
405-7 Cooper Street
Camden, NJ 08102-1521
Phone: (856) 225-6470
Fax: (856) 225-6435
Website: http://sociology.camden.rutgers.edu/

Type of Program: MA in Criminal Justice

Application Deadline: Fall: December 1; Spring: May 1

Requirements: GRE scores; official transcripts showing a minimum cumulative GPA of 3.0; three letters of recommendation; a brief résumé with any work experience relevant to the application; and a personal statement about your qualifications for graduate level work, as well as your reasons for pursuing an advanced degree.

Admission Date: Fall and Spring

In-state and Out-of-state Tuition Costs: Resident: $7,776 per semester (full-time), plus all applicable fees; nonresident: $12,456 per semester (full-time), plus all applicable fees

Availability of Internships and Scholarships: Not available

Orientation and Emphasis of Department/Program (Program Description): The graduate program builds on the multidisciplinary strength of the faculty. The criminal justice faculty emphasizes a comprehensive understanding of crime and the justice system—including contemporary issues affecting it—and the analytic skills required to conduct and to apply research and to assess public policy. Students may also take courses in public policy and administration, whose faculty stresses the skills to oversee complex public agencies. Faculty members from the Graduate School in Camden and School of Law–Camden provide the program with a wide array of justice-related electives.

Number of Faculty: 8

Accreditation: Middle States Commission on Higher Education

Average Length of Time to Complete the Program: Not available

Rutgers, The State University of New Jersey, Newark

Address: 249 University Avenue
Newark, NJ 07102
Phone: (973) 353-5205
Website: http://www.newark.rutgers.edu/

Department: Rutgers School of Criminal Justice, Center for Law and Justice
123 Washington Street,
Newark, NJ 07102
Phone: (973) 353-3311
Website: http://rscj.newark.rutgers.edu/

Type of Program: MA in Criminal Justice; PhD in Criminal Justice

Application Deadline: MA: May 1, December 1; PhD: December 15

Requirements: Stated below

Information Required for Application:
- GRE General;
- TOEFL (International Students);
- Three letters of recommendation;
- Personal statement;
- Transcripts;
- A résumé; and
- An academic writing sample.

Admission Date: MA: Fall and Spring; PhD: Fall only

In-state and Out-of-state Tuition Costs: In-state: $7,776 per semester; out-of-state: $12,852 per semester

Availability of Internships and Scholarships: Graduate fellowships and an international research program

Orientation and Emphasis of Department/Program (Program Description): The School of Criminal Justice offers a thirty-credit program that includes five required courses (fifteen credits) and five elective courses (fifteen credits), which may include a field-work course (three credits). Students should refer to the *Criminal Justice Master's Program Handbook* for a detailed discussion of current policies, procedures, and requirements for completing the master's program of study. The PhD program is designed to provide students with a command of criminological theory, research methods, and criminal justice policy, as well as in-depth knowledge in areas of specialization within criminology and/or criminal justice. The doctoral degree is awarded based on evidence that the candidate has achieved a high level of proficiency in independent scholarship and research. This is assessed through course grades, the qualifying exam, the production of a publishable-quality empirical paper, and successful defense of the dissertation.

Number of Faculty: 32

Accreditation: Middle States Association of Colleges and Schools

Average Length of Time to Complete the Program: All requirements for the degree of master of arts should be completed within three years of the first matriculation in the criminal justice MA program. All requirements for the doctor of philosophy should be completed within five years, and must be completed within seven years of the first matriculation in the criminal justice PhD program.

Sacred Heart University

Address: 5151 Park Avenue
Fairfield, CT 06825
Phone: (203) 371-7999
Website: http://www.sacredheart.edu/

Department: Department of Criminal Justice
Academic Building
HC Suite 219
5151 Park Avenue
Fairfield, CT 06825
Phone: (203) 371-7941
Fax: (203) 365-4892
Website: http://www.sacredheart.edu/academics/
collegeofartssciences/academicdepartments/criminaljustice/

Type of Program: MA in Criminal Justice

Application Deadline: Not available

Requirements: Not available

Information Required for Application: A completed graduate application, official transcripts from all colleges and universities attended, two letters of recommendation, a one-page personal statement, a current résumé, and a $60 nonrefundable application fee.

Admission Dates: Not available

Tuition costs: $675 per credit hour

Availability of Internships and Scholarships: Students may participate in an internship as part of the elective course required for the degree. This is a three credit course. Students will be placed in criminal justice agencies. There are a limited number of research and staff assistantships available to full-time graduate students on a competitive basis.

Orientation and Emphasis of Department/Program (Program Description): The purpose of an advanced degree program is to pursue a greater knowledge then is possible in an undergraduate program. This program will prepare students to go from the acquisition of knowledge to the application of knowledge. It will provide individuals with the knowledge necessary to solve the problems related to crime and justice within our society. This program is not limited to teaching students stop-gap measures for dealing with crime and justice related issues. It does not simply focus on counting the number of crimes occurring at any given time or in any given place. Rather, the focus is on how to prevent such incidents from occurring in the first place.

Number of Faculty: 7

Accreditation: New England Association of Schools and Colleges

Average Length of Time to Complete the Program: Not available

St. Ambrose University

Address: 518 West Locust Street
Davenport, IA 52803
Phone: (563) 333-6000
Website: http://www.sau.edu/

Department: Department of Sociology Criminal Justice
Phone: (563) 333-6166
Website: http://www.sau.edu/mcj/

Type of Program: MA in Criminal Justice

Application Deadline: Not available

Requirements: Students with a bachelor's degree from an accredited institution may apply for admission.

Information Required for Application: A completed graduate application form, official transcripts from the institution granting the bachelor's degree, a professional goals statement, two letters of recommendation, and a nonrefundable $25 application fee.

Admission Date: Not available

Tuition costs: $488 per credit hour

Availability of Internships and Scholarships: A limited number of graduate assistantships and fellowships are available on a competitive basis.

Orientation and Emphasis of Department/Program (Program Description): The master of criminal justice program is ideal for those interested in upper-level careers in law enforcement, security, corrections, and human services. The degree provides a theoretical basis for topics that apply to the field, for example, using political theories and policy analysis research techniques to improve crime policy. The program's academic focus also prepares those who want to teach criminal justice or to serve as personnel and training specialists in justice-related organizations. The curriculum addresses social justice topics, including race, class, and gender, and their impact on the criminal justice system—from arrest through sentencing.

Number of Faculty: 9

Accreditation: North Central Association of the Higher Learning Commission

Average Length of Time to Complete the Program: Two years

St. Cloud State University

Address: 720 4th Avenue South
St. Cloud, MN 56301
Phone: (320) 308-0121
Website: http://www.stcloudstate.edu/

Department: Department of Criminal Justice Studies
Phone: (320) 308-4101
Website: http://www.stcloudstate.edu/criminaljustice/

Type of Program: MS in Criminal Justice

Application Deadline: June 1, October 1, May 1

Requirements: The master of science degree in criminal justice is intended for persons who have undergraduate degrees in criminal justice or other undergraduate majors. It is a portfolio-project or thesis degree that consists of core courses, elective courses, and a possible internship with a criminal justice agency. An applicant must meet one of the following grade point average (GPA) standards to be eligible for academic admission consideration to the School of Graduate Studies:

- Possess at least an overall 2.75 GPA (4.0 scale) in your previous undergraduate work; or
- Possess at least an overall 2.75 GPA (4.0 scale) in the last half of your undergraduate work.

Information Required for Application:
- Upload unofficial transcripts.
- Unofficial documents will be used for the admission review process. If admitted, you will need to submit official documents before coursework commences.
- Upload your statement of intent, résumé, and a writing sample.
- Applicants may also submit unofficial copies of GRE/GMAT scores, TOEFL/IELTS/PTE, and International transcript evaluations for the review process. If admitted, you will need to submit official documents before coursework commences.
- Through an online system, request your recommenders to submit an online recommendation form.
- Pay a $40 application fee.

Admission Date: Fall, Spring, Summer

In-state and Out-of-state Tuition Costs: In-state (off campus): $393.46 per credit hour; out-of-state $538.86 per credit hour

Availability of Internships and Scholarships: Graduate assistantships and scholarships

Orientation and Emphasis of Department/Program (Program Description): This master's degree is sometimes called the traditional master's degree in the Department of Criminal Justice Studies. It is course-centered, including research courses, core courses, and seminar or specialization courses required for all students. The specialization courses may focus on a specific sub-system of criminal justice. The master of science in criminal justice degree may be completed with a thesis (Plan A) or a professional portfolio of projects and papers (Plan C). Each plan requires a preliminary conference and a final oral examination. All graduate coursework must be completed within the seven years prior to the awarding of the degree.

Number of Faculty: 28

Accreditation: The Higher Learning Commission: North Central Association and the American Association of State Colleges and Universities

Average Length of Time to Complete the Program: Three semesters

St. John's University

Address: 8000 Utopia Parkway
Queens, NY 11439
Phone: (718) 990-2000
Website: http://www.stjohns.edu/

Department: College of Professional Studies
Phone: (718) 990-5991
Website: http://www.stjohns.edu/academics/schools-and-colleges/college-professional-studies/programs-and-majors/criminal-justice-leadership-masters-professional-studies/

Type of Program: Master's of Professional Studies in Criminal Justice Leadership

Application Deadline: Not available

Requirements:
- Evidence of a bachelor's degree from a regionally accredited college or university;
- A record of scholarly achievement with, in general, an overall undergraduate average of at least B (3.0/4.0);
- Two letters of recommendation (one should preferably be from an academic who has taught and evaluated the candidate at the undergraduate level); and
- An essay of approximately 300 words describing the applicant's reason for applying.

Information Required for Application: Stated above.

Admission Date: Not available

In-state and Out-of-state Tuition Costs: $1,100 per credit hour

Availability of Internships and Scholarships: Not available

Orientation and Emphasis of Department/Program (Program Description): Offered through St. John's College of Professional Studies, this innovative thirty-six-credit program is designed to prepare criminal justice and other public and private sector professionals to meet the emerging leadership challenges. The thematic core of the graduate program addresses the study of leadership in all the components of the criminal justice system and other related public sector agencies and corporate security. Courses address the multifaceted challenges leaders face in these agencies. The study of leadership pervades the entire curriculum and is the thematic link that provides the graduate program with its unique analytical approach to organizational decision making.

Number of Faculty: Not available

Accreditation: Middle States Association of Colleges and Schools

Average Length of Time to Complete the Program: Not available

Saint Joseph's University

Address: 5600 City Avenue
Philadelphia, PA 19131
Phone: (610) 660-1000
Website: http://www.sju.edu/

Department: Department of Criminal Justice
Website: http://www.sju.edu/int/academics/cas/grad/criminaljustice/

Type of Program: MS in Criminal Justice

Application Deadline: Rolling admissions

Requirements: 3.00 GPA

Information Required for Application: A completed graduate application, official sealed transcripts of undergraduate coursework, a personal statement outlining professional goals and educational objectives for attending the program, a résumé, and $35 application fee.

Tuition costs: $774 per credit hour, plus applicable fees

Availability of Internships and Scholarships: Applicants who wish to be considered for a graduate assistantship must complete the above application process and submit a letter directly to Dr. Raquel Bergen, Department Chair of Sociology, by March 1 before the Fall semester for which they are applying for admission. Students who are awarded assistantships are required to be enrolled in the program on a full-time basis (three courses per semester) and to work with their assigned faculty member(s) twenty hours per week. Additional employment outside the university is not permitted while the student holds an assistantship. Assistantships are awarded for one academic year (Fall/Spring). Successful applicants may subsequently reapply for a second year. In such cases, the selection decision will be based on the student's original undergraduate grade point average and credentials.

Orientation and Emphasis of Department/Program (Program Description): The master's program in criminal justice is designed to meet the graduate educational needs of practitioners and students pursuing careers in criminal justice, in both the public and private sectors. The thirty-credit curriculum requires degree candidates to take four core courses. The student selects the remainder of the courses. This arrangement allows individuals to create unique plans of graduate study that are compatible with their interests and career objectives in the field of criminal justice. The program is flexible enough to allow students to concentrate on the theoretical and methodological knowledge needed to pursue a degree beyond a master's or to focus on the management skills necessary to succeed as upper-level decision makers.

Number of Faculty: 6

Accreditation: Middle States Association of Colleges and Schools

Average Length of Time to Complete the Program: Not available

Saint Leo University

Address: 33701 State Road 52
St. Leo, FL 33525
Phone: (352) 588-8200
Website: http://www.saintleo.edu/

Department: Department of Criminal Justice
Website: http://www.saintleo.edu/academics/graduate/criminal-justice.aspx

Type of Program: MS in Criminal Justice

Application Deadline: Not available

Requirements: Stated below

Information Required for Application:
- Fill out the online application.
- Submit the one-time $80 nonrefundable application fee.
- Submit a transcript release form for each regionally accredited college or university you attended or in which you were enrolled, even if you did not complete a full academic term. You must have earned a bachelor's degree from a regionally accredited college or university with a minimum GPA of 3.0 on a 4-point scale, unless otherwise approved by the director of the program. Submit your transcript release form(s) directly to the Office of Graduate Admission. Graduates or former students of Saint Leo University do not need to submit transcripts if they have been previously submitted and are on file.

Admission Date: Not available

In-state and Out-of-state Tuition Costs: $422 per credit hour

Availability of Internships and Scholarships: Internships: Find an internship close to home or work, or with federal agencies such as the U.S. Secret Service, U.S. Customs, the Drug Enforcement Administration, U.S. District Court, and Florida Department of Law Enforcement.

Orientation and Emphasis of Department/Program (Program Description): The MS in criminal justice is a blended program that combines traditional, in-person classes—offered on alternating weekends—with a variety of delivery formats, including online options and video conferencing. Saint Leo also offers online-only concentrations in corrections, critical incident management, forensic psychology, forensic science, and legal studies.

Number of Faculty: Not available
Accreditation: Southern Association of Colleges and Schools Commission on Colleges

Average Length of Time to Complete the Program: Not available

Salem State University

Address: 352 Lafayette Street
Salem, MA 01970
Phone: (978) 542-6000
Website: http://www.salemstate.edu/

Department: Department of Criminal Justice
Website: http://www.salemstate.edu/academics/schools/620.php

Type of Program: MS in Criminal Justice

Application Deadline: February 14

Requirements:
- A bachelor's degree in criminal justice or related field;
- A cumulative undergraduate 2.5 GPA and 2.7 GPA in the major; and
- An undergraduate basic statistics course.

Information Required for Application:
- A $50 nonrefundable application fee;
- Complete, official transcript documenting the award of a bachelor's degree in criminal justice or a cognate field, cumulative undergraduate 2.5 GPA and 2.7 GPA in the major, and successful completion of a course in basic statistics;
- Official transcripts of any graduate courses taken or degrees held;
- Three references (your references will be asked to submit their comments online via the online application);
- Official copy of scores from either the Graduate Record Examination (GRE) or Miller Analogies Test (MAT) taken within the last five years (those who already hold a master's degree or higher are exempt from this requirement);
- Test of English as a Foreign Language (TOEFL) or International English Language Testing System (IELTS) scores (for students for whom English is not a first language); and
- A statement of purpose (500- to 1,000-words, double-spaced) addressing the following questions: What factors in your personal and professional history have influenced you in the past and now lead you to seek admission to this program at Salem State? What are your long-term professional goals, and how will this program help you meet them? Is there any other information that you think would help the admissions committee to evaluate your application?

Admission Date: Fall

In-state and Out-of-state Tuition Costs: In-state: $140 per graduate credit hour; out-of-state: $230 per graduate credit hour

Availability of Internships and Scholarships: Internships

Orientation and Emphasis of Department/Program (Program Description): Salem State's graduate program in criminal justice is designed for professionals currently working in the criminal justice system, college graduates who want to enter the criminal justice field and students who may wish to continue study toward a doctoral degree. The program is Quinn Bill–approved and adheres to the university's guidelines for graduate programs and the standards of the Academy of Criminal Justice Sciences for graduate programs.

Number of Faculty: 16

Accreditation: New England Association of Schools and Colleges

Average Length of Time to Complete the Program: Not available

Sam Houston State University

Address: 1806 Avenue J
Huntsville, TX 77340
Phone: (936) 294-1111
Website: http://www.shsu.edu/

Department: Department of Criminal Justice and Criminology
Department Address: 816 17th Street
Huntsville, TX 77340
Phone: (936) 294-1635
Website: http://www.shsu.edu/academics/criminal-justice/
departments/criminal-justice-and-criminology/

Type of Program: MS in Criminal Justice (online); MA in Criminal
Justice and Criminology; MS in Criminal Justice Leadership and
Management; MS in Victim Services Management (online); PhD
in Criminal Justice

Application Deadline: MA: February 1 and September 1; MS
in Criminal Justice Leadership and Management: May 1: PhD:
February 1

Requirements: Stated below

Information Required for Application:
MA and MS in Victim Services Management
- Graduate admissions application;
- Application fee;
- Official transcript from the baccalaureate degree–granting
  institution;
- Official transcripts of all college-level coursework;
- Undergraduate degree in an allied field;
- Two recommendation letters from undergraduate professors;
- Personal essay; and
- Official GRE scores.

MS in Leadership and Management
- Graduate admissions application;
- Application fee;
- Official transcript from the baccalaureate degree–granting
  institution;
- Official transcripts of all college-level coursework;
- Current résumé;
- Three years employed as a criminal justice professional (pro-
  bation officer, police officer, corrections counselor, etc.) is
  preferable;

- Official GRE scores may be requested to demonstrate graduate study readiness if the GPA is inordinately low;
- An acceptable undergraduate GPA. A prima facia acceptable GPA is a 3.0 for the final sixty baccalaureate credits.
- Applicant questionnaire;
- Personal essay;
- Employer endorsement form; and
- Letter from chief of police (if applying for 100 Club scholarship).

PhD
- Graduate admissions application;
- Application fee;
- Official transcript from the baccalaureate degree granting institution;
- Official transcript from the master's degree granting institution;
- Master's degree in criminal justice or an allied field;
- Doctoral application;
- Essay, as described in the doctoral application;
- Three recommendation letters, preferably from faculty who are sufficiently acquainted with the student to comment on potential for success in the doctoral program;
- Current résumé or vita;
- Official GRE scores; and
- In some instances, a personal interview may be requested.

Admission Date: MA: Fall and Spring; MS: Fall; PhD: Fall only

In-state and Out-of-state Tuition Costs: In-state: $4,111 per twelve credit hours; out-of-state: $8,359 per twelve credit hours

Availability of Internships and Scholarships:
Alpha Phi Sigma Criminal Justice Scholarship: The Alpha Phi Sigma-Phi Chapter Scholarship is awarded to a male or female member of the criminal justice organization who has completed forty-three hours (twelve are in criminal justice), is enrolled in twelve semester hours, and has an overall grade point average of 3.0 with a 3.2 grade point average in criminal justice courses.
ASIS International Houston Chapter John Tullie Brady Scholarship in Security Management Studies: The John Tullie Brady Scholarship is available to a full-time graduate or undergraduate student in good standing enrolled at Sam Houston State University whose area of study is security studies, who plans to work in the area of industrial security, or who has a security profession and maintains an overall GPA of 2.5 or above.
Dan Richard Beto Endowed Scholarship in Correctional Leadership: The Dan Richard Beto Endowed Scholarship is available to a full-time graduate or doctoral student in good standing

enrolled at Sam Houston State University whose area of study is institutional or community corrections. The student must be from a foreign country and plan to teach at an institution of higher learning or work for an institutional or community corrections agency. Financial need will be a consideration, but not a determining factor.

George J. Beto Memorial Scholarship: The George J. Beto Memorial Scholarship is available to an international student or a member of a minority group (including women) who has demonstrated financial need and has satisfactorily met the standard entrance requirements established by the university. The student must be enrolled as a full-time criminal justice student at Sam Houston State University. Preference is given to especially needy students from lower-income families. Special consideration will be given to first-generation college students. Preference will be given to undergraduate students, although graduate students will not be precluded. Students must maintain a grade point average of 3.0.

Tom Broussard, PhD, Memorial Endowed Scholarship: The Thomas Broussard, PhD, Memorial Scholarship was established in May 1991 by Ms. H. Pamela Schoch, the wife of the late Dr. Broussard, in his memory and as a tribute to Dr. Broussard's accomplishments in criminal justice. The Broussard may be granted for the Fall and Spring semesters to academically deserving graduate and/or undergraduate students at Sam Houston State University, preferably a student interested in the field of probation and maintaining a 2.5 grade point average.

Susan L. Canfield Memorial Endowment Scholarship: The Susan L. Canfield Memorial Endowment Scholarship was established in 2008 in memory of Ms. Canfield, who lost her life while trying to apprehend two prisoners. Fellow officers of the Wynne Unit resolved to establish an endowed scholarship in her memory in order that her sacrifice in the line of duty would never be forgotten. The Canfield Scholarship may be granted to a full-time or part-time (minimum of nine hours per semester) undergraduate or graduate student (minimum of six hours per semester) in good standing enrolled at Sam Houston State University, majoring in criminal justice, demonstrating financial need, and maintaining a minimum overall GPA of 2.0. Preference given to children or grandchildren of Ms. Canfield; employees of Texas Department of Criminal Justice or their children or grandchildren; or retired employees of Texas Department of Criminal Justice or their children or grandchildren.

Diane Cochran Criminal Justice Scholarship: Recipient must be an undergraduate or graduate student in good standing at SHSU entering an internship at a criminal justice agency, having completed two long semesters at SHSU. Applicants must demonstrate financial need as determined by the coordinator of the criminal justice internship program and the College of Criminal Justice student development committee. Requires a 2.5 grade point average.

Rolando V. del Carmen Criminal Justice Scholarship: The del Carmen Student-Endowed Criminal Justice Scholarship was established by graduate students in honor of Dr. del Carmen as a means of expressing their sincere gratitude for his encouragement and mentorship. Recipient must be a current full-time graduate student enrolled in the College of Criminal Justice at SHSU; demonstrate financial need; and demonstrate strong academic achievement.

Rolando V., Josefa, and Jocelyn del Carmen Endowed Criminal Justice Scholarship: The del Carmen Family Scholarship was established by Dr. and Mrs. Rolando del Carmen and their daughter Dr. Jocelyn del Carmen to provide financial assistance to academically deserving undergraduate and graduate students in criminal justice. Recipient must be a current full-time student enrolled in the College of Criminal Justice at SHSU; demonstrate financial need; and demonstrate strong academic achievement.

O. B. Ellis and Philip Gibbs, MD, Memorial Scholarship: The Ellis-Gibbs Memorial Scholarship is available to criminal justice majors between 21 and 45 years of age who have attained a minimum of junior level undergraduate standing or are candidates for or working toward master's or doctoral degrees. Preference will be given to scholarship candidates with experience in the criminal justice profession. Students must maintain a grade point average of 3.0.

Charles M. Friel Scholarship: The Charles M. Friel Scholarship may be awarded for the Fall and Spring semesters to academically deserving graduate students in the College of Criminal Justice at Sam Houston State University. Students must maintain a grade point average of 3.0.

R. W. Gordy Memorial Scholarship Endowment Fund: The R. W. Gordy Memorial Scholarship was established in 2007 for a full-time student majoring in criminal justice who is a citizen of the United States; pursuing a career in law enforcement in the United States; maintaining a minimum of 2.5 GPA; and demonstrating financial need.

George G. Killinger Memorial Scholarship: These scholarships are granted for the Fall and Spring semesters to academically deserving undergraduate or graduate students in the College of Criminal Justice at Sam Houston State University. Students must maintain a grade point average of 3.0.

Merlyn D. Moore Criminal Justice Scholarship: The Merlyn D. Moore Scholarship was established by Dr. and Mrs. Merlyn D. Moore to provide financial assistance to an entering freshman or current undergraduate or graduate student who is a full-time student in good standing enrolled at Sam Houston University and majoring in criminal justice. Student must be able to demonstrate financial need and demonstrate a strong academic background. Preference will be given to those students who are actively participating in any criminal justice organization.

Victor G. Strecher Criminal Justice Scholarship: The Victor G. Strecher Scholarship was established to provide a scholarship for the Fall and Spring semesters to academically deserving undergraduate or graduate student in the College of Criminal Justice at Sam Houston State University. Preference will be given to a student from a working class background and first generation to attend college.

Donald J. Weisenhorn Criminal Justice Scholarship: The Donald J. Weisenhorn Scholarship was established with the donor's intent to provide one or more scholarships to a full-time sophomore or above undergraduate or graduate student in good standing enrolled at Sam Houston State University majoring in criminal justice. Recipient must maintains an overall GPA 3.0 and 3.5 in major. Financial need will be a consideration with equal weight as academics.

Marcus Zaruba Memorial Criminal Justice Scholarship: The Marcus Zaruba Scholarship was established to provide financial assistance to a full-time undergraduate or graduate student in good standing enrolled at Sam Houston State University, majoring in criminal justice; maintaining a minimum GPA of 3.0 overall, and demonstrating financial need.

Correctional Management Institute of Texas Scholarship: CMIT will provide tuition costs each year for selected employees accepted into the master's of criminal justice leadership and management online/weekend programs. Applicants for the scholarships must first be accepted into the MS in leadership and management program and be active professionals in the criminal justice field with a minimum of five years' experience. Continued financial support of selected students is contingent upon their maintaining at least a 3.3 grade point average and making satisfactory progress toward completing the degree program in two years.

LTC Michael A. Lytle Academic Prize in Forensic Science: Michael A. Lytle ('77) was the recipient of the SHSU Distinguished Alumni Award in 2003. He is a decorated military intelligence and foreign area officer, distinguished forensic educator, and consulting criminologist providing technical and policy advisory assistance on law enforcement intelligence, terrorism, and transnational crime to state, local, federal, and international agencies. This prize was established to recognize an outstanding graduating graduate student in forensic science.

Orientation and Emphasis of Department/Program (Program Description): The online master of science in criminal justice program combines the convenience of an online education with the prestige of a criminal justice degree from SHSU's College of Criminal Justice. The master of arts in criminal justice and criminology is designed to prepare graduate students in conducting research and actively participating in the development of knowledge in the areas of criminological theory, crime control, and correctional and police administration. The curriculum is broad enough to satisfy these various interests. Students who are planning careers in law enforcement, corrections, or rehabilitation, or who wish for a deeper understanding of crime and the criminal justice system should confer with the graduate program advisor to develop a combination of elective courses that will support their particular career interests. The master of science in criminal justice leadership and management is designed for persons in mid-management positions in criminal justice agencies, or for those who have a reasonable expectation of being promoted to such a position. It serves practitioners whose jobs and family commitment prevent them from returning to campus as full-time students. The master of science in victim services management is designed to prepare graduates to work in various areas of victim services, including but not limited to direct service provision (e.g., rape crisis centers or victim service providers), organizational management, and social policy development. This degree will benefit persons with or without previous employment experience in the field of victim services. Courses are sequenced so that students can complete the degree in two years, enrolling in two fifteen-week courses per semester. The doctor of philosophy in criminal justice is designed to produce students of crime and justice who possess a deep and extensive awareness of the body of knowledge in the field of criminal justice and the intellectual and methodological skills necessary for the continuing process of discovery and understanding of crime and justice related issues. The graduate should be capable of integrative and analytical thinking, competent at transmitting knowledge, able to engage in various accepted modes of research, and possess skills in problem-solving.

Number of Faculty: 36

Accreditation: Southern Association of Colleges and Schools Commission on Colleges

Average Length of Time to Complete the Program: Two years for the MS in Victim Management (not available for others)

San Diego State University

Address: 5500 Campanile Drive
San Diego, CA 92182
Phone: (619) 594-5200
Website: http://www.sdsu.edu/

Department: School of Public Affairs
San Diego State University
PSFA 100
5500 Campanile Drive
San Diego, CA 92182-4505
Phone: (619) 594-6224
Website: http://spa.sdsu.edu/index.php/academic_programs/
criminal_justice_overview/

Type of Program: Master's in Criminal Justice and Criminology
(MCJC)

Application Deadline: March 1. The MCJC program does not
accept Spring applications. All supporting documentation including transcripts, test scores, letters of recommendation, and personal statement must be received by April 1, although it is best to
apply earlier.

Requirements: The master of criminal justice and criminology
admits students from a variety of backgrounds. We look for evi-
dence of knowledge and/or experience in the following areas:
- The criminal justice system;
- Sociology and criminological theory;
- Research methods; and
- Knowledge of statistics.

Information Required for Application:
- Two letters of academic recommendation from two persons
  familiar with the applicant's academic ability;
- Personal statement (a 500-word essay about your professional
  and educational goals);
- GRE Scores; and
- Transcripts.

Admission Date: Fall only

In-state and Out-of-state Tuition Costs: $8,032 per year tuition
for both in-state and out-of-state students

Availability of Internships and Scholarships: Not available

Orientation and Emphasis of Department/Program (Program Description): The master of science in criminal justice and criminology program, offered jointly with the Department of Sociology, gives students a unique opportunity to integrate knowledge from the fields of sociology, criminology and criminal justice. The program emphasizes research methods and theoretical perspectives in criminal justice and criminology with substantive course work in international criminal justice, social control systems, and criminal justice policy.

Number of Faculty: 7

Accreditation: Western Association of Schools and Colleges

Average Length of Time to Complete the Program: Not available

Seattle University

Address: 901 12th Avenue
Seattle, WA 98122
Phone: (206) 296-6000
Website: https://www.seattleu.edu/

Department: Criminal Justice Department
Contact: Dr. Jacqueline Helfgott, Chair
Phone: (206) 296-5477
E-mail: jhelfgot@seattleu.edu
Website: http://www.seattleu.edu/artsci/departments/criminal/

Type of Program: MA in Criminal Justice; MA in Criminal Justice with Victimology Specialization; MA Criminal Justice with Investigative Criminology Specialization; MA in Criminal Justice with Research and Evaluation Specialization; MA/JD Joint Degree

Application Deadline: March 15

Requirements: Not available

Information Required for Application:
- Completed application for graduate admission (apply online);
- A nonrefundable application fee of $55;
- Official transcripts from the last two years of the baccalaureate degree and any post-baccalaureate course work. A completed undergraduate degree must be verified prior to enrollment. Doctoral students should only submit all graduate-level transcripts unless non-graded. Exceptions to the policy are noted with the degree requirements; and
- Students who have earned degrees from institutions issuing non-graded transcripts must submit official results from GRE (Code 4695), GMAT (Code 5613), or MAT (Code 2287) tests as determined by your program.

Admission Date: Fall only

In-state and Out-of-state Tuition Costs: $651 per credit hour

Availability of Internships and Scholarships: Student internships are highly recommended but optional. Our students have interned a variety of federal, state, and local agencies, including the Drug Enforcement Administration, the FBI, King County Prosecutor's Office, King County Medical Examiner's Office, King County Sheriff's Office, Pioneer Human Services, police departments in Seattle, Redmond, and Bellevue, U.S. Marshal, U.S. Secret Service, Washington State Department of Corrections, State Patrol Crime Lab, and Office of the Attorney General.

Orientation and Emphasis of Department/Program (Program Description): The master of arts in criminal justice (MACJ) is an interdisciplinary program that offers a comprehensive, rigorous, analytic study of crime and the societal responses to it. Our focus is on the application of theory and research methods in the development of initiatives, policies, and practice. In addition, we give special emphasis to criminal justice ethics, issues of diversity in criminal justice, critical thinking, and leadership. Our students go on to successful careers in all sectors of the criminal justice system, including law enforcement, courts, corrections, social service, policy, and research.

Number of Faculty: 31

Accreditation: Northwest Commission on Colleges and Universities

Average Length of Time to Complete the Program: Two years

Shippensburg University of Pennsylvania

Address: 1871 Old Main Drive
Shippensburg, PA 17257
Website: https://www.ship.edu/
Phone: (717) 477-7447

Department: Department of Criminal Justice
321 Shippen Hall
Shippensburg University of Pennsylvania
1871 Old Main Drive
Shippensburg, PA 17257-2299
Phone: (717) 477-1558
Department Website: http://www.ship.edu/Criminal_Justice/

Type of Program: MS in Administration of Justice

Application Deadline: Not available

Requirements:
- A baccalaureate degree in criminal justice, administration of justice, or related social science field from a regionally accredited college or university;
- Minimum grade point average of a 2.75 on a 4.0 scale. Applicants with less than a 2.75 undergraduate GPA will be required to take the Graduate Requisite Examination (GRE) and provide a sufficient score before they are eligible for admission. They may also take the Miller Analogies Test (MAT) and provide a sufficient score;
- In 500 words or fewer provide a statement of interest indicating your reasons for pursuing this program, your professional goals, and how this degree will help fulfill said goals; and
- Students are invited to provide an optional résumé.

Information Required for Application: Stated above

Admission Date: Not available

In-state and Out-of-state Tuition Costs: In-state: $442 per credit hour; out-of-state: $663 per credit hour

Availability of Internships and Scholarships: Not available

Orientation and Emphasis of Department/Program (Program Description): In response to local and regional needs, the Department of Criminal Justice developed the master of science degree program in administration of justice in 1983. In 1999, the program was significantly revised to make it more consistent with its contemporaries yet distinct enough to serve our special populations. The program is designed for in-service and pre-service students.

Practitioners raise their level of education while adding research and theory to the in-field experiences. Pre-service students gain direct and indirect benefits from the program as they study and interact with experienced professionals. The program enhances career potentials for both groups of graduate students.

The program's major strengths are its applied perspective and strong emphasis on theory, policy, research, and analysis. Philosophy, format, and implementation stress the practical application of a higher level of knowledge, skills, and strategies. The methodological and theory components are highly suitable as a preparation for entering advanced graduate studies and other professional programs.

Number of Faculty: 10

Accreditation: Middle States Association of Colleges and Schools

Average Length of Time to Complete the Program: Not available

Southeast Missouri State University

Address: 1 University Plaza
Cape Girardeau, MO 63701
Phone: (573) 651-2000
Website: http://www.semo.edu/

Department: Department of Criminal Justice and Sociology
Brandt 329
Phone: (573) 651-2541
Website: http://www.semo.edu/criminaljustice/

Type of Program: MS in Criminal Justice

Application Deadline: Not available

Requirements: Undergraduate GPA minimum of 2.75 on a 4.0 scale.

Information Required for Application:
• Letter of intent
• $40 application fee

Admission Date: Not available

In-state and Out-of-state Tuition Costs: In-state: $285.50 per credit hour; out-of-state: $505.50 per credit hour

Availability of Internships and Scholarships: For more information on endowed and sponsored scholarships, information on other available scholarships, and instructions on how to apply for scholarships, please consult the Southeast Scholarships page provided by the Department of Student Financial Services. Graduate assistantships also available.
Bill Ferrell Endowed Scholarship: Awarded to a Scott County, Missouri, resident with a 3.0 GPA and a criminal justice or pre-law major. Awarded to a new student each year. Deadline is March 1.
Neil Keeney Memorial Scholarship: Candidates should be U.S. citizens working toward degrees granted by the College of Science and Mathematics, the College of Health and Human Services, or the Harrison College of Business. Selection of the scholarship recipient should be prioritized in the following order: African-American biracial, Hispanic-American, Native American, and non-minorities. Single parents should be given priority, if single parents are present in the eligible pool. Preference should be given to Crawford, St. Francois, Ste. Genevieve, and Washington County candidates in that order. If there are no qualified candidates from these counties, the award may be made to a qualifying candidate from another rural SEMO county. Deadline is March 1.

Tri-County Citizens Advisory Board: Open to residents of Scott, New Madrid, and Mississippi Counties who are majoring or minoring in criminal justice and have completed sixty semester hours with a minimum GPA of 2.5. Financial need is a determining factor. Deadline is July 15.

William K. Nyberg Memorial Criminal Justice Scholarship: The recipient of this scholarship shall be a student enrolled at Southeast Missouri State University majoring in criminal justice. This scholarship is renewable, but applicants must reapply each year.

Orientation and Emphasis of Department/Program (Program Description): The purpose of the master of science in criminal justice is to provide a high-quality graduate program that prepares competent individuals with the skills and knowledge necessary to meet the criminal justice needs of the region, including such aspects of criminal justice as law enforcement, courts, corrections, and crime prevention. The goals of the program are to prepare graduates who are able to:

- Assess and understand criminal justice problems and issues;
- Conduct basic and applied research in criminal justice, particularly evaluation research;
- Use computer technology to locate information and use statistics and software to analyze problems, particularly with respect to criminal justice agencies;
- Understand legal issues which affect criminal justice professionals; and
- Integrate the findings concerning the psychological, sociological, economic and cultural roots of crime.

The program provides an internship option, a thesis option, or a capstone experience.

Number of Faculty: 8

Accreditation: North Central Association

Average Length of Time to Complete the Program: Not available

Southern Illinois University Carbondale

Address: Carbondale, IL 62901
Phone: (618) 453-2121
Website: http://www.siu.edu/

Department: Department of Criminology and Criminal Justice
Faner Hall, Mail Code 4504
Carbondale, IL 62901
Phone: (618) 453-5701
Website: http://cola.siu.edu/ccj/

Type of Program: MA in Criminology and Criminal Justice; PhD in Criminology and Criminal Justice

Application Deadline: MA: May 1, November 1; PhD: February

Requirements:
Master's
- Have completed a four-year bachelor's degree by the time you are admitted to the program;
- Have an undergraduate degree in criminology and criminal justice or related major (e.g., administration of justice), or have a minimum of twelve units in sociology, psychology, political science, or other social science; and
- Earn a grade point average of at least 2.70 or better (A = 4.00) on approximately the last sixty hours of undergraduate coursework.

Doctoral
- Have completed a four-year bachelor's degree;
- Have completed a master's degree in criminology and criminal justice; if you do not have an MA in criminology and criminal justice, then have a minimum of twelve graduate units in sociology, psychology, political science, or other social science; and
- Earn a grade point average of at least 3.00 or better (A = 4.00) in all prior graduate coursework and in the last sixty credit hours of undergraduate study.

Information Required for Application:
Master's
- Have the Educational Testing Service (ETS) submit your scores from the Graduate Record Exam (GRE), aptitude portion only, to SIU's Graduate School.
- Have your undergraduate institution submit an official copy of your transcript. We will review a copy of a transcript, but admission is contingent on having an official transcript sent from the institution to SIU's Graduate School.

- Have three letters of recommendation, preferably from your college instructors or other professionals in a position to relay your potential as a scholar, sent through the Apply Now website (instructions will be sent to the persons writing your letters). There is also an evaluation form they will need to complete. Evaluations coming from other professionals will be considered, but the committee will want to have feedback on your academic potential. We recommend that you waive your right to review the letters so that the authors feel they can write a candid assessment.
- Submit a personal statement. The statement should highlight your academic achievements as well as your goals for completing our master's program. The goals should include academic and professional aims. Address how our department can assist you in your professional aims.
- Be sure to indicate whether you want to be considered for a paid graduate assistantship for the academic year. Graduate assistants help faculty members with teaching and research tasks.
- If you are an international student, you will need to take the TOEFL English proficiency test and have that submitted with your application.

Doctoral
- Have ETS submit your scores from the Graduate Record Exam (GRE), aptitude portion only, to SIU's Graduate School. Even with a master's or other graduate degree in hand, students will need to submit GRE scores.
- Have your undergraduate and graduate institutions submit an official copy of your transcript. We will review a copy of a transcript, but admission is contingent on having an official transcript sent from the institution to SIU's Graduate School.
- Have three letters of recommendation, preferably from your college instructors or other professionals in a position to relay your potential as a scholar, sent through the Apply Now website (instructions will be sent to the persons writing your letters). There is also an evaluation form they will need to complete. We recommend that you waive your right to review the letters so that the authors feel they can write a candid assessment. Letters of recommendation for the doctoral program should speak to the applicant's academic abilities as well as potential as a scholar.
- Submit a personal statement. The statement should highlight your academic achievements as well as your goals for completing the doctoral program. The doctoral program in criminology and criminal justice is research intensive; therefore,

a successful personal statement will specifically address the research goals of the applicant. Also, you should address how our department can assist you in your professional and academic aims.

- If you are an international student, you will need to take the TOEFL English proficiency test and have that submitted.

Admission Date: MA: Fall and Spring; PhD: Fall

In-state and Out-of-state Tuition Costs: Not available

Availability of Internships and Scholarships: Graduate internships, assistantships, and scholarships.

Orientation and Emphasis of Department/Program (Program Description): The Department of Criminology and Criminal Justice offers a master of arts degree and a doctoral degree. The graduate programs prepare students for advanced positions throughout criminal justice, and the MA provides the foundation for students who intend to continue with the PhD. Within the curriculum, students can choose courses among various substantive specializations and elect to work with faculty whose research most closely fits their own areas of interest. Job prospects are plentiful with a graduate degree in criminology and criminal justice. We have successful alumni from this program working in all areas of criminal justice, in several countries, and some prominent criminology faculty at other universities.

Number of Faculty: 13

Accreditation: The Higher Learning Commission

Average Length of Time to Complete the Program: Not available

Southern University and Agricultural and Mechanical College

Address: 801 Harding Boulevard
Baton Rouge, LA 70807
Phone: (225) 771-4500
Website: http://www.subr.edu/

Department: Mandela School of Public Policy and Urban Affairs
416 Higgins Hall
Southern University
Baton Rouge, LA 70813
Phone: (225) 771-0033
Website: http://www.subr.edu/index.cfm/page/282/n/356

Type of Program: Master's in Criminal Justice (MCJ)

Application Deadline: Not specified

Requirements:
- Admission into the Graduate School;
- Baccalaureate degree from an accredited institution of higher learning;
- Minimum GPA of 2.70;
- GRE score (within the last 5 years);
- Three letters of recommendation from academic sources (professors, deans, etc.);
- A typed double-spaced personal essay of not more than 1,000 words; and
- A TOEFL score for international students.

Information Required for Application: Stated above

Admission Date: Not specified

In-state and Out-of-state Tuition Costs: Full-time general fees: $3,792: out-of-state additional fees: $3,737

Availability of Internships and Scholarships: Assistantships, scholarships, and fellowships

Orientation and Emphasis of Department/Program (Program Description): The criminal justice master's program is designed to provide students with advanced knowledge, research, and analytical skills that should contribute to their educational and professional development, and to provide the students the theoretical knowledge and professional, leadership, and management skills that should enable them to function effectively in criminal justice agencies, such as the police, prisons, juvenile justice, probation, and private security.

Number of Faculty: 3

Accreditation: Southern Association of Colleges and Schools

Average Length of Time to Complete the Program: Not available

Suffolk University

Address: 73 Tremont Street
Boston, MA 02108
Phone: (617) 573-8000
Website: http://www.suffolk.edu/

Department: Department of Sociology
8 Ashbuton Place
Boston, MA 02108
Phone: (617) 573-8485
Website: http://www.suffolk.edu/college/departments/9897.php

Type of Program: MS in Crime and Justice Studies

Application Deadline: Not available

Requirements:
- Hold a bachelor's degree from an accredited college or university;
- Complete the application form; and
- Successfully complete the TOEFL, IELTS, or PTE-Academic (for international applicants).

Information Required for Application:
- Goal statement
- Résumé
- Two letters of recommendation
- Official transcripts

Admission Date: Not available

In-state and Out-of-state Tuition Costs: Full-time: $13,128; part-time: $1,094 per credit

Availability of Internships and Scholarships: Graduate internship and practicum

Orientation and Emphasis of Department/Program (Program Description): The four core courses provide a foundation in the areas of criminology and applied research. The optional requirements allow students to choose their own areas for specific application of theories and research methods. Finally, free electives or concentrations allow students to specialize in areas that are particularly important for crime and justice professionals, including victim advocacy, substance abuse, counseling, and public administration.

Number of Faculty: 17

Accreditation: New England Association of Schools and Colleges

Average Length of Time to Complete the Program: Not available

Sul Ross State University

Address: East Highway 90
Alpine, TX 79832
Phone: (432) 837-8011
Website: http://www.sulross.edu/

Department: Department of Political Science
Website: http://www.sulross.edu/page/1038/political-science/

Type of Program: MA in Public Administration; MS in Criminal Justice joint degree; also offers a joint program option combining both degrees

Application Deadline: Not available

Requirements: A 2.5 GPA on a 4.0 scale calculated on the last sixty hours prior to the issuance of the bachelor's degree and a GRE score of at least 850 (verbal and quantitative) or a minimum GMAT score of 400; or a bachelor's degree with a 3.0 or higher GPA; or a master's degree from an accredited college or university and the approval of the department in which they propose to work.

Information Required for Application:
- Application for admission (apply using the Texas Common Application at http://www.applytexas.org; list all previously attended colleges or universities);
- A one-time, nonrefundable application fee of $25 ($50 for international students);
- Official college/university transcripts from all institutions attended (previously-attended colleges/universities other than Sul Ross must send official transcripts by mail; an English-language interpretation must accompany transcripts for international students); and
- Any documentation required by the major department. This documentation may include the GRE, GMAT, GRE subject examination, professional certifications, etc. Check with the department in which you plan to seek a degree.

Admission Date: Not available

In-state and Out-of-state Tuition Costs: Not available

Availability of Internships and Scholarships: Scholarships

Orientation and Emphasis of Department/Program (Program Description): The master of arts degree in public administration is designed to serve the needs of students who are preparing for political or administrative careers in public or governmental service, careers in secondary education, or continued graduate studies. Students can choose from a public administration option, a general political science option, or a joint degree in public administration and criminal justice. The dual master of arts degree in public administration/master of science degree in criminal justice allows students to simultaneously earn two degrees by completing fifty-four total semester credit hours.

Number of Faculty: Not available

Accreditation: Commission on Colleges of the Southern Association of Colleges and Schools

Average Length of Time to Complete the Program: Not available

Tarleton State University

Address: 1333 West Washington Street
Stephenville, TX 76401
Phone: (254) 968-9000
Website: http://www.tarleton.edu/

Department: Department of Criminal Justice
Box T-0665
Stephenville, TX 76402
Phone: (254) 968-9024
Website: http://www.tarleton.edu/COLFAWEB/criminaljustice/

Type of Program: Master's in Criminal Justice (MCJ; online)

Application Deadline: Not available

Requirements:
- Bachelor's degree from a regionally-accredited U.S. institution (or equivalent from a foreign institution);
- At least a 3.0 GPA on the last sixty hours of completed coursework;
- Completed graduate application with essay and $30 fee;
- All official transcripts; and
- Other applicable program prerequisites.

Information Required for Application:
- Two letters of recommendation

Admission Date: Not available

In-state and Out-of-state Tuition Costs: Must submit a form for calculation

Availability of Internships and Scholarships: Scholarships

Orientation and Emphasis of Department/Program (Program Description): Welcome to Tarleton State University. Your interest in a graduate degree in criminal justice is consistent with a growing national trend of criminal justice professionals seeking career advancement and academic credentials. Our online graduate program provides you with a broad-based education and is designed to give you the skills and knowledge required to successfully navigate the competitive process to advance your objectives.

Number of Faculty: 20

Accreditation: Commission on Colleges of the Southern Association of Colleges and Schools

Average Length of Time to Complete the Program: Not available

Temple University

Address: 1801 North Broad Street
Philadelphia, PA 19122
Phone: (215) 204-7000
Website: http://www.temple.edu/

Department: Department of Criminal Justice
Gladfelter Hall, 5th Floor
Temple University
1115 Polett Walk
Philadelphia, PA 19122
Phone: (215) 204-7918
Website: http://www.temple.edu/cj/contact/

Type of Program: MA in Criminal Justice; PhD in Criminal Justice

Application Deadline: December 15 (November 30 for international students)

Requirements: Successful applicants to the graduate programs will usually have at least the following credentials:
* GRE scores of at least 153 on the verbal section and 144 on the quantitative section;
* An overall undergraduate GPA of at least 3.0 on a 4-point scale, and an average in the major of at least 3.2; and
* Applicants to the PhD program who have completed graduate level coursework should have at least a 3.0 average for that coursework.

Information Required for Application:
* The Temple University graduate application form;
* Transcripts from all graduate and undergraduate study;
* Official GRE score report;
* A brief résumé;
* Letters of recommendation from three persons familiar with the applicant's abilities and scholarly potential;
* A biographical statement explaining the applicant's purpose for graduate study (2-3 pages is usually fine);
* At least one sample of the applicant's writing (previous academic work is preferable); and
* A nonrefundable application fee of $60 if submitted electronically ($75 for paper applications)

Admission Date: Fall only

In-state and Out-of-state Tuition Costs: In-state: $745 per credit; out-of-state: $1,043 per credit

Availability of Internships and Scholarships: Limited research opportunities for MA students, teaching assistantships reserved for PhD students.

Orientation and Emphasis of Department/Program (Program Description): Our graduate program comprises a faculty that is diverse in background and academic interests. At Temple you will experience a dynamic research environment in which faculty with students and in teams conduct research on the local, regional, national, and international levels. You can assess for yourself the evidence of our success to date—review the wide variety of research grants we receive, the range of publications we (and our students) produce, the reputations of our faculty, and the quality of the graduate students we develop.

Number of Faculty: 30

Accreditation: Middle States Commission on Higher Education

Average Length of Time to Complete the Program: Not available

Tennessee State University

Address: 3500 John A. Merritt Boulevard
Nashville, TN 37209
Phone: (615) 963-5000
Website: http://www.tnstate.edu/

Department: Department of Criminal Justice
Crouch Hall, 3rd Floor
Phone: (615) 963-5571
Website: http://www.tnstate.edu/criminaljustice/

Type of Program: Master's in Criminal Justice (MCJ)

Application Deadline: July 1, November 1, April 1

Requirements:
- An application for admission on the approved application form (paper-based or online), accompanied by a $35 nonrefundable application fee;
- A baccalaureate or post-baccalaureate degree from an accredited college or university that offers programs that are prerequisites for the degree program at Tennessee State University; and
- Official transcripts from all colleges or universities previously attended, indicating the year in which the bachelor's degree was awarded.

Information Required for Application: All applicants, whether degree-seeking or not, must submit an official transcript of all post-secondary work, including TSU, with the application. These transcripts must be obtained from the registrar of your college or university in sealed envelopes and attached to your application.

Admission Date: Fall, Spring, Summer

In-state and Out-of-state Tuition Costs: In-state: $866 per hour; out-of-state: $1,015 per hour

Availability of Internships and Scholarships: Scholarships

Orientation and Emphasis of Department/Program (Program Description): The department offers the master of criminal justice degree jointly with Middle Tennessee State University in Murfreesboro. The degree program was developed by Dr. Douglas Morgan, TSU department head at the time, and the late Dr. J. Frank Lee, department head at MTSU. The program first graduated students in 1978. Since it began, students have earned the MCJ degree and scattered across the United States and the world. Some have pursued even more study and earned doctorate degrees or law degrees. Many are working in local, state, or federal agencies and a few are college professors of criminal justice.

Number of Faculty: 13

Accreditation: Southern Association of Colleges and Schools Commission on Colleges

Average Length of Time to Complete the Program: Not available

Texas A&M International University

Address: 5201 University Boulevard
Laredo, TX 78041
Phone: (956) 326-2001
Website: http://www.tamiu.edu/

Department: Department of Public Affairs and Social Research
5201 University Boulevard
301 Canseco Hall
Laredo, TX 78041-1900
Phone: (956) 326-2475
Website: http://www.tamiu.edu/coas/pasr/

Type of Program: MS in Criminal Justice (online)

Application Deadline: April 30, November 30

Requirements:
- Application for graduate admission;
- Graduate application fee of $35 (late fee, $25; international graduate student application fee of $50; refer to admissions deadlines section);
- Official college/university transcript(s) from institutions other than Texas A&M International University must be sent directly from each institution attended. Degree must be posted on transcript. The degree must be from a college or university of recognized standing, with degrees from institutions outside the U.S. evaluated for equivalency to U.S. degrees; and
- The Test of English as a Foreign Language (TOEFL) or International English Language Testing System.

Information Required for Application: Stated above

Admission Date: Fall, Spring, Summer I, and Summer II

In-state and Out-of-state Tuition Costs: In-state: $2,376 per ten hours; out-of-state: $8,033 per ten hours

Availability of Internships and Scholarships: Fellowships, assistantships, scholarships, and grants

Orientation and Emphasis of Department/Program (Program Description): The master of science in criminal justice (MSCJ) is an online comprehensive program designed to prepare you to actively participate in the development of knowledge and policy responses to contemporary crime problems. A focus is placed on criminological theory, research in criminal justice, and the administration of criminal justice. It is also designed to prepare you to conduct research and policy analysis, and to take an active leadership role as a professional in the field of criminal justice. You may pursue either a thesis or non-thesis degree.

Number of Faculty: 31

Accreditation: Southern Association of Colleges and Schools Commission on Colleges

Average Length of Time to Complete the Program: Not available

Texas Southern University

Address: 3100 Cleburne Street
Houston, TX 77004
Phone: (713) 313-7011
Website: http://www.tsu.edu/

Department: Department of the Administration of Justice
Website: http://www.tsu.edu/academics/colleges__schools/
publicaffairs/aj/

Type of Program: MS in Administration of Justice; PhD in Administration of Justice

Application Deadline: November 15, May 1, July 15

Requirements:
1. Graduation with a bachelor's degree or its equivalent from an accredited college or university (an example of the "equivalent" as indicated above may be an international student who has graduated from a college university that issues a diploma or certificate instead of a degree);
2. A satisfactory undergraduate sequence of courses in the proposed major;
3. A grade point average in all undergraduate work of 2.5 (C+) or better or a grade point average of 3.0 on the last sixty semester hours of undergraduate course work;
4. A score on the aptitude section of the Graduate Record Examination (GRE) or Graduate Management Admission Test (GMAT), which will be used in conjunction with other admission factors;
5. A score of at least 550 on the paper-based test, 213 on the computer-based test, or 79 on the internet-based test of the TOEFL (if the applicant is an international student); and
6. An analytical writing score of 3.5 or above on GRE or GMAT exam to fulfill the English proficiency requirement.

Information Required for Application: Stated above

Admission Date: Fall, Spring, Summer

In-state and Out-of-state Tuition Costs: *Master's:* In-state: $13,094: out-of-state: $15,694. *Doctoral:* In-state: $13,183: out-of-state: $14,579 (for 2013–2014)

Availability of Internships and Scholarships: Assistantships by department

Orientation and Emphasis of Department/Program (Program Description):

Master's: The graduate program is designed to advance students' understanding of justice in the contemporary era and prepare them for challenges in law enforcement, corrections, and judicial administration. The program will prepare academicians, policy makers, top administrators, and researchers by advancing their knowledge of theory, research, and data analysis. In addition, the program places emphasis on the historical and contemporary issues in administrative and policy matters, including race and crime, homeland security, and the application of geographic information systems. In order to accommodate the needs of our professional graduate students, the Department of Administration of Justice offers its courses in the evening.

Doctoral: The purpose of the doctor of philosophy of administration of justice is to prepare individuals for: (1) leadership and managerial positions in justice agencies; (2) faculty positions in higher education that require advanced knowledge of theory, administration, research, and data analysis; and (3) research positions in private and public research institutions specializing in the administration of justice issues, policy, and data analysis. The doctor of philosophy in administration of justice will educate future leaders needed to assume administrative and policy positions at all levels of government, and in the private sector in the State of Texas, nationally and globally.

Number of Faculty: 13

Accreditation: Southern Association of Colleges and Schools

Average Length of Time to Complete the Program: Not available

Texas State University—San Marcos

Address: 601 University Drive
San Marcos, TX 78666
Phone: (512) 245-2111
Website: http://www.txstate.edu/

Department: School of Criminal Justice
Hines Academic Center
601 University Drive
San Marcos, TX 78666
Phone: (512) 245-2174
Website: http://www.cj.txstate.edu/

Type of Program: MS in Criminal Justice

Application Deadline: June 15, October 15, April 15

Requirements:
Master's: All applicants must hold either a baccalaureate degree in criminal justice or a degree in a related field from a regionally accredited university, with a minimum of a 3.0 GPA on the last sixty undergraduate semester hours of letter-grade work earned at a four-year college or university before receipt of a bachelor's.
Doctoral: Applicants to Texas State's Doctoral Program in criminal justice must have the following:
- A master's degree in criminal justice or closely related field;
- GPA of 3.5 or higher on all completed master's work; and
- Completion of the Graduate Record Exam (GRE), with a combined verbal and quantitative score of 1,000 or higher on GRE (suggested minimum). Note: Applicants for Spring and Fall will need to take the new (revised) GRE unless they have taken the old GRE within the last five years. The preferred minimum score on the verbal section of the new GRE is 150, and it is also 150 on the quantitative section.

Information Required for Application:
Master's
- $40 application fee;
- Official transcripts from all four-year universities or secondary schools attended; and
- GRE Scores.

Doctoral
- An official Texas State Graduate College doctoral online application (domestic and international applications);
- A $40 application fee (check or money order in U.S. currency should be made payable to Texas State or payable during

online application). A $50 (U.S. currency) international/evaluation fee is required if the application is considered for admission based on foreign credentials.

- One official transcript from each senior-level post-secondary institution attended. Transcripts must be mailed directly from the university or college attended or submitted in a sealed university envelope with the university's registrar's signature on the back of the envelope. (If you are a Texas State University degree recipient or are currently enrolled, you need to request transcripts from any colleges not listed on your Texas State transcript. The Graduate College will provide Texas State transcripts.);
- Official scores of your Graduate Record Examination (GRE);
- Three letters of recommendation indicating your skills and capacity to be successful in the PhD program; and
- Letter outlining your personal history and life goals that are relevant to obtaining a doctoral degree.

Admission Date: Fall, Spring, Summer

In-state and Out-of-state Tuition Costs: In-state: $637.63 per hour; out-of-state: $991.63 per hour

Availability of Internships and Scholarships: Graduate and doctoral assistantships

Orientation and Emphasis of Department/Program (Program Description):

Master's: The School of Criminal Justice offers a master of science in criminal justice (MSCJ) degree, and also participates in the master of science in interdisciplinary studies program. The curriculum provides for the development of skills in criminal justice program planning, implementation, and evaluation to ensure a meaningful contribution to this important area of community and human services.

Doctoral: The School of Criminal Justice at Texas State University offers a doctoral program for criminal justice professionals who seek advanced education as well as students who will pursue academic appointments at colleges and universities in Texas and around the nation. Texas State University is located in the heart of the central Texas corridor, near sixteen state criminal justice offices and thirteen Texas counties, including Travis (Austin) and Bexar (San Antonio). The university's geographic proximity to state criminal justice agency headquarters for law enforcement, criminal courts, and corrections—and to managers and executives in these agencies—makes it an ideal location for offering a doctoral-degree program.

Number of Faculty: 24

Accreditation: Commission on Colleges of the Southern Association of Colleges and Schools

Average Length of Time to Complete the Program: Not available

Tiffin University

Address: 155 Miami Street
Tiffin, OH 44883
Phone: (800) 968-6446
Website: http://www.tiffin.edu/

Department: School of Criminal Justice and Social Sciences
Phone: (419) 448-3292
Website: http://www.tiffin.edu/criminaljustice/

Type of Program: MS in Criminal Justice with concentrations available in
- Criminal behavior;
- Crime analysis;
- Forensic psychology (seated);
- Justice administration (online);
- Homeland security administration; and
- Justice administration (seated).

Application Deadline: Not available

Requirements: Applicants must have an accredited bachelor's degree. Applicants with at least a 3.0 GPA will be accepted.

Information Required for Application:
- Personal statement
- Official transcripts
- Current résumé

Admission Date: Not available

In-state and Out-of-state Tuition Costs: $700 per credit hour

Availability of Internships and Scholarships: Not available

Orientation and Emphasis of Department/Program (Program Description): The master of science in criminal justice (MSCJ) is a professional practical degree program that attracts skilled managers, agents, and clinicians from many components of the criminal justice and juvenile justice systems. Combined with the faculty who direct and facilitate the educational experiences in the MSCJ program, the school's talented and multifaceted students complete the mixture and create an intellectual synergy that's found in very few graduate programs.

Note: There is no thesis track. Instead, the program offers a capstone project.

Number of Faculty: 32

Accreditation: Higher Learning Commission of the North Central Association of colleges and Schools

Average Length of Time to Complete the Program: Not available

Troy University

Address: 600 University Avenue
Troy, AL 36082
Phone: (334) 670-3100
Website: http://www.troy.edu/

Department: Department of Criminal Justice
Website: http://www.troy.edu/college-of-arts-and-sciences/criminal-justice.html

Type of Program: MS in Criminal Justice

Application Deadline: Not available

Requirements:
- Hold a master's or higher degree from a regionally accredited university. No test score is required. An official transcript showing completion of a master's or higher degree is required.
  or
- Hold a baccalaureate degree from a regionally accredited college or university with a minimum overall undergraduate grade point average of 2.5 (4.0 scale) or a 3.0 grade point average on the last thirty semester hours. All hours attempted in the term in which the thirty semester hours were reached will be used to calculate the grade point average. All transcripts from all colleges or universities attended are required.
  and
- Have an acceptable score on the appropriate entrance exam [GRE 290 (850 on the old exam) (verbal plus quantitative), MAT 385, or GMAT 380].

Information Required for Application:
- Official transcript
- Recommendation form

Admission Date: Not available

In-state and Out-of-state Tuition Costs: $460 per credit hour

Availability of Internships and Scholarships: Not available

Orientation and Emphasis of Department/Program (Program Description): The master of science degree in criminal justice is designed to broaden and enhance each student's ability to understand, analyze and evaluate issues that confront the American criminal justice system. The objectives of the program's core coursework are: (1) to prepare students to understand, analyze, and evaluate the principles and functions of personnel administration in criminal justice applications; (2) to prepare students to understand, analyze, and evaluate trends and developments affecting the interpretation of the U.S. Constitution in light of historical case precedent; (3) to prepare students to understand, analyze, and evaluate issues that affect the structure and functioning of the criminal justice system; and (4) to understand, analyze, and evaluate criminological theories that explain criminal behavior and its application to organizational management.

Number of Faculty: Not available

Accreditation: Southern Association of Colleges and Schools Commission on Colleges

Average Length of Time to Complete the Program: One year

University at Albany, State University of New York

Address: 1400 Washington Avenue
Albany, NY 12222
Phone: (518) 442-3300
Website: http://www.albany.edu/

Department: School of Criminal Justice
135 Western Avenue
Draper Hall 219
Albany, NY 12222
Phone: (518) 442-5210
Website: http://www.albany.edu/scj/

Type of Program: MA in Criminal Justice; PhD in Criminal Justice

Application Deadline: MA: July 1, December 1; PhD: December 31

Requirements: Not available

Information Required for Application: MA and PhD
- Three official transcripts
- Statement of goals
- GRE Scores

Admission Date: MA: Fall and Spring; PhD: Fall only

In-state and Out-of-state Tuition Costs: In-state: $11,295 annually: out-of-state: $19,775 annually

Availability of Internships and Scholarships: Fellowships, assistantships, and internships (most funding is awarded to doctoral students)

Orientation and Emphasis of Department/Program (Program Description): The MA degree provides research and statistical skills that allow students to appreciate, design, and evaluate effective policy and practice. Students learn about the structure of the criminal justice system and the nature of successful crime prevention programs. Students in the MA program may complete a formal concentration in criminal justice information technology through courses focused on the collection, protection, storage, manipulation, interpretation, and communication of data. They also have the option to pursue a joint MA/MSW degree or a degree with a concentration in public administration.

Number of Faculty: 32

Accreditation: Not available

Average Length of Time to Complete the Program: Not available

The University of Alabama

Address: Tuscaloosa, AL 35487
Phone: (205) 348-6010
Website: http://www.ua.edu/

Department: Department of Criminal Justice
University of Alabama
Box 870320
Tuscaloosa, AL 35487-0320
Phone: (205) 348-7795
Website: http://cj.ua.edu/

Type of Program: Master's in Criminal Justice (MCJ)

Application Deadline: June 15, June 15 (Early admissions: October 1, November 15)

Requirements:
• Minimum GPA of 3.0

Information Required for Application:
• A statement of purpose (tell us about your interest in criminal justice and your exciting career plans—no more than one page, single-spaced);
• Undergraduate transcripts;
• Test score from the GRE; and
• Three letters of recommendation.

Admission Date: Fall, Spring

In-state and Out-of-state Tuition Costs: In-state: $4,725 for nine to fifteen credits: out-of-state: $11,975 for nine to fifteen credits

Availability of Internships and Scholarships: Graduate assistantships

Orientation and Emphasis of Department/Program (Program Description): At the master's level, our mission is the development of research skills and expansion of the conceptual and practical knowledge critical for leaders in criminal justice or in the social services. We fulfill this mission in several ways:
• Low student-faculty ratio allows personal academic and career advising, and ensures enough different courses are offered to meet your needs.
• Diverse research opportunities equip you to pursue specific interests.
• Strong employer network gives you an edge in job searching.
• Classes provide thorough preparation for PhD programs.

Number of Faculty: 10

Accreditation: Commission on Colleges of the Southern Association of Colleges and Schools

Average Length of Time to Complete the Program: Not available

University of Alabama at Birmingham

Address: 1720 2nd Avenue South
Birmingham, AL 35233
Phone: (205) 934-4011
Website: http://www.uab.edu/

Department: Department of Justice Sciences
1201 University Boulevard – 210
Birmingham, AL 35294-4562
Phone: (205) 934-2069
Website: http://www.uab.edu/cas/justice-sciences/

Type of Program: MS in Criminal Justice; MS in Forensic Sciences; MS in Computer Forensics and Security Management

Application Deadline: Not available

Requirements: Not available

Information Required for Application:
- Application fee ($45)
- One official transcript
- Letter of recommendation
- GRE Scores

Admission Date: Not available

In-state and Out-of-state Tuition Costs: In-state: first semester hour $562, each additional hour of coursework $355: out-of-state: first semester hour $1,042, each additional hour of coursework $835

Availability of Internships and Scholarships: Not available

Orientation and Emphasis of Department/Program (Program Description): The Department of Justice Sciences offers a program of study leading to the master of science degree in criminal justice (MSCJ). The program is divided into two tracks: the thesis track training program, which is designed to prepare students to pursue doctoral-level study in criminology, criminal justice, or a related field; and the non-thesis program, geared toward working professionals and designed to provide to them advanced training in such areas as research methods, program evaluation, and policy analysis. The required core curriculum for both tracks includes courses in criminological theory, research methods, statistics, and criminal justice policy. The master of science in forensic science program is designed to prepare individuals for careers in various forensic science and conventional analytical laboratories, emphasizing the application of scientific methods and technologies to legal proceedings. With thoughtful planning, many students have found the program offerings helpful in building a strong foundation to pursue doctoral (PhD and MD) studies. The program also offers, in conjunction with the Department of Computer and Information Sciences, the opportunity for students to pursue a graduate certificate in computer forensics that involves additional, elective coursework. Students may also pursue a certificate in forensic accounting, offered in conjunction with the Department of Accounting and Information Systems.

The master of science in computer forensics and security management (MSCFSM) is an interdisciplinary professional practice graduate program involving faculty from the Departments of Computer and Information Sciences and Justice Sciences (College of Arts and Sciences), and the Departments of Management, Information Systems and Quantitative Methods (School of Business), and Accounting and Finance (School of Business). The program prepares students with backgrounds in criminal justice, computer and information sciences, information systems, information technology, and forensic accounting to practice in the fields of computer forensics and security management including information security and IT auditing.

Number of Faculty: 20

Accreditation: Commission on Colleges of the Southern Association of Colleges and Schools

Average Length of Time to Complete the Program: Not available

University of Alaska Fairbanks

Address: 505 South Chandlar Drive
Fairbanks, AK 99775
Phone: (907) 474-7034
Website: http://www.uaf.edu/

Department: Justice Department
501 Gruening Building
P.O. Box 756425
Fairbanks, AK 99775-6425
Phone: (907) 474-5500
Website: http://www.uaf.edu/justice/

Type of Program: MA in Administration of Justice (online)

Application Deadline: April 15

Requirements: In general, applicants may be admitted to a graduate program if they have a bachelor's degree from an accredited institution with at least a 3.0 (B) cumulative undergraduate GPA and a 3.0 (B) GPA in your major.

Information Required for Application:
- Official transcripts
- Official GRE Scores
- Résumé
- A statement of goals
- Three letters of recommendation

Admission Date: Fall

In-state and Out-of-state Tuition Costs: In-state: $7750 per semester; out-of-state: $11,422 per semester

Availability of Internships and Scholarships: Graduate assistantships, teaching assistantships, and research assistantships

Orientation and Emphasis of Department/Program (Program Description): The MA in administration of justice has been designed as a web-based degree program to accommodate the needs of justice professionals for whom a two-year leave of absence from their profession is not feasible. Since relocation to the Fairbanks area is not necessary, the MA degree program has attracted justice professionals from throughout the country who have found the flexibility of a web-based format useful.

Number of Faculty: 7

Accreditation: Northwest Commission on Colleges and Universities

Average Length of Time to Complete the Program: Not available

University of Arkansas at Little Rock

Address: 2801 South University Avenue
Little Rock, AR 72204
Phone: (501) 569-3000
Website: http://www.ualr.edu/

Department: Department of Criminal Justice
Ross Hall, 5th Floor
Phone: (501) 569-3195
Website: http://www.ualr.edu/criminaljustice/

Type of Program: MA in Criminal Justice; MS in Criminal Justice (online); PhD in Criminal Justice

Application Deadline: February 18, March 18, April 22, July 22 (reviewed over the duration of four separate meeting times)

Requirements:
Master of Arts
- Baccalaureate degree from an accredited institution, with a cumulative grade point average of at least 2.75 (4.0 scale);
- Score of at least 50 on the Miller Analogies Test or 900 on the Graduate Record Examination verbal and quantitative sections; and
- Transfer credit: up to six hours of credit may be transferred into the program, with a limit of twelve hours under unusual circumstances.

Master of Science
- Baccalaureate degree from an accredited institution, with a cumulative grade point average of at least 2.75 (4.0 scale);
- Score of at least 50 on the Miller Analogies Test or 900 on the Graduate Record Examination verbal and quantitative sections; and
- Statement of purpose detailing current employment in the criminal justice system and the significance of attaining the MSCJ.

Doctoral
- Applicants are required to score at least 1,000 on the combined verbal and quantitative portions and at least 4 on the written portion of the Graduate Record Exam (GRE).
- Applicants must have a cumulative GPA in their master's program of at least 3.5.
- International students must take the TOEFL exam and score at least 550 on the paper-based test, 213 on the computer-based version, or 79 on the Internet-based version.

- Admission to the doctoral program requires a master's degree in criminology/criminal justice or a closely related field. Applicants from other disciplines may be admitted after taking one or more courses in the MACJ program to establish knowledge in criminal justice issues.
- Three courses in statistics and research methods at the master's level are also required.

Information Required for Application: Stated above

Admission Date: Fall only

In-state and Out-of-state Tuition Costs: In-state: $284.50 per hour; out-of-state: $651.50 per hour

Availability of Internships and Scholarships: Assistantships and fellowships

Orientation and Emphasis of Department/Program (Program Description): The master of arts in criminal justice program prepares graduates for positions of responsibility in the criminal justice system and related areas, facilitates the professional and intellectual development of in-service students, and provides foundation work for those planning careers in research or teaching. The curriculum provides a distinctive melding of professionally structured knowledge and the ethical imperatives of criminal justice in a constitutional democracy. The master of science in criminal justice is a professionally oriented terminal master's degree offered completely online. It provides students with advanced academic training, special expertise in advanced issues within the criminal justice system, supervisory and administrative proficiency, and the methodological and statistical skills necessary to understand research and new developments in criminal justice. Graduates of this program will gain applied knowledge enabling them to rise toward the highest levels in criminal justice organizations. Students in the PhD program in criminal justice are guided through an intense, supervised course of study of the history, current issues, and research related to criminology and criminal justice. This program requires extensive work in qualitative and quantitative methods, statistical analysis, and research design. Students will be trained to be prolific writers and skilled at obtaining grants. Coursework and mentoring will provide students with other aspects of professional development, including teaching and pedagogy, service to the discipline, and program administration.

Number of Faculty: 13

Accreditation: The Higher Learning Commission

Average Length of Time to Complete the Program: Not available

University of Baltimore

Address: 1420 North Charles Street
Baltimore, MD 21201
Phone: (410) 837-4200
Website: http://www.ubalt.edu/

Department: Criminal Justice Department
Phone: (410) 837-5372
Website: http://www.ubalt.edu/cpa/graduate-programs-and-certificates/degree-programs/criminal-justice/

Type of Program: MS in Criminal Justice

Application Deadline: December 1

Requirements:
- A bachelor's degree with a minimum 3.0 GPA from a regionally accredited college or university; and
- Successful completion of undergraduate courses in research methods, statistics, and criminological theory.

Information Required for Application:
- Online application
- Official transcript
- Writing sample

Admission Date: Rolling Fall admissions, Spring

In-state and Out-of-state Tuition Costs: In-state: $6,262 for nine credits: out-of-state: $8,764 for nine credits

Availability of Internships and Scholarships: Not available

Orientation and Emphasis of Department/Program (Program Description): In this thirty-six- to thirty-nine-credit master of science program, you'll:
- Apply research theory, methods, planning and statistics to the daily decisions you'll encounter in your work;
- Interact with field professionals through our partnerships with the Baltimore City Police Department, state government agencies, and victim advocacy programs such as the House of Ruth; some are federal agents, while others work in middle management in either corrections or the courts; and
- Choose to specialize in law enforcement, courts and law, corrections, or juvenile justice.

Number of Faculty: 11

Accreditation: Middle States Commission on Higher Education

Average Length of Time to Complete the Program: Not available

University of California, Irvine

Address: Irvine, CA 92697
Phone: (949) 824-5011
Website: http://www.uci.edu/

Department: Department of Criminology, Law, and Society
2340 Social Ecology II
Irvine, CA 92697-7080
Website: http://cls.soceco.uci.edu/

Type of Program: MAS in Criminology, Law, and Society (online);
PhD in Criminology, Law, and Society

Application Deadline: MAS: June 2; PhD: January 15

Requirements:
- Hold a bachelor's degree (or equivalent) from a recognized academic institution with degree standards equivalent to those of the University of California; and
- Have a minimum cumulative undergraduate GPA of 3.0.

Information Required for Application:
Master's
- Two formal statements demonstrating your writing ability and clarity of thought, which includes a personal history (one page) describing your previous professional and academic achievements, and a formal statement of purpose (two-three pages) detailing current goals and specifically how and why the MAS program will help you achieve them;
- Official transcripts from each college or university attended indicating you have attained at least a bachelor's degree. Admission standards to UC Irvine require a 3.0 GPA, but some special considerations may apply; and
- Three confidential letters of recommendation.

Doctoral
- An application fee;
- One official transcript from each college or university attended (electronic transcripts which are securely transmitted from official sources are accepted);
- Three letters of recommendation;
- Scores from the GRE; and
- Statement of purpose.

Admission Date: Fall

In-state and Out-of-state Tuition Costs: In-state: $5,184.50 per semester; out-of-state: $10,218.50 per semester

Availability of Internships and Scholarships: Not available

Orientation and Emphasis of Department/Program (Program Description): The master of advanced study (MAS) degree in criminology, law, and society is designed to meet the needs of working professionals and traditional students by providing educational access and flexibility in an online format. It is well suited to meet the goals of individuals who are seeking leadership positions within their organizations in a variety of fields, including but not limited to criminal justice, legal, and social services. The curriculum emphasizes both theoretical and practical applications and an interdisciplinary approach that serves not only as an excellent pathway to career advancement but also provides a solid foundation from which to pursue doctoral study in related fields. The PhD program in criminology, law, and society is consistently ranked within the top five in the *U.S. News and World Reports'* annual rankings. The program focuses on the causes, manifestations, and consequences of crime; the impacts of crime on society; social regulation; the civil justice system; the social and cultural contexts of law; and the interactive effects of law and society. With high caliber faculty and an interdisciplinary perspective, the program aims to develop students' theoretical and methodological sophistication to prepare them for faculty positions at major universities and colleges or for research, training, and administrative work in the justice system.

Number of Faculty: 13

Accreditation: Senior Commission of the Western Association of Schools and Colleges

Average Length of Time to Complete the Program: Not available

University of Central Florida

Address: 4000 Central Florida Boulevard
Orlando, FL 32816
Phone: (407) 823-2000
Website: https://www.ucf.edu/

Department: Department of Criminal Justice
College of Health and Public Affairs
University of Central Florida
12805 Pegasus Drive
Orlando, FL 32816-1600
Phone: (407) 823-2603
Website: http://www2.cohpa.ucf.edu/crim.jus/

Type of Program: MS in Criminal Justice

Application Deadline: January 15 (Fall Priority), July 15, December 1, April 15

Requirements:
- Hold a bachelor's degree from a regionally accredited U.S. institution or its equivalent from a foreign institution, and a GPA of 3.0 or more (on a 4.0 maximum) in all work attempted while registered as an undergraduate student or while registered as an upper-division undergraduate student (normally based on the last sixty attempted semester hours); or, a graduate degree or professional degree or equivalent from a regionally accredited U.S. institution or its equivalent from a foreign institution in a field related to the discipline of the program to which the student is applying.
- Students applying to doctoral programs must submit an official competitive score on the general tests of the Graduate Record Examination (GRE) (or an official competitive score on the General Management Admission Test [GMAT] as required), or an equivalent score on an equivalent measure approved by the graduate program and the university.
- Students applying to doctoral programs must also submit three letters of recommendation, a résumé or curriculum vita, and a written essay.
- International students must demonstrate their proficiency in the English language. International students, except those who are from countries where English is the only official language, those who have earned a degree from a regionally accredited U.S. college or university, or those who have earned a degree from a country where English is the only official language or from a university at which English is the only official

language of instruction, are required to submit a score on the TOEFL or IELTS before they can be admitted to the university. A computer-based TOEFL score of 220 or 80 on the internet-based TOEFL (or equivalent score on the paper-based test) or 6.5 on the IELTS is required unless otherwise specified by the program.

- International students applying to master's programs that do not require a GRE (or GMAT), must submit a course-by-course evaluation of their official transcripts from a credential evaluation service recommended by UCF. This course-by-course evaluation must show a GPA that is equivalent to a 3.0 from an earned degree that is equivalent to a U.S. bachelor's degree.

Information Required for Application: Stated above

Admission Date: Fall, Spring, Summer

In-state and Out-of-state Tuition Costs: In-state: $367.94 per hour; out-of-state: $1,192.34 per hour

Availability of Internships and Scholarships: Fellowships and assistantships

Orientation and Emphasis of Department/Program (Program Description): The benefits of an advanced graduate degree in criminal justice are self-evident and are being increasingly recognized by employers in central Florida and throughout the United States. Federal, state, and local criminal justice agencies benefit from an informed and innovative workforce that is aware of the complex issues and problems faced by the system regardless of geographic locale. Furthermore, graduates of the program are grounded in the latest theories and learn how these theories affect each individual or organization within the system. The Department of Criminal Justice offers a master of science in criminal justice with two tracks of study: the professional track and the research track.

Number of Faculty: 33

Accreditation: Southern Association of Colleges and Schools Commission on Colleges

Average Length of Time to Complete the Program: Not available

University of Central Missouri

Address: 108 West South Street
Warrensburg, MO 64093
Phone: (660) 543-4111
Website: http://www.ucmo.edu/future.cfm

Department: Criminal Justice Department
P.O. Box 800
Warrensburg, MO 64093
Phone: (660) 543-4950
Website: http://www.ucmo.edu/cj/

Type of Program: MS in Criminal Justice

Application Deadline: March 1, October 1

Requirements:
- The applicant must have earned an undergraduate degree in criminal justice or a related field prior to enrollment at UCM in the coursework for the program, submitted a complete graduate program application, and earned a minimum grade point average of 3.0 on all undergraduate course work and 3.0 on all graduate course work.
- A student without a criminal justice degree may be required to complete up to fifteen hours of background courses in criminal justice prior to taking graduate level courses.
- Students with a cumulative undergraduate grade point average of 2.75 to below 3.0 may be considered for admission by the criminal justice graduate committee.
- Students must take the Graduate Record Examination (GRE) and submit a minimal combined score of 300 points on the general test (quantitative and verbal reasoning), and a minimal score of 4.0 on the analytic writing test.

Information Required for Application: Not available

Admission Date: Fall, Spring

In-state and Out-of-state Tuition Costs: In-state: $6,400 per academic year; out-of-state: $11,900 per academic year

Availability of Internships and Scholarships: Scholarships

Orientation and Emphasis of Department/Program (Program Description): This program is designed for those students who wish to enter and/or progress in the criminal justice fields of law enforcement, corrections, and juvenile justice, or who plan to seek positions in leadership.

Number of Faculty: 26

Accreditation: The Higher Learning Commission

Average Length of Time to Complete the Program: Not available

University of Central Oklahoma

Address: 100 North University Drive
Edmond, OK 73034
Phone: (405) 974-2000
Website: https://www.uco.edu/

Department: School of Criminal Justice
100 North University Drive
Edmond, OK 73034, Box 209
Phone: (405) 974-5501
Website: http://www.uco.edu/la/criminal-justice/

Type of Program: MA in Criminal Justice Management and Administration; MA in Crime and Intelligence

Application Deadline: September 15, February 15

Requirements: To be admitted, students must meet at least one of the following criteria.
- 2.75 GPA overall or 3.00 GPA in the last sixty hours attempted;
- An index score of 5.00 or higher on the GRE using the formula GRE/400 + GPA for the last sixty undergraduate hours; and/or
- A master's degree from an accredited university/ college with an overall GPA of 3.00.

Information Required for Application:
- All applicants must complete a statement of purpose paper.

Admission Date: Fall, Spring

In-state and Out-of-state Tuition Costs: In-state: $230.90 per credit hour; out-of-state: $542 per credit hour

Availability of Internships and Scholarships: Scholarships

Orientation and Emphasis of Department/Program (Program Description): The master of arts in criminal justice management and administration program is designed to meet Oklahoma's needs for graduate education in the area of criminal justice management and administration. The curriculum has been developed to provide opportunities to individuals interested in acquiring specialized skills and knowledge within the criminal justice field. The master of arts in criminal justice management and administration curriculum further encourages the development of the students critical, analytical, and creative abilities related to the subject area. This is further accomplished by the enhancement of research skills, class work, out-of-class projects, and field studies. The criminal justice management and administration program has non-thesis and thesis options. Students who opt for the non-thesis must complete thirty-two hours of academic work. The credit hour requirements are reduced to thirty hours for those students who elect the thesis option. Students who were accepted into the program in the Summer of 2004 and thereafter will be required to complete thirty-six hours regardless of the thesis or non-thesis option. If you plan on pursuing a doctoral degree, it is strongly recommended that you complete a master's thesis. The master of arts in crime and intelligence analysis is a new program designed to offer students a foundation of comparative studies, statistical analysis, and technological courses that have an emphasis on information/intelligence evaluation and reporting. The classes present both a theoretical and practical approach to develop general tools of research, writing, and analysis. A selection of elective courses allows students to investigate particular areas of interest, and the interdisciplinary nature of the electives provides additional skill sets necessary for developing a global perspective.

Number of Faculty: 22

Accreditation: Higher Learning Commission

Average Length of Time to Complete the Program: Not available

University of Cincinnati

Address: 2600 Clifton Avenue
Cincinnati, OH 45220
Phone: (513) 556-6000
Website: http://www.uc.edu/

Department: School of Criminal Justice
University of Cincinnati
P.O. Box 210389
665 Dyer Hall
Cincinnati, OH 45221-0389
Phone: (513) 556-4307
Website: http://cech.uc.edu/criminaljustice.html

Type of Program: Master's in Criminal Justice (MCJ); PhD in Criminal Justice

Application Deadline: Applications accepted throughout the year (MCJ online)

Requirements:
Online Master's
- Have a bachelor's degree (in any field of study) from a regionally accredited institution;
- Provide at least one professional or academic letter of recommendation; and
- Have achieved previous academic performance that meets any one of the following criteria:
  - 3.0 GPA (4.0 scale) in the last two years of college work (sixty semester hours/ninety quarter hours);
  - 2.75 GPA in all college work (120 semester hours/180 quarter hours);
  - 2.5 GPA in the last two years of college (sixty semester hours/ninety quarter hours) and five years of work experience in criminal justice;
  - 3.25 GPA in nine hours of graduate credit from another university or universities and five years' work experience in criminal justice; or
  - 3.5 GPA in six hours of graduate credit in the MS program at the University of Cincinnati as a non-degree student and five years' work experience in the field of criminal justice.

Master's
- A baccalaureate degree (any major) from an accredited institution;
- For undergraduate applicants, a minimum grade point average of 3.0 on a 4.0 scale;

- For applicants with an MA, a minimum graduate grade point average of 3.5;
- GRE scores; and
- At least two letters of reference and a personal statement.

Information Required for Application:
- A completed online university graduate application;
- Official collegiate transcript(s);
- Letters of recommendation submitted through the online recommendation system;
- Test scores from qualifying exams, such as the Graduate Record Exam (GRE) or the Graduate Management Admission Test (GMAT);
- Test scores from English proficiency tests such as TOEFL or IELTS; and
- A personal statement or letter of intent.

Admission Date: Continuous for online program; Fall only for MCJ and PhD

In-state and Out-of-state Tuition Costs: In-state: $7,091 per semester; out-of-state: $12,848 per semester

Availability of Internships and Scholarships: Not available

Orientation and Emphasis of Department/Program (Program Description):
Online Master's: The online master of science in criminal justice programprovides you with a comprehensive degree designed for criminal justice and social service professionals who need additional knowledge and skills to advance to a higher-level position, have a desire to teach at a community college or university, and/or seek an advanced degree as a prerequisite for entry into the criminal justice field.

Master's: Graduate training is growing in significance in the field of criminal justice. Agencies are equating professionalism with higher educational training, and for many careers the master's in criminal justice is becoming the minimum qualification for employment. The master of science in criminal justice is both an entry-level degree to middle-management careers and an avenue for advancement for persons already employed in some phase of the criminal justice system.

Doctoral: The PhD program in criminal justice began in September 1992 and had its first graduate in 1996. The doctoral program is designed to develop social scientists' ability to consume, transmit, and independently produce research knowledge on crime and criminal justice to prepare them for careers in academia and/or agency-based research. The criminal justice faculty at the University of Cincinnati is very serious about the education of our graduate students. We are demanding but also supportive. Our goal is to motivate students to achieve new intellectual levels and to maximize opportunities for success within and beyond the graduate program. We want our students to play an integral role in shaping the future of criminal justice research and education.

Number of Faculty: 43

Accreditation: North Central Association of Colleges and Schools

Average Length of Time to Complete the Program: MCJ: one year; PhD: not available

University of Colorado at Colorado Springs

Address: 1420 Austin Bluffs Parkway
Colorado Springs, CO 80918
Phone: (719) 255-8227
Website: http://www.uccs.edu/

Department: School of Public Affairs
1420 Austin Bluffs Parkway
Colorado Springs, CO 80918
Phone: (719) 255-4993
Website: http://www.uccs.edu/spa/

Type of Program: Master of Criminal Justice (MCJ)

Application Deadline: Rolling admissions

Requirements: Not available

Information Required for Application:
- GRE scores
- $60 application fee
- Official transcripts

Admission Date: Rolling admissions

In-state and Out-of-state Tuition Costs: $612 per credit

Availability of Internships and Scholarships: Internships

Orientation and Emphasis of Department/Program (Program Description): The master of criminal justice (MCJ) program is designed for students interested in comprehensive professional graduate education in the field of criminal justice. It is intended to develop in the student a fundamental understanding of the basic fields within criminal justice and of background material from supporting disciplines, which would enable the student to adapt to many operational specializations.

Number of Faculty: 19

Accreditation: North Central Association of the Higher Learning Commission

Average Length of Time to Complete the Program: Not available

University of Colorado Denver

Address: 1250 14th Street
Denver, CO 80202
Phone: (303) 556-2400
Website: http://www.ucdenver.edu/

Department: Department of Criminology and Criminal Justice
Campus Box 142
P.O. Box 173364
Denver, CO 80217-3364
Phone: (303) 315-2228
Website: http://www.ucdenver.edu/academics/colleges/SPA/
Academics/programs/CriminalJustice/Pages/index.aspx

Type of Program: Master of Criminal Justice (MCJ)

Application Deadline: April 1, October 1

Requirements: Not available

Information Required for Application:
- A completed application from the Graduate School office on the Downtown Denver Campus;
- Two copies of all graduate and undergraduate transcripts, and transcripts for any non-degree courses previously taken;
- Three letters of recommendation, in which the recommender specifically addresses the candidate's ability to pursue successfully the program chosen (forms for recommendation letters are available with the online application);
- The Graduate Record Exam, including the analytical, verbal, and quantitative portions. GRE score average should be 155 or higher. Analytical writing score should be 4 or higher. The English literature subject test is not required;
- Evidence of a 3.0 grade point average in previous courses;
- A one-page statement of purpose in which the applicant carefully describes reasons and motivation for pursuing the program chosen and career aspirations upon completing the degree; and
- A critical writing sample of approximately ten pages in length.

Admission Date: Fall, Spring

In-state and Out-of-state Tuition Costs: In-state: $4,308 per semester; out-of-state: $13,440 per semester

Availability of Internships and Scholarships: Required internship, scholarships, and grants

Orientation and Emphasis of Department/Program (Program Description): The master's degree in criminal justice, founded in 1972, is a rigorous academic program. It helps students develop their critical thinking skills and provides them with an interdisciplinary perspective on criminology and the criminal justice system. It focuses on law enforcement, the judiciary, correctional systems, juvenile justice, and the formulation of laws and codes. A special benefit of the program is that it prepares students not only to administer the current system but also to become pioneers in evaluating and changing the system so that it is more responsive to the needs of the community.

Number of Faculty: 8

Accreditation: Higher Learning Commission of the North Central Association

Average Length of Time to Complete the Program: Not available

University of Delaware

Address: Newark, DE 19716
Phone: (302) 831-2792
Website: https://www.udel.edu/

Department: Department of Sociology and Criminal Justice
325 Smith Hall
Phone: (302) 831-1236
Website: http://www.udel.edu/soc/

Type of Program: MA in Criminology; PhD in Criminology

Application Deadline: February 1

Requirements: Stated below

Information Required for Application:
- Online application;
- GRE (competitive scores for admissions are 156 for the verbal section and 146 for the quantitative section; scores cannot be over five years old);
- Unofficial transcript containing GPA;
- Three letters of recommendation;
- Statement of objectives (why you want an MA or PhD and what you plan to do with it; one to five pages in length);
- TOEFL (minimum 600/250/100) or IELTS (7.5) for foreign students; and
- A writing sample (strongly encouraged).

Admission Date: Fall only

In-state and Out-of-state Tuition Costs: In-state and out-of-state tuition: $1,578 per credit

Availability of Internships and Scholarships: Fellowships, assistantships

Orientation and Emphasis of Department/Program (Program Description): The Department of Sociology and Criminal Justice offers master of arts and a doctor of philosophy degree programs in both sociology and criminology. The graduate program in criminology was added in 1986 and granted permanent status by the university in 1992. The primary focus of the program is the preparation of members of the next generation of sociologists and criminologists by emphasizing systematic training in theory and research methodology as well as teaching. These advanced education degrees are intended for persons interested in careers in academia, public service, or private enterprise. The department has a large number of full-time distinguished faculty (28) from the disciplines of sociology, psychology, law, criminology, history, and criminal justice. This allows students to work closely with faculty members while preserving a reasonable breadth of interests. Thus, while both the sociology and criminology degrees rely on strong theoretical and methodological foundations, they also allow students to tailor a program that meets their individual needs.

Number of Faculty: 28

Accreditation: Middle States Commission on Higher Education

Average Length of Time to Complete the Program: Not available

University of Detroit Mercy

Address: 4001 West McNichols Road
Detroit, MI 48221-3038
Phone: (313) 993-1000
Website: http://www.udmercy.edu/

Department: Department of Criminal Justice
Website: http://liberalarts.udmercy.edu/programs/depts/cjs/

Type of Program: MA in Criminal Justice

Application Deadline: Not available

Requirements:
- Applicants must have a bachelor's degree from an accredited college and must have demonstrated intellectual competence for graduate study.
- Selection is based on such factors as previous academic record (at least a 2.7 GPA) and/or relevant experience.
- Also, as prerequisites, applicants must have had at least fifteen hours of basic course work in the behavioral/social sciences.
- Applicants should solicit three letters of recommendation.

Information Required for Application: Stated above

Admission Date: Not available

In-state and Out-of-state Tuition Costs: $1,385 per credit hour

Availability of Internships and Scholarships: Not available

Orientation and Emphasis of Department/Program (Program Description): The master of arts in criminal justice is designed for professional workers (law enforcement, corrections officers, security personnel) and others who desire to further their knowledge of the criminal justice system and its related disciplines. It provides the student an opportunity to broaden and deepen his/her perspective in the criminal justice profession. Problem solving, leadership, critical thinking, and the prudent application of theory to practice are skills that the program is designed to foster. It is developed to meet the need for specialized training for criminal justice suited to its unique functions. Students interested in a generalist's approach to criminal justice will find the course of study appropriate. Law enforcement and corrections personnel acquire a broad background in administrative theory and current concerns of the criminal justice system.

Number of Faculty: 4

Accreditation: Higher Learning Commission of the North Central Association

Average Length of Time to Complete the Program: Not available

University of Florida

Address: Gainesville, FL 32611
Phone: (352) 392-3261
Website: http://www.ufl.edu/

Department: Sociology and Criminology and Law
3219 Turlington Hall
P.O. Box 117330
University of Florida
Gainesville, FL 32611-7330
Phone: (352) 392-0265
Website: http://soccrim.clas.ufl.edu/

Type of Program: MA in Criminology, Law, and Society; PhD in Criminology, Law, and Society

Application Deadline: Not available

Requirements:
Master's: Admission to graduate study is competitive and is based on evaluation of the total record of the applicant: statement of purpose, career plans, letters of recommendation, GPA, and GRE scores. Applicants generally have an undergraduate major or MA in criminology or a related discipline.
Doctoral: Admission to graduate study is competitive and is based on evaluation of the total record of the applicant: statement of purpose, career plans, letters of recommendation, GPA, and GRE scores. Applicants generally have an undergraduate major or MA in criminology or a related discipline.

Information Required for Application:
- The statement of purpose should describe the applicant's reasons for undertaking graduate study in criminology, including both educational and personal experiences that have influenced the decision to attend graduate school. It should also describe the applicant's future career plans. The statement should describe the planned area of concentration within criminology if it has already been chosen.
- The most useful letters of recommendation are from college instructors who can address the applicant's readiness to do graduate work in criminology.
- Submit official GRE and TOEFL scores sent by ETS.
- Official transcripts for each undergraduate, graduate, and professional degree completed or in progress should be sent by the university or college where the degree was earned.
- Upload a copy of your CV or résumé.
- Upload a statement of purpose.

Admission Date: Fall only

In-state and Out-of-state Tuition Costs: Not available

Availability of Internships and Scholarships: Awards and Scholarships

Orientation and Emphasis of Department/Program (Program Description): Master's students at the University of Florida take a sequence of five required courses plus elective courses to complete the required thirty-six hours for the degree. Students may select either a thesis or non-thesis option. In both options, the graduate student must meet the graduate council requirement that MA candidates have a broad interdisciplinary understanding of criminology and law and society. The hours taken to complete the MA will count toward the total of ninety hours required for the PhD, if admitted to that program. The doctoral program consists of ninety semester hours of credit beyond the BA degree. Students with a criminology or closely related MA received within the last seven years from an accredited U.S. university may request up to thirty hours credit from their MA work toward this total. Those with an MA from this department may apply thirty-six hours. The department requires PhD students to complete at least sixty-six hours of course work, including the MA hours. Qualifying exams in crime and justice, law and society, and methods take place at the end of a student's course work. The twenty-four hours remaining to complete the required ninety hours usually consist of individual pre-doctoral and doctoral dissertation research. In addition to the MA requirements, the graduate program in CLS requires additional criminology courses, nine elective courses, and dissertation credits. Each PhD student must indicate an area of specialization in either crime and justice or law and society.

Number of Faculty: 38

Accreditation: Southern Association of Colleges and Schools Commission on Colleges

Average Length of Time to Complete the Program: Not available

University of Houston–Clear Lake

Address: 2700 Bay Area Boulevard
Houston, TX 77058
Phone: (281) 283-7600
Website: http://prtl.uhcl.edu/

Department: Department of Criminology
Phone: (281) 283-3416
Website: http://prtl.uhcl.edu/portal/page/portal/HSH/HOME/
HSH%20Programs/Criminology/

Program Type: MA in Criminology

Application Deadline: January 6, May 20, August 11

Requirements: Not available

Information Required for Application:
- Transcripts
- GRE scores
- $45 application fee

Admission Date: Fall, Spring, Summer

In-state and Out-of-state Tuition Costs: In-state: $7,244 for nine hours; out-of-state: $10,583 for nine hours

Availability of Internships and Scholarships: Not available

Orientation and Emphasis of Department/Program (Program Description): Not available

Number of Faculty: 5

Accreditation: Commission on Colleges of the Southern Association of Colleges and Schools

Average Length of Time to Complete the Program: Not available

University of Illinois at Chicago

Address: 2035 West Taylor Street
Chicago, IL 60612
Phone: (312) 996-7000
Website: http://www.uic.edu/

Department: Department of Criminology, Law, and Justice
1007 West Harrison Street, MC 141
Chicago, IL 60607-7140
Phone: (312) 996-5290
Website: http://clj.las.uic.edu/

Program Type: MA in Criminology, Law, and Justice; PhD in Criminology, Law, and Justice

Application Deadline: MA: March 15; PhD: February 1 (priority by January 1)

Requirements:
Master's
- Baccalaureate field applicants must have a baccalaureate degree in criminology, law, and justice or a related field from an accredited college or university.
- Have a grade point average at least 3.00/4.00 for the final sixty semester hours (ninety quarter hours) of undergraduate study.
- Take the GRE general (verbal, quantitative, and analytical). The combined verbal and quantitative scores on the GRE should be at or above the 50th percentile.
- Obtain a minimum English competency test score. This can be achieved with the following scores: TOEFL 550 (paper-based); 80, with subscores of reading 19, listening 17, speaking 20, and writing 21 (iBT Internet-based); or IELTS 6.5, with scores of 6.0 for all four subscores.
- Three letters of recommendation are required, preferably from professors familiar with the student's recent work or, in case of the applicants with professional experience, from supervisors.
- A one-page personal statement is required. The statement should address the applicant's reasons for wanting to take graduate work in criminology, law, and justice and the relationship of this advanced training to the applicant's professional and other goals.
- Applicants must submit a sample of their academic writing.
- The department will consider applicants for non-degree status who hold a baccalaureate degree from an accredited college or university and meet the admission requirements of the Graduate College.

Doctoral:

- Baccalaureate field students may enter either with an MA or a BA. If applicants received their criminology, law, and justice MA from UIC, then they must have received a high pass (3.50) on their MA comprehensive exam.
- A grade point average of at least 3.00/4.00 for the final sixty semester hours (ninety quarter hours) of undergraduate study, with a GPA of at least 3.25 in all graduate courses taken.
- GRE scores (verbal, quantitative, and analytical) are required with a minimum combined verbal and quantitative score at or above the 50th percentile.
- Obtain a minimum English competency test score. This can be achieved with the following scores: TOEFL 550 (paper-based); 80, with subscores of reading 19, listening 17, speaking 20, and writing 21 (iBT Internet-based); or IELTS 6.5, with scores of 6.0 for all four subscores.
- Three letters of recommendation addressing the applicant's academic accomplishments and potential are required.
- A personal statement of academic and professional goals in required.
- A writing sample (an MA thesis or other major research paper) should be submitted.

Information Required for Application: Stated above

Admission Date: Fall only

In-state and Out-of-state Tuition Costs: In-state: $3,689 for six to eleven credit hours; out-of-state: $7,688 for six to eleven credit hours

Availability of Internships and Scholarships: Assistantships

Orientation and Emphasis of Department/Program (Program Description): The Department of Criminology, Law, and Justice offers work leading to the master of arts and the doctor of philosophy in criminology, law, and justice. The master of arts is organized into four curricular areas that include: the nature and development of rules, rule-breaking behavior, rule application, and research methodology. It is designed for careers in research, evaluation, and criminal justice administration. The interdepartmental concentration in gender and women's studies is available to students in this program. Building on the above general curricular areas, the doctor of philosophy degree offers additional course work in theory, substantive specialties, and research methods. Concentrations are offered in law and society, criminology, and organizations and administration.

Number of Faculty: 13

Accreditation: Higher Learning Commission of the North Central Association of Colleges and Schools

Average Length of Time to Complete the Program: Not available

University of Louisiana at Monroe

Address: 700 University Avenue
Monroe, LA 71209
Phone: (318) 342-1000
Website: http://www.ulm.edu/

Department: Department of Criminal Justice
Stubbs 208
The University of Louisiana at Monroe
Monroe, LA 71209-0330
Phone: (318) 342-1443
Website: http://www.ulm.edu/criminaljustice/

Type of Program: MA in Criminal Justice

Application Deadline: Not available

Requirements: Applicants may be admitted to the Graduate School on regular status if they have earned a baccalaureate degree from a regionally accredited institution with a grade point average (GPA) of 2.5 on all undergraduate work pursued based on a 4.0 scale, have met undergraduate prerequisites for their major and minor fields, have met departmental admission requirements, and have submitted satisfactory Graduate Record Examination/ Graduate Management Admission Test scores. The minimum requirements for regular status are two of the following:
* Minimum GRE (verbal + quantitative) converted score of 750 or GMAT of 450
* Minimum cumulative undergraduate GPA of 2.5 (based on a 4.0 scale)
* Minimum formula score of 1875 (GPA * GRE) or 1,000 (GPA * 200 + GMAT)

Information Required for Application:
* Application fee $20
* Official transcripts
* Official GRE scores

Admission Date: Not available

In-state and Out-of-state Tuition Costs: Not available

Availability of Internships and Scholarships: Scholarships and graduate assistantships/work study

Orientation and Emphasis of Department/Program (Program Description): Thirty-three semester-hour (thesis option) or thirty-six semester-hour (non-thesis option) program. The enrollment of this program ranges between twenty-five and thirty-five, with an average of approximately thirty enrolled in any given semester. All graduate courses are offered both online and in the classroom, with offerings alternating between classroom and online delivery. Classroom courses are held primarily in the evening hours. A student can obtain this degree within a one- to two-year time frame; most complete in eighteen to twenty-four months. The degree can be obtained through online courses, but the time to complete the course of study may extend to twenty-four to thirty-six months, depending upon self-imposed limitations and the availability of appropriate coursework. See the graduate catalog for entry requirements.

Number of Faculty: 2

Accreditation: Commission on Colleges of the Southern Association of Colleges and Schools

Average Length of Time to Complete the Program: One to two years

University of Louisville

Address: 580 South Preston Street
Louisville, KY 40202
Phone: (502) 852-5555
Website: http://www.louisville.edu/

Department: Justice Administration
Brigman Hall
Louisville, KY 40292
Phone: (502) 852-6567
Website: https://www.louisville.edu/justice/

Type of Program: MS in Administration of Justice

Application Deadline: July 1, December 1, April 1

Requirements: Stated below

Information Required for Application:
- Complete application for admission;
- Payment of nonrefundable $60 application fee (check or money order made payable to the University of Louisville);
- Baccalaureate degree or its equivalent earned from a regionally-accredited institution;
- Official transcripts of all undergraduate and graduate work completed;
- Minimum 3.0 (GPA) on a 4-point scale;
- Minimum 282 combined quantitative and verbal scores on the Graduate Record Examination (GRE) or completion of twelve hours of applicable graduate course credit with a minimum of a 3.0 (GPA) on a 4.0-point scale (accepted on a case-by-case basis);
- Two recommendation forms from individuals who can speak to the applicant's academic or professional capabilities; and
- An original essay identifying the applicant's background, professional interest and goals, and the applicant's motivation and potential for successful completion of graduate work.

Admission Date: Fall, Spring, Summer

In-state and Out-of-state Tuition Costs: In-state: $599 per credit hour; out-of-state: $1,247 per credit hour

Availability of Internships and Scholarships: Financial aid

Orientation and Emphasis of Department/Program (Program Description): The master of science in justice administration (MSJA) online degree gives you the knowledge and training you need to move forward and up in your career. Our program focuses on the criminal justice system, theories of crime and delinquency, legal issues in criminal justice, and advanced statistics and research methods. Our innovative curriculum and award-winning faculty provide an educational experience you won't find anywhere else. You can choose from several elective courses that allow you to gain specialized knowledge in areas such as emergency management, computer applications in criminal justice, capital punishment, and homeland security.

Number of Faculty: 17

Accreditation: Commission on Colleges of the Southern Association of Colleges

Average Length of Time to Complete the Program: Not available

University of Maryland, College Park

Address: College Park, MD 20742
Phone: (301) 405-1000
Website: http://www.umd.edu/

Department: Department of Criminology and Criminal Justice
2220 Samuel J. LeFrak Hall
College Park, MD 20742
Phone: (301) 405-4699
Website: http://www.ccjs.umd.edu/

Type of Program: MA in Criminology and Criminal Justice; PhD in Criminology and Criminal Justice

Application Deadline: December 1

Requirements: In order to be considered for admission, the Graduate School at the University of Maryland has established a set of minimum admission criteria:
- Applicants must have earned a four-year baccalaureate degree from a regionally accredited U.S. institution or an equivalent degree from a non-U.S. institution.
- Applicants must have earned a 3.0 GPA (on a 4.0 scale) in all prior undergraduate and graduate coursework.
- Applicants must provide an official hard copy of a transcript for all of their post-secondary work.

Information Required for Application:
- Official transcripts of all previous academic work at institutions of higher learning;
- Three letters of recommendation from professors, if possible, or employers who are acquainted with the applicant's qualifications; and
- Statement of goals and purpose (if not completed with online application).

Admission Date: Fall

In-state and Out-of-state Tuition Costs: In-state: $551 per credit; out-of-state: $1,188 per credit

Availability of Internships and Scholarships: Assistantships, fellowships, grants

Orientation and Emphasis of Department/Program (Program Description): Our traditional master's program is designed to give students a strong foundation in criminology and criminal justice research so that they can pursue research positions in government and private non-profit agencies, or research institutes. Further, this program gives students a firm foundation to continue their education in PhD programs. Our PhD program is designed to give students well-rounded experiences as scholars and teachers through coursework, research experience, and teaching opportunities. Our PhD students are mentored by faculty as they participate in on ongoing research projects and as they develop their own scholarly interests. The coursework is designed to give them a firm grounding in the historic progression of research in key areas and to keep them engaged in the latest developments. Finally, they are given opportunities to teach through teaching assistantships and, if wanted, as instructors.

Number of Faculty: 32

Accreditation: Middle States Commission on Higher Education

Average Length of Time to Complete the Program: Not available

University of Maryland Eastern Shore

Address: 11868 Academic Oval
Princess Anne, MD 21853
Phone: (410) 651-2200
Website: http://www.umes.edu/

Department: Department of Criminal Justice
Hazel Hall, 3rd Floor
University of Maryland Eastern Shore
Princess Anne, MD 21853
Phone: (410) 651-6585
Website: http://www.umes.edu/Criminal/Default.aspx?id=12288

Type of Program: Master of Criminal Justice (MCJ)

Application Deadline: April 15, October 15

Requirements:
- A baccalaureate degree from a regionally accredited four-year college or university, or the equivalent from a foreign country;
- A minimum cumulative grade point average (GPA) of 3.0 (on a 4.0 scale) on undergraduate coursework;
- Successful completion of the Graduate Record Examination (GRE) [general test] with a combined score of 1,000 or above on both quantitative and verbal scores;
- Three letters of recommendation from persons capable of adequately assessing the applicant's potential for success in the program; and
- An interview by the admissions committee.

Information Required for Application: Stated above

Admission Date: Fall, Spring, and Summer

In-state and Out-of-state Tuition Costs: In-state: $287 per credit; out-of-state: $511 per credit

Availability of Internships and Scholarships: Not available

Orientation and Emphasis of Department/Program (Program Description): Not available.

Number of Faculty: 7

Accreditation: Middle States Commission on Higher Education

Average Length of Time to Complete the Program: Not available

University of Massachusetts Lowell

Address: 1 University Avenue
Lowell, MA 01854
Phone: (978) 934-4000
Website: http://www.uml.edu/

Department: School of Criminology and Justice Studies
113 Wilder Street
HSSB, 4th floor
Lowell, MA 01854
Phone: (978) 934-4139
Website: http://www.uml.edu/FAHSS/Criminal-Justice/

Type of Program: MA in Criminology and Justice Studies; PhD in Criminology and Justice Studies

Application Deadline: Not available

Requirements: Not available

Information Required for Application:
- An application
- Application fee
- A statement of purpose
- Three letters of recommendation
- Official transcripts
- Official test score report
- Résumé

Admission Date: Not available

In-state and Out-of-state Tuition Costs: In-state: $12,039 per year; out-of-state: $21,874 per year

Availability of Internships and Scholarships: Scholarships and fellowships

Orientation and Emphasis of Department/Program (Program Description): The master's degree program offers courses in two formats: on-campus and online. Students may take courses in either of the formats or a combination. Requirements are the same for all course formats. Once the majority of required courses have been completed, students are free to choose the remaining courses in their program of study. Students should meet with their advisor to develop an individualized course of study that best meets their interests and needs. Selected specialty courses will be taken during the second or subsequent year. With the approval of the academic advisor, students may select up to nine credits of graduate level courses in other programs at the university.

Students will be assigned an academic advisor, usually the graduate coordinator, when entering the program. The doctoral degree at UMass Lowell is an interdisciplinary, research-oriented degree. The program is designed to provide a theoretically grounded, methodologically sophisticated, and statistically rigorous education. As such, the curriculum provides for a sequence of courses in theory, methodology, and statistics. The curriculum also builds upon faculty research strengths and offers substantive courses that address the incidence of crime, the prevalence and correlates of criminals and victims, and the effectiveness of current strategies in the areas of crime prevention, policing, the courts, and the corrections system (both institutional and community based). Throughout the five concentrations or specialty areas in which students can specialize, the curriculum stresses evidence driven and "best practices" approaches to numerous substantive topics that are key areas in contemporary criminology and criminal justice.

Number of Faculty: 25

Accreditation: New England Association of Schools and Colleges

Average Length of Time to Complete the Program: Not available

University of Memphis

Address: 3641 Central Avenue
Memphis, TN 38111
Phone: (901) 678-2000
Website: http://www.memphis.edu/

Department: Department of Criminology and Criminal Justice
311 McCord Hall
Memphis, TN 38152-3530
Phone: (901) 678-2737
Website: https://www.memphis.edu/cjustice/

Type of Program: MA in Criminal Justice

Application Deadline: Not available

Requirements:
- Possess a baccalaureate degree from an accredited college or university.
- Have earned a grade point average of at least 3.00 on a scale of 4.00 and achieved an acceptable score on the GRE. The admissions committee reserves the right to make exceptions for candidates presenting special circumstances.
- Submit a letter of purpose for graduate study to the coordinator of graduate studies in criminology and criminal justice that is no more than one typed single-spaced page in length.
- Submit two letters of recommendation.

Information Required for Application: Stated above.

Admission Date: Not available

In-state and Out-of-state Tuition Costs: In-state: $535 per credit; out-of-state: $1,156.50 per credit

Availability of Internships and Scholarships: Assistantships, fellowships

Orientation and Emphasis of Department/Program (Program Description): The graduate program of the Department of Criminology and Criminal Justice, which is part of the School of Urban Affairs and Public Policy, seeks to serve students who are interested in the criminal justice system, with a focus on those who seek careers in this area. Faculty conducts research and participates in program development relevant to the many different facets of criminology and criminal justice. A significant emphasis of the program is on developing partnerships with policymakers, program developers, and other community groups. The graduate program provides students with a solid foundation of knowledge about criminology and criminal justice. The required course work provides students with the skills necessary for conducting and evaluating research. Graduate students have the opportunity to learn in both classroom and community settings and to work closely with faculty in all facets of research.

Number of Faculty: 12

Accreditation: Commission on Colleges of the Southern Association of Colleges and Schools

Average Length of Time to Complete the Program: Not available

University of Missouri–Kansas City

Address: 5100 Rockhill Road
Kansas City, MO 64110
Phone: (816) 235-1000
Website: http://www.umkc.edu/

Department: Department of Criminal Justice and Criminology
5215 Rockhill Road
Kansas City, MO 64110-2447
Phone: (816) 235-2751
Website: http://cas.umkc.edu/cjc/

Type of Program: MS in Criminal Justice and Criminology

Application Deadline: November 1, March 15

Requirements:
- Complete an undergraduate degree from an accredited university of college with a program major in the socio-behavioral sciences sufficient to prepare for graduate-level study in the criminal justice and criminology field.
- Achieve a cumulative GPA of 3.0 in all undergraduate work.
- Complete undergraduate courses in statistics, research methods, and theories of crime.
- Submit two letters of recommendation. Applicants should ask at least two individuals to provide references on their behalf. Please note that references may also include a written letter of reference that speaks to the applicant's scholastic aptitude, and their level of preparation for graduate-level education. References should be provided by individuals who are not related to the applicant, and ideally will come from individuals who have direct knowledge of the applicant's academic credentials and preparedness

Information Required for Application:
- Official transcripts from the school where the bachelor's degree was obtained, and other schools where course work has been taken or degrees have been obtained after completion of the bachelor's degree, should be sent directly to the UMKC Admissions Office.
- Submit a writing sample to the department admissions committee. This writing sample should take the form of a two- to three-page letter requesting admission to the program. Within the letter, applicants should identify how their undergraduate education—and perhaps their work or personal experience—has prepared them for graduate study in the area of criminal

justice and criminology. Also, the letter should address how the applicant views study in our graduate program as fitting with his or her future career and/or educational goals.

Admission Date: Fall, Spring

In-state and Out-of-state Tuition Costs: In-state: $434.59 per credit hour; out-of-state: $968.29 per credit hour

Availability of Internships and Scholarships: Assistantships

Orientation and Emphasis of Department/Program (Program Description): The MS-CJC degree requires successful completion of thirty credit hours of graduate work. Within these thirty hours, students may elect to complete a thesis or pursue the non-thesis option. A core of six courses is required of all students.

Number of Faculty: 18

Accreditation: Higher Learning Commission: A Commission of the North Central Association

Average Length of Time to Complete the Program: Not available

University of Missouri–St. Louis

Address: 1 University Boulevard
St. Louis, MO 63121
Phone: (314) 516-5000
Website: http://www.umsl.edu/

Department: Department of Criminology and Criminal Justice
Website: http://www.umsl.edu/ccj/

Type of Program: MA in Criminology and Criminal Justice; PhD in Criminology and Criminal Justice

Application Deadline: MA: April 1; PhD: February 1

Requirements: Stated below

Information Required for Application:
Master's
- Application;
- Statement of Purpose (briefly explain why an advanced degree in criminology and criminal justice is of interest and why the applicant merits serious consideration);
- Official transcripts from all universities attended;
- Minimum grade point average of 3.0 on a 4.0 scale. Students whose overall GPA is 2.75 to 2.99 may be admitted under some circumstances; and
- Two letters of recommendation.

Doctoral
- Application;
- Statement of Purpose (briefly explain why an advanced degree in criminology and criminal justice is of interest and why the applicant merits serious consideration);
- Writing sample (should show your ability to write a research paper; if you've written a master's thesis, please submit a chapter);
- Official transcripts from all universities attended;
- Minimum grade point average of 3.0 on a 4.0 scale. Students whose overall GPA is 2.75 to 2.99 may be admitted under some circumstances;
- GRE scores above the 50th percentile; and
- Three letters of recommendation.

Admission Date: Fall

In-state and Out-of-state Tuition Costs: In-state: $412.35 per credit; out-of-state: $551.30 per credit

Availability of Internships and Scholarships: Teaching and research assistantships, fellowships, and tuition and fee waivers

Orientation and Emphasis of Department/Program (Program Description): The department offers a master of arts degree in criminology and criminal justice, which provides students with advanced theoretical and methodological training for research and management careers in criminal justice.

Number of Faculty: 29

Accreditation: Higher Learning Commission of the North Central Association of Colleges and Schools

Average Length of Time to Complete the Program: Not available

University of Nebraska at Omaha

Address: 6001 Dodge Street
Omaha, NE 68182
Phone: (402) 554-2800
Website: http://www.unomaha.edu/

Department: School of Criminology and Criminal Justice
University of Nebraska at Omaha
6001 Dodge Street, 218 CPACS
Omaha, NE 68182-0149
Phone: (402) 554-2610
Website: http://criminaljustice.unomaha.edu/

Type of Program: MS in Criminology and Criminal Justice; MA in Criminology and Criminal Justice; PhD in Criminology and Criminal Justice

Application Deadline: MS/MA: July 30; PhD: February 1

Requirements:
- Quality of previous undergraduate and graduate work. The Graduate College requires as a minimum standard a B average of 3.0 on a 4.0 scale, in a program of study resulting in the award of a baccalaureate degree from a regionally accredited college or university. If an applicant has studied at the graduate level and performed satisfactorily, less weight may, but not necessarily, be placed on the quality of the undergraduate academic record. Some programs require a higher minimum grade point average for admission.
- Strength of letters of recommendation from persons competent to judge the applicant's probable success in graduate school. These letters are usually from the applicant's former professors who are able to give an in-depth evaluation of the applicant's strengths and weaknesses with respect to academic work. Additional recommendations may come from employers or supervisors who are familiar with the applicant's work experience. Applicants should instruct their references to send all letters of recommendation directly to the program in which they desire entrance.
- Official scores on required aptitude or advanced knowledge examination(s).
- Statement by the applicant of academic career objectives and their relation to the intended program of study. These statements help the department/school identify students whose goals are consistent with its objectives.

- Other evidence of graduate potential. Some programs require other evidence of graduate potential, such as a portfolio of creative work, completion of specialized examinations, or personal interviews.

Information Required for Application: Stated above

Admission Date: Fall

In-state and Out-of-state Tuition Costs: In-state: $245.25 per credit; out-of-state: $665 per credit

Availability of Internships and Scholarships: Scholarships

Orientation and Emphasis of Department/Program (Program Description): What do a number of administrators in criminal justice and other social service agencies in the Omaha Metropolitan Area have in common? They have a master's degree. Obtaining a professionally oriented master's degree can help students advance their careers, improve their professional skills, develop new competencies, and change careers. A master's degree can also help students obtain a job and earn a higher income. According the Bureau of Labor Statistics, the unemployment rate in 2010 for individuals 25 and over with a master's degree as their highest degree was 4 percent, compared to 5.4 percent for individuals with a bachelor's degree, and 10.3 percent for individuals with a high school diploma. The median annual salary of master's degree recipients was over $12,000 higher than the median salary for individuals who only held a bachelor's degree. The master of arts degree in criminology and criminal justice is designed to emphasize research activity and scientific inquiry. The master of arts degree is designed to prepare students for work in a research agency or admission into a PhD program. The doctor of philosophy in criminology and criminal justice is designed to train the next generation of criminologists to develop and conduct basic and applied research regarding the causes of crime and societal responses to crime. Successful graduates often obtain faculty positions at universities or research positions in criminal justice and social service agencies.

Number of Faculty: 37

Accreditation: North Central Association, Higher Learning Commission

Average Length of Time to Complete the Program: Not available

University of Nevada, Las Vegas

Address: 4505 South Maryland Parkway
Las Vegas, NV 89119
Phone: (702) 895-3011
Website: https://www.unlv.edu/

Department: Department of Criminal Justice
Box 455009
4505 Maryland Parkway
Las Vegas, NV 89154-5009
Phone: (702) 895-0236
Website: http://criminaljustice.unlv.edu/

Type of Program: MA in Criminal Justice

Application Deadline: April 15 (February 1 for priority and for consideration for a graduate assistantship position)

Requirements:
- An undergraduate degree from an institution with regional or national accreditation is required. Students are encouraged to complete some undergraduate course work related to criminal justice/criminology and statistics in social sciences.
- A minimum of a 2.75 GPA for all undergraduate work and a 3.0 GPA for the last two years of undergraduate work are required. A student who has met the minimum GPA requirements is not guaranteed admission. A student with less than the minimum GPA may be provisionally admitted if there is compelling evidence to indicate a reasonable likelihood of success in the program.

Information Required for Application:
- Official transcript
- GRE scores
- Two letters of recommendation

Admission Date: Fall

In-state and Out-of-state Tuition Costs: In-state: $264 per credit; out-of-state: $527.50 per credit

Availability of Internships and Scholarships: Scholarships and assistantships

Orientation and Emphasis of Department/Program (Program Description): The Department of Criminal Justice offers a broad-based graduate program leading to a master of arts degree. The program addresses issues of crime and criminal justice within an analytical framework and emphasizes theory, research, and their implications for social policy. The curriculum is grounded in the social and behavioral sciences and in legal approaches to crime and social control. It draws from contemporary research and theoretical developments across a spectrum of academic disciplines. The graduate program in criminal justice offers two degree options: a traditional master's degree and a professional master's degree. The traditional master's degree is designed to prepare students for doctoral studies in the field and in related areas of the social and behavioral sciences, as well as for those who want to teach at the community college level. The professional master's degree is designed to serve the needs of professionals currently working in justice-related agencies by providing the knowledge and skills to enhance their performance in current positions and/ or prepare them for career advancement.

Number of Faculty: 14

Accreditation: Northwest Commission on Colleges and Universities accreditation

Average Length of Time to Complete the Program: Not available

University of Nevada, Reno

Address: 1664 North Virginia Street
Reno, NV 89557
Phone: (775) 784-1110
Website: http://www.unr.edu/

Department: Department of Criminal Justice
Ansari Business Building, 6th Floor
1664 North Virginia Street, MS/214
Reno, NV 89557-214
Website: http://www.unr.edu/cla/cjweb/

Type of Program: MA in Criminal Justice

Application Deadline: Not available

Requirements: Minimum admission requirements for the Graduate School are:
- A bachelor's degree or recognized equivalent from a regionally accredited institution;
- A satisfactory scholastic average, usually a minimum grade point average (GPA) of 2.75 on a 4.0 scale if applying for a master's degree; or a minimum GPA of 3.0 on a 4.0 scale if applying for a doctoral degree; and
- Enough undergraduate training to do graduate work in your chosen field.

Information Required for Application:
- Complete required admissions questionnaire.
- As part of the Admissions Questionnaire, you will also need to submit a writing sample (see instructions in the questionnaire).
- Complete GRE Examination.
- Request three letters of recommendation, preferably from professors who can talk about your ability to do MA level work. Letter writers should complete a letter of recommendation form.
- Complete graduate school application, which includes graduate assistant application.

Admission Date: Not available

In-state and Out-of-state Tuition Costs: In-state: $264 per hour; out-of-state: additional fee of $290.50/1-6 credit hours

Availability of Internships and Scholarships: Assistantships

Orientation and Emphasis of Department/Program (Program Description): The Department of Criminal Justices has offered a master of arts in criminal justice designed for individuals already in justice-related careers interested in advancing in their professions, for students desiring to pursue doctoral study, and individuals wishing to expand their knowledge of criminal justice and to pursue justice-related careers. Within these interests, students are offered the flexibility to pursue their individual goals. While most students attend full time, some attend part time so they can maintain employment. Many required classes are offered in the late afternoon or evenings to accommodate working students.

Number of Faculty: 23

Accreditation: Northwest Commission on Colleges and Universities

Average Length of Time to Complete the Program: Not available

University of New Haven

Address: 300 Boston Post Road
West Haven, CT 06516
Phone: (203) 932-7000
Website: http://www.newhaven.edu/

Department: Henry C. Lee College of Criminal Justice and Forensics
Website: http://www.newhaven.edu/lee-college/

Type of Program: MS in Criminal Justice; MS in Criminal Justice (online), PhD in Criminal Justice

Application Deadline: Not available

Requirements: Not available

Information Required for Application:
- Application fee
- Official transcripts
- Two letters of recommendation
- GRE scores
- Résumé

Admission Date: Not available

In-state and Out-of-state Tuition Costs: $800 per credit hour

Availability of Internships and Scholarships: Student fellowships

Orientation and Emphasis of Department/Program (Program Description): The criminal justice graduate program is a program stressing a broad understanding of the social and behavioral sciences, the institutions of the criminal justice system, and the development of methodological tools and skills. The criminal justice doctoral program is designed to be a small, selective program to enable every student to receive the individualized instruction and mentoring necessary in doctoral education.

Number of Faculty: 63

Accreditation: New England Association of Schools and Colleges

Average Length of Time to Complete the Program: Not available

University of North Alabama

Address: 1 Harrison Plaza
Florence, AL 35632
Phone: (256) 765-4100
Website: http://www.una.edu/

Department: Department of Criminal Justice
7 Willingham Hall, UNA Box 5194
Phone: (256) 765-5045
Website: http://www.una.edu/criminaljustice/

Type of Program: MS in Criminal Justice

Application Deadline: July 1, November 1

Requirements: In addition to the general requirements for admission to graduate studies (see General Regulations and Procedures), admission to the MSCJ program also requires the following:
Unconditional Admission
- Hold a master's or higher degree from a regionally accredited university. Official transcript must reflect that degree was awarded. No test scores are required; or
- Hold a bachelor's degree and possess a minimum GPA of 2.5 on all attempted undergraduate course work; and
- Receive a minimum a score of 800 (verbal plus quantitative) on the Graduate Record Exam or a minimum score of 380 on the Miller Analogies Test.

Information Required for Application:
- Application and $25 application fee'
- Official transcripts from all colleges and universities attended; and
- Official GRE or MAT scores.

Admission Date: Fall, Spring

In-state and Out-of-state Tuition Costs: $276 per credit hour

Availability of Internships and Scholarships: Scholarships and work study

Orientation and Emphasis of Department/Program (Program Description): Not available

Number of Faculty: 5

Accreditation: Southern Association of Colleges and Schools Commission on Colleges

Average Length of Time to Complete the Program: Not available

The University of North Carolina at Charlotte

Address: 9201 University City Boulevard
Charlotte, NC 28223
Phone: (704) 687-8622
Website: http://www.uncc.edu/

Department: Department of Criminal Justice and Criminology
Colvard 5062
Phone: (704) 687-0740
Website: http://criminaljustice.uncc.edu/

Type of Program: MS in Criminal Justice

Application Deadline: May 1, October 1, April 1

Requirements:
• A completed application submitted online to the Graduate School;
• A preferred undergraduate grade point average of at least 3.0 on a 4.0 scale; and
• A preferred combined score of at least 1,000 using the older scoring scale or approximately 300 using the new scoring scale, on the verbal and quantitative sections of the Graduate Record Examination.

Information Required for Application:
• Undergraduate and graduate grades;
• Scores on the Graduate Record Examination;
• Letters of recommendation (preferably from academic sources);
• Specific previous coursework;
• Statement of purpose; and
• Work history

Admission Date: Fall, Spring, Summer I, or Summer II

In-state and Out-of-state Tuition Costs: In-state: $501 for zero to two credit hours; out-of-state: $2,037 for zero to two credit hours

Availability of Internships and Scholarships: Graduate assistantships and scholarships

Orientation and Emphasis of Department/Program (Program Description): The master's degree program in criminal justice and criminology has four major objectives:
1. To provide present and future criminal justice personnel with the educational background necessary to function effectively in the dynamic field of criminal justice;

2. To familiarize students with the nature, functions, and methods of research and with the existing body of knowledge on criminal justice;
3. To provide criminal justice agencies with qualified candidates for careers in administration, law enforcement, planning and analysis, juvenile justice, corrections, and teaching in community colleges; and
4. To prepare students for entry into doctoral programs.

Number of Faculty: 19

Accreditation: Commission on Colleges of the Southern Association of Colleges and Schools

Average Length of Time to Complete the Program: Not available

The University of North Carolina Wilmington

Address: 601 S. College Road
Wilmington, NC 28403
Phone: (910) 962-3000
Website: http://www.uncw.edu/

Department: Department of Sociology and Criminology
Contact: Dr. Leslie Hossfeld, Chair
Phone: (910) 962-7849
E-mail: hossfeldl@uncw.edu
Website: http://www.uncw.edu/soccrm/masters.html

Type of Program: MA in Criminology and Public Sociology

Application Deadline: April 15 (March 15 to be considered for assistantship funding)

Requirements: Stated below

Information Required for Application:
- An application for graduate admission;
- Official transcripts of all college work (undergraduate and graduate);
- Official scores on the Graduate Record Examination (GRE);
- Three recommendations by individuals in professionally relevant fields; at least two must be from academics;
- A writing sample in the form of an essay explaining how the MA in criminology and public sociology may assist the candidate in meeting her or his personal goals; and
- A 3.0 overall undergraduate GPA.

Admission Date: Fall

In-state and Out-of-state Tuition Costs: In-state: $520.34 for zero to two credit hours; out-of-state: $2,020.34 for zero to two credit hours

Availability of Internships and Scholarships: Scholarships, teaching, research, and graduate assistantships

Orientation and Emphasis of Department/Program (Program Description): The MA in criminology and public sociology is designed for students with a passion for public involvement and a desire to understand the values, assumptions, and social structures within national societies and global systems.

Number of Faculty: 30

Accreditation: Commission on Colleges of the Southern Association of Colleges and Schools

Average Length of Time to Complete the Program: Not available

University of North Dakota

Address: Grand Forks, ND 58202
Phone: (701) 777-3000
Website: http://www.und.edu/

Department: Department of Criminal Justice
O'Kelly Hall, Room 305
221 Centennial Drive, Stop 8050
Phone: (701) 777-2066
Website: http://arts-sciences.und.edu/criminal-justice/

Type of Program: PhD in Criminal Justice

Application Deadline: March 31, November 1

Requirements:
- Master's degree in criminal justice or related field;
- A cumulative GPA of 3.0 for all coursework taken for graduate credit; and
- A minimum combined score of 300 on the verbal and quantitative components of the GRE or a minimum combined score of 1,000 on the earlier versions of the GRE.

Information Required for Application:
- Submit official transcripts.
- You are strongly encouraged to provide at least two academic references which can speak to your ability to successfully complete a vigorous doctoral program within a supportive environment.

Admission Date: Fall, Spring

In-state and Out-of-state Tuition Costs: In-state: $332.27 per credit; out-of-state: $793.30 per credit

Availability of Internships and Scholarships: Assistantships and tuition waivers

Orientation and Emphasis of Department/Program (Program Description): Drawing on a broad array of multi-disciplinary resources, the Department of Criminal Justice at the University of North Dakota—in partnership with the Department of Criminal Justice at Minot State University—offers a graduate program of study leading to the degree of doctor of philosophy in criminal justice. The program is designed to prepare students for academic teaching and research, research in government and non-profit agencies, and higher-level administrative positions in criminal justice agencies. The program retains a traditional core of theory, research methods/statistics, and study of national and international issues in the administration of criminal justice. The program places special emphasis on the operation and administration of criminal justice agencies and systems in rural and/or American Indian tribal jurisdictions. The program also offers a specialized program of study for individuals holding a juris doctorate and wishing to meet educational requirements for teaching and research positions in criminal justice higher education programs.

Number of Faculty: 7

Accreditation: Higher Learning Commission of the North Central Association of Colleges and Schools

Average Length of Time to Complete the Program: Not available

University of North Florida

Address: 1 University of North Florida Drive
Jacksonville, FL 32224
Phone: (904) 620-1000
Website: http://www.unf.edu/

Department: Department of Criminology and Criminal Justice
Building 51, 2310
1 University of North Florida Drive
Jacksonville, FL 32224
Phone: (904) 620-1724
Website: https://www.unf.edu/coas/ccj/

Type of Program: MS in Criminal Justice

Application Deadline: August 1, December 1, March 15

Requirements: A baccalaureate degree from a regionally accredited U.S. institution or its equivalent from a foreign institution with a GPA of 3.0 or higher in all work attempted in the last sixty credit hours of undergraduate study.

Information Required for Application:
- Official transcripts from all attended institutions;
- A letter of intent discussing academic and relevant employment experiences, areas of interest in the field, and reasons for seeking an MSCJ degree; and
- Two letters of recommendation.

Admission Date: Fall, Spring, Summer

In-state and Out-of-state Tuition Costs: In-state: $492.30 per credit; out-of-state: $1043.04 per credit

Availability of Internships and Scholarships: Graduate assistantships and scholarships.
The Auzenne Fellowship is designed to assist Florida's State Universities in increasing the enrollment of students who are enrolled in graduate study in disciplines in which there is under-representation. Under this program, graduate students are nominated to receive awards of $5,000 each ($2,500 per semester; Fall, Spring, or both) for year-long, full-time study. Awards will not be granted to the same Auzenne Fellows for more than two academic years for those in master's programs or four academic years for doctoral students.

Orientation and Emphasis of Department/Program (Program Description): Public concerns about crime and the dramatic expansion of the criminal justice system in recent decades have spurred a proliferation of courses in this field in colleges across the country. Jobs that did not exist at all two decades ago—such as victim advocates or police computer mapping specialists—continue to develop. There is a growing demand for persons with graduate level education in all sectors of the system. The master of science in criminal justice at UNF provides an opportunity for advanced academic work in this expanding field of study. As a discipline, criminal justice draws together all the social and behavioral sciences, natural sciences, mathematical and computer sciences, history, law, and jurisprudence to focus on the problem of crime in society. The graduate program at UNF builds upon the unifying interdisciplinary nature of the field it seeks to address. Furthermore, the program at UNF is vitally concerned with the interrelationship between theory, practice, and research, based on the firm conviction that none of these can stand alone. Sound practice requires a firm theoretical and research base, while advances in theory and research arise from the realities of practice. The program emphasizes the acquisition of professional skills that will enable students to keep abreast of research and developments in the field long after they have completed their formal studies.

Number of Faculty: 23

Accreditation: Commission on Colleges of the Southern Association of Colleges and Schools

Average Length of Time to Complete the Program: Not available

University of North Texas

Address: 1155 Union Circle
Denton, TX 76203
Phone: (940) 565-2000
Website: http://www.unt.edu/

Department: Department of Criminal Justice
1155 Union Circle #305130
Denton, TX 76203-5130
Phone: (940) 565-2562
Website: http://pacs.unt.edu/criminal-justice/

Type of Program: MS in Criminal Justice

Application Deadline: August 1, December 1

Requirements: Minimum GPA of 2.8 overall or 3.0 in the last sixty hours of undergraduate work – We also assess verbal and analytical writing scores on the GRE.

Information Required for Application:
- Completed application on file with the graduate school;
- Verbal and analytical writing GRE scores on file with the graduate school;
- Personal statement; and
- Transcripts on file with the graduate school with a minimum 2.8 GPA overall or minimum 3.0 GPA on the last sixty hours of undergraduate work.

Admission Date: Fall, Spring

In-state and Out-of-state Tuition Costs: In-state: $7,128 for nine credit hours; out-of-state: $13,446 (plus additional instruction fees) for nine credit hours

Availability of Internships and Scholarships:
Scholarship: Applications for the Tory J. Caeti Memorial Scholarship are accepted from new students entering the MSCJ program in the Fall.
Internship: The Department of Criminal Justice offers an internship program for pre-professional and research oriented CJUS master's students. CJUS master's students can apply up to six credit hours of internship coursework back to their elective requirements, although students may want to check with Dr. Fritsch to see where these credit hours will be applied on your individual degree plan. Please contact Prof. Kawucha, the Internship Coordinator, for more information at (940) 565-4475 or Soraya.Kawucha@unt.edu.

Orientation and Emphasis of Department/Program (Program Description): A master of science degree in criminal justice from the University of North Texas improves your ability to take informed and thoughtful actions as an administrator, researcher, police officer, probation officer, or caseworker in the criminal justice system. Our exceptional curriculum provides you with an understanding of the nature and scope of problems posed by crime and the operation and administration of the criminal justice system. You'll examine these areas from theoretical, practical and empirical standpoints. We also offer:

- Opportunities to participate in research under a faculty member's direction;
- Prospects for earning academic credit through an internship;
- Specialized electives so you can tailor your degree to your professional and personal goals; and
- Study abroad opportunities.

Number of Faculty: 19

Accreditation: The Commission on Colleges of the Southern Association of Colleges and Schools

Average Length of Time to Complete the Program: Not available

University of Pennsylvania

Address: 3451 Walnut Street
Philadelphia, PA 19104
Phone: (215) 898-5000
Website: http://www.upenn.edu/

Department: Department of Criminology
483 McNeil Building
3718 Locust Walk
Philadelphia, PA. 19104-6286
Phone: (215) 573-9097
Website: http://crim.sas.upenn.edu/

Type of Program: MS in Criminology; PhD in Criminology

Application Deadline: The department will accept applications on a rolling basis for the MS program from October 1 through June 30. Application to the PhD program will be accepted from October 1 through December 16.

Requirements: Not specified

Information Required for Application: Applications to the master's program or to the PhD program must include the following:
- Completed application forms, including a personal statement;
- Official transcripts from all undergraduate and graduate institutions attended;
- Three letters of reference, with at least two from former professors or individuals who can evaluate academic preparation;
- Results from a Graduate Record Examination (GRE) taken in the last five years. LSAT scores may be accepted in lieu of GRE scores if the test was taken in the last five years. Please note that we can no longer accept GMAT scores. (Individuals with an undergraduate degree from Penn are not required to submit GRE or LSAT scores in order to apply to the MS program.); and
- Results from the Test of English as a Foreign Language (TOEFL) for those who do not have transcripts with one year of study at an English-speaking university.

Admission Date: Rolling

In-state and Out-of-state Tuition Costs: Full-time tuition and fees are $22,316 per semester (total $44,632); health insurance fees are $1,623 per semester (total $3,258).

Availability of Internships and Scholarships: Loans and assistantships

Orientation and Emphasis of Department/Program (Program Description): Penn's unique master of science in criminology program aims to shape criminal justice "change agents," preparing students to spend their career applying criminological research in public and non-profit domestic and international organizations. It is also designed for those research-oriented students who are preparing themselves for graduate or professional education at the University of Pennsylvania or other leading research universities. Penn's highly interdisciplinary PhD in criminology combines the traditional concerns of criminologists with concepts, theories, and empirical research from a wide variety of academic disciplines. Working closely with faculty, students are encouraged to design their own curriculum and begin research very early in their graduate education. The program seeks to produce scholars of unusual breadth who can work creatively in academic or policy settings.

Number of Faculty: 10

Accreditation: Middle States Commission on Higher Education

Average Length of Time to Complete the Program: Not available

University of Phoenix

Address: Not available
Phone: (866) 766-0766
Website: http://www.phoenix.edu/

Department: College of Criminal Justice and Security
Website: http://www.phoenix.edu/colleges_divisions/criminal-justice.html

Type of Program: Master of Public Administration; MS in Administration of Justice and Security; MS in Administration of Justice and Security with a concentration in Global and Homeland Security; MS in Administration of Justice and Security with a concentration in Law Enforcement Organizations

Application Deadline: Not available

Requirements:
- Have an undergraduate degree from an approved, regionally accredited or nationally accredited college or university, or hold a comparable degree from a recognized institution outside the United States.
- Have a cumulative GPA of 2.5 (on a 4.0 scale) as shown on the undergraduate degree posted transcript.
- Meet work experience requirements or have access to an organizational environment, depending on your selected degree program, in order to successfully complete program objectives and apply concepts you learn in our courses. Please contact an Enrollment Advisor to learn if your program has such a requirement.
- Be a citizen or permanent resident of the United States or hold an approved, valid visa if residing in the United States.
- Not have been expelled from a previous institution.
- Complete all required forms for admission and submit an official undergraduate degree posted transcript.

Information Required for Application: Not available

Admission Date: Not available

In-state and Out-of-state Tuition Costs: $740 per credit hour

Availability of Internships and Scholarships: Scholarships, institutional grants, cash plans, third party billing plans

Orientation and Emphasis of Department/Program (Program Description):
Master of Public Administration: The University of Phoenix master of public administration degree program helps you develop the

skills necessary to create and implement public policy. Courses such as Law and Public Administration, and Public Budgeting help you go beyond theory and gain real-world insight into how governments operate. Discover how the University of Phoenix can help you cultivate the skills you need to manage in the public service arena.

Master of Science/Administration of Justice and Security: If you're ready to take the next step in becoming a leader in the world of criminal justice and security, then you've come to the right place. The master of science in administration of justice and security at the University of Phoenix focuses on developing leadership and administrative skills. While criminal justice and security are at the center of our master's degree program, you'll also study other important areas such as cybercrime, forensics, public policy, profiling, and more. Additionally, our criminal justice and security degree programs are continually updated, ensuring you learn the most current knowledge and skills from our experienced faculty who have a pulse on the world of criminal justice and organizational security.

Master of Science in Administration of Justice and Security with a concentration in Global and Homeland Security: Day in and day out, you're confronted with issues that threaten local communities. Leverage your law enforcement experience to play a role in protecting the nation from larger threats and in leading the response to these dangers. Earning a master of science in administration of justice and security with a concentration in global and homeland security may put you on the path to a new career as a command officer, private security director, or intelligence analyst. Learn how to work together with other law enforcement agencies to solve problems, and gain the skills you need to manage critical incidents, intelligence, cybercrime, and technology while getting a foundation in criminology.

Master of Science in Administration of Justice and Security with a concentration in Law Enforcement Organizations: Throughout your career in law enforcement, you've seen opportunities to do things better. Put yourself in a position to make change happen by earning a master of science in administration of justice and security with a concentration in law enforcement. Gain the skills you need to manage critical incidents, intelligence, cybercrime, and technology while getting a foundation in criminology.

Number of Faculty: 3

Accreditation: Higher Learning Commission

Average Length of Time to Complete the Program: Not available

University of Phoenix–Colorado Campus

Address: 10004 Park Meadows Drive
Lone Tree, CO 80124
Phone: (303) 755-9090
Website: http://www.phoenix.edu/campus-locations/co/colorado-campus/colorado-campus.html

Department: College of Criminal Justice and Security
Website: http://www.phoenix.edu/colleges_divisions/criminal-justice.html

Type of Program: Master of Public Administration; MS in Administration of Justice and Security; MS in Administration of Justice and Security with a concentration in Global and Homeland Security; MS in Administration of Justice and Security with a concentration in Law Enforcement Organizations (online and on campus)

Application Deadline: Not available

Requirements:
- Have an undergraduate degree from an approved, regionally accredited or nationally accredited college or university, or hold a comparable degree from a recognized institution outside the United States.
- Have a cumulative GPA of 2.5 (on a 4.0 scale) as shown on the undergraduate degree posted transcript.
- Meet work experience requirements or have access to an organizational environment, depending on your selected degree program, in order to successfully complete program objectives and apply concepts you learn in our courses. Please contact an Enrollment Advisor to learn if your program has such a requirement.
- Be a citizen or permanent resident of the United States or hold an approved, valid visa if residing in the United States.
- Not have been expelled from a previous institution.

Complete all required forms for admission and submit an official undergraduate degree posted transcript.

Information Required for Application: Not available

Admission Date: Not available

In-state and Out-of-state Tuition Costs: $740 per credit hour

Availability of Internships and Scholarships: Scholarships, institutional grants, cash plans, third party billing plans

Orientation and Emphasis of Department/Program (Program Description):

Master of Public Administration: The University of Phoenix master of public administration degree program helps you develop the skills necessary to create and implement public policy. Courses such as Law and Public Administration, and Public Budgeting help you go beyond theory and gain real-world insight into how governments operate. Discover how the University of Phoenix can help you cultivate the skills you need to manage in the public service arena.

Master of Science/Administration of Justice and Security: If you're ready to take the next step in becoming a leader in the world of criminal justice and security, then you've come to the right place. The master of science in administration of justice and security at the University of Phoenix focuses on developing leadership and administrative skills. While criminal justice and security are at the center of our master's degree program, you'll also study other important areas such as cybercrime, forensics, public policy, profiling, and more. Additionally, our criminal justice and security degree programs are continually updated, ensuring you learn the most current knowledge and skills from our experienced faculty who have a pulse on the world of criminal justice and organizational security.

Master of Science in Administration of Justice and Security with a concentration in Global and Homeland Security: Day in and day out, you're confronted with issues that threaten local communities. Leverage your law enforcement experience to play a role in protecting the nation from larger threats and in leading the response to these dangers. Earning a master of science in administration of justice and security with a concentration in global and homeland security may put you on the path to a new career as a command officer, private security director, or intelligence analyst. Learn how to work together with other law enforcement agencies to solve problems, and gain the skills you need to manage critical incidents, intelligence, cybercrime, and technology while getting a foundation in criminology.

Master of Science in Administration of Justice and Security with a concentration in Law Enforcement Organizations: Throughout your career in law enforcement, you've seen opportunities to do things better. Put yourself in a position to make change happen by earning a master of science in administration of justice and security with a concentration in law enforcement. Gain the skills you need to manage critical incidents, intelligence, cybercrime, and technology while getting a foundation in criminology.

Number of Faculty: Not available

Accreditation: Higher Learning Commission

Average Length of Time to Complete the Program: Not available

University of Phoenix–Hawaii Campus

Address: 745 Fort Street
Suite 2000
Honolulu, HI 96813
Phone: (808) 536-2686
Website: http://www.phoenix.edu/campus-locations/hi/hawaii-campus/hawaii-campus.html

Department: College of Criminal Justice and Security
Website: http://www.phoenix.edu/colleges_divisions/criminal-justice.html

Type of Program: Master of Public Administration; MS in Administration of Justice and Security (only one on campus); MS in Administration of Justice and Security with a concentration in Global and Homeland Security; MS in Administration of Justice and Security with a concentration in law Enforcement Organizations

Application Deadline: Not available

Requirements:
- Have an undergraduate degree from an approved, regionally accredited or nationally accredited college or university, or hold a comparable degree from a recognized institution outside the United States.
- Have a cumulative GPA of 2.5 (on a 4.0 scale) as shown on the undergraduate degree posted transcript.
- Meet work experience requirements or have access to an organizational environment, depending on your selected degree program, in order to successfully complete program objectives and apply concepts you learn in our courses. Please contact an Enrollment Advisor to learn if your program has such a requirement.
- Be a citizen or permanent resident of the United States or hold an approved, valid visa if residing in the United States.
- Not have been expelled from a previous institution.
- Complete all required forms for admission and submit an official undergraduate degree posted transcript.

Information Required for Application: Not available

Admission Date: Not available

In-state and Out-of-state Tuition Costs: $740 per credit hour

Availability of Internships and Scholarships: Scholarships, institutional grants, cash plans, third party billing plans

Orientation and Emphasis of Department/Program (Program Description):

Master of Public Administration: The University of Phoenix master of public administration degree program helps you develop the skills necessary to create and implement public policy. Courses such as Law and Public Administration, and Public Budgeting help you go beyond theory and gain real-world insight into how governments operate. Discover how the University of Phoenix can help you cultivate the skills you need to manage in the public service arena.

Master of Science/Administration of Justice and Security: If you're ready to take the next step in becoming a leader in the world of criminal justice and security, then you've come to the right place. The master of science in administration of justice and security at the University of Phoenix focuses on developing leadership and administrative skills. While criminal justice and security are at the center of our master's degree program, you'll also study other important areas such as cybercrime, forensics, public policy, profiling, and more. Additionally, our criminal justice and security degree programs are continually updated, ensuring you learn the most current knowledge and skills from our experienced faculty who have a pulse on the world of criminal justice and organizational security.

Master of Science in Administration of Justice and Security with a concentration in Global and Homeland Security: Day in and day out, you're confronted with issues that threaten local communities. Leverage your law enforcement experience to play a role in protecting the nation from larger threats and in leading the response to these dangers. Earning a master of science in administration of justice and security with a concentration in global and homeland security may put you on the path to a new career as a command officer, private security director, or intelligence analyst. Learn how to work together with other law enforcement agencies to solve problems, and gain the skills you need to manage critical incidents, intelligence, cybercrime, and technology while getting a foundation in criminology.

Master of Science in Administration of Justice and Security with a concentration in Law Enforcement Organizations: Throughout your career in law enforcement, you've seen opportunities to do things better. Put yourself in a position to make change happen by earning a master of science in administration of justice and security with a concentration in law enforcement. Gain the skills you need to manage critical incidents, intelligence, cybercrime, and technology while getting a foundation in criminology.

Number of Faculty: Not available

Accreditation: Higher Learning Commission

Average Length of Time to Complete the Program: Not available

University of Phoenix–Las Vegas Campus

Address: 3755 Breakthrough Way
Las Vegas, NV 89135
Phone: (702) 638-7279
Website: http://www.phoenix.edu/campus-locations/nv/las-vegas-campus/las-vegas-campus.html

Department: Criminal Justice and Safety
Website: http://www.phoenix.edu/colleges_divisions/criminal-justice.html

Type of Program: Master of Public Administration (only one not on campus); MS in Administration of Justice and Security; MS in Administration of Justice and Security with a concentration in Global and Homeland Security; MS in Administration of Justice and Security with a concentration in Law Enforcement Organizations

Application Deadline: Not available

Requirements:
- Have an undergraduate degree from an approved, regionally accredited or nationally accredited college or university, or hold a comparable degree from a recognized institution outside the United States.
- Have a cumulative GPA of 2.5 (on a 4.0 scale) as shown on the undergraduate degree posted transcript.
- Meet work experience requirements or have access to an organizational environment, depending on your selected degree program, in order to successfully complete program objectives and apply concepts you learn in our courses. Please contact an Enrollment Advisor to learn if your program has such a requirement.
- Be a citizen or permanent resident of the United States or hold an approved, valid visa if residing in the United States.
- Not have been expelled from a previous institution.
- Complete all required forms for admission and submit an official undergraduate degree posted transcript.

Information Required for Application: Not available

Admission Date: Not available

In-state and Out-of-state Tuition Costs: $740 per credit hour

Availability of Internships and Scholarships: Scholarships, institutional grants, cash plans, third party billing plans

Orientation and Emphasis of Department/Program (Program Description):

Master of Public Administration: The University of Phoenix master of public administration degree program helps you develop the skills necessary to create and implement public policy. Courses such as Law and Public Administration, and Public Budgeting help you go beyond theory and gain real-world insight into how governments operate. Discover how the University of Phoenix can help you cultivate the skills you need to manage in the public service arena.

Master of Science/Administration of Justice and Security: If you're ready to take the next step in becoming a leader in the world of criminal justice and security, then you've come to the right place. The master of science in administration of justice and security at the University of Phoenix focuses on developing leadership and administrative skills. While criminal justice and security are at the center of our master's degree program, you'll also study other important areas such as cybercrime, forensics, public policy, profiling, and more. Additionally, our criminal justice and security degree programs are continually updated, ensuring you learn the most current knowledge and skills from our experienced faculty who have a pulse on the world of criminal justice and organizational security.

Master of Science in Administration of Justice and Security with a concentration in Global and Homeland Security: Day in and day out, you're confronted with issues that threaten local communities. Leverage your law enforcement experience to play a role in protecting the nation from larger threats and in leading the response to these dangers. Earning a master of science in administration of justice and security with a concentration in global and homeland security may put you on the path to a new career as a command officer, private security director, or intelligence analyst. Learn how to work together with other law enforcement agencies to solve problems, and gain the skills you need to manage critical incidents, intelligence, cybercrime, and technology while getting a foundation in criminology.

Master of Science in Administration of Justice and Security with a concentration in Law Enforcement Organizations: Throughout your career in law enforcement, you've seen opportunities to do things better. Put yourself in a position to make change happen by earning a master of science in administration of justice and security with a concentration in law enforcement. Gain the skills you need to manage critical incidents, intelligence, cybercrime, and technology while getting a foundation in criminology.

Number of Faculty: Not available

Accreditation: Higher Learning Commission

Average Length of Time to Complete the Program: Not available

University of Phoenix–Louisiana Campuses

Baton Rouge Campus
Address: 2431 South Acadian Thruway
Baton Rouge, LA 70808-2300
Phone: (225) 927-4443
Website: http://www.phoenix.edu/campus-locations/la/baton-rouge-campus/baton-rouge-campus.html

New Orleans Learning Center
Address: 1 Galleria Boulevard
Suite 825
Metairie, LA 70001-2082
Phone: (504) 613-1500
Website: http://www.phoenix.edu/campus-locations/la/baton-rouge-campus/new-orleans-learning-center.html

Lafayette Campus
Address: 425 Settlers Trace Boulevard
Lafayette, LA 70508
Phone: (337) 354-4700
Website: http://www.phoenix.edu/campus-locations/la/lafay-ette-campus/lafayette-la-campus.html

Shreveport-Bossier Campus
Address: 350 Plaza Loop Drive, Building E
Bossier City, LA 71111-4390
Phone: (318) 549-8920
Website: http://www.phoenix.edu/campus-locations/la/shreve-port-bossier-campus/shreveport-bossier-campus.html

Department: Criminal Justice and Safety
Website: http://www.phoenix.edu/colleges_divisions/criminal-justice.html

Type of Program: Master of Public Administration (only one not on campus); MS in Administration of Justice and Security; MS in Administration of Justice and Security with a concentration in Global and Homeland Security; MS in Administration of Justice and Security with a concentration in Law Enforcement Organizations

Application Deadline: Not available

Requirements:
- Have an undergraduate degree from an approved, regionally accredited or nationally accredited college or university, or hold a comparable degree from a recognized institution outside the United States.

- Have a cumulative GPA of 2.5 (on a 4.0 scale) as shown on the undergraduate degree posted transcript.
- Meet work experience requirements or have access to an organizational environment, depending on your selected degree program, in order to successfully complete program objectives and apply concepts you learn in our courses. Please contact an Enrollment Advisor to learn if your program has such a requirement.
- Be a citizen or permanent resident of the United States or hold an approved, valid visa if residing in the United States.
- Not have been expelled from a previous institution.
- Complete all required forms for admission and submit an official undergraduate degree posted transcript.

Information Required for Application: Not available

Admission Date: Not available

In-state and Out-of-state Tuition Costs: $740 per credit hour

Availability of Internships and Scholarships: Scholarships, institutional grants, cash plans, third party billing plans

Orientation and Emphasis of Department/Program (Program Description):

Master of Public Administration: The University of Phoenix master of public administration degree program helps you develop the skills necessary to create and implement public policy. Courses such as Law and Public Administration, and Public Budgeting help you go beyond theory and gain real-world insight into how governments operate. Discover how the University of Phoenix can help you cultivate the skills you need to manage in the public service arena.

Master of Science/Administration of Justice and Security: If you're ready to take the next step in becoming a leader in the world of criminal justice and security, then you've come to the right place. The master of science in administration of justice and security at the University of Phoenix focuses on developing leadership and administrative skills. While criminal justice and security are at the center of our master's degree program, you'll also study other important areas such as cybercrime, forensics, public policy, profiling, and more. Additionally, our criminal justice and security degree programs are continually updated, ensuring you learn the most current knowledge and skills from our experienced faculty who have a pulse on the world of criminal justice and organizational security.

Master of Science in Administration of Justice and Security with a concentration in Global and Homeland Security: Day in and day out, you're confronted with issues that threaten local communities. Leverage your law enforcement experience to play a role in protecting the nation from larger threats and in leading the response to these dangers. Earning a master of science in administration of justice and security with a concentration in global and homeland security may put you on the path to a new career as a command officer, private security director, or intelligence analyst. Learn how to work together with other law enforcement agencies to solve problems, and gain the skills you need to manage critical incidents, intelligence, cybercrime, and technology while getting a foundation in criminology.

Master of Science in Administration of Justice and Security with a concentration in Law Enforcement Organizations: Throughout your career in law enforcement, you've seen opportunities to do things better. Put yourself in a position to make change happen by earning a master of science in administration of justice and security with a concentration in law enforcement. Gain the skills you need to manage critical incidents, intelligence, cybercrime, and technology while getting a foundation in criminology.

Number of Faculty: Not available

Accreditation: Higher Learning Commission

Average Length of Time to Complete the Program: Not available

University of Phoenix–New Mexico Campus

Address: 5700 Pasadena Northeast
Albuquerque, NM 87113
Phone: (505) 821-4800
Website: http://www.phoenix.edu/campus-locations/nm/new-mexico-campus/new-mexico-campus.html

Department: Criminal Justice and Safety
Website: http://www.phoenix.edu/colleges_divisions/criminal-justice.html

Type of Program: Master of Public Administration (only one not on campus); MS in Administration of Justice and Security; MS in Administration of Justice and Security with a concentration in Global and Homeland Security; MS in Administration of Justice and Security with a concentration in Law Enforcement Organizations

Application Deadline: Not available

Requirements:
- Have an undergraduate degree from an approved, regionally accredited or nationally accredited college or university, or hold a comparable degree from a recognized institution outside the United States.
- Have a cumulative GPA of 2.5 (on a 4.0 scale) as shown on the undergraduate degree posted transcript.
- Meet work experience requirements or have access to an organizational environment, depending on your selected degree program, in order to successfully complete program objectives and apply concepts you learn in our courses. Please contact an Enrollment Advisor to learn if your program has such a requirement.
- Be a citizen or permanent resident of the United States or hold an approved, valid visa if residing in the United States.
- Not have been expelled from a previous institution.
- Complete all required forms for admission and submit an official undergraduate degree posted transcript.

Information Required for Application: Not available

Admission Date: Not available

In-state and Out-of-state Tuition Costs: $740 per credit hour

Availability of Internships and Scholarships: Scholarships, institutional grants, cash plans, third party billing plans

Orientation and Emphasis of Department/Program (Program Description):

Master of Public Administration: The University of Phoenix master of public administration degree program helps you develop the skills necessary to create and implement public policy. Courses such as Law and Public Administration, and Public Budgeting help you go beyond theory and gain real-world insight into how governments operate. Discover how the University of Phoenix can help you cultivate the skills you need to manage in the public service arena.

Master of Science/Administration of Justice and Security: If you're ready to take the next step in becoming a leader in the world of criminal justice and security, then you've come to the right place. The master of science in administration of justice and security at the University of Phoenix focuses on developing leadership and administrative skills. While criminal justice and security are at the center of our master's degree program, you'll also study other important areas such as cybercrime, forensics, public policy, profiling, and more. Additionally, our criminal justice and security degree programs are continually updated, ensuring you learn the most current knowledge and skills from our experienced faculty who have a pulse on the world of criminal justice and organizational security.

Master of Science in Administration of Justice and Security with a concentration in Global and Homeland Security: Day in and day out, you're confronted with issues that threaten local communities. Leverage your law enforcement experience to play a role in protecting the nation from larger threats and in leading the response to these dangers. Earning a master of science in administration of justice and security with a concentration in global and homeland security may put you on the path to a new career as a command officer, private security director, or intelligence analyst. Learn how to work together with other law enforcement agencies to solve problems, and gain the skills you need to manage critical incidents, intelligence, cybercrime, and technology while getting a foundation in criminology.

Master of Science in Administration of Justice and Security with a concentration in Law Enforcement Organizations: Throughout your career in law enforcement, you've seen opportunities to do things better. Put yourself in a position to make change happen by earning a master of science in administration of justice and security with a concentration in law enforcement. Gain the skills you need to manage critical incidents, intelligence, cybercrime, and technology while getting a foundation in criminology.

Number of Faculty: Not available

Accreditation: Higher Learning Commission

Average Length of Time to Complete the Program: Not available

University of Phoenix–Oregon Campus

Address: 13221 Southwest 68th Parkway
Tigard, OR 97223
Phone: (503) 403-2900
Website: http://www.phoenix.edu/campus-locations/or/oregon-campus/oregon-campus.html

Department: Criminal Justice and Safety
Website: http://www.phoenix.edu/colleges_divisions/criminal-justice.html

Type of Program: Master of Public Administration (only one not on campus); MS in Administration of Justice and Security; MS in Administration of Justice and Security with a concentration in Global and Homeland Security; MS in Administration of Justice and Security with a concentration in Law Enforcement Organizations

Application Deadline: Not available

Requirements:
- Have an undergraduate degree from an approved, regionally accredited or nationally accredited college or university, or hold a comparable degree from a recognized institution outside the United States.
- Have a cumulative GPA of 2.5 (on a 4.0 scale) as shown on the undergraduate degree posted transcript.
- Meet work experience requirements or have access to an organizational environment, depending on your selected degree program, in order to successfully complete program objectives and apply concepts you learn in our courses. Please contact an Enrollment Advisor to learn if your program has such a requirement.
- Be a citizen or permanent resident of the United States or hold an approved, valid visa if residing in the United States.
- Not have been expelled from a previous institution.
- Complete all required forms for admission and submit an official undergraduate degree posted transcript.

Information Required for Application: Not available

Admission Date: Not available

In-state and Out-of-state Tuition Costs: $740 per credit hour

Availability of Internships and Scholarships: Scholarships, institutional grants, cash plans, third party billing plans

Orientation and Emphasis of Department/Program (Program Description):

Master of Public Administration: The University of Phoenix master of public administration degree program helps you develop the skills necessary to create and implement public policy. Courses such as Law and Public Administration, and Public Budgeting help you go beyond theory and gain real-world insight into how governments operate. Discover how the University of Phoenix can help you cultivate the skills you need to manage in the public service arena.

Master of Science/Administration of Justice and Security: If you're ready to take the next step in becoming a leader in the world of criminal justice and security, then you've come to the right place. The master of science in administration of justice and security at the University of Phoenix focuses on developing leadership and administrative skills. While criminal justice and security are at the center of our master's degree program, you'll also study other important areas such as cybercrime, forensics, public policy, profiling, and more. Additionally, our criminal justice and security degree programs are continually updated, ensuring you learn the most current knowledge and skills from our experienced faculty who have a pulse on the world of criminal justice and organizational security.

Master of Science in Administration of Justice and Security with a concentration in Global and Homeland Security: Day in and day out, you're confronted with issues that threaten local communities. Leverage your law enforcement experience to play a role in protecting the nation from larger threats and in leading the response to these dangers. Earning a master of science in administration of justice and security with a concentration in global and homeland security may put you on the path to a new career as a command officer, private security director, or intelligence analyst. Learn how to work together with other law enforcement agencies to solve problems, and gain the skills you need to manage critical incidents, intelligence, cybercrime, and technology while getting a foundation in criminology.

Master of Science in Administration of Justice and Security with a concentration in Law Enforcement Organizations: Throughout your career in law enforcement, you've seen opportunities to do things better. Put yourself in a position to make change happen by earning a master of science in administration of justice and security with a concentration in law enforcement. Gain the skills you need to manage critical incidents, intelligence, cybercrime, and technology while getting a foundation in criminology.

Number of Faculty: Not available

Accreditation: Higher Learning Commission

Average Length of Time to Complete the Program: Not available

University of Phoenix–Philadelphia Campus

Address: 30 South 17th Street
Philadelphia, PA, 19103-4001
Phone: (610) 989-0880
Website: http://www.phoenix.edu/campus-locations/pa/phila-delphia-campus/philadelphia-campus.html

Department: Criminal Justice and Safety
Website: http://www.phoenix.edu/colleges_divisions/criminal-justice.html

Type of Program: Master of Public Administration (only one not on campus); MS in Administration of Justice and Security; MS in Administration of Justice and Security with a concentration in Global and Homeland Security; MS in Administration of Justice and Security with a concentration in Law Enforcement Organizations

Application Deadline: Not available

Requirements:
- Have an undergraduate degree from an approved, regionally accredited or nationally accredited college or university, or hold a comparable degree from a recognized institution outside the United States.
- Have a cumulative GPA of 2.5 (on a 4.0 scale) as shown on the undergraduate degree posted transcript.
- Meet work experience requirements or have access to an organizational environment, depending on your selected degree program, in order to successfully complete program objectives and apply concepts you learn in our courses. Please contact an Enrollment Advisor to learn if your program has such a requirement.
- Be a citizen or permanent resident of the United States or hold an approved, valid visa if residing in the United States.
- Not have been expelled from a previous institution.
- Complete all required forms for admission and submit an official undergraduate degree posted transcript.

Information Required for Application: Not available

Admission Date: Not available

In-state and Out-of-state Tuition Costs: $740 per credit hour

Availability of Internships and Scholarships: Scholarships, institutional grants, cash plans, third party billing plans

Orientation and Emphasis of Department/Program (Program Description):

Master of Public Administration: The University of Phoenix master of public administration degree program helps you develop the skills necessary to create and implement public policy. Courses such as Law and Public Administration, and Public Budgeting help you go beyond theory and gain real-world insight into how governments operate. Discover how the University of Phoenix can help you cultivate the skills you need to manage in the public service arena.

Master of Science/Administration of Justice and Security: If you're ready to take the next step in becoming a leader in the world of criminal justice and security, then you've come to the right place. The master of science in administration of justice and security at the University of Phoenix focuses on developing leadership and administrative skills. While criminal justice and security are at the center of our master's degree program, you'll also study other important areas such as cybercrime, forensics, public policy, profiling, and more. Additionally, our criminal justice and security degree programs are continually updated, ensuring you learn the most current knowledge and skills from our experienced faculty who have a pulse on the world of criminal justice and organizational security.

Master of Science in Administration of Justice and Security with a concentration in Global and Homeland Security: Day in and day out, you're confronted with issues that threaten local communities. Leverage your law enforcement experience to play a role in protecting the nation from larger threats and in leading the response to these dangers. Earning a master of science in administration of justice and security with a concentration in global and homeland security may put you on the path to a new career as a command officer, private security director, or intelligence analyst. Learn how to work together with other law enforcement agencies to solve problems, and gain the skills you need to manage critical incidents, intelligence, cybercrime, and technology while getting a foundation in criminology.

Master of Science in Administration of Justice and Security with a concentration in Law Enforcement Organizations: Throughout your career in law enforcement, you've seen opportunities to do things better. Put yourself in a position to make change happen by earning a master of science in administration of justice and security with a concentration in law enforcement. Gain the skills you need to manage critical incidents, intelligence, cybercrime, and technology while getting a foundation in criminology.

Number of Faculty: Not available

Accreditation: Higher Learning Commission

Average Length of Time to Complete the Program: Not available

University of Phoenix–Sacramento Valley Campus

Address: 2860 Gateway Oaks Drive
Sacramento, CA, 95833-4334
Phone: (800) 266-2107
Website: http://www.phoenix.edu/campus-locations/ca/
sacramento-valley-campus/sacramento-valley-campus.html

Department: Criminal Justice and Safety
Website: http://www.phoenix.edu/colleges_divisions/criminal-justice.html

Type of Program: Master of Public Administration (only one not on campus); MS in Administration of Justice and Security; MS in Administration of Justice and Security with a concentration in Global and Homeland Security; MS in Administration of Justice and Security with a concentration in Law Enforcement Organizations

Application Deadline: Not available

Requirements:
- Have an undergraduate degree from an approved, regionally accredited or nationally accredited college or university, or hold a comparable degree from a recognized institution outside the United States.
- Have a cumulative GPA of 2.5 (on a 4.0 scale) as shown on the undergraduate degree posted transcript.
- Meet work experience requirements or have access to an organizational environment, depending on your selected degree program, in order to successfully complete program objectives and apply concepts you learn in our courses. Please contact an Enrollment Advisor to learn if your program has such a requirement.
- Be a citizen or permanent resident of the United States or hold an approved, valid visa if residing in the United States.
- Not have been expelled from a previous institution.
- Complete all required forms for admission and submit an official undergraduate degree posted transcript.

Information Required for Application: Not available

Admission Date: Not available

In-state and Out-of-state Tuition Costs: $740 per credit hour

Availability of Internships and Scholarships: Scholarships, institutional grants, cash plans, third party billing plans

Orientation and Emphasis of Department/Program (Program Description):

Master of Public Administration: The University of Phoenix master of public administration degree program helps you develop the skills necessary to create and implement public policy. Courses such as Law and Public Administration, and Public Budgeting help you go beyond theory and gain real-world insight into how governments operate. Discover how the University of Phoenix can help you cultivate the skills you need to manage in the public service arena.

Master of Science/Administration of Justice and Security: If you're ready to take the next step in becoming a leader in the world of criminal justice and security, then you've come to the right place. The master of science in administration of justice and security at the University of Phoenix focuses on developing leadership and administrative skills. While criminal justice and security are at the center of our master's degree program, you'll also study other important areas such as cybercrime, forensics, public policy, profiling, and more. Additionally, our criminal justice and security degree programs are continually updated, ensuring you learn the most current knowledge and skills from our experienced faculty who have a pulse on the world of criminal justice and organizational security.

Master of Science in Administration of Justice and Security with a concentration in Global and Homeland Security: Day in and day out, you're confronted with issues that threaten local communities. Leverage your law enforcement experience to play a role in protecting the nation from larger threats and in leading the response to these dangers. Earning a master of science in administration of justice and security with a concentration in global and homeland security may put you on the path to a new career as a command officer, private security director, or intelligence analyst. Learn how to work together with other law enforcement agencies to solve problems, and gain the skills you need to manage critical incidents, intelligence, cybercrime, and technology while getting a foundation in criminology.

Master of Science in Administration of Justice and Security with a concentration in Law Enforcement Organizations: Throughout your career in law enforcement, you've seen opportunities to do things better. Put yourself in a position to make change happen by earning a master of science in administration of justice and security with a concentration in law enforcement. Gain the skills you need to manage critical incidents, intelligence, cybercrime, and technology while getting a foundation in criminology.

Number of Faculty: Not available

Accreditation: Higher Learning Commission

Average Length of Time to Complete the Program: Not available

University of Phoenix–San Diego Campus

Address: 9645 Granite Ridge Drive
Suite 200
San Diego, CA 92123
Phone: (800) 473-4346
Website: http://www.phoenix.edu/campus-locations/ca/san-diego-campus/san-diego-campus.html

Department: Criminal Justice and Safety
Website: http://www.phoenix.edu/colleges_divisions/criminal-justice.html

Type of Program: Master of Public Administration (only one not on campus); MS in Administration of Justice and Security; MS in Administration of Justice and Security with a concentration in Global and Homeland Security; MS in Administration of Justice and Security with a concentration in Law Enforcement Organizations

Application Deadline: Not available

Requirements:
* Have an undergraduate degree from an approved, regionally accredited or nationally accredited college or university, or hold a comparable degree from a recognized institution outside the United States.
* Have a cumulative GPA of 2.5 (on a 4.0 scale) as shown on the undergraduate degree posted transcript.
* Meet work experience requirements or have access to an organizational environment, depending on your selected degree program, in order to successfully complete program objectives and apply concepts you learn in our courses. Please contact an Enrollment Advisor to learn if your program has such a requirement.
* Be a citizen or permanent resident of the United States or hold an approved, valid visa if residing in the United States.
* Not have been expelled from a previous institution.
* Complete all required forms for admission and submit an official undergraduate degree posted transcript.

Information Required for Application: Not available

Admission Date: Not available

In-state and Out-of-state Tuition Costs: $740 per credit hour

Availability of Internships and Scholarships: Scholarships, institutional grants, cash plans, third party billing plans

Orientation and Emphasis of Department/Program (Program Description):

Master of Public Administration: The University of Phoenix master of public administration degree program helps you develop the skills necessary to create and implement public policy. Courses such as Law and Public Administration, and Public Budgeting help you go beyond theory and gain real-world insight into how governments operate. Discover how the University of Phoenix can help you cultivate the skills you need to manage in the public service arena.

Master of Science/Administration of Justice and Security: If you're ready to take the next step in becoming a leader in the world of criminal justice and security, then you've come to the right place. The master of science in administration of justice and security at the University of Phoenix focuses on developing leadership and administrative skills. While criminal justice and security are at the center of our master's degree program, you'll also study other important areas such as cybercrime, forensics, public policy, profiling, and more. Additionally, our criminal justice and security degree programs are continually updated, ensuring you learn the most current knowledge and skills from our experienced faculty who have a pulse on the world of criminal justice and organizational security.

Master of Science in Administration of Justice and Security with a concentration in Global and Homeland Security: Day in and day out, you're confronted with issues that threaten local communities. Leverage your law enforcement experience to play a role in protecting the nation from larger threats and in leading the response to these dangers. Earning a master of science in administration of justice and security with a concentration in global and homeland security may put you on the path to a new career as a command officer, private security director, or intelligence analyst. Learn how to work together with other law enforcement agencies to solve problems, and gain the skills you need to manage critical incidents, intelligence, cybercrime, and technology while getting a foundation in criminology.

Master of Science in Administration of Justice and Security with a concentration in Law Enforcement Organizations: Throughout your career in law enforcement, you've seen opportunities to do things better. Put yourself in a position to make change happen by earning a master of science in administration of justice and security with a concentration in law enforcement. Gain the skills you need to manage critical incidents, intelligence, cybercrime, and technology while getting a foundation in criminology.

Number of Faculty: Not available

Accreditation: Higher Learning Commission

Average Length of Time to Complete the Program: Not available

University of Phoenix–Southern Arizona Campus

Address: 300 South Craycroft Road
Tucson, AZ 85711
Phone: (520) 881-6512
Website: http://www.phoenix.edu/campus-locations/az/
southern-arizona-campus/southern-arizona-campus.html

Department: Criminal Justice and Safety
Website: http://www.phoenix.edu/colleges_divisions/criminal-
justice.html

Type of Program: Master of Public Administration (only one
not on campus); MS in Administration of Justice and Security;
MS in Administration of Justice and Security with a concentra-
tion in Global and Homeland Security; MS in Administration of
Justice and Security with a concentration in Law Enforcement
Organizations

Application Deadline: Not available

Requirements:
- Have an undergraduate degree from an approved, regionally
  accredited or nationally accredited college or university, or
  hold a comparable degree from a recognized institution outside the United States.
- Have a cumulative GPA of 2.5 (on a 4.0 scale) as shown on the
  undergraduate degree posted transcript.
- Meet work experience requirements or have access to an organizational environment, depending on your selected degree
  program, in order to successfully complete program objectives and apply concepts you learn in our courses. Please contact an Enrollment Advisor to learn if your program has such a
  requirement.
- Be a citizen or permanent resident of the United States or hold
  an approved, valid visa if residing in the United States.
- Not have been expelled from a previous institution.
- Complete all required forms for admission and submit an official undergraduate degree posted transcript.

Information Required for Application: Not available

Admission Date: Not available

In-state and Out-of-state Tuition Costs: $740 per credit hour

Availability of Internships and Scholarships: Scholarships, institutional grants, cash plans, third party billing plans

Orientation and Emphasis of Department/Program (Program Description):

Master of Public Administration: The University of Phoenix master of public administration degree program helps you develop the skills necessary to create and implement public policy. Courses such as Law and Public Administration, and Public Budgeting help you go beyond theory and gain real-world insight into how governments operate. Discover how the University of Phoenix can help you cultivate the skills you need to manage in the public service arena.

Master of Science/Administration of Justice and Security: If you're ready to take the next step in becoming a leader in the world of criminal justice and security, then you've come to the right place. The master of science in administration of justice and security at the University of Phoenix focuses on developing leadership and administrative skills. While criminal justice and security are at the center of our master's degree program, you'll also study other important areas such as cybercrime, forensics, public policy, profiling, and more. Additionally, our criminal justice and security degree programs are continually updated, ensuring you learn the most current knowledge and skills from our experienced faculty who have a pulse on the world of criminal justice and organizational security.

Master of Science in Administration of Justice and Security with a concentration in Global and Homeland Security: Day in and day out, you're confronted with issues that threaten local communities. Leverage your law enforcement experience to play a role in protecting the nation from larger threats and in leading the response to these dangers. Earning a master of science in administration of justice and security with a concentration in global and homeland security may put you on the path to a new career as a command officer, private security director, or intelligence analyst. Learn how to work together with other law enforcement agencies to solve problems, and gain the skills you need to manage critical incidents, intelligence, cybercrime, and technology while getting a foundation in criminology.

Master of Science in Administration of Justice and Security with a concentration in Law Enforcement Organizations: Throughout your career in law enforcement, you've seen opportunities to do things better. Put yourself in a position to make change happen by earning a master of science in administration of justice and security with a concentration in law enforcement. Gain the skills you need to manage critical incidents, intelligence, cybercrime, and technology while getting a foundation in criminology.

Number of Faculty: Not available

Accreditation: Higher Learning Commission

Average Length of Time to Complete the Program: Not available

University of Phoenix–Southern California Campus

Address: 3090 Bristol Street
Costa Mesa, CA, 92626-3099
Phone: (800) 888-1968
Website: http://www.phoenix.edu/campus-locations/ca/south-ern-california-campus/southern-california-campus.html

Department: Criminal Justice and Safety
Website: http://www.phoenix.edu/colleges_divisions/criminal-justice.html

Type of Program: Master of Public Administration (only one not on campus); MS in Administration of Justice and Security; MS in Administration of Justice and Security with a concentration in Global and Homeland Security; MS in Administration of Justice and Security with a concentration in Law Enforcement Organizations

Application Deadline: Not available

Requirements:
- Have an undergraduate degree from an approved, regionally accredited or nationally accredited college or university, or hold a comparable degree from a recognized institution outside the United States.
- Have a cumulative GPA of 2.5 (on a 4.0 scale) as shown on the undergraduate degree posted transcript.
- Meet work experience requirements or have access to an organizational environment, depending on your selected degree program, in order to successfully complete program objectives and apply concepts you learn in our courses. Please contact an Enrollment Advisor to learn if your program has such a requirement.
- Be a citizen or permanent resident of the United States or hold an approved, valid visa if residing in the United States.
- Not have been expelled from a previous institution.
- Complete all required forms for admission and submit an official undergraduate degree posted transcript.

Information Required for Application: Not available

Admission Date: Not available

In-state and Out-of-state Tuition Costs: $740 per credit hour

Availability of Internships and Scholarships: Scholarships, institutional grants, cash plans, third party billing plans

Orientation and Emphasis of Department/Program (Program Description):

Master of Public Administration: The University of Phoenix master of public administration degree program helps you develop the skills necessary to create and implement public policy. Courses such as Law and Public Administration, and Public Budgeting help you go beyond theory and gain real-world insight into how governments operate. Discover how the University of Phoenix can help you cultivate the skills you need to manage in the public service arena.

Master of Science/Administration of Justice and Security: If you're ready to take the next step in becoming a leader in the world of criminal justice and security, then you've come to the right place. The master of science in administration of justice and security at the University of Phoenix focuses on developing leadership and administrative skills. While criminal justice and security are at the center of our master's degree program, you'll also study other important areas such as cybercrime, forensics, public policy, profiling, and more. Additionally, our criminal justice and security degree programs are continually updated, ensuring you learn the most current knowledge and skills from our experienced faculty who have a pulse on the world of criminal justice and organizational security.

Master of Science in Administration of Justice and Security with a concentration in Global and Homeland Security: Day in and day out, you're confronted with issues that threaten local communities. Leverage your law enforcement experience to play a role in protecting the nation from larger threats and in leading the response to these dangers. Earning a master of science in administration of justice and security with a concentration in global and homeland security may put you on the path to a new career as a command officer, private security director, or intelligence analyst. Learn how to work together with other law enforcement agencies to solve problems, and gain the skills you need to manage critical incidents, intelligence, cybercrime, and technology while getting a foundation in criminology.

Master of Science in Administration of Justice and Security with a concentration in Law Enforcement Organizations: Throughout your career in law enforcement, you've seen opportunities to do things better. Put yourself in a position to make change happen by earning a master of science in administration of justice and security with a concentration in law enforcement. Gain the skills you need to manage critical incidents, intelligence, cybercrime, and technology while getting a foundation in criminology.

Number of Faculty: Not available

Accreditation: Higher Learning Commission

Average Length of Time to Complete the Program: Not available

University of Phoenix–Southern Colorado Campuses

Fort Collins Campus
Address: 2720 Council Tree Avenue
Suite 200
Fort Collins, CO 80525-6306
Phone: (970) 226-1781
Website: http://www.phoenix.edu/campus-locations/co/colorado-campus/fort-collins-learning-center.html

Turnpike Learning Center
Address: 8700 Turnpike Drive
Westminster, CO 80030-7030
Phone: (303) 755-9090
Website: http://www.phoenix.edu/campus-locations/co/colorado-campus/turnpike-learning-center.html

Colorado Springs Downtown
Address: 2 North Cascade Avenue
Suite 100
Colorado Springs, CO 80903-1620
Phone: (719) 527-9000
Website: http://www.phoenix.edu/campus-locations/co/colorado-campus/colorado-Springs-downtown.html

Department: Criminal Justice and Safety
Website: http://www.phoenix.edu/colleges_divisions/criminal-justice.html

Type of Program: Master of Public Administration (only one not on campus); MS in Administration of Justice and Security; MS in Administration of Justice and Security with a concentration in Global and Homeland Security; MS in Administration of Justice and Security with a concentration in Law Enforcement Organizations

Application Deadline: Not available

Requirements:
- Have an undergraduate degree from an approved, regionally accredited or nationally accredited college or university, or hold a comparable degree from a recognized institution outside the United States.
- Have a cumulative GPA of 2.5 (on a 4.0 scale) as shown on the undergraduate degree posted transcript.

- Meet work experience requirements or have access to an organizational environment, depending on your selected degree
  program, in order to successfully complete program objectives and apply concepts you learn in our courses. Please contact an Enrollment Advisor to learn if your program has such a
  requirement.
- Be a citizen or permanent resident of the United States or hold
  an approved, valid visa if residing in the United States.
- Not have been expelled from a previous institution.
- Complete all required forms for admission and submit an official undergraduate degree posted transcript.

Information Required for Application: Not available

Admission Date: Not available

In-state and Out-of-state Tuition Costs: $740 per credit hour

Availability of Internships and Scholarships: Scholarships, institutional grants, cash plans, third party billing plans

**Orientation and Emphasis of Department/Program (Program
Description):**
Master of Public Administration: The University of Phoenix master
of public administration degree program helps you develop the
skills necessary to create and implement public policy. Courses
such as Law and Public Administration, and Public Budgeting
help you go beyond theory and gain real-world insight into how
governments operate. Discover how the University of Phoenix can
help you cultivate the skills you need to manage in the public service arena.
Master of Science/Administration of Justice and Security: If you're
ready to take the next step in becoming a leader in the world of
criminal justice and security, then you've come to the right place.
The master of science in administration of justice and security at
the University of Phoenix focuses on developing leadership and
administrative skills. While criminal justice and security are at
the center of our master's degree program, you'll also study other
important areas such as cybercrime, forensics, public policy, profiling, and more. Additionally, our criminal justice and security
degree programs are continually updated, ensuring you learn the
most current knowledge and skills from our experienced faculty
who have a pulse on the world of criminal justice and organizational security.
*Master of Science in Administration of Justice and Security with a
concentration in Global and Homeland Security:* Day in and day
out, you're confronted with issues that threaten local communities. Leverage your law enforcement experience to play a role

in protecting the nation from larger threats and in leading the response to these dangers. Earning a master of science in administration of justice and security with a concentration in global and homeland security may put you on the path to a new career as a command officer, private security director, or intelligence analyst. Learn how to work together with other law enforcement agencies to solve problems, and gain the skills you need to manage critical incidents, intelligence, cybercrime, and technology while getting a foundation in criminology.

Master of Science in Administration of Justice and Security with a concentration in Law Enforcement Organizations: Throughout your career in law enforcement, you've seen opportunities to do things better. Put yourself in a position to make change happen by earning a master of science in administration of justice and security with a concentration in law enforcement. Gain the skills you need to manage critical incidents, intelligence, cybercrime, and technology while getting a foundation in criminology.

Number of Faculty: Not available

Accreditation: Higher Learning Commission

Average Length of Time to Complete the Program: Not available

University of South Carolina

Address: Columbia, SC 29208
Phone: (803) 777-0169
Website: https://www.sc.edu/

Department: Department of Criminology and Criminal Justice
Currell College
1305 Greene Street
Columbia, SC 29208
Phone: (803) 777-7097
Website: http://artsandsciences.sc.edu/crju/

Type of Program: MA in Criminology and Criminal Justice; PhD in Criminology and Criminal Justice

Application Deadline: July 1 (March 1 to be considered for funding), November 15

Requirements:
- A baccalaureate degree (or the international equivalent) from an accredited college or university;
- Standardized test scores (consult the program to which you are applying for particular test requirements);
- Official transcripts;
- Two or more letters of recommendation;
- Application;
- Application fee; and
- English proficiency requirement.

Information Required for Application:
Master's
- University application through the Graduate School website (online), including a written statement describing prior education, relevant work experiences, and purpose in pursuing a masters degree in criminology and criminal justice (500 words);
- Two letters of academic reference from faculty members or other persons qualified to evaluate applicant's abilities to undertake graduate–level studies;
- Scores obtained within the last five years on the Miller Analogies Test (MAT) or Graduate Record Examination (GRE, both verbal and quantitative sections of the general exam); and
- Official grade transcripts from all previous institutions.

Doctoral
- University application through The Graduate School website (online), including a written statement describing prior education, relevant work experiences, criminal justice interests

and purpose in pursuing a doctoral degree in criminology and criminal justice (500-1,000 words);

- A sole-authored writing sample, such as a course paper or thesis chapter, written during your previous degree program (please limit the sample to no more than twenty-five pages and include course number, date, and name of professor). Writing samples are uploaded electronically by applicants at the time they complete the online application;

- Three letters of academic reference from faculty members or other persons qualified to evaluate applicant's abilities to undertake graduate-level studies;

- Scores obtained within the last five years on the Graduate Record Examination (GRE, both verbal and quantitative sections of the general exam; we only accept GRE scores for the doctoral program); and

- Official grade transcripts from all previous institutions.

Admission Date: Fall, Spring

In-state and Out-of-state Tuition Costs: $22,801 for fifteen to eighteen credit hours

Availability of Internships and Scholarships: Graduate assistantships, graduate school fellowships, and awards

Orientation and Emphasis of Department/Program (Program Description): Established in 1974, the Department of Criminology and Criminal Justice at the University of South Carolina is one of the oldest programs in the nation. Our Columbia campus is centrally located in South Carolina's capital city, which provides graduate students access to a wide array of state and federal agencies, and abundant opportunities for research. Our faculty members contribute significantly to USC's designation as an institution of "very high research activity" by the Carnegie Foundation for the Advancement of Teaching. They are engaged in scholarship that spans many facets of criminal justice practice and policy as well as criminological theory. Their work is published in the most prestigious journals in the field and also informs local, state, and national criminal justice agencies. You are part of a vibrant department and should expect numerous rewarding experiences from your graduate program as you are prepared for an exciting future in criminal justice practice, research, or higher education.

Number of Faculty: 18

Accreditation: Western Association of Schools and Colleges

Average Length of Time to Complete the Program: Not available

University of Southern Mississippi

Address: 118 College Drive
Hattiesburg, MS 39406
Phone: (601) 266-1000
Website: http://www.usm.edu/

Department: School of Criminal Justice
Arthell Kelley Hall 123
118 College Drive, Box #5127
Hattiesburg, MS 39406
Phone: (601) 266-4509
Website: http://www.usm.edu/criminal-justice/

Type of Program: MA in Criminal Justice, MS in Criminal Justice, MS in Forensic Science, PhD Criminal Justice

Application Deadline: March 1, September 1

Requirements:
Master's
- Admission decisions are based on a balancing of a variety of factors. These include: scores on the verbal, quantitative, and analytical portions of the Graduate Record Examination's general test; undergraduate grade point average (both overall and in criminal justice); and evidence of related field training and work experience.
- In addition, applicants are to submit for consideration three letters of recommendation from members of their undergraduate faculty and to have such faculty members forward examples of written work which they are able to identify as original work by the applicant submitted in their courses. The letters should be sent to the department.
- Applicants granted regular admission that have an undergraduate major in criminal justice or criminal justice—including non-degree graduate students—must have achieved a grade point average of 3.0 overall and in their criminal justice courses.
- Applicants may be granted conditional admission in cases where other than grade point averages indicate. In these cases the department may, at its discretion, grant conditional admission to undergraduate criminal justice majors and non-degree graduate students in criminal justice with a GPA of less than 3.0 but more than 2.75 overall and in criminal justice courses.
- Applicants who are not criminal justice or criminal justice undergraduate majors who meet all other criteria may be granted conditional admission if the department is satisfied that their grade point average overall and in their particular major indicates

the potential to perform acceptably in the program. Students should see the appropriate graduate advisor for requirements to achieve regular admission. All prospective students with other than an criminal justice undergraduate major or strong professional training in criminal justice will be admitted conditionally until after completion of twelve hours of undergraduate criminal justice courses with a B or better in each course. These course hours are CJ 325, CJ 330, CJ 352, and either CJ 341 or CJ 360. All such supplemental undergraduate work must be completed prior to beginning graduate course work.

Doctoral
- A minimum of eighty-four semester hours beyond the bachelor's degree or fifty-four semester hours beyond the master's degree, with a minimum of thirty semester hours completed in specified 600- and 700-level course work in administration of justice and the remainder in approved cognates. A minimum grade of B is required in each course credited toward the degree;
- A qualifying examination;
- A combination of course work that may include proficiency in a foreign language, statistics, or computer science as determined by the department;
- A written comprehensive examination;
- Presentation and oral defense of dissertation; and
- Residency (students must meet the residency requirements specified in the bulletin).

Information Required for Application: Stated above

Admission Date: Fall, Spring

In-state and Out-of-state Tuition Costs: In-state: $375 per semester hour; out-of-state: $835 per semester hour

Availability of Internships and Scholarships: Fellowships, grants, assistantships

Orientation and Emphasis of Department/Program (Program Description):
The master of arts in criminal justice consists of a minimum of thirty-three hours of criminal justice course work, or a minimum of twenty-four hours of criminal justice course work with nine hours of additional course work in an approved minor (with eighteen hours of 600 level or higher). The master of science in criminal justice consists of a minimum of thirty-nine hours of criminal justice course work, or a minimum of thirty hours of criminal justice course work with nine hours of additional course work in

an approved minor area, plus successful completion of a written comprehensive examination (with eighteen hours at the 600 level or higher). The doctoral program is designed to prepare students for productive careers as teachers and practitioners of justice administration and research. This doctoral degree is normally taken after a student has earned a master's degree, but exceptional students who have earned only a baccalaureate degree are admitted at the discretion of the doctoral admissions committee. In both cases applicants must meet all university and departmental requirements for regular admission.

Number of Faculty: 25

Accreditation: Commission on Colleges of the Southern Association of Colleges and Schools

Average Length of Time to Complete the Program: Not available

University of South Florida

Address: 4202 East Fowler Avenue
Tampa, FL 33620
Phone: (813) 974-2011
Website: http://www.usf.edu/

Department: Criminology Department
University of South Florida
4202 East Fowler Avenue, SOC107
Tampa, FL 33620-7200
Phone: (813) 974-7197
Website: http://criminology.cbcs.usf.edu/

Type of Program: MA in Criminology; PhD in Criminology

Application Deadline: MA: January 15, September 30; PhD: January 15

Requirements:
Master's
- Have a bachelor's degree from a regionally accredited university;
- Take the GRE within five years preceding application; and
- Meet at least one of the following criteria:
    1. A graduate degree earned from a regionally accredited university;
    2. At least a B average (3.0 on a 4.0 scale) on all work as an upper division student seeking a bachelor's degree; and/or
    3. A minimum verbal score of 153 (500 on old GRE scale) and a minimum quantitative score of 144 (500 on old GRE scale) or the equivalent total (verbal plus quantitative on new GRE scale) of 1,000 or higher on the old GRE scale to be competitive. GRE Scores are mandatory. All applicants must submit GRE scores.

Doctoral
- A bachelor's degree from a regionally accredited university or college and a GPA of at least 3.0; or a master's degree from a regionally accredited university or college and a GPA of at least 3.4 (on a 4.0 scale) during graduate study;
- A minimum verbal score of 153 (500 on old GRE scale) and a minimum quantitative score of 144 (500 on old GRE scale) or the equivalent total (verbal plus quantitative on new GRE scale) of 1,000 or higher on the old GRE scale to be competitive. GRE Scores are mandatory. All applicants must submit GRE scores.

Information Required for Application:

Master's: Applicants will be selected for admission on a competitive basis based on the following:

- GPA on all work as an upper division student seeking a bachelor's degree;
- Verbal plus quantitative scores on the GRE;
- Three letters of recommendation addressing applicant's ability to do graduate work;
- Sample of written work indicating applicant's writing, research, or critical thinking skills (this sample should consist of at least three typed pages on a topic related to criminology or the applicant's undergraduate major);
- A statement of purpose, highlighting the applicant's credentials and indicating his/her (a) reasons for seeking the MA degree, (b) areas of interest in criminology/criminal justice, and (c) future career plans; and
- Proof of language proficiency.

Doctoral

- Official transcripts for all previous academic work at institutions of higher education;
- Official report of GRE scores;
- Three letters of recommendation speaking to the applicant's academic capabilities;
- A statement of purpose highlighting the applicant's qualifications and indicating applicant's (a) reasons for seeking a PhD degree in criminology, (b) research interests, and (c) future career plans;
- A sample of written work providing evidence of the applicant's scholarly abilities (for persons who have completed the MA/MS, a sample chapter from your thesis or area paper is most appropriate);
- Proof of language proficiency.

Admission Date: MA: Fall, Spring; PhD: Fall

In-state and Out-of-state Tuition Costs: In-state: $431.43 per credit; out-of-state: $877.17 per credit

Availability of Internships and Scholarships: Graduate assistantships, fellowships, awards

Orientation and Emphasis of Department/Program (Program Description): The master of arts in criminology is a two-year program designed to provide the student with an in-depth understanding of the major ideas and issues in criminology and criminal justice. Students will master both theoretical and methodological tools of inquiry used in the field of criminology and criminal justice.

The doctor of philosophy is granted in recognition of high attainment in a specific field of knowledge. It is a research degree conferred when a student has demonstrated proficiency and distinctive achievement in a specified field. Beyond minimum hours of course work, examination, and residency requirements, the doctor of philosophy degree requires a student to complete a dissertation that provides evidence of the ability to do original and independent research that contributes to a body of knowledge.

Number of Faculty: 30

Accreditation: Commission on Colleges of the Southern Association of Colleges and Schools

Average Length of Time to Complete the Program: MA: two years; PhD: not available

The University of Tennessee at Chattanooga

Address: 615 McCallie Avenue
Chattanooga, TN 37403
Phone: (423) 425-4111
Website: http://www.utc.edu/

Department: Criminal Justice and Legal Studies
100 Davenport, Department 3203
615 McCallie Avenue
Chattanooga, TN 37403
Phone: (423) 425-4135
Website: http://www.utc.edu/criminal-justice/

Type of Program: MS in Criminal Justice

Application Deadline: Not available

Requirements:
- Hold a baccalaureate degree from a regionally accredited college or university.
- Have a minimum GPA of 2.7 (based on a 4.0 scale) on all undergraduate work or 3.0 in the senior year.
- Be approved by the Criminal Justice Department

Information Required for Application:
- A supplemental admissions form;
- Payment of the $30 nonrefundable application fee ($35 for international students);
- An official transcript from each college or university previously attended (sent directly from the institution to the Graduate School office);
- An official report of the applicant's score on the Miller Analogies Test (MAT) or the Graduate Record Exam (GRE) that is not more than five years old. Applicants who took the MAT may also be required to submit a writing proficiency essay prescribed test. for admission; and
- Two letters of recommendation.

Admission Date: Not available

In-state and Out-of-state Tuition Costs: Not available

Availability of Internships and Scholarships: Scholarship, internships, and graduate assistantships

Orientation and Emphasis of Department/Program (Program Description): The MS in criminal justice prepares graduates for leadership in management positions in criminal justice and social service agencies or for entry into doctoral study. The program places emphasis on the development of skills in critical thinking, communication, and applied research.

Number of Faculty: 11

Accreditation: Not available

Average Length of Time to Complete the Program: Not available

The University of Texas at Arlington

Address: 701 West Nedderman Drive
Arlington, TX 76019
Phone: (817) 272-2011
Website: http://www.uta.edu/

Department: Department of Criminology and Criminal Justice
Box 19595
Arlington, TX 76019-0595
Phone: (817) 272-3318
Website: http://www.uta.edu/criminology/

Type of Program: MA in Criminology and Criminal Justice

Application Deadline: October 15, April 1, June 15

Requirements:
- Must have successfully completed a baccalaureate degree in criminology/criminal justice or related discipline.
- A minimum GPA of 3.0 in the last sixty hours of undergraduate work as calculated by the Graduate School.
- A minimum of 149 on both verbal and quantitative subtests of the GRE (minimum of 440 on both verbal and quantitative subsets under old scoring system). The GRE is not required of an applicant who satisfies all of the following requirements:
  - Has three or more years of professional experience with increasing responsibility in a criminal justice (or closely related) occupation and provides a detailed work history documenting this experience;
  - Submits an acceptable sample of professional writing authored solely by the applicant. This will be evaluated to assess writing and analytical skills; and
  - Successfully completes a personal interview with the graduate advisor, where credentials, goals and objectives of graduate studies, and views related to the study and profession of criminology/criminal justice will be discussed.
- Must submit three letters of recommendation addressing the applicant's potential for success in the graduate program from persons knowledgeable of the applicant's abilities.

Information Required for Application: Stated above.

Admission Date: Fall, Spring, Summer

In-state and Out-of-state Tuition Costs: $1300 per credit hour

Availability of Internships and Scholarships: Fellowships, scholarships

Orientation and Emphasis of Department/Program (Program Description): The CRCJ on-campus graduate program—offered exclusively at UT Arlington—is a comprehensive examination of the criminal justice system with a foundation in research and statistics. The program is designed for pre-professional students, criminal justice professionals, and students who wish to pursue further relevant post-graduate studies. The thirty-six-hour program offers both thesis and non-thesis options. With the approval of the graduate advisor, students may use their elective hours to concentrate on a particular field of study.

Number of Faculty: 13

Accreditation: Commission on Colleges of the Southern Association of Colleges and Schools

Average Length of Time to Complete the Program: Not available

The University of Texas at Dallas

Address: 800 West Campbell Road
Richardson, TX 75080
Phone: (972) 883-2111
Website: http://www.utdallas.edu/

Department: Department of Criminology
Contact: John Worrall, Program Head and Graduate Director
E-mail: worrall@utdallas.edu
Phone: (972) 883-4893
Website: http://www.utdallas.edu/epps/criminology/

Type of Program: MS in Criminology; MS in Criminology (online);
PhD in Criminology

Application Deadline: MS: February 1; PhD: February 15 (with full
documentation) for funding consideration, otherwise July 1

Requirements:
- A GRE combined score of 300 is advisable based on our experi-
  ence with student success in the program;
- Three letters of recommendation; and
- An admissions essay:
  - Include any current or long-range interests in research,
    teaching or other professional objectives.
  - Please describe any publications or other evidence of schol-
    arly endeavor you have achieved.
  - List academic and professional organizations in which you
    are active and any fellowships, scholarships, or other hon-
    ors you have received.

Information Required for Application: Stated above.

Admission Date: Fall

In-state and Out-of-state Tuition Costs: In-state: $1,343 per credit
hour; out-of-state: $1,918 per credit hour

Availability of Internships and Scholarships: Not available

**Orientation and Emphasis of Department/Program (Program
Description):** The criminology master's degree program provides
a multidisciplinary mix of theoretical and applied research, and
delivers a high-quality education on the etiology, control, and
variation of crime across space and time. The program also serves
local, regional and national communities through professional
development programs, public policy analysis and evaluation
research, and program and policy design. It also offers a forum for
new ideas and approaches to the study of crime. Graduates pursue

analytic, managerial, and research positions in various sectors of the criminal justice system.

The doctoral program in criminology is an interdisciplinary, research-oriented program that emphasizes theories of criminal behavior, research methodologies in criminology, and society's response to crime. Doctoral students graduate prepared for an academic, analytical, or administrative appointment as a university professor or manager of research and development within a criminal justice organization, at a policy institution, or in the private sector.

Number of Faculty: 14

Accreditation: The Southern Association of Colleges and Schools

Average Length of Time to Complete the Program: Not available

The University of Texas at San Antonio

Address: 1 UTSA Circle
San Antonio, TX 78249
Phone: (210) 458-4011
Website: https://www.utsa.edu/

Department: Department of Criminal Justice
501 West Cesar E. Chavez Boulevard
San Antonio, TX 78207
Phone: (210) 458-2535
Website: http://copp.utsa.edu/criminal-justice/home/

Type of Program: MS in Justice Policy

Application Deadline: Not available

Requirements: To qualify for unconditional admission, applicants must satisfy university-wide graduate admission requirements and submit all transcripts and Graduate Record Examination (GRE) general test scores, as well as two letters of recommendation and a personal statement. An applicant admitted unconditionally as a degree-seeking student must possess a baccalaureate degree from an accredited university or equivalent training at a foreign institution; have a grade point average of 3.0 or better in the last sixty semester credit hours of undergraduate work as well as all previous graduate work; have eighteen hours in criminal justice, criminology, or a closely-related discipline, or professional experience in the justice system; be in good standing at the last institution attended; have a valid GRE test score and the recommendation of the justice policy graduate admissions committee. Students who do not meet these criteria may be admitted conditionally or on probation as degree-seeking depending on the nature of the deficiency. Admission as a special student may be considered by the admissions committee upon request of the applicant.

Information Required for Application: Not available

Admission Date: Not available

In-state and Out-of-state Tuition Costs: $7,152 (for 2013-2014)

Availability of Internships and Scholarships: Scholarships and internships

Orientation and Emphasis of Department/Program (Program Description): The master of science (MS) degree in justice policy is designed to provide students with competency in policy planning, evaluation, and criminal justice agency management, and preparation for continued graduate study in criminal justice and criminology. The program assists students to develop and apply research expertise toward the resolution of contemporary justice practice and policy issues.

Number of Faculty: 14

Accreditation: Commission on Colleges of the Southern Association of Colleges and Schools

Average Length of Time to Complete the Program: Not available

The University of Texas at Tyler

Address: 3900 University Boulevard
Tyler, TX 75799
Phone: (903) 566-7000
Website: https://www.uttyler.edu/

Department: Criminal Justice Division
3900 University Boulevard
Tyler, TX 75799
Phone: (903) 566-7426
Website: http://www.uttyler.edu/criminaljustice/

Type of Program: MS in Criminal Justice

Application Deadline: May 1, November 1

Requirements: Not available

Information Required for Application: GRE scores (no letters of recommendation are necessary, and no essay is required)

Admission Date: Fall, Spring

In-state and Out-of-state Tuition Costs: In-state: $713 per credit hour; out-of-state: $1,064 per credit hour

Availability of Internships and Scholarships: Scholarships

Orientation and Emphasis of Department/Program (Program Description): The UT Tyler criminal justice MA degree program is designed to meet the needs of several types of students, including existing and prospective criminal justice professionals seeking to advance their knowledge and credentials. The program also provides excellent preparation for doctoral-level work.

Number of Faculty: Not available

Accreditation: Southern Association of Colleges and Schools Commission on Colleges

Average Length of Time to Complete the Program: Two years

The University of Texas of the Permian Basin

Address: 4901 East University Boulevard
Odessa, TX 79762
Phone: (432) 552-2020
Website: http://www.utpb.edu/

Department: College of Arts and Sciences
The University of Texas of the Permian Basin
4901 East University Boulevard
Odessa, TX 79762
Phone: (432) 552-2220
Website: http://cas.utpb.edu/

Type of Program: Not available

Application Deadline: Not available

Requirements: Not available

Information Required for Application: Not available

Admission Date: Not available

In-state and Out-of-state Tuition Costs: In-state: $580 per credit; out-of-state: $1,440.75 per credit

Availability of Internships and Scholarships: Not available

Orientation and Emphasis of Department/Program (Program Description): Not available

Number of Faculty: 5

Accreditation: Commission on Colleges of the Southern Association of Colleges and Schools

Average Length of Time to Complete the Program: Not available

The University of Texas–Pan American

Address: 1201 West University Drive
Edinburg, TX 78539
Phone: (866) 441-8872
Website: http://www.utpa.edu/

Department: Criminal Justice Department
Phone: (956) 665-3566
Website: http://portal.utpa.edu/utpa_main/daa_home/csbs_home/cj_home

Type of Program: MS in Criminal Justice

Application Deadline: August 1, December 1, May 1, June 1

Requirements: Stated below

Information Required for Application:
- Online application;
- Application fee of $50;
- Official transcripts;
- Three letters of recommendation;
- Personal statement; and
- Previous education:
  - Undergraduate coursework in research methods and criminological theory
  - Students who meet the graduate school admissions without a 3.0 GPA must have a GPA of 2.75 or higher on a 4.0 scale for the last sixty semester hours of undergraduate courses completed.

Admission Date: Fall, Spring, Summer I, Summer II

In-state and Out-of-state Tuition Costs: In-state: $5,488; out-of-state: $12,568 (for 2013–2014)

Availability of Internships and Scholarships: Financial aid, scholarships, assistantships

Orientation and Emphasis of Department/Program (Program Description): The master of science in criminal justice is an intensive graduate-level program that is designed for students who want to pursue further studies beyond the bachelor's degree and to prepare candidates for the doctoral degree.

Number of Faculty: 8

Accreditation: Southern Association of Colleges and Schools Commission on Colleges

Average Length of Time to Complete the Program: Not available

University of West Florida

Address: 11000 University Parkway
Pensacola, FL 32514
Phone: (850) 474-2000
Website: http://www.uwf.edu/

Department: Department of Criminal Justice
Building 85, Room 160
Phone: (850) 474-2336
Website: http://www.uwf.edu/cops/departments/criminal-justice/

Type of Program: MS in Criminal Justice

Application Deadline: June 1, October 1, March 1

Requirements:
- Submission of graduate application and processing fee; and
- Submission of official transcripts.

Information Required for Application:
- Submission of one of the following graduate admission test scores: GRE or MAT;
- Undergraduate cumulative GPA;
- Academic preparation as demonstrated by quality and relevance of undergraduate degree major;
- Submission of personal statement written by the applicant, which outlines future career goals in criminal justice and how the degree will help him/her to achieve the goals. Additional contents of the statement should include the applicant's academic preparation, work-history, volunteer experience, activities, and honors or awards received; and
- Submission of three letters of recommendation from individuals familiar with the applicant's ability to succeed in a graduate program. At least two of the letters should be from former professors.

Admission Date: Fall, Spring, Summer

In-state and Out-of-state Tuition Costs: In-state: $372.91 per credit hour; out-of-state: $1,032.55 per credit hour; Alabama residents: $477.91 per credit hour

Availability of Internships and Scholarships: Internships and graduate assistantships

Orientation and Emphasis of Department/Program (Program Description): The University of West Florida offers a program of study leading to the master of science in criminal justice. This program, taught by a dynamic faculty committed to high-quality graduate-level education, is designed to provide students with the knowledge and skills in theory, administration, research, and data analysis necessary for careers in the practice and administration of criminal justice, research, education, and policy analysis, or for pursuing doctoral-level studies. The master of science in criminal justice is designed to fit the demands of contemporary students' diverse schedules. Classes are offered evenings, some weekends, and in online and blended delivery formats. Full-time students can complete the degree in four semesters (one-and-a-half years). Students can also complete the program entirely on line over an extended period of time.

Number of Faculty: 12

Accreditation: Southern Association of Colleges and Schools Commission on Colleges

Average Length of Time to Complete the Program: One-and-a-half years

University of West Georgia

Address: 1601 Maple Street
Carrollton, GA 30118
Phone: (678) 839-5000
Website: http://www.westga.edu/

Department: Department of Criminology
Pafford Building
Phone: (678) 839-5199
Website: http://criminology.westga.edu/

Type of Program: MA in Criminology

Application Deadline: July 31, November 30, May 15

Requirements: For admission to the program, a student is expected to have a bachelor's degree in criminology, criminal justice, or another social or behavioral science. However, other complimentary degrees may be considered. Students can be admitted without the expected degree with the stipulation that selected undergraduate- and/or graduate-level courses must be completed. Applicants for graduate study in criminology must meet the College of Social Science's requirements and:
- Submit official Graduate Record Examination (GRE) scores.
- Obtain three strong letters of recommendation.
- Submit a 750-word intellectual autobiography including reasons for seeking the degree.
- Have a minimum overall 2.50 GPA.

Information Required for Application: Not available

Admission Date: Fall, Spring, Summer

In-state and Out-of-state Tuition Costs: In-state: $1,728 for nine credit hours; out-of-state: $6,705 for nine credit hours

Availability of Internships and Scholarships: Graduate research assistantships

Orientation and Emphasis of Department/Program (Program Description): The MA in criminology program at UWG is designed to provide the background necessary for criminal justice practice and/or to prepare students for doctoral study and work in academic settings. It is offered with two tracks. The criminal justice administration track addresses issues of crime and criminal justice within a framework that emphasizes theory and research and their implications for criminal justice policy and practice. The crime and social justice track trains students in understanding and applying theory and research in academic settings. Both curricula are grounded in the social, behavioral, and natural sciences. Students admitted to the program choose a plan of study that best matches their practical and academic interests.

Number of Faculty: 16

Accreditation: Commission on Colleges of the Southern Association of Colleges and Schools

Average Length of Time to Complete the Program: Not available

University of Wisconsin–Milwaukee

Address: University of Wisconsin–Milwaukee
P.O. Box 413
Milwaukee, WI 53201
Phone: (414) 229-1122
Website: http://www4.uwm.edu/

Department: Criminal Justice Department
2400 East Hartford Avenue
Enderis Hall
Milwaukee, WI 53211
Phone: (414) 229-4851
Website: http://www4.uwm.edu/hbssw/criminal_justice/

Type of Program: MS in Criminal Justice

Application Deadline: July 1, November 1, April 1

Requirements:
- Undergraduate degree from an accredited university in criminal justice, a related social science, or other relevant educational experience;
- Undergraduate cumulative grade point average of 3.00, to be admitted in good standing (students with less than a 3.00 GPA may be admitted on probationary status);
- Satisfactory scores on the verbal quantitative sections of the Graduate Record Examination or the Miller Analogies Test;
- Three letters of recommendation from persons who are familiar with the applicant's academic record; and
- Satisfactory completion of a research methods course and a statistics course. Lacking these, an applicant may be admitted on the condition that these courses will be taken prior to receiving the MS degree. Credits for such courses will not count toward the degree.

Information Required for Application: Stated above

Admission Date: Fall, Spring, Summer

In-state and Out-of-state Tuition Costs: In-state with eight or more credits both semesters: $11,596: out-of-state with eight or more credits both semesters: $24,062

Availability of Internships and Scholarships: Teaching assistantships and project assistantships; scholarships through the Helen Bader School of Social Welfare

Orientation and Emphasis of Department/Program (Program Description): This program prepares students for leadership positions in the field of criminal justice. It provides a strong foundation for students who anticipate advanced study at the doctoral level. The curriculum offers criminal justice professionals a broad foundation for understanding criminal justice policy. Legal, organizational, political, and behavioral frameworks are used to analyze the operation of the U.S. criminal justice system. Students are introduced to advanced knowledge on the nature and causes of crime, the justification and means of social control, the administration of the justice system, and the evaluation of criminal justice programs.

Number of Faculty: 9

Accreditation: Higher Learning Commission: A Commission of the North Central Association

Average Length of Time to Complete the Program: Not available

University of Wisconsin–Platteville

Address: 1 University Plaza
Platteville, WI 53818
Phone: (608) 342-1491
Website: http://www3.uwplatt.edu/

Department: Department of Criminal Justice
1 University Plaza
Platteville, WI 53818
E-mail: banachoc@uwplatt.edu
Phone: (608) 342-1622
Website: http://www.uwplatt.edu/cj/

Type of Program: MS in Criminal Justice (online)

Application Deadline: December 1, April 15, July 15

Requirements:
- Have earned a bachelor's degree from a regionally or nationally accredited institution that meets UW-System standards and is recognized by the Council for Higher Education Accreditation (CHEA). International degrees are evaluated on an individual basis.
- Have a cumulative undergraduate grade point average (GPA) of 2.75 or above, or 2.90 for the last sixty credits taken at your degree-granting institution. If you do not qualify for admission in full standing, you may be admitted on a trial enrollment if recommended by the admitting department and approved by the dean of the School of Graduate Studies.
- Provide a copy of your Test of English as a Foreign Language (TOEFL) scoring report if English is not your native language. Program admission requires a minimum score of 500 for the paper-based exam, 173 for the computer-based exam, or 61 for the Internet-based exam. If you prefer, you may also submit scores from the International English Language Testing System (IELTS). You must have a band-level score of 6 or higher.

Information Required for Application:
- Complete the online University of Wisconsin System application for graduate admission.
- Pay the $56 application fee at the secure website when you apply online, or you may mail a check payable to University of Wisconsin–Platteville.
- Request an official transcript be sent directly from the undergraduate degree-granting institution to the Distance Learning Center using the transcript request form. We cannot accept or evaluate unofficial transcripts.Official transcripts must be sent

directly from the institution(s) where the coursework was completed. Your application is not complete until we receive your transcript(s). All transcripts become the property of the University of Wisconsin–Platteville.

- Provide official transcripts for any previously earned graduate credits to be considered for transfer.
- Applicants may be contacted on an individual basis for additional information to support their admission.

In addition, applicants must submit the following materials to the criminal justice program director:

- A detailed résumé;
- Two letters of support from professional sources who can comment on the applicant's ability to be successful in graduate coursework;
- A personal statement of purpose and goals;
- A portfolio containing evidence of the applicant's writing skills consisting of research papers or projects undertaken as part of undergraduate or graduate coursework, or as part of employment.

Admission Date: Fall, Spring, Summer

In-state and Out-of-state Tuition Costs: $630 per credit, regardless of residency

Availability of Internships and Scholarships: Not available

Orientation and Emphasis of Department/Program (Program Description): The online master of science in criminal justice programprovides you with a comprehensive degree designed for criminal justice and social service professionals who need additional knowledge and skills to advance to a higher-level position, have a desire to teach at a community college or university, and/or seek an advanced degree as a prerequisite for entry into the criminal justice field.

Number of Faculty: 13

Accreditation: Higher Learning Commission

Average Length of Time to Complete the Program: Not available (may take up to seven years to complete)

Valdosta State University

Address: 1500 North Patterson Street
Valdosta, GA 31698
Phone: (229) 333-5800
Website: http://www.valdosta.edu/

Department: Department of Sociology, Anthropology, and Criminal Justice
Address: University Center
1500 North Patterson Street
Valdosta, GA 31698
Phone: (229) 333-5943
Website: http://www.valdosta.edu/colleges/arts-sciences/sacj/

Type of Program: MS in Criminal Justice

Application Deadline: July 15, November 15, and April 15

Requirements:
- A bachelor's degree from a regionally- accredited institution;
- Minimum cumulative undergraduate GPA of 2.75 on 4.0 scale calculated on all attempted coursework;
- Minimum GRE requirements of 146 verbal and 140 quantitative with a 3.5 analytical score (for GRE's taken before October 2002, a minimum score of 800 on any two combined sections: verbal plus quantitative, or verbal plus analytical); and
- Miller Analogies Test requirement of 387.

Information Required for Application:
- Application fee of $35
- Two recommendation letters
- Two-page essay

Admission Date: Fall, Spring, Summer

In-state and Out-of-state Tuition Costs: In-state: $230 per credit hour; out-of-state: $828 per credit hour

Availability of Internships and Scholarships: Scholarships

Orientation and Emphasis of Department/Program (Program Description): The master's degree in criminal justice is focused on integrating criminal justice theory with criminal justice practice. Students in this program will:
- Develop an understanding of major criminological theories, their strengths and weaknesses, their role in explaining crime and delinquency, and their role in informing public policy;
- Develop a familiarity with the structure and function of systems of criminal justice in the United States and in other countries;

- Develop the use and application of scientific research methods to the study of crime as well as to solving crimes; and
- Integrate criminal justice theory and research findings with criminal justice practice, and develop an understanding of the development of contemporary criminal justice issue in modern societies and how such issues may be informed by systematic research and analysis.

Number of Faculty: 10

Accreditation: Southern Association of Colleges and Schools Commission on Colleges

Average Length of Time to Complete the Program: Not available

Virginia Commonwealth University

Address: 821 West Franklin Street
Richmond, VA 23284
Phone: (804) 828-0100
Website: http://www.vcu.edu/

Department: School of Government and Public Affairs
923 West Franklin Street
P.O. Box 842028
Richmond, VA 23284
Phone: (804) 828-2292
Website: http://www.wilder.vcu.edu/

Type of Program: MS in Criminal Justice

Application Deadline: April 1 (March 1 for funding consideration), October 1

Requirements:
- An undergraduate GPA that exceeds 2.7 overall;
- A satisfactory score on the GRE; and
- Previous evidence of ability to perform graduate-level work (where applicable).

Information Required for Application: Above

Admission Date: Fall, Spring

In-state and Out-of-state Tuition Costs: In-state: $4,955.50 for nine to fifteen credits: out-of-state: $10,189 for nine to fifteen credits

Availability of Internships and Scholarships: Not available

Orientation and Emphasis of Department/Program (Program Description): The graduate program in criminal justice is designed to provide advanced educational preparation for students and criminal justice professionals pursuing careers in the field of criminal justice. Such preparation includes understanding the range of theory, research, and policy in criminal justice. The curriculum is directed especially toward assisting students in developing the advanced knowledge, skills, and abilities required by criminal justice professionals.

Number of Faculty: 12

Accreditation: Commission on Colleges of the Southern Association of Colleges and Schools

Average Length of Time to Complete the Program: Not available

Walden University

Address: 100 Washington Avenue South
Suite 900
Minneapolis, MN 55401
Phone: (866) 492-5336
Website: http://www.waldenu.edu/

Department: Criminal Justice and Emergency Management
Website: http://www.waldenu.edu/programs/study-area/
criminal-justice/

Type of Program: MS in Criminal Justice, MS in Criminal
Justice Leadership and Executive Management

Application Deadline: Not available

Requirements: A bachelor's degree or higher

Information Required for Application: Not available

Admission Date: Not available

In-state and Out-of-state Tuition Costs: $470 per credit hour

Availability of Internships and Scholarships: Not available

**Orientation and Emphasis of Department/Program (Program
Description):**
MS in Criminal Justice: Modern criminal justice professionals must be equally savvy to stay at the forefront with the ever-
changing landscape of domestic and international crime. In
Walden's master of science in criminal justice program, you will
study a unique blend of criminal behavior theory along with
technology, homeland security, and management skills applicable to the challenges facing the law enforcement community. You
will evaluate the root causes of crime and its impact on criminal
justice practices and procedures, and analyze how law enforcement, courts, and corrections function and interact at the local,
state, and federal level.
MS in Criminal Justice Leadership and Executive Management:
Walden's master of science in criminal justice leadership and
executive management will help law enforcement professionals prepare for executive management roles in criminal justice
or to transition into a career in education or as a consultant.
In this program, you will study management philosophies as
well as the budgeting and communication skills that criminal
justice professionals require in order to create and influence
policy makers.

Number of Faculty: Not available

Accreditation: The Higher Learning Commission

Average Length of Time to Complete the Program: Not available

Washburn University

Address: 1700 Southwest College Avenue
Topeka, KS 66621
Phone: (785) 670-1010
Website: http://www.washburn.edu/

Department: Criminal Justice and Legal Studies Department
Benton Hall, Room 201 B
1700 Southwest College Avenue
Topeka, KS 66621
Phone: (785) 670-2057
Website: http://www.washburn.edu/academics/college-schools/
applied-studies/departments/criminal-justice-legal-studies/

Type of Program: Master of Criminal Justice (MCJ)

Application Deadline: April 1, November 1

Requirements:
- Applicants must complete and submit an application for formal admission to Washburn University. In addition, the application for admission to the MCJ program must be completed and submitted to the Criminal Justice Office.
- Applicants must have all official transcripts of all undergraduate and graduate course work sent directly to the Washburn Admissions Office from the institution(s) where the credit was earned, and the applicant must send copies of the official transcripts to the master of criminal justice program coordinator in the Department of Criminal Justice Office. Note: If all the applicant's undergraduate course work was completed at Washburn, he or she is not required to submit a transcript.
- Applicants must have three persons—who are in position to attest to the applicant's academic abilities and potential for graduate study—complete the three reference forms attached to the program application. References from former professors are preferred, but must not be from the MCJ coordinator, criminal justice chairperson, or members of the admissions committee.
- Applicants must submit a personal biographical statement explaining (a) personal philosophy of the criminal justice system and (b) reasons for entering the program.
- If applicable, applicant's scores from the GRE must be attached to the application or sent to the graduate program coordinator.

- A $35 nonrefundable application fee is required at the time of application and should accompany the completed application for admission form. The check should be made out to Washburn University with the notation at the bottom of the check of "MCJ Application Fee."
- Obtain the recommendation of the criminal justice graduate admissions and retention committee and the graduate program coordinator.

Information Required for Application: Stated Above

Admission Date: Fall, Spring

In-state and Out-of-state Tuition Costs: In-state: $325 per credit hour; out-of-state: $662 per credit hour

Availability of Internships and Scholarships: Not available

Orientation and Emphasis of Department/Program (Program Description): The master of criminal justice (MCJ) degree program at Washburn University was established in the Fall semester of 1996 and is accredited by the North Central Association of Colleges and Schools. This graduate degree program is designed to meet the needs of criminal justice professionals and pre-professionals who desire to enhance their knowledge, skills, and talents in the field of criminal justice. For the professional currently employed in the field, advanced knowledge and skills acquired in the program can enhance opportunities for career advancement. The degree program can prepare the pre-professional graduate for a variety of criminal justice positions. The MCJ degree program can also prepare students for teaching positions in community colleges and training academies, and for admission to doctoral programs in criminal justice related fields. Course work emphasizes the application of theory and research to contemporary practices in law enforcement, courts, and corrections administration. Washburn University is located in the state capital of Kansas, within minutes of several state, federal, and local criminal justice agencies. Course scheduling and delivery methods are flexible and designed to meet the scheduling needs of in-service and pre-service students. During the regular Fall and Spring semesters, courses are offered during daytime and evening hours, online, and on weekends. Some courses are offered during the Summer semesters.

Number of Faculty: 42

Accreditation: North Central Association of Colleges and Schools

Average Length of Time to Complete the Program: Not available

Washington State University

Address: Pullman, WA 99164
Phone: (509) 335-3564
Website: http://www.wsu.edu/

Department: Department of Criminal Justice and Criminology
P.O. Box 644872
Washington State University
Pullman WA 99164-4872
Phone: (509) 335-8611
Website: http://libarts.wsu.edu/crimj/

Type of Program: MA in Criminal Justice; PhD in Criminal Justice

Application Deadline: MA: January 10, July 1; PhD: the program does not allow Spring admission, so applicants must submit their materials by February 1 to be considered for admission the following Fall.

Requirements:
- A bachelor of arts or bachelor of science degree or equivalent;
- An undergraduate grade point average of at least 3.0 from the last sixty semester hours (ninety quarter hours) or a graduate GPA of at least 3.30 for twelve semester credit hours at a recognized graduate school;
- Satisfactory scores on the Graduate Record Examination (GRE); and
- For students entering from a foreign university, evidence of English proficiency (i.e., Test of English as a Foreign Language) and financial resources.

Information Required for Application:
- A complete application, including the $75 application fee;
- A letter of intent and introduction, outlining areas of interest in criminal justice, career objectives, and any academic or professional experiences that recommend you as an applicant;
- Three original letters of recommendation from persons qualified to speak to your academic qualifications and potential. References will be contacted automatically through the online application system and asked to submit a recommendation form electronically. These letters are used to help assess the quality of your academic and work experiences;
- Official copies of transcripts (including all colleges or universities from which you have earned or expect to earn a degree, and all colleges or universities at which you have taken graduate level course work; transcripts for coursework taken at

Washington State University are not required; official transcripts are those mailed directly from the registrar of the institutions you attended);

- An official copy of your GRE scores sent to our department (scores must be less than five years old); and
- Official TOEFL score.

Admission Date: Fall, Spring

In-state and Out-of-state Tuition Costs: Not available

Availability of Internships and Scholarships: Teaching assistantships

Orientation and Emphasis of Department/Program (Program Description): Both the MA and PhD are designed to offer students a complete overview of the criminal justice system, criminological theory, and methods of analysis. The department is large enough to offer the range of specializations necessary for a flexible graduate program, yet small enough to retain a sense of community among students and faculty.

Number of Faculty: 15

Accreditation: Northwest Commission on Colleges and Universities

Average Length of Time to Complete the Program: Not available

Wayne State University

Address: 42 West Warren Avenue
Detroit, MI 48202
Phone: (313) 577-2424
Website: http://www.wayne.edu/

Department: Department of Criminal Justice
3291 Faculty/Administration Building
656 West Kirby
Detroit, MI 48202
Phone: (313) 577-2705
Website: http://clasweb.clas.wayne.edu/CRJ/

Type of Program: MS in Criminal Justice

Application Deadline: June 1, October 1, February 1

Requirements:
- Applicants must hold a baccalaureate degree from an accredited U.S. institution or a degree equivalent to a four-year U.S. baccalaureate degree from a college or university of government-recognized standing.
- For regular admission consideration, master's degree applicants should have a minimum undergraduate grade point average of 2.75 (C+) or its equivalent in upper division coursework, and doctoral applicants should have a minimum of 3.0 (B).

Information Required for Application:
- No application fee
- Official transcripts

Admission Date: Fall, Spring, Summer

In-state and Out-of-state Tuition Costs: In-state: $554.15 per credit; out-of-state:$1,200.35 per credit

Availability of Internships and Scholarships: Internships, Scholarships

Orientation and Emphasis of Department/Program (Program Description): The Department of Criminal Justice at Wayne State University offers a comprehensive and flexible program leading to the degree of master of science in criminal justice. The Department of Criminal Justice curriculum provides an integrated appreciation of the entire criminal justice system and its relationship to crime in contemporary society.

Number of Faculty: 12

Accreditation: Higher Learning Commission of the North Central Association of Colleges and Schools

Average Length of Time to Complete the Program: Not available

West Chester University of Pennsylvania

Address: 700 South High Street
West Chester, PA 19382
Phone: (610) 436-1000
Website: http://www.wcupa.edu/

Department: Criminal Justice Department
200A Ruby Jones Hall
West Chester University
West Chester, PA 19383
Phone: (610) 436-2647
Website: http://www.wcupa.edu/_ACADEMICS/sch_sba/
criminaljustice/

Type of Program: MS in Criminal Justice

Application Deadline: Not available

Requirements: Not available

Information Required for Application: Not available

Admission Date: Not available

In-state and Out-of-state Tuition Costs: In-state: $548.24 per credit; out-of-state: $779.24 per credit

Availability of Internships and Scholarships: Graduate assistantships

Orientation and Emphasis of Department/Program (Program Description): The master of science in criminal justice offers a multidisciplinary curriculum to give students the sophisticated working knowledge of the major systems within the field. Students will take challenging and rigorous courses rooted in history, law, philosophy, research, psychology, management, and political science that involve critical analysis of complex issues.

Number of Faculty: 20

Accreditation: Middle States Commission on Higher Education

Average Length of Time to Complete the Program: Not available

Western Connecticut State University

Address: 181 White Street
Danbury, CT 06810
Phone: (877) 837-9278
Website: http://www.wcsu.edu/

Department: Justice and Law Administration
Website: https://www.wcsu.edu/asb/jla/

Type of Program: MS in Justice Administration

Application Deadline: Not available

Requirements: Stated below

Information Required for Application:
- Graduate admission application form and fee;
- Official transcripts for all undergraduate and graduate courses and degrees;
- An entrance examination score from one of the following:
  - Miller Analogies Test (MAT);
  - Graduate Record Examination (GRE);
  - Law School Admission Test (LSAT); or
  - Graduate Management Admission Test (GMAT).
- Two letters of recommendation;
- Current résumé or curriculum vitae; and
- Interview with program coordinator.

Admission Date: Not available

In-state and Out-of-state Tuition Costs: In-state: $5,692 per semester; out-of-state: $11,419 per semester

Availability of Internships and Scholarships: Scholarships

Orientation and Emphasis of Department/Program (Program Description): The master of science (MS) in justice administration program at WestConn is designed to meet the needs of both practicing justice professionals and other graduate students preparing to enter this field. Most students attend this program on a part-time basis, although some pursue this degree full-time. Opportunities exist for networking with and learning from the experiences of other students. Current students and graduates of this program include: correctional professionals at the federal and state levels; other offender rehabilitation specialists; law enforcement officers at all levels (from the rank of patrol officer through chief, in both federal and local agencies); other public safety and security professionals; counselors; and computer security specialists.

Number of Faculty: 8

Accreditation: New England Association of Schools and Colleges

Average Length of Time to Complete the Program: Not available

Western Illinois University

Address: 1 University Circle
Macomb, IL 61455
Phone: (309) 298-1414
Website: http://www.wiu.edu/

Department: School of Law Enforcement and Justice Administration
Stipes Hall 403
1 University Circle
Macomb, IL 61455
Website: http://www.wiu.edu/coehs/leja/

Type of Program: MA in Law Enforcement and Justice Administration

Application Deadline: Not available

Requirements: Applicants for admission to the School of Graduate Studies must hold a bachelor's degree from an institution that is accredited by the appropriate U.S. Department of Education regional institutional accrediting agency. Applicants usually apply for admission to a degree program simultaneously with admission to the School of Graduate Studies. Once all admission materials are received, a GPA calculation is completed and application materials are forwarded to the program of interest for consideration.

Information Required for Application: Not specified

Admission Date: Not available

In-state and Out-of-state Tuition Costs: In-state and residents of IA, IN, MO, WI: $308.96 per credit hour; out-of-state: $617.92 per credit hour

Availability of Internships and Scholarships: Not available

Orientation and Emphasis of Department/Program (Program Description): Established in 1976, the School of Law Enforcement and Justice Administration offers a master of arts in law enforcement and justice administration. The law enforcement and justice administration (LEJA) graduate program is internationally known for academic excellence. It provides students with a rich blend of theoretical, administrative, and practical knowledge as well as research skills. Those who have earned the degree occupy positions of responsibility across the United States and in several foreign countries. The program is designed to provide a balanced, interdisciplinary course of study for those currently employed in criminal justice and related fields, as well as for those wishing to pursue careers in these fields of academia. Courses provide students with current information in the areas of administrative/ organizational behavior, law, research and quantitative skills, and specialized areas such as policing, corrections, security, and multiculturalism/diversity in criminal justice.

Number of Faculty: 40

Accreditation: Higher Learning Commission: North Central Association

Average Length of Time to Complete the Program: Not available

Western Oregon University

Address: 345 North Monmouth Avenue
Monmouth, OR 97361
Phone: (503) 838-8000
Website: https://www.wou.edu/

Department: Criminal Justice Department
Website: http://www.wou.edu/provost/extprogram/cj_online/

Type of Program: MA in Criminal Justice

Application Deadline: Year round

Requirements:
- If the applicant's GPA for the last ninety quarter hours (sixty semester hours) is less than 3.0, passing test scores from the Miller Analogies Test (MAT) or Graduate Record Exam (GRE) are required. Minimum required scores are 395 for the MAT and an average of 450 on the verbal and quantitative sections and 3.5 on the analytical writing section of the GRE.
- Hold an undergraduate degree, preferably with a concentration of study in the social or behavioral sciences. If this requirement is not met, applicant must provide evidence that he or she is currently a supervisor in a criminal justice agency or has successfully completed two years of full-time employment in a criminal justice agency, and submit a letter of recommendation from his or her unit supervisor indicating that the applicant has the potential for advancement to a supervisory or administrative position. Applicants who do not hold an undergraduate degree in a related field may be expected to complete additional hours in addition to the forty-five required hours.
- Complete the criminal justice graduate program application.
- Submit a biographical letter explaining why you are seeking a graduate degree and how it meets your professional or academic goals.
- Submit a current résumé.
- Send transcripts from all college/universities attended (unofficial transcripts are acceptable).

Information Required for Application:
- Completed WOU application for graduate admission form. Submit this form to the Graduate Office, Administration Building, Office 202. Students must be admitted to the WOU Graduate School before being considered for admission to the program. Submit all WOU Graduate School application materials to the Graduate Office at least one week prior to the program admission deadline.

- Sealed official transcripts from the university that granted your bachelor's degree and from all other institutions of higher education where you completed coursework. A GPA of 3.0 in the last ninety quarter hours (sixty semester hours) of undergraduate coursework is required. Those with less than a 3.0 GPA can be admitted with MAT or GRE scores (see below for requirement).
- Miller Analogies Test (MAT) or Graduate Record Exam (GRE) score. If the applicant's GPA is 3.0 or higher, the test requirement is waived. If the GPA is less than 3.0, minimum required score for the MAT is 395 or higher. For the GRE, the minimum quantitative score is 147, the minimum verbal score is 148, and a 3.5 or higher is required on the analytical writing section.
- $60 nonrefundable application fee.

Admission Date: Year round

In-state and Out-of-state Tuition Costs: $360 per graduate credit

Availability of Internships and Scholarships: Assistantships

Orientation and Emphasis of Department/Program (Program Description): The graduate program is designed specifically for individuals currently working in the field of criminal justice and its ancillary professions, although well-qualified non-practitioners are welcome. The primary mission of the program is to provide students with an academic foundation for managerial and other advanced professional roles in the field of criminal justice. A student in the CJ program can choose one of two formats for earning their degree: (1) completely online, or (2) as a mix of online and face-to-face coursework. All of the required professional core courses are only offered online. Students can choose to complete their elective courses online or on-campus.

Number of Faculty: 7

Accreditation: Northwest Commission on Colleges and Universities

Average Length of Time to Complete the Program: Not available

Westfield State College

Address: 577 Western Avenue
Westfield, MA 01085
Phone: (413) 572-5300
Website: http://www.westfield.ma.edu/

Department: Department of Criminal Justice
Website: http://www.westfield.ma.edu/prospective-students/
academics/criminal-justice/

Type of Program: MS Criminal Justice

Application Deadline: Not available

Requirements:
In order to be considered for admission to the program, a complete application must be presented for review, including:
- Bachelor's degree with a major or minor in any of the social sciences with a 2.7 GPA or a 3.0 for the last two years of undergraduate studies (class ranking will also be considered);
- Three professional or academic letters of reference;
- An official GRE with a combined score of 950 on two sections or a MAT score of 45 or better (for WSU students with a GPA of 3.3 or higher this requirement is waived); and
- A narrative statement about your professional goals, academic experience, and factors which support your future endeavors.

For the BS/MS option for high-achieving students, students must meet all three criteria listed below:
- Westfield State University students with a GPA of 3.3 entering into their final semester or after completing their undergraduate degree would be considered for the program.
- Students who are entering into their final semester at Westfield State University may be eligible to take two courses from graduate credit, assuming the 120 credits needed to complete their BS will be fulfilled independently of the MS coursework.
- All students will be required to complete the entire graduate application packet, with the exception of the standardized test requirement.

Information Required for Application: Stated above

Admission Date: Not available

In-state and Out-of-state Tuition Costs: $280 per credit

Availability of Internships and Scholarships: Graduate assistantships

Orientation and Emphasis of Department/Program (Program Description): The graduate program in criminal justice focuses on theoretical and applied issues in law enforcement, corrections, administration, and public law. Its goal is to further critical thinking about significant issues in crime and criminal justice. Judges, lawyers, managers, and criminal justice researchers supplement the faculty, bringing many practical considerations to the study of the discipline.

Number of Faculty: 14

Accreditation: New England Association of Schools and Colleges

Average Length of Time to Complete the Program: Not available

West Texas A&M University

Address: 2501 4th Avenue
Canyon, TX 79016
Phone: (806) 651-0000
Website: https://www.wtamu.edu/

Department: Department of Political Science and Criminal Justice
Website: https://www.wtamu.edu/academics/political-science-criminal-justice.aspx

Type of Program: MA in Criminal Justice Studies

Application Deadline: August 1, December 1, May 1

Requirements:
- Undergraduate grade point average (GPA) of 3.00 or higher;
- Official transcripts; and
- Condition admission requirements also accepted.

Information Required for Application: Stated above

Admission Date: Fall, Spring, Summer

In-state and Out-of-state Tuition Costs: In-state: $489.66 for three credit hours; out-of-state: $579.66 for three credit hours

Availability of Internships and Scholarships: Not available

Orientation and Emphasis of Department/Program (Program Description): The criminal justice program provides you the opportunity to make a difference in the criminal justice system. You will learn about ethics, the rights of people accused of a crime, and the justice system in classroom and real-world settings.

Number of Faculty: 9

Accreditation: Southern Association of Colleges and Schools Commission on Colleges

Average Length of Time to Complete the Program: Not available

Wichita State University

Address: 1845 Fairmount Street
Wichita, KS 67260
Phone: (316) 978-3456
Website: http://www.wichita.edu/

Department: Criminal Justice Program
School of Community Affairs
1845 Fairmount
Box 135
Wichita, KS 67260-0135
Phone: (316) 978-7200
Website: http://www.wichita.edu/thisis/home/?u=criminaljustice

Type of Program: MA in Criminal Justice

Application Deadline: July 15, December 1

Requirements: Applicants are evaluated with respect to (1) undergraduate grade point average; a minimum GPA of 3.0 based on the last sixty hours is required for consideration of admission to degree status; (2) amount, type, and scope of undergraduate preparation; and (3) reference letters.

Information Required for Application:
- Three letters of reference from people acquainted with the applicant's background and potential; and
- A brief autobiographical statement describing particular interests, experiences, and goals related to academic and professional work in criminal justice.

Admission Date: Fall, Spring

In-state and Out-of-state Tuition Costs: In-state: $253.05 per credit hour; out-of-state: $637.70

Availability of Internships and Scholarships: Graduate teaching assistantships

Orientation and Emphasis of Department/Program (Program Description): The criminal justice program at Wichita State University is one of the oldest in the United States. Founded by renowned police chief and scholar O.W. Wilson in 1937, only one other active criminal justice department has a longer history. Through the years, the program at Wichita State has evolved from strictly a police science program into a program that encompasses the entire criminal justice system, including criminological theory. Faculty in the program have an international reputation and have conducted research and published books and academic papers that have contributed to our growing understanding of crime, criminals, and the criminal justice system. The interdisciplinary faculty holds degrees in criminology, criminal justice, psychology, sociology, law, and public administration.

Number of Faculty: 10

Accreditation: Higher Learning Commission of the North Central Association of Colleges and Schools

Average Length of Time to Complete the Program: Not available

Widener University

Address: 1 University Place
Chester, PA 19013
Phone: (610) 499-4000
Website: http://www.widener.edu/

Department: Criminal Justice Department
Website: http://www.widener.edu/academics/schools/arts_
sciences/criminal_justice/

Type of Program: MA in Criminal Justice

Application Deadline: July 15, November 15, April 15

Requirements: Not available

Information Required for Application:
- Official transcripts;
- Two letters of recommendation; and
- A personal statement

Admission Date: Fall, Spring, Summer

In-state and Out-of-state Tuition Costs: $684 per credit

Availability of Internships and Scholarships: Graduate assistantships and fellowships

**Orientation and Emphasis of Department/Program (Program
Description):** In our part-time, traditional graduate program in
criminal justice, the areas you will study in obtaining your master's degree (MACJ) include the nature of crime and delinquency,
distinctions between law and criminal justice, organizational
behavior, planning and program development, research methodology, and data analysis.

Number of Faculty: 5

Accreditation: Middle States Association of Colleges and Schools
Accreditation

Average Length of Time to Complete the Program: Not available

Wilmington University

Address: 320 North DuPont Highway
New Castle, DE 19720
Phone: (877) 967-5464
Website: http://www.wilmu.edu/

Department: Department of Criminal Justice
Website: http://www.wilmu.edu/behavioralscience/crimjust.aspx

Type of Program: MS in Administration of Justice

Application Deadline: Not available

Requirements: Not available

Information Required for Application:
• Submit graduate application.
• Submit official transcripts.
• Attend an orientation or schedule a program planning conference.
• Complete a writing assessment.

Admission Date: Not available

In-state and Out-of-state Tuition Costs: $424 per credit

Availability of Internships and Scholarships: Graduate assistantships

Orientation and Emphasis of Department/Program (Program Description): The Wilmington University master of science in administration of justice positions students to be leaders in the field of criminal justice. Students will gain the knowledge and skills to address the problems and issues that will challenge agencies in the future.

Number of Faculty: 17

Accreditation: Commission on Higher Education of the Middle States Association

Average Length of Time to Complete the Program: Not available

Xavier University

Address: 3800 Victory Parkway
Cincinnati, OH 45207
Phone: (513) 745-3000
Website: http://www.xavier.edu/

Department: Criminal Justice (Graduate)
Website: http://www.xavier.edu/criminal-justice-grad/

Type of Program: MS in Criminal Justice

Application Deadline: Not available

Requirements: Not available

Information Required for Application:
- The graduate application form;
- $35 application fee;
- One official transcript sent directly from the college/university to graduate services from all previous undergraduate and graduate course work;
- Official test scores from the Miller Analogies Test (MAT), the Graduate Record Exam (GRE), or the Law School Admission Test (LSAT); and
- Two letters of recommendation.

Admission Date: Not available

In-state and Out-of-state Tuition Costs: $575 per credit hour

Availability of Internships and Scholarships: Assistantships, scholarships

Orientation and Emphasis of Department/Program (Program Description): The master of science in criminal justice program is designed for those persons who are interested in studying the theory and practice of criminal justice in law enforcement, courts and corrections. Students graduate with an understanding of the dynamics of criminal and delinquent behavior, the nature and scope of crime and delinquency in contemporary society, and the current efforts by the criminal justice system to address these issues.

Number of Faculty: 3

Accreditation: Higher Learning Commission of the North Central Association of Colleges and Schools

Average Length of Time to Complete the Program: Not available

Youngstown State University

Address: 1 University Plaza
Youngstown, OH 44555
Phone: (330) 941-3000
Website: http://www.ysu.edu/

Department: Department of Criminal Justice and Forensic Sciences
Website: http://web.ysu.edu/bchhs/cj/

Type of Program: MS in Criminal Justice

Application Deadline: Not available

Requirements:
- A bachelor's degree from a college or university certified by a regional accrediting agency (e.g., North Central Association of Colleges and Schools) approved by the U.S. Department of Education;
- An recalculated cumulative grade point average in undergraduate work of at least 2.7 on a 4.0 scale (some programs require higher GPAs). If an undergraduate course has been repeated, all grades received will figure in the calculation of the grade point average;
- Satisfactory preparation for the graduate program in which the student wishes to enroll as specified by the department of the major;
- A test of written/spoken English, which the university reserves the right to request of any entering graduate student whose primary language is not English; and
- Degree-seeking students having an undergraduate GPA below 2.7 must present a satisfactory score on the general test of the Graduate Record Exam, the Miller Analogies Test, or graduate level subject-specific exam as specified by the department of the major.

Information Required for Application: Not available

Admission Date: Not available

In-state and Out-of-state Tuition Costs: In-state: $1,110.42 per year; out-of-state: $1,377.90 per year

Availability of Internships and Scholarships: Scholarships

Orientation and Emphasis of Department/Program (Program Description): The master of science in criminal justice at YSU provides professional education of criminal justice personnel. The graduate program in criminal justice adheres to the position that the administration of criminal justice is a continuous integrated process from prevention of crime through completion of all legal intervention. The program is designed to provide society with individuals who have both a substantial awareness of the overall system and the essential competencies required to perform professional roles within the system. To achieve this objective, the program broadens the student's knowledge of the total criminal justice process and provides professional education so that its graduates may assume positions of leadership within the criminal justice system. The program has two options. The thesis option requires thirty semester hours. The thesis project itself counts as six of those thirty semester hours. The graduate research paper option requires thirty-five semester hours.

Number of Faculty: 5

Accreditation: Higher Learning Commission

Average Length of Time to Complete the Program: Not available

PART III

LIST OF GRADUATE PROGRAMS IN CRIMINAL JUSTICE AND CRIMINOLOGY IN CANADA, ALPHABETICAL BY SCHOOL NAME

(Information taken directly from school/department websites)

Simon Frasier University

Address: 8888 University Drive
Burnaby, BC V5A 1S6
Phone: (778) 782-3111
Website: http://www.sfu.ca/

Department: School of Criminology
Saywell Hall 10125
Phone: (778) 782-3213
Fax: (778) 782-4140
E-mail: crimgo@sfu.ca
Website: http://www.sfu.ca/criminology/contact.html

Type of Program: MA in Criminology; PhD in Criminology

Application Deadline: February 1

Requirements:
Master's
- Students holding a baccalaureate or equivalent from a recognized institution must meet the admission requirements for graduate studies. See graduate general regulation 1.3.2 and also see graduate general regulation 1.3.8.
- Normally, an applicant should have completed at least one course in social science research methods and one undergraduate introductory course in statistics.

- Official transcripts and a short statement of interest, which includes a description of previous employment and research or other relevant work, are required. Letters of recommendation from those who are familiar with the student's work are required.
- Application fees are set by the dean of graduate studies office, and are subject to change each year.

Doctoral

The minimum admission requirements to this doctor of philosophy (PhD) program are stated in graduate general regulation 1.3.4. Normally, an applicant should have at least one course in social science research methods and one undergraduate introductory statistics course. Direct admission may be approved for those with an MA in criminology, an MA in a discipline other than criminology, or an MSc and—under exceptional circumstances—with an undergraduate degree or its equivalent with a minimum 3.5 cumulative grade point average (CGPA). Applicants submit a research interest statement and at least two previous academic work examples. In exceptional circumstances, those with a bachelor of arts (BA) (or equivalent) may be admitted if university regulations are met, original undergraduate research is demonstrated, and the applicant is recommended for direct entry by at least two criminology faculty who are eligible to teach or supervise in the PhD program. Those who meet the GPA requirement and have demonstrated research ability through field criminal justice experience may also be considered on recommendation of at least two program faculty members. Those so admitted will have their status reviewed by the end of the second term after admission. The graduate program committee determines the candidate's ability to complete the PhD by direct entry. The student will either be confirmed as an approved PhD candidate or directed to seek master's program admission. Because many disciplines are allied to criminology, the graduate program committee reserves the right to determine equivalent courses already completed in the applicant's master's program. At the time of admission, the graduate program committee may waive up to fifteen units of requirements.

Information Required for Application: Stated above

Admission Date: Fall only

In-state and Out-of-state Tuition Costs: $1,728.80 per semester

Availability of Internships and Scholarships: Not available

Orientation and Emphasis of Department/Program (Program Description): The School of Criminology offers graduate programs leading to the degrees of master of arts and doctor of philosophy that are designed for, but not restricted to, individuals graduating with a bachelor's or master's degree in criminology, or students with a background in one or more of the behavioral or social sciences, or with legal training, who are interested in becoming specialists in criminology. There are a number of options for students interested in pursuing a master's degree within the School of Criminology. Students may complete a traditional MA by coursework and thesis. Alternately they may choose to do an MA by coursework, practicum, and project paper. (Note, however, that since this alternative does not include completion of a thesis, it is not acceptable as a precursor for entrance to the PhD program.) An MA in applied legal studies is also available through collaboration with the Society of Notaries Public of British Columbia. The doctoral program involves coursework, preliminary examinations, and completion of a dissertation. The School of Criminology has both a strong national and international focus. Undergraduate and graduate students come from all parts of Canada. At the international level, persons enrolled in the MA and PhD programs have come from Australia, Belgium, China, Denmark, Ethiopia, Ghana, Guatemala, India, Japan, Jamaica, Nigeria, Norway, South Africa, the United Kingdom, and the United States.

Number of Faculty: 36

Accreditation: Not available

Average Length of Time to Complete the Program: Not available

University of Guelph

Address: 50 Stone Road East
Guelph, ON, N1G 2W1
Phone: (519) 824-4120
Website: http://www.uoguelph.ca/

Department: Criminology and Criminal Justice Policy
5th Floor Mackinnon Building
50 Stone Road East
Guelph, ON, N1G 2W1, Canada
Phone: (519) 824-4120
Website: http://www.uoguelph.ca/cjpp/

Type of Program: MA in Criminology and Criminal Justice Policy

Application Deadline: Not available

Requirements:
Applicants are required to have completed a four-year honors degree or equivalent from a recognized post-secondary institution with a minimum B- average over the last two years of full-time equivalent study.

Information Required for Application:
Applicants interested in applying to graduate studies at the University of Guelph are required to provide two academic references as part of their application package. Each referee must submit a Referee Assessment Form on behalf of the applicant. You can learn more about references, how to choose a reference, and the referee submission process on our application documents website.

Admission Date: Not available

In-state and Out-of-state Tuition Costs: $5,367.85

Availability of Internships and Scholarships:
Scholarships and awards

Orientation and Emphasis of Department/Program (Program Description):
The CCJP MA program is a collaborative program between the Department of Sociology and Anthropology and the Department of Political Science. The program distinguishes itself from other MA programs in criminology by having a strong emphasis on criminal justice and governance, while still providing students with the necessary background for continued studies in criminology, sociology, or political science.

Number of Faculty: 12

Accreditation: Not available

Average Length of Time to Complete the Program: Not available

University of Ontario Institute of Technology

Address: 2000 Simcoe Street North
Oshawa, ON, L1H 7K4
Phone: (905) 721-8668
Website: http://www.uoit.ca/

Department: Faculty of Social Science and Humanities
Bordessa Hall
55 Bond Street East
Oshawa, ON, L1H 7K4
Phone: (905) 721-3234
Fax: (905) 721-3372
E-mail: ma.crim@uoit.ca
Website: http://socialscienceandhumanities.uoit.ca/graduate/index.php

Type of Program: MA in Criminology

Application Deadline: April 15

Requirements:
- Hold a four-year honors degree or its equivalent from a recognized institution in the same area of graduate study or a closely related subject; and
- Overall academic standing of at least a B average (GPA: 3.0 on a 4.3 scale or 73 to 76 percent), with a minimum B average in the last two full-time years (four semesters) of undergraduate work or equivalent.

Information Required for Application:
- A minimum of two letters of recommendation;
- Proof of English language proficiency;
- One official or certified copy (certified by the institution) of each previous undergraduate and graduate transcript;
- A one- to two-page statement of academic intent;
- A photocopy of your degree parchment(s); and
- Required program-specific documentation (if required).

Admission Date: Fall

In-state and Out-of-state Tuition Costs: $2,697.63 per term

Availability of Internships and Scholarships: Not available

Orientation and Emphasis of Department/Program (Program Description): The MA in Criminology program provides students with a solid foundation of advanced knowledge in criminological theory, sophisticated research methodologies, complex quantitative and qualitative applications, and contemporary substantive issues in criminology. Specifically, the MA program seeks to provide students with an in-depth and broad understanding of contemporary criminological issues and debates, and the critical thinking and practical skills necessary to conduct criminological research in the public and private sectors. This includes—but is not limited to—public policy agencies, social services, and government and non-government organizations. The program trains both mid-career and pre-career students for careers in analysis and research in criminal justice agency settings. It also prepares students for advanced graduate work in criminology at the PhD level. Special emphasis in the MA program is placed on the study of two fields: 1) inequality and crime; and 2) cybercrime. The requirement that students learn and apply both quantitative and qualitative research skills is also unique to this program.

Number of Faculty: 64

Accreditation: Not available

Average Length of Time to Complete the Program: Twenty-four months/two years if enrolled full time

University of Ottawa

Address: 550 Cumberland Street
Ottawa, ON, K1N 6N5
Phone: (613) 562-5700
Website: http://www.uottawa.ca/en/

Department: Department of Criminology
Faculty of Social Sciences
120 University
Social Sciences Building, Room 14002
Ottawa, ON, K1N 6N5
Phone: (613) 562-5303
Fax: (613) 562-5304
E-mail: crimino@uottawa.ca
Website: http://socialsciences.uottawa.ca/crm/graduate-studies/

Type of Program: MA in Criminology

Application Deadline: January 15

Requirements:
- Students must hold a bachelor's degree with a major in criminology or equivalent with a minimum average of 75 percent (B+).
- Their previous studies must have included CRM4304 (Qualitative Research in Criminology, three credits) and CRM3334 (Quantitative Research in Criminology, three credits) or the equivalent. If not, they will have to take them as additional courses during their first session in the MA program.
- The qualifying program: If the student has an honors degree in a related field (e.g., sociology, psychology, law, social work, political science, history, philosophy) but is considered to have insufficient training in the theoretical and methodological traditions of the criminological discipline, the student may be offered a qualifying year involving up to twenty-four credits in order to render the student eligible to pursue studies in the master's program. To successfully complete the qualifying year, the student must pass all courses (passing grade is C+) and have an average of B+. It is necessary to submit a new application during the qualifying year for admission to the master's program to be considered. The student will receive an offer of admission to the master's program that will be conditional on the successful completion of the qualifying year.

Information Required for Application: Not available

Admission Date: Spring

In-state and Out-of-state Tuition Costs: Not available

Availability of Internships and Scholarships: Scholarships, assistantships, and awards. Excellence Scholarships include:

- Tuition fees for the duration of the external award; and
- An assistantship during each year of the award (to undertake an assistantship, the student must be able to work at the University of Ottawa).

Orientation and Emphasis of Department/Program (Program Description): Criminology is devoted to the scientific analysis of crime, justice, and social control. It focuses on four broad questions: the social construction of norms and the notion of crime; the criminalization of specific behaviors, individuals, and groups in our society; the analysis of the goals and functioning of the criminal justice system; and the examination of contemporary forms of intervention. The master's program consists of three distinct thirty-credit options: one with a major research paper, one with a thesis, and one with a thesis and field placement. These three options are intended to equip students with knowledge of the major theoretical and methodological frameworks in criminology so that they will be able to analyze them critically and apply this knowledge to describe and explain conceptual and empirical problems of crime, justice, and social control. Students acquire theoretical, substantive, and methodological knowledge, as well as research and analytical skills, through a core curriculum of required courses and by undertaking one of the following options:

- Thesis and three elective courses;
- Thesis, field placement, and field placement seminar; or
- Major research paper and five elective courses. This option allows the student to complete the program on a part-time basis beginning in the fourth semester of registration.

Number of Faculty: 31

Accreditation: Not available

Average Length of Time to Complete the Program: Not available

University of Toronto

Address: 563 Spadina Crescent, Toronto, ON, M5S 2J7
Phone: (416) 978-2011
Website: http://www.utoronto.com/

Department: Centre for Criminology and Sociolegal Studies
14 Queen's Park Crescent West
Toronto, ON, M5S 3K9
Phone: (416) 978-7124
Fax: (416) 978-4195
Website: http://criminology.utoronto.ca/

Type of Program: MA in Criminology; PhD in Criminology; also a combined Juris Doctor/Master

Application Deadline: MA: February 1; PhD: February 1, for domestic students and international students

Requirements:
Master's (and full-time special students)
- An appropriate bachelor's degree, or its equivalent, with a final year average of at least mid-B from a recognized university.

Doctoral
- An appropriate master's degree, or its equivalent, with an average of at least B+, or demonstrated comparable research competence. Some departments admit directly to the doctoral program from a bachelor's degree for highly qualified candidates (minimum average A- required).

Information Required for Application:
- Completion of your current program with a specific average and confirmation of degree conferred. This condition has two elements that must be satisfied: 1) proof that you have obtained the specified average; and 2) proof that you have received your degree. You must arrange to have a transcript of your final official academic record forwarded to your home graduate unit once you have completed your coursework and received your degree. If your transcript is forwarded before it has been updated to indicate conferral of degree, the second part of the condition will not be cleared. To save time and expense, ensure that your academic transcript includes the confirmation of degree conferred. If you satisfy your requirements during the summer but will not receive your degree until after your graduate program commences, then you must arrange to have the following two documents forwarded to

your graduate unit: 1) an official transcript of your academic record which indicates final standing; and 2) an official statement from your registrar that confirms that the degree requirements have been satisfied and indicates the expected date of degree conferral.

- Authentication of self-reported grades. This condition requires you to authenticate self-reported grades by providing your graduate unit with official transcript(s) of your academic record directly from the issuing institution(s) by the specified date; and

- Certified English translation of academic record or diploma. You must arrange to have the document translated by an authorized translation service or your embassy or consulate.

Admission Date: Not available

In-state and Out-of-state Tuition Costs: $8,460.28 full-time students per semester

Availability of Internships and Scholarships: Not available

Orientation and Emphasis of Department/Program (Program Description): The Centre for Criminology and Sociolegal Studies, founded in 1964, offers advanced interdisciplinary study in two closely related, overlapping areas: criminology and sociolegal studies, leading to the MA and PhD degrees in criminology. MA graduates find employment in government (in areas such as child and youth services or addiction, as well as criminal justice fields), in governmental organizations in the criminal justice field, in social science research, or in other positions for which a background in criminology and legal studies is useful. Some choose to go to law school, and many have gone on to other post-graduate work, such as in criminology, sociology, law, and social work. PhD graduates have mainly found employment in tenure-track positions, most often in sociology departments or in criminology programs. Both the MA and PhD degree programs are academic rather than professional/vocational.

Number of Faculty: There are 26 faculty members including the director. Eight core faculty are based at the Centre; the other 18 are cross-appointed and adjunct faculty from other departments and universities.

Accreditation: Not available

Average Length of Time to Complete the Program: Not available

University of Windsor

Address: 401 Sunset Avenue
Windsor, ON, N9B 3P4
Phone: (519) 253-3000
Website: http://www.uwindsor.ca/

Department: Department of Sociology, Anthropology, and Criminology
Windsor, ON, N9B 3P4
Phone: (519) 253-3000 ext. 2188
Fax: (519) 971-3621
Website: http://www1.uwindsor.ca/criminology/

Type of Program: MA in Criminology

Application Deadline: February 28

Requirements:
• Minimum TOEFL: 220;
• Minimum IELTS: 6.5;
• Two academic letters of reference;
• Statement of interest or plan of study; and
• A CV or résumé.

Information Required for Application: Stated above

Admission Date: Fall only

In-state and Out-of-state Tuition Costs: $3,180.49 per semester

Availability of Internships and Scholarships: Not available

Orientation and Emphasis of Department/Program (Program Description): The Department of Sociology, Anthropology, and Criminology now offers a formal criminology MA. The criminology MA is designed to meet the clear and growing demand for highly qualified personnel in criminology. The program prepares students for research and leadership roles in related industry fields and academia. The program will provide students with an opportunity to acquire—through coursework and thesis research, seminars, and networking—academic and professional knowledge in the multi-faceted areas of crime, security, social justice, and related subjects. The program develops applied research skills that will enable students to become independent research investigators capable of disseminating knowledge and research results through their engagement in criminal justice and related fields. The MA thesis project emphasizes student training and the development of research competencies and skills demanded of criminology professionals. It will enable graduates to review, problem-solve, report on, and disseminate current research in terms relevant to various policy stakeholders within the field, and to develop ideas, propositions, and plans to redress concerns related to criminology. The criminology MA aims to foster excellence in areas that are at the forefront of research and innovation within criminology. The program provides students the necessary research tools and facilities for their intellectual development within a scholarly, dynamic, and collaborative research environment.

Number of Faculty: 22

Accreditation: Not available

Average Length of Time to Complete the Program: Not available

Wilfrid Laurier University—Brantford

Address: 73 George Street
Brantford, ON, N3T 2Y3
Phone: (519) 756-8228
Website: http://www.wlu.ca/homepage.php?grp_id=37

Department: Department of Criminology
Grand River Hall, Room 121
Phone: (519) 756-8228 ext. 5623
Website: https://www.wlu.ca/homepage.php?grp_id=1726

Type of Program: MA in Criminology

Application Deadline: January 15

Requirements: B+ average GPA

Information Required for Application:
- A completed application (applicants must submit the printed [pdf] Application Summary available from the online application);
- A completed Personal Information Form;
- A résumé of your academic and work experience; include a history of your publication and scholarly paper activity and any other information you feel will interest the admissions committee;
- Official transcripts and degree certificates (where applicable) of all undergraduate and graduate work;
- Completed reference forms (these forms will be produced for you when you create your online application); two academic references are required;
- A sample of your scholarly writing (ten to twenty pages in length); this may be a paper written for a senior undergraduate course; note that this document will not be returned to you;
- For international applicants, an official statement of your acceptable English-language test results; and
- If you are a permanent resident, evidence of your status in Canada is required; you must provide a photocopy of your signed "Record of Landing" or photocopies of both sides of your Permanent Resident card.

Admission Date: Fall

In-state and Out-of-state Tuition Costs: $2,641.64 per term

Availability of Internships and Scholarships: In addition to teaching assistantships, internal and/or external scholarship awards, and research assistantships, Wilfrid Laurier University provides competitive guaranteed funding to students enrolled in full-time graduate studies.

Research-intensive Master's Programs: Eligible students admitted to study on a full-time basis in research-based master's programs are guaranteed financial support averaging approximately $13,000 for each eligible year of study. Such support is made up of teaching assistantships and internal and/or external scholarship awards. Some research assistantship support is also available; students are encouraged to contact their academic program for more information. Major award holders (OGS, CIHR, NSERC, SSHRC) in the research master's programs are eligible for the Dean's Scholarship, valued at up to $7,500.

Orientation and Emphasis of Department/Program (Program Description): Our new two-year master's program in criminology provides prospective students with a degree that creates flexibility and choice in their potential career paths. The program offers three fields of specialized study: international crime and justice; media criminology, and; culture, crime, and policy. These three fields are underpinned by core courses in criminological theory and methods.

Number of Faculty: 16

Accreditation: Not available

Average Length of Time to Complete the Program: Two years

PART IV

POTENTIAL EMPLOYMENT OPTIONS WITH A MASTER'S OR DOCTORAL DEGREE IN CRIMINOLOGY OR CRIMINAL JUSTICE

As stated at the beginning of this book, the criminal justice system involves three distinct agencies and systems that work together to preserve order and maintain the rule of law within the United States and Canada: law enforcement, courts, and corrections. Additionally, as academic disciplines, criminal justice and criminology examine a variety of topics related to the criminal justice system as well as the phenomenon of crime itself. Education in these disciplines prepares students for employment in a multitude of professions and occupations. A graduate degree in criminology or criminal justice can lead to employment in the field of academia performing teaching or research, in the field of criminal justice in administrative positions, or in research departments with various federal, state, and local criminal and juvenile justice agencies. Additionally, certificates with a specific focus in law enforcement, corrections, investigations, and security administration are often accessible to individuals in the field. Jobs may require a degree alone or coupled with other training or experience. Other factors that may also be considered for employment within the criminal justice system are personality, skills, and interests.

The latter will eventually dictate what job a student chooses to pursue once they have obtained their graduate degree. A master's degree in criminology or criminal justice may be used as a stepping-stone toward a doctoral degree or to obtain an adjunct teaching position at a college. It can also pave the way for a job within the criminal justice system. Typically, individuals with master's degree are utilized in higher-tier administrative jobs, but this may not always be the case. Many local, state, and federal agencies—such as state and federal law enforcement agencies, state and federal prisons, or international criminal justice organizations—recommend a master's degree for upper management positions. Examples of such institutions include state troopers, state bureaus of investigation, superintendent/warden of a prison, the Federal Bureau of Investigations (FBI), the Secret Service, the Bureau of Alcohol, Tobacco, Firearms, and Explosives (ATF), U.S. Immigration and Customs Enforcement (ICE), the Drug Enforcement Agency (DEA), the Transportation Security Administration (TSA), the U.S. Fish and Wildlife Service, Interpol, and the United Nations. Additionally, many jobs deal with the social services side of the criminal justice system, but these may also require knowledge, experience, or a degree from another discipline. Examples include probation/parole officer, case manager in either a prison or community setting, crime prevention specialist, victim's advocate, and personnel of nongovernmental organizations (NGOs) such as Amnesty International, the Children's Defense Fund, the Human Rights Action Center, or the Simon Wiesenthal Center. A doctorate typically prepares students for teaching at the university level and conducting research. Research positions may be at universities, although this type of research is predominately performed in order to secure tenure for a professor position. Other research positions include working for large cities such as Los Angeles, New York, Chicago, or Atlanta; at private think tanks such as Rand Corporation, the Sentencing Project, or the Urban Institute; or at federal or state agencies, such as state sentencing and policy commissions, the National Bureau of Economic Research, the National Institute of Justice, or the U.S. Sentencing Commission. A PhD in criminal justice can prepare a student for a job in several law concentrations, such as criminal, environmental, and international law, as well as jobs in international relations. Additionally, many of the jobs that require a master's degree are also open to individuals who possess a doctorate.

A variety of employment opportunities are open to someone with a graduate degree in criminology or criminal justice. While salary may rank as one of the most important factors to many people when selecting a job within the field of criminal justice, other factors are in play that should also be considered, such as the cost and time associated with the education requirements, whether the position will demand geographic mobility or extended travel, any hazards or danger inherent to the position, and whether the job calls for nontraditional hours or on-call periods/duties. Not all jobs in the criminal justice field will be affected by each of these elements, but employment in this discipline can sometimes require many sacrifices that jobs in other fields do not. It is wise to consider all characteristics of an education and occupation when making a decision.

History of the clan Macrae with genealogies

Alexander MacRae

Rowena J. Burton

March 11 1911.

LARGE PAPER EDITION

———

THE HISTORY OF THE CLAN MACRAE

The Rev. ALEXANDER MACRAE, M.A. (Author)

HISTORY

OF THE

CLAN MACRAE

WITH GENEALOGIES

BY

THE REV. ALEXANDER MACRAE, M.A.

"Seallaibh ris a' charraig o'n do ghearradh a mach sibh."
"Look unto the rock whence ye are hewn."

DINGWALL: GEORGE SOUTER
1910.

PREFACE TO THE LARGE PAPER EDITION.

— o —

The delay which for various unavoidable reasons has occurred in the publication of the large paper edition of this book has afforded an opportunity for making considerable additions to it, as it first appeared. These additions are the work mainly of my fellow-clansman and namesake Mr Alexander Macrae, M A., Bushey, Hertford-shire, a gentleman who adds ripe scholarship and high literary attainments to an intimate knowledge of the Gaelic language and of the people of Kintail among whom his youth was passed.

In the preface to the original edition, I dealt at some length with the rival claims of the Inverinate, Conchra, and Torlysich families to contain the senior lineal representation of Fionnla Dubh Mac Gillechriosd, whom I there described as the founder of the Clan. This question was gone into with great fulness during the hearing of the "Macrae Chieftainship" case in the Court of the Lord Lyon King of Arms in 1908-9; but it still remains un-settled, while it is claimed on behalf of the Clann Ian Charrich branch, not without valid reason, that they are an older family than Fionnla Dubh's, and that their progenitor, Ian Carrach, and not Fionnla Dubh, was the real founder of the Clan Macrae of Kintail. The decision of the Lord Lyon did not upset the statement contained in the opening paragraph of the first chapter of the book, (a paragraph which was first written as far back as 1893, and that after long and careful inquiry), to the effect that the Macraes were under the Chieftainship of the Barons Mackenzie of Kintail, as the evidence submitted to the Court did not show that the Macraes ever acknowledged any other Chief

But although the Lord Lyon's judgment left the question of Chieftainship as it was before, yet the great interest, called forth by this famous case, has brought a "fierce light" to beat upon the history of the Clan, with the result that additional information about its past history is being slowly but surely gleaned from various sources, and it is hoped that, at no distant date, it may be found possible to bring out a thoroughly revised and re-arranged issue of this book with further additions, and, possibly, corrections also. The number of inquiries constantly received, and the fact that there have been many more applications for the large paper edition, than could be supplied, would seem to show that there will soon be room for another issue.

A. M.

WANDSWORTH COMMON, LONDON.
19th November, 1910

SUBSCRIBERS TO LARGE PAPER EDITION.

1 Barrett, F T , for the Mitchell Library, Glasgow
2. Bind, Mrs J. M., 13 Lower Maze Hill, St Leonards on-Sea, Sussex
3. Burford, Mrs E H , 318 N Pennsylvania Street, Indianapolis, Indiana, U S A
4 Cadell, George, 20 Murrayfield Drive Murrayfield, Midlothian
5 Cole, Miss M Ward Glanderston, Normanby Street, Brighton, Victoria, Australia
6 Finlayson, Miss C M , Heathfield Bridge-of-Weir
7 Forrester, R Bookseller, 1 Royal Exchange Square, Glasgow
9 Matheson, Sir Kenneth, Bart , of Lochalsh (2 copies)
10 Mackenzie, Colonel J A F H Stewart, of Seaforth
11 Mackenzie, Sir Arthur, Bart , of Coul
12 Mackenzie, Mrs, 1 Albany Street Oban
13 Mackenzie, Mrs 22 Newbattle Terrace, Edinburgh
14. Melville & Mollen, Proprietary, Ltd , Booksellers, 12 Ludgate Square London, E C
15 Melvin Bros , Booksellers, Inverness
16 Macrae, Duncan, Ardintoul House, Kyle
18 Macrae, Sir Colin George, Edinburgh (2 copies)
19 MacRae, Dr Farquhar, 27 Lowndes Street, Belgrave Square, London, S W
20 Macrae, The Rev Donald, B D., Edderton, Ross shire
21 Macrae, John, 22 West Nile Street, Glasgow
22 Macrae, Miss F , High'and Orphanage, Inverness
23 Macrae, J M Chattanooga, Tennessee, U S A
24 Macrae, H R., Esq., of Clunes, 14 Gloucester Place, Edinburgh
25 Macrae, Colonel R , C S I , Nairn
26 Macrae, Wm. S , 700 Cherry Street, Chattanooga, Tennessee, U S A
27 Macrae, Malcolm, Lochluichart, Ross-shire
28 Macrae, C C , 93 Onslow Gardens, London, S W
33 Macrae, Hugh Investment Trust Company, Wilmington, North Carolina (5 copies)
34 Macrae, J D., M D , Bonar-Bridge.
35 Macrae, R., Merchant, Sheldaig, Lochcarron
39 Macrae, The Rev Alex., M A., London (4 copies)
41 Macrae, Alex M A , Bushey, Herts (2 copies)
42 Macrae, G W , 700 Cherry Street, Chattanooga, Tennessee, U S A
43. Macrae, D J Borpukhuri Tea Estate, Sootea P.O , Assam, India
44 Macrae, Farquhar, Reno, Nevada
47 Macrae, A W., Calheut, India (3 copies)
48 Macrae, Miss Jane, Box 296, Glencoe Ontario, Canada
49. Macrae Finlay, 902 Ninth Avenue, Helena, Montana, U S A
50 Signet Library, Edinburgh (John Minto, Librarian), per G P Johnston Booksellers, 33 George Street, Edinburgh

CONTENTS.

— — —

— — —

LIST OF ILLUSTRATIONS.

PREFACE.

———:o———

THE preparation of this History has been prompted by a desire to put on record, before it is too late, the fast diminishing oral and traditional information with which it is still possible, in some degree, to supplement such meagre written records of the Clan Macrae as we happen to possess, and, though it probably contains little which can be of interest to the general reader, yet my purpose will be fulfilled, and my labour amply rewarded, if it proves of interest to the members and connections of the Clan itself.

The work of collecting information was first begun as a recreation during a brief visit to Kintail in August, 1890, when I had the good fortune to make the acquaintance of an excellent folk-lorist and genealogist, the late Mr Alexander Macmillan, Dornie, from whom I received much of the traditional and oral information recorded in this book. By 1893, I had succeeded in collecting sufficient matter for a series of " Notes on the Clan Macrae," which appeared in *The North Star* at intervals between July, 1893, and June, 1896, when the writing of this volume was commenced.

The difficulty of the work was greatly increased by the fact that it was possible to carry it on, only at long intervals during occasional periods of freedom from the labours of an exceptionally busy life. Another great disadvantage was the fact that a large part of the information received from the Country of the Macraes had to be collected by correspondence. I am, therefore, well aware that, though the greatest care has been taken to obtain correct information, and to verify every statement, yet there are undoubtedly many blemishes and defects in the book which might have been avoided if the work had been of a more continuous nature, and if it had been possible for me to have direct oral communication, more freely, with the genealogists and folk-lorists of the Macrae Country.

The genealogical portion of the book, up to page 224, is based mainly upon the MS. History of the Clan, written by the Rev. John Macrae, of Dingwall, about two hundred years ago, including the additions made to it by various transcribers down to about the year 1820. In the case of several families the genealogy is continued down to the present time, from family Bibles, family letters, registers, and other sources of information, and where there are continuations from oral sources great care has been taken in selecting the names and particulars to be included, and much matter has been left out because it could not be sufficiently authenticated and confirmed to warrant its publication. The result is that a great many families are incomplete, but there are very few genealogies of which this cannot be said.

In any case, omissions are a less evil than mistakes, and my endeavour throughout the book has been, as far as possible, to be correct in my information, however meagre it might be.

The Roman numerals up to page 234 represent in every case the number of generations from Fionnla Dubh Mac Gillechriosd, the reputed founder of the Clan Macrae of Kintail, and it is hoped that the genealogical portions of the book are otherwise arranged clearly enough to be easily followed.

A controversy has recently arisen as to which family contains the lineal representation of Fionnla Dubh Mac Gillechriosd. Such controversies are far from uncommon in old families, even when for many generations they have possessed estates and titles to which the lineal succession has always been recorded with greater care than was ever done in the case of any family of the Macraes. The lineal succession of Fionnla Dubh Mac Gillechriosd is usually held to be in the Inverinate family, and that is the opinion of the Kintail genealogists whom I have had the opportunity of consulting.

At the same time, the lineal representation of the founder of the Clan is claimed by two other families. The Macraes of Conchra claim, on the strength of family traditions and old family letters, that the founder of their branch of the Clan, the Rev. John Macrae of Dingwall (page 142), and not Alexander of Inverinate (page 69), was the eldest son of the Rev. Farquhar Macrae of Kintail.

The Torlysich family, again, claim that their progenitor, Farquhar (page 186), was the eldest son of Christopher (IV.), Constable of Ellandonan (page 24), and that the reason why John of Killin refused to give Farquhar the post of Constable (page 28) was, that the appointment of the eldest son to a post formerly held by his father might lead the Macraes to regard the office of Constable as hereditary in their own family, and that they might thus become inconveniently powerful for the Mackenzie family, which at that time was small and comparatively unimportant.

In all the copies of the Rev. John Macrae's history that I have seen, Duncan, the first of the family who settled at Inverinate (page 30), is stated to have been older than his brother Farquhar, and Alexander of Inverinate is stated to have been the eldest son of the Rev. Farquhar Macrae of Kintail; and as the Rev. John Macrae's MS. history formed the chief written authority at my disposal, I have felt justified in continuing the genealogy of the Inverinate family as the direct lineal representatives of Fionnla Dubh Mac Gillechriosd.

It might seem hardly worth while recording some of the lists of names given, without dates or any other particulars, in the genealogical portions of the book, but no such list has been given without satisfactory reasons for believing it to be correct, as far as it goes. Some of those lists will probably be recognised, as their own families, by readers in the Colonies and also in the United States, where the descendants of Macrae emigrants from Kintail are both numerous and prosperous, and the interest taken by some of them in the preparation of this book shows that they have not yet lost the traditions of their Clan or forgotten the home of their fathers.

It is hoped the Appendices will add somewhat to the interest of the book. Very much more might have been written about Kintail did space permit, and for the same reason the collection of poetry is much smaller than was originally intended. The Royal descents in Appendix F are given on the authority of Burke's genealogical publications, and various Mackenzie genealogies. It has not been found possible to identify all the place names in Appendices H and M, probably because of the way they are spelled, but though the spelling of the original documents has been in almost every case retained, most of the names will be easily recognised.

It is needless to say that this book could not have been written without the help of many generous friends, some of whom are no longer within reach of this expression of my gratitude—among them Sir William Alexander Mackinnon, K.C.B., Captain Archibald Macra Chisholm, Mr Alexander Mackenzie, the Clan Historian, and Mr Alexander Matheson, shipowner, Dornie, one of the best read and most intelligent of Highland seannachies, whose acquaintance it was my misfortune not to have made until only a few weeks before his death, which occurred on the 14th of October, 1897. In addition to the help acknowledged from time to time throughout the book, I am specially indebted to Mrs Mackenzie of Abbotsford Park, Edinburgh (now of Portobello), for much information and help, and for many interesting recollections of more than one Kintail family; to Mrs

Alister MacLellan (of Ardintoul); to Mrs Farquhar
Finlayson, Rothesay; to Major John MacRae-Gilstrap
of Ballimore, who was one of the first to take an
interest in this work, and who, in addition to old
family papers, placed also at my disposal a large
quantity of material collected at his own expense in
the Register House, Edinburgh; to Sir James Dixon
Mackenzie of Findon, Bart., for the use of old and
interesting documents in his possession; to Mr
William Mackay of Craigmonie, Inverness, for much
help, given on many occasions, with a readiness and
kindness, which to me will always form a pleasant
recollection; to Mr Horatio Ross Macrae of Clunes
for the fac-simile of signatures to the Macrae-Campbell
Bond of Friendship, as well as for the use of documents bearing on the history of the Inverinate
family; to the Rev. Donald Macrae, B.D., minister
of Lairg, for much help and many valuable suggestions; to Professor Donald Mackinnon, M.A.,
Edinburgh, for information about the Fernaig MS.,
and for valuable suggestions about the extracts from
it in Appendix J; to Mr Charles Fraser-Mackintosh,
LL.D., of Drummond, for the Kintail Rent Roll of
1756 in Appendix H; to Mr John H. Dixon of
Inveran for Appendix K; to Mr P. J. Anderson,
librarian of Aberdeen University, for Appendix L;
to Mr Alexander Macbain, M.A., Inverness, for the
fac-simile page of the Fernaig MS.; to Mr Farquhar
Macrae, Dornie; to Dr Donald Macrae, Beckenham;
to Major Frederick Bradford McCrea, London; to
Lieutenant-Colonel J. H. Carteret Carey of Castle
Carey, Guernsey; to Mr Farquhar Matheson, Dornie,

who prepared the map, which is interesting as recording some old Kintail place-names now no longer in use; to my brother, Mr John Macrae, for help in the transcription of old documents; to my mother for help in the translations given in Appendix J; and to the publisher, Mr A. M. Ross, and his foreman, Mr John Gray, not only for putting up with inconveniences and delays caused by the fact that, in almost every case, the proofs were sent for revision to some members of the families whose histories are here recorded, but more especially for the never-failing courtesy and kindness which have made the passing of the book through the press a work of interest and pleasure.

ALEXANDER MACRAE.

WANDSWORTH COMMON, LONDON,
15th March, 1899.

Macrae.

(Conchra.)

The Badge of the Macraes was the Fir Club-Moss (*Lycopodium Selago*):
Gaelic – Garbhag an t-sleibh.

THE HISTORY OF THE CLAN MACRAE.

CHAPTER I.

Country of the Macraes.—Meaning and Probable Origin of the Name — Its First Appearance as a Surname.— Traditional Origin of the Clan Macrae.— Macraes in the Districts of Clunes and Glenurquhart.—Migration to Kintail.—Campbells of Craignish said to be of Macrae Origin.—The Connection of the Macraes with the House of Kintail —Also with the House of Gairloch — The Macraes were Episcopalians and Jacobites —Macraes in the Seaforth Regiments.—The Rev. John Macrae's MS. History of the Clan.

THE Macraes were a small but important clan in the district of Kintail, in the south-west of the county of Ross, where they are said to have settled in the fourteenth century, under the chieftainship of the Barons Mackenzie of Kintail.

According to the most competent authorities, the name Macrae or Macrath, as it is written in Gaelic, means "son of Grace or Luck," [1] and, so far as at present known, it occurs first in *The Annals of the Kingdom of Ireland by the Four Masters*, under

[1] Macbain's Gaelic Dictionary.

A

the year of our Lord 448, a certain " Macraith [1] the Wise" being mentioned in that year as a member of the household of St Patrick.   We meet with it occasionally in Ireland from that date onwards, and in the eleventh and twelfth centuries it was frequently used in that country as the personal name of lords, poets, and more especially ecclesiastics.

The name first appears in Scotland at a somewhat later date.   In a Gaelic manuscript of the eleventh century, called *The Prophecy of Saint Berchan*, we find the term Macrath applied to one of the successors of Kenneth Macalpin,—King Gregory who reigned at Scone during the last quarter of the ninth century, and was one of the greatest of the early Scottish Kings.   This seems to be the first instance of the name Macrae or Macrath in Scotland. Gregory the Macrath was not only prosperous in worldly affairs and in his wars against his enemies, but was also a sincere supporter and benefactor of the Scottish Church, which he delivered from the oppression of the Picts, and favoured with his support and protection.[2]   Considering the meaning of the name, and the connection in which it first appears both in Ireland and in Scotland, it is not unreasonable to suppose that it may have been first given as a distinguishing personal name to men who were supposed to be endowed with more than an ordinary measure of sanctity and grace.   The name Macrae had thus in all probability an ecclesiastical origin.

[1] Raith in Macraith is the old genitive form of Rath

[2] Appendix B,

In a genealogy of the Mackenzies contained in *The Black Book of Clanranald*, we find it stated that Gilleoin of the Aird, from whom the old Earls Gillanders of Ross and the Mackenzies of Kintail are traced, was the son of Macrath (McRrath).[1] Supposing the genealogy to be correct, this Macrath would have lived not earlier than the tenth century. By that time Christianity was fairly established in the Highlands of Scotland, and as the name Gilleoin means the servant of St John, it is not at all unlikely that Macrath also may have been so named from some family connection with the early Church in the Highlands.[2]

The name Macrae (McRaa) occurs also in *The Dean of Lismore's Book* under circumstances which might well have entitled the bearer of it to be called, if not a son of grace, at all events a son of luck.[3]

In those times there were no family or hereditary surnames in this country. Family surnames appear in England about the twelfth century, but it was not until much later that they became common in the Highlands of Scotland. For instance, the surname Mackenzie, which is a comparatively old one, arose in the early part of the fourteenth century. The use of Macrae as a surname is probably of an earlier date than the surname Mackenzie, and that

---

[1] *Reliquiae Celticae*, Vol II, page 300.

[2] In a Gaelic MS. of 1450, containing genealogies of several Highland families, and published with an English translation in The Transactions of the Iona Club, an ancestor of the Macleans is also mentioned as Gilleoin, son of Macrath (Gilleain mc Icrait). This helps to confirm the tradition mentioned below, that the Macraes, Mackenzies, and Macleans were of the same ancestry, but it is not easy to make anything satisfactory out of those old genealogies.

[3] Appendix B.

it grew in the first instance out of a personal name
is evident from the fact that in Gaelic the Macraes
are always spoken of as " Clann Mhicrath," that is
the " descendants of Macrath."

So far as at present known, the name Macrae is
first mentioned as a surname in the year 1386, in an
agreement made, at Inverness, between the Bishop
of Moray and Alexander Stewart, Earl of Buchan,
better known as the Wolf of Badenoch, with regard
to some land in Rothiemurchus, in Inverness-shire,
which was formerly occupied by a certain Cristinus
M'Crath (Christopher Macrae), who was then dead.[1]
From that date onwards the name is frequently met
with as a surname in various parts of Scotland, not
only in the Highlands, but also in Ayrshire and in
the south of Perthshire.

Tradition relates that the Macraes came originally
from Ireland, and were of common ancestry with the
Mackenzies and the Macleans, and it is said that a
company of them fought at the battle of Largs in
1263, under the leadership of Colin Fitzgerald, the
reputed progenitor of the Mackenzies of Kintail.
The Fitzgerald origin of the Mackenzies is now
discredited by Scotch historians; but, whatever
their origin may have been, it is extremely probable
that the Macraes were in some way connected with
the same stock, as a strong friendship and alliance
existed between the two clans from early traditional
times, and continued without intermission so long as
the Mackenzies held the ancestral lands of Kintail.
The Macraes who settled in Kintail are said to have /

---

[1] *Registrum Episcopatus Moraviensis* (Baunatyne Club), page 196.

lived originally at Clunes, on the Lordship of Lovat, near the southern shore of the Beauly Firth, where the site on which stood the house of their chief is still pointed out.[1] So far as the date to which these traditions refer can be fixed, this would be about the middle of the thirteenth century. It is also said that the name was known in Glenurquhart[2] in the twelfth century, which is an earlier date than can well be assigned to any traditions that have come down to us with regard to the settlement at Clunes, but there appear to be no existing traditions connecting the origin of the Macraes of Kintail with the district of Glenurquhart. There are, however, many traditions connecting them with the district of Clunes, and explaining the cause of the migration to Kintail.[3]

According to the Rev. John Macrae, the most probable cause of the migration of the Macraes to Kintail, or, at all events, of that branch of them which afterwards became the most important, was that, though they do not appear to have been very numerous, they were becoming too crowded in the old home at Clunes. At the same time Lovat's own kindred and friends were becoming so numerous that the country could not accommodate them all,

---

[1] The site of Macrae's house (Larach tigh Mhicrath) is on the southern slope of the Hill of Clunes, and is marked by a number of large stones, which are supposed to have formed the foundations of the house Tradition says that the house was originally built in the course of one night by supernatural agencies, and the place has always been regarded as a favourite haunt of the fairies.

[2] Mackay's Urquhart and Glenmoriston, p. 12 ; and also the Rev. John Macrae's Account of the Origin of the Macraes, Appendix A.

[3] See chapter on legends and traditions of the clan, and Appendix A.

and this was an additional reason for the Macraes
to move to other places, as favourable opportunities
arose. Three of the sons of Macrae of Clunes are
said to have left home in this way, but the old man
himself remained in Clunes all his days, enjoying
the esteem and confidence of the Lords of Lovat,
four of whom were fostered in his house. Of these
three brothers, one settled at Brahan, near Dingwall,
where there was a piece of land in the time of the
Rev. John Macrae, called Cnoc Mhicrath (Macrae's
Hill), and the well which supplied Brahan Castle
with water at that time was called Tobair Mhicrath
(Macrae's Well). The descendants of this man were
then to be found in Strathgarve, Strathbran,
Strathconon, Ardmeanach, and one of them, John
Macrae, was at that time a merchant at Inverness.

Another son went to Argyleshire, where he
married the heiress of Craignish. His successors afterwards adopted the name Campbell, and maintained a
friendly intercourse with the Macraes of Kintail for
many generations. A contract of friendship, drawn
up between the Campbells of Craignish and the
Macraes of Kintail about two hundred years ago,
has been kept in the family of Macrae of Inverinate
ever since, and is now in the possession of Horatio
Ross Macrae, Esq. of Clunes.[1]

Another of the sons of Macrae of Clunes is said
to have gone to Kintail. This was probably during
the first half of the fourteenth century, before the
family of Mackenzie was very firmly established
there. He might have been attracted to Kintail,

[1] Appendix C.

perhaps by family connections, but quite as likely
by the fact that, as the Chief of Kintail was still
struggling to establish his family there, the circumstances of the country might afford opportunities of
distinction and advancement for a man of enterprise.
It is a singular fact that each of the first five Barons
of Kintail had only one lawful son to succeed him.
Mackenzie being thus without any male kindred of
his own blood, earnestly urged Macrae to remain
with him in Kintail. Mackenzie's proposals were
accepted, and Macrae settled in Kintail, where he .
married one Macbeolan or Gillanders, a kinswoman
of the Earls of Ross, by whom Kintail was held
before it came into the possession of the Mackenzies.
As the Macraes and Mackenzies were said to be of
common ancestry, the Baron of Kintail expected
loyal and faithful support from his newly arrived
kinsman, and he was not disappointed. The Macraes
were ever foremost in the cause of the chiefs of
Kintail, and by their prowess in battle, their industry in the arts of peace, and in many instances
by their scholarly culture and refinement, they were
mainly instrumental in raising the Barony of Kintail,
afterwards the Earldom of Seaforth, to the important
position it occupies in the annals of Scottish history.

There do not appear to have been any Macraes
settled in Kintail as landholders before this, but it
is more than probable that several of them had
already been in the service of Mackenzie. It is said
that Ellandonan Castle was garrisoned by Macraes
and Maclennans during the latter part of the
thirteenth century, when it was first taken possession

of by Kenneth, the founder of the House of Kintail.[1] The newly arrived Macrae of Clunes, however, took precedence of the others, and he and his family gradually assumed a position of great importance in the affairs of Kintail. So loyal were the Macraes in the service of Kintail that they became known as Mackenzie's "shirt of mail." This term was generally applied to the chosen body who attended a chief in war and fought around him. It would thus appear that the bodyguard of the Barons of Kintail was usually composed of Macraes. But in addition to the important services they rendered as mere retainers of the House of Kintail, the Macraes were for many generations Chamberlains of Kintail, Constables of Ellandonan Castle, and sometimes Vicars of Kintail, so that the leading members of the Clan may be said to have taken, from time to time, a much more prominent part in the affairs of Kintail than the Barons themselves did. This continued to be the case until Kintail passed out of the possession of the Mackenzies in the early part of the present century.

It was always the privilege of the Macraes to bear the dead bodies of the Barons of Kintail to burial. At the funeral, in 1862, of the Honourable Mrs Stewart Mackenzie, daughter and representative of the last Lord Seaforth, the coffin was borne out of Brahan Castle by Macraes only.[2] The scene was not without a pathetic and historic

---

[1] Appendix E.

[2] On this occasion the coffin was first lifted by Donald John Macrae of Inversheil, Donald Macrae of Achnagart, Peter Macrae of Morvich, and Ewen Macrae of Leachachan

interest.   This lady was the last of Seaforth's race, who was a Mackenzie by birth, and it is a remarkable fact that at the funeral, in 1881, of her son, Colonel Keith William Stewart Mackenzie, in whose case the name Mackenzie was only an adopted one, the Macraes, although they claimed their old privilege, did not muster a sufficient number to bear the coffin, and the vacant places had to be supplied by the Brahan tenantry.   With the funeral of Mrs Stewart Mackenzie, then, may be said to have ended for ever the intimate and loyal connection which existed for five centuries between the Macraes and the house of Kintail and Seaforth.

But the loyal and valiant support which the Macraes gave the Mackenzies was not limited to the house of Kintail.   They were mainly instrumental also in establishing the family of Gairloch. About 1480 Allan Macleod, laird of Gairloch, with his two young sons, was barbarously murdered by his own two brothers.   His wife was a daughter of Alexander Ionraic (Alexander the Just), sixth Baron of Kintail, who died about 1490, and sister of Hector Roy Mackenzie, a younger son, who became progenitor of the lairds of Gairloch.   Hector Roy took up the cause of his sister, and obtained from the King a commission of fire and sword for the destruction of the Macleods of Gairloch.   In this task, which proved by no means easy, Hector received his main support from the Macraes, one of whom had meanwhile encountered the two murderers and killed them both single-handed in fair fight at a spot in Gairloch, which is still pointed

out.[1] In 1494 Hector Roy received a grant of
Gairloch by charter from the Crown, but it was
not until the time of his grandson, John Roy
(1566-1628) that the Macleods were finally expelled, and the supremacy of the Mackenzies fully
established.

It was in Gairloch that the Mackenzies obtained
their first important footing outside of Kintail. At
that time they were only a small clan, and the
struggle which led to the conquest of Gairloch
taxed all their strength, and was both fierce and
prolonged. Hence the great number of legends and
traditions connected with it. After the conquest of
Gairloch their power and influence rapidly increased,
and the other lands which they afterwards held
in the counties of Ross and Cromarty came into
their possession by easier and more peaceful means.
Consequently there are no such stirring traditions
in connection with the acquisition of those other
lands as we find in the case of Gairloch, but
wherever the Mackenzies settled some Macraes
accompanied them, and some of the descendants
of these Macraes are still to be found on all the
old Mackenzie estates. It is in Gairloch, however,
next to Kintail and Lochalsh, that we find the
best and most interesting Macrae traditions and
legends, and it may be mentioned that one of the
Gairloch Macraes, called Domhnull Odhar[2] (Sallow
Donald), who was a contemporary of John Roy, is
represented as the crest of the Gairloch coat-of-arms.
The Macraes were also very renowned archers, and

---

1 J. H. Dixon's Gairloch, p. 26.   2 Appendix K

the scene and range of some of their famous shots are still pointed out, both in Gairloch and Kintail.[1]

During the long period of religious and civil warfare which preceded and followed the Revolution of 1688, the Macraes supported the Episcopal Church and the House of Stuart, and as a result they suffered much, not only in property, but also in life and limb. In the Rising of 1715 a great many of them fell at the battle af Sheriffmuir, and tradition relates, as a proof of the loss they then sustained, that in the parish of Kintail alone fifty-eight women were made widows on that fatal day. In 1745, notwithstanding the fact that Seaforth[2] remained loyal to the House of Hanover, a number of young and resolute Macraes left Kintail to join the army of Prince Charles, and it is said that many more would have followed if they had not been restrained by force. Of those who went no one ever again returned, and thus ended for ever their connection as a Clan with the fortunes of the ancient Scottish House of Stuart.

During the closing decades of the last century, when the Highland regiments were raised, the Macraes entered loyally and readily into the military service of their country. Two regiments (in all four battalions) of Highlanders were raised on

---

[1] Appendix K.

[2] William, 5th Earl of Seaforth, having joined the Rising of 1715, his estates were forfeited, and his title passed under attainder. The estates were bought from the Crown in 1741 for the benefit of his son, Kenneth, who was known by the courtesy title of Lord Fortrose, which was the subordinate title of the Earls of Seaforth. Lord Fortrose was the "Seaforth" of the time of Prince Charles, but, notwithstanding his well known Jacobite sympathies, he considered it more prudent to remain loyal to the House of Hanover

the Seaforth estates between 1778 and 1804,[1] and
the Macraes were numerous in both. Many of them
served also as officers, and frequently with distinction,
in other Highland regiments, and during the Indian
wars of that period, and the great European wars
which followed the French Revolution, the Macraes,
like so many of the other Highland Clans, added their
full share of lustre to the honour of British Arms.

The chief written authority for the early history
of the Macraes is the MS. genealogy of the Clan,
which was written towards the close of the seventeenth century by the last Episcopalian minister
of Dingwall, the Rev. John Macrae, who died in
1704. The original MS., which appears to be now
lost, is believed, without any apparent evidence,
however, to have been at one time in the possession of the late Dr W. F. Skene. A copy of
it, with additions, was made by Farquhar Macrae of Inverinate in 1786. This transcript copy
appears to have been taken to India by Farquhar's
son, Surgeon John Macrae, where a copy of it,
which is now in the possession of Captain John
MacRae Gilstrap of Ballimore, was made by Colonel
Sir John Macra of Ardintoul about 1816. Several
copies of Sir John's transcript appear to have been
made from time to time in Kintail and Lochalsh,
and are still occasionally met with. A copy of it
was printed at Camden, South Carolina, in 1874 ;
and another copy, which belonged to the late Miss
Flora Macra of Ardintoul, was published in *The
Scottish Highlander* in 1887. The additions made

1 Appendix D.

by Farquhar of Inverinate appear to have been limited to his own family, and there is some reason to believe that the valuable additions now found in some copies of this MS., with regard to other families, were made by one of the Ardintoul family. At all events, Archibald of Ardintoul says, in a letter written in 1817 to his son, Sir John, then in India, that he will endeavour to add to the genealogy down to his own day. The oldest copy now known to exist is in the possession of Horatio Ross Macrae, Esq. of Clunes, and bears on the fly-leaf of it the date 1760, but this is probably the transcript which was made by Farquhar of Inverinate, and which, though said to have been finished only in 1786, may have been commenced much earlier. It is certainly not the original copy. The style of the MS., though somewhat quaint, is clear and forcible, showing considerable literary power and a perfect mastery of the English language, and there is about it a sobriety of tone which gives an impression that the writer was thoroughly acquainted with his facts, and that his statements may be accepted with confidence.

CHAPTER II.

I. FIONNLA DUBH MAC GILLECHRIOSD.

According to the Rev. John Macrae, the founder of
the Clan Macrae of Kintail was Fionnla Dubh Mac
Gillechriosd (Black Finlay, the son of Christopher),
who was removed by two or three generations from
the man who came from Clunes. Finlay Dubh was
a contemporary of Murdo Mackenzie, fifth chief of
Kintail, who died in 1416, leaving an only child to
succeed him. This child's name was Alexander, and
is known as Alister Ionraic (Alexander the Upright).
Alexander being a minor at the time of his father's
death, was sent as a ward of the King to the High

School in Perth, probably after the Parliament which
was held at Inverness by James I. in 1427. During
his absence at school, the Constable of Ellandonan
Castle, whose name was Macaulay, appears to have
been left in charge of affairs, but through the
misconduct and oppression of certain illegitimate
relatives of the young chief, serious troubles arose
in Kintail. The Constable's position becoming now
somewhat difficult, he became anxious for the return
of his young master, and as he was himself unable
to leave his post he proposed Finlay Dubh as the
most suitable person to go to Perth to bring the
young chief home, " who was then there with the
rest of the King's ward children." This choice was
approved by the people   Finlay accordingly went
to Perth, and prevailed upon Alexander to escape
from school without the consent or knowledge of the
master. To avoid pursuit they went to Macdougal
of Lorn instead of going straight home. Macdougal
received them kindly, and Alexander made the
acquaintance of his daughter, and afterwards married
her. In due time they arrived in Kintail, and by
Finlay's counsel and help, the oppressors of the
people were soon brought under subjection, and
order established throughout Mackenzie's land. The
good counsel and judicious guidance of Finlay Dubh
was not lost upon Alexander, who became a good,
just, and prosperous ruler, and greatly increased the
power and the influence of the House of Kintail.
Finlay Dubh had two sons—

1. CHRISTOPHER, of whom below.

2. JOHN, who was educated at Beauly Priory,

took holy orders, and became priest of Kintail,[1] in Sutherlandshire He married, as priests in the Highlands often did in those days, and had a daughter Margaret, who was lady-in-waiting to the Countess of Sutherland, and who appears to have married John Gordon of Drummoy, son of Adam Gordon, Dean of Caithness, son of Alexander, 1st Earl of Huntly.[2] From this marriage descended the Gordons of Embo, and for that reason we are told that "there was of old great friendship and correspondence betwixt the Gordons of Sutherland, come of this family, and the Macraes of Kintail."

II. CHRISTOPHER, eldest son of Finlay Dubh, of whom very little is known, had four sons—

1. FINLAY, of whom below.

2. DONALD, whose descendants lived at Fortrose, where one of them, Alexander Macrae, was a well-known writer whose name appears frequently in legal documents from 1629 to 1673.

3. DUNCAN, who was the most noted of Christopher's sons, is known in the traditions of Kintail as Donnacha Mor na Tuagh (Big Duncan of the Battle-axe). He was a man of great valour and personal strength, and many legends have been preserved of the brave deeds he performed in the

---

1 Kintail was the old name of a district in the north-west of Sutherlandshire, which was divided, about the middle of the last century, into the parishes of Tongue and Durness The name Kintail—Gaelic, *Cintaille*, or *Ceanntaile*—is said to mean the head of the two seas—a description which applies to the Sutherland Kintail as well as to the Ross-shire one.

2 Reference is made at some length to this Margaret in The Earls of Sutherland by Sir Robert Gordon, who speaks of her in the highest terms. The Rev John Macrae's account of the marriage does not agree with Sir Robert's in every point, but there is no doubt that Margaret was related to the Macraes of Kintail.

contests of the Mackenzies and the Macraes with
their common enemies. He greatly distinguished
himself with his battle-axe at the Battle of Park,
which was fought at Strathpeffer between the Macdonalds and the Mackenzies shortly before the death
of Alexander Ionraic, which took place in 1488.[1]
The circumstances which led to this famous fight
were the following :—Coinneach à Bhlair (Kenneth
of the Battle), the son and heir of Alexander Ionraic,
had married Margaret, daughter of John Macdonald
of Islay, who laid claim to the lordship of the Isles
and the earldom of Ross. One Christmas eve
Kenneth was insulted by Alexander Macdonald of
Lochalsh, the nephew and heir of John of Islay.
In revenge for the insult Kenneth sent his wife
back to her father. The lady, who was blind of
one eye, was sent away mounted on a one-eyed
horse, attended by a one-eyed servant, and followed
by a one-eyed dog. John of Islay and Alexander
of Lochalsh, roused to fury by this outrageous
insult, mustered all their followers, to the number
of more than fifteen hundred warriors, and set out
on an expedition to punish the Mackenzies. The
Macdonalds, plundering and destroying as they
went, directed their march to Kinellan, in Strathpeffer, where the Baron of Kintail was then residing.
They arrived at Contin one Sunday morning and
burned the church, together with the priest and a

---

[1] The exact date of the Battle of Park does not appear to be known, the
official records relating to the Highlands at this time being exceedingly
meagre   Sir Robert Gordon, in his History of the Earls of Sutherland, a book
written about the close of the sixteenth century says it was fought shortly
after 1476.

large congregation of aged men, women, and children, who were worshipping in it at the time.

Meantime, on the approach of the enemy, Kenneth and his two brothers, Duncan and Hector Roy, sent their aged father for safety to the Raven's Rock, a prominent and precipitous hill overhanging the Dingwall and Skye Railway between Strathpeffer and Garve. They then led their followers, who numbered only six hundred men, against the Macdonalds, and the battle was fought on the moor which is still known as Blar-na-Pairc, a well-known spot about a mile west of the Strathpeffer wells. The Mackenzies were led by Kenneth himself, and Alexander of Lochalsh seems to have acted as leader of the Macdonalds, while their chief warrior was Lachlan Maclean of Lochbuy, called Lachlan Mac Thearlaich (Lachlan, son of Charles). Duncan Mor, who was one of the personal attendants of Kenneth, thinking that he had been somewhat slighted in the arrangements made for the battle, showed unmistakable signs of sulkiness. He was persuaded, however, by Hector Roy to take up a battle-axe and join in the fight. With his battle-axe he did so much havoc that the Macdonalds began to give way before him. Lachlan Mac Thearlaich, seeing this, put himself in Duncan's way in order to check his murderous career. The two champions met in deadly combat. Lachlan being a powerful man, clad in mail and well trained in the use of arms, seemed at first to be having the best of the fight, but, in an unguarded moment, he exposed himself to his opponent's battle-axe, which at one deadly stroke severed his head from his body.

The superior strategy of Kenneth was already telling severely against the much larger army of the enemy, and the Macdonalds, seeing their champion killed, gave up the struggle as lost, and fled. Duncan Mor took a foremost part in the pursuit, which was continued on the following day as far as Strathconon, until most of the Macdonalds were either slain or taken prisoners. Both John of Islay and his nephew, Alexander of Lochalsh, were among the prisoners, but within six months they were both magnanimously released. This victory, to which Duncan Mor had so greatly contributed, "put Kenneth in great respect throughout the North," and he was afterwards knighted by James IV. "for being highly instrumental in reducing his fierce countrymen to the blessings of a civilised life."

Duncan Mor afterwards took a very prominent and active part in the great feud between Hector Roy and the Macleods of Gairloch. We are told that " Duncan, with his son Dougal, who was a strong, prudent, and courageous man, with ten or twelve other Kintail men, were always, upon the least notice, ready to go and assist Hector whenever, wherever, and in whatever he had to do, for which cause there was a friendly correspondence between the family of Gairloch and the Macraes of Kintail." The greatest defeat that Hector Roy inflicted on the Macleods was at the battle of Bealach Glasleathaid near Kintail. Both Duncan and his son Dougal took part in this fight, in the course of which Dougal was attacked by four men at once. On being informed that his son was in great danger, Duncan calmly

replied, "Leave him alone, if he is my son there is no
fear of him," and so it turned out, for Dougal killed
the four Macleods without receiving any serious hurt
himself. At the battle of Druim a Chait[1] (the
Cat's Back), which was fought on a subsequent
occasion at the place so called on the west side
of Knockfarrel, in Strathpeffer, between the Mackenzies under Hector Roy, and the Munros, Ding-
walls, and Maccullochs, under Sir William Munro of
Foulis, Duncan once more distinguished himself
and largely contributed to the defeat of the Munros
and their allies, which was so complete that few of
them escaped alive. "It is said of this Duncan that
he was in many conflicts and combats, and always
came off victorious, but never without a wound.
He was a facetious and yet a bloody man."

Duncan Mor na Tuagh is sometimes spoken of
as Mackenzie's ploughman, but it is not at all likely
that a member of what appears at this time to have
been the leading family in Kintail next to the Baron
himself should occupy such a position. The Gaelic
term *Scallag*, which in this case has been translated
ploughman, formerly meant any servant or retainer.
In the MS. history of the Mackenzies, which was
written by Rev. John Macrae, author of the Macrae
Genealogy, it is stated that Duncan Mor happened
accidentally to be present the day of the Battle
of Park, on some other business, and that he was the

---

1 This battle is sometimes called the Battle of Tobair nan-Ceann (the well
of heads). It is said that Hector and his men, being armed with battle axes
and two edged swords, did so much execution among their enemies that no fewer
than nineteen heads rolled down into a well in a hollow below a spot where
they overtook a party of the enemy during the pursuit—hence the name
Tobair-nan-Ceann.

principal officer of Kintail. Comparing the various traditional and MS. accounts of this remarkable man, perhaps the most natural conclusion to arrive at is that at this time he may have been young and untried; that he first gave proof of his valour and prowess at the Battle of Park, and that he afterwards became either the factor of Kintail or perhaps the principal officer of the Baron's fighting men. It is not at all unlikely that Duncan Mor began his career as a page or personal servant, that is as the *scallag* of Mackenzie, probably of Sir Kenneth à Bhlair, but whatever the commencement of his career may have been, it is quite certain that a man around whose memory so many legends and traditions of a heroic kind have gathered must have been, in spite of possible eccentricities, an important and leading man among his own countrymen.[1]

The male succession of Duncan Mor na Tuagh failed in the person of Duncan Roy Macrae, who died at Conchraig of Tollie in 1679

4. MAURICE, married and left issue.

✗ III. FINLAY, eldest son of Christopher, was the contemporary and chief counsellor of John of Killin, ninth Baron of Kintail, who fought at Flodden in 1513, and at Pinkie in 1547. John of Killin was a minor at the time of the death of his father, Sir Kenneth à Bhlair, in 1491. He was still a minor when, in consequence of the death of his eldest brother, Kenneth Og (Kenneth the younger), in 1497, he became Baron of Kintail. Kenneth Og

---

[1] For a more detailed account of the exploits of Duncan Mor na Tuagh, see chapter on legends and traditions of the clan.

was the only child of Kenneth à Bhlair's first wife,
Lady Margaret Macdonald, of whom her husband
disposed in the ignominious manner already described. A few days after sending Lady Margaret
away, Kenneth, at the head of a large body of his
followers, went to Lord Lovat to demand his
daughter, Agnes Fraser, in marriage. Lord Lovat,
having no friendly feeling towards the Macdonalds
at that time, delivered his daughter over to Kenneth,
and they lived together ever after as husband and
wife. John of Killin was the first issue of this
irregular marriage, and although the marriage is
said to have been legitimised by the Pope, Hector
Roy declared his nephew, John of Killin, illegitimate,
and seized the estates for himself. Hector being a
well known and a very popular man, appears to have
received all but the unanimous support of the people
of Kintail, and one of the Clann Ian Charrich Macraes, called Malcolm, was made Constable of Ellandonan Castle. Finlay, however, took up the cause
of John of Killin, between whose supporters and
those of Hector Roy there arose a feud which lasted
for some years.

In course of time, however, John of Killin,
young as he was, proved quite a match for his uncle,
Hector Roy, whom he surprised one night at
Fairburn, by a clever stratagem, and took prisoner.
It was agreed between them that night that Hector
should hold the estates until John attained the
age of twenty-one, after which Hector promised to
restore the estates, 'and to acknowledge John ever
afterwards as his chief. John's supporters insisted

that Ellandonan Castle, being the principal residence of the family, should be given up to him at once. As Malcolm Mac Ian Charrich refused, however, to surrender the Castle, John's supporters laid siege to it, and had Malcolm's cattle brought down to the seaside and there slaughtered to feed the besiegers. Malcolm, however, would not surrender without Hector's consent, and even when this was obtained, Malcolm still refused to surrender until compensated for the loss of his cattle. Hector eventually persuaded Malcolm to yield, whereupon John of Killin dismissed him from the Constableship, to which he appointed Finlay's son, Christopher. It is said that the Clann Ian Charrich family of Macraes did not afterwards assume much importance in Kintail.

Finlay is said to have had four sons.

1. CHRISTOPHER, of whom below.

2. JOHN, called Ian Mor nan Cas (Big John of the feet), a name which he is said to have received under the following circumstances: Roderick,[1] brother of John of Killin, being charged with manslaughter, King James V. ordered him to be given up to justice. John of Killin accordingly set out with a party of men to apprehend him in Kintail, but Roderick, being a very powerful man, "and unwilling to be brought as a prisoner, while the party were struggling to bring him, and could not, this John took him by the feet, and so got him down, when each man having a leg, an arm, or some other hold of him, they carried him along until he consented to walk on his feet with them to the presence

[1] This Roderick was progenitor of the Mackenzies, Achilty, Fairburn, &c.

of his injured brother." John Mor nan Cas left sons, and his descendants appear to have settled in Lochcarron and Kishorn, where several of them are said to have been living in 1786.

3. GILPATRICK is also said to have left issue.

4. MILES or *Maolmuire* was killed at Kinloch-ewe shortly before 1539 by the followers of Donald Gorm Macdonald, of Sleat. Part of a monument erected on the spot where Miles was killed is said to have been standing about 1700. Miles left numerous issue, some of whom appear to have lived in Gairloch, and others in Tain.

IV. CHRISTOPHER, eldest son of Finlay, was appointed Constable of Ellandonan Castle, as already stated, probably about 1511. Very little is known about him except that he held the office with trustworthiness and success, until shortly before Donald Gorm's invasion of Kintail in 1539. His sons were—

1. CHRISTOPHER, called Christopher Beg (Little Christopher), whose male succession terminated in 1685.

2. DUNCAN, of whom below.

3. FARQUHAR, progenitor of the Torlysich family, of whom hereafter. The descendants of this Farquhar were called the *Black Macraes*, as distinguished from the descendants of his brother Duncan, who were called the *Fair Macraes*.

4. FINLAY, called Finlay Dubh. He married Isabel, daughter of Sir Dougal Mackenzie, Priest of Kintail, who is spoken of as a very beautiful woman, but of doubtful character. Finlay lived

at Aryngan, near Ardintoul. While his brother
Duncan, who married Sir Dougal's widow, was
living in Strathglass, as mentioned below, Finlay
went to see him, and his wife went along with him
to see her mother. During this visit Finlay's wife
made the acquaintance of a man called Alister
Dubh, a son of Chisholm of Comer. Alister Dubh
afterwards followed her to Kintail, and, taking
advantage one day of Finlay's absence from home,
eloped with her to Strathglass. She had a
young boy called Christopher, whom she took with
her. This Christopher settled in Strathglass, where
he became a man of importance and means, and
from him the Macraes of Strathglass were
descended. Finlay, believing that his wife had
encouraged Alister Dubh's plot, did not attempt to
bring her back, and disowned her henceforth.

5. JOHN.

6. DONALD.

V. DUNCAN, second son of Christopher IV.,
was called Donnacha Mac Gillechriosd. He was in
his own day a prominent man in the affairs of
Kintail, and gained great renown for himself by
killing Donald Gorm Macdonald, of Sleat, at the
siege of Ellandonan Castle, in 1539.[1] The circumstances which led to that event were the following:
Some time before this, Donald Gorm, having
devastated the lands of Macleod of Dunvegan, who

---

[1] There seems to be some doubt as to the date of this siege. 1539 is the
date usually given, but 1537 is also mentioned. As the feud appears to have
continued for some time, and as Donald Gorm made more than one raid into
Kintail, it is possible that 1537 may have been the date of the first raid, and
1539 the date of the one which resulted in his death.

was an ally of John of Killin, passed over to the mainland, laid waste the district of Kinlochewe, and killed, among others, Miles, son of Finlay Macrae, as already mentioned.   John of Killin, naturally exasperated by this unprovoked invasion of his own territory, as well as by the raid against his friend and ally, Macleod of Dunvegan, sent his son Kenneth to Sleat with a large body of followers to retaliate on the Macdonalds.   Thereupon Donald Gorm invaded Kintail with a strong party, carried off a great deal of booty, and aggravated matters further still by killing Sir Dougal Mackenzie,[1] Priest of Kintail, who was then living at Achyuran, in Glensheil.   It would appear that both parties made more than one raid into each other's territories, and that the feud continued for some time.

At all events, on a subsequent occasion, Donald Gorm, hearing that Ellandonan Castle was but very weakly garrisoned, made a sudden raid upon it with a number of birlins or galleys, full of his followers, in the hope of being able to take it by surprise   The Constable of the Castle at this time was John Dubh Matheson, of Fernaig, who had married Sir Dougal Mackenzie's widow,

1 Sir Dougal Mackenzie appears to have been a member of the House of Kintail.   A certain Sir Dougal Mackenzie is said to have been one of the Commissioners sent to the Pope in 1491 to procure the legitimisation of Kenneth à Blilair's marriage with Agnes Fraser of Lovat.   It is not impossible that this may have been the man who was killed by Donald Gorm nearly fifty years afterwards, even though he left a young and marriageable widow. The Sir Dougal who went to Rome is said to have been made a " Knight to the boot of Pope Clement VIII."   The title *Sir*, however, as formerly applied to the Clergy, did not imply any superiority of rank   It simply meant that the bearer of it had taken only the degree of Bachelor of Arts, whereas the title *Mr* indicated the higher degree of Master of Arts.

and had recently been appointed to the Constableship in succession to Christopher Macrae. The
rumour that reached Donald Gorm with regard to
the unprotected state of Ellandonan was only too
true, for John Dubh and the watchman were the
only two in the Castle The advance of the
boats was noticed by the watchman, who gave
the alarm; but there was no time to gather
men from the mainland before the enemy arrived
It so happened, however, that Duncan Mac Gillechriosd was passing by on his way from Lochalsh,
and, hearing the cry of alarm, he made for
the Castle with all speed. He arrived there before
the enemy, and thirsting for revenge against the
Macdonalds for having lately killed his uncle Miles
at Kinlochewe, he took his stand at the postern
gate of the tower and killed several of the crew of
the first galley as they were landing. As the
enemy crowded upon him in increasing numbers,
he made his way into the tower, and barricad-
ing the gate behind him, joined the Constable and
the watchman in defending the Castle.

Donald Gorm immediately began a furious
battering of the gate, but the dauntless three had
so strongly secured it with iron bars on the inside,
and they harassed the besiegers so much by throw-
ing stones among them from within, that he was
obliged to withdraw his men. Both sides now
began to use their bows and arrows. The Macdonalds, who were suffering heavily themselves,
aimed at the embrasures, and in this way they
unfortunately succeeded in killing the Constable.

Duncan was now left alone with the watchman and his last arrow to defend the fort. This arrow he resolved to save until a favourable opportunity occurred for making effective use of it. The opportunity soon arrived, for at this stage Donald Gorm had the masts of some of his galleys taken down for the purpose of trying to make a breach in the wall or to mount it, and as he moved round the Castle to discover the weakest and most suitable point of attack, Duncan, thinking the opportunity a favourable one, took aim with his last arrow, and struck him on the foot. The arrow was a barbed one, and in pulling it out of the wound an artery was severed. Every possible effort was made to stop the bleeding, but without avail. The wounded chief was then conveyed by his men some distance away from the Castle to a reef, which is still called *Larach tigh Mhic Dhomhnuill*, or the site of Macdonald's house, where he died.

For this service against the Macdonalds, James V. gave John of Killin considerable additions of land in the county of Ross, and the Macraes were thus once more instrumental in increasing the substance and the honours of the House of Kintail.

Duncan now thought, with some reason, that he had a good claim to succeed John Dubh Matheson as Constable of Ellandonan, but John of Killin thought him too rash and passionate for the post. He then put in a claim for his brother Farquhar, but, to avoid quarrels and bitterness between the Macraes and the Maclennans, who were also claimants for the post, it was decided to give it to John MacMhurchaidh Dhuibh (John, the son of Black Murdoch), priest of Kintail. Duncan was so much offended at the treatment he received in return for the excellent service he had rendered that he left Kintail in disgust, and went to the country of Lord Lovat, by whom he was kindly and hospitably received Lord Lovat gave him the lands of Culigeran, in Strathglass, but Duncan killed so many deer in the neighbouring forest of Ben Vachart that Lovat was soon obliged to move him some miles away to a place called Crochel, where he lived for several years. While living at Crochel the Baron of Kintail paid him several visits, and frequently invited him to return to Kintail. Duncan, who had all along retained an affection for his native place, at last decided to accept Kintail's offers.[1] Lord Lovat, however, being anxious to retain him, offered him for a small feu-duty the lands of Clunes which Duncan's predecessors formerly held. Duncan agreed to this proposal, and Lord Lovat being about to proceed to the south, promised him to have the necessary legal documents drawn up there before his return. When Lovat departed

[1] The year 1557 was probably the date of Duncan's return to Kintail. It was not until after the siege of Ellandonan Castle in 1539 that Duncan left Kintail and the first Lord Lovat, who died after that date, was Hugh, who was killed at the battle of Blar-na-leine near Loch Lochy in 1544 The news of his tragic end in such a famous battle could hardly have circulated as a rumour that he died at Braemar. Hugh's successor, Alexander, the fifth Lord Lovat, died at Aigas Island, in the Beauly River, in 1557. For some months previous to his death he had been travelling for his health, and it is quite possible that rumours of his death may have circulated during his travels, and may have influenced Duncan's decision to remain in Kintail.

for the south, Duncan went to Kintail to inform his friends of the offer he had received and his intention of accepting it; but while on this visit a rumour reached him that Lord Lovat had died at Braemar, and doubting whether Lovat's successor would be willing to confirm the agreement, he finally resolved to return to Kintail, where he received the quarter land of Inverinate and Dorisduan. At Inverinate, a romantic spot on the north shore of Loch Duich, he lived for the rest of his days, as did also his descendants after him for more than two centuries. Duncan married the widow of John Dubh Matheson, Constable of Ellandonan. She was a daughter of Duncan Ban of Glenmoriston, and was first married to Sir Dougal Mackenzie, as already stated. By her Duncan had two sons and a daughter, who was carried away from her father's sheiling in Affric, by John Macintaggart from Strathglass, who married her, and by whom he had several sons and daughters. Duncan lived to a good old age. His sons were—

(1). CHRISTOPHER, of whom below.

(2). JOHN, who was "a resolute and warlike man," and took a very active part in the great feud which raged at this time between the Macdonalds of Glengarry and the Mackenzies of Kintail. It is said that "few parties were sent out on desperate attempts to infest or annoy the enemy but John was commander, and he seldom or never returned without bloodshed. He might be called an Hazael for speed of foot." His brother Christopher used to tell him that his cruelty and bloodshed would bring judgment upon himself or upon his family; and it is stated that, although he had three sons who lived to old age, their progeny were of no great consequence. His sons were—

a. Christopher.

b. Duncan, who was also a warrior like his father, was an old man in 1654, when General Monk visited Kintail. It is said that, some time before this, Duncan consulted a local seer as to the manner in which he should end his days, and was informed that he would die by the sword. This appeared so improbable in the case of an old warrior who had taken part in so many bloody frays, and invariably escaped unhurt, that the question was referred to " Coinneach Odhar,"[1] the Brahan Seer, who confirmed the first seer's prediction. Duncan, however, gave the matter no credit, but one day, while Monk and his army were in Kintail, the old man left his house in Glensheil, and went up among the hills, where he was met by some soldiers who were wandering about in search of plunder, and who spoke roughly to him in English, which he

[1] Kenneth Mackenzie, better known as Coinneach Odhar (Dun Kenneth), or the Brahan Seer, was one of those prophets of former times whose mystic utterances have so frequently puzzled and startled people by their literal fulfilment. He is said to have been born in Lews about the commencement of the seventeenth century, and to have subsequently moved to the neighbourhood of Brahan, where he worked on a farm as a common labourer. Having brought upon himself, by certain unguarded utterances, the resentment of Lady Seaforth, he was by her orders apprehended, brought to trial as a wizard, and sentenced by the ecclesiastical authority to be burnt to death at Fortrose This is said to have happened while he was still a young man. (For an interesting collection of the prophecies ascribed to him by the traditions of Ross shire, see *The Prophecies of the Brahan Seer*, by Alexander Mackenzie, Inverness.)

did not understand.   Unable to brook such an insult the old man drew his sword, but was immediately overpowered and killed by the soldiers. This, we are told, was all the bloodshed committed by General Monk and his soldiers in Kintail.

c. Finlay.

J. V. Wilson & Co.]

RUINS OF ELLANDONAN CASTLE.

[_Aberdeen._

Elizabeth R. Newt[?]

B. Feb. 4 - 1845

D. Feb. 19 - 1935

Married Sept. 8 - 1868

Wm [?]jackant Newt

July - 8 - 1831

July - 4 - 1906

Elizabeth Maria Newt ([?] . . . .

Dec - 20 - 1870

Christopher Pg - 447 = D { See.
[?]Ross [?] Kindail   { Ellen
                            { Pg - 3 .

CHAPTER III.

VI. Christopher.—Constable of Ellandonan Castle.—Origin of Feud between Kintail and Glengarry. — Kenneth, Lord Kintail, obtains Crown Charter for Glengarry's Possessions in Lochcarron and Lochalsh.—Christopher and his Family contributed to Kintail's success. — Christopher an enterprising Cattle Dealer.—His Convivial Habits. — His Friendship with Sir Donald Macdonald of Sleat. — Christopher's Marriage and Family.—Duncan called Donnacha Mac Gillechriosd.—One of the Biggest Men in the Highlands.—Ian Mor a Chasteil.—Duncan and a Companion take part in the Fight of Leac na Falla, in Skye.—Angus Og of Glengarry invades Lochcarron. —Lady Mackenzie and the Kintail Men prepare to intercept Angus Og on his return —Fight at the Cailleach Rock.—Death of Angus Og —His Burial at Kilduich.—Duncan robbed at Elycht Fair.—The Rev. John, son of Christopher VI.—Tutor or Governor to Colin, Earl Seaforth.—Other Descendants of Christopher VI. — The Rev Finlay Macrae of Lochalsh.—Jacobite and Episcopalian.—Supports Rising of 1715.—Deprived of his Living.—His Marriage.—His Descendants.—Maurice, son of Christopher VI.—Christopher Og.—Domhnul na Smuich, and Donald Beg.

VI. CHRISTOPHER, eldest son of Duncan V., was for some time Constable of Ellandonan Castle. He is said to have been "prudent and solid in counsel and advice, bold, forward and daring when need required, yet remarkably merciful during the bloody wars 'twixt Mackenzie and Glengarry." The circumstances which led to the great feud between Kintail and Glengarry[1] appear to have been somewhat as follows:— Donald Macdonald, who was Chief of Glengarry about 1580, when the feud broke out, inherited parts of Lochalsh, Lochcarron, and Lochbroom from his grandmother, Margaret, one of the sisters and co-heiresses of Sir Donald Macdonald of Lochalsh, while Mackenzie of Kintail acquired the portion of the other co-heiress, by purchase, in 1554. With the territories of two such rival clans as the Mackenzies and the Macdonalds, not only closely adjoining, but in some instances mixed up together, as those territories now were, trouble was bound to arise. Men were constantly coming and going between Lochcarron and Glengarry, and it appears that in passing through Mackenzie's territories they frequently committed acts of violence against the people. In such circumstances it was not difficult to find an excuse for a quarrel, and an incident soon occurred which brought matters to a crisis. One of Glengarry's men, having found it necessary for some reason to leave his old home, settled, with his family and cattle, in Glenaffric. Being a great hunter, he frequently resorted to the neighbouring deer forest of Glasletter, which then belonged to Mackenzie of Gairloch. One day, while hunting there, accompanied by a servant, he was surprised by Gairloch's forester, who called upon him to surrender. The forester was a Macrae called Fionnla Dubh Mac Ian Mhic Dhomh'uill Mhoir, or Fionla Dubh nam Fiadh

---

[1] For an exhaustive account of this feud, see Mackenzie's History of the Mackenzies, new edition, chapters on Colin Cam and Kenneth, first Lord Kintail.

(Black Finlay of the Deer),[1] and he also was accompanied by a gillie or servant. The hunter refused to surrender, whereupon Finlay Dubh and his companion killed both the hunter and his servant, and buried them under a bank. As soon as the murdered men were missed, suspicion fell upon the forester and his gillie, both of whom were brought to trial by Mackenzie of Kintail, but nothing could be proved against them. Shortly afterwards, however, the bodies of the murdered men were found by their friends, and, very little doubt being now left as to who were the perpetrators of the dark deed, a party of the Macdonalds set out to take vengeance. Arriving at Glenstrathfarrar, which then belonged to Mackenzie of Redcastle, they plundered the place and killed a brother of Finlay Dubh, the forester, called Duncan Mac Ian Mhic Dhomh'uill Mhoir, whom they found ploughing in his own field. When tidings of this outrage reached Roderick Mor, who was then the Laird of Redcastle, and who had old grievances of a similar kind against the Macdonalds, he resolved at whatever cost, and in spite of the advice of more cautious friends, to take up the quarrel. Such, then, was the commencement of this feud, which lasted, with little intermission, for more than a quarter of a century, and which ended in favour of Mackenzie, who obtained a Crown charter for Glengarry's possessions in Lochcarron and Lochalsh in 1607, and the superiority of all his other possessions. To this result, which added still further

[1] For the Kintail tradition of Fionula Dubh nam Fiadh and his exploits on this occasion, see chapter on the legends and traditions of the clan.

to the power and influence of the House of Kintail,
Christopher and his family greatly contributed, and
we read that Kenneth, Lord Kintail, "did always
ask his advice in any matter of consequence he had
to do in the Highlands."

Not only was Christopher a bold and stout
warrior, he was likewise an enterprising man of
business.   He was the first man in that part of
the country whc sent cattle to the markets of the
South.   For that purpose he bought cattle yearly
from the neighbouring estates, and made so much
money in his cattle-dealing that "if he was as
frugal in keeping as he was industrious in acquiring,
he had proven a very rich man in his own country."
But he appears to have been a man of decidedly
convivial habits, and to have spent his money very
freely, for when he went to Inverness, or to Fortrose,
which was then a very important place and much
frequented, "the first thing he did was to call his
landlord the vintner, and with him pitched upon
and agreed for the hogshead of wine that pleased
him best, resolving to drink it all with his acquaint-
ances before he left the town."   He was on very
friendly terms with Sir Donald Macdonald of Sleat,
commonly called Donald Gorm Mor, grandson of
Donald Gorm, who was killed by Christopher's father
at the siege of Ellandonan Castle in 1539.   This
Sir Donald was married to a sister of Kenneth, Lord
Kintail, and being on one occasion in the South,
along with his lady, he was detained there much
longer than he expected, with the result that he
ran short of money.   There were no banking trans-

actions in those days, and the credit of Highland
Chiefs, at all event in the South, was not always
good. In consequence of all this, Sir Donald was
obliged to go home for more money in order to
enable his lady to travel in a manner suitable to
her rank, and meantime she remained behind in
Perth, to await the return of her husband. It so
happened, however, that Christopher was at this
time in the South with cattle, and hearing that
Lady Macdonald, the sister of his own Chief, was
in Perth, he went to pay her his respects. On
learning the cause of her delay, he told her that he
had with him money and men enough to meet all
expenses, and to escort her safely and suitably to
her home, if she would do him the honour of
accepting his services. Christopher's offer was
gladly accepted, and starting immediately for the
North, they arrived at Sleat the next day after Sir
Donald himself. Sir Donald, who was greatly surprised and much delighted, persuaded Christopher
to remain with him for some days, with the result
that a fast friendship was established between the
two families, notwithstanding the fact that on one
occasion during the visit, while the cups were
circulating far too freely, Christopher made an ill-
timed reference to the death of Donald Gorm, and
so greatly roused the resentment of some of the
Macdonalds who were present, that they would
probably have killed him but for the interference
and protection of his host. Christopher was afterwards greatly ashamed of what he said, and Sir
Donald and he continued to be very fast friends.

Christopher married a daughter of the Rev. Murdoch Murchison,[1] Priest of Kintail, and Constable of Ellandonan Castle, who died in 1618, and by her he had seven sons, all of whom were prosperously settled before the death of their father.

1. DUNCAN, called Donnacha Mac Gillechriosd, is said to have been one of the biggest and strongest men in the Highlands. "He was equal in height and bulk of body" to John Grant, the contemporary Laird of Glenmoriston, commonly called Ian Mor a Chasteil (Big John of the Castle).[2] We are told that Duncan could pass through the doorway of the Church at Kintail only by turning sideways, and it appears, from what the clan historian relates of him, that he was no less remarkable for his prowess and force of character than for his bodily size "He was a stout, forward, and bloody man, and delighted much in arms."

The following incident, which is related of Duncan, not only shows the pleasure which he himself found in fighting, but the light-heartedness and delight with which the Highlanders of those days joined in any affray, whether they were concerned in the quarrel or not. On a certain occasion Duncan and another Kintail man, called Ian Og Mac Fhionnla Dhuibh (Young John, the son of Black Finlay), were in the Isle of Skye buying horses. On their way home, by the Coolin Hills, they observed bands of Macleods and Macdonalds,

[1] See Footnote, page 56

[2] For an interesting account of Ian Mor a Chasteil, who was Laird of Glenmoriston from 1581 to 1637, see Mackay's Urquhart and Glenmoriston— page 125.

between whom there was a feud at the time,
gathering together and making preparations for
battle. Neither Duncan nor John was in any way
concerned in the quarrel, but Duncan thought
that such an opportunity of exercising themselves
in the art of war was too good to be thrown away,
and he easily persuaded his companion to join in
the fight. In order to avoid every appearance
of injustice or partiality they resolved to take
sides. John joined the Macleods, because his
mother was of that clan, while Duncan joined
the Macdonalds, and was no doubt very glad to
do so because of the friendship which had been
established between his father and their Chief.
Duncan had the support of a powerful servant,
who managed to get possession of a pass across
a rough stream for which both parties were con-
tending. This position he held against the Macleods until the Macdonalds came up in full force,
with the result that the Macleods were defeated
with great slaughter. Tradition relates that this
was a very fierce and deadly struggle, and a
large flag-stone, which was covered with blood
at the close of the fight, is still pointed out and
known as Leac na falla[1] (the flag-stone of blood).
As soon as the victory was decided, Duncan,
who received the hearty thanks of the Macdonalds,
went in search of his companion, John Og, and,
when he found him, they resumed and continued
their homeward journey as if nothing had hap-

[1] The fight at Leac na falla has been powerfully depicted on canvas
by the well-known Highland artist, Mr Lockhart Bogle.

pened. Both had the good fortune to escape without hurt or wound. Such were the stern amusements in which our bold Highland forefathers took most delight.

In his youth Duncan took a prominent part in the great Glengarry feud. On one occasion, during the temporary absence of Kenneth, Lord Kintail, in Mull, Angus Og, son and heir of Macdonald of Glengarry, and one of the bravest and most daring of all his warriors, made a raid on Lochcarron in November, about 1602, and put to death as many of Kintail's supporters—men, women, and children —as he could lay hold of, seized the cattle and drove them to Slumbay on the north coast of Lochcarron, where his followers had left their boats. Meantime news of the raid reached Kintail, and a number of men immediately set out for Lochcarron, but before they arrived Angus Og had already put out to sea, and was beyond reach even of their arrows. The Kintail men now returned to Ellandonan, but a few of the swiftest runners among them took the shortest cut to Inverinate, where they launched a newly-built twelve-oared galley belonging to Duncan's father, and proceeded with all speed to Ellandonan, their plan being, if possible, to intercept Angus Og before he could pass through Kylerea. At Ellandonan they found Kintail's lady superintending preparations for the expedition. The galley was quickly manned by eighteen of the best and the bravest men available, besides the rowers, and placed under the command of Duncan. They had also a small boat to attend on them, and

on board the galley they had two small brass
cannons and some ammunition, which the lady served
out with her own hands, and before they started
she gave them an eloquent exhortation to play their
part bravely, and to maintain the honour of their
clan and their absent Chief like good and true men.
She then mounted the Castle wall and watched
them as they sailed away under cover of the fast
gathering shades of the winter night.

They had not gone far when they met a boat
coming to tell them that the Macdonalds were at
Kyleakin, apparently waiting for the turn of the
tide to help them through Kylerea, where the tidal
current is usually so strong that a boat can make
little headway against it. Shortly afterwards there
passed by the Kintail men, without observing them,
a small boat which they concluded to have been
sent on by the Macdonalds to see whether Kylerea
was clear. They allowed this boat to pass un-
challenged lest any alarm should be raised. It was
a calm moonlight night, with a covering of snow on
the ground, which added to the light and made it
easy to sail about even in narrow waters. The
Kintail men, therefore, decided to direct their course
at once towards the fleet of the Macdonalds, and
having filled their row-locks with seaweed to prevent the pulsing noise of their oars, they steered
towards Kyleakin. As they approached the Cailleach Rock, which lies off the coast of Skye, and not
far from the Lochalsh end of Kylerea, they observed
the first of Macdonald's galleys drawing near. They
soon discovered that this was Angus Og's great

thirty-two oared galley, sailing some distance ahead of the rest of his fleet with "his best men and gentlemen" on board. Upon observing the Kintail galley, which was quickly approaching him, Angus challenged it two or three times, but the only answer he received was a broadside from the brass cannon, which, breaking some of the oars, disabled his galley and threw it on the Cailleach Rock. His men, thinking they were driven ashore, crowded on to the rock. When they discovered their mistake, and found a stretch of water lying between them and the mainland, they became completely confused and fell easy victims to their assailants. Some of them attempted to escape by swimming, but they no sooner reached the shore than they were dispatched by men whom Duncan landed by the little boat for that purpose. Angus had about sixty men on board his galley, every one of whom was either killed or drowned. He himself was taken on board the Kintail boat alive, but was mortally wounded in the head and in the body, and died before the morning. The remainder of his fleet, to the number of about twenty galleys, hearing the sudden uproar and firing at the Cailleach Rock, turned back in confusion, and landing on the coast of Skye they made their way to Sleat, and thence crossed to the Mainland. "At this skirmish or little sea fight," says the Rev. John Macrae in his history of the Mackenzies, "not one drop of blood was shed of the Kintail men's, except of one called John Gauld Mac Fhionnla Dhuibh (John the Stranger, son of Black Finlay), whose dirk, being slippery with blood, ran through his fist and cut his four fingers. Certainly their skill and dexterity in that expedition and their unexpected victory and success ought not to be ascribed to them, but to God, whose vengeance justly followed those persons for their bloody murders of men, women, and children, and who can make any instrument prove powerful and effectual to bring His own purpose to pass."

Meantime Lady Mackenzie was anxiously waiting at Ellandonan for the result of the expedition. She heard the firing of the cannon in the night, and from this she concluded that an engagement had taken place. At daybreak she saw her protectors returning, leading Angus Og's great galley along with them She rushed down to the shore to salute them, and when she inquired if everything had gone well with them, Duncan replied, "Yes, madam, and we have brought you, without the loss of a single man, a new guest whom we hope is welcome to you." On looking into the galley she at once recognised the body of Angus Og of Glengarry, and immediately gave orders that it should be properly attended to. On the following day Angus Og was buried in a manner suitable to his rank at Kilduich, in the same grave as some of Lady Mackenzie's own children. The common tradition in Kintail used to be that he was buried in the doorway of the church at Kilduich, but in a MS. history of the Mackenzies, written about the middle of the seventeenth century,[1] and which may be regarded as

---

[1] This MS., which is frequently quoted in Mackenzie's History of the Mackenzies as the "Ancient MS.," together with Rev. John Macrae's History

conclusive on this point, the writer tells us that to say he was buried in the church door is a "malicious lie," because he himself had seen "the head raised out of the same grave and returned again, wherein there were too small cuts, noways deep."

Duncan, like his father, appears to have engaged in cattle dealing, and from the record of a meeting of the Privy Council held in Edinburgh on the 11th December, 1600, it appears that at the Fair of Elcyht (Alyth ?), on the 1st of November, 1599, he was robbed by a certain Oliver Ogilvy and others of twenty-six cows and four hundred silver marks. Duncan died without male issue, but left several daughters.

2. THE REV. FARQUHAR, second son of Christopher, will be mentioned hereafter.

3 THE REV. JOHN, third son of Christopher VI., was "a man of an able and strong body, a sharp and sagacious mind, and somewhat more curious in his learning than his elder brother, Mr Farquhar." Mr John was governor or tutor to Colin Mackenzie, first Earl of Seaforth, at the University of Edinburgh, and appears to have gained a great influence over his pupil, whose "early and unexpected death (in 1633) did so dispirit him that he afterwards lived in the Highlands more obscurely than was expected of him." He also studied medicine, and left behind him a great reputation among his

of the Mackenzies, which is known as the Ardintoul MS, form the chief authorities for this account of the death of Angus Og.

own countrymen for his skill as a physician. He was married to a daughter of Dugald Matheson of Balmacarra, and lived to a great age. He left three sons—Christopher, Donald, and Duncan. The following extract, from the Rev. John Macrae's history, is interesting as showing what an expensive luxury tobacco was in the days of Mr John :—
"I remember that after Mr John's death, when his friends were examining his papers, there was among them a letter directed to him at Edinburgh from Alexander Mackenzie, the first of the family of Kilcoy, and son of Colin Cam, XI. of Kintail, telling he had received the pound of tobacco sent him, and blaming Mr John for not sending him more of it, as he got it so cheap as twenty pounds Scots the pound," that is £1 13s 4d sterling. It need hardly be added that this sum meant much more then than it does now.

4. FINLAY, fourth son of Christopher VI., and VII. from Finlay Dubh Mac Gille Chriosd, is said to have been a handsome man, and of good ability according to the education he received. He was frugal and industrious, and left considerable means to his children. He did not live long, but left four sons, the eldest of whom was

(VIII.) DONALD, called Domhnull Dubh. He is spoken of as an able, strong man, of good sense, and well to live. He had five sons and three daughters—

(1.) CHRISTOPHER, "a well-humoured, free-hearted gentleman," died young and without issue.

(2.) DONALD, mentioned below,

(3.) FINLAY.

(4.) DUNCAN.

(5.) FARQUHAR.

(6) A daughter, who married Alexander Macrae of Achyark, son of Alexander of Inverinate.

(7.) MARGARET, who married Farquhar, son of Alexander of Inverinate.

(8.) A daughter, who married Alexander, brother-german of Murdoch Mackenzie of Fairburn.

(IX.) DONALD, son of Donald Dubh, was called Donald Og (Donald the Younger) He is said to have been well known in the North, and in many parts of the South, for an "affable, generous gentleman." He was endowed with great natural parts and ready wit, and though he got little education, he was Chamberlain of Kintail for several years, and discharged the duties of the post with exactness and success. He married, first, Anne, daughter of Alexander Macrae of Inverinate, who died within a year of her marriage, without issue He married, secondly, Isabel, daughter of John Grant of Corrimony, by whom he had several sons and daughters, though the names of only three are recorded—

(1.) ALEXANDER, for whom he made liberal provisions.

(2.) THE REV. FINLAY, mentioned below.

(3.) THE REV. DUNCAN, who was a youth of great promise, and an eloquent preacher. He was educated at Aberdeen, and was tutor in the family of Mackenzie of Findon, where he died in November, 1690. He was buried in Dingwall.

(X.) THE REV. FINLAY, second son of Donald Og,

was educated at St Leonard's College, St Andrews, and obtained his degree on the 24th July, 1679. He officiated for a time in the Island of Cumbray, in the Firth of Clyde, which he left at the time of the Revolution in 1688. He was afterwards presented to the parish of Lochalsh by Frances, Countess of Seaforth, in 1695. Being a strong Jacobite and Episcopalian, he refused to conform to Presbytery, or to take the prescribed oaths, and was consequently looked upon as an intruder by the Presbyterians. In 1715 he strongly urged his parishioners to take up arms on behalf of the House of Stuart, under William, Earl of Seaforth, and it was, no doubt, to some extent owing to his influence that so many of the men of Lochalsh joined in that rising. His sympathy with the House of Stuart cost him his parish, of which he was deprived on the 21st September, 1716. The Rev. Finlay is said to have been "a great philosopher and divine, a clear preacher, of ministerial and dignified appearance, and much given to hospitality and charity." He married Margaret, daughter of Duncan Macrae of Inverinate, with issue, and died not later than 1728, as his son, John, was served heir on the 15th October of that year. So far as it can now be traced, the succession of the Rev. Finlay is as follows—

(1.) JOHN, mentioned below.

(2.) HECTOR, who was tacksman of Ardelve, and was alive in 1761, as he is said to have been tutor or guardian to the family of John Macrae of Conchra, who died in that year

(3.) DONALD, called Donald Bane, married Barbara Macrae, widow of John, son of the Rev. Donald Macrae of Kintail, with issue—

(a.) Finlay, called Finlay Fadoch, a well-known schoolmaster in Fadoch, and afterwards in Ardelve, about the close of the last and beginning of the present century. He afterwards went, when a very old man, to America. He married a daughter of John Macrae (Ian Mac Mhurachaidh), the Kintail poet, and had issue—(a1) Duncan, born 1803; (a2) Anne, who married Duncan Macrae, Drudaig, and went to America; (a3) Barbara, who married Kenneth Mackenzie, Lochcarron, with issue—Kenneth, Malcolm, and Thomas.

(b.) Jane, who married Murdoch Macrae, who had a son, Malcolm, who married Janet Macrae and had a son. John, now living at Dornie, and a daughter, Isabella, married to Roderick Matheson at Totaig Ferry.

(4.) MARION, daughter of the Rev. Finlay, married John Matheson, and had, with other issue, a son,

(a.) Alexander, who was for some years tenant of Reraig, in Lochalsh, and afterwards merchant and schoolmaster at Dornie. He married Catherine Matheson of the Bennetsfield family, and had with other issue—

(a1.) John, who married Isabella, daughter of Donald Macrae, and had a large family, of whom are Alexander Matheson, shipowner, and Betsie Matheson, shopkeeper, both living at Dornie.

(a2.) Farquhar, who married Isabella, daughter of Kenneth Mackenzie, Kishorn, of the Applecross

family, and had a large family, one of whom is
Kenneth Matheson, merchant, Salen, in Argyllshire,
who is married, with issue. Another is the well-
known Dr Farquhar Matheson, of London. After
studying at the Universities of Glasgow and Aberdeen, and graduating in medicine, Dr Farquhar
Matheson went as a young man to London, where
he has risen to eminence in his profession, and is
particularly recognised as an experienced and skilful specialist in diseases of the ear, nose, and throat.
He is one of the surgeons to the Royal Ear and
Throat Hospital, London. For many years he has
been one of the best known and most influential
Highlanders in London, and is at the present time
(1896) President of the Gaelic Society of London,
Joint Secretary of the Highland Society, Governor
and Surgeon to the Royal Scottish Hospital, a
Justice of the Peace for the County of London, and
a Fellow of several learned and scientific Societies.
Dr Matheson is married and has issue, two daughters, Isabel and Barbara, and a son, Farquhar, at
present a student of Cambridge University.

(a3). Margaret married Farquhar Matheson, and
had, with other issue, a daughter, Margaret, who
married Duncan Matheson, innkeeper, Dornie, and
had issue :—Donald, now living in Glasgow, married
Christina Macpherson, with issue ; Farquhar, now
living at Dornie, married Jane Macrae (Auchtertyre
family), Mary married Andrew Ross ; Margaret
married Farquhar Macrae now living at Inversheil.[1]

1 This statement of the descendants of Marion, daughter of the Rev.
Finlay Macrae, is taken from a full and interesting account of her descendants,
given to the author by the above-mentioned Miss Betsie Matheson of Dornie,
in August, 1896.

(5). ISABEL, who married Duncan, son of Alexander Macrae of Conchra, with issue.

(XI). JOHN, eldest son of the Rev. Finlay, was served heir on the 15th October, 1728. Tradition says he was one of the best swordsmen of his time in the Highlands,[1] and he appears to have been a man of mark in his own country. He had a son—

(1). ALEXANDER, who married, as his first wife, Isabella Macrae, and had issue,

(a). Hector married Anne Macrae, with issue; Alexander, now a blacksmith at Bundalloch, married with issue; and John, who died about 1890, leaving issue.

(b). Isabella.

Alexander, son of John, son of the Rev. Finlay, married, as his second wife, Kate Macrae, and had issue.

(c). Duncan, who married Flora, daughter of John Macrae by his wife, Catherine, daughter of John Og, son of the Rev. Donald Macrae of Kintail, and by her had issue —(c1) John, married with issue, in America; (c2) Alexander, who died unmarried; (c3) Donald, now living at Fadoch, married a daughter of the late Alexander Macrae, commonly known as Alister Mor na Pait (Big Alexander of Patt), and has issue .—Duncan, Helen, Alexander, John, now living in London, and by whom this statement of the descendants of his grandfather, Duncan, was given to the author in November, 1896. Catherine, Duncan, Farquhar, James, Donald, Flora; (c4) Anne, married with issue, in America;

[1] See chapter on legends and traditions of the clan

(c5) Isabella; (c6) Flora; (c7) Helen, married in Strathglass; (c8) Catherine, married Donald Macdonald, with issue—

(d). John; (e). Farquhar, married with issue, and went to America; (f). Mary; (g). Catherine; (h). Rebecca

5. MAURICE, fifth son of Christopher VI., is said to have been a strong and industrious man, who loved Kintail better than any other place. He had advantageous offers from Earl Colin to go to Kinlochewe; but he would not go, and the Earl, appreciating his devotion to his native place, gave him his choice of a tack in it. He was a man of means, and gave money to the Laird of Chisholm, for which he and his successors had grazing in Glen Affric till the principal was paid. Maurice was drowned in Strathglass on his way home from Inverness, and was buried in Kintail. He left issue.

6. CHRISTOPHER, sixth son of Christopher VI., was called Christopher Og. He left sons and daughters.

7. DONALD, seventh son of Christopher VI., was called Domhnull na Smurich,[1] or Domhnull Beg. He was of short stature, "but so remarkable for strength and nimbleness that few would venture to compete with him, since all that did were worsted in such exercises as required strength and dexterity. He was a great drover, lived well but not long, and left no male issue."

[1] Smurich, genitive of smurach, which means dross or dust.

CHAPTER IV.

VII.—THE REV. FARQUHAR MACRAE, second
son of Christopher (VI.), was born at Ellandonan
Castle in 1580. He was a delicate child, but grew
up to be a man of good physique and great bodily
strength. His father, perceiving that he possessed
good ability and a talent for learning, sent him to
school at Perth, where he remained for four or five
years, and became very proficient in Latin. Some

of his exercises and discourses in that language are mentioned as being still preserved in the year 1704. From Perth he proceeded to the University of Edinburgh, where he studied under James Reid, one of the Regents or Professors of the University, and soon surpassed all his fellow students in the study both of classics and of philosophy. His repute for learning and scholarship was so great at the University that he was unanimously chosen in 1603 to succeed James Reid as Regent, but Kenneth, Lord Kintail, who was in Edinburgh at the time, earnestly opposed the appointment, as he was anxious to secure Mr Farquhar's services for his own people in the Highlands. Mr Farquhar himself was not anxious to accept the appointment either, as his great desire was to become a preacher of the Gospel, and with a view to that calling he had already studied divinity at the University. He therefore fell in readily with Lord Kintail's proposal, and about this time left the University to fill the post of headmaster of the Fortrose Grammar School, which then enjoyed a great reputation in the North, and where he remained for about fifteen months. He appears to have passed his "trials" or examinations for the Church while he was at Fortrose, and having been admitted to Holy Orders he very soon acquired celebrity as a "sound, learned, eloquent, and grave preacher."

About this time some ironworks[1] were commenced at Letterewe, on Loch Maree, in the parish of Gair-

[1] For an interesting account of the historic ironworks, not only in Gairloch but in other parts of the Highlands, see J H Dixon's Gairloch, page 75, &c.

loch, by Sir George Hay, who afterwards figured prominently in Scottish history as the Earl of Kinnoull and High Chancellor of Scotland. Sir George introduced a colony of Englishmen to carry on the works. It therefore became necessary to provide for that parish a clergyman who could preach well in English, and Bishop David Lindesay, who then held the diocese of Ross, selected the young Mr Farquhar as the most suitable man at his disposal. He was accordingly appointed Vicar of Gairloch in 1608, and continued to hold that office until 1618. We read, however, that another Vicar, the Rev. Farquhar Mackenzie, was admitted to the parish of Gairloch about the year 1614. The probability is that the two clergymen shared the work of the extensive parish between them, and that the Rev. Farquhar Macrae restricted his ministrations to the English-speaking ironworkers, and to the part of the parish which lies to the north of Loch Maree, and which was then regarded as part of the parish of Lochbroom. Mr Farquhar's ministrations gave great satisfaction, not only to the native people of Gairloch, but also to the ironworkers, and more especially to Sir George Hay himself, who found great pleasure in his society, and became much attached to him. Sir George was a learned lawyer and a man of science, and probably did not find the contemporary Laird of Gairloch—John Roy Mackenzie[1]—such congenial company as the scholarly and cultured Vicar. John Roy does not appear to

---

[1] John Roy Mackenzie was Laird of Gairloch from 1566 to 1628 He was a warrior of renown, and among his bravest followers were some of the Macraes of Kintail See chapter on the legends and traditions of the clan.

have been a very loyal supporter of the Church, for in 1612 we find Mr Farquhar raising an action. against him for payment of the teinds or tithes. The action went on for several years, and was won by Mr Farquhar, who, in 1616, let the tithes of Gairloch to Alexander Mackenzie, Fiar of Gairloch, for the yearly sum of £80 Scots.[1] Mr Farquhar lived at Ardlair, which is only about four miles from Letterewe,[2] where Sir George lived, and as there were probably very few men of scholarly and scientific tastes in Gairloch in those days, Sir George and Mr Farquhar were, no doubt, a good deal in one another's company.   There is a large and prominent rock of a peculiar shape at Ardlair called the " Minister's stone," which is still pointed out as one of the places where Mr Farquhar used to preach, both in Gaelic and in English.[3]

About 1616 Sir George Hay left Letterewe for the south, in 1622 he was appointed High Chancellor of Scotland, and was afterwards created Earl of Kinnoull His subsequent career was one of great distinction and usefulness until his death in 1634, at the age of sixty-two. So much was Sir George attached to Mr Farquhar, that when he was leaving Letterewe he strongly urged him to leave Gairloch and seek a wider field for his talents in the south. Sir George offered him a choice of several parishes which were in his own patronage.   He also promised

[1] Mackenzie's History of the Mackenzies, New Edition, pages 415-416.

[2] Both Ardlair and Letterewe are situated on the North-East Coast of Loch Maree.

[3] There is an illustration of this stone in Mr J. H Dixon's book on Gairloch (page 81), which also contains several interesting and appreciative references to Mr Farquhar.

him a yearly pension, and undertook to get him ecclesiastical promotion. Mr Farquhar decided to accept this liberal offer, and to accompany Sir George to the south, and considering his own ability and the great influence of his patron, it is quite possible that if he had done so his career in the Church would have been a very successful and distinguished one. But Colin, Lord Kintail, or more probably his uncle Roderick, the celebrated "Tutor of Kintail"—for Colin was then a minor—interposed, as Lord Kenneth had done in Edinburgh, being resolved at whatever cost to retain Mr Farquhar's services for his own people, and promising him the vicarage of Kintail in succession to the occupying incumbent, the Rev. Murdoch Murchison, Mr Farquhar's uncle,[1] who at this time must have been well advanced in years. Mr Farquhar once more sacrificed bright and promising prospects out of a sense of loyalty to the House of Kintail, and remained in Gairloch.

It was during Mr Farquhar's incumbency of Gairloch that Kenneth, Lord Kintail, finally brought the island of Lews under his rule.   In 1610 his lordship

---

[1] It would appear from *Fasti Ecclesiæ Scoticanæ* that Mr Farquhar succeeded his grandfather as Constable of Ellandonan and Vicar of Kintail, as it is there stated that Christopher Macrae, that is Mr Farquhar's father, married a daughter of Murdoch Murchison, Constable of Ellandonan and Vicar of Kintail, Mr Farquhar's predecessor, who would thus be also his grandfather; but according to the Rev. John Macrae, Mr Farquhar succeeded his uncle in the Vicarage of Kintail. There are three men of the name Murchison mentioned in connection with Kintail during this period :—(1) John Murchison, called John Mac Mhurchaidh Dhuibh (John, the son of Black Murdoch), Priest of Kintail, who was made Constable of Ellandonan, in succession to John Dubh Matheson, who was killed by Donald Gorm in 1539 ; (2) John Murchison, who was Reader of Kintail from 1574 to 1614 (the Reader was a man appointed to read the Scriptures and the new Protestant Service Book of this period), (3) Murdoch Murchison, who was Vicar of

visited the island, and with a view to revive the
religious life of the people, which was then at a very
low ebb, he took Mr Farquhar along with him.   The
state of matters in Lews may be imagined from the
fact that for forty years previous to Mr Farquhar's
visit no one appears to have been baptised or married
in the island.   The people had practically lapsed into .
heathenism, but Mr Farquhar's visit worked a change
and his mission proved thoroughly successful.   Large
numbers of the people were baptised,[1] some of them
being fifty years of age, and many men and women
were married who had already lived together for
years.   The success of this mission went far to re-
concile the inhabitants of Lews to Lord Kintail's
rule, to which they all the more cheerfully and
readily submitted upon his promising that he would
provide for the permanent settling among them of
such another man as Mr Farquhar.   Having succeeded in establishing good order and contentment
in the island, no doubt largely by the aid of Mr
Farquhar, who appears to have remained there for
some time, his lordship, who was seized by sudden
illness, returned to Fortrose, where he died shortly

Lochalsh from 1582 to 1614, when he became Vicar of Kintail, until his death
in 1618.   These men were undoubtedly members of the same family, but it is
not clear what their relationship was to one another   From an examination of
the dates it would seem probable that the last two were brothers, and the sons
of the first.   In that case, if Murdoch was Mr Farquhar's uncle, as he almost
certainly was, Mr Farquhar's mother would be a daughter, not of the Rev.
Murdoch Murchison, as stated on page 38 of this book, but of John Murchison,
Priest of Kintail, who was made Constable of Ellandonan in 1539.

[1] According to one of the traditions of Kintail, the number that came to
be baptised by Mr Farquhar was so great that, being unable to take them
individually, he was obliged to sprinkle the water at random on the crowd with
a heather besom

afterwards, in 1611, and was succeeded by his son Colin, who was subsequently created first Earl of Seaforth.

In 1618 the vicarage of Kintail became vacant by the death of the Rev. Murdoch Murchison, who was also Constable of Ellandonan Castle, and Mr Farquhar was appointed to fill both offices. The deed by which those appointments were conferred upon him was drawn up at Fortrose in that year.[1] At Ellandonan Castle he lived for many years in "an opulent and flourishing condition, much given to hospitality and charity." Colin, Earl of Seaforth, lived most of his time at Fortrose, but made periodical visits to Ellandonan in "great state and very magnificently." Referring to these visits, the Rev. John Macrae, of Dingwall, grandson of Mr Farquhar, says—"I have heard my grandfather say that Earl Colin never came to his house with less than three and sometimes with five hundred men. The Constable (of Ellandonan) was bound to furnish them victuals for the first two meals, till my lord's officers were acquainted to bring in his own customs." When Earl Colin visited his West Coast estates the lairds and gentlemen of the neighbourhood and of the Isles, including Maclean, Clanranald, Raasay, and Mackinnon, used to come to pay him their respects at Ellandonan Castle, where they feasted in great state, and consumed "the wine and other liquors" that were brought from Fortrose in the Earl's train. When these lairds and gentlemen left the castle Earl Colin called together all the principal

1 The Rev. John Macrae's history of the Macraes,

men of Kintail, Lochalsh, and Lochcarron, who went
with him to the forest of Monar, where they had a
great hunt, and from Monar he used to return to
Fortrose.

Earl Colin died at Fortrose in 1633, and was
succeeded by his brother, Earl George, who confirmed Mr Farquhar in his various appointments
and offices, and renewed his wadset rights to the
lands of Dornie, Inig, Aryugan, Drumbnie, and other
places in Kintail. Not only did Mr Farquhar secure
these rights during his own lifetime, but on payment
of a certain sum of money to the Earl he received
an extension of them for some years in favour of his
son, the Rev. John Macrae, of Dingwall, while the
wadset rights of Inverinate, Dorisduan, and Let-
terimmer, which appear to have been already in the
family for some generations, were confirmed in favour
of his son Alexander on payment of a sum of six
thousand merks Scots.

When Earl George's son and heir, Kenneth, who
was born at Brahan Castle in 1635, was about six
years of age his father placed him under the care of
Mr Farquhar of Ellandonan, where the sons of
neighbouring gentlemen were brought to keep him
company. Here the young heir remained for several
years without suffering any disadvantage, for we
read that under the wholesome rather than delicate
diet prescribed by Mr Farquhar, he began to have
a "healthy complexion," and grew up so strong that
he was able to endure much labour and fatigue,
and so great in stature that he became known as
Coinneach Mor—big Kenneth. He also became so

thoroughly acquainted with the language and circumstances of the people, that he was considered, in his own time, to be the best chief in the Highlands and Islands of Scotland. Nor was his book learning neglected, for when he was taken from Ellandonan to be placed in a public school, he gave every evidence, not only of ability, but of good training also. He entered King's College, Aberdeen, in 1651, but the troubles of the Civil War prevented him from finishing his course, which, as far as it went, did full credit to Mr Farquhar's tuition.

But the influence and prosperity of Mr Farquhar excited the envy and jealousy of some of his neighbours, who made complaint to Patrick Lindesay, Bishop of Ross, that he was becoming too worldly and was neglecting his ministerial duties. Upon receiving these complaints the Bishop called upon Mr Farquhar to preach before the next provincial Assembly of the Diocese or Synod. The Bishop himself preached on the first day from the text, " Ye are the salt of the earth." It was Mr Farquhar's turn to preach the second day, and he had unfortunately chosen the same text as the Bishop. Mr Farquhar told some of his brother clergymen of this fact, and it eventually came to the ears of the Bishop, who sent for Mr Farquhar and told him on no account to change his text. Mr Farquhar acquitted himself on this occasion with such eloquence and ability that it was " a question among his hearers whether the Highland salt or Lowland salt savoured best," and the Bishop himself was so impressed with the sermon that he not only dismissed the complaints as ground-

less but received Mr Farquhar into special favour.
This must have occurred comparatively early in Mr
Farquhar's incumbency of Kintail, as Bishop Patrick
Lindesay's rule of the Diocese of Ross terminated in
1633, and it was probably some time before that
date, as we are told that he was " held in esteem by
the Bishop ever after "—a phrase which would seem
to imply that the Bishop's personal acquaintance
with him extended over several years.   Bishop
Patrick Lindesay was succeeded by Bishop John
Maxwell, who invited Mr Farquhar on more occasions
than one to preach before him.   His brother clergymen were always greatly pleased with his performances in the pulpit, and on one occasion when the
Bishop himself was asked for his opinion, he declared
Mr Farquhar to be "a man of great gifts, but unfortunately lost in the Highlands, and pity it were
his lot had been there."   Had Mr Farquhar chosen
to carry his services to the more tempting fields of
work afforded by the large towns of the South, no
doubt his career might have been very much greater
and more distinguished from a worldly point of view,
but the memories which he left behind him in Gairloch, and more especially in Lochalsh and Kintail,
where his name is still remembered with affection
and pride, clearly proves that his talents were not
lost even in the Highlands, and that his work among
the people bore rich fruit.

In 1651, Mr Farquhar left Ellandonan Castle,
after a residence of thirty-three years, under circumstances described as follows by the Rev. John
Macrae in his history of the Mackenzies :—After

the defeat of the supporters of King Charles II. at Dunbar, on the 3rd September, 1650, and while Earl George was absent in Holland, we find his son, Kenneth, then a lad of about sixteen, raising men in Kintail for the Royalist service. He was accompanied by his two uncles, Thomas Mackenzie of Pluscardine and Simon Mackenzie of Lochslin,[1] Roderick Mackenzie of Dochmaluag, and others. For some reason or other, not explained, Mr Farquhar incurred the displeasure of Lochslin, who was acting as leader, and who would not march off with the men until Mr Farquhar was removed from Ellandonan Castle. Mr Farquhar, however, "refused to go without violence, lest his going voluntarily might be interpreted as an abdication of his right, a yielding to the reason pretended against him, and when all the gentlemen of my lord's friends there refused to put hands on him, and the young laird (Kenneth), his foster, refused to lay his commands on them to remove him, Young Tarbat,[2] being vexed for delaying the march of the men for the King's service, and Lochslin himself, led him to the gates of the Castle, and then Mr Farquhar told them he would go without further trouble to them, for he was well pleased to be rid of the Island, because it was a bad habitation for a man of his age and corpulency." It is said, also, that he found it too

---

[1] Simon Mackenzie of Lochslin was the father of Sir George Mackenzie of Rosehaugh, Lord-Advocate of Scotland, a well-known historian and lawyer, and who, in consequence of his severe administration of the law against the Covenanters, has sometimes been called the "Bloody Mackenzie."

[2] Young Tarbat was George Mackenzie, afterwards first Earl of Cromartie, and at this time about twenty years of age.

cold for his old age, which is not unlikely, considering the exposed nature of the site on which the
castle stood, nor is it unlikely either that the duties
of Constable were becoming too heavy for a man
of his advanced years.   The question of Mr
Farquhar's expulsion from Ellandonan Castle came
before the Presbytery of Dingwall on the 5th July,
1651,[1] when a letter was read from Mr Farquhar,
who excused himself from attending, " being unable
to travel so far"; while Simon of Lochslin excused
his absence from the same meeting on the ground
that he was employed in the " present expedition "
—that is the expedition which ended in the defeat
of the Royalist Army at Worcester on the 3rd
September, 1651.   The collapse of the Royalist
party at Worcester led to fresh ecclesiastical
developments in the Presbytery of Dingwall, and
this case does not appear to have come under
consideration again. On leaving the castle Mr
Farquhar took up his residence at a sheltered spot
in the neighbourhood, called Inchchruter, " where
he lived very plentifully for eleven years, some
of his grandchildren, after his wife's death,
alternately ruling his house, to which there was
a great resort of all sorts of people, he being very
generous, charitable, and free-hearted."   When
General Monk's army visited Kintail in 1654,[2] they
took away three hundred and sixty of Mr Farquhar's cattle, for which his friends strongly urged
him to put in a claim for compensation when King

---

1 Inverness and Dingwall Presbytery Records, edited by William Mackay.
2 For an account of General Monk's visit to Kintail, see Appendix E

Charles II was restored in 1660, but the old man refused to do so, being so loyal to the House of Stuart that he considered the successful restoration of the King sufficient compensation for any loss he might have suffered in the Royalist cause.

In 1656 Mr Farquhar, who was then seventy-six years of age, is described as "being now aged and infirm, and so unable to do duty as formerly, or as is necessary to embrace or exercise the office and function of the ministry at the said kirk (of Kintail) as their lawful and actual minister." Accordingly the Presbytery of Dingwall, at a meeting held on the 14th February in that year,[1] granted an Act of Transportation to Kintail on behalf of Mr Donald Macrae of Urray (Mr Farquhar's son), who had received a call from the congregation of Kintail with the consent of Mr Farquhar himself and the approval of the Earl of Seaforth. Mr Donald was admitted to Kintail as fellow-labourer and "conjunct" minister with his father, on the 20th July following, by the Rev. Alexander Mackenzie of Lochcarron. A lengthy document, drawn up on the 24th June by the Presbytery, after "long and mature deliberation," and setting forth in great detail the conditions of this "conjunct ministrie," is preserved in the Records of the Presbytery of Dingwall. Notwithstanding the care with which this document was drawn up, difficulties arose between the father and the son with regard to the possession of the vicarage, and the matter was discussed, privately, by Mr Donald's request, at a

---

[1] Inverness and Dingwall Presbytery Records, edited by William Mackay.

meeting of the Presbytery of Dingwall, held on the 29th of December, 1657, when Mr Donald promised to abide by the decision of the Presbytery. The Presbytery gave its decision in favour of Mr Farquhar, who appears to have spent the remainder of his days in peace.

It is so frequently the custom to speak only of what was wild and unsettled in the Highlands of two or three centuries ago that, to anyone interested in the social history of that part of the country, it must be very pleasant to contemplate the life-long work of such a man as Mr Farquhar in a parish so Highland and so outlying as Kintail, but there were many such men in those days—men whose scholarly and cultured refinement was a source of sweetness and light to the community among whom their lot was cast; and though the memory of many of them may have passed away in the great social changes which the Highlands have been undergoing for the last century and a half, yet they were the salt of the earth to their own generation, and the silent and hidden influence of their lives and their labours may still be seen in the politeness and culture which is sometimes to be found even in the humble cottage of the Highland crofter. In the days of Mr Farquhar, Kintail was well peopled, and, being the ancestral home of one of the most powerful noblemen in Scotland, it was a place of considerable importance. The principal men of the district came into very frequent personal contact with the Earl himself, with the natural result that they also became keenly interested in the great religious and political

movements with which the Chiefs of Kintail were
in various ways so intimately associated Consequently we find among the people of Kintail, in a
very marked degree, the high political and religious
tension which so frequently marks a period of civil
and revolutionary warfare.   Perhaps in no other
district of the Highlands was the religious and
political feeling of the people more pronounced
at this time than in Kintail and the neighbourhood This fact is fully borne out by the
tone of the *Fernaig Manuscript*, which is a
collection of Kintail poems of this period, and to
which reference is made elsewhere in this book.
Such, then, were the circumstances of the Highland
community of which Mr Farquhar was for nearly
half-a-century the central figure, and the chief guide
not only in spiritual things, but in things temporal
as well.   Though the sphere of his work and
activity was limited to a remote Highland parish,
his long life was thus a very eventful and anxious
one, and covered one of the most stirring periods of
Scottish history.   It was during his University
career that James VI. succeeded to the throne of
England, and the Royal House of Scotland rose to
the zenith of its ill-starred greatness.   Then, in the
course of time there came the Covenanter movement
and the Civil War, which ended in the execution of
Charles I. and the exile of his family.   Mr Farquhar
himself was a staunch Royalist and an Episcopalian,
so that he belonged to the losing cause of what, so
far as Scotland as a whole was concerned. was
only the minority ; but though the army of the

enemy overran his country and plundered his property, he held stoutly to his principles like a good man and true. Those principles were doomed in course of time to be all but totally renounced and rejected by the people of the Highlands, and this is not the place to discuss whether in doing so they did rightly or wrongly, but the steadfastness with which Mr Farquhar and his family supported the Scottish Episcopal Church and the Scottish Royal Family must call forth the admiration of all who appreciate what is loyal and true in human nature. He lived for two years after the restoration of King Charles II., and thus had the satisfaction in his old age of seeing the Royal House of Stuart enjoying a fitful return of power and popularity, and then he died before the true character of the restored King had time to become generally apparent. And so his end was peace. He died in the midst of a prosperous grown-up family, regretted and mourned by all his countrymen, and leaving behind him memories of goodness and worth which the lapse of more than two centuries have not effaced.

Mr Farquhar married on the 1st December, 1611, Christina, eldest daughter of Macculloch of Park, Strathpeffer, and by her, who died before him, he had eight sons and two daughters, viz :—Alexander, John, Donald, Miles, Murdoch, John, Christopher, Thomas, Isabel, and Helen. He died in January, 1662, at the age of eighty-two, and was buried with his ancestors at Kilduich, in Kintail.

CHRISTOPHER and THOMAS died apparently without issue, as their nephew, Finlay, son of John, is

mentioned as their heir on the 28th July, 1696.[1]
The other sons of the Rev. Farquhar Macrae will
be mentioned hereafter.

ISABEL, eldest daughter of Mr Farquhar, married
Malcolm Macrae, son of Ian Og Mac Fhionla Dhuibh,
" a pretty, young gentleman, bred at school and
college," who was killed at the battle of Auldearn
in 1645   After his death, she married William, son
of the Rev. John Mackenzie, of the Dochmaluag
family.

HELEN, second daughter of Mr Farquhar, married
John, younger son of John Bayne of Knockbain.

1 Register of Retours.

CHAPTER V.

VII. Alexander of Inverinate.—Chamberlain of Kintail.—His Marriages and Family.—Rev John Macrae, last Episcopalian Minister of Dingwall.—Difficulties Connected with the Appointment of his Successor.—Author of Histories of the Mackenzies and of the Macraes.—His Marriage and Family.—Rev. Alexander Macrae founds a Roman Catholic Mission in Kintail.—Alexander Macrae, merchant, Bristol, leaves Money for the Education of Boys of the name Macrae.—Other Descendants of the Rev. John Macrae of Dingwall.—The Rev Donald Macrae, last Episcopalian Minister of Kintail.—He supports the Jacobite Cause.—Battles of Sheriffmuir and Glenshiel.—Kintail Church Destroyed by the Crew of a Man-of-War.—Episcopalianism in Kintail.—The Rev Donald Macrae's Marriage and Descendants.—Farquhar of Morvich and his Family.—Ian Mac Mhurachidh, the Kintail Poet.—Murdoch, son of Alexander of Inverinate.—His Tragic End.—The Glenlic Hunt.—Traditions and Poems connected therewith

VIII ALEXANDER, son of the Rev. Farquhar VII., is commonly known as Alexander of Inverinate. His father procured for him a wadset of the lands of Inverinate, Dorisduan, and Letterinimmer, for the sum of six thousand marks, and he is mentioned in the Valuation Roll of the County of Ross in 1644, as possessed of lands in the parish of Kintail of the yearly value of £266 13s 4d Scots. He was Chamberlain of Kintail under Kenneth Mor, third Earl of Seaforth, who, as already stated, received his early education at Ellandonan Castle, from Alexander's father, and by whom Alexander himself was much esteemed.   It is stated in the Rev John Macrae's History of the Mackenzies, that when General Middleton and Lord Balcarres were in the Highlands raising an army to support Charles II. against Cromwell, probably about 1651, they paid a visit to Seaforth, who welcomed Balcarres in a special manner, and sent Alexander of Inverinate to bring Lady Balcarres, who was a daughter of Colin, first Earl of Seaforth, to Kintail, which, "with some hazard and difficulty, Alexander performed," bringing the lady safe to Ellandonan Castle, where she lived for some time with her husband.   Alexander married, as his first wife, Margaret, daughter of Murdoch Mackenzie, second laird of Redcastle, by whom he had two sons, Duncan and John, and two daughters, Catherine (or Christina) and Mary.   He married, as his second wife, Mary, daughter of Alexander Mackenzie, fourth laird of Dochmaluag, by whom he had seven sons, Alexander, Donald, Christopher, Farquhar, Murdoch, Allan, and Hugh, and at least two daughters, Isabel and Margaret.   The descent of both his wives can be traced to the Royal Houses of Stuart and Plantagenet.[1]

1. DUNCAN, eldest son of Alexander by his first wife, Margaret Mackenzie of Redcastle, will be mentioned hereafter

2. THE REV. JOHN, second son of Alexander by his first wife, was educated at Aberdeen University, and was laureated, that is, took his degree, on the

[1] See Royal Pedigrees Appendix F,

12th July, 1660. When the first school was opened in Dingwall he was appointed master of it. This was before the 21st July, 1663, as he is mentioned on that date as schoolmaster of Dingwall and Clerk to the Session. He was ordained in 1667 to the parish of Kilmorack, and was translated in 1674 to the parish of Dingwall, where he lived and laboured for thirty years, and of which he was the last Episcopalian minister. He is mentioned in various documents of the period as Treasurer of Ross. He is said to have been a great favourite in the family of the Earl of Seaforth, who gave him a wadset of the lands of Dornie, Dronaig, Aryugan, &c., in Kintail, for the sum of seven thousand five hundred marks. His influence in Dingwall and the neighbourhood appears to have been very great, and so loyal was the feeling of the people, both to his memory and to the Church to which he belonged, that on his death they so persistently opposed the introduction of Presbyterianism among them, that, in spite of repeated attempts, it was found impossible to settle a Presbyterian minister in Dingwall until 1716, twenty-eight years after the Revolution, and this settlement was made not by patronage or by a "call" from the people, but by the Presbytery acting under warrant from the Privy Council.[1]

[1] From the record of a meeting of the Privy Council of Scotland, on the 25th April, 1704, and under the heading "The Agent for the Kirk against Macraes and others," we learn something of the first attempts made to introduce Presbyterianism into the Royal burgh of Dingwall after the death of the Rev. John Macrae. The Rev. William Stewart of Kiltearn, having been delegated by the "United Presbyteries of Ross and Sutherland" to supply the vacancy, repaired to Dingwall accordingly, on Sunday the 16th January. Finding the aspect of affairs on his arrival rather threatening, he decided to appeal to the magistrates

The Rev. John Macrae was the author of an important History of the Mackenzies, to which frequent reference is made in this book. The clan historian, Alexander Mackenzie, frequently refers to it also, in his History of the Mackenzies, as the Ardintoul MS. He was also the author of a History and Genealogy of the Macraes, which has already been described in the first chapter of this book.

The Rev. John married, before the 21st July, 1673, Janet Bayne, of Knockbain. There is a sasine of that date to Mr John Macrae, Treasurer of Ross, and Janet Bayne, his spouse. By her he had issue as below. He died in January, 1704.

a. Alexander, eldest son of the Rev John, was educated for the Church, but, as the Episcopal Church was proscribed in Scotland after the Revolution of 1688, he threw in his lot with the Roman Catholics rather than become a Presbyterian. For many years he discharged the duties of a Roman Catholic priest between Brahan and Strathglass,

for protection. The magistrates, however, could not be found, and meantime the ringleaders of the mob surrounded the house in which the minister was, and made the outer door fast with nails. The minister then made a strong appeal to the people from the window of the house, and eventually succeeded, by the help of Sir Robert Munro of Fowlis and others from Kiltearn, in regaining his liberty and effecting an entrance into the church. But when the "worship was begun and almost finished," there arrived a company of armed men from the country, among whom the chief ringleaders were John Macrae vic Alister Oig, Hugh Macrae, father (it ought to be brother) to the said deceased Mr John Macrae, late incumbent at Dingwall ; Kenneth Macrae, brother german to Farquhar Macrae of Invermate ; and —— Macrae, son to Christopher, brother german to the said deceased Mr John Macrae, all in the parish of Kintail. These men having entered the church "upon pretence that they were coming to attend the worship," the said John Macrae vic Alister went up to the door of the pulpit and "presented a pistol to the

and was probably the last who said mass in Brahan
Castle.   He was the first Macrae who became a
Roman Catholic after the Reformation, and was the
founder of the mission which that Church still
carries on in Kintail   His first converts were his
own cousins, Alexander Macra of Ardintoul and
John Og, son of the Rev. Donald Macrae, last Episcopalian minister of Kintail, and another man called
Ian Buidhe Mac Dhonnachaidh (Yellow John, the
son of Duncan).   In his old age he retired to the
Scotch Roman Catholic College at Douai, in France,
and there died   The Kintail Mission was well supported by the Macraes, and was afterwards carried
on by the Rev. John Farquharson, a celebrated
priest of Strathglass, the Rev. Norman Macleod, and
others.

b. John, who married Margaret, daughter of the
Rev. Roderick Mackenzie, minister and Laird of
Avoch.   He is also said to have married, as her
second husband, Anne, daughter of Alexander
Mackenzie, third Laird of Applecross, who survived

minister, threatening to kill him until stopped by the hearers, whereupon the
rest of the armed men approached nearer, and scrambling over the seats to
the pulpit with menacing countenances and arms in their hands, they commanded Mr Stewart to come down and begone, which constrained him to
retire." The disturbance continued as he passed out through the churchyard,
until at last ' the minister, finding himself like to faint through the violence
he had suffered, prayed some gentlemen, his friends, to carry him off any way,
which was done" Nor did Sir Robert Munro and his friends escape without
blows, and "further, these rabblers cried loudly and frequently King Willie is
now dead and their King is alive" The ringleaders were summoned by the
Privy Council, but failed to compear, whereupon they were declared rebels,
and their goods and gear forfeited to the Crown   Various other unsuccessful
attempts were made to introduce Presbyterianism into Dingwall, and though
the Rev. Daniel Bayue was appointed to the living in 1708, it was not until
1716 that he was able to enter upon possession of it.

him, and afterwards married, as her third husband, Colin Mackenzie of Inverness.[1]

*b*1. Alexander, who was served heir to his grandfather, the Rev. John Macrae, minister of Dingwall and Treasurer of Ross, on the 24th of June, 1741. Having afterwards recovered from Seaforth the money for certain wadsets which he held in Kintail, and sold some property which he held about Dingwall, he went into business in Bristol, where he became a prosperous and wealthy merchant, and died without issue in April, 1781. He left a sum of fifty thousand marks[2] to the King's College, Aberdeen, for educating boys of the name Macrae who could be traced in the male line from his great-grandfather, Alexander of Inverinate, "in preference to all others "[3] Several students of the name Macrae held this bursary in past times

*b*2. Margaret, who married John Matheson, Durinish.[4]

*b*3. Mary, married to James, son of Alexander Matheson of Bennetsfield,[4] and had, with other issue, Catherine, who married Alexander Matheson, some

1 Only the first marriage is mentioned in the MS history of the Macraes, but both are mentioned in Sir James Dixon Mackenzie's Genealogical Tables of the Mackenzies   The probability is that he was twice married, and that his family was by the first wife

2 Fifty thousand merks Scots mortified by the late Alexander Macrae, of Dornie, and left under the management of the King s College of Aberdeen, for educating the children of the nearest descendants from Alexander Macrae, son of Mr Farquhar Macrae, the first Protestant minister in the parish of Kintail. —*Old Statistical Account.*

3 Appendix L

4 For the descendants of this marriage, see Mackenzie's History of the Mathesons

time schoolmaster, Dornie, who has been already mentioned on page 48.

c. Christopher, baptised at Dingwall in November, 1682.

d. Roderick, baptised at Dingwall, 18th August, 1692, and mentioned, in 1763, as the deceased Mr Roderick Macrae in the will of his nephew, Alexander Macrae, some time of Bristol. He married a daughter of Alexander Mackenzie, Chamberlain of Ferintosh, and had issue—

*d*1. John

*d*2. Duncan, who went to Maryland in America, was a lieutenant in the "Provincials" during the American War of Independence, and was killed in the expedition under General Forbes against Fort Duquesne in 1757.

*d*3. Helen, married to Thomas Maclean, a schoolmaster at Ord.

*d*4. Janet.

e Mary, who married Roderick Dingwall of Ussie. There is a sasine on disposition by Roderick Dingwall of Ussie in favour of Mary Macrae, relict of the said Roderick, in liferent of the lands of Wester Ussie and Bogachro, &c., in the parish of Fodderty, 6th January, 1745 They had issue, at least one son, called John.

f Janet, baptised at Dingwall, 8th October, 1693, married John Tuach of Logereit.

A daughter of the Rev. John Macrae, last Episcopalian minister of Dingwall, was married to John Og, son of John Mackenzie, second laird of Applecross, and had issue.[1] This John Og was one

[1] Sir James Dixon Mackenzie's Genealogical Tables of the Mackenzies,

of the famous " Four Johns of Scotland" who were killed at Sheriffmuir in 1715.

3. ALEXANDER, eldest son of Alexander of Inverinate by his second wife, Mary Mackenzie of Dochmaluag, was called Alister Og, and lived at Achyark, in Kintail. He married a daughter of Donald, son of Finlay, son of Christopher VI , and had issue—

a. John, who was a well educated man and was one of the Seaforth Captains at Sheriffmuir. He was probably the John Macrae vic Alister Oig who took part as ringleader in the riot at Dingwall church in 1704, which has been already referred to. He married and had a son John, who had a daughter Isabel, who married William Morrison, farmer of Baloagie, on the Fairburn estate.

4. THE REV. DONALD, second son of Alexander of Inverinate by his second wife, Mary Mackenzie of Dochmaluag, and IX in descent from Finlay Dubh Macgillechriosd, was for some time schoolmaster at Fortrose, and became Vicar of Kintail in 1681. He was an ardent Jacobite and Episcopalian, and at the revolution of 1688 he refused to conform to Presbytery, so that Kintail remained Episcopalian for at least another quarter of a century. His name is mentioned in a list of " Episcopal Ministers who enjoy Churches or Benefices in Scotland" in March, 1710, and of whom it is said ; " Some of them pray for the Pretender ; others do not refuse to pray for the Queen (Anne), and some pray only for their sovereign without naming anybody. but it is generally thought they mean the Pretender."[1]   The

1 The Case of Mr Greenshields—printed in 1710

Rev. Donald and his family took a prominent part in the Rebellion of 1715, and he had two sons and a son-in-law killed at Sheriffmuir. He appears also to have been involved in the attempt which was made to revive the cause of the Stuarts in Kintail in 1719, and which ended in the defeat of the Jacobite party at the battle of Glenshiel, on the 10th of June in that year, for we read that his church was destroyed by the crew of one of the ships of war that sailed into Loch Duich at that time.[1] He died shortly afterwards, and with him ended the Episcopal Church in Kintail. The Episcopal form of worship in the Highlands at this time differed very little, if any, from the Presbyterian form, as there appears to have been no prayer book used, so that the Rev. Donald would conduct his services after the abolition of Episcopacy and the establishment of Presbyterianism exactly as he did before. This no doubt explains to a great extent the apparent readiness with which the common people of those times seem to have passed from the one form of worship to the other. The leading men of Kintail, however, were not to be satisfied with the mere outward appearance of things. Many of them looked at the underlying principles of their religion as well. The heavy loss sustained at Sheriffmuir, and the treatment to which they had so recently been subjected at the time of the Battle of Glenshiel, had produced among them a particular dislike of the Whig party, with which Presbyterianism was so closely associated, and rather than conform to Presbyterianism, after the

[1] Appendix E.

death of the Rev. Donald Macrae, many of them joined the Roman Catholic Mission which had recently been established among them by the Rev. Alexander Macrae already mentioned. The Rev. Donald Macrae married Catherine Grant[1] of Glenmoriston, by whom he had issue.

(1) ALEXANDER, mentioned below.

(2) MR JOHN, who married a daughter of the Laird of Chisholm, but left no issue. The Mr prefixed to his name suggests that he was a University graduate He appears to have been well educated, and was tutor to Norman Macleod of Macleod, with whom he is said to have travelled abroad, and who settled on him and his heirs the sum of " 1000 pounds Scots per bond " Mr John died in 1741, leaving this sum to his youngest brother, John Og

(3). DUNCAN married and left issue.

(4). COLIN ; (5). CHRISTOPHER, both killed at Sheriffmuir.

(6). JOHN OG, who, on the death of his father, and the final suppression of Episcopacy in Kintail, became a Roman Catholic, and was the fourth to join the mission referred to above. He died young,

---

[1] The tradition in Kintail is that this Catherine Grant was a daughter of John Grant, Laird of Glenmoriston, 1703-1736, commonly called *Ian a' Chragain*, by his second wife, Janet, daughter of Sir Ewen Cameron of Lochiel Janet died in 1759, aged 80 years. This places her birth in 1679, so that in 1715, the year of the Battle of Sheriffmuir, she was 36 years of age Now, the Rev Donald Macrae had two sons and a son-in-law killed at Sheriffmuir. These, according to the Kintail tradition, would be the grandchildren of Janet Cameron, who, at the time of their death, was only 36 years of age The son in-law (John of Conchra), who was killed at Sheriffmuir, left two children ; this would make Janet Cameron a great grandmother at the age of 36, and, therefore, if the Rev. Donald was married only once, the probability is that Catherine Grant was a sister, and not a daughter, of *Ian a' Chragain.*

and was attended by Father Farquharson of Strathglass on his death-bed. He married Barbara Macrae, daughter of Farquhar, son of Christopher, son of Alexander of Inverinate, and by her had issue—

(*a*). ISABELLA, who married Alexander Macrae of Achtertyre, of whom hereafter.

(*b*). HELEN, who married Duncan Macrae, Fadoch, also mentioned hereafter.

(*c*). CATHERINE, who married John Macrae, a descendant of John Breac, son of the Rev. Farquhar Macrae.

(*d*). CHRISTINA, married with issue.

John Og's widow afterwards married Donald, son of the Rev. Finlay Macrae of Lochalsh, with issue

(7). MARY

(8). ISABELLA, who married, first, John Macrae of Conchra, who was killed at Sheriffmuir, and of whom hereafter. She is said to have married, secondly, Alexander Mackenzie of Applecross, son of John, who was killed at Sheriffmuir, and thirdly, George Mackenzie of Fairburn.

(9). KATHERINE married Donald Macrae of Torlysich.

On the other hand, it is stated in an old Genealogical Tree of the Macraes, that the Rev. Donald had a daughter, Mary, by "his first marriage with Chisholm's daughter" In that case, it may be possible that he was twice married, and that his second marriage was with Catherine, daughter of *Ian a' Chragain*. The disparity of their years, however, would be very great, and they might have had one child, John Og, mentioned below. This explanation may be regarded as not altogether improbable, as the tradition is certainly an old one, and was related to the writer in a very circumstantial manner by one of John Og's descendants, a man whose information he has invariably found reliable Janet Cameron must have married at a very early age, and some of her descendants must have done so also, because we read that there were great great-grandchildren at her funeral

(10). CHRISTINA married Donald Macrae of Morvich, son of Farquhar, son of Alexander of Inverinate.

(X.) ALEXANDER, eldest son of the Rev. Donald Macrae, appears to have lived at Ruroch in Kintail. He married Florence, daughter of Ewen Mackenzie VII of Hilton, by whom he had two sons —

(1). FARQUHAR.

(2). JOHN, who married a daughter of Chisholm of Muckarach. His circumstances becoming reduced, he, along with many others from Kintail, emigrated to North Carolina in 1774, where he died, shortly after his arrival, from the bite of a snake, which he received while clearing some ground for a plantation He left one son there, called JOHN.

Alexander had three daughters.

(XI) FARQUHAR, eldest son of Alexander, by Florence Mackenzie of Hilton, married, first, the widow of John Macrae of Achyark, by whom he had one daughter. He married, secondly, Margaret (or Mary), daughter of Duncan Macrae of Balnain, by whom he had three sons.

(1) CHRISTOPHER, a sergeant in the regiment which was raised by Lord Seaforth in 1778 (the 78th, afterwards the 72nd). He served abroad, and died in India. He was the author of several Gaelic songs, which used to be very popular, and may still be heard in Lochalsh and Kintail.

(2). COLIN married with issue—ALEXANDER and four daughters

(3). ALEXANDER was tacksman of Inchcro, in Kintail He married Mary, daughter of Duncan

Macrae, Fadoch, who was descended from Miles, son of the Rev. Farquhar Macrae, with issue—

(a) Christopher, who, along with his brother, was for some time tacksman of Inchcro. He was married, but died, without issue, in or near Dingwall about 1860.

(b). Duncan, who died, unmarried, in New Zealand about 1882.

(c). A daughter, who married John Macrae, Dornie, who was commonly called Ian Dubh Nan Dorn (Black John of the Fists), so called from the extraordinary strength he possessed in his hands.

5 CHRISTOPHER, third son of Alexander of Inverinate and Mary Mackenzie of Dochmaluag, is mentioned hereafter.

6. FARQUHAR, fourth son of Alexander of Inverinate and Mary Mackenzie of Dochmaluag, lived at Morvich. He married with issue, one of whom—

a. Murdoch, who is mentioned as taking a prominent part in the skirmish at Ath nam Muileach (the ford of the men of Mull), in Glenaffric, on the 2nd October, 1721, when Donald Murchison of Auchtertyre, with about three hundred followers, met and repulsed William Ross of Easter Fearn, near Tain, who was proceeding to Kintail under the escort of a company of soldiers to collect rents on the Seaforth Estates on behalf of the Forfeited Estates Commissioners.[1] Murdoch married Mary, daughter of Farquhar X , and left with other issue—

John. the celebrated Kintail poet, commonly called Ian Mac Mhurachaidh, whose Gaelic songs are

[1] Appendix E.

F

still well known in Kintail and Lochalsh. These
songs are of very high poetical merit, and this,
together with the strong and effective local colour-
ing they possess, helps to account for the deep
and lasting impression which the poet made on
his countrymen, and the prominent place which
his name occupies among the traditions of Kintail.
The poems deal chiefly with the pursuits and de-
lights of such a country life as he himself led among
his native glens and mountains, many of which he
has invested with associations which must continue
classic and sacred to his countrymen so long as any
of them are left in Kintail to speak the Gaelic
tongue. About 1770 a great many of the people
of Kintail emigrated to America, and the poet
resolved to seek his fortune there also His friends
endeavoured to persuade him to remain at home,
but nothing could shake his resolution. It is said
he was so greatly esteemed in the Highlands that,
when his intention to leave the country became
known, several neighbouring lairds offered him valuable lands on their estates if he would only remain
in the country. But the spirit of adventure was
then abroad in Kintail, and, notwithstanding the
prospects held out to him at home, the poet was
as much as anyone under its influence There are
various traditions as to the motives which induced
him to leave the country, but the chief motive was
undoubtedly the adventurous desire to seek fortune
in a new field beyond the Atlantic, as so many of
his countrymen did at this time. On the day of his
departure, many of his friends accompanied him to

the heights of Auchtertyre in Lochalsh, and the spot is still pointed out where he took his farewell of them   But things went hard with him in America. When the War of Independence broke out, he cast in his lot with the Loyalists, whose cause soon became the losing one, and, after sharing in the hardships and defeat of the British armies, he at last perished a fugitive among the primeval woods. During the time of his adversity in America, he composed several songs, which were brought back to Kintail, and in which he expresses with much beauty and pathos the yearning of his soul to return to the scenes and the friends of happier days.[1]   He married before he left Kintail   It is doubtful who his wife was, but the tradition in Kintail is that she was Christina Macrae, daughter of Alexander Roy of the Torlysich family.[2]   He had three sons, Charles, Murdoch, and Donald.   He also had a daughter whom he left behind him a child in Kintail, and who afterwards married Finlay Macrae, who was schoolmaster at Fadoch, in Kintail, a grandson of the Rev. Finlay Macrae, with issue, as already mentioned.

b. Farquhar, called Farquhar Og (Farquhar the younger), had, with other issue, a son called Donald Ban, who had a son Murdoch, who had a son, the Rev. Donald Macrae, who was born in 1802,

---

[1] Appendix J.

[2] In Sir J. D Mackenzie's genealogical tables of the Mackenzies, it is stated that about this time Winifred Mackenzie, of the Dochmaluag family by her father and the Fairburn family by her mother, married John Macrae, a poet of Kintail. At all events, the poet lived on terms of the closest friendship with the Fairburn family.

ordained a minister of the Free Church by the
Presbytery of Lews in 1844, and died at Cross, in
Lews, on the 15th November, 1876, with issue, six
children.

c Alexander is mentioned as taking part in the
affair of Ath nam Muileach.   He appears to have
had a son John, who is also mentioned in connection
with the same affair

d. Anne, married Alexander Mac Gillechriosd
Macrae, in Strathglass, and had issue—Christopher;
Isabel, who married as his second wife Alexander
Macra of Ardintoul; Margaret, who married Dun-
can MacAlister Mac Gillechriosd, and had a son a
priest.

7 MURDOCH, fifth son of Alexander of Inverinate and Mary Mackenzie of Dochmaluag, came to an
ultimely and tragic end.   He was out hunting in
Glenlic one day in the early winter, and, according
to tradition, found a man stealing his goats   Having captured the thief, Murdoch was leading him
along, but as they were passing the brink of a
precipice called the Carraig (Rock), the prisoner succeeded in pushing Murdoch over the rock, at the foot
of which his body was found after a search of fifteen
days.   The death of Murdoch was such a mysterious affair that there arose a belief in Kintail that
the dark deed was the work of an evil spirit,
and the spot where the body was found was
long believed to be haunted, but it is said that, many
years afterwards, an old man in Strathglass con-
fessed on his deathbed that he was the murderer,
and gave a full account of the event.   Another

version of the same tradition says that the goat-
stealer was accompanied by his little grandson, who
was a witness of the murder, and who afterwards
went to America, where he lived to a very advanced
age, and related the circumstances of the murder on
his deathbed. The Glenlic hunt and the death of
Murdoch occupy a very prominent place in the traditions of Kintail.[1] Several elegies composed on the
occasion have been preserved, and some of them are
of a very high order. The traditions with regard to
those elegies are somewhat vague, and it is not
easy to arrive at definite facts, but some of them
are believed to have been composed by John Macdonald, Ian Lom,[2] the Lochaber Bard, who was the
contemporary of the sons of Alexander of Inverinate.
It is said that Ian Lom's life being at one time in
danger in his own country, he fled for refuge to Kintail, where he was living with the Inverinate family
at the time of Murdoch's death, and that on each of
the fifteen days during which the search lasted, he
composed an elegy. Another tradition says that
some of the elegies were composed by Murdoch's
brother, Duncan. In any case, the fragments that
have been preserved are of great merit, and not un-
worthy even of such poets as Ian Lom and Donnacha
nam Pìos. One of the elegies contains a verse in
which all Murdoch's brothers are mentioned, except

---

[1] See chapter on legends and traditions of the clan

[2] John Macdonald, or Ian Lom (Bare John), was a celebrated Gaelic poet
of the family of Keppoch He was a personal friend and a devoted supporter of
the Earl of Montrose One of his chief productions is a descriptive poem on
the victory gained by Montrose over the Earl of Argyll at Inverlochy, in 1645.
Ian Lom died at a very advanced age about 1710.

Alexander, who may possibly have died before :

> 'S tùirseach do sheachd bráithrean giáidh,
> Am *parson* ge h-árd a leugh,
> Thug e, ge tuigseach a cheaird,
> Aona bharr-tùins air cách gu lèir
>
> Bho thus dhiubh Donnachadh nam Piòs.
> Gillecriosda, 's an dithis de'n chléir,
> Fearachar agus Ailean Donn,
> Uisdean a bha trom 'n ad dhéigh [1]

The *parson* mentioned in the first of these verses was undoubtedly Murdoch's brother — the Rev. Donald of Kintail, who, from the reference here made to him, seems to have written an elegy on this occasion, but the manner in which Donnacha nam Piòs is mentioned would seem to imply that he himself was not the author, at all events of the poem from which these verses are quoted

Murdoch left a young widow, and at least two sons, who grew up and married with issue.

8. ALLAN, sixth son of Alexander of Inverinate and Mary Mackenzie of Dochmaluag, left no male issue

9. HUGH, seventh son of Alexander of Inverinate and Mary Mackenzie of Dochmaluag, will be mentioned hereafter

10 Christina, daughter of Alexander of Inverinate by his first wife, Margaret Mackenzie of Redcastle, married Alexander Matheson of Achtaytoralan, in Lochalsh, an ancestor of the Ardross family.

---

[1] Sad are thy seven beloved brothers,— the parson though profound is his learning,—though his office is one of giving comfort, yet he surpassed the others in his grief   •

First among them is Duncan of the silver cups, then Christopher and the two clergymen, Farquhar, Allan of the auburn hair, and Hugh, who was sad after thee.

CHAPTER VI

IX. Duncan, called Donnachadh nam Piòs.—His Character and Attainments —Traditions about Him.—The Silver Herring — The Oak Trees at Inverinate —Duncan as a Poet.—The Fernaig Manuscript. — A Valuable Contribution to Gaelic Literature.—Religion and Politics of the Poems contained in it —Professor Mackinnon's Estimate of Donnachadh nam Piòs and his Work.—His Tragic End —His Marriage and Family — X Farquhar.—His Marriage and Family.—XI. Duncan —His Marriage and Family.

IX. DUNCAN, eldest son of Alexander of Inverinate (VIII.), by his first wife, Margaret Mackenzie of Redcastle, was commonly known as Donnachadh nam Piòs, which means Duncan of the silver cups, a name said to have been given to him probably because of the magnificence of his table service. He was a man of high character, a poet, and a skilful mechanician, and many anecdotes and traditions illustrative of his attainments are still related about him in Kintail and Lochalsh. It is said that when he was a student in Edinburgh he assisted in forming a plan for bringing the water into that city. There is a tradition that on one occasion a strange ship had her mast broken in passing through Kyle Rea. The captain, unable to proceed any further, was advised to appeal to Duncan for help.

Duncan took the matter in hand himself, and spliced the broken mast so skilfully that the joining could hardly be seen, and in return for this service the grateful captain gave him a silver herring, which remained for a long time an heirloom in the family, and which was commonly believed by the people of Kintail to possess the magic power of attracting herring into Loch Duich.   It is also said that the oak trees at Invermate were reared by him from acorns that he brought from France.   There is reason, however, to believe that Duncan's trees have been cut down, and that the present trees are not so old as his time

It is, however, as a poet that Duncan achieved his greatest distinction.   Fragments of poetry ascribed to him still survive orally among the people of Kintail, and Professor Mackinnon of Edinburgh University, has proved[1] beyond any reasonable doubt that he was the compiler of the *Fernaig Manuscript* and the author of many, if not of most, of the poems contained in it   This manuscript which has recently been printed[2] consists of two small volumes of paper in pasteboard covers, about eight inches long and three broad.   The two volumes together consist of one hundred and twenty-eight pages, of which about one hundred and five are closely and neatly written upon in the handwriting of the period   It contains about

1 Transactions of the Gaelic Society of Inverness, Volume XI

2 Reliquiæ Celticæ, left by the late Rev. Alexander Cameron, LL D , edited by Alexander Macbain, M A and the Rev John Kennedy and published by the Northern Counties Newspaper and Printing and Publishing Company, Limited, Inverness, 1894.

four thousand two hundred lines. It was commenced in the year 1688, and the latest date
mentioned in it is the year 1693. The spelling
is phonetic and very difficult, if not quite un-
readable, for one who is accustomed only to the
modern Gaelic spelling. In addition to poems by
Duncan himself, the manuscript contains poems also
by writers who can easily be identified as his
relatives and kinsmen, such as his great-grandfather, Macculloch of Park; his father-in-law, Macleod of Raasay; his brother, the Rev. Donald
Macrae of Kintail There are poems also by Bishop
Carswell of the Isles; Alexander Munro. teacher,
Strathnaver, and others. The history of the
manuscript from the time of the writer until the
present century is unknown. In the year 1807, it
was in the possession of Mr Matheson of Fernaig,
father of the late Sir Alexander Matheson of
Ardross. Hence the name by which it is now
known. We afterwards find it in the possession of
Dr Mackintosh Mackay, on whose death, in 1873,
it was handed over to Dr W. F. Skene It is
now in the keeping of Mr Alexander Macbain, of
Inverness.

The Fernaig Manuscript is a valuable contribution to Gaelic literature, and next to the Dean of
Lismore's book it is said to be the most important
document we possess for the study of older Gaelic.
But it possesses more than mere philological value.
Its poetry, which is mainly religious and political,
affords an agreeable glimpse of the religion and the
politics of the remote Highlands at the time of the

Revolution. In Politics the authors of these poems are Jacobites, in Religion they are ardent Episcopalians, and they evidently had a clear, intelligent, and comprehensive grasp of the great questions of the day, not simply as those questions affected their own local interests, but as they affected the kingdom as a whole. Though the poems deal with the state of the country in unsettled times of warfare and revolution, they nevertheless breathe, even against political and religious opponents, a spirit of kindly toleration which must afford, at all events to patriotic Highlanders, a pleasing contrast with the narrow bigotry and religious intolerance which formed so striking a feature of this period in the south of Scotland.

"He (Donnachadh nam Piòs) was undoubtedly," says Professor Mackinnon, "a remarkable man and a character pleasant to contemplate. I have no reason to doubt that there were many like-minded Highland gentlemen living in those days—cultured, liberal, and pious men; but undoubtedly Duncan Macrae, the engineer and mechanician, the ardent ecclesiastic, the keen though liberal-minded politician, the religious poet, and collector of the literature of his countrymen, is as different from the popular conception of a Highland Chief of the Revolution as can well be conceived. We have it on the testimony of Lord Macaulay that Sir Ewen Cameron of Lochiel was not only a great warrior, not only eminently wise in council, eloquent in debate, but also a patron of literature. It is a high character to attain in that rude age, and from

4

Ere Vaghky fea gi fhojlt
and i nows Vattaelvin
Lea Viftias di Rhohus
fi hroiltis gi reaungji
ba lea fhijgg i feukab
gfea fhood oii the fa gu agin
fhrafft phallotnis Loonh
Lea mots sym l nj ftcnnon

5

Eiiimig ogaragh fhiyrh
lviit fi noahis so go tallii
Si gfy ffist Chhan durjll
Chlaid Rhamromeg, hjfst Ellen
ath nj hojrigns bo hiiyh
Lingi sad ronhar fea Haungii
tra pas magh i rateift
Lea fhijtt oggins ffea faingvine

6

Che di nuiffias Lgo dju
Mand di fhhthit grafftill
ath toip fo fheilt
Lea boimli fhoih agad Chajh
ath gin gnaghis sad rateift
Lea nost thon nj haugrie
Soi dogghto rodin
Si tiifs oid no ly

7

Bi Lyivos fi nonhrs oid
Corphm i ghuitis fea huipt
Boin, aidd agad gruhggin
ffore gin rhloiisin gm rhoig
Cha rhloiint and i godo
ath, alloff agnd bo id ma
guardon for fofub
Bi bonel guay rumgis

8

Ma hjnorhlos nj hauhnos
Bi ghaihodso I hhiyh
bbh nj miftias no ly
Lia and faift gmlosios
Va ghty dou gm hauhnos
Bsoildo pi fhahos gobighh
Sno monvug i Laf
Si ghagg mia rhoig gi bjg ghin

Smb

so severe a judge of Highlanders as Lord Macaulay undoubtedly was. Duncan Macrae did not possess the great gifts, mental and physical, of Eoghan Dubh.[1] With kindly exaggeration the English historian calls Lochiel the Ulysses of the Highlands. By no figure of speech would we be justified in claiming such a high sounding title as this for Donnachadh nam Pìòs. And yet, the Highland chief who, among the distractions of Civil War and in the scanty intervals of leisure wrested from a useful, honoured, and industrious life, sat down to compose Gaelic verse and to collect the poems composed by his countrymen and neighbours, is highly deserving of our affection and admiration. Such a man was Duncan Macrae.

Altogether, the Fernaig Manuscript appears to me to be an important contribution to our stock of Gaelic literature; the political and religious intelligence, the devout and tolerant spirit, the strong sense and literary power displayed by the various writers in rude and turbulent times, are creditable to our people, while the enlightened compiler is a Highland Chief of whom not only the Macraes, but all his countrymen, may well be proud."[2]

But Duncan was not merely a mechanician and a poet, he was also a practical man of the world, and prospered in his affairs. His end, however, was

[1] Eoghan Dubh (Black Ewen) is the name by which Sir Ewen Cameron of Lochiel was usually known in Gaelic

[2] Professor Mackinnon, on the Fernaig Manuscript in the Transactions of the Gaelic Society of Inverness, Volume XI

tragic.   Having gone on one occasion to the " Low Country " to negotiate the purchase of the lands of Affric from The Chisholm, he was returning home accompanied by a single attendant, who possessed the fatal and involuntary power of causing anyone whom he might happen to see in the act of fording a river to be drowned.[1]   The homeward journey was accomplished by Duncan and his servant without accident or mishap, until they reached Doirsduan in the Heights of Kintail.   Here it was necessary to cross the River Conag, which happened to be in flood.   The servant forded the river in safety, and then threw himself on his face on the ground lest he might chance to see his master in the water.   Having remained in that attitude long enough, as he thought, for his master to gain the bank, he turned round and caught sight of his master, who was still struggling in the water, and who immediately lost his footing in the stream.   Duncan succeeded, however, in recovering himself, and in getting sufficiently near the bank to seize hold of the branch of a tree, but the unfortunate servant, losing all presence of mind in his anxiety, still felt

1 This fatal power was called, at all events in some parts of the Highlands " Or na h'aoine " (the charm of the fast or of Friday), and was believed to be possessed by some men in Kintail within very recent times.   A man well known to the author was, on one occasion about forty years ago, returning home from church, with his wife, on a wet afternoon, in Strathconon.   They were accompanied by a shepherd from Kintail, and on the way they had to ford a stream which was in high flood   When they reached the stream the shepherd plunged in, waded to the other side, and then stood still on the opposite bank, with his back to the stream, until the other man and his wife, who had great difficulty in crossing, came up to him   The man, struck by the strange behaviour of the shepherd, said to him—" You were going to allow my wife and myself to get drowned without offering to help us "   " Perhaps,"

constrained to look at his master, who vainly
struggled for some time to gain the bank, but finally
lost his hold and was drowned.   By this accident
the family is said to have lost " much property,"[1] as
Duncan had valuable papers on his person at the
time, and among them the title deeds of Affric.
Many local traditions have grown round the death
of Donnachadh nam Piòs, and the sad and tragic
event has been commemorated both by elegies and
pibrochs.   The exact date of Duncan's death is not
known, but it was some time between 1693 and
1704.

Duncan married Janet, daughter of Alexander
Macleod, fifth laird of Raasay, and sister of John,
sixth laird, commonly called Ian Garbh.   Ian Garbh,
who was drowned off the north coast of Skye while
returning from a visit to the Lews, left no issue,
and so the succession to the estates of Raasay came
to Janet and her sister, Giles, who were served heirs
in 1688.   But Janet and her sister, being anxious
to maintain the dignity of their own clan, resigned
or sold their rights in 1692 to their cousin, Alexander Macleod, who succeeded as the seventh chief

replied the shepherd, "it is a good thing for you and your wife that I did not
offer to help you"   The shepherd believed that he possessed the same fatal
power as the servant who accompanied Donnachadh nam Piòs, and that if he
saw the man and his wife in the stream they would both be drowned

1 Though there seems to be no documentary evidence of this loss, yet
Duncan undoubtedly held lands in the Chisholm country   There is a sasine on
charter of apprising under the Great Seal in favour of Duncan Macrae of
Invernate, of the lands of Meikle Comer, Comerroy, and others, in the parish
of Kilmorack and shire of Inverness   At Edinburgh 10th July, 1674, and
sasine on 12th September, 1674, in presence of Christopher Macrae, in Beolak,
in Kintail, and others   Alexander Macrae in Achachaik (Achyark ?) as Sheriff
and Bailie in that part, gives sasine

of the family. It is said that the words of the satirical ditty known in the west of Ross-shire as Cailleach Liath Rasaidh (the greyhaired old woman of Raasay) were composed, on hearing of this transaction, by a Kintail wit, who was probably zealous for the dignity of the Inverinate family, and had perhaps hoped that Raasay might come into their possession. Janet herself appears to have possessed poetic talent, and is said to have composed an elegy on the death of her husband. By her Duncan had issue—

1. FARQUHAR, mentioned below.

2. KENNETH, who was one of the ringleaders of the riot at Dingwall Church in 1704, which has been already referred to. He married and left issue.

3. JOHN married and left issue. There is a John Macrae of Inverinate mentioned as taking a prominent part in the affair of Ath nam Muileach, and this was probably the man

4. MARGARET, who married the Rev. Finlay Macrae of Lochalsh, with issue, as already mentioned.

5. Another daughter, whose name is not recorded.

X. FARQUHAR, eldest son of Duncan IX., about whom very little is known, married, in 1694, Anne, daughter of Simon Mackenzie, first laird of Torridon, and died in 1711, with issue—

1 DUNCAN, mentioned below.

2. CHRISTOPHER, who married and had issue, at least one son, Farquhar, called Ferachar Ban (Fair Farquhar) of Fadoch. He married Mary, a sister of Archibald Macra of Ardintoul. This Mary

died shortly before the 6th June, 1823, after a married life of sixty-two years. Her husband was alive at the time of her death, but he was completely blind and almost deaf with age. He died before 1826.   They left issue — Hector ; Duncan ; Alexander, who appears to have been educated at at Aberdeen, and to have graduated M.A. in 1803 ; John ; and several daughters, one of whom, Isabel, was married to a Duncan Macrae, who was dead in 1826

3. JOHN, who is said to have been a man of great physical strength, and of whom it is related that on one occasion, at Loch Hourn, he carried away from a boat, across the beach, a large barrel of salt under each arm, one of which a man of ordinary strength could, with difficulty, lift from the ground.[1] John is witness to a sasine by his brother, Duncan Macrae of Inverinate, to Florence Mackenzie, his spouse, at Coul, 10th August, 1725.

4 JANET. married Christopher Macrae, at Drudaig, a descendant of the Rev. Donald, son of the Rev. Farquhar Macrae VII.

[1] The following extract from a letter written in Kintail in 1826 refers to this incident, and is worth quoting as an instance of the usual tendency to magnify the "good old days". "I have heard my father remark that the people of his native country are much degenerated in strength, as many anecdotes, still well known, will show.   One trial of strength he often spoke of as being particularly well authenticated   John Macrae, uncle to Farquhar Macrae, late Fadoch, was at Loch Hourn with Simon Murchison, brother of Alexander of Auchtertyre, when they observed a man carrying up salt from the seaside to the beach, a barrel at a time. ' Do you see,' says Macrae, ' that man is boasting.'   He then went and took up a barrel under his arm. ' Will you,' says he, ' help me to take up this other to my haunch ?'   Simon did so with very great difficulty, and Macrae swaggered away with both up to the beach   This was related to my father by the above Simon Murchison "

5. MARY, who married Murdoch, son of Farquhar Macrae of Morvich, and had, with other issue, John, the Kintail poet, already mentioned

6 ANNE, who married Duncan Macrae, son of Donald, in Glensheil.

XI DUNCAN. eldest son of Farquhar X., was served heir on the 19th March, 1725. He married Florence, daughter of Charles Mackenzie of Cullen (Kilcoy family), by his wife, Florence, daughter of John Mackenzie, second laird of Applecross, and died in 1726, leaving issue—

1. FARQUHAR, mentioned below.

2. ANNE, who married Captain Horne and resided with him in France. Mrs Horne is said to have been the first to bring tea to Kintail. The caddy in which the tea was brought is now in the possession of Mrs Mackenzie, of Abbotsford Park, Edinburgh, the great-granddaughter of Mrs Horne's brother, Farquhar of Inverinate

CHAPTER VII.

XII. FARQUHAR, son of Duncan XI , was the
last of the family who held Inverinate and acted as
Chamberlain of Kintail.   Like so many more of his
Clan, he was an ardent Jacobite, and narrowly
escaped trouble in 1745.   Considering all that the
people of Kintail had suffered at the hands of the
supporters of the House of Hanover, both in 1715
and again in 1719, it is no matter for surprise that
in 1745 they once more showed signs of strong
Jacobite sympathies.   It is said that, notwithstanding Seaforth's loyalty to the House of
Hanover at that time, the army of the Prince was
joined by a number of Macraes, not one of whom

ever again returned to Kintail, and that Farquhar, who was then a very young man, was so strongly suspected of Jacobite sympathies that he was placed for some time under arrest.   There is a tradition that on one occasion he was mistaken by a party of the King's soldiers for the Prince himself, who had recently passed a day or two in Kintail in the course of his wanderings after the battle of Culloden, and that they took him to Fort-William, where his mother succeeded in satisfying the authorities as to his identity, and so secured his release.   Farquhar made some additions to the Rev. John Macrae's Manuscript History of the Clan, but those additions appear to have been limited to the merest outline of his own family.   He married first, on the 22nd April, 1755, Mary, daughter of Alexander Mackenzie, eighth laird of Dochmaluag, on whose death he married, as his second wife, Elizabeth, widow of Richard Ord, of Inverness, and daughter of John Mackenzie, son of Alexander, seventh laird of Dochmaluag, by whom he had no issue.   He died at Inverness in December, 1789, and was buried in Kintail.   By his first wife, Farquhar left numerous issue—

1. ALEXANDER, born 10th May, 1756, and died unmarried in Demerara.

2. DUNCAN, born 8th June, 1757.   He received an Ensign's Commission in the 78th Highlanders, which was raised by Lord Seaforth in 1793, and served with that regiment in India.   He was promoted Captain in 1797, and retired on half-pay in 1805.   He was connected at various times with

other regiments than the 78th.   He died about 1825.   Captain Duncan is said to have been a man of very handsome personal appearance, a good Highlander, and a generous man.   He married first, on the 4th August, 1784, Janet, daughter of Alexander Murchison of Tarradale.   He married, as his second wife, Christina, daughter of the Rev. William Bethune of Kilmuir, Skye.   By his first wife he had issue—

a. Kenneth, born 19th May, 1785.   He was educated at King's College, Aberdeen, and went to London in 1803 "to be placed in a mercantile house."   He was afterwards a planter in Demerara.

b. Mary, born 20th August, 1786, died in infancy.

c. Alexander, born 28th August, 1787.   He was educated at Aberdeen, and was afterwards a planter in Demerara, where he was resident for half a century.   He is the author of a "Manual of Plantership in British Guiana," which was published in 1856.   Alexander married and left three daughters —Christina, Mary, and Flora—but no male issue. He died at Southampton in 1860 from the effects of an accident he met with on the homeward voyage from Demerara.

d. Mary and Margaret, born 1st February, 1789, died in infancy.

Captain Duncan had issue also by his second wife, as follows—

e. John

f. Duncan, who entered Aberdeen University in 1820, and attended for four sessions, but did not graduate.   He died unmarried in Demerara.

g. Mary, who was born at Inverinate, and married Lieutenant John Robertson Macdonald of Rodel, in Harris, with issue, one daughter, Jane, unmarried.

h. Jessie, who married Hector Mackinnon of the Island of Egg, with issue :—

*h*1. Duncan, died in Australia.

*h*2. Lachlan also died in Australia.

*h*3. Jessie, who married a Mr Crawford.

*h*4. Flora, who married a Mr Morrison, with issue.

*h*5. Alexandrina, who married a Mr Finlayson.

i. Flora, who, on 2nd February, 1826, married Alexander Macdonald of Vallay, North Uist, with issue—

*i*1. Alexander Ewen, in Australia, married, with issue.

*i*2. William John, a Senator of Vancouver Island, married, with issue—Flora; Edith; Christina; Reginald, in the Royal Artillery; William, in the Royal Navy; Douglas.

*i*3. Duncan Alexander Macrae, in Australia.

*i*4. Colin Hector, in Australia, married, with issue.

*i*5. Duncan, in Australia.

*i*6. Christina Mary, married the Rev. John William Tolmie, of Contin, with issue :—(1) John, married Alexandrina, daughter of Donald Macrae, Luskintyre, in Harris, son of the Rev. Finlay Macrae; (2) the Rev. Alexander Macdonald Cornfute of Southend, Kintyre; (3) Margaret, married the Rev. Archibald Macdonald of Kiltarlity, joint author of the *History of Clan Donald*, with issue, Marion

Margaret Hope; Christina Mary; Flora Amy Mac-ruari; (4) Mary Macrae; (5) Flora, married Charles Hoffman Weatherall, M.R.C.V.S., in India, with issue; (6) Hugh Macaskill, in New Zealand; (7) Gregory, in New Zealand; (8) Williamina Alexandrina.

*i*7. Harriet Margaret married Alexander Allan Gregory, of Inverness, with issue :—(1) Alexander, married Miss Stewart (of Murdostoun, Lanarkshire), with issue; (2) Margaret Maclean, married Francis Foster, with issue; (3) Harriett, married William Lindsay Stewart (of Murdostoun); (4) Catherine Christina, married Charles William Dyson Perrins, Esq. of Davenham, Worcestershire, and of Ardross Castle, with issue; (5) William; (6) Neil; (7) Mary; (8) John, in the Royal Navy; (9) Reginald.

*i*8. Mary Isabella married the Rev. Kenneth Alexander Mackenzie, LL.D., of Kingussie, with issue :— John, died young; Mary Flora, married Walter Frederick Rodolph De Watteville, M.B., &c., of Edinburgh University; Elizabeth.

3. KENNETH, born 16th July, 1758. He received a Commission in the old 78th, afterwards the 72nd Highlanders, which was raised by the Earl of Seaforth in 1778. He afterwards served in the 76th Foot, in which regiment he was promoted Major in 1795, and Lieutenant-Colonel in 1804. He served with his regiment in India with much distinction. In one of his dispatches from India, dated 26th December, 1804, and giving an account of the capture of Deig, General Lake says —" I myself feel under the greatest obligation to

Lieutenant-Colonel Macrae, to whose conduct on this occasion I attribute the ultimate success of the attack" (on Deig, on the 23rd December, 1804). Colonel Kenneth also took a prominent part in the siege and capture of Bhurtpore in the following year. Among the casualties at the siege at Bhurtpore, there was a Lieutenant D. Macrae of the 76th killed, and a Lieutenant J. Macrae of the same regiment wounded, on the 21st January, 1805. Colonel Kenneth Macrae was afterwards Paymaster-General of Jamaica, where he died about 1814. He married a Miss Mackay in Jamaica, but left no issue.

4. JEAN, born 23rd August, 1759. She married, in 1781, the Rev. John Macqueen, of Applecross, and died in 1847. She was called in Kintail "The Sunbeam of Tullochard" because of her beauty. She left issue—

a Donald, a planter in Demerara.

b. John, a Major in the Army; married a daughter of Judge Bliss, of New Brunswick, and left a son, John, a Lieutenant in the Rifle Brigade, and other issue.

c. George, a Captain in the Rifle Brigade.

d. Archibald, who was Clerk of Arraigns in Demerara, and died unmarried.

e. Dr Kenneth, H.E.I.C.S., married, but left no surviving issue.

f. Farquhar, a Captain in the Indian Navy, married and left issue.

g. Mary ; *h*, Jane ; *i*, Jessie ; *k*, Beatrice.

5. JOHN, born 3rd November, 1760, was a Doctor of Medicine, H.E.I.C.S. (Calcutta and Chittagong).

He married the daughter of a Colonel Erskine, with issue—

a. John, also a Doctor of Medicine, H.E.I.C.S., married and left one daughter. He died at Monghyr, in India, early in 1864.

b. Farquhar, who was a Lieutenant in the Indian Army, served in the first Burmese War, 1824-6, and died in 1847.

c. Ellen married Mr Lee Warner, without issue.

d. Dora married James Fraser of Achnagairn, in Inverness-shire, with issue—

*d*1. Dora, who married Robert Reid, brewer, London, without issue.

*d*2. Jane, who married Eyre Lambert, without issue.

*d*3. Helen, who married, first, Huntly George Gordon Duff of Muirtown, with issue :—(1) Emily Dora, who died young; (2) Georgina Huntly, who married Francis Darwin of Elston, Notts, and of Muirtown, Inverness, without issue. Helen married, secondly, Charles Middleton of Middleton Lodge, Ilkley, Yorkshire, with issue; (3) Charles Marmaduke; (4) Reginald Charles; (5) Lionel George; (6) Mary Hilda.

e. Georgina, who married, 3rd March, 1831, Edmund Currie of Pickford, Sussex, with issue—

*e*1. The Very Rev. Edward Reid Currie, D.D., Dean and Vicar of Battle, in Sussex, married, first, Geraldine Dowdeswell, only child of Richard Tyrrell, Esq., with issue; Edward George. He married, secondly, Frances Emma, only daughter of the Rev. William Frederick Hotham.

*e*2. Georgina married Sir Augustus Rivers Thompson, K.C.S.I., Lieutenant Governor of Bengal.

*e*3. Eliza Fredrica married George William Moultrie, of the Bank of Bengal.

*e*4. Mary Catherine.

*e*5. Dora married Nathaniel Stewart Alexander, Bengal Civil Service.

6. CHARLES, born 26th June, 1762, died young.

7. FARQUHAR, born 30th March, 1764. He was a Doctor of Medicine, and was appointed Medical Officer to Lord Macartney's Embassy to China in 1792-4. He was afterwards killed in a duel with a Major Blair in Demerara in 1802. He left no issue. He is said to have been "handsome and comely in personal appearance, and strong in proportion." His portrait is represented as Colin Fitzgerald, the reputed founder of the House of Seaforth in Benjamin West's celebrated deer hunt painting in Brahan Castle. There is an interesting tradition with regard to the manner in which Farquhar came to be chosen as the model for Colin Fitzgerald. It is said that the artist accidentally saw him one day in Hyde Park, and, being struck by his appearance, asked him if he would sit as a model for the founder of the House of Seaforth, which he readily consented to do. Farquhar was not only a native of the ancestral country of the Seaforths, but was also closely related to that family, and it is a remarkable fact that he should have struck the artist, to whom he is said to have been a perfect stranger, as a suitable representative for the hero of the painting.

8. MADELINE, born 2nd October, 1765. She

married, on the 27th June, 1782, the Rev. John Macrae, M.A., minister of Glensheil, and died on the 21st January, 1837. The Rev. John Macrae, who was a native of the neighbourhood of Dingwall, was educated at Aberdeen. He was ordained to the parish of Glensheil in 1777, and died there in 1823, aged seventy-five years. By him Madeline had issue—

a. Alexander, born in 1783, died young.

b. Mary, born in 1785, married in 1814, Donald Munro (of the family of Lealty, in Ross-shire), and died in 1844, leaving issue—

*b*1. Madeline, who married the Rev. Alexander Fraser Russell, M.A., Free Church minister of Kilmodan, in Argyleshire, with issue :—(1) Sir James Alexander Russell, M.D., LL.D., &c., Lord Provost of Edinburgh, 1891-94. He married Marianne Rae, daughter of James Wilson, Esq., of Edinburgh, and niece of Professor Wilson (Christopher North), without issue ; (2) The Rev. John Munro Russell, M A., B.D., minister of the Scottish Church, Cape Town. He married Nancy Eliza, daughter of the Rev. Robert Elder, D.D., Free Church minister of Rothesay, with issue—Alexander Fraser ; Robert Elder ; Madeline Mary ; Ian Robson ; (3) Donald George, a tea planter in India, died in Edinburgh in 1897 ; (4) William John, M.B., died at Wandsworth in 1883 ; (5) Duncan Kenneth Campbell, a Civil Engineer ; (6) Tindal Mackenzie, died young ; (7) Alexander Fraser, M.A., M.B., &c., Army Medical Department, married Laura Charlotte, daughter of Colonel Frederick Prescott Forteath of Newton,

Elginshire, with issue—James Forteath, Margaret Marianne; (8) Mary Florence Beatrice, died young.

*b*2 Isabella, now (1897) residing at Abbotsford Park, Edinburgh, married John Mackenzie, Leguan, British Guiana, with issue : — (1) Gilbert Proby, Surgeon - Major Indian Medical Service, married Jane Scott, and died in 1890, leaving issue—John, Indian Staff Corps; Thomas Rennie Scott; George Kenneth; Isabella; Emma; Gilbert Proby; (2) Donald George, Captain, Indian Staff Corps, married Mary Ruth, daughter of Captain G. M. Prior, R.A., and died in India in 1885, leaving issue — Isabella Florence Ruth; Ethel Lucy; (3) Charles Tindal Grant, died young.

*b*3. John died unmarried in Australia.

*b*4. Anne married Allan Cameron, with issue.

*b*5. Christina Flora married George Ross in Demerara, with issue.

*b*6. Donald married Maggie Muir, with issue.

c. Isabella, born 1786, married John Campbell, farmer, Duntulm, in Skye, and died in 1849, leaving numerous issue.

d. Florence, born 1788, married Duncan Macrae of the Torlysich family, and died in 1865, with issue, one son, Francis Humberston, who married in Tasmania, and left issue, two sons and one daughter.

e. Beatrice, born 1790, married the Rev. Alexander Campbell, minister of Croy, and died in 1877, with issue—

*e*1. Rev. Patrick Campbell, minister of Killearnan, in Ross-shire, died unmarried.

*e*2. Madeline married James M'Inroy, with issue.

*e*3. Jane married the Rev. James M. 'Allardyce, D.D., minister of Bowden, in Roxburghshire, with issue, one son, who died young.

*e*4. Duncan died in Calcutta.

*e*5. Charlotte married Captain Hamilton, H.E.I.C.S., with issue, one son, Dr Archibald Hamilton.

*e*6. Rev. Colin A. Campbell, minister of Lyne, Peeblesshire.

f. Duncan, born 1796, died in Florida.

g. Christina, born 1798, married Lieutenant Farquhar Macrae of the 78th Highlanders, Torlysich family, of whom hereafter.

h. Rev. John Macrae, born 21st November, 1799. He succeeded his father as minister of Glensheil in 1823, became minister of Glenelg in 1840, and died on the 7th July, 1875. He married in 1826 Jamesina Fraser, daughter of Norman Macleod of Ellanriach, Glenelg, and by her, who died in 1852, he had issue—

*h*1. John Kenneth, who was Deputy-Commissioner at Rangoon, and married Elizabeth Dunbar, with issue; John Dunbar; Norman Farquhar; Hugh; Madeline; Catherine; Florence.

*h*2. Norman James, an Indian missionary, married Jessie, daughter of Dr John Junor, Peebles, without issue.

*h*3. Alexa married Hugh Bogle, Esq., of Glasgow, with issue :—(1) Margaret Kennedy married Frank Crossman ; (2) Madeline Macrae married Harry Calthorpe, with issue; (3) Gilbert married Alice

Galloway, with issue; (4) John Stewart Douglas; (5) William Lockhart, a distinguished artist, whose paintings of Highland subjects are well known at the annual exhibitions of the Royal Academy. He is married to Margaret, daughter of Peter Maclean of Dunvegan, Skye; (6) Rosalind De Vere; (7) Mary Innes married George Kynoch; (8) Norman Archibald died in Burmah in 1894.

*h*4. Madeline Charlotte married the Rev. Colin A. Campbell, minister of Lyne, Peeblesshire, without issue.

*h*5. Forbes.   *h*6. Catherine Christina Sibella.

i. Kenneth, born in 1802, died unmarried in Florida.

9. ANNE, born 21st March, 1768, married in 1794 Lachlan Mackinnon, Esq. of Corriechatachan, in Skye, who died in 1828, aged 56 years, leaving issue—

a. Lachlan, who married, first, Catherine, daughter of Duncan Macdougall of Ardentrive, by whom he had issue, five daughters, one of whom married Archibald Roberts Young, of the Bengal Civil Service, with issue. He married, secondly, Charlotte, daughter of General Sir John Hope, without surviving issue.

b. Anne, who in 1815 married the Rev. John Mackinnon, minister of Strath, in Skye, with issue—

*b*1. The Rev. Donald Mackinnon, D.D., also minister of Strath. He married, first, Flora, daughter of Dr Farquhar Mackinnon of Kyle, in Skye, and secondly, Emma Flora, daughter of

Colonel William Macleod, of the Madras Army, and by her had issue—John William Macleod; Lachlan Kenneth Scobie; Donald; Charles John; Archibald; Godfrey William Wentworth; Emma Flora; Annie Emily.

*b*2. Lachlan, of Melbourne, in Australia, and of Elfordleigh, in Devonshire, who was one of the original founders of *The Melbourne Argus*. He married, first, Jane, daughter of Robert Montgomery, of Belfast, and secondly, Emily, daughter of Lieutenant Bundock, R.N.

*b*3. John Murray Macgregor of Ostaig House, Skye, who married Christina, widow of Archibald Smith, Esq.

*b*4. Charles Farquhar, of Melbourne, Australia, died unmarried.

*b*5. Surgeon-General Sir William Alexander Mackinnon, K.C.B., LL.D., &c., Knight of the Legion of Honour in France, &c., who was born in 1830, and educated at Edinburgh and Glasgow Universities. He joined the army in 1853, and was appointed Assistant-Surgeon to the Forty-Second Highlanders. He served with that regiment during the Crimean War, being present at Alma, Balaclava, Kertch, and Sebastopol, for which he received the medal with three clasps; was appointed Knight Commander of the Legion of Honour; and received the Turkish medal. He afterwards served on the personal staff of Lord Clyde in the Indian Mutiny in 1857, taking part in the campaigns of Rohilcund and Oude, and in the actions of Bareilly and others. He served in New

Zealand from 1862 to 1866 as Surgeon of the Fifty-Seventh Regiment; was appointed Sanitary Officer and Field-Surgeon to the New Zealand forces, and was present at various engagements. For these services he received the Companionship of the Bath. He was Assistant-Professor of Clinical and Military Surgery at the Army Medical Hospital from 1867 to 1873. In 1874, he was appointed principal Medical Officer in the Ashantee War, and was promoted to be Deputy-Surgeon-General. He was principal Medical Officer also at Aldershot and Colchester, and in China, Malta, and Gibraltar, and is Honorary Surgeon to the Queen. In 1889, he attained the highest rank in his profession, being appointed in that year Director-General of the Army Medical Department. In 1891, he was created a Knight Commander of the Bath, and finally, after forty-three years of service, retired from the army on the 7th May, 1896. His career has thus been one of great distinction. Lord Clyde, General Sir Duncan A. Cameron, and others have borne the strongest testimony to his fearless and efficient devotion to duty on active service; and on the 3rd July, 1894, the Secretary for War declared in Parliament that " there could be no more efficient or just chief of the Army Medical Department than Sir William Mackinnon."[1]

*b*6. Colin Macrae married Anne, daughter of Robert Saunders Webb, Esq., with issue.

*b*7. Godfrey Bosville, of Melbourne, Australia,

---

[1] A portrait and biographical sketch of Sir William Mackinnon appeared in the *Celtic Monthly* for August, 1896,

married Maggie, daughter of Charles Macdonald, Esq. of Ord, Skye, with issue :—John ; Annie ; Mary Anne ; Charles Macdonald ; William ; Neilly.

*b*8. Ann Susan, died young.

*b*9. Mary Jane, died young.

*b*10. Catherine Charlotte, died in 1890.

*b*11. Louisa Houptoun, married John Henry Stonehouse Lydiard, son of Admiral Lydiard, R.N., with issue, and is now living in Melbourne.

*b*12. Flora Downie, now of Duisdale House, Skye.

c. Mary, married Lieutenant-Colonel Duncan Mackenzie, with issue :—George and Lachlan, both in the Indian Service.

d. Charles, married Henrietta, daughter of Captain Studd, H.E.I.C.S., with issue—

*d*1. Victoria, married Major-General Colin Mackenzie, of the Indian Army, with issue :—(1) Colin John, Major 2nd Battalion Seaforth Highlanders (Ross-shire Buffs). He served in the Egyptian Campaign, the Burmese Campaign, the Black Mountain Expedition, and the Hunga Nagar Campaign in Cashmere. (2) Charles Alexander ; (3) Ronald Pearson, M.D.; (4) Mary Charlotte ; (5) Henrietta Studd ; (6) Victor Herbert, of the British East Africa Company, died in 1892 ; (7) Kenneth Lascelles ; (8) Frederick William, R.N.; (9) Henry Studd ; (10) Morna ; (11) Annie Stuart.

*d*2. Anne, married General John Stewart, of the Indian Army.

*d*3. Flora Jane, married Dr Clarke, of the Indian Army, with issue.

*d*4. Harriet, married Colonel Prinsep, of the Indian Army, with issue.

*d*5. Jessie, married Captain Poynter, with issue.

*d*6. Mary, married Captain Murray, with issue.

*d*7. Susan Margaret, married, in 1877, Algernon St Maur, fifteenth Duke of Somerset.

*d*8. Henrietta, married a Mr Sargent, with issue.

e. Farquhar, Lieutenant H.E.I.C.S., died at the Cape of Good Hope in 1825.

f. Flora, died unmarried.

g. Margaret, married Captain D. Macdonald, of the 42nd Highlanders, with issue :—

*g*1. Farquhar ; *g*2 Archibald ; *g*3 Lachlan ; *g*4 Christina.

*g*5. Catherine, married, first, Donald Reid, Esq., and secondly, General Macleod.

*g*6. Ann Mary, married M. H. Court, Esq., of Castlemans, Berks.

h. Alexander Kenneth, married, first, Flora, daughter of the Rev. Alexander Downie, D.D., of Lochalsh, with issue—

*h*1. Alister, died in India in 1860.

*h*2. Annabella, married Admiral Rutherford, R.N.

Alexander Kenneth married, secondly, Barbara, daughter of Captain Daniel Reid, R.N., with issue—

*h*3. Flora Downie. *h*4. Catherine.

*h*5. Annie Flora, married · Robert Currie, H.E.I.C.S., with issue.

*h*6. Charlotte.

*h*7. Lachlan Charles, of *The Melbourne Argus*, married, as his second wife, Emily Grace Bundock.

Mackinnon, adopted daughter of his cousin, Lachlan Mackinnon, of Elfordleigh, with issue.

*h*8. Daniel, died unmarried.

*h*9. Charles, married Constance, daughter of Colonel Wright, with issue.

*h*10. Thomas Mackenzie.

i. Kenneth, a Doctor H.E.I.C.S., married Jessie, daughter of Captain Kenneth Mackenzie, of Kerrisdale, with issue—

*i*1. Catherine Mary, married Robert Scott Moncrieff, with issue:—(1) Jessie Margaret, married George Scott Moncrieff, Sheriff of Inverness, with issue—Colin; John. (2) Charlotte, married Charles Watson, grandson of the Rev. Thomas Chalmers, D.D., with issue; (3) Susan; (4) Mary Catherine, married Wellington Ray, M.A., with issue; (5) Robert Lawrence, in Buenos Ayres, married Victoria Troutbeck; (6) Kenneth, an electrical engineer in India; (7) William Elmslie, Indian Medical Service; (8) Catherine, B.A., of London University; (9) David.

*i*2. Flora Anne, married Major John Ross, of Tilliscorthy, Aberdeenshire, with issue:—(1) John, British Consul, Fiji Islands; (2) Alexander, British Consul at Beira; (3) Helen, married W. J. Bundock Mackinnon; (4) Jessie; (5) Charles; (6) Robert.

*i*3. Jessie, married Dr A. Halliday Douglas, Edinburgh, with issue ·—(1) Kenneth Mackinnon, M.D., married Florence Amy Leslie, with issue— Jessie Margery; Kenneth; Archibald. (2) Rev. Andrew Halliday Douglas, M.A., Presbyterian minister, Cambridge, married Isabel Lumsden Love, with issue, Margaret Isabel Mackinnon ; (3) Charles Mackinnon, D.Sc., Lecturer, Edinburgh University, married Anne Tod.

*i*4. Charles Kenneth, Colonel in the Indian Army, married Miss Broadfoot.

*i*5. Kenneth Hector, died unmarried.

j. Jessie, married Hugh Macaskill, of Mornish.

k. Johanna, married the Rev. James Morrison, of Kintail, with issue—

*k*1. Rev. Roderick Morrison, born 1839, also minister of Kintail, who died at Kintail Manse 11th June, 1897.

*k*2. Annie, married William Dick, Esq.

*k*3. Jane.

l. Susannah and Jane (twins), died unmarried.

10. HECTOR, born September, 1722, died young.

11. FLORENCE married Captain Kenneth Mackenzie of Kerrisdale, in Gairloch, younger son of Sir Alexander Mackenzie, third baronet of Gairloch, with issue—

a. Alexander, a Captain in the 58th Regiment, married Ellen, daughter of William Beibly, M.D., President of the College of Physicians, Edinburgh, with issue—

*a*1. Kenneth, a planter in Bengal.

*a*2. William, Deputy Postmaster-General in India—retired.

*a*3. Julius, an engineer in Birmingham, married, with issue.

*a*4. Frank, a planter in India, married, with issue.

b. Hector died unmarried in Java.

c. Farquhar went to Victoria, where he married and left issue:—Hector; John; Violet; Mary; Flora.

d. Jean married William H. Garrett, of the Indian Civil Service, with issue—

*d*1. Edward.   *d*2. William.

*d*3. Eleanor, married, first, Dr Calder, H.E.I.C.S., with issue :—(1) William, died without issue; (2) Edward, Captain, Mercantile Service, married, with issue.

Eleanor married, secondly, Gershom Gourlay, Esq., of the firm of Gourlay Brothers, engineers, Dundee, with issue; (3) Henry, of the firm of Gourlay Brothers; (4) Jane, died young; (5) Miriam, died young; (6) Frederick, a civil engineer, married Agnes, daughter of the Venerable Archdeacon John Edward Herring, with issue; (7) Florence, died young; (8) Charles, of the firm of Gourlay Brothers, married Fanny Gordon; (9) Morris, died young; (10) Margaret, married J. Campbell Penney, with issue; (11) Kenneth Mackenzie married Grace, daughter of D. M. Watson of Greystone, with issue; (12) Frank, a Doctor of Medicine.

*d*4. Flora died young.   *d*5. Emily.

*d*6. Elizabeth married James Bell, Esq., Dundee, with issue :—(1) James, merchant in Dundee, married, with issue; (2) Morris, a civil engineer, married, with issue; (3) Grace married, with issue; (4) Jane married, with issue; (5) Thomas; (6) William; (7) Son.

e. Mary married, first, Dr Macleod, Dingwall, without issue, and secondly, Murdo Mackenzie, Calcutta, also without issue.

f. Christian Henderson married John Mackenzie, solicitor, Tain, a son of George Mackenzie, third of Pitlundie, with issue :—George ; Kenneth.

g. Jessie married Dr Kenneth Mackinnon, of the Corriechatachan family, H.E.I.C.S., Calcutta.

12. COLIN, of whom next.

XIII. COLIN, youngest son of Farquhar Macrae of Inverinate and Mary Mackenzie of Dochmaluag, was born on the 14th March, 1776. He was a merchant and planter in Demerara, where he rose to a position of importance and prominence. He was Colonel Commandant of the Colonial Militia, a member of the Colonial Legislation, and one of the negotiators of the cession of Demerara to England after the Peace of 1814. He married Charlotte Gertrude, daughter of John Cornelius Vandenheuvel,[1] Esq , of Demerara, who was for some time Governor of that Colony when it belonged to the Dutch, and by her had issue, as below. Colin died in Edinburgh on the 25th October, 1854.

1. CHARLOTTE married Captain Edward Brook Vass, with issue—Charlotte Gertrude ; Catherine Murat ; Maria Cornelia.

---

1 The Vandenheuvel family came originally from Germany, which they were obliged to quit at the time of the Reformation in consequence of their adhesion to the Protestant cause. This they did, however, with the permission of the Emperor Charles V , and settled for a time in Brabant. Shortly afterwards the head of the family rendered an important military service to the Emperor, for which he received a patent of nobility, the addition of a sword to his coat-of-arms, and a medal which was recently, and is probably still, in the possession of his descendants. One of his sons eventually returned to Germany, and, having made profession of the Roman Catholic religion, he obtained possession of the old family estates. The eldest son, however, remained in the Netherlands, and from him was descended in a direct line the said John Cornelius Vandenheuvel, of Demerara.

2. FARQUHAR, drowned in 1838 off Cape Hatteras, in America, while trying to rescue another man.

3. MARIA CORNELIA married Dr James Sewell, son of Chief Justice Sewell, of Quebec, with issue— James; Justine; Colin; Edward; Hope; Horace.

4. JOHN ANTHONY, who succeeded as representative of the Inverinate family, and of whom hereafter.

5. COLIN WILSON married Louisa Elliott, without issue.

6. JUSTINE HENRIETTE married, 26th December, 1833, Horatio Ross, Esq. of Rossie, Forfarshire, and Wyvis, Ross-shire, Captain in the 14th Light Dragoons, and some time M.P. for Aberdeen and the Montrose Burghs. She died at Southsea in 1894, leaving issue—

   a. Horatio Senftenberg John, Esq., of the Indian Civil Service, married Caroline Latour St George, daughter of Sir Theophilus St George, Bart., with issue.

   b. Hercules Grey, Esq., of the Indian Civil Service, who distinguished himself during the Indian Mutiny, married, with issue.

   c. Colin George, Esq , sometime of Wyvis, and later of Gruinards, Ross-shire, married, with issue.

   d. Edward Charles Russell, who was winner of the Queen's prize at the first Wimbledon Meeting in 1860, Chairman of the Board of Lunacy, &c., married Margaret Seymour Osborne, with issue.

   e. The Rev. Robert Peel, a clergyman of the Church of England, some time Rector of Drayton Bassett. in Staffordshire, married, with issue.

7. ALEXANDER CHARLES, M.D., formerly In-

spector-General of Hospitals, Army Medical Department, married Charlotte Reid, with issue—

a Fanny Catherine Ousley married on the 26th April, 1866, Robert George, son of Sir Frederick Larkins Currie, Bart., and died on the 17th September, 1870, leaving issue, a son and two daughters.

b. Charles Colin, born 1843, M.A. University College, Oxford, barrister-at-law in London, and of Oakhurst, Oxted, Surrey, formerly Secretary of the Legislative Council of Bengal, married Cecilia, daughter of Samuel Laing, Esq., M.P., with issue— Charles Alexander; Frank Laing.

c. Louisa.

8. ISAAC VANDENHEUVEL, born 12th June, 1819, a clergyman of the Church of England, and now (1897) Vicar of Brassington, in Derbyshire. He married Elizabeth Johnson, with issue—

a. Christina Elizabeth married, 6th September, 1894, John Eaton Fearn, with issue — Francis; Russel Colin.

b Colin John.

9. ROBERT CAMPBELL married, 25th October, 1853, Jane Eliza, eldest daughter of Vice-Admiral Mark John Currie, and died 11th February, 1896, with issue—

a. Farquhar Campbell.

b. Mark Reginald married Nancy Dill, with issue

c. Junita Gertrude married Harry William Antill, with issue.

d. Justine Alice married William Mathias Lancaster,

e. Harold John married Maggie von Broda.

f. Colin Tisdall.

g. Horace Duncan died unmarried in 1885.

h. Marshall.

i. Hilda married William Arthur Warwick Herring, with issue.

j. Mary Edith married Peter Felix Mackenzie-Richards, with issue.

10. MARGARET ELIZABETH married John Kennedy, Esq. of Underwood, Ayrshire, and died in 1893, leaving issue—

a. John, D.L. for County of Ayr, W.S., and a Parliamentary solicitor, Westminster, married and has issue.

b. Neil James, B.A., LL.B. and advocate in Edinburgh, married, 10th September, 1895, Eleonora Agnes, only surviving child of Robert William Cochran Patrick, Esq. of Woodside and Ladyland, in the County of Ayr, some time M.P. for North Ayrshire, on whose death, in 1897, Mrs Kennedy having succeeded to the estates, Mr Neil J. Kennedy assumed the name of Cochran Patrick.

c. Charlotte Maria died unmarried, 1896.

d. Justine Henriette married, 1884, Alan John Colquhoun, C.B., son of John Colquhoun, author of "The Moor and the Loch," a nephew of the late Sir James Colquhoun of Luss, Bart. He was formerly Captain in "The Black Watch," and is now (1897) Lieutenant-Colonel Commanding the Duke of Edinburgh's Own Edinburgh Artillery Militia, and has issue

e. Elizabeth Theodora Mary married John

William M'Kerrell Brown, of the Bank of Scotland, Dunfermline.

f. Adelaide Emily Jane.

XIV. JOHN ANTHONY, LL.D., Esquire of Wellbank, Forfarshire, J.P., and a Writer to the Signet in Edinburgh, second son of Colin XIII., was born on the 1st February, 1812. Mr Macrae raised the first Volunteer Company in Scotland in 1859, and, at his death, was Major of the Queen's R.V. Brigade. He married Joanna Isabella Maclean, daughter of John Maclean of Dumfries estate, in the Island of Carriacou, West Indies, and died on the 23rd May, 1868, leaving issue—

1. John Anthony, born 23rd November, 1842 ; died 5th March, 1852.

2. Colin George, of whom below.

3. Horatio Ross, Esquire of Clunes,[1] Inverness-shire, is a Justice of the Peace for the County of Inverness, a writer to the Signet in Edinburgh, and Lieutenant-Colonel of the Queen's Rifle Volunteer Brigade. He married Letitia May, daughter of Sir William Maxwell of Cardoness, Bart., with issue— Alexander William Urquhart, born 18th April, 1885.

4. Jessidora married in 1884, Sir William Francis Maxwell of Cardoness, Bart., Kirkcudbright-shire, with issue—

William Francis John, born 7th July, 1885 ; Joanna Mary ; Dorothea Letitia May.

---

[1] Mr Macrae's estate of Clunes is situated in the district which, according to tradition, was the original home from which the Macraes migrated to Kintail.—See Chapter I,

Sir COLIN GEORGE MACRAE (Inverinate)

XV. COLIN GEORGE, eldest surviving son of John Anthony XIV., is now the lineal representative of the Macraes of Inverinate, and is fifteenth in descent from Fionnla Dubh Mac Gillechriosd, the founder of the Clan Macrae of Kintail. He was born 30th November, 1844, is a writer to the Signet in Edinburgh and a Justice of the Peace for the City of Edinburgh and for the County of Forfar. He was educated at the Edinburgh Academy and at the University of Edinburgh, where he had a distinguished career and graduated Master of Arts. As a student, he was for two years President of the University Conservative Club, and since his entry upon public life has taken a prominent part in the affairs of his native city At the present time (1897) he is Chairman of the School Board of Edinburgh, a position which he has occupied for the past seven years with conspicuous success and with the cordial support of his fellow-citizens.[1] He is also a loyal member and supporter of the Church of Scotland, in connection with which he has done much active and valuable work, having sat in the General Assembly almost continuously for twenty years. His interest in the Highlands, and more especially in young Highlanders coming to Edinburgh, has always been great, and has frequently been shown in a kindly and practical manner.[2] Mr Macrae

---

[1] . . . He is a man who, as an educationist, has done much sterling and unselfish work for the city, and his opinions must command respect even from those who disagree with him . . . It is undeniable that the Edinburgh Board has done admirable public work, and never more than in the time of Mr Macrae himself. . . . —*The Scotsman*, 19th February, 1897

[2] A portrait and biographical sketch of Mr Colin George Macrae appeared in *The Celtic Monthly* for November, 1896.

married, 23rd June, 1877, Flora Maitland, daughter
of John Colquhoun, Esq., author of the well-known
work entitled "The Moor and the Loch," and has
issue—

1. JOHN ANTHONY, born 19th May, 1883.
2. FRANCES MAITLAND DOROTHEA.

CHAPTER VIII.

Christopher, son of Alexander of Inverinate. — Tacksman of
Aryugan.—His Marriage and Descendants —Mathesons of
Lochalsh and the Rev. Dr Kennedy of Dingwall Descended
from him.—Other Descendants of Christopher.—John, son of
Christopher.—His Marriage and Descendants.

IX. CHRISTOPHER, son of Alexander of Inverinate
and Mary Mackenzie of Dochmaluag, and ninth in
descent from Fionnla Du Mac Gillechriosd, was
tacksman of Aryugan, in Kintail, and was commonly
known as "Gillecriosd Mor a Chroidh" (Big Christopher of the Cattle). He was alive on the 15th
August, 1723, as his signature appears on a bond of
caution drawn up on that date for the protection
of their rights by the wadsetters on the estates of
Macdonald of Sleat, which the "Forfeited Estates
Commissioners" were then proposing to sell. It is
uncertain who his wife was, but it is said that he
was twice married, and that his first wife was of the
Murchisons of Auchtertyre, and that his second wife
was a Chisholm. He left a large family, all of whom
are said to have married and to have left issue.
Many of his descendants are still living in Kintail
and Lochalsh.

1. DUNCAN. He is witness to a sasine on the
19th March, 1700, and was killed at the Battle of
Sheriffmuir in 1715. He is said to have married

Margaret, daughter of John Mackenzie of Lochbroom, and left issue, as below, so far as it has been found possible to trace them—

a. John, who had a son.

*a*1. Duncan, who married Janet, daughter of Christopher, son of Finlay, son of John Breac, son of the Rev. Farquhar Macrae, and had (1) John, who had issue—John ; Donald , Farquhar ; Kenneth ; Christopher.   (2) A son called Christopher Tailor ; (3) Isabella ; (4) Christina.

*a*2. John, who had issue—John, Christopher, Alexander, Duncan.

*a*3. Anne, who married Christopher, at Druidaig.

*a*4. Christina, who married Ian Mac Callum.

b. Alexander, called Alister Ruadh (Red Alexander), who had issue—

*b*1. John, called the Red Smith, who had sons—(1) Alexander, who was a blacksmith at Ardelve ; (2) Finlay.

*b*2. Finlay, who went to America.

2. ALEXANDER had a son Duncan, who had a son Christopher, a priest, and other issue.

3. DONALD, who had a son Duncan, who had a son John, who had a son Alexander, admitted to the Grammar School, Aberdeen, with a Macra bursary in 1806, entered the University in 1809, and graduated M.A. in 1813.

4. CHRISTOPHER, mentioned as taking part in the affair of Ath nam Muileach on the 2nd October, 1721.

5. MURDOCH, also present at the affair of Ath nam Muileach,

6. FARQUHAR, who was also present at the affair of Ath nam Muileach, married, it is said, a Macdonald of Sleat, and had a daughter, Barbara, who married, first, John Og, son of the Rev. Donald Macrae of Kintail, with issue, and secondly Donald, son of the Rev. Finlay Macrae of Lochalsh, also with issue.

7. JOHN, mentioned below.

8. FINLAY.

9. MARY married, in 1695, Farquhar Matheson of Fernaig, and had, with other issue—

a. John, who, in 1728, married, as his second wife, Margaret Mackenzie of Pitlundie, and died in 1760, leaving issue—Alexander, who, about 1763, married Catherine Matheson, and died in 1804, leaving issue—John, who, in 1804, married Margaret, daughter of Captain Donald Matheson of Shiness, and died in 1826, leaving, with other issue—Sir Alexander Matheson, Bart. of Lochalsh, who married, as his second wife, Lavinia Mary, daughter of Thomas Stapleton of Carlton, Yorkshire, and died in 1886, leaving, with other issue—Sir Kenneth James Matheson, Bart. of Lochalsh.

b. Donald, who married Margaret, daughter of Roderick Mackenzie, Sanachan, of the Applecross family, and had a daughter—Mary, who married Donald Kennedy of Kishorn, by whom she had, with other issue—the Rev. John Kennedy of Redcastle, one of whose sons was the Rev. John Kennedy, D.D., who was Free Church minister of Dingwall from 1844 until his death in 1884, and occupied throughout his whole career a foremost place among the greatest preachers of Scotland.

10   MARIAN married John Macrae, a descendant of Miles, son of the Rev. Farquhar.

11. ANNE.

12. CHRISTINA.

13. CATHERINE married Colin Mackenzie, ninth laird of Hilton.   There is a sasine by Colin Mackenzie of Hilton[1] in favour of Catherine Macrae, his spouse, in liferent of his pecklands of Easter Casichan in the parish of Contin and shire of Ross, on the 26th August, 1749.   Catherine left issue—

a. John, who died before his father.

b. Alexander, tenth of Hilton.

c. A daughter who married, as his first wife, John Macdonell, twelfth of Glengarry, and had, with other issue—Alexander, who carried on the representation of that family.

14. JANET.   15. ISABEL.

16. MARGARET, who married Finlay Macrae, Strathglass.

X. JOHN,[2] son of Christopher of Aryugan, called Ian Ban, was educated at Aberdeen, and is mentioned in some copies of the MS. history of the Clan as "Mr John, graduate in Aberdeen."   He is said to have married Annabella, daughter of Duncan Macrae, tutor of Conchra, by his wife Isabel, daughter of the Rev. Finlay Macrae, with issue—

---

[1] The property of this family, which was formerly known as Hilton, was situated in Strathbran, and is now traversed by the Dingwall and Skye Railway between the stations of Achnanlt and Achnasheen.

[2] The succession of Christopher of Aryugan is continued here in his son John only for convenience of arrangement, and not because John's descendants are the oldest lineal representatives of Christopher.

1. FINLAY, who lived at Achmore, and married Isabella Macrae, daughter of Farquhar Mac Ian of the Torlysich family, with other issue—

a. Alexander.

b. John, who married Kate, daughter of Duncan Macrae, and had, together with several daughters, the following issue—

b1. Christopher, who married Mary, daughter of Christopher Macrae, Cari, with issue—(1) Alexander; (2) John, married Isabella, daughter of Duncan Maclennan, Sallachy, with issue—Mary; Jemima; Christopher; Ewen; Mary Anne; Duncan; (3) Christopher; (4) Janet; (5) Isabella; (6) Mary.

b2. Finlay. b3. Alexander.

b4. Duncan, who was for many years a farmer at Kirkton, Lochalsh, and is now (1897) living at Durinish, Lochalsh. He married Jessie, daughter of Alexander Maclennan by his wife Mary, daughter of Alexander Macrae, Achtertyre, and by her, who died 11th April, 1882, aged sixty-seven, had issue—(1) Mary, who married John Maclennan, Strathglass, with issue—Duncan; John; Donald Ewen; Jessie; Annie; Catherine; Mary; Mary Anne; Margaret; Lexy; (2) Catherine, who married Captain William Mackenzie of the Merchant Service, with issue—William; (3) Mary Anne, who died unmarried on the 19th January, 1893.

b5. Annabella, married Duncan Macrae, with issue—(1) John, married Mary, daughter of Thomas Macrae, with issue; (2) Finlay married Annabella Macdonald, with issue; (3) Duncan; (4) Annabella married, with issue.

2. DUNCAN married and had issue—at least one son—

. *a.* John, who married, and had, with other issue—

*a*1. Duncan, who married Grace, daughter of Colin Mackenzie, Kishorn, and died at Dingwall on the 19th December, 1895, aged seventy-nine, leaving issue.—(1) Donald, in America, married Jessie Kennedy, with issue, (2) Marjory married Andrew Robertson, with issue; (3) Catherine married John Murchison, builder, Dingwall.

*a*2. Alexander, in Kishorn, married a daughter of Duncan Mackenzie of Lochcarron, and sister of the Rev. Murdoch Mackenzie of the Free Church, Inverness, with issue :—(1) Duncan, living at Kyleakin; (2) Murdoch, a minister of the Free Church of Scotland. Alexander has also three daughters.

*a*3. Murdoch, living at Strome Ferry, married, without issue.

3. FARQUHAR married Mary Macrae, with issue—

a. Duncan married Christina Mackenzie, and died in 1864, with issue—

*a*1 Alexander, a schoolmaster in Lochcarron, married, first, Mary Mackenzie, without surviving issue. He married, secondly, Catherine, daughter of John Macpherson, and died in 1892. By his second wife he had issue :—(1) John, a doctor, married Sarah Wilson, and died at Gateshead-on-Tyne in 1889, leaving issue—Ethel, Charles; (2) Alexander married Agnes Reid; (3) Farquhar, Lieutenant, Army Ordnance Department, married Martha Bessie Rafuse, with issue—Albert Edward; William Farquhar; Catherine Macpherson; James

Norman ; (4) the Rev. James Duncan, minister of Contin, married Catherine, daughter of Peter Robertson, with issue—Catherine Macpherson ; James Peter Robertson ; (5) Mary Elizabeth married John Macleod, with issue.

*a*2. Farquhar, married Mary Macrae and died in 1894.

*a*3. John was holder of the Macra bursary at the Grammar School, Aberdeen, in 1831, and afterwards entered the shipbuilding business and was drowned at the launching of the Daphne, on the Clyde, on the 3rd July, 1883. He married Margaret Gillies, with issue—(1) Alexander, a joiner in Glasgow, married, with issue ; (2) Mary, married, with issue.

*a*4. Donald, married Margaret Macrae, with issue—Colin , John ; Farquhar.

*a*5. Kenneth, married Flora Macmillan, with issue—Donald; John; Helen; Jane; Christina Anne.

*a*6. Margaret, married Lachlan Matheson, with issue.

*a*7. Helen, married Christopher Macrae, with issue.

*a*8. Christina, married John Macrae, with issue.

b. John, married, first, a Macdonald, with issue —(*b*1) Kenneth, who went to Australia ; (*b*2) Mary, (*b*3) Jane ; (*b*4) Anne, married John Galt, Elgin.

John married, secondly, Catherine Mackenzie and died in 1867. By his second marriage he had a son.

*b*5. The Rev Farquhar Macrae, who is now a Presbyterian minister in Manitoba, and is married, with issue—

I

c. Christopher married in 1839, Mary Finlayson, who died on the 17th August, 1897, aged ninety-two. He died in 1872, aged eighty-one years, leaving issue—

*c*1. Alexander, born 15th October, 1843. He married, in 1872, Catherine Maclean, and is now living in New Zealand, with issue—John; Catherine; Mary; Alexandrina; Margaret.

*c*2. Farquhar, born 12th November, 1845, and is now living at Dornie. He is a good genealogist, and is well versed in the legends and traditions of the Macrae country. He married, first, Mary Maclennan, and secondly Margaret, daughter of Duncan Matheson, Dornie.

*c*3. John, born on the 27th June, 1848, married 18th May, 1877, Williamina Macdonald, with issue —Farquhar; Mary Finlayson; Catherine Finlayson, died in infancy; Christopher; Ninian Finlayson; Alexander; Catherine Finlayson; Jessie Isabella Anne Finlayson; Malcolm John Duncan Finlayson.

*c*4. Duncan, born 18th January, 1851, married, in 1883, Catherine Finlayson, with issue — Farquhar; Alexander; Mary; Christopher, Catherine, Donald Roderick; Anne.

d. The Rev. Farquhar Macrae, born at Camuslunie on the 25th November, 1805. He received his early education from a well-known Kintail schoolmaster, Finlay Macrae, commonly called Finlay Fadoch. In 1816 he was admitted to a Macra bursary at Aberdeen Grammar School, where he had for his teacher the celebrated classical

scholar and Gaelic poet, Ewen Maclauchlan. He
entered the University in 1819, and after a distinguished career, graduated M.A. in 1823. He studied
Divinity from 1823 to 1827. From 1825 to 1833
he was schoolmaster of Lochcarron, and was licensed
by the Presbytery of Lochcarron in 1829. In 1833
he was ordained to the charge of South Uist, where
he remained for eight years, and in 1841 became
minister of Braemar. At the Disruption of the
Church of Scotland in 1843 he cast in his lot with
the Free Church, and in 1849 became minister of
the Free Church in Knockbain, in succession to his
well-known fellow-clansman, the Rev. John Macrae.
Here he lived and laboured, trusted and respected
by his people until his death, which occurred at
Nairn on the 20th December, 1882. He was a man
of much culture and sound scholarship, and an able
and eloquent preacher, equally good both in Gaelic
and in English. The Rev. Farquhar married Anne
Murray and had issue, one surviving son—Francis
Farquhar.

e. Christina married Roderick Mackenzie at
Camusluinie, with issue.

f. Isabel married Thomas Macrae at Camusluinie,
with issue.

CHAPTER IX.

IX Hugh, son of Alexander of Inverinate —X Alexander of
Ardintoul —Was at the Battles of Sheriffmuir and Glensheil
Traditions about Him —IX Archibald of Ardintoul.—His
Marriage and Descendants —Colonel Sir John Macra.—Alex-
ander of Hushinish — His Marriage and Family.

IX HUGH, the youngest son of Alexander of
Inverinate by his second wife, Mary Mackenzie
of Dochmaloaig. He is mentioned as one of the
leaders of the disturbance in connection with the
vacancy at Dingwall church in 1704,[1] and took part
in the Jacobite rising of 1715. He was wounded
in the battle of Sheriffmuir, and his name appears on
a list of "Gentlemen Prisoners" taken to Stirling
on the following day. It is said that he was
removed from Stirling to Perth, where he remained
in hospital until he was sufficiently recovered from
his wound to be able to accomplish the homeward
journey. Hugh was living at Sallachy in 1721.
He married Margaret Macleod of Swordlan, in
Glenelg, and by her had issue—

1. ALEXANDER.
2. JOHN, went to America 1774.
3. RODERICK, went to America 1774.
4. DUNCAN

[1] See note page 71.

5. BARBARA, married Farquhar, son of Alexander, with issue.

6. MARY, married G. Macculloch.

X. ALEXANDER, eldest son of Hugh, was appointed local factor of Kintail, and lived at Aryugan or Ardintoul. He was one of the first to join the Roman Catholic Mission, which has already been referred to. As a young man he fought on the Jacobite side, both at Sheriffmuir and at Glensheil, and is mentioned as taking part in the affair of Ath nam Muileach in 1721. After the battle of Glensheil, he was for three days among the hills without any food except one drink of milk. It is said that on one occasion when "Colonel Alexander Mackenzie, the next Protestant heir to the Seaforth estates, had come to the country with a view to take up the rents, but finding that the people would not come into his views nor pay him the rents they judged belonged to Lord Seaforth, he went up from Ardelve to Kintail with a large boat well manned, that he might arrest some of the people and send them to Fort-William. Alexander was up in Kintail at the time, and observing a fellow carrying his own father on his back to put him into the boat, his indignation was roused. 'You silly, dastardly rascal,' said Alexander, 'is it putting your own father in you are,' and he set the old man at liberty The Colonel was in the stern of the boat and came up to him. They grappled, and Alexander getting hold of his thumbs, held him there until he yielded,"[1] and

[1] Old letter from Kintail.

left the people alone. Alexander married, first, a daughter of Fraser of Guisachan (or Culbokie), and by her had a daughter, who married John Macrae, Strathglass. On one occasion Alexander sustained such heavy losses through a severe winter that he became somewhat straitened in his circumstances, and it is said that his wife, who was unwilling to share the lot of a poor man, took advantage of a temporary absence of her husband from home, to pack up her effects and leave him. Circumstances, however, turned out more favourable for Alexander than his wife anticipated, and the tide of his prosperity soon turned. His wife hearing of this, decided to join him once more, and returned to his sheiling at Glasletter, but he refused to receive her On her death, which occurred shortly afterwards, he married, as his second wife, Isabel, daughter of Alexander Macgilchrist (Macrae) of Strathglass, by his wife, Anne, daughter of Farquhar Macrae of Morvich, and by her had issue—

1. ARCHIBALD.

2. ALEXANDER.

3. FARQUHAR, who went to America.

4 JOHN, a doctor. He went as surgeon of an emigrant ship to America about 1817. The vessel was wrecked on the return voyage off Prince Edward Island, but no lives were lost. In 1821 Dr John himself left for Canada, along with "Alexander, a brother of Mr Macrae, Dornie," and several others from Lochalsh and Kintail, and he is mentioned as being at Glengarry in Canada in 1826.

5. ANNE married John Macrae of Conchra.

6. MARGARET married Donald Macrae, Torly-sich.

7. MARY married Farquhar Macrae, Fadoch. She died in 1823, leaving issue.

XI. ARCHIBALD, eldest son of Alexander by his second wife, Isabel Macrae, was born in 1744. He was educated in the house of Archibald Chisholm of Fasnakyle, probably by a priest, to whose instructions he did no small credit. He was a devout Catholic, a man of sound judgment and high character, " a courtly old gentleman, shrewd. practical, but warm-hearted and unobtrusively religious ; able, too, to face difficulties, the common lot of all mortals, with the clear conscience and stout heart of a strong and upright man." For fully half-a-century he occupied a foremost place in the affairs of the Seaforth estates, of which he was for many years chamberlain. He was created a free Burgess and Guild Brother of the Burgh of Dingwall on the 16th October. 1789. Archibald married on the 9th September, 1783, Janet, daughter of John Macleod, the tenth chief of Raasay. John Macleod was one of the Highland chiefs who entertained Dr Samuel Johnson in the course of his celebrated tour in the Hebrides in 1773. Writing of his host on that occasion, Dr Johnson says :—" The family of Raasay consists of the laird, the lady, three sons, and ten daughters. For the sons there is a tutor in the house, and the lady is said to be very skilful and diligent in the education of her girls. More gentleness of manners, or a more pleasing appearance of domestic society is not found in the most polished countries."[1] Archibald died about 1830, leaving issue—

1. FLORA, born 9th September, 1783, died unmarried in 1852.

2. Colonel Sir JOHN MACRA, K.C.H., who was born on the 14th February, 1786. He obtained an Ensign's commission in the 79th Highlanders in 1805, and was promoted to the rank of Lieutenant in the same year. His subsequent promotions were as follows :—Captain, 1812 ; Major, 1818 ; Lieutenant - Colonel, 1821 ; Colonel, 1837. He was created a Knight of the Order of Hanover (K.C.H.) in 1827. His military career was both distinguished and eventful. He was present at the siege and surrender of Copenhagen in 1807, and went to Sweden with the army under Sir John Moore in 1808. Later on in the same year he accompanied the British force which was sent to Portugal, and was present in all the operations of that campaign, including the retreat of Sir John Moore and the battle of Corunna, on the 16th January, 1809. From Spain he accompanied his regiment in the Walcheren expedition, and was present at the siege and capture of Flushing in August the same year. At Walcheren he suffered from the fever which caused so much havoc among the British troops, and from the effects of which he never completely recovered. The following year, however, he was in

---

[1] The China tea service used by the Raasay family at the time of Dr Johnson's visit is now in the possession of Captain John MacRae-Gilstrap of Balhmore, Tigh-na-bruaich, Argyllshire, great grandson of the above-mentioned Janet Macleod.

the Peninsula, and served with his regiment throughout the campaigns of 1811 and 1812, being present at all the operations in which his regiment took part, including the battles of Fuentes D'Onoro, on the 5th May, 1811, and Salamanca, on the 22nd July, 1812, the siege of Burgos in September and October, 1812, and many smaller engagements. In 1813 he joined the staff of the Marquis of Hastings, then Lord Moira, who in that year was appointed Governor-General of India, and who was married to Sir John's cousin, Flora Campbell, daughter of the fifth Earl of Loudon, by his wife Flora, daughter of John Macleod, tenth chief of Raasay. The Marquis of Hastings was one of the ablest and most successful of our Indian statesmen, and his rule, which extended from 1813 to 1823, was a period of great importance in the history of that country. In 1814 and 1815, after some severe fighting, he succeeded in subduing the Goorkhas, who had established a power of considerable strength in Nepaul. But the circumstances and events to which Lord Hastings owes his great celebrity as an Indian ruler and statesman arose in another quarter. The centre of India was at this time occupied by the great Princes of the Mahratta nation, who, although partly subdued, were still powerful, and evidently preparing to make an effort to recover their former greatness. Besides these restless and active enemies there existed also a formidable body of freebooters called the Pindarees, who had established themselves along the south of the Vindhya Mountains. During the Goorkha War the Pindarees, secretly supported by the Mahrattas, crossed the British frontiers and plundered and destroyed more than three hundred villages. Lord Hastings resolved to put an end to these robbers, and having obtained permission to proceed against them on a great scale, he collected forces from all parts of India, and brought into the field the "grand army," with which, after a war of two years' duration—1817-18—the Pindarees and the Mahrattas were completely conquered. Other native powers were subdued at the same time, and Lord Hastings had thus the honour of being the first to render British authority absolutely supreme in India. In all these operations Sir John Macra, who held the post of Military Secretary to the Governor-General, took an important part. He was in the field throughout the war against the Goorkhas in 1814 and 1815, and was with the grand army in 1817 and 1818. At the end of 1818 he was sent home with despatches announcing the successful termination of the war, and returning immediately to India, he continued to serve under the Marquis of Hastings, who was now in a position to rule in peace and to effect wise and useful changes for the good of the people of India. The importance of Lord Hastings' measures, which have been fully justified by time, was not then appreciated by the Directors of the East India Company, and this, together with failing health, for he was now an old man, induced him to leave India in 1823. In the following year he was appointed Governor of Malta, where Sir John, after a short visit home, joined him once more in the capacity of Military Secretary, until the death of the Marquis, which took place in 1825. Sir John retired in May, 1826, after a most distinguished career of more than twenty years, which were nearly all passed in active service. After his retirement he lived chiefly at Ardintoul and Raasay, where he is still remembered by old people as a man of frank and generous disposition and a genuine Highlander. He was an excellent performer on the bagpipes. He was also an amateur maker of bagpipes, and it is said that some of those which he made are still to be found in the West Highlands. He died on the 9th August, 1847, and was buried in Kintail. A plain iron cross, which has been placed by his nephew, Captain A M. Chisholm, on the wall of the old ruined church of Kilduich, marks the place of his last rest.

3. ALEXANDER was born on the 3rd of May, 1787. He obtained an Ensign's commission in the 75th Highlanders in 1806. He joined that regiment the following year and served with it for some time. He was for many years tacksman of Hushinish in Harris, and was a Justice of the Peace and a Deputy-Lieutenant of the county of Inverness. He was a good Catholic, and was well known in the West Highlands as a liberal and large-hearted man. He was " pre-eminently a man without guile," and it was said of him at the time of his death, that the poor on the West Coast lost in him "a friend who always kept his heart open to their wants, and assisted them without ostentation." As an amateur musician he possessed

unusual taste and cultivation, and was an excellent violinist. He had also a keen appreciation of the national music and poetry of the Highlands, and was himself an excellent type of the old Highland gentleman, dignified, cultured, generous almost to a fault, and in full and kindly sympathy with all that was best and noblest in the character and traditions of his countrymen. He died on the 25th January, 1874, and was buried at Kilduich. He married Margaret, daughter of Farquhar Macrae, and by her, who died at Strathpeffer on the 10th July, 1896, and was buried at Kilduich, had issue—

a. Janet Macleod.

b. Isabella Christian married Alister Macdonald Maclellan of Portree, Ceylon.

c. Archibald Alexander.

d. John.

e. Marion Flora.

4. ISABELLA was born on the 6th April, 1789, and married, in 1808, Major Colin Macrae (75th Highlanders), Conchra family, with issue.

5. JANE was born on the 8th April, 1791, and married, at the end of 1816, or beginning of 1817, Donald Macrae of Achtertyre, with issue.

6. CHRISTINA, born 11th January, 1793, died unmarried.

7 MARY, who was born in June, 1794, married in 1821, Dr Stewart Chisholm, of the Royal Artillery, who was at the battle of Waterloo, and attained the rank of Deputy Inspector-General of Army Hospitals He died at Inverness in 1862, leaving issue—

a. Archibald Macra, born 6th July, 1824, late Captain 42nd Royal Highlanders, now of Glassburn. He is a J.P. for the counties of Ross and Inverness. He married, 14th October, 1853, Maria Frances, only daughter of William Dominic Lynch, and granddaughter of the late Lewis Farquharson Innes of Balmoral and Ballogie,[1] without issue.

b. Loudon, who served in the 43rd Regiment H.E.I.C.S., and was killed in the Burmese War in 1853.

c. Mary Stewart, who married Philip Skene, Esquire of Skene, and died at Inverness on the 4th January, 1895, aged 72 years, without issue.

d. Jessie Macleod married Charles O. Rolland of Ste. Marie Monnoir, near Montreal in Canada, with issue.

8. JAMES, born 30th October, 1796, was an Army Surgeon, and died, unmarried, in India, in 1832.

9. ANNE, born 1st October, 1798, married Captain Valentine Chisholm, with issue, John and Jessie.

---

[1] A biographical sketch, with a portrait, of Captain Chisholm, appeared in the *Celtic Monthly* for February, 1893

CHAPTER X.

VIII. JOHN, son of the Rev. Farquhar Macrae of
Kintail, was born at Ardlair on the 13th March,
1614. He received his early education at Fortrose
Grammar School, and thence proceeded to St
Andrews, where he studied under Mr Mungo
Murray, and became one of the most distinguished
students of the University. We read that he had
for his "antagonist" at St Andrews the Duke of
Lauderdale, who afterwards played so prominent a
part in public affairs during the reign of Charles II.
Upon completing his course, and taking the degree
of M.A. at St Andrews, he went to Aberdeen, where
he studied Divinity for three years under Dr Robert
Barrow, and became "a great divine and profound
schoolman." In 1638, when the Presbyterians
gained the ascendancy in the Church of Scotland

and deposed the clergy who would not subscribe the National Covenant,[1] Mr John wished to leave the country, but was prevented by his father, who kept him with himself in Kintail. He had several offers of a living at this time, but refused to accept any because of the necessity of signing the National Covenant, an act which would mean the abjuration of Episcopacy. In 1640 the severity of the Presbyterian measures was somewhat relaxed, and George, Earl of Seaforth, presented Mr John to the living of Dingwall, from which the previous incumbent had been ejected for refusing to acknowledge the Acts of the General Assembly of the Church of Scotland, which met in Glasgow in 1638. Mr John entered into possession of the living of Dingwall without subscribing the Covenant, and continued a staunch Episcopalian until his death. His learning and force of character soon brought him to the front, and he became the leader of his own party in the Presbytery, so that there was frequent and sharp contention between himself and the Presbyterian party. In 1654 the noted Covenanter, Mr Thomas Hogg, became minister of Kiltearn, and three years later his almost equally noted friend, Mr John Mackillican, became minister of Fodderty. To Mr John and his followers these two men and their

---

[1] In 1638 the Presbyterians of Scotland drew up and signed *The National Covenant*, by which they bound themselves to defend their religion and their freedom of conscience with their lives Hence the term *Covenanter*. In 1643 this term received a further meaning in consequence of an alliance entered into by the Covenanters and the English Parliament, called *The Solemn League and Covenant*, by which both parties pledged themselves to mutual defence against the king

views on Church government were specially objectionable, and the strife between the opposing parties soon became very bitter. In 1658 Hogg's party appear to have been in the majority. He himself was Moderator of the Presbytery, while his friend Mackillican was Clerk, and they took their revenge on their opponents by recording against them in the minutes several entries which show much personal animosity and very little of that spirit of Christian charity which is sometimes claimed in Ross-shire for Mr Hogg and his party. In these entries they record Mr John's "needless strife, his great miscarriage deserving censure, his litigiousness, needless contention and intractableness, his stubbornness and wilfulness, his wearying tediousness, his misapplication of scripture, and his pertinacity and loquaciousness."[1] Matters had come to such a pass that some of the brethren were forced to declare that the meetings of Presbytery were "bitterness to them," and to wish the Presbytery to be dissolved and annexed to other Presbyteries It was probably as a result of this quarrel that there was no meeting of the Presbytery from April, 1658, to May, 1663 The restoration of Charles II. led to the establishment of Episcopacy once more. One result of the change was the deposition of Hogg and Mackillican, and when the Presbytery met again in 1663[2] the objectionable

---

[1] Inverness and Dingwall Presbytery Records, edited by William Mackay.

[2] The clergy still continued to meet as a Presbytery after the Restoration of Charles II and the re-establishment of Episcopacy, but it appears that their acts, in order to have any force, had to receive the sanction of the Bishop.

minutes recorded against Mr John were deleted and
marked on their margin as "shameless lying" and
"the spirit of lieing and malice."   Mr John's party
was now in the ascendant, and as far as ecclesiastical matters were concerned the remainder of his
days were passed in peace.   It is said of him that
"he was more fit for the chair" of a Professor "than
for the pulpit," and that " he gave such evidence of
his learning as the place wherein and the society he
was among would allow, and of his piety and vigilance such as they could desire or expect from any,"
while his public life was creditably fiee from that
religious intolerance which formed so marked a
feature of the age in which he lived.   He appears
also to have been a man who prospered in his
worldly affairs.   He held the wadset rights of
Dornie, Aryugan, Inig, and other places in Kintail
for some yeais in succession to his father, and there
is a sasine in his favour, on the 18th April, 1672, of
three Oxgates of the town and lands of Craigskorrie
and several others, including the quarterlands of
Balnain in the parishes of Contin, Fodderty, and
Urray.   Mr John married, first, Agnes, daughter
of Colin Mackenzie, first laird of Kincraig, and,
secondly, Florence Innes,[1] heiress of Balnain.   He
died in 1673, and was buried in Dingwall.   His
tombstone was to be seen in Dingwall Churchyard
until very recently, but a search made in 1897
failed to discover any trace of it.   By his first wife
he had issue—

After the death of Mr John, Florence Innes married, as her second
husband, Colin Mackenzie, uncle of Murdoch Mackenzie of Fairburn.

1. ALEXANDER, mentioned hereafter.

2. DUNCAN, who was some time Bailie of Dingwall. He was attorney for his father in the abovementioned sasine on the 18th April, 1672. He appears to have been the father of Harry Macrae, Bailie of Dingwall, who is mentioned in 1697, and also subsequently, as lawful son of the late Duncan Macrae. Bailie Harry Macrae is frequently mentioned in the Burgh Records of Dingwall. He is said to have left no male issue.

3. CATHERINE married Donald Ross of Knockartie. By the marriage contract, dated 25th March, 1672, " the said Donald Ross disposed to the said Catherine Macrae in liferent the lands of Culrichics, in the parish of Kilmuir and shire of Ross." There is a " renunciation by Catherine Macrae, with consent of Donald Ross, late of Knockartie, and now of Rosskeen, her spouse, in favour of the Laird of Balnagown, of her liferent right by contract of marriage of the lands of Tormore, Gartie, and Knockartie, &c. At Apidale, 26th February, 1699."

4. ISABEL, married Lachlan Mackinnon of Corriechatachan, with issue. There is a tombstone to her memory in the old Church of Kilchrist, in the parish of Strath, Skye, bearing the date 1740.

Mr John is said to have had another daughter by his first wife, who married Mr George Tuach.

By his second wife, Florence Innes, Mr John had issue—

5. JOHN, of whom below.

6. JAMES, who succeeded, in right of his mother, to the estate of Balnain, his elder brother John

being for some reason passed by. There is a sasine on the 11th June, 1673, on disposition by his father, dated at Fortrose, 15th August, 1672, to James and the "heirs male to be gotten of his body, whom failing, to return to any other son to be gotten betwixt the said Mr John Macrae and his said spouse (Florence Innes), and the heirs to be gotten of that child's body; whom failing, to John Macrae, eldest lawful son procreated between the said Mr John Macrae and his said spouse, his heirs male and assignees whomsoever, of the Quarterland of Balnain, in the parish of Urray and shire of Ross." James married Isabel, third daughter of Alexander Mackenzie of Ballone. Contract dated 29th June, 1697. He is mentioned in 1703 as having been invited to the funeral of Hugh Munro of Teaninich, which took place on the 23rd September of that year. He left no issue.

On the death of James, the estate of Balnain passed to a Murdoch Macrae, who, in the manuscript history of the Clan, is said to have been a brother of James. On the other hand, it is stated in the above-mentioned contract of marriage between James and Isabel Mackenzie, dated 29th June, 1697, that James was the "only lawful son now on life pro-created between the late Mr John Macrae, minister of Dingwall, and Florence Innes, his second spouse." Again, in Mr John's disposition of the lands of Balnain, in favour of his son James, dated 15th August, 1672 (that is to say, a few months before Mr John's death), only two sons by Florence Innes are mentioned, viz., John and James, and James at that time was, or very nearly was, of age, as he was infefted in the lands of Balnain the following June, so that in all probability Mr John had only two sons by his second wife, Florence Innes. Taking these documentary evidences into consideration, and comparing them with the traditions of Kintail, which are very clear on this point, the probability is that the Murdoch who is said to have succeeded to Balnain was a son of John, the eldest son of Mr John and Florence Innes.

(x.) MURDOCH, who was probably tenth in descent from Fionnla Dubh Mac Gillechriosd, "finding the lands of Balnain much encumbered, was tampering about the disposal of them to Seaforth when he died." Murdoch is said to have married Mary, daughter of Donald Mac Fhionnla Mhic Gillechriosd, by whom he had issue—

(1). DUNCAN, who disposed of the estate of Balnain to Seaforth "for a verbal promise of a free liferent tack of Fadoch, in Kintail, which he held rent free only for five years, though he lived about forty years thereafter. Thus the estate of Balnain fell into the family of Seaforth for little money." He appears to be the Duncan Macrae of Fadoch who is mentioned in the Valuation Roll of the Seaforth estates in 1756. Duncan married and left a large family—

(a). John.

(b). Donald, who had sons :— (b1) Donald, whose descendants are still living in Kintail; (b2) Farquhar, who is mentioned in a genealogical tree of about 1820 as " Dr Downie's herd."

(c). Farquhar.

(d). Mary or Margaret, who married Farquhar, son of Alexander, son of the Rev. Donald Macrae.

(e). Isabel, who married Alexander Macrae, called Alister Buidh, in Fadoch, a descendant of Miles, son of the Rev. Farquhar Macrae, of whom hereafter.

(2). FARQUHAR.

(3). DONALD, of whom next.

(4). CHRISTOPHER. ✓

(XI.) DONALD, son of Murdoch of Balnain, was called Donald Ban. He is said to have married Mary, daughter of Alexander Macrae, with issue—

(1). JOHN married, with issue.

(2). CHRISTOPHER married, with issue.

(3). FINLAY, of whom next.

(XII.) FINLAY, who was called Fionnla Buidh (yellow-haired Finlay), was a farmer at Coilrie about 1760, and was married, with issue—

(1). DONALD, of whom below.

(2). CHRISTOPHER.

(3). ALEXANDER, who married and left issue—

(a). Donald, who lived at Bundalloch, married and left issue, at least one son—Donald, also at Bundalloch, who married Christina, daughter of Duncan Macrae, Camusluinie, with issue.

(b). Finlay, went to America.

(c). Duncan, who lived at Carndu, near Dornie, and married Christina, daughter of Murdoch Macrae.

4. MALCOLM, who left issue—

(a) Donald, who had (a1) Kenneth, who lived at Sallachy; (a2) John, who went to America.

(*b*). John died unmarried.

(XIII.) DONALD, son of Finlay, was called Donald Ban. He married Christina, daughter of Angus Macmillan, at Killelan, and by her, who died in 1836, had issue as below. Donald died at Sallachy in 1840, and was buried at Killelan.

(1). DONALD, called Domhnull Ruadh (Red-haired Donald), married, with issue, and went to Canada

(2). DUNCAN, a farmer at Sallachy. He gave evidence before Lord Napier's Crofter Commission at Balmacara in 1883, and died at the advanced age of ninety-four in 1890. He married Margaret Macrae, with issue—(*b*1) Alexander; (*b*2) Donald; (*b*3) John; (*b*4) Christina; (*b*5) Anne; (*b*6) Margaret.

(3). FINLAY

(4). ANGUS, born at Coilrie. He was for many years tacksman of Achnault, and subsequently leased the farms of Newhall Mains and Kinbeachie, in the Black Isle. He married Isabel, daughter of Donald Mackenzie, Lochcarron, who died at Kinbeachie on the 17th April, 1892, aged seventy-five years, and was buried at Cullicudden, by whom he had issue as below. Angus died at Kinbeachie on the 8th August, 1877, aged seventy-two years, and was buried at Cullicudden.

(*a*). Murdoch, who by purchase acquired the estate of Kinbeachie in 1897.

(*b*). Christina, married John Macniell, and died in Australia in 1891, without issue.

(*c*). Helen, married Roderick Tolmie, and died in Queensland in 1890, with issue—(*c*1) Isabella;

(c2) James ; (c3) Christina ; (c4) Mary ; (c5) Ella ; (c6) Sarah ; (c7) Agnes ; (c8) Maggie ; (c9) Roderick.

(d). Margaret, married on the 7th February, 1868, John Macdonald, Invergordon, with issue— (d1) Donald Alexander ; (d2) Isabella Christina Mackenzie Macrae ; (d3) Margaret Jane, married a Mr Graham, and died at Belize, British Honduras, 27th February, 1895, aged twenty-three years ; (d4) Angus, died young ; (d5) Hannah ; (d6) John Evan ; (d7) Duncan Donald ; (d8) Grace Maclennan, died in infancy ; (d9) Joseph ; (d10) Helen, died in infancy ; (d11) Murdoch Evan Macrae.

(e). Donald, married Jeannie Hooper without issue, and died in New Zealand.

(f). The Rev. Duncan Mackenzie, M.A., minister of the Free Church, Lochearnhead, married, 27th August, 1890, Jeanie Cooper, only daughter of Andrew Watters, Esq. of Inchterf, Glenample, Perthshire, with issue—(f1) Jean Cooper McWhannell ; (f2) Angus ; (f3) Andrew Thomas Watters ; (f4) Duncan Mackenzie.

(g). Sarah.

(h). Evan Mackenzie, now of Brahan Mains.

(i). Jane, married, first, John Macdonald, of Achnacloich, Nairnshire, without issue. She married, secondly, the Rev. Duncan Finlayson, Free Church, Kinlochbervie, Sutherlandshire, with issue—Isabel Mary.

(5). CHRISTINA married Donald Macrae, and went to Canada about 1849.

(6.) MARY married Ewen Maclennan, and went to Australia.

IX. ALEXANDER, eldest son of the Rev. John of Dingwall and his first wife, Agnes Mackenzie of Kincraig, received a wadset, dated 13th and 24th January and 26th February, 1677, of the lands of Conchra and Ardachy, in the parish of Lochalsh, which was held by his family for some generations There is a sasine on the 6th March, 1683, in favour of Alexander, eldest son and heir, "served and retoured" to the late Mr John Macrae, minister of Dingwall, of a portion of the lands of Easter Rarichies, in the parish of Nigg.   There is also a sasine by Alexander, on the 14th April, 1699, in favour of Hugh Baillie, writer in Fortrose, and John Tuach, writer in Dingwall, of the towns and lands of Little Kindease, in the parish of Nigg.   He appears to have been a man of considerable means, and is said to have been "a sensible, good countryman," and to have lived to an advanced age.   He married Florence Mackinnon of Corrichatachan, by whom he had at least two sons—

1. JOHN, who succeeded him.

2. DUNCAN, commonly called the "Tutor of Conchra," because he acted as guardian to the children of his brother John, who was killed at Sheriffmuir.   In this capacity his name appears frequently in connection with the proceedings of the Forfeited Estates Commissioners in Lochalsh and Kintail, after the Rebellion of 1715.   Duncan married Isabel, daughter of the Rev. Finlay Macrae of Lochalsh, with issue—

a. Farquhar.

b. Alexander.

c. Isabel, said to have married Duncan, son of the Rev. Donald Macrae of Kintail.

d. Annabel.   *e.* Mary.

f. Janet, who married Alexander Matheson, at Sallachy, where he died in 1793, leaving a son, Roderick, who was farmer of Immer, in Lochcarron, and wrote a manuscript history of the Mathesons. He married and left issue.

X. JOHN, eldest son of Alexander, succeeded to the wadset rights of Conchra, and is commonly known as "John of Conchra." He took a prominent part in the Jacobite rising of 1715, and was Captain in one of Seaforth's regiments on that occasion. He was one of the famous "Four Johns of Scotland"[1] who so greatly distinguished themselves at the battle of Sheriffmuir, where he fell along with many of his clansmen. The memory of John of Conchra still enters largely into the traditions of Lochalsh and Kintail, and many anecdotes about his strength and prowess are preserved in that country. It is said that on the march to Perth, where the Highlanders assembled in 1715, a horse carrying provisions fell into a hole. The men who were near at the time endeavoured to lift it out, but all their efforts were in vain until the arrival of John of Conchra, who succeeded in pulling the horse out by himself. This incident made him known at once to the Highlanders as one of the strongest men

[1] The "Four Johns of Scotland," *Ceither Ianan na h' Alba*, were so called by Highlanders from their valour at the battle of Sheriffmuir. They were John Macrae of Conchra, John Murchison of Auchtertyre, John Mackenzie of Applecross, and John Mackenzie of Hilton. All of them were officers in Seaforth's regiments, and fell in the battle.

among them, and a man of whom great deeds would be expected in the day of battle. The Highlanders, however, were but poorly supplied with firearms, and while discussing the expectations formed about him, with Alexander of Ardintoul, John of Conchra remarked—" If it was to measure manly strength of arm that we were going to meet the Whig rabble I should meet them with good courage, but I fear the little bullets." [1] It is said that on the day of the battle the herdsmen of Conchra saw an apparition of their master walking about among the cattle, and that when they went home and told his wife about it, she at once concluded that he was slain. The fate of the " Four Johns of Scotland " is lamented in a Gaelic elegy by Kenneth Macrae of Ardelve, who was an old man when the battle of Sheriffmuir was fought, and who makes the following reference to John of Conchra .—

G'un thuit an t' oganach anns an t' sreup,
An t' Ian o Chonchra 's bu mhòr am beud,
An curaidh laidir le neart a ghairdean,
A cur nan àghannan diubh gu feur.
Be sud Ian Chonchra a bha gun sgàth,
Bé 'n duine marbhteach e anns a' bhlar,
Ri sgoltadh cheann fhad's a mhair a lann da
'S bha fir gun chaint ann as deigh a laimh [2]

[1] Old letter from Kintail.

[2] And there fell in the combat the young hero, John of Conchra, and great was that loss , the strong warrior who by the strength of his arm laid heaps of them down on the grass Such was John of Conchra, the dauntless, a deadly man was he in the fight, cleaving skulls as long as his blade lasted, and behind him lay men made speechless by the work of his hand.

See also Appendix J.

The dirk worn by John of Conchra at Sheriff-muir has been preserved by his descendants. It was taken to America about 1770 by one of his grandsons, in whose family it remained until 1894, when it came into the possession of Duncan Macrae. Esq. of Kames Castle   John of Conchra married, as her first husband, Isabel, daughter of the Rev. Donald Macrae of Kintail, by his wife Catherine Grant of Glenmoriston, with issue.

1. ALEXANDER, who died young and unmarried. His name is frequently mentioned in connection with the proceedings of the Forfeited Estates Commissioners on the Seaforth estates, after the Rebellion of 1715.   He is mentioned as a minor under the guardianship of his uncle, Duncan, Tutor of Conchra, on the 29th July, 1728, and probably lived for some years after.

2. JOHN, of whom next.

XI. JOHN is said to have been an active, industrious man who prospered in his affairs. There is, under date 12th April, 1754, a renunciation by him in favour of Kenneth, Lord Fortrose, of the town and lands of Conchra, Croyard, &c., in which he is described as John Macrae of Conchra, eldest son and heir of the late John Macrae of Conchra, and grandson and heir of the late Alexander Macrae of Conchra, eldest lawful son of the late Mr John Macrae, Minister at Dingwall. He married[1]

[1] There is some confusion in the Mackenzie Genealogies with regard to this marriage, and also with regard to the marriage of James Macrae of Balnain with another Isabel Mackenzie of Ballone (page 147). See Sir J D Mackenzies' Genealogical Tables, sheet 10, and Mackenzie's History of the Mackenzies, pages 575-6

Isabel, daughter of Alexander Mackenzie, third of Ballone, and died in 1761, with issue :—

1. JOHN, described in an old "Tree" as last of Conchra, a Captain in the 80th Regiment, was killed on the 8th February, 1804, on board the Admiral Applin, in the Bay of Bengal, by the French, while returning as a passenger to India to join his regiment. His son, James, who was with him at the time, was taken prisoner to Mauritius, along with the ship. Captain John married Anne, sister of Archibald Macra of Ardintoul, who, on the death of her husband, received two pensions, one from the Government and another from the East India Company. By her Captain John left issue :—

a. James, Captain in the 11th Devon Regiment, was drowned off the Lizard on the 21st February, 1811, while on his way to the Peninsular War.

b. Florence, married Captain James Grant, with issue :—*b*1. Patrick James, Major 7th Fusiliers, married Sarah Graham ; *b*2. Anne, married Allan Ord, with issue :—Thomas, Captain 2nd Dragoon Guards, died 1870 ; Jane , Patrick ; Catherine.

2. DUNCAN, born at Conchra, 26th April, 1754, and died 27th November, 1824. He married, first, in 1785, Sarah Powell, with issue :—

a. Flora, born 1786.

b. Powell, born 1788.

He married, secondly, in 1789, Mary Chesnut, with issue :—*a.* Isabella Scota, who married John Macrae of Conchra ; *b.* Margaret ; *c.* Harriet ; *d.* Flora ; *e.* Duncan ; *f.* Sarah ; *g.* Mary ; *h.* Sarah ; *i.* John.

3. COLIN, of whom below.

4. FLORENCE, married Murdoch Matheson, with issue :—

a. Alexander, who settled in Charleston, U.S.A., about 1830, and married a daughter of Captain Bate, with issue :—Murdoch ; Alexander ; John ; Flora.

XII. COLIN, son of John of Conchra and Isabella Mackenzie of Ballone, was Major in the 75th (Abercromby's) Highlanders. He served in India, and came home in command of the regiment in 1806. He married, in 1808, Isabella (who died in 1827), daughter of Archibald Macra of Ardintoul, by his wife Janet, daughter of John Macleod, tenth Baron of Raasay, with issue as below. Major Colin died at Banff on the 10th March, 1821, and by his own dying request was buried with his forefathers in Kintail. His father-in-law, Archibald Macra of Ardintoul, and his brother-in-law, Donald Macrae of Auchtertyre, went to Banff to arrange the funeral. The men of Lochalsh and Kintail went as far as Cluanie to meet the hearse, and bore the coffin for the rest of the way on their shoulders.[1]

1. JOHN went to South Carolina about 1828. He married his cousin, Isabella Scota, daughter of Duncan Macrae and his wife, Mary Chesnut, and died without issue.

2. ARCHIBALD lived at Bruiach, in Inverness-shire, married Fanny Taylor of Alding Grange, Durham, and died at Kemerton Priory, in Gloucester-shire, with issue, Mary and Flora, both of whom died young.

[1] Letter from Kintail, 1821.

3. James died young at Banff, and was buried there.

4. COLIN went to South Carolina about 1850, and lived with his brother John until the death of the latter, when he succeeded as lineal representative of the Conchra family, and thirteenth in descent from Fionnla Dubh MacGillechriosd, the founder of the Clan Macrae of Kintail. He lives at Camden, in South Carolina, and is unmarried.

5. DUNCAN, born 8th October, 1816. He served in the H.E.I.C.S., and married, November, 1852, Grace, daughter of Donald Stewart, representative of the Stewarts of Overblairich (cadet of the Stewarts of Garth), with issue as below. Mr Macrae resides at Kames Castle, Rothesay, and is a J.P. and D.L. for the County of Bute.

a. Stewart, married December, 1891, Ethel Evelyn, eldest daughter of Martin Ridley Smith, of Hayes Common, Kent, and his wife, Emily, daughter of Henry Stuart of Montford, Bute, with issue :—*a*1. Kenneth Stewart; *a*2. John Nigel; *a*3. Grace Emily.

b. Sophia Fredrica Christina Hastings, married 13th November, 1879, R. P. Henry-Batten-Pooll, of Road Manor, Somersetshire, and Timsbury, Wiltshire, with issue :—*b*1. Robert Duncan, died 12th August, 1894; *b*2. Walter Stewart; *b*3. Mary Margaret; *b*4. John Alexander; *b*5. Arthur Hugh.

c. John MacRae-Gilstrap, of Ballimore, Argyleshire, Captain Forty-Second Royal Highlanders, The Black Watch, served in 1884 and 1885 in Egypt, the Soudan, and the Nile Expedition, was

Major JOHN MacRAE-GILSTRAP, of Ballimore,
(Conchra)

present at all the engagements in which his regiment took part, and was mentioned in dispatches. Captain MacRae-Gilstrap[1] married on the 4th March, 1889, Isabella Mary, daughter of the late George Gilstrap of Newark-on-Trent, and niece of the late Sir William Gilstrap, Bart. of Fornham Park, Suffolk, under whose will he assumed, 9th January, 1897, by Royal Licence, the additional surname and arms of Gilstrap, and has issue.— c1. Margaret Helen; c2. Janet Isabel; c3. Ella Mary; c4. Elizabeth Barbara Katherine; c5. Flora Sybil; c6. John Duncan George.

d. Anna Helena.

e. Isabella.

f. Colin William, Lieutenant in the Forty-Second Highlanders, The Black Watch. Lieutenant Colin, who is an accomplished performer on the bagpipes, is possessor of the "fedan dubh" or Black Chanter of Kintail.[2] This chanter, which was one of the heirlooms of the "High Chiefs" of Kintail, was given by the last Earl of Seaforth to the late Colonel Sir John Macra of Ardintoul. By him it was given to his nephew, Captain Archibald Macra Chisholm of Glassburn, late of the Forty-Second Royal Highlanders, The Black Watch, who, in 1895, gave it to Lieutenant Colin.

6. FRANCIS died young.

7. JESSIE died young at Banff, and was buried there.

---

[1] A portrait and biographical sketch of Captain MacRae-Gilstrap, and also a portrait of Mrs MacRae-Gilstrap, appeared in the *Celtic Monthly* for July, 1896,

[2] Appendix I,

CHAPTER XI.

VIII The Rev. Donald Macrae, son of the Rev. Farquhar.—Vicar
of Urray.—Chaplain to Seaforth's Regiment —Commissioner to
the General Assembly.—Vicar of Kintail.—His Marriage and
Descendants —The Drudaig Family.

VIII. REV. DONALD, son of the Rev. Farquhar
Macrae of Kintail, became Vicar of Urray in 1649.
He was chaplain to the regiment contributed by
Seaforth to the expedition which ended in the
defeat of the Royalist troops at Worcester on the
3rd September, 1651, but does not appear to have
accompanied it to England, as he was chosen
Commissioner to the General Assembly of the
Church of Scotland in that year, and was present,
after his return from the Assembly, at a meeting of
the Dingwall Presbytery at Contin on the 19th
August in that year, when the brethren expressed
their satisfaction with the manner in which he had
performed his duties as their Commissioner. In
1656 he was translated to Kintail as fellow labourer
and "conjunct" minister with his father, under
circumstances which have already been referred to
in some detail.[1] On the death of his father in 1662
Mr Donald became sole Vicar of Kintail until his
own death, which occurred about 1681. Mr Donald

1 See page 64,

married Isabel, daughter of Murdoch Mackenzie, fifth of Hilton, and by her had issue—

1. ALEXANDER, of whom below.

2. JOHN, who left one son, Kenneth, who married and had two sons. After the death of their father these two sons went to North Carolina in 1774 with their mother, who had married a second husband.

3. COLIN married and left, together with daughters—

a. Kenneth.

b. Alexander was tacksman of Achantighard, where his widow was living in 1756. He married Janet, daughter of Donald Macrae, and had issue—

*b*1. Christopher, who was for some time tacksman of Leachachan. He afterwards lived at Kyle-akin. He married Janet, daughter of Donald Macrae, Dornie, with issue :—(1) Christopher; (2) Alexander, died in Demerara, leaving issue; (3) Colin, died in Demerara; (4) Donald; (5) James; (6) Christina, who married Christopher Macrae, Kyleakin; (7) Janet,[1] who, on the 13th March, 1838, married Malcolm Macrae, Dornie, and died on the 25th October, 1893, leaving issue—Jean, died young, Jessie; Barbara, married Thomas Paton, Glasgow; Christopher, died in America; Jane; Murdoch, died young; Christina; Isabella, married Roderick Matheson, Totaig; John, now living at Dornie; Christina; Mary Anne.

*b*2. Mary, married Murdoch Macrae.

*b*3. Christina, married Fionnla Og Mor of Corrie-dhomhain.

---

[1] Mentioned also on page 18.

L

*b*4. Anne, married Duncan Macrae.

4. MARY, married John Matheson of Bennets-field, with issue.

IX. ALEXANDER, son of the Rev. Donald, was settled by his father in the lands of Drudaig, where his descendants lived for some generations. He is said to have married a daughter of Fraser of Belladrum, and had issue—

1. CHRISTOPHER, of whom below.

2. DONALD, who married Anne Matheson of Fernaig, with issue—

a. Donald, who had at least four sons—Alexander; Donald; Christopher; Duncan.

b. Duncan, who was living at Achantighard in 1756. He married Isabel, daughter of Maurice Macrae, with issue—

*b*1. Donald, who had at least four sons—Christopher; Duncan; Allan; John.

*b*2. Farquhar.

*b*3. Alexander, who was in the Seventy-Eighth Highlanders.

*b*4. Christopher, also in the Seventy-Eighth Highlanders, was killed in India on the 29th November, 1803.[1]

X. CHRISTOPHER, son of Alexander, is mentioned in an old letter, as having been at the Battle

---

[1] The following extract is from a letter written by a cousin of Christopher at Bombay, and refers to his death —"You will no doubt be sorry for poor Christopher's fate, who was killed in battle on the 29th November, 1803 You heard, I daresay, of his marriage. He left a promising young daughter, with a pretty good fortune of £600 sterling His fate was unexpected, so that he left his affairs unsettled. His wife is now married to another man in the military service, and has the guardianship of the child."

of Sheriffmuir. He is described as "a tall, slender man, but very spirited." He was one of the first adherents of Presbyterianism in Kintail, and was one of the first and firmest supporters of the Rev. John Bethune, who was appointed first Presbyterian minister of the newly-formed parish of Glenshiel in 1727. Christopher married Janet, daughter of Farquhar Macrae of Inverinate, and died in 1765, leaving issue—

1 CHRISTOPHER, of whom below.

2. MARGARET married Farquhar Macrae.

3. FLORENCE married Christopher Macrae at Dall, son of Finlay, son of John Breac, with issue.

4. ANNE married Duncan, son of Maurice Macrae of Achyuran, with issue.

XI. CHRISTOPHER, son of Christopher, was tacksman of Drudaig and Glenundalan.[1] He married Anne, daughter of John Macrae, son of Duncan, and died young, leaving issue—

1. DONALD, who lived at Drudaig, and afterwards went to America. He married Margaret, daughter of Farquhar Macrae, Fadoch.

2. DUNCAN married Christina Macrae, with issue at least three sons—John; Christopher; Alexander.

3. CHRISTOPHER married Margaret, daughter of Alexander Macrae of Auchtertyre, and went to Canada about 1816, where he died, leaving issue—

a. Donald, married Mary Macgregor about 1841, and died at Woodside, Manitoba, on the 18th July, 1886, leaving a large family, one of whom is called Duncan, by whom the information here given about

---

[1] Glenundalan is in Glenshiel, above Sheil House,

the family of Christopher and Margaret Macrae was communicated to the author in 1896.

b. Alexander, who went to France as a young man and was never again heard of.

c. Margaret, married Kenneth Macgregor, and died at Ashfield, Ontario, leaving issue—two sons and two daughters.

d. Isabella, married Donald Macgregor, and died also at Ashfield, Ontario, leaving a large family.

e. Duncan, married and had a large family. He died about 1891, and was the last survivor of the family.

f. Annie, married John Macrae, with issue.

g. John, died in Indiana about 1866, leaving a large family.

4. ALEXANDER, married Flora Macrae, with issue—

a. Duncan. *b.* Donald.

c. Alexander, who was living in 1887 with his son, a chemist in Edinburgh.

5. ANNE, married Donald Macrae at Achnagart, and had, with other issue, the Rev. John Macrae of Knockbain, of whom hereafter.

6 MARGARET

7. MARY.

8. JANET.

9. ISABEL.

CHAPTER XII.

VIII. Miles, son of the Rev Farquhar Macrae.—Receives a joint
wadset of Camusluinie — His Marriage and Descendants —The
Camusluinie Family.—VIII. Murdoch, son of the Rev. Farquhar
Macrae —His Descendants

VIII. MILES or MAOLMOIRE, son of the Rev.
Farquhar Macrae of Kintail, received, about 1646, a
joint wadset with his brothers Murdoch and John
Breac, of Camusluinie, which the family held until
1751, when the wadset was redeemed.   He married,
it is said, a Murchison, and left issue, at least one
son.

IX. DONALD, who is said to have been "an
active and spirited man."   He married and left
issue, at least one son.

X. JOHN, who married Marian, daughter of
Christopher Macrae of Aryugan, by whom he had
issue—

1 ALEXANDER, of whom below.

2. FARQUHAR, who had two sons, Donald and
Farquhar.

3. DUNCAN died unmarried.

XI. ALEXANDER, son of the above-mentioned
John, was called Alister Buidh.   He married, first,
Isabel, daughter of Duncan Macrae of Balnain, by
whom he had issue—

1. DUNCAN, of whom below.

2. JOHN, called Ian Ruadh (Red-haired John), married Isabella Macrae, with issue—

a. Donald, who married, first, Christina Maclennan, by whom he had a son.

*a*1. Duncan, who went to New Zealand He married Isabella, daughter of Farquhar Maclennan, Camusluinie, with numerous issue.

Donald married, secondly, Christina, daughter of Christopher Macrae, Carr, and died in 1883, leaving issue.

*a*2 John, a farmer at Ardelve, married Mary Macrae, with issue—Jessie ; Donald; Isabel; Christina ; Alexander ; Duncan ; John.

*a*3. Christopher died at Ardelve in 1887.

*a*4. Alexander, a farmer at Ardelve, married 16th December, 1886, Zeller, daughter of Donald Macrae, Auchtertyre family, with issue—Farquhar ; Frederick ; Donald ; Margaret ; Duncan.

b. Farquhar died unmarried at Ardelve in 1887.

Alexander, called Alister Buidh, married, secondly, Mary, daughter of Alexander Macrae, Camusluinie, with issue—

3. FARQUHAR, called Ferachar Ban. He was a Sergeant in the Seventy-Eighth Highlanders, served in India, and afterwards lived as a Pensioner at Dornie He married Anne, daughter of Murdoch Murchison, with issue—

a. Alexander, a Roman Catholic Priest, was for some time at Beauly, and was afterwards drowned at Cape Breton.

b. Janet ; *c.* Mary.

XII. DUNCAN, eldest son of Alister Buidh, is spoken of as "an industrious and religious man." He lived at Fadoch, and afterwards at Ardelve. He married Helen, daughter of John Og, son of the Rev. Donald Macrae of Kintail, with issue.

1 MARY, born 14th September, 1774, married Alexander Macrae, Inchcro, with issue.

2. ALEXANDER, who went to Canada in 1821. He married Anne, daughter of John Mackenzie, by his wife, Christina, daughter of Alexander Macrae, Auchtertyre, and had, with other issue—

a. Duncan.

b. John Alexander, an American Railway Contractor, now living at Niagara Falls He married, first, Agnes Anne Ross, who died on the 22nd August, 1891, and was buried at St Catherine's Cemetery, Ontario. She left one son, William. John Alexander married, secondly, Julia Perham.

c. Christopher.

3. JOHN, called Ian Ban, born at Ardelve 30th January, 1777, died 14th August, 1848, and was buried at Kilduich. He married Isabel, daughter of Alexander Macpherson, Gairloch, and by her, who died on the 6th March, 1861, had issue—

a. Duncan, died unmarried 8th May, 1886, aged seventy-two years.

b. Anne, died unmarried 18th July, 1858, aged forty-one years.

c. Kate, died unmarried 10th February, 1883, aged sixty-two years.

d. Hannah, died unmarried.

c. Margaret, died unmarried.

d. Alexander, for many years Postmaster at Strome Ferry, died unmarried on the 25th June, 1896, aged seventy-one years.

VIII MURDOCH, son of the Rev. Farquhar Macrae of Kintail, had a joint wadset with his brothers, Miles and John Breac, of Camusluinie. He married and had issue, at least one son.

IX. DONALD, who married and left issue, at least one son.

X. MURDOCH, who married Giles or Julia, daughter of Kenneth Mackenzie, merchant, Dingwall, by whom he had issue two sons, as mentioned below, and four daughters, of whom nothing appears to be known.

1. DONALD, who married Anne, daughter of Alexander Mackenzie of Lentran, second son of Simon Mackenzie, first laird of Torridon. Donald died at an advanced age about 1790, and had issue—

a. Murdoch, who emigrated to North Carolina in or about 1773 He was engaged on the Loyalist side in the American War of Independence, and "was killed in the engagement 'twixt the Loyalists and the Americans at More's Bridge in that country in February, 1776."

b. John, who was a planter in Jamaica.

c. Colin, who was a printer in London.

d. Alexander, who was a merchant in New York.

e. Abigail ; *f*, Giles or Julia ; *g*, Florence. These three daughters were married. *h*, Janet.

2. ALEXANDER, who married a Maclean, niece of the Rev. John Maclean, first Presbyterian Minister

of Kintail, by whom he is said to have had issue, one son and four daughters.

It has been found impossible, so far, to trace the descendants of Murdoch, son of the Rev. Farquhar Macrae, any further.

CHAPTER XIII.

VIII. John Breac, son of the Rev Farquhar.—Foster Brother of Kenneth, third Earl of Seaforth.—Under Factor or Chamberlain of Kintail —His Marriage and Descendants.—The Auchtertyre Family.—Finlay, son of John Breac —Killed at the Battle of Glensheil.—His Marriage and Descendants —The Carr Family.

VIII. JOHN, probably the youngest son of the Rev. Farquhar Macrae of Kintail, was called Ian Breac. He was tacksman of Achyaragan in Kintail, and is spoken of as " an active and successful farmer, who left means behind him." He also had a joint wadset of Camushuinie with his brothers Miles and Murdoch, for which his father gave ten thousand marks to George, second Earl of Seaforth. With regard to this wadset the clan historian says that " whether the other two paid off John or not, his successors got none of the money when the wadset was redeemed in 1751." In addition to being an " active and successful " farmer, John Breac was under factor or chamberlain of Kintail under Kenneth Mor, third Earl of Seaforth, who, it will be remembered, was brought up as a boy and received his early education in the family of the Rev. Farquhar Macrae.[1] John Breac was Kenneth Mor's

[1] See page 59.

foster brother, and there is some reason to believe
that the reputation which Kenneth had of being the
best chief in the Highlands of Scotland was in some
measure due to the influence of his foster brother,
to whose strong sense of justice and kindly consideration for the rights and the feelings of the
people the traditions of Kintail and Lochalsh still
testify. It is said that about the year 1670, while
there was a rearrangement of farms and a revision
of leases being made on the Seaforth estate of
Kintail, John Breac was ill of a fever and unable to
take any part in the proceedings On hearing,
however, that a certain Kenneth Mackay of Sallachy
was to be removed against his own wish from a
farm which his family had held for several generations, John Breac, ill as he was, got out of bed,
wrapped himself well up in a blanket and set out
across the hills of Attadale in pursuit of Seaforth,
who had, only that day, left Kintail for Brahan.
John Breac overtook him at Camalt Inn, Attadale,
and refused to part with him until he promised to
let Mackay remain in undisturbed possession of his
ancestral home. It is said that this Mackay's
descendants are still living at Sallachy. From all
accounts John Breac was a man of weight and
influence among his countrymen, and his death was
lamented in an elegy, of which a few fragments
have been orally preserved in Lochalsh and Kintail
to the present day.[1]

John Breac was married, but it is uncertain who
his wife was He had at least three children, and

1 Appendix J.

his eldest son, Duncan, was born before his marriage. One tradition says that the mother of this Duncan was a daughter of Munro of Foulis, who was living at the time with Lady Seaforth at Ellandonan Castle. Another tradition, which can be traced back among Duncan's descendants for more than a hundred years, and which, for other reasons also, appears to be a more authentic one, says that Duncan's mother was a daughter of Mackenzie of Hilton, and that she afterwards became John Breac's wife. This tradition is to a certain extent supported by the Manuscript History of the Clan, in which it is stated that John Breac "had a son by his wife before marriage," but does not say who his wife was. In any case it was Finlay, the second son, who was served heir to John Breac, who died before the 28th of July, 1696, that being the date of the service. John Breac left at least the following issue—

1. DUNCAN, of whom below.

2. FINLAY, of whom hereafter.

3. CATHERINE, who married Murdoch Matheson, and had a son John, who had a son Kenneth, who married a daughter of Roderick Mackenzie of Rissel, Lochcarron, and had a son John, who died without issue at Kishorn in 1849, aged seventy-two years.

IX. DUNCAN, son of John Breac, is mentioned on an old genealogical tree as "Mr Duncan," and was probably educated for the Church. There is a tradition that he occupied some post of importance[1] on the Seaforth estate of Kintail. He lived at Coilrie, was married, and left issue—

1 Gaelic, "Fear drèachd," which means a man holding an office of trust and rank

1. ALEXANDER, of whom below.

2. MURDOCH, who had issue—

a. Alexander, mentioned as a Schoolmaster in Easter Ross.

b. John.

3. DONALD, married and had issue—

a. John, who had a son called John Roy Og, who had two sons, viz., Thomas, who was drowned, and John, who had two sons, John and Thomas, who resided at Dornie in the first half of the present century.

b. Alexander.　c. Duncan Roy.

4. BEATRICE, who married Donald Macrae, and had a son Alexander, who had a son Alexander Og, who lived at Dornie.

X. ALEXANDER, son of Duncan, married and had issue—

1. DONALD, of whom next.

2. DUNCAN, married with issue.

3. MARY.

4. CATHERINE, married with issue.

5. REBECCA, married with issue.

XI. DONALD, son of Alexander, was called Domhnull Mhic Alister. Having quarrelled for some reason with Seaforth, he left Kintail and went to Rannoch, in Perthshire. After a brief and apparently not very satisfactory sojourn in that part of the country he returned home, and afterwards took a grazing farm on Bein na Caillich, in Skye, where he lived for some time. He was drowned while crossing Kylerea Ferry during a storm, and his body was never found. He married Flora, daughter of

Kenneth Mackenzie, Culdrein, Attadale (Dochmaluag family), by his wife Flora Mackenzie, whose
father was Roderick, son of John, second laird of
Applecross. and whose mother was Isabel, daughter
of Kenneth Mackenzie, sixth laird of Gairloch.   By
her he had issue—

1. ALEXANDER, of whom below.

2. DUNCAN, who married, and had issue.

a Flora, who, on the 17th March, 1788, married
John Macrae, Sallachy, with issue—Duncan; Donald;
Isabel.

b. Isabel, who married Malcolm Macrae, with
issue—

b1. Duncan, who went to America, married, and
had issue.

b2. John, who died young.

b3. Margaret.   b4. Kate.

b5. Flora, who married George Finlayson at
Avernish, with issue—Duncan ; Kenneth, now living
at Avernish ; John.

XII. ALEXANDER, eldest son of Donald, was
called Alister Donn (Brown Alexander).   He was
co-tacksman of Auchtertyre, with the famous Coll
Macdonell, fourth of Barisdale,[1] and was in his own
day one of the leading men of the parish.   He had a
house built for himself at Auchtertyre, which is said
to have been the first " white house" in the parish
of Lochalsh, except the Minister's Manse.   He married Isabel,[2] daughter of John Og, son of the Rev.

---

1 For several references to Coll of Barisdale, see Antiquarian Notes (Second
Series) by Charles Fraser Mackintosh, LL D.

2 See page 79,

Donald, son of Alexander of Inverinate, and by her had issue as below. He lived to a very advanced age, and was the oldest man in the parish for several years before his death, which occurred in June, 1832. He was buried at Kirkton, Lochalsh.

1. DUNCAN, of whom below.

2. DONALD, born at Auchtertyre in 1775. He was a planter at Demerara, and afterwards tacksman of Auchtertyre, and factor for Macleod of Raasay and Matheson of Attadale He married, about the end of 1816 or the commencement of 1817, Jane, daughter of Archibald Macra of Ardintoul, by whom he had issue as below. He died on the 15th November, 1843, and was buried at Kirkton.

a. John, a Doctor of Medicine, was surgeon in the East India Company's service, and died unmarried at Cawnpore on the 21st January, 1857.

b. James died unmarried.

c. Archibald died unmarried.

d. Jessy, who, in 1849, married John Stewart of Ensay (of the Stewarts of Garth), and died on the 26th of October, 1860, leaving issue—

d1. Jane Macrae.

d2. William, a Captain in the 91st Highlanders.

d3. Isabella Christian married, in 1882, Gordon Fraser, and has issue.

d4. Mary died in 1891.

d5. Donald Alexander married, in 1894, Isabella Mary Anderson, with issue—Mary.

d6. Jessy Chisholm married, in 1888, Thomas Scott,

*d*7. Archibald died in childhood.

3. ALEXANDER, who died while studying medicine at Aberdeen on the 14th June, 1810, aged twenty-two years, and was buried at Kirkton.

4. JOHN, died unmarried, and was buried at Kirkton.

5. FARQUHAR went to Canada about 1833, and was for some time a schoolmaster there. He is spoken of as "an excellent teacher and a most loveable man."[1]   After a few years spent in Canada he returned to Lochalsh, and died unmarried on the 4th October, 1839.   He was buried at Kirkton.

6. CHRISTINA married John Mackenzie, Auchmore, and had, with other issue, Anne, who married Alexander Macrae in America, a descendant of Miles, son of the Rev. Farquhar Macrae of Kintail, with issue as already mentioned.[2]

7. MARY married Alexander Maclennan, and had, with other issue, a daughter Jessie, who married Duncan Macrae, farmer, Kirkton, with issue as already mentioned.[3]

8. MARGARET married Christopher Macrae (Drudaig family), went to America, and had issue as already mentioned.[4]

9. BARBARA married Malcolm Ross, a native of Easter Ross.   He was a road contractor, and made, among other roads, the one leading from Strome Ferry to Lochalsh. Barbara and her husband subsequently went to America.   She died on the 11th February, 1870, and her husband died on the

---

[1] Letter from one of his old pupils.
[2] Page 167.   [3] Page 127.   [4] Page 163.

22nd April, 1877, both at a very advanced age. They left issue—

a. John, who was born at Auchmore, in Lochalsh, before his parents emigrated. He is a railway contractor in America.

b. Catherine died at the age of twenty-one, on the 9th May, 1846, and was buried at Russelton Flats, Quebec.

c. Alexander, married with issue.

d Isabella.

e. Christina, married with issue.

f. Donald Walter married Susan Macdonald. He died on the 26th December, 1877, and was buried at St Catherine's Cemetery, Ontario.

g. Agnes Anne married John Alexander Macrae of Niagara Falls, with issue, and died on the 22nd August, 1891,[1] as already mentioned.

10. FLORA died unmarried.

XIII. DUNCAN, eldest son of Alexander of Auchtertyre, was for some time a Sergeant in the Seventy-Eighth Highlanders. He was a farmer at Auchmore, and afterwards lived at Auchtertyre, where he died at a very advanced age on the 13th February, 1860, being for some time before his death the oldest man in the parish. He was buried at Kirkton. He married Christina, daughter of Murdoch Mackenzie, farmer at Braintra,[2] and by her, who died on the 10th of October, 1874, aged

---

[1] See page 167

[2] The family to which this Murdoch Mackenzie belonged lived at Braintra for many generations, and is said to have been descended from Sir Dougal Mackenzie, Priest of Kintail, who was killed by Donald Gorm Macdonald of Sleat in 1539.—See page 26.

M

ninety years, and was buried at Kirkton, he had issue—

1. DONALD, born at Auchmore on the 15th of January, 1808. He lived at Avernish, where he died on the 3rd of April, 1888, and was buried at Kirkton. He married, on the 23rd of January, 1845, Margaret, daughter of Murdoch Matheson, and by her, who died on the 22nd of April, 1893, aged seventy-two years, had issue—

a. Margaret, born on the 12th of November, 1845, married on the 31st July, 1873, Ewen Matheson, at Plockton, with issue—

*a*1. Annabella Mary ; *a*2, Margaret Mary ; *a*3, Farquhar ; *a*4, Frederick Donald ; *a*5, Hectorina.

b. Donald, born on the 22nd of January, 1847, a Sergeant of Police in Glasgow, married on the 5th of April, 1870, Janet, daughter of Thomas Maclennan, with issue—

*b*1. Margaret, born on the 27th of March, 1871, married on the 15th October, 1896, Colin Campbell, in Glasgow, with issue.

*b*2. Jessie, born on the 22nd of April, 1873.

*b*3. Jane, born on the 14th of September, 1876.

*b*4. Catherine, born on the 18th of October, 1880.

*b*5. Frederick Donald, born on the 4th of April, 1883.

. *c.* Murdoch, born on the 25th of May, 1849, died unmarried in Minnesota, in the United States, in 1872.

d. Catherine, born on the 10th of October, 1851.

e. Frederick George, born on the 7th of December, 1853 ; a Captain in the Merchant Service, drowned at sea in 1882.

f. John Alexander, born on the 11th of March, 1856.

g. Farquhar, born on the 17th of October, 1858.

h. Zeller, born on the 26th of October, 1860, married Alexander Macrae, at Ardelve, with issue as already mentioned.[1]

2. MARGARET, married on the 25th of April, 1844, John Matheson, and died on the 2nd of January, 1846, without surviving issue

3. JOHN, born at Auchmore in March, 1814. He lived for many years at Aultdearg in Kinlochluichart,[2] and afterwards moved to Easter Ross. He died at Bridgend of Alness, in the parish of Rosskeen, on the 15th of April, 1865, and was buried at Kirkton, in Lochalsh. He married, on the 10th April, 1851, Flora,[3] born 13th September, 1825, daughter of Alexander Gillanders, some time tacksman of Immer and Attadale in Lochcarron, and left issue—

a. Rev. Alexander, born on the 23rd of April. 1852, a clergyman of the Church of England, now (1898) Assistant Master of Emanuel School, Wandsworth Common, and Curate of St Helen's Church, Bishopsgate, in the City of London. He is the author of this book.

b. Margaret, born on the 12th October, 1853.

c. Duncan, born on the 29th of July, 1855, and

1 Page 166.

2 Kinlochluichart is a quoad sacra parish situated near the centre of the county of Ross, and traversed by the Dingwall and Skye Railway.

3 Appendix F.

now in America, married on the 19th July, 1887, Mary Anne, daughter of Roderick Macdonald, Dingwall, and by her, who died the following year at Toronto, Canada, had issue, one son, Roderick John, born on the 15th of March, 1888.

d. Annie, born on the 14th of June, 1857, married, on the 3rd of December, 1886, Ivan Ingram Mavor, of Newcastle-on-Tyne (son of the Rev. James Mavor, M.A., Glasgow) who was shortly afterwards killed in an accident at Birkenhead, and by whom she had issue, one son, Ivan, born on the 12th of September, 1887.

e. Jeannie, born on the 20th of August, 1859, married, on the 12th of August, 1896, Farquhar Matheson, Dornie.

f. Farquhar, born on the 20th of October, 1862, M.B. and C.M., of Aberdeen University, now living at Alness.

g. John, born on the 31st of October, 1865.

IX. FINLAY, son of John Breac, son of the Rev. Farquhar Macrae He was served heir to his father in July, 1696.[1]

Finlay is said to have " lived in plentiful circumstances at Dullig," and was killed in the battle of Glensheil in 1719, fighting on the Jacobite side. " During the retreat he loitered behind to have a shot at two troopers who were following up close behind.

---

[1] Finlaus M'Cra in Achgargan haeres Joannis M'Cra nuper in Achgargan, filii legitimi quondom Magistri Farquhardi M'Cra aliquando Ministri verbi Dei apud ecclesiam de Kintaill patris —*Register of Retours*, 28th July, 1696.

Under the same date Finlay is entered as heir to his uncles Christopher and Thomas, legitimate sons of Mr Farquhar Macrae, formerly Minister of Kintail.

He killed one of the troopers, but the other killed him."[1] It is uncertain who his wife was, but she is mentioned on an old genealogical tree as Janet Nighean Lachlain Mhic Thearlich (daughter of Lachlan, the son of Charles), and by her he had issue—

1. FARQUHAR, of whom hereafter.

2. Christopher, who lived at Dall, and is mentioned as "a religious, honest man." He married Florence, daughter of Christopher Macrae, Drudaig, with issue—

a John, called Ian Ban, a carpenter or builder. He married Catherine, daughter of John Og, son of the Rev Donald Macrae, with issue—

*a*1. Christopher, who had sons—(1) Farquhar, who had a son, Alexander; (2) Donald, (3) John.

*a*2. Flora, who married Duncan Macrae,[2] a descendant of the Rev. Finlay Macrae, Lochalsh.

b. Janet, who is said to have married Duncan, grandson of Christopher of Aryugan[3]

c. Flora, married Alexander Macrae, of the Merchant Service. He was called the Captain Dubh (the Black Captain).

d. Anne, is said to have married "Farquhar of the Smith family."

3. Flora, married Neil Mackinnon of Kyleakin, and had issue at least a son—

a. John, who married a Miss Macdonald, and had a son—

*a*1. Dr Farquhar Mackinnon of Kyleakin, who married and had issue—(1) John, who lived at Kyleakin. (2) The Rev. Neil Mackinnon of Creich,

---

[1] Old letter from Kintail.   [2] Page 50.   [3] Page 121.

who married Elizabeth Flora Anne, daughter of James Thomas Macdonald of Balranald, with issue— Farquhar; Catherine, married James Ross, Pollo, Kilmuir, Easter Ross, with issue; James Thomas; Jane; Jemima; Christina. (3) Margaret.

4. ISABEL, married, first, Kenneth Macleod of Arnisdale, Glenelg, commonly called Kenneth Mac Alister, with issue. She[1] married, secondly, Neil Mackinnion of Borreraig, one of the Corrichatachan family. From this marriage were descended the Mackinnons of Strath

X. FARQUHAR,[2] son of Finlay, married, first, a daughter of Duncan Macrae of Aryugan,[3] who was killed at the Battle of Sheriffmuir, and had issue—

1. FINLAY, called Fionnla Ban, lived at Bundalloch; married, and had issue.

2. DONALD, who went to America in 1774.

3. DUNCAN, who also went to America in 1774.

Farquhar married, secondly, a daughter of Alister Mor Mac Ian Mhic Dhonnachidh, and had issue.

4. CHRISTOPHER, of whom below.

5. ISABEL, who married Christopher Macrae, Achyark, with issue—

a. Farquhar, who lived at Ardelve and married Anne, daughter of John, son of Alister Ruadh Macrae, already mentioned,[4] and had issue—

1 There is some reason to believe that this, and not the daughter of the Rev John Macrae of Dingwall, is the Isabel whose name is mentioned on the tombstone referred to on page 146

2 The succession of Finlay is continued here in his son Farquhar only for convenience of arrangement It is not maintained that he was the eldest son,

3 Page 123   4 Page 124.

*a*1. Duncan, now living at Ardelve, by whom this statement of the descendants of his grandparents, Christopher and Isabel Macrae, was given to the author in 1890. Duncan gave evidence before Lord Napier's Crofter Commission in 1883. He married Mary, daughter of Duncan Macrae, with issue :—Anne ; Anne ; Duncan, who died at Dornie in 1883 ; Kate ; Farquhar ; Maggie.

*a*2. John.

*a*3. Farquhar, married Janet Macrae, with issue : —Anne ; Janet ; Maggie ; Isabel ; Mary ; Alexander.

*a*4. Christopher, married Kate Macrae, with issue :—Anne ; Duncan ; Margaret married Hector Macdonald ; Farquhar ; Christina ; Catherine ; Mary.

b. Farquhar.

c. Duncan, who was a soldier and served in India.

d. Alexander.

e. John, who was for many years a schoolmaster at Sleat, and a well-known Gaelic scholar, folklorist, and genealogist. He married Catherine Macrae of the Torlysich family, and had issue—

*e*1. John ; *e*2, Christopher ;

*e*3. The Rev. Godfrey, Minister of Cross, in the Island of Lews ;

*e*4. Isabel ; *e*5, Annabel ; *e*6, Christina ; *e*7, Flora.

f. Finlay, married a Miss Finlayson, with issue : —Mary ; Christopher ; Roderick ; Kenneth ; Farquhar ; Duncan ; Annabel ; Isabel.

6. CHRISTINA, married Duncan Macdonald, at Carr, with issue.

7 MARY, married Farquhar Maclennan, a native of Kintail, and had issue at least one son.

a. Roderick, called Ruaridh Mor (Big Roderick), who lived in Glenurquhart, and died in 1884. He married Mary Grant, and had, with other issue—

*a*1. Alexander, who lived in Kingussie, where he died in 1892. He married Helen, daughter of Duncan Macrae,[1] with issue ; (1) The Rev. Duncan, M.A. of Edinburgh, Free Church, Laggan, married, in 1893, Isabella, daughter of Donald Macpherson, Factor of the Island of Eigg, by his wife, Mary, daughter of Farquhar Macrae of Camusfunary, with issue, Norman ; (2) Mary, died young ; (3) Roderick, M.A of Aberdeen, now Headmaster of the Public School, Kingussie, married Flora, eldest daughter of the Rev Neil Dewar, Free Church, Kingussie ; (4) John ; (5) Jane ; (6) Helen ; (7) Kenneth, M.A. of Aberdeen ; (8) Mary Anne ; (9) Alexander.

XI. CHRISTOPHER, son of Farquhar, was a farmer at Carr. He married Isabel Macrae, with issue—

1. WILLIAM, lived at Carr. He married Anna-

---

[1] Some time during the last century two brothers of the name Macrae migrated from Kintail to Badenoch, where their descendents, who were men of good position, were known as Na Talich (the Kintail Men) From one of these brothers is descended the Rev. Alexander Macrae, Minister of the Scottish Church, Crown Court, London From the other brother were descended, in the second or third generation—(1) the above-mentioned Duncan, who, in addition to his daughter, Helen, had two sons · (*a*) John, S S C., Procurator-Fiscal of Kirkwall, who died a comparatively young man, in 1890, leaving a widow and family, one of whom, Robert, is in the Indian Civil Service ; and (*b*) Kenneth, now living in London (2) Kenneth, who had a son, John, a Doctor of Medicine, for many years Medical Officer of the Parish of Laggan, and now living with his family in Edinburgh

bel, daughter of Murdoch Macrae, Achnagait, and died in July, 1879, leaving issue—

a. Alexander, went to South America; b, Mary; c, Donald;

d. Isabel, married Murdoch Macrae at Camuslunie, with issue—William; Elizabeth; Alexander; Donald;

e. Christopher;

f. Murdoch, now living at Seabank, in Gairloch.

2. CHRISTOPHER, a farmer at Carr, died in 1895. He left a son, Alexander.

3. FINLAY, a farmer a Carr. He married Mary, daughter of Donald Macrae, with issue—a, Mary; b, Kenneth; c, Christopher; d, Isabel; e, Jessie; f, Donald.

4. CHRISTINA, married Donald Macrae at Ardelve, as already mentioned.[1]

5. CATHERINE, married Farquhar Macrae, Camusfunary, with issue, of whom hereafter.

6. JANET, married Donald Macrae, Inverness, without issue.

7. MARY, married Christopher Macrae, Durinish, with issue—a, Alexander; b, John; c, Christopher; d, Mary; e, Isabel; f, Janet.

[1] Page 166.

CHAPTER XIV

V. Farquhar, son of Constable Christopher Macrae of Ellandonan Castle —Progenitor of the Black Macraes —Fearachar Mac Ian Oig —The Rev Donald Macrae of Lochalsh —Tradition about Ancestry of Governor James Macrae of Madras —Domhnull Og —High-handed proceedings of Garrison placed in Ellandonan by the Parliament after the Execution of Charles I.—Fight between the Garrison and the Kintail men.—Domhnull Og's Descendants —Donnacha Mor Mac Alister killed at Sheriff-muir.—Maurice of Achyman.—His Marriage and Descendants. —The Rev John Macrae of Knockbain.—Eonachan Dubh and his Descendants —Domhnull Mac Alister, Progenitor of the Torlysich Family —Killed at Sheriffmuir —His Marriage and Descendants

V. FARQUHAR, son of Christopher,[1] who was fourth in descent from Fionnla Dubh Mac Gille-chriosd, and was Constable of Ellandonan Castle in the time of John of Killin, ninth Baron of Kintail, was progenitor of the branch of the clan which was known as Clan 'ic Rath Dhubh (the Black Macraes). He married and had issue—

1. DONALD, of whom below.

2. MAURICE, who left issue.

3. CHRISTOPHER, whose descendants appear to have been well known in Kintail about the end of the seventeenth century, and of whom the Rev.

---

[1] Page 24.

John Macrae of Dingwall says, in his manuscript history of the clan, that others in Kintail could give a more satisfactory account than he could.

VI. DONALD, eldest son of Farquhar, married a daughter of Alexander Bain of Inchvanie, and by her had five sons, who are spoken of as "all bold, pretty, forward men."

1. ALEXANDER, mentioned as "an understanding active man." For some time he was "principal officer" or Chamberlain of Kintail, "a desirable and lucrative post." It is said that Sir Kenneth Mackenzie, first Baronet of Coul, was fostered and brought up in his house, and that this led to "a friendship 'twixt the family of Coul and the Macras." Alexander left no lawful son, but he had two illegitimate sons—John, who lived and died at Leault in Kintail, leaving numerous issue; and Murdoch, who lived and died with Sir Kenneth Mackenzie at Coul.

2. JOHN, called Ian Og, married, and had issue—

a. Alexander, who had issue:

a1. John, who had a son, John, who lived at Coul.

a2. Duncan, who had several sons, one of whom, John, was a gunsmith in Kintail.

a3. Alexander, who left issue.

b. Duncan, who was killed in the Battle of Auldearn in 1645, leaving issue, one son, Christopher, who was for some time principal officer of Kintail, and left issue.

c Farquhar, called Fearachar Mac Ian Oig, whose name figures prominently in the traditions of

Kintail.   It is said that on one occasion, while
Farquhar was out hunting, the ground officer or
bailiff of Kintail entered his house, and seized some
of his chattels in payment of certain dues, which the
bailiff was endeavouring to levy on his own account,
and which Farquhar strenuously opposed.   When he
returned home his wife tauntingly informed him of
what had happened, and he, giving way to the
impulse of the moment, immediately set out in pursuit
of the bailiff, whom he soon overtook and killed
For this deed of blood he was obliged to flee the
country, but he soon returned, and for seven years
concealed himself among the hills of Kintail.   At the
end of that time he made peace with the bailiff's
friends, and paid them a ransom   He was now able
once more to appear in public among his friends and
his countrymen, who welcomed him back with great
delight.   The chief of Kintail, perhaps Colin, first
Earl of Seaforth, refused, however, to allow Farquhar
to come into his presence, but during a rebellion in
the Lews, of which there were more than one at this
time, Farquhar joined the expedition sent there,
unrecognised, and, being a man of great valour, he
conducted himself in a manner which led to a complete reconciliation between himself and his chief.
Farquhar possessed considerable poetic talent, and is
said to have composed several songs during his exile.[1]
Whatever truth there may or may not be in this
tradition of Farquhar's exile, we know that during
the chieftainship of Colin, first Earl of Seaforth, who
lived in far greater state than any of his predecessors,

1 Appendix J,

the people of Kintail suffered greatly from the excessive rents which were then levied upon them, and as Farquhar Mac Ian Oig is specially mentioned as one of those who suffered from the exorbitant raising of rent, it is quite possible he may have been a leader of resistance and opposition to the exactions of the chief and his officials, and may have been obliged in consequence to spend part of his life as an outlaw.   The Rev. John Macrae of Dingwall, in his Manuscript History of the Mackenzies, explains, as an instance of the "grievous imposition" of Earl Colin's time, how the yearly rent of the tack of land called Muchd in Letterfearn, which was held by Farquhar Mac Ian Oig, was in a short time raised from sixty merks Scots to two hundred and eighty. It appears that while this process of rent-raising was going on, Farquhar left Muchd and moved to Achyark.   At all events tradition says it was at Achyark he was living when the bailiff seized his property.   In the poem ascribed to Farquhar, as mentioned above, he calls his wife Nighean Dhonnachidh (Duncan's daughter), and by her he had, with other issue, a son.

c1. The Rev Donald of Lochalsh, who was educated at Aberdeen, where he graduated M.A in 1653.   He was minister of Lochalsh before the 11th August, 1663, and was still there on the 12th April, 1688.   He is said to have lived until 1710.   He married Annabel, daughter of William Mackenzie of Shieldaig, and by her had issue:—Mr John; Donald; Duncan ; Farquhar ; Maurice ; and Christopher.

d. John, called Ian Dubh Mac Ian Oig, who

went to Greenock, and was, according to a Kintail tradition,[1] the grandfather of Governor James Macrae of Madras, of whom hereafter.

3. DONALD, mentioned below.

4. DUNCAN, left a daughter but no male issue. "He was a pretty man and lived to a great age."

5. FINLAY, left issue, and his descendants were numerous in Kintail and Lochalsh.

VII. DONALD, son of Donald VI., had five sons, "all pretty men, who outlived their father."[2]

1. JOHN, was "bred a scholar," but does not appear to have profited much by his learning, as he became one of Earl Colin's menial servants. He had a son called John, who married and had issue.

2. CHRISTOPHER, mentioned below.

3. DUNCAN, who was eighth in descent from Fionnla Dubh Mac Gillechriosd, married and had issue at least three sons—John, who is described as "a great natural orator," and was accidentally killed in Strathconon in 1698 ; Ronald ; and

(IX.) FARQUHAR,[3] who left a son.

(X.) CHRISTOPHER, who is said to have married a Maclennan, with issue—

---

1 Tradition communicated to the author by Mr Alexander Matheson, shipowner, Dornie, in 1897.

2 It is interesting to note how frequently the Clan historian refers to the good looks and handsome personal appearance of the different members of this branch of the Clan, who were his own contemporaries, and with whom he was perhaps personally acquainted This is a characteristic which some members of this branch of the Macraes are said to have retained until the present time.

3 The Rev. John Macrae's account of this family terminates with Farquhar (IX.) The continuation of the genealogy here given was communicated in outline to the author in August, 1896, by Councillor Alexander Macrae, Invernate.

(1) FARQUHAR, of whom below.

(2) CHRISTINA, who married Donald Macrae, a farmer at Inverinate, and had, with other issue—

(*a*). Duncan, commonly called Donnacha Sealgair (Duncan the Hunter), who married and had issue.

(*b*). Alexander, who was Quarter-Master Sergeant in the Seventy-Eighth Highlanders. He served with his regiment in India, and took part in the Battle of Assaye on the 23rd of September, 1803, and several other engagements. He was also present at the capture of Java in 1811, and retired from active service in 1815, "after twenty-five years of faithful, zealous, and gallant good conduct."[1] On the occasion of his retirement he was presented by his regiment with a valuable gold watch, in recognition "of his long and faithful services to his good King and country." Sergeant Macrae afterwards lived at Kirkton, Lochalsh, where he died at the age of eighty-four, on the 16th of June, 1855, and was buried in Kirkton Churchyard. He married Elizabeth, daughter of Alexander Mackenzie,[2] fifth laird of Cleanwaters, by whom he had issue—

[1] Letter from Lieutenant-Colonel D Forbes, Commanding 1st Battalion 78th Highlanders, dated Java, 1st March, 1815.

[2] Cleanwaters was formerly the name of a small estate on the south side of Dingwall. The above-mentioned Alexander was a son of Alexander, fourth of Cleanwaters, son of Charles, son of John, son of Colin, second laird of Kilcoy, son of Alexander, first laird of Kilcoy, younger son of Colin, eleventh baron of Kintail, son of Kenneth, tenth baron of Kintail, by his wife the Lady Elizabeth Stewart of Athole, for whose descent from the Royal families of England and Scotland see Appendix F. For some account of the Mackenzies of Cleanwaters see Mackenzie's History of the Mackenzies, new edition, page 584.

(*b*1.) Alexander, who married Jane Macdonald, and died in Australia, leaving issue.

(*b*2.) Donald, who died at Inverness in 1891, unmarried.

(*b*3.) Jessie married Robert Forbes, with issue.

(*b*4.) David, in Australia.

(*b*5.) Christina married Alexander Macintosh, with issue—(1) John died unmarried in Dingwall in 1896; (2) Elizabeth married Thomas Nicol, a well-known citizen and Magistrate of Dingwall, and has issue; (3) Margaret married John Macrae, a solicitor and Magistrate of Dingwall, with issue; (4) Annie; (5) Alexander; (6) Mary; (7) Donald, who was in the Seaforth Highlanders, and was killed in India; (8) Robert; (9) Charles; (10) David.

(*b*6.) Charles, a supervisor of Inland Revenue, died at Rothesay on the 16th of September, 1885, aged fifty-four years, and was buried in Rothesay Cemetery. He was twice married. By his first wife he left a daughter, and by his second wife two sons and five daughters.

(XI.) FARQUHAR lived at Inchcro. He married Margaret (?), sister of Alexander Macrae of the Merchant Service, commonly called the Captain Dubh (the Black Captain), and by her had issue—

(XII.) CHRISTOPHER, who lived at Fadoch, married Isabella Macrae. He was drowned in one of the rivers of Kintail, and left issue.

(1). DUNCAN, who died at Glenose, in Skye, on the 19th August, 1877, aged seventy-two years. He married Margaret Maclennan, with issue—

(*a*). Alexander in Australia.

(*b*). Christopher, also in Australia.

(*c*). Jessie Hannah.

(2). ALEXANDER, who married Flora, daughter of Duncan Macrae (the above-mentioned Donnacha Sealgair), and had issue—

(*a*). Alexander, living at Inverinate, and now the County Councillor for the Parish of Kintail. He married Anne Maclennan, and has issue :—Mary ; Alexander ; Donald ; Farquhar , Duncan ; Flora.

(*b*). Donald married Mary Anne Macrae, with issue : — Anne ; Farquhar ; Duncan ; Alexander ; Duncan ; Alexander ; Flora.

(*c*). Isabella.

(3). JOHN died in Australia in 1888, married with issue.

(4). JAMES, who was commonly known as Seumas Ban (James the Fair). He was the author of several Gaelic songs[1] which are well known in Lochalsh and Kintail. He lived for many years at Ardroil, in Lews, where he was the neighbour and friend of the Rev. John Macrae, some time of Carloway, Lews, and formerly of Knockbain. James died at New Kelso, Lochcarron, on the 16th January, 1888, aged seventy-five years, and was buried in Lochcarron Churchyard. He married Flora, daughter of Duncan Mackenzie, by his wife Christina, daughter of John Macrae,[2] and by her, who died at Hemel

---

[1] Appendix J.

[2] This John Macrae, commonly known as Ian Mac a Gobha—John the Son of the Smith—was the man who brought Ian Mac Mhurachaidh's poems and songs from America (page 83). He died at Carndu, Dornie, in 1839, aged ninety-three years. See also Appendix J.

Hempstead, Hertfordshire, on the 18th of March, 1895, and was buried in Lochcarron, had issue—

(*a*). John, who is also a Gaelic poet[1] of considerable talent, now living at Timsgarry in Lews. He married Elizabeth Fraser, with issue—John Fraser; Duncan; James; Isabel Anne; Alexander.

(*b*). Isabella married Kenneth Murchison, Lochcarron, with issue—Margaret; Roderick Impey; James Alexander; Flora; Christina; Isabella; Finlay; Kenneth; Barbara.

(*c*). Flora.

(*d*). Christina, whose name was included in the Women's Roll of Honour for the Victorian Era in the Earl's Court Exhibition of 1897, for having been the means of saving the crew of a Danish ship—the Grana—which was wrecked on the coast of Lews on the 21st of October, 1896. For her conduct on that occasion the Danish Government presented her, through the Prime Minister, Lord Salisbury, with a marble clock, bearing a suitable inscription.[2] Christina is married to Donald Mackay, Mangersta, Lews, and has issue — Flora Helen; Andrina; John; Jemima; Farquhar Alexander.

(*e*). Barbara.

(*f*). Farquhar, a graduate of Aberdeen University, now a Medical Practitioner in London.

(*g*). Alexander Mackenzie, now a student at the Presbyterian College, London.

4. DONALD, called Dahitar or Dyer, so called

---

1 Appendix J.

2 An account of the heroic conduct of Mrs Mackay on this occasion, together with a portrait of herself, appeared in *The Strand Magazine*, December, 1897.

because he was taught the trade of dyeing, though he never followed it.   He left sons and daughters.

5. DONALD, who was eighth in descent from Fionnla Dubh Mac Gillechriosd, being the second member of the family who bore this name, was called Donald Og.   He greatly distinguished himself in a skirmish which took place in 1650 between the men of Kintail and a garrison which had been placed in Ellandonan Castle by the Scottish Parliament after the execution of Charles I., with whose cause George Earl of Seaforth, after much wavering, finally cast in his lot.   The garrison treated the people with great insolence, and among other things, as the autumn drew to a close, they insisted that the people should furnish them with a sufficient store of fuel for the winter.   Accordingly, a party of soldiers, under a certain John Campbell and a Sergeant of the name Blythman, proceeded to the residence of the Chamberlain at Inverinate in order to enforce their commands.   The soldiers were met by a small party of ten men, probably a deputation appointed to remonstrate against this new imposition.   The remonstrance soon gave place to high words, and the officer in command ordered the soldiers to fire.   This the soldiers did, but without doing the men any injury.   The Kintail men, however, had old scores to settle, especially against John Campbell, who, it seems, had on a former occasion attacked and wounded some people at Little Inverinate, so they immediately drew their swords, fell upon the soldiers, killed several of them, including John Campbell and Sergeant Blythman, and put the rest to flight.

Donald Og, who was evidently the leader of the Kintail men, singled out Campbell for attack, and with one fierce stroke of his sword, "cut off his head, neck, right arm, and shoulder from the rest of his body." The place where this occurred was long known as Campbell's Croft. Sergeant Blythman was killed while attempting to cross a stream of water between Little Inverinate and Meikle Inverinate, at a spot which was afterwards called Blythman's Ford. Thus the ten Kintail men, without losing any of their own number, fought against the thirty soldiers, and put them to flight. After this the garrison made no further demand for fuel, nor did they make any effort to avenge their defeat. On the contrary, they felt so uneasy and so much afraid of the men of Kintail that shortly afterwards they left the country, and no further notice was ever taken of the matter. Donald Og left issue,[1] Duncan, and

(IX.) ALEXANDER, who had a son.

(X.) DUNCAN, called Donnacha Breac, who had a son.

(XI.) JOHN, who had a son.

(XII.) JOHN, who had a son.

(XIII.) KENNETH, who had a son.

(XIV.) ALEXANDER, who lived in Lochcarron, and married Anne Macrae, with issue.

(1) ALEXANDER, who married, and had issue.

(2) DONALD, who married Helen, daughter of

1 The succession of Donald Og, as here given, was communicated to the author in 1897, in Kintail, by two independent genealogists, whose statements were in entire agreement, and were further confirmed by some family notes in the possession of the Rev. Donald Macrae of Lairg.

Joseph Riddoch of Skeith, near Cullen, and afterwards of Fowlwood, Grange, and died in 1889, leaving issue.

(*a*). Joseph Riddoch, born on the 4th of July, 1855, and died on the 27th of August, 1874.

(*b*). Anne, married Hugh Stewart, who died in 1889, leaving issue—Jane; John; Nelly, who died in childhood.

(*c*). The Rev Donald, born on the 10th of January, 1864, M.A. of St Andrews, B.D. of Aberdeen, Minister of the Parish of Lairg in Sutherlandshire, to which he was ordained in 1890. He married on the 15th of January, 1891, Anne, daughter of William Stephen of Culrain House, and has issue :—

(*c*1). Donald Alastair, born on the 26th of October, 1891.

(*c*2). Ronald Stephen Bruce, born on the 15th March, 1893.

(*c*3). Colin Frederick, born on the 19th of February, 1895.

(*c*4). Charles Eric, born on the 16th of February, 1897.

(*d*). Alexander, born on the 18th September, 1866, married Marie Don, and is now living in East Liverpool, Ohio, in the United States.

(*e*). Helen.

(3). KENNETH, in Kansas in the United States, married, with issue.

(4). FLORA married John Macdonald, in Skye, with issue.

VIII. CHRISTOPHER, son of Donald VII., is said to have been " a prudent and facetious man." He married and left a son.

IX. ALEXANDER, who lived about the time of the Revolution of 1688. He married Margaret, daughter of Alexander Macdonald, of the Glengarry family, by whom he had six sons, " all pretty men."

1. DONALD, who was killed at the Battle of Sheriffmuir, and of whom hereafter.

2. DUNCAN, who was called Donnachadh Mor or Donnachadh Mac Alister. He was noted for his prowess and strength, and was killed at the Battle of Sheriffmuir. It is said that as the Kintail men were passing through Glensheil, under the leadership of Duncan, to join the Jacobite Rising which ended in that battle, they came upon six men who were struggling to place a large stone in a wall they were building. Duncan told the men to stand aside, and, seizing hold of the stone, lifted it up and placed it in the desired position, and at the same time expressed a fervent hope that the Macraes would never be without a man who could lift that stone as he had done. This stone is still pointed out at Achnagart. Duncan's sword was picked up on Sheriffmuir after the battle, and was exhibited for many years in The Tower of London as " the great Highlander's sword." There are men still alive who remember seeing this sword in The Tower. It is not there now, however, and what has become of it is no longer known, though the probability is that it may have been lost in the fire by which The Tower Armoury was destroyed in 1841. In the time of William Earl of Seaforth, Duncan was Captain of the Freiceadan or Guard, whose duty it was to protect the marches of the Seaforth estates

from the plundering raids of the Lochaber cattle-lifters, and many are the traditions of his adventures and feats of arms against the Fir Chaola (the thin or lean men), as the Lochaber marauders were usually called in Kintail.[1]   Duncan was also a poet, but it has been found impossible so far to recover any more than the merest fragments of his productions.[2]   He was married, and left issue.

3. MAURICE, son of Alexander, was tenth in descent from Fionnla Dubh Mac Gillechriosd.   He lived at Achyuran, in Glensheil, and is said to have married Christina, daughter of Alexander Macrae, Camusluinie, with issue at least two sons, Alexander and Duncan.

(XI.) ALEXANDER, son of Maurice, was called Alister Ruadh (red-haired Alexander), and was ground officer of Kintail.   It is said that while at school at Fortrose he married a Margaret Fraser of Belladrum, by whom he had one daughter, who married Duncan Macrae, Achnashellach.   Alexander married, secondly, a daughter of John Macrae, Inversheil, with issue :—

(1) DONALD, called Domhnull Ruadh, who was a farmer at Achnagart, and in 1794 moved to Ard-elve, in Lochalsh, where he lived for nineteen years. In 1813 he moved to Morvich, in Kintail, where he died the same year.   He married Anne, daughter of Christopher Macrae of Drudaig,[3] and by her had a large family, of whom at least four sons reached manhood, and there was a daughter alive and

1 See chapter on the legends and traditions of the clan.
2 Appendix J.   3 Page 164.

unmarried in 1830. The four sons had the farm of Immer, in Lochcarron, between them for some time, and they were there as late as 1823.

(*a*). Alexander is mentioned as the eldest of Donald Roy's sons in a letter written by himself to the Honourable Miss Mackenzie of Seaforth, on the 22nd May, 1830. He married Isabella Crichton, who was descended from a Covenanting family, and had issue : — Marion, Donald, William Crichton, Alexander, John, Farquhar.

(*b*). Christopher married and left a son, Donald, who is now living at Bundalloch, in Kintail, and is married with issue.

(*c*). Farquhar.

(*d*). The Rev. John, some time of Knockbain, and better known in the Highlands as Macrath Mor a Chnuicbhain (the great Macrae of Knockbain), said to have been the youngest of the sons, was born either at Achnagart or at Ardelve in May, 1794. In his youth he was noted not only for physical strength but also for his mental capacity and intelligence, and numerous anecdotes about his great personal strength and courage are still floating about the Highlands. While living at Immer with his brothers he made the acquaintance of the Rev. Lachlan Mackenzie, of Lochcarron, who is said to have formed a high opinion both of his character and of his abilities. After leaving Immer he received a share in the farm of Ratagan, on the south side of Lochduich, and while there he acted for some time as superintendent of the workmen who were engaged on the construction of the road leading from Kintail across Mam Ratagan to Glenelg and Kyle Rhea. He afterwards held an appointment as teacher in a school at Arnisdale, in Glenelg, where he became a centre of much influence for good. Upon deciding to enter the Church he succeeded in obtaining a bursary for Mathematics at Aberdeen University. In this subject he took a high position during his course, but failed to make a good appearance in Latin and Greek, having commenced the study of those languages too late in life to be able to acquire the familiarity which is necessary for a complete mastery of their construction and idiom. He was, however, a very proficient student of Hebrew. On completing his college course and obtaining licence, he acted for some time as assistant to the Rev. James Russell, of Gairloch. He became minister of Cross, in Lews, in 1833. Here he continued until 1839, when he became minister of the parish of Knockbain, in the Black Isle.[1] The great controversy which led to the Disruption of the Church of Scotland in 1843 was then at its height, and Mr Macrae soon became one of the ablest and most energetic of the leaders of the popular party in the Highlands. In 1843 he cast in his lot with the Free Church, and remained at Knockbain for some years longer. In 1847, the death of his intimate friend, the Rev. Alexander Stewart, of Cromarty, made him wish for a change of locality, and in 1849 he accepted the Gaelic Church at Greenock, where he continued until town

[1] The Black Isle is the peninsula lying between the Beauly and Cromarty Firths, on the north-east coast of Scotland.

life and labour began to tell so much on his health
that he found it necessary to move to a quieter
scene.   Accordingly in 1857 he moved to the parish
of Lochs in Lews, and then in 1866 to Carloway,
also in Lews.   Here he remained until 1871, when
he retired from active duty, generously declining to
accept the retiring allowance to which he was
entitled from the Church.   He died at Greenock on
the 9th October, 1876, leaving behind him a
memory and a name which Gaelic-speaking Highlanders will not readily allow to perish.   Mr
Macrae's powers as a preacher were undoubtedly of
the very highest order, and his influence among the
people and his brother clergy was very great.   It
was said of him at the time of his death that no
minister in the Highlands during the last two
hundred years had made so great an impression on
so large a number of people.   One writer says that
Mr Macrae, " who was of fine personal appearance,
was the type of a genuine Kintail man, well propor-
tioned, beautifully shaped head and shoulders,
herculean limbs, and deep chest, an excellent' voice,
and an impressive manner.   The effects he produced
upon his hearers were such as no preacher of the
time except Dr Chalmers was known to produce.
In Gaelic his powers came fully out, yet in English
he often thrilled his hearers as he did when he
spoke in his native tongue.   His preaching was
characterised by richness of thought, beauty and
simplicity of illustration.   He was a large-hearted
man, sound in doctrine, liberal in sentiment, and
esteemed by all."   Another writer says that " His

appearance as he presented himself before a congregation at once arrested attention, it suggested to his hearers the thought that this was a messenger from God." · The Rev. John Macrae married Penelope, daughter of Captain Mackenzie of Bayble in Lews, and by her, who died on the 9th December, 1859, aged fifty-four years, he had four sons and two daughters.

(*d*1). John went to Australia, married.

(*d*2). Donald went to New Zealand.

(*d*3). Jane married the Rev. Donald Macmaster of Kildalton, in Islay, with issue :—John ; Donald ; Mary ; Hugh ; Æneas ; Alexander ; Ebenezer ; Jane.

(*d*4). Ebenezer, in New Zealand, married, with a large family.

(*d*5). Annie married the Rev. Alexander Macrae of Clachan, in Kintyre, with issue .—John ; Alexander ; Ebenezer James , Duncan Graham.

(*d*6). Alexander Stewart.

(2). FARQUHAR, married Finguela, daughter of Duncan Macrae of the Torlysich family, with issue—

(*a*). Donald, married Catherine Maclennan, with issue—

(*a*1). Donald.

(*a*2). Murdoch,[1] now living at Cairngorm, in Kintail, married Margaret Finlayson, with issue— Donald ; John ; Alexander ; Murdoch ; Farquhar ; Duncan.

[1] Mr Murdoch Macrae's name came into considerable prominence throughout the Highlands during the crofter agitation about 1884, in connection with proceedings instituted against him for damage alleged to have been done by a pet lamb belonging to him, in the deer forest of Kintail, then leased by a wealthy American, the late Mr W. L. Winans.

(*a*3). Farquhar, now living at Sallachy, married Anne Mackay.

(*a*4). Isabella.

(*b*) John married, and had issue.

(*c*). Alexander, killed in Egypt.

(*d*). Farquhar married Catherine Maclennan, and had issue.

(*d*1). Alexander, who died at Strome Mor, Lochcarron, on the 28th August, 1895, aged 80 years. He is the author of a treatise on "Deer Stalking," published by Blackwood & Sons, Edinburgh. He married Anne, daughter of Duncan Macrae of Leachachan, with issue — Catherine; Mary; Christina, married Alexander Macrae, in New Zealand; Duncan, at Strome Mor, Lochcarron; the Rev. Farquhar, M.A., minister of the parish of Glenorchy, in Argyllshire; Donald, in New Zealand; Flora, married Joseph Ramsay, in Glasgow; Alexander, in Western Australia; Kate Anne; Ewen.

(*d*2). Flora, married Duncan Maclennan, with issue—

(*d*3). Catherine; (*d*4). Farquhar.

(3). Christina (?), who, according to the traditions of Kintail, married Ian Mac Mhurachaidh, the poet.[1]

(4). Anne, who married Donald Macrae, of the Torlysich family, and had issue—a son, Maurice, and daughters.

(XI.) DUNCAN, son of Maurice, son of Alexander IX., married Anne,[2] daughter of Christopher Macrae of Drudaig by his wife Janet, daughter of Farquhar Macrae of Inverinate, son of Duncan

1 Page 83.   2 Page 163.

of Inverinate, son of Alexander of Inverinate by his first wife, Margaret Mackenzie of Redcastle,[1] and by her had issue at least one son—

.   (1). DUNCAN, called Donnachadh Og. He lived at Carr, and married Anne, daughter of Duncan Maclennan, Inchcro, and by her had issue—

(a). Donald lived at Fernaig, and died 2nd December, 1858.   He married Janet, daughter of Alexander Macrae of Morvich, and by her, who died on the 20th of May, 1897, aged seventy-eight years, had issue—

(a1). Peter, late of Morvich.

(a2). Catherine, married Dr Cameron.

(a3). Mary, married Roderick Macrae.

(a4). Anne, married Duncan Maclennan of Achederson, in Strathconon.

(a5). Jessie, married Dr Duncan Macintyre, of Fort-William. She died in Edinburgh on the 30th of January, 1898.

(a6). Duncan Alexander, late of Fernaig and Monar, married Barbara Mitchell, with issue—

(b). Farquhar, who was tacksman of Camusfunary, in Skye, married Catherine, daughter of Christopher Macrae, Carr, with issue—

(b1). Alexander, married Madeline, daughter of Captain Farquhar Macrae of Inversheil, with issue, a son, Farquhar, who is married, with issue ; and three daughters.

(b2). Duncan, died in America.

(b3). Ewen, now at Fernaig, in Lochalsh.

(b4). John, also at Fernaig.

[1] Appendix F,

(b5). Thomas, in Leith.

(b6). Donald, in Australia.

(b7). Mary, married Donald Macpherson, Eig, with issue—(1) John ; (2) Catherine, married the Rev. John Smyth Carroll, M.A., Glasgow ; (3) Isabella, married the Rev. Duncan Maclennan, M.A., Laggan[1]; (4) Mary, married David Boyd, Aberdeen ; (5) Farquharina, married John Macrae, Portree.

(b8). Jane, married Mr Mackintosh, with issue.

(b9). Anne. (b10). Catherine.

(c). Ewen, died at Fernaig.

(d). Duncan, was a farmer at Leachachan. He married Mary, daughter of Donald Maclennan, Conchra, and died on the 15th of January, 1862, aged sixty-four years, leaving issue—

(d1). Christina, married Alexander Macrae, Achlorachan, in Strathconon.

(d2). Ewen, now at Borlum, near Fort-Augustus.

(d3). Anne, married Alexander Macrae, with issue.

(d4). Isabella, married Robert Blair, with issue.

(d5). Lachlan, in Inverness, married, with issue.

(d6). Christina.

(d7). The Rev. Duncan, now minister of the parish of Glensheil.

(d8). Donald, a doctor, died in Bristol in 1889.

(e). John, was tacksman of Braintra, in Lochalsh, where he died on the 1st of May, 1874, aged seventy-three years. He married Flora, daughter of Roderick Finlayson, Achmore, and by her, who died on the 6th of May, 1867, aged forty-five years, had issue—

1 Page 184.

Colonel RODERICK MACRAE (Torlysich)

(e1). Anne, married Murdoch Matheson, of the Hudson Bay Company, with issue, Flora Catherine; Joan Alexandrina Mary.

(e2). Duncan, J.P., of Ardintoul.

(e3). Roderick, M.D. of the University of Edinburgh, Surgeon-Lieutenant-Colonel in the Indian Medical Service. He served in the Afghan War in 1878-1880, at the close of which he received a special staff appointment "for excellent services in the field," and now holds the important appointment of Chief Medical Officer of the District of Dacca, under the Bengal Government.[1]

(e4). Ewen, in New Zealand, married in 1891, Mary Eleanor Fantham, with issue—Flora Mary; Annie Ethel Frances; Robert Cunningham Bruce.

(e5). Donald John, in Assam, married, 12th October, 1894, Catherine Isabella Gibbs, Daisy Bank, Portobello.

(e6). John Farquhar, M.B. and C.M., Brighton, married, in 1886, Edith Lily Johns.

4. CHRISTOPHER, son of Alexander IX., and tenth in descent from Fionnla Dubh Mac Gillechriosd, was called Gillecriosd Glas (Pale Christopher). He married and left issue—

(XI.) DONALD, who is said to have married Marion (?), a sister of the poet Ian Mac Mhurachidh, and had a son.

(XII.) JOHN, called Ian Dubh na Doiraig (Black John of Doiraig). He married Catherine Macrae, and had with other issue—

---

[1] A biographical sketch, with a portrait of Surgeon-Lieutenant-Colonel Macrae, appeared in the *Celtic Monthly* for December, 1896.

(1). Donald, who was a farmer in Glengarry, where he died in 1860.

(2). Alexander, who was a soldier in the Seventy-Eighth Highlanders.

(3). Duncan, of whom next.

(XIII). DUNCAN,[1] called Donnacha Ban Brocair (Fair Duncan the Foxhunter), lived for many years at Tulloch, near Dingwall, and was afterwards a farmer at Kernsary, near Poolewe, where he died in November, 1851. He married Margaret, daughter of John Macrae, farmer and miller in Lochbroom, by his wife Catherine, daughter of Alexander Macvinish of Achilty, in the parish of Contin, and by her, who died in Dingwall in 1859, aged fifty-three years, had issue—

(1). CATHERINE, born in 1827, married Charles Macleod, a Free Church missionary, with issue, two daughters.

(2). ISABELLA, born in 1829. She married Duncan Mackenzie, and died in 1891, leaving issue, two sons and three daughters.

(3). DUNCAN, born in 1832, now of Strathgarve, Dalveen, Queensland. He married on the 21st of September, 1869, Charlotte Jane, daughter of Loudon Hastings Macleod, with issue[2]—

(a). Margaret Jane.

(b). Addie Sophia.

(c). Loudon Hastings Duncan, born on the 1st of August, 1876.

---

[1] The descent of this Duncan from the above-mentioned Christopher, son of Alexander IX., was communicated to the author in August, 1897, by Mr Alexander Matheson, shipowner, Dornie.

[2] A biographical sketch, with a portrait of Mr Duncan Macrae, appeared in the *Celtic Monthly* for May, 1897.

(4). ALEXANDER, born in 1834, now of Brixham, Devonshire, married in 1871, Anne Lorrimer, who died on the 5th of December, 1897, aged sixty-seven years, without issue.

(5). FARQUHAR, born in 1836, now of Killiemore, in the Island of Mull. He married, in 1870, Maggie, daughter of Donald Macdougall of Port Ellen and Tyndrum, in the Island of Islay, and by her, who died in 1887, aged forty-two years, had issue—(*a*). Duncan ; (*b*). Kate Cameron ; (*c*) Grace Maclennan.

(6). JOHN, born in 1838, was for some time a farmer at Ardlair, on the shores of Loch Maree. He went to Queensland in 1873, and was killed there by a horse in 1880. He married and left issue—(*a*). Duncan ; (*b*). Ian ; (*c*). Grace.

(7). COLIN, born in 1843, married, in 1880, a Miss Young, and died in 1892 without issue.

5. FARQUHAR, son of Alexander IX., was severely wounded at the battle of Sheriffmuir, and brought home by his nephew, John, who is mentioned below. Next day as this John was going over the field of battle he found his father and his uncle Duncan among the slain, and his uncle Farquhar lying wounded with a fractured leg. John tried to catch one of the stray horses that were wandering over the field in order to carry his wounded uncle away, but without success. It is said that the wounded man succeeded, however, by hailing one of the horses in English, to draw it near enough to seize it by the bridle, which he held until his nephew came up to him. But the horse, on hearing the beating of drums in the distance, became very restive, and the young man

had great difficulty in managing it.   He succeeded,
however, at last in getting his uncle mounted.   They
then set out on the homeward journey, and never
halted until they reached Fort-William, where Farquhar remained for three months, until his wound
was quite healed.   He then returned to Kintail,
taking the horse along with him.   The horse was
carefully kept until it became weak with age and at
last died through sinking accidentally in a bog.
The iron shoes it wore at Sheriffmuir were kept for
many years in the Torlysich family as an heirloom,
and were last in the possession of the late Alexander
Macrae of Morvich.

6. JOHN, who was known as Eonachan Dubh
(Black little John), is said to have been the youngest
of the sons of Alexander IX.   He was tenth in descent
from Fionnla Dubh Mac Gillechriosd.   He is said to
have been a man of short stature, but of great
strength, and there are traditions still preserved
of his deeds of daring and prowess against the Lochaber marauders, with whom, in his time, the men of
Kintail had many a stout contest.[1]   John married,
and had issue at least one son.

(XI.) CHRISTOPHER, who lived at Malagan, in the
Heights of Kintail, and in whose house Prince
Charles passed a night, or part of a night, during
his wanderings in that part of the country about the
end of July, 1746.   He is said to have married
Anne,[2] daughter of Christopher Macrae of Aryugan,
and had issue at least one son—

1 See chapter on the legends and traditions of the clan.
2 Page 126,

(XII.) ALEXANDER, who married Anne Macrae, Camusluinie, and had issue.

(1). MURDOCH, of whom below.

(2). CHRISTOPHER, who married Janet Macrae, with issue.

(a). Isabel married Alexander Macrae at Reraig, in Lochalsh, and had issue.

(a1). Christopher died in Canada, married, with issue.

(a2). Malcolm died in Canada.

(a3). Christina married Alexander Finlayson, Lochcarron.

(a4). Duncan, who was ground officer of Lochalsh, and died in 1866, aged fifty years.

(a5). Mary, married James Macrae, Kirkton, Lochalsh, without issue.

(a6). Hugh, in the Inland Revenue, died at Kirkton, Lochalsh, in 1891. He was married, but left no issue.

(a7). Agnes, married Murdo Finlayson, of Kyle Inn, Lochalsh, with issue :—Catherine, who married Alexander Maclennan, of whom hereafter.

(a8). Roderick, married Mary, daughter of Donald Macrae, Fernaig,[1] with issue, and died in 1893.

(a9). Flora married Alexander Mackenzie, Oban.

(a10). Alexander died young.

(b). Annabella married Kenneth Maclennan, Sallachy.

(c). Alexander, who died at Reraig, Lochalsh, and left a son.

---

[1] Page 205.

(c1). John, living in Paisley, and married with issue, a son, Alexander, and several daughters.

(3). ALEXANDER, married and had issue at least one son.

a. John, who married Isabella, daughter of Farquhar Macrae of Torlysich, and had, with other issue—

a1. Christopher, who lived in Glensheil, married and had issue.

a2. Alexander, who was a farmer in Glenmoriston from 1844 to 1868, when he removed to another farm in Badenoch, which he occupied until 1884. He married Anne, daughter of Duncan Macrae, Attadale, and died in Edinburgh, leaving issue—(1) John, living at Islip, New York, by whom this information about his own family was communicated to the author in 1898.   (2) Duncan, living in North Wales, married with issue, a son, James Alexander. (3) Jane, married Colin Maclennan, Islip, New York. (4) Catherine, married William Russell, New York.

(XIII.) MURDOCH, lived at Sheil House, and died at Achnagart on the 17th of December, 1846, aged eighty-six years.   He married Annabella, daughter of the Rev. Donald Mackintosh, of Gairloch, by his wife Catherine, daughter of William Mackenzie, fourth laird of Gruinard,[1] and by her, who died on the 15th of April, 1861, aged seventy-eight years, had issue—

(1). CATHERINE, died young.

(2). ALEXANDER, died in Montgomery County, in Ohio, about 1856.   He was married and left issue.

1 Mackenzie's History of the Mackenzies, new edition, page 618.

(3). ANNE, married Donald Macrae, a merchant in Jeantown, Lochcarron.

(4). DONALD, of whom next.

(5). ANNABELLA, married William Macrae, Carr, with issue.[1]

(6). ALEXANDRINA, died unmarried on the 31st of January, 1860, aged forty-two years.

(7). ISABELLA, died at Seabank, Gairloch, on the 2nd of November, 1896.

(8). CHRISTOPHER, a wool broker in Liverpool, died on the 15th of January, 1856, aged thirty-five years.

(9). CHRISTINA, married John Mackenzie, Ardroil, Lews.

(XIV.) DONALD, was for some time tacksman of Achnagart, and afterwards became proprietor of the estate of Kirksheaf, near Tain. He was a Justice of the Peace for the County of Ross. He married Anne Magdalen Gordon, only daughter of Thomas Stewart, J.P., of Culbo, and died in 1884, with issue one son.

(XV.) CHRISTOPHER ALEXANDER of Kirksheaf, born in 1864, Captain in the 3rd Battalion Seaforth Highlanders. He died at Dover, while on the way to Algiers, on the 20th of December, 1894, and was buried in the St Duthus Cemetery, Tain. He married, in 1888, Helena Margarette, third daughter of the late Edward Griffith Richards, J.P., of Langford House, Somerset, with issue—

(1). DONALD CHRISTOPHER, born on the 3rd of March, 1889.

---

1 Page 184.

(2). KENNETH MATHESON, born on the 11th of September, 1890.

(3). ELEANOR MARJORIE, born on the 2nd of August, 1893.

X. DONALD, son of Alexander IX., and his wife, Margaret Macdonald, was the first of this family who lived at Torlysich. He married Rebecca (?), daughter of John Macrae, a former occupier of the lands of Torlysich, called Ian Mac Ian,[1] and was killed at the Battle of Sheriffmuir. By his wife Donald had issue—

1. DONALD, of whom below.

2. JOHN, who as a young man was at the Battle of Sheriffmuir, and brought his wounded uncle, Farquhar, home, as already mentioned. John was afterwards tacksman of Inversheil, and lived to a very advanced age, his descendants to the fourth generation being at his funeral in Kilduich He married Anne Macrae, and had issue at least four sons—

a Alexander, who married Marion, probably a sister of Ian Mac Mhurachaidh the poet, and lived at Achyuran. He had a son.

*a*1. Duncan, who had two sons, Duncan and Farquhar.

b. Donald, called Domhnull Buidh (yellow-haired Donald), who married and had issue :—

---

[1] Ian Mac Ian of Torlysich was the Chief of the Clann Ian Charrich Macraes (see pages 22-23). He is said to have been killed in a fight between the Kintail men and the Lochaber cattle lifters, at a place called Carndhottum, between Glenmoriston and Glengarry. His body was brought back to Kintail for burial, and Donald married his daughter and took possession of Torlysich.

*b*1. John, who married Isabella, daughter of Farquhar Macrae of Sheil Inn, and went to Canada.

*b*2. Donald, who married and went with his family to Australia.

*b*3. Duncan.

c. Christopher, was a farmer at Achnagart, and married a daughter of John, son of Duncan Macrae of Glenelchaig, with issue at least three sons :—

*c*1. Farquhar, and *c*2, John, who both went with their families to Canada.

*c*3. Alexander, who was for some time a farmer at Achnagart, and married a daughter of Donald Macrae, Inchcro, with issue :—(1), Christopher ; (2), Alexander ; (3), Donald ; (4), Catherine, who married John Maclennan, with issue—Alexander, tacksman of Linassie, in Kintail, of whom hereafter; (5), Mary, who married John Macrae (Ian Ruadh) of the Torlysich family ; and (6) Isabella, who married his brother Allan. Both Mary and Isabella went to Australia with large families.

d. Farquhar married and had issue—

*d*1. Donald, a soldier.

*d*2. Malcolm, who was sheriff-officer for Kintail.

3. DUNCAN lived in Glensheil. He married, first, a Macrae, without surviving issue.

He married, secondly, Annabella, daughter of Donald Matheson of Craig, Lochalsh, by whom he had issue—

a. Donald, who married Anne, daughter of Alexander, son of Maurice of Achyuran,[1] and by her had issue, a son Maurice and several daughters.

[1] Page 204.

Duncan married, thirdly, a daughter of Christopher Macrae, by whom he had, with other issue— b, Christopher; c, Alexander; d, John, a soldier, who served in India, and obtained a pension. He married and left issue.

XI. DONALD, son of Donald X, succeeded his father in Torlysich, and had Glenquaich in joint wadsett with some cousins from Glengarry. He married Katherine,[1] daughter of the Rev. Donald Macrae of Kintail, with issue—

1. FARQUHAR, of whom below.

2. DUNCAN married and left issue.

3. JOHN married Abigail Macrae, Camusluinie, with issue—

a. John married Mary, daughter of Donald MacLennan, with issue—

a1. Christopher died in the West Indies.

a2. Donald, who lived for several years at Avernish, Lochalsh. He married Elizabeth, daughter of Donald Macrae, and died at Carnoch, in the Heights of Kintail, on the 22nd of March, 1892, aged eighty-five years, leaving issue :—(1) Mary married Donald Mackenzie, with issue, and died on the 5th of July, 1878 ; (2) John, in Wales, married Lilla Andrews; (3) Donald, at Killelan, married Janet Maclennan ; (4) Farquhar, in New Zealand ; (5) Christopher, at Carnoch; (6) Anne married, on the 6th of January, 1898, John Macrae, of Dornie, son of Malcolm and Janet Macrae.[2]

a3. Farquhar went to Australia.

*a*4. Catherine married John Macrae,[1] schoolmaster at Sleat, in Skye, with issue.

*a*5. Helen, married Malcolm Macrae, and went to Australia in 1852 with her husband and family. She died there shortly after their arrival, and her husband died in 1872. They left, with other issue, a son Duncan, now a farmer at Donnybrook, in Victoria.

b. Donald, married Hannah, daughter of John Macrae, with issue—

*b*1. John, who married Isabel, daughter of Roderick Matheson, with issue.

*b*2. Farquhar.

*b*3. Donald, a gamekeeper at Cailleach, in Skye, married Catherine Munro, with issue.

c. Alexander, married Anne, daughter of John Macrae, with issue.

*c*1. John, went to Australia.

*c*2. Donald, lived at Inversheil. He married Catherine, daughter of John Macrae, Durinish, with issue.

*c*3. Farquhar, went to Australia.

*c*4. Catherine, went to Australia.

d. Christopher, died without issue.

John and Abigail Macrae had two other sons in the Seventy-Eighth Highlanders. He had also some daughters.

4. MARGARET, married Duncan, son of Alexander, son of Farquhar.

5. HELEN, married Kenneth Maclennan, in Morvich.

[1] Page 183

XII. Farquhar, son of Donald XI., succeeded his father at Torlysich. He married "Helen Grant of Dundreggan, in Glenmoriston, whose mother was a daughter of Colonel Grant of Shewglie, whose wife was a daughter of John Grant, commonly called Ian a Chragain,[1] by his second wife, Janet, daughter of Sir Ewen Cameron of Lochiel,"[2] and by her had issue—

1. Duncan, called Donnacha Mor, succeeded to Torlysich, and was extensively engaged in cattle dealing. When Seaforth sold the south side of Glensheil to Mr David Dick, Duncan left the old family home at Torlysich, about 1820, but got the farm of Achnagart, which still formed part of the Seaforth property. He married Florence,[3] daughter of the Rev. John Macrae, of Glensheil. with issue one son, Francis Humberston, who married in Tasmania, and left issue, now the lineal representatives of the old Torlysich family.

2. Donald, tacksman of Cluanie, in the Heights' of Kintail. He married Margaret, daughter of Alexander Macra of Ardintoul, with issue—

a. Alexander, some time tacksman of Glenquaich, died unmarried in Australia.

b. Hannah married Donald Macdonald, Lochaber.

c. Isabella married Donald Stewart of Luskintyre, in Harris, with issue—

---

1 For an interesting account of Ian a Chragain, who was Laird of Glenmoriston from 1703 to 1736, see Mackay's "Urquhart and Glenmoriston."

2 Letter.   3 Page 106.

*c*1. John, now of Ensay, married Jessy Macrae of Auchtertyre, with issue as already mentioned.[1]

*c*2. Donald died unmarried.

*c*3. William died unmarried.

*c*4. Robert died unmarried.

*c*5. Alexander married Anne, daughter of Captain Mackenzie.

*c*6 Grace married Duncan Macrae of Kames Castle, with issue as already mentioned.[2]

*c*7. Mary married, first, the Rev Robert Mackintosh of Kirkmichael, and, secondly, Robert Anderson of Lochdhu, with issue.

*c*8. Helen Grant married, in 1846, William Hill Brancker of Athline, in the Island of Lews. She died in October, 1897, and left with other issue, William Stewart, barrister-at-law, of the Inner Temple.

*c*9. Richmond Margaret married John Macdougall of Lunga, with issue :—Stewart, now of Lunga, late Major in the Ninety-Third Highlanders, and married with issue.

*c*10. Hannah married Captain Ronald Macdonald (Aberarder family) of the Ninety-Second Highlanders.

d. Janet married Duncan Macrae of Linassie, who went with his family to Canada.

Donald of Cluanie had also a natural son, John, who was a Sergeant in the Seventy-Eighth Highlanders, and was killed after greatly distinguishing himself at the battle of El Hamet, in Egypt, in 1807. Sergeant John Macrae is mentioned by

[1] Page 175. [2] Page 153

General David Stewart of Garth in his *Sketches of the Highlanders*.[1]

3. ALEXANDER, tacksman of Morvich, married Jessie Cameron of Clunes, in Lochaber, who died on the 12th of March, 1858, aged eighty-two years. Alexander died on the 27th of January, 1852, aged ninety-two years, and by his wife left issue—

a. Janet married Donald Macrae, Fernaig, with issue as already mentioned,[2] and died at a very advanced age on the 20th of May, 1897.

b. Helen, married Ewen Maclennan of Killelan, with issue—

*b*1. Alexander, in Canada.

*b*2. Anne Charlotte, married Alexander Maclennan,[3] tacksman of Linassie, with issue—Ewen Donald; Percy Cameron; Katie Christina; John.

Alexander of Morvich had also two natural sons —(1) Alexander, who was for many years a farmer

---

[1] In Volume II, page 317, General Stewart, in speaking of the battle of El Hamet, says.—Sergeant John Macrae, a young man about twenty-two years of age, but of great size and strength of arm, showed that the broadsword, in a firm hand, is as good a weapon in close fighting as the bayonet. . . Macrae killed six men, cutting them down with his broadsword (of the kind usually worn by sergeants of Highland corps), when at last he made a dash out of the ranks on a Turk, whom he cut down, but as he was returning to the square he was killed by a blow from behind, his head being nearly split in two by the stroke of a sabre. Lieutenant Christopher Macrae, whom I have already mentioned as having brought eighteen men of his own name to the regiment as part of his quota of recruits for an ensigncy, was killed in this affair, with six of his followers and namesakes, besides the Sergeant. On the passage to Lisbon in October, 1805, the same sergeant came to me one evening, crying like a child, and complaining that the ship's cook had called him English names, which he did not understand, and thrown some fat in his face. Thus, a lad who in 1805 was so soft and childish, displayed in 1807 a courage and vigour worthy a hero of Ossian.

[2] See page 205, where her age is erroneously stated to have been seventy-eight—she was much older.   [3] Page 215.

at Achlorachan, in Strathconon. He married, first, Maria Margaret, daughter of Kenneth Mackenzie of Langwell and Corrie, in Lochbroom, with issue, a son, Kenneth Farquhar, late of Achlorachan, and now living in the State of Oregon, in America, and a daughter, Alice, who married Murdoch Mackenzie of Glenbeg, Kishorn. He married, secondly, Chistina, daughter of Duncan Macrae, Leachachan.[1] (2) Duncan, who married and had issue.

4. John, called Ian Ruadh, was for some time tacksman of Dalcataig, in Glenmoriston. He married Mary, daughter of Allan Grant of Dundreggan, and sister of Captain Grant of Reraig, Lochalsh, with issue—

a. John, married Mary Macrae of Achnagart, with issue, and went to Australia.

b. Allan, married Isabella Macrae of Achnagart, with issue, and went to Australia.

c. Duncan, died unmarried.

d. Angus, died unmarried.

e. Jessie, married Duncan Macrae of Sheil House, and went as a widow to Australia with her three sons—Duncan; Christopher, who died on the voyage; Alexander.

f. Donald, who died at Inversheil in 1896, at a very advanced age, and whose portrait was painted some years before his death by Mr William Lockhart Bogle.

5. Christopher, was a Lieutenant in the Second Battalion of the Seventy-Eighth Highlanders, which was raised in 1804, and joined by many young men

[1] Page 206.

from Kintail.   Coming back to the district as a
recruiting officer, Christopher brought twenty-two
recruits to his battalion, and, in recognition of his
services, obtained an Ensign's Commission for his
brother Farquhar.   The departure of these men
was commemorated in a pibroch called Lochduich.
Lieutenant Christopher was killed, along with seven
other Macraes, as already, mentioned, at the battle
of El Hamet, in Egypt, in 1807.

6. FARQUHAR joined the Seventy-Eighth Highlanders at a very early age, and obtained an Ensign's
Commission, as stated above, shortly after the raising of the Second Battalion.   He was promoted
Lieutenant in 1808.   He was present at the battle
of Maida, in Italy, in 1806, and at El Hamet the
following year.   He served also in India and in
Java, and was with the portion of his regiment
which was wrecked in the Bay of Bengal while
sailing from Java to Calcutta in November, 1816,
and had to remain nearly five weeks on the Island of
Preparis, where they suffered great hardships before
they were finally rescued.[1]   He retired about 1825.
On returning home he lived first at Cluanie, and
afterwards became tacksman of Inversheil.   He
married, on the 12th of January, 1826, Christina,
daughter of the Rev. John Macrae of Glensheil,[2] and
died on the 18th of November, 1858, aged about
seventy-two years, leaving issue as below.   His wife
died in Bute on the 4th of August, 1887, and was
buried at Kilduich.

1 Historical Records of the 78th Highlanders, by James Macveigh, page 84.
2 Page 107.

a. Donald John, born on the 18th of April, 1830, who was tacksman of Inversheil and Cluanie, and who, according to the obituary notices of him which appeared at the time of his death, was one of the best known and most highly esteemed farmers in the North of Scotland. He married Margaret, daughter of Archibald Wallace, Esq. of Conrick, in Dumfriesshire, and died on the 14th of June, 1877, leaving issue—

*a*1. Margaret Wallace.

*a*2. Farquhar, in India.

*a*3. Christian Isabella Stewart married, in 1894, R. D. Tipping, in India, with issue—Richard Percy Macrae.

*a*4. Archibald Wallace.

*a*5. Fanny.

*a*6. Donald John.

*a*7. William Alexander Mackinnon.

*a*8. Agnes Wallace.

b. Helen Elizabeth Grant, born 13th of March, 1828, married Farquhar Finlayson, of Rothesay, with issue—Christina Madeline; Duncan; Mary Catherine.

c. Madeline, born 18th of April, 1832, married Alexander Macrae, as already mentioned.[1]

7. ISABELLA, married John Macrae, as already mentioned.[2]

8. JANET, married John, son of Duncan Macrae, farmer, Conchra, with issue at least one daughter, Mary, who married a Mr Fraser, with issue.

9. CATHERINE, married Alexander Maclennan Culagan, Lochcarron, with issue—

[1] Page 205.   [2] Page 212.

a. John, died in Trinidad. He was married and left issue, a son and a daughter.

b. Farquhar, lived in Lochcarron, where he died in 1869, aged fifty-eight years. He married Janet, daughter of Kenneth Mackenzie, Morvich, by his wife, Anne Macrae, and left issue—

*b*1. Alexander, now living at Craig House, Lochcarron. He married Catherine, daughter of Murdoch Finlayson, as already mentioned,[1] and has issue—Farquhar, now a Medical Student at the University of Aberdeen; Agnes; John; Murdo Roderick Finlayson; Duncan Lachlan.

*b*2. Hannah, married James Macleod in Australia.

*b*3. John, died in Australia in 1869.

*b*4. Lachlan, in Queensland.

*b*5. Kenneth, at Monar.

*b*6. Annie, married to Joseph Williams in Hereford. *b*7. Catherine.

c. Christopher, died in Australia, was married, and left issue.

d. Duncan, died in Australia, unmarried.

e. Lachlan, living at Clunes, Victoria, in Australia, is married, and has a large family.

[1] Page 211.

CHAPTER XV.

Finlay, son of Christopher of Aryugan —Settled in Lochcarron.
—Fionnla nan Gobhar.—His Family.—Donald Macrae of
Achintee.—Ruling Elder of the Parish of Lochcarron.—His
Marriage and Descendants.

X. FINLAY,[1] son of Christopher of Aryugan,
and tenth in descent from Fionnla Dubh Mac
Gillechriosd, left Kintail and settled in the neighbourhood of New Kelso, in Lochcarron, and there is
no reasonable doubt that this was the Finlay Macrae
known in Lochcarron as Fionnla nan Gobhar (Finlay
of the goats), who lived at a place called Frassan,
near New Kelso, during the first half of the eighteenth
century, and was a man of means.   This identity is
further confirmed by the traditions of Fionnla nan
Gobhar's descendants, who claim Christopher of
Aryugan as their ancestor.   Fionnla nan Gobhar
married, and left issue at least two sons—

1. DUNCAN, of whom next.

2. FINLAY, who married, and had issue at least
one son, Duncan, who married Rebecca Macaulay,
and had a daughter, Mary

XI. DUNCAN, son of Finlay, married, and had
issue—

1. DONALD, of whom next.

[1] Page 125.

P

2. CHRISTOPHER, who emigrated to North Carolina about the end of the last century, and was living there in 1810. He married, and had issue at least one son and several daughters.

XII. DONALD lived at Achintee in Lochcarron, He is said to have been a man of " great piety and much force of character," and was ruling elder of the parish of Lochcarron under the ministry of the well-known Mr Lachlan Mackenzie. He married Mary, daughter of his cousin, Duncan Macrae, who is mentioned above, and by her had issue as below. He died on the 3rd of January, 1821, aged eighty years, and was buried in Lochcarron.

1 DUNCAN, who died unmarried in 1804.

2. THE REV. FINLAY, born in 1792. He was educated at King's College, Aberdeen, graduated Master of Arts in 1812, and became minister of North Uist in 1818. "Amid the bitterness and strife engendered by the veto controversy he was accused of maintaining erroneous opinions in a sermon preached at the opening of the Synod (of Glenelg). The case came before the General Assembly (of the Church of Scotland) in 1841, who referred it to a committee, who reported on the 31st of May, unanimously, that unsoundness of doctrine was not chargeable."[1] He was not only acquitted of the charge of heresy, but was also complimented by the Assembly on the general ability of the sermon. He continued minister of North Uist until his death on the 15th of May, 1858. He married on the 16th of July, 1824, Isabella Maria (born 1800, died in

---

[1] Fasti Ecclesiæ Scoticanæ.

Edinburgh 1882), daughter of Colonel Alexander Macdonald of Lynedale, Skye, and Balranald, North Uist, and by her had issue—

a. Donald, born at Baleloch, in North Uist, in August, 1825. He married in March, 1851, Annabella, daughter of Captain David Miller, Royal Marines, of Pow, Perthshire, and died in 1893, leaving issue—

*a*1. David Miller, born in 1851, and died unmarried in 1893.

*a*2. Annabella Douglas, born in 1853.

*a*3. Isabella Maria, born in 1855, died in childhood.

*a*4. John Miller, born in 1857, died, unmarried, in 1882.

*a*5. Elizabeth Anne, born in November, 1859, married, in 1887, Charles Gordon Mackay, M.B., Lochcarron, with issue.

*a*6. Alexandrina Cornfute, born in November, 1859, married, in 1887, John Tolmie,[1] of H.M. Register House, Edinburgh.

*a*7. Isabella, born in 1861, died in infancy.

*a*8. Finlay Alexander, born in 1863, of the firm of Jackson, Gourlay, Taylor, & Macrae, Chartered Accountants, London and Glasgow. He married, in 1886, his cousin, Mildred Augusta, daughter of Surgeon-Major Alexander Macrae, of whom below, with issue—(1) Florence Annabella, born in 1887; (2) Rita Mildred, born in 1888; (3) Dorothy Mary, born in 1890; (4) John Finlay Noel, born in 1891; (5) Nina Elizabeth, born in 1893.

*a*9. Mary Jane Harris, born in 1865.

[1] Page 100.

*a*10. Caroline Isabella Craigdaillie, born in 1867, married Percy Maclean Rogers, London, with issue.

*a*11. Somerled James, born in 1870, died unmarried, in 1893.

b. Alexander, born at Baleloch, in North Uist, in 1828, a Doctor of Medicine. He was surgeon in the Army, first in the Ninety-Third Highlanders, and afterwards in the Ninth Lancers, with which regiment he served in the Indian Mutiny. He was afterwards promoted Surgeon-Major of the Ninety-Seventh Regiment, and died in London on his return from India, in May, 1862. He married, in 1851, Florence, daughter of Dr William Henry Maclean of the Royal Hospital, Greenwich, with issue—

*b*1. Lachlan, born in 1858, married, with issue.

*b*2. Mildred Augusta, born in 1859, married her cousin, Finlay Alexander, as mentioned above.

*b*3. Eva Florence Impey, born in 1862, married, in 1894, Thomas Southwood Bush, Bath.

c. Duncan, born at Vallay, in North Uist, in 1829, went to Australia, was married, and died in 1866, leaving issue, two sons, Duncan and Finlay.

d. John Alexander, born at Vallay, in 1832. He succeeded his father as minister of North Uist, and died unmarried in 1896.

e. James Andrew, born at Vallay in 1834, Major in the Inverness Highland Light Infantry, died unmarried in 1873.

f. Jane Ann Elizabeth, born at Vallay in 1838, married Captain Edward William Hawes, R.N., who served in the Crimean War and died in December, 1874, and by whom she had issue :—Isabella Georgina

Emily; Mary Margaret; Elizabeth Alexandrina Macdonald.

g. Godfrey Alexander, born at Vallay in 1840,
a Doctor of Medicine, died unmarried in Edinburgh
in 1884.

3. CHRISTOPHER, who in his youth was a great
favourite of the Rev. Lachlan Mackenzie, succeeded
to his father's farm, and in 1842 became tacksman
of Glenmore, in Kishorn, where he lived for many
years.   He was extensively engaged in cattle dealing,
and was the first man who sold cattle on the present
site of the Muir of Ord Market.   He married
Margaret, daughter of John Gillanders, of Kishorn,
and by her had issue as below.   Christopher died
on the 5th of October, 1875, aged over eighty years.
His wife died on the 26th of July in the same year,
aged seventy-five, and both were buried in Lochcarron.

a. Mary, married John Maclennan, and succeeded
to her father's farm at Achintee.   She has issue—.

*a*1. Duncan, married with issue.

*a*2. Anne, married Alexander Maclennan, with
issue.

*a*3. John, died while studying at the University.

*a*4. Christopher.

*a*5. Christina, married, with issue.

b Flora, married Alexander Mackenzie, with
numerous issue, one of whom is the Rev. Colin
Mackenzie, of the Free Church, St Ninians, Stirling.

c. Margaret, married Kenneth Macdonald, factor
for Lord Dunmore, in Harris.   She died on the 22nd
October, 1863, without issue.

d. Rebecca, died unmarried in Liverpool.

e. Donald, a Doctor of Medicine, of The Firs, Beckenham, Kent, and a Justice of the Peace for the county of Inverness. He married on the 2nd of June, 1874, Harriet Parker Garth, daughter of Arthur Michel, Esq., of Eaton Square, London, with issue, one daughter.

Emily Elizabeth Mary, married, on the 15th of September, 1897, Edward Oliver Kirlew, B A., of Christ Church, Oxford.

f. Jane, married William Coghill, of the Royal Engineers, without surviving issue.

g. John, died in New Zealand on the 12th of July, 1895.

h Kate ; *i.* Isabella.

4. JOHN, a farmer at Achintee, married Kate Maciver, and died in 1835, leaving issue—

a. Donald, born in 1826, succeeded to his father's farm. " He was a religious and a highly respected man." He married in 1850 Margery, daughter of Donald Macdonald, Lochcarron, by whom he had issue as below. He died in 1887.

*a*1. John, died young.

*a*2. Mary, born in 1852, married, in 1877, John Mackenzie, Lochalsh.

*a*3. Donald, born in 1854, was a schoolmaster at Dunblane, and died in 1879.

*a*4. John, born on the 25th of June, 1856, ordained minister of the Free Church at Aberfeldy in 1884 He married on the 20th of April, 1887, Catherine Campbell Mackerchar, with issue, Donald, born on the 16th of September, 1888.

*a*5. Margaret, born in 1858, died in 1867.

*a*6. Catherine, born in 1861, married, in 1882, to Murdoch Mackenzie, Auchnashellach, Lochcarron.

*a*7. Isabella, born in 1865, married, in 1894, to John Stewart, Slumbay, Lochcarron.

*a*8. Alexander, born in June, 1867, a minister of the Free Presbyterian Church at Kames, in Argyll-shire.

*a*9. William, born in 1869, succeeded to his father's farm at Achintee.

*a*10. Margaret Isabella, born in October, 1873.

b. Alexander, born in 1828, went to Australia in 1852, settled near Ballarat, and died in 1890. He was married, and left a large family.

c. Mary, born in 1830, died young.

5. THE REV. DONALD, born on the 12th of January, 1801. He was educated at King's College, Aberdeen, and graduated Master of Arts in 1823. He became minister of Poolewe, in Ross-shire, in 1830. At the Disruption of the Church of Scotland in 1843, he cast in his lot with the Free Church, and was followed by his entire congregation. In 1845 he became minister of the Free Church at Kilmory in Arran, where he continued until his death on the 6th of August, 1868. He married on the 2nd of August, 1834, Jessie, daughter of the Rev. James Russell, M.A., of Gairloch, and by her had issue—

a. Mary Johanna, married the Rev. John Stewart, for many years Free Church minister of Pitlochry, who died in 1882, and by whom she had issue—

*a*1. Jessie Russell.

*a*2. Alexander, in South Africa.

*a*3. Donald Macrae, a Presbyterian minister in Melbourne.

*a*4. Margaret, married James Arthur Thompson, Lecturer in Biology in Edinburgh University.

*a*5. William, in the United States.

*a*6. Ella ; *a*7. Douglas ; *a*8. Ian.

b. Donald, a medical practitioner in the city of Council Bluffs, Iowa, U.S.A., was for three years Mayor of that city.   He married Charlotte Angelica, daughter of Joseph Bouchette, Surveyor-General of Canada, with issue, one son, Donald, who is also a medical practitioner, in partnership with his father, and is married, with issue.

c. Isabella, died young in 1855.

d. Jessie Russell, married the Rev. John Teed Maclean, minister of the Free Gaelic Church, Govan, Glasgow.   She died in 1888, leaving issue.

e. James Russell, a farmer near Council Bluffs, U.S.A., married, with issue.

f. Rev. John Farquhar, sometime minister of the Free Church, Cockpen, near Edinburgh, and afterwards of the Free Church, St Andrews.   He is now minister of the Toorak Presbyterian Church, Melbourne, one of the most important Presbyterian Churches in Australia.   He married Bertha, daughter of Thomas Livingstone Learmmouth, of Park Hall, Polmont, with issue—Frederick ; Norman ; Ethel ; Muriel ; Marjory Bertha.

g. Rev. Duncan, now minister of the Presbyterian Church, Wood Green, London.   He married Alice, daughter of Alfred Hawkins, solicitor, London, with issue—Irene, died in childhood ; Russell Duncan ; Winifred Alice ; Kathleen Doris.

h. Finlay Alexander, now living at Wood Green,

London, married Myra, daughter of the Rev. Colin Campbell, minister of the parish of Lamlash, in Arran.

6. ANNE, married George Mackenzie, with issue.

7. JESSIE, married Finlay Matheson, a Senator of Canada, with issue.

8. REBECCA, married Kenneth Macleod, with issue.

9. MARY, married in 1806, Christopher Macdonald, Lonellan, Kintail, with issue—

a. Kate, married, first, in 1826, Alexander Macrae, shipowner, Dornie, with issue.

a1. Donald, born in 1827, died in Australia.

a2. Margaret Catherine, married in 1859, Alexander Bremner, of the Inland Revenue, now in Dunblane, with issue, three sons, one of whom is Dr A. M. Bremner, Alyth, Perthshire.

Kate, married, secondly, in 1841, John Murdoch, of the Inland Revenue, with issue—

a3. John; a4. Mary; a5. Christopher; a6. Caroline.

b. Duncan, born in 1809, died in 1831.

c. Mary, married Roderick Mackenzie, shipowner, Shieldaig, with issue—

c1. Isabella, married Duncan Macrae, Dornie, with issue.

c2. Mary, married Christopher Macdonald, New Zealand, with issue.

c3. Anne.

c4. Christopher, merchant, Shieldaig.

c5. Margaret, married Roderick Macrae, Lochcarron.

d. Christina, married, in 1841, Charles Mackenzie, Lonellan, with issue—

*d*1. Alexander Colin, born in 1842, schoolmaster, Maryburgh, near Dingwall, Major, First Volunteer Battalion Seaforth Highlanders, and a Justice of the Peace for Ross and Cromarty.

*d*2. Christopher Duncan, born 1843, now in business in Middlesbrough, Yorkshire, married, in 1870, Margaret Sclanders, daughter of John Macmillan, Glasgow, with issue.

*d*3. Annabella, married, in 1875, John Bell, at Bishop Auckland, Durham, with issue.

*d*4. Mary, died in 1894; *d*5. Margaret.

e. Finlay of Drudaig, a Justice of the Peace for the County of Ross, married, in 1860, Jessie Margaret, daughter of Lieutenant John Macdonald, North Uist, and died in 1892, leaving issue—

*e*1. John Christopher, a planter in India.

*e*2. Johanna Matheson.

*e*3. Alexina Flora, married Dr Robert Moodie, of Stirling, with issue.

*e*4. Mary Catherine, married James Gerrard, of Coorg, in India.

*e*5. Jemima Margaret.

*e*6. Duncan Alexander, died young.

*e*7. James Andrew, died young.

f. Alexander, born in 1820, drowned in 1834.

CHAPTER XVI.

Governor James Macrae of Madras.—Tradition about his Ancestry.
—His Humble Birth.—Boyhood.—Goes to Sea.—Mission to
Sumatra —Governor of Madras.—Return to Scotland.—His
Death —His Heirs.—Their Marriages and Descendants.

THERE have been very few men who had a more
romantic or a more successful and honourable career
than Governor James Macrae of Madras, who, though
by birth a native of the County of Ayr, is sometimes
claimed as a descendant of the Macraes of Kintail.
There is a Kintail tradition to the effect that some
time during the first half of the seventeenth century a
certain John Macrae, known in Kintail as Ian Dubh
Mac Ian Oig[1] (Black John, son of John the younger),
migrated to the south and settled for some time at
Greenock, that either he or one of his sons afterwards moved farther south to the town of Ayr or
its neighbourhood, and that he was the grandfather
of Governor James Macrae of Madras. At the same
time, the name Macrae or M'Cra appears more than
once in connection with Ayr [2] many generations
before the time to which this tradition refers, and it
is quite possible that, notwithstanding the Kintail

[1] Pages 189-190.

[2] In the Register of the Great Seal, 25th August, 1534, mention is made
of Thomas M'Cra, Sergeant or Constable of the Sheriff of Ayr, but the name
occurs in Ayr as far back as 1477.

tradition, Governor Macrae may have belonged to an old Ayrshire family of that name. But, on the other hand, it may be mentioned that, besides this Kintail tradition, there are traditions[1] also among other families of the name to the effect that they are descended from certain Macraes who left Kintail and settled in the south-west of Scotland about the middle of the seventeenth century.

Of Governor Macrae's ancestry, however, nothing beyond the Kintail tradition appears to be known. He was born in the neighbourhood of Ayr about the year 1677. His parents were in poor circumstances, and at an early age James was employed in herding cattle. He lost his father while still very young, and his mother then moved to a small thatched cottage in one of the suburbs of Ayr. Here she earned her living as a washerwoman, while her son added to the earnings by serving as an errand boy in the town. By some means or other he contrived to acquire an education—perhaps through the kindness of a fiddler of the town of Ayr called Hugh Macguire, and about 1692 went to sea. It is generally supposed that he was not heard of again in Ayr until he returned home after an absence of about forty years. In 1720 he is mentioned as Captain Macrae, then serving under the Honourable East India Company, and conducting a special mission to the English settlement on the West Coast of Sumatra. So successfully did he fulfil the object of that mission, and deal with certain commercial abuses which prevailed there at the time,

---

1 These traditions are again referred to in Chapters XX., XXI.

that he was appointed Deputy-Governor of Fort St David, with reversion of the Governorship of Fort-George. He was afterwards appointed Governor of the Presidency of Madras, and assumed charge of office on the 15th of January, 1725. His rule is said to have been stern and arbitrary, but highly acceptable to the Company, as he reformed many abuses, reduced expenditure, and greatly increased the Company's revenues. The first Protestant Mission was inaugurated at Madras during his rule in 1726, and in the following year a general survey of the town and suburbs was made under his direction. He is said to have been emphatically a commercial Governor, effecting fiscal reforms on all hands, correcting various abuses and greatly developing and increasing the commerce of the Presidency, while many improvements of various kinds were carried out as the result of his intelligent and energetic policy. The old records of Madras reveal many facts most creditable to the rule of Governor James Macrae, who thus occupies a high and honourable place in the long list of eminent statesmen who have made our Indian Empire what it is. He resigned the Governorship on the 14th of May, 1730, and on the 21st of January, 1731, set sail for Scotland.

On his return to Scotland he found himself a perfect stranger, but a diligent search led to the discovery of some relatives or friends, whom he treated with great kindness, and among whom he made a liberal distribution of his wealth. He bought several estates in the West of Scotland, and fixed his own residence at Orangefield, in Ayrshire. He was admitted a

burgess of Ayr on the 1st of August, 1733, and in
1735 he presented Glasgow with a bronze statue of
William III.   He died on the 21st of July, 1744,
and was buried in Monktoun Churchyard, where he
is commemorated by a monument which was erected
in 1750. Governor Macrae died unmarried, and the
exact degree of relationship between himself and the
family which he adopted appears to be somewhat
doubtful.   They were the grandchildren of Hugh
Macguire, to whose kindness, as already mentioned,
Governor Macrae is said to have been indebted for
such education as he received in his childhood, and
they are also mentioned as his sister's children.   It
is quite possible that a son of Hugh Macguire, also
called Hugh, may have married Governor Macrae's
sister.   In that case, then, both descriptions might
be correct.[1]

On obtaining some information about her,
Governor Macrae is said to have written to his
sister, Mrs Hugh Macguire, at Ayr, enclosing a
large sum of money, and offering to provide for
herself and family.   The surprise of Mrs Macguire and her husband, who is said to have
been a poor man, earning his living partly as
a carpenter and partly as a fiddler, was, of course,
unbounded, and "they are said to have given
way to their delight by indulging in a luxury

---

[1] The writer of the article on Governor Macrae in the *Dictionary of
National Biography* speaks of the family he adopted simply as the grandchildren of his old benefactor, Hugh Macguire, but in J Talboys Wheeler's
Madras in the Olden Time (a work to which the author is indebted for most of
the information contained in this chapter) they are mentioned as the children
of Governor Macrae's sister, Mrs Hugh Macguire,

which will serve to illustrate both their ideas of happiness, and the state of poverty in which they had been living. They procured a loaf of sugar and a bottle of brandy, and scooping out a hole in the sugar loaf they poured in the brandy, and supped up the sweetened spirit with spoons until the excess of their felicity compelled them to close their eyes in peaceful slumber."[1] Governor Macrae made liberal provisions for the Macguire family, as follows :—

1. The eldest daughter married Mr Charles Dalrymple, Sheriff-Clerk of Ayr, and received the estate of Orangefield.

2. MARGARET married Mr James Erskine, who received the estate of Alva, and was afterwards elevated to the bench under the title of Lord Alva.

3. ELIZABETH married William Cunningham, thirteenth Earl of Glencairn, in August, 1744, and died at Coats, near Edinburgh, on the 24th of June, 1801, leaving issue—

a. William, Lord Kilmaurs, died unmarried in 1768.

b. James, fourteenth Earl of Glencairn, died unmarried on the 30th of January, 1791. This was the Earl of Glencairn so frequently referred to in the works of Robert Burns, and on whose death the poet wrote his well-known "Lament for James, Earl of Glencairn."

c. John, fifteenth and last Earl of Glencairn, born in 1750, was an officer in the 14th Dragoons, but afterwards took orders in the Church of England. He married, in 1785, Lady Isabella Erskine,

[1] J. Talboys Wheeler's *Madras in the Olden Time.*

second daughter of the tenth Earl of Buchan, and widow of William Leslie Hamilton. He died without issue on the 24th of September, 1796, when the title became extinct.

d. Harriet married Sir Alexander Don, Bart. of Newton-Don, Roxburgh, and had a son—Sir Alexander Don, Bart., who succeeded to the barony of Ochiltree on the death of his grandmother, the Countess of Glencairn, in 1801.

4. The fourth daughter married James Macrae, of whom next.

JAMES MACRAE, who married the fourth daughter of Hugh Macguire, received the barony of Houston, in Renfrewshire. He appears to have been a young gentleman of doubtful origin, said to have been the nephew of Governor Macrae, but supposed to have been his natural son.[1] He was a Captain in the Army, and on the 4th of April, 1758, was served heir general to Hugh Macguire of Drumdow, who is there mentioned as his father, and who died in 1753. Captain Macrae died on the 16th of October, 1760, leaving issue, at least, one son—

JAMES, of Houston, and afterwards of Holmains, in Dumfriesshire, was also a Captain in the Army. In consequence of an insult which Captain Macrae received, or thought he had received, one night at the theatre door in Edinburgh, from one of the

---

[1] This account of James Macrae is from J Talboys Wheeler's *Madras in the Olden Time*, but the writer of the article in the *Dictionary of National Biography* says that he was the son of Hugh Macguire (in which case he was probably the nephew of Governor Macrae), and that he adopted the name Macrae as one of Governor Macrae's heirs. This would seem to be borne out by his service of heirship, and in that case he could not, of course, have married a daughter of Hugh Macguire, as stated by J. Talboys Wheeler.

servants of Sir George Ramsay, Bart. of Bamff, in Perthshire, a quarrel arose between Sir George and himself. The quarrel led to a duel between them on Musselburgh Links, in which Sir George Ramsay was killed, in 1790. After this Captain Macrae appears to have lived abroad. He married, about 1787, Maria Cecilia, daughter of Judge Le Maistre, of the Supreme Court of Judicature in India, and by her, who died in 1806, had issue as below. Captain Macrae died in France on the 10th of January, 1820.

1. JAMES CHARLES, Esq. of Holmains, J.P. and D.L., was born on the 2nd of January, 1791. He married on the 26th of June, 1820, Margaret Elizabeth, daughter of Sir Alexander Grierson, Bart. Mr Macrae sold Holmains, and went to live at Reading, where he died about 1876. He appears to have been the last representative in the male line of this family.

2. MARIE LE MAISTRE married J. P. Davis, Esq., of London.

\

CHAPTER XVII.

A Romance of Sheriffmuir.—The Rev. James Macrae of Sauchieburn.—The Rev. David Macrae of Oban, and afterwards of
Glasgow.—The Rev. David Macrae of Gourock, and afterwards
of Dundee.

AMONG the Macraes who fought at the battle of
Sheriffmuir, a certain young man, covered with
wounds and apparently dead, with his sword still
in his grasp, was found on the field after the battle.
On its being discovered that life was still in him, he
was taken to a neighbouring farm house, where he
was kindly cared for until his wounds were healed.
Instead of returning home he settled in the neighbourhood and married the farmer's daughter.   By
her he had at least one son,

DUNCAN, who joined the Highland army in
1745 on its way south under Prince Charlie.   Duncan married and had at least one son,

JAMES, who became a carpenter in the Perthshire Highlands, married and had issue, at least one
son,

JAMES, who was trained for the ministry of the
Established Church, but, owing to his objections to
the Confession of Faith, left and became an Independent minister at Sauchieburn, in the parish of
Fettercairn, in 1775.   During the latter part of the

century he made considerable stir in the Scottish ecclesiastical world as a vigorous and able champion of religious freedom and equality.   He was in many respects considerably in advance of his times.   His preaching is said to have been evangelical and full of power, and people flocked to his church from all the adjacent parishes.   After a long and honourable course of labour he was forced by the increasing infirmities of old age to resign his pastorate, and shortly afterwards died at Laurencekirk in 1813. He had married Jean Low of Fettercairn in 1777, by whom he had a large family, one of whom was

DAVID, born on the 14th of October, 1796.   He was educated at Aberdeen University, and graduated M.A. in 1820.   For some time he was teacher of Mathematics in one of the schools of Aberdeen, where he had as one of his pupils the late Professor John Stuart Blackie of Edinburgh University.   He joined the Presbyterian (Secession) Church in Aberdeen; was trained for the ministry of that denomination, and on the 6th of March, 1827, was ordained minister of the Secession (now United Presbyterian) Church at Lathones, in Fife.   Here he laboured for eleven years, when he accepted a call from the congregation of the United Presbyterian Church at Oban, and was inducted there on the 25th of April, 1838.   At Oban Mr Macrae engaged in many important labours, and the energy and ability with which he set himself to work among the people during the famine which visited the Highlands in 1845-47, had the effect not only of providing for the poor during a time of great trial and destitution, but also of creating habits of industry and independence among them. The memory of his good works is warmly cherished by the people of that district, and many anecdotes of the earnestness and saintliness of his life may still be heard among them. Mr Macrae continued at Oban until 1852, when, at the urgent solicitation of the United Presbyterian Presbytery of Glasgow, he transferred the scene of his labours to that city. He commenced his work in Main Street, Gorbals, where he built up a large and flourishing church, and laboured with much success until 1873, when he moved along with his congregation to a new church in Elgin Street. The jubilee of his ministry was celebrated in Glasgow amid many signs of respect, gratitude, and devotion by his congregation and numerous friends in April, 1876. He died on the 19th of July, 1881, and was buried at Craigton, Glasgow. He had married on the 15th of April, 1828, Margaret, daughter of Gilbert Falconer, of Aberdeen, and sister of Forbes Falconer, the distinguished Orientalist, and Professor of Oriental Languages in King's College, London, and by her (who died on the 29th of November, 1874, aged seventy-four years) had issue as below—

1. JAMES GILBERT, born at the Manse of Lathones in 1833; was at Umballa, in India, at the time of the Mutiny. He married, but without issue, and died in London on the 22nd of September, 1886.

2. JANE FALCONER, born at the Manse of Lathones in 1835. At a pic-nic party on the Island of Kerrara, in Argyllshire, on the 30th of July, 1875, she slipped down a steep place, ruptured a blood vessel,

and died on the hillside.   A cross was erected to
mark the spot where she expired.

3. REV. DAVID, who is now one of the best known
and ablest of the ministers of Scotland, was born at
the Manse of Lathones on the 9th of August, 1837,
and taken to Oban when he was only seven months
old.   At Oban he spent his boyhood, and received
the rudiments of a liberal education, which was
afterwards continued at the Universities of Glasgow
and Edinburgh.   In 1859 he was lamed for life by
a fall on Arthur Seat.   A serious illness followed,
but he was able to resume his studies the following
year   While going through the Theological course
of the United Presbyterian Hall in Edinburgh,
he travelled abroad between the Sessions, and to
those early travels he no doubt owes in some degree
the sympathetic and enlightened knowledge of men
and things which has formed so marked a feature
both of his public life and of his writings.   He was
ordained minister of the United Presbyterian Church
at Gourock, in Renfrewshire, on the 9th of April,
1872.   He very soon came into prominence as a
leading man in his own denomination, and in 1873
he commenced a movement which resulted in a
reform of the United Presbyterian Theological Hall.
In 1876 he commenced another movement for the
Revision of the Confession of Faith, which led to
the adoption of what is now known in Scotland as
the Declaratory Act, first by his own denomination,
afterwards by the Presbyterian Church of England,
and more recently by the Free Church of Scotland.
For going further still, and demanding a right to set

aside the dogma of eternal punishment, Mr Macrae
was expelled from the United Presbyterian Church,
at a special meeting of its Supreme Court in Edinburgh, in May, 1879. In the meantime he had been
called to Dundee as successor to the Rev. George
Gilfillan, who died in 1878, and, on being expelled
from his own denomination, the call was renewed,
Gilfillan's congregation declaring itself ready to leave
the denomination with him. The call was accepted,
and Mr Macrae commenced his ministry in Dundee
in October, 1879, when the Rev. Baldwin Brown,
Chairman of the Congregational Union of England
and Wales, travelled specially from London to
preach the induction sermon. In Dundee Mr
Macrae organised a large congregation of more
than thirteen hundred members, built the Gilfillan
Memorial Church, and laboured there for eighteen
years. From this ministry he retired in November,
1897, and is now living in Glasgow. When leaving
Dundee, he was presented with a remarkable testimonial by his congregation, and with a public address
from the citizens, which was presented to him in the
Town Hall by the Lord Provost. In 1880, and subsequently, he took a leading part in the movement
for the maintenance of Scotland's National Rights, including the petition addressed to the Queen in 1897,
and signed by over one hundred thousand Scottish
people of all ranks and classes, protesting against
"the violation of the Treaty of Union in the un-
warrantable substitution of the terms 'England' and
'English' for 'Britain' and 'British,' even in official
utterance and in treaties with foreign powers." Mr

Macrae is the author of numerous books and pamphlets, including *The Americans at Home*, originally published in two volumes by Edmonston & Douglas, Edinburgh, giving the results of his observations during a long tour in America, from Canada to the Gulf States, at the close of the war, and when the coloured people had newly emerged from slavery, —and recording also his interviews with Longfellow, Emerson, Lowell, Henry Ward Beecher, General Grant, Confederate General Lee, and other noted soldiers both of the North and South. This book, which was most favourably reviewed by the press, both at home and in America, has passed through several additions, and has been translated into French and Italian. Amongst his other works are *George Harrington; Dunvarlich; Diogenes among the D.D.'s*, a book of ecclesiastical burlesques, beginning with the " Trial of Norman Macleod for the murder of Moses Law;" *Quaint Sayings of Children; Voices of the Poets; Reminiscences of George Gilfillan; Lectures on Robert Burns; New Parables;* &c. Mr Macrae married, on the 23rd of February, 1875, Williamina Burton Craig, without issue.

4. MARGARET FORBES, born in Oban in 1839, a lady of "rare gifts and far-reaching sympathies." She was intimately associated in after years with her brother, David, in his work, and died suddenly of heart disease at Maryland House, Glasgow, on the 20th of October, 1881.

CHAPTER XVIII.

The Macraes of Wilmington.—Connection with the Macraes of
Kintail.—Ruari Donn.—His Descendants.—General William
Macrae.

ABOUT the year 1770, a certain Roderick Macrae
emigrated from Kintail to America, and landed at
Wilmington, in North Carolina. He was only one
of many who left Kintail for America at that time,
but he was a man of importance among them, and
his descendants have since occupied a prominent
and honourable place in the affairs of his adopted
country. What his exact connection with the main
stock of the Clan may have been is not fully known,[1]
but he was closely related to the Rev. Donald
Macrae,[2] the last Episcopalian Minister of Kintail.
He may have been a son of Alexander, eldest son of
the Rev. Donald, or he may have been a son of Hugh,[3]
youngest brother of the Rev. Donald. At all events,
Hugh is said to have had a son, Roderick, who went
to America about 1770 or 1774, and he is the only
Roderick Macrae of whom there appears to be any

---

[1] An American account of the Macraes of Wilmington says that they are
descended from a certain Rev. Alexander Macrae of Kintail, who had two sons
killed at Culloden. This, of course, is incorrect, and is clearly a mistake for
the Rev. Donald Macrae who had two sons killed at Sheriffmuir.

[2] Page 76.   [3] Page 132.

record as having gone from Kintail to America about that time. The Roderick who landed at Wilmington, and of whom below, is said to have been accompanied by a brother and two sisters, viz.:—

PHILIP (or Finlay), who is said to have served as a Lieutenant in the Army of Prince Charles in 1745, and who cherished such a hatred of the English, in consequence of the atrocities of the Duke of Cumberland, that he would never speak the English language, but spoke only Gaelic as long as he lived.

MARY, who married a Macrae (?) with issue, and settled in Moore County.

CATHERINE, who married Donald Macrae, who settled with his family in Georgia, where their descendants still live.

RODERICK, called Ruari Donn (Brown Roderick), landed at Wilmington, about 1770, as mentioned above. Thence he proceeded to Chatham County, and lived for a time at Pocket Creek. Soon afterwards he moved to Crane's Creek, in the same County, and eventually settled at Little Rockfish, a few miles south of Fayetteville, in Cumberland County, North Carolina. Roderick married, first, Catherine Burke, apparently a widow, and by her had issue—

1. COLIN, of whom below.

2. JOHN, settled at or near Augusta, in Georgia. He married, and left issue.

Roderick married, secondly, Christina Murchison, with issue.

3. JOHN, who was for a number of years teller of

the Commercial Bank of Wilmington, and died unmarried in 1863.

COLIN, son of Roderick, was a farmer at Little Rockfish, where all his family were born. He was a man of sound sense and good education, was for many years a prominent Magistrate of his County, and " was esteemed by all who knew him as an independent, upright, and honest man." He married Christian, daughter of Duncan Black, and sister of John Black, some time Sheriff of Cumberland County, by whom he had issue as below. He died at a very advanced age on the 8th of July, 1865—

1. ALEXANDER, of whom below.

2. ARCHIBALD, born on the 17th of January, 1798.

3. ISABELLA, born on the 9th of January, 1800.

4. DONALD, born on the 19th of January, 1802.

5. ANNE, born on the 26th of January, 1804.

6. JOHN, born on the 26th of July, 1806, died in 1883.

7. CATHERINE, born on the 6th of July, 1808.

8. RODERICK, born on the 11th of October, 1810, died in 1882.

ALEXANDER, son of Colin, was born at Little Rockfish, North Carolina, on the 26th of March, 1796. When he was about eighteen years of age he moved to Wilmington, where he engaged in various pursuits. He was for many years president of the Wilmington and Weldon Railroad Company, and being a man of great energy and much public spirit was connected with most of the affairs of Wilmington during his long, useful, and honourable life. He volunteered as a private in the war of 1812-14, was soon made Sergeant, and was about to be promoted to a lieutenancy when the war ended. When the War of Secession broke out in 1861, although he was then sixty-five years of age, he was called upon because of his popularity and influence to raise a company to aid in the defence of Wilmington. So ready was the response to his appeal for recruits that instead of a company he raised a whole battalion, which became known as " Macrae's Battalion of Heavy Artillery," and which served under him with much distinction throughout the war. He died at Wilmington on the 27th of April, 1868.

Alexander married first, on the 30th of April, 1818, Amelia Ann, daughter of John Martin. She died on the 24th of August, 1831, leaving issue—

1. JOHN COLIN, born at Wilmington, on the 10th of March, 1819, was a Colonel in the Confederate Army, and died unmarried on the 9th of February, 1878.

2. ARCHIBALD, born at Smithville, on the 21st of September, 1820, was a Lieutenant in the United States Navy, and died on the 17th of November, 1855.

3. ALEXANDER, born at Wilmington, on the 1st of March, 1823, and died on the 18th of December, 1881. He married Elizabeth Chambers, with issue—

a. Caroline Amelia.

b. Elizabeth, married J. Fairfax Payne, with issue.

4. DONALD, born at Wilmington on the 14th of October, 1825, and died on the 15th of September, 1892. He married, first, Mary Savage, with issue—

a. Mary Savage, born on the 11th of December, 1851, and died on the 10th of May, 1896.

He married, secondly, Julia Norton, with issue—

b. Norton, died in childhood.

c. Agnes, born on the 20th of November, 1859, married Walter Linton Parsley, with issue—

*c*1. Julia, born on the 2nd of March, 1882.

*c*2. Anna, born on the 14th of January, 1886.

*c*3. Mary, born on the 25th of March, 1890, died in infancy.

*c*4. Walter Linton, born on the 12th of January, 1892, died on the 8th of December, 1897.

*c*5. Donald Macrae, born on the 5th of October, 1895.

d. Donald, born on the 3rd of May, 1861, now living at Wilmington, and by whom most of this information about the Macraes of Wilmington was communicated to the author in 1898.

e. Julia, born on the 15th of December, 1862, died in infancy.

f. Hugh, born on the 30th of March, 1865, now living in Wilmington. He married Rena Nelson, with issue—

*f*1. Dorothy, born on the 26th of December, 1891.

*f*2. Nelson, born on the 5th of June, 1893.

*f*3. Agnes, born on the 7th of October, 1897.

5. HENRY, born at Wilmington on the 8th of May, 1829. He was a Major in the Confederate Army, and died on the 22nd of April, 1863. He was married and left issue—Alice; Mary.

Alexander married, secondly, on the 15th of March, 1832, Anna Jane, daughter of John Martin (his first wife's father) and his wife, Zilpah Mac-Clammy, and by her, who died on the 17th of October, 1842, aged thirty-five years, had issue—

6. ROBERT BURNS, born at Wilmington on the 15th of December, 1832. He was a Major in the Confederate Army, and died on the 28th of December, 1864. He was married, but left no issue.

7. WILLIAM, born at Wilmington on the 9th of September, 1834. He was a Brigadier-General in the Confederate Army, and one of its most distinguished soldiers. At an early age he displayed great aptitude for mathematics and mechanics, and, having received an excellent education, he took up the profession of Civil Engineer. In this capacity he was employed for some time in surveying lines for projected railways in North and South Carolina, and also in Florida. On the outbreak of the war between North and South, in 1861, he volunteered as a private, but was soon elected Captain of a company of the Fifteenth North Carolina Regiment, which was placed at first in General Cobb's Brigade, and transferred the following year to General Cook's Brigade. Macrae was promoted Lieutenant-Colonel in 1862, Colonel in 1863, and Brigadier-General in August, 1864. His brigade consisted of five North Carolina regiments, and had already become famous in the war. Macrae never left it from the day he took over the command of it until the fighting ceased, with the surrender of General Lee, at Appomattox on the 9th of April, 1865. Under his command it attained the very highest degree of discipline and efficiency, and so unbounded was the confidence of the men in their

leader, that they considered no foe too numerous to be attacked, nor any position too strong to be assailed, if the order came from General William Macrae. He fought in almost all the great battles of the war, and was repeatedly complimented by General Lee in general orders for personal valour and able handling of his troops. At the battle of Malvern Hill, he led into action a regiment three hundred strong, and came out with only thirty-five. At the battle of Fredericksburg, he was posted on a hill under terrific fire, but held the ground though he lost nearly half his men. He was in the great battles of the Wilderness in May, 1863. At the battle of Ream's Station, on the 25th of August, 1864, he captured nine pieces of artillery and more men than he had in his own command. In April, 1865, when General Lee, with the remnants of his brave army, was attempting to make his way from Petersburg to the mountains, Macrae's Brigade covered the retreat near Farmville, and, while advancing towards Appomattox, where preparations for surrender were already being made, he attacked and drove off a Northern force which had fallen on the waggon trains. This is said to have been the last fight in Virginia, and his brigade was the last of the Confederate troops to stack arms and surrender. General Macrae was undoubtedly a soldier of the highest order, and a born leader of men, possessing in an eminent degree the power of imparting his own courage and enthusiasm to others. Though indifferent to danger himself, he was most careful of the lives of the soldiers who fought under him and were always ready to follow him with implicit trust.   He was a stern disciplinarian, yet not one murmur was ever heard in his brigade against the most stringent orders issued by him.   " It was said of his company, when he was Captain, that it was the best company in the regiment.   It was said of his brigade, when he was Brigadier-General, that it was the best brigade in the division.   It was truthfully said of Macrae that the higher he rose the more magnificent his character appeared." [1]

After the close of the war General Macrae filled some important appointments as superintendent of railways.   In these positions he displayed the highest order of ability, both as an engineer and as an organiser of men, and was widely known and universally respected as a man of humane and generous disposition, and wide and enlightened sympathies.   He died unmarried at Augusta, Georgia, on the 11th of February, 1882, and was buried at Wilmington. [2]

8. MARION, born on the 30th of November, 1835, died in childhood.

9. RODERICK, born on the 13th of September, 1838.

10. WALTER GWYN, born on the 27th of January, 1841, Captain in the Confederate Army.

Alexander married, as his third wife, Mary Herring, without issue, and as his fourth wife, Caroline A. Price, also without issue.

[1] Memorial Address on General William Macrae, delivered at Raleigh, North Carolina, by the Honourable B H. Bunn.

[2] The above sketch of the career of General William Macrae is compiled mainly from a " Memorial Address " delivered at Wilmington, North Carolina, on the 10th of May, 1890, by the Honourable Charles M Stedman, and from the Rev. David Macrae's book on " The Americans at Home,"

CHAPTER XIX.

Ian Mac Fhionnla Mhic Ian Bhuidhe.—A Sheriffmuir Warrior —
    His Descendants.

AMONG the Kintail warriors who fought at Sheriffmuir, and around whose names have gathered traditions of that fatal day, was a certain John Macrae,
known as Ian Mac Fhionnla Mhic Ian Bhuidhe
(John, son of Finlay, son of Yellow John).   In the
course of the fight, he received no fewer than seven
sword cuts on his head, and was left for dead on
the field.   But during the night he revived, and
resolved to make an effort, under cover of the darkness, to commence the homeward journey.   Having
had the misfortune to lose his shoes in the battle, he
began to search for another pair with which to equip
himself for the journey, and while thus engaged, came
across Duncan Mor Mac Alister,[1] who was lying near
him mortally wounded, and suffering from intense
thirst.   John recognised him by his voice, and having
no other means of fetching water, he took one of
Duncan's shoes and brought him a drink in it.
Before Duncan expired he gave John an account of
how he received his wounds, and this account is

1 Page 198,

still preserved in the traditions of the Clan.[1]
John recovered from his own wounds, and made
his way back to Kintail, where he lived to a
very advanced age. He was a great hunter, and
possessed a famous gun called An Nighean Alainn
(the beautiful daughter), which he always carried
with him, even in his old age, wherever he went.
On one occasion, as he was passing down the hills,
probably about Scatwell, on his way to Brahan
Castle, he observed a magnificent stag, which he shot
and carried on his shoulders all the way to Brahan
as a present to Seaforth. John was married, and
had issue at least one son,

DONALD, who was a soldier, and was killed in
battle in the Netherlands, probably at Fontenoy, in
1745. He was married, and left one son,

DUNCAN, who married, and left also an only son,

JOHN, who was twice married. By his first wife
he had a large family, all of whom went to Canada
and settled in the district of London. By his second
marriage also he had a family, the eldest of whom was

ALEXANDER, who lived at Dornie, and went
to Australia in 1852. He married in 1842 Christina,
daughter of Donald Macmillan (a connection of the
Torlysich family), and his wife, Helen, daughter of
Alexander, son of Farquhar Macrae, a younger son of
the Inverinate family,[2] and by her had issue—

[1] See chapter on legends and traditions of the clan.

[2] A comparison of dates leads to the conclusion that Alexander, the grandfather of the above-mentioned Christina, who married in 1842, could hardly
have been Alexander, son of Farquhar of Morvich, mentioned on page 84 as
having been present at the affair of Ath nan Muileach in 1721. He might
possibly have been a grandson of Farquhar of Morvich, that is to say, a son of
Farquhar Og (page 83), son of Farquhar of Morvich, younger son of Alexander
of Inverinate.

R

1. JOHN, living in Victoria, Australia, married, with issue, four sons and one daughter.

2. DONALD, living at Gelantipy, near Melbourne, and by whom the information contained in this chapter was communicated to the author in 1898. He is married to Agnes, daughter of Hector Armour of Stewarton, Ayrshire, without issue.

3. JOHN (the younger), living in Victoria.

4. DUNCAN, living in Victoria.

5. ALEXANDER, living in Victoria.

6. HELEN, married Angus Gillies, in Victoria, with issue.

McCrea.

CHAPTER XX.

The McCreas of Guernsey.—Descended from the Macraes of Kintail.—Connection with Ulster.—Emigrated to America.—Jane McCrea, "The Bride of Fort Edward."—Major Robert McCrea in the American War of Independence.—Governor of Chester Castle. — Connection with Guernsey. — His Marriages and Descendants.

THE McCreas of Guernsey are descended from the Macraes of Kintail, and their connection with the main branch of that Clan, though now lost, was known so recently as sixty or seventy years ago.[1] This connection is borne out, not only by the traditions of the family, but also by their personal appearance and features, which, in many instances, are strikingly typical of the Macraes of Kintail. The family tradition is that in the time of the Covenanters a certain Macrae of Kintail, who had adopted Puritanic principles, left his own country, where those principles were held in great disfavour, and eventually made his way to Ireland and settled among the Puritans of Ulster.   It may be pointed out

[1] Mrs Carey, who was born in 1819, and of whom mention is made hereafter, a daughter of Major Robert McCrea of Guernsey, was shown her own name on a family tree while on a visit as a young girl to the country house of a gentleman of the name Macrae in Scotland.   Mrs Carey died in 1878, and there does not appear at present to be any possibility of ascertaining who that gentleman was.

that this tradition is not at all without an appearance of probability, for, although no trace of Puritanism appears in Kintail until well into the eighteenth century, yet the Macraes of Kintail were closely associated with Dingwall during the whole of the Covenanter period, and as they were deeply interested in the political and religious movements of the time, it is not at all unlikely that some of them might come under the religious influence of the neighbouring family of Munro of Fowlis, who were among the most active supporters of the Covenanter movement in the Highlands, and to whom the chief Macrae families of the time were closely related.[1]   The adoption of Puritanic principles would, of course, be extremely distasteful not only to the Macrae vicars of Dingwall, but also to the leading Macrae families of Kintail, who were such ardent Episcopalians. A Macrae holding such principles could hardly feel comfortable among his own people, and would not unnaturally seek a new home among people to whom his views would be more acceptable than they were to his own countrymen. Whether it was the man, who left the Highlands, himself, or one of his descendants that afterwards went to America, is uncertain, but it was probably one of his descendants. At all events, some members of the family remained behind in Ulster, where their descendants are still living. There is a tradition among the McCreas of Guernsey that one of their ancestors took part in the defence of Londonderry during the famous siege

---

[1] Appendix F.—Alexander Macrae of Inverinate married as his second wife a granddaughter of Hector Munro of Fowlis, who died in 1603.

of 1689, but this ancestor may have been on the female side, as there is a further tradition of some family connection with the Rev. George Walker,[1] who organised the defence of Londonderry on that occasion, and was afterwards killed at the Battle of the Boyne, in 1690, shortly after being nominated to the Bishopric of Derry by King William III. From Ulster a certain William McCrea[2] emigrated to America, and from him the Guernsey family trace their descent as below.   The McCreas of Guernsey are a family of soldiers, and have served with much distinction in every war we have been engaged in during the present century.   There is perhaps no other family in the United Kingdom that has held a greater number of commissions in the Army and Navy during the reign of Queen Victoria than the descendants of Major Robert McCrea of Guernsey.

WILLIAM McCREA went to America about 1710 or 1715, and was an elder in White Clay Creek Church, near Newark, Delaware.   His watch and seal were in the possession of his descendants in America in 1831.   He married a Miss Creighton, and had a son,

THE REV. JAMES McCREA, who was born at Lifford, in the county of Londonderry, in Ireland,

---

[1] One version of this tradition is, that the Rev. George Walker himself was a McCrea by birth, and that the surname Walker was only an adopted one.

[2] There is a tradition in the family that the ancestor who fled from Ross-shire changed his name from Macra or Macrae to McCrea, as a mark of his complete religious severance from his family, but the spelling of the name is a matter of no genealogical consequence whatever.   At that time there was frequently no fixed spelling of names, and this name appears in various forms, M'Crea included, in Ross-shire documents of the period.

before his father left that country. He is mentioned as a Presbyterian Clergyman of Scotch descent and devoted to literary pursuits. He married, first, a Miss Graham, who was dead before 1754, and, secondly, Catherine Rosebrooke, who, after his death, married Richard Macdonald. She died in July, 1813, and was buried next her son Philip at Sanaton. By his first marriage the Rev. James had issue—

1. JOHN, who was educated for the law, and settled in the city of Albany. " A man highly respected in his day." He was a Colonel in the American Army during the War of Independence, and was the Colonel John McCrea mentioned in connection with the murder of his sister Jane, of whom below. He died in May, 1811. He married Eva Bateman, by whom he had issue—

a. Sally, who was dead in 1831.

b. James, a Councillor at Law. He settled on a large estate at Balston, Central Saratoga, in the Province of New York, about 1816, and was alive in 1842, but appears to have left Balston for Ohio. He married and had issue—

*b*1. John Beckman (or Bateman), who was a lawyer at Balston in 1831.

*b*2. James, who was living at Balston in 1831, and was then twenty-four years of age.

*b*3. Catherine Mary, who was living at Balston in 1831, and was then eighteen years of age.

*b*4. Stephen, who was also living at Balston in 1831. He was then fourteen years of age, and was the possessor of a watch and seal which had belonged to his great-great-grandfather, William McCrea.

2. MARY, who married the Rev. Mr Hanna, an American, and had with other issue—

a. James, who was "settled in Pensylvania" in 1816, an Attorney-General.

b. John, who was a "Member of Congress." He had a house and land "three miles south of Balston Spayor Springs," and was dead in 1816.

3. WILLIAM, who also had a house and land three miles from Balston Spayor Springs, and was dead in 1816. He married "General Gordon's sister." She was alive in 1816, and had two children, one of whom was called

a. Maria. She married a Mr Macdonald, who was dead in 1833, and by whom she had two children, who appear to have both died young. She married, secondly, a Mr Staat, apparently without issue. She was living in 1842.

4. JANE, died young.

5. JAMES, who was born in 1745. He lived at Balston, and died on the 7th May, 1826. He married, and his wife was dead in 1816. He had issue, at least, one son,

a. John, who was a Clergyman in Ohio in 1831, and was married and had daughters.

6. SAMUEL, married a Miss Sloane, of New Jersey, who was dead in 1816. He settled at Balston, and had issue—

a. Samuel, who with his wife and four daughters were living at Balston in 1842. He is mentioned in that year as the only member of the McCrea family then living at Balston. According to another account, there were descendants of the McCrea family still living at Balston and in other parts of the State of New York in 1888.[1] In 1842 he had issue—Mary Ann, Caroline, Elizabeth, Jane.

b. William, dead in 1830.

c. John, living in Virginia in 1831.

d. Mary, married Judge Betts.

e. Another daughter, unmarried in 1831.

7. GILBERT, married a Miss Meshet, and had several children. He settled in Kentucky, and was dead in 1816. His widow was alive in 1842.

8. JANE, who is said to have been born at Bedminster (now Leamington), New Jersey, in 1753, though there is some reason to believe that she was born before that date. She is known as "The bride of Fort Edward," and was killed on the 27th of July, 1777, at Fort Edward, near Albany, on the Hudson River, by an Indian, under circumstances which have given her name a very prominent place in Anglo-American history. She is described, on the authority of persons who knew her, as "a young woman of great accomplishments, great personal attractions, and remarkable sweetness of disposition. She was of medium stature, finely formed, and of a delicate blonde complexion. Her hair was of a golden brown and silken lustre, and, when unbound, trailed on the ground." It would be quite impossible in the limited compass of the present notice to give even a summary of all that has been written about the death of this young woman, or of the various versions which exist of that tragic occurrence. The outstanding facts

---

[1] Appleton's Cyclopædia of American Biography, published at New York in 1888.

are as follows :—After the death of her father, Miss McCrea, who was engaged to a young man named David James, an officer in the British Army, appears to have lived with her eldest brother, John, who, as already mentioned, was a Colonel in the American Army. As a natural result of opposite sympathies with regard to the war, there arose an estrangement between Colonel McCrea and David James.[1] Miss McCrea resolved, however, to remain faithful to her lover, and when the time appointed for their marriage arrived, he sent a body of loyal Indians to escort her safely from her home to the British Camp, where the marriage was to take place. But on the way two of the Indians appear to have quarrelled as to who should have the honour of presenting her to the bridegroom and receiving the promised reward. In the course of the quarrel one of the Indians became furious, and resolving that if he himself could not receive the reward neither should his opponent, struck Miss McCrea on the head with his tomahawk, and killed her on the spot. He then carried the scalp of his victim into the British Camp, where it was soon recognised by the length and the beauty of the hair. On the following day her body was recovered, and buried by her brother, Colonel John McCrea. David James never recovered from the shock caused by the tragic death of his bride. Shortly afterwards he resigned his Commission in the Army, and though he lived for many years he

[1] In " The Tartans and the Clans of Scotland," with historical notes by James Grant, he is named " Jones" See also " Pictorial Field Book of the American Revolution," by B. J. Lossing

never married. Miss McCrea's remains were removed in 1852 to the Union Cemetery, between Fort Edward and Sandy Hill, where their resting-place is marked by a marble tombstone erected by her niece, Sarah Hanna Payne, and bearing a suitable inscription.

9. STEPHEN, a Surgeon-General in the American Army. He married a Miss Rudyers, and was dead in 1816. He had two children, one of whom died young; the other, a daughter, married and appears to have had issue.

By his second marriage, also, the Rev. James McCrea had issue—

10. ROBERT, of whom below.

11. PHILIP, "killed in the war." He married and had a son Philip, who was living in Ohio in 1831, and had a daughter.

12. CREIGHTON, formerly of New Jersey. He was a Captain in the 75th Highlanders, and was at the capture of Seringapatam. The family possesses a jewelled watch said to have been given to Captain Creighton by Tippoo Sahib. He also served on the Loyalist side in the American War of Independence, and was an Ensign in the 1st American Regiment (or Queen's Rangers) in 1782. At one time he resided at Guernsey, where he made a will, but he died in America on the 10th December, 1818.

13. CATHERINE, who married a Mr Macdonald, son of a Colonel Macdonald, of the British Army, and was alive in Ohio in 1842. She had a large family, and her husband was "just dead" in July, 1813.

ROBERT, son of the Rev. James McCrea by his second wife, Catherine Rosebrooke, was born on the 2nd November, 1754. He fought on the Loyalist side in the American War of Independence, and was Major in the 1st American Regiment (or Queen's Rangers) in 1782. He was severely wounded at the battle of Brandywine in 1777, and received a "pension for wounds." He was for some time Governor of Chester Castle, and in 1788 was Captain of one of six Companies of Invalides stationed in Guernsey. He afterwards became Major Commanding the 5th Royal Veterans. He is mentioned as a man of fine presence, and at the age of seventy-five years is said to have looked like a man of fifty.[1] He died at Paris on the 2nd July, 1835, and was buried at Père la Chaise, Paris. He married, first, Jane Coutart, a Guernsey lady of Huguenot descent, who was born on the 20th December, 1767, and died on the 8th April, 1796. He married secondly, on the 12th June, 1804, Sophia Le Mesurier, who was born on the 23rd January, 1780, and died on the 8th March, 1860. She was a sister of General William Le Mesurier,[2] of Old Court, Guernsey, who served in the Peninsular War. Major McCrea had issue by both marriages as below. By the first wife he had—

1. CATHERINE MARIA, born on the 28th December, 1786, married Colonel Frederick Barlow, of the Sixty-First (Gloucestershire) Regiment, at the head

---

[1] Letter dated 1831.

[2] A branch of these Le Mesuriers were formerly Hereditary Governors of the Island of Alderney.

of which he was killed at the Battle of Salamanca, on the 22nd of July, 1812, and by him had issue one daughter,

a. Jane, who married Philip de Sausmarez, Captain R.N., a younger brother of the Seigneur de Sausmarez, a fief for centuries in the possession of the family.[1]   Captain Philip de Sausmarez entered the Royal Navy on the 18th of June, 1823, saw much service, including the China War, and retired on the 31st of March, 1866.   By him Jane Barlow had issue—

*a*1. Philip Algernon, born 1841, Captain West African Mail Service, and afterwards Consul at Rouen.   He is married, and has issue—

*a*2. William Howley, born 1845, died young.

*a*3. Lionel Andros, born 1847, entered the Royal Navy 1860, Sub-Lieutenant 1866, and was for some time engaged in the suppression of the slave trade in South East Africa.   He was present at the Bombardment of Alexandria in 1882, was mentioned in despatches, and received the Egyptian medal with the clasp for Alexandria, the Khedive's bronze star, and the Order of Osmanjeh (fourth class)   He received special promotion, and the Albert and Royal Humane Society's medals for having, while acting as officer of the watch on the 1st of June, 1868, on H.M.S. Myrmidon, lying in Banana Creek, River Congo, jumped overboard into the shark-infested river and rescued a seaman who could not swim.   He retired

---

[1] The founder of the De Sausmarez family received from Henry II. the fief of Jerbourg, in the Island of Guernsey, and was appointed hereditary Captain of Jerbourg Castle, which was situated within the limits of the fief.

with the rank of Commander in 1883. He married his cousin, Mary, daughter of Frances Charlotte McCrea and George Bell, and has issue—

Lionel Wilfred, Lieutenant in the King's Royal Rifles, and daughters.

*a*4. Frederick Barlow, born in 1849, M.A., Pembroke College, Oxford, appointed one of Her Majesty's Inspectors of Schools in 1878.

2. MARY AUGUSTA, born on the 9th of February, 1788, married at Kinsale on the 27th of December, 1814, Lieutenant-Colonel Chilton Lambton Carter,[1] of the Forty-Fourth Regiment, by whom she had issue—

a. John Chilton Lambton, Captain in the Fifty-Third Regiment, sold out in 1852, and went to New Zealand. He married and left issue.

b. William Frederic, Lieutenant-Colonel of the Sixty-Third Regiment, Knight of the Legion of Honour and of the Order of Medjidie, served in the Crimea in 1854-5, including the Battles of the Alma, Balaclava, and Inkerman, the Expedition to Kerch, the Fall of Sebastopol, succeeding to the command of his Regiment at the last attack and the capture of Kimburn. He married, with issue, and died in 1867.

3. RAWDON (so named after his godfather, Francis Rawdon, Marquis of Hastings[2]), born on the 5th of

---

[1] Colonel Carter was descended from Robert Chilton of Houghton-le-Spring, who married Anne Lambton—See Burke's Peerage, Earl of Durham.

[2] Francis Rawdon, Marquis of Hastings, known successively through his career as Lord Moira and Earl of London, was descended from Sir Arthur Rawdon, Bart. of Moira, in County Down, a man who distinguished himself in the defence of Londonderry and Enniskillen in the reign of William III. The Marquis of Hastings was not only a distinguished soldier, but also one of the most eminent of our Indian statesmen. Born 1754, died 1825. For his connection with the Macraes of Kintail, see page 137.

April, 1789, Captain in the Eighty-Seventh Regiment, served in the Peninsular War.   He was one of the storming party at the taking of Monte Video in 1807, where he received five wounds.   He was killed at the battle of Talavera on the 28th of July, 1809.

4. ROBERT COUTART,[1] born on the 13th January, 1793.   He was an Admiral in the Royal Navy.   He was at the battle of Trafalgar, 21st October, 1805, on H.M.S Swiftshire, and saw much other service. He married, on the 10th of April, 1822, Charlotte, daughter of the Rev Nicholas Dobrée, Rector of Ste. Marie-de-Castro, Guernsey (by his wife, who was a sister of the first Lord de Saumarez), and by her, who died on the 8th December, 1897, in her 103rd year, had issue—

a. Robert Barlow, born on 9th of January, 1823, Major-General Royal Artillery.   He was present in the Revolution in Hayti, in 1859, when he landed in command of three batteries of the Royal Artillery and a detachment of the Forty-First Regiment, for the protection of Europeans.   For his conduct on that occasion he received the brevet rank of Major, and the thanks of both the English and French Governments.   He married, on the 9th August, 1850, Harriet, daughter of John Maingay of Grange Villa, Guernsey, and died at Ewell, Surrey, on the 11th February, 1897.   He was buried at Candie Cemetery, Guernsey.

b. Frances Charlotte, married on the 3rd Febru-

1 Admiral McCrea acquired land in Australia known as McCrea Creek, Victoria, and still held by the family.

ary, 1848, George Bell, of The Merrienne, Guernsey, eldest son of Thomas Bell, mentioned below, and died on the 11th July, 1854, leaving issue—one daughter, Mary, who married her cousin, Commander L. A. de Sausmarez, as already stated.

c. James, born on the 19th of February, 1825, a Captain in the Forty-Fifth Regiment, served in the Kaffir Wars of 1846-7 and 1852-3. He was Colonel Assistant-Adjutant-General of the Royal Guernsey Militia, and died at Grange Villa, Guernsey, on the 2nd September, 1885, in his 65th year. He married Mary Brock Potenger, and by her, who died at Guildford on the 27th January, 1886, had issue—

*c*1. Victor Coryton Dobrée, died in infancy.

*c*2. De la Combe, born 15th March, 1857, died unmarried in Ceylon in 1878.

*c*3. Flora, married Henry Roome, with issue.

*c*4. Constance, died unmarried.

d. Richard Charles, born on the 18th of Apr l, 1826, Captain in the Sixty-Fourth Regiment. He was killed in action near Cawnpore on the 28th November, 1857. He is mentioned in Major-General Windham's despatch on that occasion as " that fine gallant young man," and was promised the Victoria Cross, had he lived to receive it. He married, on the 5th June, 1850, Anne De la Combe, daughter of Thomas Bell, of The Merrienne, Guernsey, and by her had issue—

*d*1. Rawdon, born 28th February, 1851, late Captain 28th Regiment, now living in Guernsey.

*d*2. Julia, married Colonel Anthony Durand,

Bombay Staff Corps, who served in the Indian Mutiny, 1857-8; Abyssinian Expedition, 1867-8; and the Afghan War, 1880. She died in India.

*d*3. Charles Brooke Potenger, born in 1855.

e. John Dobrée, an Admiral in the Royal Navy, saw much war service, including the Baltic, 1855 (medal). He married, on the 9th May, 1857, Marion, daughter of J. Anderson, of Cox Lodge Hall, Northumberland, and died on the 18th March, 1883, leaving issue—

*e*1. Richard Francis, a Major in the Royal Artillery, married Mabel Romney.

*e*2. Charles Dalston, died young.

*e*3. Charles, a Lieutenant in the Royal Navy, died at Gibraltar in 1896.

*e*4. John Henry, married Olive Macdonald, with issue—John Dobrée, died young; Lena Marion, born 1893; Francis Dobrée, born 1894.

*e*5. Frederic, died young.

*e*6. Alfred Coryton, Lieutenant Indian Staff Corps, served in the Hazara Expedition in 1891, medal with clasp; and in Chitral in 1895, was with the Relief Force at the storming of the Malakand Pass, and in the action at Khar—medal with clasp. He married Emma Priestley.

*e*7. Florence Marian.

*e*8. Mary Evelyn, married Frederick W. D. Fisher, of the India Forest Service.

*e*9. Frances Edith, died in 1890.

f. Katharine Carterette, married on the 17th April, 1854, Major-General John Cromie Blackwood de Butts, R.E, son of the late General Sir A. de Butts, R.E., K.C.H., with issue, *f*1. Arthur John, born 1855, M.D., formerly Captain Third Royal Guernsey Light Infantry Militia, married Alice, daughter of Colonel Martindale, R.E., C.B., with issue.   He died at Folkestone in February, 1898, and was buried at Ewell, Surrey.

*f*2. Katharine Mary McCrea, born in 1855, married, in 1880, Edward Kenyon,[1] Major Royal Engineers, with issue—Herbert Edward ; Roger de Butts, died in childhood ; Kenneth, died in childhood ; Catherine Mary Rose ; Ellen Blackwood ; Winifred Lillian ; Frances Margaret.

*f*3. Harriet Olivia, born in 1856, married E. Fairfax Taylor, Principal Clerk and Taxing Officer, House of Lords, with issue.

*f*4. Annie Georgina Louisa, born in 1858, married Major Norton Grant, R E., with issue.

*f*5. Alice Maud Martindale, born in 1860, married Major James Henry Cowan, R.E., with issue.

*f*6. Frederick Robert McCrea, born in 1863, Captain Royal Artillery, served in the Burmese War in 1886-7, was with the Indian Contingent at Suakim in 1896, and was killed in action at the Sampagha Pass, on the North-West Frontier of India, on the 29th of October, 1897.   He married Katharine, daughter of Captain Travers of the Seventeenth Regiment, with issue.

*f*7. Brownlow Stanley Cromie, born in 1865, M.D., M.R.C.S.

*f*8. Isobel Rhœta, born 1867.

*f*9. Ellen Dobrée, born 1872.

g. Rawdon, died young.

---

[1] See Burke's Peerage, Kenyon.

h. Mary Coutart, married on the 10th September, 1856, the Rev. Haydon Aldersey Taylor, M.A., St John's College, Oxford, Army Chaplain, who served in the Crimea. She died on the 13th of September, 1890, leaving issue—

*h*1. Lilian Aldersey, died on the 4th of June, 1873.

*h*2. Charlotte McCrea, married Commander Edward Lloyd, R.N.

*h*3. Anna Katharine De Sausmarez.

*h*4. Haydon D'Aubrey Potenger, Major in the Gloucestershire Regiment, married.

*h*5. Oswald Albon Aldersey, Captain in the Duke of Wellington's Regiment, married.

*h*6. Marion Louise, married Lieutenant-Colonel Davidson, of the Black Watch.

*h*7. Harriette Mary, married the Rev. William Philip Hurrell, M.A, Oriel College, Oxford, St James' Vicarage, Northampton.

*h*8. Frances Arabella Joyce, married George Adams Connor of Craigielaw, Long Niddry, N.B.

*h*9. Coutart De Butts.

*h*10. Leonora Eliot.

i. Harriet Amelia, married, on the 4th of September, 1861, Brownlow Poulter, M.A., Barrister-at-Law of Lincoln's Inn, a Justice of the Peace, and formerly Fellow of New College, Oxford, and has issue—

*i*1. Rev. Donald Francis Ogilvy, M.A., of Lincoln College, Oxford.

*i*2. Mabel Catherine, M.B., Ch.B.

*i*3. Creighton McCrea, Captain Indian Staff Corps, died March, 1896.

*i*4. Aline Marian.

*i*5. Arthur Brownlow, Cape Mounted Rifles.

*i*6. Muriel Alice.

*i*7. Douglas Ryley, Lieutenant in the Royal Artillery.

*i*8. Julia Harriette.

*i*9. Richard Charles McCrea, solicitor.

5. JANE, born 9th March, 1794, married on the 5th October, 1815, Colonel George Augustus Eliot, who held a command in the British service in the American War of 1812, believed to have been then attached to the Royal Engineers.   He left one son, who died young.

6. JAMES CREIGHTON, died in infancy in 1796.

By his second wife, Sophia Le Mesurier, Major Robert McCrea had issue—

7. SOPHIA MARIA CREIGHTON, born on the 19th June, 1805, married Sir Charles Payne, Bart., Captain 25th Regiment of Light Dragoons, with issue one son, died young.

8. ROBERT BRADFORD, born on the 18th of June, 1807.   He was Captain in the Forty-Fourth Regiment, and was killed at Cabul on the 17th of November, 1841.   He married, on the 7th of August, 1832, Margaret Bushnan, and had issue—

a. Frederick Bradford, born on the 4th of December, 1833, a Major in the Eighth (The King's) Regiment, who served at the taking of Delhi in 1857, and was afterwards present in the following actions, viz., Bohundshur, Ackabad, Mynpoorie, Battle of Agra, actions of Karonge and Alumbagh, relief of the garrison of Lucknow, battles of the 2nd and 6th December at Cawnpore, action of Fattehghur, and the Oude campaign of 1858. Also, was in command of details of a force of about two thousand strong at Meerun-ka-Serai for about four months, and prevented the Nana Sahib and Feroh-Shah, the son of the King of Delhi, each, on two occasions, from crossing the Ganges, and so getting into Central India. For the services rendered on those two occasions, he was thanked by the General Officers of three Divisions. He has the Indian Mutiny medal with clasps for Delhi and the Relief of Lucknow, and is a F.R.G.S , F.R.H.S., and F.I.I. In 1871 Major McCrea founded "The Army and Navy Co-operative Society," of which he has been a Managing Director ever since, and with a capital of £60,000 the Society has up to the 31st of January, 1898, paid in bonuses and interest, £1,297,508, and accumulated reserve funds amounting to £270,449. Major McCrea married, on the 24th of January, 1864, Frederica Charlotte (who died on the 10th of June, 1894), only daughter of Captain John Francis Wetherall, 41st Regiment, and has issue—

*a*1. Frederick Augustus Bradford, born on the 8th of October, 1865, late Captain in the Hampshire Militia.

*a*2. Robert George, born on the 24th of February, 1867.

*a*3. Francis Bramston, born on the 3rd of November, 1868 ; married, on the 2nd October, 1897, Edith, daughter of Charles Arthur Patton, Marpole House, Ealing.

*a*4. Henrietta Mary, born on the 3rd of June, 1872.

b. Osborn Leith.

c. Henry Nepean died young.

9. HENRY TORRENS (so called after his godfather, Sir Henry Torrens[1]), born 15th June, 1812, Ensign 2nd Queen's Royals, was drowned at Bombay on the 21st April, 1831, unmarried.

10. ELIZABETH CAREY, born 10th June, 1813, married, on the 14th June, 1854, William Jones (an author) of Brent House, Brentford, Middlesex. He was Vice-Consul at Havre, and was instrumental in helping the flight of Louis Philippe, King of the French, in 1848.   She died in London on the 31st of December, 1856, without issue.

11. LOUISA CREIGHTON, born on the 3rd of May, 1816, and married H. M. Arthur Jones, who afterwards took the name of Owen, a Welsh squire of Wepré Hall, near Flint.   Issue—Lewis, who died young.

12. HALE SHEAFF (so called after his godfather, Sir Hale Sheaff), born on the 17th of April, 1817, and died on the 20th September, 1820.

13. MARTHA ELIZA, born on the 3rd of December, 1819, and married, on the 29th of June, 1850, the Rev. Carteret Priaulx Carey, M.A., Oxon, eldest son of John Carey[2] of Castle Carey, Guernsey.   She died on the 15th of April, 1878, leaving issue—

---

[1] Major-General Sir Henry Torrens, K.C.B., a native of Londonderry, who was, in 1798, Aide-de-Camp to Lieutenant-General Whitelock, second in command to the Earl of Moira (Note, page 269) at Portsmouth, was Secretary to the Duke of Wellington during the Peninsular War   He was afterwards appointed Adjutant General, and, while holding that office, he revised the Army Regulations and introduced many important improvements   Born 1779, died 1828.

[2] The Careys of Guernsey have held a leading position there for upwards of six hundred years.

a. John Herbert Carteret of Castle Carey, Guernsey, born on the 11th of April, 1851. He was for some time a Lieutenant in the Sixtieth Royal Rifles, afterwards Captain and Adjutant First Royal Guernsey Infantry, and was engaged in the reorganisation of the Royal Guernsey Militia; retired on War Office pension as Major (Army rank) in 1894; Honorary Lieutenant-Colonel of the Royal Guernsey Militia, 1894. He is a member of the Societé Jersiaise and a member of the Council of the Guernsey Historical and Antiquarian Society. He married, on the 24th of February, 1877, Isabella Anne, sole surviving child of the late James S. Scott, J.P., formerly of Lawnsdowne, Queen's County, Ireland, with issue, twin daughters, Eleanor Katherine Matilda and Marguérite Blanche Isabel.

b. Abdiel Archibald McCrea, born on the 4th of July, 1852, died young.

c. Carteret Walter, born on the 13th December, 1853, Lieutenant in the Seventy-Fourth Highlanders, 12th November, 1873, Equery to H.R.H. the Duchess of Edinburgh in Malta, Captain 1882, Major 1890. He served in the Egyptian Expedition in 1882 as Adjutant of his battalion, and was present at the Battle of Tel-el-Kebir, where his horse was wounded. He received the Egyptian War medal with clasp, the Khedive's bronze star, and the Order of Medjidie, Fourth Class. In 1892, out of eighty competitors, he received the first prize—£100— awarded by Lord Wolseley for the best essay on the "Reorganisation of the Volunteer Forces." He served as Second in Command of the Second Bat-

talion of the Highland Light Infantry (74th Highlanders), in the North-West Indian Frontier War,
1897-98, including operations against the Boners,
commanding the infantry in the reconnaisance in
the Milandri Pass, operations against the Mah-
munds, Pelarzais, and Shamozais, and was with the
Reserves during the operations against the Utman
Khels ; also in the Bonewal Campaign, 1898, including storming and capture of the Tangu Pass,
and the capture and occupation of Kingergali, Jowar,
Tursak, and Ambeyla.   He married, on the 11th
December, 1890, Florence Margaret, daughter of
William Ravenhill Stock, with issue—Vera Carteret
Priaulx.

d. Samuel Robert, born on the 16th of March,
1855, died young.

e. William Wilfred, born on the 23rd of August,
1856.   Formerly Major in the First Royal Guernsey
Light Infantry Militia. He was appointed Secretary
to the British Commissioners, Egyptian States
Domains, 1882, was present at the bombardment of
Alexandria, and was attached to the Intelligence
Department under Sir J. Goldsmid from July to
September, 1882, receiving the thanks of Her
Majesty's Government for his services.   In 1883 he
was appointed Inspector, and in 1897 Inspector-
General of the Egyptian States Domains. He holds
the Egyptian War medal, the Khedive's bronze
star, the Order of Osmanlieh, Fourth Class, and the
Order of Medjidie, Fourth Class. He married, in
1880, Louisa Sophia, daughter of the late General
Broadly Harrison, Colonel of the Thirteenth Hussars.

14. CHARLOTTE, born on the 9th of January, 1822, and died on the 16th of January, 1884. She adopted the three orphan children of her brother, Herbert Taylor.

15. HERBERT TAYLOR (so called after his god-father, Lieutenant - General Sir Herbert Taylor, K.C.B.), born on the 3rd of May, 1827. He was a Lieutenant in the 94th Regiment and Paymaster in the 43rd Light Infantry. He served in the Kaffir War 1851-52-53. He married, on the 5th of January, 1851, Elizabeth, daughter of John Carey, Castle Carey, Guernsey, and died at the Cape of Good Hope, on his way home from India, on the 8th of April, 1855, leaving issue as below. His wife died in the Neilgherry Hills, Kotagherry, on the 28th July, 1855—

a. Herbert Carey Howes, born on the 28th of October, 1851. He married Maria, daughter of General Rolandi, of the Spanish Army, and has issue—Constance Isabella Rolandi.

b. John Frederick, born on the 1st of April, 1854, at Fort George, Madras. He was Surgeon-Major in the Cape Mounted Rifles. He saw much service in the Cape, won the Victoria Cross in the Basuto War, and was severely wounded in the action at Twee Fontein. He married, in 1887, Miss E. A. Watermeyer, and died on the 16th July, 1894, without issue.

c. Elizabeth Charlotte, born on the 20th of June, 1855, and died on the 20th of December, 1896.

CHAPTER XXI.

A Tradition of the Time of Montrose.—Macraes in Galloway.—
Alexander Macrae of Glenlair married Agnes Gordon of
Carleton —Their Descendants.

There is a tradition to the effect that after the
defeat of Montrose at Philiphaugh, near Selkirk, on
the 12th of September, 1645, two Highland brothers
of the name of Macrae who served in his army,
sought refuge in Galloway because it was the nearest
place where Gaelic was then spoken. There they
settled down and prospered. The same tradition
relates that from one of these brothers was descended a certain

ALEXANDER MACRAE, who, in 1744, married,
as his first wife, Agnes, daughter of Alexander Gordon, fifth of Carleton, by his wife Grizzell, daughter
of Sir Alexander Gordon, Baronet of Earlston,[1] by
his wife Marion, daughter of Alexander Gordon,
fifth Viscount Kenmure, and sister of William, Earl
of Kenmure, who was executed in 1716. Agnes
Gordon brought him as her dowry the farm of
Glenlair, in the parish of Parton, in Kirkcudbright.
He is said to have married three other wives, and
to have had issue, at least by some of them. By his
first wife, Agnes Gordon, he had a son,

[1] See Burke's Peerage and Baronetage, Gordon of Earlston.

ALEXANDER, born in 1745, in the parish of Parton, in Kirkcudbright, of Moreland estate, in the Island of Jamaica, where he lived for many years. He married, on the 17th of September, 1767, Mary, daughter of Thomas Harvie, Professor of Greek in the University of Glasgow, and by her, who died in Jamaica, and was buried at Old Harbour, parish of St Dorothy, had issue as below.   Alexander himself died in Edinburgh on the 14th of March, 1796, a few months after his return from Jamaica—

1. WILLIAM GORDON, of whom next.

2. ALEXANDER, a Captain in the First Royals.

3. JAMES, in the Thirteenth Light Dragoons, killed at Martinique in 1821.

4. THOMASINE married the Rev. Mr Maddison.

WILLIAM GORDON McCRAE[1] was born near Ayr in 1768.   He married Margaret Morison,[2] who was descended from the family of Lord Forbes of Pitsligo, and by her had issue—

1. MARY HARVIE, born 1797, married Dr Cobham, Barbadoes, with issue—

a. Francis McCrae married, with issue.

b. Richard married, with issue.

---

[1] He changed the spelling of the name from Macrae to McCrae.

[2] Margaret Morison was connected with the Pitsligo family as follows :—Rev. John Forbes (born 1643, died 1708), described on a marble slab on the wall of the old church of Kincardine O'Neill, Aberdeenshire, as of the noble family of Pitsligo (ex nobile Dominorum de Pitsligo oriundus familia), married Margaret Strachan, and had issue one daughter, Nichola Helen, who, on the 30th October, 1707, married John, youngest son of Sir John Forbes, Bart. of Craigievar, and had a daughter, Margaret (baptised 17th October, 1710), who married George Herdsman, factor to the Earl Marischal, and had a daughter, Mary (born on the 28th of July, 1740), who married Andrew Morison, Clerk to the Court of Session, and had, with other issue, the above-mentioned Margaret, who married William Gordon McCrae.

c. Elizabeth married Hon. Mark Nicholson, with issue.

d. Mary married Hon. James Graham, with issue.

2. ALEXANDER, born in 1799, Captain in the Eighty-Fourth Regiment, commanding the Grenadier Company, and afterwards Postmaster-General of Victoria, in Australia.   He married Susanna Dannay, with issue—

a. Alexander died unmarried.

b. George died unmarried.

c. Margaret married Edward Graham without issue.

d. Sarah Agnes married Dr W. G. Howitt with issue :—Sarah Muriel Susanna ; Phœbe ; Godfrey ; William Godfrey ; Alexander McCrae ; John Bakewell ; George Ward Cole ; Charles Hugh.

e. Katherine Susannah married Thomas W. Palmer with issue :—Catherine Wrangham married H. R. Anthony ; Ethel McCrae married George Ogle Moore ; Agnes McCrae married Charlton Howitt ; Margaret Annie.

f. Mary Harvie married W. F. Freeman with issue :— Susanna McCrae ; Clara Annie married George Jennings ; Alfred William ; Marion Kate ; Harry Randall.

g. William Gordon died unmarried.

h. John Morison, born 1848, now living at Perth, West Australia, and by whom this information about his own family was communicated to the author in 1898.   He married, first, in 1870, Eleanor Harrison Atkin, with issue—Alexander ; John Morison.   He married, secondly, in 1893, Bessie Fraser Brock, widow of F. A. Brock.

i. Union Rose died in infancy.

j. Thomasanne Cole married Maurice Blackburn with issue :—Maurice McCrae; James; Gertrude; Elsie.

k. Agnes Bruce married George Loughnan with issue :—Marion; Muriel; John Hamilton; George Richmond; Agnes; Valory.

3. ANDREW MURISON, born in 1800. He was a Writer to the Signet in Edinburgh, and practised for some time as a Parliamentary Agent in London. He went to Australia in 1838. On arriving in Melbourne (after staying some time in Sydney) he was admitted a solicitor, and practised there for several years. He was afterwards a Stipendiary and Police Magistrate, and in that capacity served on several stations. He was also a Warden of the Gold Fields, a Commissioner of Crown Lands, and Deputy Sheriff. He died in 1874. He married, in 1830, Georgina Huntly Gordon, and by her, who died on the 24th of May, 1890, aged eighty-six years, had issue—

a. Margaret Elizabeth Mary, born in 1831, died young.

b. George Gordon, born in Scotland in 1833, a retired Civil Servant, now living at Hawthorn, near Melbourne, and by whom most of the information contained in this chapter was communicated to the author in 1896. Mr George Gordon McCrae is a poet of recognised merit and standing. He married Augusta Helen Brown, with issue.

c. William Gordon, born in Scotland in 1835, now living in West Australia.

d. Alexander Gordon, born in Scotland in 1836, now living in New South Wales.

c. Farquhar Peregrine Gordon, born in England in 1838, Inspector, Bank of Australasia, Sydney, New South Wales. He married Emily Aphrasia Brown, and has issue.

f. Georgina Lucia Gordon, born in Australia in 1841, married Robert Hyndman, with issue.

g. Margaret Martha, born in Australia, married Nicholas Maine, with issue—Margaret Isabella.

h. Octavia Frances Gordon, born in Australia, married George Watton Moore, with issue.

i. Agnes Thomasina, died in infancy.

4. AGNES, born 1802.

5. JOHN MORISON, born in 1804, Lieutenant Seventeenth Native Infantry, Bengal.

6. FARQUHAR, born in 1806, Surgeon in the Enniskillen Dragoons. He afterwards went to Australia, and died in Sydney. He married Agnes Morison, with issue.

7. AGNES, born in 1808, married William Bruce, and had issue.

8. THOMAS ANNE, born in 1810, married Commander George Ward-Cole, R.N., with issue.

9. MARGARET FORBES, born in 1812, married Dr David John Thomas, with issue.

CHAPTER XXII.

Legends and Traditions of the Clan Macrae —How the Macraes
first came to Kintail —How St Fillan became the Greatest of
Physicians and made the Inhabitants of Kintail Strong and
Healthy.—How Ellandonan Castle came to be built —How
Donnacha Mor na Tuaigh fought at the Battle of Park —
How the Great Feud between Kintail and Glengarry began.—
How Ian Breac Mac Mhaighster Fearachar made Lochiel
retract a vow against the Men of Kintail.—Tradition about
Muireach Fial —Tradition about Fearachar Mac Ian Oig —
Tradition about the Glenlic Hunt —Traditions about Donnacha
Mor Mac Alister.—Traditions about Eonachan Dubh.—How
Ian Mor Mac Mhaighster Fionnla killed the Soldiers —A
Tradition of Sheriffmuir —How a Kintail Man was innocently
hanged by the Duke of Cumberland.—Some Macrae Traditions
from Gairloch.

Like every other clan, the Macraes of Kintail had
their own legends and traditions, and in olden time
their country was more than usually rich, even for
the Highlands, in poetry, legend, and historic lore.
It was formerly a well-known and universal custom
in the Highlands for the people of a township to
meet together in some central house in the long
winter evenings, and pass much of the time in
singing songs and reciting tales. This custom, which
has survived to a certain extent in some districts
down to our own times, was called the Ceilidh, a
word which means a meeting for social intercourse

and conversation, and it is needless to say that at such meetings the Seanachaidh or reciter of ancient lore, who could relate his tales in fluent, sonorous language, and with a due admixture of homely, dramatic dialogue, a thing to which the Gaelic language so effectively lends itself, was a man whose company was always welcome. The Seanachaidh has now given place very largely to the political newspaper and other cheap forms of literature, and it may be questioned if, in itself, the change is altogether for the better. At all events, the reciter of Highland folklore endeavoured to entertain his listeners with tales of the courage, devotion, and chivalry which go to make a true hero, and to young, impressionable minds the effect of this could hardly fail to be, at least, as wholesome as the ceaseless appeal to human selfishness and covetousness which too frequently forms the chief stock-in-trade of the political newspaper.

In this chapter an effort is made to preserve a few of the old legends and traditions of Kintail, and they are given almost in the very words in which they were communicated to the author by men who know Kintail and its people, and who, in almost every case, heard them related by old men at the Ceilidh many years ago.[1] There is no attempt made

---

[1] The author has great pleasure in acknowledging his indebtedness for most of the information contained in this chapter to Mr Alexander Matheson, shipowner, Dornie (p. 48), Mr Farquhar Macrae, Dornie (p 130); Mr John Alexander Macrae, Avernish (p. 179), Mr Farquhar Matheson, Dornie (p 49), Mr Alexander Maclennan, Craig House, Lochcarron (p 224); Mr Donald Macrae, Gelantipy, Victoria (p. 258); Mr John Macrae, Islip, New York (p. 212); and Mr Alexander Macmillan, an old man of Dornie, who died on the 13th May, 1896.

to harmonise them, even when possible to do so, with the actual facts of the historic incidents to which they refer, and the reader will readily recognise some of them as local versions of legends which may be found in other lands as well as in the Highlands, but they are interesting as showing the light in which the people of the country looked upon their own history, and they serve to illustrate the wholesome pride of the clan in its own heroes, as well as their appreciation of the man of courage, presence of mind, and prompt action, who was bold and fearless in the face of a foe, loyal to his chief, true to every trust, as well as humane and gentle to the weak and helpless who were in any sense dependent upon him. It is not pretended for a single moment that such traits of character were universal in the Highlands any more than in other places, but they constituted the standard of life and conduct at which the true man was expected to aim, and it was only in as far as he succeeded in reaching that standard that his memory was held worthy of an honoured place in the traditions of his clan and country.

HOW THE MACRAES FIRST CAME TO KINTAIL.

Once upon a time, in Ireland, three young men of the Fitzgerald family, called Colin Fitzgerald,[1] Gilleoin na Tuaigh, and Maurice Macrath were present at a wedding, and partook somewhat freely of the

---

[1] Colin Fitzgerald was the reputed founder of the Clan Mackenzie, and Gilleoin na Tuaigh of the Clan Maclean.

good cheer which was provided for the guests.   On
the way home they got so seriously implicated in a
quarrel that they thought it prudent to seek safety
in flight.   While crossing a ferry they took violent
possession of the ferryman's boat, and putting out to
sea with it they sailed across to Scotland.   They
landed at Ardnamurchan, and gradually made their
way across the country to the Aird of Lovat.   On
arriving there late in the night, and very tired, they
lay down under a hedge to rest until the morning
before deciding what their next step was to be.   But
in the early morning they were awakened from their
sleep by the clang of arms, and found two men
engaged in a fierce fight quite near them.   It turned
out that one of these men was Bissett, the Lord of
Lovat, while his antagonist was a redoubtable bully
who, in consequence of some dispute, had challenged
him to mortal combat.   Maurice, observing that
Bissett was on the point of being vanquished, proposed to go to his aid, but the other two thought it
would be wiser and more prudent not to do so, as
they did not know the merits of the case, and had
already been obliged to leave their country through
thoughtless interference in a quarrel which did not
concern them.   Maurice, however, would not be
persuaded, and going to Bissett's assistance he cut off
the bully's head with one blow.   Bissett then invited
his unexpected deliverer to his house, and being
favourably impressed by him he offered him an
important post in his service, and gave him the lands
of Clunes to settle on.   When the Frasers became
Lords of Lovat the Macrae family was still living at

Clunes, and the head of the family was appointed
Lord Lovat's chief forester.   One day there happened to be a great hunting expedition in the Lovat
forest, and among those who took part in it was a
bastard son of Lovat, who began to abuse Macrae for
not giving his hounds a better chance.   One of
Macrae's sons, called John, who happened to be
present at the time, took up the quarrel on behalf of
his father, who was an old man, and settled the
matter by killing the bastard.   As the old man had
rendered him so much loyal and valuable service in
the past Lovat decided to overlook this unfortunate
mishap, but at the same time advised him to send his
sons out of the country, at all events for a time, for
fear of the vengeance of the Fraser family.   The four
sons took the hint and quietly left the Lovat country.
They journeyed together as far as Glenmoriston, and
at a place called Ceann a Chnuic (the end of the
hillock) they parted.   One of them, called Duncan,
went to Argyllshire, married the heiress of Craignish,
and became the ancestor of the Craignish Campbells.
Another, called Christopher, went to Easter Ross.
The third, who was called John, went to Kintail and
spent his first night there in the house of a man
called Macaulay, at Achnagart.   He was such a
restless man that they called him Ian Carrach, which
means twisting or fidgety John.   Macaulay's
daughter, however, fell in love with him and persuaded him to remain there.   In course of time they
were married.   Their first child was born at Achnagart, and he was the first Macrae born in Kintail.
The family of Ian Carrach was one of the chief families

of Kintail until Malcolm Mac Ian Charrich, Constable of Ellandonan, lost his influence by supporting Hector Roy's claim for the estates of Kintail against John of Killin.[1]   A fourth son of Macrae of Clunes, called Finlay, after wandering about for some time, finally made his way to Kintail and settled there near his brother John.   He was called Fionnla Mor nan Gad.[2]   Fionnla Mor nan Gad was the ancestor of Fionnla Dubh Mac Gillechriosd, with whom the recorded genealogy of the Macraes of Kintail commences.

HOW ST FILLAN BECAME THE GREATEST OF PHYSICIANS, AND MADE THE INHABITANTS OF KINTAIL STRONG AND HEALTHY.

While St Fillan was travelling on a pilgrimage in France with a hazel staff from Kintail in his hand, he went one day into the house of an alchemist. The alchemist told the Saint he would give him a fortune if he would bring him to France what was under the sod where the hazel staff grew.   Upon being questioned by St Fillan the alchemist explained that under that sod there was a white serpent, of which he wished very much to get possession.   St Fillan then undertook to go in search of the serpent, and the alchemist gave him the necessary instructions how to capture it.   When St Fillan reached the

---

[1] Pages 22, 23, and Footnote page 214.

[2] The meaning of Gad here is doubtful, it usually means a withe or switch, but in this case it may possibly mean spear.   See Macbain's Gaelic Dictionary.

spot where the hazel staff had been cut, at the north-east end of Loch Long, he kindled a fire and placed a pail of honey near it. The warmth of the fire soon brought a large number of serpents out of their holes, and among them the white serpent, which was their King. Being attracted by the smell of the honey, the white serpent crawled into the pail. Fillan then seized the pail and ran away with it, followed by an ever-increasing number of serpents, anxious to rescue their King. The saint knew he would not be safe from their pursuit until he had crossed seven running streams of water. The river Elchaig was the seventh stream on his way, and when he crossed it he felt that he was now safe. When he reached the top of a small hill called Tulloch nan deur (the hill of tears) he paused for a short rest, and composed a Gaelic hymn or song, of which the following verse is all that appears to be known—

'S mi 'm sheasidh air Tulloch nan deur,
Gun chraicionn air meur na bonn,
Ochadan [1] a rhigh nan rann,
'S fhada 'n Fhraing bho cheann Loch Long [1]

St Fillan then continued his journey, and when he arrived at the end of it, the alchemist took the pail containing the honey and the serpent, put it in a cauldron to boil, and left the Saint alone for a little to watch over it, giving him instructions at the same time that if he saw any bubbles rising to the surface he was on no account to touch them. The alchemist was not long gone when a bubble rose, and Fillan

[1] Standing on the hill of tears with skinless soles and toes,
Alas ! O King of verses, far is France from the head of Loch Long.

thoughtlessly put his finger on it. As the bubble burst it gave out such a burning heat that he suddenly drew his finger back and put it in his mouth to allay the pain, but no sooner did he do so than he felt himself becoming possessed of miraculous healing powers. This was how St Fillan became the greatest physician of his age. The alchemist intended to get this power from the white serpent for himself, but when he returned to his cauldron he found that all the virtue had gone out of it. St Fillan then returned to Kintail with his newly-acquired power, which he used among the people in such a way that in watching over their spiritual health he remembered their bodily health also, and so made them strong and well-favoured among their neighbours.

HOW ELLANDONAN CASTLE CAME TO BE BUILT.

In olden times there lived in Kintail a wealthy chief of the same race as the Mathesons, who had an only son. When the son was born he received his first drink out of the skull of a raven, and this gave him the power to understand the language of birds. He was sent to Rome for his education, and became a great linguist. When he returned to Kintail his father asked him one day to explain what the birds were saying. "They are saying," replied the son, "that one day you will wait upon me as my servant." The father was so annoyed at this explanation that he turned his son out of the house. The son then

joined a ship which was bound for France. Having
learned on his arrival in France that the King was
very greatly annoyed and disturbed by the chirping
of birds about the palace, he went and offered to help
the King to get rid of them. The King accepted
the offer, and the adventurer explained to him that
the birds had a quarrel among themselves, which
they wished the King to settle for them. By the
help of his visitor the King succeeded in settling the
dispute to the entire satisfaction of the birds, and was
troubled by them no more. In gratitude for this
relief the King gave his deliverer a fully-manned
ship for his own use, and with this ship he sailed to
far distant lands, but no land was so distant that he
could not understand and speak the language of the
people.

On one occasion, in the course of a very long
voyage, he met a native King, whom he greatly
pleased with his interesting conversation. The King
invited him to dine at the royal palace, but when he
got to the palace he found it was so infested with
rats that the servants had the very greatest difficulty
in keeping them away from the table. Next time
the adventurer visited the palace he brought a cat
from the ship with him, under his cloak, and when
the rats gathered round the table he let the cat
loose among them. The King was so pleased with
the way in which the cat drove the rats away, that
in exchange for the cat he gave his guest a hogshead
full of gold. With this gold the wanderer returned
to Kintail, after an absence of seven years, and
anchored his ship at Totaig. The arrival of such a

magnificent ship caused a considerable sensation,
and when the owner presented himself at his father's
house, as a man of rank from a distant country, he
was received with great hospitality. His father,
who failed to recognise him, waited upon him at
table, and thus fulfilled the prophecy of the birds.
The son then made himself known to his father, and
a birth mark he bore between his shoulders proved
his identity to the entire satisfaction of the people,
who received him with enthusiasm as the long lost
heir.   His ability and knowledge of the world afterwards brought him into the favour and confidence of
King Alexander II., who commissioned him to build
Ellandonan Castle to protect the King's subjects in
those parts against the encroachments of the Danes.

HOW DONNACHA MOR NA TUAIGH DISTINGUISHED HIMSELF AT THE BATTLE OF PARK.[1]

Shortly before the battle a raw but powerful looking
youth from Kintail was seen staring about among
the Mackenzies in a stupid manner as if looking for
something. He ultimately came across an old, rusty
battle axe of great size, and setting off after the
others he arrived at the scene of strife just as the
combatants were closing with each other.   This
youth was Donnacha Mor na Tuaigh, and Hector
Roy, observing him, asked him why he was not
taking part in the fight and supporting his chief
and clan.   Duncan replied : " Mar a faigh mi miadh

[1] Page 17.

duine, cha dean mi gniomh duine" (Unless I get a man's esteem I will not perform a man's work) This reply was meant as a hint that he had not been provided with a proper weapon. Hector answered him, "Dean sa gniomh duine 's gheibh thu miadh duine" (Do a man's work and you shall get a man's esteem). Duncan at once rushed into the combat exclaiming, "Buille mhor bho chul mo laimhe 's ceum leatha, am fear nach teich romham teicheam roimhe" (A heavy stroke from the back of my arm and a step to enforce it; he who does not get out of my way let me get out of his). Duncan soon killed a man, and, drawing the body aside, coolly sat down on it. Hector Roy, observing this strange proceeding, asked Duncan why he was not still engaged along with his comrades. Duncan answered: "Mar a faigh mi ach miadh aon duine cha dean mi ach gniomh aon duine" (If I get only one man's due, I will do only one man's work). Hector told him to do two men's work and he would get two men's reward. Duncan, returning again to the combat, soon killed another man, and pulling the body aside placed it on the top of the first one, and again sat down. Hector repeated his question once more, and Duncan replied that he had killed two men, and earned two men's reward. "Do your best," replied Hector, "and let us no longer dispute about your reward" Duncan instantly replied: "Am fear nach biodh a cunntadh rium cha bhithinn a cunntadh ris" (He that would not reckon with me, I would not reckon with him), and rushed into the thickest

of the battle, where he did so much execution among
the enemy that Lachlan Maclean of Lochbuy (Lach-
lainn Mac Thearlaich), the most redoubtable warrior
on the other side, placed himself in Duncan's way to
check him in his destructive career. The two met
in mortal strife, and Maclean being a very powerful
man, clad in mail, and well trained in the use of
arms, seemed likely to prove the victor; but Duncan, being lighter and more active than his heavily
mailed opponent, managed, however, to defend
himself, watching his opportunity, and retreating
backwards until he arrived at a ditch. His opponent, now thinking that he had him in his power,
made a desperate stroke at him, which Duncan
parried, and at the same time jumped over the ditch.
Maclean then made a furious lunge with his weapon,
but instead of entering Duncan's body it got fixed
in the opposite bank of the ditch. In withdrawing
his weapon Maclean bent his head forward, and thus
exposed the back of his neck, upon which Duncan's
battle axe descended with the velocity of lightning,
and with such terrific force as to sever the head from
the body. This, it is said, was the turning-point of
the battle, for the Macdonalds, seeing the brave
leader of their van killed, gave up all for lost, and
began at once to retreat. Duncan was ever afterwards known as "Donnacha Mor na Tuaigh" (Big
Duncan of the Battle Axe). That night as Mackenzie sat at supper he inquired for Duncan, who
was missing and could nowhere be found. "My
sorrow." said Mackenzie, "for the loss of my scallag
mhor (big servant) is greater than my satisfaction for

the success of the battle." "I thought," replied one of those present, "that as the Macdonalds fled I saw him pursuing four or five of them up the burn." The words were hardly spoken when Duncan came in with four heads bound together with a rope of twisted twigs. "Tell me now," said Duncan, as he threw the heads down before his master, "if I have not earned my supper."

HOW THE GREAT FEUD BETWEEN KINTAIL AND GLENGARRY BEGAN.[1]

There was once a famous archer of the Clan Macrae called Fionnla Dubh nam Fiadh[2] (Black Finlay of the Deer). He was forester of Glencannich. While Finlay was occupying this position, a certain Macdonald of Glengarry, who had fled from his own home for murder, took refuge in the forest, having obtained permission from one of the chief men of the Mackenzies, not only to take refuge there, but even to help himself to anything he could lay his hands on unknown to Finlay. One day Finlay and another man went out to hunt in a part of the forest which was the usual haunt of the best and fattest deer. To their great surprise they found Macdonald hunting there also. Finlay asked him who gave him

1 Pages 34, 35.

2 Fionnla Dubh nam Fiadh belonged to a tribe of Macraes called Clann a Chruitear (the descendants of the harper) Those belonging to this tribe were generally of a very dark complexion. It is said they were not of the original stock of Macraes, but were descended from a foreign harper, who was brought into the country by one of the Mackenzies, and who settled down there and adopted the name Macrae.

permission to be there. "That's none of your business," replied Macdonald; "I mean to kill as many deer as I please, and you shall not prevent me." Thus a quarrel arose between them, and the end of it was that Finlay shot Macdonald through the heart with an arrow, and cast his body into a lake called Lochan Uine Gleannan nam Fiadh (the green lake of the glen of the deer). After a time Macdonald's friends in Glengarry began to wonder what had become of him, but at last a rumour reached them that he had been killed by Fionnla Dubh nam Fiadh.

On hearing this they formed a party of twelve strong and able men to go to Glencannich to make inquiries, and, if necessary, to take vengeance on Finlay. On arriving at Glencannich the first house they came to was Finlay's. His wife met them at the door, and as they did not know that this was Finlay's house, they stated the object of their visit, and asked if she could give them any directions or information. She told them to come in and rest. They did so, and as they were tired and hungry they were not sorry to see her making preparations to show them hospitality. Meantime Finlay, who was in the other end of the house, began to amuse himself by playing on his trump or Jews' harp. The Glengarry men were so engrossed and interested in the conversation of their hostess that they took no notice of Finlay's music. She, however, listened attentively to it, and from the tune he was playing she understood that he wished her to poison her guests. She accordingly contrived to mix a certain kind of poison, used by her husband to kill foxes, in the rennet with which she was preparing some curds and cream which she set before them. They partook freely of this dish, and eleven of them died from the effects of the poison shortly after they left the house. Finlay then went out and buried them. The twelfth man, however, managed to make his way back to Glengarry, where he told his fellow clansmen what had happened.

The chief, hearing of it, chose eleven strong and brave men to return to Glencannich with this survivor, who undertook to act as their guide and lead them straight to Finlay's house. Now, though this man had already been to Finlay's house, he had not actually seen Finlay himself, and would therefore be unable to recognise him. In due time the Glengarry men reached the brow of a hill opposite to Finlay's house, where they found a man cutting turfs. This was Finlay himself, but he received them with such calm indifference that they never suspected who he was. They asked him if he knew where Finlay was, or if he was at home. " Well," replied Finlay, pointing to his own house, " when I was at that house just now, Finlay was there too." The Glengarry men, thinking the prize was now within their grasp, hurried to the house without looking behind, and so did not observe that Finlay was following after them. As they crowded in at the door, Finlay called to his wife through the back window to hand him out his bow and quiver. His wife did so, and Finlay then took his stand in a convenient position with his bow and arrows. " Come out," shouted he

to the Glengarry men, "the man you want is here."
They rushed out, but he shot them dead one after
another before they were able to reach him. He
then buried them along with his former victims, and
shortly afterwards moved down to his winter quarters
at Achyaragan in Glenelchaig.

After a time Glengarry began to wonder what
had become of his messengers, and so he sent yet
another twelve to make enquiries about them and to
punish Finlay. As these men were passing by
Abercalder, in the neighbourhood of Fort-Augustus,
on their way to Glencannich, they got into conversation with a man who was ploughing in a field.
The man innocently told them that he was Finlay's
brother, whereupon they immediately struck their
dirks into him and left him dead in the shafts of the
plough. On finding that Finlay had left Glencannich they followed him to Glenelchaig, where
it so happened that the first man they met was
Finlay himself, who was out hunting on Mamantuirc.
They began to ask him questions about the man
they were in search of, which he answered to their
satisfaction, and as they walked along he conversed
with them with a freedom which prevented any
suspicion on their part. But on parting with them
he quickly took up his stand in a favourable position,
and shouting out that he was the man they wanted,
killed them all with his arrows before they could lay
hands on him. The last of the twelve took to flight
and was killed while in the act of leaping across a
waterfall. His name was Leiry, and the waterfall
is called Eas leum Leiridh (the waterfall of Leiry's

leap) to this day   When Mackenzie of Kintail
heard of the murder of Finlay's brother at Abercalder he applied for a commission of fire and sword
against Glengarry, who was also making preparations
on his own account to retaliate for the slaughter of
his men by Finlay   The Mackenzies and the Macdonalds met and fought their first battle at the Pass
of Beallach Mhalagan, in the heights of Glensheil.
During the fight Finlay took shelter with his bow
and quiver behind a large stone, which is still
pointed out, and continued to pour a deadly shower
of arrows among the Macdonalds until at last they
took to flight.   After the fight was over, Mackenzie
made his men sit down to rest and to partake of
some food.   Observing Finlay among them he turned
round to him and charged him with cowardice
for taking shelter behind the stone during the fight.
" You are very good," said he, " at raising a quarrel,
but you are a very poor hand at quelling it."
" Don't say more," replied Finlay, " until you have
examined your dead foes."   When the dead Macdonalds were examined it was found that no fewer
than twenty-four of the chief men among the slain
had fallen to Finlay's arrows.

One day, as Finlay lay ill in bed at Fadoch,
suffering from a wound in the head, a travelling
leech from Glengarry happened to visit the district.
He was called in to see Finlay, who felt much
relieved by his treatment.   As the leech continued
his journey in the direction of Camusluinie, he met
a woman, who asked him how the patient was.
" He is much better, and will soon be quite well,"

replied the leech. "Agus leigheis thu Fionnla Dubh nam Fiadh" (And you have cured Black Finlay of the Deer), replied the woman. The leech did not know until now who his patient was, and upon learning that it was Fionnla Dubh nam Fiadh, he returned again to the house, and on a pretence of having neglected something that ought to have been done, in order to make the cure certain, proceeded to examine the wound in the patient's head once more. In the course of the examination he drove a probing needle through the wound into his brain, and as the blood gushed out some of it flowed into Finlay's mouth. "Is milis an deoch a thug thu dhomh" (Sweet is the drink you have given me), said he, and with these words he expired. The leech then left the house, and continued his journey. When the sons of Duncan returned and found their father dead, they set out at once in pursuit of the leech. They overtook him among the hills above Leault, killed him, and buried him on a spot which is still pointed out. Finlay himself was buried at Killelan.

HOW IAN BREAC MAC MHAIGHSTER FEARACHAR MADE LOCHIEL RETRACT A VOW HE HAD MADE AGAINST THE MEN OF KINTAIL.

John Breac[1] used sometimes to go in attendance on Seaforth to the meeting of the Scottish Parliament at Perth, and on one of those occasions Seaforth's sword was stolen from the hall of the house where

[1] Page 170.

he was living in the town.   The next time Seaforth
went to the meeting of Parliament John Breac, who
was with him, recognised the stolen sword in the
possession of one of the followers of Lochiel.   John
charged the man with the theft, beat him soundly,
and took the sword from him.   When Lochiel heard
of the ignominious treatment to which his man had
been subjected he swore that he would execute summary vengence on any Kintail man afterwards found
among the Camerons in Lochaber.   Shortly after his
return to Kintail John Breac missed three of his
horses from his farm at Duilig.   He at once set out
on their track, and traced them all the way to Lochaber, where he found them in a field, and some men
trying to catch them.   John went into the field and
helped the men to catch the horses, for which they
thanked him, but they had no suspicion who he was,
nor did he tell them the object of his visit.   He
asked them, however, if Lochiel was at home, and
they told him he was.   He then went to the house,
but it was early morning and Lochiel was still in
bed. · John told the servant that his business was
very urgent, and desired to be conducted to Lochiel's
bedroom   " Who are you, and where do you come
from ?" asked Lochiel when he saw the stranger
entering his bedroom.   " I come from Kintail," replied John.   " From Mackenzie's Kintail or Mackay's
Kintail ?"[1] asked   Lochiel.   " From   Mackenzie's,"
replied John.   " Then you are a very bold man,"
continued Lochiel.   "Are you not aware that I have
vowed vengence against any Kintail man found in

1 See Note, page 16,

my country?" "I am well aware of it," replied John, "and what is more, I believe I was the cause of your vow." John then quietly took possession of Lochiel's sword, which was hanging on the wall by the bedside, and, explaining who he was, swore that he would deal with him as he dealt with his man in Perth if he did not at once retract his vow against the men of Kintail, and order the stolen horses to be sent back to Duilig. Lochiel, who clearly saw that John Breac was a man who meant what he said, readily granted both requests, rather than run the risk of being ignominiously beaten like a dog.

TRADITION ABOUT MUIREACH FIAL.

About the time of the battle of Sheriffmuir there lived in Kintail a certain Maurice Macrae, known as Muireach Fial (Maurice the Generous). He was a man of some means, and lent money to the Chisholm of Strathglass, in return for which he received certain grazing rights on the lands of Affric. Maurice and his wife used to go once a year to Inverness to sell butter and cheese, which they carried on horseback through the Chisholm country. On one occasion, as they were returning home, they were met by a party of Strathglass men, who invited Maurice to drink with them in Struy Inn. Maurice accepted the invitation, and being of a convivial disposition, was in no hurry to leave. His wife, having vainly endeavoured to induce him to resume his journey, started leisurely alone, expecting that her husband would soon overtake her. But Maurice did not follow, and his wife, at last becoming anxious on his account, hurried home to Kintail, where a party was immediately organised to go in search of him. They searched all over Strathglass, and having made many inquiries without obtaining any information, they returned back to Kintail. On returning home one of their number disguised himself as a poor idiot, and went to Strathglass, where he wandered about begging his way from door to door, but at the same time keeping a careful watch for any trace or talk of the missing Maurice. One night, while lying at the door of a house, he heard someone tapping at the window. He listened attentively, and soon heard the man at the window and the master of the house talking about the bradan tarragheal (the white-bellied salmon), which was tied to a bush and concealed in a certain pool in the river. When the conversation ceased and the visitor took his departure, the Kintail man, wondering what was meant by the salmon, stole quietly away to the pool mentioned, and there found the body of Maurice, who had been murdered by some of the Strathglass men, and whose body had been hidden in the river in a dark pool under a thick bush. He drew the body out of the water, carried it some distance away to a safe hiding-place, and then set out in all haste to Kintail.

When the people of Kintail heard what had happened they formed a large party and went to fetch the body home to Kilduich. As they were passing by Comar churchyard, in Strathglass, on the way back to Kintail, they came upon a large funeral party who were in the act of burying one of the principal men of Strathglass. As the stone was being placed on the grave, four of the Kintail men stepped into the churchyard and carried the stone away. This was done in order to provoke a fight, that they might have an opportunity of avenging the death of Maurice. As the challenge was not accepted they carried the stone all the way to Kilduich and placed it over Maurice's grave, where it is still pointed out. Maurice might have been murdered for the sake of the money he was carrying home with him from Inverness, but the people of Kintail suspected that the murder was instigated by some one connected with the Chisholm, who did not like to see a stranger's cattle grazing on the hills of Affric, and the tradition further says that as soon as Maurice was dead all his cattle were stolen from their grazing by the Chisholm's men. Years afterwards, when Maurice's son, then an old man, was lying on his death-bed, a certain neighbour called Murachadh Buidh nam Meoir (yellow Murdoch of the fingers) went to see him. It was a cold day, and as Murdoch, who was asked to replenish the fire, was in the act of breaking up an old disused settle for fuel, he found concealed in it the parchment bond of the above-mentioned agreement between the Chisholm and Muireach Fial.

TRADITION ABOUT FEARACHAR MAC IAN OIG.

Fearachar Mac Ian Oig[1] lived at Achyark, and was a man of note in Kintail. It was in the time of Colin Earl of Seaforth, and the rents were very

[1] Page 187.

heavy. To make matters worse, the bailiff who collected them was a very unpopular man, and was in
the habit of exacting certain payments on his own
account. A quarrel having arisen about a certain
tribute which Farquhar refused to pay, the bailiff
went to Achyark one day while Farquhar was out
hunting, and, taking advantage of his absence,
carried away a cow and a copper kettle in payment
of the disputed tribute. When Farquhar returned
home, his wife told him that if he were half a man
the bailiff would not dare to do what he did. This
taunt roused him to such fury that he immediately
set out with his loaded gun in pursuit of the bailiff,
whom he overtook at the river Conag. As the
bailiff was crossing the river, with the kettle on his
back, Farquhar shot him dead. When he returned
home he told his wife what he had done. " You
silly woman," said he, "you have caused me to work
my own ruin. I must now look to my safety, and
you must take care of yourself the best way you
can." He then fled for safety in the direction of
Loch Hourn, where he had an uncle living. When
he reached Coalas nam Bo (the strait of the cows),
on Loch Hourn, in the dead of the night, he began
to shout across the ferry to his uncle, who was living
on the other side. When the uncle heard him he
recognised his voice, and roused his own sons, who
were asleep in bed. "Get up," said he, "I hear
Farquhar, my brother's son, shouting to be ferried,
with a tone of mischief in his voice." The young
men at once got up, and brought Farquhar across
the ferry. When his uncle asked him what the

matter was, Farquhar told him that he had killed
Domhnull Mac Dhonnachaidh Mhic Fhionnlaidh
Dhuibh nam Fiadh (Donald, the son of Duncan, the
son of Black Finlay of the Deer). "If that is all,"
replied the uncle, "it does not matter much, for if
you had not killed him, I should kill him myself."
Farquhar hid with his uncle for some months, and
then took up his abode in a cave in Coire-Gorm-a-
Bheallaich, in Glenlic. This he made his hiding-
place for seven years, careful never to appear to any
but his most trusted friends. He never left his
hiding-place without placing a copper coin in a
certain position on a stone at the mouth of the cave,
his idea being that if anyone had visited and dis-
·covered his hiding-place in his absence they would
be sure either to take the coin away or, at all events,
to handle it, and move it from the position in which
he had left it. It is said that in those times, if
a murderer succeeded in evading the law for seven
years, he could not afterwards be punished, and so,
at the end of seven years, Farquhar, considering
himself a free man, suddenly appeared one day at a
funeral in Kilduich. His friends were delighted to
see him again, and having paid a ransom to the
representatives of the murdered man, he was henceforth able to go about the country in safety. On
one occasion, when taunted on being a murderer by
one of the bailiff's friends, Farquhar replied, "Ma
mharbh mis 'e nach d' ith sibh fhein e?" (If I killed
him, have you not eaten him yourselves?) This
reply referred to the ransom which in those days
would probably consist of food and cattle. Seaforth,

however, would not forgive the murderer of his bailiff, and so he sent a message to caution Farquhar never on any account to come into his presence. Shortly afterwards, Seaforth was fitting out an expedition for the Lews, and gave instructions that his men should meet on a certain day at Poolewe. When Seaforth arrived there he was disappointed to find so few of his men waiting for him. "How," said one of the Kintail men, "can you expect your men to respond to you, when you won't allow the bravest of them to come into your presence?" "And who is the bravest of them?" asked Seaforth. "Fearachar Mac Ian Oig," was the reply, "and he would soon be here if you would only restore him to the position he occupied before the murder of the bailiff." Seaforth consented to do this, and Farquhar, who was in concealment near by, was immediately introduced, and became reconciled to his chief there and then. The tradition says that in the course of this expedition Farquhar proved himself one of the bravest and best of Seaforth's followers.

TRADITION ABOUT THE GLENLIC HUNT.

There was hardly any event in the past history of Kintail around which there gathered more legendary and traditional lore than the famous Glenlic hunt, in which Murdoch, son of Alexander of Inverinate, lost his life, and which has been already referred to.[1] The reason for this was no doubt the mystery surrounding Murdoch's death, and the series of

[1] Pages 84-85.

elegies composed during the fifteen days that the search for his body continued. His death was supposed by many people to have been the work of some evil spirit, and for many generations it was considered unsafe to pass at night by the spot where the body was found, as strange sights were seen there and strange noises heard, and, most convincing of all, mysterious marks, as of a round foot with long claws, used to be seen on the otherwise smooth unbroken surface of the snow that fell there in winter. But there was one man in the district who was proof, at all events, against any fear of the evil spirit by which the scene of the tragedy was believed to be haunted. This was a redoubtable weaver called Am Breabadair Og (the young weaver), who lived at the Cro of Kintail. and who always carried a brace of pistols with him wherever he went. Having resolved to challenge the evil spirit to meet him, he carefully loaded his pistols with silver buttons—silver being, according to a well-known belief of olden times, a metal which for shooting purposes was proof against the power of witches and evil spirits alike. Thus fortified, he set out as the night came on to the haunted spot, determined to challenge and shoot any thing, whatever it might be, that chanced to come across his path. Nothing happened, however, the first night, and so he repeated his watch the second night also without any result. This went on for fourteen nights in succession, and still the weaver's watches were disturbed by neither voice nor vision. But on the fifteenth night, which, it may be observed, corre-

sponded with the number of days the search for
Murdoch's body lasted, the weaver returned home
crestfallen, exhausted, and silent.   Nobody was
ever told what he saw or heard on that night, but
he had evidently failed to drive away the evil spirit,
which continued to haunt the place as before.

TRADITIONS ABOUT DONNACHA MOR MAC ALISTER.

Of all the Macrae heroes there is no one whose name
enters so largely into the later traditions of Kintail
as Donnacha Mor Mac Alister.[1] It is said that when
Duncan was a mere lad he went on one occasion
with his mother to sell butter and cheese at Inverlochy (Fort-William). On the way home Duncan
sulked and fell behind, because his mother refused
to give him money to buy a "bonnet" for himself.
As they continued the homeward journey along
Locharkaig side the mother was attacked by three
Lochaber robbers, who not only took her money
from her, but also a silver brooch, an heirloom which
she prized very greatly. The conduct of her son,
who refused to give any help, annoyed her so much
that she called out to one of the robbers that she
had still one coin left, and she would give it to him
if he would thrash her son for her. " Easan am bog
chuilean" (he, the soft whelp), contemptuously replied the robber, and going up to Duncan, struck
him on the face with the back of his hand. This
was more than the sulking lad could stand, and

[1] Page 198.

being now roused to action, he fell upon the robbers, beat them, and recovered his mother's money and brooch.

Duncan once went to see his aunt in Lochaber, and after wading the Garry river, he continued his journey across the Pass of Coire 'n t' Shagairt. As the darkness came on he arrived at a lonely sheiling, and asked permission to pass the night there. The mistress of the sheiling received him very coldly, and refused his request, but Duncan had made up his mind to remain, and refused to go. Presently the daughter of the mistress came in from the milking of the cows, and proceeded to turn Duncan out by force. A struggle ensued, but Duncan's chivalry led him to acknowledge himself beaten. His strength, however, gained him the respect of the mistress, and he received permission to remain overnight. He then sat down and took off his shoes and stockings to cool his feet. When the mistress of the sheiling saw his feet she recognised him, by some mark or peculiarity about them, as a connection of her own family. It turned out that she was the aunt he had come to Lochaber to see. Next morning his cousin, who wanted to put his skill as a hunter to the test, told him there was a herd of deer among the cattle. Duncan went out, killed two of them, and brought them in for breakfast. On returning home, after spending a few pleasant days with his aunt and her daughter, he found the Garry river in flood. At the river he met his mother's foster brother, Dugald Macdonald, who, on being asked by Duncan if the river was

fordable, taunted him for hesitating to wade across.
Duncan then plunged in, but was very nearly
drowned before he got to the other side. Dugald
afterwards went to Glensheil to see Duncan's mother.
He met Duncan fishing on the River Sheil, which
was in flood, but did not recognise him. Dugald
told him where he was going, and asked him to show
the way. Duncan pointed out his own father's
house on the other side of the river. Dugald then
attempted to ford the river, but would have been
drowned if Duncan had not come to his rescue
Thus Duncan proved himself to be the stronger of
the two. When Dugald was leaving Glensheil,
Duncan's father gave him a thrashing for tempting
Duncan to run the risk of wading the Garry river
when it was in such high flood, and reminded him
that if Duncan had been drowned then, he would
not be alive to save Dugald from drowning in the
River Sheil. Duncan's mother always used to say
ever after this that though her husband was so good
to her she could not forget how he thrashed her
foster brother.

It has already been mentioned[1] that William
Earl of Seaforth appointed Duncan Captain of the
Freiceadan or Guard, whose duty it was to protect
the marches of Kintail from the plundering raids of
the Lochaber cattle lifters. Seaforth had heard of
Duncan's strength and courage, but before entrusting
him with such a difficult and responsible post he
resolved to satisfy himself as to the truth of what
he had heard about him. He accordingly invited

1 Page 198.

Duncan to come to see him in Brahan Castle. When Duncan arrived at Brahan, Seaforth received him alone in a room in the Castle. After some conversation, Seaforth locked the door of the room, drew his sword, and called upon Duncan to clear himself at once of some imaginary charge, or he would take his life. Duncan, who had left his sword in the hall of the Castle, had no weapon to defend himself with, but Seaforth's hound was lying on the floor close by. Duncan seized it by the legs and threw it at Seaforth, and, before Seaforth could recover from his surprise, Duncan took his sword from him. Seaforth was so pleased with Duncan's promptness and coolness that he at once decided to make him the Captain of his Guard.

At one time a band of Camerons came to Lochalsh and stole a large number of cattle from Matheson of Fernaig. When this became known, Duncan and his men set out in pursuit. They soon discovered the track of the spoilers, and they overtook them on the borders of Lochiel's country. A fight ensued, in which the Camerons had the worst of it. Not only was the cattle recovered, but in the course of the fight Duncan, assisted by his brother Eonachan and Matheson of Fernaig, the owner of the cattle, overcame Lochiel's three chief warriors, and led them prisoners to Kintail. When Seaforth heard of this he sent a bantering message to Lochiel asking him to come and ransom his champions from their prison. Lochiel sent for the prisoners, but at the same time replied to Seaforth that the Kintail men could never have taken the Cameron champions prisoners in fair

fight. Seaforth then offered to send three men from
Kintail to Lochiel to challenge any three of the
Camerons to a friendly contest of feats of strength.
Seaforth wanted the same three men to go, but his
father would not allow Eonachan to be one of the
three because he was too young, and because his
impulsive and hasty temper might cause the friendly
contest to end in a quarrel. Eonachan's place
had to be taken by his brother Donald. Duncan,
Donald, and Matheson of Fernaig then set out for
Lochiel's castle at Achnacarry. On the way it
occurred to Duncan that his brother Donald had
not yet tried the strength of any of the Cameron
champions, and so, when next they stopped to rest,
Duncan proposed to his brother that they should
wrestle together. They did so, and Duncan was
soon satisfied that his brother was equal to the best
of the Camerons. When they arrived at Achnacarry Castle they were received with much hospitality, and liberally supplied with food and drink.
In due time the hall of the castle was cleared, and
a large number of men who had come together to
witness the contest were brought in. The opposing
champions stood forth and began a wrestling match.
The Camerons in each case had the worst of it, and
Lochiel was so much disgusted with his champions
that he kicked them out at the door. He then invited the Kintail men to join in the feast with his
other guests, which they did. As the cup circulated
freely and the evening wore on, some of the Camerons began to betray their real feelings towards the
vanquishers of their champions, and occasionally cast

threatening glances at Duncan and his companions. But Lochiel's lady, being anxious to avoid bloodshed, contrived to warn the Kintail men of their danger. Duncan took the hint, and taking advantage of the first favourable opportunity, he quietly got his companions out without exciting any suspicions, while he himself was engaged in conversation with Lochiel. Shortly afterwards he slipped out also and joined them. The night was dark and stormy, but they betook themselves to the mountains of Glengarry. When they reached the river Garry towards break of day, they found the Camerons in close pursuit with firearms. The Kintail men plunged into the flooded river and with much difficulty gained the other side; but the Camerons would not venture to try the river, and so they returned home after following the Kintail men for many miles to no purpose.

Another version of this legend says that during the feast some of the Camerons made the door fast to prevent the escape of the Macraes, and that a servant girl (perhaps from Kintail) made them aware of this by whispering to one of them to get out by the window, and that on a signal from Duncan they rushed for the door, broke it open, and escaped into the darkness, challenging the Camerons at the same time to follow them.

When Duncan was a young man, he lived for some time at Killechuinard, and at night used to swim across Lochduich to Inverinate to see his sweetheart. On one occasion, as he was half-way across, he suddenly came into collision with a bull swimming in the opposite direction. The angry bull tried to gore him, and though Duncan was a powerful swimmer, he did not think he could swim against a Highland bull. So he cleverly contrived to get on the bull's back, and, seizing hold of his horns, he compelled the animal to swim back with him to Inverinate.

Though Duncan was a warrior of renown and a mighty hunter, he was also very tender-hearted, and always ready to help anyone in distress. On one occasion a servant at his father's sheiling at Caorun, in the Heights of Cluanie, was taken ill of a virulent fever, and while others were afraid to go near her, Duncan took her in his arms and carried her all the way down to Glenshiel, where she received proper attendance and recovered from her illness. She afterwards composed a song about Duncan's kindness, of which the following is the only verse that now seems to be known :—

> Se nigh'n Alastair Rhuaidh
> A rug a bhuaidh,
> 'S cha be na fuar mhic greananach ;
> Se fear mo ghaoil
> A macan caomh,
> A rinn sa Chaorun eallach dhiam.[1]

It has already been stated[2] that Duncan was killed at Sheriffmuir, where, according to tradition, he fought in command of the Kintail contingent of

[1] It was the daughter of Alister Roy (Duncan's maternal grandfather) that brought forth virtue (or blessing) and not cold and surly sons—the man of my love is her gentle son, who took me up as a burden at Caorun.

[2] Page 198.

Seaforth's regiments.   Mention has also been made of the stone which he set up at Achnagart as he and his followers were leaving Kintail on that occasion. It is said that in the retreat after the battle he killed seven troopers, one after another, with his claymore, until at last one of them came upon him with a pair of loaded pistols, shot him, and left him for dead on the field.[1]   During the night another Kintail man called John Macrae, and commonly known as Ian Mac Fhionnla Mhic Ian Bhuidhe,[2] who had lost his shoes in some marshy ground, and was also severely wounded, revived sufficiently to think of leaving the fatal field under cover of the darkness, and commence the homeward journey.   He accordingly began to search among the dead for a pair of shoes.   In the course of the search he came upon Duncan, who was still alive and able to speak, and whose voice John immediately recognised.   "Oh, Dhonnachaidh bhoc," said John, "'n tusa tha so, ciod e a thachair riut?" (O, poor Duncan, is that you; what has happened to you?)   "Thug iad a nasgaidh mi le 'n cuid peileiran beag" (They have done for me without any trouble with their little bullets, replied Duncan.)   He then asked for a drink, and John, having no other means

---

[1] In *British Battles on Land and Sea*, James Grant, in his description of Sheriffmuir, gives a slightly different account of the death of Duncan Mor. He says that :—"Under Duncan Mor the Macraes made a desperate resistance, and are said to have died almost to a man.   During the struggle, and while his people were falling around him, and ere he fell himself, he was frequently seen to wave his reeking sword on high, and heard to shout, "Cobhair! Cobhair! an ainm Dhe agus Righ Seumas" (Help! Help! in the name of God and King James).   Before Duncan fell he slew fifteen with his own hand, which was so much swollen in the hilt of his claymore that it could with difficulty be extricated."

[2] Page 256.

of fetching a drink, took one of Duncan's shoes, and brought it to him full of water. The water revived him so much that he was able to give John a full account of his adventures during the battle, but before the morning dawned Duncan was numbered among the slain. John lived to accomplish the homeward journey, and it was he who brought to Kintail an account of the manner of the death of Donnacha Mor Mac Alister. There is a tradition in Kintail that a sketch of Duncan in the battle was made by one of the officers of the Royalist troops, and that it was exhibited along with his sword in the Tower of London.

TRADITIONS ABOUT EONACHAN DUBH.

Eonachan Dubh,[1] Duncan's youngest brother, is also frequently mentioned in connection with Duncan's adventures with the Lochaber cattle lifters. It is related of Eonachan that on one occasion he pursued a party of Lochaber raiders who had stolen cattle from Macleod of Glenelg, and recovered the spoil single handed. As the Glenelg men were returning home from an unsuccessful pursuit they met Eonachan, and when they told him where they had been, and how they had failed to discover any trace of the raiders, Eonachan volunteered to set out at once, and alone, in search of them. Late at night he discovered them in an empty sheiling house, where they had arranged to take shelter for the night, and were then roasting a huge piece of beef on a spit

[1] Page 210,

for their supper. Eonachan presented himself as a benighted traveller, and asked to be allowed to share the shelter of the hut for the night. This request was readily granted. After sharing in their hospitality he entertained them for some time with his conversation, and at last went out to the door to see what the night was like. It was very dark, and as soon as he got outside he shouted to the men within that the cattle had all gone away. One of the men then went out to see, but no sooner was he outside the door than Eonachan, who was prepared for the occasion, threw his plaid over his head, knocked him down, and gagged and bound him before he had time to utter a word. Shortly afterwards another went out to see what had become of their companion, but Eonachan dealt in the same manner with him also. After a little time a third man went out, but only to receive the same treatment as his companions. There were now only two men left in the hut, and Eonachan, knowing that he was quite a match for both of them together, called upon them to yield, which they did without further resistance. These two men he gagged and bound also. The Lochaber men had some guns, which Eonachan rendered useless by breaking off the stocks. He then told them to make their way the best they could, with gagged mouths and bound hands, to their chief, Lochiel, with Eonachan's compliments. Having thus disposed of the thieves, he collected the cattle and drove them back to their owner in Glenelg.

Eonachan was once on a visit to Brahan Castle,

V

and while talking with the Countess, who had a fire
of cinnamon in her room, she asked him if ever he
saw such a fine fire as that. " No," replied Eonachan,
" the fragrant smell of that fire reaches all the way
to the cattle folds of Kintail." " How is that?"
asked the Countess. Eonachan pointed out to her
that her extravagant ways had make it necessary
for her husband to increase the rents which his Kintail tenants paid for their cattle folds. The Countess
took Eonachan's pointed reply in good part and dis-
continued the cinnamon fires. When Seaforth heard
of this he told Eonachan that the Countess insisted
on having a fresh ox tongue on her table at dinner
every day of the year, and that if Eonachan could cure
her of this extravagance, as he had done in the matter
of the cinnamon, he should feel deeply indebted to him.
Shortly afterwards Eonachan was going to Dingwall
with a large herd of cattle, and, as he approached
Brahan, he directed his herdsmen to drive three
hundred and sixty-five of the cattle past the front
of the Castle, in such a way as to make the number
appear as large as possible. Having given these
instructions, he himself hurried on in advance.
When he arrived at the Castle he was kindly
welcomed by both Seaforth and his lady. As he
sat by one of the windows talking with the lady the
herd of cattle began to pass by. "What a very large
herd of cattle," remarked the lady. " Not at all,"
replied Eonachan, "it is only as many as you require
for your own dinner in the course of the year." She
could not believe that she required so many, and she
asked Eonachan what he meant. He explained to

her that as she wanted an ox tongue every day for her dinner, and as an ox had only one tongue, it was necessary to kill three hundred and sixty-five oxen every year for her dinner, and that was exactly the number of the herd then passing by.

Eonachan once dreamt that his sister, who was married in Lochaber, was dead.   He was so impressed by this dream that he tried to persuade his brothers to go with him to Lochaber to see how she fared   His brothers made light of his fears and refused to go, so he set out alone.   When he arrived at his sister's house he found that she was not only dead, but that she was being buried on that same day.   He then started after the funeral party, and overtook them as they arrived at the churchyard. Here there arose a dispute as to where she ought to be buried, which greatly annoyed her brother. " What are you disputing about ? " said he; " if there is no room in Lochaber for her, there is plenty of room in Kintail; lift the coffin on my back." They did so, thinking he could not carry it very far. For a long time they watched him, expecting every moment to see him lay down his burden, until at last he disappeared over the crest of a hill.   They then set out in pursuit of him to recover the body and bring it back to the proper place of burial, but before they could overtake him he accidentally fell in with some men from Kintail, who helped him to carry the body all the way to Kilduich, where it was buried with all due ceremony.

HOW IAN MOR MAC MHAIGHSTER FIONNLA KILLED THE SOLDIERS.

John, son of the Rev. Finlay Macrae of Lochalsh, was considered one of the best swordsmen of his own time in the Highlands. One Sunday, while Mr Finlay was conducting divine service in Lochalsh Church, a party of four or five soldiers came across from Glenelg,[1] and began to plunder his house. While this was going on John, who was returning home from a journey, arrived at an inn above Auchtertyre, and went in to rest. But he had hardly sat down when word reached him of what was going on at his father's house, and, setting out at once with all speed, he overtook the soldiers on the way to their boat with the plunder. He told them to return everything they took, and that they would be allowed to depart without being further interfered with. It so happened, however, that as John was hurrying along to catch the soldiers, one of his garters came undone, and, instead of returning their booty, the soldiers began to make fun of his hose, which had slipped down about his ankle. This was more than John could stand, and falling upon the soldiers with his sword, he killed them one after another before they could reach their boat. The place where the soldiers were buried is still pointed out. It is quite near Lochalsh Parish Church, and is known as Blar nan Saighdear (the Soldiers' Field).

1 The military barracks at Glenelg were built in 1722, but in all probability there were soldiers stationed in that neighbourhood from the time of the battle of Glensheil in 1719 onwards,

A TRADITION OF SHERIFFMUIR.

Many years after the Battle of Sheriffmuir, a Highland drover, who was conducting his herd of cattle to the Southern markets, arrived late one night near a gentleman's house in the Braes of Stirling. The gentleman was a Captain Macdougall, who had fought on the Royalist side at Sheriffmuir. The drover called on the Captain to ask permission to halt with his cattle for the night on the terms which were then usual in such circumstances. The permission was granted, and the Captain being struck by the manner and appearance of the old drover, invited him to pass the night as his guest. The invitation was accepted, and, in the course of conversation, the Captain, learning that his guest was from Kintail, asked him if he knew a place called Corriedhomhain. The drover replied that he did, and the Captain then proceeded to relate the following incident of the Battle of Sheriffmuir : " In the course of the pursuit after the battle," continued the Captain, " I followed a stout Highlander with three well-mounted troopers. The Highlander, perceiving our approach, faced about, took off his plaid, and, carefully folding it, placed it on the ground that by standing on it he might have a firmer footing. My desire being to take him prisoner and not to kill him, we closed upon him with brandishing swords, and commanded him to surrender. This, however, he was not disposed to do, and one of the troopers, approaching too near, had his skull cleft in two by a stroke of the

Highlander's claymore. As another instantly shared a similar fate, the third trooper and myself thought it prudent to keep at a more respectful distance. I was so greatly struck by the Highlander's bearing and swordsmanship that I asked him who he was, but the only information he would give me was that he was from Corriedhomhain, in Kintail." " I know the man as well as I know myself," replied the drover, " his name is Duncan Macrae." " Well then," replied the Captain, " give him my compliments, tell him I commanded the troopers who attacked him in the retreat from Sheriffmuir, that I have ever since been curious to know the name and condition of such an excellent swordsman and brave man, and that I wish him well." " I will do so with much pleasure," replied the drover, who was himself the same Duncan Macrae, of Corriedhomhain, who had fought the four troopers.

This Duncan Macrae, of Corriedhomhain, was known in Kintail as Donnacha Mor nan Creach (Big Duncan of the Spoils). He belonged to a family called Clann a Chruiter (the descendants of the Harper), and said to be descended from a minstrel, probably of Irish origin, who settled in Kintail and adopted the name Macrae. Fionnla Dubh nan Fiadh was of the same tribe.[1]

HOW A KINTAIL MAN WAS INNOCENTLY HANGED BY THE DUKE OF CUMBERLAND.

There was once a lady in Assynt who owned a piece of land which she proposed to give to some neigh-

[1] Page 298.

bouring laird, on condition that he should maintain her in comfort for the rest of her life. Seaforth offered to maintain her in Brahan Castle on the terms she proposed, but the old lady, preferring to remain near her own home, rejected Seaforth's offer and came to terms with Macleod of Assynt. Seaforth was annoyed at this, and, by way of retaliation, sent Murdoch Macrae[1] (Murrachadh Mac Fhearachair), one of his under factors, and Coll Ban Macdonell of Barisdale, with a party of Kintail men, on a harrying expedition to Macleod's estates of Assynt. In the course of their raid they plundered Macleod's house, and, among other things, they carried away a web of beautiful tartan. They also took away two mares, which were afterwards found and recognised on the farm of Barisdale. When Macleod heard of this he commenced proceedings against Coll of Barisdale for the theft of the horses. When the trial came on, the horses were brought to Fort-Augustus to be identified, and were kept there in the military stables. But when it became known to the men of Kintail, among whom Coll of Barisdale was very popular, that the horses were being taken to Fort-Augustus to be used as evidence against him in the trial, they resolved to make some effort to put the horses out of the way. Accordingly, Ian Mor Mac Mhaighster Fionnla (Big John, son of the Rev. Finlay), Ian Mac Fhearachair (John, son of Farquhar) of Morvich, and Donnacha Dubh Mac Dhonnachidh Mhic Choinnich Mhic Rhuari (Black Duncan, son of

---

[1] This Murdoch (see page 81) was the father of the Kintail poet, Ian Mac Mhurachaidh.

Duncan, son of Kenneth, son of Roderick), a Mackenzie of Lochcarron, set out for Fort-Augustus. Passing through Strathglass, they arrived at Tomich Inn early in the evening and went to bed. They then called the innkeeper to come in to them and offered him a glass of whisky. In the morning, before they got up, they called him in again and offered him another glass. This they did that in the event of any trouble he might be a witness that they spent the whole night in his house. But as soon as the people of the inn retired to rest, the three visitors quietly got up and set out in all haste to Fort-Augustus. They entered the stables by a hole which they made in the roof, and when they found Macleod's stolen mares they cut off their heads, which they took away with them and sank in Loch Ness. They then returned to Tomich Inn and went to bed again before daylight, without having been missed by the innkeeper or any of his people. The trial of Coll of Barisdale fell through because the headless horses could not be identified as Macleod's lost property.

One day, a long time after, Murdoch Macrae was in Inverness, and had on a pair of hose made out of Macleod of Assynt's stolen web of tartan. It so happened that Macleod was in Inverness on the same day, and, meeting Murdoch in the street, he recognised the stolen tartan in the hose, and naturally concluded that Murdoch was one of the Seaforth party by whom his house had been pillaged. Macleod resolved to be avenged upon him, and communicated the matter to Macleod of Dunvegan and

Sir Alexander Macdonald of Sleat, both of whom were on the Government side, and there the matter rested for some time.   But one night, about a month after the Battle of Culloden, when Murdoch happened to be in the house of Macdonald of Leck, in Glengarry, where a party of the Skye Militia was stationed at the time, he was suddenly seized by a party of soldiers under Macleod of Dunvegan, and sent with a letter from Sir Alexander Macdonald to Lord Loudon, who was then stationed at Fort-Augustus   Loudon sent him to Inverness in charge of an escort of soldiers.   On his arrival at Inverness, Murdoch was brought before the Duke of Cumberland, who, at the instigation of Macleod of Assynt, ordered him to be hanged at once as a spy from the Pretender.   Murdoch was hanged on an apple tree which grew at the Cross of Inverness, and which immediately afterwards withered.   His body, which, after his death, had been stripped naked, was left hanging on the tree for two days, and then buried at the back of the Church.[1]   While thus exposed, he is said to have " appeared all the time as if he had been sleeping, his mouth and eyes being shut close—a very uncommon thing in those who die such a death."   This execution of a man, believed to have been innocent, appears to have made a deep impression in Inverness.   There are several contemporary references to it, and in a poem entitled " The Lament of the Old Cross of Inverness," in 1768, reference is made to the withering of the tree,

---

[1] For a fuller account of the hanging of Murdoch Macrae, see Charles Fraser-Mackintosh's *Antiquarian Notes*, first series, pp. 206 210.

and Murdoch himself is mentioned "as a man of fame and reputation," who enjoyed the esteem of men of rank and worth, and had never deserted his King or his country.

MACRAE TRADITIONS OF GAIRLOCH.

The early connection between the Macraes and the Mackenzies of Gairloch has been already referred to (pages 9, 10), and some Macrae traditions from Gairloch will be found in Appendix K.

APPENDIX A.

As to the origin of the Macras, tradition tells us of a desperate engagement 'twixt two of the petty Princes of Ireland, in which a certain young man signalized himself by his prowess, defending himself from a particular attack of the enemy, which others, observing, said in Irish words signifying he was a fortunate man if he could award the danger; from whence he was afterwards called Macrath, *i.e.*, the fortunate son.

It is allowed this clan were an ancient race of people in Ireland, and had of old great estates there, have produced eminent men, and are still numerous in that island

The pronunciation of the name here spelled Macra, varying with the dialect of the country where any of the clan generally reside, has occasioned various ways of spelling this word, as is the case with several others, thus in Ireland they use Macrath and Magrath, in the North of Scotland, Macrah, Macrae, Maccraw, Macrow   In England and the south of Scotland the Mac is left out, from an ill-founded prejudice, and the name Rae, Craw, Crow, and such like, retained as being of the same stock.   A more particular account might be had from such as conversed with and have known those historians and genealogists, such as Fergus, Macrourie, Mildonich, Maclean, &c., who were good scholars, and acquainted with the manuscripts and records of Ireland kept for giving an account of the tribes who came from Ireland to Scotland, and became heads of families and chiefs of clans; and from them I heard it confidently said and affirmed, that the Mackenzies, Macleans, and Macraes were of the same people in Ireland.   Yea, I heard Sir Allan Maclean of Doward, who was curious and taught in these things, being at Dingwall in the year 1663, say no less, and it is as certain as tradition and the authorities of the fore-mentioned antiquaries can make it, that a Macra had his tomb, as well as Mackenzie and Maclean, in Icolumbkill, and that close by one another.   Doctor George Mackenzie, who has wrote a genea-logical and historical account of the Mackenzies, mentions that when Colin Fitzgerald came from Ireland in the year 1263, a number of the Macras were of his party at the battle of Largs, in Ayrshire, which, it is natural to think, was in consequence of a friendly attachment then known to have been 'twixt their ancestors, as is since continued 'twixt their descendants   But whether there were any Macras before then in Scotland I cannot determine, only that tradition says there were some of them on the estate of Lovat, when the Bizets were lords of that place, which titles and estate they forfeited and lost, according to Buchanan, in the following manner.—Anno 1242.—King Alexander the Second, with many of the nobility, being at Haddington, Patrick Cuming, Earl of Athole, his lodging was burnt in the night time, and he, with two of his servants, perished in the flames   This fire was judged not to be accidental, and because of an enmity 'twixt him and William Bizet, nephew to King William The Lyon, and eldest son of John Bizet, the first Lord Lovat of that name, the suspicion was fixed upon him.   William endeavoured to exculpate himself by offering to prove his being in Forfar the night of the burning, and also offered to vindicate himself by combat, as the custom then was   But neither would do, so that he was summoned criminally to a certain day, when, finding the interest and power of his adversaries too great for him, or being conscious of his own acces-sion to the crime, he did not appear, so was sentenced and forfeited, but, by reason of his connection with the Royal Family, the King gave him a reprieve, with liberty to go to Ireland, where he had an estate in a place called Glenns of Glenmores, the rents of which estate were on certain occasions before this forfeiture col-lected by persons sent on purpose from the estate of Lovat, as they were in like manner sent to' raise the rents of Glenelg when in possession of this family.

The ruin of this William Bizet did not satisfy the Cumings. They level next at his brother, John, Lord Lovat, who, by his own folly, hastened what they desired, for in the next year, 1243, he joined Macdonald in his rebellion against the King, and when

Macdonald was forced to return to the Isles, the King commanded
the Earl of Ross to apprehend John Bizet, Lord Lovat, which he,
having heard, went and lurked in Achterlies, but a price being set
on his head, he was taken by George Dempster of Moorhouse in
the wood of Achterlies, and sent to the King, by whom he was
sentenced and forfeited, but was reprieved, as was his brother
William, with liberty to go to Ireland   This John Bizet had no
children but three daughters, on whom the King bestowed the
estates as their portions because of their relation to the Royal
family—Agnes, the daughter of King William the Lyon, being the
mother of this John.   The eldest daughter, Mary, with the greatest
part of the lordship of Lovat and title of Lord Lovat, was given
by the King to Sir Simon Fraser of Kinnel, second son of
Alexander Fraser of Tweedale, Anno 1247.   Elizabeth, the second
daughter, was married to Andreas Aboses of Spitewood, and
Cecilia, the youngest, to William Lord Fenton, whose portion of
the estate with her was the Braes of the Aird, Ercliss, Strathglass,
Buntaite, Guisachan, and Glenelg, all which fell in again to the
next Lord Fraser of Lovat with Janet, daughter to Lord Fenton,
Anno. 1279.

When I lived at Kilmorack, in the year 1672, a strong wind
having cast down the top stone of the easter gable of the Kirk of
Beauly, it fell on the altar and broke to pieces, whereof I laid most
together, and found the letters M. B., supposed to be the initials
of Mary Bizet, raised on it in large letters.   She was thought to
have caused build or at least finish this gable and side walls
adjoining the length of St Catherine and St Cross' Chapels.

In the year 1249, King Alexander the Second died, and William
and John Bizet having gone to Ireland and settled their families
there, their three brothers, Walter, Malcom, and Leonard, who
lived in Killiechuimen and Abertarff, finding the Bizets greatly
hated, followed them to Ireland.

All this time the Macras continued on the lordship of Lovat,
and Mary Bizet having been fostered in the house of Macra of
Clunes, had a kindness for him, and a deference to his counsel and
advices, which was a means of bringing him to the favour of her
husband, Simon, the first Lord Fraser of Lovat, and from him
continued 'twixt their successors till the Macras removed.   Nor
was it afterwards forgot, as will appear in the sequel.

The Macras were faithful and serviceable adherents of the family, an instance of which was thus.—There was in Ardmeanach about this time a man of numerous kindred and followers called Loban, agnamed Gillgorm, who had a claim or quarrel against the family of Lovat, and in their repeated attacks, and while Lord Lovat was frequently from home and at Court, the Macras opposed them valiantly and with open hostility. But the second or third Lord Fraser of Lovat, judging it for his interest to put an end to so troublesome a quarrel, brought from the south country twenty-four gentlemen of his name, some of whose posterity, as I'm informed, live yet in the Aird. With these and the Macras, and such others as he could get and thought necessary, he marches directly against Gillgorm, who, with all the forces he could make ready, were prepared to receive him, and after some proposals of peace made and rejected, did in end engage in set fight upon the Moor of Drimderfit, above Kessock, called since, from the dismal effects of that fight, Drimdeair, *i e*, the Ridge of Tears

Both parties fought resolutely, and Gillgorm being killed, his kindred and followers were almost totally cut off [1] Lovat carried away the spoil, and Gillgorm's relict, who was with child, and thought was related to the family of Lovat, where it was resolved, if she would bring forth a male child, he should be destroyed lest he should remember and revenge his father's death. But by the time she was delivered, and that of a son, humanity prevailed over their first intended cruelty so far as that they were satisfied with having his back broken that he might not be a man of arms. He was given to the monks of Beauly to be taught and learned there. He made a good progress, and, coming to perfect age, entered into Orders and became a priest, and was called Croter or Cratach Mac Gillgorm. He travelled to the West Coast and the Isle of Skye. He laid the foundation of, and built the church of Kilmore, in Slate, and of Kilchoinen, in Glenelg, and though he lived about the time of Pope Innocent the Third, who possessed the Chair in the beginning of the 13th century, he did not observe his decree against the marriage of the clergy, for this Pope was the first who made that law, and although before his

---

[1] In a note added to a transcript copy of the Rev. John Macrae's MS., in 1785, it is stated that there were several cairns of stones then on the site of the battle, and that the largest of them was believed to mark the grave of Gillgorm himself.

time many churchmen did abstain from marriage and led a single life, yet it was free for any churchman of the Superior or Inferior Order to marry, as appears by the story of St Hylarie. He was Bishop of Poictiers, in France, and having gone to the East to reform the Arian Heresy, heard that a young nobleman treated with his daughter, Abra, for marriage, he wrote to his daughter not to accept of the offer, since he had provided for her a far better husband The daughter obeyed, and before he returned the father prayed that his daughter might die quietly, wherein God heard his prayer, which, when his wife, her mother, understood, she never ceased importune him till she obtained the like favour, as Baptista Mantuanns writes of him

But, to return to Croter MacGillgorm, he did not, I say, observe the Pope's said decree, but married and had children; and in memory of Finanus, then a renowned saint, called one of his sons Gillifinan, usually pronounced Gillinan, the letters turning quiescent in the compound, and the son of that man again was patronimically called MacGillinan, whose successors are now in the North of Scotland called Maclinans

Now, to compensate for this long and, perhaps you may think, needless digression, there are two vulgar errors discovered. The first is that the battle of Drumderfit was fought 'twixt the Macras and Maclinans, and that Lovat had sent his men only to assist the Macras, whereas there were not such a race of men then in being as Maclinans, and what the Macras did was only as followers of Lord Lovat. The other error is that the Macras came to Kintail as soon as Colin Fitzgerald, of whom the Mackenzies are descended, which cannot hold, as Simon, the first Fraser Lord Lovat, married Mary Bizet, Anno. 1247, which was but nineteen years before Colin Fitzgerald got his charter of Kintail from the King, Anno. 1266; and the Macras, living on the Lordship of Lovat, during the time at least of three Lords of that name, cannot be supposed to have come to Kintail till a considerable time thereafter But why or how the Macras removed so totally from the Lordship of Lovat and from Urquhart, where, being in alliance with the Macleans, they likewise possessed several lands, is not at this distance of time easily accounted for, especially as it was never known that there was any misunderstanding betwixt Lovat or his friends and them. On the contrary such of the Macras as lived in the neighbourhood of the Frasers still kept up a good and friendly correspondence, and Lovat likewise had a grateful remembrance of their good services and fidelity to him and his family, so that we may conclude they did not remove at once, but at different times, as circumstances favoured them."

The Rev John Macrae then proceeds to give an account of the migration of the Macraes to Kintail. This account is summarised in Chapter I.

THE MACLENNANS OF KINTAIL.

The name Maclennan (in Gaelic Mac Gillinnein), the traditional origin of which is incidentally given in the above extract, means son of the servant of Finnan. St Finnan, who flourished about A D 575, was a native of Ireland, and one of the companions of St Columba. Others derive the name Maclennan from Mac Gille Adhamhnain. Adamnan, who became Abbot of Iona in 679, was the author of a famous life of St Columba   The first derivation, which is the one given by the Rev. John Macrae in the above extract, seems the more probable,[1] though the name of Adamnan appears in so many different forms that it is difficult to say what names may or may not be derived from it.   The Maclennans were at one time numerous in Kintail, and tradition has preserved the name of Domhnull Buidhe Mac Gillinnein as one of the chief of the Kintail warriors in the feud with Glengarry   There is a well-known tradition that eighteen of the chief Maclennans of Kintail were killed in the Battle of Auldearn, in 1645, and that their widows were afterwards married by Macraes, who thus acquired possession of the Maclennan holdings, and so became the leading name in Kintail. But it is a tradition that has no trace of any foundation in fact. We have full contemporary accounts of the Battle of Auldearn, where only four Kintail men were killed, two Maclennans and two Macraes, viz. ·—Roderick Maclennan, called Ruari Mac Ian Dhomh'uill Bhain, the chief standard-bearer of Kintail , his brother, Donald Maclennan , Malcolm Macrae,[2] son-in-law of the Rev Farquhar Macrae , and Duncan Macrae, called Donnacha Mac Ian Oig[3]   It had been arranged before the battle that Sea-

1 See Macbain's Gaelic Dictionary.   2 Page 68.   3 Page 187.

forth, who was ostensibly fighting against Montrose, but had already resolved to change sides, should withdraw his men without fighting. But the men themselves were not aware of this, and consequently, when they received the order to retreat, many of them refused to do so. Maclennan, the standard-bearer, indignant at the thought that the banner which had so often been victorious should flee in his hands, fixed the staff in the ground, and stood by it with his two-handed sword drawn. A number of Seaforth's men rallied round him and refused to surrender until the brave standard-bearer was shot. Several others were killed during this incident, but only the above-mentioned four were from Kintail.

There is a tradition that when Colin, first Earl of Seaforth, built Brahan Castle and fixed his residence there, most of the Maclennans left Kintail and settled in the neighbourhood of Seaforth's new home [1] This is not at all improbable, as the name Maclennan was, and still is, fairly common in the country round about Brahan. There are only a few Maclennans mentioned in the Rent Rolls given in Appendix H, so that at that time they could not have occupied a very important position in Kintail. We are told that there were several Maclennans in Glensheil about 1790, and that though there were many points of difference between themselves and the Macraes, yet they were always ready to join the Macraes in defence of their common country against every foe. [2]

---

[1] Tradition communicated to the author by Mr Alexander Maclennan, Craig House, Lochcarron

[2] Old Statistical Accounts of Kintail and Glensheil

APPENDIX B.

THE following account of Gregory, or, as he is called in The Prophecy of St Berchan, Grig the Mac Rath, a contemporary of Alfred the Great, and one of the greatest of the early Kings of Scotland, is abridged from Chronicles of the Scots, edited by William Forbes Skene, LL D :—

The Prophecy of St Berchan consists of two Irish manuscripts, written probably about the time of Donald Bane, who was King of Scotland from 1093 to 1098.   It contains a list of Kings of Scotland from Kenneth Macalpin to Donald Bane in the form of a prophecy attributed to St Berchan, who lived towards the end of the seventh century   The names of the kings are concealed under epithets, and Grig, the son of Dungal, who reigned during the last quarter of the ninth century, is called Mac Rath   The following is a translation of some of the parts of the prophecy which refer to him :—

> Till the Mac Rath shall come,
> He shall sit over Alban as sole chief ;
> Low was Britain in his time,
> High was Alban of melodious cities

> Pleasant is it to my heart and body,
> My spirit relates good to me,
> As King the Mac Rath in the Eastern land,
> Under ravenous misfortune to Alban

> Seventeen years of warding valour,
> In the sovereignty of Alban ;
> There shall be slaves to him in the house—
> Saxons, Galls, and Britons.

Grig founded a church among the Picts of Maghcircin (or Mearns).

Long afterwards there was a church in Mearns dedicated to St Cyricus, and called in old charters Ecclesgreig (Grig's Church) Grig and St Cyricus were probably not the same, but they appear to have been in some way connected

In the Chronicle of the Scots and Picts we find the following entry :—

Grig Mac Dungal xii annos regnavit et mortuus est in Dundurn et sepultus est in Iona insula   Hic subjugavit sibi totam Yberniam et fere totam Angliam et hic primus dedit libertatem ecclesiae Scoticanae que sub servitute erat usque ad illud tempus ex consuetudine et more Pictorum [1]

After a reign, variously stated from eleven to eighteen years, of great prosperity and dutiful devotion to the interests of the Church, Gregory is said to have been slain in battle at Dundurn, which, according to Skene, was situated somewhere about the east end of Lochearn, but as a matter of fact, the place and manner of his death, as well as the date of it, are somewhat uncertain.   The time in which he lived is roughly fixed by a great eclipse of the sun, which, according to the Pictish Chronicle, occurred in the ninth year of his reign.   The eclipse is known to have occurred on the 16th June, 885.   This, so far as known, is the earliest recorded instance of the name Mac Rath in Scotland.   He was a Son of Grace in his devotion to the Christian Church, and he was also a Son of Fortune in his wars with the neighbouring tribes, as well as with the Danes, whom he drove out of his kingdom.   Though he was nominally King of Scotland, his actual rule was probably limited to the countries round about Scone, in Perthshire, which was the Capital of those early Scottish Kings, and it is interesting to note that the name Mac Rath appears to have been somewhat common in that part of Perthshire in the fourteenth and fifteenth centuries.   Gregory is also said to have built the city of Aberdeen

---

[1] "Grig, son of Dungal, reigned twelve years and died at Dundurn and was buried in the Island of Iona.   He subdued to himself Ireland and nearly all England, and he first gave freedom to the Scottish Church, which until that time was in servitude according to the constitution and custom of the Picts."   There is some reason to believe that he invaded the Kingdom of Northumbria, which at this time was harassed by the Danes, but there does not appear to be any foundation for the statement with regard to Ireland.

The following legend is from the Dean of Lismore's Book —
On one occasion Fionn and six of the chief princes were all
drinking together at Alvie They were accompanied by their
wives, and as the cup circulated and took effect the women began
to talk among themselves of their chastity.   No women on earth
could be more chaste than they   While this talk was going on a
maid was seen approaching the company.   Her covering was a
single seamless robe of spotless white from end to end.   Fionn
asked what virtue was there in her seamless robe.   She replied—
" My seamless robe has the strange power, that such women as are
not chaste can find no shelter in its folds   It shields none but the
spotless wife " The princes then insisted that their wives, each
one in her turn, should try on the seamless robe.   They did so, but
the robe would not fit them or spread out over them or cover their
persons.   " Give my wife the seamless robe," said M'Raa,[1] " for I
have no fear as to the result."   M'Raa's wife took the robe, which
fitted her and spread over her so easily that no part of her person
remained exposed.

1 The name is so spelled in the original text ; in the English translation it
is rendered MacRea.   It has been questioned on competent authority whether
this is the same as the modern name Macrae.

APPENDIX C.

BOND OF FRIENDSHIP BETWEEN THE MACRAES OF KINTAIL AND THE CAMPBELLS OF CRAIGNISH, 1702.

"At Ballachulish, in Lochaber, upon the eighth day of October, one thousand seven hundred and two years, it is condescended and agreed to betwixt the parties following, viz '—George Campbell of Craignish, on the one part, and Farquhar Macra of Inverinate ; Master Donald Macra, minister of the Gospel, in Kintail ; Donald Macra of Camuslumy ; John Macra, in Achyark ; Duncan Macra, son of Christopher Macra, in Aiiyugan ; and Kenneth Macra, brother german to the said Farquhar Macra of Inverinate, all in Kintail, in name and behalf of the hail remnant, gentlemen and others of the said name of Ra, in Kintail and elsewhere, lineally descended of their forbearers and predecessors on the other part , that is to say—Forasmuch as the said George Campbell of Craignish, and the saids Farquhar, Mr Donald, Donald, John, Duncan, and Kenneth Macras, have at date hereof seriously considered what relation, firm friendship, and correspondence has been of old and hitherto continued betwixt the Campbells of Craignish, the said George Campbell, now of Craignish, his predecessors, and the forebearers and predecessors of the said Farquhar Macra of Inverinate, and others above written, and all others of the said name of Ra, and the great love and favour each of them did bear to other, both by the said George Campbell of Craignish and his predecessors, taking the part of any of the said name of Macra, in all lawful causes, defending the samen against others when occasion required, and the firm, stable, and sure love and favour the said Farquhar Macra and others foresaid, of the said name of Macra, and their predecessors, did and doth bear to the said George Campbell of Craignish and his predecessors, and the acts of kindness and friendship done by the said name of Macra to the said family of Craignish, when occasion offered, in all time bygone. And now for the more firm and sure upholding and maintaining of the said relationship, friendship, and correspondence, and for the better keeping and preserving the samen on record, in all time coming, the said George Campbell of Craignish, by their presents, binds and obliges him, his heirs and successors, to maintain, and in hand take the part of any of the said name of Macra in all lawful causes, and defend the samen, to the uttermost of their power, against any other person, their duty to Her Majesty and Her Highness' successors and Council, and their immediate lawful superiors, alwise excepted   And sicklike the saids Farquhar Macra, Mr Donald, Donald, John, Duncan, and Kenneth Macra, in name and behalf foresaid, for them, their heirs, and all others lineally descending of their bodies, by their presents, binds and obliges them and their foresaids, so far as they may do by law, to own, maintain, and in hand take the part of the said George Campbell of Craignish or his foresaids, or any others lineally descending of his family, in all lawful causes, and defend any of the said family, to the utmost of their power, against all other person or persons, their duty to Her Majesty and Her Highness' successors and Council, and their immediate lawful superiors, all is excepted   And both the said parties obliges them and their foresaids to renew and reiterate their presents, as oft as they will be required thereto, that the samen may be kept in record and memory ad futuram rei memoriam.

"In testimony hereof (written by John Campbell, younger of Balmillin), both parties have subscribed their presents, place, day, month, and year, foresaid, before these witnesses — Ronald Campbell of Lagganlochta, Ronald Campbell, brother german to the said George Campbell of Craignish; Archibald Campbell, merchant in Kilvoran, in Islay, and the said John Campbell, writer hereof.

(Signed)	"GEO. CAMPBELL.	FARQR. MACRA.
	"MR DOND MACRAH.	D. MACKRA.
	"JOHN MACRAH	DUN. MACRA.
	"KEN. MACRA.	

"RON. CAMPBELL, Witness	RON. CAMPBELL, Witness.
"ARCH. CAMPBELL, Witness.	J CAMPBELL, Witness."

FAC-SIMILE OF SIGNATURES TO THE BOND OF FRIENDSHIP

APPENDIX D.

THE SEAFORTH HIGHLANDERS.—THE AFFAIR OF THE MACRAES

THE two regiments now linked together as the Seaforth Highlanders are the 72nd Highlanders (the Duke of Albany's Own
Highlanders) and the 78th Highlanders (the Ross-shire Buffs)
The 72nd, now the First Battalion of the Seaforth Highlanders,
was raised by Kenneth, Earl of Seaforth. It was inspected and
passed at Elgin on the 15th of May, 1778, and was numbered
the 78th. In 1786 it was re-numbered the 72nd, and in 1822
received the additional name of The Duke of Albany's Own
Highlanders, Albany being the second title of the Duke of York,
then the Commander-in-Chief of the British Army. It is usually
stated that this regiment was recruited largely from the Macraes,
but an examination of the muster roll of the men who were
inspected and passed in Elgin in May, 1778, shows that although
there were several Macraes among them, yet they formed but a
small proportion of the whole regiment The Ross-shire names on
the roll are comparatively few, and so far as can be judged from
names, the recruits might have been brought together from all
parts of the United Kingdom. The majority were in all probability Highlanders, and the Macraes became so prominent in this
regiment, not because of their number, but because of the part
they took as ringleaders in the Mutiny, which is known as "The
Affair of the Macraes."

From Elgin the regiment proceeded to Edinburgh, where it
was ordered to be kept in readiness to embark for India
During their sojourn in Edinburgh, many of the men were billeted
in the Canongate and other parts of the city, and among them
there arose a rumour that the regiment had been sold to the East

India Company But this was not the only grievance. The
bounty money promised, and also their pay, were in arrears, and
the result was that on Tuesday, the 22nd of September, 1778,
when the regiment assembled, and were about to proceed to Leith
to embark there, a large number of men refused to march until
their grievances were attended to.   The officers were insulted and
stoned by the populace, who were in complete sympathy with the
men. A scene of great confusion ensued, and, notwithstanding
Seaforth's efforts to allay the mutinous feeling by promising that
their demands should be complied with as soon as possible, five
hundred Highlanders shouldered their arms, set off at a quick
pace, with pipes playing and two plaids fixed on poles for colours,
to Arthur's Seat, where they took up a position of such natural
strength that, with the arms of those days, it would be no easy
matter to compel them to surrender.   Here they remained for
some days, being liberally supplied with food and even ammunition by the people of Edinburgh and Leith, among whom they
had many sympathisers.   They appointed officers, and placed
sentries in regular order, so that any attempt to surprise them was
seen to be clearly hopeless.   Two accidents occurred among them.
One man was killed by falling over a rock, and another man, who
was accidentally shot through the thigh, was removed to the
Royal Infirmary.   Meantime the authorities were assembling a
considerable force in the city, but at the same time efforts were
being made to induce the mutineers to come to terms.   On the
second day, General Skene, who was second in command in
Scotland, visited them, but they insisted on their former conditions,
and the dismissal of certain officers.   On the third day they were
visited by the Duke of Buccleuch, Lord Dunmore, Lord Macdonald, and several gentlemen and clergymen, but with the same
result.   On the next day, however, a settlement was arrived at, and
the following conditions were accepted by them, viz. —A general
pardon for all that had passed ; that all arrears should be paid
before embarkation , and that they should never be sent to the East
Indies.   These are the conditions as stated in the newspapers of
the day, but it is quite possible the third condition may have
been that they were not to be disposed of to the East India Company, as they readily sailed to India three years afterwards.   The
conditions were signed by the Duke of Buccleuch, Lord Dunmore,

Sir Adolphus Stoughton, Commander-in-Chief for Scotland, and General Skene, second in command in Scotland.

On Friday, the 25th of September, at 11 a.m., they marched down from Arthur Seat, headed by Lord Dunmore, and assembled in St Anne's Yard, near Holyrood, where they were addressed by General Skene, who gave them some good advice, and promised that a Court would be held next day to inquire into the complaints against some of the officers These complaints were pronounced by the Court to be without foundation, but not one of the mutineers received punishment of any kind. After the meeting in St Anne's Yard, the men were billeted in the suburbs of Edinburgh, and on the following Monday they embarked at Leith.

This amicable settlement did not give satisfaction to all the officers, some of whom blamed Lord Dunmore for acting as he did on behalf of the mutineers, and urged the necessity of severe measures as the only guarantee for the maintenance of discipline. The public, however, applauded the wisdom and prudence of the reconciliation, as there was a general feeling that the mutineers were not without some real grievances. Several disturbances of a similar nature had recently taken place in the Highland regiments, and all about breaches of the conditions of enlistment It is quite possible that, in the anxiety to gain recruits, promises were sometimes made which could not easily be fulfilled ; but the fact that the disputes were frequently about arrears of pay, which the Government were well able to afford, shows an inexcusable carelessness with regard to one of the most practical of all the conditions of employment. And when, in addition to these grievances, the men had to serve under officers who neither knew their language nor appreciated their character, it can easily be understood that their lot was not always free from provocation [1]

1 " A Highland regiment, to be orderly and well disciplined, ought to be commanded by men who are capable of appreciating their character, directing their passions and prejudices, and acquiring their entire confidence and affection. The officer to whom the command of Highlanders is entrusted must endeavour to acquire their confidence and good opinion. With this view he must watch over the propriety of his own conduct. He must observe the strictest justice and fidelity in his promises to his men, conciliate them by an attention to their disposition and prejudices, and at the same time by pre-

Of these disturbances, "The Affair of the Macraes" was by far the most formidable, and had it not been so wisely and so judiciously settled, it might have had a very disastrous effect on the efforts being then made to recruit the army from the High-lands It showed once for all that Highland soldiers meant to insist at whatever cost upon being dealt with in good faith, and henceforth we hear less about breaches of the conditions of enlistment.

The idea of sending the regiment to India was for a time abandoned, and from Leith they sailed to Jersey and Guernsey, where they were stationed for some time to resist any attempt at invasion by the French. In 1781 they proceeded to India, ac-companied by the Earl of Seaforth as their Colonel The voyage, which lasted from the 12th June, 1781, to the 2nd April, 1782, proved a disastrous one. Illness broke out among the men, and before they arrived at St Helena, to their utter dismay, their Colonel died His death had a most depressing effect upon the men, of whom no fewer than two hundred and forty-seven died before they reached India. Traditions of this disastrous voyage still survive in Kintail. The subsequent career of the 72nd Highlanders is a matter of history, which it is not necessary to repeat here.

The 78th Highlanders (the Ross-shire Buffs), now the Second Battalion of the Seaforth Highlanders, was raised by Francis, Earl of Seaforth It was inspected and passed at Fort-George in July, 1793, and proceeded to Jersey and Guernsey The follow-ing year another battalion was raised, which was inspected and passed at Fort-George in June, and received the distinctive name of the "Ross-shire Buffs" From the Channel Islands, the first battalion went on active service to Holland, while the second battalion proceeded at once to the Cape of Good Hope, and took part in the capture of the Colony from the Dutch. In 1796 it

serving a firm and steady authority, without which he will not be respected Officers who are accustomed to command Highland soldiers find it easy to guide and control them when their full confidence has been obtained, but when mistrust prevails, severity ensues, with a consequent neglect of duty, and by a continuance of this unhappy misunderstanding the men become stubborn, disobedient, and in the end mutinous.—*Sketches of the Highlanders, by Major-General David Stewart of Garth*

was joined by the first battalion, and the two battalions, incorporated into one, proceeded to India, where the regiment saw
much service before it returned home again in 1817   In 1804
another second battalion was raised   This battalion fought with
great distinction at the battle of Maida, in Italy, in 1806   The
next year it was in Egypt, and suffered very heavily at El Hamet
It saw some further arduous service in Holland, and was
incorporated with the other battalion of the Ross-shire Buffs in
1817.   The subsequent history of the Ross-shire Buffs is well
known   A large number of Macraes from Kintail served in each
of these three battalions.

The 72nd and the 78th (Ross-shire Buffs) were linked together
in 1881 as the Seaforth Highlanders.

APPENDIX E.

KINTAIL.

THE old parish of Kintail, including Glensheil, which was made into a separate parish by the Lords Commissioners of Teinds on the 30th December, 1726, is situated in the south-west of the County of Ross A considerable portion of its boundary runs along the sea coast, its inland boundaries being the parishes of Lochalsh, Kilmorack, Kiltarlity, Kilmonivaig, and Glenelg. The present parish of Kintail is about eighteen miles long, and varying in breadth from five to six miles. Glensheil is about twenty-six miles long, and from two to six miles in breadth. The combined area of the two parishes is rather more than two hundred square miles, a great portion of which consists of moorland and mountain From the sea coast the country opens up in three large valleys or glens—Glenelchaig, Glenlic, and Glensheil These glens are surrounded by steep and lofty mountains, which are frequently covered with green pasture from base almost to summit. The richness of its pastures was no doubt the reason why, in the pastoral age of the Highlands, Kintail was so noted for its cattle It was often called Cintaille nam Bo (Kintail of the cows), and, needless to say, was one of the happy hunting grounds of the cattle lifters of Lochaber. The natural pastoral richness of the country helped also to rear a race of men who, according to all accounts, were at least as robust in mind and body, and as well favoured as any of their neighbours The men of Kintail were usually of good physique and strong, full features.[1] They had large chests and deep voices, and in mimick-

---

[1] There are some excellent representations of Kintail faces in Benjamin West's painting of the rescue of King Alexander III. from the fury of a stag by Colin Fitzgerald, the reputed founder of the House of Kintail, the original of which is in Brahan Castle. See also page 104.

ing the speech of a Kintail man in Gaelic it is still the custom to adopt as deep a tone of voice as possible. In an old Gaelic song they are spoken of as, " Fir ghearra dhonna Chintaille " (the thick-set auburn-haired men of Kintail). They were known among their neighbours as Na Domhich, which may mean either the bulky ones, or the barrels, while the Lochaber men were usually called —at all events in Kintail—Na Fir Chaola, which means the lean or sharp-featured men.

The earliest glimpses we get of the history of Kintail comes to us, as in the case of most Highland parishes, through legends connected with some of the early Scottish Saints, and two at least of the contemporaries of Columba, St Oran[1] and St Donan,[2] have left traces of their names in the country. Scurran, or Oran's Peak, is the highest and most prominent of the mountains of Kintail, and near the foot of it is a place called Achyuran, or Oran's field, while the small island on which the ruins of the stronghold of the Barons of Kintail still stand is called Ellandonan, or Donan's Island So far as at present known, not even a legend has survived to explain what connections those two Saints may have had with the country, but that they were connected in some way with the places which bear their names, may be regarded as extremely probable.

About the middle of the seventh century the country was visited by an Irish Saint called Congan He was a son of the King of Leinster, and was trained as a soldier. On succeeding to his father's dominions he ruled well, but was unfortunate in war with his enemies, and having been wounded and conquered, he

[1] Oran, a well-born Irishman, came to Iona with Columba. When Oran arrived, Columba told him that whoever willed to die first should not only go more quietly to Christ, but should confirm and ratify the right of the community to the Island by taking corporal possession of it Oran consented, whereupon Columba not only assured him of eternal happiness, but said that none who came to pray at his own sepulchre should receive his petition till he had first prayed at Oran's. Oran was thus the first man to be buried in Iona There are many traces of Oran's name to be met with in the West Highlands. Columba came to Iona in A.D. 563.

[2] Donan was also a disciple of Columba He founded a Monastery in the Island of Eigg, where he was put to death, together with his community of about fifty persons, by a band of pirates, probably Picts from the neighbouring mainland, on the 17th of April, A.D. 617.

was forced to flee from his native country   Taking with him his sister Kentigerna and her three sons, one of whom was the celebrated St Fillan, he sailed for Scotland, and eventually settled in Lochalsh, where he led a religious and ascetic life, and lived to an old age. He is said to have died in Lochalsh, and to have been buried in Iona. St Fillan afterwards built a Church in Lochalsh, and dedicated it to his uncle Congan   It was called in Gaelic, Kilchoan, that is, St Congan's Church, and stood very near the present site of the Parish Church.

St Fillan, whose name is associated with Kintail, flourished early in the eighth century. He was the son of an Irish nobleman called Feradach, by Kentigerna, sister of St Congan, and fled with his uncle from Ireland to Lochalsh, as already stated   The chief scene of this Saint's labour, however, was in Perthshire, but tradition says that, in addition to the church he built in Lochalsh, he built another at Kilellan (Fillan's Church), in Kintail, which, as the name implies, was called after himself. There is a burying-place still at Kilellan, and there is a local tradition that St Fillan himself was buried there. It is said that, when he felt his end was drawing near, he went to Iona, and there died, kneeling before the high altar. His body was then sent in a birlinn or galley to Kintail, and buried at Kilellan under a sod that had been brought from Iona

The next Saint whose name enters prominently into the traditions of Kintail is St Duthac, to whom the old Parish Church at Kilduich was dedicated   He was Bishop of Ross, and flourished about the middle of the thirteenth century. His name is associated more especially with Tain, which in Gaelic is called Baille Dhuthich, that is, Duthac's Town. The Kintail tradition is that Farquhar Mac an t' Shagairt, Earl of Ross, who founded the Abbey of Fearn, and died in 1257, sent two Irish monks to Kintail to minister to the spiritual wants of the people   One of these was Duthac, who had charge of the north side of Lochduich, which has ever since been so called after him. The other monk was called Carrac, and had charge of the south side. The two monks used to meet together from time to time at the west end of the Loch. On one occasion, at the time of driving their cattle to the Sheiling, they arranged that on the way they should hold a meeting at the usual place, but when Duthac arrived there he found Carrac lying dead on the knoll where they used to meet, and which still bears Cairac's name.   Duthac was so grieved at the death of his friend that he did not care to live in Kintail any longer.   It was then he went to Tain, where, we are told, he "taught publicly with all gentleness," and became noted for his miraculous powers.   His day was celebrated on the 8th of March, and his shrine at Tain became a famous resort for pilgrims.   How far these Kintail legends may have any foundation in fact it is, of course, impossible to say   The legend of the death and burial of St Fillan, probably refers to some other ecclesiastic who may have been connected with the old church at Kilellan, but the name of St Fillan was such an honoured one in Kintail[1] that it would not be surprising if legends of other saints gradually gathered around it   There is no reason to believe that St Fillan was buried in Kintail.   There were other early Celtic ecclesiastics of the name Fillan, but they do not appear to have been connected with Kintail   Some trace of another Saint survives in the place name, Killechuinard,[2] on the south side of Lochduich, where the remains of some ruins and of a disused burial-place are still to be seen, but of their history nothing appears to be known beyond a vague tradition that a monastery once stood there.

The stronghold of Ellandonan, around which most of the history of Kintail centres, is believed to have been built in the time of Alexander II ,[3] who reigned from 1214 to 1249, as a place

---

[1] Page 291.

[2] It is difficult to say which Saint it was whose name is here preserved A certain Cyneheard was Bishop of Winchester from 754 to 780, and there is some record also of a Scottish Monk or Abbot called Kineard, who visited Gaul with the great British scholar, Alcuin, about the end of the eighth century, and wrote a life of Charlemagne.   It is more likely, however, that Cille-Chuinard means the Church of Donort, which in Gaelic would be Cille-Dhomort, and would be pronounced almost exactly the same as Cille Chuinard. Donort was Abbot of the great Celtic Monastery of Murthlac, in Banffshire, from about 1056 to 1098.   According to some authorities, there was for some time a Diocese of Murthlac, of which Donort was Bishop   It is on record that at the beginning of the twelfth century King David I. of Scotland gave to the newly-formed Bishopric of Aberdeen five churches which had been founded by the missionary zeal of the Monks of Murthlac, and which had belonged to their monastery.   It is quite possible that one of those churches, dedicated to Donort, may have stood on the spot now known as Killechuinard.

[3] See page 293 for the Kintail legend of the Building of Ellandonan Castle.

of defence against the Danes.   At that time Kintail formed part of the Earldom of Ross, and is said to have been inhabited by three different tribes—the Mac Beolans, who inhabited Glensheil and the south side of Lochduich and Lochalsh, as far as Kylerea; the Mac Ivors, who inhabited Glenlic, and the Mac Thearlichs, who inhabited Glenelchaig.[1]   Sometime during the latter part of the thirteenth century, the Earl of Ross appointed a kinsman of his own, called Kenneth, to the government of Ellandonan Castle, which is said to have been garrisoned by a number of Macraes and Maclennans   Kenneth was an able and ambitious man, and, having quarrelled with the Earl of Ross, whom he set at defiance during the unsettled times which followed the death of King Alexander III., in 1286, he succeeded in establishing himself in a position of independence as lord and ruler of Kintail.   It is said that he ruled well, and that his influence was felt over most of the Western Isles   He died in 1304, and was buried in Iona   He was the founder of the great Clan Mackenzie, and from him they derive their name.[2]   The Earls of Ross, however, still continued superiors of the lands of Kintail, as part of their Earldom, and the Mackenzies occupied the lands and the Castle as their vassals for about two hundred years.   King Robert Bruce confirmed to the Earl of Ross all his lands, including Borealis Ergadia, that is, North Argyle, as the west of Ross, Lochalsh and Kintail included, was then called.   We find many other references to the overlordship of the Earls of Ross until 1463, when Alexander Mackenzie, sixth of Kintail, obtains a charter direct from the Crown.

Meantime we find various contemporary references to the circumstances and affairs of Kintail.   In 1331, Randolph, Earl of Moray, who was then Warden of Scotland, despatched a Crown officer to Ellandonan to prepare the Castle for his reception and to arrest misdoers.   Fifty of these misdoers were put to death, and their heads were exposed on the top of the Castle walls. As Randolph sailed up towards the Castle in his barge and saw those heads, he declared, in his zeal for the cause of law and order, that he loved better to look upon them then than on any garland of roses he had ever seen.[3]   In

---

[1] Mackenzie's History of the Mackenzies, New Edition, page 45.

[2] Appendix G.   [3] Sir Walter Scott's Tales of a Grandfather.

1503, Alexander Gordon, Earl of Huntly, undertook to reduce Ellandonan and other castles on the west coast " for the daunting of the Isles," and to furnish or raise men to keep them when reduced, King James IV engaging to provide a ship and artillery for the purpose.   In 1504 there was a general insurrection in the Highlands, which it took the King's forces two years to quell, and in the course of which Ellandonan Castle was occupied by the Earl of Huntly.   In 1539, Donald Gorm Macdonald of Sleat invaded the country and attempted to take the castle, but was killed during the siege by a Macrae, called Duncan Mac Gille-chriosd.[1]   Donald Gorm and his followers succeeded, however, in setting fire to the castle, for we find that in 1541 James V. granted remission to Donald's accomplices for their treasonable burning of the Castle of Ellandonan and the boats there.   The great feud which broke out between Kintail and Glengarry about 1580, and in which the Macraes took such a leading part, has been already referred to.[2]   This feud, which lasted for about twenty-five years, ended in the complete discomfiture of Glengarry, whose possessions in Lochcarron and Lochalsh were made over to Kintail by a Crown charter in 1607.   The House of Kintail had now practically reached the zenith of its greatness.

Meantime the Barons of Kintail and their people took a prominent part in the national affairs of Scotland.   John, the second Baron of Kintail, fought on the side of Bruce at Bannockburn, and is said to have had a following of five hundred men   John of Killin, ninth Baron, who was one of the Privy Councillors of James V., fought with his followers at Flodden in 1513, and at Pinkie in 1547.   Colin, the eleventh Baron, fought as a young man at the head of his vassals on the side of Queen Mary at the battle of Langside in 1568

In the unsettled times of the reign of Charles I , with whose cause George, second Earl of Seaforth, finally cast in his lot, the men of Kintail played an important part.   Seaforth fought at the battle of Auldearn in 1645, nominally against Montrose, but it had been arranged beforehand that his men should retire without fighting, and that Montrose should be allowed an easy victory[3]   Shortly afterwards Seaforth publicly avowed himself a supporter of Mon-

[1] Page 25.   [2] Chapter III.   [3] Page 336.

X

trose, who was then joined by a large number of the men of Kintail.   Henceforth the people of Kintail continued to be staunch supporters of the House of Stuart until the final defeat at Culloden in 1745.   In 1650 the Parliament placed a garrison in Ellandonan Castle to overawe the country, but the insolence of the soldiers becoming intolerable, they were summarily turned out by the people, and no attempt was made to restore or to replace them [1] A number of Kintail men fought on the Royalist side at Worcester in 1651.   In 1654, on the 26th of June, General Monk, Cromwell's lieutenant in Scotland, visited Kintail with an army, and remained there for two or three days.   The names of the places mentioned in the account of his visit at the time were evidently written by men who knew no Gaelic, and are not easily identified now   One Kintail man was killed by the soldiers,[2] the houses and huts were burnt wherever they went, and a large spoil of cattle was taken by them,[3] "which made some part of amends for the hard march."[4]

A large number of Macraes took part in the rising of 1715, and suffered heavily at the battle of Sheriffmuir.   Tradition relates that this battle made fifty-eight widows in Kintail.   The Macraes of Kintail and the Mathesons of Lochalsh were in the centre of the second line of Mar's army, and a writer of the last century says that they were the only part of Seaforth's men that behaved well at Sheriffmuir, for when the rest ran away the Macraes and Mathesons held their ground until a large number of them was left dead on the field [5]   The same writer, who was a

---

[1] Page 195.   [2] Page 31.   [3] Page 63

[4] The events which led to Monk's visit to Kintail were as follows :—In 1653 a Stuart rising took place in the Highlands under the Earl of Glencairn, whose place was soon taken by General Middleton   It was to quell this rising that Monk made his march through the Highlands in 1654.   Having heard that Middleton was in Kintail, Monk led his forces there, only to find, on arriving, that Middleton had left the day before and gone to Glenelg.   Monk did not follow Middleton to Glenelg, but plundered the people of Kintail and then departed by way of Glenstrathfarrar.   The rising shortly afterwards collapsed.   For a more detailed account of General Monk's visit to Kintail, see a paper by Mr William Mackay in Volume xviii. (1892) of the Transactions of the Gaelic Society of Inverness.

[5] The Highlands of Scotland in 1750, from a MS. in the British Museum, with introduction by Andrew Lang

bigoted Whig, and very much biased in most of his remarks on the Jacobite clans, tells us that the common people in Kintail are "the Macraes, who are by far the most fierce, warlike, and strongest men under Seaforth." He then goes on to say that until quite recently the Macraes were little better than heathen and savages, but his only excuse for such a statement seems to have been his Whig prejudices, and his desire to make it appear that, as a result of Whig influences in Kintail, there was a "surprising alteration in the people even in point of common civility, decency, and cleanliness." As a matter of fact, there was hardly any district in the Highlands where Whig influences made way more slowly than in Kintail.

Early in 1719, Cardinal Alberoni, Prime Minister of Spain, with which country we were then at war, fitted out a powerful expedition under the Duke of Ormonde[1] to support the Jacobite cause in the Highlands of Scotland. But scarcely had the expedition left the coast of Spain when it was overtaken by a terrible storm in the Bay of Biscay. The storm lasted for twelve days, and so completely dispersed the fleet that only two vessels were able to reach Scotland. These two vessels had on board the Earl of Seaforth, the Earl Marischal, the Marquis of Tullibardine, and about three hundred Spaniards, with arms and ammunition for two thousand men. They landed in Kintail on the 5th of April, and encamped on the mainland opposite to Ellandonan. Here they lay quiet for some time in the hope that Ormonde might still be able to effect a landing, but they were soon joined by several Highlanders, including the famous Rob Roy Macgregor and a party of his followers.

Shortly afterwards three ships of war—the Worcester, the Enterprise, and the Flamborough—sailed up Lochalsh under the command of Captain Boyle of the Worcester. On the 10th of May, early in the morning, Captain Boyle drew up the Worcester and the Enterprise in front of Ellandonan Castle, which was garrisoned by forty-five Spaniards, commanded by Irish officers, and at nine

---

1 James Butler, Duke of Ormonde, a distinguished soldier of the reigns of William III. and Anne. On the accession of George I. he embraced the cause of the Stuarts, and was henceforth obliged to live abroad. Born, 1665, died, 1747.

o'clock sent his lieutenant with a boat under a flag of truce to demand the surrender of the Castle, which was refused.   About four in the afternoon Captain Boyle was informed by a deserter from the Jacobite side that the number of men in their camp was more than four thousand, and was daily increasing.   One thousand would probably be nearer the truth.   He therefore resolved to delay action no longer, and at eight o'clock in the evening he opened upon the Castle "a great fire," under cover of which he despatched two boats, manned and armed, under two lieutenants, to whom the Spaniards, who had mutinied against their officers, readily surrendered   To prevent the Jacobites, whose camp lay near the Castle, from taking possession of it again, Captain Herdman of the Enterprise was sent to blow it up   This duty he effectually performed after having first sent off the prisoners with three hundred and forty-three barrels of gunpowder, fifty-two barrels of musket shot, and some bags of meal.   At the same time he burnt several barns on the mainland near the Castle, where quantities of corn had been stored for the use of the camp. Such was the end of Ellandonan Castle.

Meantime Captain Hedesley of the Flamborough sailed up Lochduich, where a large quantity of ammunition, belonging to the Spaniards, was stored under a guard of thirty of their men, but on his first appearance within sight the Spaniards set fire to it.   This store was situated at Loch nan Corr, near the site of the Manse of Kintail, and, for many years afterwards, cannon balls and other relics of ammunition used to be found on the glebe in great abundance.   It was at the same time that the old church of Kintail was destroyed,[1] the only possible excuse for such an act of sacrilege being the fact that the incumbent of the parish was that ardent Episcopalian and Jacobite, the Rev. Donald Macrae, who was now an old man, and who died shortly afterwards.   After destroying the church, the troops landed, and, according to their custom, plundered the unfortunate, defenceless people.

On hearing of these events, the Commander-in-Chief of the Forces in Scotland ordered General Wightman, who was then stationed at Inverness, to proceed to Kintail with the troops under his command—about 1200, which included 136 Highlanders,

[1] Old Statistical Account.

chiefly Munros and Mackays.   The Jacobite force consisted of about 1100, which included about 200 Spaniards [1]

The battle was fought on the 10th of June, at a place now called Eas-nan-arm (the waterfall of arms).   The fighting began at five o'clock in the afternoon, and lasted for about three hours.   The King's troops made three unsuccessful attempts to dislodge the Highlanders, but in the fourth attack Seaforth was wounded, and the heather in which the Highlanders were posted having caught fire, they began to fall into a state of confusion. Recognising the hopelessness of further resistance, the Highlanders dispersed and retired to the mountains, and next morning the Spaniards surrendered as prisoners of war.   The King's troops lost twenty-one killed, and one hundred and twenty-one wounded. The loss of the Highlanders is not known, but was probably not very heavy.   Seaforth, Marischal, and Tullibardine, with the other principal officers, succeeded in making their escape to the Continent.

Major-General Wightman spent some days in the neighbouring country, plundering and burning the houses of the guilty, and on the 28th of June he writes from Lochcarron to say he is on his way to Inverness.   The local tradition of a Dutch Colonel, who was killed in the battle, and whose ghost used to revisit the scene of the conflict, appears to have no foundation in fact.   The only officer in the Royalist side who is returned as killed in the official list of casualties is Captain Downes of Montagu's regiment, who was buried on the south side of the river, and whose grave is still pointed out [2]

After the Rebellion of 1715, the Seaforth estates, being forfeited, were placed by Parliament under the management of the Forfeited Estates Commissioners.   The Commissioners did not find their task an easy one, for the tenants as a rule adhered loyally to their old landlords or chiefs, and refused to pay any rent to the factors whom the Commissioners appointed.   For several years the Kintail rents were regularly paid to Seaforth's Chamberlain, Donald Murchison, who continued to send them to his

[1] Tullibardine, in a letter to the Earl of Mar, gives the number as 1120, including 200 Spaniards.

[2] For a full account of the battle of Glensheil, see " The Jacobite Attempt of 1719," edited for the Scottish History Society by W. K. Dickson.

master on the Continent. At last two Whigs of Easter Ross—William Ross of Easter Fearn, and his brother, Robert Ross, a Bailie of Tain—undertook to collect the rents on the estates of Seaforth, Chisholm, and Glenmoriston, and started from Inverness on the 13th September, 1721, with an escort of soldiers under Lieutenant John Allardyce. Having visited Glenmoriston, they proceeded to Strathglass and Kintail, but a young lad, Patrick Grant, son of Ian a Chragain, the Chief of Glenmoriston, took a short route to Kintail, and informed Donald Murchison of the approach of the Whig factors. Though Murchison had been " bred a writer," he had also some military training, and held a Lieutenant-Colonel's commission in the Jacobite army of 1715. Part of the funds collected from the people he used in keeping on foot a company of armed Highlanders, whom he always held in readiness for the protection of Seaforth's interests in Lochalsh and Kintail. With these and several other followers, amounting in all to 300 men, Murchison set out, accompanied by Patrick Grant, to meet the Whig factors and their military escort. They met on the 2nd of October, at a place called Ath nam Muilach, a narrow pass in the mountains between Glenaffric and Kintail. After some skirmishing, in which several were wounded, a meeting was arranged between Easter Fearn and Murchison, with the result that the factors retreated, leaving their commission in Murchison's hands, and promising, it is said, not to act again in the service of the Commissioners. Among the wounded was Easter Fearn himself and his son Walter The son died on the following morning, and his body was carried by the soldiers to Beauly Priory for burial.[1]

In the following month the Sheriff-Depute of Inverness held Courts of Inquiry at Inverness with the view of ascertaining who were Murchison's followers. Among the witnesses examined was a soldier in the Royal Regiment of North British Fusiliers, called Donald Macrae, who was one of the escort that accompanied the factors, and who recognised from fifty to sixty Kintail men, whose names and patronymics are stated in his evidence[2] They were

[1] Fuller accounts of the affair of Ath nam Muilach are given in Mackenzie's History of the Mackenzies (new edition), pp. 305-310, and Mackay's Urquhart and Glenmoriston, pp 295-296.

[2] For a full account of these inquiries see a paper on "Donald Murchison and the Factors on the Forfeited Estates," by William Mackay, published in the Transactions of the Gaelic Society of Inverness, Vol. xix. (1893). See also Appendix M.

nearly all Macraes, most of them belonging to the chief families of Kintail.   Nothing appears to have come of this inquiry.

Shortly afterwards another attempt was made to obtain possession of Seaforth's estate for the Government.   A company of soldiers, under Captain Macneill, formerly of the Highland Watch, proceeded from Inverness to Kintail by Dingwall, Garve, and Lochcarron   But while crossing the hills of Attadale, between Lochcarron and Lochalsh, they were met by Donald Murchison and his dauntless followers at a place called the Coille Bhan (the white wood).   A skirmish ensued, in which one soldier was killed and several wounded.   Captain Macneill himself was severely wounded, and, withdrawing his men, shortly afterwards made his way back to Inverness as well as he could.[1]   After this the Forfeited Estates Commissioners appear to have made no further attempt to collect rents in Kintail.[2]

In 1725 General Wade,[3] in his report to the King, states that the Seaforths still pay their rents to Donald Murchison, and in the same year the Forfeited Estates Commissioners report that they had not sold the estate of William, Earl of Seaforth, as they had not been able to obtain possession of it.   The constant fighting in which the men of Kintail had been engaged almost since 1640 told against their material circumstances, and General Wade states, in

[1] Mackenzie's History of the Mackenzies (new edition), p. 311.

[2] In Appendix H. will be found a list of the tenants on Seaforth's Kintail estate in 1719 and 1756, and the rents they paid.   Considering the high value of money at those dates, it will be found that the difference between the rents paid in the Highlands then and now was not so great as is generally supposed.

[3] George Wade, Field Marshal of His Majesty's forces, and Privy Councillor, was a distinguished soldier whose name is still well known in the Highlands in connection with his roads and bridges   He joined the army in 1690, served in the Continental wars of his time, and eventually rose to the highest military rank   In 1724 he was appointed to a command in Scotland, and while holding that command he employed his soldiers in making roads in the Highlands   The roads gave rise to a famous couplet —

> If you had seen these roads before they were made,
> You would hold up your hands and bless General Wade.

In 1745 he commanded an army in the North of England to oppose the Southward march of the Highlanders, but was too old and infirm to be of much service. He died in 1748, at the age of 80.   Wade was an officer of great vigour and sound judgment, and is well entitled to a high place among the chief benefactors of the Highlands.

1725, that though they were formerly reputed the richest of any tenants in the Highlands, they had now become poor through neglecting their business and applying themselves to the use of arms. Consequently they were no longer able to pay their rents with their former readiness and regularity In 1726 Seaforth was pardoned for his share in the Rising of 1715, and permitted to return to his native land. He received a grant of the feu-duties due to the Crown out of his forfeited estates, which were held by the Government until his death in 1741, when they were purchased from the Crown—by his mother—for the benefit of his son Kenneth, Lord Fortrose.[1]

For some time after these events, the country enjoyed peace Law and order were more firmly established, and there was a gradual return of prosperity Simon, Lord Lovat, then an active supporter of the Hanoverian Government, raised a company of Highlanders to keep in check the Lochaber cattle lifters, and Kintail profited to some extent from this protection. In 1722, barracks was erected in Glenelg, and a few companies of soldiers were usually stationed there until after the battle of Culloden, when the building was gradually allowed to fall into disuse Shortly afterwards the country was opened up by one of General Wade's military roads, running from Fort-Augustus to Glenmoriston, thence down through Glensheil to the head of Lochduich, and across the hills of Ratagan to Glenelg.

In 1726, as already stated, and while the Seaforth estates were still in the hands of the Government, the south side of Kintail was formed into the separate parish of Glensheil, and shortly afterwards a Presbyterian minister — the Rev. John Beton—was settled there in spite of considerable opposition from the people, to whom Presbyterians and Whigs were equally hateful, but the

---

[1] The restored Earl did not show Donald Murchison the gratitude to which his loyal services entitled the latter Donald shortly afterwards left the country, and died in the prime of life near Conon A monument erected to his memory on the Lochalsh side of Kyleakin bears the following inscription — " Tullochard.—To the memory of Donald Murchison, Colonel in the Highland Army of 1715. He successfully defended and faithfully preserved the lands of Kintail and Lochalsh from 1715 to 1722 for his Chief, William, the exiled Earl of Seaforth.—Erected by his great-grand-nephew, Sir Roderick I. Murchison, K.C.B.—1863."

Parish Church was not built until 1758. The old Parish Church of Kintail was at this time vacant for several years. The Rev Donald Macrae, the last Episcopalian minister, died about 1721, but his Presbyterian successor, the Rev John Maclean, was not appointed until 1730.

The Rising of 1745 brought fresh trouble upon Kintail. Though Seaforth remained loyal to the House of Hanover, yet it was well known that the sympathies of the people were on the other side. Sheriffmuir and Glensheil were not yet forgotten. A writer of the period[1] states that "some of the wild Macraes" were out in that year, and there is a local tradition to the effect that of those who joined in that rising not one ever again returned to Kintail. After the battle of Culloden, Lord George Sackville[2] entered Kintail by Glenaffric, and with the brutal cruelty so characteristic both of himself and of his chief, the Duke of Cumberland, plundered the defenceless people, and drove away a large number of cattle and other booty[3] In the course of his wanderings after the defeat at Culloden, Prince Charles came to

[1] The Highlands in 1750, edited by Andrew Lang.

[2] The subsequent career of Lord George Sackville (born 1716, died 1785) was far from creditable. He was in command of the British horse at the battle of Minden in 1759, when his conduct was so unsatisfactory that he was tried by Court-Martial and dismissed from the army. In 1775, under the title of Lord Germaine, he became Secretary of State for the American Colonies, and directed the American War, with the disastrous result that we lost our American Colonies. The career of William, Duke of Cumberland (born 1721, died 1765), son of George II, was no less discreditable. In 1745 he was in command of the British army which was defeated by the French in the great battle of Fontenoy, in the Netherlands. Next year he defeated the army of Prince Charles Edward at the battle of Culloden, after which he fixed his headquarters at Fort-Augustus, and harried the neighbouring country with every species of military execution. The barbarous cruelty with which he treated the defenceless people gained for him the nickname of "The Butcher" From Scotland he returned to the command of the army in the Netherlands, and was again defeated in 1746 by the French, with great loss, at the battle of Laufeldt. In the Seven Years' War he held an important command, and suffered a great defeat at the battle of Hastenbach in 1757. Shortly afterwards he made a humiliating surrender to the French at Klosterseven, for which he was recalled and degraded from his rank in the army. Culloden was his only victory, and the very fates seemed to exact grim vengeance for the cruel and cowardly use he made of it.

[3] Old Statistical Account of Kintail.

Glensheil on the 27th of July, 1746, and remained there until the following afternoon.[1]

With the defeat of Culloden it may be said of Kintail, as of the rest of the Highlands, that the old order of things came to an end, and began gradually to make way for the modern conditions of life. There arose a greater security of life and property as people learned to look to the law for protection rather than to the sword. Cattle-lifting and clan feuds came to an end, schools were established, and means of communication with the great commercial and industrial centres of the South greatly improved But although settled peace and security thus brought many benefits, yet there came, on the other hand, many unavoidable social and economic changes which did not always prove an unmixed blessing.

In the Old Statistical Accounts of Kintail, by the Rev. Roderick Morrison, and of Glensheil, by the Rev. John Macrae, we have a fairly full description of the circumstances of the country during the fifty years following the battle of Culloden. About 1769-1774, a large number of the people emigrated to America, chiefly to Carolina Their descendants are still numerous there and in the neighbouring States, and many of them have since been honourably associated with the affairs of their adopted country. These emigrants belonged, as a rule, to the well-to-do farmers of the country. They were not unfrequently young men to whom the idle life imposed upon them by the peace and the altered conditions which followed the battle of Culloden, was not always agreeable. Many were prompted to seek new homes, partly by love of adventure, and partly by a desire to share in the rumoured wealth of the New World It would seem, too, that even in those days the rent question was not altogether free from difficulties, and that the more spirited of these men disliked a connection with their Chief, in which valour was no longer of any account, and of which the chief feature was the paying of rent

We find difficulties about the rent as far back as the time of Colin, first Earl of Seaforth, who lived in far greater state than any of his predecessors, and was, therefore, obliged to raise the rents accordingly.[2] The relations set forth in Ian Mac Mhur-

[1] Page 210.   [2] Page 189.

achaidh's poems,[1] as existing between the people and their chief, may reasonably be regarded as somewhat exaggerated. The poems containing references to such relations were evidently composed with a view to induce as many people as possible to emigrate with him to America, and it is but natural that he should dwell somewhat emphatically on the disadvantages of life in the old country, as compared with the advantages of the promised land beyond the seas. But the pointed and practical advice he gives to the landlords themselves reasonably pre-supposes some excuse for offering it, and it is interesting as showing what the class of men to whom he belonged held to be the landlord's wisest and most practical policy to adopt toward his people.

> Cum na clachan steibhe
> Dh'fhag na daoine gleusda 'n coir dhut.

> Bidhe aoidheal ris a cheathairne,
> Cum taobh nan daoine matha riut,
> 'S gur mor an cliu gun chleith
> A choisininn t-athar air an t-sheol sin.

> Gur iomadh bochd 'us diunleachdan
> Thug beannachd air do shinnseara,
> Gur maireanach an dilib sin,
> 'S gur cinntiche na 'n t-or e.[2]

On the whole, however, the relations existing between the Sea-forths and the people of Kintail were usually very cordial, thanks to the pastoral richness of the country, and the tact and sense of justice evidently possessed by some of the Macrae Chamberlains, who were so frequently the real rulers and administrators of the affairs of Kintail, for during the last two hundred years of their power the Earls of Seaforth were hardly ever resident in Kintail themselves. The traditions of the country have preserved frag-ments of songs in which the virtues of more than one Chamber-

---

[1] Appendix J.

[2] Preserve the foundation stones left to you by able and generous men. Be courteous to the yeomanry, keep the good men on your side, great and evident was the renown gained by your father in that way. Many a poor man and many an orphan invoked blessings on your ancestors. Such things are an enduring heritage, and more to be relied on than gold.

lain are set forth, and of which the lament for Ian Breac Mac
Mhaighster Fearacher[1] may be taken as an example.

But the social stagnation which seemed to be setting in after
the battle of Culloden was not destined to last long   A change
was rapidly approaching, and scarcely had the emigration commenced when the Highlanders were called upon to fight the battles
of their country in all quarters of the globe.   To this appeal the
men of Kintail, like the rest of their compatriots, gave a ready and
willing response   A fair number of Highlanders fought in the
great wars of the last century, such as the War of the Austrian
Succession (1740-1748), and the Seven Years' War (1756-1763),
and there were certainly a few Kintail men among them, but it
was not until towards the end of the century that Highlanders
were either encouraged or invited to join the army in large numbers, and that the famous Highland Regiments were enrolled.
Between 1778 and 1804, four battalions of about a thousand men
each were raised by the Earls of Seaforth,[2] and each battalion
contained a large number of men from Kintail.

It would seem from the Old Statistical Account that the forty
years following the battle of Culloden was, on the whole, a period
of prosperity for Kintail.   There was a steady increase of population in spite of emigration, and so well off were the people that the
famine of 1782, which was felt so severely in many parts of the
Highlands, was not felt at all in Kintail   In 1792 there were only
fifteen poor persons in Kintail and twenty-one in Glensheil. These
were supported by the weekly collections in the churches and by the
charity of their neighbours.   There was no confirmed drunkard in
either of the two parishes, and no thieves.   A baron-bailie or judge
visited the country quarterly to settle such differences as might
arise among the people.   Those differences were usually questions
connected with encroachments on marches, trespassing, and pen-
folding.   From the beginning of June to about the middle of
August the cattle were moved from the arable fields and lower
pastures to the sheilings on the upper moorlands.   A number of
people went along with the cattle as herds and dairymaids, and
huts were erected for shelter and sleeping accommodation.   In fine
summer weather life under such circumstances would not be un-

1 Appendix J.   2 Appendix D.

pleasant, and the season spent in the sheiling was usually regarded as a time of much enjoyment.   It was a time of mirth and love making, and the praise of nighean na h'airidh (the maid of the sheiling) forms the theme of many a Gaelic love song.   The stock consisted mainly of Highland cattle.   There were hardly any sheep, but there were about three hundred horses at this time in the parish of Kintail alone, and probably a corresponding number in Glensheil.   There was a parish school at Cro and another near the Church of Glensheil.   There was a third school in Glenelchaig supported by subscriptions from the farmers, many of whom were Roman Catholics, nearly a third of the people of Kintail at that time being of that creed.[1]   It is to the credit of Protestants and Roman Catholics alike that religious differences did not prevent them from combining to support the cause of education.   Considering all circumstances, it would appear that at the close of the last century the people of Kintail were in fairly prosperous circumstances, and quite as advanced in their views and ways as any of their neighbours

But there was evidently a marked change for the worse during the next forty years.   The population, which was almost stationary during the period of the Napoleonic War, when so many of the men were serving in the army, began to increase rapidly after the peace of 1815, without any corresponding increase in the means of sustenance, and we learn from the New Statistical Account in 1836 that at that time there was a considerable amount of poverty in the country.   But the increase of population was not the sole cause of this change.   Francis, Earl of Seaforth, having got into debt, was obliged to sell considerable portions of his West Coast estates.   When his people came to know of the state of his affairs they offered to pay his debts if he would reside among them, but their offer was disregarded.   Lochalsh was sold under value in 1803, Kintail and a large portion of Glensheil followed in 1807, and the long connection of the Seaforth family with that country was all but ended before the death of the last Earl of Seaforth, which occurred at Warriston, near Edinburgh, on the 11th of January, 1815—the last of the direct male representatives of the House of Kintail. The remainder of the old Kintail estate was sold by his

---

1 For an account of the founding of the Roman Catholic Mission in Kintail see page 73.

grandson, Keith William Stewart-Mackenzie, in 1869, and the last connecting link between the Seaforth family and Kintail was thus finally severed.

With the severing of the old Seaforth connection, there came other changes also, changes of an unavoidable nature, which were only a part of the great social change which, during the last hundred years, has gradually transformed, either for better or worse, the circumstances and the condition of the people of the Highlands. Farms on a larger scale were let to strangers from the South ; sheep took the place of cattle   The smaller tenants were gradually dispossessed of their holdings in order to make way for large sheep farms, and in many instances poverty was the result.   Those who had attained to middle age in the midst of the free and primitive surroundings to which they had hitherto been accustomed, could not be expected to take kindly to a change either of abode or occupation, and when they left the country in search of a new home, as many of them did, it was only to experience failure, disappointment, and poverty.

The young and the enterprising emigrated in large numbers, chiefly to Canada, and between 1831 and 1841 there began a steady decrease of the population, which has continued ever since. The decrease of population, however, is not to be attributed solely to the formation of large farms.   It was observed during the early decades of the present century that the spread of education and the increased facilities of communication with the South induced many of the more enterprising young people to seek opportunities of improving their circumstances elsewhere.   This is equally true at the present time, and small though the population is, positions of honour and trust, both at home and abroad, are occupied by more than one of the sons of Kintail, who could have found no possible career in their own native parish.

It has already been mentioned that the old church in Kintail was destroyed in 1719.   Another church was built some time afterwards.   Part of the roof of this church fell in during divine service on Sunday, the 7th October, 1855, without injuring any one.   It was then declared unsafe, and the present church built. The following is a list of the ministers of Kintail since the Reformation, with the dates of the commencement of their ministry :—

John Murchison (Reader)	1574
Murdoch Murchison	1614
Farquhar Macrae	1618
Donald Macrae	1662
Donald Macrae	1681
John Maclean	1730
Donald Maclean	1774
Roderick Morison	1781
James Morison	1825
Roderick Morison	1877
Roderick Mackenzie	1898

The Free Church principles of the Disruption of 1843 did not meet with much favour in Kintail, which is one of the very few Ross-shire parishes in which the Free Church has no place of worship The failure of the Free Church movement in Kintail was, to a certain extent, owing to the traditional dislike of the people to the Whigs with whom they believed the movement to be in some measure associated , but the chief cause was the popularity of the two parish ministers of the time, the Rev James Morrison of Kintail and the Rev John Macrae of Glensheil, whose fathers, as ministers of the same two parishes, had succeeded in winning the people over to the Presbyterian Church, and who were themselves, both of them, men of ability and sound judgment, and of light and leading among the people with whom, by family and other associations, they had been so long connected.

The Roman Catholic Mission, which is still conducted in Kintail, was founded, as already mentioned,[1] by the Rev. Alexander, son of the Rev John Macrae, last Episcopalian minister of Dingwall.   For many years the mission was conducted by priests who visited the country from time to time, but towards the close of the last century a native of Kintail, the Rev Christopher Macrae, was appointed priest in charge, and since then there has been a regular succession of priests resident at Dornie.   The present priest in charge is the Rev Archibald Chisholm   The handsome Roman Catholic premises at Dornie were built by the late Duchess of Leeds, and consist of a church, presbytery, convent, and school.   The church, which is dedicated to Saint Duthac, was opened in 1861.

Although the district of Glensheil was made into a separate parish in 1726, and a minister appointed in 1730, there was no

1 Page 73.

permanent church built until 1758, when the present Church was erected. The following is a list of the ministers of Glensheil, with the dates of the commencement of their ministry.—

John Beton (or Bethune) - - - - - -	1730
John Macrae - - - - - - -	1777
John Macrae - - - - - - -	1824
Farquhar Maciver - - - - - -	1840
Alexander Matheson - - - - . -	1864
Duncan Macrae - - - - - - -	1891

There is now a Free Church in the parish of Glensheil, which was built in 1865. The first minister of it was the Rev Angus Mackay, and he was succeeded by the Rev. Kenneth Macrae, who was ordained in 1898.

Population of Kintail and Glensheil at various periods :—

	Kintail.	Glensheil.	Total.
1755 ..	693	509	1202
1790 ...	840	721	1561
1801 ...	1038	710	1748
1811 ..	1058	728	1786
1821 ...	1027	768	1795
1831 ...	1240	715	1955
1841 ...	1168	745	1913
1851 ...	1009	573	1582
1861 ...	890	485	1375
1871 ...	753	463	1216
1881 ...	688	424	1112
1891 ...	588	394	982

APPENDIX F.

ROYAL LINEAGE OF CERTAIN FAMILIES OF THE CLAN MACRAE.

I. Descent of Margaret Mackenzie, first wife of Alexander Macrae of Inverinate (page 70) :—

EDWARD I of England had, by his second wife, Margaret, daughter of Philip III. of France, a son,

1. EDMUND PLANTAGENET, who married Margaret, daughter of John, Lord Wake, and was beheaded in 1329. He had a daughter,

2. JOAN, the "Fair Maid of Kent," who died in 1385. She married Sir Thomas Holland, Earl of Kent, and afterwards the Black Prince. By Sir Thomas Holland she had

3 THOMAS HOLLAND, Earl of Kent, who married Alice Fitzalan, and died in 1397. He had a daughter,

4 MARGARET, who married John Beaufort (died 1410), son of John of Gaunt, son of Edward III., and had a daughter,

5 JANE BEAUFORT, who married King James I of Scotland, and, secondly, Sir James Stewart, the "Black Knight of Lorn" She died in 1445, leaving by her second marriage a son,

6. JOHN STEWART, first Earl of Athole, who married, first, Margaret, daughter of Archibald, fifth Earl of Douglas He married, secondly, Eleanor, daughter of William Sinclair, Earl of Orkney, and died in 1512. By his second marriage he had a son,

7 JOHN STEWART, second Earl of Athole, killed at Flodden in 1513. He married MARY, daughter of ARCHIBALD CAMPBELL, second Earl of Argyll (killed at Flodden), son of COLIN CAMPBELL, first Earl of Argyll (died 1493), son of ARCHIBALD CAMPBELL (died before his father), son of Sir Duncan Campbell (died 1453), by his wife, MARJORY STEWART, daughter of ROBERT, Duke of Albany, Regent of Scotland (died 1420), son of Robert II. (died 1390),

Y

son of Walter, Lord High Steward of Scotland, by his wife MARJORY, daughter of ROBERT BRUCE (died 1329) By his marriage with Mary Campbell, John, Earl of Athole, had a daughter,

8. ELIZABETH STEWART, who married Kenneth Mackenzie, tenth Baron of Kintail, who died in 1568, leaving a younger son,

9. RODERICK MACKENZIE, first of Redcastle, who married Florence, daughter of Robert Munro of Fowlis, and died shortly after 1608. He had, with other issue, Colin, of whom below, and a son,

10 MURDOCH MACKENZIE, second of Redcastle, who, in 1599, married Margaret, daughter of William Rose, eleventh of Kilravock, and died before 1629 He had, with other issue, Finguala, of whom below, and

11. MARGARET, who married Alexander Macrae of Invernate.

II. Descent of Mary Mackenzie, second wife of Alexander Macrae of Invernate (page 70), from Jane Beaufort (No. 5 in the first Table).

JANE BEAUFORT, as mentioned above, married, first, JAMES I. of Scotland (died 1437), son of ROBERT III (died 1406), son of ROBERT II. (died 1390), son of MARJORY, daughter of ROBERT BRUCE. By this marriage Jane Beaufort had a daughter,

6 ANNABELLA, who married George Gordon, second Earl of Huntly (died 1502), and had a son,

7. ALEXANDER GORDON, third Earl of Huntly, who commanded the left wing of the Scottish army at Flodden in 1513, married Joan, daughter of John Stewart, first Earl of Athole (No. 6 in the above Table), by his first marriage, and died in 1524. He had a son,

8. JOHN GORDON, who married Margaret, natural daughter of King James IV by Margaret, daughter of John Lord Drummond, and died before his father, leaving a son,

9. GEORGE GORDON, fourth Earl of Huntly, "the most powerful subject in Scotland," who was killed at Corrichie, near Aberdeen, in 1562. He married Elizabeth, daughter of Robert, Lord Keith, who was killed at Flodden, and had a daughter,

10. ELIZABETH GORDON, who married John Stewart, fourth Earl of Athole (died 1579), and had a daughter,

11. ELIZABETH STEWART, who married Hugh Fraser, Lord Lovat (died 1576), and had a daughter,

12. ANNE FRASER, who married Hector Munro of Fowlis (died 1603), and had a daughter,

13. MARGARET MUNRO, who married Alexander Mackenzie of Dochmaluag, Strathpeffer (died 1636), and had a daughter,

14 MARY MACKENZIE, who married Alexander Macrae of Inverinate.

III. Descent of Agnes Mackenzie, first wife of the Rev John Macrae of Dingwall (page 145), progenitor of the Conchra family, from Roderick Mackenzie of Redcastle (No 9 in the first Table) :—

RODERICK MACKENZIE of Redcastle had, as mentioned above, a younger son,

10. COLIN MACKENZIE, first of Kincraig, who married Catherine (sasine to her, 15 Sept, 1617), daughter of the Rev. John Mackenzie of Dingwall, and had a daughter,

11. AGNES, who married, as his first wife, the Rev John Macrae of Dingwall.

IV. Descent of Flora Gillanders, wife of John Macrae (page 179), from Murdoch Mackenzie of Redcastle (No 10 in the first Table):—

MURDOCH MACKENZIE, second of Redcastle, had, as mentioned above, a daughter,

11. FINGUALA MACKENZIE, who married Roderick Mackenzie, first of Applecross (died 1646), and had a son,

12. JOHN MACKENZIE, second of Applecross (sasine 1663), married a daughter of Hugh Fraser, third of Belladrum, and had a son,

13 KENNETH MACKENZIE, first of Auldenny, married Isabel, daughter of John Matheson of Bennetsfield, by Mary, daughter of the Rev. Donald Macrae of Kintail (p. 162), and had a son,

14 RODERICK MACKENZIE, second of Auldenny (sasine 1709),

married Margaret (or Catherine), daughter of Simon Mackenzie of Torridon, and had a daughter,

15. JANET MACKENZIE, who married John Mackenzie, of the Dochmaluag family, and had a son,

16. KENNETH MACKENZIE, of Torrancullin, near Kinlochewe (died 1837), who married Kate Mackenzie, of the Torridon family (died 1848), and had a daughter,

17. MARGARET MACKENZIE, who was born in 1797, and died at Strathpeffer, 1888. She married Alexander Gillanders, born at Kishorn, 1792, died at Strathpeffer, 1877, and had, with other issue,

18. FLORA GILLANDERS, who married John Macrae.

Colonel J. A. STEWART-MACKENZIE of Seaforth

APPENDIX G.

THE HOUSE OF KINTAIL.

I. KENNETH, or in Gaelic, Coinneach, who gave their name to the great Clan of Clann Choinnich or Mackenzie. He married Morbha, daughter of Alexander Macdougall of Lorn. Kenneth died in 1304, and was buried in Iona. He was succeeded by his son,

II. JOHN, the first of the race, who was called Mackenzie, led 500 of his vassals at Bannockburn in 1314. He married Margaret, daughter of David de Strathbogie, Earl of Atholl, by Joan, daughter of the Red Comyn who was killed by Robert Bruce in 1306. John died in 1328, and was succeeded by his son,

III. KENNETH, known as Coinneach na Sroine (Kenneth of the Nose), who was executed by the Earl of Ross at Inverness in 1346. He was succeeded by his son,

IV. MURDOCH, called Murachadh Dubh na' h'Uaigh (Black Murdoch of the Cave) He died in 1375, and was succeeded by his son,

V. MURDOCH, called Murachadh na Drochaid (Murdoch of the Bridge). It was in his and his son's time that Fionnla Dubh Mac Gillechriosd, the founder of the Clan Macrae of Kintail, lived. He died in 1416, and was succeeded by his son,

VI. ALEXANDER, called Alister Ionraic (Alexander the Upright) to whom, during his minority, Fionnla Dubh Mac Gillechriosd was guardian. He died in 1488, and was succeeded by his son,

VII. KENNETH, called Coinneach a Bhlair (Kenneth of the Battle). He died in 1491, and was succeeded by his son,

VIII. KENNETH, who was treacherously killed by the Laird of Buchanan, in 1497, and was succeeded by his brother,

IX. JOHN, of Killin, who fought at Flodden in 1513, and at Pinkie in 1547.   He died in 1561, and was succeeded by his son,

X KENNETH, called Coinneach na Cuirc (Kenneth of the Whittle)   He died in 1568, and was succeeded by his son,

XI COLIN, called Cailean Cam (One-eyed Colin). He died in 1594, and was succeeded by his son,

XII KENNETH, Lord Mackenzie of Kintail   He died in 1611, and was succeeded by his son,

XIII COLIN, first Earl of Seaforth   He died in 1633, and was succeeded by his brother,

XIV. GEORGE, second Earl of Seaforth, a leading Royalist in the Civil War, died in Holland in 1651, and was succeeded by his son,

XV KENNETH, third Earl of Seaforth, called Coinneach Mor (Big Kenneth), also a firm Royalist. He died in 1678, and was succeeded by his son,

XVI KENNETH, fourth Earl of Seaforth, died in Paris in 1701, and was succeeded by his son,

XVII WILLIAM, fifth Earl of Seaforth, known as Uilleam Dubh a Chogidh (Black William of the War). For the prominent part he took in the Jacobite Rising of 1715, he was attainted, and his estates forfeited   He died in Lews in 1740, and was succeeded by his son,

XVIII KENNETH, for whom the estates were bought from the Crown in 1741, and who was known by the courtesy title of Lord Fortrose. He was the Seaforth of the time of Prince Charles, but, notwithstanding his well-known Jacobite sympathies, he considered it more prudent to remain loyal to the House of Hanover   He died in London in 1761, and was buried in Westminster Abbey. He was succeeded by his son,

XIX. KENNETH, created Baron Ardelve and Earl Seaforth (Ireland)   He died near St Helena in 1781 while on the way to India as Colonel of the old 78th Regiment, raised by him on his own estates, and now known as the 1st Battalion of the Seaforth Highlanders.   He left no male issue   He was succeeded by

XX. THOMAS FREDERICK MACKENZIE-HUMBERSTON, Colonel of the Hundredth Foot, son of William, son of Alexander, son of Kenneth, third Earl of Seaforth   He was killed in India in 1783, and, leaving no issue, was succeeded by his brother,

XXI. Francis Humberston Mackenzie, created Lord Seaforth of the United Kingdom. He sold the greater portion of the Kintail estates, died in 1815 without surviving male issue, and was succeeded by his daughter,

XXII Mary Elizabeth Fredrica, who married, first, Admiral Sir Samuel Hood, without issue She married, secondly, the Honourable James Alexander Stewart, with issue, and died at Brahan in 1862 She was succeeded by her son,

XXIII Keith William Stewart Mackenzie, who sold what remained of Kintail in 1869. He died in 1881, and was succeeded by his son,

XXIV. James Alexander Francis Humberston Stewart-Mackenzie, Colonel of the Ninth Lancers, and lineal representative of the Earls of Seaforth

When Francis Humberston Mackenzie, Lord Seaforth, died without surviving male issue, in 1815, there was no known male representative left of any head of the house of Kintail since Kenneth, Lord Mackenzie of Kintail, who died in 1611 Kenneth had seven sons, but the male issue of the first six had, so far as known, become extinct. The seventh son was

Simon, of Lochslin, who died in 1666, having had, with other issue—

Simon, who died in 1664, leaving an only son,

Simon, first of Allangrange, who died in 1730, and was succeeded by his son,

George, second of Allangrange, who died in 1773, and was succeeded by his son,

John, third of Allangrange, who died in 1812, and was succeeded by his son,

(xxii.) George Falconer, who was served heir male to the House of Kintail in 1829 He died in 1841, and was succeeded by his son,

(xxiii) John Falconer, fifth of Allangrange, who died unmarried, in 1849, and was succeeded by his brother,

(xxiv) James Fowler, now of Allangrange, lineal representative of the Chiefs of the great Clan Mackenzie, and heir male to the dormant honours and ancient titles of the historic family of Kintail.

APPENDIX II.—The Forfeited Estates Commissioners collected particulars about the rental of Kintail and Lochalsh in September, 1718, and there are some lists of tenants for that and subsequent years contained in the Forfeited Estates papers in the Register House, Edinburgh. The following appears to be the most complete list as regards Kintail.

Rental of the Seaforth estate of Kintail, taken from the depositions of the tenants, as certified by Kenneth Mackenzie of Dundonel, Deputy to Edmund Burt, Esq., Receiver-General of the Rents and Profits of the unsold Forfeited Estates in North Britain, at Inverness, on the 22nd July, 172(7?) (last figure torn in original):—

TENANTS' NAMES.	HABITATIONS.	Mut-tons.	BUTTER. Stone.	BUTTER. Lb.	CHEESE. Stone.	CHEESE. Lb.	VICCARAGE. £ s. D.	RENT IN SCOTS MONEY. £ s. D.
KINTAIL—BARONY OF ARDELF.								
John M'Rae	Achnagart of Glensheel	2	1	...	2	...	16 0 0	223 6 8
Donald M'Rae	Torluishich	2	1	...	2	...	20 0 0	266 13 4
Maurice Macra	Easter Achyuran	1	...	10	2	...	15 0 0	200 0 0
John M'Rae	Wester Achyuran	1½	...	5	1	...	7 10 0	100 0 0
Evan M'Lennan	Ditto	⅔	...	5	1	...	7 10 0	100 0 0
Murdo M'Vic Wuirich	Achnasheallach	1	1	10	2	...	13 0 0	173 13 4
Farquhar M'Rae	Mickle Ratigan	1	1	...	2	...	17 10 0	233 6 8
Christopher M'Rae	Little Ratigan	1	1	...	2	...	17 10 0	233 6 8
Malcolm M'Rae	Little Achyark	2	1	...	2	...	15 0 0	213 6 8
Murdo M'Rae								
Christopher M'Rae, junr.	Kilchuinort	1	1	...	2	...	16 0 0	197 6 8
Murdo M'Rae	Muck	1	...	10	2	...	7 0 0	86 11 8
Ann M'Rae	Mickle Achyark	2	1	...	2	...	19 17 8	245 3 4
Duncan M'Rae								
John M'Rae, junr.								
Duncan M'Rae	Inshchroe	...	...	...	...	...	9 0 0	111 0 0
John M'Ean vic Eulay	Limasy	...	...	...	...	...	...	40 0 0

TENANTS' NAMES.	HABITATIONS.	Muttons.	BUTTER.		CHEESE.		VICCARAGE.	REST IN SCOTS MONEY.
			Stone.	Lb.	Stone.	Lb.	£ s. d.	£ s. d.
KINTAIL.—(Continued).								
Kenneth M'Rae	Achniterd Easter	...	...	...	...	...	2 0 0	24 13 4
William Mackenzie	Achinterd Wester	...	...	...	...	...	2 10 0	30 16 8
Christopher M'Rae	Easter Druidaig	...	...	...	...	...	6 0 0	80 0 0
Finlay M'Rae	Wester Druidaig	1	...	10	1	...	6 0 0	72 16 8
Duncan M'Rae	Tollie	...	...	...	...	...		17 15 8
Donald M'Rae	Dale	1	1	...	2	...	10 0 0	131 6 8
Christopher M'Rae	Arieyugan	1	1	...	2	...	10 10 0	129 19 0
Mary M'Rae, widow	Cambusnagoul	...	...	...	...	...	...	80 0 0
Alexander M'Rae	}	...	...	...	...	...	...	40 0 0
John M'Rae-Smith	} Rowrach, divided into	...	...	...	...	...	...	10 0 0
Dond. M'Rae	} Mickle Oxgate, Middle	...	...	...	...	...	...	30 0 0
Angus M'Huiston	} Oxgate, and Culmadin	...	...	...	...	...	...	20 0 0
Dond. Bayne	}	...	...	...	...	...	...	60 0 0
John M'Rae		...	...	...	...	...	...	10 0 0
Donald M'Finlay Duy		...	...	...	...	...	...	10 0 0
Donald M'Rae	Artullich and Clachan(?)	...	...	...	...	...	4 10 0	55 10 0
Farquhar M'Rae	Morrich	2	1	10	3	...	28 9 0	351 1 4
Alexander M'Rae	Innersheal	7-10ths	...	14	1	8	13 10 0	167 2 0
Waste	Do., one penny and half	3-10ths	...	6	...	12	5 16 0	71 12 0
John M'Crimmon	Easter Leakichan	⁴	...	3	...	6	1 17 6	21 15 10
Rory M'Lennan	Wester Leakichan	1	...	10	1	...	4 0 0	53 6 8
Florence Mackenzie, widd. of Dn. M'Rae	Achidren (where the Manse is now) }	...	...	...	...	...	...	84 0 0
Farquhar Finlay	}							
Finlay M'Rae	} Mickle Innerinnit	2	1	...	2	...	17 0 0	226 13 1
Alexander M'Rae	}							
John M'Rae	}							

KINTAIL—(Continued).

Tenants' Names	Habitations	Muttons	Butter Stone	Butter Lb.	Cheese Stone	Cheese Lb.	Viccarage £ s. D.	Rent in Scots Money £ s. D.
Donald M'Ley								
Murdo M'Coilire								
Donald M'Coilvue								
Alexander M'Rae	Keppoch Mickle	1	...	10	...	10	4 4 0	52 1 0
Duncan M'Rae	Carr	...	...	10	1	...	5 4 0	69 6 8
Donald M'Aulay	Little Keppoch	1	...	...	1	...	1 17 6	23 2 6
Rory M'Rae	Clinbow (below Cerr)	2	...	5	...	10	2 12 0	34 13 4
James Mackenzie	Fadoch	1	...	10	1	...	9 0 0	120 0 0
Kenneth M'Eau vic Illechallim	Half Craigag (?)	1	...	10	...	...		12 12 0
John M'Couchie	Leault	1	...	10	1	...	6 14 8	88 12 0
George Mackenzie	Achyargan	1	...	10	2	...	17 4 0	212 2 8
Christapher MacRae								
Farquhar MacRae	Bundalloch	1	1	...	2	...	10 10 0	129 10 0
Murdo M'Crae	Biolaig	4	2	...	4	...	9 16 0	127 10 8
John M'Crae	Upper Killilan	2	1	...	2	...	12 10 0	166 13 4
Alexander M'Crae	Neather Killillan	2	1	...	2	...	13 0 0	173 6 8
Murdo Murchison	Keillins (?)	...	...	10	1	...	6 0 0	74 0 0
Duncan M'Crae	Achig Chuirn	...	...	10	1	...	11 0 4	132 6 4
Finlay M'Crae	Upper Mamaig	...	...	10	1	...	5 0 0	59 0 0
Finlay M'Crae, above mentioned, and Kenneth M'Crae	For half of Craigag (?)	...	...	10	1	...	1 0 0	11 0 0
Alexander M'Crae	Duyleg	1	...	10	2	...	17 4 0	212 2 8
Alexander M'Crae								
Duncan M'Crae	Neather Mamaig	...	...	10	1	...	5 16 0	72 2 8
Donald M'Illichallum								
Murdoch M'Rea								
John Bane M'Ra, for half, with	Coridhoin	...	...	10	1	...	9 0 0	111 0 0
Murdo M'Ra								

The following Macraes were landholders in the parish of Lochalsh in 1718, and paid together, with other dues, the under-mentioned rents :—

Alexander M'Cra, wadset of Conchra, &c., for 4000 marks—

feu-duty (Scots)	- - - -	£106	13	4
Duncan M'Cra - - - -	Innerskinnaig (*near Conchra*)	73	6	8
Duncan M'Cra - - - -	Ardelve - - -	77	6	8
Donald Macra - - - -	Ardelve - - -	77	6	8
Hugh M'Ra - - - -	Salchy - - -	88	18	0

Rental of Seaforth Estates—Kintail and Glensheil, 1756 :—

		Scots		
Alexander M'Rath, - - -	Aryugan - -	£4710	9	4
Malcolm M'Rath - - - John M'Rath - - -	Cambusnagawl Ardintowl - - }	1417	9	4
John M'Rath - - -	Dall - - -	1206	8	0
Christopher M'Rath - -	{ Easter and Wester Drui- daig, Glenundalan }	1919	2	0
The Widow, Alexander Mac- Challan, and Duncan M'Rath }	Wester Achintyart -	705	3	4
Duncan MacMillan - - -	Easter Achintyart -	705	3	4
Rorie MacLinan - - -	Leckichan - - -	502	2	8
Mr John Beaton, Minister of { Letterfearn - - {	Leckichan, Muck, Achi- gichuirn - - }	2309	6	8
Christopher M'Rath - -	Kilchuinort - - -	1911	8	0
Kenneth M'Rath, Alexander M'Rath, John's son, and Alex- ander, Christopher's son }	Little Ratagan - -	2211	4	8
Donald M'Rath's widow, Finlay Roy M'Rath - - }	Meikle Ratagan - -	2211	4	8
Donald Oig M'Rath - - -	Torlysich -	2111	1	4
Duncan M'Rath - - -	Achnashelach -	1616	5	4
Donald M'Rath, Christopher M'Rath - - }	Achnagart - - -	2012	2	8
Duncan M'Rath, Alexander Roy M'Rath - - }	Easter Achiguran -	1818	4	0
Donald M'Rath, Farquhar M'Rath }	Wester Achiguran -	1807	2	8
John M'Rath, Alexander M'Rath	Innershcall - -	2201	1	4
Donald Derg Maclennan, John and Donald Buy M'Lennan }	Morvich - - -	3609	5	4
Alexander M'Lennan, Donald Maclennan, Donald M'Leod }	Little Achyark -	1913	10	8
Duncan M'Lennan, Farquhar M'Lennan, Donald M'Rath }	Meikle Achyark -	2215	3	4
Four Tenants - - -	Inchchrow - -	1911	1	4
Mr John M'Lean, Minister of Crowe - - - }	Lienassie, &c - -	2908	3	4

		Scots		
Three Tenants	Ardhullich (?)	£2501	1	4
Farquhar M'Rath	Little Invernate	2317	9	4
Alister, Farquhar's son, Alister, John's son	Meikle Invernate	2018	10	8
Duncan M'Rath	Leault	805	6	8
John Cuthbert, Finlay Beg	Little Keppoch	407	9	4
Three Tenants	Karr	1304	3	4
Five Tenants	Dornie	2607	9	4
Two Tenants	Bundaloch	1217	9	4
Donald M'Rath	Cambuslyne	3306	8	0
Alexander M'Rath, &c	Nether Mamaig	614	4	0
Christopher M'Rath	Duilig	1911	1	4
Duncan M'Rath	Fadoch	1613	7	4
Duncan M Rath	Upper Killilan	2018	6	0
Three Tenants	Nether Killilan	1603	10	8
Duncan M'Rath	Conryoine	1007	6	0

The following Macraes appear on the Rental Roll for Lochalsh :—

Alexander M'Rath	Altnasou and Dronaig	£2912	1	4
John M'Rath	Conchra	3413	4	0
Hector M'Rath	Ardelve	2704	5	8

APPENDIX I.

FEADAN DUBH CHINTAILLE.

THE Feadan Dubh, or Black Chanter of Kintail, which, for several generations, was one of the heirlooms of the Mackenzies of Kintail, is now in the possession of Lieutenant Colin William MacRae[1] of the Black Watch A full description of the chanter and the drones accompanying it appeared in the *Inverness Courier* of the 29th May, 1894, from which the following account is mainly taken

The chanter is considered to be much older than the drones, and the note holes are very much worn. It was badly broken at some time or another, and is now held together by no less than seven silver rings. The two top rings have engraved on them the words, "A smeorach aigharach" (the merry thrush) The other rings have "Scur Oiam," the slogan of the Macraes; "Caisteal Donain," "Cinntaille," "Loch-Duich," and on the bottom ring "Tulloch Aird," the slogan of the Mackenzies. On the chanter stock is fixed a stag's head and horns in silver, the Mackenzie crest, surmounted by a baron's coronet, and underneath it the inscription, "Lord Seaforth, Baron Mackenzie, High Chief of Kintail, 1797," and below this inscription the words, "Tulloch Aird."

The stock of the blowpipe has the following inscription.— " This silver-mounted black ebony set of bagpipes, with the Feadan Dubh Chintaille, was the property of Lord Seaforth, Baron Mackenzie, High Chief of Kintail, 1797," and on the blowpipe itself is the figure of a Highlander, in silver, in full costume, with drawn claymore, surmounted by the motto, "O Thir nam Beann" (from the land of the mountains).

1 Page 159.

The stock of the big drone has the following inscription :—
"From Lord Seaforth, Baron Mackenzie, High Chief of Kintail,
to Lieutenant-Colonel Sir John Macra, K.C.H, of Ardintoul, Kintail, late 79th Cameron Highlanders." The big drone has three
shields, and the top shield has the following inscription :—"All
Highland bagpipes, till after the Battle of Waterloo, had but two
or three short or treble drones." The second shield has, "Lieut.-
Colonel Sir John Macra, K C.H, late 79th Cameron Highlanders,
was the first to introduce (and it was on this set of pipes) the use
of a big or bass drone," and the third shield has, "The big or
bass drone was pronounced a great improvement in the harmony
and volume of sound."

The stock of the second drone has the following :—"From
Lieut.-Colonel Sir John Macra, K C.H., to his nephew, Captain
Archibald Macra Chisholm, late 42nd Royal Highlanders, the
Black Watch" The shield on the second drone has, "The intro-
duction of the big or bass drone was approved, and the example
was soon followed in the making of military bagpipes."

The stock of the third drone has the following inscription :—
"From Captain A M Chisholm, late 42nd Royal Highlanders, Black
Watch, Freicadan Dubh to *(present possessor)* The shield on the third
drone has "Lieut -Col Sir John Macra was an excellent performer
on the bagpipes. He made pipes and chanters, and when military
secretary to his relative, the Marquis of Hastings, Viceroy of
India, he taught the natives of India to play on the Highland
bagpipes."

Captain Archibald Macra Chisholm was put in possession of
the Kintail bagpipes soon after the death of his uncle, Sir John
Macra, in 1847. When the late Keith Stewart-Mackenzie, of Seaforth and Brahan Castle, became aware of this, in 1849, he wrote
to Captain Chisholm expressing his most anxious desire to possess
this old Mackenzie heirloom He made a handsome offer for
them, but Captain Chisholm declined it. Captain Chisholm was
himself an excellent performer on the bagpipes, and for over thirty
years acted as judge of pipe music at the Northern Meetings in
Inverness. Some time before his death, which occurred on the
19th October, 1897, while this book was in the press, he presented
the Kintail bagpipes to his cousin, Lieutenant Colin William
MacRae, as already mentioned,

APPENDIX J.

THE following poems are given as specimens of the language and poetry of the Macraes, and as illustrations of their social, political, and religious views in olden times —

I

This song, composed by Fearachar Mac Ian Oig, during his exile (page 188), was given to the author in 1890 by Alexander Macmillan, Dornie   It is given also in The Transactions of the Gaelic Society of Inverness, Leaves from My Celtic Portfolio, by Mr A. W. Mackenzie.

Cha ne direadh na bruthaich
Dh'fhag mo shiubhal gun treoir.

Na teas ii la greine
'Nuair a dh' eifeadh i oirnn.

Laidh a' sneachd so air m' fheusaig
'Us cha leir dhomh mo bhiog

'S gann is leir dhomh in 's fhaisge,
Ceann a bhata nam dhorn.

Se mo thigh moi na cieagan,
Se mo dhaingean gach frog

Se mo thubhailte m' osan,
Se me chopan mo bhrog.

Ge do cheanaichinn am buideal
Cha 'n fhaigh mi cuideachd 'ni ol.

'S ged a cheanaichinn a' seipein
Cha 'n fhaigh mi creideas a' stoip

Ged a dh' fhadinn an teine,
Chi fear foille dheth ceo.

'S i do inghean-sa Dhonnachaidh
Chuir an iomagain so oirnn.

Te 'g am beil an cul dualach
O guallainn gu brog.

Te 'g am beil an cul bachlach
'S a dhreach mar an t'or.

Dheoin Dia cha bhi gillean
Riut a' mire 's mi beo.

Ged nach deaninn dhut fidhe
Bhiodh iasg a's sitheinn ma d'bhord.

'S truagh nach robh mi 's tu 'ghaolach
Anns an aonach 'm bi 'n ceo.

Ann am bothan beag barraich
'S gun bhi mar rium ach d' fheoil

Agus paisdean beag leimbh
A cheileadh ar gloir

'S mi a shnamhadh an caolas
Air son faoilteachd do bheoil.

Nuair a thigeadh am foghar
Be mo roghainn bhi falbh,

Leis a' ghunna nach diultadh
'S leis an fhudar dhu-ghorm.

Nuair a gheibhinn cead frithe
Bho 'n righ 's bho 'n iarl og,

Gum biodh fuil an daimh chabraich
Ruith le altaibh mo dhorn,

Agus fuil a bhuic bhiorich
Sior shileadh feadh feoir.

Ach 's i do nighean-sa Dhonnachaidh
'Chuir an iomagain so oirnn.

It is not the climbing of the hills that has made my walk listless. Nor the heat of a sunny day when it rose upon us. The snow has settled on my beard, and I cannot see my shoe. Hardly can I see, nearer still, the head of the staff in my hand The rocks are my big house, and the holes are my stronghold. My hose is my towel, my shoe is my drinking cup If I were to buy a bottle, I could get no company to drink it. If I were to buy a chopin, I should not get credit for a stoup If I were to light a fire, some treacherous man would see the smoke. It was your daughter, Duncan, that brought this anxiety upon us. She

who has beautiful hair from her shoulders down to her shoe. She
who has curling hair of the hue of gold. God forbid that young
men should make love to you while I live. Though I cannot
weave for you, yet there would be fish and venison on your table.
Would that you were with me, my love, on the hill of the mist.
In a small brushwood hut with no one with me but you And a
little child that would not betray our talk. I would (gladly)
swim the ferry for a welcome from your mouth. When the
autumn would come, my desire would be to wander with a gun
that would not miss fire, and with dark blue gunpowder. When I
should receive permission for the forest from the King and the
young Earl, the blood of the antlered stag would flow by the skill
of my hand, and the blood of the roe-buck would flow continually
into the grass. But your daughter, Duncan, has brought this
anxiety upon us.

II

The following lament on Ian Breac Mac Mhaighster Fearachar
(page 170) was taken down by Mr Alexander Macrae, farmer,
Ardelve (page 166), from the recitation of Mr Duncan Macrae,
Ardelve (page 183), and communicated to the author in 1896.
The author of this poem is unknown :—

Gu 'm beil m' inntinn se trom,
'Us cha shcinnear leum fonn
Thionndaidh disne rium lom
    'S na clairibh.

Gu 'm beil m' aigneadh fo ghruaim,
'S cian gur fada o'n uair
M'an aitreabh 's an d'fhuair
    Mi m' arach.

An deigh cinneadh mo ruin
Air an d' imich an chu,
'S tric mi 'n ionad fir dhiubh
    O'n dh' fhas mi.

Cha b'e bhi 'n dubhar gun ghrein
Fath mo mhulad gu leir,
Thuit mi cumha luchd speis
    Mo mhanrain.

z

'S ann sa chlachan od shios
Dh' fhag sinn ceannas nan chiar
'S am fear buile na 'n iarrta
    'N airidh.

Duin' uasal mo ghaoil
Chaidh a bhualladh le aog
'S ann 'n ad ghnuis a bha aoidh
    A chairdeas.

'S n' am b' fhear ealaidh mi fein
Mar mo bharail gu geur
'S ann ort a b' fhurasd dhomh ceatachd
    Aireamh

Gu n robh geurchuis ni's leor
Ann an eudan an t' sheoid
'S bu cheann reite do ghloir
    An Gailig.

'S mor an gliocas 's an ciall
Chaidh sa chiste leat sios,
Thug sud itean a sgiath
    An alaich.

Bhun an geamhradh rinn teann
Cha robh aoibhneas dhuinn ann
'S neo shubhach an gleann
    Bhon la sin.

'S lom an snaidheadh bhon tuath
Bhi cuir Ian san uaigh
'S bochd a naigheachd do thuath
    Chintaille.

Tha do chinneadh fo ghruaim
Dol air linne leat suas,
Air an tilleadh bu chruidh leo
    D' fhagail.

Tha do dheirbhleinean broin
Mar ghair sheillein an torr
'N deigh na mel, na mar eoin
    Gun mhathair.

Nise 's turseach an eigh
Gun am furtachd ac fhein
'S mor a thuiteas dhuibh 'n deigh
    Do laithean,

'S mor an aireamh, 's a chall
Cha do thearuinn mi ann
'S cia mar thearnas mi 'n am
    A phaidhidh.

Ghillean glacibh se ciall
Tha n ur cuid air an t sheibh
'S iommadh fear bhios ag iarridh
    Fath air.

Tha na taice 's na treoir
Ann an caol chiste bhord
Anns a chlachan an Cro
    Chintaille.

Tha do cheile fo sprochd
'S i neo eibhin gun toirt,
Rinn creuchdan a lot
    Gun tearneadh

B' fhiach a h' uidheam sa pris
Fhad 's a luighigeadh dh' i
Gus na ghuidheadh le Righ
    N an gras thu.

A Mhic Mhoire nan gras
A dhoirt d'fhuil air nar sgath
Gu 'm a duineil 'n a aite
    Phaisdean.

Heavy minded am I, nor can I raise the song (of gladness), the die has fallen for me inauspiciously as to its sides. My mind is in sadness, and for a long time, on account of the home in which I was reared   On account of my beloved clan, whose fame has travelled far, often have I been in the place of some of them since I grew up.   Being in a sunless shade is not the sole cause of my sadness, I have fallen into mourning for those who are the esteemed ones of my mirth.   It was down in that graveyard that we left the chief of the heroes, and the head of the township if they were being counted.   My beloved nobleman, who has been struck by death, in thy face was the expression of friendliness.   If I were a man of talent, keen as to my wit, it would be easy for me to record thy praises   There was intelligence enough in the face of the hero, and a subject of agreement would be thy praises in Gaelic.   Great is the wisdom and the understanding that went

down with thee in thy coffin, this has plucked feathers from
the wing of thy tribe. The winter visited us severely, there was
no pleasure for us in it, and joyless is the glen since that day. A
keen bereavement for the people, putting John in the grave; sad
tidings for the tenantry of Kintail. Sad were thy clansmen as
they carried thee West on the water, hard for them was it to
have left thee as they returned. Thy sad orphans are like the
noise of bees on a mound for their honey, or like fledglings without a mother. Sad now is their cry without a time of comfort
for them; many of them will fall after thy days. Great is their
number, nor did I escape the loss, how can I be saved in the day
of reckoning (or rent paying). Young men, be prudent, your property (cattle) is on the mountain; many a man will try to take
advantage of it. Our support and strength is in a narrow wooden
coffin in the graveyard in Cro of Kintail. Thy wife is downcast,
joyless, listless, wounded with sores from which she had no escape.
Prosperous were her surroundings and her lot as long as thou wast
vouchsafed to her, until thou wast asked for by the King of
Grace. Son of Mary of Grace, who shed Thy blood for our sake,
may his boys be worthy of his place

III.

The following Lament for Murdoch Macrae of Inverinate, who
was killed in Glenlic (page 84), is still well known in Kintail. It
is given in The Transactions of the Gaelic Society of Inverness
(Vol. VIII.), Leaves from My Celtic Portfolio. by Mr William
Mackenzie.[1] The author is not known :—

> Si sealg geamhraidh Ghlinn-Lic
> A dh' fhag greann oirn tric 'us gruaim,
> 'N t-og nach robh teann 's a bha glic
> 'S an teampull fo'n lic 's an uaigh.
>
> A cheud Aoine de 'n geamhradh fhuar
> 'S daor a phaigh sinn buaidh na sealg,
> An t-og bo chraobhaiche snuagh
> Na aonar bhuainn 'us fhaotainn marbh.

---

[1] On page 383, line 8, for Mr A. W. Mackenzie read Mr William Mackenzie.

Tional na sgire gu leir
Ri siubhal sleibh 's ri falbh bheann
Fad sgios nan coig latha deug
'S am fear direach treun air chall.

Murachadh donn-gheal mo run
Bu mhin-suil 's bu leannan mnai
A ghuuis anns an robh am ball-seire
'S a bha tearc air thapadh laimh.

Chuala mise clarsach theud,
'S fiodhall do rear a co-sheinn—
Cha chuala 's cha chluinn gu brath
Ceol na b' fhearr na do bheul binn,

Bu tu marbhaich' bhalla-bhric-bhain,
Le morbh fhada dhireach gheur,
Le cuilbheir bhristeadh tu cnaimh
'S bu shilteach fo d' laimh na feidh.

Bhean uasal a thug dhut gaol
Nach bi chaoidh na h-uaigneas slan,
'S truagh le me chluasan a gaoir
Luaithead 's tha 'n snaim sgaoilt le do' bhas.

Gur tuirsach do chaomh bhean og
'S i sileadh nan deoir le gruaidh
'S a spionadh a fuilt le dorn
Sior chumha nach beo do shnuagh.

'S tursach do chinneadh mor deas
Ga d' shireadh an ear 's an iar
'S an t-og a b' fhiughantaich beachd
Ri slios glinne marbh 's an t-sliabh.

Tha Crathaich nam buailtean bo
Air 'n sgaradh ro-mhor mu d'eug,
Do thoir bho bheatha cho og
A ghaisgich ghlan choir nam beus.

'S tuirseach do sheachd braithrean graidh
Am *parson* ge hard a leugh
Thug e, ge tuigseach a cheard,
Aona bharr-tuirs air cach gu leir.

Bho thus dhiubh Donnachadh nam Pios,
Gillecriosd 's an dithis de'n chleir,
Fearachar agus Ailean Donn,
Uisdean a bha trom 'n ad dheigh.

'S math ain fear rannsaichidh 'n t-aog,
'S e maor e thaghas air leth,
Bheir e leis an t-og gun ghiamh
'S fagaidh e 'm fear liath ro shean

The winter hunt in Glenlic has made us often shudder in our sadness about the youth who was not parsimonious, yet was prudent, now lying in a grave under a stone in the temple. The first Friday of the cold winter dearly did we pay for the success of our hunt—the young man of most comely appearance alone missing, and to be found dead   All the people of the parish searching on moor and mountain during the weariness of fifteen days, for the athletic brave man who was missing.   The fair complexioned Murdoch of my choice, of gentle eye, the beloved of woman, of a countenance with the expression of kindness, and rare for prowess of arm   I have heard the stringed harp and the violin in harmony playing with it, I have neither heard, nor shall ever hear sweeter music than (the converse of) thy melodious mouth   Thou couldst kill speckled white trout, with long straight and sharp spear, thou couldst break bones with the gun, and the deer bled freely at your hand.   The gentle woman who gave thee her love, and who can never be well in her solitude—it pains my ears to hear her lamenting how soon the marriage knot has been undone by thy death.   Sad is thy gentle young wife, with tears flowing down her cheek, plucking her hair with her hand in bitter grief that there is no longer any life in thy countenance. Sad was thy great and accomplished clan, searching for thee east and west, while the youth of most sympathetic judgment was (dead) on the moor on the side of the glen.   The Macraes of the cattle folds are grievously afflicted by thy death—taken out of life so young, thou generous hero of becoming conduct.   Sad are thy seven beloved brothers—the parson, though profound is his learning, though his office is one of giving comfort, yet he surpassed the others in his grief   First among them is Duncan of the silver cups, then Christopher and the two clergymen, Farquhar, Allan of the auburn hair, and Hugh, who was sad after thee.   Death is an excellent searcher, a messenger who chooses in a special way, he removes the unblemished young man, and leaves the grey-haired and very old man.

IV.

The author of the following poem was Donnachadh nam Pios (page 87), writer of the Fernaig MS   It has been transliterated from the Fernaig MS. into modern spelling by Professor Mackinnon [1]

Aon a rinneadh leis an Sgriobhair air lath a' bhreitheanais.

Smaoineamar an la fa dheoidh
Is coir dhuin a dhol eug,
Smaoineamar peacaidh na h'òig,
Smaoineamar fòs na thig 'n a dheigh.

Smaoineamar na thig 'n a dheigh.
Gur e la na mor bhreith ;
Gach ni rinneadh leinn 's an fheoil
Cha'n fhaodar na's mo a chleith

Cha'n fhaodar na's mo a chleith,
Maith no sath a rinneadh leinn ;
'N uair chi sinn Breitheamh nan slogh
Teachd oirnn s na neoil, tromp 'g a seirm.

'N uair sheirmear an trompaid mhor,
Cruinnicheadar na sloigh ma seach ;
Gach neach a tharlas duibh beo
Caochlaidh iad an doigh 's am beachd.

Caochlaidh muir agus tir,
Caochlaidh gach ni as nuadh,
Liobhraidh an talamh suas,
Gach neach a chaidh anns an uir.

Gach neach a chaidh anns an uir
Eiridh iadsan 'n an nuadh chorp,
Is gabhaidh gach anam seilbh
'S a choluinn cheilg an robh chlosd.

Nior chlosd an sin do na chuan,
Gluaiseadar e fa leth ;
Na bhathadh bho thoiseach tim
Liobraidh se air chionn na breith.

Breith bheir buaidh air gach breith ,
Cha Bhreitheamh leth-bhreitheach an Righ
Shuidheas air cathair na breith
'S a bheir ceart bhreith air gach ti.

[1] Transactions of the Gaelic Society of Inverness, Vol. XI.

Gach tı a bha cur ri olc
Tearbar a nochd air an lamh chlı ,
Caırear air a laımh dheis,
Gach ti bhios deas air a chinn.

Gach ti bhios deas air a chinn
Labhraidh 'm Breitheamh rıu gu ceart ;
Bho 'n is buidheann bheannaicht' sıbh,
Maitheam-sa dhuibhs' 'ı 'ur peac'.

Maitheam-sa dhuibhs' 'n 'ur peac' ;
Gabhaıdh-s' seılbh cheart 's an rio'chd
Chomharraich m' Athair bho thos,
Dhuıbhse ann an gloir gun chrıch.

Oir aır bhi dhomhsa fo thart,
Fo fhuachd, fo acras, chum bais,
'M prıosan gun treoir gun neart,
Dh' fhuasgaıl sıbh ceart aır mo chas.

Air bhi dhomh a'm choıgreach cein
'S a'm *thraveller* anns gach bail',
Fhreasdaıl sıbh dhombsa 'n am fheum ;
Cha robh ar deagh-bheus dhomh gann.

Ach freagraidh iadsan am Breitheamh,
Cuın chunnaiceamar sıbh fo thart,
Fo fhuachd, fo acras, chum baıs,
'S a dh' fhuasgail sinn do chas ceart ?

Bheirim-sa dearbhadh dhuibh,—
Dh' fhuasgail 's gur ann duıbh nach olc,
Mheud 's gu'n d' rinneadh leibhse dhiol,
Rı piantaıbh mo bhraithre bochd-s'.

Sin labhraıdh 'm breitheamh os n' aıı d
Rıu fhuair ait' air a laimh chli,
Imichibh uamsa gu brath,
Dh' ionusuidh cais is craidh gun chrich.

Far am bi 'n t-Abharsaır am pein,
Aingle 's a chleir air fad,
Mheud 's nach d' rınneadh leibhse dhıol
Rı piantaibh mo bhraithre lag-s'.

Imichidh iad so gu truagh
Dh' Ifrinn fhuair am bi fuachd is teas,
Dhoibh-san ge duilich an cas,
Nior faıgh iad bas ann am feasd.

Ach imichidh buidheann a ghraidh
A fhuair ait air an lamh dheis
Do fhlaitheanas nam flath feile ;
O ! cibhinn doibh-san an treis.

O ! cibhinn doibh-san an treis,
Eibhinn doibh-san gach ni chi,
Eibhinn bhi 'n cathair nan gras,
Eibhinn bhi lathair a Bhreithimh.

Eibhinn bhi lathair a Bhreithimh,
Eibhinn a shiochai' 's a bhuaidh ;
Cha'n fhaodar a chur an ceill
Meud eibhneis an aite bhuain.

Eibhneas e nach faca suil,
Eibhneas e nach cuala cluas,
Eibhneas e nach teid air chul,
Dhoibh-san d'an toirear mar dhuais.

Duais is mo na gach duais,
Ta shuas air neamh aig mo Righ ;
Eibhinn do gach neach a ghluais,
Air chor's gu'm buaidhaichear i

Air chor's gu'm buadhaichear i
Smaoneamar air crich an sgeoil,
Smaoneamar ar peacaidh bath,
Smaoneamar an la fa dheoidh.

One by the writer on the Day of Judgment.

Let us meditate on the last day when it must fall to our lot to die, let us meditate on the sins of youth, let us meditate still further on what must come hereafter. Let us meditate on what must come hereafter, that is on the great Day of Judgment, when nothing done by us in the flesh can any longer be concealed. No longer can be concealed the good or the evil done by us, when we see the judge of all people coming to us in the clouds, with the sound of the trumpet. When the great trumpet is sounded, all people shall assemble from every quarter ; those who happen to be still alive shall change in manner and in mind. Sea and land shall change, all things shall be changed anew, the earth shall yield up all who are buried in the dust. All who are buried in the dust shall rise in their new bodies, and each soul shall take possession of the false body in which it formerly rested.

No rest then for the ocean, it shall be agitated on its own account; all who were drowned from the beginning of time it shall yield up for the judgment A judgment that will surpass every judgment; no partial judge is the King who shall sit on the judgment seat, and give righteous judgment to all. Those who gave themselves up to evil will, on that day, be banished on the left hand; on the right hand will be placed those who are prepared for His coming To those who are prepared for His coming the Judge will openly say : " Because you are a blessed company I will pardon your sins I will pardon your sins; take you rightful possession of the kingdom set apart from the beginning by my Father for you in glory everlasting. For when I was thirsty and cold and hungry unto death in prison, without energy or strength, you brought true relief to my trouble. Being a stranger far away, and a sojourner in many places, you waited on me in my necessity ; your deeds of kindness towards me were not few." But they will answer the judge, " When did we see thee thirsty, cold, and hungry unto death, and brought true relief to your trouble ?" " I will give you a proof—you brought relief, nor will it be to your hurt, inasmuch as you showed compassion for the suffering of my poor brethren " Then will the judge openly speak to those placed on the left hand—" Depart from me, for ever, to everlasting trouble and torment ! Where the Adversary will continue in torment, together with his angels and ministers for ever, inasmuch as you showed no compassion for the sufferings of my feeble brethren " Miserably will they depart to dismal Hell, where there will be cold and heat ; however agonising for them may be their trouble, they can never die there. But the company of beloved ones, placed on the right, will depart to the paradise of the hospitable princes ; Oh ! joyful will it be for them the while. Oh ! joyful will it be for them the while, joyful for them all that they behold, joyful to be in the city of grace, joyful to be in the presence of the judge. Joyful to be in the presence of the judge, joyful his peace and his glory ; it is not possible to declare the greatness of the joy of the everlasting place. Joy which eye never beheld, joy which ear never heard, joy that will not cease for those to whom it will be given as a reward. Greater than all rewards is the reward up in Heaven with my King ; joyful for everyone who has so conducted him-

self as to attain to it.   That it may be deserved, let us think of
the end of the tale, let us think of our deadly sin, let us think
of the last day.

V.

The following poem, also by Donnachadh nam Pios, has been
transliterated from the Fernaig MS. into modern spelling by
George Henderson, Ph D [1] :—

Gne orain do rinneadh leis a sgriobhair, anno 1688.

Ta saoghal-sa carail,
Tha e daondau da 'r mcalladh gu geur ;
Liuthad caochladh th' air talamh
Is daoin' air an dalladh le bhreig ;
Chreic pairt duibh-s' an anam
'S do chaochlaidh iad barail chionn seud,
Fhir chaidh ann sa chrannaig,
Dhoirt t' fhuil da ar ceannach,
O ! aoin Righ Mhoire beannuich nar creud.

O ! Athair nan gras
Na failing sinne 'nar cruas,
Ach amhraic oirnn trath
Le tlaths o d' fhlathas a nuas.
Mar thug thu le d' mhioraild
Clann Israel gun dhiobhair sa chuan,
Dionn t' eaglais da rireadh,
Ga ghuidh le luchd a mi ruin,
Bho 'sgriob-s' ta teachd mu' cuairt.

'S coir dhi-s' a bhi umhailt
Gad tha i fo dhubh ann san am ;
Gur h-iad ar peacaunan dubhar
Tharruing oirnn pudhar is call ;
Ach deanmar trasg agus cumha
Ris an fhear dh' fhag an t-iubhair sa chrann,
Chon s' gu 'n ceannsuich e' bhuidheann
Chleachd an cu-coir as duibhe,
Mar tha breugan is luighean is feall.

Dhe churanta laidir
Dh' alaich muir agus tir,
Tha thu faicsinn an drasda
Mar dh' fhailing am prabar-s' an Righ ;

[1] See Leabhar nan Gleann, p. 271.

Ach reir 's mar thachair do Dhaidh,
Nuair ghabh Absolon fath air go dhith,
Beir dhachaigh 'na dhail leat,
Dh' aindeoin am pairtidh,
Nar Righ chon aite le sith.

Fear eil' 's math is eol domh
Tha 'n ceart uair air fogaireadh 'na phairt,
Shliochd nan cuireannan seolta
Da thogradh 's nach obadh an spairn ;
Ga tamull leinn bhuainn thu
Cha toireamar fuath dhut gu brach ;
Sann da 'i seors bu dual sin,
Eatar mhith agus uaislean,
Bhi air do dheas-laimh an cruadal 's an cas

Truagh nach fhaicinn thu teachd
Mar b' ait le mo chridh san am,
Far ri Seumas le buidheann
Nach geill a dh' iubhair nan Gall,
Tha 'n drasda ro bhuidheach
Mheud s gu 'n shuidhich iad feall,
Le 'n seoladh 's le'n uidheam
Anns na modaibh as duibhe,
Chuir fa dheoidh sibh air suibhail do'n Fhraing.

Ach thamar an duigh
Gu'n caochail an cursa seo fothast,
Gu'm faic mi le m' shuilibh
Bhi sgiursadh gach tnu bha 's na moid,
'S gach Baron beag cubach
'Mhealladh le caraibh 's le luban Priounns Or ;
Gheibh Mac Cailein air thus duibh,
Dh' aindeoin a chuirte,
'Galair bu duthchasach dho.

B'e dhuthchas bho sheanair
Bhi daondan r'a melladh gach ti,
Cha b'fhearr e 'thaobh athair
Ga b' mhor a mhathas bho' Righ ;
Ma 'se seo an treas gabhail
Thug eug bhuaith 'bhathar gu pris,
Le maighdinn sgoraidheach sgathail
Cha d' cheannsuicheadh aisith ;
Ged thuit thu cha'n athais duit i.

Iomah Tighearn is *post*
Nach eol domh-s' a nis 'chur an dan
Tha'n drasda gu moiteil
Le phrabar gu bosdail a' d' phairt ;

'S ann diubh sin Cullodar,
Granntaich is Rosaich a chail,
Nuair thionndas an rotha
Chon annsachd bho thoiseach
Gur teannta dhaibh 'chroich 'miosg chaich.

Ach fhearaibh na h' Alba
Ga dealbhach libh 'drasda 'n ur cuirt,
Gad leught' sibh bho'r leanabachd
'S bho la 'gheil sibh a dh' Fhergus air thus,
Thuit gach fine le toirmeasg
Do threig 's nach robh earbsach do'n chrun,
Ach seo t'eallach a dhearbhas
Gur h-airidh an seanchas,
Gun eirich mi-shealbhar da'n cliu.

Cha chan mi na's leir dhombh
Ri 'ur maithibh, ri'r cleir, ri'r por,
D'eis ur mionnan a Shearlas
Gu seiseamh sibh-p fhein 'n aghaidh deoin,
'S an t-oighre dlighcach na db'eis
Thuit nis go Righ Seumas r'a bheo,
Ach dh'aindeoin ur leirs'
Ga mor 'ur cuid leugh',
Ar liom-s gu'n 'reub sibh a choir.

. . . . . air coir dhirich
Le masladh na dhiobair do phairt,
Bha uair a staid iosal
S tha air direadh le uchd math an drasd ;
Seann fhacla 's gur fior e
Bha riamh eadar Chriostuidhean graidh,
Gur miosa na ana-spiorad
Duine mi-thaingeil
Ghabh na's leoir dhuibh-s an aim air na chas.

Càs eile nach fas'
Dheirich mar fhasan sa ruaig' s',
Chlann feinn bhi na'n taic
Do gach neach tha cur as da mu cuairt ;
Do threig iad 's cha 'n ait daibh
'N cuigeamh faithn' bha 'chasgadh an t-sluaigh ;
'N aghaidh nadur a bheart seo
Do neach 'ghabb baisteadh
Ann an ainn nan tri pearsan ta shuas.

Ach fhir 'dh'oibrich gach mioraild
Bha miosg Chlainn Israel bho thus,
Nach soilleir an giamh seo
Dh'aon neach ghabh 'Chriosdachd mar ghrund?

Bho laigh geilt agus fiamh mor
Air gach Marcus, gach Iarl 's gach Diuc,
Casg fein an iorghalt-s
Mas toil leat-s a Dhia e,
Mu tuit sinn fo fhiabhrus do ghnuis.

Is mor dh' eireas dhut a Bhreatunn
'S nach d'fhaodadh do theagasg na am,
Cha leir dhut fath t'eagla,
Gu'n tharruing ana-creidimh ort call;
Bho'n la mhurtadh libh Searlas
Tha fhuil-san ag eigheachd gu teann,
Gabh aithri a t' eucoir,
Thoir dhachaigh Righ Seumas,
Neo thig sguirsa bho Dhe ort a nall.

Ghaidhealu gasda
Na laighidh fo mhasladh sa chuis,
Ach faighear sibh tapaidh
'S Righ Seumas na thiac air ur cul;
Ge ta Uilleam an Sasunn
Na geillibh a feasda do chrun;
Liom is cinnteach mar thachras
Thaobh innleachd a bheairtean,
Gu pilltear e dhachaigh gun chliu.

Na ma h'ioghnadh libh-p fhein seo
'S gun ghlac es' an eucoir air cheann,
Bha *manifesto* ro eitigh,
Nach faic sibh gur breugach a chainnt;
'S gach gealladh do rinn se
Do Shasunn do threig se gu teann,
Tha iad nis 'n aghaidh cheile,
Nuair thuig siad an reusan,
Ach na tha Phresbiterianich ann.

Na ma lughaid 'ur misneachd
Gu robh iad seo bristneach na curs,
Fo sgaile *religion*
B'e 'n abhaist s an gliocas bho thus;
Co dhiubh alach a nise
Nach . . . . le mi-ruin,
Ach tha'n aite le fios dhuinn,
Ged dh'fhailing righean tric iad,
Aig gach armunn bha tiorcadh a chruin

Gu ma h'-amhluidh seo dh' oireas
'Mhaithibh Alba s na h' Eire san am,
Tha 'coitheamh le Seumas
'S nach d' amhraic iad fein air an call;

Ach b' fheall am bathais 's an eudan
Fo gach neach bha ri eiginn 's u feall,
Ghabh an *test* a bha citigh,
Eadar mhaithibh is Chleire,
Thoir an anman dha 'n eucoireach mheallt.

Ach tba mi dall na mo bharail
Mar ceannsuich Dia 'charachd-sa trath,
'S mar mhealtar leis barail
'Chleamhuais fhuair alloil gun bhlath ;
Is mairg a thoisich mar ealaidh
Athair-ceile chur ealamh bho bhair,
Ach seo ordugh nam balach,
Far ri dochus nan cailleach,
San t-saoghal chruaidh charail-s' a ta.

Song composed by the writer in the year 1688.

   This world is deceitful, it constantly deceives us bitterly, many
changes there are on earth and many men blinded by its falsehood.
Some have sold their souls and have changed opinion for the sake
of gain.   Thou who suffered on the Cross and spilt Thy blood for
our redemption, Oh ! Thou only King (son) of Mary, bless our creed.
Oh ! Father of Grace, do not fail us in our sore distress, but look
upon us soon with tenderness from Thy Heaven above.   As Thou
didst miraculously lead the children of Israel, without the loss of
any, through the sea, so do Thou in very deed defend Thy Church
(though her ill-wishers pray for her downfall) from the evil now
fallen upon her   It is her duty to be humble, though she is at
this moment under a cloud.   Her sins are the cause that have
brought upon us harm and loss, but let us fast and mourn to Him
who went to the Cross without faltering, that He may subdue
them who have been practising the blackest deeds, falsehood,
sacrilege, and treachery.   O God, mighty and strong, who peopled
land and sea, Thou seest how at this juncture the rabble has disappointed the King ; but as it happened in the case of David,
when Absalom took advantage of him (to try) to ruin him, do
Thou, in Thy appointed time, lead the King home in peace to his
own place in spite of their factions.   Another man[1] I know full
well, who at this moment is in exile for his (King James's) cause—

----

[1] Perhaps Kenneth, fourth Earl of Seaforth, who accompanied James II,
to France after the Revolution of 1688.

of the race of the capable heroes, who would accept and never refuse the strife.   Though for a little thou art away from us, we
shall never feel indifferent towards thee.   It is in the blood of our
race, commons and nobles alike, to stand by thy right hand in the
time of difficulty and trouble.   Would that I might see thee coming as my heart at this moment would desire, along with King
James with a host that would not yield to the bows and arrows of
the Lowlanders, who are rejoicing at having planned their treachery
with the cunning and resources of their dark councils, which have
at last driven you an exile into France.   But I am in hopes that
the course of events will yet change, and that I may see with my
own eyes the discomfiture of every wretch who took part in their
councils, and of every petty, cringing baron, who, by his tricks and
wiles, deceived Prince Orange; Argyll, in spite of his rank, will, as
one of the first, be smitten with the disease that comes natural to
him.   It comes natural to him from his grandfather to deceive
everyone, nor is he better from his father, though he (the father)
received so much kindness from his King.   If this is the third
occasion on which the disease was caught from a "maiden" sharp-
toothed, clear-cutting, disgrace has not been quelled though he
were to fall by her, to him it would be no disgrace.   There are many
lords and officials whom I cannot now mention in my verse, who at
the present time, together with their rabble, boast with affected
modesty of their connection with thee (Argyll)   Among them are
Culloden, the Grants, the Rosses of the cabbage.   When the wheel
turns round to its first love they will find themselves among the
rest quite close to the gallows.   But, ye men of Scotland, though
your court (i e , your political situation) may now seem satisfactory
to you, still, if your story be read from your infancy even as far
back as the day when you first submitted to Fergus, it will be
found that every clan has fallen by appointed decree—who
deserted and proved faithless to the Crown.   But this is a forge that
will test unfailingly the truth of the saying that " a stain may fall
on their honour."   I am not going to speak about all I know, to
our nobles, our clergy, our people, after your oath to Charles that
you would stand by him, come what may, and by his legitimate
heir, who is now King James, for life ; but in spite of your sagacity,
and wide though your learning may be, you are certainly violating
the right.   (Not to speak of his) undoubted right, it is a disgrace

that so many have forsaken his cause, who were once in lowly
estate, but have now climbed by good fortune upwards. There is
a proverb, and a true one, which has ever been in use among lov-
ing Christians—that worse than a hostile spirit is the ungrateful
man ; many such have taken advantage of him (the King) in his
trouble. Another matter, not less sad, which has come into prominence in this affair—his own children supporting those who are
everywhere opposing him. They have forsaken, and not to their
joy, the fifth commandment given for the guidance of people
Such conduct is unnatural in anyone who has received baptism in
the name of the Trinity on high. But Thou, the worker of all the
wonders that were seen from the first among the children of Israel,
is not this a very apparent guilt for anyone professing Christian
principles ? Since a great fear and cowardice has fallen upon every
Marquis, every Earl, and every Duke, do Thou thyself check their
turbulence, if it be Thy will, O God, lest we fall under the wrath
of Thy countenance. Much may happen to thee, O Britain, since
thou didst refuse to receive warning in time Thou dost not see
the cause of thy fear, for unbelief has brought disaster upon thee.
Since the day King Charles was murdered, his blood is constantly crying out. Repent of thy guilt, bring King James home,
or destruction from God will surely come down upon thee. Ye
worthy Gaels, don't rest under disgrace, but be of courage with
King James to back you up. Though William is in England,
never yield allegiance to his Crown. Certain it seems to me what
will happen from the deceitfulness of his schemes, he will be driven
back in disgrace. Let this not surprise you, seeing that he has
seized injustice by the head (i.e., has acted upon it from the out-
set). His manifesto was altogether perjured Don't you see how
false his words are, and how he instantly renounced every promise
he made to England. They (his supporters) are now at variance
among themselves since they have understood his object, except
such Presbyterians as there are among them. Let not your
courage be any the less that these (the Presbyterians) have
always been unstable in their allegiance. Under the veil of
religion it has been their custom and their policy from the first
. . . . . . But we know that each hero who succoured the
Crown holds his position, though Kings may often have failed them.
So may it happen to the nobles of Scotland and Ireland who are

fighting for James without thinking of their loss, but treacherous were the countenance and face of each one engaged in mischief and deceit, who accepted the perjured "test," whether nobles or clergy, giving up their souls to the crafty evil one. But I am blind in my opinion if God will not soon check this treachery, and bring to nought the schemes of cold, unnatural, sterile blood-relationship. Woe to him who commenced his career by suddenly making war upon his own father-in-law ; but such is the way of clowns and the hope of carlines in this callous and deceitful world.

VI

Of the poets of Kintail, no one is better remembered than Ian Mac Mhurachaidh (pp. 81-83), or has left behind him a greater wealth of song. Though in comfortable circumstances, he disliked the purely mercenary relations which were beginning to grow up between landlord and people, and therefore resolved to emigrate to Carolina. The following is one of several songs which he composed in order to induce as many as possible of his countrymen to accompany him :—

> Thanig leitir bho Ian Beitean
> Chuir eibhneas air fear nach fhac i.
>
> Beagan do mhuinntir mo dhuthcha
> Triall an toabh am faigh iad pailteas.
>
> Far am faigh sinn deth gach seorsa
> An t-sealg is boidhche tha ri fhaicinn.
>
> Gheabh sinn fiadh is boc is moisleach
> 'S comas na dh' fhaodar thoir asda.
>
> Gheabh sinn coileach-dubh is liath chearc
> Lachan, ialtan agus glas gheoidh.
>
> Gheabh sinn bradan agus ban iasg
> 'S glas iasg ma 's e 's fhearr a thaitneas.
>
> B' fhearr na bhi fuireach fo uachd'rain
> 'S nach fuiligeadh iad tuath bhi aca.
>
> A ghabhadh an an aite 'n t' sheoid
> An t' or ged bann a spog a phartainn.
>
> A ghabhadh an an aite 'n diunloaich
> Siogaue sgugach 's e beartach,

Falbhamaid 's bitheadh beannachd Dhia leinn
Triallamaid, riadhamaid barca.

Falbhamaid uile gu leir
'S gur beag mo speis do dh' fhear gun tapadh.

Thogainn fonn, fonn, fonn,
Dh' eireadh fonn oirn ri fhaicinn.

There came a letter from John Bethune, which has given joy
to one who has not seen it. A few of my country people about to
depart to a land of plenty, where we can find every kind of the
most delightful hunting that could be seen. We shall find deer,
buck and doe, with permission to take as many as we want. We
shall get the woodcock and the woodhen, teals, ducks, and wild
geese. We shall get salmon and white fish, and grey fish if it
will please us better. Better far than stay under landlords who
won't suffer a tenantry with them; who would take, instead of a
good man, gold, were it from the claw of a lobster; who would
take, instead of a brave man, a sulky sneak, provided he was rich.
Let us depart, and may the blessing of God be with us, let us go
and charter a ship. Let us depart, all of us, for small is my
esteem for a man of no courage

I would raise a chorus of delight; we should be delighted on
seeing it.

VII.

When the ship, by which Ian Mac Mhurachaidh and so many
of his countrymen were about to leave Kintail, arrived at Caileach,
where it anchored, the poet invited the captain of the ship to
dinner with him. When the captain saw the good cheer provided,
he told the poet that he would not be able to fare so sumptuously
in America, and strongly advised him to remain at home. The
poet's wife and some other friends who were present also urged
him to the same effect with such earnestness that his resolution
was almost overcome, but he felt that, after all he had done and
said, he could not desert the people he had induced to join him,
and who looked up to him as their leader, so he decided, at whatever sacrifice, to go along with them, and the next song, which was
probably less applicable to the poet's own circumstances than to

those of some of his fellow-emigrants, was composed to cheer and encourage them as the ship was sailing away :—

> Nise bho na thachair sinn
> Fo's cionn an stoip 's na creachaige,
> Gu'n ol sinn air na faicinn e
> 'S na cairtealan san teid sinn
>
> Mhnathan togaidh an turrus oirbh
> 'Us sguiribb dheth na h-iomadan,
> Cha bharail leum gun tillear mi
> Bho'n sguir mi dh 'iomain spreidhe.
>
> Mhnathan sguiribh chubarsnaich
> Bho'n char sibh fo na siuil a stigh,
> Cha bharail leam gu'n lubar sinn
> Ri duthaich bhochd na h-eiginn.
>
> H-uile cuis dha theannachadh,
> An t' ardachdainn se ghreannaich sinn,
> Lin-mhora bhi dha'n tarruin
> 'S iad a sailleadh na cuid eisg oirn.
>
> Gur iomadh latha saraicht'
> Bha mi deanamh dige 's garraidhnean,
> An crodh a faighinn bais oirn
> 'Us mi paidheadh mail gu h-eigneach.
>
> 'S iomadh latha dosguineach
> A bha mi giulan cosguis dhuibh,
> 'N uair reidheadh a chuis gu osburnaich
> Bhi 'g osunaich ma deighinn.
>
> 'S beag mo speis d' an uachdaran
> A chuir cho fad air cuan sinn,
> Air son beagan do mhal suarach
> 'S cha robh buanachd aige fhein deth.
>
>> Tha tighinn fotham, fotham, fotham,
>> Tha tighinn fotham eiridh.

Now that we have met over a stoup and drinking-shell, let us drink in anticipation of seeing the quarters whither we are going Women, take courage for the voyage, and stop your mourning; I don't think I can be induced to return, now that I have ceased to herd cattle. Women, restrain your anxiety, now that you have gone under the sails; I don't think I can be bent backwards to the poor country of destitution. Every thing is being tightened, the raising (of rents?) is what has embittered us, trawling with

great nets, and salting our fish.   Many a hard day was I making
dykes and walls, my cattle dying, while I paid rent with difficulty.
Many an unfortunate day have I borne expenses on your account,
and when the matter fell into ruin, I sighed over them.   Small is
my esteem for the landlord who has sent us so far over the ocean,
for the sake of a little wretched rent, which he did not long enjoy.

I feel inclined to go.

VIII.

Among those who accompanied Ian Mac Mhurachaidh was a
certain John Macrae—a blacksmith—called Ian Mac a Ghobha
(page 193)   The American War of Independence began almost
immediately after the arrival of the Kintail emigrants in Carolina,
and they unhesitatingly cast in their lot with the Loyalists.   The
poet now became one of the foremost, by his songs and his example,
in urging his brother Highlanders to stand up in defence of what he
considered to be the just rights of their King and country, and
consequently, when the Americans got him into their hands they
treated him with unusual severity.   Ian Mac a Ghobha lost his
arm in the war, and, making his way back to Scotland, eventually
succeeded, after considerable difficulty, in obtaining a pension for
his services.   He appears to have been a man of mark in more
ways than one.   He possessed an excellent voice and an excellent
memory, and brought back with him to Kintail several of Ian
Mac Mhurachaidh's songs, which he was never tired of singing.
He died at Carndu, near Dornie, in 1839, aged ninety-three.   The
morning after his death an old woman, who lived by herself on
the other side of the sea, opposite to Kilduich, told the first neighbour she met : "'S mi a chuala an t-sheinn bhreagh a dol a stigh a
Chlachan Duthaich an raoir, 's mar eil mi air mo mhealladh se
guth binn Mhic a Ghobha a bhann."—("What beautiful singing I
heard going into Kilduich churchyard last night ; if I am not mistaken, it was the sweet voice of Mac a Ghobha."   Soon afterwards
the news of his death arrived.[1]

The following song, perhaps Ian Mac Mhurachaidh's last, was
composed by him while wandering a fugitive in the primeval
forest, evidently before the close of the war, as he still looks

[1] Tradition communicated to the author by Mac a Ghobha's great-grandson,
Dr Farquhar Macrae, London.

forward with hope to the arrival of Lord Cornwallis, who was forced to surrender to the French and the Americans at Yorktown on the 18th of October, 1781. It has been the song of many a Kintail emigrant since the days of Ian Mac Mhurachaidh :—

'S mi air fogradh bho 'n fhoghar,
Togail thighean gun cheo unnta.

Ann am bothan beag barraich,
'S nach tig caraid dha 'm fheorach ann

Ged a tha mi s' a choille
Cha'n eil coire ri chnodach orm.

Ach 'bhi cogadh gu dileas
Leis an righ bho'n bha choir aige.

Thoir mo shoraidh le durachd,
Gus an duthaich 'm bu choir dhomh bhi

Thoir mo shoraidh Chuitaille
Am bi manran is oranan.

A'n tric a bha mi mu'n bhuideal
Mar ri cuideachda sholasach.

Cha be 'n dram 'bha mi 'g iarraidh
Ach na b'fhiach an cuid storaidhean.

Ceud soraidh le durachd
Gu Sgur-Urain, 's math m' eolas innt'.

'S tric a bha mi mu'n cuairt di
'G eisdeachd udlaich a cronanaich.

A bheinn ghorm tha ma coinneamh
Leum bo shoilleai a neoineanan.

Sios 'us suas troimh Ghleann-Seile
'S tric a leag mi damh crocach ann.

Gheibhte bric air an linne
Fir ga 'n sireadh 'us leos aca.

Tha mi nis air mo dhiteadh
An am priosan droch bheolaintcach.

Ach na 'n tigeadh Cornwallis
'S mise d' fhalbhadh ro-dheonach leis.

A thoirt sgrios air na beistean
Thug an t' eideadh 's an storas bhuam.

Tha mi sgith 'n fhogar sa
Tha mi sgith 's mi leam fhein
'S cian bho thir m' eolas mi.

I am an exile since Autumn, building houses without smoke in them.   In a little hut of brushwood, where no friend will come to inquire for me.   Though I am in the wood (an outlaw) no fault can be charged against me, except fighting loyally for the King because he was in the right.   Take my sincere farewell to the country where I ought to be.   Take my farewell to Kintail, the place of mirth and songs.   Where I often sat round a bottle with a happy company.   It was not the drink I desired but the worth of your stories.   A hundred sincere farewells to Scur Ouran, well do I know it.   Often was I in its vicinity listening to the bellowing of an old stag.   The green mountain opposite to it, bright to me were its daisies   Up and down Glensheil often did I lay an antlered stag low.   Trout might be found on the pool, men seeking them with a torch.   I am now condemned to a prison of bad fare.   But if Cornwallis came, gladly would I join him.   To scourge the wretches who have robbed me of my clothes and property.

I am tired of this exile, I am tired in my loneliness,—far am I from the land of my acquaintance.

NOTE—Several of Ian Mac Mhurachaidh's poems will be found in *The Celtic Magazine* (Inverness), April-August, 1882.

The following are some other Macrae poets whose Gaelic songs were at one time and in some instances still are known among Gaelic-speaking Highlanders :—

DUNCAN MACRAE, commonly called Donnachadh Mac Alister (page 198).   Only fragments of a lament for his mother and of a song to his gun appear to be known now.

KENNETH MACRAE,[1] of the Clann Ian Charrich tribe, and a

[1] Kenneth had a son, Alexander, about whom the following paragraph appeared in *The Courier* (London) of the 28th November, 1807 :—"The oldest man now living in Scotland is supposed to be a Highlander of the name of Alexander Macrae.   He was born in the parish of Kintail in the year 1687, and is now, of course, just 120 years old.   In the year 1719 he fought under Lord Seaforth at the battle of Glensheil, and in 1724 he enlisted as a private in the Scots Brigade, serving in Holland, where he continued seven years, the last two of which were spent in prison in some town of France, the name of which he does not remember.   In 1731 he returned to his farm and married a second wife, who died a few years after.   In 1765 he fell into such low circumstances that he was forced to procure a subsistence by going about from house to house reciting Ossian's poems in Gaelic   In 1773 he married his present wife, by whom he has three children, the last when he was aged ninety-six.   About

relative of Ian Mac Ian of Toilysich (foot note, page 214). He lived at Ardelve, and was an old man at the time of the battle of Sheriffmuir, at which he was present On his return home he composed a celebrated lament, or ballad, on the "Four Johns of Scotland" (foot note, page 153), which is given in "The Transactions of the Gaelic Society of Inverness," Vol. VIII.—Leaves from my Celtic Portfolio, by Mr William Mackenzie.

CHRISTOPHER MACRAE, Sergeant in the 78th Highlanders (page 80). Some of his songs are still well known in Kintail and Lochalsh.

DONALD MACRAE, a weaver in the parish of Petty in Invernessshire, where he was born in 1756, and died in 1837. His father was a native of Glenclchaig in Kintail. He was the author of several religious poems, which are spoken of very highly in *The Literature of the Highlanders* by the Rev Nigel Macneill.

JOHN MACRAE, schoolmaster at Sleat in Skye (page 183).

THE REV. DONALD MACRAE of Ness in Lewis (page 83) is mentioned in Macneill's *Literature of the Highlanders* as a true poet, though he did not produce much. His best known song is "The Emigrant's Lament," written on the occasion of the departure of many of his congregation for Canada.

JOHN MACRAE (page 130, c3) composed, among other Gaelic songs, one on the late Professor Blackie of Edinburgh.

JAMES MACRAE of Ardroil in Lews (page 193) composed several good, and sometimes humorous, Gaelic songs

twelve years ago, while still very stout, he was deprived of the use of his limbs by a violent fever, and ever since has been unable to walk. He is now bedridden, deaf and blind, but his memory is still very correct. His general amusement is singing and repeating Ossian's poems in Gaelic, but he repeats so fast that it is impossible to write them down, and, if interrupted, must again return to the beginning of the poem. He appears to have been a stoutmade, middle-sized man, and still looks uncommonly well." The old man lived at Ardelve, and this paragraph is believed to have been communicated to the *London Courier* by the Rev. Lachlan Mackenzie of Lochcarron, who on one occasion, while attending a meeting of his Presbytery at Ardelve, visited him at his home. It is said that in the course of the conversation, Mr Lachlan asked the old man if he was not afraid of death. "O dhuine bhoc," replied the old man, "nam faicadh d'thu Ceither Ianan na h' Alba folbh gu Sliabh an t' Shiorradh 's ann orra nach robh feagal roimh 'n bhas."—(Poor man, if you had seen the four Johns of Scotland setting out for Sheriffmuir, little did they fear death).

JOHN MACRAE of Timsgarry in Lews (page 194).

DUNCAN MACRAE[1] of Isle Ewe in Gairloch, a faithful follower of Prince Charlie, whom he accompanied throughout the Rising of 1745, and whose retreat he assisted to cover after the defeat of Culloden, composed a well-known Gaelic song called "Oran na Feannaige" (the song of the crow). It consists of an imaginary dialogue between himself and a crow which he saw in Edinburgh while there with the Prince.

[1] This Duncan Macrae was believed to possess the gift of the Sian. This gift was supposed to enable a man, by means of an incantation, to render an object invisible until the charm was removed, except for a short time at regular intervals usually of seven years. Shortly after the Battle of Culloden, a French ship, which put in at Poolewe, left a cask of gold for the use of the Prince. According to the traditions of Gairloch, this cask was entrusted to Duncan's care, and being unable at that time to escape the vigilance of the King's troops, and convey the gold to the Prince, he hid the cask in a place in Gairloch called the Fedan Mor, making use of the Sian to render it invisible. The cask never reached the Prince. On one occasion, about 1826, the cask suddenly became visible to a shepherd's wife who was spinning there with a spindle and distaff while herding her cattle. She stuck the spindle in the ground to mark the spot, and ran home for help to remove the treasure, but when her friends arrived at the spot neither the cask nor the distaff could be discovered.—*Dixon's Gairloch*, p. 165.

APPENDIX K.

It has already been stated, in Chapter I, that the district of Gairloch is rich in Macrae traditions. The following traditions are taken from Mr John H. Dixon's book on Gairloch, with the kind permission of the author :—

HOW THREE MACRAES FROM KINTAIL ATTEMPTED TO DRIVE THE MACBEATHS FROM GAIRLOCH AND PUT THE COUNTRY IN POSSESSION OF MACKENZIE OF KINTAIL.

Once upon a time there lived a powerful man—Ian Mac Ian Uidhir (John the son of Sallow John)—in the Carr of Kintail, and when he heard such aliens (the Macbeaths) resided in the island of Loch Tollie (in Gairloch) he thought within himself, on New Year's night, that it was a pity such mischievous strangers should be in the place, raising rents on the land which did not of right belong to them, while some of the offspring of gentlemen of the Clan Mackenzie, although a few of them possessed lands, were without possessions.

Some time after this, when the snow was melting off the mountains, he lifted his arrow bag on his back, sent word for Big Donald Macrae from Invernate, and they walked as one together across Killelan. Old Alastair Liath (Grey Alexander) of Carr accompanied them. They walked through the mountains of Lochcarron. They came in by the mountains of Kinlochewe. They came at a late hour in sight of Loch Tollie, and they took notice of Macbeath's castle in the island, and of a place whence it would be easy for them to send their arrows to the castle. There was a rowan tree alongside the castle, which was in their way, but when the darkening of night came they moved down to the shore in such a way that the heroes got near the bank of the loch, so that they might, in the breaking of the sky, be opposite Macbeath when he came out.

When Macbeath came out in the morning, the other man said to Donald Mor, " Try how true your hand is now, if it is not tremulous after the night, try if you can hit the seed of the beast, the hare, so that you make a carcase of him where he is, inasmuch as he has no right to be there." Donald shot his arrow by chance, but it only became flattened against one of the kind of windows in the kind of castle that was in it.

When the man from Carr saw what happened to the arrow of the man from Invermate, he thought that his companion's arrow was only a useless one. The man from Carr got a glimpse of one of the servants of Macbeath, carrying with him a stoup of water to boil a goat buck, which he had taken from Craig Tollie the night before ; but, poor fellow! it was not he who consumed the goat buck. Old Alastair Liath of Carr threw the arrow, and it went through the kidneys of him of the water-stoup.

Macbeath suspected that a kind of something was behind him which he did not know about. He thought within himself not to wait to eat the goat buck, that it would be as well for him to go ashore—life or death to him—as long as he had the chance to cross. He lifted every arrangement he had, and he made the shore of it. Those who would not follow him he left behind him ; he walked as fast as was in his joints, but fast as Macbeath was, the arrow of the son of Big Donald fixed in him in the thickest of his flesh. He ran with the arrow fixed, and his left hand fixed in the arrow, hoping always that he would pull it out. He ran down the brae to a place which is called Boora to this day, and the reason of that name is, that when Macbeath pulled the arrow out a buradh, or bursting forth of blood, came after it.

When the Kintail men saw that the superior of the kind of fortress had flown, they walked round the head of Loch Tollie, sprawling, tired as they were ; and the very ferry-boat which took Macbeath ashore took the Macraes to the island. They used part of the goat buck which Macbeath was to have had to his meal. They looked at the man of whom they had made a corpse, while the cook went to the preparation for the morning meal. Difficulty nor distress were not apparent on the Kintail men. The fearless heroes put past the night in the castle. They feared not Macbeath ; but Macbeath was frightened enough that what he did not get he would soon get.

Although the pursuit of the aliens from Mackay's [1] country was in the minds of the Kintail men, they thought they would go and see how the lands of Gairloch lay. They went away in the morning of the next day, after making cuaranan (untanned shoes) of the skin of the goat buck by putting thongs through it, as they had worn out their own on the way coming from Kintail. They came through Gairloch ; they took notice of everything as they desired. They walked step by step, as they could do, without fear or bodily dismay They reached Mackenzie's Castle, they saluted him. They said boldly, if he had more sons, that they would find more land for him. Mackenzie invited them in and took their news. They told him about the land of Gairloch, the way in which they saw Macbeath, and the way in which they made him flee, and the time on which they lived on the flesh of the goat buck. "And Kenneth," says Donald (addressing the chief), "I shall remember the day of the foot of the goat buck as long as Donald is (my name) on me."—*Dixon's Gairloch*, pp. 21-23

HOW IAN LIATH MACRATH (GREY JOHN MACRAE) BROUGHT JOHN ROY MACKENZIE OF GAIRLOCH INTO POSSESSION OF HIS HEREDITARY RIGHTS.

John Roy grew up a tall, brave, and handsome young Highlander. When he could carry arms and wear the belted plaid, he went to the Mackay country to visit his mother. None but his mother knew him, and neither she nor he made known who he was. In those days any stranger who came to a house was not asked who he was until he had been there a year and a day. John Roy lived in the servants' end of the house, and slept and fed with them. Mackay had two rare dogs, called Cu-dubh and Faoileag (black dog and sea gull), and they became greatly attached to John Roy, so that they would follow no one else. Near the end of the year Mackay told his wife that he suspected the stranger was a gentleman's son. Her tears revealed the truth.

---

[1] The Macbeaths were said to have come from the country of the Mackays in Sutherlandshire, probably in the thirteenth century. They had, at least, three strongholds in Gairloch, one of which was the island in Loch Tollie, as mentioned above. There are still some families of the name Macbeath both in Gairloch and in Applecross.

John Roy was then kindly received at the table of the laird, who asked him what he could do for him John Roy begged that Mackay would give him a bodyguard, consisting of the twelve of his men whom he might choose, and the two dogs, Cu-dubh and Faoileag.   He got these, and they went away to Glas Leitire in Kintail, taking with them an anker of whisky.   Arriving there, John Roy placed his twelve men in concealment, and went himself to the house of Ian Liath Macrath (Grey John Macrae).   It was the early morning, and the old wife was spinning on the distaff.   She looked out, and saw a man there.   She called to Ian Liath, who was still lying down, "There is a man out yonder sitting on a creel, and I never saw two knees in my life more like John Roy's two knees."   Ian Liath got up, went to the door, and called out, "Is that you, John?"   John Roy answered that it was "Have you any with you?"   "Yes, I have twelve men."   "Fetch them," said Ian Liath.   He killed a bull, and feasted them all.   Then he told John Roy that Mackenzie of Kintail was coming that very day to hunt on the Glas Leitire hill of his (John Roy's) fathers.   John Roy, with his twelve men and Ian Liath, went to the hill, taking the whisky with them Mackenzie arrived to hunt the deer, and when he saw John Roy and his men, he sent a fair-haired lad to inquire who they were.   John Roy bade the boy sit down, and gave him whisky.   Whenever he rose to go, more whisky was offered, and he was nothing loath to take it.   Mackenzie, thinking the lad was long in returning, sent another boy, who was treated in the same way.   Mackenzie then saw that John Roy had returned, so he went back with his followers to his castle, and John Roy was not further molested by the lords of Kintail.

John Roy came back with Ian Liath to his house, when the latter told him that he had Hector Roy's chest with the title-deeds of Gairloch, and that John Roy must claim the estate. Ian Liath took all his belongings, and accompanied John Roy and his twelve men to Gairloch They came to Beallach a Chomhla, at the side of Bathais (Bus) Bheinn Coming down the mountain they found a good well, and there they rested and left the women and the cattle The well is called to this day "Ian Liath's Well." They met people who informed them that Ian Dubh Mac Ruaridh Mhicleoid, or Black John the son of Rorie

Macleod, who was governor of the old castle of the Dun, was accustomed to walk every day across the big sand and to lie on the top of the Crasg to spy the country. The party went to the Crasg, and Ian Liath told Ian Dubh Mac Ruaridh Macleod, whom they met there, that unless he left the castle before that night he would lose his head. Macleod took the hint, and sailed away in his birlinn, with all his valuables, except one chest containing old title-deeds, which came into John Roy's possession along with the castle.—*Dixon's Gairloch,* pp. 39-40.

HOW THE MACRAE ARCHERS DEFEATED THE MACLEODS AT LEAC NAN SAIGHEAD.[1]

It was after the expulsion of the Macleods that the affair of Leac nan Saighead occurred. Many of the Macleods who had been driven from Gairloch had settled in Skye. A number of young men of the clan were invited by their chief to pass Hogmanay night in his castle at Dunvegan. There was a large gathering. In the kitchen there was an old woman, who was always occupied in carding wool. She was known as Mor Bhan, or Fair Sarah, and was supposed to be a witch. After dinner was over, at night the men began to drink, and when they had passed some time thus they sent in to the kitchen for Mor Bhan. She came and sat down in the hall with the men. She drank one or two glasses, and then she said it was a poor thing for the Macleods to be deprived of their own lands in Gairloch and to live in comparative poverty in Skye. "But," says she, addressing the whole party, "prepare yourselves and start to-morrow for Gairloch, sail in the black birlinn, and you shall regain Gairloch I shall be a witness of your success when you return." The men being young and not overburdened with wisdom, believed her, because they thought she had the power of divination. They set sail in the morning for Gairloch, and the black galley was full of the Macleods It was evening when they came into the loch, and they dare not risk landing on the mainland, for they remembered that the descendants of

---

[1] Leac nan Saighead is on the south coast of Gairloch, and not far from Shieldaig.

Domhnull Greannach (a great Macrae) were still there, and they
knew their powers only too well.   They, therefore, turned to the
south side of the loch and fastened their birlinn to Fraoch Eilean,
in the shelter opposite Leac nan Saighead, between Shieldaig and
Badachro.   They decided to wait there till morning, then disembark
and walk round the head of the loch.   But all the movements of
the Macleods had been well watched.   Domhnull Odhar Mac Ian
Liath and his brother, Ian Odhar Mac Ian Liath, the celebrated
Macrae archers, sons of Ian Liath, mentioned in the last extract,
knew the birlinn of the Macleods, and they determined to oppose
their landing.   They walked round by Shieldaig and posted themselves before daylight at the back of the Leac, a projecting rock
overlooking Fraoch Eilean.   The steps on which they stood at the
back of the rock are still pointed out.   Donald Odhar, being a
short man, took the higher of the two steps, and Iain the other.
Standing on these steps they crouched down in the shelter of the
rock, from which they commanded a full view of the island on
which the Macleods were lying here and there, while the Macrae
heroes were invisible from the island.   They were both celebrated
shots, and had their bows and arrows with them   As soon as the
day dawned they opened fire on the Macleods, a number of them
were killed before their comrades were even aware of the direction
whence the fatal arrows came.   The Macleods endeavoured to
answer the fire, but not being able to see their foes, their arrows
took no effect.   In the heat of the fight one of the Macleods
climbed the mast of the birlinn for a better sight of the position
of the foe.   Ian Odhar took his deadly aim at him when near the
top of the mast.   The shaft pierced his body and pinned him to
the mast.   "Oh," says Donald, "you have sent a pin through his
broth."   So the slaughter continued, and the remnant of the Macleods hurried into the birlinn.   They cut the rope and turned her
head seawards, and by this time only two of them were left alive.
So great was their hurry to escape that they left all the bodies of
their slain companions on the island.   The rumour of the arrival
of the Macleods had spread during the night, and other warriors
such as Fionnla Dubh nan Saighead and Fear Shieldaig were soon
at the scene of action, but all they had to do was to assist at the
burial of the dead Macleods.   Pits were dug, into each of which a
number of the dead bodies were thrown, and mounds were raised

over them, which remain to this day, as anyone may see. The
name Leac nan Saighead means "The flat stone of the arrows."
—*Dixon's Gairloch*, pp. 45-46.

HOW FIONNLA DUBH NAN SAIGHEAD (BLACK FINLAY OF THE ARROWS) FOUGHT AND DEFEATED THE MACLEODS OF ASSYNT.

Fionnla Dubh nan Saighead was a relative of Donald Odhar and
Ian Odhar, and was also of the Macraes of Kintail. Finlay
usually lived at Melvaig. As a marksman, he was on a par with
Donald Odhar. In his day, young Macleod, laird of Assynt, came
to Gairloch in his birlinn to ask for a daughter of John Roy in
marriage. He was refused, and set off northwards on his return
voyage in his birlinn, which was manned with sixteen oars. They
rowed quite close to the land round Rudha Reidh, the furthest out
headland of the north point. Rudha Reidh was then known as
Seann Rudha, a name which is still sometimes given to it. Fionnla
Dubh nan Saighead sat on a rock as the birlinn passed He called
out, " Whence came the heroes ?" They replied, " We came from
Gairloch." " What were you doing there ?" said Finlay. " We
were asking in marriage the daughter of Mackenzie of Gairloch for
this young gentleman." " Did you get her ?" said Finlay. They
replied, " Oh, no." Finlay dismissed them with a contemptuous
gesture and an insulting expression They passed on their way
without molesting him, because they had no arms with them.
Young Macleod brooded over the insult he had received from
Finlay Macrae, who was well known to him by repute. He soon
returned with his sixteen-oared birlinn, manned by the choicest
warriors of Assynt, to take vengeance on Finlay, who noticed the
galley, and guessed who were its occupants. He called for one,
Chisholm, his brother-in-arms, and the two of them proceeded to
the leac, or flat stone, close to the edge of the low cliff about a mile
north to Melvaig; the leac is still pointed out. They reached this
place before the Macleods could effect a landing. On the way, the
Chisholm said to Finlay, " You must leave all the speaking to
me." As the birlinn drew near, Chisholm called out, " What do
you want ?" " We want Fionnla Dubh nan Saighead." " You
won't get him, or thanks," said Chisholm ; " Go away in peace,"

The Macleods began to threaten them. "If that is the way," said Chisholm, "let every man look out for himself." The contest began. Finlay and Chisholm were well sheltered at the back of the leac. A number of the Macleods were killed by the arrows of the two heroes on shore, whilst they themselves remained uninjured. The Macleods, finding their losses so severe, soon thought that discretion was the better part of valour, and, turning their birlinn northwards, departed for their own country. They never again molested Finlay.—*Dixon's Gairloch*, pp. 46-47.

NOTE.—In speaking of the Macrae archers, Mr Dixon says that the arrow fired at the serving man on the Loch Tollie Island, by Alastair Liath, must have killed its victim at a distance of fully five hundred yards. Donald Odhar and Iain Odhar, the heroes of Leac nan Saighead, slew many Macleods with their arrows nearly four hundred yards away. Lest any reader should doubt the authenticity of these performances on account of the marvellous range attained, Mr Dixon gives several instances of wonderful shots made by Turks, including one of four hundred and fifteen yards, against the wind, by Mahmood Effendi, the Turkish Ambassador's secretary, in a field near Bedford House, in 1791, and one of nine hundred and seventy-two yards by the Sultan himself, in 1798, in the presence of Sir Robert Ainslie, British Ambassador to the Sublime Porte.—*Dixon's Gairloch, p. 20.*

APPENDIX L.

THE MACRA BURSARIES.

THE following information has been kindly supplied by Mr P. J. Anderson, librarian of the University of Aberdeen, from the old Minute Books of the Macra foundation :—

Alexander Macra, ironmonger in Bristol, who died on 24th August, 1780, sets forth in his quaintly-worded last will and testament (dated at Edinburgh, 8th November, 1763), his desire "that a considerable portion of such share of worldly substance as I shall at the time of my death be entrusted with by the providence and bounty of Almighty God, my gracious Creator and Supporter, may be employed in perpetuity for the maintenance, education, and instruction of indigent children, with preference to male children or boys, of the Surname of Macra, natives of that part of Great Britain called Scotland" For this purpose he appoints as his executors the President of the Court of Session, the Dean of the Faculty of Advocates, the Senior Baillie of Edinburgh, the Senior Manager of the Orphan Asylum in Edinburgh, the Principal of King's College in Aberdon, the Professor of Divinity, the senior Professor of Philosophy, and the Professor of Humanity there, the Senior Minister, the Senior Baillie, the Dean of Guild, and the Deacon Convener of Aberdeen· directing them to allow his estate to accumulate until of the value of £20,000 Scots.   Subject to an annuity of £150 Scots payable to each of his sisters (Margaret, spouse to John Matheson in Duriness, and Mary, spouse to John Matheson in Rairaig), and to a perpetual payment of the interest on 7300 merks Scots to John Macra, son of the testator's late uncle Mr Roderick, and his heirs male, whom failing, the interest on 2000 merks Scots to the heir male of the testator's great grandfather, Alexander Macra of

Inveriuet: the yearly produce of the said £20,000 Scots is to be spent "on the decent cloathing, mantenance, education, and instruction of as many indigent boys or male children of the Sirname of Macra, and all natives of Scotland, as the said nett yearly produce can sufficiently support."

The boys are to be above the age of nine, and under the age of twelve, and preference is to be given to descendants of the testator's said great grandfather. On attaining the age of thirteen, each boy, if "he is found to have an extraordinary genius for Letters," is to come to Aberdeen to attend one of the burgh schools, "until he be fit for the Humanity class in the King's College in Aberdon . . . . and for as long thereafter as is usually allowed there, for being instructed in the Latin, Greek, and Hebrew Languages, Mathematics, Philosophy, and Divinity, if he so inclines."   If not found "quite acute for Letters," a boy may be bound apprentice to some handicraft.

"And I hereby ordain that any boy's father's or other of his predecessors' using to add the letter e, h, w, or y to his surname of Macra . . . . shall not be sustained an objection to the admission of such boy, but the addition of any of these four letters to the proper surname of Macra is to be construed an inattentive complyance with the pronunciation of the word Macra, which is as various as the accent of the language is different in the several countrys wherein the father and other predecessors of such boy resided."

An action in the Court of Session for reduction of the will was unsuccessful, and the duties of the Trust were undertaken by the eight last named executors, the others declining to act.

In 1794, by which time the required sum of £20,000 Scots (£1666 13s 4d sterling) has been realised, "in consequence of information sent to Ross-shire, where the relations of the mortifier reside, sundry applications from them, supported by the clergymen of these parishes, are transmitted to the agent at Aberdeen, along with certificates of the propinquity of several familys who had children qualified in terms of the mortification to be admitted to the benefit of it."

Kenneth, son of Duncan Macra, in Linasee, Kintail, late lieutenant in the 78th Foot, and Alexander, son of Farquhar Macra, at Fadoch, Kintail, are admitted as "nearest in degree to Alex-

ander Macra of Inverinet," and come to Aberdeen, being entrusted
to the care of Professor Macleod   Alexander, another son of
Lieut. Duncan, accompanies his brother.

In 1796 the testator's sisters and his cousin John are reported
dead, and in 1798 "Captain" Duncan, who visits Aberdeen, is
recognised as heir male of the mortifier's great grandfather, " which
is proved by the genealogys transmitted by the ministers of the
parishes where the several branches of the family reside."

1799 Alexander, son of Farquhar, enters bajan class at King's
College · graduates M.A. in 1803.   (*Officers and Graduates of
King's Coll*, 1893, p 268)   A fourth boy, Duncan, son of John,
in Morvich, is admitted.

1800. Kenneth, son of Duncan, enters bajan class at King's
Coll.: in 1803 goes to London " to be placed in a mercantile
house "

1804 Alexander, son of Duncan, enters semi-class at King's
Coll

1805. Duncan, son of John, in Morvich, " has not much
genius," and is bound apprentice for five years to Mr Littlejohn,
wright in Aberdeen

1806 Admitted, and comes to Aberdeen to attend Grammar
School Alexander, son of John, son of Duncan, son of Donald,
son of Christopher, lawful son of Alexander of Inverinet.   Enters
bajan class 1809 ; M A 1813.

1813. Admitted · Duncan, son by a second marriage of Captain
Duncan   Enters bajan class in 1820, and attends four sessions,
but does not graduate.

1816 Admitted · Farquhar, son of Farquhar in Camuslunie
Enters bajan class in 1819 , M A 1823 , appointed schoolmaster
at Lochcarron , student of divinty 1823-27 , minister of Free
Church, Knockbain

1824. Admitted . Christopher, whose propinquity is certified
by Archibald Macra of Ardintoul and many respectable persons
of the clan, " the boy being in a state of absolute nakedness and
starvation " , proved to be over age.

1826 Admitted . Farquhar, son of Alexander , proved to be
over age.   Duncan, son of Murdoch, in Stornoway , proved to be
over age   John, son of Duncan, in Camuslunie.   Donald, son of
John, in Conchra.

1831. A. Mitchell, Headmaster of the Grammar School, Old Aberdeen, reports, 1st September, that John and Donald "have attended the Grammar School of Old Aberdeen for the space of three years and ten months Their attendance has upon the whole been sufficiently regular; but their application has by no means been such as to ensure success in the study of the Latin language, consequently they are both very deficient I cannot say that there is much difference between them, but on the whole I think Donald the better scholar. Neither the one nor the other appears to have any 'extraordinary genius for letters'" To be sent home to their parents.

1832 John and Donald wish to follow some liberal profession, but this is not sanctioned. The former is apprenticed to Mr Rennie, shipbuilder; the latter to Mr Simpson, wright.

Mr Alexander Macrae, only surviving son of late Captain Duncan, authorises payment of the annuity to his mother (?stepmother).

1833 Admitted Alexander, son of Finlay, Auchtertyre. Dies of smallpox, has not been vaccinated; this to be a *sine qua non* in future.

1834. Applications from John, son of Christopher, Drudaig; Donald, son of Finlay, Auchtertyre; Kenneth, son of John, Camuslunie; James, son of Donald, Kintail; the first is admitted, and is subsequently apprenticed to Mr William Henderson, builder.

1839. Applications from Colin, son of Christopher, Inchroe; Donald, son of Farquhar, Glenshiel; Donald, son of Finlay, Lochalsh; Donald, son of Farquhar, Glenshiel: the second is admitted, subsequently apprenticed to Messrs Blaikie & Son.

1843. Finlay Macrae admitted, subsequently apprenticed to Mr Cook, tailor.

1847. In this year the trustees authorised their agent, Mr James Nicol, advocate, to uplift the funds from the Northern Investment Company, in whose hands they then lay, and to lend them on heritable security, which he reported had been found. The money, however, Mr Nicol retained in his own hands unsecured, and in 1850 his firm, Nicol & Munro, became bankrupt.

Mr Alexander Anderson, advocate, who was appointed judicial factor on the Macra Trust, was able to recover £419 14s 3d from the sequestrated estate, and £1246 19s 1d from the Macra Trustees, who were held to have been guilty of gross negligence. In 1862 he reported that the fund had now been restored to its original amount of £1666 13s 4d; and a body of trustees was constituted *de novo* · those accepting office being the Principal, the Professor of Divinity, the Senior Minister, the Senior Baillie, the Dean of Guild, and the Deacon Convener

During the succeeding twenty-six years a considerable number of applications were received by the Macra Trustees, accompanied usually by proofs of descent from Alexander Macra of Inverinet; but of those admitted to the benefits of the Fund, no one seems to have proved himself worthy of a University education   Under the scheme of administration of the Aberdeen Educational Trust, dated 17th November, 1888, two bursaries at the Grammar School "shall be known by the name of the Macra bursaries, and these two bursaries shall be awarded to any candidates properly qualified in the opinion of the Governors to avail themselves of the education given at the Grammar School of Aberdeen, who shall satisfy the Governors that they are of the lineal descendants of Alexander Macra of Inverinet, the great grandfather of the said Alexander Macra, ironmonger, Bristol."

On the death of Mr Alexander Macra, Demerara, son of Captain Duncan, the right to the perpetual annuity seems to have passed to Dr John Macrae, H E.I C.S ,[1] son of Dr John Macrae, younger brother of Captain Duncan , but no payments were ever made to him   On his death in 1864, a claim was put forward by John Anthony Macrae, W.S., son of Colin, younger brother of Dr John, senior.   On 31st March, 1865, the Trustees having considered the proofs advanced by him, find that he "is now the heir male lineally descended from the testator's said great grandfather."   On 1st October, 1868, Colin George Macrae, W.S., was served heir to his father, John Anthony; and he now represents the family.

[1] Page 103.

APPENDIX M.

EXTRACT FROM MINUTES OF COURT HELD AT INVERNESS TO INQUIRE
INTO THE AFFAIR OF ATH NAM MUILEACH [1]

INVERNESS, 20th November, 1721.   In presence of Master Robert
Gordon of Haughs, Sheriff-Depute of Inverness,

Compeared Donald McRae, soldier in the Royal Regiment of
North British Fusiliers, who, being solemnly sworn in a precogni-
tion, maketh oath that he was of the detachment of His Majesty's
Forces, appointed to attend the Factors on the Forfeited Estates,
when the insult and murder was committed on the saide Forces
and Factors at Loch Affrick, upon the Second day of October last
by several Bodies of Highlanders, and that he knew and seed the
persons following amongst the saide Bodies of Highlanders, viz. —
Donald Murchison, Chamberland to the late Earl of Seaforth.
Donald Murchison of Auchtertyre.
John McRae of Inverinat.
John Dow McAlister Vic Gilchrist, in Achyark.
Christopher, Ferquhar and Murdo McRaes, sons to Christopher
     McRae, in Arivugan
Don McRae in Glensheil, nephew to the said Christopher.
John McUrchie Vic Alister Vic Vinister, in Killelan.
John McFinlay Vic Ean, in Killelan.
Duncan McEan Vic Conchie, in Killelan.
Alexander McEan Vic Conchy, in Killelan
John McEan Vic Conchy, in Killelan.
John McEan Vic Conchy Vic Alister, in Glenelchak.
John Dow McAlister Vic Gilchrist, in Achayouran of Glensheall.
Donald McAlister Vic Gilchrist, in Achyouran-begg

---

[1] Page 358.   See also paper on " Donald Murchison and the Factors on
the Forfeited Estates," by Mr William Mackay, published in " The Transactions of the Gaelic Society of Inverness," Vol. XIX

Alexander McConchy Vic Gilchrist, in Rategan of Glensheal.

Alexander McRae, son to Master Donald McRae, minister of Kintail.

John McRae, son to Alexander McFerquhar Vic Rae, in Morvich.

John McKenzie, in Invermat, son to Kenneth Roy, brother to the late Aplecross

Ferquhar Oig McFerquhar Vic Alister, in Inversheile.

Murdo McFerquhar Vic Alister, in Croe of Kintail

Alexander McFerquhar Vic Alister, in Morvich, in Croe of Kintail.

John McRae Vic Vinister, in Letterfearn.

John McRae, eldest son to Donald McRae of Drindaig, living in Letterfearn

Murdo McAlister Vic Vinister, in Camboslynie.

Alexander McAlister Vic Vinister, in Glenelchak

Alexander McHuistan Vic Rae, in Meikle Salachy of Lochalsh, nephew to Aryvogan.

Donald Oig McLennan, in Achnafearn of Lochalsh.

Murdo McRae, in Coriloyne of Glenloyne.

John McRae, son to the said Murdoch McRae, in Coriloyne of Glenloyne.

Ferquhar McConchy Voir Nakaime, in Glenloyne.

Alexander McHutchan Vic Rae, in Sallachy More.

Duncan McHutchan Vic Rae, in Sallachy More.

John Dow McLennan, in Achnaguiran

Colline McEan Vic Iver, in Inversheal.

Murdo McEan Vic Iver, in Inversheal.

Duncan McConchy Vic Gilchrist, in Islandonanbeg

Evander Murchison, son to John Murchison McEan Vic Conil, in Achnabein.

Donald Roy, son to the ground officer of Glenmoriston.

John McAlister Vic Rae, in Cambouslyne of Glenelchak, one of the baggage men to the Rebells.

Donald McRae further maketh oath that the said John McAlister Vic Rae, baggage man, and others of the party who conducted the troops and factors back through the wood, informed him that the persons following were amongst the committers of the said insult and murder, viz :—

John Dow McAlister Vic Gilchrist, in Achyark

Duncan McConchy Vic Charlich, in Sallachy More

Alexander McFinlay Vic Ean, in Achnabein

Duncan McAlister Vic Conchy Matheson, in Achnachen of Lochalsh

Murdo McConchy Vic Ean, in Killelan.

Alexander McConchy Vic Vinister, in Aglachan of Lochalsh.

Christopher McFerquhar Oig, in Letterfearn.

Alexander McAlister Vic Gillichrist Vic Ferquhar Oig, in Mamaig of Glenelchaig.

Alister McAlister Vic Gilchrist, in Kilaric.

John McEan Vic Conchy, in Ratigan.

Donald McAlister Vic Gillichchrist, in Achyark of Glensheal.

Donald Murchison, in Achachoraran, brother to the deceast Achtertoir

Murdo Murchison, brother to the deceast Achtertoir

Alexander Murchison, brother to the deceast Achtertoir

John McGilchrist McRae, in Comer of Strathglesh.

Christopher McEan Vic Conil Vic Vinister, in Conchraig of Cambouslyne.

Christopher McUrchie Vic Vinister, in Glenelchack.

Alexander and Myles Murchison, sons to John Murchison McEan Vic Conil, in Achnabein

John McDonald Reach Vic Conchy Oig, in Meikle Salachie.

John Dow McEuan Gou, in Meikle Salachy.

John McLennan Vic Conchy Voi, in Mid Ausgett of Kintail.

Donald McEan Doi Brebater, in Mid Ausgett of Kintail.

Finlay McEan Doi Brebater, in Mid Ausgett of Kintail

Duncan Mac Ean Glas, in Achnasou of Lochalsh.

Donald Matheson, in Conchra of Lochalsh.

Duncan Matheson, in Achnashew

Donald McDonald Oig, in Ardmai.

Finlay McCoil Reach Vic Conchie Oig, in Letterwhile of Kintail.

Donald McRae furthur maketh oath that he seed Patrick Grant, son to the late Glenmoriston, with the saids companies of Highlanders; all which he declares to be truth, as he shall answer to God, and declares he cannot write, and further maketh oath that he seed Kenneth McConchy Vic Alister, in Ratigan of Glensheall, in company with the saids Highlanders.

ADDENDUM I.

——:o——

The following version of the Gaelic poem given on page 388 was sent to the author by Mr William Mackay, Craigmonie, Inverness, but it was too late to be included in Appendix J. It was written down in 1877 by a well-known Gaelic scholar and poet, the late Mr Farquhar Macdonell, of Plockton, Lochalsh, and sent by him to the Rev. Alexander Stewart, LL D., of Nether-Lochaber, by whom it was afterwards sent to Mr Mackay. According to Mr Macdonell, it was composed immediately after the burial of Murdoch Macrae in Kilduich. The author considers this the best, as it is also the most complete, of several versions of the same poem that he has come across :—

Deanam na marbhrainn s' as ur
Air miann suilean Chloinn 'ic Rath,
Air Murachadh donna-gheal mo ruin
A bha lan do chliu gun chleith.

A dheagh mhic Alasdair uir,
Togamaid do chliu an tos,
Sud an laoch fo'n robh a' mhuirn,
'Shliochd Fhearachair nan cuirt 's nan corn.

Si sealg geamhraidh Ghlinne-lic
Chuir greann oirn gu tric 'us gruaim,
M' an og nach robh teann 's a bha glic,
Bhi 's an teampull fo'n lic 's an uaigh.

Chiad aoine de 'n gheamhradh fhuar,
'S daor a phaigh sinn duais na sealg,
An t-og bo chraobhaiche snuagh
Na aonar bhuainn 'us fhaotainn marbh

Tional na sgire gu leir
A suibhal sleibh 's a falbh bheann,
Fad sgios nan coig latha deug,
'S am fear dileas, treun air chall.

'S turseach do chinneadh mor deas,
Ga d' shireadh an ear 's an iar,
'S an t-og a b' ionmholta beachd
Ri shos glinne marbh 's an t-shabh

Clann 'ic Rath nam buailtean bo
Air an siarradh gu mor mu d'eug,
Mu d' thoirt as a bheatha so oirn,
Mhic athair nan corn 's nan teud.

'S turseach do dheas bhraithrean graidh
'S am *parson* ge h-ard a leugh,
Thug e, ge tuigseach a cheaird,
Barr tuinse air cach gu leir.

Air thus dhiubh Donnachadh nam Pios,
Gillecriosd 'us dithis na chleir,
Fearachar agus Ailean Donn
'S Uisdean a tha trom do dheigh.

Bu tusa an t-ochd shlat ghraidh
Dh'ios nam braithrean glana coir,
A' nochd gur dosgach an cradh,
Gu 'n fhioiseadh am blath dhiubh og.

Gur tursach do cheud bhoan og,
'S fliuch frasach na deoir le gruaidh,
I 'spionadh a fuilt d' a deoin,
Sior chumha nach beo do shnuagh.

Bhean uasal a thug dhut gaol,
Nach bi chaoidh na h-uigneas slan,
'S truagh le mo chluasan a gaoir,
Luaithead 's a sgaoil an t-aog a snaim.

Bu tu 'n t-slat eibhinn, aluinn, ur,
Bu mhiann suil 's bu leanan mua,
A ghnuis an robh am breac seirc,
Bha cho deas air thapadh lamh.

Bu tu marbhaich' a bhalla-bhric bhain,
Le mordha 's le lan chrann geur,
'S le cuilbheir bhristeadh tu cnaimh,
'S bu shilteach 'o d' laimh na feidh.

Do chul buidh' fainneach ri lic,
Bha ruthaidh, 's e gle gheal, dearg,
'Ghnuis an robh 'n gliocas gun cheilg,
Air nach d'fhiosraicheadh riamh fearg.

Chuala mise clarsach theud,
Fiodhall 'us beus a cu-sheinn,

'S cha chuala, 's cha chluinn gu brath,
Ceol a b'fhearr na do bheul binn.

'S math am fear rannsachaidh 'n t-aog,
Gun maor e dh'iarras gu mean,
Bheir e leis an t-og gun ghiamh,
'S fagaidh e fear liath bhios sean.

Bha thu fearail anns gach ceum,
Bu bharant thu 'n deirce bhochd,
'S tha thu air deas laimh do Righ,
Le lughad 's chuir thu 'm pris an t-olc

Tha sluagh taght' aig deagh Mhac Dhe,
Gun easbhuidh, gun fheum air ni,
'S tha thus' a nis 'an aoibhneas mor,
'An cathair cheoil aig Righ nam righ.

ADDENDUM II.

——'o:——

Page 109.—Surgeon-General Sir William Alexander Mackinnon died in London on the 28th of October, 1897.

Page 141.—Captain Archibald Macra Chisholm of Glassburn died on the 19th of October, 1897.

Page 158 —Colin Macrae, Camden, South Carolina, lineal representative of the Macraes of Conchra, died on the 20th of September, 1898. He was succeeded as representative of that family by his brother,

Duncan Macrae of Kames Castle, who died on the 14th of December, 1898, and was buried on the 21st at Kilduich, his clansmen in Kintail making his funeral the occasion for a remarkable display of clan sentiment and loyalty. His eldest son,

Stewart Macrae (page 158), of Newark-on-Trent, is now lineal representative of the Macraes of Conchra

Page 281.—In addition to the marriage of Alexander Macrae and Agnes Gordon, there appears also to be some record of a marriage, about the same time, between a William Macrae and a Thomasine Gordon of Carleton. It is not impossible, however, that a confusion of names may have occurred with regard to one and the same marriage.

ERRATA

——:o:——

Page 67	-	line	2	-	-		Comma after property.
,, 67	-	,,	22	-	-		Read has.
,, 69	-	,,	1	-	-	,,	VIII.
,, 84	-	,,	17	-	-	,,	untimely
,, 87	-	,,	25 (last)	-		,,	farther.
,, 193	-	,,	1 of footnote 2			,,	Ghobha
,, 269	-	,,	2	,,	2	,,	Loudon
,, 282	-	,,	8	,,	2	,,	Herdman.
,, 283	-	,,	7	-	-	,,	Dunnay.
,, 284	-	,,	19	-	-	,,	Georgiana.
,, 335	-	,,	12	-	-	,,	Mantuanus.
,, 383	-	,,	8	-	-	,,	Mr William Mackenzie.

Map.—Achyark, inadvertently left out in preparation of block for map, is at the foot of Glenlic.

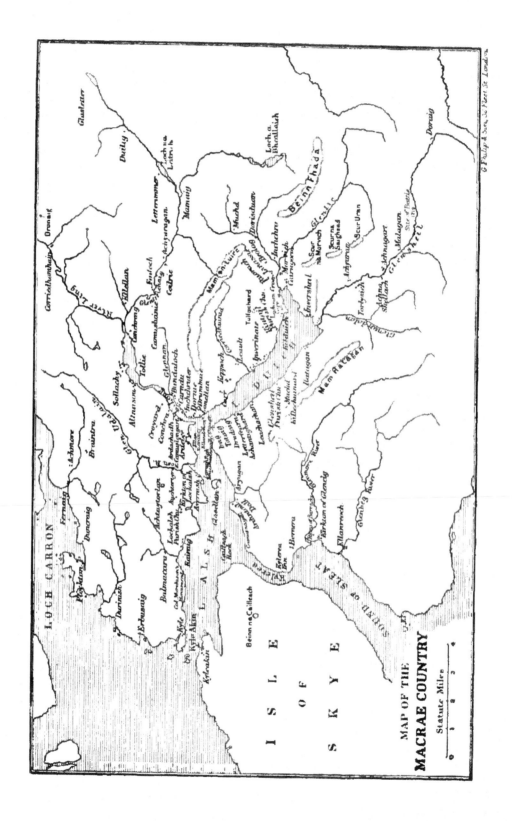

MAP OF THE

MACRAE COUNTRY

Statute Miles

INDEX.

——:o:——

NOTES AND ADDITIONS.

NOTES AND ADDITIONS.

Page 80, line 4 from bottom—

(*a*) Alexander, son of Colin, married Janet Mackay, Avernish, with issue. Isabel married John Macrae Camusluinie, without issue, and Mary married John Macrae, Ardelve, with issue as mentioned on p. 166, ll. 12, 13, 14.

(*b*) Flora married Duncan Macrae, Camusluinie, without issue.

(*c*) Isabel married Farquhar Macrae, Kintail, with issue, and went to America.

(*d*) Janet married John Macrae, Sallachy, with issue, and went to Canada.

(*e*) Margaret married Donald Macrae, blacksmith, Ardelve, with issue, and went to Canada.

Page 102, for the Descendants of the Rev. John Macqueen and Jean Macrae, read as follows :—

a. Son died young.

b. Mary died unmarried in 1871.

c. Donald John, born in 1786. Ensign in the 74th Highlanders 1800; Lieutenant 1803; Captain 1810; Major 1830. Served in the Peninsular War, and was wounded seven times. He was a Knight of the Order of Hanover, and a Military Knight of Windsor. He married Mary Bliss, daughter of the Honourable Judge Bliss of Fredericton, New Brunswick, and died in 1865, with issue.

e1. John, Lieutenant in the 60th Rifles, died young in India.

c2. Sarah Jean, married first David Reid with issue :—(1) Mary died in childhood. (2) Donald Norman

married first Emana Pugh with issue—(a) Mary, born
1871, who married Farquhar Mackinnon of Kyle with issue,
Flora, John, Donald, Sheila; (b) Jessie, born 1872, married
Ross Palmer with issue, Mary, Jessie, Dorothy, Eileen,
Donald Horsley; (c) Donald James, born 1873, married.
Donald Norman Reid married, secondly, Lilian Wright
with issue (d) Florence, born 1878, married Denis Calnan,
Indian Civil Service; (e) Norman born 1881; David born
1884.   (3) John Alexander, born 1844, died unmarried in
India, 1883.   (4) Catherine Barbara, born 1846, died
1865.   Sarah Jean married, secondly, Hugh Bliss John-
ston, son of the Honourable Hugh Johnston of St John,
New Brunswick, with issue.   (5) Hugh, born 1856, died
unmarried in India, 1889.   (6) Harriet, born 1858.   (7)
George, born 1860, M.D. of Edinburgh University,
Physician in London, married Alice Merryweather with
issue (a) Hugh Kenneth born 1886, Alec Leith born 1889

c3. George Bliss, Captain in the 60th Rifles, and
afterwards in the 51st King's Own Light Infantry, served
in the Indian Mutiny, married, without issue.

c4. Minnie, died young.

c5. Madeline, married James Grant, with issue (1)
Donald, married with issue; (2) Margaret; (3) James.

c6. Frances Anne.

d. Archibald, died unmarried in 1872.

e. Jean, died unmarried.

f. Elizabeth, married Alexander Sutherland, and died
without issue in 1879.

g. Kenneth, Surgeon H.E.I C.S., married Margaret
Bairnsfather, without surviving issue, and died in 1879.

h. Jessie, married Major Milne, without surviving
issue.

i. Farquhar, Captain in the Indian Navy, married
Maria Shuttleworth, with issue—Farquhar.

k. Maria, married Colonel Campbell, R.A., with issue.

l. David, died young.

Page 103, *for the Descendants of Georgina Macrae and Edward Currie, read as follows :—*

e. Georgina married at Patna, Bengal, on the 3rd March, 1831, Edward Currie, who died at Ticehurst, Sussex, 8th January, 1889. Georgina died at Boulogne, 16th April, 1860, leaving issue—

*e*1. Helen Eliza, born 7th July, 1832, died 24th August, 1833.

*e*2. Georgina, born 14th July, 1834, married 14th April, 1859, Sir Augustus Rivers Thompson, who died at Gibraltar, 29th November, 1890. She died in London, 13th December, 1892, with issue—(1) Ruth, born 11th October, 1864, married 15th November, 1888, Richard Arthur Bosanquet, with issue — Arthur Rivers, born 12th July, 1890; Cecily Ruth, born 25th September, 1892; Raymond Francis, born 3rd September, 1895. (2) Dora Georgina, born 28th September, 1866, married 18th June, 1891, Colin McLean, with issue—Lachlan, born 29th September, 1892; Eila Beatrice, born 3rd January, 1894; Mona Rivers, born 13th March, 1895; Dora Elizabeth, born 9th July, 1899. (3) Rachel Mary, born 26th November, 1868, married 3rd October, 1899, the Rev. Arthur Davis. (4) Bertha, born 18th July, 1870.

*e*3. Eliza Fredrica, born at Cobham 2nd October, 1835; married 10th January, 1857, George William Moultrie of the Bank of Bengal. He died at Surbiton, Surrey, 12th February, 1904, leaving issue—(1) James Edward, born 16th November, 1858; married 31st October, 1898, Ethel Mowbray Fergusson, with issue— Frederick James Fergusson, born 26th August, 1899; Lionel Geoffrey Fergusson, born 9th June, 1901. (2) Amy Frederica, born 20th August, 1860; married 27th November, 1879, the Right Rev. Louis George Mylne, D.D., Oxford, late Bishop of Bombay, now Rector of

Alvechurch, Worcestershire, with issue—Edward Graham, born 19th January, 1883; Alan Moultrie, born 2nd January, 1886; Ronald Heathcote, 28th June, 1887; Kenneth Macnaughton, born 15th May, 1890; Athol Wordsworth, born 11th December, 1894; Euan Louis, born 16th June, 1897; Angus Fletcher, born 24th March, 1899. (3) Fendall Alexander, born 1st October, 1863. (4) Helen Georgina, born 11th April, 1866; died 31st December, 1893. (5) Hugh Crawford, born 23rd September, 1868; married 6th January, 1904, Mary Reid, with issue— Amy Frances Heather, born 2nd April, 1905. (6) Steuart Bullen, born 6th November, 1872; married 14th November, 1904, Lilian Murray. (7) Constance Minnie, born 4th May, 1877; died 8th January, 1886.

*e*4. Edward Hamilton, born at Bath 24th December, 1836; died at sea 27th August, 1837.

*e*5. Edward, born at Calcutta 31st August, 1838; died 19th August, 1839.

*e*6. John, born at Calcutta 1st September, 1839; died 6th April, 1840.

*e*7. Mary Katharine, born at Calcutta 24th January, 1841; died 27th April, 1883.

*e*8. Dora, born at Calcutta 23rd March, 1842; married Nathaniel Stuart Alexander, Bengal Civil Service, with issue—(1) William Nathaniel Stuart, born 8th May, 1874. (2) Edward Currie, born 15th September, 1875. (3) Mary Bethia Isabel, born 20th May, 1878. (4) Robert Dundas, born 29th August, 1880.

*e*9. The Very Rev. Edward Reid Currie, D.D., born at Calcutta 16th February, 1844 See p. 103.

Page 107, *line* 9 *from bottom :—*

Norman Farquhar married January, 1907, in Melbourne, Aileen Marguirite Ann, eldest daughter of Andrew Rowan of that city, with issue—John Kenneth Andrew Farquhar, born 5th June, 1908..

Page 124, *line* 10 *from bottom* :—

3. DONALD, who had a son Duncan, who married with issue.

a. John, married with issue.

*a*1. Alexander, M.A., Aberdeen, went as a school-master to Canada.

*a*2. Donald (called Domhnull Ruadh, Red-haired Donald), married Anabella Macrae, with issue—(1). Mary, died unmarried at Fadoch. (2) Margaret, married Christopher Mackenzie, Ardelve, an elder, died in 1905, with issue—one son, Donald.

*a*3. Kate married Alexander Macrae (MacIan), Inverinate, with issue—(1) Farquhar. (2) John, police-constable in Edinburgh, died unmarried in Edinburgh. (3) Flora, died unmarried. (4) James, police-constable in Glasgow, married, first, a Macdonald from Camusluinie, with issue—Alexander, married in Greenock; James married a second time. (5) Maggie married Murdoch Macrae, Letterfearn, with issue—John, married in America; Christopher, at Drudaig, married Christina Macaulay, with issue—Murdo, Elizabeth, Margaret, Jane; Farquhar, at Drudaig; Lilias; Kate, married Charles Macaulay in America ; James, at Drudaig.

b. Murdoch, son of Duncan, lived at Dornie, married Mary Macrae, sister of Farquhar, mentioned as Dr Downie's herd (page 148), with issue.

*b*1. Donald married Kate Macdonald Carr, with issue—(1) Mary married John Fraser in America, with issue—Christina, Alexander, Duncan, Farquhar, Catherine, Donald, Annie. (2) Farquhar lived at Fort-Augustus, married Anne Macgregor, Strathglass, with issue—Kate ; Mary married Murdoch Mackenzie, Lochalsh, and went to London ; Donald married a Macrae at Fort-Augustus; Christina ; Annie. (3) Christina married Duncan Macrae, Inverinate, with issue in America—Alexander, Donald, Catherine, Christina, Ellen. (4) James

Morrison, lived at Auchtertyre, married Isabel Mackay, Altnasuth, with issue—Catherine married Murdoch Mackenzie, Lochalsh, with issue; Christina married Duncan Sinclair, schoolmaster, Lochalsh, with issue; Farquhar, postmaster, Kyle of Lochalsh, married Mary Murchison, with issue—Isabel, Annie; Mary Ann married Alexander Davidson, schoolmaster, Plockton, with issue; Jane married, first, Andrew Chisholm, with issue, and, secondly, George Young, bookseller, Inverness. (5) Murdoch, at Torcullin, Kintail, married Kate, daughter of Finlay Macrae, who served in the Seaforth Highlanders, with issue— Duncan went to Canada, where he married Maggie Macrae, with issue—Murdoch Finlay, Alexandrina, Kate; Finlay served in the Seaforth Highlanders in Afghanistan and Egypt, then went to America, now in Helena, Montana, married Kate, daughter of Duncan Macrae, Ratagan, with issue—Duncan, Murdoch, Helen Kate; Christopher married Catherine Macrae, Bundaloch, daughter of Donald, *a*4, page 129, and went to America, issue — Christina, John Farquhar, Duncan Murdoch, Mary Margaret, Catherine; Catherine married William Senogles, Kendal, Westmoreland, with issue—Murdoch David, Christina, Catherine, Sarah Ann; Annabella married George Hood, Glasgow, who died, 1901, without issue; Christina died young; John Tait, at Inverinate, was for some time piper at The Alhambra, London, married Mary Anne Mackenzie, with issue— Catherine, Murdoch, George Hood. (6) Christopher died unmarried in New Zealand.

*b*2. Christina married Alexander Macrae, Ardintoul, with issue, and went to America.

*b*3. Janet married Farquhar Macrae, Lochalsh, with issue, and went to America.

*b*4. Isabella married John Macrae, Dornie, with issue—Alexander, who died unmarried.

*b*5. Jane married Mr Fraser, Inverness, with issue

*b*6. Catherine married Mr Ross, Glasgow.

*b*7. Isabella died unmarried.

c. Duncan, son of Duncan, lived at Dornie, married with issue.

d. Colin, son of Duncan, lived at Dornie, married with issue.

*d*1. Duncan married without surviving issue.

*d*2. Christopher, innkeeper at Tomdoun, in the Heights of Kintail, married Catherine Macrae with issue— (1) Alexander, in Arisaig, married to Mary Macdonald, with issue—Duncan, Colin, Catherine. (2) Colin, in Lochaber, married Sophia Campbell, with issue—Christopher, John, Flora, Isabella, Louisa. (3) Donald, at Cluanie, in Kintail, married Ellen Macrae. (4) John, in Sutherlandshire, married Margaret Gillies, with issue—Duncan, Flora, Catherine, Jessie, Christina, Ellen. (5) Flora married Alexander Macrae, Cro, Kintail, with issue— Alexander, at Moy Hall, Inverness, married Mary Rose, with issue—Alexander, Lily, Mary, Flora, Lousia; Mary married John Macaulay, Ardelve, with issue—John, Alexander, Duncan, Flora married Farquhar Macrae, Auchtertyre, already mentioned (page 183), Christina, Helen ; Catherine married Duncan Macrae, Loch Hourn, with issue—Alexander, Catherine, Flora, Mary Harriet, Christina ; Isabella married John Macintyre, Pitlochry ; Jessie married James Brethowe, with issue. (6) Mary married Alexander Macrae, Lochcarron, with issue. (7) Christina married Alexander Macrae, with issue—Duncan, living at Arnisdale, Glenelg ; Flora ; Catherine ; Annie.

Page 127, to come in at foot :—

*b*6. Mary married John Murchison, Lochcarron, with issue.

*b*7. Isabella died unmarried.

*b*8. Maggie died unmarried.

*b*9. Annie married John Macrae of the Balnain family, mentioned hereafter.

*b*10. Kate married John, son of Murdoch Macrae, of the Balnain family, with issue.

*b*11. Janet married Farquhar Macrae, Sallachy, with issue in America.

*b*12. Mary died young.

Page 128, *line* 11 :—

*a*2. Alexander, in Kishorn, &c., issue—(1) Duncan, at Kyle, married Catherine, daughter of John Macrae, Lochcarron, with issue—John, Bella, Mary, Johan, Alexander, Jessie Anne. (2) Rev. Murdoch, United Free Church, Edderton. (3) Annie, married John Burnet, with issue. (4) Annabella. (5) Isabella. (6) Donald.

Page 129, *line* 15 :—

*a*4. Donald married Margaret Macrae, with issue— (1) Colin married Kate Macdonald. (2) John Farquhar, in the Argentine Republic, married Helen Stevenson, with issue—Rudolph John. (3) Farquhar married Annie Macpherson, with issue—Maggie Anne, John Farquhar, Mary, Donald. (4) Catherine married Christopher, son of Murdoch Macrae, Torchullin, as already mentioned (page 450), with issue, and went to America.

Page 148, *line* 4 *from bottom* :—

(*b*). Donald, married with issue.

(*b*1). Donald married Isabel Grant, Glenmoriston, with issue—(1) John married Lilias Macrae, Camusluinie, with issue—Isabel; John; Donald, farmer, Attadale, married Hannah Macrae (Strome Ferry), with issue— Lilias, John, Proby died 1895, Farquhar, M.A., Glasgow (1906); Alexander died unmarried in Australia; Annie married John Matheson, Patt, Lochalsh, and went to Manitoba, issue—Catherine, Alexander, Lilias, Euphemia, Lachlan, John, Isabel, Charles. (2) Elizabeth married Thomas Macrae, Camusluinie, with issue, as given hereafter. (3) Flora died young. (4) Mary married John Mackenzie, Glengarry, with issue.

(*b*2). Murdoch married Marion, daughter of Christopher Macrae (Roy), Achnagart, and had, with other issue— (1) Duncan married a Matheson, with surviving issue, a daughter, who married Kenneth Matheson, Balmacarra, with issue.   (2) John married Catherine, one of the "several daughters" mentioned, page 127, line 6, with issue, and went to America.

(*b*3). Farquhar (*b*2 on page 148) married Isabella, daughter of Alexander Macrae (page 152, last line), with issue (all of whom went to America about 1849).   (1) Malcolm married Helen Macrae (page 217), with issue. (2) John, called "Ian Mor," married Anne, one of the "several daughters," page 127, line 6, with issue, one daughter.   (3) John married Christina Macrae (Roy), Dornie, with issue.   (4) Alexander.   (5) Flora, who married Alexander Macrae.

(*b*4). Janet married Christopher Macrae, Kyleakin (page 161).

(*b*5). Mary married Murdoch Macrae (Page 449).

(*b*6). Finlay.

(*c*). Farquhar married with issue, at least one daughter, who married Malcolm Macrae of Corriedhoin.

Page 149, *last line :—*

(*a*2). John married a daughter of Murdoch Macrae, Sallachy (and went to America), with issue—Evan Hugh Douglas, Donald Kenneth, Maggie, Mary, and others.

Page 150, *line* 7 ·—

(1). DONALD (Domhnull Ruadh) died on the way to America, leaving issue—Donald married, with issue, in Toronto.

Page 150, *line* 13 :—

(*b*1). Alexander married Janet Finlayson, with issue— Maggie, Christina.

(*b*2). Donald married Maggie Barr, living in Leeds, with issue—Maggie, Annie, Duncan.

(*b*3). John married Marion Smith, also in Leeds, with issue—Kenneth, Maggie.

(*b*5). Annie married Farquhar Macrae, Lochlonghead, with issue; John, innkeeper, Lochlonghead, married Betsy Maclean, with issue—Jessie, Maggie, Williamina; Farquhar at Lochlonghead; William in Leeds; Annie married Murdoch Macrae, Dornie; Maggie married Donald Campbell, Glenelg; Christina; Kenneth died unmarried in 1900.

Page 159, *line* 13 :—

Anna Helena married in 1906 Sir Alan John Colquhoun, Bart., of Luss.

Page 162, *line* 12 :—

a. Donald lived first at Carr, and afterwards at Achantighard, where he died in 1811. He married in 1748 Christina, daughter of Alexander, son of Farquhar Macrae, with issue—

*a*1. John, died in India.

*a*2. Donald, born 1752, died 1831, lived first at Totaig, and afterwards at Dornie. He married in 1787 Anabella, daughter of Farquhar Macrae of the Duilig Family, with issue—Alexander, John, Donald, Colin, Duncan, Isabella, Anne, Flora, all as already mentioned.

*a*3. Alexander, a tenant at Ruorach, married Christina, daughter of Duncan, son of Donald Macrae of Torlysich, with issue—(1) Alexander, died unmarried. (2) Murdo resided in Glenelg, and married Catherine, daughter of Murdo Maclennan, with issue—Alexander married a Maclennan in Carolina, with issue; Murdo married in Carolina, with issue; Flora married Farquhar Maclennan, Cluny, with issue; Jessie married James Mackerchar; Catherine married Alexander Morrison, and emigrated to Carolina. (3) Donald lived in Immergraddan, Glenelg, and married a daughter of John Macrae, with issue. (4) John married Effie, daughter of Murdo Maclennan, Immergraddan, with issue; Alexander married a Macrae from Plockton, with issue, in Australia; John in Glenelg; Donald in Glenelg; Catherine in Glenelg.

*a*4. Christopher, a tenant in Letterfearn, married Flora Macdonald, with issue — (1) John, married Janet, daughter of Alexander Macrae, Letterfearn, with issue—Mary, Janet, Christina. (2) Donald died unmarried. (3) Murdo married Margaret, daughter of John Macrae, Sarraig, Letterfearn, with issue—John, in Oregon, U.S., married Isabella Murchison, with issue—Hugh, Christopher, Murdo, and others; Christopher, at Letterfearn, married Christina MacAulay, with issue—Murdo, Elizabeth, Margaret, Jane; Farquhar; James; Lily; Catherine, in Vancouver, B.C., married Charles Welsley Macaulay. (4) John married Anne, daughter of Donald Macrae, Drudaig, with numerous issue of sons and daughters in Australia.

*a*5. Duncan lived at Ruorach, Kintail. He married Mary, daughter of Malcolm Macrae, Letterfearn, with issue—Donald, John, Hugh, Helen, Flora, who all emigrated with their father to Upper Canada.

*a*6. Mary married John Macrae, Inverinate, with issue.

*a*7. Margaret married Donald Maccrimmon, Glenelg.

*a*8. Elizabeth married Donald Buie Macrae, Nonach, with issue—Duncan, who lived in Portchullin, and others.

Page 162, *line* 17 :—

*b*1. Donald married Mary, daughter of Christopher Macrae, Drudaig, with issue—(1) Christopher married Christina, daughter of Christopher Macrae, Leckachan, with issue—Christopher, Donald, Colin, Janet. (2) Duncan lived at Carndue, and married Anne, daughter of Malcolm Macrae, with issue—Donald, Malcolm, Alexander, Mary, John. (3) John died unmarried. (4) Alexander died unmarried. (5) Isabella married Christopher Macrae. (6) Janet. (7) Flora married a Macrae.

*b*2. Farquhar married Isabella, daughter of Alexander Macrae, Ardintoul, with issue—(1) Christopher married Marion, daughter of John Macrae, Glenshiel, with issue—James, Alexander, Farquhar, Catherine, and another daughter. (2) Archibald. (3) Donald lived at Letterfearn, and married Anne Maccrimmon, Glenelg, with issue—Farquhar, in Tain; Archibald; John married Betsie, daughter of John Macrae, Plockton, with issue— Isabella, Mary Anne; Alexander married Margaret, daughter of Alexander Macrae (Page 193, 4th line from top), with issue—Elizabeth married John Macrae, Glasgow, with issue—Alexander, Mary, Maggie, Farquhar. Duncan, Donald John, Anne; Donald married Christina, daughter of Farquhar Macrae, Letterfearn, with issue; Isabella married a Mr Martin, Glenelg. (4) James was drowned. (5) James emigrated to Upper Canada about 1842. (6) Duncan emigrated to Upper Canada about 1842. (7) Anne married Malcolm Macdonald, Letterfearn. (8) Isabella married Donald, son of Christopher Macrae, and emigrated to America. (9) Jane married Angus Macaulay, Letterfearn.

*b*3. Alexander, who was in the 78th Highlanders.

*b*4. Christopher, in 78th Highlanders, killed in India 29th November, 1803.

*b*5. Elizabeth married Farquhar, son of John Roy Macrae of the Dulig family, with issue as already mentioned.

*b*6. Christina married Roderick Mackenzie, Plockton, with issue.

*b*7. Mary married Donald Macrae of Nonach, with issue.

68. Isabella married Donald Macmillan, Dornie, with issue.

Page 165, line 4 from bottom :—

XI. ALEXANDER, called Alister Buidh, had by his second wife a fourth son—

ALEXANDER (*to come at foot of page* 166), married, with issue.

a. Christopher married Anne, daughter of Donald and Julia Macrae, Camusluinie, with issue—

a1. John married in Ontario, with issue; Anne married in 1905 Angus Mackintosh; Mary; James Donald.

a2. Donald Alexander, Roman Catholic priest, in Goderich, Ontario.

Christopher married, secondly, Anne (page 50, last line), daughter of Duncan Macrae, with issue—

a3. Duncan.

a4. John.

a5. Alexander.

a6. Kenneth, a priest in Canada.

a7. Christopher ; and one daughter.

b. Alexander married Flora Stewart, and went to America.

Page 166, line 6 :—

a1. Duncan, who went to New Zealand, has issue— Christina Bella, married Donald Macrae, son of Alexander Macrae, author of a book on " Deer Stalking," p. 204, with issue ; Isabella married a Mr Thompson with issue ; Farquhar; Mary; Catherine; Duncan; Annie Jane; Jessie.

Page 166, line 18 :—

Farquhar, eldest son of *a4*, Alexander and Zeller Macrae, a youth of great ability and promise, after a highly creditable career at Aberdeen Grammar School, died on the 23rd of September, 1907, aged 20 years.

Page 168, 8th line from top :—

IX. DONALD married a daughter of Charles Mackenzie of Letterewe, with issue.

X. MURDOCH married Julia Mackenzie, as already mentioned, with issue.

1. DONALD was the last of the family to live in Camusluinie, where the site of his house is still pointed out. He married Anne Mackenzie of Lentran, who survived him by several years. He died at an advanced age in 1790 leaving issue—

a. Murdoch, as already mentioned.

b. John, as already mentioned.

c. Colin, as mentioned.

d. Alexander, as mentioned.

e. Abigail married John Breac Macrae (page 216, 13th line from top), with issue, as mentioned.

f. Janet married John Macrae, called Ian Ard, with issue, at least two daughters—

*f*1. Isabella married Farquhar Macrae, Sallachy, with issue.

*f*2. Janet died unmarried.

g. Julia married Alexander, son of Donald Macrae, with issue—

*g*1. Alexander lived in Camusluinie. He married Janet, daughter of Alexander Macrae of the Duilig family, with issue—Alexander, for some time hotelkeeper at Reraig, Lochalsh, married Isabella, daughter of Duncan Finlayson, Plockton, with issue—Duncan ; John married and left issue—Duncan Hector, and Jessie; William, now living in Glasgow ; Jessie.

h. Flora or Florence.

i. John, a natural son, who lived at Patt, in the Heights of Lochalsh. He married Catherine, daughter of Donald Macrae, Glenshiel, with issue—

11. Murdo, called Murachadh Beg, lived for several years in Glenundalan, and afterwards in Bundaloch. He married Martha Mackenzie, with issue—(1) Duncan, who was an excellent folklorist and genealogist, and who died unmarried at Bundaloch in 1884. (2) Flora married Murdo Macrae, Lochcarron, with issue. (3) Catherine married Colin Macrae, Dornie, with issue, as mentioned elsewhere. (4) Anne married John Macrae, son of Duncan, with issue, among others—Alexander emigrated to Canada; Mary; Catherine; Duncan married with issue; Murdo, now living in Inverness, married Mary Anne, daughter of Farquhar Maclennan, with issue—Jessie, Catherine, Farquhar, a medical student of Aberdeen University, Mary, John, Murdo. (5) Janet married Roderick Macrae, Letterfearn. (6) Mary married James Nett of Melbourne, Australia, who afterwards resided in England.

12. Donald lived in Fernaig, Lochalsh. He married Catherine, daughter of Alexander Macaulay, with issue—Duncan, Donald, John, Christopher, Farquhar.

13 John; *14* Duncan; *15* Donald; *16* Anne; *17* Julia; *18* Catherine.

2. ALEXANDER married Catherine Maclean, niece of the Rev. John Maclean, first Presbyterian Minister of Kintail, with issue—

a. Murdo, a tenant in Camusluinie, and afterwards in Ellan-na-goine, Sallachy. He married Mary, daughter of Alexander Macrae, Camusluinie (page 50, 8th line from top), with issue.

a1. Alexander died unmarried.

a2. John married Catherine Matheson, Lochalsh, with issue—(1) Mary. (2) Julia married Samuel Cameron, Sallachy, with issue. (3) Helen.

a3. Alexander Og died unmarried.

a4. Catherine married Alexander Macrae, Bundaloch, without issue.

*a*5. Julia died unmarried.

*a*6. Janet married Alexander Mackay, Bundaloch, with issue.

*a*7. Mary married Alexander, son of John Mor Macrae of the Duilig family, with issue hereafter mentioned.

*a*8. Isabella married Alexander Maclennan, Sallachy, with issue in Australia.

*a*9. Catherine died unmarried.

3. ANABELLA or ANNE married Alexander Macrae (page 211, line 1), with issue, as there mentioned.

4. ANNE married Thomas Macrae at Carr, a descendant of Ferachar MacIan Og, with issue—

a. Murdoch, a soldier in the 78th Highlanders. After serving with his regiment in India, he returned to Kintail and married a daughter of Murdo, son of Duncan Macrae, Achnagart, with issue.

*a*1. Thomas, who lived at Camusluinie, and married Isabella Macrae (Page 131, last line), with issue—(1) Alexander, lived at Applecross. He married Isabella Mackenzie, with issue—Donald; Bella; Anne married John Leed Macleay, Wanganui, New Zealand, with issue; Farquhar; Murdo, M.B. and C.M. (1908) of Glasgow University; Christina, died 1908; Thomas in New Zealand. (2) Isabella in New Zealand. (3) Helen died unmarried. (4) Anabella died unmarried. (5) Mary married John Moir, Culigeran, Struy, Beauly, with issue—Mary Jane, who married Donald Martin of Tarbert, Harris, with issue.

*a*2. Duncan lived in Raasay. He married Anne Nicolson, with issue—(1) Archibald married Maggie Cameron, Morven, with issue—Kate. (2) Neil married Kate Macrae, Skye, with issue—Duncan, Murdo, Thomas, John. (3) Murdo unmarried. (4) Isabella married Donald Gillanders, Garve, with issue—Mary.

*a*3. Donald drowned in Loch Duich. He was married, without issue.

*a*4. Anne married Archibald Ninnie Finlayson with issue in New Zealand.

*a*5. Margaret married Duncan Matheson, with issue.

*a*6. Isabella died unmarried.

*a*7. Alexander died unmarried.

b. Donald lived at Carr. He married Anne Macrae with issue.

*b*1. Thomas lived at Carr. He married Maggie, daughter of John Macrae, and emigrated to Australia, with issue—(1) Donald, who lived at Port Campbell, Victoria, Australia ; and others.

*b*2. Christopher married, but died without issue.

*b*3. Isabella married Colin Macrae, Inchcro, with issue as given (page 80, 4th line from foot).

*b*4. Anabella married Roderick Macrae, son of Malcolm of the Duilig family, with issue as hereafter mentioned.

*b*5. Christina married Duncan Macrae, Bundaloch.

*b*6. Lilias died unmarried.

*b*7. Janet died unmarried.

*b*8. Mary died unmarried.

c. Lilias married Donald, son of George Macrae of the Duilig family, with issue as hereafter mentioned.

d. Anne married Duncan, son of Farquhar Macrae, Killilan, with, among others, the following issue—

*d*1. Finlay, a soldier in the 78th Highlanders, married with issue Catherine, who married Murdo Macrae, Torchullin, with issue mentioned on page 450 ; Duncan married with issue ; Mary ; and others.

*d*2. Murdo lived at Letterfearn. He married and left issue, one daughter.

5 ISABELLA.

6. MARGARET.

Page 179, *line* 18 :—

Flora Gillanders, wife of John Macrae, died at Strathpeffer, 12th December, 1900, buried at Kirkton, Lochalsh.

a. Rev. Alexander Macrae married, 7th August, 1901, Winifred Baliol, daughter of James Beeby Scott, of the Bank of England, by his wife Ada Sarah, daughter of James Beeby, Accountant General of the Navy, with issue —Duncan, born 17th October, 1902, died 15th February, 1903, and buried at Brompton Cemetery; Farquhar Baliol, born 2nd October, 1903.

b. Margaret married 15th December, 1904, as his second wife, without issue, Torquil Nicolson, who died 15th June, 1906.

Page 180 :—

e. Jeannie, who married Farquhar Matheson, Dornie, died 7th June, 1901, leaving issue—Margaret Mary, born 5th November, 1898, and Flora Gillanders, born 13th March, 1900.

f. Farquhar Macrae, M.B. and C.M., married 12th July, 1899, Margaret Mann, daughter of Hugh Ross, Bridgend of Alness, with issue—Hugh Ross, born 25th May, 1901; John Alexander, born 21st February, 1903; Flora Gillanders, born 10th November, 1908.

Page 182, *line* 15 :—

1. FINLAY, called Fionnla Ban, married Margaret Macrae, Camusluinie, with issue.

a. Christopher died unmarried.

b. John lived at Stromeferry, married Isabella, sister of Christopher Roy of Morvich (page 212, line 8), and went to Australia, issue—

b1. Donald married in Australia with issue, two daughters.

b2. Finlay married a daughter of John Macrae, schoolmaster, Sleat (p. 183), with issue in Australia.

b3. Farquhar married without issue in Australia.

b4. Duncan married a sister of Duncan Mor of Totaig, in Australia.

*b*5. Margaret married with issue in Australia.

c. Alexander married Kate, daughter of Christopher Macdonald, Lonellan, Kintail, with issue as given on page 233.

d. Duncan married Anabella Macrae (page 127, *b*5).

*d*1. John married Mary, daughter of Thomas Macrae, Camusluinie, with issue—(1) John married with issue, in Lochinver. (2) Duncan married Margaret Macleod, Raasay, with issue—John, Charles, Donald, Donald, Mary, Murdoch. (3) Margaret married William Gillies, Plockton. (4) Lilias married John Gillies, Plockton, and went to California, issue—William, Donald, Mary Anne, John, Annie, Margaret Mary. (5) Thomas in California.

*d*2. Anabella married Roderick Macaulay, Durinish, Lochalsh, with issue—(1) John married Mary (p. 127, l. 11), daughter of John Macrae, with issue—Roderick John. (2) Kate married Donald Maclennan, with issue. (3) Mary died young. (4) Duncan. (5) Roderick.

*d*3. Finlay married Anabella Macdonald, Applecross, with issue—(1) Jessie (2) Matilda. (3) Duncan, M.A. of Aberdeen (1896), married Agnes. daughter of the Rev. Walter Ross, Nethy Bridge, Inverness-shire. (4) Maggie. (5) Finlay.

*d*4. Duncan unmarried.

*d*5. Margaret died young.

e. Anabella married a Maclennan without issue.

f. Mary died unmarried.

Page 183, *line* 8 :—

Farquhar, living at Auchtertyre, married Flora Macaulay, Camuslongart, with issue—Duncan John.

Maggie married John Duff, with issue—John, Mary, Donald.

Page 183, *line* 11 :—

Anne married Kenneth Matheson with issue ; Maggie married Donald Macrae, Bundaloch (page 200, line 12), with issue—Donald ; Mary married Donald Reid in Glasgow ; Alexander, in Manitoba, married Isabel Macrae, with issue—Farquhar.

Page 183, *line* 19 :—

d. Alexander married with issue.

*d*1. Duncan died unmarried.

*d*2. Christopher died unmarried.

*d*3. Alexander married with issue—Mary married in England ; Catherine married in Glasgow ; John in Glasgow ; Alexander married with issue ; Donald in Glasgow ; Flora.

*d*4. Colin in Falkirk.

*d*5. Christina died unmarried.

*d*6. Catherine married Christopher Macrae, Ardelve, with issue—Annie, Duncan, Maggie, Christina, Mary, Farquhar.

*d*7. Christina married in Islay.

Page 191, *line* 2 :—

2. CHRISTINA married Donald Macrae, a farmer at Inverinate, with issue—

a Duncan, called Donnacha Sealgair, married Margaret Macrae, with issue.

*a*1. John Roy married with issue—(1) Alexander died in Armadale, Australia, and left issue. (2) Roderick died in Armadale, Australia, and left issue. (3) Duncan in Australia.

*a*2. Donald died young.

*a*3. Donald died in Edinburgh.

*a*4. Duncan died young.

*a*5 Ninnie died in America.

*a*6. Margaret died in Australia. She married Farquhar Macrae, with issue—(1) Christopher married Elizabeth Maclennan, with issue.

*a*7. Catherine married Ivy Macovil, with issue.

*a*8. Flora married Alexander Macrae, Inverinate (page 193, line 4).

*a*9. Alexander married Flora, daughter of Farquhar (page 148, line 2 from foot).

b. Farquhar, known as Ferachar Buie, married Isabella Maclennan, with issue.

*b*1. Donald went to Australia.

*b*2. Alexander died at Letterfearn.   He married, with issue—(1) Alexander.   (2) Kenneth, a detective in Perth. (3) Kate married Kenneth Macrae; and two other daughters.

*b*3. Roderick lived at Inverinate.   He married Anabella Matheson, Dornie (a daughter of John Matheson and of Isabella Macrae, mentioned on page 48, line 6 from foot), with issue—(1) Christina married in America with issue. (2) Kate married Peter Campbell, headmaster, Abriachan Public School, Inverness-shire, with issue. (3) John died young.

c. Donald Roy Macrae lived at Carndu, Dornie. He married Annie Macmillan, Dornie, with issue.

*c*1. John lived at Ardintoul, and afterwards in Broadford   He married Flora Macrae, with issue—(1) Donald Macrae, Applecross. (2) Alexander married in Glasgow, with issue. (3) John in Broadford. (4) Christina married a Mr MacColl, Glasgow, with issue—John, Mary, Flora, Joan, Christina. (5) Flora married in Broadford.

*c*2. Donald lived at Inverinate.   He married Mary Macdonald, Carr, with issue—(1) Farquhar married with issue. (2) Donald went to Australia.   He married, and left numerous issue. (3) Kate married Donald Macrae, gamekeeper, Killilan, with issue—Catherine married John Fraser; John, in London, married Alice Adams, with issue—Donald William, Catherine Ellen, Ian Alexander; Mary Anne married a Mr Buxton with issue; Christina married Duncan Macmillan, Dornie; Flora married Joseph

Tritton with issue; Bella died; Donald, a gamekeeper at Inverinate, married Christina, daughter of Alexander Cameron, Sallachy, with issue—Mary, Catherine Bella, Alexander, Joan. (4) Duncan, a farmer and shoemaker at Dornie, married Isabella, daughter of Roderick Mackenzie, shipowner, Shieldaig, with issue—Donald at Dornie; Roderick a farmer and merchant in Shieldaig; James died when a student at the Raining School, Inverness; Mary. (5) Mary married Roderick Matheson, Lochcarron, with issue. (6) Kenneth married Kate Macrae, mentioned above, with issue, Donald and Alexander and seven daughters. (7) Alexander married Margaret Matheson, Avernish, with issue—Donald, John, Hector, Duncan, Mary, Mary Anne, Christina, Bella. (8) Donald married Effie Mackintosh, Portree, with issue.

*c*3. Alexander died in Australia. He married Ellen Macrae, with issue.

*c*4. Duncan lived for some time at Ardintoul, and afterwards emigrated to Australia, where he died.

*c*5. Donald died in Australia.

*c*6. Kenneth died in Australia.

*c*7. Christopher died in Australia; was married, and left issue.

*c*8. Christina married Kenneth Macrae, Achmore.

d. Alexander, Quartermaster and Sergeant in the 78th Highlanders (page 191, line 8).

Page 200, *line* 11 :—

Donald, son of Christopher, married Maggie, daughter of Farquhar Macrae (*a*3, page 183), with issue—Donald.

Page 212 :—

Delete the whole of lines 3 and 4.

In line 5, *a*. John, being a son of XII. ALEXANDER (mentioned on page 211, line 1), should be entered as (3). JOHN, and his family enumerated (*a*), (*b*), &c., as follows :—

(*a*). Christopher married Christina Macrae, with issue.

(*a*1). Hannah married Finlay Macdonald, Inverinate, with issue.

(*a*2). John married Mary Macrae, with issue, and went to Australia.

(*a*3). Annie married Kenneth Macdonald, Glenelg, with issue—Duncan, in Australia.

(*a*4). Kate died unmarried.

(*a*5). Alexander died unmarried.

(*a*6). Christopher died unmarried.

(*b*). Alexander as on page 212.

(*c*). Annie married Alexander Macrae, Glenshiel, with issue.

(*d*). Kate married John Macrae, Glenshiel, with issue.

(*e*). Helen married Donald Macmillan, with issue—Christopher, Christina, Isabella, John, Helen, Kate, Isabella, Flora married Kenneth Macrae, page 129.

(*f*). Isabella married John Macrae, son of Christopher (page 212, line 8), with issue.

(*g*). Janet married William Morrison, schoolmaster, Letterfearn, with issue.

(*h*). Hannah married Donald Macrae, Cro of Kintail, with issue.

Page 214, line 4 from foot :—

*a*1. Duncan married Christina, daughter of Alexander Macrae, Auchtertyre, with issue.

(1). John (not Duncan, as on page 214) married Isabella, daughter of Murdo, son of Duncan Macrae, Achnagart, with issue—

(*a*). Donald died unmarried.

(*b*). Duncan married Anne, daughter of Roderick Finlayson, with issue ; Alexander married a Miss Bain, and emigrated to Oregon, U.S , where he died in 1879, leaving numerous issue.

(*c*). Murdo married a Miss Mackenzie of Newcastle, without issue.

(*d*). Alexander married a Miss Bain, and emigrated with his family to America.

(*e*). Farquhar, who was for many years proprietor of the Strome Hotel, married Proby Mary, daughter of Kenneth Mackenzie, Kishorn, with issue—

(1). Malcolm, living in Salen, Mull, married Flora Murchison, Lochcarron, with issue—Farquhar, Proby Mary.

(2). John married in Melbourne, Australia, with issue —Farquhar Colin, John.

(3). Isabella married William Mackenzie, with issue— William; Hector; Isabella married George Mackinlay, Edinburgh, with issue; Jessie married John Macdonald with issue; Proby Mary died.

(4). Annie married Murdo Leed, shipowner, Inverness, with issue—Murdo; Proby Mary married Ronald Fletcher, Laggan, Mull; Catherine married John Macnair, New York; Elizabeth.

(5). Elizabeth married John Kennedy, Lochcarron, with issue—Farquhar; Donald; Anne; Proby Mary married Rev. John Macdonald, Free Church, Sleat, Skye; Bella Anne.

(6). Hannah married Donald Macrae of the Balnain family, with issue as mentioned elsewhere.

(7). Isabella married Bailie John Mackenzie, Inverness, with issue—Alistair; Farquhar; Annie Maria.

(*f*). Hannah married Donald Macrae, with issue— Isabella married Donald Matheson with issue—Christopher; Bella; Hannah married Herr Hoeckling.

(*g*). Christopher died unmarried.

(*h*). Alexander died unmarried.

(*i*). Isabella died young.

(2). Farquhar, called Ferachar Post, married Eliza, daughter of Alexander Macrae, tenant of Ruarach, Kintail, with issue—Duncan; Farquhar married with issue; Donald married Elizabeth Sutherland with issue; Alexander.

(3). Marion married Farquhar Macrae, Carr, with issue—Christina died unmarried; Mary, unmarried; William died unmarried; John married Grace Mackay, Ardnarff, without issue; Alexander married a daughter of Duncan Macrae, Fernaig, with issue, a son, Ewen, in Glengarry, and a daughter.

Page 285, *line* 10 *from bottom :—*

6. FARQUHAR, born 1806, &c., had issue—

a. Jean Farquhar. *b.* Margaret Morison. *c.* William Gordon. *d.* John Morison. *e.* Mary Amelia Morison, born 1844, married George Cadell of the Indian Forest Department, with issue—George Ward Cole, born 1872; Agnes Morison, born 1873; William Farquhar, born 1874, Florence St John, born 1877; Muriel McCrae, born 1887.

f. Farquhar.

CLANN IAN CHARRICH.

(pp. 22, 23, 214, 288.)

———— · ⚫ · ————

I. JOHN, called Ian Carrach, the progenitor of the Clann Ian Charrich family of Macraes, was the eldest son of Macrae of Clunes, and was the first Macrae to migrate to Kintail, as narrated on page 288 of this book. His descendants, whose names cannot at present be traced, lived in the old home at Achnagart for some generations, and one of them is said to have been married to one of the Grants of Glenmoriston. By her he had numerous issue, all of whom died young, except one named John. This John who was also called Ian Carrach married, and had issue, at least two sons, Finlay and Malcolm.

1. FINLAY of whom hereafter.

2. MALCOLM was constable of Ellandonan Castle in the early years of the 16th century. He espoused the cause of Hector Roy of Gairloch in the great feud between Hector and his nephew, John of Killin. After a struggle which lasted several years, and in which Malcolm took a very prominent part, the supporters of Hector Roy had to yield, and Malcolm Mac Ian Charrich was dismissed by John of Killin from the Constableship. He thus lost his influence, and his family did not afterwards assume so much importance in Kintail (pages 21-23). One of his descendants, Malcolm, called Callum Mac Urichcian (probably Malcolm, son of Murdo, son of John), was living at Letterfearn, Kintail, in the early part of the 19th century, and was married to Anne Macdonald with issue.

1. CHRISTINA married Alexander Macrae, Ardelve, with issue.

ALEXANDER MACRAE, M.A. (Clann Ian Charrich.)

2. MARTHA married John MacColl, farmer, Glen-finnan, in Inverness-shire, with issue.

a. Alexander, born 1825, died at Bolton, in Lanca-shire, in 1892. He married Anne Baxter, with issue—Ralph, Margaret, John, Annie, Alexander.

b. John, born 1827, M.A., Oxford, died in Australia in 1893, was twice married, with issue.

c. Christina died unmarried in Australia.

d. The Rev. Malcolm, D.D., born 1834, Canon of Ripon Cathedral, an intimate friend of the Right Hon. William Ewart Gladstone, and a well known theological and controversial writer. He married Consuelo Albinia, daughter of Major-General Crompton Stansfield of Esholt Hall, Yorkshire, without issue, and died in 1907.

e. Janet, born 1835, unmarried.

f. Hugh, born 1837, B.A. of London. Author of several mathematical and philosophical works. Married first, in 1865, Mary Elizabeth Johnson, and by her, who died in 1884, has issue—Mary Janet ; Martha Christina ; Flora ; Hugh Ernest, a judge in Burma, married with issue ; Anne Louise, married with issue. Hugh married, secondly, in 1887, Lina Hortense Marchal, and is now (1909) living at Boulogne, in France.

3. CATHERINE died unmarried.

4. ANNE died unmarried.

5. DONALD went to Australia in 1854. Married Barbara Forbes with issue.

6. DUNCAN went to Australia in 1854. Married Catherine, daughter of Farquhar Macrae, with issue.

7. HUGH died unmarried in India.

II. FINLAY Mac Ian Charrich was a farmer in Ardintoul, Kintail. Tradition says that he lost his life in defence of his home against a band of spoilers from Sleat in Skye. He left issue, at least one son, Donald.

III. DONALD, known as Domhnull Duilig (Donald of Duilig), was but a child at the time of his father's death, but when he grew up to be a man, he gathered together a strong party of Kintail warriors, and making his way to Sleat, he put to the sword the only survivor of his father's murderers. He then returned to his home in Ardintoul, but fearing sudden attacks from parties of revenge from Skye, he moved inland to Duilig in the heights of Kintail. Here he lived in plentiful circum- stances for many years, and was looked upon as a man of outstanding merit, not only among members of his own family, but among the Clan as a whole. Round his memory have gathered many interesting stories, legends, traditions, and songs, most of which have, unfortunately, been lost, but a few of them may still be heard among the older people in Kintail. Donald was married, and had at least three sons—Finlay, of whom hereafter, Donald, John.

IV. DONALD, of whom little is known, lived for some time in Duilig. He married, and had issue, at least one son :—

V. DONALD, who was fifth in descent from Ian Carrach, and was known as Domhnull Og (Young Donald). He took a prominent part in the great feud between Mac- kenzie of Kintail and Macdonald of Glengarry in the end of the 16th and the beginning of the 17th century. In the spring of the year 1606 Mackenzie, after he had seized the lands of Lochcarron, laid siege to Strome Castle, which was at that time held by the Macdonalds. In the opera- tions round the Castle Donald Og was taken prisoner. An account of his escape is given thus in an old manu- script :—" Mackenzie, having no hope of taking the Castle by storm, resolved to raise the siege. Then Donald Og, hearing confidentially from one of the servants within the Castle how things were moving on both sides, and that Mackenzie was preparing to raise the siege, bribed one of the attendants to give him admittance into the room in the Castle where the gunpowder was kept. Finding that only one barrel remained, he got it destroyed by pouring water over it.   He afterwards returned to his own room in the Castle, and maintained that he felt unwell and would be the better of fresh air.   He was then escorted under two sentinels to the battlements of the Castle. Here he walked backwards and forwards till a suitable opportunity for action presented itself.   At last he threw his plaid over the heads of the two sentinels, and then with one spring leaped off the battlements to the ground below.   Mackenzie's party rushed forward expecting to find him dead.   He was, however, only stunned by the fall, and soon recovered.   He made known to Mackenzie the state of the besieged, and persuaded him to renew the attack, with the result that the Castle was surrendered a few days afterwards in 1606.   Mackenzie ordered it to be blown up in case it might fall again into Glengarry's hands."   In recognition of his faithful services and his brave action on this occasion Mackenzie allotted to Donald Og free lands for life in Killilan.   He married and had at least two sons :—

1. JOHN of whom hereafter.

2. DUNCAN was a tenant at Ratagan.   He married, and had issue, at least one son, Donald, who had a son Ronald, who married Julia Macrae (a niece of Murdo XIII., page 212), with the following issue—

a. Alexander emigrated to Australia in 1849.   He married Catherine Macdonald, Drudaig, with issue—

a1. Ronald married in New South Wales, with numerous issue.

a2. Julia married twice in Victoria with issue

b. Duncan emigrated to America.   He married with issue.

c. Christopher married a Mackenzie from Letterfearn, and emigrated to America.

d. Murdo emigrated to America.

e. John in America.

f. Another son also in America.

VI. JOHN, son of Donald Og, and sixth in descent from Ian Carrach, was called Ian Ban, and succeeded to his father's farm in Killilan. He married Margaret, daughter of John Murchison, Auchtertyre, and sister of Colonel Donald Murchison, who acted so zealously on Seaforth's behalf after the Rebellion of 1715. He left a son—

VII. DONALD, who married Flora, daughter of Farquhar Macrae, Inchchro, with issue—

1. DUNCAN Roy, a tenant at Ardelve, married Catherine, daughter of John Ban Macrae, Aird, Lochalsh. He died about the year 1840, leaving issue—

a. Christopher married Mary, daughter of Murdo Maclennan, Aird, Lochalsh. He was tenant of the farm of Mangaridh, Skye. He left issue—

*a*1. Duncan married with issue, two daughters in British Columbia.

*a*2. Flora married Donald Macrae, Skye, with issue— Christopher, who is married with issue, one son; Margaret; Mary, married with issue; Catherine.

*a*3. Catherine married Alexander Finlayson, Kyleakin, Skye, with issue—Donald; Christopher; Alexander; Finlay; Marion, who married John Gillies, Plockton, with issue; Maggie.

*a*4. Flora married John Murchison, Skye, with issue— Mary; Christopher, married a Miss Mackenzie, Kyle; Margaret married Donald Macrae, Carr, Kintail (page 185, line 4), with issue—Anabella Mary, Johan Flora.

b. Donald Roy was for some time blacksmith at Dornie. He married Margaret, daughter of Colin Macrae, tacksman, of Inchchro (page 80, line 4 from foot), and emigrated to America in 1848. He left issue—

*b*1. Colin married in Canada.

*b*2. John in Ontario.

*b*3. Alexander married Isabella Campbell, with issue, and lives now in Assiniboia, Canada.

*b*4. Janet in Ontario.

*b*5. Mary in Ontario.

*b*6. Catherine married in Assiniboine, Canada.

c. Duncan was a tenant in Ardelve in 1862. He married Isabella, daughter of Donald Macrae, Nostie, Lochalsh, with issue—

*c*1. Donald married Mary Macdonald in Arisaig with issue—Alexander, Margaret.

*c*2. Duncan in Glasgow, married Catherine Macrae, with issue—Duncan, Donald, Alexander-Angus.

*c*3. Alexander lives at Lochluichart. He married Catherine Murchison, Portchullin, iwth issue—Duncan, Lauchlin, Malcolm, John, Donald, Alexander, Mary Kate, Roderick, Isabella, David.

*c*4. John lives in Glasgow. He married Anne Mackenzie with issue—Isabella, Kenneth, John Duncan, Christina.

*c*5. Catherine married Donald Mackenzie, Ardelve, with issue—Duncan, Christopher, Donald, Jessie.

*c*6. Janet now living at Auchtertyre.

*c*7. Annie married Donald Macpherson, Sleat, Skye.

*c*8. Maggie married Donald Macintyre, Wishaw, with issue—Thomas, Donald, Catherine.

d. Colin died in Ardelve.

e. Flora married a Mr Sinclair, and emigrated to Australia.

f. Mary married Duncan Macrae, Ardelve (page 183, line 1), with issue as already mentioned.

g. Janet married Duncan Macqueen, Ratagan, with issue—(1) Father Macqueen, Inverness. (2) John Macqueen, Ardelve, married with issue. (3) Donald in America. (4) Archibald in America.

2. JOHN, son of Donald VII., was called John Roy, and lived for some time in Inverness. He married and had issue, at least one son, whose descendants lived a few years ago in Inverness; and one daughter, Isabella, who died at Dornie in Kintail.

3. ANNE married George, son of Donald, son of Alexander of the Duilig family, with issue, as mentioned hereafter.

4. CATHERINE married Malcolm Macrae, tenant at Cragaig, with issue. (a) Donald died unmarried at Bundaloch. (b) Farquhar married a daughter of Duncan Macrae, Bundaloch. He had issue, and emigrated to America. (c) Mary married a Mackerlich, with issue.

IV. JOHN, youngest son of Domhnull Duilig, and fourth in descent from Ian Carrach, left two sons—

1. KENNETH, who was a tenant in Ardelve. When an old man he joined Earl William of Seaforth's army, and was present at the Battle of Sheriffmuir in 1715. On his return home he composed a celebrated elegy on the "Four Johns of Scotland" who fought and fell in the battle. He left one son, Alexander, who lived for some time at Cragaig, and afterwards at Ardelve, and was said to have attained to the age of 120 years. A sketch of his life appeared in the *London Courier* of the 28th November, 1807 (page 407). None of his descendants can be traced now in Kintail or Lochalsh, and it is probable that no male issue survived him.

2. JOHN (probably the Ian MacIan mentioned on pp. 214, 408), married and left issue, at least one son—

a. Malcolm, who was noted for his loyal adherence to Seaforth after his estates were forfeited in 1715. Malcolm took an active part in resisting the attempts of the Forfeited Estates Commissioners to collect the rents on the Seaforth estates. He was present at the skirmish at Coille Bhan (page 359), and fired the shot which severely wounded Captain Macneill, who was in charge of the detachment. When Seaforth obtained a pardon from the King, and returned to his Estates in 1726, Malcolm was offered the farm of Reraig in Lochalsh. He, however, refused this offer, and chose, in preference, part of the farm of Drudaig in Kintail. Here he died in the year 1731, leaving two sons—

*a*1. John, who was tacksman of Ardelve, and who married a daughter of Duncan Macrae of Drudaig, with issue—(1) Kenneth, who was for a long time tacksman of Ardelve and afterwards innkeeper at Jeanton, Lochcarron. He died at the age of 57, on the 19th July, 1819, and was buried in Kintail. He married Jane Mackenzie with issue; Hector emigrated to Upper Canada; John emigrated to Upper Canada; Alexander died in the West Indies; Christina; Helen; Isabella. (2) Isabella, who married John Ban Macrae, Camusluinie, with issue—(*a*) John married Margaret Macrae, Camusluinie, with issue— John married Isabella Macrae of the Inchchro family, and died at Camusluinie in 1904, without issue; Kenneth died unmarried in Camusluinie in 1905; Catherine married Kenneth Maclennan, Letterfearn, with issue. (*b*) Christopher married Helen Macrae, Camusluinie, and removed with his family to Barra, where one of them, John, is now living with issue. (*c*) Janet married John Mackerlich, Ardnarff. (3) Mary married Farquhar Macrae, Camusluinie, with issue as already mentioned (page 128, line 14 from foot).

*a*2. Alexander lived in Glenshiel. He married a granddaughter of Eonachan Dubh (page 210, line 14), and is said to have had issue at least three sons, two of whom are said to have emigrated from Letterfearn to Australia. The other son (1) John married Catherine Maclennan with issue. (*a*) Margaret married John, son of John Macrae, Camusluinie, with issue, John married Isabella Macrae without issue; Kenneth died unmarried; Catherine married Kenneth Maclennan, Letterfearn, with issue as mentioned elsewhere. (*b*) Alexander lived in Camusluinie, and married Catherine, daughter of Alexander Macrae of Cnoc-na-carn, Camusluinie, with issue, David, born 18th April, 1846, and now living at Camusluinie; Alexander, died in New Zealand; Catherine, married Duncan Macrae, with issue, Christopher, in New Zealand, married Rebecca Carr, with issue—(Duncan, Catherine Margaret,

Christina Grace), Kate, Alexander, in New Zealand, John
in New Zealand, Donald, Alexander, David; Bella now in
Camusluinie. *(c)* Donald lived in Camusluinie and
Killilan, and married Catherine Macrae, Inverinate, with
issue—Kate, married John Fraser, without issue; John,
now living in London, married Alice Adams, with issue—
Donald, Kate, John; Mary Anne, married a Mr Buxton,
with issue—Donald, John; Christina, married Duncan
Macmillan, Dornie; Flora, married Joseph Tritton, with
issue—Donald, Christina, Edward; Bella died. *(d)*
Christina, married Allan Cameron, Sallachy, with issue.

IV. FINLAY, eldest son of Domhull Duilig, and
fourth in descent from Ian Carrach, succeeded his father
as tacksman of Duilig in the year 1580 He left at least
three sons—1. Alexander of whom hereafter, Donald,
Roderick.

V. DONALD, second son of Finlay IV., lived at Duilig.
He married and left issue two sons—John, Finlay.

VI JOHN, called John Roy, eldest son of Donald V.,
was "remarkably handsome in his personal appearance."
He lived at Conchra, and married Isabella, daughter of
John Macrae, one of the famous "Four Johns of Scotland"
(page 153), who fell in the Battle of Sheriffmuir. He left
issue three sons and two daughters, viz—

1 FINLAY, was tenant of Duart, Lochalsh, in 1772.
He married Mary, daughter of Donald Macmillan, Coilree,
Kintail, with issue—

(a) John, drowned at Point of Sleat, in 1817. *(b)*
Donald, married Anabella, daughter of Ewen Mackenzie,
Strome. He was drowned in 1847. He left issue—

*b*1. John, who was a shipowner, married Isabella,
daughter of John Macrae, Dornie, on the 23rd of March,
1848, with issue—Donald, John Farquhar, Isabella
married Kenneth Finlayson, Plockton, with issue, Eliza,
Anne, Anabella married Gillian Currie, with issue, Betsie
married John Macrae, Letterfearn, with issue. *b*2. Alexander. *b*3. Ewen went to California. *b*4. Isabella

married John Mackenzie, son of Alexander Mackenzie, Ardelve, and emigrated to America in 1848. *b*5. Jane married Farquhar Matheson, Achnadarroch, Lochalsh.

c. Colin was a sailor. He married Florence, daughter of John Matheson, Plockton, with issue and emigrated to Cape Breton in 1827.

2. DONALD, died without issue.

3. FARQUHAR, the third son of John Roy, was for some time tenant at Western Achadhantighard, Letterfearn, but removed to Dornie in 1794, where he died in 1825 aged 75 years. He married in 1772, Elizabeth, eldest daughter of Duncan Macrae, son of Donald of Drudaig, (page 162, line 14), and had issue—

a. John, born 1776, was "a very ingenious man and a handy craft." He married in 1809 Elizabeth, daughter of Alexander Matheson, schoolmaster, Dornie, (page 48, 11th line from foot). He died at Dornie on the 15th of February, 1858, aged 82 years. He left issue—*a*1. John, who was born in 1812. *a*2. Farquhar, died in 1836. *a*3. Alexander, born 14th March, 1829. *a*4. Anne, married Christopher Macrae, Bundaloch, in 1839, and emigrated to Australia in 1852. *a*5. Isabella, married John Macrae, Plockton, with issue as already mentioned. *a*6. Mary, married in April, 1849, Duguld Matheson, Avernish, Lochalsh, and emigrated to America in the following June.

(b) Donald, born 1784, married in 1818, Mary, daughter of Captain Duncan Macrae of Inverinate, with issue—*b*1. Duncan, born on 22nd January, 1819 ; died unmarried. *b*2. Kenneth, died unmarried. *b*3. John Roy, was for several years tacksman of the farm of Bundaloch. He died unmarried at Dornie. *b*4. Farquhar died unmarried. *b*5. Mary, married Finlay Macrae, Carr, with issue as already mentioned, (page 185, line 12). *b*6. Magdalen, now (1909), living at Dornie. *b*7. Florence, married Alexander Macnair, Accountant in the City Chambers, Edinburgh. She died in 1905, leaving issue— Annie, Donald, Mary, Flora.

(c) Duncan died unmarried. *(d)* Anabella, married in 1787, Donald, son of Donald Macrae, tacksman of Achadhantighard, who was Innkeeper at Totaig, but in 1796 removed to Dornie where he died leaving issue—*(d1.)* Alexander, died unmarried at Dornie. *(d2.)* John, died in New Orleans, leaving issue, *one* daughter, Sarah Anabella Eliza. *(d3.)* Donald, died unmarried. *(d4.)* Colin, married Catherine, daughter of Murdo Macrae, and emigrated to America, where he left issue—Alexander, Donald, John, Colin, Isabella, Christina. *(d5.)* Duncan, died in Carolina, America. *(d6.)* Annie, married John Roy Macrae, son of Finlay, son of Duncan Macrae, Camusluinie, and has issue of thirteen sons and daughters in Ontario. *(d7.)* Isabella, married in 1818, John Matheson, Dornie, (page 48, 6th line from foot), with issue—(1) John, died at Dornie ; (2) Flora, married Farquhar Maclennan, and is now (1909), living at Dornie; (3) Annie, married James Turnbull, with issue in America; (4) Marion, married James Murchison, Oregon, with issue; (5) Mary, died at Dornie ; (6) Roderick, now (1909), living at Dornie ; (7) Anabella, married Roderick Macrae, Inverinate, with issue—John ; Christina, married D. Macmillan, Oregon, with issue ; Catherine, married Peter Campbell, headmaster of the Abriachan Public School, Inverness-shire, with issue ; (8) Donald, died at Dornie ; (9) Alexander, shipowner at Dornie.   He was an excellent folklorist and genealogist, and wrote manuscript notes on the Clan Macrae, the Clan Matheson, and the Clan Mackenzie.   He died on the 14th of October, 1897 ; (10) Betsie, now (1909), living at Dornie.

(e) Isabella, married Donald Mackerlich, and emigrated to Cape Breton, where she left issue.

(f) Florence, married Finlay Macrae, shoemaker, Dornie, with issue of three sons and four daughters, who emigrated to Canada in 1845.

(g) Isabella, married Duncan Macrae, Bruaich, Dornie, She emigrated with her husband to Cape Breton in 1822.

4. ANNIE, daughter of John Roy, married Alexander Stewart, miller, Nostie, Lochalsh, with issue.

5. MARY.

VI. Finlay, younger son of Donald V., married and left a son.

VII. DONALD, who lived at Cnoc-na-carn, Camusluinie, in 1700. He married Catherine, daughter of Murdoch Murchison, Caiplach, Lochalsh, and had issue, two sons, each named Alexander.

VIII. ALEXANDER, born 1728; lived at Cnoc na-carn. He married Anne, daughter of Alexander Macrae, Camusluinie, with issue—

a. Finlay, who served in the 78th Highlanders, and was killed in India in 1794.

b. Alexander, married Isabella, daughter of Murdo Roy Macrae of Corriedhoin, with issue—

b1. Mary, married Malcolm Macrae, Ardelve, with issue—(1) Murdo in Stornoway; (2) Maggie, married Roderick Morrison, Harris, with issue; (3) Alexander, Preventive Officer, Inland Revenue, Lochcarron, married with issue—Mary Catherine; (4) Roderick, died unmarried; (5) John, in Glasgow, married with issue—Malcolm Alexander, (6) Barbara married a Mr Morrison, Lewis, with issue; (7) Bella, unmarried.

b2 Catherine married Alexander Macrae, Camusluinie, a descendant of Ian Carrach, with issue, as already mentioned.

b3. Isabella, married Farquhar Maclennan, Camusluinie, with issue—(1) Isabella, married Duncan Macrae, New Zealand, with issue, as already mentioned, (page 166, line 6). (2) Mary, in New Zealand; (3) Catherine, died in Camusluinie; (4) Alexander, in New Zealand, married Jane Leishman, with issue—Bella, Farquhar, Sarah, Robert. (5) Annie, married Alexander Maclennan, Camusluinie, with issue—Ewen, Mourdina, Farquhar Alexander, Flora Jane, Bella Kate, Duncan. (6) Murdo, died in Camusluinie; (7) Jane, married Alexander

Maclennan, Plockton, with issue—Murdo, Maggie; (8) John, in New Zealand; (9) Ewen, in New Zealand, married with issue.

c. Donald, married Catherine, daughter of John Macrae, Camusluinie, with issue—

c1. Alexander, died unmarried.

c2. John, married, Maggie Macinnes, Drumbuie, Lochalsh, with issue—Donald, John, Kate, Donald, Alexander, Duncan, Bella.

c3. Duncan, in Glenelg. He married a Miss Morrison, with issue—one son, Malcolm.

c4. Catherine, married Malcolm Morrison, Glenelg, with issue.

c5. Isabella, married Duncan Macrae, son of Duncan Roy, Ardelve, with issue, as already mentioned.

d. Margaret, married Duncan Macdonald, Camusluinie, with issue.

e. Catherine, married Alexander Macrae, Ardnarff, Lochalsh, with issue—(1) Alexander, went to Mull, where he married with issue—John, a farmer in Kerrera, and two daughters, one of whom is named Rebecca ; (2) Rebecca, married George Maculloch, Dornie, with issue ; (3) Anne died unmarried.

f. Catherine, married John Mackay, Camusluinie, with issue—Maggie, Kate, Anne, Donald in Stirling.

g. Janet, married Alexander Macrae, Camusluinie, with issue, three daughters, and a son Alexander, married Isa-bella Finlayson, with issue—William, in Glasgow ; John lived for several years in China and died in Glasgow leaving issue—John Hector, Jessie ; Duncan ; Jessie.

h. Janet, married Duncan Macmillan, Dornie, with issue—Alexander, who was one of the best genealogists in Kintail, (see preface, page v.); Farquhar, died in Greenock; Annie ; Christina ; Annie.

i. Christina, married Farquhar Macrae, Letterfearn, with issue—

i1. Farquhar, married Catherine Macrae, with issue—

Farquhar, Parochial Inspector, Broadford, who married a Miss Macleod, with issue; Christopher married Helen Paterson, with issue; Catherine; Christina, married Donald Macrae, with issue; Duncan.

i2. Donald, married a Macrae from Inverinate, with issue, Farquhar, married Mary Macdonald, with issue—Kate; Donald, married with issue, in Glasgow.

i3. Finlay married Mary Macdonald, Letterfearn, with issue—Murdo, who married Anne Murchison, with issue; Christina, married William Renwick, with issue, one son Finlay; Catherine, married a Mr Ferguson, with issue; Mary; Maggie, married a Mr Currie, with issue; Farquhar, married Christina Macrae, in Glasgow, with issue.

i4. Alexander married Catherine Macrae, with issue—Duncan, married in New Zealand, with issue; Christina, married Robert Macrae, with issue; Alexander, married Jane Matheson, with issue; Farquhar; Maggie; Patrick.

j. Mary, married a Macrae from Bundaloch, with issue.

VIII. ALEXANDER, second son of Donald VII., married and left issue, two sons. One of them was a tailor, and is said to have gone to America. The other, Alexander, married Catherine Macrae, daughter of Donald Macrae of Nonach (page 455, 7th line from foot), and went, about the year 1850, to Lochalsh, Ontario, Canada. He had issue—

1. Duncan Roy, married Margaret Macdonald, with numerous issue, in Ontario.

2. Donald Buidh, married in Lochalsh, Ontario, and left numerous issue.

3. Donald Roy, married Catherine Matheson, with issue—

a. Donald, a merchant in Erbusaig, Lochalsh, Ross-shire, where he died in October, 1909. He married Anne Gillies, with issue—

a1. Catherine Mary; *a2.* Dolina; *a3.* John Duncan; *a4.* William John, now a student at the Dingwall Academy.

b. Rev. Kenneth, Free Church minister of Glenshiel.

c. John died unmarried.

d. Duncan died unmarried.

e. Catherine.

f. Flora, married John Finlayson, with issue.

4. Christina, married, with issue, in Ontario.

5. Janet, in Ontario.

6. Mary, married, with issue, in Ontario.

7. Isabella, married a Mr Finlayson, in Ontario, with issue.

V. RODERICK, third son of Finlay, son of Domhull Duilig, "was a brave, handsome man, and exceedingly tall in stature." As a young man he joined the forces of Seaforth, and was present at the Battle of Auldearn in 1645   He afterwards became in a romantic manner the confidential friend and adviser of Mackenzie of Fairburn, a near relative of whom he married. When a very old man he was drowned while fording the river Elchaig in Kintail.   He left numerous issue, of whom only a few can now be traced.   One of his sons lived in Easter Ross, from whom was descended the Rev. William Macrae, chaplain of the 78th Highlanders, and afterwards minister of Barvas in Island of Lewis, where he died in 1855, leaving issue Dr Charles Macrae, Stornoway, who married a daughter of John Mackenzie, Strome, with issue. Another descendant of Roderick was the late Rev. John Macrae, Stornoway, Lewis. One of Roderick's sons was—

VI. JOHN, who lived in Kintail, and married with issue —two sons, Malcolm, Roderick.

VII. MALCOLM, eldest son of John, married and left issue, at least one son.

VIII. ALEXANDER, who lived in Bundaloch, and was an old man in 1772.   He married and left issue—

1. DUNCAN, who emigrated to America with issue.

2. JOHN, died of fever while crossing to America.

3. MALCOLM, called Callum Ruadh, married with issue.

a. Annie married Roderick Finlayson, with issue.

ai. Alexander married Catherine, daughter of Donald

Macrae, Portchullin, Lochalsh, with issue—Catherine married Duncan Macrae, Bundaloch, with issue, (page 130, 11th line from first); Anne; Mary; Bella; John.

*a*2. Donald, married in Lossiemouth, with numerous issue.

b. Donald, emigrated to America.

4. Donald married and left issue.

a. Donald, called Domhuill Beg (Little Donald), married Helen, daughter of Alexander Macrae, Ardelve, with issue. *a*1. Mary, died unmarried; *a*2. Maggie, died unmarried; *a*3. Anabella, married Duncan Mackenzie, Coigach, Lochbroom, emigrated to Canada where she has issue, one son, Donald; *a*4. Catherine, married Donald. McLaren, with issue; *a*5. Bella, married Roderick Maclennan, Letterfearn, with issue.

b. Margaret, married Murdo Macrae, Bundaloch, with issue; *b*1. Kenneth; *b*2. Christina; *b*3. Anabella; *b*4. Mary, married John Maclennan, Ruorach, Kintail, with issue—Duncan; John; Maggie married Duncan Macrae with issue; Mary married Mr Kennedy, Plockton, with issue.

c. Christina, married Finlay Mackerlich, Bundaloch, with issue—*c*1. John, married Catherine Mackay, Aultnasuth, with issue; *c*2. Mary; *c*3. Maggie; *c*4. Finlay, married Maggie Macrae, Bundaloch, with issue—Farquhar, who is now living in Bundaloch.

5. RODERICK, married Anabella, daughter of Domhuill MacThomais Macrae of Chriamphall, Carr, Kintail, a descendant of Ferachar MacIan Og, with issue—

a. John, married Maggie Macrae, Dornie, with issue—John at Bundaloch; Joan; Grace, at Bundaloch, with issue—John Macrae and Margaret Macrae.

b. Alexander, died unmarried.

c. Christopher, married Isabella, daughter of John Macrae, (called Ian Soar, John the Carpenter), who is mentioned hereafter, with issue—*c*1. Marion; *c*2. Roderick who is now (1909), headmaster of the Public School, Glenconvinth, Inverness, and married to Anne, daughter of Donald Mackenzie, Coigach, Lochbroom, with issue—Christopher Donald, Isabella.

d. Duncan, lived at Horsham, Victoria, Australia. He married Anne Maclennan, with issue, now in Victoria—Anabella, married the Rev. Mr Fowler; Roderick; Christina; Catherine; Flora.

e. Roderick, married Flora Maclennan, with issue—*e*1. Isabella, married Mr Mackinnon, Bridge of Allan, with issue; *e*2. Roderick, now a farmer in St Louis, America; *e*3. Anabella, married in St Louis; *e*4. Mary, married Mr Cameron, Greenock, with issue; *e*5. Grace, in St Louis; *e*6. John, a farmer in Alberta, Canada; *e*7. Murdo, a farmer in Alberta, Canada.

f. Bella, married Thomas Macrae, Dornie, as his first wife without issue.

g. Donald, married Jessie, daughter of Duncan Macmillan, Bundaloch, with issue—Roderick, emigrated to America; Duncan, emigrated to America; Anne, married Mr Watson, Glenbrittle, Skye, with issue; Bella, Catherine.

VII. RODERICK, son of John, son of Roderick, married Mary Murchison, with issue—

1. JOHN Mor, (Big John), lived at Attadale. He married and left issue—

a. Alexander, called the Moar Dubh, (The Black Ground Officer,) married Mary Macrae, Sallachy, with issue—

*a*1. Duncan, emigrated to Australia about 1850. He married with issue, two sons in Melbourne; *a*2. John married a Maclean in Skye; *a*3. Donald, died young; *a*4. Anne, married with issue in Australia; *a*5. Kate, married with numerous issue in South Uist; *a*6. Christina, married in Glasgow, with issue.

b. Donald, lived in Attadale, and married Kate Macdonald, Camuslunie, with issue; Duncan, died unmarried; Bella, married Mr Cameron with issue; Anne, married John Macaulay, Inverinate, with issue.

c. Mary, married Kenneth Maclean, Lochcarron, with issue.

d. Catherine, married Murdo Macrae, Attadale, with issue, Kate, married Christopher Macrae, Inverinate, with issue, one daughter in Melbourne.

2. DONALD, married Christina, daughter of John Mackerlich, with issue—

a John, called Ian Soar (John the Carpenter), married Marion, daughter of Duncan Macrae, Sallachy, Lochalsh, with issue—

*a*1. Donald, died at Park, Bundaloch; *a*2. Donald Buidh, married Margaret, daughter of Archibald Macrae, Bundaloch, with issue—John, married Mary Maclennan, Camuslongart; Annie in New Zealand; Archibald; Duncan, married in New Zealand, with issue; Marion, married Hugh Mackenzie, Lochbroom, with issue; Alexander, in New Zealand, married first Mary Matheson, with issue—Mary Anne, and secondly Jessie Rogerson, with issue—Donald and Jessie; Mary.

b. Donald Soar, married a Mackenzie, daughter of the Gobha Ban (the Fair Blacksmith), Ardelve. He emigrated to America where he left issue—*b*1. Roderick, married with issue; *b*2. Mary married Neil, son of John Ban Mackenzie, Lochcarron, with issue— Donald, in Laurier; Christina, in Lochalsh, Canada; Margaret, died young; John, in Laurier; Niel Gault; Johan, died young; Mary Ann; Roderick, the gigantic Drum-Major of the famous Canadian " Kilties Band," which visited this country a few years ago.   His height is 7 feet 1½ inches.   *b*3. Isabella, married Mr Mackay, Laurier, Ontario.

c. Roderick Soar, lived at Ardnarff, Lochalsh. He married Julia, daughter of Donald Macrae, son of George of the Duilig Family with issue; *c*1. John, died unmarried at Ardnarff in 1905; *c*2. Jock died unmarried at Ardnarff in 1904; *c*3. Donald married Anne, daughter of John Mackerlich, Ardnarff. He died in Southland, New Zealand, where he left issue—Julia married to a Mac-

gregor with issue ; Donald ; Roderick ; John ; Jessie ; c4.
Donald, married Marion Cameron, Aultnasuth, with issue,
Mary married Archibald Weir, Glasgow, with issue—
George, Donald, Archibald ; Duncan, married as his first
wife Flora Macdonald, Fernaig, Lochalsh, with issue—
Christina, Donald, and as his second wife Annie Maccoll,
Appin, with issue—Catherine ; Roderick, married Marjory
Maclennan, with issue—Sarah, Kate ; Anabella, married
Donald Macrae, Portchullin, and lives now in Plockton ;
c5. Anabella, married Donald Cameron, Sallachy, and
left issue—Mary, married Joseph Macpherson, Ord, Skye,
with issue—Neil, who was drowned, Anabella, Jane, Mary,
Ewen, Norman, in Kyleakin ; Roderick, married Mary,
daughter of Malcolm Macrae, Glenelg, with issue—Jessie,
Malcolm, Anabella, Donald ; c5. Mary died young ; c6.
Janet, now (1909), living at Ardnarff ; c7. Christina, now
(1909), living at Ardnarff.

d. Catherine, married John, son of Murdo Mackenzie,
Aultnasuth, with issue—Christina, John, Donald, who is
a good genealogist.

V. ALEXANDER, eldest son of Finlay, eldest son of
Domhuill Duilig, and fifth in descent from Ian Carrach,
succeeded his father to the lands of Duilig. He was
married and left issue at least one son.

VI. DONALD, who held the lands of Duilig and part
of Killilan. He married Elizabeth, daughter of George
Mackenzie of Dochmaluak, by whom he had issue six sons
and some daughters, viz.—John, George, Alexander,
Donald, Roderick. The names of the rest of the family
cannot now be traced.

1. JOHN, eldest son of Donald VI. was known as Ian
Ruadh. He was a gentleman of considerable learning
and accomplishments, being when young educated in the
Chanonry of Ross (Fortrose). He had most of
Glenelchaig under stock and used to send droves of cows
and horses to the Southern markets. He died in 1720 in
Strathglass on his way home from the Contin market, but

his body was brought to Kintail and was buried in Kilduich. It is said that John left more wealth behind him than any of the Macraes of Duilig, who lived in Kintail. He married a daughter of Captain John Murchison Auchtertyre, by whom he had issue only one daughter, who married a Macrae of Aryugan, Kintail.

2. GEORGE, of whom hereafter.

3. ALEXANDER, was called Alistair Caol, (slender Alexander). He was a great hunter, and is said to have obtained special permission from Seaforth to hunt on his forests at his will. He lived in Coilree in Glenelchaig, and when an old man he emigrated in 1774 to Carolina with a family of sons and daughters, one of whom Roderick was married to a daughter of Colin, son of the Rev. Donald Macrae, junior minister of Kintail. Roderick is known to have had descendants in good circumstances dispersed through the State of Carolina, and he was evidently the Roderick Macrae, who landed at Wilmington in 1774, and from whom the Macraes of Wilmington are descended. (Page 248).

4. DONALD, was called Domhuill á Chogidh (Donald the Fighter), on account of his spirited and fiery disposition. He was a farmer and married with issue—

a. Malcolm, called Callum Ruadh, lived for some time in Glencannich. He married a Macrae from Kintail, and had issue—a1. Malcolm, called Callum Og, who when a young man emigrated to America; a2. A son, who was for several years a tailor in Strathglass. He married a daughter of Farquhar, son of Donald Macdonald, Camusluinie, and emigrated to America; a3. A daughter, who lived till recently at Crasg in Strathglass.

5. RODERICK, was a farmer at Altnabrahan in Glenling, Lochalsh. He was married and left issue.

a. Donald, who was a soldier in the 78th Highlanders, and was present at the "Affair of the Macraes" in Edinburgh in 1778. He went with his regiment to India and was present at several engagements. He returned to

Kintail and is known to have lived as an old man at Ridh-Breac, Glenling, in the year 1810. He married Mary, daughter of Kenneth Maclennan, Kintail, and by her had issue.

*a*1. Alexander, a poet of considerable talent. He lived for several years in the Ling Valley, Lochalsh, and about the year 1837 he emigrated to Carolina. From there he removed to Louisville, Kentucky, where he lived for many years. When the Civil War broke out, he remained neutral and suffered imprisonment for about a year. At the conclusion of the war he removed to Pollard, Barber County, Alabama, where he was Postmaster for some time. He married a lady of German extraction with issue—(1) Mary Ann, married a Mr Sutherland. (2) Donald, was Captain in one of the regiments of the Federal Army. (3) Alexander, served in the Federal Army and was severely wounded in one of the engagements.

*a*2. Roderick, lived for some time in Sallachy, and afterwards removed to Applecross. He married Barbara Macrae, with issue—(1) John, married Mary Macdonald, Torridon, and died in Inverness in 1906, leaving issue—Alexander, in South Africa; Roderick, in New Zealand; John, in Inverness; Catherine, married in Inverness. (2) Mary, died young.

*a*3. Annie, died unmarried in Aultnasuth.

*a*4. Christina, married John Maclennan, Aultnasuth, with issue—(1) Donald, now living in Maryburgh, Ross-shire. He married Annabella Macinnes, with issue—John Alexander, died young; Murdo in Vancouver; Donald in Vancouver; Caleb; Jessie. (2) Murdo, died in Plockton.

*a*5. Alexander, died young. *b*. Lilias, died unmarried. *c*. Anne, died unmarried.

6. Another son of Donald VI, whose name cannot now be traced, lived for many years in Ishcean, in Strathfarrar, but afterwards removed to Munlochy, where he died. He was married and left issue. Two of his grandsons, Roderick and Thomas, died unmarried a few years ago.

VII. GEORGE, the second son of Donald VI., was tacksman of Duilig in his young days, and was the last of the family of Domhuill Duilig to live in the old home. He removed to Camusluinie in 1772, and a few years afterwards he accompanied his son, Donald to Gairloch, where he and his wife died, and were buried in the Churchyard of Tournaig. George is said to have been married to Anne, daughter of Donald, son of John Ban, son of Donald, son of Donald of Duilig, and by her he had issue, some daughters and one son.

VIII. DONALD, who was a farmer in Camusluinie. About 1778 he went with his aged parents and young family to Tournaig in Gairloch, but returned to Kintail about the year 1815. He was drowned in Loch Long in the spring of 1827, at the age of 72, and was buried in Killilan. He married Julia, daughter of Thomas Macrae of Carr, a descendant of Ferachar MacIan Oig (Page 187), and by her he had issue.

1. DONALD, of whom below.

2. THOMAS, who was a farmer in Camusluinie. He married Elizabeth, daughter of Donald Ban Macrae of Nonach, Lochalsh, of the Balnain family with issue.

a. Murdoch, born in 1824, lived in Camusluinie, Kintail, where he died on the 5th of September, 1909 He married Isabella, daughter of William Macrae, Carr, (page 185, line 5), with issue.

a1. William, in Camusluinie

a2. Elizabeth, in Camusluinie.

a3. Alexander, educated at the Grammar School of Aberdeen, and graduated M.A. of Aberdeen University in 1904. He is now (1910) a Master at the Royal Masonic School, Bushey, Hertfordshire, and is the author of this chapter on the *Clann Ian Charrich Macraes*

a4. Donald, of Messrs A. Dow & Company, Edinburgh.

b. Mary, was born in 1826. She married John, son of

Duncan, son of Fionnla Ban, (page 182, 13th line from foot), with issue as already mentioned. (Page 463).

3. JOHN, emigrated when a young man to Ontario, Canada. He lived for many years as a prosperous merchant in the town of Port Colborne. He married first a Macgregor (daughter of *c*. Margaret or *d*. Isabella, page 164), with issue.

a. Bella, who died unmarried at Port Colborne in 1868, aged 24 years. John, married as his second wife, Mary Grabel, with issue.

b John Cyrus Matthew Fraser, who died unmarried at Port Colborne in January, 1904.

c. Edward Grabel, who died unmarried at Port Colborne in 1898.

4. JESSIE, married Malcolm, son of Farquhar Macrae, (Ferachar Buidh nan Fiadh), with issue.

a. Annie, married Alexander Murchison, Drumbuie, Lochalsh with issue.

b. George, married and emigrated to America, where he left issue

c. Maggie. died unmarried in Ardelve in 1905.

d Mary, died unmarried in Ardelve.

e. Catherine, married in South of Scotland with issue, one daughter.

5. JULIA, married Roderick Saor, son of Donald Macrae, Ardnarff, with issue as already mentioned.

6. MARY, married Finlay Mackay, Avernish, Lochalsh, with issue.

a. Donald died in Cardiff, was married without issue.

b. John, now living unmarried at Avernish.

c. Christina, died unmarried in Avernish.

d. Mary, died unmarried in Avernish.

e. Janet married Alexander Macrae, Kintail (page 80, 4th line from foot), with issue as mentioned on page 445.

f. Flora, now living in the United States.

g. Annie died unmarried in Avernish.

h. Isabella married Hector, son of Farquhar Macrae, Ardelve (Ferachar Buidh nan Fiadh), and went to the United States. She now lives in Morgan, Minnesota, with issue.

7. Annie was drowned with her father in Loch Long in 1827.

8. Lilias married John, son of Donald Ban Macrae of Nonach, of the Balnain family, with issue as given on page 452.

9. Annie married as his first wife Christopher Macrae, son of Alexander, fourth son of Alexander Macrae. (Page 165, 4th line from foot), with issue, as given. (Page 457).

IX. DONALD, eldest son of Donald VIII., was a farmer at Portchullin, Lochalsh, where he died on the 16th of May, 1862, aged 81 years. He married Catherine, daughter of Duncan Macrae, Nonach, Lochalsh, with issue—

1. DUNCAN, of whom below.
2. DONALD, died unmarried in New Zealand.
3. BELLA, died young in Portchullin.
4. MARY, died young in Portchullin.
5. ANNIE married Duncan Finlayson, Lochalsh, with issue—*a.* Donald, died unmarried; *b* Kate married John Mackenzie, Plockton, with issue; *c.* Bella; *d.* Kate married in South Africa; *e.* Mary; *f.* Christina.
6. ISABELLA married John, son of Murdo Macrae, Ardneaskan, Lochcarron, with issue—

a. Donald married Barbara Finlayson, Kelso, Lochcarron, with issue—Bella, Roderick, Catherine, John, Duncan Donald.

b. Murdo married Maggie, daughter of Duncan Maclennan, Sallachy, Lochalsh, with issue—Bella, John, Jemina, Duncan, William.

c. Donald married Christina Mackenzie, Plockton, with issue—Bella, Donald, John, Jessie, Duncan.

d. Catherine married Duncan Macrae. (Page 128, line 14).

e Jessie.

7. CATHERINE married Alexander Finlayson, Kintail, with issue, as already mentioned.

X. DUNCAN, eldest son of Donald IX. lived for some time in Portchullin, and afterwards emigrated to New Zealand, where he died. He married Janet, daughter of Alexander, son of Christopher Ban Macrae, Portchullin, Lochalsh, with issue—Donald of whom next, Flora married in 1907 James Robertson, Alexander, Thomas, Jessie.

XI. DONALD, now (1910), living in Otaperi, Southland, New Zealand. He married in 1906 Madeline, daughter of Arthur Devery and Madeline Bailey, with issue. He is so far as now known the lineal representative of Ian Carrach, the founder of this family of Macraes.

THE KILLEARNAN MACRAES

From the earliest times in the History of the Clan there were Macraes living in the Black Isle (or Ardmeanach, as it was then called, page 6); and a prosperous family of Macraes in Killearnan, had at one time, the control of Kessock Ferry. There is a tradition in Kintail, however, that this family belonged to the Clann Iain Charrich Macraes Like the rest of the Macraes, the family was Jacobite and Episcopalian.

At the commencement of the eighteenth century, the head of this family was Thomas Macrae, who had a son

ALEXANDER, born August, 1734, and, was as a boy, an eye witness of the battle of Culloden. He married Margaret Davidson, with issue—

1. DONALD, born 1762, married Isabella Young, and had with others who died young, the following issue—

a. Margaret.

b. Isabella married John Maclean, who settled in Canada, where his family prospered.

c. Murdoch.

d. Donald married with issue, a son and a daughter who died unmarried.

e. William, a lawyer of talent and promise, who died young and unmarried.

f. Rev. John born in 1802, a minister of the Church of Scotland. In 1828 he went as a minister to Pictou in Nova Scotia, and remained there for 17 years, eventually becoming minister of Stornoway where he died much respected and honoured in 1877. In 1829 he married Julia Macdougall.

*f*1. William born 1830, died 1831.

f2. Isabella born 1832, married the Rev. J. Macdonald, with issue :—(1) Peter, a doctor, married Agnes Raintree with issue—James. (2) John, a doctor. (3) Elsie, living in Edinburgh.

f3. Rev. Donald, D.D., born 1833, and died in 1909, a leading Presbyterian minister in Canada, married C. H. Macleay, with issue—(1) Bessie married Rev. James Mackenzie with issue—Alexander Macrae ; Morell Macrae ; Norman Archibald ; Catherine Sybil Isabel ; Arthur Dundonald ; Jean Euphemie Ross ; Elizabeth Violet. (2) Alexander, at St John, New Brunswick, married Gertrude Gregory with issue—Donald Alexander ; Catherine Edith Maria ; George Frederick Gregory ; Alexander Kenneth. (3) Sylla, married Owen Campbell with issue—Donald Arthur Rede ; Charlotte Mary; John Astley Douglas. (4) John Kenneth, lawyer at St John, New Brunswick. (5) Rev. Archibald, Principal, Residential College, Calgary. (6) Violet. (7) John, married Elsie Jacques. (8) Rev. Donald, married Isabel Richardson. (9) Colin, banker, Canada.

f4 Archibald born 1835, died 1910, was a planter at Tirhoot in India, married B. A. Bertram with issue—(1) Katherine married R. M Williamson, Aberdeen, with issue—George, Archibald Bertram, Margaret Lesley ; (2) Ronald at Tirhoot in India ; (3) Julia Macdougall ; (4) Beatrice Bertram married W. Mellis, Aberdeen ; (5) Archibald Campbell.

f5. Alexander born 1837, died unmarried.

f6. John born 1839, died unmarried

f7. William born 1841. After a brilliant career at Aberdeen University, he entered the Indian Medical Service. He married C. A. Maciver, with issue—(1) John Lewis, Major, I M.S. ; (2) Norman died young ; (3) Isabel married the Rev. J. Cameron with issue—John Norman, Lewis Charles ; (4) William in the Army.

*f*8.   Elizabeth born 1843, married Andrew Smith, now living at Bellingham, Washington, U S.A , and has issue— David, John, Julia, Harry, George, Alister, Annie, James.

2   RONALD born June, 1764, lived at Craigie House, in the parish of Knockbain, and married Isabella, daughter of John Paterson, Artafallie, Knockbain, and niece of the Rev. Dean Paterson of the Scottish Episcopal Church with issue—

a.   Margaret married Peter Angus, with issue—Bella, Catherine.

b.   Elizabeth married William Paterson, with issue— Lachlan, Donald, William, Elizabeth, Bella, Catherine.

c.   Anne married Alexander Dingwall, with issue—

*c*1.   John, died without issue.

*c*2.   Bella.

*c*3.   Rev. Ronald married Marion Grant, with issue— (1) Alexander, a doctor in Glasgow ; (2) William, in India; (3) Donald, a doctor in Alloa ; (4) Marion Grant ; (5) Anne married the Rev J. Macintosh ; (6) Jessie married the Rev. Evan Grant.

*c*4.   Mary, and four other daughters.

d.   Bella.

e.   Betty married Roderick Macdonald, with issue— Colin, Ronald, Donald, Bella, William, Alexander, Jessie.

f.   Jessie ; *g.* Alexander ; *h.* William.

i.   Helen married William Macintosh, with issue in America—Andrew, William, Williamina.

j.   Catherine married Alexander Chisholm, with issue —Roderick, Ronald, Bella, Alexander, Martha, Catherine, Helen, Jane, William.

3.   ALEXANDER born August, 1766, settled at Black Mill Bay, and married with issue—Alexander, John.

4.   MARGARET born January, 1769.

5.   JOHN born August, 1771.

6.   REV. WILLIAM born December, 1774, a minister of the Church of Scotland.   He was for some time an

Army Chaplain at Fort Augustus, and became minister of his native parish Killearnan, in 1806. On the 12th May, 1813, he was admitted to the charge of the parish of Barvas in Lewis, where he lived and laboured, honoured and loved by all who knew him for the long period of 43 years. He is spoken of as a " very talented man " and " possessing in addition great charm of manner." He married at Fort Augustus Mary Macdonald with issue as below, and died on the 9th July, 1856.

a. Margaret born at Fort Augustus, 10th November, 1811, married Evander Maciver of the Coll family, with issue—

*a*1. John Kenneth, planter at Tirhoot in India, and went afterwards to America, married with issue—Evander, Jessie.

*a*2. Mary died unmarried.

*a*3. Colin married in America.

b. Eliza born at Barvas, 6th March, 1816, married John Mackenzie, Galson, indigo planter, Tirhoot, India, with issue—

*b*1. John Francis born 11th February, 1835, indigo planter, died 30th November, 1906. He married at Geneva in 1864, Lucy Sisson, with issue—Francis, Kenneth, Evander, Kathleen married Alfred Murray, indigo planter ; Mabel, Dora, Mary, Lucy.

*b*2. Janet Mary born 25th October, 1836, married in 1856, Minden James Wilson at Mozufferpore in India, with issue James, Arthur Melville, John, Harry, Janet, Margaret, Eliza, Matilda, Adele, Blanche, Minnie.

*b*3. Charlotte Eliza Flemming born 10th August, 1839, married May, 1858, Major-General Hardress Edmund Waller of the Indian Army, with issue—William, John, Hardress, Edmund, Richard, Julia, Kathleen Emma.

*b*4. Wilhelmina Felicia born 14th March, 1841, married 23rd January, 1865, Lachlan Macdonald of Skeabost, Skye, with issue—Charles, Kenneth, Somerled, Lachlan, Raoul, Lizabel.

*b*5. Blanche Gertrude born 11th January, 1843, married 8th November, 1864, General Theodore William Hogg, with issue—Theodore G. McK. Trower, John McK. Trower, Rudolph Edward Trower, Cyril Minden Trower, Blanche Edith Trower, Annie Louisa Trower, Helen Margaret Trower, Mary Kathleen Trower, Minnie Trower, Claudine Trower, Ida Christabel Trower.

*b*6.   Julia born 16th September, 1844, married 15th November, 1867, Dr Cameron, and died on the 28th December, 1906, leaving issue—Kenneth and John.

*b*7.   Walter Scott born 13th December, 1845, and died 21st March, 1883, married M. Macdonald, with issue—Alistair and Johanna.

*b*8.   William born 12th July, 1848, married in 1874 Lucy Cosserat with issue—Alan, Kenneth, John, Daisy, May.

*b*9.   Eliza Annabella born 17th April, 1852, married in 1872 Frank Murray, with issue—Frank, Walter, Teanie Gertrude, Flossie, Lilla.

*b*10.   Evander born 9th July, 1855, died 8th May, 1857.

*b*11.   Minden Hardress born 25th October, 1858, married Alice G. Watkin Williams, with issue—Walter Scott and Hilda.

c.   Charles Mackenzie born 18th February, 1818, M.D. of Edinburgh, of which University he was a distinguished alumnus.   A medical practitioner in Stornoway for over 50 years.   On the 25th December, 1895, he was presnted with a handsome public testimonial as a mark of appreciation of his public services, and of the esteem and honour in which he was held.   In his youth he was a powerful athlete, and is described as an intellectual man of refined and cultured manner, and a brilliant conversationalist.   " No man in the island (of Lewis), among clergy or laity, was ever honoured and loved as he was."   Dr Charles Mackenzie Macrae married 8th November, 1855, Anabella Jane Mackenzie, and died on 3rd May, 1909, leaving issue—

*c*1.   William Alexander born 31st December, 1856, manager of the Bank of California in Portland, Oregon ; married Janet Henshelwood, with issue — Thomas Henshelwood, deceased.

*c*2.   Alexander William born 15th June, 1858, was for some time a planter in India, and afterwards managing director in India of Pierce Leslie & Co., East India Merchants.   He joined the Malabar Volunteer Rifles when first raised, and commanded them for many years. While he occupied that post, he raised and temporarily commanded the Southern Provinces Mounted Rifles— a corps *d'élite.*   He was Honorary Aide-de-camp to Lord

Kitchener, and was offered a similar appointment by Lord Ampthill, Governor of Madras, and holds volunteer officers decoration. On giving up his command in 1906 was promoted from the rank of Lieutenant-Colonel to that of Honorary Colonel. He married at Calicut, South India, on the 10th September, 1890, Sylvia Frances Ferguson, with issue—Shena Anabella Mackenzie and Frances Evelyn Mackenzie, both died in infancy ; Charles Mackenzie born 28th September, 1893 ; Dorothy Mackenzie born 25th November, 1895 ; Kenneth Norman Mackenzie born 9th July, 1899.

*c*3.   Anabella Mackenzie born 7th April, 1860.
*c*4.   Mary Anne born 2nd November, 1868.
*c*5.   Caroline Mackenzie born 7th November, 1873.
*c*6.   Daniel Mackinlay born 13th May, 1878. Was

for some time a medical student, served in the Boer War, and settled in the Transvaal.

d.   Mary born 14th November, 1819. Married James Mackenzie, 4th June, 1839, with issue as given below, and died 4th September, 1876.

*d*1.   Mary married James Mackenzie, Sydney, Cape Breton, with issue—Jeannette.
*d*2.   John.
*d*3.   Margaret married Donald Mackenzie, without issue.
*d*4.   Wilhelmina married the Rev Daniel Nicholson with issue—Mary May, Minna Maria.
*d*5   James Alexander. *d*6.   William.
*d*7.   Rev. Charles Evander married with issue—William Nicolson, Christina.
*d*8.   Malcolm Macaulay married with issue—James Macaulay, Malcolm Ayres
e.   John born 28th September, 1821, an indigo planter in India, married with issue—William, Nellie, Mary, Annie
f.   Jean born 11th September, 1823, married Murdo Macdonald, with issue.
*f*1.   Rev. William, M.A., Kirkcaldy, married a daughter of the Rev. Dr Macmillan, with issue—Aluin Jane, Somerled, Ronald.
*f*2.   Roderick. *f*3.   John Robert.

g. Anne born 20th July, 1825, married Alexander Grant, Tongue, with issue—William, Robert, Anna Margaret.

h. William born 1828, died 4th March, 1850.

i. Alexander born 23rd July, 1832, deceased.

7. RODERICK born May, 1777.

8. THOMAS born November, 1779.

9. BETSY born March, 1782. Married Mr Leitch with issue, the Rev. Mr Leitch, minister at Fort Augustus.

Alexander of Killearnan, had by a second marriage

10. ALEXANDER, who went to Canada.

11. RONALD, who went to Australia.

12. MARGARET.

13. CATHERINE.

THE MACRAES OF CORRIED-HOMHAIN.

This family of Macraes trace their descent from Fionnla Dubh nam Fiadh, a famous archer of the Clan, who lived probably in the latter end of the sixteenth century, and whose adventures and deeds of daring and prowess are narrated on pages 298 to 303 of this book.

I. Finlay, called Fionnla Dubh nam Fiadh (Black Finlay of the Deer), married and had issue, at least three sons—1. Duncan ; 2. Donald ; 3. Murdo.

II. Donald, second son of Finlay, married and left issue, at least one son.

III Duncan, who married and had issue, at least one son.

IV. John, who married Janet Mackerlich, with issue—

1. Murdo, who married as his first wife Mary, daughter of Alexander, son of Colin Macrae, of the Inverinate family, with issue—

a. John married Julia, daughter of Murdo Mackenzie, Braintra, with issue.

*a*1. Murdo died unmarried.

*a*2. Mary married John Macrae, Applecross, son of Kenneth, son of Donald of the Ardintoul family, with issue—

(1) Donald, who was for several years a schoolmaster in Harris, where he died on the 26th April, 1907. He married Margaret, daughter of Christopher, son of John, son of Duncan Macrae, with issue—Margaret, Nellina.

(2) Alexander died unmarried in Sydney, Australia.

(3) Kenneth married Isabella Shoesmith, with issue—Mary, Kenneth John, and others.

(4) John married Mary Macintyre, with issue—Nellina, Catherine Mary, Annie, Margaret, John.

(5) Niel died unmarried in Manitoba.

*a*3. Christopher died unmarried.

*a*4.   Alexander died unmarried.

*a*5.   Margaret died unmarried.

*a*6.   Janet married Murdo Mackay, with issue in New Zealand.

*a*7.   Annie now living unmarried, at Ardelve.

b.   Duncan married Margaret Macrac, Carnduc, with issue—

*b*1.   Duncan married with issue—Margaret, Flora, Marion, Donald drowned in Labrador, Charles died un-married.

*b*2.   Christopher was a soldier in the Black Watch. He married a daughter of Donald Macrae (page 464, 6th line from foot), with issue—Donald now living in Perth, and some daughters.

*b*3.   Murdo married Mary Mackenzie, without issue.

*b*4.   John married in Glenurquhart, with issue.

c.   Christina married Malcolm Macrae (son of Feracher Buidh Brocair), with issue of several daughters.

Murdo married as his second wife Barbara, daughter of Duncan Macrae of Corriedhoin, with issue—

d.   Malcolm married Mary, daughter of Alexander Macrae, Cnoc na-carn, Camusluinie, with issue as already given.

e.   Roderick married Catherine Mackay with issue— Alexander married in New Zealand Christina Mackay with issue—Murdo, Malcolm, George, Jessie, Jane, and others.

f.   Margaret married first John Macrae, Ardelve, with issue—

*f*1.   Murdo married without issue.

*f*2.   Alexander died without issue.

Margaret married as her second husband Alexander Maclennan, with issue—

*f*3.   John who went to America.

*f*4.   Bella.

*f*5.   Alexander who married Jane, daughter of Farquhar Maclennan, Camusluinie, with issue as already mentioned.

2.   Donald (called Domhuill Buie of Nonach), married Elizabeth Macrae (page 455, 7th from foot), with issue—

a.   Donald died unmarried.

b.   Duncan lived at Portchullin, and married Mary Macrae, with issue—

*b*1.   John, living unmarried at Portchullin.

*b*2.   Mary, living unmarried at Portchullin.

*b*3.   Donald, who now lives at Plockton, married Anabella, daughter of Donald Macrae of the Clann Iain Charrich family without issue.

*b*4.   Finlay died unmarried.

c.   Catherine married Alexander Macrae, Righe Breac, Lochalsh, with issue as already mentioned.

d.   Janet married Alexander Macrae, Ardelve, with issue, in America and in Australia.

e.   Annie married John Macrae (page 128, 3rd from top), with issue.

f.   Isabella married Finlay Maclennan, with issue in America.

3.   Duncan married with issue.

a.   Duncan died unmarried.

b.   Christina married Malcolm, son of John Macrae, Avernish, with issue.

*b*1.   Duncan married Isabella, daughter of Donald Macrae, Plockton.

*b*2.   Flora married George Finlayson, with issue.

c   Janet married John Bain Macrae, with issue.

d.   Catherine married Donald Bain Macrae of Duilig family, with issue, as already given.

4.   John married a Matheson, with issue.

a.   Farquhar lived in Edinburgh.   He married Elizabeth Moncrieff Veitch, with issue—Henry and others.

b.   Donald married Catherine Maclennan, with issue, in Hawke Bay, New Zealand.

*b*1.   John.

*b*2.   Another son.

c.   Betsie married Alexander Macrae (page 211, 2nd from foot), with issue.

*c*1.   John married with issue.

*c*2.   Janet was married without issue.

II.   Duncan, eldest son of Black Finlay of the Deer, married and had issue, at least two sons.

1.   Malcolm of whom next.

2.   Donald served for some time as bailiff under Colin, Earl Seaforth, and lost his life under tragic circumstances, as described on page 307 of this book.

III   Malcolm eldest son of Duncan, was a farmer in Corriedhomhain.   He married and had issue, at least three sons—

1. Duncan of whom next. 2. Donald. 3. Alexander.

IV. DUNCAN, known as Donnacha Mor nan Creach (Big Duncan of the Spoils), succeeded his father as farmer in Corriedhomhain, and also acted for some time as forester to Alexander Mackenzie of Fairburn. He was present at the battle of Sheriffmuir in 1713, and some of his adventures there are described on page 325 of this book. Duncan married and had numerous issue, most of whom settled in Strathconon, where some of their descendants now live. The eldest son

V. DUNCAN, succeeded his father in Corriedhomhain. He married Margaret, daughter of George Mackenzie, Faddoch, a son of Mackenzie of Fairburn, with issue—

1. MALCOLM, of whom hereafter.

2. MURDO Roy lived at Dornie. He married Jane, daughter of Donald, son of the Rev. Finlay Macrae, with issue—a. Malcolm married Janet, daughter of Christopher Macrae, Kyleakin, with issue—

a1. Christopher died unmarried.

a2. John married Anne, daughter of Donald Macrae of Carnoch (page 216) with issue—Mary Eliza, Malcolm, Janet. a3. Janet married Farquhar Matheson, Plockton, with issue. a4. Barbara married in Glasgow, with issue. a5. Christina died unmarried. a6. Jane married with issue. a7. Bella married Roderick Matheson, with issue. a8. Mary Anne. a9. Christina married with issue.

b. John Ban left issue one daughter Bella, married a Macrae with issue, in Washington, America.

c. Elizabeth married Farquhar, son of Alexander, son of John Macrae, and emigrated to America with issue.

d. Barbara died unmarried.

e. Isabella married Alexander Macrae of Cnocnacarn, Camuslumie, with issue, as given elsewhere.

f. Mary married a Mr Morrison with issue.

g. Christina. h. Margaret.

3. Alexander (called the Saor, i.e. Carpenter), married a daughter of Donald Ban Macrae of Drudaig, with issue —a. Duncan died unmarried. b. Janet married Farquhar, son of Farquhar Macrae (page 183, 10th from top), with issue as mentioned. c. Christina died unmarried. d. Maggie married a Macaulay with issue. e. Another daughter.

4. Finlay og Mor lived in Bundaloch. He married and had issue—

a. Roderick lived at Bundaloch; he married Janet Campbell, Glenelg, with issue—*a*1. Duncan lived in Islay. He married there and left issue. *a*2. Finlay died unmarried in Bundaloch. *a*3. John now (1910), living in Achnashellach. He is married with issue—Duncan, Jessie, Marion, Mary, Donald, Grace, George, Roderick, Catherine *a*4 Christina married in Islay with issue.

b. Malcolm called Callum Dall (Blind Malcolm), lived at Bundaloch. He married Rebecca, daughter of Duncan Macrae, with issue—

*b*1. Murdo lived in Bundaloch, married Jessie, daughter of John Macaulay, with issue—Finlay, Farquhar, Rebecca, Mourdina.

c. Duncan married a daughter of Donald Ban Beg Macrae with issue. He and his family emigrated to Australia

d. Catherine died unmarried.

5. CHRISTOPHER lived at Carndue. He married Mary, daughter of Alexandar Macrae, with issue—

a. John died unmarried.

b. Janet died unmarried.

c. Another daughter who married John Macrae with issue—

*c*1. Alexander married Elizabeth Mackay, Jeantown, with issue, who are living near Invergordon in Black Isle.

6. RODERICK lived in Sallachy. He married Catherine, daughter of Donnacha Ban MacFerachar Ruadh with issue—

a. Duncan Ban married Flora, daughter of Colin Macrae, Inchcro (page 80, line 4 from foot), without issue.

b. Thomas emigrated to Australia, where he died unmarried.

c. George.

d. Margaret married John, son of Ferachar Ban Macrae, Faddoch, with issue.

e. Julia died unmarried.

7. Barbara married as his second wife Murdo Macrae of Corriedhomhain family, with issue, as already mentioned (page 503).

8. Helen married Christopher Macrae with issue, and emigrated to America.

VI. Malcolm, eldest son of Duncan V. lived in Corriedhomhain. He married Christina, daughter of Farquhar, son of Duncan og Macrae of the Balnain family (page 149, line 1), with issue

a. Alexander Ban lived for some time in Balmacara, Lochalsh. He married Isabella, daughter of Christopher Macrae, Achnagart, with issue, as given on page 211.

b. Farquhar emigrated to America. He married a daughter of Christopher, son of Finlay Buidh Macrae with issue—John, Donald, and others in Canada.

c George lived at Sallachy, Lochalsh. He married Mary, daughter of Donald, son of Duncan Macrae with issue—

    *c*1. John, died unmarried

    *c*2. Duncan, died unmarried.

    *c*3. Christina, now (1910), living at Sallachy

    *c*4. Donald, unmarried.

    *c*5. Malcolm, died unmarried.

    *c*6. Murdo, who lived at Sallachy, married Margaret, daughter of Duncan Mackay, Fearn, Easter Ross, with issue—Duncan George, now (1910) in General Post-Office, Glasgow; Malcolm at Sallachy, married in March, 1910, Mary Maclennan, Durinish, Lochalsh; George in U.S. America; Mary married Duncan Maclennan, and went to U.S. America; Alexander in U S. America; Anne at Sallachy.

d. Margaret married Alexander Mackay, Plockton, with issue.

THE DESCENDANTS OF MUIREACH FIAL.

Page 51, line 7.

VII. Maurice, known as Muireach Fial (Maurice the Generous), was, according to a tradition among his own descendants, not the fifth son of Christopher VI., but the twin brother of the Rev. Farquhar Macrae. He married, and left issue, at least one son.

VIII. Duncan, who married and left issue, at least one son.

IX. Murdo, who married and left issue, three sons—Duncan, John, Farquhar.

X. Duncan, eldest son of Murdo IX., married Annie Roy, daughter of Eonachan Dubh (page 210), with issue—

1. Donald, known as the " Comastair," married, and had issue.

a. Margaret.

b. Donald (called " Drobhair ") who died unmarried at Bundaloch about 1870.

2. Murdoch, known as Murachadh Buidh nam Meoir (yellow Murdoch of the fingers), died without issue.

3. Annie married John Macrae, Killechuinard, son of Malcolm, son of Donald, son of John, with issue.

a. Mary died unmarried

b Isabella died unmarried.

c. Alexander, called Alasdair Dhu (Black Alexander), married Christina, daughter of Malcolm, son of Finlay Buidh Macrae, Coilree, with issue.

c1. Annie, who married Donald MacDonell, Letter-fearn, without issue.

d. Duncan, called " Fear an Duin," married Mary, daughter of Farquhar Mackerlich, Glenelchaig, with issue.

d1. Anne.

d2. Annie.

4. Margaret married Alexander Macrae, son of Malcolm of the Clann Iain Charrich family, with issue as already mentioned.

X. John, called John Donn (Brown John), second son of Murdo IX., married, with issue—Alexander, of whom hereafter ; Christopher.

XI. Christopher married Julia, daughter of Alexander Macrae of Achnagart (page 211), with issue.

1. Farquhar married Mary, daughter of Duncan Macrae, with issue—a. Alexander, died young. b. Finlay, died young. c. Duncan, died unmarried. d Julia. e. Anne, married Duncan Matheson, Plockton. f. Alexandrina, died unmarried.

2. Alexander, went to Canada about 1860, married, with issue.

3. Murdo Roy, died in 1876. He married Elizabeth Mackenzie, with issue.

a. Duncan, went to Canada.

b. Christopher, lived in Forres, married, with issue.

c. Murdo, drowned when young.

d. Roderick, now (1910) living in Tulloch, Lochcarron.

e. Julia, married, and left issue, who live in Alness.

f. Elizabeth, deceased.

4. Anne married Donald Cross, Gairloch, with issue.

a. Anne married John Murchison, Torridon, with issue.

a1. Donald, married in Rothesay. a2. James, married in Forres, with numerous issue. a3. Murdo, married with issue in Glasgow. a4. Jeanette, married Donald Macrae, Invershiel, with issue.

(1). Julia, married in Strathconon. (2). Hannah, married with issue in Dornie. (3). Duncan. (4). Helen.

b. Anabella, married Donald Macrae, as mentioned hereafter.

5. Mary, died young.

6. Anabella, married a MacNair, without issue.

XI. Alexander, eldest son of John X., was a soldier in the 78th Highlanders, and was present in several engagements in India, and also in the Peninsula, where he served under Sir John Moore. He died in Bundaloch, Kintail, about 1845. He married Barbara Macrae, a descendant of Duncan Mor of Torlysich (page 198), with issue.

1. Duncan, called Donnacha Donn (Brown Duncan), married Anne, daughter of Roderick MacLean, Morvich, Kintail. He and all his family, except one daughter, Isa-

bella, died on the way to America in 1849. Isabella married Farquhar, son of Malcolm Macrae of Cragaig, Glenelchaig, with issue, now living in Glengarry, Canada.

2. Donald lived in Bundaloch, Kintail, where he died in 1884 He married Anabella, daughter of Donald Cross, Gairloch, with issue.

a. Donald, died unmarried

b. Catherine, died unmarried.

c. Christopher, now (1910) living at Carndue, Kintail. He married in 1874 Catherine Macrae, a descendant of Muireach Fial, with issue.

*c*1. Catherine, married John Gray, Dundee, with issue.

*c*2 Alexander, now living in U.S. America.

*c*3. Donald.

*c*4 Bella.

*c*5 John Duncan, educated at the Grammar School, Aberdeen, and now a student in Arts at Aberdeen University.

*c*6. Flora.

d. Duncan, died young.

e. John, married Mary Maclaine, with issue.

*e*1. Donald, married in Ardrossan, with issue— William, Alexander.

*e*2. Alexander, died in 1901.

*e*3. Malcolm.

*e*4. Catherine.

*e*5 Kenneth.

f. Donald, died unmarried.

g. Barbara, died young.

X. Farquhar, the youngest son of Murdo IX., married with issue, at least one son.

XI. John, who married with issue.

1. John, married with issue.

a. Anne, died unmarried.

b. Murdo, married Flora Macdonald, Inverinate, with issue.

*b*1. Christina, died unmarried.

*b*2. Farquhar, now living unmarried at Inverinate.

*b*3. Catherine, now living unmarried at Inverinate.

c. Alexander, married Mary Macrae, Lochalsh, with issue.

*c*1. Duncan, married, and went to Australia.

*c*2. Lily, married, and went to Australia.

*c*3. Donald, married in Easter Ross.

*c*4. Alexander, died young.

2. Alexander married Catherine Maclennan, Kintail, with issue.

a. Farquhar married Margaret Macleod, with issue—Finlay, Malcolm, John, and several daughters. He emigrated about 1859 to Prince Edward Island, where his descendants now live.

b. Anne, died unmarried.

c. Catherine went to Canada, and married a Mr Garvice of the Free Church College, Halifax, with issue.

d. Margaret married a Mr Burke in Canada, with issue.

e. Alexander died in 1881. He married Isabella Macdonald, with issue.

*e*1. Duncan married Christina Macrae, with issue.

(1). Alexander, now living in Kyle. He married Mary Murchison, with issue. (2). Duncan, married in Dundee. (3). Margaret, now living in Balmacara. (4). Finlay, married with issue in Glasgow.

*e*2. Flora married John Mackay, Ardelve, with issue.

*e*3. John married Catherine Polson. He went about 1860 to Canada, where he died in 1895. He left one daughter, Catherine, who married a Mr Mackie, with issue.

*e*4. Alexander went to Canada. He married Mary Ann Sutherland, with issue.

(1). Thomas, an Inspector on the staff of the Canadian Pacific Railway, married with issue. (2). Flora married a Mr Craig, a banker, with issue. (3). Hugh.

*e*5. Finlay married a Mackenzie in Elgin, with issue Bella and Grace.

*e*6. Donald died in 1873. He married Jessie Macmillan, with issue, in Liverpool.

*e*7. Catherine married in 1874 Christopher Macrae, a descendant of Muireach Fial, with issue as already mentioned.

*e*8. Allan went to Canada in 1864. He married Catherine Finlayson, with issue—Finlay, Grace, Bella, Mary, Alexander.

ERRATA TO NOTES AND ADDITIONS.

Page 453, line 10 from top —After 1849 insert except Malcolm who went
to Australia.
,, 455, ,, 1 ,, —For Carolina read Australia.
,, 459, ,, 13 ,, —For a medical student read M.B. and C.M
,, 463, ,, 12 ,, —For Donald read Donald John Delete Anne
,, ,, ,, 13 ,, —Delete John.
,, 467 ,, 5 from foot—Delete Alexander, who is given on page 468,
line 1.
,, ,, ,, 2 ,, —For Newcastle read Muncastle
,, 468 ,, 10 ,, — Before Isabella insert f1.
,, ,, ,, 8 ,, — For (g) read f2.
,, ,, ,, 7 ,, —For (h) read f3.
,, ,, ,, 6 ,, —For (i) read f4
,, 471 ,, 7 ,, —After this line insert 8. Mary married Duncan
Macrae (page 455).
,, 474 ,, 10 ,, —After Johan Flora insert—William Murdoch.
,, 475 ,, 8 ,, —For Father read Rev. Duncan.
,, 485 ,, 12 ,, —After Bundaloch insert —d. Mary married
James Macrae with issue in America.
,, 487 ,, 19 ,, —After Mary insert A 3. Isabella married
Christopher Macrae (page 485).
,, ,, ,, 12 ,, —Delete Gault
,, 489 ,, 11 ,, —For America read Australia.
,, ,, ,, 8 ,, —For America read Australia.
,, ,, ,, 7 ,, — Insert A 4 John married with issue in New
Zealand. A 5 Duncan in America
,, 490 ,, 8 from top—For Kentucky read Alabama.

NOTE.

Page 104, line 24; also page 348, foot note

The central figure representing the founder of the House of Seaforth
in this painting is not Farquhar Macrae, as stated in the text, but
Francis Lord Seaforth who died in 1815. Farquhar is probably represented as one of the younger men in the group

Page 351, foot note 2.

Killechuinard ought to be Cille chaoin teort, which is shown in Mr W.
J. Watson's Place names of Ross and Cromarty to be Kentigerna's Church
or cell

INDEX TO NOTES AND ADDITIONS

Lightning Source UK Ltd.
Milton Keynes UK
UKOW05f1558010816

279677UK00003B/65/P

Masques et bouffons; comédie italienne

Maurice Sand

MASQUES ET BOUFFONS

(COMÉDIE ITALIENNE)

— —

TOME SECOND

PARIS. TYPOGRAPHIE DE HENRI PLON, IMPRIMEUR DE L'EMPEREUR

8, rue Garancière.

BOUFFO

PANTALON.

LE DOCTEUR, IL BISCEGLIESE, CASSANDRE, CASSANDRINO, FACANAPPA, IL BARONE, GAULTIER-GARGUILLE, GUILLOT-GORJU.

Depuis les comédies grecques jusqu'à nos vaudevilles modernes; depuis le *vieux satyre* barbouillé de raisin jusqu'à Cassandre barbouillé de tabac, depuis Aristophane, Plaute, Térence, Machiavel, Beolco, Molière et Goldoni, le vieillard de la comédie comme celui de la farce a toujours été plus ou moins chiche, crédule, libertin, dupé et raillé, mouchant, toussant, crachant, et, par-dessus tout, mécontent :

Qu'il s'appelle *Stepsiade, Philocléon, Blephurus,* dans les comédies d'Aristophane;

Theuropide, Euclion, Demiphon, Demenète, Stalinon, Nicobule, dans celles de Plaute;

Messer ANDRONICO, PASQUALE, PLACIDO, CORNELIO, TOMASO, dans celles d'A. Beolco;

PANTALONE, ZANOBIO, FACANAPPA, IL BERNARDONE, LE DOC-
TEUR, IL BARONE, CASSANDRO, IL BISCEGLIESE, dans la *Commedia
dell' arte;*

COLLOLONIO, PANDOLFO, DIOMEDE, DEMETRIO, COCCOLIN,
GERONTIO, BARTOLO, dans la comédie italienne *sostenuta,*

GAULTIER GARGUILLE, JACQUEMIN JADOT, dans la farce française,

ORGON, GORGIBUS, ARPAGON, SGANARELLE, dans les pièces
de Molière : c'est toujours le PAPPUS ou le CASNAR des
atellanes.

« Le Pappus, » dit M. Ferdinand Fouque, « que les Grecs
appelaient Παππος, est tantôt un vieillard avare, libidi-
neux, méticuleux, pénétrant et rusé; tantôt un vieillard
simple, de bonne foi et toujours dupe soit d'une maîtresse, soit d'un rival, soit d'un fils, d'un valet ou de
quelque autre intrigant. Il répond au Docteur bolonais et
au Pantalon vénitien. Une cornaline nous en donne le
masque barbu ... Son vêtement est de pourpre. Les Osques
avaient un autre vieillard appelé Casnar; il ne différait pas
du Pappus. »

Dans la *Mostellaire* de Plaute, en l'absence de Theuropide, vieux marchand athénien, son fils devient éperdument amoureux d'une musicienne; il l'achète, puis l'amène
dans la maison paternelle et s'y livre, avec elle et ses amis,
à toutes sortes d'orgies.

Un jour que nos convives joyeux avaient bu « à la
grecque », c'est-à-dire jusqu'à ne pouvoir plus remuer,
même pour fuir, le vieux Theuropide arrive. Tranion,

véritable Scapin, l'esclave dévoué du jeune homme, invente une fourberie pour éloigner le vieillard de la maison. Il en fait fermer et verrouiller la porte principale, et attend Theuropide de pied ferme.

THEUROPIDE. Mais qu'est-ce que cela signifie? Ma maison fermée en plein jour! (*Il frappe.*) Hola! hé! quelqu'un! Qu'on m'ouvre la porte!

TRANION *feignant de ne pas le reconnaître.* Quel est cet homme-là qui s'approche si près de la maison?

THEUROPIDE. Personne ne vient! Mais il me semble, si je n'ai pas perdu toute connaissance, que c'est là Tranion, mon esclave?

TRANION. Oh! seigneur Theuropide, mon bon maître! quel bonheur! Est-il possible que ce soit vous? Permettez-moi de vous saluer et de vous souhaiter le bonjour. Votre santé a-t-elle toujours été bonne dans ce pays lointain, seigneur?

THEUROPIDE. Je m'y suis toujours porté comme tu vois que je me porte maintenant.

TRANION. Vous ne pouviez mieux faire.

THEUROPIDE. Et vous autres? Est-ce que la cervelle vous a tourné en mon absence?

TRANION. Pourquoi, s'il vous plaît, demandez-vous cela, seigneur?

THEUROPIDE. Pourquoi? parce que vous sortez tous à la fois vous promener, et que personne ne reste pour surveiller la maison : peu s'en est fallu que je n'aie enfoncé ces portes à coups de pied.

TRANION. Oh! monsieur! sérieusement, avez-vous touché cette porte-là?

THEUROPIDE. Et pourquoi ne la toucherais-je pas? Non-seulement je l'ai touchée, mais, comme je te l'ai déjà dit, je l'ai presque enfoncée.

TRANION. Je ne reviens pas de mon étonnement. Encore une fois, avez-vous touché à cette maison-là?

THEUROPIDE. Ah çà! me prends-tu pour un menteur? Puisque je te dis que j'y ai touché et que j'y ai frappé bien fort!

TRANION. Ah! grands dieux!

THEUROPIDE. Qu'est-ce qu'il y a?

TRANION. Par Hercule! vous avez eu tort.

THEUROPIDE. Quelle invention me dis-tu là?

TRANION. On ne peut pas dire tout le mal que vous avez fait. Il est atroce, irréparable. Vous avez commis un affreux sacrilége!

THEUROPIDE. Pourquoi?

TRANION. Oh! monsieur! retirez-vous d'ici, je vous en prie, éloignez-vous de cette fatale maison. au moins, venez de mon côté. Mais, tout de bon, avez-vous touché la porte?

THEUROPIDE. Certainement! il faut bien que j'y aie touché puisque j'y ai frappé, l'un ne va pas sans l'autre.

TRANION. Ma foi! vous êtes perdu, vous et les vôtres!

THEUROPIDE. Fassent les dieux que tu périsses par ton augure! car tu es aussi des miens. Mais pourquoi cela? Que veux-tu dire?

TRANION. Sachez, monsieur, qu'il y a sept mois que nous sommes tous partis de cette maison, et, depuis, personne n'y a remis les pieds.

THEUROPIDE. Dis-m'en donc vite la raison.

TRANION. Je vous en prie, monsieur, regardez bien autour de vous si personne ne nous écoute.

THEUROPIDE. Il n'y a pas une âme, tu peux parler en toute sécurité.

TRANION. Donnez-vous la peine de regarder encore une fois.

THEUROPIDE. Je te dis qu'il n'y a personne; tu peux sans crainte me dire ton secret.

TRANION. Il faut qu'un crime horrible ait été commis dans cette maison.

THEUROPIDE. Si tu veux que je te comprenne, parle plus naturellement.

TRANION. Je veux dire qu'il s'est passé, il y a longtemps, dans votre maison, un ancien crime de la plus noire scélératesse. Mais nous l'avons découvert depuis peu.

THEUROPIDE. Quel est donc ce forfait? Qui peut en être l'auteur? Dis-le, malheureux, sans me faire languir davantage!

TRANION. L'ancien propriétaire de la maison, celui qui vous l'a vendue, après s'être saisi de son hôte, l'a poignardé de sa propre main.

THEUROPIDE. Et il l'a tué?

TRANION. Bien plus! après lui avoir pris son argent, il l'enterra dans la maison même.... Un soir que monsieur

votre fils avait soupé dehors, lorsqu'il fut revenu il se
coucha, nous en fîmes autant; quand tout d'un coup....
je dormais déjà profondément, et même j'avais oublié
d'éteindre la lampe . quand tout à coup j'entends notre
jeune maître crier de toute sa force J'y cours, il m'assure que le vieux mort lui était apparu pendant qu'il
dormait.

THEUROPIDE. Mais c'était en songe, en rêve, enfin il
dormait !

TRANION. Vous avez raison, mais écoutez-moi. notre
jeune maître me dit que le mort lui avait dit ceci...

THEUROPIDE. Toujours en dormant ?

TRANION. Cela est vrai; il a eu grand tort, et je suis très-
étonné qu'une âme qui depuis soixante ans est séparée
de son corps, n'ait pas songé à prendre le moment où
votre fils serait éveillé pour venir le voir. Je suis fâché de
vous le dire, monsieur, mais vous avez parfois des absences
qui ne font point honneur à votre jugement.

THEUROPIDE. Je me tais.

TRANION. Voici ce qu'a dit mot à mot ce vieux spectre :
« Je m'appelle Diaponce, je suis un étranger d'au delà de
la mer. C'est ici ma demeure, et cette maison est en mon
pouvoir. Caron n'a pas voulu de moi dans les enfers; il
m'a renvoyé brutalement parce que, bien que mon corps
ait été enterré, il n'a pas reçu les honneurs de la sépulture. J'ai été trompé par mon hôte, il m'a attiré et égorgé
ici pour avoir mon argent. Il m'a à peine couvert de terre
et je reste caché dans cette maison. Il n'y a que moi qui

sache qui je suis. Ce que j'exige de toi, c'est que tu quittes cette maison » Voilà ses paroles, monsieur. La maison est maudite, elle est vouée à la vengeance divine. Je ne saurais vous dire toutes les apparitions qui s'y montrent chaque nuit. Chut! chut! entendez-vous?

THEUROPIDE *effrayé*. Qu'est-ce que c'est? Ah! mon pauvre Tranion, je t'en prie, par Hercule, dis-moi ce que tu as entendu

TRANION. La porte a remué et je suis pourtant sûr que personne ne l a poussée.

THEUROPIDE. Je suis transi de peur : en ce moment on ne me trouverait pas une goutte de sang dans le corps Peut-être que les morts viennent me chercher, pour me faire descendre tout vivant dans les enfers.

TRANION *à part, entendant remuer dans la maison* Je suis perdu! ils gâteront toute ma comédie de fantômes et de spectres par leur étourderie! (*A Theuropide*) J'en tremble de peur! Eloignez-vous, seigneur, éloignez-vous de cette porte; fuyez, au nom d'Hercule! fuyez, je vous en prie.

THEUROPIDE Tranion!

TRANION *feignant de prendre son maître pour le fantôme*. Monsieur le spectre! ne m'appelez point.... je n'ai rien fait! Je vous assure que ce n'est pas moi qui ai tant frappé à la porte.

THEUROPIDE *tremblant*. Mais à qui en as-tu?.. à qui parles-tu?

TRANION. Comment, monsieur, est-ce vous qui m'aviez appelé? En vérité, j'ai cru de bonne foi que c'était le mort

qui se plaignait du bruit que vous avez fait. Mais comment
êtes-vous encore là ? Partez ! enveloppez-vous la tête ; fuyez,
et ne vous avisez pas de regarder derrière vous.

THEUROPIDE *se sauvant* Grand et puissant Hercule ! assiste-
moi contre ces coquins de fantômes qui veulent m'enlever !
(*Il part.*)

Pantalon et Cassandre ne sont pas moins crédules et poltrons que leur ancêtre Theuropide l'Athénien.

Angelo Beolco, dans sa comédie de *la Rhodiana* (écrite
vers 1550), fait agir deux vieillards. L'un, *messer* DEMETRIO,
médecin, jurant par les savants docteurs anciens, Asclé-
piade, Hippocrate, Esculape et Galien, l'autre, *ser* COR-
NELIO [1], avocat vénitien, amoureux malgré ses années et
ses infirmités, crachant du latin à chaque instant quand il
se trouve en société de messer Demetrio, parlant avec prétention, mais employant son dialecte vulgaire avec une
certaine *Prudentia* qu'il veut faire agir auprès de la jeune
Béatrice dont il est amoureux

« CORNELIO *seul.* Depuis que je suis sorti du ventre de ma
mère, et jeté au beau milieu de ce monde, je ne crois pas
m'être jamais trouvé plus dépourvu d'idées, plus abattu
(comme si j'étais enfermé, sans manger ni boire, dans la
caverne d'un affreux monstre, ou pris dans les toiles d'araignée) que je ne me trouve présentement depuis que je suis

---

[1] Les noms de Demetrio et de Cornelio restèrent adoptés au théâtre pour
les rôles des vieillards, surtout dans les comédies apprises, comme dans *la
Vedova, comedia farctissima* de Nicolo Buonaparte, *cittadino Fiorentino*, 1643.
Cornelio, dans *la Sbratta* de da Cagli, 1553, etc.

ici, *ita et taliter quotiens*. Il me semble être abandonné dans une barque vide, et resté seul au gouvernail sur une mer en fureur. Mais si l'Espérance veut bien m'ouvrir un peu sa fenêtre, je sortirai de ces embarras, et je ferai tant avec l'argent, les cadeaux et mes vertus, que j'obtiendrai les faveurs de cette belle, digne du ciseau de Sansovino. Je vais aller trouver Prudentia, la mappemonde de la galanterie... mais la voici à propos.

Que le bonjour te soit donné. Où vas-tu ainsi, galante Prudentia?

PRUDENTIA. Vous ferez bien de ne pas m'ennuyer; si vous avez la tête pleine de fantaisies, je n'ai pas le temps de m'en occuper. Vous n'êtes qu'un ladre engraissé de la misère du pauvre monde, car vous ne donneriez rien à un mendiant.

CORNELIO. Prudentia, je ne veux pas me vanter, mais si tu savais les aumônes que je fais, tu en serais émerveillée. Entre autres choses, j'entretiens tous les hôpitaux de ce pays de mes vieux habits que je ne porte plus, et il ne se passe pas un jour de carème que je ne donne moi-même aux pauvres tous les liards (*bagatini*) usés que j'ai rognés dans l'année.

PRUDENTIA. De cette manière vous ne vous faites pas de mal! Vous en agissez ainsi avec les intrigues d'amour, vous offrez ce que vous n'avez pas, pour être aidé, et, l'obstacle une fois franchi (*passato il ponto*), vous ne connaissez plus personne, vous tournez la tête d'un autre côté, et nous vous avons servi pour l'amour du ciel.

CORNELIO. Aide-moi, Prudentia, tu sais que je suis tendre des entrailles et doux du poumon. Attends, je veux te prouver toute mon amitié, et si tu me promets de m'aider, je te promets de mon côté de te donner une paire de chausses en drap rouge que je n'ai portée que quatre fois, et un quarteron de fèves excellentes, à condition que tu parleras à cette jeune fille (*sta zovene bella à muò un papagà in stampa d'Aldo*), belle comme un perroquet imprimé par *Aldo* [1], blanche comme un linge, légère comme un lapin, je crois qu'elle s'appelle Béatrice et sa mère Sofronia, m'a-t-on dit, car je ne les connais pas autrement, étant étranger.

PRUDENTIA. Il me semble que je les connais; je ferai ce que je pourrai pour leur parler, et je leur dirai tant de petits riens (*festuche*) de vous, que je pense d'avance que vous aurez la belle à votre désir. Mais comment ferez-vous avec les infirmités que vous avez?

CORNELIO. Va, tu n'es qu'une girafe! tu cherches toujours à te moquer des gens. Crois-tu donc que je sois si détérioré que je ne sache mettre un cheval au galop quand je veux? Va, tu ne me connais pas encore!

PRUDENTIA. Ne vous glorifiez pas de cela, je connais votre grande et vénérable bêtise. Quand vous serez près d'elle, n'allez pas lui dire que vous avez tant d'années sur les reins, entendez-vous?

CORNELIO Si ce n'étaient les maladies, j'aurais envie de dire mille gaillardises, et, tout maigre que je suis, je te

---

[1] Aldo Manuce, célèbre imprimeur vénitien du quinzième siècle

ferais vingt cabrioles sur une main ; et, tout fatigué que je
suis, à pieds joints, courbette sur courbette, et à la course
tu verrais bien que je ne suis pas un lourdaud !

PRUDENTIA. Or donc, messer Cornelio, puisque vous êtes
si chaud pour cette affaire, fiez-vous à moi, j'agirai de
telle sorte que vous aurez ce que vous désirez. En attendant, je vous prie de me donner quatre *bolognini* (cinq
sous) que je ne pourrai vous rendre qu'en disant beaucoup
de bien de vous.

CORNELIO. Puisses-tu chausser mes savates (*le suole de i
miè zoccoli*) si j'ai plus de deux *quattrini* (six centimes).
Ma femme ne veut pas que je porte d'argent sur moi,
parce que, dit-elle, je le sème par terre. Mais je te promets, si tu m'apportes une bonne réponse, de te donner,
sans marchander, trois *bolognini* en vieil argent ancien,
qui ont un trou au milieu pour passer au cou de la
chatte, et qui sont dans mon coffret. Maintenant je m'en
vais, je ne suis resté que trop longtemps avec toi. cela
suffit, tu m'as compris (*Il sort*)

PRUDENTIA *seule* Va-t'en au diable ! tu n'auras pas de
peine à y arriver ! Regardez-moi, de grâce, cette vieille
bête mal accoutrée, admirez, je vous prie, quelle galante
aventure m'est tombée entre les mains ! Je le servirai pour
son argent. Ce vieux teigneux, goutteux, catarrheux, qui
s'est mis dans la tête d'être amoureux d'une aussi belle et
honnête jeune fille ! Oh ! le joli poupon à tenir dans ses
bras ! »

Plus loin, Cornelio rencontre Truffa, et, poursuivant
toujours son idée amoureuse, il veut employer la sor-

cellerie et lui fait des offres pour obtenir les faveurs de
la jeune fille

« Va, » lui dit-il, « si je peux avoir cette colombe par
les grimoires et incantations, sans employer cette carogne
de Prudentia qui est toujours pendue à ma ceinture, je
promets de te donner mon chapeau . tu sais, celui que tu
as acheté dans le temps, et que je porte à remettre en
forme. »

PANTALON.

PANTALONE, qui donna son nom aux culottes et aux
chausses faites tout d'une pièce, est un des quatre masques
de la *Commedia dell' arte.*

« A Venise, dit M. Paul de Musset, quatre masques bouffons et improvisateurs revenaient dans toutes les pièces :
le *Tartaglia*, bredouilleur, le Truffaldin, caricature bergamasque; le Brighella, représentant les orateurs de places
publiques et d'autres types populaires; et enfin le célèbre
Pantalon, le bourgeois vénitien personnifié avec tous ses
ridicules, et dont le nom a une étymologie digne d'un
commentaire. Ce mot vient de *pianta-leone* (plante-lion);
les anciens marchands de Venise, dans leur fureur d'ac-
quérir des terres au nom de la république, plantaient à
tout propos le lion de Saint-Marc sur les iles de la Méditer-
ranée; et comme ils venaient se vanter de leur conquête,
le peuple se moquait d'eux en les baptisant *plante-lion.* »
Selon d'autres auteurs, Pantalon tire simplement son nom
de San Pantaleone, l'ancien patron de Venise.

Pantalon est tantôt père, époux; tantôt veuf ou vieux garçon, songeant encore à plaire, et fort ridicule par conséquent; tantôt riche et tantôt pauvre, tantôt avare et tantôt prodigue. C'est toujours un homme d'un âge mûr. Originaire de Venise, il représente ordinairement le marchand, le négociant rangé, père de deux filles fort difficiles à garder. C'est ISABELLE et ROSAURE, ou CAMILLE et SMERALDINE, qui s'entendent avec leurs soubrettes FIAMETTA, ZERBINETTE, OLIVETTE ou CATTE, pour tromper l'impuissante vigilance du bonhomme

Dans cette situation, il est fort avare et fort méfiant; on peut lui appliquer ce que l'esclave Strobile dit de son maître Euclion dans l'*Aululaire* de Plaute ·

« La pierre-ponce n'est pas si sèche que ce vieillard-là! Il est si avare, que, lorsqu'il va se coucher, il prend la peine de lier la gueule du soufflet pour l'empêcher de perdre son vent pendant la nuit Quand il se lave, il pleure l'eau qu'il est obligé de répandre. Il y a quelque temps, le barbier lui coupa les ongles · il ramassa soigneusement toutes les rognures, et, pour ne rien laisser perdre, les emporta précieusement. »

Aujourd'hui encore, les sobriquets de claque-dent, de pince-maille, pleure-pain, Pantalon *dei bisognosi*, Pantalon *cagh'in aqua*, lui vont à merveille. Les Bolonais et les Vénitiens se moquent de l'avarice de Pantalon et du docteur Balanzoni. « Ils les représentent, » dit M Frédéric Mercey, « lorsqu'ils se mettent en débauche, assis à une table rase, mangeant de la soupe de lévrier, buvant du vin clairet puisé à la fontaine du coin, et se régalant d'un œuf de cane, dont ils gardent le jaune pour eux, donnant le blanc à leurs femmes, et l'eau lactée à leurs enfants, repas qui, à ce qu'ils assurent, n'engendre ni crudités ni pesanteurs d'estomac. »

Mais il n'est pas toujours aussi ladre; il se contente parfois d'être ridicule Vêtu de ses pantalons rouges, de sa robe d'indienne, coiffé de son bonnet de laine, chaussé de ses pantoufles turques, il représente bien l'antique marchand vénitien courant à ses affaires, grasseyant, achetant, vendant, avec force discours, serments et gesticulations, sur la place Saint-Marc.

Il prend toujours l'honneur à témoin; sa vieille probité est connue, et s'il entend s'élever quelque différend, il y court La discussion dégénère-t-elle en dispute, il s'en mêle et veut intervenir comme médiateur, mais Pantalon est né sous une mauvaise étoile : il fait si bien qu'il est rare qu'on n'en vienne pas aux coups, et il a la chance d'en attraper bon nombre.

Pantalon a toujours du guignon à Venise comme en terre ferme. Ayant, un jour, loué un *bœuf sans cornes* (un cheval) pour une promenade, il emmena son valet Arlequin. La rosse s'étant arrêtée tout court, Arlequin, pour la faire avancer, lui allonge une volée de coups de bâton. La pauvre bête, impatientée, lui lance une ruade dans le ventre Arlequin, furieux, ramasse un pavé et veut le jeter au cheval; mais il s'y prend si maladroitement que la pierre va frapper rudement maître Pantalon, qui ne bronchait pas de sa monture. Il se retourne, et aperçoit Arlequin qui se tient le ventre en beuglant. « Quelle méchante bete nous a-t-on donnée là? dit-il d'un air piteux à son valet. Croirais-tu qu'en même temps qu'elle t'a attrapé dans le ventre, elle m'a allongé un grand coup de pied au milieu du dos? »

Pantalon est toujours exploité par quelqu'un, et son valet Arlequin a pour emploi, comme on l'a vu, de lui faire avaler des bourdes fantastiques Arlequin, le voyant si naïf, se déguise en marchand et s'imagine de lui présenter des mémoires comme celui-ci

« Deux douzaines de chaises de toile de Hollande,

Quatorze tables de massepain,

Six matelas de faïence, pleins de râclure de bottes de foin;

Une couverture de semoule,

Six coussins garnis de truffes;

Deux pavillons de toile d'araignée, garnis de franges faites de moustaches de Suisses,

Une seringue de queue de cochon, avec son manche de velours à trois poils. »

Chaque article est coté à des prix fabuleux; mais Pantalon envoie le faux marchand et sa note à tous les diables.

L'avarice donne parfois de l'esprit à Pantalon. Il a entendu un jour Arlequin dire seul, et tout haut, en faisant ses comptes et en écrivant ses chiffres : « Toi, tu n'as pas de queue, tu en auras une! » et tous les zéros devenir des 9. Pantalon prend le mémoire, l'examine, et dit devant son valet : « Toi, tu as une queue, tu n'en auras pas. » Et de convertir tous les 9 en 0, à la grande mortification d'Arlequin.

Arlequin lui présente dès lors ses mémoires au plus juste prix

« Pour un quartier de veau rôti et un emplâtre d'onguent pour la gale, ci. . . . . 5 livres 10 sols.

Pour un chapon et un brayer tout neuf pour monsieur Pantalon, ci. . . . . . . 12 livres.

Pour un pâté pour Arlequin et deux mesures d'avoine pour le maître, ci. . . 1 livre 10 sols.

Pour une livre de beurre frais, et pour avoir fait ramoner la cheminée, ci. . . . 12 sols.

Pour des tripes et pour une souricière, ci . . . . 10 sols.

Pour trois saucisses et le ressemelage d'une paire de vieux souliers, ci. . . . . 15 sols.

Pour avoir fait la barbe au patron, et avoir raccommodé les commodités, ci. . 1 livre 10 sols.

Total. . . . . . 20 livres 7 sols.

Pantalon ne trouve rien à redire au prix, seulement il fait l'homme offensé de voir accolés si ridiculement ces divers articles, jette le papier au nez d'Arlequin et ne paye point.

Dans *Pantalon spetier* (apothicaire) de Giovanni Bonicelli, ce personnage se querelle avec son ami le Docteur, savant homme de loi, sur l'excellence de leurs professions respectives La conversation finit par des gourmades, mais bientôt on songe à se réconcilier, *a far pase*. Le Docteur fait les avances et envoie à son compère deux perdrix dans un panier. Son valet Arlequin est chargé du message.

Pantalon est flatté de cette démarche, et donne un quart de ducat de *buona mano* à Arlequin Celui-ci l'accable de bénédictions, fait une fausse sortie, revient, et raconte que, dans son zèle, il est venu si vite que ses chausses se sont rompues. Pantalon se sent en humeur de faire le magnifique; il lui donne un autre quart de ducat, en lui disant . « Fais bien attention, garçon! je ne te le prête pas, je te le donne en toute propriété. » Arlequin rebénit Pantalon, s'éloigne un peu, et revient encore. Il doit quelque chose au tailleur qui doit rapetasser ses chausses; ce tailleur, avare et cruel, l'a menacé, s'il ne lui apportait un quart de ducat, de lui enlever de dessus la tête, la première fois qu'il le rencontrerait, son petit chapeau, son gentil *capellino*. Pantalon souffrira-t-il qu'on fasse pareille injure à son ami le Docteur, dans la personne de son valet? Pantalon s'exécute encore. Mais Arlequin revient encore, et demande de quoi payer la couturière de sa mère, qui a commandé une robe et ne peut payer la façon La couturière veut garder l'étoffe, quelle infamie! Pantalon donne encore, mais en déclarant que, cette fois, c'est un prêt. Arlequin se le tient pour dit, et s'en va tout de bon. Pantalon ouvre le panier, et, au lieu de perdrix, trouve une tête de bouc avec ses cornes. Il rappelle Arlequin : « Je crains, dit-il, de t'avoir donné quelques pièces fausses... Rends-les-moi toutes pour que je te les échange contre un bon ducat. » Arlequin, aussi crédule que rusé, rend toute la monnaie, après quoi Pantalon lui jette la tête de bouc dans les jambes, en lui disant de remporter « la tête de son père », et le menace de le bâtonner s'il reparaît devant lui.

« Dans sa boutique, l'apothicaire Pantalon joue à sa clientèle les plus vilains tours. Il vend pour de la noix muscade des noix de Mestre, pour de la poudre de girofle de la terre des paludes séchée au soleil, pour du baume de vipère de la décoction d'anguilles. Aussi ses valets Nane et Mantecha, qu'il laisse mourir de faim, lui dévorent ses drogues inoffensives, sous prétexte que tout fait ventre. Il discute avec ses ouvriers pour une minute de temps qu'ils lui doivent. Quand il est question de les payer, il n'a jamais le son, il ne peut même pas leur donner de quoi dîner. Enfin, quand ils en viennent aux menaces, il les autorise à aller demander, de sa part, quelque chose au cabaret, dans un petit mortier de fer grand comme le creux de la main, en leur recommandant bien de ne pas le casser. Il chasse son petit apprenti Mantecha à l'heure du dîner. Tolole, le père de Mantecha, vient lui demander grâce pour l'enfant; Pantalon consent à le reprendre, mais à condition qu'il ira dîner chez ses parents. »

Il n'oublie pas les tours qu'on lui a joués, car, à l'ouverture de son testament, on trouve : « Je lègue à mon valet vingt-cinq bons coups de fouet bien sanglés, pour avoir fait un trou au fond de mon *orinale* et m'avoir tout fait répandre dans mon lit. »

Mais Pantalon est quelquefois dans une haute et brillante position. Il est si noble et si riche alors, qu'il pourrait bien faire un doge. Il a des villas magnifiques, des millions dans ses coffres, c'est *don Pantalcone!!!* Il est alors vêtu de velours, de soie et de satin; mais il conserve la forme de ses habits à la mode à Venise, où il a paru dès le commen-

cement du seizième siècle. Il est le confident des princes, le
conseiller des doges, il est peut-être du tribunal des Dix.
C'est alors qu'il grasseye son érudition à tout propos, qu'il
éclaire de ses lumières et de ses conseils les plus hauts
marquis italiens. Il est appelé à trancher leurs différends;
mais, qu'il soit noble ou bourgeois, il embrouille si bien
les cartes qu'on finit par en venir aux épées, et que, réduit
à employer la force pour apaiser les querelles, il joue de
son poignard damasquiné à tort et à travers.

Il est curieux et intéressant de trouver la description du
Pantalon dans Shakespeare :

« Le sixième âge offre un maigre Pantalon, en pantoufles, avec des lunettes sur le nez et des poches sur le
côté; les chausses bien conservées de sa jeunesse se trouvent maintenant trop larges pour sa jambe amaigrie; sa
voix, jadis forte et mâle, aiguisée en fausset d'enfant, ne
fait plus que siffler aigrement d'un ton grêle : (*As you like it.*) »

Pantalon est toujours en grande vogue dans toute la
Vénétie, le Bolonais et la Toscane.

« Une chose surprenante, » dit M. Frédéric Mercey, « c'est
que notre siècle, qui a sinon tout détruit, du moins tout
changé, n'a pu arracher le masque d'aucun des quatre bouffons italiens. Ils ont bravé l'inconstance du public, la tyrannie
de la mode, les caprices des auteurs. Ils ont vu mourir cette
aristocratie vénitienne qui les méprisait; ils ont survécu
à la République, au conseil des Dix; Pantalon, Arlequin
et Brighella, les trois masques de Venise, ont enterré les
trois inquisiteurs d'État. Qui donc les a sauvés au milieu
de ces révolutions et de ces catastrophes? Leur popularité. »

Pantalon a été mis à toute sauce en Italie, surtout vers la fin du siècle dernier. il a eu toutes sortes de nuances de caractère, toutes sortes d'états, comme le Pulcinella napolitain. Il a été joué avec et sans son masque brun à moustaches grises, bien que la tradition l'exige avec le masque

Voici ce que Riccoboni dit du type de Pantalon au commencement du siècle dernier. « Pour le caractère du personnage de Pantalon, dans son principe, on en a fait un marchand, homme simple et de bonne foi, mais toujours amoureux, et qui est la dupe, ou d'un rival, d'un fils, d'un valet, ou d'une servante; quelquefois, et surtout depuis près d'un siècle, on en a fait un bon père de famille, un homme plein d'honneur, extrêmement délicat sur sa parole et très-sévère envers ses enfants. On lui a laissé toujours la qualité d'être dupe de tous ceux qui l'environnent, ou pour lui tirer de l'argent de sa poche, malgré son économie, ou pour le réduire, par adresse, à donner sa fille en mariage à son amant, malgré des engagements qu'il avait faits. Enfin, on s'est servi du personnage de Pantalon selon l'intention de la fable : lorsqu'il a fallu en faire un homme vertueux, il a été l'exemple des vieillards pour la sagesse; mais lorsque l'intention de la fable a porté le poète à en faire un homme faible, il a été le modèle d'un vieillard vicieux On a suivi en cela la méthode de Plaute, qui a fait les vieillards de ses comédies tantôt vertueux et tantôt vicieux, selon l'intention de la fable qu'il traitait Depuis cinquante ans, on s'est avisé, dans la ville de Venise, de corriger certaines mœurs du pays, et de les appliquer au

personnage de Pantalon Suivant cette idée, on en a fait
tantôt un mari, ou un amant très-jaloux, tantôt un débauché, tantôt un bravache et autres »

Le costume de Pantalon en 1716 avait un peu changé
de forme. Il ne portait plus son long caleçon à pieds,
mais une culotte courte et des bas; il avait conservé
les couleurs traditionnelles, mais il jouait souvent dans sa
longue *zimara*, qui avait été rouge d'abord, puis noire
ensuite C'est lorsque la république de Venise eut perdu le
royaume de Nègrepont que l'on prit le deuil dans tout
l'État Pantalon, en bon citoyen, ne voulut pas aller contre
les lois et usages de sa patrie; il adopta la simarre noire,
qu'il a toujours portée depuis (*planche 26*).

Cependant, de nos jours, Pantalon a quitté ses vêtements vénitiens, il s'est modernisé. Il porte la perruque
poudrée et s'habille comme Cassandre, c'est-à-dire comme
au temps de Louis XV.

En 1578, Giulio Pasquati, né à Padoue, fut engagé dans
la troupe des *Gelosi*, alors à Florence, pour jouer les rôles
de Pantalon et de MAGNIFICO

En 1580, ces rôles furent remplis dans la troupe des
Uniti par un acteur nommé Il Braga,

En 1650, dans la troupe des *Fedeli*, Luigi Benotti, né à
Vicence;

En 1645, Cialace Arrighi dans la troupe de Mazarin;

En 1655, au Petit-Bourbon, Turi, né à Modène, joua
jusqu'en 1670, année de sa mort.

     « Tous les acteurs de cette troupe,
      Qui maintenant ont vent en poupe,

Compris leur nouveau Pantalon,
Rouge, ma foi, jusqu'au talon,
Y font à l'envi des merveilles »

En 1670, la troupe n'ayant plus personne pour remplir ce rôle de Pantalon, Louis XIV fit demander un acteur au duc de Modène, lequel choisit Antonio Riccoboni (père de Louis Riccoboni (Lelio) qui vint en France en 1716). Mais Antonio refusa, préférant rester au service du duc de Modène.

C'est alors que les rôles changèrent de nom sur la scène italienne de Paris, et que cet emploi fut rempli par Romagnesi (Cinthio). Dans les canevas de Gherardi, il n'y a pas un seul Pantalon. Ce type devient *Géronte, Oronte, Gaufichon, Trafiquet, Persillet, Sonnet, Brocantin, Tortillon, Goguet, Grognard, Jacquemart, Boquillard, Prudent.*

Voici, dans Gherardi, une scène de Brocantin avec ses filles :

BROCANTIN. Quel ouvrage faites-vous là, vous ?

COLOMBINE. C'est une pente de lit pour moi. Mais je crains de la faire trop petite, on n'y pourra jamais coucher deux.

BROCANTIN Et quel besoin, s'il vous plaît, que vous couchiez avec quelqu'un ?

COLOMBINE. Non, mais si, par bonheur, je venais à être mariée....

BROCANTIN *en colère.* Si, par bonheur ou par malheur, vous veniez à être mariée, vous vous presseriez. Hé! je sais de vos fredaines Vous n'avez pas toujours une aiguille et de la tapisserie entre les mains, et vous vous escrimez de la plume! Mais ce n'est pas pour cela que nous sommes ici. Laissez votre ouvrage et m'écoutez. (*Ils prennent des siéges.*) Le mariage.... (*A Colombine.*) Oh! oh! vous riez déjà! tuchoux! il ne faut que vous hocher la bride ... Le mariage, dis-je, étant un usage aussi ancien que le monde, car on s'est marié avant vous et on se mariera encore après....

COLOMBINE. Je le sais bien, mon papa. Il y a longtemps qu'on m'a dit cela.

BROCANTIN. J'ai résolu, pour éterniser la famille Brocantine... Vous voyez où j'en veux venir? J'ai donc résolu de me marier.

ISABELLE et COLOMBINE *ensemble.* Ah! mon père!

BROCANTIN. Ah! mes filles! vous voilà bien ébaubies! Est-ce que je ne me porte pas encore assez bien? Regardez cet air, cette taille, cette légèreté! (*Il saute et fait un faux pas.*)

ISABELLE. Vous allez donc vous marier, mon père?

BROCANTIN. Oui, si vous le trouvez bon, ma fille.

COLOMBINE. A une femme?

BROCANTIN. Non, c'est à un tuyau d'orgue.... Voyez, je vous prie, la belle demande!

ISABELLE. Vous épousez une femme?

BROCANTIN. Mais je crois que vous avez toutes deux l'esprit en écharpe! Est-ce que je suis hors d'âge d'avoir lignée? Savez-vous bien qu'on n'a jamais que l'âge qu'on paraît! Et M. Visautrou, mon apothicaire, me disait encore ce matin, en me donnant un remède, que je ne paraissais pas quarante-cinq ans.

COLOMBINE Oh! mon papa, c'est qu'il ne vous voyait pas au visage!

BROCANTIN. J'ai ce que j'ai, mais je sens bien que j'ai besoin d'une femme. Je crève de santé, et j'ai trouvé une fille comme je la souhaite : belle, jeune, sage, riche. Enfin une fille de hasard.

ISABELLE. Une autre fille que moi, qui ne saurait pas vivre, vous dirait, mon père, que vous risquez beaucoup en vous mariant : mais moi, qui sais le respect que je vous dois, je vous dirai que, puisque vous crevez de santé, vous faites parfaitement bien de prendre une femme.

BROCANTIN. Oh! oh! vous prenez la chose du bon biais! Puisque vous êtes si raisonnable, apprenez donc que je suis en pourparlers de mariage; mais c'est pour vous

ISABELLE et COLOMBINE *ensemble*. Ah! mon père!

BROCANTIN. Ah! mes filles! » etc.

En 1705, Antonio Colalto, *le Vieux*, et sa femme vinrent à Paris jouer sur les théâtres forains.

En 1712, le Pantalon de la troupe foraine d'Octave se nommait Luigi Berlucci. Sa réputation fut éclipsée par celle de Giovanni Crevilli, qui, après avoir longtemps joué en Italie, vint sur nos théâtres forains et s'y fit remarquer sous le nom du *Pantalon vénitien*.

Alborghetti, né à Venise, avait déjà joué longtemps en Italie, sous le masque, l'emploi des pères, maris jaloux et tuteurs, toujours sous le nom de Pantalon, lorsqu'il vint en France avec la troupe du régent, en 1716. Il avait beaucoup de moyens et « joignait à ses talents pour le théâtre des mœurs irréprochables et beaucoup de vertu; mais son caractère un peu sévère lui faisait traiter quelquefois avec trop de dureté une épouse estimable. » Alborghetti mourut le 4 janvier 1751, âgé de cinquante-cinq ans.

En 1752, Fabio Sticotti prit cet emploi. Il était dans la troupe depuis 1716, et avait suivi sa femme Ursula Astori, chanteuse de la troupe. « Sticotti, gentilhomme du Frioul, sur les terres de la république de Venise, était bien fait de sa personne et n'était pas moins désiré dans la société par son extrême gaieté qu'accueilli au théâtre par son talent. Il eut pour enfants Antonio et Micaelo Sticotti, qui jouèrent à la Comédie-Italienne, et Agathe Sticotti, qui a paru quelquefois sur le théâtre, mais qui a été plus connue par ses qualités estimables et par l'attachement invincible d'un homme de mérite qui l'a épousée malgré les persécutions d'une famille irritée. » Fabio Sticotti mourut à l'âge de soixante-cinq ans, à Paris, le 5 décembre 1741.

Le 6 mai 1744, Carlo Véronèse, père de Coraline et de Camille, fut lui-même un bon acteur; mais sa réputation fut éclipsée par celle de ses filles, pour lesquelles il composa un grand nombre de pièces, il remplit jusqu'à sa mort (1759) l'emploi des Pantalons.

Colalto débuta en 1759, mais il ne fut reçu que l'année suivante. Grimm parle ainsi de son talent :

« Le 7 décembre 1774, les comédiens italiens ont donné la première représentation des *Trois Frères jumeaux vénitiens*, pièce italienne et en prose, du sieur Colalto (*Pantalon*).

» Cette pièce a eu un succès prodigieux et très-mérité. L'idée en est prise du conte des *Trois Bossus*.. La ressemblance qu'elle peut avoir avec *les Ménechmes* de Goldoni n'ôte rien au mérite de l'auteur, qui a surpassé ses modèles;

mais le point sur lequel on ne saurait lui donner trop d'éloges est la perfection incroyable avec laquelle il joue lui-même les trois rôles des trois frères Zanetto. Le changement de sa figure, de sa voix, de son caractère, qu'il varie de scène en scène, suivant que chacun des trois personnages l'exige, est une chose incompréhensible et ne laisse rien à désirer. Cette pièce, qui n'est point écrite, qui n'est qu'un canevas, est parfaitement jouée par presque tous les acteurs, mais surtout par le sieur Colalto, par la dame Bacelli, qui fait le rôle d'Éléonore, et par le sieur Marignan, qui joue le Commissaire avec une vérité et un comique bien au-dessus de Préville. Ils ont, de plus, l'avantage de varier leur jeu et leurs discours à chaque représentation, et l'ivresse soutenue du public pour cette pièce entretient encore la verve des acteurs. »

Colalto mourut en septembre 1777. « Son caractère personnel était d'une modestie et d'une simplicité peu communes à son état. Il ne connaissait d'autre bonheur que celui de vivre paisiblement au sein de sa famille, et de faire du bien aux malheureux que le hasard offrait à sa générosité. Il est mort d'une maladie fort longue et fort douloureuse. Ses enfants, qui n'ont point quitté son chevet, l'ont vu s'éteindre dans leurs bras. Il a senti tous leurs soins, et ses derniers mots ont été l'expression de sa reconnaissance. Ses yeux s'étaient arrêtés sur l'estampe du *Paralytique servi par ses enfants*. On lit ces vers au bas de la gravure :

Si la vérité d'une image
Est la vérité de l'objet,

Que le sage artiste a bien fait
De mettre la scène au village !

« Mes enfants, leur dit le mourant d'une voix faible, l'auteur de ces vers ne vous connaissait pas. »

En Italie (vers 1750) Darbes fut remarqué comme bon *Pantalon*. Darbes était directeur d'une troupe italienne. Il alla un jour trouver Goldoni pour avoir une pièce de sa façon, il obtint, non sans peine, la comédie *Tonin, Bella grazia*. Il jouait le rôle de Pantalon, et, comme le caractère de ce père était sérieux, Darbes jugea à propos de jouer sans masque. La pièce de Goldoni tomba à plat. D'où venait cela ? Était-ce la faute de la pièce ou de l'acteur ? Goldoni en fit une autre pour Darbes, qui reprit le masque traditionnel. La pièce réussit au delà des espérances de l'auteur et du chef de troupe. Darbes ne quitta plus jamais le masque, et défia, ayant Goldoni pour auteur, tous les Pantalons de l'Italie · Francesco Rubini à Saint-Luc et Corrini à San-Samuel de Venise, Ferramonti à Bologne, Pasini à Milan, Luigi Benotti à Florence, Golmetti et Garelli, Giuseppe Franceschini, etc.

LE DOCTEUR.

Tel qu'il est encore aujourd'hui, LE DOCTEUR, bien qu'un peu passé de mode en Italie, fut apporté sur la scène, en 1560, par Lucio. C'est tantôt un savant, un homme de loi, quelquefois grand jurisconsulte, rarement un médecin. Le docteur GRAZIANO ou BALOARDO GRAZIAN, est originaire de Bologne. Il est membre de l'Académie *della Crusca*, philosophe, astronome, grammairien, rhétoricien, cabaliste, diplomate. Il parle de tout, décide de tout, mais, bien qu'il ait étudié fort longtemps, il ne sait absolument rien, ce qui ne l'empêche pas de citer, hors de propos, « des textes latins qu'il estropie », dit M. F. Mercey, « ou des traits de fable qu'il dénature, changeant Cyparisse en fontaine, Biblis en cyprès; faisant trancher par les trois Grâces le fil de nos destinées et présider les Parques à la toilette de Vénus, et cela avec un aplomb sans pareil et toute l'intrépidité de la sottise ».

S'il est avocat, il ne voit clair que dans les affaires dont il n'est pas chargé, et ses plaidoyers sont si intéressants que le tribunal s'endort et que le public se sauve, ce qui le force, à son grand regret, d'abréger un peu ses discours. Il est souvent père de famille : alors sa fille, Colombine ou Isabelle, marquée contre son avarice qui l'a fait surnommer le Docteur *Rince-Pot*. Il fait souvent ce qu'il peut pour plaire aux dames, même il est parfois soupirant, malgré ses années et malgré son ventre, qui devrait lui donner à réfléchir. Lourd et ridicule dans ses manières comme dans son langage, il est mystifié par ses valets, à moins, chose difficile, qu'ils ne soient plus bêtes que lui. Veut-il être plaisant, ses plaisanteries tournent à la méchanceté : c'est alors *pain bénit* que de le tourmenter et berner.

De 1560 au milieu du dix-septième siècle, le Docteur, toujours vêtu de noir de la tête aux pieds, portait la robe des gens de science, des professeurs et des avocats du seizième siècle; par-dessus cette longue robe il en portait une plus

courte, ne venant qu'au genou, et les chausses noires. Ce
ne fut que dans la troupe italienne venue à Paris en 1653
qu'Augustin Lolli prit la culotte courte, la grande fraise à
molle, tailla son pourpoint de dessous en veste à la
Louis XIV et se coiffa du feutre à bords extravagants pour
remplacer la toque, qui avait trop d'analogie avec celle
des valets (planche 27)

    « La ville de Bologne, en Italie, qui est le centre des
» sciences et des belles-lettres, et où il y a une université si
» fameuse et tant de collèges des nations étrangères, nous
» a toujours fourni un grand nombre de savants, et surtout
» de docteurs, qui avaient les chaires publiques de cette
» université. Ces docteurs avaient une robe qu'ils portaient
» dans l'école et par la ville, l'on pensa très-sagement de
» faire d'un docteur bolonais l'autre vieillard qui put figu-
» rer auprès du Pantalon, et ces deux habits deviennent
» très-comiques l'un à côté de l'autre.... Le Docteur est un
» babillard éternel et qui ne saurait ouvrir la bouche sans
» cracher une sentence ou une citation latine. Il ne serait
» pas impossible qu'on eût copié ce caractère d'après
» nature. Nous voyons encore aujourd'hui des pédants et
» des médecins en faire de même. Il y a eu des comédiens
» qui ont pensé différemment sur le caractère du Docteur.
» Les uns ont entrepris de bien parler et de déclamer des
» tirades qui exposaient au public tout le savoir et toute
» l'érudition possible, et cela orné des citations latines des
» auteurs les plus graves D'autres ont tourné ce caractère
» plus au comique: au lieu de faire un Docteur savant, ils
» en ont fait un ignorant, qui parlait le latin macaronique

» de Merlin Coccaie, ou dans ce goût-là. Les premiers
» étaient engagés par force à savoir quelque chose, pour
» ne pas lâcher des solécismes de bonne foi. Les autres
» avaient la même obligation de savoir; mais il leur fal-
» lait du génie, car je suis persuadé qu'il faut avoir plus
» d'esprit pour mal appliquer une sentence, que pour la
» débiter dans son vrai sens. » (L. Riccoboni.)

Le masque noir qui ne couvre que le front et le nez du
Docteur, ses joues aux couleurs exagérées, sont une personnalité contre un jurisconsulte de Bologne du seizième
siècle, qui avait une large tache de vin sur toute une partie
du visage

Le docteur BALANZONI *Lombarda* (surnom qui fut appliqué à ce personnage parce que Bernardino Lombardi et
Roderigo Lombardi jouèrent ce rôle en Italie, le premier
au seizième siècle, le second au siècle dernier), porte, comme
Basile, un grand chapeau relevé des deux côtés. Il est de
Bologne comme le précédent. Il a beaucoup d'analogie
avec lui, ou plutôt c'est le même personnage dans une
autre position sociale. Il est alors particulièrement médecin, ce qui ne l'empêche pas de pratiquer l'alchimie et les
sciences occultes. Il est avare, égoïste et très-faible pour
résister à ses appétits sensuels et grossiers. Va-t-il voir un
malade, il cause de toute autre chose que de la maladie,
s'intéresse à mille riens, touche à tout, casse les vases, tâte
le pouls du malade par acquit de conscience, en parlant du
minois chiffonné de Colombine ou de la taille de Violette.
Le moribond finit par s'endormir de lassitude aux exploits
amoureux que bredouille cet ignorant Docteur au nez

rubicond, aux joues bourgeonnées et à l'œil brillant. Le malade endormi, il cherche à lutiner la servante ou à faire le damoiseau auprès de la fille ou de la maîtresse de la maison. Il n'y a pas d'exemple qu'il ait jamais guéri qui que ce fût, excepté Polichinelle, qui ne peut pas mourir, et qui avait fait semblant d'être malade, un jour, pour l'attirer chez lui, et lui donner une verte correction à propos d'une petite rivalité d'amour ou de gourmandise, on n'a jamais bien su laquelle.

Ce type de médecin ridicule a été, de tout temps, l'objet de la satire. Ainsi, à Athènes, déjà bien avant Aristophane, les bateleurs doriens, comme nous l'avons dit dans l'Introduction, attiraient la foule en jouant des farces sur leurs tréteaux, et c'était souvent un personnage de médecin qui amusait le plus, par son baragouin, ses embrouilla-minis, ses périodes interminables, interrompues par quelques bons coups de pied de la part d'un autre mime.

> Du fameux docteur Balouarde
> Le nez souffle mainte nazarde
>
> . . . . .
>
> Quand le docteur parle, l'on doute
> Si c'est latin ou bas-breton,
> Et souvent celui qui l'écoute
> L'interrompt à coups de bâton.

Dans *Arlequin empereur dans la lune* (1684) :

Nous sommes dans un jardin, auprès d'un télescope immense qui sert au Docteur pour consulter les astres. Le Docteur quitte son instrument, et, parlant un langage mi-parti qui lui est propre, il dit à Pierrot : « *E possibile, Pierò, che tu non vogha chetarti ?* Tais-toi, je t'en prie !

Pierrot. Mais, monsieur, comment voulez-vous que je me taise? Je n'ai pas un moment de repos! Tant que la journée dure, il faut que je travaille après votre fille, votre nièce et votre servante, et à peine la nuit est-elle venue qu'il faut que je travaille après vous! Dès que je suis couché, vous commencez d'abord votre carillon « Pierrot! Pierrot! lève-toi vite, allume la chandelle, et me donne ma lunette à longue vue je veux aller observer les astres! » Et vous voulez me faire accroire que la lune est un monde comme le nôtre! La lune! par la jernibieu! j'enrage!

Le Docteur. Pierrot, *ancor una volta, taci, ti bastonaro!*

Pierrot. Parbleu, monsieur, quand vous devriez me tuer, il faut que je débagoule mon cœur! Je ne serai pas assez sot pour convenir que la lune soit un monde; la lune, la lune, morbleu! qui n'est pas plus grande qu'une *œumelette* de huit œufs!

Le Docteur *Che impertinente!* Si tu avais tant soit peu d'entendement, j'entrerais en raison avec toi: *Ma tu sei una bestia, un ignorante animale che non sa dove s'habbia la testa se non se la tocca; e però chiudi la bocca!* Tais-toi, encore une fois, tu feras mieux.... As-tu remarqué ces certains nuages qu'on voit autour de la lune? ces nuages s'appellent des crépuscules Or voici comme j'argumente....

Pierrot. Voyons?

Le Docteur. Donc, s'il y a des crépuscules dans la lune, il faut qu'il y ait *una* génération et *una* corruption, s'il y a corruption et génération, il faut qu'il y ait des *animali* et des *vegetabili*, *ergo*, *la luna è un mondo abitabile com' il nostro*

PIERROT. *Ergò*, tant qu'il vous plaira ! Pour ce qui est de moi, *nego*, et voici comment je vous le prouve. Vous dites qu'il y a dans la lune les tres... cus... tres... pus... les trois pousse-culs.

LE DOCTEUR *Crepuscoli*, et non pas pousse-culs, bête !

PIERROT. Enfin les trois... vous m'entendez bien, et que, s'il y a les trois puscuscules, il faut qu'il y ait une génération et une corruption ?

LE DOCTEUR. *Certissimo*.

PIERROT. Or voici ce que dit Pierrot...

LE DOCTEUR. *Vedemo ?*

PIERROT S'il y a une génération et une corruption dans la lune, il faut qu'il y naisse des vers · or serait-il que la lune serait véreuse ? Qu'en dites-vous ? Il n'y a, mordi, point de réplique à cela !

LE DOCTEUR *riant*. Oh non assurément ! Et dis-moi, Pierrot, *in questo nostro mondo*, y nait-il des vers ?

PIERROT. Oui, monsieur.

LE DOCTEUR. S'ensuit-il pour cela que notre monde soit véreux ?

PIERROT. Il y a quelque raison à cela. »

Après l'entretien sur la lune, le Docteur fait part à Pierrot de ses projets de mariage pour sa fille, Arlequin survient et embrouille la cervelle de Pierrot, qui répond au Docteur sur ce qu'Arlequin lui demande. Le Docteur, impatienté des impertinences de son domestique, lui allonge un soufflet à lui casser les dents; Pierrot tombe, se relève et sort en disant : « C'est un effet de la lune ! »

Dans la troupe dite des *gelosi*, qui vint en France

en 1572, le rôle du Docteur Graziano était rempli par Lucio Burchiella, acteur plein de verve et d'esprit, qui fut remplacé, en 1578, par Lodovico, de Bologne.

En 1572, Bernardino Lombardi vint en France, dans la troupe des *confidenti*. Il avait l'emploi des Docteurs. Aussi bon poète qu'acteur distingué, il publia à Ferrare, en 1583, une comédie en cinq actes, plusieurs fois réimprimée, *l'Alchimista*. On y retrouve, comme dans les pièces de ce temps-là, divers dialectes italiens, entre autres, le vénitien et le bolonais.

Le Docteur GRATIAN BALOARDO était joué dans la troupe de 1655 par Angelo-Augustino Lolli, de Bologne. De Tralage parle avec éloge de ses mœurs. Ses camarades l'appelaient *l'Ange*, sans doute à cause de son nom d'Angelo. Il épousa mademoiselle Adami, qui jouait les soubrettes dans la même troupe. Il mourut, fort âgé, le 29 août 1694.

Loret parle d'une querelle qui aurait eu lieu entre Turi (*Pantalon*) et Ange Lolli (*le Docteur*), et qui se serait terminée par un duel :

> Baloardo comédien,
> Lequel, encor qu'Italien,
> N'est qu'un auteur mélancolique,
> L'autre jour, en place publique,
> Vivement attaquer osa
> Le Pantalon Bisognoza,
> Qui pour repousser l'incartade
> Mit soudain la main à l'espade,
> Et se chatouillèrent longtemps
> Devant quantité d'assistants,
> Qui, croyant leur combat tragique
> N'être que fiction comique,

Laissèrent leurs grands coups tirer
Sans nullement les separer
Si le conte ou l'histoire n'erre,
Baloarde, tombant par terre,
S'ecria « Dieux ! quelle pitié !
» Les Français ont peu d'amitié !
» Ayant commencé de combattre,
» Nous pensions qu'on nous tint à quatre,
» Sans cet espoir, nous n'eussions pas
» Pour nous battre fait un seul pas. »

En 1694. Marc-Antonio Romagnesi (Cinthio), ayant pris dans la troupe les rôles de Pères, joua aussi parfois les *Docteurs* sous des noms francisés, comme celui de *Bassinet*.

En 1690. Giovanni Paghetti et Galeozzo Savorini remplissaient les rôles de Docteurs en Italie. Paghetti vint en France jouer sur les théâtres forains.

En 1716. Dans la troupe du Régent, Francesco Matterazzi, mort en 1758, à l'âge de quatre-vingt-six ans. A la même époque, Ganzachi et Luzi, de Venise, allèrent jouer les Docteurs dans la troupe improvisatrice allemande de Vienne.

En 1752, Bonaventure Benozzi, frère de la célèbre Silvia, prend l'emploi des Docteurs; Pietro Antonio Veronese, fils de Carlo Veronese (*Pantalon*), le 17 juillet 1754. Savi, le 15 octobre 1760 jusqu'en 1767.

IL BISCEGLIESE.

Les Napolitains ont sur leur théâtre un type qui ressemble beaucoup, comme caractère et comme costume,

aux vieillards de l'ancienne comédie italienne en France,
tels que Pandolfo, Geronzio, lesquels portaient le même
habillement que les vieillards du théâtre de Molière. C'est
PANGRAZIO IL BISCEGLIESI (*planche* 28), ainsi nommé parce
qu'il est originaire de Biscegla.

« Il faut savoir, dit M. Paul de Musset, que Bisceglia est
une petite ville de la Pouille où l'on parle un patois qui
jouit du privilége de mettre en joie les Napolitains, du plus
loin qu'ils en reconnaissent l'accent. De temps immémo-
rial, le personnage de don Pancrace, au théâtre de San-
Carlino, est rempli par des Biscéhais, ou par des Napolitains qui savent imiter à merveille le parler de la Pouille.
Leur succès de ridicule ne tient pas moins à l'accent qu'au
talent des artistes, qui du reste sont des comédiens incom-
parables. Le public rit de confiance dès que Pancrace paraît. L'affiche ne manque jamais d'ajouter au titre de la
pièce ces mots d'un attrait particulier pour la foule : *Con
Pangrazio bisceghese* (avec Pancrace biscéhais). L'effet produit sur nos théâtres par les jargons de paysans n'approche
point du fou rire qu'excite ce Pancrace; il faudrait remonter au temps de Gros-Guillaume et du gentilhomme gascon
pour trouver un équivalent de ce personnage à caractère,
qui soutient encore, avec l'illustre Polichinelle, la comédie
nationale *dell' arte*, tradition précieuse et charmante dont
le bouge de San-Carlino est le dernier asile. Ce goût populaire est pourtant cause d'une injustice amère et cruelle, un
Biscéhais ne peut plus se montrer à Naples sans que tout
le monde pouffe de rire aussitôt qu'il ouvre la bouche; la
tyrannie de l'habitude et du préjugé le condamne au métier

de bouffon, car il ne lui servirait à rien de se fâcher, on ne
s'amuserait pas pour si peu à la bagatelle du point d'honneur, et les rieurs ne feraient que s'égayer davantage d'un
accès de colère biscéhaise »

Le mérite de *Pangrazio Biscegliese* consiste dans l'intona-
tion pleurarde du dialecte particulier de sa localité et dans
l'exhibition des ridicules habituels qu'apportent les bourgeois de province dans les capitales. La vie des grandes
villes, le luxe, les usages, les mœurs un peu relàchées, lui
font pousser à chaque pas des exclamations de surprise qui
dérangent ses idées bornées. « Cela ne se fait point ainsi
chez nous, » dit-il à chaque instant, ou bien encore .
« Chez nous, il ne se fait pas tant de bruit, il n'y a pas
tant de gens qui vous coudoient comme ici, mais au moins
tout le monde vous connaît. Ce n'est déjà pas si beau, votre
Naples! Si vous aviez vu Biscegha, bâtie sur un rocher, à
la bonne heure! voilà un joli pays, couvert de riches villas
et renommé pour ses vins et ses raisins secs, vous n'en
pouvez dire autant. Et puis, à Biscegha, vous ne voyez pas
tant d'immondices et d'ordures que par toute votre ville de
Naples. Enfin, si je pouvais avoir fini mes affaires, je ne
serais pas longtemps sans m'en aller loin de votre tumulte,
de vos puces, de vos lazzaroni et de vos filles perdues. » Le
Biscegliese a parfois grandement raison, mais on lui passe
ses critiques, qui, sous l'égide de ses nombreux ridicules
et de son comique langage, passent encore pour être
bêtise de sa part.

Comme Pantalon, il représente encore plusieurs types
provinciaux, marchands, bourgeois, vieux paysans; mais

le fond de son caractère est toujours tant soit peu avare,
crédule et facile à tromper.

Il est vêtu d'un pourpoint et d'une culotte à la mode
ancienne, en velours noir. Les manches de son habit et sa
calotte sont de drap rouge; ses bas, de coton rouge.

Aujourd'hui, le Biscehais, que les Napolitains appellent
aussi *Pangrazio Cucuzziello* (Pancrace le Cornichon), a
changé de costume, comme la plupart des autres masques
italiens. Il porte une perruque rousse ornée d'une queue *en
salsifis*, un gilet à la Louis XV, broché et brodé, ressemblant à un morceau de tapisserie; la veste et la culotte
noires, les bas rouges et les souliers à boucles.

Le Jettatore, avec Pancrace biscelhais. Tel est le titre d'une
pièce dans laquelle M. Paul de Musset nous montre Bisceghese agissant sur la scène de San-Carlino, à Naples.

« On avait frappé les trois coups. Le petit orchestre
jouait l'ouverture. Enfin la toile se leva, et l'on vit arriver
don Pancrace affublé de tous les préservatifs des mauvais
sorts : les cornes de bœuf, les mains de corail, le rat en
lave du Vésuve, le cœur, les fourches et le serpent. Un
éclat de rire l'accueillit à son entrée, selon l'usage, et puis
il s'avança d'un air piteux au bord de la rampe, pour confier au public ses frayeurs superstitieuses.

« Messieurs, dit-il, si j'ai oublié quelque chose, aver-
tissez-m'en, par charité. Ces grosses cornes que je porte
sous chaque bras préservent mon front d'un pareil ornement. Ce n'est pas ce qui me tourmente le plus; dame
Pancrace est incapable de me manquer de fidélité. En tour-
nant cette main de corail, dont l'index et le petit doigt sont

ouverts du côté des gens de mine suspecte, j'éviterai les
influences pernicieuses .. Mon attirail est complet, et l'on
m'a dit qu'à présent je pouvais me hasarder dans la rue
de Tolède Je vois avec satisfaction qu'on est en sûreté à
Naples... un homme prudent ne court aucun risque dans
cette capitale; cependant je ne suis pas sans inquiétude. J'ai
fait un mauvais rêve, et j'ai grande envie de retourner à
Bisceglia. »

« Sur ce, don Pancrace raconte son rêve, d'où il tire
toutes sortes de pronostics.... En effet, tous les incidents
possibles viennent fondre en un jour sur le pauvre Pancrace. Tandis qu'il s'embrouille dans ses amulettes, un
filou lui vole son mouchoir, un autre sa tabatière, un troisieme sa montre. Polichinelle se déguise en huissier pour
lui signifier un faux exploit. Une fille délurée feint de le
prendre pour son amant que des Corsaires avaient emmené
en Barbarie; elle l'embrasse et l'obsède de ses caresses.
Pancrace veut s'enfuir, un fiacre le renverse dans la boue.
Il se relève furieux, maugréant contre les embarras, les
filous et les filles délurées de Naples, lorsque deux jeunes
gens charmants, en gilet jaune, avec breloques, chaînes
d'or et lorgnons, l'abordent poliment et l'aident à se nettoyer.... Une si heureuse rencontre enchante le Biscéliais,
qui s'extasie sur les belles manières et la politesse des élégants de Naples.... Ils frappent sur les tables du traiteur
avec leurs badines, et commandent au garçon de servir au
seigneur Pancrace ce qu'il y a de meilleur et de plus cher :
du riz aux petits pois, des côtelettes frites à la milanaise,
des œufs à la coque, des raves, de la salade de concom-

bres. Pancrace préfère à tout cela le macaroni classique;
on lui en sert un *rotolo*, qu'il absorbe en le dévidant avec
ses doigts. Pendant ce temps-là, les deux élégants déjeu-
nent et vident les plats raffinés, dont le Biscéhais n'a pas
voulu, puis ils échangent un signe d'intelligence, se lèvent,
prennent leurs chapeaux, se confondent en salutations et
s'éloignent ... Le vieillard ne peut croire qu'il soit encore
dupe de sa crédulité. Avec les conjectures bizarres qu'il
imagine sur l'absence des jeunes *don Limone*, il divertit le
public, et finit par payer la carte, non sans marchander. »

CASSANDRE.

Une vieille perruque jaunâtre, dont on voit la trame,
surmontée d'un bonnet de nuit au ruban gras, sur un chef
chauve, dont elle cache à peine les oreilles rouges; deux
sourcils velus et grisons ombrageant de petits yeux vairons,
au regard soupçonneux et méfiant; une trogne rubiconde
barbouillée de tabac, des lèvres charnues, grossières, s'ou-
vrant bêtement quand il écoute ou regarde ce qui se passe
autour de lui; le cou gros et court, dénotant un tempérament sanguin, irascible, l'abdomen proéminent, retenu
dans un gilet jadis brodé et dans une vieille culotte de reps.
le tout enveloppé dans une prétendue robe de chambre,
sale guenille jaune qui fut de la peluche il y a cinquante
ans, de grosses jambes, chaussées de bas drapés, terminées
par des pieds d'une largeur et d'une longueur malséantes,
enfouis dans des souliers qui rappellent les bateaux de

charbon; une démarche lourde, un grognement continuel
voilà Cassandre à son petit lever.

Personne n'est encore debout dans la maison, il faut à
peine jour, et Cassandre se plaint déjà de la paresse de son
valet et de ses filles. Tant mieux, après tout! il aura le
temps de regarder son argent. Ayant pris dans sa large
tabatière, qui crie comme un rouage mal graissé, une dis-
crète prise de tabac, il ouvre prudemment une cachette
connue de lui seul; mais une mouche a volé, et Cassandre
a refermé prudemment l'ouverture de son trésor. Puis,
c'est son valet, Pierrot, qui dort tout debout, qui ne voit
rien, et qui, en bâillant, s'en va donner de la tête dans son
maître, en écrasant les cors et durillons que protégent mal
ses grands souliers. Un splendide coup de pied administré
à Pierrot, qui riposte au hasard par un large soufflet tombant toujours à point sur la face de Cassandre, c'est l'affaire
d'un instant.

Pierrot reconnaît son erreur et se repent de sa précipi-
tation. Il demande grâce à son bon maître, et tout est
oublié. « Il est déjà tard, dit Cassandre, il faut que je sorte;
apporte-moi mes affaires, et surtout mes lunettes, que j'ai
oubliées chez moi. Va vite! » Cassandre n'est plus seul, il
doit paraître sourd et myope devant les autres. Finesse fort
vieille, mais qui réussit toujours.

Tout en recommandant à son valet de ne rien faire pour
déjeuner et d'enfermer sa fille à double tour, il se revêt de
son bel habit (*planche* 29). Il prend son chapeau gansé,
sa canne à pomme d'ivoire, ses gants verts, sa montre colossale, qu'il a raccommodée lui-même pour éviter des frais

inutiles; montre dont le mouvement fait un tel tic-toc, que, lorsqu'il passe sur la chaussée, les voisins désœuvrés, attirés par le bruit, se mettent sur le pas de leurs boutiques et se disent : « Voilà M. Cassandre qui passe! — Où va-t-il? — Chez sa maîtresse, » disent des plaisants. Qu'importe? A le voir venir du bout de la rue, malgré sa toilette de soupirant, vous lui feriez bien l'aumône, et, qui pis est, il l'accepterait. C'est cependant l'homme le plus riche de sa paroisse, mais le plus avare aussi. Il n'y a rien qu'il ne fasse pour de l'argent. Il donnerait sa fille à Polichinelle!!! Il le trouve cependant un peu débauché. Il préfère Léandre, l'hidalgo, le riche, le bellâtre. C'est chez lui, son futur gendre, qu'il va déjeuner pour épargner, dit-il, la peine de ses valets. « Et puis, nous causerons mieux de nos petites affaires à table. »

Pendant ce temps, que se passe-t-il chez lui? Sa fille Colombine a usé de ses charmes pour corrompre Pierrot; elle y a ajouté un pâté de venaison et une bouteille de vieux vin, qui ont endormi tous les scrupules de son geôlier, et elle se livre à la joie et à la danse avec son amoureux Arlequin.

Il est rare que Cassandre ne revienne pas, en ce moment, accompagné de son amphitryon, qui marche en coq et qui apporte des présents à la séduisante Colombine. Alors, les amoureux s'envolent. Colombine va être sacrifiée; mais Arlequin, protégé par une fée dont il a sauvé le talisman, tient tête au bonhomme Cassandre et lutte de richesses avec Léandre. Cassandre n'hésite pas. C'est le plus riche qui aura sa fille, sa pouponne, le fruit de ses entrailles, et, comme

les trésors des fées sont incalculables, Léandre éconduit se
retire furieux, en reprochant au vieillard son manque de
foi. Cassandre hausse les épaules, rit sous cape et bénit les
amants

Le personnage de Cassandre fut créé vers 1580, dans la
troupe des *Gelosi*, sous le nom de CASSANDRO *da Sienna*. Il y
remplissait les rôles de père sérieux, tandis que *Pantalon*,
dans les mêmes intrigues très-compliquées, faisait, avec le
Docteur, les personnages ridicules, les maris jaloux, battus
et contents. Le *Zanobio* jouait aussi en même temps, mais
avec des nuances encore différentes. Ce personnage de
Cassandre disparut des canevas italiens pendant plus d'un
siècle, car ce ne fut qu'en 1752 que Périer prit ce nom pour
jouer les pères ridicules sur les théâtres forains. Desjardins,
en 1756, et Garnier, en 1759, l'imitèrent. Sur la scène
italienne française, Robert des Brosses, né à Bonn, en
Allemagne, entra d'abord en qualité de musicien dans
l'orchestre « Il débuta, en 1744, dans les rôles de pères
dans le comique français. Cet acteur, estimable par ses
mœurs et par ses talents, y joint celui de compositeur pour
la musique. Il a fait celle d'un grand nombre de ballets et
d'opéras-comiques. »

En 1780, Rozière joua les mêmes rôles sur le Théâtre-
Italien. Mais le plus célèbre de tous les Cassandres fut Chapelle, dont la crédulité et la naïveté étaient proverbiales au
théâtre. « Chapelle était gros et court, ses yeux, qui s'ou-
vraient et se fermaient continuellement, étaient couronnés
d'un épais sourcil noir, sa bouche, toujours entr'ouverte,
lui donnait un air stupide, ses jambes ressemblaient à des

pieds d'éléphant. Si vous ajoutez à cela une tournure pesante, vous aurez une idée de Chapelle. On aurait pu croire en le voyant que la nature, après l'avoir formé, lui avait dit : Je voulais te faire homme, je t'ai fait Cassandre; pardon, Chapelle. »

C'est à Chapelle que Seveste père racontait qu'en revenant d'une tournée qu'il avait faite en Normandie, pendant son séjour à Rouen, il avait apprivoisé une carpe qui le suivait partout comme un chien, mais qu'il venait malheureusement de la perdre, ce qui le chagrinait beaucoup « Et comment avez-vous perdu cette carpe? lui demanda Chapelle. — Mon Dieu! dit Seveste, j'ai eu l'imprudence de l'amener un soir au théâtre, dans ma loge, il survint un orage épouvantable après le spectacle. Ma carpe m'avait très-bien suivi jusque dans la rue, mais sur la place de la Comédie, la pauvre bête se noya en voulant sauter un ruisseau — Quel malheur! s'écria Chapelle, je croyais que les carpes nageaient comme les poissons. »

On lui avait fait croire tant de choses, que, dans les dernières années de sa vie, il était devenu méfiant et sceptique au point que lorsqu'un garçon de théâtre lui disait : « Vous répétez demain, » il répondait : « Va te promener, je ne donne plus là dedans! » Quand on lui demandait comment il se portait, il vous tournait le dos en disant. « Ça n'est pas vrai! » Chapelle, qui cumulait la profession d'épicier avec celle d'acteur, se retira en 1816 chez un oncle, chanoine à Versailles, et mourut à Chartres en janvier 1824.

CASSANDRINO.

Les Romains ont un type appelé Cassandrino, qui est le
même que leur Pasquin. C'est un bon bourgeois de Rome,
déjà mûr, cinquante ans à peu près, mais encore jeune de
manières. leste, bien poudré, bien frisé, tiré à quatre épin-
gles, ayant toujours du linge irréprochable, des bas blancs
sans une maculature, des souliers à boucles d'argent, bien
cirés. Coiffé d'un léger tricorne, il porte habit et culotte de
fin drap rouge, qui font ressortir un gilet de satin blanc
pailleté aux amples basques. Son caractère est charmant,
ne se mettant jamais en colère quoi qu'il arrive, faisant la
sourde oreille aux quolibets et aux plaisanteries qui le con-
cernent. Courtois, bien élevé, très-fin, très-spirituel, il n'est
pas difficile de voir dans ce type une personnification des
beaux *monsignori*, comme le fait remarquer Beyle. « Hier,
vers les neuf heures, dit l'auteur de la *Chartreuse de
Parme*, je sortais de ces salles magnifiques, voisines d'un
jardin rempli d'orangers, qu'on appelle le *café Rospoli*.
Vis-à-vis se trouve le palais *Fiano*. Un homme, à la porte
d'une espèce de cave, disait : « *Entrate, o signori!* Entrez,
Messieurs, voilà que ça va commencer! » J'entrai, en effet,
dans ce petit théâtre pour la somme de 28 centimes. Ce
prix me fit redouter la mauvaise compagnie et les puces.
Je fus bientôt rassuré; j'avais pour voisins de bons bourgeois de Rome .. Le peuple romain est peut-être celui de
l'Europe qui aime et saisit le mieux la satire fine et mordante.... La censure théâtrale est plus méticuleuse que celle

de Paris, aussi rien de plus plat que les comédies. Le rire
s'est réfugié aux marionnettes, qui jouent des pièces à peu
près improvisées... J'ai passé au palais Fiano une soirée
fort agréable; le théâtre, sur lequel les acteurs promènent
leur petite personne, peut avoir dix pieds de large et quatre
de hauteur . Les décorations sont excellentes et soigneusement calculées pour des acteurs de douze pouces de haut .
Le personnage à la mode parmi le peuple romain est Cassandrino.., vieillard coquet de quelque cinquante-cinq à
soixante ans, leste, ingambe, à cheveux blancs, bien
poudré, bien soigné, à peu près comme un cardinal De
plus, Cassandrino est rompu aux affaires et brille par
l'usage du monde le plus parfait, ce serait, en vérité, un
homme accompli, s'il n'avait le malheur de tomber régulièrement amoureux de toutes les femmes qu'il rencontre....
Vous conviendrez qu'un pareil personnage n'est pas mal
inventé pour un pays gouverné par une cour oligarchique,
composée de *célibataires,* et où le pouvoir est aux mains de
la vieillesse. .. Il va sans dire qu'il est séculier, mais je
parierais que, dans toute la salle, il n y a pas un spectateur
qui ne lui voie la calotte rouge d'un cardinal, ou tout au
moins les bas violets d'un *monsignore.* Les *monsignori* sont,
comme on sait, les jeunes gens de la cour du pape, les
auditeurs de ce pays, c'est la place qui mène à toutes les
autres .. Rome est remplie de *monsignori* de l'âge de Cassandrino, qui n'ont pas fait fortune, et qui cherchent des
consolations en attendant le chapeau. »

M Frédéric Mercey nous donne dans son *Théâtre en Italie*
plusieurs rendus-comptes des pièces qui se jouaient sur le

théâtre Fiano · *le Voyage à Civita-Vecchia*, *Cassandrino dilet-
tante*, *impresario*, etc.

En 1840, ce théâtre était dirigé et manœuvré par un
joaillier du Corso, homonyme par hasard du héros de ses
improvisations, M. Cassandre, maintenant mort depuis
plusieurs années Cassandrino existe toujours à Rome
comme principal personnage de la baraque portative de
Gaetanaccio.

FACANAPPA.

La malice et la fantaisie vénitiennes semblent être per-
sonnifiées aujourd'hui dans le masque Facanappa, premier
sujet des troupes de marionnettes. Son succès à Venise est
égal à celui du Bisceghese à Naples. Les affiches indiquent
toujours qu'il est de la pièce, c'est *Arlecchino mercante fallito
con Facanappa*, *Pantalone spetier con Facanappa*, etc, etc.
Chacune de ses entrées en scène est accueillie par des
applaudissements et des trépignements de joie. C'est lui
qui vient faire part au public des changements survenus
pendant la représentation, et qui, à la fin du spectacle,
vient encore annoncer les pièces du lendemain.... toujours
con Facanappa Il a le privilége de tout dire, et il ne se gêne
pas pour faire de nombreuses allusions, employant dans son
dialecte vénitien les mots populaires les plus usités, et en
fabriquant de nouveaux au besoin.

Arlequin et Facanappa attendent un navire qui doit leur
apporter des Indes une fortune considérable en denrées
coloniales. Tous les deux sur le port, ils passent en revue
les vaisseaux qui entrent en rade « *Facanappa*. Que disent

les gens qui montent celui-ci? — *Arlequin.* Ils disent : *Yes, yes.* — *Facanappa.* Ce sont des amis. Et cet autre? — *Arlequin.* — Ils disent : *Oui, oui.* — *Facanappa.* Ce sont aussi des amis. Et ce troisième? — *Arlequin.* Ceux-là disent : *Ja, ja.* — *Facanappa* (imitant l'accent allemand). *Ja, ja.* Ce sont des porcs. » Cette plaisanterie soulève un tonnerre d'applaudissements. Après quoi Facanappa, dont le nez, vu sa petite taille, est toujours au niveau du derrière de son interlocuteur, s'écrie en voyant arriver un nouveau navire : « Le voilà! le voilà! bien sûr, car ça sent le poivre! »

Un long nez de perroquet surmonté d'une paire de lunettes vertes comme celles de Tartaglia, un chapeau plat à larges bords, une cravate rouge, un vaste gilet à boutons de clinquant et une longue redingote blanche dont les pans traînent à terre : tel est ce personnage, dont l'emploi est très-varié, mais qui, pour le fond du caractère, semble être un *monsieur Prud'homme* vénitien.

Au commencement du siècle dernier, ce type portait le nom de BERNARDONI. L'acteur Leinhaus joua, en 1705, sur le théâtre improvisateur de Vienne, les rôles de père ridicule, sous ce nom, avec l'accent vénitien, pour rappeler autant que possible le classique Pantalon.

Le ZANOBIO est encore un type de vieillard dans le même genre, mais qui date du quinzième siècle. Ce personnage parodiait les bourgeois de Piombino et avait un rôle très-caractérisé alors, puisque dans la troupe des *Gelosi*, qui jouait à Florence en 1578, Girolamo Salimbeni, Florentin, fut engagé par Flaminio Scala pour remplir exclusivement cet emploi.

IL BARONE.

Il y avait autrefois à Palerme un théâtre national comme celui de Naples, mais dont les types étaient tout à fait différents. Ainsi le père de famille, il Barone, seigneur sicilien, dupe de ses valets, trompé par sa fille, était la personnification de la noblesse du pays, et celle de la bourgeoisie visant aux distinctions nobiliaires. Nous ne savons si Lappaauo et son successeur Pasquimo, deux célèbres acteurs siciliens, ont continué ce type, mais il n'y a pas encore maintenant de pièces de marionnettes siciliennes sans le Baron.

GAULTIER-GARGUILLE.

Sous le nom de *Fleschelles* dans les rôles sérieux, et sous celui de *Gaultier-Garguille* dans les farces, Hugues Guéru, né en Normandie, jouait les rôles de père et de vieillard, d'abord sur le théâtre du Marais en 1588, puis à l'hôtel de Bourgogne.

Son nom de Gaultier-Garguille vient de gaultier, qui veut dire bon vivant, du vieux verbe français gaudir (se réjouir) et de garguille qui veut dire gargouille, gueule grande. Guéru épousa la fille de Tabarin vers 1620. Il devait avoir au moins cinquante ans (il était du même âge que son beau-père), tandis que sa femme était jeune et fort riche. Après la mort de Gaultier-Garguille, elle put, avec son propre bien et celui dont son mari l'avait avantagée, épouser un seigneur de Normandie. Gaultier fut un bon et honnête mari, et quand venaient les beaux jours, il quittait sa maison de la rue Pavée-Saint-Sauveur pour aller à sa maison de campagne de la porte Montmartre, vivre en « franc bourgeois », disait-il.

Il avait le corps maigre, les jambes longues et la face large. Il portait un demi-masque verdâtre à long nez, à moustaches en poils de chat, les cheveux roides et blancs, la barbe en pointe comme celle de Pantalon, la calotte noire, les souliers noirs, le pourpoint noir à manches de frise rouge, les chausses de frise noire, la ceinture, la gibe-cière, la dague et la canne.

En 1622, l'hôtel de Bourgogne, où

« Gaultier, Guillaume et Turlupin
Font la figue au plaisant Scapin, »

était alors à l'apogée de ses succès de fou rire. Les plus belles farces étaient, selon les critiques du temps : *la Malle de Gaultier, le Cadet de Champagne, Tire la corde, j'ai la carpe, Mieux que devant, la Farce joyeuse de maistre Mimin,* etc.

Gaultier-Garguille avait surtout une réputation comme chanteur de balivernes, aussi, vers 1630, parut-il un Recueil de chansons, assez obscènes pour la plupart, approuvées par Turlupin et Gros-Guillaume. Hugues Guéru mourut en 1633.

Avant sa réception à l'hôtel de Bourgogne, les rôles de pères de la farce furent remplis par Agnan en 1615

« Quand Agnan, à la laide trogne,
Jouait à l'hôtel de Bourgogne
Quelque histoire du temps jadis. »

Après la mort de Gaultier-Garguille, Jacquemin Jadot le remplaça dans les farces; mais il ne le surpassa jamais :

« Jacquemin avec sa posture,
Sa grimace et son action,
Nazarde à la perfection,
Et rend quinaud la nature
On ne peut assez admirer
Les bons contes qu'il nous vient dire,
Qui font qu'à force de trop rire,
Nous sommes contraints de pleurer »

GUILLOT-GORJU.

Au théâtre de l'hôtel de Bourgogne, en 1634, dans la troupe française, Guillot-Gorju était la personnification des *Docteurs*. Ce rôle était rempli par Bertrand Haudouin de Saint-Jacques, qui avait été doyen de la Faculté de médecine, assure Guy-Patin. Il joua pendant huit ans à l'hôtel de Bourgogne, se retira et alla s'établir à Melun, où il recommença à exercer sa profession de médecin. Mais « la mélancolie le prit », et il revint à l'hôtel de Bourgogne.

« C'était un grand homme noir, fort laid : il avait les » yeux enfoncés et un nez de *pompete,* et quoiqu'il ne ressem- » blât pas mal à un singe et qu'il n'eût que faire d'avoir » un masque sur le théâtre, il ne laissait pas d'en avoir » toujours un. »

Le docteur *Guillot-Gorju* était vêtu de noir de la tête aux pieds. Il portait le costume ancien du temps de Henri IV. Le pourpoint boutonné jusqu'au menton, la trousse à côtes de melon et les chausses collantes, deux jarretières, ou plutôt deux ficelles à la jambe gauche, l'une au-dessus, l'autre au-dessous du genou.

> « Guillot-Gorju, chacun admire
> » Et le savoir et le bien dire
> » Que tu débites en te moquant,
> » Et, par ta haute rhétorique,
> » Le plus souvent tu fais la nique
> » Au plus docte et plus éloquent »

Il mourut en 1643, à l'âge de cinquante ans.

Le sieur *Boniface* remplissait en 1633, à l'hôtel de Bourgogne, les mêmes rôles de Docteurs que Guillot-Gorju. Ce personnage de comédie prit alors le nom de « Docteur BONIFACE », nom qui lui fut conservé par la suite

LA CHANTEUSE.

Les Grecs n'eurent pas de poésie qui ne fût chantée, pas de pièces de théâtre qui ne fussent chantées et accompagnées d'instruments.

« Aux temps homériques, dit M. Charles Magnin, les chanteurs allaient, comme nos jongleurs du moyen âge, célébrer les exploits des héros dans les fêtes, les assemblées publiques et les palais des rois, préférant toujours *la chanson la plus nouvelle.* »

Thespis, dans les canevas qu'il composait, faisait chanter ses chansons par des chœurs, comme, par exemple, les chansons à Bacchus et à Silène dans le canevas intitulé *la Vendange.* Les acteurs déclamaient ensuite. Le premier, il tira des chœurs un chanteur qui fut appelé *le coryphée.* Eschyle ajouta un second personnage chantant, et Terpandre ayant introduit l'accompagnement avec la lyre, ces chants, ces *scolies,* furent l'origine de l'opéra.

Les Latins n'eurent pas le goût et la passion qu'avaient les Grecs pour la musique. Les chants et les accompagnements furent séparés de la poésie. On sait que les atellanes étaient composées de farces, de pantomimes, de danses et de musique. Certaines de leurs pièces devaient avoir beaucoup de ressemblance avec nos opéras-comiques modernes, surtout avec les pièces appelées autrefois *intermèdes* en Italie, aujourd'hui *opera buffa*. Dans l'antiquité, ce nom d'*intermède* fut donné à toutes les pièces qui étaient jouées ou chantées pendant les grandes représentations. Les chœurs tragiques ou comiques venaient sur le *proscenium* entre chaque acte. Peu à peu, on les remplaça par des mimes, des bouffons, des danseurs, puis des petites pièces courtes, mêlées de chants, qui faisaient prendre patience aux spectateurs pendant l'entr'acte.

« A l'imitation des anciens, » dit M. Castil-Blaze dans son *Histoire de l'opéra italien*, « qui faisaient arriver le chœur pendant les entr'actes de leurs drames, les Italiens exécutèrent des madrigaux et des chansons placés en même lieu. Ces intermèdes chantés au repos, et qui n'étaient amenés et liés par aucun dialogue, n'obtinrent pas longtemps la faveur du public. *La Flora* d'Alamanni, *il Granchio* (l'Écrevisse) de Salviati, *la Cofanaria* (le Couffin) d'Ambra, représentés et imprimés à Florence en 1566, avec les intermèdes-concerts écrits par Lori, Nerli, Cini pour ces joyeuses comédies, firent imaginer quelque chose de mieux. *Il Mogliazzo fatto da Bogio et Lisa, la Cattrina (atto scenico rusticale)*, de Francesco Berni, produits à Florence en 1567, eurent d'autant plus de succès qu'une action dramatique, simple, à deux ou trois personnages, se déployait en ces intermèdes harmonieux. C'était l'aurore de l'*opera buffa*, un reflet de *li Gieus de Robin et de Marion*, un prélude heureux de la *Gallina perduta* de Francesco Escolani, qui mit bientôt l'Italie en rumeur, de *la Serva padrona* que l'Europe entière salua d'un cri d'admiration. »

En parlant de ce petit chef-d'œuvre de Pergolèse, le président de Brosses disait :

« Surtout il y a un bouffon et une bouffonne qui jouent
» une farce dans les entr'actes, d'un naturel et d'une
» expression comique qui ne se peuvent ni payer, ni ima-
» giner. Il n'est pas vrai qu'on puisse mourir de rire, car, à
» coup sûr, j'en serais mort, malgré la douleur que je
» ressentais de ce que l'épanouissement de ma rate m'em-
» pêchait de sentir, autant que je l'aurais voulu, la musique
» céleste de cette farce. »

Aujourd'hui, entre un *baisser* et un *lever* de rideau, l'en-tr'acte existe dans toute la plénitude de son ennui. C'est de cet ennui d'attendre que vient souvent le mauvais vouloir du public, qui passe au moins un tiers de sa soirée à bâiller. Il faut qu'une pièce soit bien bonne pour résister à ses entr'actes. Je ne sais pas pourquoi nous avons cessé en France de remplir ce vide des représentations, comme on le faisait au dernier siècle. L'orchestre jouait des morceaux de musique *ad hoc*. C'est dans ces intermèdes que les Italiens montrent, plus que dans les drames et tragédies, combien ils sont grands compositeurs, imitateurs de la nature, bons acteurs, grands pantomimes et excellents chanteurs. « Les Italiens, » dit le président de Brosses, « ont le goût des spectacles plus qu'aucune autre nation, et, comme ils n'ont pas moins celui de la musique, ils ne séparent guère l'un de l'autre; de sorte que, le plus souvent, la tra-gédie, la comédie et la farce, tout chez eux est opéra. »

Le premier opéra buffa fut exécuté à Rome, au commencement du seizième siècle, à l'occasion des fêtes que donna Julien de Médicis, frère de Léon X. La comédie de Plaute, *Penulus*, fut mise en musique et représentée deux jours de suite dans un immense théâtre, bâti exprès sur la place du Capitole.

Aux seizième et dix-septième siècles, il n'y avait guère de canevas improvisés ou de pièces régulières qui ne se terminassent par des danses ou des chants, soit populaires, soit tirés des tragédies mises en musique par des compositeurs célèbres, tels que Peri, Corsi, Monteverde, Soriano, Emilio del Cavaliere, Marco Antonio Cesti, Giovanelli, Cavalli, qui firent alors pour le théâtre ce qu'au siècle suivant firent Scarlatti, Pergolèse, Jomelli, Piccinni, Paesiello, Cimarosa, et, de nos jours, Cherubini, Rossini, etc.

Au commencement du seizième siècle, en 1526, la Barbera faisait fureur en Italie. Elle était Florentine, et voyageait de ville en ville, accompagnée de chœurs qu'elle tenait à ses gages, et avec lesquels elle exécutait des intermèdes dans les représentations dramatiques, dont le goût était alors une véritable passion. Machiavel parle beaucoup d'elle dans ses lettres. « La Barbera doit être en ce moment à Modène », écrit-il à Guicciardini à la fin d'une longue lettre politique, « et si vous pouvez lui être agréable en quoi que ce soit, je vous la recommande, car elle m'occupe beaucoup plus que l'empereur. »

Florence, Turin, Venise, Bologne, Rome, Naples, furent les premières villes où l'opéra italien s'établit, et là brillèrent par la beauté de leurs voix les *signore* Catarina Marti-

nella, à Rome, Archilei, Franceschina Caccini, Giulia et
Vittoria Lulle, la Moretti, Adriana Baroni et sa fille Leonora, de Mantoue; Checca della laguna, Margherita Costa,
Petronilla Massini, Francesca Manzoni. Toutes ces *virtuoses*
étaient actrices et joueuses de divers instruments tout
autant que chanteuses : car, dans la *farsa* ou *festa teatrale*
de Jacopo Sannazaro, exécutée à Naples chez le prince de
Calabre, en 1492, une actrice représentant *la Joie* chantait
en s'accompagnant de la viole, tandis que ses trois sui-
vantes jouaient de la cornemuse, de la flûte et du rebec.
Cet usage de cumuler les talents et de s'accompagner parfois soi-même d'un instrument s'est perpétué chez les
chanteuses italiennes jusqu'au milieu du siècle dernier : à
preuve Rosalie Astraudi qui, pour ses débuts en 1744,
chanta un duo, dans *les Talents déplacés*, avec Rochard,
en s'accompagnant en même temps sur le violoncelle

Mais la plupart de ces *opere* étaient mélangées de scènes
improvisées et de lazzis avec les personnages de la *commedia
dell' arte*. Dans l'*Anfiparnasso, opera armonica*, d'Orazio
Vecchi, jouée à Modène en 1594, Brighella, Pantalon, un
valet nommé Pirolino, un Capitan, agissent comme dans
leurs farces improvisées « Pantalon appelle Pirolin. Le
valet gourmand lui répond de loin, avec la bouche pleine.
Pantalon crie : — Holà, Pirolin! où es-tu donc? Pirolin!
Pirolin! Ah! voleur, que fais-tu donc à la cuisine? — Je
m'emplis l'estomac avec des oiseaux, dit Pirolin, des
oiseaux qui chantaient jadis : *Pipiripi! cucurucu!* »

Le 14 décembre 1645, le cardinal Mazarin fit représenter
à Paris *la Festa teatrale della finta Pazza*, de Giulio Strozzi,

musique de Francesco Socrati, et machines de Torelli, sur le théâtre du Petit-Bourbon.

Margarita Bartolazzi était *chanteuse* de cette troupe Sa voix était si ravissante, dit un auteur contemporain, « qu'on ne saurait la louer assez dignement »

Luigia Gabriella Locatelli et Giulia Gabrielli faisaient aussi partie de la troupe en qualité de cantatrices. Cette troupe donna ses représentations jusqu'en 1652.

Loret nous apprend qu'une troupe nouvelle, composée en partie de chanteurs et de cantatrices, vint à Paris en décembre 1654 :

« J'appris hier en mangeant ma soupe
Qu'une belle et gaillarde troupe
De très-rares comédiens
Et même grands musiciens
Arriva lundi de Mantoue,
Naples, Turin, Rome et Padoue,
Pour être du ballet royal
Qu'on doit danser en carnaval »

En 1658 eut lieu au Petit-Bourbon la grande représentation de *Rosaura*, tragédie lyrique d'Antonio Arcoleo, musique d'Antonio Perti, d'abord représentée à Venise. Les intermèdes étaient remplis par Fiurelli (Scaramouche) C'est ainsi que Loret en parle :

« C'est la table de Scaramouche,
Contenant fruit, viande et pain,
Et pourtant il y meurt de faim,
Par des disgraces qui surviennent,
Et qui de manger le retiennent »

Le nom d'*opera*, mot qui ne passa dans notre langue
qu'en 1671, était employé alors dans sa véritable acception
d'œuvre. On disait *opera musicale, tragica, sacra, comica
scenica, armonica*, etc. Les œuvres comme *la Rosaura, Orfeo,
Ercole amante, Serse*, portaient en tête des annonces le
mot *machines*, et la salle du Louvre où se représentaient
ces opéras italiens portait le nom de *Salle des machines.*
L'opéra de *Serse* (Xerxès) (22 novembre 1660) dura plus
de huit heures.

> « Car moi, qui suis monsieur Loret,
> Fus sur un siége assez duret,
> Sans aliment et sans breuvage
> Plus d'huit heures et davantage »

Les acteurs de cette pièce étaient la signora Anna Berge-
rotti, il signor Melone, qui était abbé et qui jouait les rôles
de femme, Bordignone, Atto, Tagliavacca, Zanetto, Chia-
rini, Piccinni, Assalone, Rivani, Augustino.

Dans les entr'actes, « *Scaramouche* Tiberio Fiurelli, travesti,
danse entre deux docteurs, il est reconnu par ses compagnons, les Trivelins et les Polichinelles, qui le dépouillent
et le houspillent vertement. » Dans un autre intermède :
« Danse de matassins. » Louis XIV réunissait dans ces
représentations la troupe des chanteurs et celle des bouffons italiens, ainsi que les danseurs et tous les musiciens
français. De ces fantaisies royales devaient bientôt sortir
l'opéra français, la comédie française et italienne installée
régulièrement.

Après la démolition du Petit-Bourbon, Louis XIV prêta

la salle du Palais-Royal à Molière et à la troupe des comiques italiens, qui à leur tour chantèrent, mais font simplement des couplets.

Dans le recueil des scènes de Gherardi, nous voyons qu'à la fin du dix-septième siècle les airs adaptés aux comédies sont les uns italiens, les autres français. Ce sont pour la plupart des airs tirés de vieux opéras italiens du commencement du siècle, des ponts-neufs et des rigaudons français, des couplets italiens dont quelques-uns ont beaucoup de *maestria*. Les airs de quelques pièces cependant, comme *les Originaux* (1693), musique de M. de Masse, furent composés pour la circonstance.

Le rôle de LA CHANTEUSE ou CANTATRICE (*planche 50*) y était fort restreint et ne demandait qu'une jolie voix et une jolie figure. Telle était Élisabeth Danneret, connue alors sous le nom de *Babet la chanteuse*, qui débuta à la Comédie-Italienne, le 8 juillet 1694, dans *la Fontaine de sapience*.

Son rôle consistait à venir, vêtue en bergère comme on les rêvait dans ce temps-là, offrir une coupe d'eau merveilleuse en chantant

> « Qui goûte de ces eaux ne peut plus se méprendre
> Quand l'amour lui demande un choix,
> Buvons-en mille et mille fois,
> Quand on prend de l'amour, on n'en saurait trop prendre »

Et, à la fin de la pièce, quand bergers et bergères se sont choisis avec *sapience* et dansent ensemble, la bergère *chanteuse* revient et leur chante :

Amanti, ci vuole costanza in amor.

Amando,

Penando,

Si speri, si si ;

Che baste sol un di,

Un' hor', un momento,

Per render contento

Un misero cor.

Dans *le Départ des comédiens* (1694), Gherardi, jouant Arlequin, disait au Docteur : « Pour vous, Monsieur, vous allez vivre de vos rentes. Je voudrais bien m'associer avec vous, mais il est défendu à un comédien italien de se reposer avant l'âge de cent vingt ans, et ce n'est que par tolérance que Scaramouche s'est retiré à quatre-vingt-quatorze. »

Il s'adressait ensuite à Babet : « Et vous, mademoiselle, qu'allez-vous devenir ? » Babet répondait alors en chanson :

« Quand une fille,

Jeune et gentille,

Voudra,

Bientôt elle parviendra

J'en connais une,

Que la fortune

Jusques aux cieux élèvera. .

Dans un nuage, à l Opéra. »

Dans cette fiction, Babet ne croyait pas si bien dire la vérité. Après la mort de Gherardi, avec lequel elle vivait maritalement et dont elle avait un fils, elle entra à l'Opéra.

D'autres fois, Babet est vêtue en sibylle, en prêtresse antique, en Bellone, déesse de la guerre, en *naiade*, en

Égyptienne, etc. Élisabeth Danneret était petite, mais très-bien prise dans sa taille et d'une jolie figure.

La nouvelle troupe de 1716 avait amené aussi comme chanteuse Ursula Astori, fille d'un horloger de Venise. Elle épousa Fabio Sticotti (Pantalon) en 1755, et mourut en 1759.

Quelques plaisants, à propos de LA CHANTEUSE, dirent qu'un abbé faisait partie de la nouvelle troupe en qualité d'aumônier « Ils ont une Chanteuse, un Docteur et un Aumônier; c'est une troupe complète. » Nous ne savons si un abbé avait accompagné les comédiens, mais ce n'eût pas été le premier cas de ce genre pour une troupe italienne. Les Italiens mêlent fréquemment les pratiques religieuses aux choses les plus profanes. Le premier registre de la nouvelle troupe était ainsi conçu : « Au nom de Dieu, de la Vierge Marie, de saint François de Paule et des âmes du purgatoire, nous avons commencé, ce 18 mai 1716, par *l'Inganno fortunato* »

Ce que raconte le président de Brosses, en parlant d'une représentation dans les arènes de Vérone, en 1740, n'est pas moins curieux . « Que je n'oublie pas de vous dire la surprise singulière que j'eus à la comédie la première fois que j'y allai. Une cloche de la ville ayant sonné un coup, j'entendis derrière moi un mouvement subit, tel que je crus que l'amphithéâtre venait en ruine, d'autant mieux qu'en même temps je vis fuir les actrices, quoiqu'il y en eût une qui, selon son rôle, fût alors évanouie Le vrai sujet de mon étonnement était que ce que nous appelons *l'Angelus* ou le *Pardon* venait de sonner, que toute l'assemblée s'était mise promptement à genoux, tournée vers l'orient; que les acteurs s'y étaient de même jetés dans la coulisse, que l'on chanta fort bien l'*Ave Maria;* après quoi l'actrice évanouie revint, fit fort honnêtement la révérence ordinaire après l'*Angelus,* se remit dans son état d'évanouissement, et la pièce continua. »

Dans la troupe de 1716, nous voyons *les Stratagèmes,* musique de Plagliardi (1716); *Alcyone,* parodie (1741), musique de M. Blaise, *la Serva padrona* (1756), musique de Pergolèse. Puis, les compositeurs de musique pour la comédie italienne sont Tarade, Kohot, Philidor, Gibert, Sodi, Monsigni, Chardini, Lamette, Duni, Clément, Grétry, le chevalier d'Herbain, Bambini, Gossec, Garnier, Desbrosses, etc.

Rosalie Astraudi débuta à l'âge de onze ans, le 30 avril 1744.

Elle fut reçue pour chanter dans les parodies, les intermèdes, jouer les amoureuses et les soubrettes, et danser dans les ballets. « Elle s'acquitta de tous ces emplois à la satisfaction du public. » Elle épousa un grand seigneur et quitta le théâtre en 1755.

Justine-Benoîte du Ronceray, dite mademoiselle Chantilly, née à Avignon en 1727, était fille de du Ronceray, ancien musicien de la chapelle du roi de France, et depuis musicien du roi de Pologne Stanislas. En 1744, étant première danseuse de ce monarque et ayant obtenu un congé pour venir en France, mademoiselle Chantilly, accompagnée de sa mère Claudine Bied, qui était aussi musicienne du roi de Pologne, débuta sur le théâtre de l'Opéra-

Comique de la foire Saint-Laurent que dirigeait Favart
Favart s'éprit sérieusement de mademoiselle Chantilly et
l'épousa à la fin de cette même année. Il fut appelé plus
tard par le maréchal de Saxe à diriger le théâtre qui devait
suivre l'armée française dans les Flandres

Il y avait toujours dans les camps du maréchal un
opéra-comique. C'était là qu'on donnait l'ordre des batailles. Entre deux pièces, la principale actrice, qui fut
assez longtemps madame Favart, venait annoncer : « Messieurs, demain, relâche au théâtre, à cause de la bataille
que donnera M. le maréchal. Après-demain, *le Coq du
village, les Amours grivois* »

Par goût autant que par système, le maréchal de Saxe
voulait de la joie dans ses armées, il disait que les Français
n'allaient jamais si bien que lorsqu'on les menait gaiement, et que ce qu'ils craignaient le plus à la guerre,
c'était l'ennui. Mademoiselle Chantilly suivit donc son
mari à Bruxelles, au quartier général; ce fut là que le
maréchal de Saxe devint amoureux d'elle (1746)

« Mademoiselle de Chantilly, » lui écrivait-il un jour,
« je prends congé de vous, vous êtes une enchanteresse
» plus dangereuse que feu Armide. Tantôt en Pierrot, tantôt
» travestie en Amour, et puis en simple bergère, vous faites
» si bien que vous nous enchantez tous. Je me suis vu au
» moment de succomber aussi, moi dont l'art funeste effraye
» l'univers. Quel triomphe pour vous, si vous aviez pu me
» soumettre à vos lois ! Je vous rends grâces de n'avoir pas
» usé de tous vos avantages, vous ne l'entendez pas mal
» pour une jeune sorcière, avec votre houlette, qui n'est

» autre que la baguette dont fut frappé ce pauvre prince
» des Français que Renaud l'on nommait, je pense Déjà
» je me suis vu entouré de fleurs et de fleurettes, équipage
» funeste pour tous les favoris de Mars. J'en frémis; et
» qu'aurait dit le roi de France et de Navarre, si, au lieu
» du flambeau de la vengeance, il m'avait trouvé une guir-
» lande à la main? Malgré le danger auquel vous m'avez
» exposé, je ne puis vous savoir mauvais gré de mon
» erreur, elle est charmante! Mais ce n'est qu'en fuyant
» que l'on peut éviter un péril si grand :

« Adieu, divinité du parterre adorée,
» Faites le bien d'un seul et les désirs de tous;
» Et puissent vos amours égaler la durée
» De la tendre amitié que mon cœur a pour vous! »

» Pardonnez, mademoiselle, à un reste d'ivresse cette
» prose rimée que vos talents m'inspirent; la liqueur dont
» je suis abreuvé dure souvent, dit-on, plus longtemps
» qu'on ne pense.

» MAURICE DE SAXE. »

Madame Favart débuta à la Comédie-Italienne le 5
août 1749. « Il n'y eut pas d'exemple d'un si grand
succès. » Grimm dit que sa célébrité venait de la passion
qu'elle avait inspirée au héros de Fontenoy.

Son talent fut différemment apprécié. Elle avait, assure-
t-on, une gaieté franche, naturelle, le jeu agréable et
piquant. Propre à tous les caractères, elle les rendait avec
une vérité surprenante : soubrettes, amoureuses, paysannes, rôles naïfs, rôles de caractère, tout lui devenait

propre; en un mot, elle se multipliait à l'infini, et l'on était
étonné de lui voir jouer, le même jour, dans quatre pièces
différentes, des rôles entièrement opposés. Elle imitait si
parfaitement les différents patois, que des personnes dont
elle empruntait l'accent la croyaient leur compatriote.
« Nous assurons hardiment, » écrivaient les frères Parfait,
en 1769, « malgré le sentiment de quelques personnes, toujours avides de la nouveauté, que cette aimable actrice n'a
point encore été remplacée dans ces rôles, pour ce qui
regarde la partie de la comédie, et nous n'avons besoin,
pour en convaincre ceux qui pourront en douter, que de
les envoyer à la première représentation qui se donnera
de *la Fée Urgèle*. »

Au mois de juin 1771, la maladie dont elle mourut se
déclara; et, bien qu'elle connût son état désespéré, elle
continua de jouer par intérêt pour ses camarades jusqu'à
la fin de cette même année.

Au mois d'avril 1772, Grimm raconte ainsi la mort de
madame Favart, et dénigre très-durement son talent

« Le théâtre de la Comédie-Italienne vient de perdre une
actrice célèbre, madame Favart; elle a montré beaucoup
de courage et de patience pendant tout le temps de ses
souffrances. Revenue, un jour, d'un long évanouissement,
elle aperçut, parmi ceux que son danger avait rassemblés
en hâte autour d'elle, un de ses voisins dans un accoutre-
ment fort grotesque; elle se mit à sourire, et dit qu'elle
avait cru voir le *Paillasse de la Mort* , mot de caractère
dans la bouche d'une fille de théâtre mourante. Jamais les
prêtres ne purent la déterminer à renoncer au théâtre. Elle

dit qu'elle ne voulait point se parjurer, que c'était son état; que si elle guérissait elle serait obligée de le reprendre, et qu'elle ne pouvait par conséquent y renoncer de bonne foi; elle aima mieux se passer de sacrements. Mais, lorsqu'elle se sentit expirer, elle dit : « *Oh! pour le coup, j'y renonce.* » Ce fut son dernier mot. Madame Favart était âgée à peu près de cinquante ans. C'était une mauvaise actrice. Elle avait la voix aigre et le jeu bas et ignoble, elle n'était supportable que dans les rôles de charge et ne l'était pas longtemps. Elle jouait supérieurement la Savoyarde montrant la marmotte. c'était tout son talent, c'était ce qui avait fait sa fortune sur ce théâtre, lors de son début en 1749. Elle s'appelait alors mademoiselle de Chantilly; elle dansait, elle chantait, et sa danse en sabots tourna la tête à tout Paris. »

Du 2 août 1752 au 7 mars 1754, Monelli, Guerrieri, Lazzari, les *signore* Anna Tonelli, Catarina Tonelli, Rossi Lazzari, vinrent chanter sur le théâtre de la Comédie-Italienne. Ils donnèrent *la Serva padrona* de Pergolèse, *il Maestro di musica* de Scarlatti, *Serpilla et Bajocco* de Ristorini, et autres intermèdes mis en musique par Cocchi, Selleti, Rinaldo di Capua, Latilla, Jomelli, Ciampi, Leo. Comme ces Italiens ne chantaient que l'*opera buffa*, le nom de *bouffons* leur fut donné. De là vient qu'aujourd'hui on appelle encore *bouffes* nos chanteurs italiens, bien que la plupart du temps il n'y ait rien de bouffon dans ce qu'ils donnent au public.

La guerre était alors déclarée entre la musique française et la musique italienne. Le parti de la musique française, ayant le roi et madame de Pompadour à sa tête, l'emporta. Les chanteurs italiens quittèrent Paris, mais la Comédie-Italienne s'empara du répertoire, sujets et musique, de la troupe chantante, et traduisit toutes les pièces, telles que *la Serva padrona* qui devint un opéra-comique français sous le nom de *la Servante maîtresse*.

Larnette, Rochard, Bouret, mesdames Favart, Rosalie Astraudi, Foulquier (*Catmon*), Superville (dite *la commère Babichon*) y chantaient en français et rachetaient la faiblesse de leur chant par la verve, l'esprit et l'entrain de leur jeu. C'est ce qui fut cause de l'insuccès de la signora Deamicis, le 20 juin 1758, quand elle vint à Paris faire une tentative auprès du public français pour faire admettre la musique italienne qui, cinq ans auparavant, avait produit tant d'opéras-comiques.

Après une seule représentation de quatre heures, qui fut donnée par ordre de MM. les gentilshommes de la chambre, et qui se composa de *la Serva padrona* et de *gli Raggieri della femina Scaltra*, la signora Deamicis et son père comprirent qu'un nouvel essai était inutile. Elle passa en Angleterre, où elle quitta son emploi de *prima comica* pour chanter la musique sérieuse de Bach.

Mademoiselle Foulquier, dite *Catmon*, avait débuté, en 1755, dans les rôles d'Angélique, et ensuite dans les rôles de Silvia. Elle joignait à la décence du maintien et aux grâces naturelles du chant et de la déclamation, le talent de la danse qu'elle possédait à un degré supérieur.

Sa sœur aînée, madame Bognoli, débuta dans les *Silvia* le 12 avril 1758.

Le 6 mai 1761, mademoiselle Piccinelli débuta dans *la Cantatrice italienne*. Favart, dans une lettre au comte de Durazzo, raconte ainsi l'histoire de mademoiselle Piccinelli : « Voici ce que l'on dit : Une pauvre villageoise trouva un jour une enfant nouveau-née exposée au milieu d'un champ ; c'était notre signora. La *contadina* en prit soin par charité, lui donna son lait, et l'éleva le mieux qu'elle put, jusqu'à l'âge de huit à neuf ans, comme sa propre fille. Une de ces femmes qui cherchent des ressources pour leur fortune dans la jeunesse et les agréments des personnes de leur sexe, passa par hasard dans le village de la bonne nourrice, aperçut la petite, fut frappée de ses grâces naturelles et proposa une somme assez modique pour l'acheter. Le marché fut passé. Cette troisième mère n'épargna rien pour donner à sa fille adoptive une éducation convenable aux desseins qu'elle avait sur elle ; la petite créature en profita au delà de toutes les espérances que l'on avait conçues. Déjà la matrone bâtit des projets de fortune ; elle fait recevoir son élève au spectacle ; elle s'arrange pour lui procurer un protecteur opulent, mais la nouvelle actrice, ne prenant point goût à ces dispositions, s'avisa de faire elle-même un choix qui fut contrarié. Pour avoir la paix, elle planta là sa troisième mère, et se mit volontairement sous la protection d'une autre plus complaisante, afin de pouvoir paraître décemment dans le monde ; celle-ci la conduisit à Paris. Mademoiselle Piccinelli reçue aux Italiens, la renommée publie partout ses succès, les différentes mères de la cantatrice se rendent auprès d'elle, chacune la revendique. La première dit : « Elle est à moi, je lui ai donné la vie » La deuxième réplique · « Je la lui ai sauvée, je l'ai nourrie, elle m'appartient. » La troisieme : « Je l'ai achetée, je lui ai donné de l'éducation, qui peut contester mes droits? » La quatrième ajoute . « Elle s'est donnée librement à moi, et je travaille journellement à sa fortune, cela vaut mieux, si quelqu'une de vous me la dispute, je lui arrache les yeux. » Notre cantatrice, pour les mettre d'accord, distribue à chacune une égale somme d'argent. Les trois premières se retirent, la quatrième reste pour lui servir de conseil. La Piccinelli, fatiguée de ces petites tracasseries de famille, renonce à toutes les mères du monde pour se mettre sous l'autorité d'un mari. Elle choisit M. Vezian, frère d'une très-jolie fille que nous avons eue pour figurante aux Italiens, et à laquelle il doit un emploi considérable. »

Mademoiselle Piccinelli joint à une figure agréable « une voix également étendue et flexible, et le son en est en même temps argentin et gracieux Elle sut plaire aux oreilles françaises. Elle réunit à ce talent celui de jouer la comédie avec beaucoup de noblesse. »

Mademoiselle Collet débuta, le 21 janvier 1761, dans *la Fille mal gardée*. « Son jeu enfantin lui obtint les applaudissements du public, qui les lui redoubla dans le rôle de Betzi de *le Roi et le Fermier*. C'est presque les seuls où elle se soit distinguée. Elle avait peu de voix et remplaçait par des minauderies ce qui lui manquait du côté de l'expression. » Morte en avril 1766.

Mademoiselle Vilette, après avoir chanté *le Devin du village* à l'Opéra, vint débuter sur la scène italienne le 7 septembre 1761. Sa voix charmante reçut les plus grands applaudissements.

En 1762, mademoiselle Colombe, Vénitienne, débuta avec le plus grand succès sur le théâtre de la Comédie-Italienne, à Paris. Elle dansait autrefois dans les ballets sur le même théâtre. Un Anglais en devint si amoureux, qu'il voulut l'enlever. Elle quitta le théâtre pour lui échapper, et n'y rentra qu'en 1772.

« Son début a été des plus brillants, dit Grimm dans sa Correspondance. Elle n'est pas de la première jeunesse, elle a du moins l'air d'avoir environ trente ans Elle n'a d'autre défaut que trop de noblesse et trop de beauté pour le caractère des rôles de l'opéra-comique, son port, sa démarche, son maintien sont ceux d'une reine. Son regard auguste, noble et tendre, ses grands yeux, les plus beaux du monde, sembleraient plutôt l'appeler à la tragédie Son jeu est tant soit peu maniéré, mais de cette manière qui plaît encore.... Elle a une voix charmante et un goût de chant excellent, plein de cette grâce, de cette douceur, de cette facilité qu'on n'a jamais su sentir en France.... Pour moi, c'est la première et peut-être la dernière fois que j'ai entendu chanter, sur un théâtre de Paris, avec ce charme et cette grâce qui produisent le ravissement »

Les comédiens italiens, pour réparer les pertes qu'ils venaient de faire par la retraite de mademoiselle Piccinelli et la mort de madame Savi, qui avait débuté en 1760 dans les rôles de première amoureuse, chargèrent, en avril 1766, Colalto, qui jouait les rôles de Pantalon, d'aller chercher en Italie deux actrices. Il revint au mois d'août et présenta les *signore* Zanarini et Bacelli, mère et fille. Elles débutèrent comme première et seconde amoureuses dans *les Amours d'Arlequin* de Goldoni. Ceux qui comprenaient l'italien applaudirent beaucoup surtout la mère, les autres se retirèrent médiocrement satisfaits. Madame Zanarini fut reçue pour jouer les amoureuses, et sa fille, mademoiselle Bacelli, pour les soubrettes.

En 1765, mademoiselle Beaupré.

En 1770, la charmante Rosalie Lafond, à peine âgée de quinze ans, débuta dans *les Ensorcelés*.

En 1770, mademoiselle Mesnard, jeune et jolie cantatrice qui fut d'abord bouquetière, puis, après son entrée au théâtre, protégée par le duc de Chaulnes, qui la fit peindre par Greuze. C'est elle qui fut aimée de Beaumarchais et qui fut cause de ce scandaleux pugilat entre « le duc et pair crocheteur » et l'auteur de *Figaro*. On sait qu'à la suite de cette affaire, Beaumarchais, bien qu'acquitté par le tribunal des maréchaux de France, qui avaient envoyé par lettre de cachet M. de Chaulnes à Vincennes, fut mis au Fort-l'Évêque par M. de la Vrillière pour le seul motif que le fils d'un horloger ne pouvait avoir raison contre un duc et pair.

En 1779, mademoiselle Guedon, fille de Carlin Bertinazzi.

Lors de la retraite de madame La Ruette, en 1777, Grimm écrivait : « Cette charmante actrice unissait à la voix la plus intéressante, à la physionomie la plus fine et la plus heureuse, un tact infiniment rare, et la sensibilité la plus naïve et la plus délicate. On n'espère plus de voir les rôles d'Isabelle, de Colombine, joués comme ils l'ont été par elle. La délicieuse scène de la Rose dans *le Magni-fique*, fut, pour ainsi dire, tout son ouvrage; elle y répandait un mélange de décence et d'intérêt dont la magie est inexplicable. C'est un mot singulier peut-être, mais plein de vérité, que celui de madame d'Houdetot qui disait que, *dans ce moment, madame La Ruette avait de la pudeur jusque dans le dos.* »

Les théâtres de la foire Saint-Laurent (Opéra-Comique) s'emparèrent des types, des pièces et de la musique des Italiens. Ils jouèrent et chantèrent des récitatifs en français avec musique italienne, des airs de contredanses françaises, des romances, des ponts-neufs. Jusqu'en 1721 nous ne trouvons que des couplets sur des airs anciens ou déjà chantés ailleurs, comme : *Réveillez-vous, belle endormie. Ramonez ci! ramonez là, la cheminée du haut en bas Va-t'en voir s'ils viennent, Jean Monsieur de la Palisse. Ton humeur est, Catherine.... Adieu paniers, vendanges sont faites La bonne aventure, ô gai! Jean Gille, Gille, joli Jean. Ma commère, quand je danse. Voilà le plaisir, mesdames! voilà le plaisir !* etc. Ce sont encore des airs tirés des opéras français, de *Joconde*, d'*Armide*, d'*Alceste*, des Cotillons, la Pavane d'été, le Branle de Metz, le Menuet d'Exaudet, ou de M. de Grandval, *les Folies d'Espagne*, etc.

En 1757, Monsigny écrit la musique de *On ne s'avise jamais de tout*, et de beaucoup d'autres opéras-comiques. En 1759, Duni compose *la Veuve indécise*; Laruette, *le Boulevard*, en 1753. Les compositeurs de musique de l'Opéra-Comique étaient aussi MM. Lacoste, Gillier, Aubert, Delacroix, etc.

L Opéra-Comique prenant trop de développement, et la troupe italienne n'en ayant plus assez, les deux troupes furent fondues ensemble en 1761. La troupe de l'Opéra-Comique était alors composée de mesdemoiselles Deschamps, Rosaline, Nessel, Luzi, Arnoult, Dezza, Florigny. Les hommes étaient Laruette, Bourette, Delisle, Audinot, Parau, Saint-Aubert, Clairval, Guignes.

Sur les théâtres forains les principales actrices, chanteuses d'opéras-comiques ou de parodies, furent :

Mademoiselle Maillard, fille d'un cuisinier, et raccommodeuse de dentelles. Elle entra en 1696 au *Jeu des marionnettes de Bertrand*, qui lui trouva des talents et l'engagea dans sa troupe, où elle resta huit ans. Elle épousa en province, à Besançon, un jeune homme nommé Cavé, qui portait alors le petit collet et qui le quitta pour elle. Il prit le nom de Maillard et se fit acteur (voyez *Scaramouche*). Elle se retira quand mademoiselle de Lisle rentra au théâtre en 1716. Étant près d'accoucher, elle se blessa, et mourut en septembre 1721.

Mademoiselle de Lisle, née en 1684, avait à peine onze ans quand elle débuta dans les soubrettes à l'Opéra-Comique. Elle reparut en 1716, joua jusqu'en 1740 et mourut en 1758.

Mademoiselle Bastolet, née à Paris, entra au *Jeu de Bertrand,* en 1698, à raison de vingt sous par jour; puis joua chez Dolet, chez le sieur Saint-Edme, chez Lalauze en 1721, chez Honoré en 1724, et se maria avec un médecin italien en 1735. Elle joua ensuite dans la troupe du sieur Pontau les rôles de mère avec un grand succès.

Mademoiselle Lambert jouait les amoureuses et chantait dans les vaudevilles; elle épousa Dolet, qui, avant d'être entrepreneur de théâtre aux foires Saint-Laurent et Saint-Germain, s'était d'abord engagé dans la troupe italienne de Constantini (*Mezzetin*), puis dans celle de Tortoretti (*Pasquariel*). Elle quitta le théâtre en 1709, se fit marchande de modes aux foires Saint-Germain et Saint-Laurent, mais, n'ayant pas réussi dans ce commerce, elle fit quitter le théâtre à son mari et monta avec lui une boutique de limonadier.

En 1700, mademoiselle Babron, fille d'une ouvreuse de loges de la Comédie-Italienne, sœur de Babron (Arlequin forain), débuta dans les rôles de *Colombine* et ceux de femmes travesties en hommes, dans la troupe de Bertrand. En 1707, elle se maria à l'acteur nommé Prevost et partit avec lui en province.

En 1710, mademoiselle d'Aigremont, connue sous le nom de *Camuson*, quitta la boutique de marchande de modes pour entrer à l'Opéra-Comique. Elle y resta jusqu'en 1723.

En 1712, mademoiselle Chateauneuf, fille de Chateauneuf, acteur et auteur, jouait les Colombines. En 1721, elle débuta, mais sans succès, au Théâtre-Français.

En 1720, mademoiselle Cochois, femme de Cochois l'acrobate, jouait les soubrettes à la foire Saint-Laurent.

Agathine-Antonie Lalauze, femme de Lalauze (Arlequin forain), joua les soubrettes jusqu'en 1721.

En 1729, Jeanneton Destouches chantait à l'Opéra-Comique.

En 1731, sa sœur, Angélique Destouches, à la foire Saint-Laurent.

Mademoiselle Joly, de 1729 à 1737.

Mademoiselle Des Aigles, en 1730.

Mademoiselle Legrand, fille de l'auteur de ce nom, après avoir débuté au Théâtre-Français, parut sur celui de l'Opéra-Comique le 12 février 1731.

Mademoiselle Lombard et son mari débutèrent à l'Opéra-Comique; puis chez Pontau, à la foire Saint-Germain, de 1733 à 1742.

En 1745, mademoiselle Beaumenard, fille de l'acteur Beaumenard, débuta à l'Opéra-Comique et y joua jusqu'en 1749, époque où elle fut reçue au Théâtre-Français.

Mademoiselle Dubois jouait les amoureuses à la foire Saint-Laurent en 1745

Mademoiselle Chevrier, actrice de l'Opéra-Comique de la foire Saint-Laurent en 1746, passa ensuite à l'Opéra, et mourut en 1758.

En 1760, mademoiselle Savi et mademoiselle Molin.

RUZZANTE.

Il n'est pas de travail inutile. Quelque aride ou frivole que paraisse un sujet, du moment qu'on l'étudie, les recherches vous conduisent toujours à une découverte sérieuse qui vous dédommage de vos peines.

Merci à toi, beau et bon Ruzzante, grand mort que nous avons trouvé couché dans la poussière de l'oubli; dont l'œuvre, rare en Italie, inconnue en France, nous a permis enfin d'envisager la *commedia dell' arte* comme une Muse du même sang et de même noblesse que celle de Shakspeare et de Molière.

On ne sait presque rien de la vie de Shakspeare, on ne sait rien de celle d'Angelo Beolco surnommé Ruzzante (le *folâtre*, le *badin*), né à Padoue en 1502. Était-il acteur de profession, ou n'était-il qu'un amateur qui faisait de l'art par vocation? Le seul renseignement sérieux qui existe est une page de Bernardino Scardeon

Bernardino Scardeon dit, dans son ouvrage *De antiquitate urbis Patavii*, 1560, « qu'Angelo Beolco, connu sous le

nom de Ruzzante, fut, à Padoue, ce que Plaute était jadis
à Rome, comme auteur, et Roscius comme acteur. Il les
a même surpassés, car il n'est aucune comédie antique,
prœtexta, *togata*, *mixta* ou *atellana*, de quelque genre
soit-elle, qui puisse soutenir la comparaison avec celles
de Ruzzante, lesquelles furent jouées dans toute l'Italie,
firent tant de plaisir et attirèrent une si grande foule
d'hommes et de femmes. Quant à lui, il était si supérieur
aux autres acteurs, que, lorsqu'il était en scène, le public
ne voyait et n'entendait que lui. »

Il est certain pour nous que Ruzzante a surpassé Plaute
en composant ses comédies, et quant à avoir été un
acteur supérieur à Roscius [1], nous sommes porté à l'admettre d'après le naturel incomparable de ses compositions
et de son langage

L'époque de Ruzzante est brillante. Ce fut à l'heure du
réveil de la comédie en Italie qu'il s'éveilla lui-même
dans la force et dans la liberté de son génie éminemment
original. Ses devanciers illustres, l'Arioste, qui, dès l'âge
de vingt ans, en 1494, avait déjà composé et fait jouer à
la cour du duc de Ferrare sa comédie intitulée *i Suppositi;*
Nicolas Machiavel (1469 à 1527), auteur de *la Mandragore*
(1504) et de *la Clizia* (1508), que le pape Léon X fit jouer
devant lui à Rome par les *sempiterni* ou les *intronati*, acteurs
académiques de Florence et de Sienne; Bernardo Dovizi,
cardinal de Bibbiena, auteur de *la Calandra*, composée

---

[1] Gennari, dans son *Saggio storico sulle accademie*, page 21, l'appelle
« le nouveau Roscius de son époque », et il traite « d'homme admirable,
prodigieux acteur et auteur de très-belles comédies ».

en 1490, lui sont très-inférieurs sous le rapport de l'individualité et de la nouveauté. Ils ne créent point un genre, ils l'exhument. Ils marchent sur les traces des maîtres de l'antiquité et ne les dépassent pas, s'ils les atteignent. Ruzzante, bien autrement hardi et créateur, complète et embellit ce qu'il traite. En outre, il crée la comédie de réalité au milieu des idylles bocagères de la convention environnante.

Ruzzante eût été certainement le Molière de l'Italie, si, au lieu de passer son temps à improviser, il l'eût consacré à écrire; car ce n'est que dans les dernières années de sa vie, qui fut très-courte (il est mort à quarante ans), qu'il mit en ordre et écrivit la plupart de ses pièces et ses charmants discours aux cardinaux Cornaro et Pisani, etc.

Il habitait pendant l'été Codevigo, villa du Vénitien Aloysio Cornelio, homme magnifique et libéral, qui fut son Mécène et l'hébergea ainsi que sa troupe comique. Aussi cette troupe lui donna-t-elle de fréquentes représentations.

D'après Scardeon, la ville de Padoue allait lui rendre de grands honneurs lorsqu'il mourut le 17 mars 1542. Ses amis et ses nombreux admirateurs lui élevèrent, en 1560, un tombeau à Padoue dans l'église San-Daniel, auprès de *Prato della Valle,* avec l'épitaphe suivante à sa louange, « en témoignage d'amitié, d'estime et d'admiration ».

V. S.

ANGELO BEOLCO.

« Ruzanti Patavino, nulli in scribendis, agendisque
» comœdus ingenio, facundia, aut arte secundo, jocis et

» sermonibus agrest. applausu omnium facetiss., qui non
» sine amicorum mœrore e vita discessit anno Domini
» MDLII die xvii martii, ætatis vero xi. Jo. Baptista Rota
» Patavin. tantæ præstantiæ admirator pignus hoc sempi-
» ternum in testimonium famæ ac nominis P. C. anno a
» mundo redempto MDLX »

Dans la suite, cette inscription ayant paru trop profane
à je ne sais qui, fut enlevée.

Bernardino Scardeon nous dit encore que « Ruzzante
était d'un caractère aimable et enjoué, toujours agréable
et affable à quelque heure que ce fût » Sa figure, d'après
le portrait qui reste de lui, dénote un esprit fin, observateur, satirique ; un caractère ferme et mélancolique
(planche 31).

Presque tous les personnages de ses comédies furent des
surnoms, qui devinrent par la suite des noms génériques
et restèrent au théâtre.

« Pour réciter ses comédies, ses compagnons scéniques,
camarades de la même troupe, et ses émules, étaient des
jeunes gens nobles de Padoue qui avaient de la réputation :
Marco Aurelio Alvarotto, qu'on appelait *Menato*; Hieronimo Zanetti, sous le nom de *Vezzo*, Castegnola, qu'on
surnommait *Bilora,* et quelques autres qui possédaient par
imitation le langage et la manière de parler des paysans. »

Aloysio Cornelio lui-même, le splendide Vénitien, protecteur du Ruzzante, se mêla-t-il à leurs jeux, et fut-il par
antithèse le créateur de l'avare *Pantalon,* qui joue sous
le nom de Cornelio un si bon rôle dans les pièces de
Ruzzante ?

Benedetto Varchi (1502-1565), le célèbre auteur de l'*Histoire de Florence*, parlant des divers genres de comédie, dit à propos des pièces antiques : « Si l'on doit s'en rapporter à l'expérience et ajouter foi aux conjectures, je crois que nos *zanni* sont plus comiques que ne l'étaient leurs mimes, et que les comédies du Ruzzante de Padoue, traitant des sujets rustiques, surpassent celles que les anciens appelaient *atellanes*. »

« Nos meilleurs écrivains, » dit Riccoboni, « ont beaucoup vanté Ruzzante. Ses comédies, au-dessus des atellanes des Latins pour le comique, admettent tous les dialectes des langues corrompues de nos Lombardies... Il a fixé sur notre théâtre le caractère ainsi que le langage du Scapin. de l'Arlequin, du Pantalon et du Docteur. »

En effet, Ruzzante fut le premier qui ouvrit les portes de la comédie aux dialectes populaires. Tous ses personnages parlent un langage différent, depuis le padouan, le bergamasque, le bolonais, le vénitien, le toscan, jusqu'au latin, l'espagnol italianisé et le grec moderne. Mais ce sont les dialectes de Padoue, de Venise et de Bergame qui sont le plus employés.

Ruzzante s'exerça d'abord dans le genre académique, et chercha à rivaliser par la pureté de son style avec le Bembo, le Speroni et les autres auteurs de son époque. Bien qu'il eût tout autant de talent que ses collègues, il était mécontent de son succès. S'apercevant, d'ailleurs, qu'il restait bien au-dessous de ce qu'il voulait rendre, il se mit à apprendre le dialecte des paysans, à en étudier les mœurs, les finesses, le caractère. Il s'appropria tellement leur langage et leurs manières, il prit si bien tout ce qu'ils avaient de naïf, d'original, de plaisant, qu'il trompait les paysans eux-mêmes qui, le voyant déguisé, le prenaient pour un des leurs.

Beolco avait pour eux une prédilection particulière, et fait à leur profit la critique des grands, des savants classiques, du luxe, des mœurs et du bel esprit.

« Ne vaudriez-vous pas cent fois mieux, dit-il dans un prologue, si vous vous contentiez, comme nous faisons dans les campagnes, de manger du bon pain, du bon fromage salé et de boire du beau vin vermeil, que de manger tant de sauces et de tant d'espèces de mets qui vous gonflent l'estomac? Vous seriez frais et roses comme des pommes, tandis que vous êtes tout affaiblis... Je jurerais que si un de vos messieurs en venait aux mains avec une de nos femmes, il aurait le dessous. Pourquoi cela? parce qu'elles ne sont point repues de douceurs, mais de choses naturelles, et que, vivant au grand air, elles ont les membres plus forts et la peau plus dure. »

Ruzzante ne perd jamais l'occasion de vanter l'emploi du langage rustique. Dans une lettre écrite en padouan, adressée *al reverendissimo cardinal Cornaro Vecchio :*

« Je ne vois pas pourquoi, dit-il, puisque je prends des types de paysans et que je les mets sur le théâtre, je les ferais plutôt parler toscan (*in lenguazo fiorentinesco*) qu'égyptien.... Maintenant le monde va tout de travers, chacun veut lever la tête plus haut qu'il ne peut. Rien ne se fait plus selon la nature; chacun se laisse éblouir par les prétentions de son voisin, au lieu de rester dans la simplicité.

On cherche aussi à changer de langage, plutôt que de parler dans sa langue propre. Chacun court à ce qui l'éblouit,
sans s'inquiéter de marcher son droit chemin, ce qui est
mal, je le dis. En ferai-je autant, moi qui suis Padouan
d'Italie (*che a son Pavàn, della Traha*)? Irai-je me faire Toscan
ou Français? Non, par le sang du cancre! non, je ne le
ferai pas. Je veux rester et marcher dans la vérité et le
naturel.

» Que personne d'entre vous ne s'étonne de m'entendre
parler une langue qui n'est pas la florentine; je ne veux
changer mon langage contre aucun autre. Je pense pouvoir vous souhaiter santé, fortune, joie et allégresse, aussi
bien dans mon grossier padouan, qu'un autre le ferait avec
une langue plus fine et plus légère. »

Beolco remplissait les principaux rôles dans ses propres
pièces, et venait toujours exposer l'argument. Parfois, vêtu
d'un costume allégorique ou de fantaisie, il faisait son petit
discours au public :

« Amusons-nous un peu. Y a-t-il quelqu'un parmi vous
qui sache qui je suis? Vous avez l'air de dire que je suis
Mercure ou un récitateur d'arguments de comédies? Non,
vous ne le devinerez jamais! Je ne veux pas vous faire
chercher davantage. Je suis un esprit follet. Savez-vous
pourquoi je me laisse voir? pourquoi je me montre? Savez-
vous d'où je viens? De l'autre monde, et je veux vous dire
pourquoi. Un de ceux qui sont là, appelé Actius par les
uns, Plaute par les autres, m'envoie vous dire que ce soir
une comédie devant être jouée, vous ne la devez pas blâmer
si elle n'est pas en latin et en vers, ou en beau langage,

parce que, s'il était aujourd'hui au nombre des vivants, il ne ferait pas ses comédies dans un autre genre que celle dont vous voici spectateurs. Il ajoute que vous ne jugiez pas par celle-ci de celles qu'il a laissées écrites; car il vous jure, par Hercule et Apollon, qu'elles furent récitées autrement qu'elles ne sont imprimées aujourd'hui, par la raison que bien des choses qui font bien sur le papier, font mal sur la scène. »

Il nous semble que toute la raison d'être de la comédie improvisée en libre dialogue, est résumée dans ce peu de mots.

Partout, soit instinct personnel, soit contagion de la mode pastorale, Ruzzante fait l'apologie de la vie rustique. Il ne faut pourtant pas le prendre pour un doucereux, pour un faiseur de *bergeries* à la Florian; il est très-réaliste dans la peinture des misères et des emportements de cette vie précaire et sauvage des paysans de son époque. La brutale passion qui le porte, dans la *Fiorina,* à enlever de force une jeune fille en la bâillonnant avec l'aide d'un ami, est probablement un trait de mœurs pris sur nature dans ces temps de guerre, de rapt et de violence. Mais s'il ose mettre de pareils drames sur la scène, avec une sorte de farouche insouciance, il fait aussitôt arriver la voix de l'indignation ou de la pitié « Par le sang du mal de la boiteuse! » s'écrie la vieille Teodosia (nous ne nous chargeons pas d'expliquer cette bizarre malédiction), « on voit aujourd'hui d'étranges choses. *Il est venu à présent un mal vivre!* et je crois qu'avant peu il n'y aura plus de sûreté dans nos chaumières. Voyez quelle jolie surprise vont avoir ce pauvre père et cette mère infortunée! L'envie de pleurer m'en vient. »

Dans une lettre qu'il adresse, sous son nom de théâtre, au cardinal Francesco Cornaro, il remercie Rome d'avoir envoyé à la bonne ville de Padoue ce bon seigneur qui lui rend l'espérance. Ces lettres, écrites en vieux dialecte padouan, sont des chefs-d'œuvre. Elles sont censées d'un paysan naïf qui a le droit de tout dire. Elles sont donc gaies, parce que, pour être lues, elles doivent faire rire. Mais cette gaieté est pleine de larmes. Ce n'est pas un histrion qui fait sa cour : c'est un homme courageux et généreux qui aime sa patrie et dit la vérité. En voici quelques fragments très-résumés, afin de ne pas trop sortir de notre sujet :

« Notre grand'mère Rome qui t'a donné ce chapeau, ô bon cardinal, ne te l'a pas donné pour te préserver du soleil et des taches de rousseur, mais pour qu'il nous abrite tous, et ce manteau de pourpre, il faut que tu nous y mettes tous contre ton cœur, comme une poule y prend ses poussins. Rends-nous la confiance et le repos. Regarde ce qu'est devenu ce pays. On n'y entend plus les jeunes garçons et les jeunes filles chanter sur les chemins et dans les champs. Les oiseaux mêmes ne chantent plus, et je crois, la peste m'étouffe! que les rossignols n'ont plus la voix aussi belle qu'au temps passé. On ne voit plus de jeux, plus de fêtes. Il est venu une telle misère en notre pays, qu'on peut bien dire : Heureux les morts qui ne sentent plus la guerre, la ruine et la peste! Nous sommes pires qu'au temps des grandes tueries où l'on voyait des choses que

l'on n'avait jamais vues, que l'on ne croyait pas possible,
où le père tuait le fils. Aujourd'hui le temps est venu si
mauvais, que mari et femme vont chacun de son côté pour
tâcher de vivre. A présent, l'amour aussi est parti. Cherche
donc à trouver un amoureux! Personne ne veut plus
prendre femme Il faudrait la nourrir, et comment faire
quand il n'y a rien à la maison? Aussi, au lieu de soupirs
d'amour, on n'entend plus rien que les pleurs de la faim.
On craint tout. La Charité va frappant de porte en porte,
personne ne veut lui donner abri sous son toit. On n'ose
plus pleurer en suivant le cercueil d'un mort, crainte de
mouiller trop de mouchoirs » Puis, reprenant le ton de la
plaisanterie : « Sois notre ami, moi, je veux bien être le
tien. Tu peux m'inviter tant que tu voudras à aller manger
avec toi, je ne te refuserai rien, pas même les bons conseils, etc. »

Il faut se rappeler que Ruzzante vivait au commencement du seizième siècle, au milieu des guerres de François Ier et de Charles-Quint se disputant l'Italie, pendant
que la terrible invasion de l'armée allemande se ruait sur
Rome, en laissant derrière elle les campagnes dévastées et
brûlées La ville sainte était prise d'assaut, saccagée et
livrée à deux mois de pillage par les luthériens, Florence
ravagée par la peste, et le propre pays de Ruzzante, le
Padouan, désolé par la famine Aussi, dans ses comédies,
il maudit énergiquement les Espagnols et les Allemands :
« Que la peste puisse les manger, dit-il, guerres et soldats,
soldats et guerres! Mais il faut rire quand même, mes
amis, il faut nous étourdir sur nos malheurs! »

Aussi, au milieu de ses plus vives bouffonneries, on retrouve souvent chez Ruzzante une situation terrible, ou un éclair de vraie passion, ou une réflexion profonde, ou un cri du cœur. Les côtés sérieux de son esprit se révèlent de la manière la plus concise, mais aussi la plus énergique, et dans les termes les plus vrais et les plus touchants, malheureusement très-souvent intraduisibles, car ces dialectes font partie de ces personnages. Il avait mille fois raison de dire et de prouver qu'en parlant autrement, ils ne seraient plus que des êtres de convention.

Mais ce qui doit nous occuper ici, c'est le côté bouffon de Ruzzante, car c'est par là qu'il appartient à la *commedia dell' arte*. Cette gaieté est bien souvent amère, tragique et hideuse comme le cadre où il esquisse ses tableaux burlesques. Quelques-unes de ses pièces ne portent pas de titre. C'est sous la dénomination de *dialogue* qu'elles sont imprimées :

« BILORA. Qui m'aurait dit que l'amour me pousserait si rudement hors de ma maison, pour me jeter au milieu de gens que je ne connais pas? Je ne sais pas où je suis. On dit que l'amour ne peut ou ne sait rien faire? Je vois bien, moi, qu'il fait ce qu'il veut. Quant à moi, c'est bien l'amour qui m'a forcé de venir voir où s'est cachée ma *chrétienne*. Sans cela je n'aurais pas marché tout hier, toute cette nuit et tout ce matin, à travers les bois, les champs, les sentiers et les ravines. Je suis si fatigué que je n'en peux plus. Un amoureux est tiré par l'amour plus fort que ne le feraient trois paires de bœufs.... Il y en a qui disent que l'amour se loge chez les jeunes gens et les fait enrager. Pour ma part,

je m'aperçois bien qu'il hante aussi les vieillards, et s'il
n'avait transpercé et enlevé le cœur de ce vieux bavard,
que le cancre puisse manger! il ne m'aurait pas emmené
ma femme dans cette ville. Ce vieil usurier ne pouvait-il
prendre plaisir de ses écus, sans chercher à en prendre de
ma femme? Par le *sang du cancre!* c'est là un tour qui ne me
plaît pas, mais je ferai si bien que, de jour, de nuit, *ou
autrement*, j'arracherai ma femme d'ici. Mais qui sait si je
la pourrai voir? J'aurais mieux fait d'aller à sa maison,
c'est ce qui serait le plus pressé... Je meurs de faim et je
n'ai pas de pain, et pas d'argent pour en acheter. Si je
savais, au moins, où elle demeure, c'est-à-dire où il l'a
menée, je la prierais tant, qu'elle me donnerait bien un
morceau de pain. »

Il va s'éloigner, quand il rencontre une ancienne connaissance. C'est Pittaro, le vieux paysan qu'il qualifie de
barba, comme qui dirait *barbon*.

« PITTARO. Eh! par la *cagasangue!* Est-ce toi, Bilora? et
que viens-tu faire ici?

BILORA. Je viens pour l'affaire de messire Andro.... Aide-
moi à dire son nom.... Androtene ou Ardochene, ce vieux
gentilhomme étranger qui a emmené ma femme chez lui....

PITTARO. Tu as eu tort de venir. Et que comptes-tu faire
de ta femme, qui paraît t'avoir oublié? Il ne suffira pas de
l'aller demander pour qu'elle retourne avec toi. Elle prend
joliment du bon temps avec lui; ni fatigues, ni soucis; à
boire, à manger tant qu'elle veut, et bien servie, car il y a
un chien de valet pour les servir tous deux. »

Il lui raconte comme quoi le vieil Andronico est amou-

reux fou de sa femme, et que celle-ci paraît avoir de l'attachement pour lui : « C'est, dit-il, messire le beau par-ci,
messire le chéri par-là. » Il lui conseille de s'en aller, il n'a
rien à faire dans cette ville; mais Bilora n'est pas de son
avis : « Ne serait-il pas mieux qu'elle s'en retournât chez
moi? Si je rencontrais le vieux, je pourrais bien le frapper
Je voudrais bien voir ma Dina! Est-elle seule à la maison? » Pittaro lui répète qu'il n'a qu'à s'en aller, qu'il ne
faut pas qu'on le voie rôder par-là. Mais Bilora resté seul
l'envoie au diable, et, quant à lui, il est si tourmenté
d'amour, de crainte et de rage, qu'il ne peut résister à
l'envie de voir sa femme. Il frappe à la porte de la maison;
Dina paraît à sa fenêtre.

Dina. Qui frappe? Qui est là? C'est vous, pauvre homme?
allez en paix.

Bilora. Oui, je suis bien pauvre, mais ce n'est pas une
raison pour m'en aller. Je suis ton ami; approche, Dina,
c'est moi!

Dina. Qui ça, vous? Quel ami! Monsieur n'est pas à la
maison, allez-vous-en.

Bilora. Ah! Dina, viens un peu ici, c'est moi. Est-ce que
tu ne me reconnais pas, folle?

Dina. Je vous dis de vous éloigner d'ici, que je ne vous
connais pas, que monsieur est absent; il est sorti pour nos
affaires, et je n'ai pas envie de jaser.

Bilora. Ah! ah! tu es bien accrétée, chère Dina! Viens
un peu ici, je veux te parler sincèrement. C'est pourtant
moi, Dina! Ne vois-tu pas que je suis Bilora ton mari, ton
chrétien (*a son el to christian*)?

Dina. Ah! quel malheur! c'est vous? Mais qu'êtes-vous venu faire ici? dites-le.

Bilora. Qu'est-ce que tu dis? Mais viens donc un peu ici que je te puisse voir.

Dina. J'y vais.

Bilora. Viens-t'en avec moi, sœur de ma foi, et je te tiendrai encore pour bonne et chère, comme tu l'étais auparavant.

Dina. Bonsoir, me voici puisque tu m'as demandée. Comment te portes-tu? Tu te portes bien?

Bilora. Moi bien, et toi? Quelle bonne mine tu as!

Dina. Avec l'aide du ciel. Je ne me trouve cependant pas trop bien, si tu veux que je te dise la vérité. Je suis assommée de ce vieillard.

Bilora. Jeunesse et vieillesse ne s'accordent guère. Moi et toi irions mieux ensemble.

Dina. Puis il est moitié malade, il tousse toute la nuit à m'empêcher de dormir. A toute heure il vient et revient me chercher pour me tourmenter, me prendre dans ses bras et m'embrasser.

Bilora. Et bien, dis-moi, ne veux-tu pas retourner dans ta maison, ou veux-tu rester ici avec ce vieux? dis!

Dina. Moi je voudrais bien revenir, mais lui ne le veut pas. Il ne veut pas non plus que tu viennes ici. Si tu savais les attentions qu'il a pour moi, les caresses qu'il me fait! Par la fièvre! il me veut joliment du bien, et j'ai grandement du bon temps avec lui.

Bilora. Mais qu'est-ce que cela fait qu'il ne veuille pas,

lui, si tu le veux? Je vois bien le manége · tu ne le veux pas non plus, et tu me contes quelque mensonge. Eh! dis?

DINA. Que te dirais-je? Je voudrais et je ne voudrais pas (*vorràe e si no vorràe*).

BILORA Le ciel me la baille belle, ce soir! Le vieux sera-t-il longtemps avant de revenir au logis?

DINA Il doit revenir tout de suite: mais je ne voudrais pas qu'il me vît avec quelqu'un. Va-t-en, cher frère, tu reviendras en cachette et nous nous entendrons.

BILORA. Oui, nous nous accorderons à coups de pieds! Prends garde, par le sang! Si je m'en mêle, je ferai pis que ne fait un soldat! »

Après plusieurs menaces de Bilora, Dina lui dit qu'elle l'avertira quand le maître sera revenu, afin qu'il la rede-mande à lui, et, qu'il le veuille ou non, Dina fera la volonté de son mari. Après quoi, Bilora lui demande un morceau de pain, parce qu'il meurt de faim et n'a pas mangé depuis qu'il est parti. Mais Dina, qui ne peut rien distraire de la maison, dit-elle, lui donne de l'argent pour aller à l'hôtellerie, où il mangera et boira à son aise, parce qu'elle ne voudrait pas être surprise donnant quoi que ce soit, et elle rentre. Bilora sort après avoir fait quelques réflexions sur la faim et l'amour, après avoir maudit le vieillard et regardé la monnaie que Dina lui a donnée, et dont les effi-gies lui fournissent des plaisanteries difficiles à traduire.

Messer Andronico arrive alors en discourant tout seul sur les femmes et l'amour dans l'âge mûr. Il éprouve le besoin de revoir Dina et de folâtrer un peu avec elle Il frappe chez lui en disant : « Ouvre-moi, ma jolie, ma

beauté ! » il va pour l'embrasser, mais c'est son valet
Tonin qui a reçu ses louanges doucereuses et qu'il traite
maintenant de brute et de cheval. Après quoi ils rentrent
tous deux.

Bilora et Pittaro reviennent. Pittaro lui demande s'il a
bien mangé, si le vin était bon, etc. Bilora, après avoir
répondu qu'il est « plein », le charge d'être médiateur entre
lui et messer Andronico, qu'il continue d'appeler *Ardoche* :
« Tu lui diras que Dina a un mari : il faut qu'il la laisse
venir, qu'il le veuille ou non, puisqu'elle le veut. Ajoute
que s'il refuse, je le tuerai, que je suis un soldat et un
brave, cela lui fera plus de peur. S'il me la rend, tout sera
bien ; dans le cas contraire, qu'il prenne garde à lui.... »

Bilora s'éloigne, et Pittaro, après avoir frappé à la porte,
et après avoir subi les interrogatoires d'usage de Dina :
« Qui êtes-vous ? Que voulez-vous ? » etc., peut enfin parler
à messer Andronico :

« PITTARO. Bonsoir, messire et Excellence.

ANDRONICO. Qui t'amène, Pittaro ? Que veux-tu ?

PITTARO. Je voudrais vous dire dix paroles en confidence,
entre vous et moi ; venez un peu par ici, messire.

ANDRONICO. Qu'est-ce qu'il y a donc de si intéressant ?

PITTARO Vous allez le savoir, messire. Vous savez bien,
sans que je vous le dise, que vous avez emmené la Dina, la
femme de ce pauvre garçon Bilora Il en a perdu la tête.
Or donc, comme je dois vous le dire, je viens vous prier,
Excellence, dans votre propre intérêt, pour que vous la
laissiez aller avec son mari. Parce que, réfléchissez, très-
cher monsieur, que c'est fièrement imprudent à vous

d'avoir enlevé la femme d'un autre. Et puis, je veux
vous dire en ami, qu'elle n'est ni vieille, ni centenaire,
et que vous êtes bien déjeté et bien vieux pour une si
jeune femme. Pardonnez-moi, messire, de vous parler si
ouvertement.

ANDRONICO. Veux-tu que je te dise la vérité? Je ne ferai
rien de ce que tu me dis, parce que je ne pourrai jamais la
quitter. M'as-tu compris? Je suis résolu à passer ma vie
avec elle Que diable! penses-tu que je laisserai cette fille
retourner à la campagne pour souffrir avec ce grand lâche
de Bilora, qui lui fait manger plus de coups de bâton que
de bouchées de pain? Me séparer d'elle? Non, non! Je
la veux tout à moi, je me ferais conscience de laisser
manger à des porcs des noix muscades. Crois-tu donc que
je l'ai emmenée, comme je l'ai fait, pour la laisser partir
si promptement? Moi qui ai endossé la cuirasse et porté
l'écu (*la falda*) tout cet été, armé comme un Rodomont,
moi qui suis resté sous les armes nuit et jour, qui ai eu tant
de fatigues et de craintes de la voir malheureuse, j'irais la
rendre? Quelle folie! Tu peux dire à Bilora qu'il cherche
ailleurs ce qu'il lui faut.

PITTARO. Par le puissant mal du cancre! que voulez-vous
donc qu'il fasse? Voulez-vous qu'il devienne enragé?

ANDRONICO. Eh bien, et moi, veux-tu donc que je me
désespère? Quelle diable de chose! Il enragera, que veux-tu
que j'y fasse? Tu m'ennuies. Tu me ferais vraiment mettre
en colère. Va-t'en au diable En voilà assez là-dessus. Je
sens les vapeurs qui me prennent.

PITTARO. Non, messire, ne vous échauffez pas. Faisons

mieux, appelons la Dina, et, après l'avoir interrogée, voyons ce qu'elle dira. Si elle veut s'en aller, laissez-la partir. Si elle ne veut pas, gardez-la et faites-en ce que vous voudrez. Qu'en dites-vous ?

ANDRONICO. Au bout du compte, tu parles bien. Mais ne va pas croire qu'elle sera de ton avis. Elle m'a encore dit, tout à l'heure, qu'elle ne me quitterait jamais pour quelque homme qui soit au monde. Je ne crois pas qu'elle ait si vite changé d'idée. Je veux bien te faire ce plaisir, et tu t'en iras alors le cœur content, quand tu sauras la vérité. (*Il appelle.*) Dina, écoute ! Est-ce que tu ne m'entends pas ? Dina ! ma jolie ! écoute ici, viens !

DINA. Vous m'appelez, mon maître ?

ANDRONICO. Écoute, ma belle, ce brave homme vient te chercher de la part de ton mari, et nous sommes convenus que si tu voulais me quitter, je te laisserais aller ; que si tu voulais rester, tu resterais. Tu sais que tu es heureuse avec moi et que je ne te laisserai jamais manquer de rien. Fais comme tu voudras et comme il te plaira. Je ne dis rien de plus.

DINA. Que j'aille avec mon mari ? Je ne le veux pas ! Pour avoir des coups de bâton ? Sur ma foi ! non. Avec l'aide du ciel, je voudrais ne l'avoir jamais connu, lui, le plus lâche de tous les lâches qui mangent du pain ! Je dis, une fois pour toutes, non ! je ne veux pas retourner avec lui.

ANDRONICO. Bien, bien, bien ! Êtes-vous content, satisfait ? Quand je vous le disais, vous ne vouliez pas me croire !

PITTARO. Mais écoutez, messire, elle a dit à Bilora lui-

même, il n'y a pas une demi-heure, qu'elle voulait bien
aller chez lui, mais que vous ne le voulez pas.

Dina. Comment! moi? je n'ai jamais dit cela. A qui
l'ai-je dit? C'est quelqu'un qui me l'a fait dire. Comme dit
la bonne femme, je laisse ce mensonge à qui l'a inventé.

Andronico. Rentre chez toi, dans ta chambre, ma belle,
et ne t'en inquiète pas davantage. (*A Pittaro*) Qu'en dites-
vous? Que voulez-vous encore?

Pittaro. Moi, messire? rien de plus. Je veux ce qu'elle
veut; mais je vous dirai que Bilora est un homme à
craindre, il ne vous veut pas de bien, et vous feriez mieux
de lui rendre sa femme.

Andronico. Que veux-tu dire par ces paroles? Explique-
toi tout de suite. Veux-tu me menacer? Ne me fais pas
mettre en colère, je suis de sang-froid, et je te dirai en peu
de mots que tu me fais l'effet d'une bête. Va-t'en d'ici! et
promptement. Une fois pour toutes, je ne veux pas rendre
Dina, m'as-tu entendu? Je rentre chez moi, fais en sorte
que je ne te retrouve plus quand je sortirai. Cela suffit, en
voilà assez »

Pittaro lui dit qu'il va s'en aller comme le vent et qu'il
ne le reverra plus Après qu'Andronico est rentré chez lui,
Bilora revient, il a probablement tout entendu, car il
reproche à son compère de n'avoir pas réussi. Sur quoi
Pittaro, impatienté et déjà rebuffé par Andronico, lui dit
qu'il *l'embête* aussi, lui (*te me n'incaghi ti ancora*), mais il
emploie des mots plus énergiques et qui étaient reçus alors
sur le théâtre. Après quoi il veut l'emmener, mais, sur le
refus de Bilora, il l'envoie au diable et s'en va.

« BILORA *seul.* Non, je ne veux pas m'en aller. Ne croi-
rait-on pas qu'il m'a rendu service? Par *le sang du mal de
la boiteuse!* mes affaires vont tout à l'envers avec les semelles
en l'air et le bonnet en bas; c'est à faire crever de rire les
écoliers! Si bien que je ne sais que faire. Ce vieux a ruiné
ma vie. Il vaudrait mieux qu'il fût mort et mis en terre. Si
j'en croyais ma rage, je l'y aiderais bien. J'y pense! quand
il sortira de chez lui, je lui dirai son fait et le malmènerai si
bien qu'il en tombera tout de suite par terre, et alors, moi
de taper dessus, en long, en travers, à lui faire sortir les
tripes et la vie. Oui, mais il criera de peur, si je fais ainsi?...
Il vaut mieux faire comme les soldats espagnols, il n'aura
pas le temps de dire huit paroles. Tirons un peu mon coutelas de sa gaîne. Voyons si la lame en est luisante. Par le
cancre! elle ne l'est guère, il n'en aura pas trop peur. Mais
moi, Bilora, je saurai bien lui dire des injures épouvanta-
bles. Vieux maudit, puisses-tu venir vite! Je te veux d'abord
enlever la peau des reins, et je te mène, et je t'en donne,
tant et tant, que je l'aurai bientôt tué! Je lui prendrai ses
vêtements, je les emporterai, et, pour n'avoir pas à craindre
les dépositions, je les vendrai, ainsi que mon manteau,
pour acheter un cheval et m'en aller bien loin. Je me ferai
soldat, je vivrai dans les camps, parce que maintenant j'ai
horreur de ma maison. Je la cède à qui la veut. Ah! que je
voudrais qu'il sortît! Chut! le voici! le voilà sorti! Oh!
que la peste te crève, vieux éreinté! Le moment est bon,
pourvu qu'il ne vienne personne! Il vient! Ah! maintenant
il ne m'échappera plus.

ANDRONICO *sur sa porte, parlant à son valet.* Quel est l'ami-mal qui rôde par ici à ces heures? Quelque ivrogne? Ne viens pas, Zane, reste au logis, je vais prendre l'air pour me calmer le sang, tu tiendras compagnie à Dina, et tu viendras me chercher sur les quatre heures de la nuit, avec la lanterne.

ZANF. Je viendrai aussitôt que je pourrai, ne vous inquiétez pas.

ANDRONICO. Zane, ferme la porte. Il vaut mieux que je prenne par là, je passerai le *traghetto* et cela me fera faire une bonne promenade.

BILORA. Que la mort te mange, vieux fini! Tiens! tiens! (*Il le frappe*)

ANDRONICO. O mon doux fils! ô mon garçon! grâce, grâce.... A moi! à moi! Au secours! Au feu! au feu! au feu! On m'assassine! Trahison! Au feu! au feu! A moi, je meurs, je suis mort! (*Il tombe*)

BILORA. Au feu!.. Oui, au feu d'enfer tu iras! Rends-moi ma femme à présent! Je t'avais bien dit de la laisser! Mais je crois bien qu'il est mort, car il ne remue plus ni pieds ni jambes. Ah!... tu as fini de rire?... Ne t'avais-je pas averti, dis! »

Ainsi finit la pièce. Ce dialogue, dont la traduction ne peut rendre l'énergie et la couleur, est, comme on le voit, une tragédie, mais une tragédie *réelle;* comme elle a pu se passer sur un *traghetto* vénitien, un de ces escaliers souvent baignés de sang que lave un instant après l'eau des *canaletti,* en emportant le cadavre. L'original est très-saisissant. Là, aucune fiction, aucun idéal. Chaque personnage pense et parle comme dans la vie positive. Mais quelle étrange gaieté, et quelle rudesse de fibres chez un public qui riait à ces scènes de désespoir et de meurtre accompagnées de *lazzi* effrayants!

Le monologue de Bilora est remarquable de vérité à une époque où la convention dramatique était pleine d'emphase· c'est un assassin qui prémédite et ne prémédite pas Lui aussi *voudrait et ne voudrait pas*. Il voudrait battre, insulter; si l'homme en meurt, tant pis. Le paysan n'est ni brave, ni méchant, ni fier, il n'a pas le point d'honneur du gentilhomme, il aime sa femme criminelle, il la regrette, il la veut, il l'aura, il la battra, il l'aimera encore C'est l'enfant de la nature. On comprend quel parti un acteur intelligent pouvait tirer d'une pareille situation entre le rire, les larmes et la terreur.

Le dialogue que nous venons d'indiquer semble être une revanche prise par la fantaisie de Ruzzante sur celui qui va suivre, et où il joue le rôle du poltron, ou, pour mieux dire, du *soldat capitan*

MONOLOGUE DE RUZZANTE *revenant de la guerre*·

« RUZZANTE. Me voilà donc enfin arrivé à cette Venise ! Il me tardait autant d'y arriver qu'il tarde à la cavale maigre et fourbue de voir pousser l'herbe du printemps. Je vais donc enfin voir ma *Gnua* (*Genoveffa*, Geneviève)! Au diable les camps, la guerre et les soldats! Je n'entendrai plus ces roulements de tambour et ces sonneries de trompette qui me faisaient trembler Je n'entendrai plus crier aux armes! Je n'aurai plus peur! Quand on criait aux armes, c'était comme si j'avais eu un pressoir dans la panse. Plus de mon quetades! Je ne tremble plus! J'ai du courage maintenant! Je pourrai dormir et rêver tant que je voudrai. Je mangerai, quand il me plaira, tant et trop si je veux. Je digérerai. J'agirai à ma guise Saint Marc! saint Marc! je suis maintenant en sûreté. Je suis venu vite, j'ai fait plus de soixante milles par jour. Je suis venu en trois jours de Crémone ici! Il n'y a pas tant de chemin que l'on dit. Ils disent que de Crémone à Brescia il y a quarante milles, il n'y a qu'une enjambée. De Brescia à Peschiera on dit trente. De Peschiera ici combien peut-il y en avoir? J'en suis venu en un jour, il est vrai que j'ai marché toute la nuit. Ma foi! les jambes m'en font mal, quoique je ne sois pas fatigué. C'est que la peur me poussait et que l'espérance me soutenait, ce sont mes souliers qui en ont porté la peine. Je les veux regarder. Le cancre me mange! en voici un qui n'a plus de semelle, je dirai que j'ai attrapé ça à la guerre. Si j'avais eu l'ennemi au derrière, je n'aurais pas mieux marché. Je suis fait comme un larron, avec ces habits que j'ai volés à un paysan. L'habit ne fait rien, je suis en sûreté.... Ensuite, je suis monté en barque à l'usine. Si j'avais été tué à la guerre, et que je ne fusse plus qu'un esprit, je ne serais pas ici! Mais non, cancre! les esprits ne mangent point. Je suis moi, je suis vivant. Il faut que je cherche Gnva, ou mon compère Menato, qui est venu aussi habiter Venise. Mais le voici. Hé! compère, c'est moi, Ruzzante!

MENATO. Est-ce vous, compère? Mais je ne vous aurais jamais reconnu! vous êtes si changé! Mais soyez le bienvenu. Venez-vous maintenant de la guerre? Avez-vous été malade ou en prison? Ah! quelle mauvaise figure, compère! Vous avez l'air d'un brigand. Pardonnez-moi, mais j'en ai vu plus de cent, qui étaient pendus, n'avoir pas si mauvaise mine que vous.

Ruzzante. Ce sont les effets et les misères de la guerre: mal boire, mal manger, la faim, la soif vous décharnent la peau; et si vous aviez été d'où je viens, moi!

Menato. Vous parlez comme un livre, l'ami. Avez-vous donc appris à parler le florentin?

Ruzzante. Celui qui court le monde n'a qu'à se dépêcher d'apprendre, je parle aussi le français, mais si je vous parlais dans cette langue, vous ne me comprendriez pas, certes. J'ai tout appris par peur en un jour, et je m'en fais gloire. »

Il y a ici plusieurs plaisanteries intraduisibles, sur des mots soi-disant florentins ou français, dits les uns pour les autres, avec explication en padouan et interprétation par Ruzzante. Menato revient à ses réflexions sur les guenilles qu'il rapporte. Ruzzante lui dit qu'il les a conquises, les armes à la main, sur un paysan qui l'avait blessé : « Le cancre à ces vauriens de paysans! dit-il, pour un *quattrin* j'en laisserai bien étrangler un.

Menato. Mais, compère, parce que vous êtes soldat à présent, vous ne croyez donc plus être de la campagne, vous?... Êtes-vous devenu si enragé que vous mangeriez du fer?

Ruzzante. Si vous aviez été où je suis allé, moi! vous auriez appris à en manger aussi du fer, des armes et du bagage, car, n'ayant plus d'argent pour vivre, j'ai vendu tout ce que je possédais dans une hôtellerie.

Menato. Est-ce tout ce que vous ont rapporté vos prises
sur l'ennemi?

Ruzzante. Je n'ai jamais voulu faire de mal à l'ennemi
Pourquoi lui en aurais-je fait? Il ne m'avait jamais rien fait
à moi? Je faisais la guerre aux vaches et aux juments, et
j'ai réussi parfois à faire des *prisonniers*.

Menato. Tu as bien la tournure d'un mauvais soldat,
tellement que personne ne croirait, en te voyant, que tu as
fait la guerre. J'avais pensé te voir revenir estropié d'une
jambe ou d'un bras, ou bien avec la figure coupée ou
un œil crevé?

Ruzzante. La bravoure ne consiste pas dans les blessures
et les estropiaisons. Croyez-vous donc que quatre hommes
me fassent peur?... Si vous aviez été où j'ai été, vous parle-
riez autrement! Vous auriez fait des choses que vous n'avez
jamais faites. Il ne faut être ni boiteux, ni manchot pour
se tirer de ces batailles où un seul ne peut rien faire contre
tant de gens! Dans ces affaires-là personne ne se connaît,
compère! on ne sait où donner de la tête. Vous entendez
tout le monde criant : Tue! tue! les roulements d'arquebu-
sades par ici, les coups de pertuisane par là. Tu vois
tomber mort ton compagnon, et puis après c'est ton tour;
et si tu veux te sauver, les ennemis te courent dessus, et
un coup d'escopette parti on ne sait d'où te casse l'échine.
Je vous dis qu'il faut avoir du courage pour chercher à
fuir ou à se cacher, et croyez-vous donc qu'on perde son
temps en se cachant? On *fait* de male peur, et cela occupe.
Tenez, moi qui vous parle, j'ai fait le mort, et toute la
cavalerie m'a passé sur le dos. Si la montagne de *Venda*

m'eût passé sur le corps, cela n'eût pas été pis Je vous dis la vérité, il faut avoir du courage pour en revenir vivant.... Un jour, en me sauvant, un cavalier et son cheval, qui se sauvaient aussi, me marchèrent sur le talon et enlevèrent toute la semelle de mon soulier, comme vous pouvez voir. »

Menato lui demande si toutes ses campagnes lui ont rapporté quelque argent. A quoi Ruzzante de lui répondre, toujours avec sa phrase sacramentelle : « *Si vous aviez été où j'ai été*, vous n'auriez pas rapporté davantage que moi. »

Mais le but de son voyage, c'est sa bien-aimée Gnva, qui, au dire de Menato, l'a oublié et qui, en ce moment, établie à Venise, vit avec le familier d'un cardinal Sur quoi Ruzzante dit que « c'est peu pour lui de tuer un homme, et qu'il le tuera, quand bien même *il serait quatre.* »

« Ruzzante. Mais voici Gnva, mon compère, c'est elle qui vient là, par ma foi ! Nous allons voir si elle me fera des caresses. Oh là ! oh là ! dis-moi donc ! compagnonne ! tu ne me vois pas ? C'est cependant moi.

Gnva. Ruzzante ! est-ce donc toi ? tu es vivant ? Mais quelles guenilles ! quelle piteuse mise ! Tu n'as rien gagné, dis, vrai !

Ruzzante. J'ai assez gagné pour toi, puisque je t'apporte ma carcasse saine et sauve, comme tu vois.

Gnva. Pour ta carcasse, je m'en passerai bien. Je pensais que tu m'aurais apporté quelque belle robe. Je m'en vais, parce que l'on m'attend. Laisse-moi partir.

Ruzzante. Au diable soit l'amour que j'ai pour toi ! Tu ne

m'as pas sitôt aperçu que tu veux t'en aller? Moi qui suis revenu de la guerre exprès pour te voir?

Gnva. Tu m'as bien assez vue. Pour te dire la vérité, je ne veux pas que tu me causes quelque désagrément, parce que j'ai quelqu'un qui m'entretient fort bien et qui ne sait rien de notre aventure passée. »

Ruzzante lui dit qu'il est capable de l'entretenir aussi bien que cet autre, mais Gnva ne veut pas mourir de faim avec lui : « Il fallait, lui dit-elle, depuis plus de quatre mois que tu es parti, rapporter quelque argent de la guerre; mais je crois bien que tu n'y as pas été; tu as la mine d'un menteur, et tu auras passé ton temps dans la boutique de quelque apothicaire. J'aimerais mieux que tu fusses revenu manchot, boiteux et borgne, le nez coupé, avec la volonté de gagner de l'argent pour moi, comme tu me l'avais promis. — Il m'avait juré, dit-elle à Menato, de mourir ou de revenir riche, et vous le voyez revenir tel qu'il est, c'est bien la preuve qu'il n'a guère songé à moi.

Ruzzante. Je te dis que j'ai eu du malheur !

Gnva. C'est possible, et moi qui n'en ai pas, et ne veux pas en avoir, je ne veux plus m'affoler de toi. Va ! fais tes affaires, je ferai les miennes. Je vais retrouver mon homme, laisse-moi m'en aller.

Ruzzante. Au diable ton homme ! Je ne connais pour ton homme que moi seul.

Gnva. Laisse-moi, malheureux, vaurien, menteur, paresseux !

Ruzzante. Viens avec moi, je te dis. Ne me fais pas mettre en colère, j'ai bien changé! C'est que tu ne me

mènerais plus par le bout du nez, comme tu le faisais
jadis

MENATO Ecoutez, ma commère, allez-vous-en ! Il serait
capable de vous tuer.

GNVA. Lui? Laissez-le donc, il n'est bon qu'à tuer ses
puces, et encore? C'est un fanfaron. »

Le *Bravo*, c'est ainsi qu'est qualifié l'amant de Gnva,
vient et donne des coups à Ruzzante, qui se laisse tomber
Le Bravo emmène Gnva. Quand il est parti, Ruzzante lève
la tête et dit à Menato :

« Compère, sont-ils partis? N'y a-t-il plus personne ?
Regardez bien !

MENATO. Non, compère, il s'en est allé avec elle, il n'y
est plus.

RUZZANTE. Mais les autres? sont-ils tous partis?

MENATO. Mais quels autres? Je n'en ai vu qu'un.

RUZZANTE. Vous n'y voyez guère bien ! Ils étaient plus
de cent.

MENATO. Eh non, par le cancre !

RUZZANTE. Eh si, par le cancre ! Voulez-vous le savoir
mieux que moi? Vous me la baillez belle. Ils n'y allaient
pas de main morte, que vous en semble? Cent contre un !
Si je n'avais pas fait le mort lestement, ils m'arrangeaient
bien !

MENATO. Vous m'aviez dit que vous étiez si brave que,
dans la bataille, vous ne connaissiez ni amis, ni parents?

RUZZANTE. Certainement. Mais que voulez-vous qu'un seul
fasse contre tant de monde? Vous auriez dû venir à mon
secours. Croyez-vous donc que je sois un Roland ?

MENATO. Je vous assure, compère, qu'il n'y en avait qu'un. Mais je croyais que vous vous laissiez maltraiter et bien battre pour vous lever et taper dessus, tandis qu'il vous aurait cru éreinté; je pensais que vous alliez l'empêcher d'emmener la Gnua.... Comprenez-vous, compère?

RUZZANTE. Ma foi non, compère; je n'y ai seulement pas songé. Je me suis jeté à terre, j'ai fait le mort, comme je faisais à la guerre, afin qu'ils me laissent la vie sauve. C'est plus sûr, quand on a tant d'ennemis sur le dos!

MENATO. Compère, sur ma foi, je vous dis que cet homme était tout seul. Que ne vous défendiez-vous avec votre lance?

RUZZANTE. Un contre cent? Il n'y a qu'à fuir dans ces occasions-là.

MENATO. Compère, il n'y en avait qu'un seul, par ma foi de compère!

RUZZANTE. Alors, s'ils n'étaient qu'un, c'est une trahison ou quelque enchantement de la Gnua, qu'en pensez-vous? Croyez-vous qu'elle soit sorcière? Jadis elle m'a bien fait croire qu'elle était la plus belle fille du monde, et cependant cela n'est pas; il y en a beaucoup de plus belles qu'elle. Maintenant, elle fait qu'un seul me paraisse cent.... Donc, que le cancre la mange! je la veux faire brûler, puisqu'elle est sorcière. Vous êtes bien sûr qu'il n'y en avait qu'un? Il faut que je sois un homme fort vaillant pour avoir supporté tant de coups de bâton!

MENATO. Par le cancre! des coups de bâton à tuer un âne, mon compère! Je n'en voyais pas le ciel, tant il y en avait. Vous ne vous en ressentez pas? Je ne sais pas comment vous êtes vivant!

II   11

Ruzzante. L'habitude, compère, j'y suis fait, je ne sens rien. Je n'ai qu'un chagrin, c'est de n'avoir pas su qu'il n'y en avait qu'un. J'aurais fait la plus belle noyade qu'on ait jamais vue. Je l'aurais attaché lui à elle, et je les aurais boutés droit dans le canal. Ah cancre! cela aurait été drôle, et nous aurions ri un peu, ma foi! Je ne dis pas que je lui aurais donné des coups de bâton, l'amour de la Gnùa n'en vaut pas la peine, mais je l'aurais jeté à l'eau, entendez-vous, compère? Et certes il y aurait eu là de quoi rire. Oh! oh! oh! oh! »

Nous terminerons nos citations par une admirable lettre de Ruzzante à son ami et camarade de théâtre, Marco Alvarotto (Menego-Menato). N'ayant aucun détail sur la vie d'un homme au premier chef remarquable et intéressant, et n'oubliant pas que, si nous faisons ici l'histoire des types de la comédie, nous faisons aussi, autant que possible, l'histoire des talents oubliés et des gloires disparues, nous croyons devoir faire connaître les aspirations et comme qui dirait l'âme de Ruzzante, résumée dans cet écrit. Nous voyons en lui un homme jeune et beau, mélancolique comme tous les grands bouffons, malade probablement d'une fatigue de l'âme et non d'une vie dissolue; car la chasteté de ses compositions est à remarquer dans une époque où le libertinage préside à tous les essais dramatiques et littéraires. Voyez le sujet de *la Mandragore* et celui de *la Calandra* ! c'est le temps de l'Arétin et de tant d'autres illustres débauchés. Le Ruzzante a, de temps en temps, le cynisme et la rudesse d'expression de son époque: mais ce cynisme, dans la bouche des paysans, choque beaucoup

moins que dans celle des *raffinés*. Le fond de ses sujets est
un enseignement moral, parfois tragique, parfois tou-
chant. L'éternel *becco* de la comédie y est terrible aussi
souvent que ridicule, et quand l'auteur met en scène une
fille pure, comme Nina, dans *la Piorana*, elle est adorable.

En outre, Ruzzante cache sous les fleurs de l'allégorie
un spiritualisme fin et délicat, comme on va voir ·

« *A Messire Marco Alvarotto.*

» Marco, mon cher maître, je me réjouis, comme vous,
du plaisir que vous avez pris à la chasse, et, pensant que,
de votre côté, vous prendrez part à celui que j'ai éprouvé
il n'y a pas longtemps, je vais vous le raconter, afin que
nous allions ainsi de divertissement en divertissement.

» Vous saurez que, trouvant ce monde le plus beau pays
du monde, je pris un jour la ferme résolution d'y rester
toujours, ou tout au moins d'être l'un des derniers à le
quitter. Sachant bien, cependant, qu'il n'est pas donné aux
hommes de bien plus qu'aux autres d'avoir une existence
qui soit plus qu'une existence, je m'entretins longuement à
ce sujet avec mes petits livres[1], qui m'affirmèrent qu'il
était possible de vivre longtemps et même éternellement,
mais qu'auparavant il me fallait trouver une certaine dame
que les uns appellent *Modestie*, les autres *Sagesse*, laquelle
peut donner autant de vie qu'on lui en sait demander.
puisque certains grands personnages, morts depuis lon-

---

[1] Ses manuscrits, qui ne furent imprimés que plusieurs années après
sa mort

gues années, vivent encore par leurs œuvres. Alors j'ouvris
la bouche pour leur dire : « Petits livres, mes frères, vous
vous moquez de moi; cette dame est comme cette herbe qui
a la vertu de rendre invisible celui qui la porte, mais qui
ne se trouve nulle part » Je me tus cependant, les sachant
véridiques et semblables aux hommes de bien qui ne
diraient pas un mensonge pour mille écus. Je résolus alors
fermement de chercher cette dame, et, fût-elle plus disgra-
cieuse que l'*Envie,* de lui faire la cour, si bien que je la
persuaderais de venir promptement avec moi. Mais, après
avoir compulsé tout mon monde d'écrits, après avoir tant
cherché et être allé plus loin avec mon cerveau que les
navires d'Espagne, et n'avoir pas même trouvé la piste de
ses pas, je me désespérai un beau jour, comme le joueur
qui a mauvaise chance au premier coup. Je maudis les
écrits, et tout en colère j'allai me reposer à la campagne.

» J'étais resté seul à la chasse, sur une de nos petites
montagnes du côté d'Este, attendant que mes chiens revins-
sent de derrière une autre colline où ils couraient un lièvre.
Ils étaient déjà si loin que je ne les entendais plus. Il me
sembla que toute chose se taisait autour de moi, et, soit à
cause de ce silence, soit fatigue de mon cerveau, le sommeil m'entra tout doucement dans les yeux, sans que je
m'en aperçusse, et il n'y fut pas plutôt entré qu'il mit pour
ainsi dire un cadenas à la porte et me chassa hors de moi-
même. Je veux et je dois lui être reconnaissant toute ma
vie, tant longue soit-elle, du songe doux et agréable qui
me fit voir et entendre des choses si belles qu'il sera beau
de les redire et plus beau de les croire. Ainsi, clos et ren-

fermé à clef comme je disais, je vis d'abord notre bon et
brave vieux Polo tel qu'il était jadis, si bien que je n'eus
pas le courage de lui demander s'il était vivant ou mort. Il
avait sa robe de fête et paraissait venir de chez le barbier,
avec une mine annonçant qu'il avait plutôt fait un bon
repas que jeûné. Je ne sais pas comment il avait connaissance de ma volonté de vivre éternellement (je crois que
l'âme est une chose divine), mais, après m'avoir souhaité
le bonjour et la bonne année, s'être frotté le nez à droite et
à gauche, avoir pris sa respiration par deux fois, sans cracher cependant, il commença à me dire : « Ruzzante, tu
t'es plus fatigué sur les livres que je n'ai fatigué mes bras
sur les animaux, et tu ne pourras jamais trouver la femme
que tu cherches, si je ne t'aide et te la montre. C'est la
manie d'appeler les choses par des noms qu'elles n'ont pas
qui te fait tromper. Tu crois qu'elle s'appelle comme tu
dis, tu me fais l'effet de celui qui, sur un livre où était
écrit *Checarello*, lisait *Balotta*. Mais viens avec moi et je te
mènerai à sa cour, où tu trouveras de bons compagnons
qui font rire autant que tu fais rire avec tes *comédies* ou
coméges (con le to comiélie, ò comiegie), je ne sais trop comment dire. »

Il serait trop long de traduire ici tout le discours que
tient à Ruzzante le vieux paysan Polo. Il lui apprend, en
résumé, que celle qu'il appelle *Sagesse* se nomme *Allégresse*,
et il sera si content de la voir, si heureux, si gai, qu'il trouvera avec elle cette existence future qu'il cherche. « Il ne
ressentira plus ces affreuses douleurs d'entrailles, il n'aura
plus de souffrance, il respirera à pleins poumons. Une

heure, une minute de cette existence bien comprise vaut
mieux que mille années d'une vie dont on ne se rend pas
compte. » Le paysan lui décrit, à sa manière rustique, le
bonheur de l'existence. Pour lui, chanter, danser, boire à
sa soif, avoir des pommes, des raves bien cuites et de
bonnes châtaignes, se promener, ne rien faire et regarder,
n'est-ce pas là l'allégresse, le bonheur, la gaieté, plutôt que
de s'alambiquer la cervelle sur les livres ? Ils vont, en causant ainsi, trouver l'*Allégresse*, et traversent une riante et
fraîche contrée, que Polo fait remarquer à Ruzzante :
« As-tu jamais vu un plus beau pays, tout entouré de
collines fleuries et ombragées de bois qui reverdissent par
l'effet des dernières pluies, ces bordures de saules éche-
velés, ces petits ruisseaux qui gazouillent sur les cailloux
en se perdant dans les herbes et les fleurs ? Entends-tu ce
petit oiseau qui chante son air, *hairo, hairo, hano* ? » Au
milieu de ce paradis terrestre, se déroule alors aux yeux
de Ruzzante tout un monde de figures allégoriques allant
et venant, que Polo lui explique à sa manière :

« Regarde tant que tu pourras regarder, nous sommes
dans le pays de l'*Allégresse*. Vois-tu d'abord cette femme qui
passe à côté de moi ? C'est la *Prudence*, la première cuisi-
nière de l'*Allégresse*. Puis le *Contentement* et le *Plaisir* qui
vont se promener en voiture, à cheval et en bateau.
Regarde celui-ci qui se roule à terre avec la bouche si
grande ouverte qu'on croirait qu'il va crever, c'est le
Rire.... Vois cette femme couverte de beaux habits, avec
tant de bijoux et de bracelets plein son tablier, c'est la
Fête; à côté d'elle son frère le *Bal* a ôté ses souliers pour

mieux sauter; tiens! regarde, il danse. Ces deux dames,
qui se tiennent par la main, c'est la *Gaieté* et la *Joie*.
Celle-ci semble ne pouvoir tenir dans sa peau, elle veut
toujours chanter, danser, jouer, lutiner. Le *Chant* les
accompagne; il paraît être à quatre, et il est cependant
seul (*le Quatuor*). Là-bas, la *Bonté*, vêtue de blanc, et
l'*Amitié* se tiennent enlacées. La *Paix* et la *Charité*, qui
marchent à cheval l'une sur l'autre!.. Vois vite l'*Heure*
qui est déjà passée, qui ne revient jamais et qui cependant
retourne et amène avec elle l'étoile du Bouvier. Un
qui s'appelle *Coq* est le premier à l'entendre; il va au-
devant d'elle et lui souhaite le bonjour en chantant.
Regarde celle-là qui est séparée de la compagnie, c'est la
Corruption, toute vêtue de noir, c'est elle qui gâte l'existence, comme les bêtes font des plantes. Voilà la *Tristesse*
les mains jointes et la tête sur ses genoux . à voir ses yeux
ternes, ne ressemble-t-elle pas à une morte? Ne t'amuse pas
à ce petit drôle qui a un arc et un carquois pendu au côté,
c'est le pire de tous, tu ne saurais jamais croire combien il
est méchant! Il n'y a si belle existence où il n'entre et qu'il
ne ruine, avec ses ruses et ses méchancetés. Son nom est
Amour, ce n'est pas le bon Amour, fils de Dieu et de la
Liberté. Je ne sais pas qui fut père de ce mauvais enfant,
mais je soupçonne bien que c'est la *Méchanceté* et le *Malheur*.
Viens-t'en, fuis-le comme la peste. Vois-tu? la *Jalousie* est
à côté de lui, avec ses habits rouges pleins de trous, afin
que puissent y entrer facilement les *mauvais desseins*. La
Douleur, qui va poussant ses lamentations, court devant
l'*Incendie*, qui se roule et déroule sur la terre comme un

chien enragé. Le *Caprice* qui ne peut rester en repos, qui
n'est pas bien où il est, qui voudrait être là où il n'est pas,
qui voudrait être et n'être pas lui, et voudrait aussi être un
autre et ne l'être pas. Ne regarde plus, parce que, à force
de regarder tous ceux-ci, nous perdrons de vue l'*Allégresse*. Qu'as-tu à regarder l'Amour? laisse-le là. »

« Pendant qu'il me parlait ainsi, il me semblait entendre
de la musique, non des chants et des sons, mais je ne sais
quoi de plus harmonieux, comme un concert. Il me paraissait que tout cela faisait une si belle chose, qu'on ne pouvait la redire en mille années, même avec mille langues. Je
voulais regarder fixement pour n'en rien perdre, tant je
prenais plaisir à ce spectacle, mais mes yeux m'en sem-
blaient empêchés par je ne sais quelle lourdeur. M'effor-
çant donc de les ouvrir, le rêve s'envola, et je me trouvai,
les yeux tout grands ouverts, dans la réalité.

» Au même instant, je vis revenir mes chiens poussant le
lièvre devant eux. Ils étaient si fatigués, qu'un d'eux vint se
reposer devant moi et que je lui ôtai de la gueule le lièvre,
encore à moitié vivant.

» Je me rappelai mon rêve et je me souvins que la
musique que j'entendais ressemblait beaucoup à la voix
de mes chiens. Il me sembla aussi que la cause de toutes
ces belles choses que j'avais vues allant et venant dans
mon songe, c'était le lièvre poursuivi par mes chiens,
lesquels, passant et repassant devant moi, finirent par me
faire ouvrir les yeux.

» Voici mon divertissement, amusez-vous-en avec quelque bon compagnon; car je sais que vous êtes plus d'une

paire. Je vous baise les mains et me recommande à vous
auprès de nos amis que vous savez, auxquels je souhaite le
bonheur et la vie aussi longue que celle que je cherchais.

» RUZZANTE.

» De Padoue, le jour de l'Épiphanie, 1535. »

Ce rêve de bonheur sur la terre, mêlé à une aspiration
de gloire, d'amour et d'activité prolongée au delà de la vie,
est encore exprimé dans un prologue de Ruzzante où, sous
les traits et toujours dans le charmant dialecte d'un paysan
padouan, il dit au public :

« La pièce que vous allez voir ne vous paraîtra pas neuve.
Tous ces contes, toutes ces nouvelles furent notre premier
métier, à nous autres gens de campagne, par la raison que
le territoire a existé avant les villes et que les maisons de
paille ont été bâties avant les maisons de pierre.... Et vous
savez bien qu'il ne se peut pas dire ou faire chose qui n'ait
pas encore été dite ou faite. Un savant (slettran) m'a dit qu'un
grand philosophe (filuorico) lui avait juré que nous qui
sommes au monde à présent, nous y avions déjà été, il y a
beaucoup de milliers d'années; moi j'étais moi, vous, vous
étiez vous, ceux-ci étaient ceux-ci, et les autres étaient les
autres. Et, dans beaucoup d'autres milliers d'années, quand
aura tourné je ne sais quelle grande roue, nous reviendrons
à être encore, moi ici debout, vous là-bas assis, moi à
parler, vous à écouter. Et moi qui aurai été moi, je serai
encore moi, et vous qui aurez été vous, vous serez encore
vous, et ceux-ci qui auront été ceux-ci, seront encore
ceux-ci, et les autres qui auront été les autres, seront
encore les autres; et ces paroles que je vous dis, qui auront

été des paroles, seront encore des paroles, et il vous semblera les avoir déjà entendues, comme il vous semble maintenant les avoir entendues déjà. »

Ce serait à tort que *la commedia sostenuta* nous disputerait Ruzzante, il appartient à notre sujet tout aussi bien que Gozzi et Goldoni, ces ingrats successeurs qui ne l'ont pas nommé et qui ne l'ont peut-être pas lu. Selon l'ancien usage italien, pour le genre comique et pour la prose, Beolco a écrit ses comédies après les avoir jouées avec ses joyeux et habiles compagnons, du moins il les a jouées en partie *à l'impromptu*, soit sur simple canevas, soit dans le genre mixte, c'est-à-dire moitié apprises, moitié improvisées D'ailleurs, dans quelques-unes de ses pièces, beaucoup de scènes ne sont qu'indiquées en quelques mots pour être mimées et improvisées par les acteurs; exemple :

« *El bravo vien e da delle tartufolle a Ruzante, etc.*

» *Qui cantano, e come hanno finito, Nale sopragiunge, e sfodrata la spada va verso Menego, dicendo, Mitti man, traittore. E Menego impaurito non mette man altramente, correndo hor quà, hor là, ricere molte botte, etc.* »

Ailleurs « *In questo, facendo il sacerdote alcuni segni, si sentono alcuni rumori, de quali Menego et Duozzo hanno paura, et dal sacerdote rassicurati, etc.* »

Une partie des œuvres de Ruzzante fut conservée dans la famille de son protecteur Cornelio, une partie fut publiée soit dans le texte original, soit traduite en italien :

1° *La Piovana, comedia, ovvero novella del Tasco da Ruzante. In Vinegia per Gabriel Giolito de' Ferrari*, 1548, *in-8° (con dedica del Giolito a Luigi Cornaro).* — Une seconde édition in-8° par le même, en 1552. — Une troisième chez *Stefano Alessi, 1558, in-8°, B. F., 1559.*

2° *L'Anconitana, comedia nuovamente venuta in luce. In Vinegia, appresso Stefano di Alessi, 1551, in-8°.* — A la fin on lit : *In Venezia, appresso Bartolomeo Cesaro, 1551, in-8°.* — Une seconde édition *per l'Alessi, 1551 et 1554, in-12.* — *1555, in-8°, B. F., per Domenico de' Ferrari, 1561, in-8°.*

3° *La Moschetta, comedia nuovamente venuta in luce. In Vinegia, presso Stefano d'Alessi, 1551 e 1554, in-4°, et 1555, in-8°, B. F.*

4° *La Vaccaria, comedia hor hora venuta in luce. In Vinegia, presso Stefano d'Alessi, 1551, 1555 et 1556, in-8°.* — *In Venezia, appresso Domenico de' Ferrari, 1561, in-8°.*

5° *La Fiorina, comedia nuovamente venuta in luce. In Vinegia, appresso Stefano d'Alessi, 1551, 1554 et 1557, in-8°.* — A Venise, chez Giov. Batt Bertacagno, 1555, avec le titre. *La Fiorina, comedia facetissima, giocosa et piena di piacevole allegrezza. Nuovamente data in luce per M. Andrea Calmo. B F* (C'est la même *Fiorina* de Beolco avec peu de changements. Le rôle de Ruzzante s'y nomme Bonelo, le soldat Tonin est remplacé par Sandrin, Bergamasque aussi. Fiore y conserve son nom.) L'aveugle Allegretio y remplace Pasquale, comme Cocolin le Marchioro de Ruzzante.

Ces cinq comédies furent imprimées en un seul volume in-8°, à Venise, par *Giovanni Bonadio, 1565.*

6° *Dialogo facetissimo et ridiculosissimo di Ruzante, recitato à Fosson alla Caccia, l'anno della carestia, 1528. Vinegia. Stefano d'Alessi, 1555, in-8°, B. F.*

7° *Tre Orationi di Ruzante, recitate in lingua rustica alli*

*illustrissimi signori cardinali Cornaro et Pisani, con un Ragio-
namento et uno sprolico insieme con una lettera scritta allo
Alvarotto per lo stesso Ruzzante, tutte opere ingeniose, argute,
et di maraviglioso piacere, non più stampate. Venetia, 1555,
appresso Stephano di Alessi con gratia et privilegio, in-8°, B. F.*

Les œuvres complètes de Ruzzante furent réimprimées
sous le titre de · *Tutte l'opere del famosissimo Ruzzante di
nuovo e con somma diligenza rivedute et corrette, et aggiuntovi
un sonetto et una canzone dello stesso autore. Al molto magnifico signor Vespasiano Zopiano gentil'huomo Vicentino. Ristam-
pate l'anno del Signore 1584, in-12* (par *Giorgio Greco*). Le
volume est divisé en huit parties. — Une autre édition *in
Vicenza, per gli eredi di Perin librero,* 1598, in-12.

La troisième et dernière édition, la plus commune, est
celle de 1617, imprimée à Vicence par Domenico Amadio :
— « Les œuvres, » dit-il dans un avant-propos *aux lecteurs,*
« du très-célèbre *signor Angelo Beolcho,* noble Padouan, surnommé *Ruzante,* sont tellement aimées et appréciées du
monde entier, par le sentiment, l'esprit, la finesse et
l'érudition dont elles sont remplies, qu'elles sont recher-
chées et demandées par chacun comme un recueil très-
savant et très-intéressant. Ayant donc eu égard à ce désir
général, je l'ai réimprimé avec soin et je le livre au public,
revu, corrigé et entièrement conforme quant à la pureté de
son style et à sa simplicité primitive et originale. En vous
délectant de ce livre, que la noblesse de votre âme prenne
en considération ma fatigue et ma bonne intention, qui
seront toujours prêtes pour le plaisir et le bien de tous, etc.

» DOMENICO AMADIO.

» De Vicence le 20 janvier 1617. »

Cette dernière édition comprend, avec les titres apologétiques de l'éditeur, les œuvres du *très-célèbre* Ruzzante, qui suivent :

La Piovana « ou l'Histoire de la bourse »

L'Anconitana, « comédie qui traite d'amour et qui ne peut donner que du plaisir. »

La Rhodiana, « comédie étonnante et très-risible, pleine de mots très-piquants, dits en diverses langues, du très-célèbre *Ruzzante,* » est attribuée aussi à Andrea Calmo, acteur et auteur vénitien, contemporain de Ruzzante. Il y a lieu de croire qu'elle a été écrite par Ruzzante, après avoir été jouée sur un canevas fourni par Andrea Calmo. C'est du moins ce que semble prouver ce fragment du prologue récité au public et placé en tête de *la Rhodiana* :

« . . . Étant dans l'usage, en temps de carnaval, de vous plaire par des divertissements et des amusements de ce genre, nous n'aurions pu le faire cette année, sans l'aide d'un de nos compagnons, qui n'a cependant pas quitté sa compagnie, mais qui nous a proposé et apporté l'œuvre que vous allez voir représenter ce soir. Nous avons donc été forcés de recourir à sa bonne mémoire qui nous a donné cette œuvre, laquelle vous plaira, si vous daignez ne pas faire trop de bruit »

La Vaccaria, « comédie non moins spirituelle qu'amusante. »

La Fiorina, « comédie non moins piquante que délectable. »

La Moschetta, « comédie non moins agréable que plaisante. »

Trois Discours de Ruzzante, « écrits et récités en langage rustique. OEuvres toutes pleines d'esprit, de saillies et d'un merveilleux plaisir. »

Deux Dialogues « en langage rustique, moraux, spirituels et plaisants. »

Un Dialogue « très-facétieux et très-drôle, joué à la chasse en 1528. »

Les personnages du théâtre de Ruzzante sont : *Messer* ANDRONICO, *messer* CORNELIO (vieillards vénitiens), DEMETRIO, PLACIDO, DIOMEDI, *ser* THOMAO, PITTARO, SIVELLO, PASQUALE, TURA et MARGALE pour les rôles de pères, maris ridicules et trompés, raisonneurs, etc.

Les amoureux : TANCREDO, THEODORO, GISMONDO, FLAVIO, ROBERTO, FEDERICO, POLIDORO (amoureux ridicule).

Les amoureuses GINEVRA, ISOTTA, FIORINETTA, BEATRICE.

Les amoureuses villageoises : GAVA, FIORE, BETTIA, NINA, GHITTA, DINA.

Les servantes BESA, GITA, BETTA, MADDALENA.

Les rôles de mère . THEODOSIA, RESPINA, RESCA, SOFRONIA, FELICITA, CLIEGA et PRUDENTIA (*Ruffiane*), DORALICE (courtisane).

Les paysans, types rustiques . RUZZANTE, MENEGO-MENATO, DUOZZO, MARCHIORO, BILORA, BELDON, TRUFFA, VEZZO, LORON, FORBINO, SITON.

Valets intrigants : TONIN le Bergamasque, NALE, SLAVERO, GARBUIO (brouillon), DALDURA, GARBINELLO, ZANE, BERTEVELLO, CAMPEGGIO, NASO, CORRADO (Allemand).

PIOLO (chanteur), IL NOTAIRE.

STENTERELLO.

—

MENEGHINO, GIANDUJA, ZACOMETO, JEANNOT, JOCRISSE.

———— —

.

Stenterello, Meneghino, Gianduja, sont ce que les Italiens appellent les *caratteristà*, c'est-à-dire, les rôles tranchés, caractéristiques, les rôles qui souvent inutiles à l'action d'une pièce, y viennent cependant prendre place et jeter, même au milieu des plus noirs mélodrames, un peu de gaieté, par leurs lazzi et leurs plaisanteries parfois incohérentes et hors de propos. Quelque pièce que l'on joue, le *caratteristà* vient y remplir son rôle, parlant son dialecte, et vêtu de son costume traditionnel, au milieu des autres acteurs qui parlent italien et sont vêtus comme la situation de la pièce le comporte. Stenterello en Toscane, Meneghino dans le Milanais, Gianduja en Piémont, sont le même type, modifié selon l'inspiration et le goût particulier de chaque province. Chacun de ces trois masques est aujourd'hui l'unique masque de sa patrie. Ils ont détrôné et remplacé,

dans tout le nord de l'Italie, Arlequin et Brighella, qui se
sont réfugiés dans les théâtres de marionnettes

« Ces messieurs de la Crusca, » dit M. Frédéric Mercey,
« et en général les puristes de Florence, sont ennemis
» déclarés du pauvre Stentarello Ils n'en parlent qu'avec
» dédain et colère, et c'est moins son inconduite que l'in-
» correction de son langage et son faible pour les patois
» qui motivent leur haine. Stentarello, en effet, est plutôt
» toscan que florentin. Vous le rencontrerez à Pérouse,
» à Arezzo, à Pistoie, à Sienne; il s'est même naturalisé
» chez les Lucquois, les Pisans et les Bolonais, ses voisins,
» et il parle à merveille la langue accentuée du peuple de
» ces villes, dont on le croirait citoyen. Mais si le langage
» varie, les actions sont les mêmes. A Bologne, Stentarello
» a pris, quelque peu, les allures de ses compagnons de
» Venise, de Milan et de Turin, Arlequin, Meneghino, et
» Gerolamo, avec lesquels il a, d'ailleurs, quelques liens de
» parenté. Ce ne sont, en effet, que les variétés d'un même
» type, que les diverses faces d'un même caractère, modifié
» par l'entourage et le climat. Ce ne sont pas des types
» différents. »

Les Florentins disent que leur Stenterello ou Stentarello,
personnage plein de fantaisie, fut créé il y a quatre-vingts
ans environ, par un acteur très-populaire nommé del
Buono La coupe de son costume, à l'instar de celui de
Jocrisse et de Jeannot, ne prouverait cependant pas qu'il
fût d'une époque si récente, Jocrisse datant déjà de 1625, et
Jeannot venant de GIANNINO, le valet florentin du seizième
siècle.

Les couleurs voyantes et mi-parties du costume de Stenterello, les trois lignes profondes et parallèles, marquées aux coins de la bouche, tradition du *rictus* antique que portent tous les masques de la renaissance, nous font l'effet de se rattacher, comme tous les autres, à un type du seizième siècle, type oublié sans doute mais ressuscité merveilleusement par l'acteur del Buono.

Cette opinion que les types se transforment et ne s'improvisent plus, est celle de M. Fréd. Mercey. « Au temps de la » république de Florence, dit-il en parlant de Stenterello, » il vivait dans les palais; il était alors dans toute la force » de l'âge et dans toute la verdeur de son esprit; il s'appe- » lait Machiavel, Boccace, l'Arétin, Poggio. Stentarello est » le petit-fils, un peu vulgarisé, de tous ces beaux esprits, » et il a hérité surtout de leurs vices et de leurs petitesses. » Je m'étonne qu'au lieu de prendre le nom de *Stentarello*, » il n'ait pas gardé celui de *Poggio*. »

Aujourd'hui le nom de *Stenterello* a prévalu, mais il dérive toujours du verbe *stentare*, souffrir : c'est-à-dire qu'il est souffre-douleur de son état.

Stenterello ne vise ni à l'esprit ni à la malice, quand il en a, c'est sans qu'il s'en doute. Cela lui échappe. Il y arrive par la naïveté; comme tous les types de la comédie italienne, il est l'image fidèle du peuple qui l'a créé.

Durant le carnaval de Florence, de grandes toiles sur lesquelles sont peints les faits et gestes de Stenterello, tapissent tous les coins de rues. Il donne ses représentations au petit théâtre de la *Piazza vecchia* et à celui de *Borgo ogni Santo*. Le bas peuple florentin encombre (en habit noir) la *platea,* et le public aristocratique les loges. La *platea* (le parterre) coûte quatre sous et les plus belles loges cinquante sous, les jours brillants. Pour le même prix, on vous donne, pendant le reste de l'année, des opéras chantés par des ténors hors de service et de jeunes créatures qui veulent quitter l'aiguille pour les beaux-arts. Tout le monde y va cependant, quand les grands théâtres sont fermés, et on y entend de la musique de Cimarosa, de Rossini, et même de Meyerbeer.

Il n'y a pas de pièces possibles à Florence sans Stenterello. Il est tantôt valet, tantôt maître, tantôt il parodie un héros de drame, de comédie ou de roman à la mode; tantôt il personnifie des passions et des caricatures politiques d'une *palpitante actualité,* et retrempe sa popularité, sous la férule de la censure ombrageuse, en allant faire quelques jours de prison, dans la personne de l'acteur qui le représente, et même de l'impresario qui lui a ouvert les portes de son théâtre. Outre les pièces spéciales dont il est le héros, il en représente encore une foule d'autres, où son personnage s'introduit comme il peut · par exemple, *Roberto Diavolo, con Stenterello; Don Giovanni, con Stenterello.* La tragédie, le drame, l'*opera seria,* ont tous une place pour Stenterello. Il y remplit de préférence les rôles des domestiques facétieux et poltrons. Il est fort amusant lorsqu'il est séduit par les nonnes, dans Robert, ou quand il reçoit à souper la statue du Commandeur.

Il change volontiers de costume, selon le besoin des pièces. Mais il conserve immuablement sa triomphante perruque noire terminée par une longue queue rouge,

à la prussienne et légèrement recourbée; ses sourcils noirs
en tire-bouchon, ou se terminant dans l'oreille comme
ceux de certains masques antiques, ses trois lignes parallèles, marquées aux coins de la bouche, et enfin ses
joues plâtrées de blanc sur lesquelles il plaque parfois un
pot de rouge, étendu en roue de carrosse. Mais ce qui le
caractérise, ce qui est le sceau sans lequel Stenterello ne
saurait exister, c'est l'absence de la plus belle de ses dents
de devant. L'acteur qui va se vouer à la reproduction de
cet amusant personnage, doit, avant tout, lui offrir ce
sacrifice. Plus le trou noir qu'il fait ainsi à sa gencive supé-
rieure est marqué, plus il a de succès. Cette dent du milieu
absente, aide du reste extrêmement l'acteur à imiter, en
charge, le dialecte du peuple toscan.

Stenterello (*planche* 52) affectionne les couleurs voyantes.
Il porte volontiers une veste de bouracan bleu clair avec
un gilet jaune serin, une culotte noire dont une jambe est
parfois d'un beau vert pomme. Les bas de coton, l'un
uni ou chiné, l'autre rayé, s'étendent sur une jambe
dont le gros genou, légèrement cagneux, atteste l'origine
florentine. (Le Florentin flageole généralement sur une
jambe molle comme du coton) Il abandonne à la cour de
Louis XIV les hauts talons; il étale son large pied dans un
bon grand soulier orné d'une gigantesque boucle d'étain.

Stenterello n'a ni la méchanceté ni la grossièreté de la
plupart des bouffons italiens. On sent qu'il appartient à
une population dont le premier besoin est un habit noir,
et le plus grand désir, qu'on lui donne du *lei*, c'est-à-dire
qu'on lui parle à la troisième personne. Les plaisanteries

assez vives de Stenterello ne sont pas indécentes. L'apparence est toujours convenable, et il a une certaine naïveté, propre au peuple toscan. Il n'est pas brave, il ne veut tuer personne, mais il a grand'peur qu'on le tue. Maigre et leste, il est toujours prêt à fuir le danger. Très-prompt à s'enflammer, il est galant auprès de toutes les femmes, mais il ne s'amuse pas à leur faire longtemps la cour, il n'en a pas la patience. Il ne recule pas devant des manières qui lui attirent souvent des soufflets dont il ne se vante guère.

Après les femmes, c'est la table qui l'entraîne. La gourmandise lui fait oublier l'amour. Pour un bon dîner, il ferait mille bassesses, il consentirait peut-être à être battu, bien qu'il n'aime pas les coups et les craigne fort pour sa santé. Sa paresse est proverbiale, et s'il avait quelques sous, il serait aussi avare que gourmand; mais n'ayant rien, il se contente de désirer les femmes et les dîners des autres, de se coucher au soleil comme un lézard tout en ayant l'œil aux aguets. Il sera heureux alors, s'il trouve une oreille indulgente pour médire des uns et des autres; il oubliera qu'il a le ventre creux, et s'amusera de ses bons mots plus encore qu'il n'en amusera les autres, bien que ceux-ci aient lieu d'être satisfaits de son esprit.

M. Frédéric Mercey, dans son *Théâtre en Italie*, parle de plusieurs canevas où Stenterello joue le premier rôle, toute l'action roule autour de lui. Ici, il est amoureux d'une princesse et ose lui déclarer sa flamme, après avoir fait une toilette exagérée, habit, veste et culotte à paillettes, la perruque frisée de frais; il a même *emprunté* le nécessaire de voyage d'un Anglais de sa connaissance afin d'être d'une propreté irréprochable. « Ce nécessaire contient une foule » de petits objets dont il ne peut deviner l'usage, et qua- » torze brosses différentes pour se nettoyer les ongles. Cette » critique de la minutieuse propreté des Anglais est tout à » fait italienne et fort drôle. Stentarello s'émerveille à la » vue de chacune des pièces du nécessaire, et, après les » avoir longuement examinées, il cherche à s'en servir. » Son embarras et ses commentaires sont à mourir de » rire; enfin, après avoir retourné dans tous les sens cette » machine si compliquée, il finit par s'éplucher le nez » avec un *coupe-cors*, et par se brosser les dents avec une » savonnette pleine de savon, ce qui lui fait faire une » horrible grimace. »

Voici un épisode des malheurs de Stenterello, où l'on voit que l'on ne s'est pas gêné pour piller les aventures de Falstaf.

Un prince surprend Stenterello aux pieds de la prin- cesse sa femme. Stenterello croit donner le change en pré- textant la recherche d'un bracelet perdu par la dame de ses pensées. La princesse, d'intelligence avec son mari, assigne un rendez-vous à Stenterello, qui, ivre de fatuité, oublie toute prudence et va se faire bafouer dans la chambre de la princesse. Le prince arrive, Stenterello de se cacher dans un coffre. Le mari prétend avoir entendu du bruit dans la chambre de sa femme, il fait le jaloux, frappe de son épée sur le coffre. Stenterello, enfermé dedans, bondit de peur. La princesse dit que ce sont les rats. Le prince veut faire jeter ce coffre dans l'Arno; Stenterello, qui tremble,

veut soulever le couvercle qui lui écrase les doigts, il crie,
il est découvert. La princesse feint de s'évanouir. Quatre
hommes arrivent, s'emparent du coupable, qui laisse sa
perruque entre leurs mains Il implore sa grâce Il ména-
geait une surprise, dit-il, à la princesse, dans le but de la
divertir, « et j'ai pris ce coffre pour la porte, en voulant
sortir de la chambre. » — « Non pas, don Stentarello, dit
» le prince, vous êtes un vieux débauché, vous allez être
» puni par où vous avez péché. »

Le prince tire un énorme couteau de chasse, affilé
comme un rasoir, et fait un geste terrible, aux grands
applaudissements du public. Stenterello demande grâce,
dit qu'il n'est pas coupable, et, que, d'ailleurs, l'eût-il
voulu tromper, il ne l'aurait pu, ce qu'il avoue piteusement
en baissant la tête.

— « Et si je te pardonnais et te rendais la liberté, que
» ferais-tu désormais ? »

« — J'ai un physique agréable, dit Stenterello en re-
» dressant sa tête chauve et balafrée, et une fort jolie voix
» flûtée; l'impresario du théâtre de *Borgo ogni Santo* m'en-
» gagerait, j'en suis sûr, comme *soprano*. »

Parfois il imite la jactance et les fanfaronnades du Capitan ou de Scaramouche. Il revêt alors le costume militaire,
fait sonner ses éperons et traine son grand sabre. Il jure
par la bombe et le canon, et il a pourfendu un cavalier
avec son cheval, d'un seul coup d'estoc « Une autre fois,
dit-il, c'était dans une bataille contre les Pandours· je vis
venir sur moi une énorme bombe; loin de trembler et de
fuir, je l'attends de pied ferme, et, la prenant au bond,

je la renvoie comme une paume dans les escadrons ennemis, je vous assure qu'elle n'y fit pas peu de dégât! » Après
avoir fait toutes sortes de métiers, comme médecin, avocat, bandit, colporteur, sans avoir jamais réussi à rien,
il revient à Florence. Il y avait laissé sa femme misérable,
dans une cabane, il la retrouve vêtue avec élégance, dans
une jolie maison. « Suis-je bien chez moi? » dit-il. Sur la
réponse affirmative de sa moitié, et après l'avoir trouvée
plus jolie qu'il ne l'avait jamais vue, il lui demande d'où
lui vient ce bien-être et ce luxe? — « Mon ami, lui dit-elle,
tu m'avais recommandée à la Providence en partant, et la
Providence ne m'a pas oubliée. » Stenterello est dans l'enchantement. Après qu'il a bu et mangé, et qu'il s'est bien
reposé dans les fauteuils de la Providence, sa femme lui
amène trois marmots qui lui sautent au cou. Mais lui de
se récrier : « *Per Bacco!* Je n'ai pas laissé un seul enfant à
Florence... pas même un projet d'enfant. Mais est-ce encore
la Providence qui s'est chargée de me rendre père? — Sans
doute, dit madame Stenterello, et tu n'y perdras rien. » —
Stenterello accepte sa position, en prenant un air de rési-
gnation comique.

Aussitôt qu'il est dans sa maison, dans ses meubles, il
devient avare. Il ne couperait pas un œuf en quatre, ce
serait du gaspillage. « Au déjeuner, dit-il, on le pique à
» l'un des bouts avec une grosse épingle, on aspire la moitié
» du contenu, et l'on réserve le reste pour le dîner. De cette
» façon, le goût est satisfait, le plaisir dure longtemps, et
» la bourse ne se vide pas. Bien plus, l'œuf n'est pas perdu,
» on reporte la coquille au poulailler, où elle invite les

» poules à pondre. Voilà ce qui s'appelle manger un œuf
» avec profit. »

En devenant avare, il est devenu spéculateur, et, voulant
doubler promptement son capital, il s'arrange de façon à
perdre tout. Mais l'âge arrive pour Stenterello et pour sa
femme; avec l'âge, celle-ci n'a plus rien à espérer de la
Providence Stenterello la chasse en lui reprochant son
inconduite, et envoie au diable les enfants qu'il appelle
bâtards.

Stenterello est souvent opprimé dans son ménage. Dans
une farce italienne, où, musicien de son état, il a pour
femme une virago criant fort et beaucoup, il prend
le parti de ne lui répondre, dans les moments périlleux,
que par une note funèbre qu'il tire du fond d'un immense
cor de chasse, beaucoup plus grand que lui. Un son, et
c'est tout! mais quel son!

Cette idée de ne répondre que par un son rappelle la scène
d'Arzigogolo, paysan florentin du seizième siècle, un ancêtre
du Stenterello moderne. Accusé de vol, Arzigogolo s'en va
trouver ser Alesso l'avocat, afin qu'il se charge de son
procès. Aux questions de l'homme de loi, le paysan répond ·
Je m'appelle Arzigogolo; mais je me nomme Beco di Meio
di Nanni dal Montale. L'affaire expliquée, ser Alesso ne
voit qu'un moyen de le tirer d'embarras, c'est de contre-
faire l'insensé. — ALESSO. Dis-moi un peu, comment feras-tu
devant le juge pour paraître fou? — ARZIGOGOLO. Oh! uh!
je ne sais pas, moi, c'est difficile! Si j'étais sage, je ferais
ainsi. (*Il lui donne un coup de bâton.*) — ALESSO. Que la mort
te mange, malheureux! tu m'as presque rompu une épaule;

je dirai que tu es vraiment fou si tu fais de telles caresses au juge Arzigogolo. J'ai entendu dire que les fous frappaient, moi, j'avais un frère dont la cervelle était dérangée qui me faisait comme ça. (*Il s'avance et cherche à le frapper.*) ALFSSO. Tiens-toi tranquille, bête, ne saurais-tu faire le fou autrement? ARZIGOGOLO. On dit encore que les fous jettent des pierres. Je vais en chercher une, et, par le sang! je vous la jetterai à la tête. » L'avocat l'ayant fait tenir en repos lui conseille de ne répondre qu'en sifflant. « Oh! dit le paysan, il me semblera que je fais boire mes bœufs. »

Arzigogolo paraît devant le juge, qui lui demande : — « Comment t'appelles-tu, paysan? D'où es-tu? etc. » — Arzigogolo ne répond que par un sifflement aigu à toutes les questions. Le juge le renvoie absous, en le plaignant beaucoup.

Vient l'avocat qui réclame son salaire, et auquel le rusé paysan ne répond aussi que par le même sifflement.

Cette scène, du théâtre de Lasca, ressemble tout à fait au *bé bé* de Guillaume l'Aignelet, dans la farce de l'*Avocat Pathelin*.

Le Stenterello de Bologne ne joue pas de rôles si importants que celui de Florence. Il est, avant tout, valet, porte sa livrée avec négligence, et s'habille tout de travers; il met, comme le Stenterello de Florence, deux bas de couleur différente, ce qui est une tradition, comme nous l'avons dit, des costumes mi-partie du seizième siècle Il est poltron et niais, mais ce qui le distingue particulièrement, c'est sa préoccupation, qui ressemble parfois à de l'idiotisme. Stenterello est, à Bologne, un être un peu fantastique. Ses distractions continuelles, sa manie de raconter des histoires qu'il ne peut jamais achever et qu'il interrompt au moment le plus intéressant, ses gestes, ses grimaces, tout lui est permis en fait de plaisanteries et d'impertinences au public. La manière même dont il se tourne pour demander pardon à son maître d'avoir fait une bévue nouvelle désarme la colère du vieux Tabarino lui-même, qui rit et prend le public à témoin, en disant d'un air résigné : *Che vogliono, c' è Stenterello !* « Que voulez-vous, c'est Stenterello. »

Un Italien, amateur passionné de Stenterello, nous disait qu'il n'y a jamais eu et qu'il n'y aura jamais deux Stenterello qui se ressemblent. C'est le personnage le plus difficile à rendre de tous les masques italiens. C'est un type tout de fantaisie dans le geste, et tout de spontanéité dans l'improvisation.

Stenterello, venant de mettre en colère son maître, qui s'est retiré pour ne pas le battre, se retourne vers le public et lui dit : « Figurez-vous... d'ailleurs, vous l'avez bien vu, n'est-ce pas ? Mon maître m'avait donné sa lettre à raccommoder et une montre à mettre à la poste... un grand trou pour mettre les lettres, vous savez bien ! comme la bouche à la Gina, qui est une jolie fille, avec des yeux plus grands que mon nez... qui pleure depuis trois jours du frais qu'il fait sur la promenade. Ah ! mais voilà que le signor Birrichino me rencontre et me dit : Stenterello !... Un drôle de nom qui me vient de mon père qui avait épousé ma mère, ce qui fait que ma mère, qui était fille de mon grand-père qui était le père de mon père qui était le père de son fils qui était le père de ma mère, avait un mari qui était le

fils de ma grand'mère. Oh! *che bestia!*... non! (Il fait une
pirouètte, va pour sortir et revient.) Où est mon maître?
C'est un drôle de maître! il est si distrait qu'il a oublié
de me donner des bas neufs! (Il allonge la jambe et perd
l'équilibre, s'accroche le pied, et feint de tomber; mais il
se rattrape, et cherche ce qui a pu le faire trébucher : il
ramasse un cheveu.) Çà! ils me tomberont tous. (Il ôte sa
perruque, et reste avec sa tête rasée, ce qui divertit toujours
le public. Prenant son cheveu, il le recolle avec précaution; après quoi il remet sa perruque sens devant derrière,
et veut continuer son discours, mais sa longue queue, qui
lui pend sur le nez et qu'il repousse à chaque instant, le fait
loucher horriblement.) Mon cheveu... qui était le fils de
ma perruque, qui était la grand'mère de la montre que
j'ai mise à la poste, mais *che diavolo* est cela? » (Et il tire le
bout de sa longue queue qui se détortille peu à peu, il tire
toujours, et il vient tant d'aunes de ruban qu'il s'empêtre
dedans et finit par se sauver en criant: *Il Diavolo, il Diavolo!* laissant le public en suspens sur l'explication qu'il
voulait lui donner de la façon dont il s'était acquitté de sa
commission.) Toutes ces idées sans suite, entrecoupées de
poses et de grimaces, sont impossibles à rendre; il faut les
voir pour comprendre les succès d'un type semblable.

On devient Arlequin, mais on naît Stenterello, nous disait
l'amateur de ce personnage, et il riait encore, vingt ans
après, en nous racontant les lazzi et postures de Domini-
cone, acteur bouffe, d'une prestance et d'une taille pareilles
à celles de Lablache. Il jouait les *caratterista* (les comiques),
et remplissant les rôles de père, le Stenterello faisant

auprès de lui les fonctions de valet La troupe de Bon et Romagnoli, qui était au service du roi de Sardaigne en 1855, possédait encore un Stenterello fort remarquable qui faisait beaucoup rire, surtout quand Gattinelli jouait le rôle de maître, au théâtre *del Corso*, à Bologne.

A Florence, Ricci est le plus célèbre des Stenterello modernes Il possède des qualités d'acteur fort au-dessus d'un bouffon. Il joue avec infiniment de verve et de goût les rôles de Bouffé et d'Arnal, en les entremêlant, comme de raison, de *lazzi* stenterellesques.

En 1855, au théâtre de San Carlino, à Naples, Altavilla était encore un *caratterista* remarquable à tous égards, jouant en dialecte napolitain. Quelle verve d'improvisation ne fallait-il pas avoir pour créer tous les deux ou trois jours un rôle nouveau? Taddei est, aujourd'hui encore, connu dans toute l'Italie comme un acteur de beaucoup de talent, jouant ces rôles de fantaisie dans l'*improvisation* aussi bien que dans le *soutenu*.

MENEGHINO.

Le Meneghino (petit Dominique) moderne, personnage, tantôt valet, tantôt maître, tantôt paysan, parlant le dialecte lombard, descend pour nous assez directement du MENICO de Ruzzante, et du *Menghino* de *la Lena* de l'Arioste.

Il est vrai que ses vêtements d'une coupe assez moderne, rappelant ceux de Stenterello, mais plus sobres pour la disposition des couleurs, ne ressemblent guère à ceux de son aïeul Menego. Mais pourquoi Meneghino aurait-il gardé la tradition du costume plutôt que les autres masques? Le Brighella moderne ressemble peu à celui du seizième siècle. Le Pantalon d'aujourd'hui n'a presque plus rien du Vénitien *Pantalone*, et tant d'autres!

Meneghino, le Milanais, porte la veste courte, et la culotte de drap vert à boutons et à galons rouges, le gilet à fleurs, les bas rayés. Sa figure d'une expression joviale, au nez retroussé, est encadrée d'une perruque à cheveux plats, se terminant par une queue ficelée de rouge, et son couvre-chef, galonné de rouge, ressemble bien plus à ces casquettes de feutre, d'une forme démesurée, que portaient les bouffons du seizième siècle (voyez FRITELLINO), qu'à un chapeau à trois cornes.

MENEGO ou MENATO sont, sous deux noms différents, le même personnage créé par Marco Aurelio Alvarotto, acteur de la troupe padouane de Ruzzante. C'est un type comique, une sorte de paysan naïf et poltron, jouant aussi des rôles de valets avec GARBINO ou GARBINELLO, TRUFFA ou TRUFFO et TONIN. Sous son apparente bêtise, Menego (Dominique) (*planche* 55), pensant et parlant à la manière des paysans, se plaint souvent des mœurs et des vices de son époque.

Voici un dialogue « très-facétieux et très-comique » du théâtre de Ruzzante, récité à Fossone pendant la chasse (*recitato a Fosson alla caccia*), en 1528.

« MENEGO. Janvier, février, mars, avril, mai et juin, le mois du blé · au diable les autres! L'année est trop longue. Pourvu que le blé devienne pain par la faucille, c'est tout

Mais qui vient là? N'est-ce pas mon compère Duozzo? c'est lui. Compère, comment va la récolte?

Duozzo Pauvrement, mon compère Trouvera la misère qui voudra cette année, et sans enseigne.

Mengo. Quant à moi, je cherche comment je pourrais faire pour manger peu. Ces maudites raves m'ont tant élargi les boyaux, que j'en mangerais encore autant et plus.

Duozzo. Pour te dire la vérité, compère, je pense que si tu avais des sorbes et que tu en mangeasses, cela rétrécirait tes pauvres boyaux; c'est mon opinion.

Mengo Mais sais-tu à quoi je pense, compère? Si on s'arrangeait de façon quand on a mangé à ne pas laisser sortir la nourriture, le ventre serait repu et la faim ne reviendrait plus si impérieuse.

Duozzo. Que dis-tu là, compère? non, malepeste! Il faut tenir tout bien ouvert, au contraire, pour se bien porter. Non, non, du diable s'il faut boucher quoi que ce soit!

Mengo. Mais, compère, ce que je cherche, c'est à me rendre malade, parce que, lorsque je suis malade, la faim ne me vient pas; et, pourvu que la faim ne vienne pas, c'est tout ce que je demande. Avez-vous compris ce que je vous dis, compère?·

Duozzo. Tu parles sagement de ces matières, compère. Mais as-tu donc peur de mourir de faim? Est-ce que tu ne connais pas le proverbe : « Que personne n'en meurt? » et cet autre qui dit : « Il faut prendre le temps comme il vient? » Tu crois donc que le blé manquera cette année? Je crois tout le contraire.

Mengo. Le proverbe est vrai, et puisse-t-il se réaliser! Mais les usuriers le font mentir, ils ne veulent ni vendre ni même montrer le blé, de manière qu'il n'y a rien à faire. Je crois bien qu'il y en aurait assez, quand même ils le vendraient à gros profits. Mais quel malheur! ils sont plus affamés du sang des pauvres, qu'un cheval maigre de l'herbe nouvelle.

Diozzo. C'est vrai ça, compère, et nous pouvons bien crier, pester, ou devenir enragés comme des chiens, avant qu'on amasse le blé pour le bien commun. Mais je te dirai que, de la manière dont s'est passé tout le mois de janvier, il y aura abondance, et les hommes s'en réjouiront.

Mengo. Sans cet espoir-là, mon compère, cela irait mal, et, quant à moi, j'ai peur que les batteurs d'estrade et les cavaliers ne mangent la récolte en herbe, avant même qu'elle soit en fleurs.

Diozzo. J'en ai grand'peur aussi, mais ils n'emporteront pas tout.

Mengo. Oui! nous mangerons ce qu'ils auront laissé, et nous en deviendrons si gras, que nous ressemblerons à des pendus, et si légers que le vent nous emportera.

Diozzo. ... Si bien, compère, que vous avez peur?

Menego. Moi, je n'ai peur de rien que de la peur, et ce n'est pas encore tant la peur que la crainte. Savez-vous, compère, que je suis homme, et s'il y en a quelques-uns qui doivent vivre, je veux être de ceux-là?

Diozzo. Quant à moi, je n'ai charge de femme ni d'enfants; je vis comme un voleur. Çà, compère, comment va l'amour? Causons un peu de choses plaisantes!

Menego. Eh! compère, comment veux-tu que marchent
l'amour et les caresses, quand on n'a rien? Conduire une
femme dans sa maison, quand on n'a qu'un seul morceau
de pain! et l'homme qui mange peu, ne peut... je ne sais
comment dire, compère? Et si elle a bon appétit, elle ne
vivra pas de paroles Ce sera là le diable, comprenez-vous?

Duozzo. Ça se comprend de reste. »

La conversation continue ainsi. Menego dit qu'il attend
la nouvelle récolte pour épouser une certaine Gnva. Duozzo
lui dit, peu à peu, qu'il connaît un *quidam* qui n'attendra pas
la récolte nouvelle pour faire manger la Gnva, et qu'il l'a
emmenée depuis trois jours chez lui...—« Je ne le crois pas, »
dit Menego, « mais c'est égal, allons toujours la voir pour
lui faire dire la vérité. » Duozzo demande la permission
d'aller chercher des armes, parce qu'il y a des loups dans
les bois, et qu'il ne se soucie pas de se battre avec Nale, le
rival de Menego. Celui-ci répond qu'il n'est pas besoin
d'armes pour aller voir la Gnva, qu'il a son couteau, que
cela suffit. (Il y a ici des plaisanteries très-équivoques et
des jeux de mots singuliers.) Il ne connaissait pas son compère pour un poltron; mais à présent, il voit ce qui en est
Il ira seul... Mais voici Gnva fort à propos.

« Menego. Bonjour, ma mie Gnva, comment vas-tu?

Gnva. J'irais bien si j'avais du pain. Cette année-ci est
encore une mauvaise année!

Menego Je t'en ai apporté un gros morceau, que je te
donnerai, sur ma foi, si tu veux me répondre sur quelque
chose que m'a conté mon compère »

Mais avant de répondre, Gnva veut chanter. Ils chantent,

et quand ils ont fini, Nale, le rival de Menego, se précipite sur lui l'épée à la main, en lui criant : « Je te tiens, je te tiens, traître! rends-toi! » Menego se sauve sans répondre, courant à droite et à gauche, recevant plusieurs coups. Il tombe par terre. Nale emmène Gnva, et Menego, resté à terre, dit : « Ai-je assez de malheur! cent pour un. Il m'a tout transpercé, et j'ai plus de trous que n'en a un crible. Quelle jolie existence j'aurais menée! j'y pense maintenant que je vais mourir. Confession! confession! je suis tout en sang, mais est-ce bien du sang? Duozzo, mon compère, va chercher le médecin; mais il demeure trop loin. Et puis, savoir s'il voudra venir, et quand bien même il viendrait, pourrait-il me guérir de mes blessures, le voudrait-il? Je suis sûr que je n'en guérirai jamais. Je resterai estropié toute ma vie, c'est sûr. Malheureux que je suis! il faut donc que je meure en ce moment-ci? J'avais bien deviné que je mourrais cette année, soit de blessures, soit de faim, dans ces pays dévastés. Et que t'importe, fou de Menego, de mourir de cela ou de faim? puisque je ne dois plus voir ma Gnva! Le cœur me dit cependant que je pourrais bien guérir! Dois-je me laisser mourir ou non? Que dois-je faire ou que ne dois-je pas faire? Si je me vengeais de ce chien de traître qui m'a ainsi mis en morceaux? Oui, j'en veux tirer vengeance! je veux qu'on sache partout qu'il m'a tué. Oh! que la peste t'étouffe, lâche! je te ferai aller aux galères! Je vais me tuer. On dira partout qu'il est mon assassin. Mais comment me tuerai-je? Voici le malheur, il y a plusieurs moyens; mais maintenant que j'en cherche, je n'en trouve plus! Où est le couteau? Maintenant que j'en ai besoin, il n'y est plus! Je trouverai bien un moyen : je vais me manger sur place. Cela dépitera la famine. Personne que moi ne le saura, et on dira que ce misérable m'a tué, que les chiens ont mangé mon corps, et, de cette façon, il ira aux galères. Vous irez aux galères, l'ami, oui, aux galères! Ne vous impatientez pas, mon compère. Je vous lègue mon couteau et mes souliers. Cela s'appelle, j'espère, faire une mort enragée que de se manger soi-même! C'est cependant dommage de mourir si jeune! Adieu, Gnya, je ne te verrai plus. Je ne veux pourtant pas me manger, cela me ferait trop souffrir. Je veux m'étrangler. »

Un magicien arrive, Duozzo lui dit que Menego est devenu fou. Le magicien, moitié prêtre, moitié médecin, le guérit et lui rend l'espoir. Il lui dit qu'il verra sa Gnya tant qu'il voudra et qu'il aura du pain abondamment. Menego réconforté le remercie, et dit qu'il ne fut jamais si gaillard.

Puis viennent des prédictions à la Mathieu Laensberg. « Vous ne mourrez point cette année de famine, quoique vous fassiez fort maigre chère. Beaucoup de femmes enceintes mourront en couches. Il se fera grosses guerres, et, quand elles seront finies, il y aura la paix. Après la disette viendra l'abondance, et les hommes de biens (c'est-à-dire les riches) vivront heureux dans ce monde. Là-dessus, je vous quitte; il faut que je m'en aille. Je reviendrai dimanche ou une autre fois. »

La pièce finit par des excuses que vient présenter à Menego son rival, il prend par la main Gnya, qui lui jure

d'être à tout jamais son amoureuse, et on se livre à la joie
en dansant et en chantant.

Le caractère du Meneghino moderne est le même, à
quelques variantes près, que celui de Stenterello ; même
costume, même emploi, même bouffonnerie, et partant
même engouement de la part de son public milanais

« Meneghino, dit M Frédéric Mercey, a remplacé Arle-
» quin et Brighella. Meneghino est l'enfant gâté des Mila-
» nais, le héros du théâtre de la Stadera, son talent con-
» siste surtout dans une espèce de gaucherie adroite, dans
» la façon plaisante avec laquelle il se heurte contre les
» murailles et trébuche contre les saillies du parquet sans
» jamais tomber, ni sans rien perdre de son sang-froid. »

Ses distractions et ses naïvetés sont pires que celles de
Pierrot Voyant passer, dans les rues de Milan, un peintre
portant deux portraits sur ses épaules, Meneghino revint
vers son maître, sans vouloir faire la commission dont il
était chargé · « Je ne sortirai plus de la journée, dit-il, il
m'arriverait malheur ; j'ai rencontré un homme à trois
têtes, cela n'est pas naturel. »

Une autre fois, rentré de nuit, Meneghino veut allumer
sa chandelle et se met à battre le briquet dans l'obscurité.
Il se cogne sur les doigts et laisse échapper pierre et amadou. Comment faire pour retrouver tout cela ? Les idées
lui viennent vite, quand elles viennent. Il cherche à tâtons
la chandelle, il la trouve, court chez son voisin l'allumer,
puis revient chercher sa pierre et son amadou. « Je savais
bien que je les trouverais comme ça, » dit-il, et le voilà
battant le briquet. L'étincelle jaillit, l'amadou pétille, et il

l'approche de la chandelle qui l'éclaire : « Tiens ! elle est allumée ! » dit-il.

Une distraction fort commune chez lui, est de se prélasser dans la robe de chambre de son maître, de chausser ses pantoufles et de se coucher dans son lit. Les nombreuses volées qu'il a reçues ne l'ont jamais guéri de ce manque de mémoire. Il faut le voir servir à table, mettre le sucre dans la soupe en guise de sel, verser à boire sur la tête des convives, puis leur enlever leurs perruques pour les faire sécher dans le feu. Servir des bûches pour de la mortadelle de Bologne, et le vase de nuit pour la soupière. Il prend la chandelle pour la bouteille au vinaigre et répand le suif dans la salade. Il met le rôti avec les bottes sur la planche au pain. Il lui est souvent arrivé de jeter les habits de son maître par la fenêtre, qu'il prenait pour l'armoire, et mille autres faits semblables.

Pantalon lui voyant un bouton à l'oreille, lui en fit la remarque : « C'est que j'aurai entendu quelque chose de sale, » lui répond son valet. C'est le mot le plus spirituel qu'il ait jamais dit.

GIANDUJA.

Gianduja ou Girolamo sont le même personnage. Au théâtre *Fiando*, à Milan, il existe encore sous le nom de Girolamo, et joue en parlant le patois lombard les mêmes rôles de paysan bavard, poltron et gourmand que le Gianduja de Turin et de Gênes. Les Piémontais craignant, en 1802, que l'on vit quelque allusion politique dans le

nom de Girolamo (Jérôme) porté par un roi, le débapti-
sèrent et l'appelèrent Gianduja (Jean-de-la-Chopine).

Ce masque est originaire de Caglianetto, de la vallée
d'Ondona, aux environs d'Asti, dont il parle le patois.
C'est un paysan finaud, faisant la bête, un faux niais,
ou plutôt un niais malin. Il a le genre d'esprit que l'on
prête en Angleterre aux Irlandais Il est beaucoup moins
fantaisiste que Stenterello, et depuis qu'il est devenu Gianduja il n'a plus rien de la distraction de Meneghino et de
Girolamo On raconte de ce dernier le fait suivant :

« Un fermier des environs de Bergame avait emmené
son valet Girolamo au marché, pour ramener le bétail
qu'il voulait acheter. Le bétail se trouva être sept ânes.
Après l'acquisition, il appelle Girolamo, et, après les avoir
comptés devant lui il le charge de les conduire au logis.
Girolamo ne fait aucune observation : « Sept ! dit-il, c'est
bien. » Il enfourche l'un et pousse les autres devant lui
Trois heures après il arrive devant la porte de son maître
et compte ses ânes sans descendre de sa monture Après
avoir compté trois fois, il n'en trouve jamais que six .
« Quel malheur! quel malheur! s'écrie-t-il avec désespoir.
Si encore c'était à moi? Mais non ! c'est le bien d'autrui et
j'ai beau être honnête on m'accusera de négligence! Il faut
absolument que je retrouve le septième. » Il pique sa monture et le voilà parti, cherchant partout, s'informant
auprès de chaque passant. Rien ! aucun renseignement.
Infatigable, il fait ce métier pendant trois jours et trois
nuits, ne prenant pas même le temps de manger. A la fin
le pauvre animal sur lequel il était monté tombe d'épuise-

ment et de fatigue. Girolamo roule avec lui dans la poussière, se relève et trouve tout à coup ce qu'il cherchait ·
« Le septième ! le voilà retrouvé, dit-il, où diable s'était-il
égaré ? » Et il s'en retourne chez son maître en laissant là
le pauvre âne crevé de faim. »

Dans son histoire des marionnettes, M Ch. Magnin dit :
« Girolamo remplit à Milan le premier rôle dans toutes les
farces, dans toutes les parodies, dans toutes les petites
pièces à allusions satiriques, triple source dont s'alimente
la fortune des *Fantoccini*. On a vu Girolamo jouer Piri-
thous, dans une parodie d'*Alceste*, poudré à blanc, avec
ailes de pigeon et bourse. Dans cette farce, il accompagne
Hercule aux enfers, et ses frayeurs pendant la route rappellent un peu les poltronneries qu'Aristophane prête, en
pareille occasion, à Xanthias dans *les Grenouilles* M Bour-
quelot, en 1841, a trouvé Girolamo très-amusant dans une
pièce en cinq actes : *Le terrible Mamo, chef de brigands*,
mélodrame avec accompagnement de poignards, d'évanouissements et de coups de pistolet.... Ajoutons que le
plastron le plus ordinaire des plaisanteries de Girolamo est
un Piémontais qu'on a grand soin de supposer parfaitement stupide, gracieuseté de bon voisinage que les Fantoccini de Turin ne manquent pas de renvoyer à leurs petits
confrères de Milan. »

Gianduja (*planche* 54) porte une veste marron galonnée
de rouge, un gilet jaune bordé de rouge, une culotte verte
ou marron, les bas rouges, la perruque noire avec la queue
rouge en trompette, dite à la Jeannot, type appelé précisément chez nous *queue rouge*. Sa physionomie est un mélange

de grossièreté et de malice. Les yeux grands, les arcades
sourcilières très-développées, le nez épaté, les lèvres
épaisses, le menton gras et les joues charnues rappellent
assez la face du Silène antique.

Je l'ai vu à Gènes, au théâtre *Delle-Vigne*, faisant, dans
son costume, le valet d'Ugolino, et venant, par ses lazzi,
jeter un peu de gaieté au milieu d'un noir mélodrame, où
Ugolino dans sa tour, avant de mourir de faim, voyait
expirer tous ses enfants autour de lui. Dans ces moments
critiques, Gianduja passait de temps en temps dans le
sombre cachot; on ne sait pourquoi il avait la liberté
d'agir ainsi, et, loin d'apporter tant soit peu de nourriture
au moribond, il faisait des jeux de mots en patois sur
cette terrible situation.

Je l'ai revu une autre fois, c'était à Cuneo, au pied des
Alpes, le théâtre était en plein vent ou à peu près. L'entrée
n'était pas chère : deux sous les premières et un sou les
secondes. Les premières étaient au fond de la salle et
voyaient fort mal, tandis que les secondes me parurent
être les places privilégiées. Bien qu'arrivé un des premiers,
je ne pus trouver de place qu'à la troisième banquette au
milieu d'une bande de *ragazzi* qui mangèrent des pommes
et des noisettes tout le temps de la représentation Je m'étais
informé d'avance auprès de l'impresario si la pièce qu'on
allait jouer et qui s'appelait *La principessa Mirabella, ô qual è
la cosa che fa di più piacer alle donne*, était une pièce écrite et
apprise, ou improvisée « *Improvisato tutto, e sempre*, » me
dit l'impresario en se redressant comme offensé de mon
doute, « le Gianduja seul parle comme les paysans, » reprit-

il en me donnant mon billet. Je m'apprêtai donc à jouir de la comédie qui, par son titre de LA PRINCESSE MIRABELLE, ou *Quelle est la chose qui fait le plus de plaisir aux Dames*, promettait beaucoup. Je vis tout de suite que j'allais avoir affaire aux *buratini* primitifs, comme les mariounettes du Guignol des Champs-Élysées.

C'était d'abord un prince habillé de satin bleu-ciel à crevés de satin blanc, le manteau de velours jaune, la toque à plumes blanches, le tout galonné d'or et des paillettes sur toutes les coutures, et Gianduja dans son costume classique, tous deux perdus dans une forêt bleue sur un ciel rose, et cherchant un moyen de se procurer de la nourriture. Gianduja trouve plusieurs expédients, comme d'aller chez le boulanger du coin et le rôtisseur d'à côté. Son maître lui fait observer débonnairement qu'ils sont perdus dans une vaste solitude, que leurs chevaux sont harassés de fatigue et de faim, et qu'il ne désire plus qu'une chose, c'est la mort, car la princesse Mirabelle ne voudra plus le revoir s'il n'a accompli ses trente-sept volontés. Gianduja ne tient pas à mourir, il dit qu'il se croyait à Cuneo, ce qui est tout à fait hors du sujet et ce qui fait crever de rire la salle entière. Après avoir peu cherché, Gianduja trouve, du côté du quinquet de gauche, une source d'eau pure et limpide : les voilà sauvés tous les deux d'une mort certaine. Mais Gianduja pense toujours à déjeuner. Cette eau merveilleuse lui a creusé l'estomac, il n'a pas mangé depuis le matin, dit-il, gros comme une noix de pain... et puis, toujours marcher, c'est être par trop traître à son pauvre corps. « C'est bon pour mon

maître qui, au bout de ses courses, trouvera la Mirabelle,
mais moi j'avalerais bien une tartine de pain avec des saucisses tout autour. » Et disant cela, la colique le prend, il
se croit mort, recommande à son maître d'enterrer son
corps après son décès, et, soit pour ne pas mourir sous ses
yeux, soit une autre cause, il sort en se bouchant le nez,
aux trépignements de joie des naïfs spectateurs.

L'action se déroule ainsi pendant quatre ou cinq tableaux
qui sont toujours la même situation. A chaque tableau le
cavalier amoureux recommence ses épreuves, jusqu'au
moment où la princesse Mirabelle, une fort belle marionnette couverte d'or et de velours et faisant toujours le
même geste, au moyen d'une ficelle tirée d'en bas par
l'impresario, dit à son chevalier qu'elle l'accepte pour
époux « parce qu'il a fait toutes ses volontés, et que ce
qui plaît le plus aux femmes c'est l'obéissance des hommes »
Après quoi, Gianduja demande la main de la première
dame d'honneur de la cour, en disant au public dans un
a parte secret qu'il lui apprendra . « *Altra cosa che piace
molto di più alle donne.* »

Sans Gianduja il n'y aurait pas eu de représentation possible. Le public bienveillant bâillait aux scènes d'amour et
de rivalité, car il y avait un traître dans cette pièce; un
traître vêtu comme Buridan, avec une barbe effroyable et
des yeux louches Aussi quand l'impresario sentait languir son public, il ne se gênait pas pour couper court
à une scène et amener au milieu de la cour Gianduja,
lequel, après s'être bien repu dans le palais, se livrait à
des incohérences amoureuses vis-à-vis de la première su-

vante venue, et lui faisant des propositions à la Jeannot,
comme celle-ci de venir boire dans un certain cabaret du
vin où il y a un berceau avec de l'épine à deux sous le cru-
chon, d'y manger du macaroni au bord de la rivière qui a
du fromage dessus, etc.

Gianduja est plus que jamais en faveur à Turin. Dans
la Prise de Delhi, long et terrible mélodrame à grand
spectacle, Gianduja, travesti en aide de camp d'un chef
indien, réjouit l'assistance par ses réflexions, ses saillies
et ses bons mots, toujours en piémontais. Il va et vient
au milieu des soldats anglais en habits rouges et en pantalons blancs, ou des highlanders cerclés de leurs jupons et
entortillés de leurs plaids classiques, aussi bien que parmi
les brahmanes en costume de Turcs de bal masqué,
vêtus de robes garnies de poil de chat et coiffés de turbans
babyloniens en forme de moule à gâteaux. Gianduja tra-
verse les champs de bataille, entre dans la place, en sort,
assiste aux conseils de guerre, écoute l'énumération des
morts et des blessés, sans s'inquiéter de rien. Il a peur
partout, et de tout, bien que personne ne s'inquiète de lui,
excepté le public.

ZACOMETO.

Zacometo, qui, en vénitien, veut dire *Giacometto* (Petit-
Jacques), et qui s'appelait encore au siècle dernier Momolo
(diminutif de Girolamo), est le *caratterista* vénitien. Vêtu ordinairement de calicot blanc, il se blanchit la figure comme
Pierrot, sauf une large tache d'un rouge sanglant posée

brutalement sur une seule joue, et un bas rouge, comme les Vénitiens du quinzième siècle. Zacometo, quelque costume qu'il prenne, garde toujours sa chausse rouge. Cette variété du type fut peut-être créée par quelque compagnon de *la Calza*.

Il y a du Scapin, de l'Arlequin et du Stenterello dans ce personnage, aussi ses faits et gestes sont-ils très-variés. Lorsqu'il joue avec Brighella, qui est fin, rusé et grand diseur de bons mots, Zacometo est un niais, un badaud, un paillasse, au costume près. Dans *les Baruffe chiozzotte* de Goldoni, Zacometo remplit le rôle du niais, du bouffon; vêtu en pêcheur de Chioggia il garde encore sa joue et son bas distinctifs.

Ce personnage vient à Venise, jeter à travers n'importe quelle pièce *sostenuta*, ses plaisantes réflexions et ses fantastiques intermèdes. Il participe donc du caractère distrait de Stenterello, disant des choses très-malicieuses, dont il a l'air de ne pas se douter, commençant une phrase qu'il achève dans un autre acte, ou qu'il n'achève pas du tout, et regardant le public, lui parlant même sans avoir jamais l'air de le voir.

On peut dire que quand l'acteur chargé de ce rôle a du talent et de l'esprit, il lui donne une physionomie propre au peuple des lagunes Plus de friandise que de gloutonnerie, plus de babil que de galanterie avec les femmes, une splendide paresse qui n'exclut pas beaucoup de vivacité, et comme qui dirait une alternative de somnolence rêveuse et de réveils soudains, enfin la pétulance et l'agilité du chat. Il représente assez bien le caractère du bar-

carole qui passe si promptement du sommeil, le ventre au
soleil ou le corps balancé par le flot paresseux des paludes, au rire, aux lazzi et surtout à l'ironie contre les
étrangers.

Ce personnage n'a jamais quitté Venise, et s'il s'absente
parfois du théâtre de *San-Samuel* ou de celui de *San-Gallo*,
c'est pour aller divertir, sous la forme de marionnette, les
marchands et les pêcheurs, sur le quai des Esclavons.

JEANNOT.

Le personnage de Jeannot, type de paysan, valet naïf;
dénaturant le sens de ce qu'il veut dire par la transposition
des mots, qui semble avoir été créé en 1779 sur les théâtres forains par l'acteur Volange, n'en est pas moins un
type fort ancien. De *Zanni* les auteurs florentins du seizième siècle ont fait GIANNI, GIANNINO et GIANNICCO, valets
de comédie dans *la Pinzochera* du Lasca, et dans *il Ser-
vigiale* de Cecchi, en 1561.

De là *Jeannin*, *Janin* (plaisant), *Jennicot*, *Janicot*, *Janot*,
badins des farces françaises qui récréaient, au seizième
siècle, le public en même temps que *Jean-de-l'Epine* ou du
Pont-Alais, surnommé *Songe-Creux*, *Jean-de-Lagny*, *Tabary*
et JEHAN-DES-VIGNES qui, « à en juger par la manière dont
en a parlé B. Des Periers, dit M. Magnin, devait être le roi
des tréteaux d'alors, et méritait d'être le héros des marionnettes. Son nom même, légèrement altéré et devenu Jean-
de-la-Ville, est encore aujourd'hui celui d'un bonhomme

de bois, haut de trois ou quatre pouces, composé de plusieurs morceaux qui s'emboîtent et se démontent, et que
nos joueurs de gobelets escamotent très-aisément. »

Jeannot (Giannino) reparaît dans les canevas et pièces
de la Comédie-Italienne à la fin du dix-septième siècle, et
dans le théâtre de Gherardi, où il joue entre autres un personnage de vieillard (1694)

Tout le monde connaît ses janotismes : il a vendu plus
de cent bottes à un homme de paille, il achète un pain à
un marchand de beurre.

> « Moi, pour leur montrer mon adresse,
> Je renversai les assiettes et les plats.
> Je fis une tache sur ma veste, de graisse,
> Sur ma culotte et mes jambes, de drap.
> Et sur les bas que mon grand-père, de laine,
> M'avait donnés avant d' mourir, violet.
> Le pauv' cher homme est mort d'une migraine,
> Tenant une cuisse dans sa bouche, de poulet »

Le triomphe de ce type fut au siècle dernier Laissons
Grimm nous mettre au courant de ses faits et gestes.

« (Mai 1779.) Un nouveau spectacle établi l'année dernière à la foire Saint-Laurent vient d'attirer depuis deux
mois et la ville et la cour, grâce au prodigieux succès
d'une espèce de proverbe dramatique, dont nous sommes
assez embarrassés de dire le sujet. Comment se dispenser
pourtant de parler d'un ouvrage qui fait les délices de tout
Paris, pour lequel on abandonne les chefs-d'œuvre de
Molière et de Racine, et qui, à la cent douzième représentation, est encore plus suivi qu'il ne l'était à la première !

L'objet d'un si bel enthousiasme, l'idole d'une admiration si rare et si soutenue, l'homme enfin qu'on peut appeler, dans ce moment, l'homme de la nation, est un certain M. Jeannot qui joue, il faut l'avouer, avec la plus grande vérité, le rôle d'un niais, que l'on arrose d'une fenêtre comme don Japhet d'Arménie, qui, par le conseil de ses amis, va faire sa plainte au clerc d'un commissaire dont il est la dupe, et qui, après avoir été bien battu pour s'être avisé de vouloir se venger lui-même, est surpris dans la rue par le guet, et se trouve enfin dépouillé du peu qu'il possède, ce qui prouve sans doute très-clairement que ce sont *les battus qui payent l'amende* Ce proverbe, qui sert de morale à la pièce, en est aussi le titre L'auteur à qui nous sommes redevables d'une si noble production est M. Dorvigny. L'auteur a rassemblé dans le rôle de Jeannot plusieurs traits confus mais vraiment comiques. Quant à l'acteur (le sieur Volange) qui l'a fait valoir avec tant de succès, il donne bien plus que des espérances. On ne peut pas avoir un masque plus mobile et plus vrai, des inflexions de voix plus variées et plus justes, un jeu plus simple et plus naturel, une gaieté plus franche et plus naïve. Messieurs les gentilshommes de la chambre ont déjà fait quelques démarches pour le faire débuter sur un théâtre plus digne de sa gloire. »

En janvier 1780, Grimm parle encore de Jeannot ·

« Jeannot ou M. de Volange, cet acteur si célèbre aux boulevards, cet homme unique qui avait fait tout l'été dernier l'admiration et les délices de la ville et de la cour, dont on avait gravé le portrait de vingt manières diffé-

rentes, qu'on trouvait en porcelaine de Sèvres sur les
cheminées de toutes nos jolies femmes, qu'on allait voir
modelé en cire dans le cabinet du sieur Curtius. entre
M. de Voltaire et M. le comte d'Estaing, cet homme enfin,
si rare et si fêté, a cru devoir déployer ses grands talents
sur un théâtre plus digne de sa gloire que les tréteaux des
Variétés amusantes. Il a débuté le 22 février 1780, jour à
jamais mémorable, sur le théâtre de la Comédie-Italienne,
par les rôles des trois jumeaux de Colalto. » (Les trois
bossus de Tabarin) « Quoiqu'il y eût ce jour-là plusieurs
autres spectacles intéressants, et notamment celui de la
première représentation d'*Atys,* on ne se souvient pas
d'avoir jamais vu à aucun de nos théâtres, dans les occasions les plus remarquables, pas même au triomphe de
M de Voltaire, une pareille affluence de spectateurs. Il
n'y avait pas moins de monde dans les coulisses et dans
les corridors qu'au parterre et dans les loges, et l'on fut
obligé de renvoyer à la porte encore plus de curieux que
l'on n'en put faire entrer. Eh bien, quel fut le succès d'un
début suivi avec un empressement si extraordinaire? A
quoi tient donc la plus brillante renommée? L'objet d'un
si bel enthousiasme, l'idole des boulevards transportée
dans ce nouveau temple y voit tomber tout à coup ses
honneurs et sa gloire éclipsée. C'est en vain que la foule
de ses adorateurs, qu'il avait entraînée après lui, ne cessait
de l'applaudir et de lui crier avec attendrissement : *Courage, Jeannot, courage....*

   » L'illusion s'était évanouie, le Roscius de la foire parut
ici confondu dans la foule des acteurs les plus ordinaires.

On trouva son maintien décontenancé, sa voix grêle, son jeu non-seulement commun et trivial, mais encore froid et dépourvu de comique. Il paraît que sa figure et son organe ne peuvent guère se prêter qu'à l'expression la plus basse et la plus niaise; c'est le caractère qu'il a su saisir avec une vérité très-piquante, mais c'est le seul aussi qui lui soit propre il n'a pas même, dans les autres rôles, le mérite d'une bonne caricature. Quoiqu'il ait été jugé ainsi dès le premier jour, tout Paris a voulu le voir, et son seul début a plus fait gagner à la Comédie-Italienne que toutes les nouveautés de l'année ensemble. O Athéniens! ce n'est pas ici la première de vos folies, et si les dieux vous sont propices, ce ne sera pas la dernière. »

« Je ne connais point, » dit mademoiselle Clairon dans ses Mémoires, « un acteur de ces spectacles forains nommé Volange, mais tout Paris convient également de la perfection de son talent aux Variétés amusantes. On l'a fait débuter à la Comédie-Italienne, où les ouvrages et les talents peut-être ne peuvent se comparer à ceux de la Comédie-Française, et, dans ce cadre, ce Volange si fameux n'a pu soutenir la comparaison du moindre des comédiens. »

JOCRISSE.

Le Jocrisse moderne, que les Piémontais et les Milanais semblent avoir copié dans leur *Gianduja*, et qui paraît être un personnage tout récent, date cependant du dix-septième siècle, puisqu'en 1625 nous le voyons parader sur les tréteaux avec toute sa bêtise traditionnelle

Il en est de même pour GRINGALET, qui, en 1634, à l'hôtel de Bourgogne, jouait les rôles de valet et servait d'interlocuteur à Guillot-Gorgu, quand celui-ci voulait s'adresser au public.

LAINCEOLE, si connu sur les théâtres de marionnettes et récemment remis au théâtre dans l'*Ours* et le *Pacha*, date aussi du commencement du règne de Louis XIII.

Nous voyons en 1656, dans l'ancienne troupe italienne, à Paris, un personnage dans le genre de Jocrisse, sous le nom de JEAN DOUCET. Voici ce qu'en disent les frères Parfait dans leur histoire du Théâtre-Italien :

« Nous ne connaissons cet acteur que par un passage de Loret que nous allons rapporter, mais ce passage laisse dans l'embarras de savoir si Jean Doucet fut un personnage imaginé par quelque acteur de la troupe, ou un rôle joué par un gagiste de la comédie. »

Muse historique de Loret du 14 février 1656.

« Mais à propos de comédie,
Il faut qu'en cet endroit je die,
Qu'un des jours passés, *Jean Doucet*,
Franc nigaut, comme chacun sait,
Pensa faire pâmer de rire
La reine et le roi, notre sire,
Et même tous les courtisans,
Par les mots naïfs et plaisants
Que proféra sa propre bouche,
Étant valet de Scaramouche
Sur le théâtre italien,
Où ce simple et naïf chrétien,
Sans avoir masque ou faux visage,
Joua fort bien son personnage »

On retrouve ce personnage dans le ballet de l'*Amour
malade*, exécuté à la cour le 17 janvier 1657.

Au commencement de ce siècle, le boulevard du
Temple a eu deux mais célèbres, BOBÈCHE et GALIMAFRÉ.
Sous sa veste rouge, son tricorne gris, surmonté d'un
papillon, Bobèche fut le roi de la parade. Sa réputation
était colossale, et ses succès étaient très-souvent dus aux
grosses vérités et aux allusions malicieuses qui lui attirèrent parfois les réprimandes de la police. Bobèche allait
jouer souvent chez les grands seigneurs, les ministres, les
banquiers. Il fit des tournées en province, donna des
représentations extraordinaires, et prit enfin la direction
d'un théâtre à Rouen.

GALIMAFRÉ n'a pas eu la renommée de Bobèche, c'était
plutôt une espèce de Paillasse, un niais balourd: aussi son
talent était-il plus apprécié par le bas peuple, qui préférait
ses grosses bêtises aux malices de Bobèche. Galimafré a
quitté le théâtre, sans pour cela quitter les planches; il
s'est fait garçon machiniste à l'Opéra-Comique. Tel le traitait avec dédain qui ne savait pas que cet homme, remuant
un châssis ou relevant un coulisseau, avait tenu la foule en
extase devant lui!

ISABELLE.

FIORINETTA, ISABELLA, AURELIA, SILVIA, FLAMINIA, CAMILLE.

FIORINETTA.

Nous voyons que dans la troupe du *famosissimo* Ruzzante, il a existé une actrice du nom de FIORINA, nom patronymique ou nom de théâtre. Le Ruzzante l'a donné plusieurs fois à ses amoureuses, ainsi que plusieurs auteurs postérieurs, comme Tarabosco en 1560, Calmo en 1553. C'est tantôt FIORE, la douce villageoise, si belle que Ruzzante se meurt d'amour pour elle dans la pièce, *la Fiorina*. C'est tantôt la Fiorinetta (*planche* 55), l'apprentie courtisane que l'amour préserve du vice et rend digne de pardon

Cette Fiorinetta, c'est la Philenie de Démophile et de Plaute remise en lumière au seizième siècle et transformée selon le goût de la renaissance[1] Il est très-curieux de suivre la transformation de ce type. Sur la scène antique, Philenie n'est qu'une courtisane amoureuse Argyrippe n'est certes pas son premier amant et ne sera probablement pas le dernier Elle se résigne à partager ses faveurs entre le père et le fils, après s'etre abaissée à flatter et à caresser deux esclaves Elle accepte ces souillures par amour pour le jeune homme.

La Fiorinetta est bien autrement intéressante, et la pièce de Ruzzante est meilleure que celle de Plaute Tout le monde connait l'*Asinaire* de celui-ci La *Vaccaria* de Ruzzante est à peu près inconnue chez nous. Nous l'esquisserons légèrement. Comme Demenète, Placido est un seigneur marié à une femme riche, qui a gardé l'administration de sa fortune et qui fait gouverner ses revenus par un *fattore,* un intendant taillé à l'instar de l'*esclave dotal* de l'*Asinaire.* Placido se plaint à son valet Truffo (le Liban de Plaute) d'avoir passé sa vie en tutelle, et d'etre encore *uomo fresco,* c'est-a-dire fringant, propre au plaisir, sans avoir jamais joui de rien au sein de l'opulence. *Madonna* Rospina le prive de tout, et, par sa vertu farouche, fait le tourment de la maison et de la famille · « Je n'ignore pas, dit-il, que mon fils Flavio est épris de la Fiorinetta, et que, depuis un an, il vit avec elle J'en suis fort aise, c'est la liaison la plus heureuse qu'il puisse avoir. Il est trop jeune pour se marier. Je veux qu'il se case le plus tard possible. Dieu le préserve

---

[1] L'*Asinaria*, de Plaute, avait été traduite (*in terza rima*) par un inconnu, quelques années avant la *Vaccaria,* et représentée au monastère de San Stefano a Venise, en 1528

d'une existence comme la mienne! Il faut qu'il profite de
sa jeunesse. La Fiorinetta n'est pas, Dieu merci! une religieuse, l'espèce d'amante la plus périlleuse qu'il y ait.
Ce n'est pas une femme mariée, autre source de dangers
quand le mari est jaloux. Ce n'est pas non plus une débau-
chée qui me donne à craindre pour la santé de mon fils,
c'est une enfant dont il a eu les premières faveurs et qui
l'aime si tendrement, qu'elle ne veut pas souffrir d'autres
hommes auprès d'elle. Mais je sais ce qui se passe maintenant dans ce jeune ménage. La mère de la Fiorina est une
ruffiana qui veut vendre sa fille au riche Polidoro, parce
que mon fils n'a plus d'argent à lui donner. Moi, je n'en
ai pas. Ma femme tient tout sous clef, et son intendant est
incorruptible. Il faut, mon cher Truffo, que, par ton art,
tu viennes à bout de me voler, c'est-à-dire de dérober à ma
femme la somme nécessaire à mon fils, pour que pendant
un an encore il puisse n'être pas troublé dans la possession
exclusive de sa maîtresse.

« Va, va, mon cher Truffo, j'autorise toutes tes fourberies.
Je ne suis pas de ces vieillards grondeurs et incommodes
qui agissent de manière à faire désirer leur mort. Je veux
être le meilleur ami de mon fils, et faire pour lui ce que
jadis mon père a fait pour moi. »

Fiorinetta aime Flavio, elle l'aime ingénument et de
toute son âme. Elle ne dit pas comme Philénie à Cléœrete.
Permettez-moi de le préférer à tous mes amants. Elle dit :
Je ne veux pas d'autre amant que lui.

« FIORINETTA. Que me voulez-vous, ma mère?

CELEGA. Tu as encore, pour mon malheur, laissé entrer

Flavio à la maison, par la porte du jardin Je ne t'ai rien voulu dire en sa présence. Mais réponds-moi, maintenant. Est-il possible que tu ne veuilles pas croire ce que je te dis? Tu sais cependant que ce que je dis est toujours vrai Quand pour la première fois tu reçus les caresses de Flavio dont tu avais si peur, n'ayant jamais reçu celles d'aucun homme, je te disais de ne pas craindre. T'avais-je trompée, quand je te trouvai tout d'un coup si éprise de lui?

FIORINETTA. Cela est plus que vrai, ma mère.

CELEGA. Eh bien, pourquoi donc ne me crois-tu pas maintenant, quand je te dis de ne plus le laisser venir? Puisqu'il n'a plus rien à nous donner, il te ruinera.

FIORINETTA. Parce que je ne peux le renvoyer ainsi. Parce que, lui voulant du bien, je ne peux pas vouloir lui faire du mal en le quittant, et qu'on ne peut vouloir en même temps à quelqu'un le mal et le bien. C'est comme si on voulait que je ne vous aime pas comme ma mère, ce serait impossible.

CELEGA. Belle affaire, si tu mets en balance l'amour que te porte ta mère avec celui d'un amoureux! Je serai forcée, jusqu'à ce que tu deviennes une grande dame, d'aller mendier, parce que ton amant ne voudra pas aller porter ses chausses ailleurs! Tu crois qu'il t'aime? Eh! c'est le plaisir que tu lui procures qu'il aime et non pas toi! Moi, c'est bien différent

FIORINETTA. Il verserait trop de larmes! Il pousserait trop de soupirs, il m'a tant de fois juré de m'aimer, il m'a fait tant de promesses .

CELEGA. Les larmes, les soupirs sont de légères preuves
d'amour. Les serments sont toujours à la bouche des amoureux. Je n'ai jamais vu répandre des larmes, pousser des
soupirs et faire des serments qu'à ceux qui ne donnent
rien. Et ceux qui dépensent ne pleurent pas. Tu veux
plaire et appartenir à Flavio tout seul. Cela, ma fille, est
bon pour une femme riche de n'avoir qu'un seul amant;
ce n'est pas ton cas.

FIORINETTA. S'il m'a fait du bien dans le passé, dois-je
donc lui en être ingrate maintenant?

CELEGA. Du moment qu'il ne t'en fait plus, le passé est
regardé comme nul. Mais supposons un peu que Flavio
t'aime : crois-tu donc, par hasard, que les choses seront
toujours ce qu'elles sont? Tu te trompes. Sitôt que tu
commenceras à changer de visage, il changera d'idée.

FIORINETTA. Oh! je ne crains rien de cela.

CELEGA. Ce qu'on ne craint pas vient plus vite que ce
qu'on craint. Voyons! Que manque-t-il à messer Polidoro
de tout ce que doit avoir un homme riche!

FIORINETTA. Il est laid, désagréable. Je n'ai jamais vu une
plus laide figure.

CELEGA. Il est si riche que cela cache tous ses défauts. Je
ne trouve rien de plus laid et de plus désagréable que celui
qui n'a pas d'argent.

FIORINETTA. Il est malade.

CELEGA. Quel malheur! Aussitôt que l'on voit un jeune
homme un peu pâle, avec une égratignure à la jambe,
ou une bosse au bras, tout de suite on dit : Il est malade!

Eh bien! supposons qu'il y ait quelque chose à dire. Est-ce qu'il n'y a pas beaucoup de tes pareilles dont on en puisse dire autant, et ce ne sont pas les plus abandonnées. Je ne te dirai plus qu'un mot. Si tu veux agir à ta guise, tu seras toujours une pauvre malheureuse, mais si tu veux m'en croire, tu seras bientôt riche et grande dame. Vois la Nina, qui jadis allait pieds nus et déguenillée, par les tavernes et autres lieux malhonnêtes, et qui aujourd'hui a tant d'habits de soie, tant de colliers de perles, et tant de domestiques pour lui obéir!

Fiorinetta. Soyez tranquille : la première fois que Flavio viendra me voir, nous parlerons de cela ensemble.

Celega. Imbécile enfant! tu ne connais pas ton mal. Sache que si tu aimes celui qui n'a rien à te donner, tous les autres tiendront les mains serrées. Notre avenir est dans la concurrence. Je t'ai déjà dit cent fois ce que tu as à faire. Si quelqu'un te fait quelque présent, soit un collier, soit un anneau, ou autre chose, montre-le vite à tous, afin que celui-ci, ne voulant pas paraître moins riche que celui-là, t'en donne un plus précieux. Il faut savoir faire bon accueil à chacun, causer avec tout le monde, et montrer que tu les aimes tous.

Fiorinetta. Vous voulez que j'aime tout le monde, comme j'aime Flavio?

Celega. Je ne dis pas que tu aimes chacun, mais que tu fasses semblant.

Fiorinetta. Ma mère, cela me serait une vie trop pénible. Je ne pourrai jamais faire le contraire de ce que je sens et de ce que j'ai dans le cœur. Je pense qu'il vaut mieux se marier. Et je veux une plus belle existence que celle que vous me proposez. »

Dans une scène suivante, Fiorinetta, avec son amant, se montre aussi passionnée qu'elle a paru douce et craintive avec sa mère.

« FLAVIO. Pourquoi ne me laisses-tu pas partir, mon cœur? Pourquoi me retiens-tu? Est-ce pour rendre plus grand le chagrin que j'aurai de l'avoir quittée?

FIORINA. Crois-tu donc que je veuille déjà laisser mon âme s'éloigner de moi?

FLAVIO. La mienne restera avec toi, car tu es l'asile de tous ses plaisirs et de tout son bonheur.

FIORINA. Comment pourra-t-elle rester avec moi, puisque je n'existe plus sans Flavio?

FLAVIO. Ta mère veut pourtant que nous nous séparions.

FIORINA. Je causerai du chagrin à ma mère, mais rien ne me séparera de toi.

FLAVIO. Quand ce nouvel amoureux se présentera à toi, avec tant d'argent, tu changeras peut-être de sentiment!

FIORINA. Ah! Flavio, il ne faut pas me dire de ces choses-là. Pourquoi parler ainsi? Sache que tout l'or du monde n'est pas suffisant pour me faire changer de sentiment pour toi. Non, mon cœur n'est pas à vendre comme une marchandise sur la place, et si l'amour que je te porte ne suffisait pas pour me faire persévérer dans mon dessein, le projet de ma mère le ferait. Elle veut me séparer de toi, toi la seule chose que j'aime au monde! Elle ne se réjouira pas longtemps de me posséder. Je me donnerai un coup de couteau dans le cœur, ou je m'arracherai la vie d'une autre façon.

FLAVIO. Non, il faut que tu vives, toi. Laisse-moi mourir, moi qui, restant privé de toi, serais privé du plus grand bonheur qu'on puisse désirer. La joie et les plaisirs ne te manqueront pas dans la vie.

FIORINA. Tu veux que je vive, mais l'existence sans toi sera pire que la mort! Dis-moi, quel plaisir sera plaisir pour moi sans mon Flavio? quelle joie me sera joie? quel délice me sera délice sans toi?

FLAVIO. Si, en mourant, ne mourait pas l'espérance de ne plus te voir jamais, ce qui est le plus grand bien qu'il y ait, sache, mon cœur, qu'aucun homme ne mourrait plus content que moi, pouvant se glorifier de mourir d'amour pour la plus belle jeune fille qu'ait jamais créée la nature.

FIORINA. Si jamais je reste vivante après toi, Flavio, sache bien que ma vie sera tellement amère et pleine de tourments que la mort me paraîtra douce en comparaison. Mais afin qu'il ne soit pas dit que j'éprouverai jamais aucun autre plaisir, après ta mort, je m'efforcerai de vivre, et de prolonger cette misérable existence si longtemps, que cette peine compensera un peu la perte d'un amant aussi charmant et tant chéri. Ecoute, Flavio, rends-moi le service le plus pieux que tu puisses me rendre : prends ton épée, et traverse-m'en le cœur. La vie ne m'est chère qu'à cause de toi; elle t'appartient, c'est ton bien : si tu veux mourir, emporte-la avec toi.

FLAVIO. Ah! ma dame chérie, si je pouvais plutôt joindre

mon âme à la tienne et n'en faire qu'une! Je m'ôterais la vie volontiers pour te la donner. Ne serait-ce pas le meilleur emploi que j'en pusse faire?

Fiorin. Tu augmenteras mon bonheur et ma vie en joignant ta bouche à la mienne.

Flavio. Ah! bouche délicieuse! Suis-je assez malheureux!...

Fiorin. Serre dans tes bras ta Fiorinetta, mon Flavio!... Flavio, je me sens mourir.... Au secours! »

Vezzo et Truffo accourent pour lui faire reprendre connaissance; mais Vezzo dit qu'il n'a pas d'eau rose; et Truffo, qui a vendu ses souliers pour en donner l'argent à Celega afin qu'elle reste tranquille, n'a pas de quoi en acheter.

« Flavio. Écoute, Fiorinetta, ma bien-aimée : est-ce donc là la preuve de l'amour que tu dis avoir pour moi, de vouloir mourir la première? Pourquoi n'ouvres-tu pas tes yeux pleins d'amour? Ne me cache pas la lumière de ma vie. N'est-ce pas déjà trop d'avoir à pleurer sur mon propre malheur, sans que tu veuilles y ajouter le tien? Fiorinetta! tu ne réponds pas à ton Flavio? Remue donc tes douces lèvres et réponds-moi! »

Truffo et Vezzo courent à droite et à gauche, cherchant un moyen de lui faire reprendre ses sens. Truffo crie tout à coup : « Revenez à la vie, nous avons l'argent! » Flavio, heureux de savoir qu'ils ont su dérober au *fattore* l'argent qui doit apaiser Celega et faire leur bonheur à tous deux, lui dit : « Nous n'avons plus raison de nous attrister.... entends-tu? ils ont apporté l'argent. »

FIORINA. Ah! mon Dieu! où suis-je?

FLAVIO. Dans les bras de ton Flavio.

FIORINA. Flavio, que ne me laissais-tu mourir? Je mourais si heureuse entre tes bras! »

Truffo et Vezzo se font part de leurs réflexions et disent que l'argent a plus de vertu que l'eau rose pour faire revenir des évanouissements.

« FLAVIO à *Fiorinetta*. Prends courage, ma vie, mon bien En dépit de la fortune adverse, nous nous réjouirons plus que jamais. (*Aux valets.*) Mais qui a l'argent de vous deux ? »

Dans la pièce de Plaute, Liban et Léonide, les deux esclaves fourbes, font longuement désirer l'argent au jeune couple. Il en résulte une scène burlesque d'une grossièreté inouïe, où le maître est forcé d'embrasser les genoux d'un de ses valets et de porter l'autre sur ses épaules. Philème est condamnée à les caresser, ce qui ne paraît pas lui coûter beaucoup, car elle leur offre d'elle-même des baisers et leur prodigue les plus tendres épithètes sans se faire prier.

La Fiorinetta est trop chaste et le Flavio trop sérieusement épris pour qu'il en soit ainsi La scène n'en est pas moins comique, à cause d'une longue histoire très-plaisante, racontée à deux, en dialecte, par Vezzo et Truffo, et qui ne sert qu'à impatienter les deux amants. Enfin, après avoir fait semblant de douter de la parole de son jeune maître, Vezzo exige que celui-ci embrasse tendrement sa maîtresse en manière de serment inviolable Après quoi, il se regarde comme assuré de sa protection dans les dangers où il s'est jeté pour le servir.

Dans l'*Asinaire*, Déménète, le père de l'amant, demande et obtient, pour prix de sa complaisance, les faveurs de Philénie. Le jeune homme y consent, pour conserver ses plaisirs. La femme acariâtre du vieillard surprend cette orgie, tance le fils, menace le père et l'emmène en le battant. Scène d'un grossier réalisme.

Ruzzante est un réaliste aussi, il appelle les choses par leur nom et ne farde point les mœurs brutales et licencieuses de son temps. Mais il appartient à la renaissance, son esprit tend à l'idéal, et il complète la destinée de la courtisane par un cinquième acte de son cru, qui est certainement le meilleur de la pièce.

Après avoir habilement adouci les monstruosités du texte antique, pour n'en conserver que le comique, comme, par exemple, de faire de la velléité du vieillard pour la courtisane une simple plaisanterie en manière de leçon à son fils, et de la soumission du fils une feinte avec l'arrière-pensée de soustraire à temps la Fiorina à cet opprobre, le Ruzzante entre dans un dénoûment romanesque.

La mère de Flavio, *madonna* Rospina, s'arrête au seuil de la Celega, au moment d'éclater. Elle rentre en elle-même, et, avec beaucoup de prudence et de dignité, elle s'accuse d'être la cause de tout le mal. Elle a manqué d'indulgence et de libéralité, elle a poussé son fils au désespoir, son époux au vice, ses valets aux rapines. Elle va trouver Celega et lui montre tant de douceur et de pitié, que cette misérable se repent et se retire dans un couvent, après avoir avoué que Fiorinetta n'est pas sa fille, mais une enfant qui lui est tombée sur les bras dans les tumultes

et les hasards de la guerre, « qui ont bouleversé les États
et amené des événements en dehors de toutes les prévisions
humaines ». Elle fait allusion aux guerres de Charles VIII
et de Louis XII. Voici déjà Fiorina purifiée de cette triste
parenté avec la Celega, et l'effet de sa constance produit de
bons fruits, le pardon de la mère de son amant, le repentir
de sa mère supposée. La manière dont la Celega s'excuse
de ses mauvais desseins est assez frappante.

« CELEGA. Sachez, madame, que sous les misères de la
vie disparaissent quelquefois les bonnes pensées. Ceci est
la faute de la fortune, qu'avec raison on dit aveugle. Je dis
ceci pour moi, qui, non pour devenir riche, mais pour me
soustraire à l'horreur de l'indigence, ai fait ce qu'on m'a
vu faire jusqu'à ce jour. Et pourtant, quand cette enfant
me tomba dans les mains, je n'avais que de bons desseins
sur elle, mais le peu de soucis que les grands et les puis-
sants prennent du pauvre monde me fit changer d'avis....
Et puis, la puissance des grands nous égare, nous ne
savons pas refuser ce qu'ils exigent. Que pouvais-je faire
pour préserver cette enfant d'un cavalier aussi volontaire
et aussi noble que votre fils ? »

La Celega disparaît et *madonna* Rospina appelle son
fils « Vous ne sauriez, lui dit-elle, être ainsi debout et
courir chaque nuit, par ces temps de carnaval, sans que
je m'en inquiète. Allez chercher votre amante et amenez-la
dans notre maison... Ce que je veux faire de bon et de
bien, tu le sauras plus tard. »

FLAVIO. Je reconnais maintenant qu'il n'est point d'amour
égal à celui d'une mère . *O madre! madre!* avec quel lan-

gage, avec quelle parole pourrai-je vous bénir autant que vous le méritez ! »

Ici vient une scène excellente, du plus haut comique, entre Placido et Rospina, le père et la mère de Flavio. Le mari se réjouit de l'heureux changement de sa femme. Il dit que les choses les plus favorables sont celles auxquelles on s'attend le moins.

« ROSPINA. Vous avez raison, Placido; car qui eût prévu il y a mille ans que Flavio prendrait femme aujourd'hui?

PLACIDO. Que dis-tu là, ma femme?

ROSPINA. Tout à l'heure, vous verrez ici Fiorinetta pour célébrer la noce.

PLACIDO. Et tu consentirais à une pareille chose ?

ROSPINA. Pourquoi non ?

PLACIDO. Est-ce donc là une femme pour notre fils?

ROSPINA. N'avez-vous pas dit mille fois qu'il faudrait faire mille fois l'épreuve d'une femme avant de l'épouser ?

PLACIDO. Ce n'est pas le cas. Je parlais des grandes dames. Mais celle-ci est une femelle de la plus basse extraction.

ROSPINA. Je vous ai entendu dire que, pourvu qu'une femme fût propre à réjouir l'âme de son mari, elle devait être choisie, sans égard à sa naissance.

PLACIDO. Mais celle-ci est sans dot!

ROSPINA. Combien de fois ne vous ai-je pas entendu maudire ceux qui cherchent une grande dot, et qui par là s'achètent une corde pour se priver de la liberté ?

PLACIDO. Je disais cela pour plaisanter.

ROSPINA. Et Flavio l'a pris au sérieux.

PLACIDO. Et tu souffriras qu'il en soit ainsi ?

ROSPINA. Je ferai envers lui comme je vous ai vu faire.

PLACIDO. Faites donc; mais quant à moi, je n'y donnerai jamais mon consentement.

ROSPINA. Si fait! et même vous ouvrirez le bal de noces s'il le faut.

PLACIDO. Non, j'irai à la campagne pendant cette fête.

ROSPINA. Allons! faites bon visage et réjouissez-vous des jours heureux qui vont venir

PLACIDO. Tu le veux ainsi? eh bien, soit ! »

On donne un grand bal, et la pièce finit, à l'italienne, par des chansons et des danses.

Cette Vaccaria de Ruzzante est excessivement remarquable, d'autant plus que, laissant de côté toute l'ordure antique de *l'Asinaire*, il a su en tirer une pièce romanesque, divertissante et d'un comique plus naïf et plus vrai. Dans l'histoire de Fiorinetta, élevée dans le mal par la Celega, et devenant par ses sentiments, sa constance et sa sincérité, l'épouse légitime du beau Flavio, on pourrait voir la réhabilitation de la courtisane. Mais on se tromperait : Fiorinetta n'est pas et n'a jamais été une courtisane, surtout une courtisane de cette époque-là. Elle n'en a ni les allures ni les sentiments. Une exploiteuse lui fait connaître, malgré elle, un homme. Il était jeune, beau, aimable, sincèrement épris. Elle s'est attachée à lui, elle serait morte plutôt que d'appartenir à un autre. La matrone Rospina, en la mariant à son fils, n'a fait que lui rendre l'honneur que son fils lui avait enlevé La mère de Flavio n'eût jamais reçu dans sa maison Philenie, la courtisane antique.

Le costume de Fiormetta devait être d'une grande
recherche et d'un grand goût. C'est le temps où les raffine-
ments de la toilette reprennent la plus grande place dans la
vie des femmes. « Je sais très-bien, dit Isotta dans *l'Anconitana* de Ruzzante, comment il faut faire les ouvrages de
chemises et de gorgerettes brodées en or et en soie; comment il faut habiller une dame, et quelles sont les couleurs
les plus avantageuses aux brunes et aux blondes; et quels
vêtements accompagnent le mieux les devises et livrées :
les couleurs qui signifient amour, espérance, jalousie, et
autres choses du même genre; comment se doivent porter
les *faldigie*, comment la coiffe à franges réussit mieux, soit
qu'elle cache tous les cheveux, soit qu'elle en laisse voir un
doigt ou deux; à quelles femmes conviennent le mieux les
boucles d'oreilles, et s'il vaut mieux les porter de perles,
ou de fil d'or, en torsades ou en anneaux; les différentes
formes de corset, pour faire paraître la gorge délicate ou
montrer plus ou moins les seins; les colliers, carcans,
chaînes d'or, rangs de perles qui font paraître la femme
plus imposante. Je sais aussi de quelles sortes d'anneaux les
doigts doivent être ornés, comment doit marcher une
femme; de quelle façon elle doit rire, tourner les yeux,
faire la révérence et les mouvements qui dénotent la grâce
et l'honnêteté, comment on doit orner un vêtement et les
nouvelles façons d'assembler les étoffes de couleurs différentes pour les faire paraître plus jolies.... Quelques femmes
portent leurs cheveux cachés ou peignés également de façon
que l'un ne passe pas l'autre, d'autres les portent comme en
désordre, ce qui les rend plus gracieuses et plus belles, etc. »

Mais à la renaissance le goût fut plus qu'à aucune autre époque tourné à l'imitation des Grecs et des Romains. Les actrices ne portaient guère les vêtements de leur temps que par force majeure dans les pièces d'actualité. Toutes les comédies antérieures de quelques années devenaient *anciennes* et étaient représentées *à l'antique*, c'est-à-dire en costumes de fantaisie, comme les employaient dans leurs tableaux les peintres de cette époque.

Rabelais raconte dans sa *Sciomachie* qu'à Rome, en 1569, au milieu des seigneurs, des hommes d'armes, des gens de pied et de cheval, qui devaient figurer un tournoi, Diane et ses nymphes paraissent tout à coup et jouent une petite scène, qui se termine par l'enlèvement simulé d'une nymphe par quelques soudards. Réclamation de Diane aux soudards enfermés dans une citadelle de carton, refus de ceux-ci, Diane et ses nymphes vont demander secours et vengeance aux chevaliers. L'assaut est donné, et le spectacle commence. « Diane portait sur le sommet du front un croissant d'argent, la chevelure blonde, éparse sur ses épaules, tressée sur la tête avec une guirlande de laurier, tout « introphiée » de roses violettes et autres belles fleurs; vêtue sur sa soutane et « verdugalle » de damas rouge cramoisi à riches broderies, d'une fine toile de Chypre toute battue d'or, curieusement plissée, comme si fût un rochet de cardinal, descendant jusqu'à mi-jambe, et par-dessus une peau de léopard bien rare et précieuse, attachée par de gros boutons d'or sur l'épaule gauche. Ses bottines dorées, entaillées et nouées à la « nymphale », avec quelques cordons de toile d'argent. Son cor d'ivoire pendant sous le bras gauche. Son carquois, précieusemet orné de perles, suspendu à l'épaule droite par de gros cordons et houppes de soie blanche et incarnat. Elle tenait en main droite une javeline argentée Les autres nymphes différaient peu en accoutrements, excepté qu'elles n'avaient le croissant d'argent sur le front. Chacune tenait un arc « turquois », bien beau, en main, et le carquois comme la première. Quelques-unes sur leurs épaules portaient des peaux d'Afrique de loups-cerviers ou de martre. D'autres menaient des levriers en laisse, ou sonnaient de leurs « trombes. » C'était belle chose les voir. »

Dans la troupe des *Intronati* (de 1550 à 1560), les amoureuses, dont nous ignorons le véritable nom, y paraissent sous les noms de LELIA (1551), BEATRICE et ISABELLA. En 1570, la belle Armani, née à Vicence, poète, musicienne et comédienne de talent, devient bientôt célèbre par toute l'Italie. La troupe des *Confidenti*, qui vint en France en 1572, avait pour amoureuse une actrice d'une grande beauté et donée de grands talents littéraires. C'était la CELIA, dont le nom était Maria Malloni. Le cavalier Marino la surnomme dans l'*Adone* « une quatrième Grâce », et Pietro Pinelli composa à sa louange tout un volume de vers. *Corona di lodi alla signora Maria Malloni, detta Celia, comica.* Elle jouait également bien la *commedia dell' arte* et la *commedia sostenuta*, la tragédie et la pastorale. Elle était surtout remarquable, selon le comte Ridolfo, dans le rôle de Silvia de l'*Aminta*.

Vers la même époque, la troupe des *Gelosi* possédait comme amoureuse « la belle et trop tendre Lidia de Bagnacavallo », dit M. Charles Magnin; « sa passion jalouse et trop peu déguisée pour son camarade Adriano Valerini fit quelque peu de scandale, chose rare à cette époque, où les comédiennes ne se piquaient de rien tant que de vertu. »

En 1577, la signora PRUDENZA, jeune actrice de Vérone, vint avec Flaminio Scala à Paris et à Blois

ISABELLA.

En 1578, Flaminio Scala engagea dans la troupe des *Gelosi*, alors à Florence, une jeune fille, née à Padoue en 1562, nommée Isabella, à peine âgée de seize ans, belle, remplie de talent et très-vertueuse. Francesco Andreini, qui jouait les Capitans dans la même troupe, devint amoureux d'elle et l'épousa. L'année suivante (1579), Isabella mit au monde un fils, G. B. Andreini (*Lelio*).

C'est d'abord sous le nom d'Accesa (l'*Amoureuse*) qu'Isabella fut admirée et applaudie dès ses premiers débuts, et nommée membre de l'académie des *Intenti* de Pavie. Elle fut la plus célèbre actrice de son temps, honorée des plus illustres suffrages, tels que ceux du Tasse, de Ciabrera, de Marino, sans parler des cardinaux, des princes et des souverains. Un portrait couronné d'Isabella fut placé entre ceux de Pétrarque et du Tasse, dans une fête qu'un de ses plus grands admirateurs, le cardinal Aldobrandini, lui donna à Rome.

Isabella (*planche* 56) était l'âme, l'honneur, le soutien de la troupe des *Gelosi* Elle vint en France avec la troupe en 1584, et là, comme en Italie, Isabella, alors âgée de

vingt-deux ans, ne se fit pas moins distinguer par sa conduite sage et réservée, qu'admirer par la diversité de ses
talents Il en fut de même quand Isabella revint en France,
appelée par Henri IV, en 1600.

Thomas Garzon dit dans sa *Place universelle* : « La gra-
» cieuse Isabelle Andreini, l'ornement le plus brillant de
» la scène et du théâtre, autant recommandable par sa
» vertu que par sa beauté, a illustré la profession de comé-
» dien de façon que, tant que le monde durera et jusqu'à
» la fin des siècles, le nom de la célèbre Isabelle Andreini
» sera en vénération. »

Du Ryer présenta à la belle Accesa, qui ne fut connue
en France que sous son nom d'Isabella (lequel devint YSA-
BELLA, YZABELLE et ZIRZABILLE), une supplique en vers au
moment de son départ en 1604.

A Isabelle, comédienne.

« Je ne crois point qu'Isabelle
Soit une femme mortelle,
C'est plutôt quelqu'un des dieux
Qui s'est déguisé en femme,
Afin de nous ravir l'âme
Par l'oreille et par les yeux.

Se peut-il trouver au monde
Quelque autre humaine faconde
Qui la sienne ose égaler ?
Se peut-il, dans le ciel même,
Trouver de plus douce crème
Que celle de son parler?

Mais, outre qu'elle s'attire

Toute âme par son bien-dire,

Combien d'attraits et d'amours

Et d'autres grâces célestes,

Soit au visage ou aux gestes,

Accompagnent ses discours!

Divin esprit, dont la France

Adorera l'excellence

Mille ans après son trépas,

(Paris vaut bien l'Italie)

L'assistance te supplie

Que tu ne t'en ailles pas »

Mais, malgré de telles instances, Isabelle quitta Paris.
Forcée de s'arrêter à Lyon par suite d'un accident, elle y
mourut au milieu d'une fausse couche, le 10 juillet 1604.
Les plus grands honneurs lui furent rendus. Pierre Mathieu
rapporte l'événement dans son *Histoire de France sous le règne
de Henri III* (Paris, 1609); et Nicolo Barbieri (Beltrame), qui
faisait partie de la troupe, raconte que le corps municipal de
la ville de Lyon honora la sépulture de la comédienne par
des marques de distinction « Les échevins », dit M. Charles
Magnin, « envoyèrent aux obsèques de la grande artiste les
bannières de la ville, avec leurs massiers, et la corporation
des marchands suivit le convoi avec des torches. Le mari de
cette femme célèbre, Francesco Andreini, fit graver sur sa
tombe une épitaphe qu'on peut lire dans Mazuchelli, et qui
existe peut-être toujours à Lyon, où on la voyait encore à
la fin du dernier siècle. Cette épitaphe se terminait ainsi :
« . . . . *Religiosa, pia, musis amica et artis scenicæ caput,*

hic resurrectionem exspectat..... » J'ajouterai qu'on frappa à l'effigie d'Isabella Andreini une belle médaille, avec son nom suivi des deux lettres C. G., qui signifie *comica Gelosa* (comédienne de la troupe des *Gelosi*), et ayant au revers une Renommée avec ces mots : « *Æterna fama....* » Elle avait mérité toutes ces distinctions non-seulement par la richesse d'imagination qu'elle déployait dans la *commedia dell' arte*, mais par plusieurs productions imprimées tant en vers qu'en prose. Pendant ses divers séjours à Paris, dont le dernier eut lieu en 1603, elle s'était acquis l'admiration de la cour et de la ville, et jouissait d'une faveur toute particulière auprès de Marie de Médicis et de Henri IV. »

On a d'elle des sonnets, des madrigaux, des chansons, la *Pastorale de Myrtille*, imprimée à Vérone, 1588. *Canzonniere*, Milan 1601. Avec elle mourut aussi la troupe des *Gelosi*.

Au commencement du dix-septième siècle, les amoureuses des différentes troupes italiennes étaient RENEMIA, LUCIA, PANDOLFINA, LUCREZIA, VIRGINIA.

LAVINIA, dont le véritable nom était Diana Ponti, *comica desiosa*, actrice et poète (1580), trouva, au rapport de L. Riccoboni, dans l'héritage de son père, comédien comme elle, un assez grand nombre de canevas, revêtus de la précieuse signature autographe de saint Charles Borromée. L'explication de ce fait curieux est celle-ci : Adriano Valerini avait été appelé à Milan. Malgré la tolérance du clergé italien pour les comédiens, le gouverneur de la ville, en proie à je ne sais quel scrupule de conscience, fit suspendre les représentations de la troupe que dirigeait Valerini. Celui-ci réclama. Le gouverneur s'en remit à la décision de l'archevêque, qui était Charles Borromée. Le bon prélat manda le comédien en sa présence, l'interrogea, l'écouta et lui permit de rouvrir son théâtre, à la condition de lui soumettre ses canevas. Il signait de sa propre main ceux qu'il approuvait. Un des plus grands saints de l'Église lisant et approuvant les canevas de la *commedia dell' arte* est un trait de mœurs qui a sa couleur. Nicolo Barbieri (Beltrame) dit dans son *Discorso alle commedie* que Braga, le Pantalon de la troupe de Valerini, ainsi que le Pedrolino, possédaient encore de son temps (1634) des manuscrits approuvés et signés par saint Charles Borromée.

En 1601, Virginia Ramponi remplissait les rôles d'amoureuses dans la troupe des *Gelosi*. G. B. Andreini devint amoureux d'elle, et l'épousa en 1601. Il composa pour elle sa première pièce sous le titre de FLORINDA, à cause du nom que portait au théâtre sa bien-aimée. Elle mourut vers 1654.

Dans la troupe française de l'hôtel de Bourgogne, une actrice italienne jouait en 1617, sous le nom francisé de FLORENTINE, les rôles d'amoureuses et les filles de Gros-Guillaume.

Dans la troupe des *Fedeli*, en 1624, Margarita Luciani, femme de Girolamo Gavarini (le capitaine Rhinocéros), mourut quelques jours après son mari et aussi dévotement que lui.

En 1655, LIDIA, actrice d'un grand mérite, seconde femme du directeur de la troupe, G. B. Andreini.

Vers 1652, Eularia Coris, jeune et charmante comé-

dienne, fut une des dernières actrices qui soutinrent par
leur talent la troupe des *Fedeli*, alors très-affaiblie. Elle
contribua, avec Lidia, au succès d'une pièce dramatique
et dévote intitulée *la Maddalena lasciva e penitente*, jouée
pour la première fois en 1607.

« La liste des personnages est curieuse », dit M. Charles
Magnin, « outre Madeleine, Marthe et Lazare, les principaux acteurs sont l'archange Michel et plusieurs anges,
la Grâce divine, trois amants de Madeleine, son page, ses
servantes, son sommelier, son cuisinier, ses deux nains et
trois vieilles de mauvaise renommée, *di bassa stima*. Dans
les trois premiers actes, il n'est question que de galanteries,
de fêtes, de festins. Madeleine, livrée à tout l'emportement
des sens, ferme l'oreille aux sages conseils que lui donne
Marthe, sa sœur. Dans le troisième acte, pénitente et
contrite, elle renonce aux plaisirs, se couvre d'un cilice,
est favorisée de visions extatiques, et monte enfin au ciel,
portée sur les bras de quinze chérubins, tandis que l'archange Michel et la Grâce divine exhortent l'auditoire à
suivre l'exemple de la pécheresse réconciliée. »

Agata Calderoni, connue sous le nom de FLAMINIA en
Italie, fut la grand'mère de Virginia Baletti, épouse de
Riccoboni (Lelio), qui prit elle-même le nom de théâtre
(*Flaminia*) devenu héréditaire dans la famille.

AURELIA.

« Est-ce vous, Aurelia? la belle Aurelia! vous dont les
richesses sont moindres que les attraits, et Dieu sait com-

bien vous êtes riche! Vous dont la beauté et la bonté égalent la richesse et la générosité, daignez me répondre, mon espoir, ma vie, mon avenir! Daignez accepter mes services, laissez-moi vous suivre, afin de lire dans vos yeux jusqu'au moindre de vos désirs. Commandez-moi tout ce qu'il est humainement possible de faire, et je suis prêt à l'exécuter, je me donne à vous corps et âme, je suis votre esclave. »

Auréha répond : « Êtes-vous Horace? Non! vous n'êtes point l'homme que j'aime, et qui ne sera mon esclave qu'en devenant mon maître. Retirez-vous, je ne dois pas vous écouter. Si vous n'avez autre chose à me demander que mon amour, réclamez de moi toute autre aumône, mais non pas celle de mon cœur. »

Tandis qu'en Italie les rôles d'amoureuses avaient pour interprète Orsola Bianchi, née à Venise, ils étaient remplis en France par sa sœur Brigida Bianchi, connue sous le nom d'AURÉLIA. Elle vint à Paris vers 1640 avec Tiberio Furelli, en repartit l'année suivante, et n'y revint qu'en 1645 avec son père Giuseppe Bianchi, directeur de la troupe, ses sœurs Luigia et Orsola et son mari Marc Romagnesi (Orazio).

Auréha composa en 1659 une pièce, l'*Inganno fortunato*, qu'elle dédia à la reine mère. Voici ce qu'en dit Loret dans sa *Muse historique* du 31 mai 1659 :

> Auréha, comédienne,
> Comédienne italienne,
> Comme elle est un fort bel esprit
> Qui bien parle et qui bien écrit,

A fait un présent à la reine

D'un livre sorti de sa veine,

En fort beau langage toscan,

Dont on a fait bien du cancan, etc.

La reine mère trouva la pièce à son gré, et en remercia Aurélia en lui faisant un cadeau dont Loret parle en ces termes :

Pour récompenser Aurélie

De la pièce belle et jolie

(Sous le nom de Comedia

Qu'à la reine elle dédia),

Cette princesse libérale,

Dont l'âme est tout à fait royale,

Au jugement des mieux sensés,

Lui fit présent, ces jours passés,

D'une paire, en pendants d'oreille,

De diamants beaux à merveille,

Ouvrage exquis, rare et brillant,

Travaillé des mieux, et valant

(Ainsi que m'a dit certain homme)

De trois cents pistoles la somme.

J'ai vu moi-même ce beau don,

Et je jure, par Cupidon,

Vainqueur des plus fameux monarques,

Que quand je vis ces riches marques

De la gratitude et bonté

De cette auguste majesté

Envers ladite demoiselle,

J'en fus ravi pour l'amour d'elle,

Car plus de deux ans il y a

Que j'aime cette Aurélia,

Pour son esprit et gentillesse,

Et je n'apprends qu'avec tristesse

Qu'icelle doit partir mardi,

Soit devant, soit après midi,

Et retourner en diligence

A Rome, Venise ou Florence,

Pour exercer en ce lieu-là

Les aimables talents qu'elle a

Auréha partit de Paris à la fin de juin 1659, mais elle ne fut qu'un an absente. Ayant appris la mort de Romagnesi, son mari, elle y revint en 1660, rentra au théâtre et ne se retira qu'en 1685. Elle resta à Paris après sa retraite, et vécut encore assez longtemps. Elle demeurait dans la rue Saint-Denis, près le couvent du grand Saint-Chaumont, où elle mourut âgée de quatre-vingt-dix ans en 1705.

C'était une fort jolie femme, qui avait un grand goût pour se mettre, et qui aimait passionnément la toilette. Mademoiselle Belmont, femme de Romagnesi de Belmont (*Léandre*), son petit-fils, dit l'avoir trouvée dans son lit, mourante, mais extrêmement parée et mise à la dernière mode.

Auréha avait été très-aimée d'Anne d'Autriche; elle avait, comme Scaramouche, ses entrées dans l'intimité de la reine.

Orsola Corteze, connue au théâtre sous le nom d'EULARIA, débuta à Paris en 1660, à l'âge de vingt-trois ans. Sa mère, Barba Corteze, connue sous le nom de FLORINDA, disait que son mari descendait de Fernand Cortez, le conquérant du Mexique. Orsola Corteze épousa, à Saint-Germain l'Auxerrois, Joseph-Dominique Biancolelli (*Arlequin*), et eut de lui douze enfants.

« Elle était grande et bien faite, sans être jolie; elle était

fort aimable. » Elle prit l'emploi des premières amoureuses
après la retraite d'*Aurélia*, et resta au théâtre jusqu'en 1680.
En 1704, elle se retira à Montargis, au couvent des filles de
la Visitation de Sainte-Marie, et y mourut en 1718, âgée de
quatre-vingt-six ans.

ISABELLE.

Françoise-Marie-Apolline Biancolelli, fille de Dominique
Biancolelli (Arlequin) et d'Orsola Corteze, naquit à Paris
en 1664 et y débuta en 1685, dans les rôles d'amoureuses, sous le nom de guerre d'Isabelle; sa sœur cadette
prit en même temps l'emploi des soubrettes sous le nom
de Colombine.

« Jamais, dit Devizé, la Comédie-Italienne n'a été si
applaudie qu'elle l'est présentement.... Si Arlequin est ini-
mitable dans les divers rôles qu'on lui voit jouer dans cette
pièce, ses deux filles ne le sont pas moins; les différents
personnages qu'elles soutiennent sont si bien remplis
qu'elles se sont attiré l'applaudissement de tout Paris, qui
ne peut se lasser de les admirer. Jamais on n'a vu tant
d'intelligence pour la comédie, avec une si grande jeunesse. Il n'y en a point dans lequel elles n'entrent, et elles
s'en acquittent de si bonne grâce que, lorsqu'elles paraissent dans quelque scène, elles semblent être uniquement
nées pour le personnage qu'elles représentent. »

Le monologue suivant, recueilli par Gherardi, résume
le caractère dominant du type d'Isabelle. C'est presque
toujours une maîtresse femme, cousine germaine, pour

l'esprit d'aventures et la rouerie sceptique, de la soubrette Colombine, avec laquelle même son emploi s'est quelquefois fondu. Elle est le type de la grande coquette, de l'intrigante, de la fille terrible.

« Messieurs, dit-elle, dans le déplorable état où la galanterie se trouve aujourd'hui, il n'est pas étrange qu'une femme soit réduite à soutenir la cause de toutes les autres. Notre sexe attendrait longtemps en vain qu'un autre prit le soin de le venger. Depuis que les cabarets et les manufactures à tabac sont devenus si fort à la mode, les femmes ont cessé de plaire ; et l'amour, tout puissant qu'il est, ne saurait plus balancer, dans l'esprit des jeunes gens, le fade et brutal plaisir d'une débauche faite à *l'Alliance* ou à *la Galère*.

» Où est le temps que le beau sexe voyait assidûment à ses pieds une jeunesse florissante ? ce temps qu'on pouvait, à bon droit, nommer l'âge d'or de la tendresse, où les cœurs venaient par escadrons reconnaître notre pouvoir ! Dans ce temps heureux il n'y eût pas eu de sûreté à nous choquer, et la peine suivait de près le moindre tort qu'on pouvait nous faire. Mais les choses ont bien changé de face, et nous éprouvons sensiblement que l'empire de la tendresse n'est point à l'épreuve des révolutions. On ne voit plus, à l'heure qu'il est, mille infatigables aventuriers arpenter d'office tout l'univers pour soutenir nos querelles ; et l'amour, qui servait autrefois à enrichir notre sexe, ne sert aujourd'hui qu'à le ruiner.

» Ce n'est pas dans notre siècle qu'il faut chercher ces héroïnes magnifiques, qui s'offraient à réparer, du revenu de leurs appas, les plus cruelles désolations de la guerre, et se mettaient par là de pair avec les plus fameux conquérants. Aujourd'hui la galanterie n'est pas reconnaissable, on lésine jusque sur les petits soins; et, bien loin de se dépouiller de tout en faveur de l'objet aimé, on ne donne son cœur qu'avec des réserves. Mais ce qui a le plus contribué à décrier la galanterie, c'est l'indigne profanation qu'on fait de nos appas, en nous unissant tous les jours à d'imbéciles vieillards, nation de tout temps réprouvée dans toute l'étendue de l'empire amoureux. Ces assortiments bizarres, que l'avarice suggère à nos pères, ouvrent la porte à des abus sans nombre; c'est la pépinière des séparations, et le revenu le plus clair de tant d'abbés coquets qui sont sans cesse à l'affût de ces sortes de mariages.

» Croit-on qu'il y ait des filles assez novices pour prendre aisément le change en fait de mariage? Et la douce idée que nous nous en faisons n'est-elle pas incompatible avec les austérités où veulent nous accoutumer les maris à lunettes? Ne savons-nous pas que l'hymen est une espèce de milice, dont les enfants et les vieillards sont également incapables? Quelle figure veut-on que fasse un vieux barbon sous la bannière de l'hymen, ou plutôt quelle figure veut-on que fasse une jeune personne auprès d'un époux qui la catéchise à toute heure, qui compte tous les pas qu'elle fait, qui n'ouvre la bouche que pour la contredire, ou pour la régaler de ses prouesses du temps passé? un bourru qui fait un crime à sa moitié d'un ruban ajouté à sa coiffure, et qui donne la question à ses serviteurs sur les démarches les plus innocentes de sa femme! Je ne parle pas de cette légion de maladies dont la vieillesse est exercée, ni de cette toux insupportable qui est la musique ordinaire d'un vieillard. Ce n'est pas que je ne trouve quelque chose d'héroïque dans la triste fidélité dont on a le courage de se piquer envers les maris faits de la sorte; mais il faut que je confesse hautement ma faiblesse. Dans une pareille extrémité, je ne puis répondre que d'une inflexibilité de rocher à ne jamais démordre de la haine que j'aurai conçue une fois pour le vieillard qui osera attenter à ma liberté. »

Quand elle est amoureuse, elle ne recule devant rien pour se débarrasser des entraves que la volonté paternelle lui suscite :

« ISABELLE *en cavalier, devant un miroir, accommodant sa cravate.* Donne-moi ce chapeau. Eh bien, Pierrot, ce cavalier-là est-il de ton goût?

PIERROT. Pardi, mademoiselle, vous voilà à charmer; on vous prendrait pour moi. Il y a pourtant un peu de différence. Est-ce que vous allez lever une compagnie de fantassinerie?

ISABELLE. Ne pense pas te moquer, je tâterais fort bien de l'armée, et je n'appréhenderais pas plus le feu qu'un autre.

PIERROT. Si tous les capitaines étaient faits comme vous, ils pourraient gagner les frais de l'enrôlement, et faire leurs soldats eux-mêmes.

ISABELLE. Je ne mets pas cet habit-ci sans raison. Tu sais que mon père veut que j'épouse M. Bassinet.

PIERROT. Votre père? bon! C'est un vieux fou qui radote, et je le lui ai dit, da!

ISABELLE. Je me sers du déguisement où tu me vois pour

détourner ce mariage. M. Bassinet ne m'a jamais vue, il
ne doit venir voir, et j'attends sa visite en cet équipage. Je
vais lui apprendre des nouvelles d'Isabelle, et je lui en
ferai, parbleu, passer l'envie.

PIERROT. Mordi, voilà une hardie tête de fille ! J'ai toujours dit à votre père que je ne croyais pas qu'il fût le mari
de votre mère quand elle vous a fait; vous avez trop d'esprit, qu'en croyez-vous?

ISABELLE. Pour moi, Pierrot, je ne m'embarrasse point
de cela. Je ne songe qu'à faire rompre, si je puis, l'imper-
tinent mariage dont je suis menacée. Mais je crois que
voilà M. Bassinet. Laisse-moi avec lui; je vais commencer
mon rôle.

PIERROT *s'en allant.* Pardi, c'est lui-même ! Il ressemble à
un marcassin !

ISABELLE *s'assied nonchalamment dans un fauteuil, le Docteur
entre.* Serviteur, monsieur, serviteur.

LE DOCTEUR *apercevant Isabelle et la prenant pour un
homme.* Ah ! monsieur, je vous demande pardon. On
m'avait dit que mademoiselle Isabelle était dans sa chambre. (*A part.*) Que diable cherche ici ce godelureau-là?

ISABELLE. Monsieur, elle n'y est pas, et je l'attends. Mais
vous, monsieur, que venez-vous faire ici? La signora Isabelle est-elle malade? Car, à votre mine, je vous crois
médecin; et vous avez toute l'encolure d'un membre de la
faculté.

LE DOCTEUR. Vous ne vous trompez pas, monsieur, je suis
un nourrisson d'Hippocrate. Mais je ne viens pas ici pour
tâter le pouls à Isabelle, j'ai bien d'autres prétentions sur....

II   24

Isabelle. Oui? Et de quelle nature, s'il vous plaît, sont les prétentions d'un docteur sur une fille?

Le Docteur. Je viens ici pour l'épouser

Isabelle *riant*. Ah! ah! ah!

Le Docteur. Mais cela est donc bien drôle?

Isabelle Point du tout; mais c'est que... ah! ah! ah!... je ris comme cela quelquefois, ah! ah! ah!

Le Docteur *allant se regarder à un miroir*. Est-ce que je serais barbouillé?

Isabelle. Non! ne voyez-vous pas bien que je ris? Ah! ah! ah!. et dites-moi un peu, monsieur, en vous déterminant à un saut si périlleux, vous êtes-vous bien tâté? N'avez-vous pas senti quelque petit mal de tête? . Vous m'entendez bien?

Le Docteur. Non, monsieur, je me porte fort bien, je ne suis point sujet à la migraine.

Isabelle *allant lui mettre la main sur le front*. Ma foi! vous porterez bien cela; et je suis plus aise que vous ayez cette fille-là qu'un autre

Le Docteur. Et moi aussi.

Isabelle. Mais quand elle sera votre femme, au moins, n'allez pas nous la gâter par vos manières ridicules; nous avons eu assez de peine à la mettre sur le pied où elle est.... Je veux être de vos amis, et je prétends, quand vous serez marié, aller sans façon chez vous manger votre chapon.

Le Docteur. Monsieur, vous me faites trop d'honneur, mais je ne mange jamais de volaille. A ce que je vois, vous connaissez parfaitement la demoiselle en question?

ISABELLE Ce n'est pas d'aujourd'hui que nous sommes toujours ensemble, et si vous étiez discret, je vous apprendrais quelque chose sur son chapitre que je suis sûr que vous ne savez pas.

Le Docteur. Ah! vous pouvez tout dire, et compter sur ma discrétion. Vous savez que les médecins.. .

Isabelle. Je passe... mais il faut voir si personne ne nous entend ... Je passe toutes les nuits dans sa chambre.

Le Docteur *stupéfait*. Dans sa chambre ?

Isabelle. Dans sa chambre Je vous dirai même... mais vous irez jaser ?

Le Docteur. Non, je me donne au diable.

Isabelle. Cette nuit, nous avons reposé sur le même chevet. Prenez vos mesures là-dessus.

Le Docteur Sur le même chevet ?

Isabelle. Et la nuit prochaine nous en ferons autant infailliblement. Elle ne saurait se coucher sans moi. Mais ce que je viens de vous dire là, au moins, ne doit pas vous empêcher de conclure l'affaire. Un homme bien amoureux ne doit pas s'arrêter à ces bagatelles-là !

Le Docteur. Bon ! voilà de belles badineries ! Je ne vois pas que rien presse encore. Adieu, monsieur, jusqu'au revoir. Le ciel m'a assisté. Voilà un jeune homme qui m'aime bien ! (*Il sort.*)

Isabelle. Je crois que ses fumées d'amour pour Isabelle sont bien passées présentement. Depuis un quart d'heure que je fais l'homme, je ne suis pas mal scélérat. »

(*Théâtre de Gherardi*)

Isabelle est généralement comique. Son emploi n'est pas

d'attendrir ni même d'intéresser. Elle embrase la scène de ses satires, de ses fantaisies et de son bel esprit. Elle parle comme un homme. Elle en a l'instruction, l'audace, le positivisme, voire les ridicules selon le temps et la mode.

« ISABELLE. Tu ne sais pas, Colombine, que la prose n'est que l'excrément de l'esprit et qu'un madrigal voiture plus de tendresse au cœur que trente périodes des mieux arrangées. Il faut être du dernier peuple pour ne pas aimer les poetes à la folie.

COLOMBINE. Eh ! vous n'en prenez pas mal le chemin.

ISABELLE. Pour moi, je suis tellement engouée de vers, qu'un poete me mènerait sans peine jusqu'aux frontières de la tendresse.

COLOMBINE. Ma foi, vous perdez l'esprit.

ISABELLE. Ah, Colombine ! qu'un homme est charmant quand il offre des vœux passés par le tamis des muses. Quel moyen de tenir contre une déclaration qui frappe l'oreille par sa cadence, et dont l'expression figurée jette la sensibilité dans l'âme la plus rebelle et la plus farouche ? Quel plaisir, Colombine, de régaler son cœur dans ces nouveautés ingénieuses qui renferment beaucoup de passion dans fort peu de vers ! Ah ! l'heureux talent de pouvoir assujettir ses mouvements et ses pensées aux pieds et aux mesures prescrites par la poésie !

COLOMBINE. Savez-vous, mademoiselle, que ces pieds-là pourraient bien vous mener droit aux Petites-Maisons !... Il est bon d'avoir de l'esprit, mais il faut encore autre chose en mariage. Toute servante que je suis, je ne voudrais d'un poete ni pour amant ni pour mari : quelle ressource y a-t-il

à être la femme d'un rimailleux ? Meuble-t-on une chambre
d'épigrammes ? Paye-t-on un boucher avec des sonnets ?
Ma foi, si j'étais à votre place, je buterais à quelque
bon financier, qui ferait rouler mon mérite en carrosse,
et qui....

ISABELLE Un financier, ah ! l'horreur !

COLOMBINE. Oh ! ne faites pas tant la sucrée. Ça n'est pas
tout à fait à votre choix, non ! »

Françoise Biancolelli, sans être d'une grande beauté,
avait le « don de plaire répandu dans toute sa personne ».
Elle était pleine de grâce, fort bien faite, et d'une physionomie douce et charmante. M. de Turgis, officier aux
gardes-françaises, en devint éperdument amoureux et
l'épousa en 1691. Elle avait vingt-sept ans et son mari
vingt et un. Le père et la mère de M. de Turgis (Charles-
Constantin) portèrent plainte en 1693 contre leur bru, en
l'accusant de rapt et de subornation. La mère de Françoise
Biancolelli, ignorant les lois de la France, et, pour débou-
ter de leur plainte les parents du mari, leur fit dire et signifier qu'il n'y avait entre sa fille et leur fils ni convention,
ni traité, ni célébration de mariage. En 1694, le père et la
mère de M. de Turgis firent un testament et déshéritèrent
leur fils, « pour le punir de son commerce honteux avec
» Françoise-Marie-Apolline Biancolelli, protestant, au
» reste, de faire déclarer nul le mariage qu'il peut avoir
» contracté avec elle, s'ils viennent à le découvrir ».

Ayant eu les preuves du mariage, ils firent reléguer leur
fils à Angers et lui enjoignirent de déclarer qu'il avait été
abusé et suborné. D'un caractère faible, il céda et signa cette

déclaration Il courut cependant, tout de suite après, chez un notaire pour protester contre ce qu'il venait de faire.

Le parlement rendit un arrêt, le 11 février 1695, qui déclare que le mariage est nul, et défend au sieur de Turgis et à demoiselle Françoise Biancolelli (dite Isabelle) « de se » hanter et fréquenter, à peine de punition corporelle, et » de contracter aucun nouveau mariage, à peine de nul- » lité ». Et cela « du vivant ou après la mort de ses père et » mère ». Constantin de Turgis fit tous les ans des protes- tations chez son notaire. On en compte sept

Françoise Biancolelli avait quitté le théâtre en 1695. Le père de M. de Turgis mourut cette année-là, mais le sort des deux époux ne s'améliora qu'en 1701. Ils se remarièrent pour la seconde fois, avec dispenses du cardinal de Noailles, dans l'église Bonne-Nouvelle, et déclarèrent « qu'il était » procréé d'eux, sous la foi du mariage, deux enfants » actuellement vivants, savoir · Charles-Dominique de » Turgis des Chaises, né en 1692, et une fille qui fut plus » tard madame Millin de Tressolles ».

« Depuis ce temps, M. de Turgis alla publiquement chez sa femme, et affecta même de paraître avec elle aux prome- nades publiques. » Bien qu'il eût conservé un logement chez sa mère, il demeurait avec sa femme rue des Petits- Pères, y recevait, et y « passait les jours et souvent les nuits ». Françoise Biancolelli portait alors publiquement son nom.

La mère de M. de Turgis mourut le 2 février 1704, et rappela dans son testament « les deux actes d'exhéréda- tion, si son fils se remariait avec la demoiselle Biancolclli », comme si elle eût ignoré qu'il se fût remarié, ce qui n'était pas probable, demeurant dans le même quartier.

M. de Turgis mourut le 29 avril 1706. Sentant sa fin prochaine, il fit venir son neveu de Turgis de Canteleu, alors âgé de quatorze ans. Il lui représenta, d'une manière touchante, la triste situation de sa femme et de ses enfants, les lui fit embrasser et les lui recommanda. Le jeune de Canteleu promit qu'il n'abandonnerait jamais ni sa tante ni ses cousins. Il tint parole, car, étant mort à vingt et un ans, il laissa à Charles-Dominique, son cousin, huit mille livres de rente pour soutenir son nom, et à sa cousine quatre mille. « Ces sommes étant distinctes, disait-il dans un écrit de sa main, des biens qui appartiennent à mes cousins de Turgis, pour leur rendre dès que je serai majeur. » Après la mort de son mari, qui n'avait laissé que des dettes, puisqu'il était mort déshérité, Françoise Biancolelli fut réduite à demander des secours, ayant dépensé son propre bien pour entretenir son mari au service. La cour rendit un arrêt, en 1709, qui lui allouait une pension viagère de mille livres pour elle et ses enfants, et en 1713, le roi, voulant récompenser les services de Constantin de Turgis en la personne de sa veuve, la gratifia d'une pension de trois cents livres.

Madame de Turgis laissa deux enfants, Charles-Dominique de Turgis, chevalier de Saint-Louis, officier au régiment royal des vaisseaux, et Marie-Anne-Reine de Turgis, épouse du sieur Millin de Tressoles.

SILVIA.

Rosa Zanetta Benozzi, célèbre sous le nom de Silvia, était venue à Paris avec la troupe appelée par le Régent en 1716. Elle joua pendant quarante-deux ans les rôles d'amoureuses avec la même vivacité, la même finesse et la même illusion : jamais le public inconstant ne se refroidit pour elle ; elle jouit des applaudissements jusqu'au moment de sa mort, et emporta les plus vifs regrets. Elle excellait surtout dans les pièces de M. de Marivaux, dont elle avait parfaitement saisi le dialogue fin et spirituel. Un volume suffirait à peine pour contenir tous les éloges qu'elle a reçus, tant en prose qu'en vers.

> « Toi que les grâces ont formée,
> Sois sûre, aimable Silvia,
> Que tu seras toujours aimée
> Tant que le bon goût durera. »

Les rôles de Silvia étaient très-différents. Dans les pièces de Marivaux, comme *le Jeu de l'amour et du hasard*, elle est maîtresse et soubrette. Dans d'autres pièces, elle est simplement soubrette, parfois simple paysanne naïve, ou bergère innocente, comme dans *Arlequin poli par l'amour*, première pièce que Marivaux donna aux Italiens.

Arlequin entre en jouant au volant, il vient de cette façon jusqu'aux pieds de Silvia ; là, en jouant, il laisse tomber le volant, et, en se baissant pour le ramasser, il voit Silvia, il demeure étonné et courbé, petit à petit et

par secousses, il redresse le corps; quand il s'est entièrement relevé, il la regarde; elle, honteuse, feint de se
retirer; dans cet embarras, il l'arrête et dit : « Vous êtes
bien pressée!

Silvia. Je me retire, car je ne vous connais pas.

Arlequin. Vous ne me connaissez pas? tant pis! Faisons
connaissance, voulez-vous?

Silvia *honteuse.* Je le veux bien.

Arlequin *s'approche d'elle et lui marque sa joie par de petits
rires.* Que vous êtes jolie!

Silvia. Vous êtes bien obligeant.

Arlequin. Oh! point, je dis la vérité.

Silvia *en riant un peu à son tour.* Vous êtes bien joli aussi,
vous!

Arlequin. Tant mieux. Où demeurez-vous? je vous irai
voir. »

Silvia lui dit qu'elle est aimée d'un berger qui pourrait
les épier, ce qui afflige Arlequin, mais elle assure qu'elle
n'aime point ce berger, et Arlequin se console. Il lui
apprend à son tour qu'il loge chez la *Fée*, ce qui cause à
Silvia de la jalousie, parce qu'elle dit que la fée est plus
belle qu'elle. Arlequin la rassure. Silvia n'a bientôt plus
d'autre inquiétude que celle de ses moutons qui s'éloignent et qu'elle est obligée de suivre. Arlequin lui prend
la main qu'il baise, en disant : « Oh! les jolis petits
doigts! je n'ai jamais eu de bonbons si bons que cela! »
et ils se quittent.

Silvia, dans un autre changement à vue, revient avec
une cousine, autre bergère, et lui demande conseil. « Arle-

qui m'a déjà baisé la main, » lui dit-elle; « il voudra me
la baiser encore. Donne-moi conseil, toi qui as eu tant
d'amants; dois-je le laisser faire? — Garde-t'en bien, » lui
dit la cousine; « sois bien sévère, cela entretient l'amour
d'un amant, et il ne faut point lui dire tant que tu l'aimes.
— Eh! comment s'en empêcher? » dit Silvia

Arlequin revient : tendresses des deux amants, jalousie
de la fée, qui fait disparaître Silvia; puis malice et ruses
d'Arlequin, à qui l'amour a donné tant d'esprit, qu'il escamote la baguette magique de la fée, devenue impuissante,
et il en fait cadeau à Silvia, laquelle évoque des esprits
et des diables qui viennent se faire rosser par Arlequin.

Dans *l'Amante romanesque* (1718), Silvia avoue à sa servante Spinette qu'elle ignore encore ce que c'est que
l'amour, bien qu'elle ait été mariée; mais, dans la solitude
où la laissait son mari, elle passait son temps à lire des
romans, ce qui lui a monté la tête. Elle déteste les hommes,
dit-elle, et veut prendre à son service une certaine Marinette, qui dit, peut-être plus qu'elle-même, beaucoup de
mal d'eux.

Cette Marinette n'est autre que Mario, qui, sous des
habits de servante, veut s'introduire auprès de Silvia qu'il
aime. Spinette s'y oppose · « Je vous souffrirais, » dit-elle,
« au lever, au coucher de ma maîtresse? L'habiller, la désha-
biller? Elle serait mal servie, vous seriez trop distrait!.... »
Mais après beaucoup de promesses de la part de Mario,
qui jure n'avoir d'autre désir que celui de voir Silvia,
Spinette le présente à Silvia, qui l'accepte pour suivante.
Mais voulant tenir parole à Spinette, Marinette (Mario)

s'excuse de ce qu'elle ne peut entrer au service de Silvia, en lui disant qu'elle vient d'hériter d'une tante qui lui laisse douze mille livres de rente : « Voilà, » dit-elle, « de quoi choisir un mari.

SILVIA. Je suis charmée de ce que tu viens de me dire, et tu n'en dois pas douter, puisque j'avais dessein de prendre soin de ta fortune et de l'attacher à moi.

MARINETTE (Mario). Madame, j'y suis attaché plus que vous ne pensez.

SILVIA. Mais tu parles déjà de choisir un mari, tu les haïssais tant!

MARINETTE. Il faut bien quelque jour finir par là, mais j'y reculerai le plus que je pourrai, et peut-être toute ma vie: j'y suis trop difficile.

SILVIA. Quel serait ton goût?... voyons.

MARINETTE. J'en voudrais un qui eût le cœur d'un Italien et les manières d'un Français. »

Silvia approuve cette manière de penser, mais elle se déchaîne toujours contre les hommes, Spinette, et plus encore Marinette, suivent son exemple : Marinette en dit enfin tant de mal, que Silvia l'embrasse avec transport.

« SILVIA. Viens, ma chère Marinette, viens, mes amours, viens que je t'embrasse! Je t'aime de tout mon cœur; je trouve en toi mes pensées, mes sentiments, mon humeur. (A Spinette qui veut l'arrêter.) Ote-toi de là, Spinette; je veux l'embrasser mille fois

SPINETTE. Madame, dispensez-moi de voir cela.

SILVIA. Pourquoi donc t'y opposer?

SPINETTE. Non, je suis jalouse.

SILVIA. Retire-toi, folle. Approche, mon héroïne, je veux t'étouffer de caresses. (*A Spinette*) Que veut dire cela? tu l'arraches de mes bras! Encore une fois, je te prie de t'ôter de là.

SPINETTE. Mais, madame, vous qui avez lu les romans, ne vous souvient-il point du déguisement de Céladon en fille pour approcher de sa maîtresse Astrée?

SILVIA. Après?

SPINETTE. Si Marinette, par hasard, était un garçon qui en eût fait autant, ferais-je bien de vous laisser faire?

SILVIA. Ah! ah! vous plaisantez encore sur mes romans! Si Marinette, avec l'esprit et les sentiments qu'elle a, était un garçon, ce garçon-là serait demain mon époux. »

Mario se jette à ses genoux, se déclare. Silvia pardonne, et l'accepte pour son chevalier en attendant qu'il soit son époux.

Dans *le Portrait* (1727), pièce de M. Beauchamp, Silvia a pris les habits de sa soubrette Colombine et fait passer Colombine pour elle-même. Elle reçoit fort mal Valère, le futur que lui a destiné son père. Valère n'est point sa dupe, il feint de la prendre pour sa femme de chambre, et lui découvre ainsi ses sentiments d'une manière plus délicate. Mais plus Valère montre sa soumission aux ordres de la belle Silvia, plus celle-ci, le croyant indifférent, essaye de le dégoûter d'elle. Dans ce dessein, elle lui fait d'elle-même ce portrait :

« D'abord, elle n'est ni grande, ni petite, ni bien, ni mal faite. Plutôt grasse que maigre, et malgré tout cela, chose rare aujourd'hui, elle a de la taille; elle a un petit

air d'étourderie et de jeunesse qui frappe. Ce n'est, si vous
voulez, ni esprit, ni éclat, cela tient pourtant un peu de
tous les deux : elle a de la blancheur et du teint, des
yeux et des dents; elle chante et danse passablement;
en un mot, elle est comme mille autres. A l'égard de sa
conduite, il n'y a rien à vous en dire; elle vit comme
vivent à présent toutes les filles. Pour son humeur, il n'est,
ma foi, pas aisé de la définir, elle est douce par réflexion,
aigre par tempérament, timide dans les choses qu'elle
sait, décisive dans celles qu'elle ignore, impérieuse avec
ceux qui ne lui doivent rien, exigeante sans amitié, jalouse
sans passion, vive jusqu'à l'emportement, distraite jusqu'à
l'oubli, inégale jusqu'à la brusquerie; enfin si difficile à
vivre, que la plupart du temps nous ne pouvons durer ensemble. Le maître, le guide, le mobile de toutes ses actions,
de tous ses discours, savez-vous ce que c'est? le caprice. »

Valère feint de croire à ce portrait, qu'il sait bien n'être pas
ressemblant, ayant l'original sous les yeux; et pour la piquer
au jeu, lui dit renoncer à Silvia, ce dont celle-ci enrage.

Parmi les nombreux madrigaux, sonnets, épîtres, etc.,
composés en l'honneur de Silvia, nous citerons cette fable,
comme caractérisant le goût de l'époque :

> Depuis qu'on a banni de la scène ennoblie
> Le comique grossier, les obscènes couleurs
>   Des premiers pinceaux de Thalie;
> Depuis que l'esprit seul produit de vrais acteurs,
> Qui de nos mœurs si bien nous traça la peinture,
>   Tant d'agrément sur la scène employa,
>   Sauva mieux l'art, rendit mieux la nature,
>   Que fait l'aimable Silvia?

D'un talent si nouveau je connais le modèle ;
    C'est un secret qu'Amour m'a déclaré,
    Non qu'en ce point le dieu m'ait préféré,
    A qui l'Amour ne parle-t-il point d'elle ?
Or, voilà le secret, peut-il être ignoré ?
    Sur une plage où règne Cythérée,
      Une des Grâces, un beau jour,
    Se promenait de ses sœurs séparée,
Prothée alors parut aux rives d'alentour,
Il la voit, il la suit, qui ne suivrait les Grâces ?
Elle fuit, et le dieu de voler sur ses traces,
Il approche, admire, aime, hésite, ose parler.
Avec colère Églé répond à cet hommage,
    Le refuser sans se troubler
Peut-être aurait été d'un plus mauvais présage
    Que fait Prothée ? Il change de langage,
Sait varier ses soins, cache ses déplaisirs ;
Encore qu'amoureux, on ne réussit guère,
Devenez séduisants, épargnez les soupirs,
Amants, tout est prouvé, alors qu'on a su plaire
Il plut aussi, bientôt un mutuel amour
Dans le sein des plaisirs éternisa leur chaîne
    Ce fut ainsi, pour l'honneur de la scène,
      Que SILVIA reçut le jour
Qui pourrait s'y tromper ? Elle a du dieu son père
    Cet ingénieux caractère
    D'enjouement, de variété,
Et la naïveté de sa charmante mère.

Silvia était née à Toulouse, de parents italiens. Elle épousa à Paris, en 1720, Joseph Baletti, connu sous le nom de *Mario*. Elle eut de ce mariage Antoine-Louis Baletti (*Lelio*), reçu au Théâtre-Italien en 1742, Louis Baletti, danseur, et Jeanne Baletti qui épousa Blondel, l'architecte du roi. Silvia mourut en 1759

FLAMINIA.

En même temps que la célèbre Silvia remplissait des rôles très-différents et qui demandaient un talent varié, FLAMINIA, l'épouse de Louis Riccoboni (*Lelio*), tenait l'emploi de première amoureuse.

Elena-Virginia Baletti naquit à Ferrare en 1686. Elle parcourut, dans son enfance, les différents théâtres d'Italie. Ses parents, bien que pauvres, lui donnèrent une éducation qui devait la mettre au-dessus du plus grand nombre de ses égales. Dès sa plus tendre jeunesse, elle passa pour une des meilleures actrices de son pays. Louis Riccoboni, déjà directeur d'une troupe à vingt-deux ans, vit dans les talents de mademoiselle Baletti un moyen de rappeler sur la scène italienne « le goût qui était perdu ». Il la demanda en mariage et l'obtint. Elle vint à Paris avec son mari en 1716, pour contribuer avec lui à la réformation *académique* qu'ils avaient vainement tentée en Italie, où les *masques* étaient restés maîtres du champ de bataille; mais le public français aimait aussi Arlequin et Scaramouche, et la représentation des chefs-d'œuvre italiens n'eût pas suffi au succès de cette nouvelle troupe. Il fallut transiger et laisser faire les masques. Flaminia se retira avec Riccoboni en 1732. On rendit justice aux talents de Flaminia, qui n'était pas seulement estimée comme excellente actrice, mais aussi comme femme très-instruite. Elle parlait l'espagnol et le français comme sa langue maternelle, et avait fait une étude

sérieuse du latin. Voici le portrait qu'on fait d'elle dans
des *Lettres historiques* sur les spectacles :

« Flaminia, épouse de Lelio, est bien faite, mais fort
» maigre. C'est une femme de beaucoup d'esprit et grande
» comédienne. Une preuve de son esprit, c'est qu'elle est
» des académies de Rome, de Ferrare, de Bologne et de
» Venise. Elle a plusieurs belles connaissances acquises,
» mais celle de son mérite semble ne lui être pas échappée.
» Elle joue ses rôles en perfection : on ne peut pas mieux
» entrer qu'elle dans les sentiments qu'ils exigent. Elle
» est non-seulement très-habile pour exprimer ses senti-
» ments, mais elle peut encore, par son esprit, en pro-
» duire autant de convenables qu'il lui plaît.... Comme
» il n'est point d'acteurs parfaits, Flaminia n'est point
» sans défauts : par exemple, elle a la voix aigre et par
» conséquent désagréable, et je voudrais qu'elle pût se
» défaire d'un air de capacité qui ne plaît pas. »

Flaminia tira du *Rudens* de Plaute le sujet de sa comédie
du *Naufrage*, qui ne réussit pas. Sa pièce d'*Abdilly, roi de
Grenade*, tragi-comédie en collaboration avec Delisle, ne
réussit pas davantage. Dégoûtée du théâtre, elle le quitta
tout à fait en 1735, et vécut retirée jusqu'en 1771, époque
de sa mort.

Marie Laboras de Mézières, née à Paris en 1713, débuta
le 25 août 1734 par le rôle de Lucile, dans *la Surprise de
l'amour.* Elle épousa François Riccoboni fils, et se retira
du Théâtre-Italien en 1761. Elle composa plusieurs scènes
françaises dans les canevas italiens, mais c'est au roman
français que madame Riccoboni dut la célébrité durable

de son nom . *Lettres de Fanny Butler, Ernestine, Histoire du marquis de Catesby,* furent ses œuvres principales. Elle traduisit aussi plusieurs pièces anglaises : *la Façon de se fixer, la Femme jalouse, la Fausse Délicatesse, Il est possédé.* Elle fut un des beaux esprits de son temps, et mourut en 1792.

Le 5 mai 1750, Anna-Elisabeta Costantini, fille de Jean-Baptiste Costantini, de Belmont (l'*Ottavio* de l'ancienne troupe), débuta à la Comédie-Italienne pour remplir les rôles d'*Isabelle* et de *Silvia*.

CAMILLE.

Giaccometta-Antonia Veronese, connue sous le nom de Camille, naquit à Venise en 1735. Elle vint en France en 1744 avec son père Veronese (*Pantalon*) et sa sœur Anna Veronese (*Coraline*), à peine âgée de neuf ans, Camille débuta par la danse, le 21 mai 1744, en même temps que sa sœur et son père débutaient dans *Coraline, esprit follet,* pièce qui fut fort à la mode. Elle débuta ensuite dans les rôles d'amoureuse en 1747, à l'âge de douze ans, dans un canevas (*les Sœurs rivales*) que son père avait composé exprès pour elle.

Panard fit ce joli madrigal, pour la remercier de lui avoir fait obtenir un grand succès avec sa comédie des *Tableaux,* en 1748 :

> « Objet de nos désirs, dans l'âge le plus tendre,
> » Camille, ne peut-on vous voir ou vous entendre,
> » Sans éprouver les maux que l'amour fait souffrir?

» Trop jeune à la fois et trop belle,
» En nous charmant sitôt, que vous êtes cruelle!
» Attendez pour blesser que vous puissiez guérir. »

« Camille, » dit un auteur du temps, « avait le geste du sentiment, qui ne s'apprend point devant un miroir, et le ton de la nature, que l'art ne peut donner, mais que le cœur donne quand il est pénétré. Sans ambition comme sans jalousie, elle ne connaissait point ces rivalités qui divisent presque toujours ceux de son état. Son caractère se peignait sur sa figure, et l'on y voyait la noblesse et la franchise, l'esprit et la gaieté; nulle femme de son état ne porta plus loin le désintéressement, et l'ingratitude ne la dégoûta point de la bienfaisance.... Avec une âme bienfaisante, on ne saurait manquer d'avoir le cœur tendre; ces qualités sont presque toujours inséparables, et si la sensibilité lui permit quelques faiblesses, elle sut les faire pardonner par la constance de son attachement.... »

« Le sieur Billioni vient de faire exécuter sur le Théâtre-Italien le ballet de *Pygmalion*, avec succès. Ce sujet est trop connu pour que j'en fasse le détail. Je remarquerai seulement que la demoiselle Camille, qui y fait le personnage de la statue, le rend avec une vérité singulière : rien n'égale la finesse de son jeu pantomime, surtout dans le temps que la statue s'anime par degrés; elle peint sa surprise, sa curiosité, son amour naissant, tous les mouvements subits ou gradués de son âme, avec une expression que l'on n'avait point encore trouvée; on peut dire de Camille qu'elle danse jusqu'à la pensée. Je crois que l'art des anciens pantomimes grecs et romains ne

pouvait aller au delà des talents de Camille en ce genre »
(25 décembre 1760). (Lettre de Favart à M. de Durazzo)

« *Thémire délivrée*, tel est le titre du ballet-pantomime
exécuté par Billon dit Bighom, ci-devant maître de ballets
de l'Opéra-Comique. Thémire (la demoiselle Camille),
au milieu d'une troupe de chasseurs, donne ses ordres,
part avec eux pour battre la campagne, et laisse le théâtre
vide (faute grossière). Deux bûcherons et une bûcheronne
dansent un pas de trois. Ils se retirent comme ils sont
venus, sans savoir pourquoi. Thémire reparait; elle s'est
séparée de la chasse involontairement Elle se trouve seule
et témoigne sa crainte. Un sauvage l'aperçoit du haut de
la colline, descend brusquement et la saisit; elle s'évanouit
de frayeur; le sauvage l'enchaîne avec des branches de
saule, et l'entraîne dans sa caverne. Les chasseurs arrivent
dans ce moment critique, ils s'aperçoivent du danger de
Thémire; ils montent la colline, des sauvages armés de
massues fondent sur eux Ah! la pauvre Thémire, que
fait-elle pendant ce temps-là? Enfin, par bonheur ou par
malheur, les sauvages sont repoussés et Thémire est délivrée. Était-il temps? n'était-il plus temps? C'est ce qu'il
reste à savoir. Quoi qu'il en soit, on ramène Thémire en
triomphe au bruit des timbales. (Pourquoi des timbales?)
On se réjouit de la délivrance de Thémire. Les sauvages
vaincus se réjouissent aussi. (Et de quoi?) Malgré ces
absurdités, le ballet fait beaucoup de plaisir : c'est qu'il
est parfaitement exécuté; c'est que Camille, qui représente Thémire, est bonne comédienne dans sa danse.... »
(Favart, 1ᵉʳ août 1760.)

Camille mourut à l'âge de trente-trois ans, en 1768.

Citons encore parmi les actrices les plus connues qui jouèrent en Italie, aux dix-septième et dix-huitième siècles, sous les noms de CLARICE, ANGELA, GRAZIOSA, ROSAURA, ELEONORA, DIANA, BEATRICE ou ISABELLA, mesdames Alborghezzi, 1600, Armelini, 1600; Andreoletti. 1602; Garziani, 1610, Aspontini, 1650; Pazzighetti, 1661; Teresa-Corona Sabolini, qui jouait en 1688 sous le nom d'OTTAVIA DIANA. Giovanna Amatis, 1695; Anziani, 1715, Malatesta, 1720; Albertini, 1706; Antonia Albani, 1760; Teodora Ricci de Padoue, qui eut une si grande influence sur le talent de Charles Gozzi, 1760; Felicita et Rosalie Bonami, 1775, Marianna Bassi, 1750; etc.

SCAPIN.

BRIGHELLA, FENOCCHIO, BELTRAME, FLAUTINO,
GRADELINO, MEZZETIN, NARCISIN, TURLUPIN,
GANDOLIN, GRATTELARD, JODELET.

BRIGHELLA.

Avec un langage mielleux, des manières avenantes, une
politesse flagorneuse, Brighella est le plus infâme scélérat
qui existe. Il n'a pas pour se racheter de la bassesse de ses
sentiments la brutale franchise de Polichinelle. c'est le chat
qui minaude, fait patte de velours et égratigne. Vif et inso-
lent avec les femmes, fanfaron et braillard avec les vieillards ou les poltrons, il rampe et se cache devant celui qui
lui tient tête. Mais alors il y a beaucoup à craindre de sa
part; plus il a eu peur, moins il vous pardonnera, et si,
dans l'ombre, vous recevez un coup de couteau, *una col-
tellata,* soyez sûr qu'il vient de lui. Chanteur, danseur,
musicien, lorsqu'il veut faire un mauvais coup, il n'est

point de maison où il ne sache s'insinuer. C'est un valet
précieux pour qui sait employer ses talents. Comme il a
beaucoup de besoins, il lui faut beaucoup d'argent, et si
vous savez ménager son amour-propre et le payer grasse-
ment, il n'y a fille ni femme, en Italie, qu'il ne sache
enjôler. Il a fait toutes sortes de métiers : soldat, clerc de
procureur, valet de bourreau. Pour détourner de lui l'attention de la potence, il préfère servir les amoureux, et
c'est plutôt par goût que par nécessité qu'il aime ce qu'il
appelle *son état;* car, s'il n'a personne à servir, il travaille
pour son compte, pour s'entretenir la main, et alors malheur aux jeunes filles sur lesquelles il met sa griffe! Elles
sont perdues à tout jamais si elles écoutent ses propos et ses
théories. Brighella ne croit absolument à rien, qu'à la
corde qui doit le pendre un jour. Aussi la vue d'un sbire le
met dans des états impossibles à décrire.

Tel est le Brighella ancien, mais, avec les siècles et la
civilisation, il s'est un peu amendé. Il a toujours les mêmes
instincts, mais il n'assassine pas tant. Aujourd'hui, bien
des femmes le regardent en face sans trembler et l'écoutent
sans le croire. Il est plus à craindre pour la bourse des vieillards, qu'il escamote avec une dextérité incroyable. Il ne
songe qu'à voler, comme l'Épidique de Plaute, dont il descend en ligne directe.

« Pour moi, » dit Épidique, « je vais assembler dans ma
tête le Sénat pour délibérer sur ce que je dois faire, car
c'est à l'argent (quoiqu'il soit notre meilleur ami) que je
dois déclarer la guerre. A quelle source pourrai-je puiser?
Il ne faut ni s'endormir, ni reculer. Je suis résolu à donner

un nouvel assaut à mon vieux maître. Je me suis muni
d'un couteau bien acéré pour éventrer la bourse du vieillard. Mais que vois-je? Deux vieux à la fois! quelle capture! Je vais me métamorphoser en sangsue, et je leur
sucerai le sang . »

Et plus tard, quand il est content de ses méfaits :

« Je ne crois pas qu'il y ait dans l'Attique une terre
d'aussi bon rapport que notre vieux bonhomme de maître.
J'escamote autant d'argent que je veux de son armoire, si
bien fermée, scellée, cachetée soit-elle. Mais si le bonhomme vient à s'apercevoir de quelque chose, gare les
verges! »

Brighella, dont le nom signifie intrigant, est aussi ancien
qu'Arlequin, son compatriote. Nous avons déjà dit qu'ils
étaient tous deux originaires de Bergame.

Le Slavèrò de *la Piovana* d'Auguste Beolco est un vrai
Brighella.

« .... Quant à moi, » dit-il, « rien ne me coûte, j'ai l'habitude des querelles. Il me faut les deux jeunes filles, et s'il
ne suffit pas de tuer un homme, j'en tuerai deux. Ne vous
souvenez-vous pas de cette dispute où j'en ai effondré un
comme on défonce une vessie, et cet autre à qui j'ai rompu
les os comme on broie une fève?... » Et ailleurs : « Maintenant je vais chercher Siton, qui doit avoir eu la jeune fille.
Avec de belles paroles, je ferai en sorte qu'il me donne les
cinquante livres qu'il m'a promises, afin que je puisse m'en
aller d'ici. Et si on vient me dire que j'ai mal agi, j'en
rejetterai toute la faute sur mon compère. »

Slavèrò ne se fait pas faute d'être parjure comme Brighella. Une bourse a été volée Bertevello le pêcheur sait qui en est le détenteur.

« BERTEVELLO. Bonjour, compagnon, comment t'appelles-tu ?

SLAVERÒ. Je me nomme Slaverò.

BERTEVELLO Slaverò, c'est bien, je le crois. Je suis résolu à ne te rien cacher, car pour aller en prison, je n'en ai que faire, puisque tu dis que la bourse est à toi, jure-moi, si je te dis qui l'a, que tu me donneras ce que tu m'as promis.

SLAVERÒ Foi d'honnête homme, je te le dis.

BERTEVELLO. Jure par ton âme.

SLAVERÒ. Puisque je te le dis, à quoi bon ?

BERTEVELLO. Tais-toi, jure comme je te dirai.

SLAVERÒ. Va, je dis comme toi.

BERTEVELLO. Dis : Moi, Slaverò, je jure....

SLAVERÒ. Moi, Slaverò, je jure. ..

BERTEVELLO Que je te donnerai ce que je t'ai promis.

SLAVERÒ Que je te donnerai ce que je t'ai promis

BERTEVELLO Par ce qui est dans cette bourse, en argent marqué ou taillé.

SLAVERÒ Par ce qui est dans cette bourse, en argent marqué ou taillé.

BERTEVELLO En livres, sous et deniers.

SLAVERÒ. En livres, sous et deniers.

BERTEVELLO. Sur des charbons ardents.

SLAVERÒ. Sur des charbons ardents

BERTEVELLO. Me brûlant et m'écorchant tout à la fois.

SLAVERÒ Me brûlant et m'écorchant tout à la fois

BERTEVELLO. Que par miracle, les vivants et les morts....

SLAVERÒ Que par miracle, les vivants et les morts....

BERIEVELLO. Me sautent aux yeux, et me les crèvent, et me les brûlent, et me sèchent les mains.

SLAVERÒ. Me sautent aux yeux, et me les crèvent, et me les brûlent, et me sèchent les mains.

BERTEVELLO. Et que le grand diable m'emporte, me transporte....

SLAVERÒ Et que le grand diable m'emporte, me transporte....

BERTEVELLO. Dans les profondeurs du malheur, dans le vent, en fusion, en bulle d'air....

SLAVERÒ. Dans les profondeurs du malheur, dans le vent, en fusion, en bulle d'air....

BERTEVELLO. Qu'il ne reste pas un brin de ma personne à tout jamais.

SLAVERÒ. Qu'il ne reste pas un brin de ma personne à tout jamais.

BERTEVELLO. Bien! Attends-moi ici dehors, je vais t'amener l'homme avec la bourse.

SLAVERÒ. Je t'attendrai. O bourse! tu vois combien j'ai envie de t'avoir! N'aie pas peur, il faudra bien que nous partions ensemble; sans cela, je n'aurais pas juré comme je l'ai fait. Et je ne me crois pas obligé de donner quoi que ce soit à celui-ci, pour m'avoir fait jurer comme je l'ai fait. D'ailleurs j'ai juré avec la langue et non avec la conscience. Est-ce que ma langue n'est pas libre? Je ne peux pas disposer d'elle. Elle peut dire ce qui lui plaît, je n'en peux mais ... »

Dans un canevas italien moderne, qui a servi sous plusieurs formes, toujours avec succès, « de jeunes seigneurs vénitiens sont dans une villa au bord de la Brenta. Pour se divertir et chasser les idées tristes que leur pourrait causer la mort de leur sommelier Meneghino, ils imaginent de se moquer de trois poltrons qui sont à leur service : Pantalon, Arlequin et Brighella. On fait semblant de se fier à la bravoure fanfaronne de Pantalon, et on le prie de passer la nuit à garder le corps du défunt. Pantalon y consent à contre-cœur ; mais c'est Arlequin que l'on a couché sur le lit mortuaire au lieu de Meneghino. On l'a couvert du linceul et tout barbouillé de blanc. Arlequin n'est guère plus rassuré que celui qui le garde. Il craint que cette farce ne lui porte malheur ; cependant il s'égaye aux dépens de son camarade, fait le saut de carpe sur son lit et pousse de gros soupirs. Mais bientôt il cesse de rire et ne songe plus qu'à imiter Pantalon, qui se cache, car Brighella arrive costumé en diable et les poursuit avec une torche. Mais Brighella, qui croyait n'avoir affaire qu'à Pantalon, et qui ne s'attendait pas à voir Arlequin à la place du mort, encore moins ce mort courir effaré par la chambre pour lui échapper, tombe à la renverse, et tous trois se roulent par terre en proie à une terreur indicible, lorsqu'enfin l'arrivée de leurs maîtres, qui se moquent d'eux, les ramène à la raison après une longue suite de lazzi que le public accueille toujours par des rires frénétiques. »

Le costume de Brighella (*planche* 58), aux seizième et dix-septième siècles, se composait d'une sorte de veste et d'un pantalon large, en toile blanche, pour indiquer son origine

rustique, d'une toque bordée d'un galon vert et d'un manteau ; la veste et le pantalon étaient déjà galonnés sur les
coutures avec des lamelles d'étoffe verte pour représenter une
sorte de livrée. Son masque olivâtre et barbu est, comme
celui d'Arlequin, la tradition des *Sanniones* antiques.

Aujourd'hui son costume est devenu un bizarre assem-
blage des modes anciennes et nouvelles. Sa veste a pris la
forme d'une redingote en laine ou en flanelle blanche à
trois collets, d'un gilet et d'un pantalon également blancs
et galonnés de vert. Il conserve sa toque traditionnelle,
blanche, bordée de vert, et son demi-masque brun, dont
la barbe est arrangée de façon à imiter de gros favoris et
une légère moustache. Le bas du visage est rasé. Il ressemble assez, avec ce costume, à un nègre qui aurait revêtu
une livrée ridicule.

Brighella est la souche des Beltrame, des Scapin, des
Mezzetin, Flautino, Gradelino, Truccagnino, Fenocchio,
Bagolino (plaisant), et de tous les valets fourbes et intrigants de la Comédie-Française, depuis *Sbrigani* (variante
du nom de Brighella), *Sganarelle*, *Mascarille* et *La Montagne*
jusqu'à *Frontin* et *Labranche ;* la livrée seule est changée. Le
caractère, c'est toujours celui de Brighella, et depuis Pseu-
dole, l'esclave grec, jusqu'à *Figaro*, le valet *da far tutto*,
ce type fut toujours menteur, ivrogne, voleur, débauché
et tant soit peu assassin.

Un comédien italien, connu sous le surnom de Briguelle,
parut en 1671 sur le théâtre de la Comédie-Italienne, pour
remplacer, dans l'emploi de premier *Zani*, Locatelli (*Trivelin*) qui venait de mourir. « Cet acteur faisait rage, »

selon Robinet, aussi, après la mort de ce bouffon, Louis XIV
voulant le remplacer, demanda-t-il un autre acteur au duc
de Modène, qui lui envoya Giuseppe Cimadori, lequel jouait
sous le nom de Fenoccino (fétu) les mêmes rôles que Brighella. Cet acteur mourut en route :

> « Briguelle fourbe fait la figue
> A tous démesleurs d'intrigue. »

On lit au bas d'un portrait de Briguelle :

> « J'aime la comédie, où, riant, je fais rire
> Ceux qui prennent plaisir d'écouter de bons mots
> Quand je suis en humeur, des traits de la satire,
> Je pique également les savants et les sots. »

Les deux plus célèbres Brighella furent, au siècle dernier,
dans les troupes italiennes, Giuseppe Angeleri, qui jouait
de 1704 à 1752 les parties improvisées dans les comédies de
Goldoni, et Atanasio Zanoni, de Ferrare, l'un des meilleurs comédiens du dix-huitième siècle. « Zanoni reçut une
très-bonne éducation, mais son goût pour la déclamation
l'ayant déterminé à embrasser la carrière du théâtre, il
entra dans la troupe du célèbre Ant. Sacchi, dont il épousa
la sœur. Personne n'égala Zanoni pour la grâce de la
prononciation, la vivacité et la finesse des reparties. Aux
qualités de son état, il joignait une âme noble. Le 22
février 1792, en sortant d'un souper splendide, il tomba
dans un canal profond et mourut peu après. » On a publié
de lui à Venise, en 1787, un *Recueil de mots brighellesques,
mordants, allégoriques et satiriques*, augmenté par Alphonse
Zanoni, son fils, en 1807 (édition de Turin).

Nous en citerons quelques fragments :

« On ne doit pas dire un voleur, mais un mathématicien ingénieux qui trouve une chose avant que son propriétaire l'ait perdue. — Les objets que l'on s'approprie sont des biens dont on hérite avant la mort de ceux qui les possèdent. — Pour faire un vol dans les règles, il faut être assisté de trois diables : un qui vous enseigne à prendre avec adresse, un qui vous montre à cacher bien secrètement, et un troisième qui vous persuade de ne jamais restituer. — Quand je suis forcé de *voyager,* c'est-à-dire de fuir, je console les poules veuves, j'adopte les poulets mineurs et les canards orphelins. Je délivre les bourses et les montres captives. — On m'appelle le galérien *à répétition.* — Je suis très-bavard, parce que mon père était muet, et qu'il a laissé un capital de paroles toutes neuves et qui n'avaient jamais servi ; au reste, je suis bâtard. — On m'a donné par charité un bouillon, mais si limpide, que le beau Narcisse s'y fût miré mieux que dans sa fontaine. — Ma chemise est devenue un roman ; elle est pleine de chevaliers errants, et la blanchisseuse ne veut pas la laver de peur de salir la rivière. — Mon souper, c'est le souper de Bertoldo : un plat de pois *ventosissimi,* avec un bouilli d'espérance, un ragoût de désirs et un rôti d'expectative. — Mes dettes ont fait de moi une étoile qui ne se laisse voir que la nuit. — Je suis si employé et si affairé, que je n'ai pas le temps de me gratter, etc. »

FENOCCHIO.

Fenocchio, variante du type de Brighella, paraît sur la scène italienne dès 1560. Il s'emploie comme lui dans les

intrigues amoureuses, et il y agit non-seulement pour le
compte de CILIO, de LEANDRO ou de ZERBINO, mais aussi
pour le sien propre. Nous le voyons dans une pièce
vénitienne du dix-septième siècle, dialoguée d'après un
ancien canevas, être amoureux d'Olivette, servante de Béatrice, fille de Pantalon. Arlequin, autre valet dans la
pièce, a la naïveté de lui faire ses confidences, ne se doutant nullement que Fenocchio est son rival. Aussi, à partir
de ce moment, Fenocchio jure de se venger d'Arlequin, et
cherche par tous les moyens à s'en débarrasser. Il commence par lui jouer de mauvais tours. Arlequin apportait
à Olivette deux oiseaux vivants, dans un panier; Fenocchio
s'en empare, remplace les oiseaux par un chat, et assiste
aux complîments d'Arlequin, aux remercîments d'Olivette, qui adore les volatiles, et à son désappointement en
voyant sortir du panier un matou furieux qui s'échappe
non sans l'avoir un peu égratignée. La colère d'Olivette
et les pleurs d'Arlequin réjouissent le cœur de Fenocchio.
Arlequin, ne sachant qui lui a fait cette méchanceté,
soupçonne son confident, qui lui jure par tout ce qu'il
y a de plus sacré (il ne se compromet pas, vu qu'il ne
respecte rien) qu'il est incapable d'une farce dont le
résultat a été de verser le sang de la jolie Olivette.

Par la force des circonstances, Arlequin ne peut plus
voir Olivette, Pantalon la tenant enfermée avec sa fille;
il a recours aux expédients de Fenocchio. Celui-ci cherche
les moyens de se débarrasser de son rival préféré : « Fais
le mort, lui dit-il, je te mettrai dans une boîte, et te por-
terai chez Pantalon l'apothicaire, sous prétexte de faire

faire ton autopsie. Pendant la nuit, quand tout le monde
dormira, tu iras trouver Olivette. » Le crédule Arlequin
y consent. Fenocchio le porte chez Pantalon, et, après lui
avoir raconté une histoire invraisemblable que celui-ci croit
parfaitement, il se retire espérant que Pantalon enlèvera
quelque bras ou quelque jambe à Arlequin. Mais Arlequin,
seul avec Pantalon, qui admire le beau cadavre qu'on lui
a confié à disséquer, ne peut résister au besoin de se gratter.
Cela étonne un peu le bonhomme, qui n'avait jamais vu
pareille chose. Tout tremblant, il prend un scalpel et se
dispose à faire une large incision à Arlequin, quand celui-ci
se lève, effrayé, et, criant au secours, tombe sur Pantalon
à grands coups de poings. Pantalon se croit assassiné par
un fantôme, et s'évanouit.

Arlequin va retrouver Fenocchio pour avoir un autre
expédient. Fenocchio lui reproche de n'avoir pas de
patience. « Il fallait te laisser saigner un peu par l'apothicaire, lui dit-il, tu aurais été voir Olivette ensuite. Je t'ai
trouvé un meilleur moyen : tu vas te déguiser en porc, et
je te conduirai à Pantalon comme un cadeau que lui fait
le Docteur. » Arlequin consent à tout; Fenocchio, déguisé
en paysan, amène son porc à Pantalon, qui admire ce bel
animal. « C'est dommage de le tuer, » dit-il. Arlequin
éprouve encore le besoin de se gratter; mais il s'y prend si
singulièrement pour un cochon, que Pantalon en est surpris. Fenocchio lui dit alors que c'est un cochon savant,
et il fait exécuter à Arlequin plusieurs tours, comme de
marcher debout, prendre du tabac dans la tabatière de
l'apothicaire, répondre par signes aux questions qu'on

lui fait Pantalon s'écrie : « Quel admirable porc! quelle rare bête! Je ne le ferai tuer que demain matin », et il fait enfermer Arlequin dans un courtil, tandis que Fenocchio se glisse dans la maison auprès d'Olivette, bien certain, cette fois, d'être débarrassé de son rival, qu'il espère voir prochainement éventré.

Arlequin, ayant trouvé moyen de sortir pendant la nuit du lieu où il était enfermé, cherche toujours, sous ce déguisement bizarre, la chambre d'Olivette; mais il est entré dans la boutique, où Pantalon dort sur son lit de sangle. En tâtonnant, Arlequin heurte quelques vases qui tombent et se brisent.

« PANTALON *réveillé en sursaut* Nane! Nane! chasse donc les chats qui sont entrés dans la boutique!

ARLEQUIN *à part* Il me prend pour un chat, je suis perdu s'il me reconnait Ah! pauvre Arlequin! qui t'aurait dit que, pour voir Olivette, il t'eût fallu faire le porc! (*tu havessi da far da porch!*) Le pire est que je ne sais pas où je vais. »

Il donne en plein dans un tas de fioles et casse tout. Pantalon se lamente: « Toute l'huile de grenouilles par terre! » dit-il, « tout mon baume d'huîtres répandu. Mon électuaire de sépia est cassé, j'en suis sûr! » Pantalon se lève, allume sa chandelle et regarde, pendant ce temps, Arlequin s'est glissé sous le lit. Pantalon, après avoir déploré la perte de ses drogues, qu'il remplacera du reste facilement, dit-il, vu que ce n'est que de la terre et de l'eau, va se recoucher et souffle sa lumière. Arlequin veut se lever, mais il soulève en même temps le lit Pantalon roule par terre avec

lui, se relève et frappe au hasard, criant : « Le porc! le
porc qui m'étrangle! au secours! »

Fenocchio, n'ayant pas réussi à se débarrasser d'Arlequin
par ce moyen, lui propose un troisième expédient : c'est d'avoir
beaucoup d'argent pour séduire Pantalon, qui lui laissera
ainsi voir Olivette. Il lui dit avoir un moyen pour s'en procurer. « Le Docteur est amateur de curiosités, nous allons
lui en vendre une. » Il fait habiller Arlequin en pendule, un
cadran au milieu du ventre, et l'apporte ainsi chez le Docteur, qui admire cette belle pièce d'horlogerie fort curieuse.
« Cela, dit Fenocchio au Docteur, représente un homme,
comme vous pouvez voir, et cela marque les minutes, les
heures, les jours, les mois, les années, les siècles; et cela
prédit le passé, cela dit papa, maman, et cela sonne. » En
disant ainsi, Fenocchio prend un marteau et démontre au
Docteur qu'il n'y a qu'à frapper sur la tête de cette méca-
nique pour la faire sonner. Mais Arlequin baisse la tête,
et le menace de tout découvrir s'il le touche. Le Docteur
heureusement n'a pas aperçu ce mouvement. Fenocchio,
qui aime encore mieux l'argent que la vengeance, entre
en marché avec le Docteur. Mais sur ces entrefaites, un
valet apporte la soupe du Docteur. Arlequin ne peut résister
à la tentation, et se jette sur le potage, qu'il avale glou-
tonnement. Le Docteur se retourne et crie : « To! to!
to! la pendule qui mange! Au secours, ce sont des
assassins! »

Truccagnino est, sous un nom différent, le même personnage que Fenocchio.

BELTRAME.

L. Riccoboni dit, en parlant du costume de Beltrame.
« Son habit n'est pas extraordinaire, et je crois que c'est un
» habit du temps, ou de peu devant. Il a un masque, et
» c'est le même que celui de Scapin.... Beltrame, qui était
» Milanais, voulant parler la langue de son pays, en por-
» tait l'habit aussi. »

Son costume est celui d'un valet de la fin du seizième
siècle; ce type, plus moderne que le Brighella, n'avait pas,
dans la troupe des *Gelosi*, d'autre emploi que celui d'un
fourbe et rusé compère, mais, comme le Mezzetin, et plus
tard le Sganarelle français, il jouait tous les rôles de maris,
feignant de croire parfois aux bourdes qu'on lui contait.
Il y a quelques années, à Bologne, ce personnage, passé
dans les marionnettes, représentait encore le bourgeois,
marchand ou vieux juif, et partageait la paternité de
Colombina avec le vieux Tabarino.

Niccolò Barbieri est le premier acteur qui ait fait connaître cette nuance de Brighella en France. Sous le nom de
Beltrame *da Milano* (*planche* 59), il vint avec Flaminio Scala
et Isabella Andreini jouer à Paris en 1600, devant Henri IV.
Après la dispersion de la troupe des *Gelosi*, Beltrame
repartit pour l'Italie et entra dans la compagnie des *Fedeli*.
En 1613 il revint à Paris avec la troupe dont G. B. Andreini
était directeur. Il resta jusqu'en 1618, revint en 1623 et
resta encore jusqu'en 1625, époque à laquelle il devint lui-
même chef d'une troupe, et se rendit célèbre en Italie et en

France, non-seulement comme acteur, mais encore comme écrivain

Son ouvrage : « *La Supplica, discorso famigliare intorno alle comedie mercenarie*, lecture pour les hommes de mérite qui ne sont pas critiqueurs de parti pris, ni tout à fait sots, » n'est qu'une plaidoirie en faveur des comédiens et de la comédie de son temps, elle est cependant assez intéressante par les anecdotes qui s'y rencontrent, et qui donnent une idée des mœurs d'alors.

« Tous les auteurs qui ont écrit contre la comédie, » dit-il, « n'ont pas toujours eu la connaissance de cet art. La science de toutes choses se trouve bien parmi tous les hommes, mais un seul n'a pas le don de tout savoir. Les auteurs sacrés ou profanes ne peuvent pas nous juger Saint Bonaventure fait une telle description des comédiens, qu'à l'en croire nous serions tous damnés. Je raconterai une petite anecdote qui procède directement de ce que je viens de dire.

« Quand je partis de Vercelli, ma patrie, en l'année 1596, je me joignis à un saltimbanque surnommé le *Montferrin*; nous passâmes par Aosta (anciennement Augusta), ville de la Savoie. Le Montferrin demanda au chef principal la permission d'établir ses tréteaux; mais comme ce n'était peut-être pas l'usage en ce pays, le chef, ne sachant comment en décider, s'en fut prendre conseil d'un supérieur spirituel, lequel refusa nettement la permission, disant qu'il ne voulait pas admettre de magiciens dans le pays. Le Montferrin, stupéfait, lui répondit que, ne sachant seulement pas lire, ce qui était vrai, il ne pouvait faire de magie. Le supérieur le fit taire : « Je sais bien comment cela se passe, » lui dit-il; « j'ai vu en Italie des charlatans prendre une boule d'une main, et la faire passer dans l'autre, ou bien se faire entrer un petit plomb dans un œil et le faire sortir par l'autre, avaler des étoupes tout enflammées et renvoyer du feu, par la bouche, en milliers d'étincelles, se traverser le bras d'un couteau et être guéris de cette blessure à l'instant même, et cela par enchantement et autres œuvres du démon. » Après quoi le supérieur renvoya le Montferrin sans vouloir écouter ses réponses, le menaçant de la prison.

» Ce supérieur était théologien, mais ne savait rien de l'adresse humaine, et en cela ressemblait à ces bienheureux saints qui parlèrent tant contre l'art de la comédie, n'ayant jamais vu que quelque farce ou quelque baliverne obscène rendue par les marionnettes (bambocci) des bateleurs et charlatans.

» Beaucoup d'ignorants, qui ne savent pas l'étymologie du mot istrio (histrion) ni sa dérivation, croient que par histrions (istrioni) on entend dire stregoni (sorciers), enchanteurs et hommes donnés au diable; et c'est pour cette raison que, dans quelques contrées d'Italie, les ignorants tiennent pour certain que les comédiens peuvent faire pleuvoir ou amener la tempête à leur volonté. Ce sont de pauvres enchanteurs ou magiciens, bien maigres, qui ont bien de la peine à faire pleuvoir sur eux-mêmes quelque monnaie pour vivre, et s'ils avaient la faculté de faire pleuvoir, ils se garderaient bien de s'en servir, puisque lorsqu'il pleut personne ne va à la comédie. »

Pour prouver que la comédie n'est pas un art vil et

méprisable, Beltrame cite un grand nombre de comédiens qui furent honorés et tenus en grande estime, parmi lesquels Roscius ami de Cicéron, Aliturus, Ésope dans l'antiquité, et ceux de son temps, comme Isabella Andreini, Pietro-Maria Cecchini (*Fritellino*), Giovanni-Battista Andreini (*Lelio*), Cintio Fidenzi, Maria Malloni (*Celia*), Nicolò Zecchi (*Bertolino*), et lui-même : « Moi, dit-il, le plus infime de tous, je fus nommé, par le roi Louis le Juste, roi très-bon et très-chrétien, soldat dans sa garde d'honneur, et je fus jaloux de me rendre digne d'un tel honneur, comme en peut rendre compte mon capitaine, l'illustre duc de la Valette. L'éminent cardinal Ubaldini peut dire aussi combien Sa Majesté Très-Chrétienne était disposée à me combler de faveurs Je ne mentionne pas les princes, princesses, rois, reines et empereurs qui ont tenu sur les fonts de baptême les enfants des comédiens de notre temps, les ont appelés compères et commères, soit de vive voix, soit par lettres, et comment, à l'occasion, ils les ont fait participer à leurs fêtes, promenés dans les carrosses de la cour ou gratifiés de cadeaux de leurs propres mains, régalés de repas somptueux ou fait participer à leurs divertissements; ou bien encore fait grâce de la prison ou de la vie, et bien d'autres faveurs. Beaucoup de princes et de grands seigneurs ont appris et joué des comédies devant leurs parents et familiers, et ont été jaloux de rendre, le mieux possible, le personnage qu'ils représentaient, et encore le faisaient-ils pour leur plaisir. Sont-ils réputés infâmes et méprisables pour cela? Non. La comédie n'est donc pas vile !

» Combien de princes, de rois et d'empereurs qui ont joué en public sur leurs théâtres! et de nos jours, j'ai vu les ducs de Mantoue, François, Ferdinand, et Vincent réciter avec nos comédiens, ainsi que le prince d'Urbin et tant d'autres dont je ne parle pas. Si un grand personnage peut se montrer par plaisir sur les planches sans déroger à sa noblesse, pourquoi les honnêtes gens sont-ils perdus de réputation en agissant de même pour vivre? Puisque les nobles ne sont pas honnis en jouant la comédie, cet art n'est donc pas méprisable.

» .... Je compare ces efforts pour médire de la comédie et des comédiens à ces chasses aux papillons que font les enfants courant à travers champs, semblables à des furieux, foulant les plantes et les fleurs des jardins sans y prendre garde, allant et venant comme des fous, fendant l'air de leurs bras, étreignant le vent de leurs mains, et suant jusqu'au sang. En désespoir de cause, lançant des pierres ou jetant leur chapeau en l'air, puis se précipitant sur leur proie, à corps perdu, sans se soucier de déchirer leurs vêtements ou de se casser un membre. Et tout cela pourquoi? pour prendre une bête qui, vivante, sert à peu de chose, et qui, morte, ne vaut rien ... En somme, les efforts de nos médisants ressemblent aux prouesses de don Quichotte de la Manche.

» Les comédiens étudient les *libretti* imprimés avec permission des supérieurs; il est vrai qu'ils inventent beaucoup de choses, mais sans sortir du sujet. Les auteurs des sujets ou des scénarios cherchent les fables les plus vraisemblables et les disposent selon les règles de facétie, comme les auteurs dramatiques font selon les règles poétiques. Les acteurs font ensuite les études nécessaires pour rendre le mieux possible le personnage qu'ils doivent représenter. Les amoureux et les femmes étudient l'histoire, la fable, les rimes et la prose, et les richesses de la langue. Ceux qui ont pour but de faire rire se creusent la cervelle pour trouver de nouvelles farces, non par volonté de pécher ou de faire pécher les autres, non pour louer le vice ou les erreurs avec des mots obscènes, mais, par l'emploi des équivoques et les bizarres inventions qu'ils trouvent, faire rire tout en faisant leur état. Le Capitan excite l'hilarité par ses extravagances hyperboliques, le Graziano, par ses citations; le premier valet, par ses intrigues, sa finesse et ses vives répliques, le second, par ses balourdises; les Arlequins, par leurs cascades (*cascate*); les Covielle, par leurs grimaces et leur langage macaronique, les rôles des vieillards, par leurs manières lourdes et leur idiome ancien, et ainsi des autres.

» J'ai lu que du temps de l'empereur Marc-Aurèle, un certain Fulvius, condamné par les médecins pour un abcès dans la poitrine, résolut, par désespoir, d'aller se faire tuer à la guerre. Il y reçut un coup de lance juste au milieu de son abcès, et cette blessure le guérit subitement de son mal incurable Tout le contraire arriva au consul Cneus Ruffinus, vieux guerrier qui mourut d'une dent de peigne qui lui entra dans la tête en se peignant. Faut-il déduire de là que qui veut se bien porter aille à la guerre et que l'on ne doive jamais se peigner, sous peine de mourir? J'ai vu des malades abandonnés par les médecins boire du vin et revenir à la santé. Donnons donc du vin à tous les malades, ils guériront tous! Un estropié qui ne marchait qu'avec des béquilles glissa et tomba, juste au moment où passait une voiture qui lui brisa les deux jambes; cela le guérit si bien qu'il marcha depuis sans béquilles. Il faut donc que celui qui est bancroche ou boiteux aille se jeter sous les voitures pour guérir? Il peut bien être arrivé quelques événements fâcheux dans les théâtres, mais ce n'est pas une raison pour n'y point aller. Deux ou trois arbres ne font pas une forêt, et ne peut-on pas mourir au théâtre aussi bien qu'ailleurs?

» En Italie, les mœurs sont très-différentes d'une ville à une autre. A Naples, les femmes appellent familièrement un homme, *mon bien* ou *mon beau visage*, et autres semblables paroles, tandis qu'en Lombardie ces mêmes mots ne se disent qu'entre amoureux, ou sont employés seulement par les courtisanes. Embrasser une femme mariée, à Naples, est une insulte qui veut du sang, et en Piémont le baiser ne signifie pas grand'chose : c'est, entre les gens qui se connaissent, une preuve d'amitié, ou une marque de salut et de révérence. Dans beaucoup de pays, il est d'usage que les femmes rendent le salut aux étrangers, ailleurs, ce serait une impolitesse. Dans certaines localités des Marches, les femmes paraissent presque ennemies du sexe masculin, elles sont enveloppées dans leurs vêtements jusqu'à cacher leur visage. A Venise, les jeunes filles s'habillent tout en blanc et les veuves tout en noir, de manière à ne pas laisser voir leur figure, qui est belle, car la sont les plus jolies âmes. En certains pays, les dames

montrent une partie de la poitrine et le commencement
de la gorge; ailleurs elles sont couvertes jusqu'au cou, et,
cependant, toutes sont femmes d'honneur. Un pêcheur va
à travers les rues à moitié nu, et un ouvrier en laine,
tout dépouillé. Ce qui serait licencieux pour certaines
gens est licite pour eux, à cause de l'usage. Voir le pied
nu et un peu de la jambe d'une belle dame paraît une
grande affaire, tandis que les lavandières et les pauvres
paysannes montrent pieds et jambes nus sans que l'on y
prenne garde, et cependant ce sont toujours des chairs de
femmes, et l'honneur des femmes est le même partout.
Pourquoi l'un scandalise-t-il, et l'autre non?—C'est l'usage.
Il en est ainsi pour les femmes qui jouent la comédie,
on sait que les discours amoureux qu'elles tiennent ne
sont qu'une fiction et ne peuvent vous corrompre l'âme,
puisque c'est l'usage de l'art. »

SCAPIN.

« Ah! ah! voici les voiturins de Ferrare et de Bologne!
Par ici, *signori, illustrissimi signori!* par ici! Où sont les
bagages? je m'en charge. Leurs Excellences veulent-elles
loger *ai Tre Mori? allo Scudo d'oro? all' Albergo reale? al
Pelicano?* où partout ailleurs? Je vous conduirai sans encombre; je suis un homme fidèle et sûr; voulez-vous me
confier votre sacoche? Prenez garde à cette flaque d'eau!
Par ici, messeigneurs! Fiqueto! Finocchio! portez donc les
malles, valises, bagages, manteaux, épées, *tutta la roba*
(toutes les affaires) de ces gentil-hommes! Désirez-vous un

valet plaisant, complaisant, s'entendant à tout? un cice-
rone? me voici, mes maîtres! prenez-moi, acceptez mes
services! Il ne me faut rien pour cela, que l'honneur d'être
votre valet, et vous ne payerez que ce que vous voudrez
Leurs Seigneuries prendront-elles de suite leurs repas?
Peut-être préfèrent-elles *una mangiata* (un goûter) avant le
souper? Holà! monsieur l'hôtelier, tous les plats sur le
feu! Je vous amène des étrangers de qualité! (Et à l'oreille ·)
Je suis de moitié dans les bénéfices, ou sinon je déconsidère
ton repaire d'empoisonneur. »

C'est ainsi que s'exprime SCAPIN. Parfois les voyageurs
l'envoient promener, lui disent qu'ils ne s'arrêtent pas, et,
pour se débarrasser de lui et de ses discours, lui donnent
une menue monnaie. Il pose alors au milieu du ruisseau
bagages et manteaux, et se retire en haussant les épaules
de mépris et de pitié. *Che cacastechi!* (Quels avares!) *Che
bisognosi!* (Quels misérables!) dit-il.

Cependant Scapin est moins *canaille* que son père Brighella Là où Brighella jouera du poignard, Scapin ne
jouera que des pieds et des mains, et encore le plus souvent ne jouera-t-il que des jambes, car il est fort lâche
et ne veut pas faire mentir l'origine de son nom Scappino,
qui vient de *scappare*, s'enfuir.

Toujours valet, il change souvent de maître; intrigant,
bel esprit, bavard et menteur, il jouit d'une fort mauvaise
réputation. C'est un brouillon, un quémandeur, tant soit
peu voleur, mais fort bien en cour auprès des soubrettes;
ces demoiselles ne peuvent se'divertir sans lui. Ce personnage a été traité de main de maître par Molière Scapin

est le nom français de Brighella. C'est le même personnage, le même costume et le même caractère. Dès le commencement du dix-septième siècle, Brighella perd son nom chez nous, et modifie son costume; mais il reste toujours le même sous une autre étiquette.

Callot, dans ses Petits Danseurs, représente le Scapino italien de son époque vêtu d'habits amples comme Fritellino, le masque et la barbe, le manteau, le grand chapeau à plumes et le sabre de bois. C'est encore ainsi que Dionis, de Milan, directeur de troupe, jouait les rôles de valet en 1650.

Mais, passant sur la scène française, avec Molière et Regnard, son costume se mélange avec celui des Beltrame, des Turlupin et des Jodelet. Il quitte le masque, prend des vêtements rayés vert et blanc, ses couleurs traditionnelles, et devient Gros-René au visage enfariné, Mascarille, La Violette, Sganarelle, etc.

Molière, que l'on querellait à propos des fourberies de Scapin, répondit à ce sujet : « J'ai vu le public quitter le *Misanthrope* pour Scaramouche; j'ai chargé Scapin de le ramener. »

Le Scapino italien (*planche* 40), qui parut sur la scène italienne de Paris en 1716, reprit le costume de Brighella, un peu modernisé, et continua les rôles créés par l'ancien Briguelle et par Mezzetin.

Giovanni Bissoni remplissait cet emploi dans la troupe de 1716 Né à Bologne, il commença son état à quinze ans, en Italie Il s'était engagé en qualité de pitre dans une petite troupe fort restreinte, sous la direction d'un certain

Gerolamo, charlatan qui débitait ses onguents au moyen de parades, en 1681. Au bout de quelque temps, Bissoni fut aussi savant que son maître, il devint son associé d'abord, et, peu après, son concurrent. Bissoni s'en alla débiter ses onguents à Milan, mais il trouva la place prise et, mourant de faim, s'avisa d'un stratagème qui lui réussit.

Il dressa ses tréteaux sur une place voisine de celle où son rival opérait. Il vanta avec emphase l'excellence de ses drogues. « Mais à quoi bon les vanter? » disait-il à la foule, « vous les connaissez tous, mes remèdes, et ceux de l'opérateur ici à côté sont les mêmes, car je suis son fils. » Il bâtit alors une histoire assez vraisemblable, comme quoi ce père rigoureux lui avait donné sa malédiction à cause de certaine petite espiéglerie de jeunesse, l'avait chassé de chez lui et ne voulait pas le reconnaître. On rapporta ce discours à l'opérateur. Bissoni profite de l'émotion de la foule et court, d'un air repentant, le visage baigné de larmes, se jeter aux genoux de son prétendu père en lui demandant pardon de ses fautes. L'opérateur soutint son caractère au delà de toutes les espérances de Bissoni : il le traita de fourbe et de coquin, et protesta que, bien loin d'être son père, il ne le connaissait même pas. Plus l'opérateur montrait une véritable colère contre la supercherie de Bissoni, plus le peuple s'intéressait à ce pauvre enfant. La foule, attendrie, acheta non-seulement toutes ses drogues, mais encore lui fit des cadeaux. Bissoni, satisfait de son succès, craignant des éclaircissements, se hâta de quitter Milan. Peu de temps après, il laissa le métier de charlatan et se joignit à une troupe ambulante pour jouer les

Scapins. Il entra ensuite, en qualité de maître d'hôtel, au service de M. Albergotti, fit un voyage en France avec lui et retourna en Italie. C'est là que Riccoboni le trouva quand il alla former la troupe du duc d'Orléans, et l'engagea pour la Comédie-Italienne, en qualité de Zanni. Il avait un médiocre talent, mais il continua à tenir l'emploi jusqu'à sa mort, qui arriva le 9 mai 1725. Il n'était âgé que de quarante-cinq ans. Il laissa par son testament tout ce qu'il possédait à Riccoboni, qui lui avait souvent rendu service.

Le 2 septembre 1759, Alessandro Ciavarelli, né à Naples, débuta à la Comédie-Italienne pour jouer les Scapins. Il mourut en 1775.

> « Ciavarelli met tant de graces
> Quand il représente Scapin,
> Qu'à ses lazzi, à ses grimaces,
> On le prendrait pour Arlequin. »

En 1769, Camerani, acteur fort médiocre, eut cependant une sorte de célébrité par ses boutades singulières et sa gourmandise, qui fut cause de sa mort : il mourut d'une indigestion de pâté de foies gras qu'il avait mangé tout seul dans la nuit. Les auteurs s'étaient concertés ensemble pour obtenir du Théâtre-Italien une augmentation de droits. Camerani, remplissant les fonctions de *semainier* perpétuel, se prononça contre eux au comité des acteurs. C'est lui qui dit ce mot superbe : « Messieurs, prenez-y garde! Il y a longtemps que je vous l'ai dit, tant qu'il y aura des auteurs, la comédie ne pourra pas aller. »

FLAUTINO

Jean Gherardi, de la ville de Prato, en Toscane, vint à Paris en 1675, pour remplacer, sous le nom de FLAUTINO, le Briguelle de la troupe italienne. J. Gherardi débuta dans *Arlequin, berger de Lemnos.*

> « On y voit leur *Flautin* nouveau,
> Qui, sans flûte ni chalumeau,
> Bref, sans instrument quelconque,
> Merveille que l'on ne vit oncque,
> Fait sortir de son seul gosier
> Un concert de flûtes entier
> A ce spectacle on court sans cesse,
> Et pour le voir chacun s'empresse »

Jean Gherardi était un bon acteur, très-comique, jouant parfaitement de la guitare et imitant plusieurs instruments à vent avec son gosier. Il faisait à lui seul tout un orchestre.

> « Avec sa guitare touchée
> Plus en maître qu'en écolier,
> Il semble qu'il tienne cachée
> Une flûte dans son gosier. »

Il resta fort peu de temps au théâtre Ses mœurs dépravées le jetèrent dans une mauvaise affaire. Il fut mis en prison et n'en sortit que pour quitter la France. Il laissa un fils, Evariste Gherardi, le célèbre Arlequin.

GRADELINO.

GRADELINO est encore une variante du type de Brighella. C'est sous ce nom, connu alors en Italie, que Constantin Constantini vint débuter à Paris en 1687.

Constantin Constantini, d'une bonne famille de Vérone, avait monté une manufacture et découvert des secrets chimiques pour la teinture des étoffes. S'étant épris d'une comédienne, non-seulement il quitta pour la suivre son état et son pays, mais encore il engagea sa femme et ses enfants à venir avec lui. Il courut ainsi l'Italie, à la suite de cette comédienne, sous le nom de *Gradelino,* accompagné de ses deux fils, Angelo Constantini (*Mezzetin*) et Jean-Baptiste Constantini (*Ottavio*). Sa maîtresse mourut, et Constantin Constantini vint à Paris pour faire apprécier son talent, qui était vrai et qui lui avait mérité de grands succès en Italie. Il eut la malheureuse idée de chanter sur la scène parisienne une chanson composée en Italie contre les Français. Il fut, malgré son talent, si bien hué et si bien sifflé, qu'il n'osa plus se montrer.

MEZZETIN.

Les premiers MEZZETIN (*Mezzetino* demi-mesure) datent de la fin du seizième siècle, et prennent naissance dans la troupe des *Gelosi.* ils portaient alors des vêtements larges en toile, le masque, le chapeau, le *tabaro* et le sabre de bois des anciens *Zanni,* tels les a représentés Callot. Ce n'était alors qu'une simple variété de Scapino et de Brighella, le costume était le même, le nom seul était différent. Mais les rôles de *Zanni* ayant pris, au commencement du dix-septième siècle, une importance plus grande, les acteurs qui les remplirent adaptèrent le costume au goût de leur époque, soit qu'ils eussent conservé, soit qu'ils eussent modifié le type.

Ce fut Angelo Constantini qui, le premier, revêtit le personnage de Mezzetin de cet habit rayé rouge et blanc qui devint caractéristique. Il avait été reçu dans l'ancienne troupe, en 1682, pour doubler Dominique Biancolelli dans le rôle d'Arlequin; mais voyant que la troupe n'avait pas de second *Zanni*, de Brighella, il en prit le caractère, et emprunta aux bouffons italiens et français ses prédécesseurs ce costume rayé (*planche* 41), tradition de celui des *Sannionnes* de l'antiquité. Il retrancha le masque qu'avaient porté Brighelle, Beltrame, Scapin, et tous les *Zanni* précédents, tant italiens que français. On sait que Molière lui-même joua longtemps les personnages de valet sous le masque. Constantini façonna à la mode du jour la coupe de ses habits, tout en conservant la couleur des étoffes.

Après la mort de Dominique, Mezzetin porta les losanges d'Arlequin, et joua les mêmes rôles jusqu'à l'arrivée d'Évariste Gherardi. Mezzetin reprit alors sa livrée et son caractère de valet fourbe, tantôt agissant pour son propre compte, remplissant des rôles de maris trompeurs ou trompés, comme Sganarelle sur le théâtre de Molière, tantôt valet d'Ottavio ou de Cinthio.

Angelo Constantini, fils de Constantin Constantini (*Gra-delino*), né à Vérone, après avoir joué dès ses plus jeunes années en Italie, vint à Paris en 1682 et débuta, dans *Arlequin Protée*, par le rôle de Glaucus-Mezzetin, tandis que Dominique jouait Protée-Arlequin.

Lorsqu'il dut remplacer Dominique, Constantini reçut des mains de Colombine, dans une scène préparée *ad hoc*, les habits et le masque d'Arlequin, rôle qu'il joua longtemps, mais toujours sous son nom de Mezzetin. Comme il était, quoique très-brun, d'une figure gracieuse et mobile, et qu'il était aimé du public, la salle entière se leva, et, pour lui manifester son estime, lui cria : « Pas de masque! pas de masque! » Constantini joua donc sans masque jusqu'à ce qu'Evariste Gherardi vint débuter dans les Arlequins et enlever la position du premier coup. Constantini reprit son emploi de Mezzetin jusqu'à la fermeture de 1697.

Les frères Parfait disent, en parlant de Constantini : « Ce qui lui arriva chez M. le duc de Saint-Agnan mérite d'être rapporté. Il avait dédié une pièce à ce seigneur, qui payait généreusement les dédicaces; dans le dessein de recevoir la récompense qu'il espérait, il se rendit un matin chez le duc; mais le suisse, se doutant du sujet de sa visite, ne voulut point le laisser entrer, Mezzetin, pour le toucher, lui offrit le tiers de la récompense qu'il recevrait de son maître, et passa au moyen de cette promesse. Il rencontra sur l'escalier le premier laquais, qui ne fut pas moins intraitable que le suisse; Mezzetin lui promit l'autre tiers, et il fut introduit dans l'appartement. Il y trouva le valet de chambre, qui se montra encore plus inflexible que les deux autres, et ne se relâcha que difficilement à la promesse du troisième tiers ; de sorte qu'il ne resta plus rien au pauvre Mezzetin, qui, dès qu'il aperçut le duc, courut à lui et lui dit : « Ah! monseigneur, voici une pièce de théâtre que je » prends la liberté de vous présenter, et pour laquelle je » vous prie de me faire donner cent coups de bâton. » Cette demande singulière étonna le duc, qui voulut en savoir la raison. « C'est, monseigneur, » lui dit Mezzetin, « que, pour » pouvoir approcher de votre personne, j'ai été obligé de » promettre à votre suisse, à votre laquais et à votre valet » de chambre, chacun un tiers de ce que vous auriez la » bonté de me donner. » Le duc fit une sévère réprimande à ses gens, et envoya cent louis à la femme de Mezzetin, qui n'avait rien promis. »

Le Mezzetin du théâtre de Gherardi, bien qu'adouci généralement dans ses mœurs, est parfois le vrai Brighella d'autrefois, avec toute sa scélératesse.

« MEZZETIN à *Isabelle*. Allons, la belle, dites la vérité ; n'est-il pas vrai que vous seriez bien aise d'être ma moitié? Voyez, regardez-moi cet air, ce port? Eh? J'enrage quand je vois ces petits embryons de cour vouloir faire assaut avec moi

ISABELLE. Il faut qu'ils aient perdu l'esprit! ce sont de plaisantes marmousettes (marionnettes)!

MEZZETIN. J'ai le derrière un peu gros, c'est vrai, tirant même sur le porteur de chaises, mais mon médecin m'a promis de faire en aller cela; il m'a ordonné de prendre du petit-lait

ISABELLE. Oh! je crois ce remède-là *sûr*

MEZZETIN. Il m'a dit que c'était une humeur àcre, répandue dans le diaphragme du mésentère et qui tombe sur l'omoplate. Mais laissons cela, et parlons du plaisir que nous aurons.

ISABELLE. On se trompe quelquefois dans ce calcul-là, et l'on n'y trouve pas souvent tout le bonheur qu'on s'y était proposé.

MEZZETIN. Je suis doux, pacifique, aisé à vivre, l'humeur satinée, veloutée. J'ai vécu six ans avec ma première femme sans avoir le moindre petit démêlé.

ISABELLE. Cela est assez extraordinaire.

MEZZETIN. Une fois seulement, après avoir pris du tabac, je voulais éternuer elle me fit manquer mon coup. De dépit, je pris un chandelier et je lui cassai la tête. Elle mourut un quart d'heure après.

ISABELLE. Ah ciel! est-il possible!

MEZZETIN. Voilà le seul différend que nous ayons eu ensemble et qui ne dura pas longtemps, comme vous voyez. Quand une femme doit mourir, il vaut mieux que ce soit de la main de son mari que de celle du médecin, qu'il faut payer cher et qui vous la traînera six mois ou un an. Je n'aime pas à voir languir le monde.

ISABELLE. Et vous n'avez point d'horreur d'avoir commis un crime aussi noir que celui-là?

MEZZETIN. Moi? pas du tout, je suis accoutumé au sang, de jeunesse Mon père a eu mille affaires en sa vie, et il a toujours tué son homme Il a servi le roi trente-deux ans.

ISABELLE. Sur terre ou sur mer?

MEZZETIN. En l'air.

ISABELLE. Comment! en l'air? je n'ai jamais entendu parler de ces officiers-là?

MEZZETIN C'est que, comme il était fort charitable, lorsqu'il rencontrait quelque agonisant qu'on menait en Grève, il se mettait avec lui dans la charrette, et l'aidait à mourir du mieux qu'il pouvait.

ISABELLE. Ah! l'horreur!

MEZZETIN. Si vous l'aviez vu travailler, il vous aurait donné envie de vous faire pendre.

ISABELLE Comme ce sont peut-être des talents de famille, vous auriez dû prendre la charge de M. votre père.

MEZZETIN. Je m'y sentais assez d'inclination; mais vous savez qu'il faut qu'un gentilhomme voie du pays.

ISABELLE. Je ne trouve qu'une petite difficulté à notre mariage, c'est que je suis déjà mariée.

MEZZETIN. Mariée? Bon, voilà une belle affaire! Est-ce là ce qui vous embarrasse? Je le suis aussi . mais il n'y a rien de si aisé que d'être veuf; cinq sous de mort-aux-rats en font l'affaire. »

Dans d'autres scènes du même répertoire, Mezzetin ne brille que par sa paillardise et sa couardise :

« ISABELLE *en servante d'auberge, recevant Mezzetin, habillé en voyageur, suivi d'Arlequin, son valet* Bonjour, messieurs; que vous faut-il ?

ARLEQUIN. Allons, ma fille, une chambre, du feu, et grande chère, je m'arrête volontiers où il y a bon vin et jolie servante.

ISABELLE. Messieurs, vous allez avoir tout ce qu'il vous faut il ne manque de rien chez nous .

Mezzetin *présentant son pied botté à Isabelle.* Allons, ma fille, viens me débotter.

Isabelle. Vous débotter? Pardi, monsieur, cherchez vos débotteuses, ce n'est pas là mon affaire.

Mezzetin. Est-ce que tu n'es pas aussi valet d'écurie?

Arlequin *à Mezzetin.* Monsieur, voilà une dondon qui me paraît assez résolue, mais il me semble qu'elle vous saboule un peu.

Mezzetin. La friponne est, ma foi, jolie; viens çà, ma fille, es-tu mariée?

Isabelle. Non, monsieur, Dieu merci! à moi n'appartient pas tant d'honneur; l'année n'est pas bonne pour les filles, tous les garçons sont à la guerre.

Mezzetin *faisant des mines auprès d'Isabelle.* Si tu voulais un peu me délasser de mes exploits guerriers?... J'ai de l'argent, oui!

Isabelle. Bon, me voilà bien chanceuse avec votre argent: ça n'a jamais été ça qui m'a tenté. J'aime mieux un homme qui me plaît que tous les trésors du monde, et si vous voulez que je vous parle franchement, j'aimerais mieux votre valet que vous. (*Elle donne un grand coup de poing dans l'estomac à Arlequin.*)

Arlequin. Ouf! La coquine est, ma foi, de bon goût. Allons, monsieur, retirez-vous, ce n'est pas là de la viande pour vos oiseaux. (*Il repousse Mezzetin.*)

Mezzetin *se rapprochant.* Cette friponne-là n'est pas prévenue de mon mérite.... Je suis pourtant drôle avec les filles. (*Il veut badiner avec elle.*)

Isabelle. Je vous prie, monsieur, encore une fois, de

vous tenir en repos. Je n'aime pas à être tarabustée. Si vous voulez entrer chez nous, la porte est ouverte; sinon, je suis votre très-humble servante. »

Elle veut rentrer dans l'auberge, Mezzetin la retient par un bras; Cinthio, qui l'a vue, sort de l'auberge, et repousse rudement Mezzetin.

« CINTHIO. En vertu de quoi, monsieur, s'il vous plaît, prenez-vous des familiarités avec cette fille-là?

MEZZETIN. En vertu de quoi?... En vertu de mon bon plaisir

CINTHIO. De votre plaisir! Croyez-moi, mon petit visage botté, ne m'échauffez pas les oreilles, car je pourrais prendre le mien à telle chose qui vous déplairait fort.

MEZZETIN. Monsieur, on ne traite pas comme cela un gentilhomme parisien qui revient de Flandre.

CINTHIO. Vous, de Flandre?

ARLEQUIN *qui s'était caché dans un coin, par peur, se rapproche.* Je veux que le diable m'emporte si nous n'y étions pas, et au camp de Fleurus, encore!

MEZZETIN *en se carrant.* Eh non, nous n'y étions pas, quand notre général fit signifier un *avenir* aux ennemis; ils ne comparurent pas le dernier juillet, à une heure de relevée, pour plaider sur le champ de bataille. .La cause fut appelée, qui dura plus de huit heures; mais, en vertu de bonnes pièces de canon, dont nous étions porteurs, nous fîmes bien vite déguerpir l'ennemi Il voulut deux ou trois fois revenir par appel, mais il fut toujours débouté de son o..... , ...'.. ' .. '.. le. dépens, dommages et intérêts, et aux frais, morbleu! aux frais!... Eh bien, y étions-nous? Non! c'est que je me moque!

CINTHIO. Je vois bien, monsieur, que vous avez vu la bataille dans quelque étude de procureur. Mais je vous prie de passer votre chemin, et de ne pas regarder derrière vous; m'entendez-vous?

MEZZETIN. Monsieur, prenez garde à ce que vous faites, si vous m'insultez.... (*Il tire son épée, Cinthio met la main sur la sienne.*)

CINTHIO. Eh bien?

MEZZETIN *se cachant derrière Arlequin* Vous aurez affaire à mon valet.

ARLEQUIN *s'enfuyant.* Je ne suis pas obligé de me faire tuer à votre place.

CINTHIO. Allez! je ne daigne pas vous répondre; mais si vous jetez les yeux sur cette fille-là, je vous ferai mourir sous le bâton. (*Il lui donne de ses gants dans le nez et s'en va.*)

MEZZETIN *après qu'il est parti.* Il s'en va, pourtant!... (*A Arlequin.*) Hé! que dis-tu à cela? Je ne lui ai pas mal rivé son clou, n'est-ce pas? »

Mezzetin chantait aussi dans les parodies, en s'accompagnant de la guitare. Watteau l'a peint jouant de cet instrument au milieu des principaux acteurs de la Comédie-Italienne : Isabelle, Ottavio, Colombine, etc. Au bas de la gravure de *Thomassin le fils* sont inscrits les vers suivants, du poëte Gacon :

« Sous un habit de Mezetin,
Ce gros brun au riant visage,

> Sur la guitare, avec sa main,
> Fait un aimable badinage.
> Par les doux accents de sa voix,
> Enfants d'une bouche vermeille,
> Du beau sexe tout à la fois
> Il charme les yeux et l'oreille »

Il dansait et chantait aussi, sous des costumes allégoriques, dans les ballets qui terminaient la plupart des pièces, comme à la fin de la pièce *les Originaux,* où, après avoir rempli le rôle du valet d'Octave pendant toute la pièce, il disparaît au dernier acte pour aller se vêtir en *costume d'Amérique.*

« Quatre Américains *dansent une entrée qui exprime le froid* Après quoi, l'Amérique s'avance et chante :

> « Je suis gelé par les frimas,
> Je grelotte de froid, je tremble, je frissonne.
> Jeune époux, ne m'imitez pas
> Une beauté mal aisement pardonne
> L'outrageante froideur qu'on fait à ses appas »

Après quoi « Quatre Africains *dansent une entrée de postures.* »

Après la suppression du théâtre et de la troupe en 1697, A. Constantini partit pour l'Allemagne, afin de trouver à s'employer Il s'était engagé dans une troupe, à Brunswick, quand Auguste Ier, roi de Pologne, qui avait entendu parler de lui, lui fit faire des propositions. Constantini les accepta et fut chargé par ce prince de composer une troupe, qui devait alternativement jouer la comédie et chanter l'opéra

italien. Il vint en France en 1698 pour recruter cette troupe,
et s'acquitta si bien de sa mission, que l'année suivante
Auguste Ier le nomma *cameriere intime*, trésorier des menus
plaisirs, et le fit noble. Mais un sort si brillant ne pouvait
pas durer. Mezzetin, entreprenant et hardi, s'éprit de la
maîtresse du roi et lui déclara son amour. Il ne s'en tint
pas là, il chercha à déconsidérer le roi dans l'esprit de cette
dame, et tint sur son compte des propos peu mesurés. La
dame fut outrée, dit-on, de l'insolence du comédien. Le
fait est que le roi sut tout, et qu'il se cacha dans la
chambre de cette dame, où rendez-vous avait été donné
à Constantini. Ce qui se passa, nul ne le sait, si ce n'est
qu'Auguste sortit furieux, le sabre à la main, et voulant trancher la tête du comédien. « Mais il sentit proba-
» blement qu'il ne lui convenait pas de souiller sa main du
» sang d'un homme qui l'avait trahi si indignement. » Il
le fit arrêter et conduire au château de Konigstein.

Mezzetin resta vingt ans dans cette prison; enfin, une
autre dame de la cour d'Auguste, qui avait alors du crédit
sur le cœur et l'esprit du roi de Pologne, engagea ce
prince à venir visiter son château-prison d'Etat. Elle fit
venir Constantini, qui parut « avec une barbe qu'il avait
» laissée croître depuis sa détention. » Il se jeta aux pieds
du roi, et, bien que la dame appuyât ses supplications,
Auguste fut inexorable et rejeta sa grâce. Mais cette dame
travailla si bien l'esprit du roi, que quelques mois après
Constantini fut remis en liberté. « On lui rendit tous ses
» effets, avec ordre cependant de sortir de Dresde et des
» Etats de Saxe. »

Mezzetin partit pour Vérone, mais il y resta peu de
temps. Désireux de revoir Paris et de remonter sur un
théâtre où il avait si longtemps joué avec succès, il vint
trouver la nouvelle troupe du régent, qui le reçut avec joie
et surprise. Il s'arrangea avec ses anciens camarades pour
jouer dans cinq ou six pièces, moyennant mille écus, et
reparut sur la scène le 5 février 1729.

On lit dans le *Mercure de France* du mois de février 1729 :

« Le sieur Angelo Constantini, natif de Vérone, connu
» ci-devant sous le nom de Mezzetin, comédien de l'ancien
» hôtel de Bourgogne, joua sur le même théâtre et débuta
» par les rôles qu'il avait joués autrefois dans la comédie
» intitulée *la Foire Saint-Germain*, représentée dans sa nou-
» veauté en 1695.

» Cette pièce fut précédée d'un prologue du sieur Lelio
» fils, dont voici le sujet :

» Momus et Arlequin paraissent d'abord. Momus se plaint
» de voir si longtemps ses jeux désertés. Il en demande la
» cause à Arlequin, qui l'impute à l'amour extrême que
» les Français ont pour la nouveauté. Momus lui promet
» de remédier à cet inconvénient par une nouveauté qui
» doit l'emporter sur toutes les autres. A son ordre, un
» vieillard vénérable s'avance : il fait entendre que c'est le
» Mezzetin de l'ancien théâtre italien. A un nouvel ordre
» du dieu qui l'introduit, et qui le prend sous sa protec-
» tion, il dépouille sa robe de vieillard et paraît sous
» l'habit de Mezzetin. Momus récite une fable, au sujet de
» la vieillesse.... Cette fable ne paraît pas d'abord favo-
» rable à un vieillard de soixante-quinze ans, mais Momus

» le console par un coup de marote qui répand sur son
» cher élève une agréable folie, qui doit tenir lieu de
» jeunesse. »

Mezzetin raconte ensuite un songe qu'il vient d'avoir.
Il se croyait, dit-il, à Paris, sur la scène italienne; il voyait
sortir une guitare du plancher et il chantait encore, malgré
son âge avancé. Pendant sa narration, une guitare sort en
effet du *premier dessous*. Il la prend, l'essaye et chante en
s'accompagnant et en s'adressant au parterre.

> « Mezzetin, par d'heureux talens,
>   Voudroit vous satisfaire,
> Quoiqu'il soit depuis très long-temps
>   Presque sexagénaire,
> Il rajeunira de trente ans
>   S'il peut encor vous plaire »

Il y eut une telle affluence de spectateurs, que, malgré
le prix des places qui avait été doublé, on renvoya autant
de monde qu'il y en avait dans la salle.

Il donna cinq représentations et, quelques jours après,
partit pour Vérone, en laissant à Paris « plus de créanciers
que de réputation, » dit un de ses détracteurs. Il mourut
en Italie à la fin de cette même année 1729.

Au-dessous du beau portrait de Constantini, peint par
de Troy et gravé par Vermeulen, on lit les six vers suivants
qui sont de la Fontaine :

> « Ici de Mezzetin, rare et nouveau Prothée,
>   La figure est représentée,
>   La nature l'ayant pourvu

Des dons de la métamorphose,
Qui ne le voit pas n'a rien vu,
Qui le voit a vu toute chose »

Cette louange parut un peu trop exagérée, car le poète
Gacon fit paraître la réponse suivante aux vers de la Fontaine, dans son *Poète sans fard :*

« Sur le portrait de Mezzetin
Un homme d'un goût assez fin
Lisant l'éloge qu'on lui donne
D'être un si grand comédien,
Que   *Qui ne le voit ne voit rien,*
Et qu'on voit tout en sa personne,
Disait · « Je ne vois pas qu'il soit si bon acteur,
» Il ne fait rien qui nous surprenne.
» — Monsieur, lui dis-je alors, pour le tirer de peine,
» Ne voyez-vous pas bien qu'un discours si flatteur
» Est un conte de la Fontaine ? »

Angelo Constantini avait épousé, en Italie, Auretta, fille
de Dorsi et de la fameuse actrice Angiola. Auretta vint à
Paris et joua sur le théâtre italien de l'hôtel de Bourgogne; mais elle n'y eut pas de succès; son talent et sa
figure étaient médiocres Elle passa en Allemagne. De
ce mariage naquirent une fille qui mourut religieuse à
Chaumont, et un fils nommé Gabriel Constantini qui joua
les Arlequins en Italie.

Sous le nom de Mezzetinone, Carot était un excellent comique qui jouait les rôles de Mezzetin, à Venise, en 1689.

NARCISINO.

Narcisino ou Narcisin est originaire de la ville de Malalbergo, entre Bologne et Ferrare. Son surnom est *dessevedo*
(valet) *di Malalbergo* Les Bolonais ayant déjà le Docteur,
qui parlait leur dialecte, celui de la classe éclairée, l'acteur
Riccont créa, vers le milieu du dix-septième siècle, un
autre personnage qui parla le patois du bas peuple, patois
qui est presque une langue différente de celle que l'on
parle encore aujourd'hui. Ce personnage était, au dix-
septième siècle, tantôt valet mais, tantôt maître, et jouait
aussi très-souvent les rôles de père, de tuteurs, ordinairement imbéciles et ignorants, entêtés et aussi malicieux que
possible. Il partageait cet emploi avec Tabarino et Fiton-
cello, rôles qui, comme Beltrame et Sganarelle, servaient
à deux fins, et qui furent créés ou plutôt renouvelés par
l'acteur Bigher, à Bologne.

Narcisin était encore tenu en grande estime et avait une
grande vogue, il y a une cinquantaine d'années, à Bologne.
Il avait alors un emploi singulier Il ne paraissait presque
pas dans les pièces, et venait seul sur le théâtre dire ou
faire quelque bouffonnerie n'ayant aucun rapport à l'action
scénique.

Coiffé d'un chapeau de paille, les cheveux longs pour
imiter les paysans, vêtu d'une veste et d'une culotte excessivement large rayée rouge et vert, parfois le tabaro sur
le bras (*planche* 42) ou un panier de fruits à la main, il
venait pendant l'entr'acte faire un intermède et causer

avec le public sur l'avant-scène, critiquait les mœurs du
temps, racontait les plaisantes aventures des faubourgs et
de la campagne. C'était une sorte de Pasquin ou de Bruscambille. Il avait le droit de tout dire, mais toujours d'une
façon générale et sans personnalités trop claires. Aujour-
d'hui encore, Narcisin se livre à ses quolibets, et moralise
même à sa manière, mais cela se passe sur les théâtres de
marionnettes.

« Messieurs! il faut avouer, et vous l'avouerez avec moi,
n'est-ce pas? que le mensonge est une étrange chose! S'il y
a dans la salle des menteurs, qu'ils prennent la peine
de s'en aller, afin de ne pas entendre ce que je vais dire.
(*Il s'arrête un instant.*) Eh bien! personne ne sort?... Je
vois, messieurs, que nous sommes tous des hommes sincères ici!.... Alors je puis vous dire entre hommes ...
Ah! j'aperçois des femmes là-bas! Ces dames, sincères et
franches, sont priées de rester; — celles qui s'adonnent au
mensonge peuvent s'en retourner chez elles voir si le vin
aigrit dans leur cave (*Une pause*). Pas une femme ne quitte
la place?... *brave signore!* je vois que je n'ai autour de moi
que franchise et loyauté! (*Il va d'un côté du théâtre, et,
contre un des côtés du manteau d'Arlequin, se baisse et du
revers de sa main, comme s'il parlait en secret à l'oreille
de chacun.*) Je n'en crois rien, mais elles veulent se faire
passer pour ce qu'elles ne sont pas! Or donc, puisque
la franchise et la vérité règnent ici, je vous dirai en
confidence qu'il faut bien que les femmes s'imaginent les
hommes plus bêtes qu'ils ne le sont, pour venir leur
raconter un tas de bourdes, qu'ils ont l'air de croire et de

prendre pour monnaie courante, jusqu'au jour où, fatigués de ce tissu d'inventions diaboliques, ils envoient promener mensonges et menteuses.

» Je vous demande un peu, mesdames (oui, c'est à vous
que je m'adresse en particulier), quand vous ne remuez
pas la langue, ne sauriez-vous encore vous passer de
mentir par vos affiquets! Je vous demande un peu si ce
n'est pas le plus gros mensonge qu'une femme puisse
inventer, de faire croire a ce qu'elle n'a pas. Tenez! j'en
vois tous les jours, et des plus maigres, se pavaner avec
des jupons de la rotondité de la coupole de Saint-Marc, à
Venise. Les rues de Bologne sont trop étroites maintenant,
car nos dames, forcées d'aller à pied, — il n'y a pas de *vettu-
rini* capables de les contenir, — garnissent et envahissent
toutes les rues, et je vous demande un peu ce qu'il résulte
de tout cela? Sous ces croupes mensongères, qu'y a-t-il?
du vent! »

Autre intermède : « Messieurs, que les avares sortent
vite! Ils pourraient user leurs oreilles à m'entendre! Personne ne bouge, je peux donc parler librement. Qu'ils
sont fous, ces gens qui passent quarante années de leur
vie à empiler l'un sur l'autre des liards, pour en faire
des sous, et des sous pour en faire des livres, et des
livres pour en faire des louis! Le jour où ils ont bien
amassé pour en jouir, ils ne peuvent s'en servir; altérés
de jouissances dans la jeunesse, ils sont exténués dans la
vieillesse. Que les exténués sortent, je vais parler pour
les jeunes gens dans la force de l'âge. O vous, jeunes
fous! qui ne pensez qu'à boire, manger et faire l'amour!

Est-ce là le but de l'existence?... Je m'arrête, messieurs; nous sommes ici au théâtre et non au sermon. » Et faisant une pirouette comme Stenterello, il disparait.

Plusieurs personnages français sont dérivés du type de Scapin, nous allons les esquisser.

TURLUPIN.

TURLUPIN (malchanceux, malheureux) fut créé à la fin du seizième siècle, à l'hôtel de Bourgogne, par Henri Legrand dit Belleville, qui le joua pendant plus de cinquante ans sous un costume ayant beaucoup de rapport avec celui de Brighella quant à la forme, et tenant un peu de l'Arlequin pour les couleurs.

Turlupin était fécond en quolibets, calembours, coq-à-l'âne, amphigouris, et en ce genre de plaisanteries qui prirent de lui le nom de turlupinades. Comme la plupart des farceurs français d'alors, il prenait son bien où il le trouvait · mais la source la plus féconde était surtout Rabelais. *Les Bigarrures et touches du seigneur des Accords, les Apophthegmes du sieur Gaulard* et *les Escraignes dijonnoises* (1560), ainsi que les *Vaillans faits d'armes de Bolorospe* (1635), durent fournir matière à Turlupin pour broder et amplifier sur des textes dans le genre de celui-ci :

« ... Habillé de vert (de gris), parfumé (comme un jambon) d'odeur (de sainteté), et enveloppé d'un manteau (de cheminée). Il rencontre une dame parée d'une belle robe (d'avocat), d'une fine fraise (de veau) et d'une riche

côte (de melon), bordée d'un filet (de vinaigre). » Ensuite
faisant la description de son héros . « Il a un corps (de
garde), une tête (d'épingle), un cou (de tonnerre), des
épaules (de mouton), des bras (de mer), une main (de
papier), un pied (de cochon), un dos (d'âne), une langue
(étrangère), une haleine (de savetier). Il était fort bien
vêtu, il avait de belles chemises de toile (d'araignée), un
rabat de point (du jour), une culotte (de bœuf).... Sa
maison était bâtie de pierres (philosophales), soutenue de
piliers (de cabaret), et on y entrait par deux cours (de
chime), d'où on montait vingt-cinq degrés (de chaleur),
et on se trouvait dans une grande chambre (de justice)....
Il courait à la chasse suivi d'une meute de chiens (-dent),
de quatre valets (de pique), montés sur des chevaux (de
frise) portant des lacs (d'amour) et des filets (de canards)....
Il visitait souvent ses châteaux (en Espagne), ses terres
et ses champs (de bataille)... et mourut d'une chute
(d'eau), etc., etc. »

 « Il était excellent farceur, » dit Sauval; « ses rencontres
étaient pleines d'esprit, de feu et de jugement: en un mot
il ne lui manquait rien qu'un peu de naïveté; et nonobstant
cela, chacun avoue qu'il n'a jamais vu son pareil.... Quoiqu'il fût roussâtre, il était bel homme, bien fait, et avait
bonne mine. Il était adroit, fin, dissimulé et agréable dans
la conversation. » Il avait débuté dès 1585 et passa sa vie
sur le théâtre, car il n'en descendit que pour entrer dans
la fosse qui lui fut accordée à l'église Saint-Sauveur
en 1637.

 Dans la troupe française de l'hôtel de Bourgogne, « Gros-

Guillaume », dit Tallemant, « était *le farmé*, Gaultier, le vieillard, et Turlupin, le fourbe. Il jouait aussi le personnage du *Zany*, qu'on regardait comme le facétieux de la bande, et pour cela il portait un habit semblable à celui de Brighella, avec le petit manteau et le pantalon. » Turlupin était un homme rangé, marié, qui ne souffrit point que sa femme montât sur le théâtre, et qui vivait en bourgeois. Il passait de longues heures dans l'étude de ses rôles. « Il étudiait son métier assez souvent, et il arrivoit quelquefois que, comme un homme de qualité qui l'affectionnoit l'envoyoit prier à dîner, il répondoit qu'il étudioit. »

Louis Legrand, fils du précédent, soutint la célébrité de son père. Il débuta sous le même nom de Turlupin le 15 décembre 1620 et vécut jusqu'en 1655.

GANDOLIN.

GANDOLIN, personnage jouant à Paris sur le théâtre du Marais en 1595 et au commencement du dix-septième siècle, semble une *doublure* de Turlupin. Il porte le masque de Brighella, le chapeau d'Arlequin, orné de sa queue de lièvre :

> « Gandolin, par sa rhétorique,
> Nous fait la rate épanouir,
> Et, pour n'avoir pas la colique,
> Il faut tant seulement l'ouïr
> Quelques fables qu'il nous raconte,
> Elles ont un si bel effet,
> Que chacun y trouve son compte,
> Et s'en retourne satisfait »

Le théâtre du Marais possédait encore, comme improvisateurs dans les farces en 1595, Santilly et Gorlay, dit *Moucheron*.

GRATTELARD.

(1620) Le *Grattelard*, bouffon français des farces tabariniques, surnommé par dérision le baron de Grattelard, est un type de valet fourbe. Son costume se rapproche beaucoup de celui de Trivelino. Il porte, comme celui-ci, un pourpoint et un pantalon à l'italienne assez large, bordé de dessins imitant des triangles, d'une couleur foncée sur un fond clair. Il porte aussi le demi-masque, la mentonnière et le serre-tête, la grande collerette plissée, la latte et les souliers de peau claire, la toque comme Brighella, mais pas de manteau. Au-dessus d'un portrait du personnage, retrouvé dernièrement à la bibliothèque des estampes, on lit le distique suivant :

« Ma mine n'est belle ny bonne,
Et je vous jure sur ma foy
Qu'on peut bien se fier à moy,
Car je ne me fie à personne »

Sur la même estampe se trouvent deux autres personnages du même théâtre : *Jasmin* (sorte de Crispin) et *Jean Broche* ou *Boche*, qui a un certain rapport avec les Docteurs italiens.

Avant Grattelard, d'autres bouffons français avaient déjà accolé à leur nom de théâtre des titres empruntés dérisoirement à la noblesse · *le comte de Salles*, boufl'on basochien du commencement du seizième siècle, *le marquis d'Argencourt*, *le baron de Plancy*, *le comte de Permission*.

Le rôle le plus brillant de Grattelard est dans la farce des Trois Bossus, conte tiré des *Facétieuses Nuits* de Straparole, qui, lui-même, l'a tiré des contes orientaux.

La farce des Bossus.

« Trostolle le bossu possède trois frères bossus, qu'il ne peut pas voir. Il a horreur des gens contrefaits. Un jour, forcé de s'absenter de chez lui, il recommande à sa femme, après avoir dîné, de tout fermer et de ne laisser entrer personne au logis. Il ne veut pas avoir à rencontrer ses frères les bossus, ou il y aura du bâton sur l'échine de madame. Après quoi il sort. Madame Trostolle a une intrigue amoureuse avec un certain Horace qui dépêche vers elle son valet Grattelard avec un billet doux.

» Le mari parti, les trois bossus arrivent avec des estomacs creux comme des puits et des dents de loup. « Il y a longtemps que nous n'avons rien mangé, » dit le premier bossu, « et mon ventre, au besoin, servirait de lanterne. — Voici le logis de mon frère, » dit le second, « entrons » Le troisième frappe à la porte. Mais madame Trostolle les reconnaît au paquet qu'ils portent sur le dos. Elle se laisse pourtant attendrir par leurs prières, les fait entrer et leur donne à repaître. Mais Trostolle arrive, elle fait cacher les trois frères, Trostolle flaire ses bossus; cependant il s'en va, sur l'affirmation de sa femme qui lui jure que personne n'est venu. Elle court alors à ses beaux-frères et les trouve ivres · « Je crois, » dit-elle, « qu'ils ont un réservoir dans le dos, ils ont bu un plein tonneau ! Il faut pourtant les faire sortir d'ici. »

» Grattelard arrive avec sa lettre : « Vois mon embarras, » lui dit madame Trostolle, « un bossu est tombé mort devant ma porte, il faut que tu le portes à la rivière. — Que me donnerez-vous ? — Vingt écus ! — Çà, entrons en besogne. — Tiens, voici le drôle. — Il est bien pesant ! » dit Grattelard ; et le voilà en route pour jeter son bossu à l'eau.

« — J'ai fait marché pour qu'il en porte un ; je vais l'affiner, il faut qu'il les porte tous les trois. »

» Grattelard revient · « Je l'ai jeté à l'eau ! » dit-il ; « mais comme il était lourd ! — Te moques-tu de moi ? » lui dit la femme ; « tu l'as bien mal jeté, car il est revenu ? Tiens, le voici !

» — Au diable le bossu ! Je vais le recharger sur mon dos et le reporter à la rivière. » Il va et revient. Mais il retrouve encore un bossu : « Ne vois-tu pas qu'il reviendra toujours ? » lui dit madame Trostolle ; « tu t'y prends mal !

» — Mordienne ! » dit Grattelard, « je me fâcherai, à la fin ! Je vais le retourner encore une fois, mais, s'il revient, je lui attacherai une pierre au cou. » Et il emporte le bossu. Madame sort aussi d'un autre côté. Trostolle revient, il a fini ses affaires et veut rentrer chez lui pour s'assurer que ses frères ne sont pas venus.

« — Comment ! mort de ma vie ! » s'écrie Grattelard en revenant de sa course et en apercevant Trostolle, « voilà encore mon bossu ! A la rivière, bossu, à la rivière ! » Et il empoigne le mari. Après quoi, il revient recevoir ses vingt écus. « Eh bien, l'avez-vous jeté dans la rivière? » lui dit madame Trostolle.

« GRATTLARD. Il m'a fallu le reprendre par quatre fois! Il revenait toujours, mais cette fois-ci....

LA FEMME. Quatre fois! N'aurait-il pas mis mon mari avec les autres?

GRATTELARD. Le dernier parlait, par ma foi!

LA FEMME. Oh! qu'as-tu fait? C'est mon mari que tu as jeté à l'eau!

GRATTELARD. Il n'y a pas grand mal! C'était un bossu qui n'a jamais dû être droit. Tenez, voici une lettre du sieur Horace.

LA FEMME. Est-il loin d'ici?

GRATTELARD. Puisque votre mari est mort, il faut vous marier ensemble. Tenez, le voici!

HORACE. Madame, si l'affection que je vous porte me peut servir de garant pour vous présenter et sacrifier mes vœux, vous pouvez croire que je suis un de vos plus fidèles sujets. »

JODELET.

JODELET, valet bouffon, naïf et niais en apparence, était joué dans la troupe française de l'hôtel de Bourgogne par Julien Geoffrin, de 1610 à 1660. Son costume est, pour la forme, celui de Beltrame, quant aux couleurs, il porte la toque noire, le pourpoint, la trousse et les chausses rayés, le masque de Brighella et la mentonnière noire, le manteau, l'escarcelle et le sabre de bois de tous les types sem-
blab¹

Scarron a composé pour le créateur de ce personnage : *Jodelet duelliste, Jodelet maître et valet*, 1645.

On a encore : *Jodelet astrologue*, comédie de d'Ouville, 1646 ; *la Femme mort de Jodelet*, comédie de Brécourt, 1660.

Julien Geoffrin fut le dernier qui joua *la farce* en France. « Pour un fariné naïf, » dit Tallemant, « il est bon acteur. Il n'y a plus de farce qu'au Marais, où il est, et c'est à cause de lui qu'il y en a. Jodelet parle du nez pour avoir été mal pansé... et cela lui donne de la grâce. »

Jodelet jouait aussi parfois avec la troupe italienne. Loret, à propos des fêtes de Vincennes en 1659, dit, dans sa *Muse historique* :

> « *Scaramouche*, à la riche taille,
> Le signor *Trivelin*, canaille,
> *Jodelet*, plaisant fariné,
> *Item* aussi le *Gros-René*,
> Et *Gratian*, le doctissime,
> Aussi bien que fallotisme. »

Il mourut à la fin de 1660. Loret lui fit cette épitaphe :

> Ici gist qui de Jodelet
> Joua cinquante ans le rolet,
> Et qui fust de mesme farine
> Que Gros-Guillaume et Jean Farine,
> Hormis qu'il parloit mieux du nez
> Que les dits deux enfarinez.

Gilotin, Tripotin et Filipin étaient des farceurs du théâtre français de l'hôtel de Bourgogne (1655). Filipin, dont le véritable nom était Villiers, jouait les mêmes rôles que

Jodelet Scarron fit pour lui *le Gardien de soi-même* Il portait le masque noir des valets italiens et la toque rouge surmontée de deux plumes.

(1635) Gogulu, masque français qui semble avoir essayé de remplacer Gros-Guillaume au théâtre de l'hôtel de Bourgogne, portait un pantalon large, un pourpoint comme celui de Brighella, le manteau, le serre-tête et la moustache exagérée des bouffons italiens.

Bruscambille, autre type de l'hôtel de Bourgogne, créé par Deslauriers, né en Champagne, acteur et auteur, débuta, dès 1598, sur les tréteaux de Jean Farine, et entra à l'hôtel de Bourgogne en 1634.

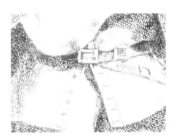

SCARAMOUCHE.

PASQUARIELLO, PASQUINO, CRISPIN.

SCARAMOUCHE est fils ou petit-fils du Matamore, car son nom, qui veut dire *petit batailleur,* et son type primitif et originaire de Naples le rangeraient dans la catégorie des Capitans, si, en France, avec Tiberio Fiurelli, ce personnage n'avait été mis à toutes sauces.

Le costume de Scaramouche n'a jamais varié quant à la couleur, il a toujours été noir de la tête aux pieds

Riccoboni dit que « pour la forme, c'est une imitation » de l'habit espagnol, qui, depuis si longtemps, dans la ‹ ville de Naples, était l'habit du palais, des magistrats » et des gens de guerre. Vers 1680, les Capitans espagnols » finirent en Italie, et le Capitan ancien, Italien, étant » oublié depuis longtemps, on fut obligé de tirer des » troupes des comédiens napolitains un acteur qui rem- » plaçàt le Capitan espagnol, le Scaramouche eń prit la » place. En Italie, ce personnage n'a jamais fait d'autre

» caractère que celui du Capitan . son caractère est d'être
» fanfaron et poltron tout à la fois. »

Ce personnage porta dans l'origine le masque, comme
tous les types qui datent de cette époque.

Dans ses *Petits Danseurs*, Callot représente le Scaramuccia
de la troupe des *Fedeli*, dont le véritable nom était Goldoni,
masqué et l'épée à la main Son costume est peu différent
de ce qu'il a été plus tard avec Fiurelli, sauf les crevés de
son pourpoint et de sa toque empanachée, qui feraient
remonter la création de ce type à la fin du seizième
siècle.

Tiberio Fiurelli, le plus célèbre de tous les Scaramouches, laissa le masque de côté, s'enfarina le visage et, par
les jeux de sa physionomie, « fut le plus grand mime du
monde ». Il porta d'abord la culotte large, puis il prit celle
qui resta traditionnelle à ce type. La ceinture a été tantôt
d'étoffe de drap, comme le costume, tantôt de cuir. Les
passementeries et les boutons furent toujours de la couleur
du vêtement (*planche* 45).

Scaramouche se dit marquis, prince et seigneur de
plusieurs contrées qui n'ont jamais existé sur aucune carte
de géographie. Il fut, dit-il, abandonné fort jeune par son
illustre père, et élevé aux frais d'un roi quelconque, qui
lui fit passer les premières années de sa jeunesse à ramer
sur ses galères. C'est certainement sur ces mêmes galères
qu'il se retirera plus tard, car c'est le plus grand voleur
qu'on ait jamais vu. Il tient de son père le Capitan pour la
vanterie, la forfanterie et la poltronnerie Comme lui, il
est amoureux de toutes les femmes, mais son visage pâle

et sa mauvaise réputation lui font beaucoup de tort auprès du beau sexe. Il se venge des rebuffades en se vantant de faveurs illusoires et en médisant des femmes qu'il prétend avoir délaissées.

Malgré ses prétentions à la noblesse, car il se dit noble comme Charlemagne, et riche comme un autre de ses aïeux nommé Crésus, il est presque toujours valet d'un fort mince seigneur ou d'un pauvre bourgeois, qui l'emploie pour servir ses amours. Mais, au lieu de faire son devoir, il s'amuse à rosser le guet et à voler les passants. Son maître rentre souvent pour lui dans cette dernière catégorie. Enfin, Scaramouche est un vaurien qui ne se plaît que dans le désordre. S'il y a quelque coup à recevoir en payement de ses fourberies, il est assez leste pour procurer au voisin l'aubaine qui lui était destinée. Il s'entend assez bien avec Pulcinella, autre gaillard de son acabit. C'est alors que, bras dessus, bras dessous, l'un parlant fort et gesticulant brutalement, l'autre beuglant et sautant, faisant tournoyer son sabre autour des oreilles des passants, ils arpentent les promenades, lorgnant les mêmes femmes et désirant les mêmes bouteilles. Il est rare qu'une dispute n'arrive pas entre nos deux compères. Polichinelle se fâche, Scaramouche se cache. « Où est ce poltron, ce lâche? » crie Polichinelle en assommant les tables des coups de son gourdin noueux. La colère passée, Scaramouche revient et fait alors à son ami une réprimande en plusieurs points sur les mauvais penchants, l'irascibilité, l'ivrognerie, l'égoïsme; discours plein de sens et de morale, que Polichinelle écoute d'un air distrait en se frottant la bosse. La plupart du temps, il ne l'écoute même pas du tout. car il n'a aucune estime pour ce poltron. Mais tout finit par des libations, et c'est le verre en main, le cerveau un peu échauffé, que Scaramouche donne carrière à sa brillante imagination. Il raconte alors tous ses exploits galants à Polichinelle, qui ne l'interrompt que par des exclamations de surprise admirative, ou de petits ricanements goguenards qui indiquent son incrédulité.

Mais tout à coup pots, verres et bouteilles volent en éclats : c'est Polichinelle qui, ennuyé des hâbleries de Scaramouche, a fait tout ce bris d'un revers de trique pour rompre la conversation, puis il se lève et, sans payer son écot, sort en ricanant.

Scaramouche s'est caché, et ne se montre plus que lorsque son camarade est fort loin. « Quel âne! » dit-il, » quel butor! des manières de rustre! La première fois, je le corrigerai d'importance; je lui tirerai les oreilles. » Sur la remarque d'un tiers, qui l'accuse d'avoir eu peur, il répond comme Panurge : « Peur? moi! j'ai du courage beaucoup, voire! De peur, bien peu; du courage, tant et plus · je n'entends pas courage de brebis, je dis courage de loup, bien plus, de meurtrier. »

Scaramouche est comme le franc archer de Bagnolet, « il ne craint rien que les dangers »

Tiberio Fiurelli naquit à Naples le 7 novembre 1608. Quoique fils d'un capitaine de cavalerie, il était, à l'âge de vingt-cinq ans, domestique de la première actrice d'une troupe alors en réputation à Naples. Il était ce qu'on appelait *gagiste,* et jouait de temps en temps de petits rôles.

Un jour, la blanchisseuse de la comédienne dit à Fiurelli que la meilleure amie de sa fille allait se marier, et elle l'invita aux noces comme garçon d'humeur joviale, sa fille devant être la demoiselle d'honneur de la mariée. La noce fut brillante · on but, on dansa beaucoup, Fiurelli surtout mangea comme deux et but comme quatre. Si bien que, au milieu des danses et des sauts, poussé par un transport amoureux où le vin n'était pas pour peu de chose, il embrassa fort vivement, et malgré sa résistance, la demoiselle d'honneur. C'était une insulte grave, surtout en public, et qui ne pouvait se réparer que par le mariage.

Dès le lendemain, la blanchisseuse, ayant réuni des témoins et les membres de sa famille, vint réclamer justice auprès de la maîtresse de Fiurelli. Lui de comparaître, et de ne rien répondre à cette scène, il ne se rappelait plus rien de ce qui s'était passé la veille La blanchisseuse lui ayant remémoré le tout, elle le menaça de porter ses plaintes devant la justice, s'il ne réparait sa faute et ne satisfaisait pas l'honneur de la famille Ayant pris conseil de l'actrice qu'il servait, il se décida à épouser la jeune blanchisseuse, qui était fort jolie, ce qui ne gâtait rien.

Quelque temps après leurs noces, Fiurelli et sa femme entrèrent dans une troupe de comédiens. Madame Fiurelli prit le nom de *Marinette,* qui était probablement le sien, car avant elle il n'est pas question de soubrettes de ce nom, lui prit celui de Scaramouche. Angelo Constantini, auteur de *la Vie, amours et actions de Scaramouche,* dit que Fiurelli fut le créateur de ce type; mais il fait erreur ici, comme dans bien d'autres passages de cette biographie Évariste Ghe-

rardi tance vertement Constantini à propos de cet ouvrage. « Que ceux, » dit-il, « qui ont parlé si indignement
» de Fiurelli, et qui se sont servis de son nom pour donner
» du débit à une infinité de quolibets et de mauvaises plaisan-
» teries, rougissent et viennent, la torche au poing, faire
» réparation aux mânes d'un si grand homme, s'ils veulent
» éviter le châtiment que leurs impostures méritent et
» devant Dieu et devant les hommes Il n'est rien de plus
» impie que de déterrer un homme pour le couvrir de
» calomnie. »

La nature l'avait doué merveilleusement, car il fut
bientôt connu dans toute l'Italie comme le mime le plus
spirituel et le plus parfait qui eût jamais existé.

Après avoir parcouru plusieurs grandes villes d'Italie, il
vint à Paris avec une troupe, sous le règne de Louis XIII,
en 1640, et il n'y eut pas moins de succès.

La reine se plaisait beaucoup à lui voir faire des grimaces. Un jour que lui et Brigida Bianchi, actrice connue
sous le nom d'*Aurelia*, étaient dans la chambre du Dauphin
(depuis Louis XIV), le prince, qui avait alors deux ans,
était de si mauvaise humeur que rien ne pouvait apaiser
sa colère et ses cris, Scaramouche dit à la reine que, si elle
voulait lui permettre de prendre l'enfant royal dans ses
bras, il se chargeait de le calmer. La reine l'ayant permis,
il fit alors tant de grimaces, tant de singeries bizarres, que
non-seulement l'enfant cessa de pleurer, mais encore qu'il
fut pris d'une hilarité dont les résultats gâtèrent les habits
de Scaramouche, aux grands éclats de rire de toutes les
dames et seigneurs présents à cette scène.

Depuis ce jour, Scaramouche reçut l'ordre de se rendre
tous les soirs auprès du Dauphin afin de l'amuser, « avec
son chien, son chat, son singe, sa guitare et son perroquet. » Scaramouche pouvait avoir alors trente-trois ans;
aussi fut-il toujours appelé particulièrement à Paris toutes
les fois qu'on y fit venir quelque troupe italienne. Bien des
années après, Louis XIV prenait plaisir à rappeler à Fiurelli leur première entrevue, et le grand roi riait beaucoup
en lui voyant mimer le récit de l'aventure.

Dans le scenario de *Colombine avocat pour et contre*, Gherardi dit au sujet de Scaramouche :

« Après avoir raccommodé tout ce qu'il y a dans la
» chambre, il prend sa guitare, s'assied sur un fauteuil,
» et joue en attendant que son maître arrive : Pascariel
» vient tout doucement derrière lui, et, par-dessus ses
» épaules, bat la mesure, ce qui épouvante terriblement
» Scaramouche. En un mot, c'est ici que cet incomparable
» Scaramuccia, qui a été l'ornement du théâtre et le mo-
» dèle des plus illustres comédiens de son temps, qui
» avaient appris de lui cet art si difficile et si nécessaire
» aux personnes de leur *caractère*, de remuer les passions
» et de les savoir bien peindre sur le visage, c'est, dis-je,
» où il faisait pâmer de rire, pendant un gros quart
» d'heure, dans une scène d'épouvante, où il ne proférait
» pas un seul mot. Il faut convenir aussi que cet excellent
» acteur possédait à un si haut degré de perfection ce mer-
» veilleux talent, qu'il touchait plus de cœurs par les seules
» simplicités d'une pure nature, que n'en touchent d'ordi-
» naire les orateurs les plus habiles par les charmes de la

» rhétorique la plus persuasive. Ce qui fit dire un jour à
» un grand prince qui le voyait jouer à Rome : « Scara-
» muccia ne parle point et dit les plus belles choses du
» monde. » Et pour lui marquer l'estime qu'il faisait de
» lui, la comédie étant finie, il le manda et lui fit présent
» du carrosse à six chevaux dans lequel il l'avait envoyé
» quérir. Il a toujours été les délices de tous les princes
» qui l'ont connu, et notre invincible monarque ne s'e t
» jamais lassé de lui faire quelque grâce J'ose même me
» persuader que, s'il n'était pas mort, la troupe serait
» encore sur pied. »

Loret dit quelque part, en parlant de Fiurelli :

> « C'est un comique sans pareil
> Comme le ciel n'eut qu'un soleil,
> La terre n'eut qu'un Scaramouche
> Alors qu'il vivait parmi nous,
> Il eut le don de plaire à tous,
> Mais bien plus aux grands qu'aux gens minces,
> Et l'on le nommait en tous lieux
> Le prince des facétieux
> Et le facétieux des princes. »

En 1659, pendant un voyage de Scaramouche en Italie,
le bruit avait couru qu'en traversant le Rhône Fiurelli
avait fait naufrage et s'était noyé. Loret célébra l'aventure
en style de complainte.

> « A péri vers les bords du Rhône,
> Par un torrent d'eau imprévu,
> Qui le prenant au dépourvu,
> Dans une vallée ou fondrière,
> Lui fit perdre vie et lumière »

Fiurelli faisait de fréquents voyages en Italie pour aller voir sa femme Marinette. Le dernier qu'il fit fut assez long : il resta sept ans absent, et ne revint à Paris qu'après la mort de sa femme. Il s'y établit et resta au théâtre jusqu'à l'âge de quatre-vingt-trois ans. S'étant retiré alors, il devint amoureux d'une jeune personne nommée mademoiselle Duval, grande, bien faite et fort jolie, fille d'un domestique du premier président de Harlay. Il la demanda en mariage et l'épousa.

Les premiers mois de la lune de miel se passèrent tranquillement, mais l'humeur jalouse et avare de Fiurelli se dévoila bientôt. Après tout, il avait peut-être raison de soupçonner et de se plaindre. Il y avait trop de différence d'âge entre les époux, et la jeune femme était coquette. Scaramouche voulut user de ses droits et de son autorité : mais la jeune dame ne voulut pas souffrir les leçons et corrections, elle se retira chez ses parents et lui intenta un procès en séparation de corps et de biens. Fiurelli, de son côté, l'accusa d'infidélité et demanda qu'elle fût rasée et enfermée dans un couvent. Cette affaire fit beaucoup de bruit, et quatre ans se passèrent à instruire ce procès. Ce fut pendant l'instruction que Fiurelli mourut, le 7 décembre 1696, âgé de quatre-vingt-huit ans.

A quatre-vingt-trois ans, il avait encore tant d'agilité que, dans ses scènes de pantomime, il donnait un soufflet avec le pied. Il joignait à une taille avantageuse une souplesse de corps, une légèreté et une force extraordinaires

On sait que Molière professa toujours pour Tiberio Fiu-

relli une admiration sans bornes. On a dit et on a raison
de croire que l'incomparable Scaramouche décida de la
vocation de l'illustre enfant qui, conduit par son grand-
père, allait le voir jouer, et qui embrassa dès lors l'idée du
théâtre avec transport. On a rapporté aussi que Molière
s'était, en tant qu'acteur comique, efforcé toujours d'imiter
les Italiens, Trivelin en particulier, mais par-dessus tout
Scaramouche. Il est bien avéré que Molière a été *Italien*
dans sa manière, et comme auteur et comme comédien,
avant d'être Français; qu'il a puisé ses premiers essais,
non-seulement ses canevas inédits, mais encore plusieurs
de ses pièces écrites, dans le répertoire italien, et que les
deux troupes jouèrent de son temps les mêmes sujets sur le
même théâtre, sans que les Italiens missent de l'affectation
à en revendiquer la priorité, et sans que Molière songeât
à la leur contester. Au reste, les emprunts devinrent réci-
proques, témoin le *Scaramouche ermite* qui eut du succès
à la cour, tandis qu'on s'y indignait contre *Tartuffe*.

On lit, au bas d'un portrait de Fiurelli, représenté en
costume de Scaramouche :

TIBERE FIORILLI, dit Scaramouche, *le grand original des
théâtres modernes.*

> « Cet illustre comédien
> Atteignit de son art l'agréable manière
> Il fut le maître de Molière,
> Et la nature fut le sien »

Voyons-le agir dans plusieurs scènes tout italiennes du
recueil de Gherardi

Le théâtre représente une rue. — *Il fait nuit.*

« Scaramouche (arrive seul d'un côté du théâtre, sans voir Pierrot et Mezzetin). Les puces m'ont éveillé plus matin que je ne voulais; et comme je ne puis plus dormir, j'ai envie de me réjouir avec ma guitare. »

Mezzetin, qui, dans la scène précédente avait déjà chanté un couplet avec Pierrot, sous les fenêtres de sa maîtresse, demande à Pierrot s'il veut en recommencer un autre.

A ce moment, Scaramouche pousse un soupir énorme.

« Pierrot *à Mezzetin*. Mezzetin?

Mezzetin. Hein, que veux-tu?

Pierrot. Je crois, mordieu! que ma maîtresse vient de soupirer. »

Scaramouche imite un certain bruit avec la bouche.

Mezzetin dit à Pierrot que sa maîtresse a l'haleine mauvaise. Après quoi, ils cherchent d'où vient ce bruit et finissent par trouver et reconnaître Scaramouche, et ils se mettent tous trois à jouer de la guitare sous les fenêtres de la belle.

Octave, après avoir donné rendez-vous à sa maîtresse Angélique dans les Tuileries, veut lui donner une collation galante pour la surprendre agréablement. Il prie Scaramouche d'y penser et s'en va. Scaramouche reste sur le théâtre et se met à rêver. Arrive Arlequin, auquel il propose de réfléchir à ce *moyen*, mais sans lui dire de quoi il s'agit. Les voilà tous deux se promenant sur le théâtre, la tête dans les mains, et revenant de temps en temps l'un auprès de l'autre, en disant . « Ma foi! je le tiens. » Ils s'en retournent, puis reviennent. « Non, cela ne vaudrait rien. » Et de recommencer leurs allées et venues sans rien dire. Tout d'un coup ils se rencontrent, et Scaramouche dit : « Oh! cela ne peut manquer de réussir! » Sur quoi, ils s'en vont, sans s'être autrement expliqués.

Autre scène : « Cinthio (s'approchant de Scaramouche): *Come vi chiamate?* (Comment vous appelez-vous?)

Scaramouche. Comment je m'appelle?

Cinthio. *Si, il vostro nome, qual è* (Oui, votre nom, quel est-il?)

Scaramouche *Il mio nome, signor, è.* (Mon nom, monsieur, est) Scaramuzza, Memeo Squaquara, Tammera, Catambera, *e figlio di* (et fils de) Cocumaro et de *madona* Papara trent' ova, e iunze, e dunze, e tiracarunze, e Stacchete, Minofla, Scatoffa, Solfana, Befana, Caiorca [1], *per servire a vossignoria* (pour servir à Votre Seigneurie).

Cinthio. *O che bel nome! in verità, non si può far di più!* (Il tire sa bourse.) Tenez, voilà pour Scaramouche. Voici pour Memeo Squaquara. Voilà pour Tammera et Catambera. (*A chaque nom il lui donne un écu.*) Et le surplus de la bourse pour le restant de votre nom.

Scaramouche *à part.* C'est quelqu'un qui va à la chasse aux noms. (*Vers Cinthio*) Monsieur, j'ai encore d'autres noms dans ma famille, aussi beaux et aussi longs que le mien. Si vous en avez affaire, vous n'avez qu'à parler? »

---

[1] Il serait curieux de savoir si tous ces noms burlesques sont une improvisation gratuite de Scaramouche, ou si tous n'appartiennent pas aux archives perdues de la *Commedia dell' arte*, comme *Memeo Squaquara*, qui est un des danseurs de Callot, une sorte de Pasquariello. Quant à *Befana*, tout le monde sait que c'est un être fantastique dont on annonce les châtiments et les récompenses aux enfants, comme chez nous le *Croquemitaine*.

Scaramouche, ayant entendu dire qu'on avait décrété d'arrestation Arlequin, son maître, sous le nom d'emprunt de marquis de Sbrufadelli, s'habille en femme pour se cacher et se sauver. Arlequin le rencontre et dit : « Ah! ah! voici quelque demoiselle du pont Neuf. Bonjour, madame, votre serviteur!

SCARAMOUCHE. Monsieur, enseignez-moi, s'il vous plaît, le chemin de la Grève?

ARLEQUIN *d'un ton railleur*. Vous n'avez qu'à suivre comme vous avez commencé.... Vous n'avez qu'à continuer toujours le même chemin, vous y arriverez tout droit.

SCARAMOUCHE. Je m'en vais donc vitement, car j'appréhende de n'y pas trouver place.

ARLEQUIN. Vous n'avez que faire de vous tant presser, il y en aura toujours pour vous.

SCARAMOUCHE. Dame, monsieur, c'est qu'on y va pendre le marquis de Sbrufadelli, qui est, dit-on, le plus drôle de corps du monde, et chacun s'empresse pour le voir.

ARLEQUIN *fâché*. Ceux qui vous ont dit cela sont des malappris. Le marquis de Sbrufadelli est homme d'honneur, et il ne sera pas pendu, entendez-vous?

SCARAMOUCHE. Je vous dis, moi, qu'il le sera, et qu'il faut absolument qu'il le soit; toutes les fenêtres sont déjà retenues!

ARLEQUIN. Belle nécessité! pendre un homme parce que les fenêtres sont retenues! Allez, madame, vous ne savez ce que vous dites.

SCARAMOUCHE. Que cela sera joli! je meurs d'envie de le voir. Il a épousé deux femmes, et on lui mettra deux quenouilles à ses côtés. La jolie chose à voir! mon Dieu, que ce sera drole!

ARLEQUIN. A la fin, je perdrai patience. Quelle insolente masque est-ce là? Je vous dis, encore un coup, que je connais le marquis de Sbrufadelli, et....

SCARAMOUCHE *se faisant connaître.* Et moi aussi je le connais.

ARLEQUIN. Scaramouche?

SCARAMOUCHE. Oui, monsieur! Je me suis déguisé de la sorte, parce que je sais que le Docteur vous cherche pour vous mettre en prison. Il est à la tête de vingt archers, et je serais fâché qu'on m'obligeât à vous tenir compagnie. Vous savez que je ne trempe point dans votre affaire, et que cela ne vous serait point arrivé si vous eussiez suivi mes conseils.

ARLEQUIN. Il n'est pas temps de moraliser . .

SCARAMOUCHE. Ah! monsieur, vous avez trop attendu, nous sommes perdus. Voici le Docteur qui vient »

En effet, on entend venir les archers et le Docteur. Arlequin, ne sachant où s'enfuir, où se cacher, se fourre sous les jupons de Scaramouche. Le Docteur est furieux, il cherche Arlequin et se trouve vis-à-vis de Scaramouche. Il lui souhaite le bonjour d'un air grognon, et, le voyant se tenir de travers et se plaindre, lui demande ce qu'il a.

« SCARAMOUCHE. Je suis grosse, monsieur, fort éloignée de chez moi, et je sens des douleurs insupportables.

LE DOCTEUR. Voilà qui est fâcheux! il faudrait pourtant bien tâcher de vous retirer d'ici, parce que je guette un certain homme que je veux faire arrêter, et, s'il venait à passer, les archers pourraient peut-être vous blesser. Dans le tumulte, on ne prend pas garde à ce qu'on fait.

SCARAMOUCHE. Et comment l'appelez-vous, monsieur, celui que vous voulez faire prendre?

LE DOCTEUR. Il s'appelle le marquis de Sbrufadelli.

ARLEQUIN *sortant sa tête de dessous les jupes.* Le marquis de Sbrufadelli, monsieur? Le marquis de Sbrufadelli est parti!

LE DOCTEUR *entendant la voix et ne voyant personne.* Qui est-ce qui parle là?

SCARAMOUCHE. C'est mon fils, monsieur, qui est dans mon ventre. (*Bas à Arlequin.*) Tais-toi, animal! tu te feras découvrir.

LE DOCTEUR *soupçonnant.* C'est votre fils que vous avez dans le ventre? Il est donc bien nourri, ce fils-là?

SCARAMOUCHE. Oh! monsieur, c'est qu'à mes enfants je n'ai jamais épargné l'étoffe.

LE DOCTEUR. Je le vois bien, puisqu'ils parlent avant que d'être venus au monde. (*Parlant au ventre de Scaramouche.*) Monsieur l'enfant, vous dites donc que le marquis de Sbrufadelli est parti?

ARLEQUIN *sortant sa tête.* Oui, monsieur, il est parti en poste. Quand on a dit une chose une fois, cela doit suffire.

LE DOCTEUR. Cela est vrai, monsieur. Je vous demande pardon de mon importunité. (*Aux archers.*) Caporal Simon! prenez-moi cet enfant-là, et me l'emmenez en prison tout à l'heure. C'est un petit débauché dès le ventre de sa mère, il faut le mettre à la correction. »

Les archers prennent Arlequin et le houspillent; Scaramouche se sauve en criant : « *Salva! salva!* »

Quand Tiberio Fiurelli se retira du Théâtre-Italien, en 1694, les rôles de Scaramouche furent remplis par Joseph Tortoretti, et qui avait joué les Pascariel jusque-là.

PASQUARIELLO.

« Le jour où Pasquariel vint au monde, les chats volèrent le rôti, la chandelle pâlit par trois fois, le vin tourna dans la cave, et, par un prodige incroyable, la marmite se répandit dans les cendres Mauvais pronostics! Aussi fut-il toujours gourmand, ivrogne et casseur, la ruine des cabarets et la terreur des cuisines. ».

Ce nom de Pascariel, ou Pasquariel comme l'écrit Gherardi, doit être un diminutif de Pasquin, cet emblème satirique des Romains.

Au seizième siècle, Pasquariello, Italien, était un danseur, un faiseur de tours de force, ainsi que Meo Squaquara, dont Scaramouche prétend descendre. Ces personnages ont été représentés par Callot Ils sont vêtus d'habits collants, ont des grelots aux jambes, portent le sabre et le *tabaro*, le masque au nez fantastiquement long, mais ils ne paraissent pas avoir de coiffure. Meo Squaquara surtout semble avoir le crâne fort dénudé. Pasquariello porte le surnom de *Truonno*, c'est-à-dire le Terrible. Ce type ne vint en France qu'en 1685; il y fut apporté par Giuseppe Tortoretti ou Tortoriti, et, comme ses aïeux, il fut surtout danseur et fort adroit équilibriste C'est toujours un rôle de valet.

Le *Mercure galant* du mois de mars 1685 dit : « La troupe italienne est augmentée d'un acteur nouveau, qui

» attire les applaudissements de tout Paris et qui n'a pas
» moins plu à la cour. Il a une agilité de corps surpre-
» nante, et seconde admirablement l'incomparable Arle-
» quin. » Mais, malgré les heureux débuts de Pasquariel,
cet acteur ne fut jamais que médiocre, et la plus grande
partie de son talent consistait dans la souplesse de ses membres Son type est une doublure de Scaramouche, qu'il
remplaça, du reste, dans la troupe italienne, après la mort
de Tiberio Fiurelli, en 1694.

Après la suppression du Théâtre-Italien (1697), J. Tortoretti (*Pasquariello*), obtint du roi un privilége pour
représenter dans toute la France les pièces de son répertoire, à condition néanmoins qu'il ne viendrait pas jouer
avec sa troupe en deçà de trente lieues de Paris.

Il composa donc une troupe et courut la province, mais
il fit de très-mauvaises affaires et mourut dans la misère.
J. Tortoretti avait épousé, en Italie, Angélique Toscano,
connue au Théâtre-Italien sous le nom de *Marinette;* elle
l'avait suivi en province, et elle partagea son mauvais sort.

Pasquariel est à peu près vêtu comme Scaramouche,
seulement il n'a pas toujours la toque et le manteau; il
remplace le drap par du velours noir, et porte parfois des
bas rouges (*planche* 44). Sa mise simple et sévère lui permet
de jouer les mêmes rôles que Scaramouche, et de remplacer
Scapin sous le nom de Pasquin.

C'est surtout dans *l'Avocat pour et contre* que Pasquariel
a un rôle important; c'est lui qui conduit l'intrigue de la
pièce . il vient à chaque instant épouvanter Arlequin,
qui est devenu grand seigneur, et son valet Scaramouche.

Tantôt il paraît en Capitan, pour forcer Arlequin d'épouser sa parente Colombine qu'il a trompée. Tantôt en danseur, en Maure, en diable, puis en peintre, car Arlequin a demandé un peintre pour faire faire son portrait.

Pasquariel entre. Il a endossé une subreveste toute couverte de taches et de couleurs; il marche tout de travers avec des béquilles, et les yeux presque fermés sous une visière verte. « Qu'est-ce que c'est que ça? demande Arlequin; c'est le peintre des invalides! Il est paralytique, et va me peindre tout de travers. » Pasquariel veut ôter son chapeau pour saluer le marquis Arlecchino, mais il tremble tellement qu'à un mouvement mal combiné les béquilles ne pouvant plus le soutenir, l'une glisse en avant, le peintre fléchit d'un côté, l'autre béquille glisse en arrière, et il tombe sur Arlequin qui tombe aussi. Tout en tombant, ce peintre poli lui souhaite le bonjour et se dit son serviteur.

Arlequin, tout estropié, se fait aider par Pierrot pour relever le peintre, et lui dit « Sans compliments, monsieur, allez-vous-en mourir auparavant et vous reviendrez après achever mon portrait. »

Mais Pasquariel ou plutôt le peintre est sourd, car sans se déconcerter davantage, il s'assied, met d'énormes lunettes sur son nez, et après avoir mêlé quelques couleurs sur sa palette avec un pinceau qui ressemble plutôt à un balai, il barbouille la figure de Pierrot qui était devant lui, la bouche ouverte, à le regarder triturer son rouge et son noir. Pierrot pleure et s'en va. Arlequin se fâche. Le peintre ne répond rien, il regarde Arlequin, et, le pinceau d'une main, la palette de l'autre, il se traîne à genoux vers Arlequin, qui, effrayé, lui demande ce qu'il va faire. « Je vais peindre *Vosignorie* », répond Pasquariel. Mais Arlequin lui fait remarquer que la toile est de l'autre côté. Le peintre se lève, veut se tourner vers sa toile, mais le pied lui manque et il tombe par terre, tout de son long. Arlequin s'écrie : « Ah ! voilà un peintre cassé ! Il me faudra payer un peintre¹ » Cependant Pasquariel se relève, et veut prendre congé pour s'en aller. Il recommence à balancer sur ses jambes, et se laisse choir sur Arlequin qui, poussé à l'improviste, tombe encore. Pasquariel tombe par-dessus en se faisant le plus lourd possible. Après quoi il se relève et s'en va poursuivi par les malédictions d'Arlequin.

Dans un autre scenario, *la Précaution inutile*, Pasquariel est valet : il a été mis de faction avec Pierrot à la porte d'Isabelle et il leur est expressément ordonné de ne pas laisser passer de billets doux. Un papillon vient voltiger devant la porte de la maison · aussitôt Pasquariel de lever le nez et de faire remarquer à Pierrot que c'est peut-être un messager d'amour qui vient apporter une lettre. Pierrot pense absolument de même. Alors voilà une chasse qui s'établit, il s'agit de le prendre pour saisir les papiers qu'il a sur lui. Ce sont des bonds, des sauts, l'un monte sur les épaules de l'autre pour l'atteindre ; mais le papillon vole toujours de plus en plus haut. Tous les deux, le nez en l'air, lui jetant leurs chapeaux, finissent par se rencontrer, et du même choc s'en vont rouler tous deux par terre.

Dans *le Grand Sophy*, Pasquariel, valet d'Octave, dit à Mezzetin : « Tu ne seras pas plutôt capitaine de dragons, que les plaisirs, la bombance et la bonne chère te suivront par tout; jamais de chagrins, jamais de tristesse, toujours en joie. Quelle félicité, morbleu! que tu es heureux! Tu reçois l'ordre de partir pour l'armée. Aussitôt tu prends la poste, et le long de ta route, les perdrix, les bécasses, les ortolans, voilà ton manger ordinaire. Goûte-moi de ce vin-là! (*Il fait semblant de déboucher une bouteille, et de verser du vin dans un verre, Mezzetin ouvre la bouche pour recevoir le vin que Pasquariel feint de verser.*) Eh bien, qu'en dis-tu? C'est le moindre de tous les vins que tu boiras en chemin. Te voilà arrivé au camp. D'abord on te donne un fort bel appartement tout de plain-pied.

MEZZETIN. Tant mieux, car je n'aime point à monter. Je prends cela pour un mauvais augure.

PASQUARIEL. Quantité d'officiers t'y viennent rendre visite. On joue, on fume, on chante, on boit des liqueurs

MEZZETIN Comment, diable! voilà une vie de chanoine! Et on disait qu'on avait tant de mal à la guerre?

PASQUARIEL. Bon, bon! Ce sont les gens qui n'y ont jamais été qui en parlent mal L'ennemi cependant s'avance, et on ordonne au capitaine des dragons de l'aller reconnaître, c'est-à-dire savoir où il est campé, les mouvements qu'il fait, et le nombre des troupes qui composent son armée. Bon! il n'y a rien de si aisé. D'abord tu marcheras en fort bel ordre à la tête de la compagnie. Oh! il me semble déjà te voir à cheval. Quel air héroïque! quelle majesté! Tu rêves? tu secoues l'oreille?

MEZZETIN Oui, c'est que je sais combien il m'en cuit pour avoir été à cheval, et pourtant je n'étais monté que sur une bourrique! Mes épaules m'en font encore mal. Ne pourrions-nous pas retrancher cela?

PASQUARIEL. Vraiment nenni, c'est un honneur. Tu t'avances donc vers l'ennemi. Aussitôt qu'il te voit paraître, il détache une compagnie de carabiniers, pour venir au-devant de toi. Quand vous êtes à portée l'un de l'autre, vous commencez à vous saluer à grands coups de pistolet, zin! van! Le capitaine des carabiniers met le sabre à la main, court vers toi, et tac!

MEZZETIN. *Hanne!*

PASQUARIEL. Oh! ce n'est rien, ce n'est qu'un bras par terre.

MEZZETIN. Vous dites que ce n'est rien? Je trouve que c'est quelque chose, moi!

PASQUARIEL. Bon, bon! Voilà une *bagatelle*, ma foi! On écrit cette action-là en cour, et on te fait colonel d'un autre régiment. Le général fait ranger tout le monde en bataille, on vient aux mains, les ennemis font un feu de tous les diables, zi, zi! pi! pa! bon! ban! tac!

MEZZETIN. Ah! je suis perdu!... encore un tac!

PASQUARIEL. C'est un coup de grenade qui vient d'emporter une jambe à notre colonel. Mais cela, bagatelle!

MEZZETIN. Le diable m'emporte si je ne m'en suis pas douté quand j'ai entendu ce vilain tac!

PASQUARIEL. Que voulez-vous? Ce sont les fruits de la guerre. On vous fait panser, on publie votre nom dans la gazette et l'on vous fait brigadier d'armée.

MEZZETIN. Charge encore plus grande?

PASQUARIEL. La malepeste! je le crois! Tous les officiers viennent vous faire leurs compliments sur votre nouvelle charge et ils envient votre bonheur. Les ennemis se rallient et reviennent à la charge D'abord, mon brigadier d'armée court de tous côtés donner les ordres nécessaires. Le combat s'opiniâtre, l'ennemi est en déroute, on crie victoire, on poursuit les fuyards l'épée à la main Dans le moment, une batterie de douze pièces de canon, que les ennemis avaient postés sur une petite hauteur, fait sa décharge, bon! don! don! tac! tac!

MEZZETIN. Miséricorde! ah! je suis mort. Il y a deux tac!

PASQUARIEL. Il faut être bien malheureux! Quelle disgrâce! Notre pauvre brigadier a son autre jambe et son autre bras emportés d'un seul coup de canon.

MEZZETIN. Je n'en suis pas étonné, moi, les tac m'ont toujours été funestes. (*S'agenouillant à terre, ses deux bras derrière le dos*) Voici un joli homme!

PASQUARIEL. Il faut avoir patience, mon ami. Ce sont des marques de ta valeur. On en écrit de nouveau à la cour, et on te fait général, la plus belle charge de toutes

MEZZETIN. Je remarque une chose plus j'augmente en charges, et plus je diminue en membres.

PASQUARIEL. Dès que tu es général, tu montes à cheval.

MEZZETIN. Attendez, s'il vous plaît. Comment voulez-vous que je monte à cheval? je n'ai ni bras, ni jambes!

PASQUARIEL. Voilà une nouvelle occasion de te signaler. Les ennemis se sont engagés dans un mauvais poste, tu les y tiens enfermés et, après avoir donné tes ordres pour le combat, tu cours de tous côtés donner courage aux soldats.

MEZZETIN. Bon! je donnerai courage aux autres pendant que je mourrai de peur!

PASQUARIEL. Le combat se donne : de quel côté qu'on se tourne, on ne voit que meurtre et carnage ; les grenades, les bombes, les carcasses, les boulets, c'est une grêle de coups. Pif! paf! zin! zan! bon! don! don! tac!

MEZZETIN. Oh! nous y voilà!

PASQUARIEL. C'est un boulet qui vient d'emporter la tête du général.

MEZZETIN. Mais cela, bagatelle?

PASQUARIEL. Vous l'avez dit.

MEZZETIN. Je suis heureux de savoir quelle charge vous me donnez après cela?

PASQUARIEL. Mais dès que tu seras guéri de tes blessures, on fera la paix, et tu iras servir en Hongrie contre le Turc.

MEZZETIN. Quand je n'aurai ni bras, ni jambes, ni tête, j'irai servir en Hongrie? Eh! va-t'en au diable avec ta compagnie! Si jamais je me fais capitaine de dragons, je veux que tous les tac du monde tombent sur moi! » (*Il s'enfuit.*)

Dans *la Fausse Coquette*, il est encore valet et au service de je ne sais quel prince polonais, qui n'est autre qu'Octave. « Il vient avec un flambeau allumé, suivi d'un de ses amis qui tient une bouteille et un verre Et comme toute l'attention de Pasquariel est tournée du côté de la bouteille, il ne songe qu'à la vider, sans prendre garde à ce que son maître lui dit : ce qui fait qu'il ne répond jamais juste aux demandes du prince, qui, lassé de ses impertinences, l'observe attentivement, et le surprenant avec un verre à la main, lui donne un coup de pied dans le ventre et s'en va. Pasquariel tombe en arrière, fait la culbute sans renverser son verre de vin, se lève, le boit et sort en disant *Gran sventura di servire un giovane senza cervello!* (Quel malheur de servir un jeune homme sans cervelle!) »

Dans la troupe du Régent (1716), Giacopo Rauzzini était chargé de l'emploi des Scaramouches. D'après les frères Parfait, « c'était un intrus dans la troupe des comédiens italiens Cent pistoles qu'il donna à celui qui avait été chargé de la part de Riccoboni (*Lelio*) d'envoyer un bon Scaramouche, firent obtenir la préférence à Rauzzini, qui n'était qu'un très-médiocre comédien et qui avait été huissier de la vicairerie de Naples. Il aimait le jeu, le faste et la dépense; il avait pris un carrosse, tenu table ouverte, par conséquent fait beaucoup de dettes. Riccoboni le père fut obligé de solliciter un ordre de la cour, pour arrêter les poursuites des créanciers de son camarade, et, comme il était plein de probité, il obligea Rauzzini de leur céder les trois quarts de sa part : ce qui fut exécuté jusqu'à la mort de ce comédien, qu'une attaque d'apoplexie surprit dans l'église de Saint-Eustache, où il mourut le 24 octobre 1751, et fut enterré le lendemain aux frais de la troupe, qui se chargea de ses funérailles. »

En 1752, Bonaventure Benozzi débuta par les rôles de Scaramouche; il était frère de la célèbre Silvia.

En 1711, Cavé dit *Maillard* débuta à la foire Saint-Germain par les rôles de Scaramouche Il courut la province et n'entra pas au Théâtre-Italien. Un jour, à la foire Saint-Laurent, Maillard était dans la boutique de Dubois, le limonadier; sa femme, qui jouait les *Colombines*, passant pour aller au théâtre, lui dit bonjour d'un air amical et coquet

— Connaissez-vous, par hasard, cette jolie comédienne? demanda à Maillard un personnage qui se trouvait aussi dans la boutique.

— Eh! cadédis, répondit-il en affectant l'accent gascon, si je la connais?

> . . . . Au gré de mes désirs,
> J'ai goûté dans ses bras mille et mille plaisirs

— Touchez-là, lui dit le particulier, qui ne le connaissait pas; je puis vous en dire autant.

Maillard quitta son ton railleur pour apprendre à l'indiscret qu'il était le mari de la Colombine calomniée.

— Ma foi, reprit l'autre, je suis fâché d'avoir été si sincère; mais je ne puis me rétracter d'un fait certain.

C'est alors que Maillard se fâcha tout de bon, et demanda raison. Les épées furent tirées, Maillard fut blessé et désarmé. Son adversaire, l'ayant lui-même conduit chez un chirurgien, le quitta, en lui disant d'un air moqueur, et en faisant allusion à ces vers de la Fontaine sur les maris trompés :

> « Quand on le sait, c'est peu de chose
> Quand on l'ignore, ce n'est rien »

En 1745, Gandini débuta au Théâtre-Italien dans *la Vengeance de Scaramouche*, et fut reçu pour ce rôle.

> L'air, la mine, la gravité,
> Tout réjouit dans Scaramouche,
> Et chacun en est enchanté,
> Même avant qu'il ouvre la bouche

Carlo Agati et Bertinelli jouaient avec beaucoup de succès les rôles de Scaramouches, en Italie, vers 1715.

PASQUINO.

Pasquin est un valet intrigant, faisant de l'esprit, parlant beaucoup et mentant davantage. Sa réputation est détestable. C'est un brouillon qui dérange toutes les affaires auxquelles il met la main, même les siennes, car il s'amuse beaucoup trop à jaser avec les servantes. Il n'est cependant occupé que d'une seule chose au monde, c'est de son propre intérêt. Pasquin n'est qu'une nuance du type de Brighella, ou plutôt c'est le même personnage que Pasquariel.

« Pasquin (en voyageur). Ah! Fortune, Fortune! feras-tu toujours faire la pirouette aux pasquinades du malheureux Pasquin, et n'embourberas-tu jamais la roue de ton inconstance dans l'ornière de mon mérite? *Partito di Roma* à coups de pied au derrière, *son venuto tramando* la savate, d'hôtellerie en hôtellerie, n'ayant d'autre monnaie pour payer mon écot que de médire libéralement de ceux qui me donnaient à manger. Enfin j'arrive ici sans argent, mais avec une faim canine, sans pouvoir apaiser les murmures affamés de mes languissants boyaux.

» O vous, *cara Olivetta,* ma chère maîtresse, dont les gentillesses et les minauderies coquettes me faisaient si souvent trouver crédit dans les hôtelleries, vous deviez rétablir ma fortune. Mais comme tout est variable, votre beauté ne faisant plus que blanchir auprès de l'inhumanité des hôteliers, j'ai été obligé de vous laisser là pour les gages. Que diriez-vous, belle abandonnée, si vous voyiez le tendre Pasquin, le ventre aussi creux que la bourse, vous qui l'avez trouvé cent fois regorgeant de vin sur le pas de votre porte, comme sur un lit mollet dont les Amours auraient remué la paillasse? C'est là qu'en venant me relever, vous saviez distinguer avec tant d'adresse les hoquets de ma plénitude vineuse, d'avec les soupirs de mon ardent amour. Ouf! cuisine, retraite charmante et délicieuse! asile favorable autrefois à mon appétit, vous qui faites le séjour ordinaire de ma charmante Olivette! Heureuses et tranquilles marmites qui êtes écurées par ses belles mains! Broches, chaudrons, poêles et lèchefrites, instruments guerriers de la mâchoire, qui servez de trophée ordinaire à ma belle maîtresse! Hélas! *per pietà*, révoltez-vous contre tous les rôtis et les ragoûts dont vous êtes les causes secondes; et, par un cliquetis universel et harmonieusement funèbre, apprenez *alla mia cara Olivetta* qu'une faim désespérée est prête à rompre les ressorts du tourne-broche de ses inclinations. »

CRISPIN.

Le costume du Crispin de la comédie française, créé par Raymond Poisson, au milieu du dix-septième siècle, est emprunté au personnage de Scaramouche, surtout au Scaramouche napolitain, qui, à l'imitation du Capitan, porte la longue rapière avec la morgue et la couardise de ce personnage Ce type, devenu valet, dévoué selon les gages qu'il reçoit, flatteur, ivrogne, menteur et voleur comme Brighella, n'en est pas moins une création tout à fait française que nous devons à Poisson Nous mentionnons cette création comme une transformation de Scaramouche qui l'a inspirée. Ce type de Crispin fut bien vite admis sur les théâtres de la foire et figura dans les mêmes pièces que Mezzetin, Arlequin, Polichinelle, Scaramouche, Pantalon, et les autres types italiens. De création plus moderne, Crispin ne porte pas le masque. vêtu de noir, chaussé de bottes ou de bottines, il porte la fraise, les gants dits à la Crispin, la large ceinture de buffle et la rapière.

R. Poisson était un homme d'une assez grande taille, et bien fait. Quelques-uns disent qu'à son habillement de Crispin, il avait ajouté des bottines, parce qu'il avait les jambes menues, mais il y a plus d'apparence qu'il paraissait ainsi sur le théâtre parce que, dans sa jeunesse, les rues de Paris, dont à peine la moitié était pavée, obligeaient les gens de pied, et surtout les domestiques, à porter des bottes pour faire leurs courses.

Raymond Poisson, mourut en 1690.

Paul Poisson, son fils, né en 1658, mort en 1735

Philippe Poisson, son second fils, né en 1682, mort en 1743.

François-Arnoult Poisson, fils de Philippe, mort en 1753.

COVIELLO.

FRITELLINO, TABARINO, BURATTINO, CAVICCHIO, FICCHETO.

Callot a gravé une série de danseurs, bouffons, mimes et masques de l'ancienne comédie italienne, dans cette série que l'on nomme *les Petits Danseurs*, mais dont le vrai titre est : *I Balli di Sfessania*, comme qui dirait *les Danses fescenniennes*. Tout le monde sait que, dans l'antiquité, les habitants de Fescennia, dont les ruines se voient encore à un quart de lieue de Galesa (Piémont), inventèrent des espèces de vers, qui eurent une si grande vogue à Rome, et où la satire, unie à une grossièreté primitive, disait les choses par leur nom. Ces vers étaient remplis de railleries, de plaisanteries et de bouffonneries, accompagnées de danses grotesques, de postures libres et de scènes improvisées, absolument comme les atellanes, mais d'un

II   36 *bis*

comique plus trivial. Horace dit dans une épître adressée
à Auguste :

Fescennina per hunc inventa licentia morem
Versibus alternis, opprobria rustica fudit

« Les peuples de Fescennie, » dit le chevalier de Jau-
court, « accompagnaient leurs fêtes et leurs réjouissances
» publiques de représentations champêtres, où des baladins
» déclamaient des espèces de vers fort grossiers et faisaient
» mille bouffonneries dans le même goût.... Ces sortes de
» vers parurent sur le théâtre, et tinrent lieu aux Romains
» de drame régulier pendant plus de six vingt ans La
» satire mordante à laquelle on les employa les discrédita
» encore plus que leur grossièreté primitive, et pour lors
» ils devinrent véritablement redoutables ... Catulle voyant
» que les vers fescennins employés par la satire étaient
» proscrits par l'autorité publique, et que leur grossièreté
» n'était plus du goût de son siècle; les perfectionna et
» les châtia en apparence du côté de l'expression.... Mais
» ils n'en furent pas moins obscènes pour le sens et bien
» plus dangereux pour les mœurs. Les termes libres d'un
» soldat gâtent moins le cœur que les discours fins, ingé-
» nieux et délicatement tournés d'un homme qui fait le
» métier de la galanterie. »

Les acteurs fescenniens étaient encore appelés à Rome
Mimi septentrionis, bouffons du nord. Ils étaient nus ou
vêtus d'habits étroits, la ceinture entourée d'une écharpe
dont les bouts flottaient au vent. « La chaussure n'est qu'un
simple chausson, qui paraît n'avoir point de coutures; la

pointe au-dessus du talon remonte assez haut, et le devant se rabat sur les cordons qui le tiennent en état. » Ils dansaient en s'accompagnant d'espèce de castagnettes, assez peu différentes des *cliquettes* d'aujourd'hui.

C'est donc sous ce titre de *I Balli de Sfessania* que Callot a reproduit cette cinquantaine d'acteurs, danseurs et bouffons de la fin du seizième siècle et du commencement du dix-septième. Ce sont, pour la plupart, des personnages d'actualités, pris indifféremment dans les diverses troupes italiennes, comme les *Gelosi*, les *Accesi*, les *Fedeli*, etc , qui vinrent à Florence à l'époque où Callot y étudiait.

On pourrait diviser ces personnages italiens, dont les noms sont francisés, en deux classes bien distinctes par les habits qu'ils portent : celle des jongleurs, sauteurs, exclusivement danseurs ou mimes; et celle des bouffons, zanni, farceurs, acteurs jouant des rôles.

La première classe de ces mimes de Callot, coiffés de serre-tête, à l'instar des pantomimes antiques, ou de toques surmontées de longues plumes, portant le demi-masque au nez très-long et pointu, sans barbe, vêtus d'habits étroits, ornés d'un rang de gros boutons, rappellent par leurs costumes collants, la mode des fous et des bouffons de cour au quatorzième et au quinzième siècle. Ces personnages ne sont, pour la plupart, que des sauteurs aux poses disloquées, aux danses échevelées, équilibristes, avaleurs de sabres et faiseurs de tours de force. Ce sont les descendants des vrais *funambuli* et *acrobates* antiques, et, comme eux, phallophores.

Grâce à Callot, nous retrouvons parmi ces types perdus :

CURLO (*pirouette*) invitant à danser, avec une pose bizarre; GIAN-FRITELLO, qui le méprise, RATSA-DI-BOIO (*fils de bourreau*), se livrant à une danse pittoresque, tandis que plusieurs de ses pareils, se tenant par les mains, forment une ronde autour d'un SMARAOLO-CORNUTO, perché sur des échasses et jouant du tambour de basque, PASQUARILLLO-TRUONNO et MEO-SQUAQUARA, imitant par leurs gestes une sorte de *cancan*; ESCANGARATO et COCODRILIO, ainsi que BELLO-SGUARDO (*Bel-OEil*), portant des bracelets de grelots aux bras et aux jambes, RAZULLO grattant, comme son nom l'indique, sa guitare, au son de laquelle CUCURUCU (nom imitant le cri du coq), aux belles lunettes, prend des poses modestes CIUCIO-SGARRA (*le Petit-Vainqueur*) menaçant COTTO-FRANCISCO, qui tremble devant lui. BABEO (*le Maladroit*) et son ami CUCIBA, comme qui dirait cornichon; CARDONI, sorte de Pourceaugnac, poursuivi par MARAMAO, matassin en tablier. GRILLO, personnage estropié, contrefait, dont le nom veut dire extravagant, qualifié de Capitan, n'était cependant que valet dans la troupe des *Gelosi*, CUCORONGNA et PLUSNOVALIA, se déhanchant à qui mieux mieux, enfin, COVIELLO (*planche 45*), renommé par ses grimaces et son langage embrouillé.

Ce personnage, d'après Salvator Rosa (1615-1673), aurait été un des sept masques de l'ancienne *commedia dell' arte*. La description qu'il en fait prouve que, déjà de son temps, le costume du bouffon avait été transformé, et probablement par lui-même; car on sait que, sous le masque de Coviello, Salvator Rosa se fit applaudir de toute la ville de Rome dans un personnage de sa création, *il signor* FORMICA. Dans le conte d'Hoffmann intitulé *Salvator Rosa*, une agréable fiction se trouve mêlée à des détails de réalité historique sur les travestissements et transformations de Salvator.

Coviello est, selon Salvator, originaire de la Calabre; « son esprit est fin et subtil, il est rusé, adroit, souple, vaniteux Il a l'accent et le costume de son pays Veste et pantalon de velours noir, bordés de galons d'argent. Il porte un masque à joues cramoisies, au front et au nez noir. » Hormis le masque, rien de semblable dans le personnage de Callot, ni dans toute cette classe de baladins, aux poses extravagantes, aux vêtements collants et ridicules, garnis d'une rangée de gros boutons tout le long du ventre; à la tête empanachée, aux membres entourés de grelots pour rendre la danse bruyante à la manière des sauvages, au masque orné d'un nez en trompe d'éléphant, qui sautant ou cabriolant, qui raclant de la guitare ou de la mandoline, qui menaçant de son sabre de bois des ennemis invisibles.

Un vieux dicton italien dit d'un sot qui fait le fanfaron : « *C'è un Coviello.* » Molière, dans le *Bourgeois gentilhomme*, a fait de son Coviello un laquais dans le genre de Scapin, qui répète sinon mot pour mot ce que dit son maître, mais idée pour idée Coviello rappelle par ses manières et ses allures le *Trasone* de Térence. C'est un sot qui fait le bravache, disent les uns; c'est un rusé observateur, disent les autres. En réalité, c'est un type bien passé de mode. Au commencement de ce siècle, on le voyait encore parfois figurer dans quelques canevas de marionnettes; il remplissait alors un rôle semblable à ceux des Capitans. Son costume était aussi fort changé. le chapeau noir empanaché de trois plumes rouges, le pourpoint à crevés rouges et les chausses noires, la trousse rouge et jaune, le manteau rouge, les gants, les bottes à entonnoir, le baudrier et l'épée des Capitans. Son masque bizarre était même remplacé par un masque couleur de chair et orné de moustaches.

FRITELLINO.

La seconde classe de ces *danseurs* se compose de ces farceurs et bouffons qui rappellent Pulcinella par leurs guenilles amples et simples, se composant d'un large pantalon et d'une sorte de chemise serrée au-dessous des hanches par une ceinture, portant le sabre de bois et cet incomparable chapeau emplumé qui prend la forme d'une casquette démesurée, comme celui de Fritellino (*planche* 46). Ils ont aussi la barbe et le masque Tels sont représentés par Callot, au commencement du dix-septième siècle, Pulcinella, causant avec la signora Lucretia, Mezzetin, grattant de la guitare et se livrant aux plus beaux entrechats avec Riciulina (soubrette dans la troupe des *Gelosi*), Guatserio (valet dans la troupe des *Fedeli*) et Mestolino (*lourdaud*), l'un vis-à-vis de l'autre, et se faisant des grimaces, des *nibes*, comme dirait un enfant de Paris, Fricasso, aux vêtements troués, cherchant, l'épée à la main, son adversaire, auquel il a le soin de tourner le dos, Bagattino (*petit bateleur*), se moquant de Spessa-Monti,

qui, furieux, essaye de dégainer sa rapière rouillée au four-
reau, FRACASSO, le sabre de bois à la main, très-différent
ici de notre Fracasse français; GIAN-FARINA, s'escrimant de
sa batte, tout en dansant avec FRACISCHINA (la célèbre Silvia
Roncagli); BERNOVALLA, danseur et *tabourinem*; TRASTULO (*le
plaisant, l'amusant*), faisant une déclaration à la signora
LUCIA, qui lui fait baiser sa pantoufle. On retrouve ce personnage du bouffon de bas étage dans les comédies de
Goldoni; mais là il joue les rôles de valet sans importance.
SCAPINO, en discussion au sujet d'un flacon avec ZERBINO,
discussion qui se termine par un duel. FRANCA-TRIPPA et
FRITELLINO dansent en s'accompagnant, l'un de son sabre
de bois, l'autre d'une mandoline.

Franca-Trippa, dont le véritable nom était Gabriello di
Bologna, s'engagea dans la troupe des *Gelosi* en 1576,
pour y tenir l'emploi des *Zanni*; il vint en France en 1577,
et joua dans les canevas qui firent les délices de la cour
de Henri III, à Blois.

Le type de Fritellino, ou bien encore Gian-Fritello, a eu
en Italie, au seizième siècle, un succès égal à celui qu'Arlequin eut au siècle suivant.

En 1560, Pietro-Maria Cecchini, connu sous le nom de
Fritellino, jouait dans la troupe des *Accesi* les mêmes rôles
que l'Arlequin de la troupe des *Gelosi*, ainsi, dans les canevas d'*Arlequin maître d'amour, Arlequin valet étourdi*, le personnage d'Arlequin est remplacé par Fritellino.

Vers 1612, Cecchini fut appelé à la cour de Mathias,
empereur d'Allemagne. Il y eut une telle faveur et un tel
succès que l'empereur l'anoblit. Il publia, en 1614, à

Vicence, un petit traité : *Discorso intorno alle commedie, commedianti e spettatori,* qu'il dédia au marquis Clemente Sanezio, et une seconde édition, en 1616, au cardinal Borghèse

Quelques années plus tard, en France, le personnage de Fritellino, appelé alors Fritrlin et Fristrlin, remplit des rôles de valet dans les farces tabariniques.

« Piphagne est accordé à la senora Isabelle et fait part de sa joie à Tabarin . « *Allegressa! allegressa!* » dit-il, « vien kà ! Tabarin, vidis to com son disposto ?

Tabarin. Nous aurons de la pluie, voilà les crapauds qui sautent; l'amour lui trotte dans la tête comme les carpes en notre grenier. Ah! mon maître, vous venez de lâcher un soupir amoureux qui est bien puant[1]

Piphagne. Adesso Tabarin voglio far una dispensa, voglio far un banquetto, et convocar tutti li miei parenti.

Tabarin Bon! vous m'en faites venir l'eau à la bouche! Jamais vous ne vites un tel gosier. Il faut donc convoquer vos parents aux noces! Vous avez Michaut Croupière, Filipo Leschandé, Guillemin Tortu, Pierre l'Eventé, Nicaise Tripesausse Il n'en faut pas tant prier, afin que je puisse remplir mes boyaux; je voudrais être tout seul aux noces. »

« Lucas a peur d'être emprisonné; Francisquine, pour se débarrasser de lui, le fait enfermer dans un sac pour le cacher des sergents qui sont, dit-elle, à la porte. Fritelin, valet du capitaine Rodomont, apportait de la part de son maître un billet à Francisquine · « Voicy un poullet que je vous apporte de la part de mon maître. » Lucas réfléchit tout haut qu'il « serait volontiers content de sortir de son sac pour en manger. »

» Francisquine, voulant se moquer du maître et du valet, dit à Fritelin qu'elle entend venir son mari Tabarin : « Ah! nous sommes perdus s'il vous trouve ici. Vite! vite! cachez-vous dans ce sac; et de deux! » Elle vend alors ces deux sacs à Tabarin, qui allait chercher de la viande. Tabarin croit avoir acquis deux porcs. Isabelle et Piphagne demandent à voir la marchandise que Tabarin leur a achetée. Ils veulent de la viande fraîche, et disent à leur cuisinier Tabarin de s'assurer si les vers ne s'y sont point mis. Tabarin tire son large coutelas au moment où il tâte les râbles de ses deux porcs, tout en disant qu'il va les égorger. Lucas et Fritelin, épouvantés, parlent et crient au secours.

« PIPHAGNE. Oi mé! Quali miracole prodigio grandé qui paraissé!

LUCAS. Au meurtre! On me veut égorger! Je suis Lucas, et non pas un pourceau!

TABARIN. *Vade, sac à nois!* Teste non pas de ma vie, voilà un pourceau qui parle!

FRITELIN. Songez à moi, mes amis, je suis mort!

TABARIN. En voici encore un qui est dans le sac?

ISABELLE. Hay! hay! voilà pour me faire avorter. »

Tabarin court après ses pourceaux, et la farce finit par des coups de bâton.

Fritellino est vêtu d'habits amples en toile, coiffé de ce « mirrificque » chapeau que nous verrons, sous la main

de Tabarin, prendre des formes si variées. Il porte le
masque brun des mimes bergamasques, et le *Tabarino*
traditionnel de tous les *Zanni* du seizième siècle, ainsi que le
sabre de bois et l'escarcelle qui, toujours vide, joue un si
grand rôle dans son existence.

TABARINO.

En 1570, une troupe italienne parcourut la France, et
vint même à Paris représenter sur ses tréteaux des farces
et des comédies moitié en français, moitié en italien, voire
même en espagnol. C'était la troupe de Juan Ganassa. On
y voyait le Docteur avec sa robe noire, Pantalon avec ses
chausses rouges, Arlequin avec ses guenilles, le Capitan et
ses longues jambes, Pagliaccio faisait *la parade* et TABARINO
était le *Zanni*. Mais ce n'était pas encore le célèbre Tabarin
qui, une cinquantaine d'années plus tard, amassait la foule
avec son maître Mondor et jouait aussi des *farces* sur la
place Dauphine.

Ce Tabarino de 1570 devait probablement remplir des
emplois doubles, comme celui de valet et celui de père
ou de mari, comme beaucoup d'autres masques de la
comédie italienne.

Il existait, il y a encore quelques années, à Bologne, un
type qui est tombé aujourd'hui dans le domaine des marionnettes, et qui représentait le vieillard, sous le nom de TABA-
RINO ou *ser Tabarin*. C'est presque toujours un marchand
retiré, ignorant, commençant toutes ses phrases en italien,
mais, faute d'usage de cette langue, les terminant en dia-

lecte bolonais. Il est presque toujours père de *Colombina* et
allié au Docteur C'est le *Cassandre* ou le *Pantalon* bolonais
Il porte la perruque poudrée et à bourse, l'habit, la veste
et la culotte courte, couleur tabac, les bas rouges, par-
dessus la culotte, les souliers à boucles et le chapeau rond.
C'est toujours un vieillard de soixante ans.

A la fin du seizième siècle, un bouffon français s'appelait
encore *Tabary*.

Le plus célèbre des Tabarins, l'associé de l'Italien
Mondor, qui, de 1618 à 1650, désopila tout Paris, était,
selon les uns, d'origine italienne et né à Milan; selon
d'autres, il était Lorrain. Mais son véritable nom est resté
inconnu[1], il fut éclipsé par la gloire du nom patronymique Est-ce par hasard qu'il prit celui de TABARINO, comme
il aurait pu adopter celui de BURATTINO ou de CAVICCHIO,
deux autres types fort en vogue au seizième siècle? Ou
choisit-il de préférence le nom déjà connu qui, avec une
partie de la troupe de Juan Ganassa, avait déjà parcouru
la France?

Une autre troupe ambulante portant la dénomination de
comédiens de Tabarin, et conduite par un certain Tabarin,
parcourut aussi une partie de la France et de l'Allemagne
sous Louis XIV, en 1659. Cette troupe italienne se fixa
ensuite à Vienne, en Autriche.

TABARIN, dont le nom vient de *tabarro*, manteau, *tabarrino*,

---

[1] Peut-être son véritable nom était-il Begot, puisque sa femme, qui jouait
avec lui sous le nom de Francisquine, s'appelait Anne Begot Mais cela ne
serait pas une preuve, puisque l'on dit aussi que cette actrice n'était sa
femme que sur les tréteaux

petit manteau (on a dit par erreur que ce nom venait de
tambourin, *tabourin*), vint donc à Paris en 1618 et s'associa
avec le charlatan Mondor, qui, à l'exemple de tous les
charlatans du seizième siècle, monta un théâtre en plein
vent, sur lequel on jouait d'abord des parades pour
amasser la foule, après quoi on débitait la marchandise
avec force gaillardises et joyeux propos. C'est ainsi que
l'Italien Cabotino (probablement l'origine du mot *Cabo-
tin*, acteur ambulant) acquit une si grande réputation,
comme opérateur nomade, au seizième siècle. Il jouait
des balivernes sur canevas, débitait ses drogues pendant
les entr'actes et arrachait les dents à la fin de la représentation, le tout avec accompagnement de violes et de
flûtes Le nombre de ces charlatans directeurs de théâtre
est considérable : les plus célèbres furent Scarniccia au
siècle dernier, en Italie, Armando Niasi, sur la place du
Châtelet, à Paris, et Mondor, qui vint remplacer, en 1618,
sur la place Dauphine, Jacques May et Duhgnac, dont la
verve d'improvisation avait récréé depuis 1598 le badaud
peuple de Paris.

C'est en 1622 que Tabarin fut à l'apogée de sa gloire
La place Dauphine, théâtre de ses exploits, était trop
petite pour contenir les spectateurs qui venaient là bien
moins dans l'intention d'acheter ses onguents que pour y
rencontrer un préservatif contre la *mélancholie*.

M Paul de Saint-Victor a décrit ainsi le vieux Paris
du dix-septième siècle avec une verve et une tournure
très-originale « Le pont Neuf au dix-septième siècle, c'était
» le caravansérail de Paris Là campait toute une peuplade

» de mendiants, de bohèmes et de bateleurs : les sept péchés
» capitaux, depuis le ruffian jusqu'au rôtisseur, tenaient
» foire ouverte; là foisonnaient ces figures excentriques,
» dont les satires et les estampes nous ont laissé de si vifs
» portraits · raffinés tordant leurs moustaches, courtisanes
» en chaises à porteurs, médicastres trottant sur leurs
» mules, pédants balayant la crotte de leurs manteaux den-
» telés.... C'était là encore que l'on rencontrait prenant
» le vent des cuisines le poète crotté, avec ses yeux de
» chouette et sa barbe en feuille d'artichaut.

Vous le voyez sur le pont Neuf
Tout barbouillé d'un jaune d'œuf.
Depuis sept heures jusqu'à onze
Faire la cour au roi de bronze
Tous ceux qui le rencontrent là
Demandent Qu'est-ce que cela ?
L'un croit que c'est un loup-garou,
L'autre un vieux singe du Pérou,
Cestuy là que c'est une autruche

» Quel pandæmonium de Callot! Ici, deux duellistes s'em-
» brochent sur le trottoir, là, un arracheur de dents fouille
» avec des tenailles de bourreau dans la mâchoire d'un
» paysan qui hurle; ailleurs, un marchand de chiens de
» chasse fouette à tour de bras sa meute affamée, plus
» loin, les tire-laine dérobent la bourse des promeneurs, et
» les mendiants, traînant leurs béquilles sur le pavé dé-
» chaussé, s'accrochent aux portières des lourds carrosses
» et aux brancards des chaises à porteurs.
» Mais le roi de cette nouvelle Cour des Miracles, c'était

» Tabarin, le valet du charlatan Mondor. Leur glorieux
» tréteau se dressait sur la place Dauphine, et, pendant dix
» ans, le peuple de Paris fit cercle autour, avalant par
» mille bouches béantes les orviétans de l'empirique et les
» lazzi du bouffon C'était une affluence, une vogue, un suc-
» cès, dont peuvent donner l'idée ces jérémiades qu'un pam-
» phlétaire prête aux femmes de la rue Dauphine, furieuses
» de voir leurs maris débauchés par ce baladin » — « Mon
mary ne bouge de ce Tabrin Je suis tout le jour sans le
voir après cette belle farce; c'est qu'il faut aller jouer avec
d'autres desbauchez comme lui. Après avoir joué, il faut
aller à la taverne. — Tout le mal vient de ce beau chien de
Tabarin, ce n'est que depuis que ce bel homme est arrivé,
qu'on a esté contrainct de donner des arrests contre les
filles desbauchées. — Et d'où pensez-vous qu'estoit venue la
maladie de l'année passée, que de ce beau bouffon? On
seschouffoit tellement à ceste place Dauphine, que l'air
en estoit tout corrompu Et cela a esté cause que le roy a
tant demeuré hors de Paris, et qu'avons eu tant de pau-
vretés. Messieurs les médecins, chirurgiens et farmatiens
n'ont garde de l'avoir oublié »

En 1625, Tabarin alla faire une tournée en province,
et se retira en 1630, pour jouir paisiblement de la fortune
qu'il avait amassée Il acheta une terre féodale près Paris,
et y mourut fort peu de temps après son acquisition. Il y a
deux versions sur sa mort : l'une qu'il succomba dans une
gageure de cabaret où il s'agissait de boire démesurément;
l'autre qu'il fut tué à la chasse. Le fait est rapporté dans
un livre intitulé *Parlement nouveau, ou centurie interlinaire*

de devis facétieusement sérieux et sérieusement facétieux, par
Daniel Martin, 1657, et dont voici un passage.

« — Me pourriez-vous bien apprendre la raison pourquoi
on appelle charlatans tous triacleurs (marchands de thé-
riaque), distillateurs, arracheurs de dents, vendeurs de
poudre de serpents, d'onguents et de baumes par les places
des villes, sur une table, ou un banc, ou un eschaffaut?

» — Oui-dà, monsieur; ce mot charlatan est à dire
proprement un homme qui, par belles paroles, vend une
mauvaise marchandise, un enjauleur, un babillard de dro-
guiste, comme était à Paris, l'an 1625, un nommé Tabarin
et un Italien nommé Montdor, qui ayant fait dresser un
eschaffaut en l'isle du Palais, amassoient la populace par
leur musique de violons et farces qu'ils jouoient, après
quoy ils se mettoient sur la louange de leurs drogues et en
disoient tant de bien que le sot et badaud peuple, croyant
qu'elles guérissent de tous maux . et plusieurs autres, il y
avoit presse à qui jetteroit le plus tost son argent noué
dans le coin d'un mouchoir ou dans un gant, sur l'eschaffaut, pour avoir une petite bouette d'onguent, enveloppée
dans un billet imprimé, contenant l'usage d'ycelui et la
façon de s'en servir.

» — On m'a dit que ce bouffon devint en peu d'années
si riche de l'argent des fols, qu'il acheta une seignéurie près
Paris, dont il n'a guères longtemps jouy.

» — Pourquoy cela?

» — Parce que ses voisins, qui estoient gentilshommes de
bonne et ancienne maison, ne pouvant endurer un Pantalon ou embabouineur de badauds, un fol qui avec son

chapeau métamorphosé en mille sortes en avoit fait rire
tant d'autres, pour leur compagnon, le tuèrent un jour à
la chasse, à ce qu'on m'a dit.

» — Son maistre ne luy avoit pas bien appris le proverbe de son pays :

« *A cader va chi troppo sale.* »

« Tabarin eut une fin tragique, dit M. de Saint-Victor,
son tréteau l'avait enrichi; les lazzi que pendant dix ans
il avait jetés à la foule étaient revenus en pluie de doublons
dans son escarcelle. L'orgueil le tenta; il acheta une terre
féodale, s'y installa et fit le seigneur. Les gentillâtres des
environs s'indignèrent de ce voisinage, et, un jour, dans
une chasse, ils tuèrent le bouffon, comme un lièvre, au
coin d'un bois. — *Poor Yorick!* »

Mondor et Tabarin avaient plusieurs concurrents,
entre autres le sieur Hieronimo et son farceur *Galinette la*
Galina, puis Desiderio de Combes et son valet *Grattelard,*
qui avaient établi leur théâtre à l'entrée du pont Neuf.
Desiderio était laid et mal bâti, et jargonnait lourdement.

« Quant à de Combes, il est grossier et rustaud; il ne
sçait ny lire, ny escrire, ny parler, et le peu d'audience
qu'on luy donne le fait tenir, comme il est, pour le plus
ignorant ciarlatan et le plus effronté menteur qui ayt
jamais monté en banc. »

On lit aussi dans la *Troisiesme après-disnée du caquet de*
l'accouchée

« C'est peut-estre la bonne mine de Montdor qui luy fait
débiter sa marchandise si promptement .. Mais l'on n'en

peut pas dire autant de Desiderio des Combes, que l'on nomme charlatan, car il n'a pas bonne trongne. »

Le peuple admirait Tabarin, qui possédait si bien le génie de la farce, les gens de condition s'en amusaient. En voyant l'empressement qu'il excitait, on conçoit que des habitués de son théâtre eurent l'idée de recueillir ses *farces* et *joyeusetés*, à l'impromptu. Mais ils ne se firent point connaître. Un seul, un nommé Guillaume, est sorti de l'obscurité. Voici comment · « Il y a cinq ou six coquins (c'est Horten-
» sius qui parle dans la *Vraye histoire comique de Francion*,
» *en* 1668) qui gagnent leur vie à faire des romans, et il n'y
» a pas jusques à un mien cuistre, qui a servi les Jésuites
» depuis moy, qui s'amuse à barbouiller le papier. Son
» coup d'essai a esté le *Recueil des farces tabariniques*, qui a
» si longtemps retenti aux oreilles du cheval de bronze,
» livre de si bonne chance, qu'on en a vendu vingt mille
» exemplaires, au lieu qu'un bon livre à peine peut-on en
» vendre six cents.... Ce cuistre s'appelle *Guillaume*, en
» son surnom... Il a bien fait encore imprimer d'autres
» œuvres.... Mais tous ses livres ne sont propres qu'à en-
» tortiller des livres de beurre. »

Les œuvres complètes de Tabarin ne contiennent donc pas une seule ligne écrite par Tabarin ou par Mondor, puisque tout leur répertoire était improvisé, mais elles furent recueillies sous les inspirations de Tabarin.

« C'eust este perte estrange
Si, perdant Tabarin des yeux,
Nous eussions perdu le meslange
De ses devis facétieux

Perte d'autant plus regrettable,
Que ses discours sont précieux,
Discours autant recommandable
Qui se soient veus dessous les cieux.

Ce sont des marques eternelles
De la gloire de Tabarin,
Qu'il a gravées sur les aisles
De la Fortune et du Destin

Parmy ces rencontres jolies
Et ce dialogue plaisant,
Vous y trouverez des saillies
D'un homme lettré et savant

Si, par quelque belle rencontre,
L'un manifeste son pouvoir,
L'autre plus docte, fera monstre
De sa doctrine et son savoir

Tous deux peut-estre feront naistre,
En refeuilletant ces escrits,
Un désir en vous de cognestre
Et d'admirer leurs beaux esprits »

Ni les comédiens de l'hôtel de Bourgogne réunis, ni
Gaultier-Garguille assisté de Gros-Guillaume, en compagnie de dame Perrine, qui ont joué les plus fameuses farces
qu'on puisse désirer, ne purent jamais, pour les cinq sous
qu'ils prenaient à chaque spectateur, récréer et désopiler
leur public comme le fit Tabarin à lui tout seul, gratis,
et avec son seul chapeau. Car c'était un maître chapeau,
qui prenait toutes les formes imaginables; une véritable

matière première, *indifferens ad omnes formas* C'était la
première pièce de toute la boutique, la pierre d'assise du
théâtre. « Ce vénérable et mirobolant feutre gris venait
directement de la succession de Saturne. Ce dieu l'avait
porté le premier, non si large qu'il était alors, mais en
forme allongée. Il le portait alors qu'il vint en Italie,
fuyant la colère de Jupiter, et lui donna la forme pointue,
afin de se déguiser. Il n'y avait eu jusqu'alors que des chapeaux ronds comme celui de Mercure. C'est depuis ce jour,
dit son panégyriste, que l'on porta des chapeaux pointus à
l'espagnole. Saturne en fit cadeau à *Tabaron*, un ancêtre
de Tabarin, qui auparavant allait nu-tête. Il fut bien aise
de trouver cet expédient pour se garantir des ardeurs du
soleil; c'est de ce feutre qu'on tira l'invention des parasols.
Ce chapeau fut gardé de père en fils avec respect et religion, comme une sainte relique, en souvenir de Saturne,
qui le portait les jours ouvriers. Mais un Tabarin quelconque, de la race tabarinienne, négligent ou distrait,
le laissa égarer. Il fut trouvé et porté à Jupiter, qui, ne
concevant pas de plus beau présent à faire à son Mercure,
l'en gratifia comme étant le seul dieu qui se servit de chapeau. Mercure, vaniteux et sot, le donna à mettre en forme,
en fit une pyramide, puis lui attacha des ailes Mais, par
malheur, la première fois qu'il s'en servit, en prenant son
élan du ciel, le vent s'engouffra dedans, et il le perdit. On
dit qu'il ne voulut plus jamais porter de chapeaux de forme
haute. Janus, qui vivait, dit-on, en ce temps-là, fut si heureux
de la trouvaille qu'il s'en coiffa; mais, ayant deux visages
et la tête fort grosse, il le déforma complétement, et il resta

depuis large comme il est maintenant sur la tête de Tabarin. Janus le cachait sous le mont Aventin. Romulus, en
batissant Rome, le trouva, et il fut longtemps conservé au
Capitole. Il n'en sortait que pour figurer dans les triomphes
des empereurs quand, chargés de dépouilles et de trophées,
ils rentraient à Rome. Les grands sacrificateurs étaient
chargés de la garde du précieux chapeau, mais un certain
quidam, de la race tabarinique, le déroba en cachette et
le transmit, de mâle en mâle, dans la famille tabarine.
Lors de l'expédition de François Ier en Italie, le grand-père
du grand-père de Tabarin le donna à un soldat français
qui revenait dans sa patrie. N'ayant, pour acheter une
drogue qui devait le guérir sûrement, que ce chapeau, ce
soldat l'échangea contre une médecine à un apothicaire de
la place Maubert, qui s'en servit, lui et ses enfants, comme
d'une chausse pour filtrer le miel.

» Tabarin, arrivé à Paris, reconnut ce chapeau, qui avait
été tenu en si grande estime dans sa famille. Indigné de
voir l'usage qu'on faisait du couvre-chef de Saturne, il le
racheta, et, s'il est le dernier qui le possède, il peut dire
qu'il fut le premier qui ait inventé de lui donner de nouvelles formes. Avec ce chapeau lunatique et fantasque, il
représente, à lui tout seul, toutes sortes de chapeaux et
apparait aux yeux de la foule qui l'admire *la gueule bée*
« Tantost en carrabin (soldat), tantost en courtisan, tan-
» tost en porteur de charbon, tantost en soldat d'Ostende,
» tantost en porteur de hotte, tantost en humeur de soupe
» dans un plat, tantost en meneur d'ours, tantost en rueur
» de pierre avec la frelonde (fronde), tantost en serviteur

» nouveau venu des champs, tantost en coureur de poulles
» maigres. »

« Bref, le chapeau de Tabarin, assisté de celui qui le portait, a fait rire plus de peuple en un jour que les comédiens
de l'hôtel de Bourgogne n'auraient su le faire avec leurs
comédies, tragicomédies et pastourelles. »

Les farces de Tabarin sont la source de tous les réper-
toires des tréteaux d'hier et d'aujourd'hui.

« Les perles y sont rares, dit M P. de Saint-Victor, mais,
» en revanche, le sel y abonde. On est tout surpris, lors-
» qu'on rôde dans ce fumier, de se rencontrer parfois nez à
» nez avec Molière et La Fontaine. Telle scène de Poquelin,
» tel apologue du Bonhomme, sont sortis d'une farce de
» Tabarin comme la perle sort de l'huître. Le sac dans
» lequel Scapin enferme Géronte figure dans trois ou quatre
» parades de la baraque du pont Neuf. »

« Tabarin propose à son maître une question burlesque,
» le maître la résout par une explication doctorale, et
» Tabarin la tranche par une calembredaine ou une gail-
» lardise. »

« Quelle différence il y a d'une eschelle à une femme?

— Combien y a-t-il de sortes de nature?

— Quelle est la chose la plus pesante du monde?

— Pourquoi on fend les marrons, les mettant cuire?

— A qui la barbe vient premier que la peau?

— A quoi ressemble l'humeur d'une femme? Etc. »

Question pour faire cinquante paires de souliers
en une demi-heure.

« TABARIN. C'est un grand secret, je ne crois pas qu'il
y ait homme au monde qui ait jamais pratiqué cette
invention.

LE MAÎTRE. A la vérité, Tabarin, ce secret doit être
curieusement recherché. C'est une des gentilles inventions
qui se soient vues de longtemps. Pour moi, je suis contraint en cela d'avouer mon ignorance, sinon que, pour
parvenir à ce but, je prendrais cent cordonniers et leur
donnerais à chacun un soulier à faire : ainsi je crois
qu'en peu de temps je viendrais à terme de ce que je
désirerais.

TABARIN. Je ne l'entends pas ainsi · je ne parle que d'un
homme seul qui en moins d'une demi-heure fera cinquante
paires de souliers Il n'y a rien de plus facile · vous avouerez vous-même, quand vous saurez le secret, que c'est une
des plus belles remarques qui se puisse imaginer; les save-
tiers des halles en tireront de grands profits. Or, pour en
avoir l'expérience, il vous faut prendre cinquante paires de
bottes toutes neuves (si vous désirez que vos souliers soient
neufs) et les couper toutes également à l'endroit de la cheville du pied, par ce moyen, au lieu de cinquante paires de
bottes que vous aviez auparavant, vous trouverez, en moins
d'une demi-heure, cinquante paires de souliers toutes
faites. N'est-ce pas une jolie invention? »

Qui sont ceux qui désirent être borgnes ?

« TABARIN. Mon maître, j'entendis l'autre jour un certain quidam qui disait qu'il voudrait avoir donné cent écus et qu'il fût borgne. Qui sont ceux qui, à juste titre, peuvent faire ce souhait ?

LE MAÎTRE. Il faut qu'un homme soit grandement hors de soi pour avoir cette cupidité dans l'âme La vue est un des premiers organes du corps et la plus délicate partie qui y soit, pour être d'une admirable et incroyable structure, où l'Auteur de l'univers a enclos ce qu'il avait de rare et d'excellent dans ce monde; car soit que nous considérions les deux paires de nerfs qui tirent leur origine du cerveau et par où sont portés les esprits visuels, dont l'une pour le mouvement est plus dure, l'autre pour la vue est plus délicate; ou que nous regardions l'humeur cristalline qui est au centre de l'œil, et la tunique, qui ressemble à la toile des araignées, qui l'enveloppe, ou les deux autres humeurs qui l'environnent et où l'œil semble nager; si nous venons, par après, à voir et contempler le reth (la rétine) admirable et les taies qui entourent tout le corps de l'œil, les muscles qui élèvent et abaissent les paupières, et l'artifice que la nature a employé en ce bâtiment admirable, nous trouverons qu'un homme est grandement imprudent de souhaiter la perte inestimable de la plus belle partie qui soit en lui.

TABARIN. Les hommes qui souhaitent et désirent d'être borgnes sont les aveugles Si vous ne me voulez croire, allez au monastère des Quinze-Vingts : je m'assure que vous n'y en trouverez pas un qui ne désire de vous *voir* pendre. »

Qui sont ceux qui se moquent des médecins et apothicaires?

« TABARIN. Qui sont ceux, à votre avis, qui se moquent
des médecins et apothicaires ?

LE MAÎTRE. Ce sont les malavisés qui, ne croyant avoir
affaire d'eux, se gabbent de leurs recettes; gens de néant,
qui ignorent que la médecine est un art tout à fait céleste
et divin, qui restitue et réintègre la nature en sa perfection et en son entier apogée. La médecine est la science
des sciences naturelles, et malappris sont ceux qui la
méprisent.

*Altissimus de cœlo creavit medicinam, et vir prudens non
abhorrebit eam.*

TABARIN. J'en disais dernièrement de même à un cou-
turier qui me fit un bas de chausses pour moi . *Homerus
et vir prudens non abhorrebit eam.*

LE MAÎTRE. Pour mon regard, je tiens que ceux qui
mécontentent les médecins, ce sont les ignorants et telle
manière de gens qui ne croient avoir affaire d'eux.

TABARIN. Vous vous trompez, car ceux qui se moquent
sont ceux-là qui ont plus besoin de leur aide : ce sont les
malades

LE MAÎTRE. Les malades, Tabarin! comment se peut-il
faire qu'un malade se moque d'un médecin, vu qu'il le
recherche et en a tant besoin?

TABARIN. N'est-ce pas une grande moquerie, quand on
tire la langue d'un demi-pied de long à celui qui vient vous
voir?

Le Maître. A la vérité, tirer la langue est un signe de dérision.

Tabarin. Or, est-il que si un médecin vient voir un malade, pour savoir la cause de son mal, le malade lui tirera la langue, c'est une pure moquerie.

Le Maître. Et l'apothicaire?

Tabarin. L'apothicaire en a bien davantage, car s'il vient de fortune pour apporter un clystère à un malade et le visiter, le malade, en se gaussant de lui, lui présentera le derrière. Ne sont-ce pas là de grandes dérisions et moqueries? »

Dialogue entre Mondor et Tabarin.

« Tabarin. Mon maître, comptons un peu tous les deux, je vous prie : il est désormais temps que je sois le maître, j'ai trop été serviteur.

Le Maître. Allez, gros coquin, gros pendard! vous voulez être le maître, marmiton que vous êtes! Vous voulez donc me commander? Et moi, que serai-je? votre serviteur? Ah! vraiment, il ferait beau voir!

Tabarin. Oui, vraiment, il ferait beau me voir. Ne suis-je pas autant que vous, et aussi grand maître que vous?

Le Maître. Ce que c'est d'un homme, quand il se persuade quelque chose et qu'il s'imprime dans l'intellect quelque insolence! Viens çà, gros maraud . qui t'entretient? qui te nourrit? qui te fournit toutes tes nécessités?

Tabarin. A la vérité, vous vous deviez bien vanter de me nourrir! vous êtes un beau maître! Quand je vins vous voir, vous fîtes un pacte avec moi et me promîtes de m'habiller, me vêtir et me nourrir, au diable si vous en avez observé la centième partie! Toutes les fois que je me suis levé, j'ai été contraint de m'habiller moi-même. Quand il m'a fallu dîner, m'avez-vous fait manger? J'ai été contraint moi-même de prendre la peine de porter la main aux plats, et de la charrier en ma bouche. J'en ai trop enduré de vous, mais dorénavant je vous apprendrai ce que c'est que d'être maître.

Le Maître. As-tu la cervelle si troublée et le jugement si louche et hors des alignements, que tu ne connaisses pas que je suis ton maître?

Tabarin. Non, dea! je vous maintiens que je suis aussi grand maître que vous. Dites-moi, s'il vous plaît, en quoi reconnaissez-vous le maître d'entre le serviteur?

Le Maître. Il est aisé de le connaître, soit à son lever, soit à son coucher, même parmi les rues : le maître marche toujours devant

Tabarin. Ah! je vous tiens au piége, venez çà. Vous dites que le maître se reconnaît à ce qu'il marche toujours devant; dites-moi, je vous supplie, toutes les fois que vous allez souper en ville et que vous revenez le soir au flambeau, qui est-ce qui marche le premier de nous deux?

Le Maître. C'est toi, Tabarin, car, portant le flambeau, tu dois m'éclairer.

Tabarin Je suis donc le maître, car je marche devant. Oh! le brave laquais qui me suit, alors! »

L'animal le plus hardi.

« TABARIN. Puisque vous avez quelque légère connaissance de la nature des animaux, me direz-vous bien quel est l'animal le plus hardi et le plus généreux des animaux ?

LE MAÎTRE. Cela est hors de doute, Tabarin, c'est le lion ; car comme il est le plus furieux de tous les autres, aussi est-il toujours le plus hardi La hardiesse et la générosité d'une chose se reconnaissent par la hauteur des entreprises et des assauts qu'elle fait. Or, parmi toutes les espèces des animaux, qui sont presque infinies en nombre, il n'y en a pas qui fasse paraître plus de générosité et de hardiesse que le lion. Il est armé d'un mâle courage qui l'accompagne en ses actions. Il n'y a bête, tant furieuse qu'elle soit, qui l'ose affronter ni aller de pair avec lui. Enfin, pour abréger, c'est le plus hardi des animaux

TABARIN. Vous vous trompez, mon maître. Je ne veux pas dire que vous ayez menti, mais cela ne vaut guère mieux. L'animal le plus hardi qui soit sur la terre, c'est l'âne des meuniers, mon maître, parce qu'il est tous les jours au milieu des larrons, et toutefois il n'a aucune peur. »

Un recueil attribué à Tabarin s'intitule : JARDIN, RECUEIL, TRÉSOR, *abrégé de secrets, jeux, facéties, gausseries, passetems,* composéz, fabriquéz, experimentéz, et mis en lumière par votre serviteur TABARIN de *Valburlesque,* à plaisirs et contentements des esprits curieux.

*Pour faire que tous ceulx qui seront en un bal, ou autre
assemblée, esternueront tous à la fois.*

« Prenez euforbe, pirètre, et ellébore blanc, de chacun
esgale portion, réduisez le tout en poudre bien subtile, et
d'icelle avec un tuyau de plume, soufflerez par la chambre
où il y aura du monde, et vous verrés l'experience. »

Pour faire gratter.

« Prenez alun de plume et le bien pulvérisez et en met-
trez dedans les linceulx, ou dans le col de quelqu'un, ou
autrement, en sorte que ladite poudre touche la chair, et
vous verrés l'effet »

*Pour faire que la viande portée sur table
semblera pleine de vers.*

« Prenez une corde de luth coupée en petites pièces, et
icelles petites pièces metterés sur la viande encor' chaude,
et la chaleur les fera mouvoir et sauter comme si c'est des
vers » Viennent ensuite les *jeux* et *secrets* suivants, pour
récréer la compagnie, ou faire des farces, comme : « recette
pour empêcher un pot de bouillir.

— Pour faire courir un œuf par la chambre sans que
personne le touche.

— Pour tuer et plumer un oyseau tout d'un coup.

— Pour couper un fil en plusieurs pièces et le faire
revenir en suite.

— Secret admirable pour couper une pomme en quatre,
huit ou plusieurs pièces, sans entamer la peau

— Pour faire que celuy ou celle que vous voudrez, s'essuyant la face à une serviette, devienne noir. C'est un secret fort plaisant.

— Pour chasser les taupes d'un jardin, pré ou autre lieu.

— Pour faire une bague, laquelle saultera sans que personne la touche, etc. »

Il parut même un almanach prophétique pour l'année 1625 sous le nom de *Tabarin*, avec des prédictions admirables sur chaque mois de ladite année. C'est un ramassis de sentences et de prédictions à la manière de *La Palisse*.

« Premièrement, s'il n'arrive point de coterets ny de fagots sur le port, nous sommes en grand danger d'acheter le charbon bien cher, etc. Le mois de mars commencera immédiatement après le dernier jour de febvrier, temps fort variable. Le mois d'avril viendra après, etc. Au mois de juin on commencera à faucher les foings et à tondre les prés.... En juillet, les lièvres auront grosse guerre avec les chiens. On verra des bœufs plus gros de la moitié que les moutons ; les ânes seront aussi lourdauds que de coutume, et ne diminueront rien de leurs longues oreilles.... Au mois d'octobre, les pommiers auront un grand combat avec les Normands.... Le mois de décembre sera le dernier de l'année, etc. Cette année, les roturiers ne seront jamais nobles. Les avaricieux qui remuent les escus par pelle, ne coucheront dans leurs draps de peur de les user. Tous recéleurs, usuriers, filous, grisons, rougets, bannis, galériens et autres de telle vacation, vivront sur la bourse d'autruy. Les taverniers, rostisseurs, mettront de l'eau dans leur vin de peur d'enyvrer le monde, et saleront la viande et la met-

tront six fois au feu. Tout marchand de drap ou de soye
auront chacun une belle femme pour attirer les chalans à
la vente. Les meusniers prendront double mouture et se
sauveront par serment, levant la main jusques au ciel, s'ils
peuvent, avec ces mots : *Le grand diable m'emporte, je n'en ay
pris que par raison* (Ils appellent leur mulet le *diable*, et le
sac, *raison*.) »

Tous ces pronostics, comme un grand nombre des *dévi-
noires* de Tabarin, viennent en droite ligne de Rabelais, qui,
lui-même, avait imité dans sa *Pantagruéline prognostication*,
le recueil de *facéties* d'Henri Bebelius.

« Cette année, les aveugles ne verront que bien peu, les
» sourds entendront assez mal, les muets ne parleront
» guère. Plusieurs moutons, bœufs, pourceaux, oisons,
» poulets et canards, mourront. Les puces seront noires
» pour la plupart. Il y aura sédition horrible entre les
» chiens et les lièvres, entre les chats et les rats, entre les
» moines et les œufs. En toute cette année ne sera qu'une
» lune, encore ne sera-t-elle pas nouvelle. En hiver, ne
» seront pas sages, selon mon petit entendement, ceux qui
» vendront leurs pelisses et fourrures pour acheter du bois.
» S'il pleut, ne vous en mélancholiez pas, tant moins vous
» aurez de poussière par les chemins. Tenez-vous chaude-
» ment. Redoutez les catarrhes et buvez du meilleur.

» RABELAIS. »

Le costume de Tabarin se composait de son « mirrificque »
chapeau en feutre plutôt roux que gris, d'un manteau court
en vieille serge verte, d'une jaquette en toile ainsi que le
pantalon (*planche* 47).

BURATTINO.

Burattino est un masque célèbre de la troupe des *Gelosi*. C'est vers 1580 que ce personnage parut à Florence et eut un tel succès, une si grande vogue qu'il passa bien vite sur les théâtres de marionnettes, et que son nom devint la dénomination de tous les *Fantoccini, Puppi, Pupazzi* et *Bamboccie*. Francesco Gattici fit même, en 1628, une pièce sur ce personnage, intitulée *le Disgrazie di Burattino*.

Dans les scenarios de Flaminio Scala, Burattino est un personnage comique, pleurard, gourmand, poltron et toujours dupe. Il est valet, tantôt du capitan Spavento, tantôt d'Isabelle, et tantôt de Pantalon. Dans les féeries, il vient au milieu de l'action faire des lazzi qui n'ont aucun rapport avec l'intrigue. C'est une sorte de Stenterello ancien. Dans *l'Innocente Persiana* (*opera regia*), Burattino est valet du prince d'Égypte, et son rôle consiste à perdre et à retrouver son maître. Ailleurs, il est courrier porteur de lettres, en bottes, un large chapeau de feutre sur la tête, le fouet à la main, il perd ses missives ou se les laisse voler, ce qui le décourage, et, maudissant le sort, il ne veut plus se charger d'aucune commission

Ailleurs, il est jardinier, père d'Olivetta, grande fille indolente qui aime peu le travail. Il lui reproche de ne savoir rien faire. « Comment, à ton âge, grande comme te voilà et, ma foi, bonne à marier, tu ne sais pas encore donner un coup de pioche ou planter un chou? » Et là-dessus de lui faire un cours comique d'horticulture, en lui nommant tous les outils de jardinage les uns après les autres et la manière de s'en servir.

Il est très-souvent hôtelier et marié à Franceschina, qui le mène par le bout du nez. Le Capitan ayant fait collation chez lui, s'en va après l'avoir payé. Burattino en est si émerveillé, qu'il prend sa broche de cuisine sur l'épaule, et, pour faire honneur au Capitan, le reconduit ainsi jusque chez lui, mais il a soin d'emmener GRILLO, son garçon d'auberge, afin de ne pas revenir seul. De retour chez lui, il aperçoit Pantalon qui parle bas à son valet Pedrolino; celui-ci ayant aperçu Burattino, dont il aime la femme, élève la voix et reproche à Pantalon de vouloir séduire l'épouse de ce pauvre homme de Burattino. Pantalon bat son valet pour avoir dévoilé ses intentions devant le mari, et s'en va. Burattino console Pedrolino tout moulu de coups pour l'honneur de son ami l'hôtelier, le fait entrer chez lui, le dorlote, et, avec la plus grande confiance, lui donne sa femme à garder pendant qu'il s'absentera.

Notre hôtelier n'est pas plutôt parti, que madame Franceschina fait des avances très-significatives à Pedrolino. Celui-ci n'est pas cruel, et ils tiennent ensemble une conversation que le mari entend malgré lui. C'est Pantalon qui veut le convaincre de la trahison de son ami et de sa femme. Furieux, il veut s'expliquer avec Franceschina, qui lui assure en se moquant de lui qu'il s'est trompé. Il veut bien le croire et retourne à ses affaires; mais Pantalon, jaloux pour son propre compte, revient à la charge auprès du mari, et lui fait surprendre une situation plus grave entre les deux amants. Burattino cherche plusieurs moyens pour se venger ; il se décide pour le poison et passe toute la moitié de la pièce à en chercher : n'en trouvant pas, il se décide pour les sbires, et c'est devant la justice et la force armée qu'il s'explique avec sa femme et Pedrolino. Le résultat c'est que Burattino a mal entendu, mal compris, et mal vu ce qui n'était qu'une plaisanterie. Il le croit, demande pardon à sa femme et la tient pour très-honnête.

L'acteur qui jouait le rôle de Burattino dans la troupe des *Gelosi* dut faire une assez longue absence, car il ne joue pas dans toute une série de canevas qui doit comprendre un espace de six à huit ans.

CAVICCHIO.

Cavicchio (*cheville*) est dans la troupe des *Gelosi*, au seizième siècle, une sorte de niais et de valet rustique. Ses rôles sont courts et consistent à venir chanter et raconter une histoire à la manière des paysans. Dans *Gli Avvenimenti comici (opera mista)*, Cavicchio porte la soupe à des moissonneurs et s'arrête devant Mezzetin et Arlequin qui, habillés en laboureurs, font la cour à Lisetta, jeune pastourelle. Il se moque d'eux ; des injures on en vient aux coups. Mais la bergère et ses compagnes, qui arrivent au bruit, les séparent et leur font faire la paix. Lisetta voulant cimenter la bonne harmonie entre Mezzetin et Arlequin, les prie, pour l'amour d'elle, de manger la soupe de Cavicchio, dans la position qu'elle leur assignera. Ils y consentent. Lisetta leur lie les bras en les mettant dos à dos, puis elle met le plat par terre en leur disant de manger, et

s'en va en recommandant à Cavicchio de leur donner à
boire après la soupe. Mezzetin et Arlequin cherchent alors
à ramasser la soupe, mais chacun d'eux enlève, chaque
fois qu'il se baisse, son compagnon sur son dos, ce qui est
une source de lazzi pour Cavicchio, qui les regarde en écla-
tant de rire. Arlequin finit par attraper l'écuelle, et tout
en mangeant se sauve en emportant Mezzetin sur son dos.
Au troisième acte, il fait nuit, Cavicchio est dans sa cabane
avec ses enfants, qui font des paniers tandis qu'il chante en
s'accompagnant de la cornemuse pour tenir sa famille en
gaieté. Entendant du bruit au dehors, il sort avec une
lumière et se trouve en face d'une ronde militaire; il crie,
appelle sa femme à son secours, mais le capitaine l'ayant
rassuré, Cavicchio reprend sa cornemuse et fait danser sa
femme, ses enfants, les soldats et jusqu'au capitaine.

CICCIALBOSCIO est encore un paysan du même genre, dans
le théâtre de Flaminio Scala.

PICCHETO.

PICCHETO est un niais, qui fatigue son maître, le caba-
retier et ses chalands, par de grosses comparaisons proverbiales et de lourdes citations qui tombent des nues.
A l'entendre, on croirait qu'il a été valet du docteur et
qu'il a profité de ses leçons. Fort timide, il craint beaucoup les voleurs, et pour les tromper, il ne couche jamais
deux fois de suite dans le même endroit de la maison,
tous les soirs, c'est un nouveau déménagement. Son maître,
intrigué de ce déplacement journalier, lui en demande la

cause » C'est à cause des voleurs, lui répond Ficcheto, ils seront bien attrapés.... — Je l'espère bien ! lui répond le patron, homme honnête et sensé. — Je dis qu'ils seront bien attrapés de ne pas me trouver. *Charogne qui roule n'amasse pas de mouches*, comme disait mon père... et puis j'aime mieux coucher loin de vous, car comme dit le proverbe *Qui couche avec les chiens se lève avec les puces*, et puis ... — En voilà assez ! lui dit son maître en le poussant rudement, couche où tu voudras » Et là-dessus Ficcheto de transporter sa paillasse.

Nous citerons encore parmi ces bouffons italiens, dont les gestes et l'emploi ne sont que vaguement connus, GIAN MANENTE et MARTINO D'AMELIA, dont les noms furent quelquefois confondus ensemble, comme dans *la Rhodiana* de Ruzzante, où Truffa, pour se moquer de son maître, feint d'être *possédé* et dit que le lutin qu'il a dans le corps s'appelle *Giovanni di Martino*. Ce qui fait beaucoup rire les assistants.

Dans *la Calandra* du cardinal da Bibbiena, le valet Fessenio compare Calandro, le mari ridicule et trompé, à ces deux bouffons. « Ce qui me fait surtout rire, dit-il, aux dépens de Calandro, c'est qu'il se croit si beau et si aimable que toutes les femmes qui le voient s'éprennent de lui aussitôt, comme si le monde ne possédait pas un pareil modèle de perfection; enfin, comme dit le proverbe populaire, s'il mangeait du foin, ce serait un bœuf; il vaut presque en son genre Martino d'Amelia ou Giovanni Manente. »

« Il est plus simple que Calandrino » est un proverbe provenant de deux nouvelles de Boccace où la simplicité du peintre Calandrino tourne à l'imbécillité. Calandriner quelqu'un (*far Calandrino qualcheduno*) signifie en faire accroire. Bibbiena donna ce nom populaire au vieillard de sa comédie, *la Calandra*.

Cortavoce, appelé aussi *Courtavoz*, fut un des premiers mimes italiens qui vinrent en France avec une troupe, en 1540. Son costume gris à capuchon, son long nez de carton, le firent surnommer *le pèlerin*.

Rabelais, décrivant dans sa *Sciomachie* (1569) les fêtes qui eurent lieu à Rome à l'occasion de la naissance d'un Dauphin de France, parle de « mimes bergamasques et autres *matachins* (matassins), qui vinrent faire leurs gestes, ruses et soubresaultx » devant la cour de Rome. Entre autres, il cite IL MORETTO, *archibouffon d'Italie*.

Ludovico Domenichi le cite plusieurs fois dans son recueil de *Facetie, motti et burle*, 1565, comme grand diseur de bons mots, et maître en son art, le surnommant le bouffon de Lucques. Il cite aussi, parmi les farceurs des quinzième et seizième siècles : IL GONELLA, Gregorio Giraldi, Astidamante, Mariano del Piombo, Fanfera, IL TOMASSONE.

Au seizième siècle, la quantité et la variété des noms qui furent employés dans les comédies tant apprises qu'improvisées sont incroyables, nous citerons les plus usités, qui sont pour la plupart des noms restés au théâtre jusqu'à nos jours et qui servent généralement à qualifier les rôles de valets :

FACELLA, VILUPPO, TOGNOLO (niais), FARFALLA, valet dans le théâtre de Girolamo Parabosco, 1560.

Braghino, Stragnacia, Cocozza, Mosca, dans Cristoforo Castelletti, 1547, ainsi que dans la troupe des *Intronati*.

Garba (1550), Garbuglio, Granda, dans Andréa Calmo, 1555.

Truffa, Stramba, Volpino (1587), Pilucca (1589), Sannione; Tofolo le Vénitien, et Tirimofolo (gros et court), Trappola, Cucurino (encapuchonné), et Grisiguino, qui fut porté sur les tréteaux français sous le nom de *Grisgoulin*.

Dans le répertoire comique des pièces florentines écrites par Cecchi, Lasca, Ambra, Salviati, Buonarroti, c'est : Guaicigna (1561); Zanauolo (1555), Tofano, Gorgoglio, Bozzacchio (1560); Vespa.

Cornacchia (bavard), Tofolo, dans le théâtre de Luigi Grotto, 1580.

Nous avons trouvé dans la riche et curieuse collection de M. Solcirol, qui possède, croyons-nous, les portraits de tous les acteurs, tant français qu'étrangers, connus depuis le quinzième siècle, une grande quantité de noms de comiques italiens, parmi lesquels nous ne citerons que ceux qui eurent le plus de succès dans leur temps : Ciucotti (*farceur*), 1550, Vincehzio Bugoni, Florentin, comique célèbre, 1560, Ariel Soldano, ayant joué à Venise, Naples, Paris, 1590 Grandi, comique de la troupe de Rosilli, 1590.

Paghetti, 1601; Lazero (*comique*), 1610; Giuseppe Dardanelli, de la troupe de la Brambilla, 1604; Petrini (*comico*), 1608; Aspontini (*comique*), 1625; Asserbini, de la troupe d'Andreini, 1650; Pancrazio Calupo, 1650; Tricano, acteur de la troupe de Jodelet, Giovanni da Pistoia, comique du théâtre des Médicis, à Florence, 1640; Bernar-

dim, 1645: Bassi de Vérone, 1646, Falchi, comique en
Italie et en Allemagne, 1651; Velene, Baratta, Ceppi,
Cattani, Zanardo, 1650, Sala (*bouffon*), 1660; Baldo,
Naples, 1670, Matteo Barra, comique, Naples, 1670;
Domenico Barzanti, Venise, Vienne, 1682, Baldo, Naples,
1696; Palestri, Venise et Paris, 1690, Behni, 1684; Parmio
(Antonio Domenico), célèbre en Italie et en Espagne, 1675,
Salviati, 1684.

Currado, farceur napolitain, 1701; Antonelli, Carlo et
Pietro Antonini, 1750, Anziani, comique à Naples, 1715;
les trois Bartoli, de 1700 à 1745, Buonamici, comique,
Florence, Naples, 1720, Antonio Bonaldi, 1740, Ber-
tocci, 1745, Battaglia, de la troupe d'Onofrio Paganini,
1772, Baldarini de Vicence, comique de la troupe de
Baldi, 1774; Ciotto, Naples, 1759, Bozzighetti, théâtres
forains, 1775; Gasparo Marzocchi de Bologne, au théâtre
de Saint-Jean-Chrysostome, 1776; Francesco Arrisi de
Modène, comique, 1770; etc., etc.

Probablement tous ces bouffons portaient des vêtements
très-tranchés et très-différents les uns des autres Les ren-
seignements sur l'ensemble de leurs costumes sont malheureusement fort rares, ce qui empêche de leur assigner une
époque bien exacte dans l'histoire du théâtre

Nous avons trouvé, en province, dans un bouquin du
seizième siècle, un recueil de gravures « sérié, colligé,
ramassié, extrait et enfagotté par Pierre Bertheau le
jeusne... demeurant à Chastelherant, 1610 » Dans cette
« collecte de diverses portraictures en taille de cuivre,
œuvres de main, paintures et portraits au naturel, » trois

planches de Geyn, *le jeune*, sont excessivement remarquables
par la finesse du travail et la rectitude du dessin. Ces gravures représentent des masques ou acteurs jouant des scènes
de théâtre, à la fin du seizième siècle ou au commencement
du dix-septième. Ces personnages ne portent pas de noms,
mais il est facile de reconnaître parmi eux un Capitan
revêtu d'une demi-armure, à la cuirasse bombée comme
le ventre de Polichinelle. Il porte un haut feutre galonné,
brodé et ombragé d'une profusion de plumes, la collerette
empesée, une longue écharpe en sautoir. Il conduit de sa
main gantée de fer une jeune femme dont le visage est
masqué. Celle-ci est coiffée d'une couronne de fleurs et de
feuillage; elle a les cheveux courts, et son cou ainsi que
sa poitrine sont perdus dans une immense collerette qui se
tient toute droite. Ce couple est conduit par un Amour
qui, vêtu d'une longue robe *à l'antique*, les yeux bandés,
le carquois au flanc, tenant de ses mains gantées une
torche de résine, marche en avant.

Dans une autre planche, une conversation est établie
entre trois personnages, dont l'un est enveloppé d'une
espèce de *domino*, et porte un demi-masque composé d'un
front et d'un nez enjolivé de trois verrues. Le personnage
du fond, coiffé d'un haut bonnet pointu, complétement
masqué, orné d'une collerette en plumes, est vêtu, comme
les *Zanni*, de la veste et du pantalon rayés horizontale-
ment et garnis de boutons. La figure de femme est habillée
à la mode du temps de Henri III. Mais le plus curieux de
ces personnages est un bouffon qui, chaussé de larges
bottes montant jusqu'au ventre et ayant sur le dos pour

tout déguisement une cape vénitienne, porte un masque dont le nez est formé par la queue d'une écrevisse; les pinces forment les moustaches. Il tient une torche et une lanterne · c'est peut-être l'Hyménée grotesque. Dans le même sujet, une sorte d'Isabelle a le visage caché sous un masque de velours noir, les cheveux relevés *à la Gabrielle* Elle est coiffée d'un diadème de plumes de paon posées sur deux rangs en éventail; son corsage, ses manches et sa jupe sont également du temps de Henri IV Elle donne la main à un personnage masqué coiffé d'un turban, et portant sur les épaules une pèlerine de fourrure très-courte qui laisse voir sa veste à brandebourgs Il est chaussé de longs bas retenus par des jarretières, et parait vouloir représenter un mahométan.

TARTAGLIA.

LE NOTAIRE, LE COMMISSAIRE, LE PROCUREUR, LE SBIRE, L'APOTHICAIRE, ETC.

Il Tartaglia (le bègue, le bredouilleur) est un masque originaire de Naples. C'est tantôt un valet bavard qui, ne pouvant venir à bout d'articuler ses mots pour formuler ses idées, se met dans une colère perpétuelle contre les autres et contre lui-même. Il est néanmoins gros et gras. De grandes lunettes lui cachent les trois quarts du visage pour exprimer qu'il a la vue basse et qu'il ne veut pas être surpris par le danger : car, bien qu'il se fasse fort de tout braver, et de tenir tête à un éléphant, il va se cacher sous des bottes de foin s'il entend le chant du coq.

Ce type fut peu employé en France. Il remplissait des rôles d'utilité, et n'avait guère plus d'une scène par canevas. Il jouait en outre les rôles de notaire, de sbire, de procureur, de juge, parfois d'apothicaire; mais c'était toujours un personnage ridicule et bafoué Tartaglia ne fut en France qu'un balourd fort bête, fort laid, tout à fait ignare, et n'eut qu'un succès de gros rire.

« On répète », dit Favart en 1761, « au Théâtre-Italien, la farce *dei Tre Gobbi*, traduite en français par Leho Riccoboni fils cette plaisanterie se dénoue mal; mais si elle réussit, ce sera un dénoûment heureux. Je crains, dans cette facétie, le personnage de Tartaglia. Un des trois bossus, bègue, s'arrête sur des syllabes indécentes. c'est beaucoup hasarder chez une nation dont les oreilles sont d'autant plus chastes que les mœurs sont plus corrompues. »

Dans *le Collier de perles*, joué en 1672, Arlequin, qui fait le rôle d'un certain marquis de Sbrofadel, après avoir avalé une médecine, s'imagine qu'il va mourir; il demande un notaire pour faire son testament. Le Docteur sort et revient avec Tartaglia, qui fait le notaire.

« TARTAGLIA. *Ser, ser, servitore illustri, tri, tri, tri, tri, trissimo.*

ARLEQUIN. C'est un notaire qui vient de Tripoli.

TARTAGLIA s'assied, tire sa plume et son papier, et commence à écrire. L'an, an, an, an. ..

ARLEQUIN. Que l'on mène cet âne à l'écurie!...

TARTAGLIA. *I, i, i, io son, son, sono, presto.*

ARLEQUIN *Va, bene!* Je laisse cette maison au Docteur.

LE DOCTEUR. Mais elle est à moi!

ARLEQUIN Je le sais bien, c'est pour cela que je vous la laisse si elle n'était pas à vous, je ne vous la laisserais pas. Je laisse mon cabinet à mon cousin.

TARTAGLIA écrivant. Mon ca, ca, ca....

ARLEQUIN. Faites vite retirer ce notaire, il va salir tous les meubles.

TARTAGLIA .... bmet! à mon cou, cou ...

ARLEQUIN. Je laisse soixante-cinq arpents de drap d'Angleterre pour habiller ma famille en deuil.

LE DOCTEUR. Vous vous trompez, on ne mesure pas le drap à l'arpent.

ARLEQUIN. Il me semble que l'on peut mesurer son bien de la manière que l'on veut.

TARTAGLIA. Pou, pou, pou, pour habiller ma famille en feuille.. .

ARLEQUIN. Je laisse à *Lallemand*, mon valet de chambre...

TARTAGLIA. Un lavement à mon valet de chambre.

ARLEQUIN criant. Lallemand! et non lavement.

TARTAGLIA écrivant toujours sous la dictée d'Arlequin. *Si, si, si, si signor*, il y a bien lavement... ent, ent, ent.

ARLEQUIN Je laisse toutes mes vieilles nippes à la fripière, ma voisine.

TARTAGLIA répétant. Tou, tou, toutes mes vieilles tri, tri, tripes, à la tri, tri, tripière, ma voisine.

ARLEQUIN. *Ohimé!* ce notaire-là n'en peut plus; il faudrait lui donner une médecine pour lui faire évacuer les paroles du ventre! Je laisse vingt écus à mon cuisinier, à condition qu'il dépendra de mon frère cadet.

TARTAGLIA. Qu'il pend, pendra mon frère cadet.

ARLEQUIN. Enfin, je laisse au notaire ci-présent, une langue de porc pour mettre à la place de la sienne.

TARTAGLIA. Po, po, po, porc toi-même! »

Arlequin lui lance un coup de pied qui l'envoie tomber

sur le nez avec ses plumes, papier, portefeuille et encrier.
Tartaglia se relève, la figure couverte d'encre, et sort si en
colère qu'il ne peut plus articuler que des sons inintel-
ligibles.

Le costume qui caractérise le Tartaglia a toujours eu
assez d'analogie avec celui des *Zanni*. Créé, dit-on, par
Beltram de Vérone, en 1650, époque où les valets tels que
Scapino et *Mezzetino* commencèrent à quitter le masque,
Tartaglia ne prit comme signe caractéristique que ces
énormes lunettes bleues, sans lesquelles il ne peut jouer.
La figure imberbe, la tête chauve, coiffée d'un chapeau
rond en feutre gris, une vaste collerette de percale; le manteau, la veste et le pantalon de couleur verte, rayés trans-
versalement de bandes jaunes; bas blancs et souliers de
cuir brun ou jaune tel fut d'abord TARTAGLIA (*planche* 48).

Mais il subit comme tous les autres les modifications
apportées par la mode En 1750, Fiorilli, acteur napolitain de grand talent, faisant partie de la troupe de Sacchi,
et pour lequel Ch. Gozzi fit plusieurs féeries, jouait ce type
en culotte courte et en toque; donnant la forme des vêtements de Scapin à ceux de Tartaglia, il retrancha les raies
jaunes et galonna sa livrée verte de brandebourgs d'argent.

Aujourd'hui, à Naples, ce personnage, dont le caractère
est de ne rien être et par conséquent de pouvoir être tout,
selon l'acteur qui le remplit, porte la perruque blanche, le
tricorne et un habit vert de forme Louis XV, les bas chinés
et les souliers à boucles. Voilà le Tartaglia moderne,
bégayant le dialecte emphatique et saccadé de Naples. Les
choses les plus libres et les plus bouffonnes sont débitées

par lui avec un sang-froid et un sérieux imperturbables. Aussi est-il fort commun que l'acteur qui joue Tartaglia aille souvent passer la nuit et parfois quatre ou cinq jours en prison. C'est chose acceptée par les acteurs et le public, et personne ne s'en préoccupe.

A chaque mot inconvenant, il s'arrête comme pour cher-cher le mot véritable, et quand il l'a trouvé, il tombe dessus avec pesanteur. Il est difficile de donner un spé-cimen des discours beaucoup trop égrillards qui le font incarcérer. Il en est un qui prit l'importance d'un fait poli-tique. Dans la pièce, Tartaglia revient d'Espagne et vient dire que la reine venait d'ouvrir les Cortès, où assis-taient les chefs de toutes les opinions politiques. La manière dont il dénatura le mot de *Cortès* et plusieurs autres est restée dans la mémoire des assistants. Ce *lazzi* fit événe-ment, d'autant plus que la reine d'Espagne était alors la belle Christine, sœur du roi de Naples. Le Tartaglia fut mis en prison pendant huit jours et privé pendant un mois de ses lunettes favorites : ce qui était la plus cruelle punition qu'on pût infliger à l'acteur et au public, car, sans ses énormes lunettes sur son nez en pied de marmite, Tartaglia est paralysé. Mais le Tartaglia n'est pas toujours un per-sonnage gras et bouffi d'une mauvaise graisse. Il est quel-quefois si sec, si long, si maigre, orné d'un nez tellement proéminent qu'il ressemble à une canne à bec de corbin. Il jouit alors d'une singulière prérogative, il est *gettatore*, il a le mauvais œil, ou plutôt il a deux mauvais yeux, car il n'y voit goutte derrière ses grandes lunettes.

« Le Tartaglia », dit M. Paul de Musset, « est un type

napolitain en grande faveur, comme le Pancrace. Il représente le Méridional usé par le climat, souffrant d'une
ophthalmie chronique et dans un état voisin du crétinisme.
Ses joues creuses, son long nez surmonté d'énormes
lunettes bleues, son air malade et son vice de prononciation constituent les signes particuliers du jeteur de sorts,
dont la rencontre est dangereuse. »

Dans la comédie du *Roi cerf* de Ch. Gozzi, Tartaglia,
bègue et stupide, est néanmoins premier ministre dans le
pays de Serendippe. Il voudrait faire épouser sa fille au roi
son maître. Le roi en aime une autre, la belle Angela. Il
l'épouse et devient jaloux. Pour contenter sa fantaisie
d'éprouver les sentiments de sa femme, le magicien Duran-
darto lui donne une formule au moyen de laquelle son
âme pourra s'introduire dans tous les corps morts qu'il lui
plaira de ressusciter.

L'imprudent monarque confie cet important secret à
Tartaglia, qui est non-seulement furieux du mariage du
roi, mais qui, par-dessus le marché, se permet d'être
amoureux de la reine. Voilà le judicieux roi et son perfide
ministre dans la forêt. Un cerf chassé tombe mort à leurs
pieds. Tartaglia persuade à son maître de faire sur cet
animal l'épreuve de sa formule magique. La formule est
terriblement bonne, car, en même temps que l'âme du roi
passe dans le corps du cerf, le corps du roi tombe privé
d'âme. Ce ne serait qu'un petit mal, car le roi, devenu cerf,
pourrait remettre son âme dans ce corps inanimé, si Tartaglia n'eût retenu la formule. Aussitôt il s'en sert pour
faire passer son âme indigne dans le corps du roi, et tandis

que celui-ci s'enfuit à travers la forêt, il se rend au palais, en ordonnant le massacre de tous les cerfs jeunes ou vieux du royaume de Serendippe.

La scène où Angela voit revenir, bègue et insupportable, l'apparence de son mari, est fort plaisante. Elle le chasse de son appartement et voit à sa porte un pauvre mendiant qu'elle se met à aimer passionnément, par la force de l'instinct, car le mendiant n'est autre que son véritable époux, qui a trouvé dans la forêt un pauvre diable mort de froid, et qui s'est emparé de son corps, jugeant peu convenable de reparaître devant sa chère moitié sous la figure d'un cerf.

Tout s'explique, et Angela, pour se débarrasser de l'odieux Tartaglia, imagine de lui promettre ses caresses s'il consent à ressusciter la petite chienne qu'elle vient de perdre. Tartaglia se soumet à ce caprice, mais à peine a-t-il quitté son corps que le roi légitime le reprend au moyen de la formule, tandis que Tartaglia jappe et frétille dans le corps de la chienne. C'est le dernier effort de son éloquence, car le roi l'étrangle aussitôt, et ainsi finit la comédie.

A Bologne, l'emploi de Tartaglia est de faire rire aux dépens de la loi. C'est tantôt M. le commissaire et tantôt un agent de police quelconque. Le *Caporale degli sbirri* est son triomphe. Vient-il pour arrêter un coupable, son bégayement le rend si ridicule, que tout le monde lui rit au nez. Sa colère devient alors de la fureur, quand il s'aperçoit que plus il parle, plus les éclats de rire augmentent. Ce sont alors des cris inarticulés, des hurlements étranges

qui sortent de son gosier. Il finit par envoyer tout au diable
et s'en va. On entend encore dans le lointain ses hoquets
bizarres et impossibles à décrire.

LE NOTAIRE.

Peut-on se passer d'un notaire? impossible. Est-ce que,
dans chaque pièce, l'amour ne joue pas un rôle, le premier rôle? Et si l'amour est suivi de l'hymen, l'hymen, à
son tour, n'est-il pas précédé du notaire?

Il faut donc, pour que le canevas d'une pièce gaie
réussisse et satisfasse le public, qu'au dénoûment Ottavio
épouse Isabelle, et le valet la soubrette. Le notaire vient
dresser le contrat et marier les jeunes gens. Les vieux ne
se marient jamais, ils n'ont besoin que de l'apothicaire,
et quand arrive le tabellion, si par hasard ils l'ont
demandé, c'est pour dresser leur testament.

Une perruque à huit marteaux, la robe noire, le nez
bourgeonné, pincé par d'énormes lunettes, le ventre puissant, le pied large, la canne dans une main pour soutenir
son gros individu, et un portefeuille dans l'autre pour en
équilibrer le poids (*planche* 49), branlant de la tête, sou-
riant à chacun, il entre, le désiré, l'indispensable, le triom-
phant notaire! Il salue la compagnie, souffle, s'essuie le
front, car c'est un homme d'importance, un affairé que
l'on s'arrache. Après la prise de tabac d'usage, que lui
offre Cassandre, il prend un siége, tire ses papiers de son
portefeuille, cherche longtemps la plume qui était à son
oreille, dérange même à ce propos toute la maison qui

cherche avec lui. Colombine finit par trouver cette précieuse plume dans la perruque de M. le garde-notes. On s'assied, on fait cercle, pendant qu'il taille cette plume, tirée, dit-il, de l'aile droite de l'Amour, et qui doit cimenter le bonheur des futurs conjoints. Enfin, après en avoir essayé le bec sur son ongle, puis coupé et recoupé encore un peu, ébarbé le haut, ôté et remis dix fois ses lunettes, comme pour éprouver la patience des clients, il se décide à recevoir les noms, prénoms et qualités d'une part et d'autre part.

La besogne est vite bâclée, surtout s'il a été prévenu d'avance D'autres fois, les discussions s'engagent, on va tout rompre. Il est là toujours impassible. Souvent il venait dresser le contrat du tuteur, et c'est l'amoureux qui signe. Il n'y voit jamais que du feu. D'ailleurs, que lui importe! pourvu qu'il ait ses deux signatures, il s'en ira satisfait, surtout s'il est bien payé, car il est tant soit peu *chiche*. Son salaire reçu, il parlera de la pluie et du beau temps en bégayant plus qu'il ne faut, se permettra quelquefois d'accepter des rafraîchissements, et même de prendre le menton de la soubrette en lui lançant par-dessus ses lunettes un regard égrillard. Il ne refuse jamais d'être de la noce, et il restera à table trois jours et trois nuits sans s'ennuyer; ne manquera pas, à chaque dessert, de chanter en fausset quelque couplet léger et badin sur les grâces et les charmes de la mariée. Après quoi, creusé par la musique et les mots soi-disant malins qu'il a décochés aux convives, il recommencera à manger. Mais il n'est si bonne compagnie qui ne se quitte. Une noce ne peut durer six ans. Le notaire s'en retournera chez lui, soutenu par quelques clients, car, son désir de revenir chez sa femme, il l'a laissé dans les flacons.

Mais il n'est pas toujours si bien accueilli. Dans les maisons où il vient contrarier par son ministère les amoureux *déboutés* de leur amour, s'il s'avise de se lever de son siége pour saluer, il se rassoira infailliblement dans le vide, à la grande satisfaction et hilarité des valets. Parfois aussi, il reçoit son salaire dans le dos, et on ne le revoit que lorsque l'orage est passé. C'est toujours un brave homme au fond, pas méchant du tout, craignant sa femme et le roi, et demeurant au coin de la rue de toutes les villes du monde.

Dans la troupe des *Intronati*, le notaire s'appelle tantôt ser NERI, tantôt ser GIULIO ou ser AGAPIO, ser CIAPPELLETO.

Dans la *Vaccaria* de Beolco (Ruzzante), Polidoro fait venir un certain notaire pour dresser un certain contrat. Polidoro, espèce de Léandre ridicule et fort riche, est amoureux de Fiorina, et, pour l'obtenir, il doit verser une somme assez ronde dans les mains de Celega, mère supposée de la pauvrette

« LE NOTAIRE. Pardonnez-moi si je vous ai fait attendre. Mais ce qui m'a retardé, c'est la rédaction de ce contrat qui sort de l'habitude.

POLIDORO Rien ne presse, rien! mais tout le monde n'est pas riche.

LE NOTAIRE. Cela est par trop évident, et, sans argent, les contrats se font mal. Or, ne serait-il pas convenable que vous écoutassiez la lecture de cet écrit, afin d'y ajouter ce qui aurait pu rester dans la plume?

Polidoro Je vous en prie, on ne saurait faire les choses trop clairement.

Le Notaire. Or donc, écoutez. L'an 1553, *et cætera*, en la maison de... *et cætera*... (Je passerai les clauses générales, venant au fait) Dame Celega, demeurant présentement au lieu dit de l'*Albarella*, donne et concède au très-riche et généreux messer Polidoro, sa fille Fiorinetta, pour une année entière, qui commencera à courir à partir de la présente publication du présent acte, et cela moyennant cinquante écus d'or qu'il (moi présent) lui compte et débourse, aux conditions ci-incluses, et convenues entre les parties contractantes · que la susdite Fiorinetta aura à être prête à toute requête de messer Polidoro. Que pendant tout le cours de la présente année, elle ne pourra avoir non-seulement la domestication de qui que ce soit, mais encore ne laissera entrer aucun autre homme dans sa maison; de cette façon, l'entrée de ladite maison doit être interdite à tous, soit amis, soit parents

Polidoro. Ajoutez-y aussi les médecins.

Le Notaire Je les y joindrai.... Qu'elle ne pourra recevoir aucune lettre, ni écrire à personne, ni tenir enfermé, ou dans la maison, aucune lettre ou sonnet d'amour à elle adressé par le passé; ni papier, ni encre pour écrire.

Polidoro. Et que je ne veux pas qu'elle essaye.

Le Notaire. Je le mettrai.... Que, pendant ce temps, elle ne puisse avoir d'amant, ou faire la courtisane en restant à la fenêtre ou sur la porte, ni aller à aucune réunion.

Polidoro. N'oubliez pas de noter que je ne veux pas qu'elle

aille aux bals ni aux mascarades, mais, par-dessus tout, je défends qu'elle aille aux comédies.

Le Notaire. J'en tiendrai compte.... En outre, que ni elle ni personne de la maison ne puisse parler par supercherie, ou à l'oreille l'un de l'autre, ni jamais dire . L'ami dit, l'ami fait; mais parler clairement, sans faire des signes en toussant, ou en crachant, ou en fermant un œil, ou un geste qui puisse faire soupçonner une entente secrète.

Polidoro. Ajoutez de plus cette note au chapitre : qu'on ne devra pas parler dans la maison. Je ne veux pas non plus qu'entre jamais au logis aucun juif avec des voiles et des brimborions, ni ces sortes d'entremetteuses qui vont par les maisons, épluchant l'honneur des femmes, sous prétexte de vendre du fil, de la laine ou du lin.

Le Notaire. Il me semble que ce sont de dures conditions et capables de ne pas être acceptées.

Polidoro. N'en prenez souci. Mes écus feront accepter mes conditions. Puisque je paye, je veux être satisfait. Mais ajoutez que je ne veux pas qu'elle aille à matines, et que, passant par la rue, elle touche ou soit touchée de qui que ce soit

Le Notaire. Vous voulez obliger les autres. Cela n'est pas possible.

Polidoro En ce cas, annulez tout ce dernier article, et mettez à la place qu'elle ne mettra pas les pieds hors de sa porte pendant toute l'année.

Le Notaire. Que si, par quelque raison ou empêchement, il arrivait que ledit messer Polidoro fût obligé de rester loin de ladite Fiorinetta pendant quelques jours ou quel-

ques nuits? Dans ce cas, l'année expirée, elle devra compléter le temps voulu, jours par jours, nuits par nuits,
devant et s'obligeant, et cetera... sous peine, et cetera...
et cetera....

POLIBORO. C'est parfait! entrons maintenant à la maison.

LE NOTAIRE Entrons! »

LE COMMISSAIRE.

Dans beaucoup de pièces italiennes, le *Podesta* ou le
Bargello vient figurer vers le dénoûment. L'un et l'autre
n'ont jamais de rôles bien longs ni bien difficiles. Leur
costume est grave, leurs manières sont insignifiantes. Ils
représentent la loi dans toute sa rigidité. Le COMMISSAIRE, étant
d'un ordre inférieur, est traité plus cavalièrement dans les
canevas italiens, comme dans les farces de Polichinelle.

« LE COMMISSAIRE *à son Clerc*. Allons, dépêchons-nous vite,
tire ton écritoire! ferme la porte, chasse les chiens, prends
une chaise, mouche ton nez, laisse de la marge et écris
gros.

LE CLERC *tirant un gros encrier et une toute petite plume*.
Monsieur, faisons vite, s'il vous plaît. J'ai un cours de
ventre, comme vous savez, qui ne me permet pas d'être
longtemps en place.

LE COMMISSAIRE. J'aurai bientôt fait. Inculpé! comment
vous appelez-vous? Dites-moi votre nom, surnom, qualité, patrie, rue, paroisse, logis, appartement. Avez-vous
un père, une mère, des frères, des parents? Que faites-vous
à Paris? Y a-t-il longtemps que vous y êtes? Qui voyez-

vous? Où allez-vous? D'où venez-vous? Écrivez donc, greffier. (*Il donne un coup sur l'épaule de son Clerc.*)

Le Clerc *laissant tomber son encrier.* Ah! j'ai l'épaule cassée... voilà un clerc estropié!

Le Commissaire. C'est *punctum interrogationis.* Quel diable d'ignorant! Et vous, inculpé, vous ne voulez donc pas répondre? Écrivez qu'il n'a rien dit.

L'Inculpé! Comment voulez-vous, monsieur, que ...

Le Commissaire. Assez! Vous croyez donc que j'ai le loisir d'entendre toutes vos sottises? Savez-vous que j'ai encore aujourd'hui trois fripons à faire pendre sans vous compter, et cinq ou six demoiselles à faire déménager.... Qu'on aille dire à la chaîne qu'elle ne parte pas encore, j'ai ici de quoi l'augmenter.

Le Clerc. Monsieur, la chaîne ne partira pas que vous n'y soyez. »   (*Recueil de Gherardi.*)

LE PROCUREUR.

Avocats, procureurs et *gens de chicane* (comme dit la chanson), ne sont pas mieux traités dans les bouffonneries italiennes que dans les farces françaises. L'homme de robe y est représenté plus avare et plus voleur que ses clients. *Chicanoux* et *Chats fourrés* furent toujours moqués, bafoués, joués avec malice par les acteurs, hués avec plaisir par le public qui les vit malmener en scène.

« Les Chicanoux gagnent leur vie à être battus, » dit Rabelais. « La manière est telle : quand un moine, prêtre, usurier ou avocat veut mal à quelque gentilhomme de son pays, il envoie vers lui un de ses Chicanoux. Chicanou le citera, l'ajournera, l'outragera, l'injuriera impudemment, selon son recors et instruction, tant que le gentilhomme, s'il n'est paralytique de sens et plus stupide qu'une grenouille, sera contraint de lui donner bastonnades et coups d'épée sur la tête, ou mieux de le jeter par les crenaux et fenêtres de son château. Cela fait, voilà Chicanou riche pour quatre mois. Comme si coups de bâton fussent ses naïves moissons. Car il aura récompense bien bonne du moine, de l'usurier ou de l'avocat, et réparation du gentilhomme, quelquefois si grande et excessive, que le gentilhomme y perdra tout son avoir, avec danger de périr misérablement en prison, comme s'il eût frappé le Roi. »

Maint spectateur, après avoir applaudi aux volées de bois vert dont Polichinelle a gratifié tel Grippeminaud ou tel Grapignan, se retirait jadis chez lui en songeant avec rage qu'un vrai grippeminaud le viendrait quérir le lendemain. En Italie, le public naïf applaudirait encore aujourd'hui aux prouesses du « seigneur de Basché daubant sur Chicanoux », surtout dans certains États, où la justice et la loi ne sont guère plus aimées ni plus respectées qu'elles ne l'étaient chez nous jadis, et ce n'est pas toujours sans danger pour l'*impresario* et pour l'acteur qu'un *homme noir* vient montrer sa vénalité et ses ridicules sur les planches. Sur la scène italienne de Paris, ces caricatures des gens de robe étaient jouées ordinairement par Arlequin ou Mezzetin, et jamais le grand Roi n'eut seulement l'idée de leur en faire la moindre observation; au contraire, il riait beaucoup de leurs farces, et les approuvait fort.

Dans la scène suivante, Grapignan était joué par l'Arlequin.

« Un Voleur. Monsieur Grapignan est-il au logis?

Grapignan. Oui, monsieur, c'est moi.

Le Voleur. Monsieur, je suis votre serviteur.

Grapignan. Monsieur, je suis le vôtre.

Le Voleur. Comme vous êtes le plus honnête homme de procureur, parmi les procureurs, je viens vous prier de m'éclairer de vos conseils, à propos d'une petite affaire qui vient de m'arriver.

Grapignan. De quoi est-il question?

Le Voleur. Monsieur, je marchais sur le grand chemin, lorsqu'un marchand, monté sur une rosse, m'a heurté fort rudement. Lui ayant dit : « A qui en a cet homme-là? » il a pris le parti de son cheval, est descendu et m'a dit que sa bête n'était pas une rosse, mais que c'était moi qui en étais une. Là-dessus, nous nous querellons, nous nous battons, et, comme il n'était pas le plus fort, je le jette à terre. Il se relève et prend la fuite. Il faut vous dire qu'en nous roulant par terre, il laissa tomber de sa poche vingt-cinq ou trente pistoles

Grapignan. Ho! ho!

Le Voleur. Que je ramassai; et, voyant qu'il avait gagné au pied, ma foi! je montai sur sa rosse et je m'en revins, comme s'il ne s'était rien passé Présentement, j'apprends que ce coquin-là, monsieur, fait informer contre moi, comme voleur de grand chemin. Voyez s'il y a la moindre apparence! Dites-moi un peu, je vous prie, où peut bien aller cette affaire?

GRAPIGNAN. Ma foi! si l'affaire est menée chaudement, cela peut bien aller tout droit à la Grève. Il faut vous tirer de là. Quelqu'un vous a-t-il vu ?

LE VOLEUR. Non, monsieur.

GRAPIGNAN. Tant mieux Il faut commencer par mettre le cheval sous clef. Car si ce marchand venait à le découvrir, n'ayant pas d'autre témoin, il ne manquerait pas de le faire interroger sur les faits, et alors vous seriez un homme perdu.

LE VOLEUR. Il n'y a rien à craindre de ce côté. C'est une rosse qui ne peut pas desserrer les dents

GRAPIGNAN. Ne vous y fiez pas. nous voyons tous les jours des témoins muets faire bravement rouer leur homme.

LE VOLEUR. Diable !

GRAPIGNAN. Çà! sans perdre de temps, il faut commencer par faire informer des premiers, et avoir des témoins, à quelque prix que cela soit

LE VOLEUR. Mais il n'y avait personne sur le grand chemin, dans ce moment-là.

GRAPIGNAN. Allez! allez! nous y en ferons bien trouver . Je songe à deux bas Normands qui travaillent pour moi; mais ils ne se rembarqueront qu'à bonne enseigne, car ils sortent d'une affaire, où sans moi... vous m'entendez bien. (*Il met la main à son cou, lui donnant à entendre qu'ils auraient été pendus.*) Aussi les témoins sont terriblement chers, cette année.

LE VOLEUR. Et d'où vient ce malheur?

GRAPIGNAN. C'est qu'on ne leur fait pas de quartier. On en pend autant qu'on en découvre.

LE VOLEUR Si ce n'est que l'argent, monsieur, voici ma bourse avec vingt-quatre pistoles.

GRAPIGNAN. Hé! hé! voilà tout au plus pour un témoin, et ils sont deux. Voyez, n'avez-vous pas quelques nippes, quelque bijou, quelque vieux diamant? Dans ces sortes d'occasions, il faut savoir se saigner.

LE VOLEUR. Voici un diamant qui vaut encore vingt pistoles, et une montre qui peut en valoir douze.

GRAPIGNAN Je pourrai bien, pour l'amour de vous, avancer cinq ou six pistoles de mon argent. Après cela, nous compterons.

LE VOLEUR. Faites, monsieur. Je remets tout entre vos mains, et je m'abandonne à votre discrétion.

GRAPIGNAN. Allez, laissez-moi faire. Ce serait bien un grand hasard si, avec mes deux témoins, je n'envoie pas votre marchand aux galères. (*Le Voleur s'en va*) Vingt-quatre pistoles d'un côté; de l'autre, une montre et un diamant : ne vaut-il pas mieux que je profite de cela que le prévôt? Car ce coquin-là va se faire rouer au premier jour! »

Tel est M. Grapignan, qui réussit à voler même les voleurs de grand chemin.

LE SBIRE.

Le Sbir est encore un type fort en vogue dans la comédie italienne, c'est le même personnage que le *Sergent du guet* de la baraque de Polichinelle, sous les noms de *caporale Rogantino* ou de *caporale Simone, Capo de gli sbirri*, etc.

Comme le *Podesta*, ce personnage terrifiant paraît peu dans les intrigues.

Un vaste feutre, un énorme manteau, de grosses bottes fortes, une longue rapière, de grandes moustaches et un nez de carton, voilà de quoi faire un Sbire Cet attirail est toujours pendu à un clou derrière la première coulisse venue Cela se passe comme une robe de chambre Car c'est souvent Arlequin, Mezzetin, Scapin ou autres valets qui se font passer pour ce qu'ils ne sont pas. Mais qu'ils prennent garde! car souvent, au moment où ils y pensent le moins, surgit tout à coup de l'autre côté de la scène un vrai Sbire qui se glisse dans l'ombre, enveloppé jusqu'aux yeux de son large *tabarro*. Mais ses grosses bottes font tant de bruit, à elles seules, qu'il faudrait être sourd comme Pandolfe pour ne pas l'entendre. A quoi sert ce sombre personnage? à faire justice des traîtres et malfaiteurs de la comédie. Il est né partout. Il a tous les âges, ou plutôt il est si vieux qu'il n'en a plus. Il demeure partout. Il est, a été et sera. Il est aussi ancien que la comédie. Mais il a l'esprit obtus et fait souvent des balourdises impardonnables. Ayant le poignet solide et serrant fort, il est redouté de tous. Arlequin le fuit comme la peste, Mezzetin le craint plus que le feu; voire le bon Pierrot, qui pourtant n'a rien fait pour *s'attirer sa connaissance*. Polichinelle seul ne le craint point. C'est son plus grand ennemi. Jamais ils ne se sont rencontrés qu'il n'y ait eu bon nombre de coups échangés, et le Sbire n'a pas toujours eu le dessus. Mais que lui importe! il est fort de sa conscience et de la loi, et ne connaît que son devoir.

L'APOTHICAIRE.

Si les médecins furent tournés en ridicule sur la scène italienne et dans les comédies de Molière, les apothicaires n'ont guère été plus épargnés. Mais ce digne corps de la science triomphe dans *M. de Pourceaugnac;* il sait garder son rang et n'empiète en rien sur les droits de la médecine. « Non, je ne suis pas médecin, dit l'apothicaire à Éraste, à moi n'appartient pas cet honneur, et je ne suis qu'apothicaire, apothicaire indigne, pour vous servir. » Dans *le Malade imaginaire*, M. Fleurant est l'apothicaire modèle, il a conscience de sa valeur et ne plaisante point avec ses remèdes. Ce n'est plus le simple Matassin qui, pour insinuer sa marchandise, cherche à étourdir son client en lui beuglant aux oreilles :

> *Piglia lo su,*
> *Signor mousu*
> *Piglia lo, piglia lo, piglia lo su.*

Dans le théâtre de Gherardi, il porte les noms les plus ridicules, comme celui de *Viseautrou*, de *Cussiffle*, de *Clistorel*, et autres du même acabit. Callot l'appelle MARIMO et l'habille fort peu différemment de ceux que l'on voit aujourd'hui dans les comédies de Molière. Il le représente la toque sur le chef, le tablier autour du ventre, et tenant en main son arme favorite, longue comme une couleuvrine et visant avec précision le dos du capitan CARDONI.

Dans la comédie italienne, l'APOTHICAIRE *(planche 50)* est

encore mieux traité que dans les comédies-ballets de
Molière. Il joue un rôle, vient s'immiscer dans l'intrigue,
et parle de son art par métaphores et emblèmes.

« Je suis persuadé, monsieur », dit-il en s'adressant au
Docteur dont il vient demander la fille en mariage,
« qu'une chaise percée dénoterait mieux un apothicaire
qu'une chaise à porteurs. (*Il est entré en chaise à porteurs.*)
Mais, comme cette voiture ne me mettrait pas en bonne
odeur auprès d'une maîtresse, et que l'équipage est un
avantageux début pour la noce, je me fais apporter chez
vous d'une manière élégante, pour vous présenter des respects accompagnés de toutes les soumissions que la phar-
macie doit à la médecine.... Je vous amène un sujet désespéré, sur lequel tous les simples ne peuvent rien, et dont
la cure seule mettra votre faculté en crédit.

C'est moi, monsieur, qui suis le malade et la maladie,
c'est moi qui suis gâté jusqu'au fond des moelles, de ce mal
affreux. C'est moi qui suis gangrené des perfections de
Colombine. C'est moi qui veux l'épouser; et c'est moi,
enfin, qui vous prie de me l'ordonner comme un apozème
savoureux, que je prendrai avec délice. Le médecin en
aura tout l'honneur et l'apothicaire tout le plaisir.

Le Docteur. Paroles ne puent point : vous êtes apothicaire ?

L'Apothicaire. Oui, monsieur, grâce au Ciel, en gros et
en détail; et à tel jour qu'il y a, on fait chez moi à la fois
de la décoction pour trente douzaines de lavements, et je
puis dire sans vanité qu'il n'est point de pays qui ne con-
naisse M. Cusiffle, .. c'est le nom de votre petit serviteur.

Hélas, monsieur, sans le procès que nous avons avec les parfumeurs, nous ne serions que trop riches! La conservation de la beauté ayant été, de tout temps, le principal emploi des femmes, vous avez fort ingénieusement imaginé que les qualités bénéfiques de quelques simples pourraient beaucoup contribuer à la fraîcheur de leur teint. Nous trouvâmes le moyen de les embellir sans les toucher, de les rafraîchir sans qu'elles en vissent rien et de leur seringuer de la beauté par derrière.

Cependant, malgré une profession si bien établie, les parfumeurs veulent nous empêcher de donner des lavements aux femmes qui se portent bien, prétendant que les agréments de la beauté doivent sortir de leur boutique, et que nous n'avons point à nous mêler des visages.

LE DOCTEUR. A qui en ont ces maroufles-là? Ils prétendent donc anéantir le clystère?.. La Faculté défendra le lavement jusqu'à la dernière goutte. »

Colombine entre, l'Apothicaire demande au Docteur la permission de la complimenter. Le Docteur, après avoir décliné les noms, profession et qualités de l'Apothicaire en le présentant à Colombine, les laisse ensemble.

« L'APOTHICAIRE. Madame, mon esprit est tellement constipé dans le bas-ventre de mon ignorance, qu'il me faudrait un sirop de vos lumières pour liquéfier la matière de mes pensées.

COLOMBINE. Ah! liquéfier des pensées! que l'expression est galante! Le joli homme d'apothicaire!

L'APOTHICAIRE. Ah! madame, vous me seringuez des louanges qui ne sont dues qu'à vous. Votre bouche est un alambic d'où les conceptions les plus subtiles sont quintessenciées. Tout le séné et toute la rhubarbe de ma boutique purgent moins mes malades que la vivacité de vos yeux ne corrige les humeurs âcres et mordicantes d'un amour enflammé dont vous serez la pilule purgative, puisque votre humeur enjouée est un orviétan souverain contre les accès mélancoliques d'un cœur opilé de vos rares vertus et de vos éminentes qualités.

Colombine. Je ne croyais pas, monsieur, être un remède si souverain contre la folie; de ce train-là, vous m'allez faire passer pour un remède à tous maux.

L'Apothicaire. Heureux le blessé à qui un pareil emplâtre sera appliqué! Adieu, catholicon de mon âme, adieu, belle fleur de pêcher! Je vais faire infuser dans la terrine de mes souvenirs les gracieux attraits dont la nature vous a pourvue. Adieu, doux antimoine de mes inquiétudes! Adieu, cher lénitif de mes pensées! »

Quand on songe que la plupart des facéties et des types de Molière sont, à l'état d'ébauche grossière mais énergique, dans la *commedia dell' arte*, c'est-à-dire dans les lazzi et parades qui, sans nom d'auteur et sans publication typographique, ont défrayé tant de siècles avant l'apparition du grand Poquelin, on doit reconnaître l'intérêt des recherches auxquelles nous nous sommes livrés sans prétention aucune d'élever notre sujet au-dessus de sa véritable valeur littéraire. C'était pour nous principalement une exploration dans les archives de la comédie éternelle. D'autres lumières viendront, par le cours des temps et la force des choses, compléter ce travail et prouver que le plus grand comique et le plus grand comédien du monde, c'est un peu tout le monde

DE QUELQUES MASQUES DE CARNAVAL

Outre tous ces types de la comédie, les Italiens possèdent encore une foule d'autres masques, lesquels se montrent par les rues et les places publiques pendant les huit jours consécutifs que dure le carnaval. Un grand nombre de ces masques ont pris naissance sur les théâtres et en ont disparu; mais la plupart ne sont que l'effet de la fantaisie ou de la mode. tels sont les *Quacqueri* ou bouffons charges, correspondant par leurs costumes à nos *Chicards* français. Un mélange de modes anciennes et modernes. Les *Matti* (fous) vêtus de longues chemises blanches, coiffés de bonnets de nuit, portant un masque blanc, le cou perdu dans une immense collerette. Hommes et femmes, ainsi vêtus, courent dans la foule par les rues en faisant mille folies; les uns avec des tambourins, les autres avec des marottes, mais la plupart du temps armés de bâtons à l'extrémité desquels pend une vessie ou une éponge mouillée qui leur sert à frapper tous les autres masques qu'ils rencontrent.

Le costume de *Bajaccio* ou Pagliaccio est encore très-usité en temps de carnaval, ainsi que celui de Pulcinella pour les hommes et les femmes. Les *Maghi* (sorciers), adoptés par les gens graves, ainsi que les *Abbatacci*, qui, vêtus de noir, sauf un seul bas blanc, vont contrefaisant les avocats et autres hommes de robe. Les *Poverelle* (mendiantes), travestissements pour les femmes. La figure cachée sous un masque blanc, les cheveux épars sur les épaules, entièrement vêtues de blanc, les *Poverelle* se réunissent en troupe et vont demander l'aumône, qui consiste en fleurs, fruits et sucreries. D'autres travestissements encore fort en vogue sont ceux de *Marinari* et de *Pescatori* (marins et pêcheurs), de *Giardinieri* et *Giardiniere* (jardiniers et jardinières), *Cascherini* (ivrognes), *Scopette* (balayeuses), etc.

Dans un recueil intitulé *Trattato su la Commedia dell' arte, ossia improvisa*, titre peu justifié par la reproduction de cinq masques de la comédie italienne (Arlecchino, Pantalone, le Docteur, Brighella, Tartaglia), Francesco Valentini a publié à Berlin, en 1826, un album contenant une grande quantité de ces costumes de carnaval. Nous ne saurions mieux faire, pour donner une idée de ces scènes de carnaval, que de traduire quelques passages de l'esquisse (*Abbozzo*) de Valentini :

« Maintenant », dit-il, « je me vois dans la nécessité, pour rendre mon petit Traité le moins incomplet possible, de représenter quelques petites scènes qui se passent dans les rues de Rome. Et pour y réussir, je vous prie de vous transporter avec moi, en imagination, sur quelque place voisine du Corso, où nous plaçons notre théâtre.

» Il est *vingt heures* (c'est-à-dire deux heures de l'après-midi), et l'on ne voit encore personne. Le temps est couvert, mais il fera beau, il ne neigera pas, nous avons quinze degrés de chaleur.

» Oh! voyez, voyez! voici déjà un *Pulcinella* sonnant dans une trompe (*lumacone*), sautant et disant mille choses. Écoutons : il se plaint de la paresse des masques. Il est deux heures passées et ils ne sont pas encore prêts! Il les battrait pour un peu. Il s'en va tout en colère, protégeant et conduisant par le bras sa chère moitié.

» Mais, silence! grande rumeur; un *Arlecchino* sur la pointe des pieds, une lanterne à la main, éclaire un *Quacquero* et sa dame la *Quacqueressa*, un *Bajaccio* porte une ombrelle.... Comment diable, cher ami, l'ombrelle et la lanterne? la nuit et le soleil? Regardez notre première connaissance, le désolé *Pulcinella* qui se lamentait, le voilà au comble de la joie, il fait mille gambades, il vient de rencontrer un confrère Pulcinella auquel il cède son épouse. Joie réciproque. Quelle heureuse rencontre! etc. Voici un *Abbataccio*, deux ou trois *Quacqueri, Poverelli, Sbirri, Micheletti*, mais surtout un capitan *Fracasso*, qui se dispute avec un Tartaglia : « Si tu ne retournes tout de suite aux galères, je te couperai en deux, morceau de voleur! — *Vo.. i. . v'in...ga...ga...gannate, io non sono...chi...chi...ricer.. ca...- ca...cacate.* » (Vous vous trompez, je ne suis pas celui que vous cherchez.) Écoutez, écoutez comme les Arlequins courent en criant de joie *Chi chi . chicchirichì chic...chinchì!*

» Laissons-les se quereller, se vanter et s'injurier. Regardez maintenant cet *Abbataccio* un livre sous le bras, qui, aidé d'autres masques, vient d'arrêter un pauvre imbécile de paysan venu pour admirer le carnaval à Rome, et ne pensant certes pas être acteur dans cette farce : « Tu es mon débiteur, lui dit-il, depuis deux ans, depuis deux siècles. Ton aïeul, bisaïeul, trisaïeul, ou si tu préfères, ton grand-père, archi-grand diable de père, qui était mon homme d'affaires, m'a fait une lettre de change,

tu ne le crois pas? Tu nies la patente vérité? Je vais te la
faire voir. » En disant cela il ouvre son livre, qui n'est
qu'une boîte à farine, souffle dedans et aveugle presque le
pauvre paysan qui le regardait la bouche béante. Tous les
assistants rient et se moquent de lui, un *Garçon d'écurie*
vient l'étriller, des *Balayeuses* l'époussètent, un *Fou* le mys-
tifie. Le paysan veut s'en aller, mais voici un *Docteur*, un
Apothicaire, des *Matassins* qui lui offrent leurs services, des
flacons d'odeur : « Il est devenu pâle (par la farine), il est
près de mourir », lui crie-t-on; mais il tourne l'angle de
la rue, et disparaît avec sa suite, dont il se débarrassera
Dieu sait quand.

» Mais d'où vient ce bruit? qu'est-ce donc? « Un Spectre!
un Spectre (*una Fantasima*)! » crie chacun de toutes ses
forces, et les Pulcinelli, Arlecchini, Brighelli, Pantaloni,
de faire mille lazzi d'épouvante. Le capitan *Ammazzasette*
(Rodomont) met l'épée à la main et court au-devant du
Fantôme, qui s'allonge indéfiniment et disparaît aux
grands cris de joie des assistants.

» Voyez cette foule, écoutez ce bruit! Regardez ce que
c'est. Un âne bien harnaché, portant le roi des Polichinelles, avec deux petits Polichinelles ses fils, assis dans les
paniers. Sa cour, composée de trente à quarante Polichinelles, l'escorte en jouant de tous les instruments. Cette
mascarade générale est étrange, capricieuse et très-drôle.
Remarquez qu'il n'y en a pas deux coiffés de même; l'un
porte une vaste perruque, l'autre un panier, quelques-uns
un mauvais chapeau, d'autres la tête rasée; il y en a qui
portent une cage avec un oiseau dedans.... »

Cette scène est représentée dans l'ouvrage Chaque Pulcinella porte en effet une coiffure de fantaisie. Mais le reste
du costume est invariable. Il se compose d'une sorte de
chemise ronde en toile bise bordée de rouge ou de bleu, ne
dépassant pas le genou, le devant de cette blouse, fendue
sur la poitrine, est terminé par un cœur de drap rouge. Le
pantalon, également bordé de rouge ou de bleu, est large
et ne dépasse pas la cheville. Ces vêtements sont retenus
à la taille par une corde servant de ceinture et à laquelle
est pendue, au milieu du ventre, une cloche de cuivre
semblable à celle que les montagnards mettent au cou de
leurs bestiaux. Le masque noir ou brun, le bonnet pointu
traditionnel, la large collerette et les souliers noirs com-
plètent le costume du PULCINELLA de carnaval tel qu'il était
en 1826.

« Le Corso, d'un bout à l'autre, du haut en bas, fourmille
de monde. Pas une fenêtre qui ne soit garnie de spectateurs. Quelle variété dans cet ensemble! les rangs, les âges,
les sexes, tout y est confondu. La joie, la gaieté, la belle
humeur, des lazzi, des plaisanteries, du bruit, des bou-
quets, des nuages de farine par-ci, une pluie de fleurs par-
là, de longues files de voitures couvertes de masques, des
chars antiques montés par la jeunesse noble, qui représente, à la course, l'enlèvement de Proserpine. Puis des
femmes travesties en *officier,* en *marin,* en *Frascatane* ou
en *Albanaise.* Deux escadrons de guerriers antiques, sur
des *chevaux de carton,* se livrant un combat acharné, etc.
La journée se termine par les courses de chevaux libres au
milieu du Corso. Tel est le carnaval à Rome jusqu'à l'heure

de l'*Ave Maria*, moment où chacun retire son masque et va
finir sa journée au théâtre, en soirée, chez lui, en ville, à
souper ou au lit. Le mardi gras étant le dernier jour, la
cloche de l'*Ave Maria* est impuissante à se faire obéir,
chacun garde son masque, et commence alors la scène des
Moccoli, trop connue pour que nous ayons à la rapporter ici. »

Après avoir parlé très-superficiellement de quelques masques du carnaval romain, nous ne devons pas passer sous
silence plusieurs types singuliers, fantastiques, religieux,
indispensables à tout canevas merveilleux, joués par les
marionnettes en Italie et un peu partout. Ce sont SATANA
OU LE DIABLE, MAGO OU L'ENCHANTEUR, L'INCANTATRICE OU LA
FÉE, LE BON GÉNIE, L'ARCHANGE MICHEL et tous les *Esprits* qui
président *aux éléments*, à la nature, etc. Ces personnages,
aujourd'hui comme au moyen âge, jouissent encore d'une
égale célébrité. Derniers vestiges des *mystères*, ils ont
toujours marché côte à côte avec les masques. Aussitôt
qu'un canevas italien sort de la réalité absolue, il tombe
infailliblement dans le merveilleux. Le genre *fiabesco*
(féerique) a été surtout monté à son plus haut diapason
au siècle dernier par Carlo Gozzi.

En même temps que la comédie italienne mourait
en France en se fondant avec l'opéra-comique et la
comédie française; après leur avoir abandonné ou inspiré
différents types, elle mourait aussi, littérairement parlant,
en Italie, à la fin du dernier siècle, mais non sans avoir
jeté un dernier éclat, le plus brillant de tous, peut-être,
depuis le Ruzzante.

CARLO GOZZI ET CARLO GOLDONI.

Carlo Gozzi fit pour la *commedia dell' arte* l'opposé de ce qu'avait fait Beolco (Ruzzante). Celui-ci avait protesté contre la langue académique de son époque. Il avait introduisé les dialectes sur la scène, et prouvé que ce langage rustique était le seul qui convînt aux pièces rustiques et bourgeoises. Environ deux cents ans plus tard, vers 1750, Carlo Gozzi, trouvant la langue italienne assouplie par tous les genres de littérature qu'elle avait traversés, la jugea propre à exprimer les idées de toutes les classes, et, après une lutte ardente et railleuse contre le théâtre de Goldoni, qui avait pourtant de l'esprit en vénitien, il devint le poète exclusif, le souverain absolu d'une excellente troupe Sacchi, chef de cette troupe, avait des acteurs précieux. Lui-même était un *Truffaldin* de premier ordre. « On ne reverra plus, » dit Gozzi lui-même, « de Truffaldin comme Sacchi, plus de Brighella comme Zanoni, plus de Tartaglia comme Fiorilli, ce Napolitain plein de feu, justement célèbre dans toute l'Italie; plus de Pantalon comme Darbès, ce comique à volonté contenu ou impétueux, majestueusement bête, et si vrai que le bourgeois vénitien croit se mirer sur la scène quand il voit ce modèle parfait de ses ridicules. La Smeralda était un ange pour la grâce, une mouche pour la légèreté. Avec trois mots, ces gens-là auraient su faire toute une scène à mourir de rire. Jamais ils n'auraient souffert qu'une pièce tombât du premier coup. Ils en auraient plutôt fabriqué une autre sur-le-

champ, et il fallait qu'on eût ri pour son argent, car
ils étaient honnêtes, et du diable s'ils voulaient rendre le
prix des billets. J'ai vécu avec eux pendant dix ans, au
milieu du bruit, des querelles, des tempêtes, des injures,
et avec tant de plaisir que je ne donnerais pas ces dix
années pour tout le reste.... Ils auraient brûlé Venise pour
moi. Hélas! tout a une fin; l'extinction et la dispersion de
la troupe a été un de mes grands chagrins. Goldoni s'est
appuyé sur un mot imposant et trompeur, et un mot est
tout-puissant sur les esprits bornés, ses pièces reviendront
peut-être sur l'eau... tandis que mes pauvres fables, si on
les oublie une fois, ne reverront plus la lumière. »

Ces pauvres fables, qui, en effet, sont fort oubliées en
Italie et fort peu connues en France, n'en sont pas moins
destinées à vivre dans les archives de la *commedia dell' arte*.
Ce ne sont pas précisément des canevas, les rôles étant
succinctement et spirituellement écrits, les parties surtout
où les acteurs avaient à exprimer des sentiments sérieux ou
passionnés qui, en général, sont difficiles à improviser.
« Je me flatte, » dit-il, « d'avoir été utile à la troupe et au
genre... Qui pourrait compter tout ce que je leur ai fait,
par complaisance, de prologues, d'adieux en vers; combien de chansons à intercaler, de quêtes de compliments
pour les jolies actrices de passage, combien de milliers d'additions aux farces, combien de soliloques, de désespoirs,
de menaces, de reproches, de prières! »

Les canevas ou pièces de Gozzi pourraient s'appeler tout
simplement des contes de fée en action. C'est le genre
fiabesco, comme qui dirait *fabulesque*. Ce sont de très-jolis

contes, et dont le principal mérite scénique est d'amener
des situations tantôt burlesques, tantôt dramatiques *Contes
de nourrices*, disait Gozzi lui-même, mais de nourrices très-
poétiques pour des nourrissons-poètes, et dont Hoffmann
s'est imprégné pour faire ses contes fantastiques.

Mélancolique, railleur et enthousiaste, Gozzi eut l'espèce
d'hallucination d'Hoffmann, sans s'y arrêter et sans y
laisser sa raison. M. Paul de Musset, dans un de ses écrits
plein de grâce et de sens sur l'Italie moderne (*Revue des
Deux-Mondes*), a parfaitement caractérisé le génie bizarre
du librettiste italien et celui du conteur allemand. Les
principales pièces de Carlo Gozzi sont : *l'Amour des trois
oranges, le Corbeau, le Roi cerf, Turandot, la Femme serpent,
les Gueux heureux, le Monstre bleu, la Zobéide, l'Oiseau vert.*
Ces sujets rendaient l'essor à l'improvisation, à la fantaisie, à cette immense part que prend une réunion d'acteurs inventifs et spirituels au succès d'une œuvre théâtrale.
Gozzi était surnommé alors l'Aristophane de l'Adriatique,
mais vint la signora Teodora Ricci · « *Amour, tu perdis
Troie!* » Gozzi, qui jusque-là s'était laissé cajoler par toutes
les charmantes comédiennes de la troupe, aima celle-ci,
qui n'avait aucun talent. Le vieux *Truffaldin* Sacchi devint
le rival du poète son meilleur ami. Les autres actrices furent
jalouses, les hommes prirent part dans la mêlée. Bref, la
troupe se dispersa. Gozzi dut changer de genre. Il fit ce
qu'avait fait Goldoni dont il s'était tant moqué, il écrivit
et arrangea pour la Ricci des pièces dans le goût étranger.
Son génie dramatique s'éteignit dans la compilation.

Heureusement le feu sacré de ce génie actif se ralluma,

et sa verve se révéla sous une autre forme. Il fit des satires,
« les meilleurs fruits qu'ait portés cet arbre si fécond »

« .... L'année 1797 », dit M Paul de Musset, « était
arrivée.... Gozzi assista à la chute de son pays, aux trahi-
sons... à l'abandon du général français, à l'entrée des
baïonnettes allemandes, à l'élection dérisoire du doge
Manin, son ami Dieu sait ce qu'étaient devenus, dans ce
conflit, les Pantalons et les Truffaldins!... L'année de la
mort de Carlo Gozzi n'est pas même connue. On ne sait
pas non plus l'année de sa naissance. Ce génie bizarre
passa comme une de ces comètes dont on n'a pas eu le
temps d'étudier la marche. »

Nous citerons encore quelques fragments des réflexions
de Carlo Gozzi sur la nature et sur l'historique de la
commedia dell' arte, et particulièrement sur le succès que
ce genre eut en Allemagne.

« La comédie improvisée, dite *commedia dell' arte,* fut de
tous temps la plus utile aux troupes de comédiens italiens.
Elle existe depuis trois cents ans Elle fut toujours com-
battue, et jamais vaincue. Il semble impossible que certains hommes, lesquels passent pour auteurs, de notre
temps, ne s'aperçoivent pas qu'ils sont ridicules en abais-
sant leur importance à une plaisante colère contre un
Brighella, un Pantalon, un Docteur, un Tartaglia, un
Truffaldin Cette colère, qui semble être l'effet de l'ivresse,
démontre clairement que la *commedia dell' arte* subsiste en
Italie, et dans toute sa vigueur, à la honte des persécutions
exercées contre elle

» Je considère les vaillants comédiens à l'impromptu

bien davantage que les poètes improvisateurs, qui, sans
dire rien qui ait un sens, captivent l'attention de ces réu-
nions qui s'attroupent pour les écouter.

» . . . . Dès le seizième siècle, un certain Cantinella fut
un célèbre comédien improvisateur,.. aux Pilotti, aux
Garelli, aux Cattoli, aux Campioni, aux Lombardi, sans
rechercher dans les temps antérieurs, succédèrent les
Darbès, les Collalti, les Zanoni, les Fiorilli, les Sacchi,
et tant d'autres.

» La comédie italienne improvisée dite *dell' arte*, est très-
ancienne, et bien plus ancienne que la comédie italienne
régulière et écrite. Elle prit son origine en Lombardie, se
répandit dans toute l'Italie, pénétra en France, où elle existe
encore. Au seizième siècle, il n'était pas plus permis aux
femmes d'assister aux comédies improvisées qu'à celles qui
étaient écrites. Ces deux genres étaient trop licencieux. On
peut juger des obscénités des pièces écrites, mais non de
celles qui étaient improvisées, ne les connaissant que par
tradition[1]. Ces deux genres furent toujours rivaux.

» Au temps de Léopold, de Joseph et de Charles VI,

---

[1] Ici Gozzi se trompe absolument en ce qui concerne Ruzzante, qu'évi-
demment il n'a jamais lu. Les pièces de Ruzzante, nous l'avons dit, ne sont
pas licencieuses, et les femmes honnêtes y assistaient « *Ad audiendas eas
hominum tam mulierum concursus* », dit B. Scardeon. Ceci est encore prouvé
par les prologues que Beolco récitait lui-même, et dans lesquels il s'adressait souvent aux belles et bonnes spectatrices, tantôt pour leur reprocher
les modes exagérées de leur toilette, tantôt pour leur parler d'amour fidèle,
d'amour conjugal, de la manière la plus naïve, et en même temps la plus
idéaliste. Dans la *Gelosia*, du Lasca (1581), un prologue est uniquement
consacré aux dames ainsi que dans *Il Granchio*, de Salviati (1566), et dans
beaucoup d'autres comédies du seizième siècle.

défunts empereurs d'Autriche, les comédiens français firent tous leurs efforts pour se maintenir sur les deux théâtres de Vienne, mais ils furent renvoyés par ces empereurs, lesquels ne voulurent que des comédiens allemands et italiens sur leurs théâtres, préférant toutefois ceux de leur nation. Les troupes de comédiens de Vienne travaillèrent avec la même méthode que celles d'Italie, et les comédies improvisées, appelées chez nous *commedie dell' arte*, eurent la préférence. Weiskern, Heindrich, Leinhaus, Prehauser, Kurz, Jaquedt, Stéphanie, Muller, Brenner, Gottlieb, la Huberin, la Nutin, la Elizonin, la Schwagerin, étaient des personnes très-habiles qui jouaient les comédies improvisées en allemand.

» Il Ganzachi, habile comédien italien, que nous connaissons et qui sait très-bien l'allemand, a été renforcer la troupe de Vienne avec le personnel et le matériel de notre théâtre. Weiskern, Heindrich, représentaient les vieillards; Leinhaus jouait Pantalon en allemand, avec la prononciation vénitienne; Prehauser jouait l'Hanswurst, espèce de second Zanni; Kurz jouait le Bernardone, Brenner faisait il *Burlino* (le farceur); Gottlieb le villageois imbécile; la Nutin, la Elizonin, la Schwagerin jouaient les rôles d'intrigantes du théâtre allemand, et étaient aimées du public autant que le sont parmi nous Sacchi, Fiorilli, Zanoni, Darbès, Coralina, Smeraldina. »

Nous citerons en abrégé d'autres curieux documents que nous fournit encore Gozzi, sur la pratique du genre qu'il préconise. « Les détracteurs du genre prétendaient l'avoir enterré. La comédie improvisée, disaient-ils, n'existe plus

même en Italie Partout on l'apprend et on la récite. »
Gozzi leur donne le plus formel démenti. « Qui voudra
voir, dit-il, le sujet qui sert de guide à ces excellents
comédiens, et qui, placé auprès d'une petite lumière pour
la plus grande commodité de toute la troupe, est contenu
tout entier sur une petite feuille de papier, sera émerveillé
d'entendre dix à douze personnes tenir en gaieté un public
pendant trois heures, et conduire à bonne fin l'argument
proposé.

» Pour donner au lecteur un spécimen du guide qui
suffit à nos comédiens improvisateurs, je transcrirai ici
un sujet que j'ai lu à la clarté de la petite lampe du
théâtre, et je le ferai sans ajouter ou retrancher un mot
C'est celui des *Contrats rompus*, que nous voyons chaque
année plusieurs fois et toujours avec plaisir. »

ACTE PREMIER.

LIVOURNE

« BRIGHELLA entre en regardant sur la scène, et ne voyant
personne, il appelle.

PANTALON. Jeu de crainte Il entre.   4

BRIGHELLA veut quitter son service, etc.

PANTALON se recommande à lui.

BRIGHELLA s'attendrit et lui promet aide.

PANTALON dit (*sous-entendu*) que les créanciers veulent être
payés, surtout Truffaldin, et qu'en ce jour expire le délai, etc.

BRIGHELLA le tranquillise.

En ce moment ·

TRUFFALDIN. Scène de vouloir être payé.

BRIGHELLA trouve un moyen de le renvoyer.

PANTALON et BRIGHELLA restent.

En ce moment ·

TARTAGLIA, à la fenêtre, écoute

BRIGHELLA s'en aperçoit. Il fait la scène des richesses avec Pantalon.

TARTAGLIA vient dans la rue. Il fait le jeu de l'aumône avec Pantalon A la fin, ils conviennent du mariage de la fille de Tartaglia avec le fils de Pantalon.

En ce moment :

TRUFFALDIN dit vouloir son argent.

BRIGHELLA fait semblant que Pantalon le lui donne. L'ayant fait trois fois, tous sortent.

FLORINDO parle de son amour pour Rosaure, et de la faim qui le tourmente Il frappe.

ROSAURE écoute son amour, veut l'éprouver, lui demande un cadeau.

FLORINDO dit que ce n'est pas le moment, et n'en pas avoir les moyens.

ROSAURE lui dit d'attendre, elle lui en fera un; et sort.

FLORINDO reste.

En ce moment :

SMERALDINA, avec un panier, le donne à Florindo et sort.

FLORINDO mange.

BRIGHELLA ayant entendu que Rosaure lui a donné le panier, le lui dérobe et s'enfuit.

FLORINDO le suit

LEANDRE parle de son amour pour Rosaure. Il cherche à tromper Pantalon.

En ce moment ·

TARTAGLIA sort en discourant seul sur les grandes richesses de Pantalon

LÉANDRE lui demande sa fille.

TARTAGLIA dit l'avoir fiancée au fils de Pantalon.

LÉANDRE est étonné; il fait une scène, » etc , etc.

« De ce feuillet textuel, reprend Gozzi, sort la comédie des *contratti rotti*, et de plus de quatre cents autres formules tout aussi concises sortent nos comédies *dell' arte*. Il n'y a pas d'acteurs malades ou nouvellement recrutés qui fassent jamais manquer de tels spectacles, et un petit accord *fait sur deux pieds*, sur le tour et le fond de l'action scénique, suffit pour que tout marche bien. Au moment de lever le rideau, il arrive très-souvent que l'on change la distribution des rôles, selon les circonstances, l'importance ou l'habileté relative des acteurs Et pourtant la comédie va heureusement et gaiement à son dénoûment. Tous les ans, on ajoute ou on retranche des scènes à l'argument, et un simple avertissement donné à la troupe suffit pour que la chose soit habilement exécutée. On voit que ces braves acteurs travaillent le fond même de leurs sujets, établissent toujours leurs scènes sur différentes bases et les dialoguent avec tant de variété qu'ils sont toujours nouveaux et à jamais durables J'ai entendu souvent ces improvisateurs se reprocher d'avoir mal établi (*piantato*) leur scène et la rétablir ensuite par d'excellents raisonnements, de manière à la motiver et à établir ainsi des avertissements pour un nouvel essai.

» Il est bien vrai que quelques acteurs sérieux dans ce
genre de comédie, et particulièrement les actrices, ont
un arsenal de matériaux différents *prémédités* dans la mémoire, matériaux qui servent aux prières, aux reproches,
aux menaces, aux désespoirs, aux sentiments de jalousie;
mais il n'en est pas moins surprenant de voir qu'en face
d'un public, et en improvisant avec des improvisateurs,
elles puissent avoir tout prêts et choisir dans cette masse
dont leur cervelle est remplie, des traits qu'elles font
tomber à propos, qu'elles expriment avec énergie, et qui
enlèvent les applaudissements des spectateurs.

» Tel est le système de notre comédie improvisée, éclat
que notre nation peut seule revendiquer, et qui durant le
cours de trois siècles n'a pas épuisé sa verve.

» Il serait trop long d'énumérer les quatre cents sujets
et plus qui se renouvellent continuellement dans les scènes
et dans le dialogue. Les habiles acteurs qui succèdent aux
habiles acteurs qui meurent, suffisent pour donner un
éternel aspect de nouveauté à ces sujets Nous voyons Roderigo Lombardi, excellent *Docteur*, remplacé par Agostino
Fiorilli, habile *Tartaglia*, d'un naturel égal tous deux,
renouveler chaque sujet, par la seule différence de leur
talent. Un seul nouveau personnage original suffit pour
ranimer l'originalité de toute sa troupe. »

Gozzi nous apprend encore que les auteurs de son temps
(et notamment Goldoni) écrivaient en dialogue, après
coup, et faisaient imprimer les canevas qui avaient réussi
entre les mains des comédiens improvisateurs. Au reste,
la plupart des auteurs comiques italiens ont agi ainsi.
Presque toutes les comédies du dix-septième siècle sont

tirées de vieux scénarios improvisés, et Gozzi en donne une
liste très-curieuse, quoique très-incomplète. Il cite entre
autres : « Le célèbre Dominique Biancolelli, qui a mis et
fait représenter, en dialogues, un très-grand nombre de
canevas italiens improvisés. Ses comédies sont imprimées,
mais sont restées infructueuses, tandis que les mêmes sujets
traités par l'improvisation sont encore très-goûtés sur le
théâtre. » Il nous apprend aussi que les comédies écrites
et récitées par les comédiens *colti* (c'est-à-dire cultivés), qui
n'avaient jamais pu réunir soixante spectateurs, attiraient
la foule, dès que les improvisateurs s'en emparaient pour
broder sur l'*ossatura*, c'est-à-dire le squelette de ces pièces.

Beaucoup de canevas arrangés après coup et publiés
sous la forme *sostenuta* n'ont servi qu'à la lecture. Les
comédiens *dell' arte* ne s'en occupaient pas; ils se conten-
taient de leurs vieux résumés secs et serrés qui les laissaient
beaucoup plus libres et plus féconds.

Mais quoi qu'en dise Gozzi, il a suivi, comme Goldoni,
un genre mixte très-heureux, moitié récité, moitié improvisé. Seulement ce genre mixte ne pouvait être traité que
par un esprit original et assez épris de ses acteurs pour
leur laisser le champ libre. Il devait donc finir avec lui.
La seule chose qui en soit restée aujourd'hui, c'est l'habitude, en Italie, de faire apparaître certains masques comiques, à travers tous les genres de spectacle.

Carlo Goldoni a commencé comme Gozzi, et avant lui,
par écrire des canevas pour la *commedia dell' arte*. Il doit
en rester de nombreuses traces en Italie, mais il n'a pas
voulu éditer ces *ossature*, dont il avait le tort de rougir,

avant de les avoir écrites à nouveau, dialoguées, chan-
gées et converties en pièces *sostenute*. Nous avons vu Gozzi
lui reprocher d'avoir gâté par ce travail à froid beaucoup
de sujets heureux, où brillaient les improvisateurs, et qui,
du reste, ne servaient pas aux comédiens de son temps
sous leur nouvelle forme, ou ne leur servaient (selon
Gozzi) qu'à jouer devant les banquettes La querelle entre
ces deux auteurs et leurs adhérents de part et d'autre,
fut très-vive. Tous deux avaient du mérite, Goldoni plus
de sagesse, d'observation et de réalité, Gozzi plus d'invention, d'esprit et d'originalité.

Tous deux commencèrent de même, par laisser l'improvisation libre Peu à peu et même très-vite, ils subirent le
besoin d'écrire les rôles et de substituer leur personnalité à
celle des comédiens

Tous deux suivirent quelque temps le genre mixte, c'est-
à-dire les rôles sérieux écrits, les rôles des masques *ad
libitum*. Enfin tous deux les firent disparaître, Gozzi, bien
malgré lui sans doute, et en regrettant toujours sa chère
troupe Sacchi; Goldoni, au contraire, avec un parti pris
de supprimer les masques et les dialectes, ou de les reléguer au dernier plan. Encore ne leur permet-il plus d'improviser, et il écrit toujours leurs dialogues C'est là où
Gozzi put l'attaquer victorieusement. Ce qu'on écrit pour
des improvisateurs est pâle, froid et lourd, et il vaudrait
beaucoup mieux ne pas voir *Truffaldin* ou *Tartaglia* que de
les voir bâillonnés par la logique de l'auteur.

L'arrêt de mort que Goldoni voulut porter contre la
comédie *dell' arte* se trouve parfaitement résumé dans une

pièce intitulée *il Teatro comico*, qu'il a placée lui-même en
tête de son recueil (édition de Turin, 1756) et déclaré être
une sorte de préface à son œuvre Cette comédie est peu
amusante, c'est une pièce critique, mais elle est curieuse
pour l'histoire du genre.

Un directeur de théâtre essaye des acteurs nouveaux,
dans une pièce nouvelle, et disserte longuement sur la
matière :

« ORAZIO, *directeur de la troupe.* Vous le voyez, il est bien
nécessaire de se procurer des acteurs liés par une convention littéraire; autrement ils tombent facilement dans l'usé
ou l'invraisemblable.

EUGENIO, *second amoureux de la troupe.* Donc il faut songer
à supprimer entièrement la comédie improvisée ?

ORAZIO Entièrement, non ! Il n'est pas mauvais que les
Italiens se maintiennent en possession de faire ce que les
autres nations n'ont pas eu le courage de faire. Les Français ont coutume de dire que les comédiens italiens sont
téméraires de se risquer à parler en public, à l'imprévu,
mais ce qui peut s'appeler témérité de la part des comédiens ignorants est une belle qualité chez les comédiens
habiles, et il y a encore des personnages excellents qui, à
l'honneur de l'Italie et à la gloire de notre art, portent
triomphalement et méritoirement l'admirable prérogative
de parler à l'impromptu avec autant d'élégance que le
poète pourrait le faire en écrivant

EUGENIO Mais les masques perdent ordinairement à dire
le prémédité ?

ORAZIO. Quand le prémédité est brillant, gracieux, bien

adapté au caractère du personnage qui doit le réciter, tout bon masque l'apprend volontiers.

EUGENIO. Est-ce qu'on ne pourrait pas retrancher les masques de la comédie de caractère ?

ORAZIO. Malheur à nous si nous faisions une telle nouveauté ! Il n'est pas encore temps de s'y risquer ! En toutes choses il ne faut pas heurter de front le goût universel. Autrefois le public allait à la comédie seulement pour rire, et il ne voulait pas voir d'autres acteurs en scène que les masques. Si les rôles sérieux faisaient le dialogue un peu long, il s'ennuyait immédiatement; aujourd'hui on arrive à pouvoir écouter les rôles sérieux, on jouit des paroles, on se complaît dans les événements, on y goûte la morale, on rit des saillies et des altercations tirées du sérieux même; mais on voit encore volontiers les masques, et il n'est pas nécessaire de les retirer tout à fait. Il faut chercher à les bien limiter et à les soutenir avec frein dans leur caractère ridicule, même en face du sérieux rendu plus agréable et plus gracieux.

EUGENIO. Mais ceci est une manière de composer très-difficile ?

ORAZIO. C'est une manière retrouvée, il n'y a pas long-temps, et à laquelle tous se sont livrés. Il ne se passera pas beaucoup de temps avant que les plus fertiles esprits s'éveillent pour l'améliorer comme le désire de tout son cœur celui qui l'a inventée. »

Malgré ce parti pris naïvement perfide, Goldoni n'osa que bien tard supprimer entièrement les masques, mais il les avait si bien ou plutôt si mal transformés, qu'ils pou-

vaient bien le regarder comme l'assassin du genre. Le
succès l'abandonna à mesure qu'il dénatura le goût
national dans la bouche de ces personnages qui, grâce à
lui, arrivaient à dialoguer *à la française*, c'est-à-dire
comme les valets et les soubrettes des imitateurs de nos
maîtres. Il abandonna la partie, se fit Français et donna
en France *le Bourru bienfaisant;* c'était là, en somme, son
véritable genre.

Il n'en est pas moins vrai, et Gozzi le reconnaît lui-
même, que Goldoni avait travaillé pour le théâtre italien,
dans les commencements surtout, d'une manière heureuse
et agréable. Ses pièces vénitiennes sont encore charmantes,
malgré l'habit plus étroit et plus empesé qu'il leur donna,
en les refaisant pour le lecteur. Forcé de laisser le dialecte
vénitien dans la bouche de ses principaux personnages
comiques, il en a fait des rôles réels pour la comédie de
mœurs. Toutefois l'ensemble de son œuvre théâtrale ne
justifie pas assez le titre qui lui fut décerné de *Molière de
l'Italie.* Si jamais génie italien mérita une telle comparaison, c'est le RUZZANTE, qui, à la fois acteur et auteur, fut,
comme notre grand Poquelin, nourri de Plaute et de
Térence, et, comme lui, les dépassa de beaucoup.

COULEURS DES COSTUMES

DES PERSONNAGES DE L'ANCIENNE COMÉDIE ITALIENNE.

— — — ——

TOME SECOND

Nº 26   PANTALON (1550). Pourpoint et pantalon de drap rouge. Grande robe de drap noir. Bonnet de laine rouge. Masque bistre. Barbe et cheveux gris. Pantoufles de maroquin jaune.

Nº 27. BALOARDO (1653) Robe, pourpoint, culotte, bas, serre-tête, chapeau et souliers noirs à nœuds de même couleur. Ceinture de cuir noir à boucle de cuivre. Collerette, sans empois, de toile blanche. Mouchoir blanc. Masque, au front et au nez noir. Les joues peintes de couleur lie de vin

Nº 28. BISCEGLIESE (1680). Pourpoint et culotte de velours noir, bordés d'un galon rouge Bonnet de drap rouge. Manches et bas rouges Souliers noirs à rubans noirs. Ceinture de cuir jaune. Cheveux blancs.

Nº 29 CASSANDRE (1780). Culotte et habit rouge amarante, doublés de gris Boutons d'acier Gilet blanc à dessins roses Bas de coton bleu clair Jarretières rouges. Souliers de cuir noir à boucles d'acier. Perruque poudrée. Cravate de mousseline Chapeau noir. Gants de laine verte. Canne à pomme d'ivoire.

NOTA — Les dates indiquent l'époque où le costume représenté sur la planche a été porté, mais non pas la date de la création du type

II

N° 30. La Cantatrice (1694) Corsage et lanières en velours rouge, brodés et passementés d'or et doublés de satin rouge-cerise. Jupe de soie blanche à dessins blancs, verts et or Nœud de la ceinture en soie blanche, rayée de rose, frangée d'or. Collier et bracelets en or Voile de dentelle. Cheveux bruns Diadème d'or à plumes blanches Souliers de satin blanc à nœuds rouge-cerise.

N° 31. Ruzzante (1525) Pourpoint violet à parements orange Manches de dessous bleu clair. Pantalon, dont une jambe mi-partie gris perle et bleue, et l'autre jambe gris foncé. Chaussures noires Bonnet violet

N° 32 Stenterello (1858). Veste de drap bleu clair, doublée de blanc Collet et parements à carreaux noirs et rouges Galons rouges. Gilet jaune à pois verts Culotte noire. Un bas rouge, l'autre rayé bleu et blanc Souliers noirs à boucles d'acier. Cravate noire avec un liséré blanc. Figure blafarde à sourcils bruns. Trois lignes brunes parallèles au coin de la bouche Une tache rouge sur chaque joue Cheveux bruns et queue rouge.

N° 33. Meneghino (1528). Robe de tricot blanc. Jambes vertes. Ceinture et souliers de cuir jaune Bonnet brun.

N° 34. Gianduja (1858) Tricorne noir bordé d'un galon rouge. Queue rouge. Cheveux bruns. Veste et culotte en drap marron à boutons et passepoils rouges. Gilet jaune bordé de rouge. Bas rouges Souliers noirs à boucles de cuivre. Jarretières rouges. Cravate verte

N° 35. Fioralisa (1533). Robe de satin blanc. Manches de dessus à crevés, en satin blanc Manches de dessous et seconde jupe à dessins lilas et roses Cheveux blonds. Chaîne et collier d'or

N° 36. Isabella (1600). Robe et corsage de satin rose à manches tailladées. Garnitures, collier et bracelets de perles Souliers de satin blanc rayé d'or. Collerette et

manchettes de guipure. Manteau de soie ou de satin
violet. Toque de velours violet à plumes blanches.
Cheveux blonds.

N° 37. Silvia (1716). Manteau à manches en satin gris perle à
revers de satin rouge-cerise. Corsage et jupes en satin
blanc à ruches et nœuds verts. Souliers de satin blanc
à nœuds verts. Collerette de gaze. Cheveux poudrés.
Rubans et plumes blanches.

N° 38. Brighella (1570). Pourpoint, pantalon et manteau blancs
à passementeries vertes. Masque brun à moustaches
noires. Barbe et cheveux noirs. Toque blanche, bordée
d'un galon vert. Bas blancs. Souliers de cuir jaune.
Escarcelle et ceinture de cuir jaune à boucle de fer.
Poignard à manche de corne.

N° 39. Beltrame (1613). Masque marron à moustaches brunes.
Toque noire. Manteau brun garni de houppes noires.
Veste, trousse et culotte de drap gris, bordées d'un
galon noir. Bas blancs. Souliers de peau jaune à
houppes noires. Ceinture de cuir jaune à boucle de
cuivre. Collerette et manchettes de toile sans empois.

N° 40. Scapino (1716). Toque, veste, culotte blanches à brandebourgs bleus. Manteau bleu à brandebourgs blancs.
Bas blancs. Souliers de peau blanche à rosettes bleues.

N° 41. Mezzetin (1682). Toque, manteau, veste et culotte de
soie rayée rouge et blanc. Doublure du manteau,
blanche. Bas blancs. Souliers de peau jaune à nœuds
rouges. Ceinture de cuir jaune à boucle de cuivre.
Serre-tête noir. Rubans du manteau et de la culotte,
rouges.

N° 42. Narcisino (1650). Chapeau de paille à rubans rouges.
Cheveux blonds. Veste et culotte rayées rouge et
vert. Bas blancs. Jarretières rouges. Souliers de cuir
jaune à nœuds rouges. Manteau gris.

N° 43. Scaramuccia (1643). Toque, manteau, pourpoint, culotte,
souliers en drap noir. Bas de soie noire. Ceinture de

cuir noir. Nœuds et bordures de satin noir   Boucle
de ceinture et rapière en fer   Collerette de mousseline
à petits tuyaux. Figure blanche, à moustaches et
sourcils peints

Nº 44. PASQUARIELLO (1685). Veste et culotte de velours noir.
Serre-tête de velours noir   Bas rouges   Souliers de cuir
noir à boucles d'acier. Collerette de mousseline. Figure
blanche. Moustaches peintes.

Nº 45   COVIELLO (1550). Masque rouge, au front et au nez noirs.
Serre-tête gris   Plumes rouges. Veste et pantalon de
flanelle grise à gros boutons rouges. Grelots de cuivre
aux bras et aux jambes.

Nº 46   FRITELLINO (1580)   Camisole et pantalon de toile blan-
châtre   Masque noir. Chapeau de feutre gris à plumes
rouges. Manteau rouge. Souliers, ceinture et escarcelle de cuir jaune   Sabre de bois

Nº 47   TABARIN (1680)   Chapeau de feutre gris à plumes de coq
Camisole et pantalon de toile blanche bordés de ga-
lons rouges, jaunes et verts. Manteau de serge verte.
Souliers de cuir jaune.

Nº 48   TARTAGLIA (1630)   Veste, manteau et culotte de drap
vert, doublés de blanc et rayés de jaune. Chapeau de
feutre gris   Grandes lunettes bleues sur le nez   Collerette, sans empois, à larges tuyaux. Bas blancs. Souliers et ceinture de cuir jaune

Nº 49. LE NOTAIRE (1725)   Perruque brune à la Louis XIV.
Robe, veste, culotte, bas noirs   Souliers de cuir noir
à boucles de cuivre. Rabat blanc. Canne et portefeuille

Nº 50. L'APOTHICAIRE (1615). Veste, culotte, bas noirs. Bonnet
noir. Souliers de cuir noir   Tablier blanc.

TABLE DES GRAVURES

DU TOME SECOND.

TABLE DU TOME SECOND.

TABLE ALPHABÉTIQUE

DES TYPES MENTIONNÉS DANS LES DEUX VOLUMES
